HEALTH PSYCHOLOGY

HEALTH PSYCHOLOGY:

Biopsychosocial Interactions

EDWARD P. SARAFINO
Trenton State College

JOHN WILEY & SONS

New York Chichester Brisbane Toronto Singapore

Acquisitions Editor: DEBORAH L. MOORE
Managing Editor: JOAN KALKUT
Copyediting Supervisor: GILDA STAHL
Production Supervisor: NANCY PRINZ
Interior Design: DAVID LEVY
Cover Design: DAWN L. STANLEY
Photo Researcher: CHRIS MIGDAL
Photo Research Manager: STELLA KUPFERBERG
Illustrations: JOHN BALBAIS with the assistance of the Wiley illustrations department

Library of Congress Cataloging in Publication Data:

Sarafino, Edward P.
Health psychology : biopsychosocial interactions / Edward P. Sarafino.
p. cm.
Includes bibliographical references.
ISBN 0-471-60606-5
1. Clinical health psychology. I. Title.
R726.7.S27 1990
610'.19--dc20 89-39798

Printed in the United States of America

10 9 8 7 6 5 4 3

Printed and bound by Malloy Lithographing, Inc.

To my mother
and in memory of my father.
They gave me life,
loved and nurtured me,
and helped me be healthy.

preface

"The first wealth is health," wrote the poet/philosopher Ralph Waldo Emerson in the nineteenth century. Although people have probably always valued good health, Americans today are becoming increasingly health conscious. This heightened consciousness generally reflects two beliefs. One is that we can do things to protect our health and prevent illness. The second is that being sick is usually unpleasant—as Emerson put it, "sickness is poor-spirited, and cannot serve anyone." If a person's health problem is serious, it can be quite distressing to the patient and his or her family and friends. These beliefs underlie psychologists' interests in helping people behave in ways that promote wellness, adjust to health problems that develop, and participate effectively in treatment and rehabilitation programs. This book was written because I share these interests.

The goal in writing this text has been to create a teaching instrument that draws from the research and theory of many disciplines to describe how psychology and health are interconnected. The resulting book is a comprehensive text that is appropriate for several courses, especially those entitled either Health Psychology or Behavioral Medicine. Two objectives were central regarding the likely audience in these courses. First, I aimed to make the content appropriate for upper-division students—mainly juniors; but the straightforward writing style also makes the material accessible to many sophomores. The content assumes that the students have already had at least an introductory psychology course. Second, I tried to make the material relevant and interesting to students from diverse disciplines—particularly psychology, of course, but also fields such as sociology, allied health, premed, and health and physical education. Undergraduate training in health psychology has developed rapidly and can play an important role in helping students from many disciplines understand the interplay of biological, psychological, and social factors in people's health (Sarafino, 1988).

The field of health psychology is enormously exciting, partly because of its relevance to the lives of those who study it and of individuals the students know or will work with in the future. The field is also exciting because it is so new, and researchers from many different disciplines are finding fascinating and important relationships between psychology and health every day. Keeping up to date in each area of such a complex field presents quite a challenge, which I have addressed by consulting thousands of articles and books. The vast majority of the roughly 1,500 references cited in this text were published within the last 10 years.

THEMES

A phrase we often hear in psychology is that we need to understand the "whole person." In approaching this goal, this book adopts the *biopsychosocial model* as the basic explanatory theme. I have also tried to convey a sense that the components of this model interrelate in a dynamic and continuous fashion, consistent with the concept of *systems*. The psychological research cited reflects an eclectic orientation and supports a variety of behavioral, physiological, cognitive, and social/personality viewpoints. In addition, *gender and sociocultural differences* in health and related behaviors are addressed at many points in the book. In these ways, this book presents a balanced view of health psychology that is squarely in the mainstream of current thinking in the field.

One additional theme makes this book unique. I have integrated a focus on *life-span development* in health and illness throughout the book, and each chapter contains information dealing with development. For example, the book discusses how health and health-related behavior change with age and describes health care issues and examples that pertain to pediatric and elderly patients. Sometimes this information is organized as a separate unit, as with the sections "Development and Health-Related Behavior," "When the Hospitalized Patient Is a Child," "Assessing Pain in Children," and "Alzheimer's Disease."

ORGANIZATION

The organization of this text is designed to focus on the major topics and problem areas in health psychology. As the table of contents shows, these topics are divided into 14 chapters in the following six parts:

- *Part 1.* Chapter 1 presents the history and focus of health psychology and describes the major concepts and research methods used in the field. Chapter 2 provides an introduction to the body's physical systems. Three reasons guided the decision to have a separate chapter on body systems, rather than introducing the needed physiological principles as they became relevant. First, this approach allows students to see how the various systems interrelate, as in the section entitled "The Endocrine and Nervous Systems Working Together." Second, each body system is mentioned at many points in the book, and students have a single place to refer back to if needed. Third, the following part of the book relies on the reader's firm knowledge of almost all body systems and discusses them in connection with people's experience of stress.

- *Part 2.* Chapters 3, 4, and 5 discuss stress, its relation to illness, and methods for coping with and reducing it. The material on body systems in Chapter 2 connects directly to discussions in Chapters 3 and 4, particularly the sections entitled "Biological Aspects of Stress," "Physiological Arousal," "Stress, Physiology, and Illness," and "Psychoneuroimmunology." This connection is one of the reasons why stress is covered early in the book. A reviewer recognized a second reason and wrote: "The issue of stress permeates all of the other topics, and it would be useful to have the students read about this first."

- *Part 3.* The third part of the book examines issues involved in enhancing health and preventing illness. Chapters 6, 7, and 8 discuss how health-related behaviors develop and are maintained, how they can affect health, and what can be done to prevent or reduce unhealthful behavior. Chapter 7 gives special attention to the topics of tobacco, alcohol, and drug use and Chapter 8 focuses on nutrition, weight control, exercise, and safety.

- *Part 4.* Chapter 9 describes the kinds of health services that are available and considers why people use, do not use, and delay using these services. This chapter also examines the patient/practitioner relationship and the problem of compliance to medical regimens. Chapter 10 discusses the hospital setting and personnel, how patients react to being hospitalized, and how they cope with stressful medical procedures.

- *Part 5.* Chapters 11 and 12 explore the physical and psychological nature of pain, ways to assess patients' discomfort, and methods for managing and controlling pain.

- *Part 6.* The last two chapters examine the impact of chronic health problems on patients and their families. The health conditions included are separated into two chapters on the basis of their mortality rates. Chapter 13 focuses on several health conditions, such as diabetes and arthritis, that have either very low or moderate rates of mortality and may lead to other health problems or disability. In contrast, Chapter 14 examines the impact of four high-mortality illnesses—heart disease, cancer, stroke, and AIDS; we then consider people's experiences with and reactions to terminal illness and loss.

Optional Organization

The underlying concept used in this overall organization of chapters involves a progression from primary, to secondary, to tertiary prevention and care. Because some instructors might like some *flexibility in the organization of chapters*, the last five chapters were written with this possibility in mind. Chapter 10, Part 5, and Part 6 are written as three independent units that may be covered in any order. Two examples of alternate sequences that would work nicely after Chapter 9 are: (1) Part 5, Part 6, and then Chapter 10; and (2) Part 6, Chapter 10, and then Part 5. Other sequences would work well, too.

LANGUAGE AND STYLE

Because the field of health psychology involves complex issues and technical information, I have made extra efforts to make the material in this book readable and clear without sacrificing content. To accomplish this, I have limited the use of jargon and have sought to write in a concrete and engaging fashion. The gradual progression of concepts, choice of words, and the structure of each sentence were all designed to aid student efforts to master and retain the material. When introducing new terms, they are defined immediately. Many examples and case studies are included to clarify concepts and bring them to life.

LEARNING AIDS

Each chapter begins with a *contents* list, giving students an immediate overview of the progression of major topics and concepts. Then a *prologue* introduces the chapter with (1) a lively and engaging vignette that is relevant to the chapter material and (2) an overview of the basic ideas to be covered. The body of each chapter includes many *figures, tables, and photographs* to clarify concepts or research findings. For example, special figures were created to show how the immune system functions and how gate-control theory explains pain perception. Important terms are printed in *boldface* type, and *italics* are used liberally for other terms and for emphasis.

Each chapter also contains two types of boxed *highlights*, each placed to fit with the surrounding content. One type of highlight is subtitled "On Issues," and focuses on applied, high-interest, and new-frontier topics. Some of these topics are: careers relating to health and psychology, breast and testicular self-examination, the effects of secondhand smoke, acute pain in burn patients, and the complex medical regimens for diabetes. The second type of highlight, subtitled "On Research," gives special attention to research methods in health psychology and to particularly unique or interesting findings. Some of the research highlighted in this way include that of (1) Janice Kiecolt-Glaser and her colleagues on stress and immune function; (2) Neil Weinstein on unrealistic optimism in health beliefs; (3) the MRFIT group on dietary modification; and (4) Edward Blanchard, Frank Andrasik, and their associates on managing headache pain.

At the end of each chapter are a substantial *summary* and a list of *key terms*, which consists of all boldfaced items from the chapter. All of these terms are redefined in the *glossary* at the back of the book.

INSTRUCTOR'S MANUAL

An instructor's manual is available for this text. It contains a test bank and information to help instructors (1) organize and present the subject matter effectively and (2) enrich the classroom experience through activities and discussion. Computer versions of the test bank are available from the publisher.

ACKNOWLEDGMENTS

Writing this book was an enormous task that took two years. During this time, I received a great deal of help and encouragement from a number of people whose contributions I gratefully acknowledge.

My thanks go to my editors at John Wiley & Sons, especially Warren Abraham, who saw merit in my plan and signed the book, and Deborah Moore, who helped establish my writing schedule, oversaw the review process, coordinated the production process, and generated the marketing plan. I also appreciate the fine work of Gilda Stahl, copyediting supervisor, and Nancy Prinz, production supervisor.

The reviewers deserve my heartfelt thanks for their helpful suggestions and favorable comments on the original plan for the book and on the major parts of the manuscript they read. These individuals are:

Tony Albiniak, Coastal Carolina College
Karen Anderson, Santa Clara University
Donald Corriveau, Southeastern Massachussetts University
Craig Holt, SUNY, Albany
Joseph Istvan, Oregon Health Sciences University
Paul Jose, Loyola University
Charles Kaiser, College of Charleston
Jacqueline Lederman, Boston University
Joseph Matarazzo, Oregon Health Sciences University
Karen Matthews, University of Pittsburgh
Barbara Melamed, University of Florida
Nancy Norvell, University of Florida
Ann O'Leary, Rutgers University
Lee Sechrest, University of Arizona
Dale Simmons, Oregon State University
Josephine Wilson, Wittenberg University
Thomas Wrobel, University of Michigan, Flint
Brian Yates, American Unviersity

Most especially, I thank my very good friend and colleague, Jim Armstrong, who read and commented on most of the chapters before they went out for review. He did this solely out of friendship and on the condition that he *not* be paid.

I am also grateful to two assistants, Sean Magill and Debra Williams who photocopied over 1,000 articles. The staff at the Trenton State College library were enormously helpful in acquiring needed materials, and the college granted me a modest amount of released time and a sabbatical leave so that I could complete this work.

Very personal thanks go to the closest people in my life—family, friends, and colleagues—for encouraging and supporting the efforts that went into writing this book and tolerating my preoccupation.

EDWARD P. SARAFINO

to the student

"I wish I could help my father stop smoking," a student in my health psychology course said. Maybe she did help—he quit by the end of the semester. This example points out two things that will probably make health psychology interesting to you: (1) the material is *personally relevant* and (2) many of the things you learn can actually be *applied* in your everyday life. Studying health psychology will also help you answer important questions you may have considered about health and psychology in the past. Does the mind affect our health—and if so, how? What effect does stress have on health and recovery from illness? What can be done to help people lead more healthful lives than they do? Why don't patients follow their doctor's advice, and what can health care workers do to help? What special needs do children have as patients, and how can parents and health care workers address these needs? How can families, friends, and health care workers help patients adjust to disabling or life-threatening health problems?

As these questions indicate, a knowledge of health psychology can be relevant both now and later when you enter *your future career.* This is so whether you are studying to be a psychologist, medical social worker, nurse or physician, physical or occupational therapist, public health worker, or health educator. You will learn in this course that the relationship between the person's health and psychology involves a "two-way street"—each affects the other. Psychological factors go hand-in-hand with medical approaches in preventing and treating illness and in helping patients adjust to the health problems they develop.

THE BOOK

This book was designed for you, the reader. First and foremost, it provides a thorough and up-to-date presentation of the major issues, theories, concepts, and research in health psychology. Throughout the book, the major point of view is "biopsychosocial"—that is, that health and illness result from the interplay of biological, psychological, and social aspects of people's lives. Because integrating these aspects involves complex concepts and technical material, I have made special efforts to write in a straightforward, clear, and engaging fashion.

To help you master the material and remember it longer, the book includes the following learning aids:

- *Chapter Contents and Prologue.* Each chapter begins with a Contents list that outlines the major topics in the order in which they are covered. The Prologue then introduces the chapter with a vignette that is relevant to the material ahead and gives an overview of the basic ideas you will read about.

- *Illustrations.* The many figures, tables, and photographs in each chapter are designed to clarify concepts and research findings and help them "stick" in your mind.

• *Summary and Key Terms.* Each chapter closes with two features: (1) the Summary, which presents the most important ideas covered and (2) the Key Terms — a list of the most important terms in the chapter, arranged in order of their appearance.

• *Glossary.* The Glossary at the back of the book gives definitions of important terms and concepts. It will be useful when you are studying or reading and are not sure of the exact meaning of a term.

STUDY HINTS

There are many ways you can use the features of this book to learn and study well, and you may want to "experiment" to find the best way for you. I will describe one method that works well for many students.

Survey the chapter first. Read the Contents list and browse through the chapter, examining the figures, tables, and photographs. Some students also find it useful to read the Summary first, even though it contains terms they may not yet understand. Then read the Prologue. As you begin each new section of the chapter, look at its title and turn it into a *question.* Thus, the heading early in Chapter 1, "An Illness/Wellness Continuum," might become "What is an illness/wellness continuum?" Doing this helps you focus on your reading. After reading the section, *reflect* on what you have just read. Can you answer the question you asked when you reworded the title?

When you have finished the body of the chapter, *review* what you have read by reading the Summary and trying to define the items in the Key Terms. If there is something you do not understand, look it up in the chapter or Glossary. Lastly, *reread* the chapter at least once, concentrating on the important concepts or ideas. You may find it helpful to underline or highlight selected material now that you have a good idea of what is important. If your exam will consist of "objective" questions, such as multiple choice, using this approach intensively should be effective. If your exam will have essay items, you will probably find it helpful to develop a list of likely questions and write an outline or a complete answer for each one.

I hope that you enjoy this book, that you learn a great deal from it, and that you will share my enthusiasm and fascination for health psychology by the time you finish the course.

EDWARD P. SARAFINO

contents

part I

AN INTRODUCTION: BASIC ISSUES AND PROCESSES

1

AN OVERVIEW OF PSYCHOLOGY AND HEALTH

PROLOGUE

Ten-year-old Anita has just arrived at a community summer recreation program and sees many unfamiliar children there. Most of them are near her age, and they vary in size and shape—tall, short, fat, and skinny. Anita is 54 inches tall, which is average for her age. But at 108 pounds, she is heavier than 90% of the children her age and height. A neighbor says that Anita "inherited a glandular problem, and you can't do anything about it," and another neighbor says Anita will lose weight easily "in a couple of years when she starts getting interested in boys." Are they right?

Anita's parents are concerned about her weight because they know that overweight people often have social problems and face special health risks, particularly for high blood pressure and heart disease. But her parents are not sure why she is so heavy or how to help her. Although her father is a bit overweight, her mother is very heavy—she has always been heavy and did not lose weight when she became interested in boys. This could support the idea of an inherited cause of her being overweight. On the other hand, they know that Anita eats a lot of fattening foods and gets very little exercise, a combination that often causes weight gains. As part of their effort to change these two behaviors, they encouraged her to join the recreation program, where she will be involved in many physical activities.

This story about Anita illustrates important issues that relate to health. For instance, being overweight is associated with the development of specific health problems and may affect the individual's social relations. Also, weight problems can result from a person's inheritance and his or her behavior. In this book, we will examine the relationships between health and a wide variety of biological, psychological, and social factors in people's lives.

This chapter introduces a relatively new and very exciting field of study called *health psychology.* We look at its scope, its history, its research methods, and how it draws upon and supports other sciences. As we study these topics, you will begin to see how health psychologists would answer such questions as: Does the mind affect our health? What role does the cultural background of individuals play in their health? How does the age of a person affect how he or she deals with issues of health and illness? But first let's begin with a definition of health.

WHAT IS HEALTH?

You know what health is, don't you? How would you define it? You would probably mention something about health being a state of feeling well and not being sick. We commonly think about health in terms of an absence of (1) *signs* that the body is not functioning properly, such as measured high blood pressure, or (2) *symptoms* of disease or injury, such as pain or nausea (Birren & Zarit, 1985; Thoresen, 1984). Dictionaries define health in this way, too. But there is a problem with this definition of health. Let's see why.

An Illness/Wellness Continuum

Consider Anita, the overweight girl in the opening story. You have probably heard people say, "It's not healthy to be overweight." Is Anita healthy? What about someone whose lungs are being damaged from smoking cigarettes or whose arteries are becoming clogged from eating foods that are high in saturated fats? Or someone who has begun to develop a cancerous tumor, but feels fine and the tumor has not yet been detected? Are they healthy? We probably would say that are not "sick"—they are just not *as* healthy as they would be if the unhealthful conditions did not exist.

What this means is that health and sickness are not entirely separate concepts—they overlap. There are degrees of wellness and of illness. Aaron Antonovsky (1979, 1987) has suggested that we consider these concepts as ends of a continuum, noting that "We are all terminal cases. And we all are, so long as there is a breath of life in us, in some measure healthy" (1987, p. 3). He also proposed that we revise our focus, giving more attention to what enables people to stay well than to what causes people to become ill. Figure 1.1 presents a model of an **illness/wellness continuum**, with premature death at one end and a high level of wellness at the other.

We will use the term **health** to mean a positive state of physical, mental, and social well-being—not simply the absence of injury or disease—that varies over time along a continuum. At the wellness end of the continuum, health is the dominant state. At the other end of the continuum is disease or illness, which involves destructive processes that lead to characteristic signs, symptoms, or disabilities.

Illness Today and in the Past

People in the United States live longer, on the average, than they did in the past, and they suffer from a different pattern of illnesses. During the seventeenth, eighteenth, and nineteenth centuries, people in North America suffered and died chiefly from two types of illness: dietary and infectious (Grob, 1983). **Dietary diseases** result from malnutrition—for example, beriberi is caused by a lack of vitamin B_1 and is characterized by anemia, paralysis, and wasting away. **Infectious diseases** are acute illnesses caused by harmful matter or microorganisms, such as bacteria or viruses, in the body.

From the early colonial days in America through the eighteenth century, colonists experienced periodic epidemics of many infectious diseases, especially smallpox, diphtheria, yellow fever, measles, and influenza. It was not unusual for hundreds, and sometimes thousands, of people to die in a single epidemic. Children were particularly hard hit. Two other infectious diseases, malaria and dysentery, were widespread and presented an even greater threat. Although these two diseases generally did not kill people directly, they weakened their victims and reduced the ability to resist other fatal diseases. Most, if not all, of these diseases did not exist in North America before the European settlers arrived—they brought the infections with them. As a result, the death toll in the Native American population was especially high because they had never been exposed to these new microorganisms and lacked the natural immunity that our bodies develop after lengthy exposure to most diseases (Grob, 1983).

In the nineteenth century, infectious diseases were still the greatest threat to the health of Americans. The illnesses of the colonial era continued to claim many lives, but new dis-

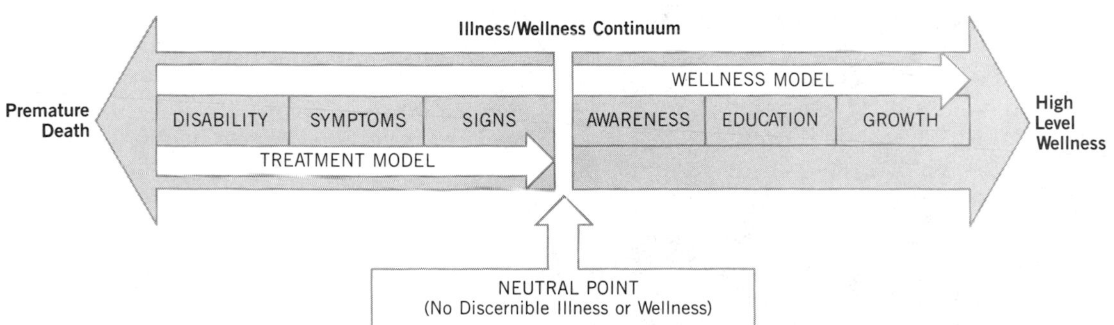

FIGURE 1.1 Moving from the center to the left shows a progressively worsening state of health. Moving to the right of center indicates increasing levels of health and well-being. The treatment model can bring you to the neutral point, where the symptoms of disease have been alleviated. The wellness model, which can be utilized at any point, directs you beyond neutral, and encourages you to move as far to the right as possible. If you are ill, then treatment is important, but don't stop there. (Ryan & Travis, 1981, p. 2.)

eases began to appear. The most significant of these was tuberculosis — or "consumption," as it was often called. In 1842, for example, consumption was listed as the cause for 22% of all deaths in the state of Massachusetts (Grob, 1983). But by the end of the nineteenth century, deaths from infectious diseases had decreased sharply. For instance, the death rate from tuberculosis declined by about 60% in a 25-year period around the turn of the century.

Did this decrease result mostly from advances in medical treatment? No, it did not. Although medical advances helped to some degree, the decrease occurred long before effective vaccines and medications were introduced. This was the case for most of the major diseases we've discussed, including tuberculosis, diphtheria, measles, and influenza (Grob, 1983; Leventhal, Prohaska, & Hirschman, 1985). It appears that the decline resulted chiefly from *preventive* measures — such as improved personal hygiene, greater resistance to diseases owing to better nutrition, and public health innovations, such as building water purification and sewage treatment facilities. Many people had become concerned about their health and began to heed the advice of health reformers like William Alcott, an advocate of moderation in diet and sexual behavior (Leventhal, Prohaska, & Hirschman, 1985). Fewer deaths occurred because fewer people contracted the diseases.

The twentieth century has seen great changes in the patterns of illness affecting people in the United States. The death rate from life-threatening infectious diseases has continued to decline as a result of advances in preventive measures and in medical care. At the same time, the average life expectancy of people has increased dramatically. At the turn of the century, the life expectancy of babies at birth was about 49 years; today it is almost 75 years (USDHHS, 1987b). Figure 1.2 shows this change and indicates an important reason for

Epidemics of deadly infectious diseases were common throughout the world before the twentieth century. There were no effective methods for prevention or treatment of the plague, for instance, which is the disease illustrated in this engraving.

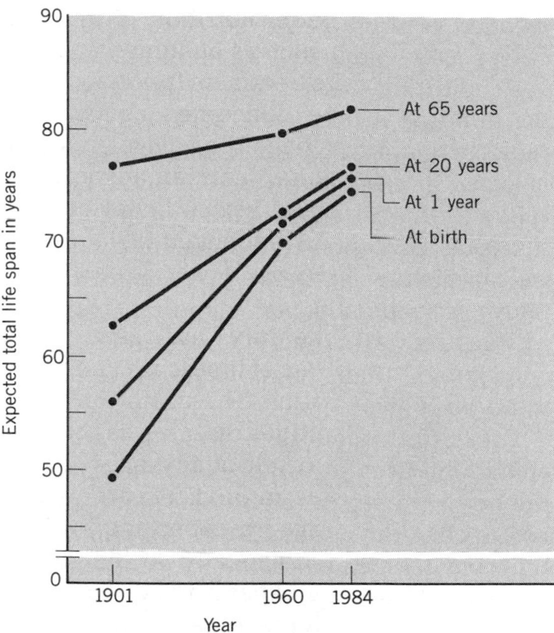

FIGURE 1.2 Expected total life span for people in the United States at birth and at 1 year, 20 years, and 65 years of age in the years 1900–1902, 1959–1961, and 1984. (Data from USDHHS, 1987b, p. 2.)

it: the death rate among children was very high many years ago. Babies who had survived their first year in 1900 could be expected to live to about 56 years of age. Surviving that first year added seven years to their expected total life span. Moreover, people in 1900 who had reached the age of 20 years could expect to live to almost 63 years of age. Today the death rate for children is much lower and the difference in the expected total life span for newborns and 20-year-olds is less than two years.

Death is still inevitable, of course, but people die at later ages now and from different causes. The main health problems and causes of death in the United States today are **chronic diseases** — that is, degenerative illnesses that develop or persist over a long period of time (Tapp & Warner, 1985). About two-thirds of all deaths in the United States are caused by three chronic diseases: heart disease, cancer, and stroke (Matarazzo, 1984). These diseases are not "new," but they were responsible for a much smaller proportion of deaths before the twentieth century. Why? For one thing, the growth of industrialization increased people's exposure to harmful chemicals. In addition: (1) a smaller proportion of the population survived to old age then and (2) chronic diseases are more likely to afflict the elderly than younger individuals. Thus, a major reason for the current prominence of chronic diseases is that larger numbers of people are living long enough to become victims of these health problems (USDHHS, 1982).

What are the main causes of death in childhood and adolescence today? The leading cause, by far, is not an illness — but death from accidental injury (Haggerty, 1986). Accidents account for about half of these deaths, and the most frequent types of accidental death involve automobiles (National Safety Council, 1983). In childhood, the next two most frequent causes of death are cancer and birth defects; in adolescence, they are homicide and suicide (Haggerty, 1986). Clearly, the role of disease in death is very different at the two ends of the life span.

VIEWPOINTS FROM HISTORY: PHYSIOLOGY, DISEASE PROCESSES, AND THE MIND

Is illness a purely physical condition? Does the mind play a role in becoming ill and getting well? People have wondered about these questions for thousands of years, and the answers they arrived at have changed over time.

Early Cultures

Although we do not know for certain, it appears that the best educated people thousands of years ago believed physical and mental illness were caused by mystical forces, such as evil spirits (Stone, 1979). Why do we think this? Researchers found ancient skulls in several areas of the world with dime-size circular holes in them that could not have been battle wounds. These holes were probably made by using

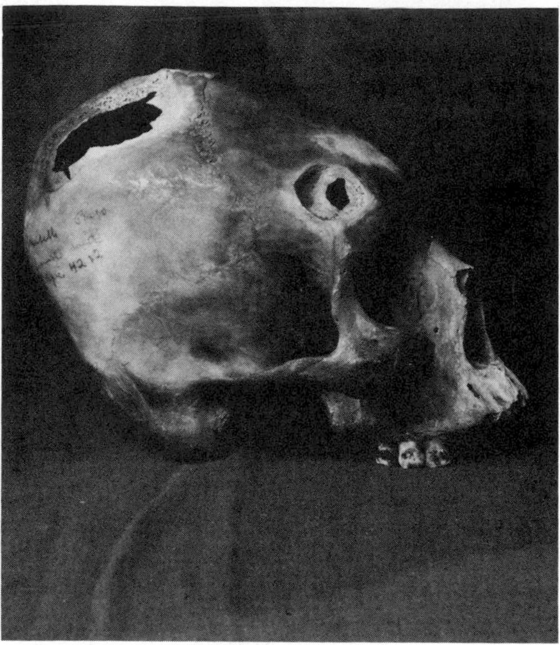

A skull with a hole probably produced by trephination. The healing of the bone suggests that the person survived the injury.

sharp stone tools in a procedure called *trephination.* This procedure was done presumably for superstitious reasons—for instance, to allow illness-causing demons to leave the head. Unfortunately, we can only speculate about the reasons for these holes because there are no written records from those times.

Ancient Greece and Rome

The philosophers of ancient Greece produced the earliest written ideas about physiology, disease processes, and the mind in the years between 500 and 300 B.C. Hippocrates, often called "the father of medicine," developed an explanation of why people get sick called the *humoral theory.* According to this theory, the body contains four fluids called *humors* (in biology, the term humor refers to any plant or animal fluid). When the mixture of these humors is harmonious or balanced, we are in a state of health. Disease occurs when the mixture is faulty (Stone, 1979). Hippocrates recommended eating a good diet and avoiding excesses to help achieve humoral balance.

People today often speak about the body and the mind as if they were separate. The *body* refers to our physical being, including our skin, muscles, bones, heart, and brain. The *mind* refers to an abstract process that includes our thoughts, perceptions, and feelings. Although we can distinguish between the mind and the body conceptually, an important issue is whether they also function independently. The question of their relationship is called the **mind/body problem**.

Greek philosophers, especially Plato, were among the first to propose that the mind and the body are separate entities (Marx & Hillix, 1963; Schneider & Tarshis, 1975). This view is reflected in the humoral theory: people get sick because of an imbalance in body fluids. The mind was considered to have little or no relationship to the body and its state of health. This remained the dominant view of writers and philosophers for more than a thousand years.

Galen was a famous and highly respected physician and writer of the second century A.D. who was born in Greece and practiced in Rome. Although he believed generally in the humoral theory and the mind/body split, he made many innovations. For example, he "dissected animals of many species (but probably never a human), and made important discoveries about the brain, circulatory system, and kidneys" (Stone, 1979, p. 4). From this work, he became aware that illnesses can be localized, with pathology in specific parts of the body, and that different diseases have different effects. These ideas became widely accepted.

The Middle Ages

After the collapse of the Roman Empire in the fifth century, much of the Western world was in disarray. The advancement of knowledge and culture declined sharply and remained at a low level during the Middle Ages, which lasted almost a thousand years. Galen's views dominated ideas about physiology and disease processes for most of this time.

The influence of the Church on the development of knowledge during the Middle Ages was enormous. According to historians, the human being

> was regarded as a creature with a soul, possessed of a free will which set him apart from ordinary natural laws, subject only to his own willfulness and perhaps the will of God. Such a creature, being free-willed, could not be an object of scientific investigation. Even the body of man was regarded as sacrosanct, and dissection was dangerous for the dissector. These strictures against observation hindered the development of anatomy and medicine for centuries. (Marx & Hillix, 1963, p. 24)

The prohibition against dissection extended to animals as well, since they were thought to have souls, too.

People's ideas about the cause of illness took on pronounced religious overtones, and the belief in demonology became strong again (Sarason & Sarason, 1984). Sickness was seen as God's punishment for doing evil things. As a result, the Church came to control the practice of medicine and priests became increasingly involved in treating the ill, often by torturing the body to drive out evil spirits.

It was not until the thirteenth century that new ideas about the mind/body problem began to emerge. The Italian philosopher St. Thomas Aquinas rejected the view that the mind and body are separate—he saw them as and interrelated unit that forms the whole person (Leahey, 1987). Although his position did not have as great an impact as others had had, it renewed interest in the issue and influenced later philosophers.

The Renaissance and After

The word *renaissance* means rebirth—a fitting name for the fourteenth and fifteenth centuries. During this period in history, Europe saw a rebirth in inquiry, culture, and politics. Scholars became more "human-centered" than "God-centered" in their search for truth and "believed that truth can be seen in many ways, from many individual perspectives" (Leahey, 1987, p. 80). These ideas set the stage for important changes in philosophy once the scientific revolution began after 1600.

The seventeenth-century French philosopher and mathematician René Descartes probably had the greatest influence on scientific thought of any philosopher in history (Schneider & Tarshis, 1975). Like the Greeks, he regarded the mind and body as separate entities, but he introduced three important innovations. First, he conceived of the body as a machine and described the mechanics of how action and sensation occurred. For example, Figure 1.3 shows his concept of how we experience pain. Second, he proposed that the mind and body, although separate, could *communicate* through the pineal gland, an organ in the

FIGURE 1.3 Descartes' concept of the pain pathway. According to Descartes: "If for example fire (*A*) comes near the foot (*B*), the minute particles of this fire, which as you know move with great velocity, have the power to set in motion the spot of the skin of the foot which they touch, and by this means pulling upon the delicate thread *CC*, which is attached to the spot of the skin, they open up at the same instant the pore, *d.e.*, against which the delicate thread ends, just as by pulling at one end of a rope one makes to strike at the same instant a bell which hangs at the other end." (Melzack & Wall, 1965, Figure 1.)

brain (Leahey, 1987). Third, he believed that animals have no soul and that the soul in humans leaves the body at death (Marx & Hillix, 1963). Thus, dissection could be an acceptable method of study—a point the Church was now ready to concede (Engel, 1977).

In the eighteenth and nineteenth centuries, knowledge in science and medicine grew quickly, helped greatly by the development of the microscope and the use of dissection in autopsies. Once scientists learned the basics of how the body functioned and discovered that microorganisms cause certain diseases, they were able to reject the humoral theory of illness and propose new theories. The field of surgery flourished after antiseptic techniques and anesthesia were introduced in the mid-nineteenth century (Stone, 1979). Before that time, hospitals were "notorious places, more likely to spread diseases than cure them" (Easterbrook, 1987, p.42). Soon the reputation of physicians and hospitals began to improve, and people's trust in the ability of doctors to heal increased.

These advances, coupled with the continuing belief that the mind and body are separate, laid the foundation for a new approach, or "model," for conceptualizing health and illness. This approach—called the **biomedical model**—proposes that all diseases or physical disorders can be explained by disturbances in physiological processes, which result from injury, biochemical imbalances, bacterial or viral infection, and the like (Engel, 1977; Leventhal, Prohaska, & Hirschman, 1985). The biomedical model assumes that disease is an affliction of the body and is separate from the psychological and social processes of the mind. This viewpoint became widely accepted during the nineteenth and twentieth centuries and still represents the dominant view in medicine today.

SEEING A NEED: PSYCHOLOGY'S ROLE IN HEALTH

The biomedical model has been very useful. Using it as their guide, researchers have made enormous achievements. They conquered many infectious diseases, such as polio and measles, through the development of vaccines. They also developed antibiotics, which made it possible to cure illnesses caused by bacterial infection (Easterbrook, 1987; Leventhal, Prohaska, & Hirschman, 1985). Does the biomedical model need improvement? Yes. Let's see why.

Problems in the Health Care System

Scarcely a week goes by when we don't hear through the mass media that health care costs are rising rapidly, particularly for prescription drugs and for hospital and nursing home care. These reports often use the phrase "escalating out of control." Between 1950 and 1978, there was a tenfold increase in the amount of money spent per capita on health care in the United States. The burden of health costs on the economy increased sharply during that same period: health care spending amounted to 4.5% of the gross national product in 1950, and over 9% in 1978 (Matarazzo, 1982). Since the late 1970s, these costs have continued to soar, rising substantially faster than the overall rate of inflation. By 1985, health care spending doubled to over $1,700 per capita and equaled 10.7% of the gross national product (Gaul, 1986). At a time when these costs are rising so rapidly, we need to consider new approaches for improving people's health.

We saw earlier that the patterns of illness affecting people have changed. The main health problems are no longer infectious diseases, they are chronic diseases. Although a great deal of progress is being made in understanding the causes of chronic diseases, improvements in techniques for treating them have been modest. For example, the General Accounting Office reported in 1987 that the gains in survival rate among cancer patients since 1950 resulted not so much from medical techniques as from other factors, especially earlier detection of the disease (Boffey, 1987).

Why does detection occur earlier today? Part of the reason is that diagnostic methods and technology have improved. But another part of the reason is that *people* have changed

—they are more aware of signs and symptoms of illness, more motivated to take care of their health, and better able to afford visits to physicians. These latter factors are clearly important. But they relate to psychological and social aspects of *the person*, and the person as a unique individual is not included in the biomedical model (Engel, 1977, 1980).

"The Person" in Health and Illness

Have you ever noticed how some people are "always sick"—they get illnesses more frequently than most people do and get well more slowly? These differences between people can result from biomedical sources, such as variations in physiological processes and exposure to harmful microorganisms. But psychological and social factors also play a role. Let's look briefly at two of these factors: the lifestyle and personality of the person.

Lifestyle and Illness

Earlier we saw that the occurrence of infectious diseases declined sharply in the late nineteenth century chiefly because of such preventive measures as improving nutrition and personal hygiene. These measures involved changes in people's lifestyles and behavior, such as in preparing and eating better balanced meals. The principal health problems today are chronic diseases. These, too, can often be prevented through people's lifestyles. How?

It is well known today, for example, that people who smoke cigarettes face a much higher risk of developing cancer and other illnesses than nonsmokers do. Characteristics or conditions that are associated with the development of a disease or injury are called **risk factors** for that heath problem. Other risk factors for cancer include eating diets high in saturated fat and having a family history of the disease. People who "do more" or "have more" of these characteristics or conditions are more likely to contract cancer than people who "do less" or "have less" of these factors. Keep in mind that a risk factor is *associated* with a health problem—it does not necessarily *cause* the problem. For example, being poor is a risk factor for cancer (Levy, 1985), but it does not cause the disease—at least, not directly.

Many risk factors are behaviors or are produced by behavior, such as smoking and unhealthful diets. Some behavioral risk factors associated with the five leading causes of death are:

1. *Heart disease*—smoking, high serum cholesterol, lack of exercise, high blood pressure, and stress
2. *Cancer (malignant neoplasms)*—smoking, high alcohol use, and diet.
3. *Stroke*—smoking, high serum cholesterol, high blood pressure, and stress.
4. *Accidents (including motor vehicle)*—alcohol use, drug abuse, driving vehicles too fast, and not using seat belts.
5. *Influenza and pneumonia*—smoking and failing to get vaccinated. (Source: Matarazzo, 1984)

Many of the people who are the victims of these illnesses and accidents live for at least a short while and either recover or eventually succumb. Part of today's high medical costs can be attributed to a failure in personal responsibility by those victims who had lifestyles that contributed to their health problems. Often society, not the individual, bears the burden of these costs through public and private health insurance programs (Birren & Zarit, 1985; Matarazzo, 1984). Because many of these health problems were preventable, a physician named John Knowles wrote:

> Over 99 percent of us are born healthy and made sick as a result of personal misbehavior and environmental conditions. The solution to the problems of ill health in modern American society involves individual responsibility, in the first instance, and social responsibility through public legislative and private volunteer efforts, in the second instance. (1977, p. 58)

Knowles proposed that people have both a moral obligation and a public duty to practice healthful lifestyles so as not to add to society's burden. He also described how individuals

HIGHLIGHT 1A: On Research
Health and Lifestyles

In 1965, Nedra Belloc and Lester Breslow began a project to study the importance of personal lifestyles on people's health. The researchers surveyed nearly 7,000 adults who ranged in age from about 20 to over 75, and asked them two sets of questions. One set asked about the health of these people over the past 12 months—for instance, whether illness had prevented them from working for a long time, forced them to cut down on other activities, impaired their continued activities, and reduced their energy level. The second set of questions asked about their health practices regarding seven issues: sleeping, eating breakfast, eating between meals, maintaining an appropriate weight, smoking cigarettes, drinking alcohol, and getting physical activity.

Were these lifestyle factors important? The survey revealed that the physical health of these people was strongly related to the following health practices:

1. Sleeping seven to eight hours a day
2. Eating breakfast almost every day
3. Never or only occasionally eating between meals
4. Being at or near the appropriate weight for their height
5. Never smoking cigarettes
6. Never or moderately drinking alcohol
7. Regularly getting physical activity

When the researchers compared the data for subjects in different age groups, they found that at each age health was typically better as the number of healthful practices increased. The impact of these health practices is suggested by the finding that the health of those who "reported following all seven good health practices was consistently about the same as those 30 years younger who followed few or none of these practices" (Belloc & Breslow, 1972, p. 419).

Were these health practices important in the future health of these people? Very much so. Breslow (1983) has described later studies of the same group of subjects. One study determined which people had died in the nine and a half years after the original survey. These data were then separated according to the age, sex, and number of healthful behaviors the people reported practicing in the original survey. Figure 1A.1 presents the results of this analysis for the men. The important finding was that the percentage dying generally decreased with increases in the number of healthful behaviors practiced, and this impact was greater for older people than for younger ones. The results for the female subjects were similar, but the impact of these health practices was not as strong.

These findings show that health and survival are strongly influenced by people's lifestyles. Practicing healthful behaviors can substantially reduce people's risk of illness and early death. Lifestyle is more critical for the health of men than women, and is particularly important as individuals get older.

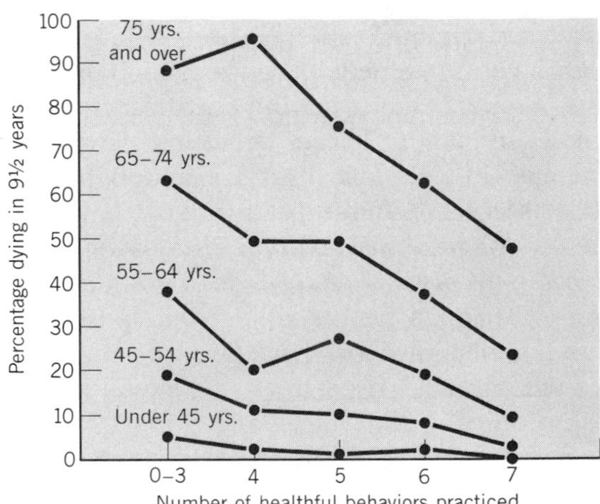

FIGURE 1A.1 Percentage of male adults who died within $9\frac{1}{2}$ years as a function of the number of healthful behaviors they reported practicing and of their ages (at the start of the study, in 1965). The findings for women were similar, but the decreases in deaths associated with increasing numbers of healthful behaviors were not as sharp. (Data from Breslow, 1983, Table 3.6.)

could reduce this burden by making several changes in their behavior, such as driving at slower speeds and eating low-cholesterol diets.

"Why don't people do what's good for them?"—we've all heard that question before. There's no simple answer—there are many reasons. One reason is that less-healthful behaviors often bring immediate pleasure, as when the person has a "good tasting" cigarette or ice cream. Long-range negative consequences seem remote, both in time and in likelihood. Another reason is that people sometimes feel social pressures to engage in unhealthful behavior, as when an adolescent begins to use alcohol or drugs. Also, some behaviors can become very strong habits—perhaps involving a physical addiction or psychological dependency, as happens with drugs and cigarettes—and quitting is very difficult. Lastly, sometimes people are simply not aware of the danger or how to change their behavior. As psychologist Carl Thoresen (1984, p. 300) has pointed out, "people need to be taught how to be more caring and more responsible for their own health and well-being, especially when the social environment commonly promotes irresponsible or nonhealthy behavior."

Personality and Illness

Do you believe, as many do, that people with ulcers tend to be worriers or "workaholics"? Or that people who suffer from migraine headaches are highly anxious? If you do, then you believe there is a link between personality and illness. Is this belief correct?

Researchers have found evidence for the view that personality plays a causal role in illness. For instance, people whose personalities include high levels of anxiety, depression, and anger/hostility seem to be "disease-prone" for developing a variety of illnesses, particularly heart disease (Friedman & Booth-Kewley, 1987). The three emotions involved in the disease-prone personality are reactions that often occur when people experience stress, such as when they have more work to do than they think they can finish or when a tragedy happens.

People differ in the way they deal with stressful situations. Many people approach these situations with relatively positive emotions. Their outlook is more optimistic than pessimistic, more hopeful than desperate. These people are not only less likely to become ill than are people with disease-prone personalities, but when they do, they tend to recover more quickly (Reker & Wong, 1985). A dramatic and well-known anecdotal example of the role of this optimistic and hopeful outlook is the case of Norman Cousins, the former editor of *Saturday Review*, who developed an "incurable" and usually fatal illness. His reaction to the prognosis was unusual: he decided he should not believe his doctors' "pronouncement of doom." Instead, he decided to supplement his medical treatment with high doses of vitamin C and lots of laughter, which he got by watching comic films like those of Groucho Marx and Laurel and Hardy. As his condition began to improve, he came to believe he was recovering because his optimism enabled him to mobilize his body's resources to fight the disease (Cousins, 1979).

The link between personality and illness is not a one-way street: illness can affect one's personality, too. People who suffer from illness and disability often experience feelings of anxiety, depression, anger, and hopelessness. But as psychologists Irwin and Barbara Sarason have pointed out:

> A physical illness does not necessarily have to be catastrophic to exert a psychological impact. Anyone who has had the flu, has a sprained ankle, or has had a toothache knows how much psychological damage these relatively minor problems can cause. Of course, the more serious the physical disorder, the greater the likelihood that it will significantly affect a person's thoughts and feelings. These psychological changes compound the detrimental effects of the person's physical condition. (1984, p. 157)

People who are ill need to overcome their negative thoughts and feelings in order to speed their recovery.

Our glimpse at the relationships of the person's lifestyle and personality in illness demonstrates why it is important to consider psychological and social factors in health and illness. Next we will see how this recognition came about.

How the Role of Psychology Emerged

The idea that medicine and psychology are somehow connected has a long history, dating back at least to ancient Greece. It became somewhat more formalized early in the twentieth century in the work of Sigmund Freud, who was trained as a physician. He noticed that some patients showed symptoms of physical illness without any organic disorder. Consistent with his psychoanalytic theory, Freud believed that these symptoms were "converted" from unconscious emotional conflicts (Alexander, 1950; Coleman, 1976). He called this condition *conversion hysteria.*

What symptoms do patients with conversion hysteria show? The symptoms can include paralysis, deafness, blindness, and the loss of sensation in part of the body, such as the hand. This last symptom is called *glove anesthesia* because only the hand has no feeling. Because the symptoms of glove anesthesia are not consistent with the nerve pathways in the arm, they cannot have an organic cause (Sarason & Sarason, 1984). Conversion hysteria was once a fairly common condition. It occurs infrequently today, probably because many people realize that medical tests can generally determine if an organic disorder exists (Coleman, 1976).

The need to understand conditions such as conversion hysteria led some researchers in the 1930s to study the interplay between emotional life and bodily processes (Alexander, 1939). The field called **psychosomatic medicine** emerged in association with the National Research Council, which began publishing the journal *Psychosomatic Medicine* in 1939. Its founders were primarily researchers trained in medicine, and their leaders included the psychoanalyst Franz Alexander and the psychiatrist Flanders Dunbar. Four years later the field was organized as a society, which is now called the American Psychosomatic Society.

During the society's first 25 years or so, research in psychosomatic medicine focused on psychoanalytic interpretations for a specific set of health problems, including ulcers, high blood pressure, asthma, migraine headaches, and rheumatoid arthritis. We can see this approach in the following case study:

> A 23-year-old university student had his first hemorrhage from a duodenal ulcer when he was eighteen years old. This was preceded by only a short period of stomach distress. When he came for psychoanalytic treatment five years later he had an active ulcer with typical symptoms and X-ray findings. The patient's most conspicuous personality trait was his extreme casualness, which reflected his marked control over the display of emotion. . . . His casualness and show of imperturbable security were but a defense against insecurity and dependence, which became overwhelming under his mother's exaggerated expectations. This conflict showed itself conspicuously in his relationship to women; he did not allow himself to become emotionally involved, had only casual sexual relationships, and terminated each affair as soon as the woman showed some personal interest in him. . . . He succeeded gradually [in therapy] in renouncing more and more of his excessive dependency and in accepting a more mature attitude. With these internal developments a profound change took place in his relationship to women. He fell in love with a young woman, and for the first time in his life a prolonged happy sexual affair ensued. He later married her. At the same time his stomach complaints diminished and he was able to live on a normal diet. (Alexander, 1950, pp. 113–114)

During the 1960s, psychosomatic medicine began to focus on new approaches and theories (Totman, 1982). It is currently a broader field, concerned with the interrelationships between psychological and social factors, biological and physiological functions, and the development and course of illness (Lipowski, 1986).

A new field was founded in the early 1970s to study the role of psychology in illness. This field, called **behavioral medicine**, initially grew out of the perspective in psychology called *behaviorism*, which focused on the learning of behavior through classical and operant conditioning. Behaviorism was in its heyday at this time, and conditioning methods had shown a good deal of success as therapeutic approaches in helping people modify problem *behaviors*, such as overeating, and *emotions*, such as anxiety and fear (Rimm & Masters, 1979). By this time, physiological psychologists had clearly demonstrated that psychological events—particularly emotions—influence bodily functions, such as blood pressure. Also, psychologist Neal Miller and his colleagues had demonstrated that physiological functions such as heart rate and intestinal contractions could be modified in animals through operant conditioning (DiCara & Miller, 1968; Miller & Banuazizi, 1968; Miller & DiCara, 1967). Researchers subsequently showed that humans often can learn to control virtually any physiological system if they are given *feedback* as to what the system is doing (Miller, 1978).

Why were these findings important? They revealed that the link between the mind and the body is more direct and pervasive than was previously thought. Soon they led to an important therapeutic technique called *biofeedback*, whereby a person's physiological processes, such as blood pressure, are monitored by the person so that he or she can gain voluntary control over these processes through operant conditioning. Biofeedback appears to be useful in treating a variety of health problems, including high blood pressure and headaches (Rimm & Masters, 1979).

In the late 1970s the field of behavioral medicine was formally launched in association with the National Academy of Sciences. The Academy of Behavioral Medicine Research was formed and the *Journal of Behavioral Medicine* was established for this new field. A separate Society of Behavioral Medicine was also founded. An important characteristic of this field is that its membership is interdisciplinary—they come from a wide variety of fields, including psychology, sociology, and various areas of medicine. As a result, the society strives to pool the talents and perspectives of this diverse membership in a "joint exploration targeted on health issues of mutual concern" (Gentry, 1984). These health issues involve all aspects of illness—prevention, diagnosis, treatment, and rehabilitation.

A third field also emerged in the late 1970s, but this one is within the discipline of psychology. It is called **health psychology**. The American Psychological Association has a large number of divisions, or subfields; the Division of Health Psychology was introduced in 1978. The journal *Health Psychology* began publication four years later as the official journal of this division. Joseph Matarazzo, the first president of the Division, has proposed the following definition of the field:

> *Health psychology* is the aggregate of the specific educational, scientific, and professional contributions of the discipline of psychology to the promotion and maintenance of health, the prevention and treatment of illness, the identification of etiologic and diagnostic correlates of health, illness, and related dysfunction, and to the analysis and improvement of the health care system and health policy formation. (1982, p. 4)

The last part of this definition describes four goals for health psychology. Let's look at some of the ways psychologists can contribute to these goals.

The first goal is to promote and maintain health. Psychologists study such topics as why people do and do not smoke cigarettes, use safety belts in cars, drink alcohol, and eat particular diets. As a result, health psychologists can help in the design of school health education programs and media campaigns to encourage healthful lifestyles and behaviors.

The second goal involves the prevention and treatment of illness. Psychological principles have been applied effectively in preventing illness, such as in reducing high blood pressure and, therefore, the risk of heart disease and stroke. For those people who become seriously ill, psychologists with clinical training can help them adjust to their current condition, rehabilitation program, and future prospects, such as reduced work or sexual activity.

The third goal focuses on the causes ("etiologic correlates") and detection of illness. Psychologists study the causes of disease; the studies we saw earlier showing the importance of personality factors in the development of illness are examples of this work. Psychologists also study physiological and perceptual processes. This knowledge has been applied to the diagnosis of problems in people's vision and hearing, for example.

The last goal is to improve the health care system and health policy. Psychologists contribute toward this goal by studying how patients are affected by characteristics or functions of hospitals, nursing homes, medical personnel, and medical costs. With the resulting knowledge, they can make recommendations for improvement, suggesting ways to help physicians and nurses become more sensitive and responsive to the needs of patients and to make the system more accessible to individuals who fail to seek treatment.

By now you are probably wondering, "Why are there three fields—aren't they basically the same?" In a sense you're right. The goals of the three fields are very similar, and the overlap in the knowledge used in these fields is extensive. Perhaps the main distinction between them is the degree to which they are interdisciplinary. Behavioral medicine has the most diverse membership, drawing knowledge directly from a wide variety of disciplines in their research. Psychosomatic medicine continues to be closely allied with medical disciplines, especially psychiatry. And health psychology is a subfield of psychology—virtually all of its members are psychologists. As a result, health psychologists are able to draw directly on the many other subfields within the discipline: clinical, developmental, experimental, physiological, and social psychology.

It is important to realize also that these three fields are separate mainly in an organizational sense. Although they have slightly different perspectives, all three fields share the view that health and illness result from the interplay of biological, psychological, and social forces. As this suggests, all three fields are interested in knowledge from a wide variety of disciplines and are engaged in a cooperative effort to enhance wellness and reduce illness. Even though the focus of this book is mainly on health psychology, we will keep in mind the overlap with and contributions of the fields of psychosomatic medicine and behavioral medicine.

CURRENT PERSPECTIVES ON HEALTH AND ILLNESS

Once we add the person to the biomedical model, we have a different and broader picture of how health and illness come about. This new perspective involves the interplay of biological, psychological, and social aspects of the person's life. As a result, this perspective is called the **biopsychosocial model** (Engle, 1977, 1980; Schwartz, 1982).

The Biopsychosocial Perspective

We saw elements of the biopsychosocial perspective in the story about the overweight girl named Anita at the beginning of the chapter. A possible biological contribution to her condition might have been her inheritance, since her mother is overweight and was heavy as a child. Psychological factors were clearly important, as we saw in Anita's behavior—she eats too much fattening food and gets little exercise. And, although we did not see how social factors played a role in her becoming overweight, they were probably there—perhaps, for example, in the dietary and exercise habits she observed in her mother's behavior. But we did see social factors as a reaction to her condition in her parents' concern and their getting her to join the recreation program. Let's look at the elements of the biopsychosocial model in more detail.

The Role of Biological Factors

What is included in the term *biological factors*? This term includes the genetic materials and processes by which we inherit characteristics from our parents. It also includes aspects of the person's physiological functioning — for example, whether the body (1) contains structural defects, such as a malformed heart valve or some damage in the brain, that impair the operation of these organs; (2) responds effectively in protecting itself, such as by fighting infection; and (3) "overreacts" sometimes in the protective function, as happens in many allergic reactions to harmless substances, such as pollen or dust.

The body is an enormously complex system. It is made up of organs, which are composed of tissues, which in turn consist of cells, molecules, and atoms. The efficient, effective, and healthful functioning of this system depends on the way these components operate and interact with each other.

The Role of Psychological Factors

When we discussed the role of lifestyle and personality in health and illness earlier, we were describing behavior and mental processes, in other words, psychological factors. Behavior and mental processes are the focus of psychology, and they involve *cognition, emotion*, and *motivation*.

Cognition is a mental activity that encompasses perceiving, learning, remembering, thinking, interpreting, believing, and problem solving. How do these cognitive factors affect health and illness? Suppose, for instance, you strongly believed "Life is not worth living without the things I enjoy." If you enjoyed smoking cigarettes, would you quit to reduce your risk of getting cancer or heart disease? Probably not. Or, suppose you developed a pain in your abdomen and you remembered having had a similar symptom in the past that disappeared in a couple of days. Would you seek treatment? Again, probably not. These examples are just two of the countless ways cognition plays a role in health and illness.

Emotion is a subjective feeling that affects and is affected by our thoughts, behavior, and physiology. Some emotions are positive or pleasant, such as joy and affection, and others are negative, such as anger, fear, and sadness. Emotions relate to health and illness in many ways. For instance, people whose emotions are relatively positive are less disease-prone and more likely to recover quickly from an illness than are people whose emotions are relatively negative. We considered these relationships when we discussed the role of personality in illness. Emotions can also be important in people's decisions about seeking treatment. People who are frightened of doctors and dentists may avoid getting the health care they need.

Motivation is a term applied to explanations of why people behave the way they do — why they start some activity, choose its direction, and persist in it. A person who is motivated to feel and look better might begin an exercise program, choose the goals to be reached, and stick with it. Many people are motivated to do what important people in their lives want them to do. Parents who quit smoking because their children plead with them to protect their health are an example.

The Role of Social Factors

People live in a social world. We have relationships with individual people — an acquaintance, a friend, or a family member — or with groups of them. As we interact with them, we affect them and they affect us. But our social worlds are larger than just the people we know or meet. The people we contact are generally part of our community, culture, society, nation, and world. There are levels of social spheres, and each level affects each other. We will look at some examples of the interrelationships between the individual's health and his or her social world.

How does our society affect the health of individuals? Society establishes certain health values. One of these values is that being fit and healthy is "good." Often the mass media — television, newspapers, and so on — reflect these values by setting good examples and urg-

Society can help prevent disease or injury in many ways, such as through advertisements against drunk driving.

ing us to eat well, not to use drugs, and not to drink and drive. The mass media can do much to promote health. But sometimes these media encourage unhealthful behavior, such as when we observe celebrities on television smoking cigarettes or drinking excessively. Can individuals affect society's values? Yes. As part of the society, we can affect its values by writing our opinions to the mass media, selecting which television shows and movies to watch, and buying healthful products, for example.

Our community consists of friends, neighbors, classmates, workmates, and a wide variety of other people we may meet. The relationships we have with these people involve relatively direct and reciprocal influences— we influence and are influenced directly by each other. Many people who exercise do so to be attractive—especially sexually attractive— to other people. Adolescents often start smoking cigarettes and drinking alcohol as a result of peer pressure (Jessor, 1984). Sometimes simply observing other teenagers engaged in these behaviors can encourage adolescents to smoke and drink. They want very much to be popular and to look "cool" or "tough." These examples involve clear and powerful motivational elements that are social in nature.

The closest and most continuous social relationships for most people occur within the family. When the person is growing up in early childhood, the family has an especially strong influence (Sarafino & Armstrong, 1986). Children learn many health-related behaviors, attitudes, and beliefs from their parents, brothers, and sisters. They learn these things when they see their parents set good examples for healthful behavior by using seat belts, serving and eating nutritious meals, exercising, not smoking, and so on. They also learn good habits when healthful behaviors, such as tooth brushing and getting dental checkups, are encouraged and not ignored. Moreover, as we have said, the individual can influence the larger social unit. The family may stop having certain nutritious foods, such as brussels sprouts or fish, because one of the children has a tantrum when these foods are served. The influence of the community, culture, and society on health continually increases as the child's world expands rapidly during the school years and later.

The role of biological, psychological, and social factors in health and illness is not hard to see. What is more difficult to understand is how health is affected by the *interplay* of these components, as the biopsychosocial model proposes. The next section deals with this interplay.

The Concept of "Systems"

The whole person—as in the sentence "We need to understand the whole person"—is a phrase we hear often. It reflects our recognition that people and the reasons for their behavior are very complex. Many health professionals strive to consider the impact of all aspects of a person's life as a total entity in understanding health and illness. This approach uses the biopsychosocial model and is sometimes called *holistic*. This term is derived from the Greek word *holos*, which means "whole" (Lipowski, 1986).

How can we conceptualize the whole person? George Engel (1980) has proposed that we can do this by applying the concept of "systems" developed by Ludwig von Bertalanffy (1968). The term **system** refers to a dynamic entity consisting of components that are continuously interrelated. A person qualifies as a system, and so do the community and society in which the person lives and various parts of the person's body, such as a group of organs (for example, the nervous system) and even cells and atoms. These are all entities that are dynamic—that is, they constantly change—and they have components that interrelate, such as by exchanging energy, substances, and information.

As you can see in Figure 1.4, the systems concept places smaller, simpler systems within larger, more complex ones. There are levels of systems. Cells are within the person who is within a society, for instance. In the previous section of this chapter, we saw that a system at one level, such as a person, is affected by and can affect a system at another level, such as the family. Looking at other levels, this means that illness in part of the body can have far-reaching effects. If you fell and seriously injured your leg, your internal systems would be automatically mobilized to help protect the body from further damage. In addition, the discomfort and disability you might experience for days or weeks might affect your social relations with your family and community.

To illustrate how the systems concept can be useful, let's use it to explain how Anita's weight problem might have come about. Let's assume that she did inherit some factor that could affect her weight. The nature of this factor might involve a preference for sweet foods, for instance (Rozin, 1984). When she was a toddler, her parents would quiet her tantrums by giving her candy, which almost always worked. Anita's parents were not concerned that she was getting heavy because they believed that "a chubby baby is a healthy baby." The meals the family ate had lots of calories and generally ended with a sweet dessert. Because Anita was heavy, she was less agile and tired more easily than children who were not overweight. So she usually preferred to engage in sedentary activities, such as playing with dolls or watching television, rather than sports. She and her friends would snack on cookies while watching television. The commercials on most children's tele-

FIGURE 1.4 A diagram of the interplay of systems in the biopsychosocial model. The person consists of biological and psychological systems, which interrelate, and each of the systems includes component systems. The person interrelates with the social systems of his or her world. Each system can affect and be affected by any of the other systems.

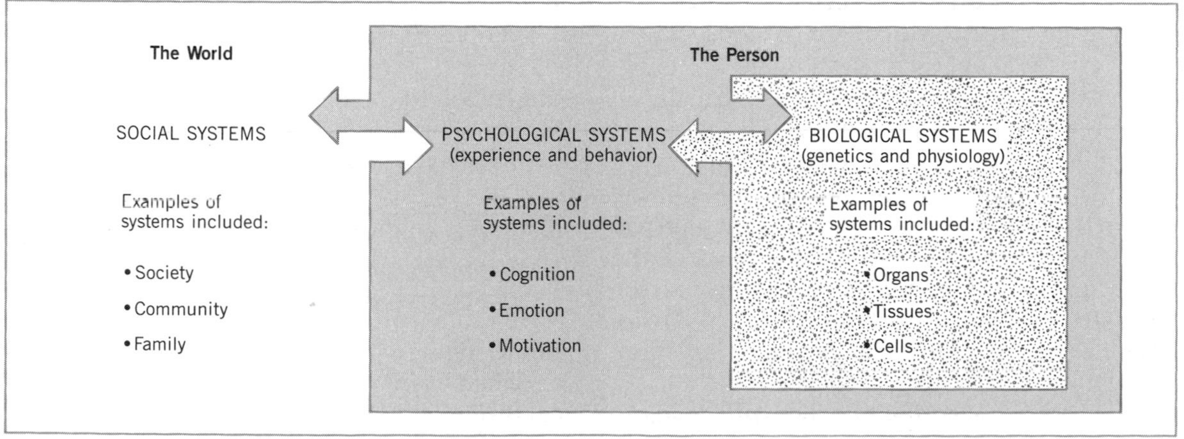

vision shows made her weight problem worse —they promoted sweet breakfast and snack foods, which she would get her parents to buy. This hypothetical account shows how different biopsychosocial systems can contribute to a person's weight problem.

The Life-Span Perspective

Have you heard the saying "I ain't what I ought to be, I ain't what I'm going to be, but I ain't what I was"? It carries several messages, one of which is that people change over time. They develop. As people develop, each portion of the life span is affected by happenings in earlier years, and each affects the happenings in years that will come. Throughout people's lives, health, illness, and the role of different biopsychosocial systems change. This is why it is important to keep the life-span perspective in mind when we examine health psychology.

The **life-span perspective** is an approach whereby characteristics of a person are considered with respect to their prior development, current level of development, and likely development in the future. How do characteristics relating to health and illness vary with development? One way is that the kinds of illnesses people have tend to change with age. Compared with older individuals, children suffer from relatively few chronic diseases (USDHHS, 1985b). Illnesses that keep children out of school tend to be short-term infectious diseases, such as colds or the flu. In contrast, many people in late adulthood and old age suffer from heart disease, cancer, and stroke.

How does the role of different biopsychosocial systems change with development? Biological systems change in many ways. Virtually all systems of the body grow in size, strength, and efficiency during childhood and decline in old age. The decline can be seen in the slowing down that older people notice in their physical abilities. They have less stamina because the heart and lungs function less efficiently and the muscles are weaker (Flynn & Mabry, 1986). They also recover from illness and injury more slowly.

Psychological systems change with development, too. As an example, we will look at the role of cognitive processes. Children's knowledge and ability to think are limited during the preschool years but grow rapidly during later childhood. Before children can assume responsibility for their health, they need to understand how their behavior can affect it. As children get older and their cognitive skills improve, they are more likely to engage in behaviors that promote their health and safety (Maddux, Roberts, Sledden, & Wright, 1986). They also become better able to understand the implications of their own illness when they are sick.

People's social relationships and social systems also change with development. How? For one thing, there are some usual progressions: Children usually become parents of their own families in adulthood, and grandparents in old age. They also progress through levels of education and employment, and retire in old age. Some changes in social relationships are related to health and illness. Children's health is largely the responsibility of adult caregivers—parents and teachers. During the teenage years, adolescents take on more and more of these responsibilities. At the same time, social relationships with age-mates in the community start to have a very powerful influence on adolescents. The strong need to be accepted by peers sometimes leads teens toward unhealthy or unsafe behavior. For example, adolescents who have a chronic illness that can be controlled—as diabetes can—may neglect their medical care to avoid looking and feeling "different" (La Greca & Stone, 1985).

The life-span perspective adds an important dimension to the biopsychosocial perspective in our effort to understand how people deal with issues of health and illness.

RELATING HEALTH PSYCHOLOGY TO OTHER SCIENCE FIELDS

Knowledge in health psychology is greatly enriched by information from a variety of medical disciplines, including psychiatry and pediatrics, and allied fields, such as nursing, nutrition, pharmacology, biology, and social work. Four other fields are especially important because they provide both information and a context for health psychology. We turn now to a description of these four related fields.

Related Fields

To understand health psychology fully, we need to know the context in which health and illness exist. Part of this context is provided by the field of *epidemiology*—the scientific study of the distribution and frequency of disease and injury. Researchers in this field determine the occurrence of illness and organize these data in terms of when the disease or injury occurred, where, and to which age, gender, and racial groups. Then they attempt to discover why specific illnesses are distributed as they are. You have probably seen the results of epidemiologists' work in the mass media. For example, news reports have described areas of the United States in which the occurrence of certain forms of cancer is linked to high or low levels of toxic substances in the environment. Another example is the spread of Lyme disease, a tick-borne illness, mainly in some eastern states.

Epidemiologists use several terms in describing aspects of their findings (Gerace & Vorp, 1985; Runyan, 1985). We will define five of these terms:

- **Mortality** means death, generally on a large scale. An epidemiologist might report a "decrease in mortality from heart disease among women," for instance
- **Morbidity** means illness, injury, or disability —basically any detectable departure from wellness.
- **Prevalence** refers to the number of cases, such as of a disease or of persons infected or at risk. It includes both continuing (previously reported) and new cases at a given moment in time—for example, the number of cases of asthma as of the first day of the current year.
- **Incidence** refers to the number of *new* cases, such as of illness, infection, or disability, reported during a period of time. An example is the number of child abuse cases in the previous year.
- **Epidemic** usually refers to the situation in which the incidence, generally of an infectious disease, has increased rapidly.

Some of these terms are used with the word *rate*, which adds relativity to the meaning. For instance, the mortality rate refers to the number of deaths per number of people in a given population during a specified period of time. An example might be a mortality rate of 10 babies per 1,000 births dying in their first year of life during the current year.

Another discipline of importance to health psychology is *public health*—the field concerned with protecting, maintaining, and improving health through organized effort in the community. People who work in public health do research and set up programs dealing with immunizations, sanitation, health education and awareness, and providing community health services (Runyan, 1985). This field studies health and illness in the context of the community as a social system. The success of public health programs and the way individual people react to them are of interest to health psychologists.

The third related field is *sociology*—the science of human social life. Sociologists study groups or communities of people and evaluate the impact of various social factors, such as the mass media, population growth, epidemics, and institutions. *Medical sociology* is a subfield of sociology. Medical sociologists study a wide range of issues related to health, including the impact of social relationships on the distribution of illness, cultural and social reactions to illness, socioeconomic factors of health care use, and the way hospital services and medical practices are organized (Adler & Stone, 1979). Knowledge from sociology gives us a broad social view and describes the social environment in which the individual exists.

The fourth field, *anthropology*, includes the study of human cultures. Its subfield, *medical anthropology*, examines the differences in health and illness across cultures: In what ways do the nature and definition of illness vary

HIGHLIGHT 1B: On Issues
Careers Relating Health and Psychology

The process of rehabilitation for a patient who is suffering from a chronic illness, serious injury, or disability involves a variety of professionals working together with the physicians as a team (USDL, 1986). Each professional has specific training for his or her special role in the rehabilitation process. Most of them also have some background in psychology. Let's look at some of these occupations.

Nurses

There are two overall categories of nurses: *registered nurses* (RNs) and *licensed practical nurses* (LPNs). RNs work in hospitals, community health clinics, physicians' offices, and industrial settings. They assess and record patients' symptoms and progress, conduct tests, administer medications, assist in rehabilitation, provide instructions for self-treatment, and instruct patients and their families in ways to improve or maintain their health. RNs often deal with mental and emotional aspects of the patient as well.

All RNs throughout the United States must be licensed to practice, have graduated from an approved training program in nursing, and have passed a national examination (USDL, 1986). There are three types of RN training programs: community and junior college programs take about two years to complete and lead to an associate degree; hospital-based programs require three years and lead to a diploma; and college and university programs take four or five years and lead to a baccalaureate degree. Although the baccalaureate degree can be important for advancement, hospitals often do not assign different activities or responsibilities to nurses from different types of training programs (Aiken, 1983).

What do LPNs do? LPNs work in hospitals, clinics, physicians' offices, and patients' homes. They perform nursing activities that require less training than those performed by RNs. For example, they take and record temperatures and blood pressures, administer certain medications, change dressings, assist physicians or RNs, and help patients with personal hygiene (USDL, 1986).

Like RNs, all LPNs throughout the United States must be licensed to practice, have graduated from an approved practical nursing program, and have passed a national examination. Training programs for LPNs take only about one year to complete and are offered through various types of institutions, such as trade and vocational schools, community and junior colleges, hospitals, and the Armed Forces (USDL, 1986).

Dietitians

Dietitians study and apply knowledge about food and its effect on the body. They do this in several kinds of settings, such as hospitals, clinics, nursing homes, colleges, and schools. The work of dietitians generally follows one of three areas—there are administrative, clinical, and community dietitians. Administrative dietitians apply principles of nutrition to meal planning and preparation for very large numbers of people. Sound management skills are essential in hiring and supervising food service workers, enforcing sanitary and safety codes, and preparing budgets and reports. Clinical dietitians work directly with patients in assessing nutritional needs, implementing and evaluating dietary plans, and instructing patients and their families on ways to adhere to needed diets after discharge from the hospital. Community dietitians usually work for social service agencies in the community, where they counsel people on nutritional practices to help maintain health and speed recovery when they are ill.

What training is required? The basic educational requirement for becoming a dietitian is a four-year college degree specializing in nutrition sciences or institutional management. To become a Registered Dietitian through the American Dietetic Association, the individual must complete a supervised internship (USDL, 1986).

Physical Therapists

Many patients need help in restoring functional movement to parts of their body and relieving pain. If they have suffered a disabling injury or disease, treatment may be needed to prevent or limit permanent disability. *Physical therapists* plan and apply treatment for these goals in rehabilitation.

To plan the treatment, physical therapists begin by reviewing the patient's records and condition. Then they perform tests or measurements of muscle strength, motor coordination, endurance, and range of movement of the injured body part. The treatment plan that comes from interpreting these data is designed to increase the strength and function of the injured part and aid in the patient's adaptation to having reduced physical abilities, which may be quite drastic. People who have suffered a severe stroke are sometimes left partially paralyzed, for instance.

What treatment techniques are applied? Probably the most universal technique used in physical therapy involves exercise, which generally begins by requiring little effort and becomes more and more challenging. Other techniques include electrical stimulation to move paralyzed muscles; application of heat, cold, massage, or ultrasound waves to reduce pain or improve muscle condition; and instruction for carrying out everyday tasks, such as tying shoelaces or cooking meals. If the patient needs to use adaptive devices, such as crutches or a prosthesis (replacement limb), the physical therapist provides training.

All physical therapists throughout the United States must have a degree or certificate from an approved training program and be licensed. Training may be obtained by pursuing one of three routes: a baccalaureate program in physical therapy, a certificate program after receiving a bachelor's degree in another field, or a master's degree program in physical therapy (USDL, 1986).

Occupational Therapists

Occupational therapists help physically, mentally, and emotionally disabled individuals gain skills needed for daily activities in a work setting, at school, in the community, and at home. Their patients are often people who had these skills at one time, but lost them because of a spinal cord injury or a disease, such as muscular dystrophy. These professionals usually specialize in working with a particular age group, such as the elderly, and a type of disability—physical, for example.

The first step in rehabilitation is to evaluate existing abilities. Then, based on the patient's age and type of disability, a program of educational, vocational, and recreational activities is designed and implemented. The program for a child, for instance, might involve academic tasks and crafts; for an adult, it might involve typing, driving a vehicle, and using hand and power tools.

Training in this field involves completing a bachelor's degree in an approved occupational therapy program. Most states also require occupational therapists to have passed a national examination and be licensed (USDL, 1986).

Social Workers

The field of *social work* is quite broad. Probably most social workers are employed in mental health programs, but many others work in hospitals, nursing homes, rehabilitation centers, and public health programs (Kane, 1983). When working with people who are physically ill or disabled, social workers help patients and their families make psychological and social adjustments to the illness and obtain needed community services, including income maintenance. These professionals are usually called medical social workers.

Some social workers help patients indirectly, for example, by administering programs, developing helping resources, and doing research. But most social workers provide direct help through counseling and by making contacts or referrals for the patients with other agencies or programs in the community. As an example, a patient whose illness or disability may require a career change may be referred for vocational counseling and occupational therapy. Or, a patient may need nursing care at home for a while after being discharged from the hospital. Or, a patient who is a single parent may need temporary help in housekeeping and child care activities. The social worker can make arrangements for these kinds of help.

What training is required for careers in social work? The minimum qualification is a bachelor's degree in a social science field. Sometimes employers prefer that the training be specialized in social work, but often a degree in psychology or sociology is sufficient. Many positions require an advanced degree, typically a master's in social work—the MSW degree.

Health Psychologists

Because the field of health psychology is so new, its full potential for careers is developing rapidly. Most health psychologists work in hospitals, clinics, and academic departments of colleges and universities. In these positions, they either provide direct help to patients or give indirect help through research, teaching, and consulting activities.

The direct help provided by health psychologists generally relates to the patient's psychological adjustment to and management of health problems. Health psychologists with clinical training can provide therapy for emotional and social adjustment problems that being ill or disabled can produce—

for example, in reducing the patient's feelings of depression. They can also help in the management of the health problem. How? One way is by teaching the patient psychological methods, such as biofeedback, that are effective in controlling pain (Holzman & Turk, 1986).

Health psychologists also provide indirect help. Their research provides information about lifestyle and personality factors in illness and injury. They can apply this and other biopsychosocial knowledge to design programs that help people lead more healthful lifestyles, such as by preventing or quitting cigarette smoking (Matarazzo, 1984). They can also educate physicians and the other health care workers we have discussed toward a fuller understanding of the psychosocial needs of patients (DiMatteo, 1985).

The qualifications for becoming a health psychologist include completion of the doctoral degree in psychology. In some cases, additional study may be needed, particularly if the doctoral program contained little training in health psychology (Matarazzo, 1983; Taylor, 1987). State licensing is required to practice clinical techniques.

---

across different cultures? How do people in these cultures react to illness, and what methods do they use to treat disease or injury? How do they structure health care systems? If health psychologists did not explore the knowledge of anthropology, our notions of health and illness would be very narrow. Medical anthropology gives us a world view of medical issues and allows us to look at different ways to interpret and treat illness (Adler & Stone, 1979).

The combined information that health psychologists receive from the fields of epidemiology, public health, sociology, and anthropology paints a broad picture for us. It describes the social systems in which health, illness, and the person exist and develop.

Health and Psychology across Cultures

The world view we get from studying health across cultures can be quite dramatic, as the following excerpt shows:

> Less than a hundred years ago the infant mortality rate in Europe and North America was as high as it is in the developing world now. In New York City in the year 1900, for example, the IMR [infant mortality rate] was approximately 140 per 1,000—about the same as in Bangladesh today. In the city of Birmingham, England, a survey taken in 1906 revealed an IMR of almost 200 per 1,000—higher than almost any country in the world in the 1980s. A look behind these statistics also shows that the main causes of infant death in New York and Birmingham *then* were much the same as in the developing world *now*—diarrheal diseases and malnutrition, respiratory infections, and whooping cough. (UNICEF, cited in Skolnick, 1986, p. 20)

Health and illness have changed across history. But these changes can also be viewed as changes across cultures, since cultures change over time. American culture in the 1800s was very different from the culture we have today. Lifestyles have changed, and so has the pattern of illnesses that afflict us.

Patterns of illness not only vary across time, they also differ from culture to culture at any given time. For instance, certain forms of cancer, particularly stomach and liver cancer, have far higher prevalence rates in Japan than in the United States today, but the reverse is true for breast (in females) and prostate (in males) cancers (Ohkura, 1981). Furthermore, large differences in rates of specific cancers even exist between regions of the same country, such as between New Jersey and Utah (Fox, 1982). In part, the differences we see in illness patterns between countries or regions result from cultural differences, such as in the diets and values of the people. Although people around the world value health and think it is "good," people in some countries, such as France and Italy, value health more positively than do people in other countries, such as Lebanon and Turkey (Diaz-Guerrero, 1984). It seems reasonable to assume that the more people value their health, the more likely they are to take care of it.

Ideas people have about the causes of illness have similarly varied across history and culture. Recall our discussion of the widespread beliefs in the Middle Ages about the causes of illness: They thought evil spirits were responsible. Today educated people in technological societies generally reject such ideas. But less sophisticated people often do not, as the following excerpt shows:

> I've heard of people with snakes in their body, how they got in there I don't know. And they take 'em someplace to a witch doctor and snakes come out. My sister, she had somethin', a snake that was in her arm. She was a young woman. I can remember her bein' sick, very sick, and someone told her about this healer in another little town. And I do know they taken her there. This thing was just runnin' up her arm, whatever it was, just runnin' up her arm. You could actually *see* it. (Snow, 1981, p. 86).

Although this account was given by a disadvantaged person in the United States, it is typical of the level of knowledge generally found in people in underdeveloped countries. This is an important thing to recognize because the large majority of people in the world live in underdeveloped societies.

The United States has been described as a "melting pot" for immigrants from every corner of the world. Immigrants carry with them health ideas and customs from their former country. Chinese Americans provide an example of such importation (Campbell & Chang, 1981). Many Chinese immigrants have entered their new country with the belief that illness results from an imbalance of two opposing forces, *Yin* and *Yang*, within the body. According to this view, too much Yin causes colds and gastric disorders, for instance, and too much Yang causes fever and dehydration. Practitioners of traditional Chinese medicine treat illnesses by prescribing special herbs and foods or by using *acupuncture*, in which fine needles are inserted under the skin at special locations of the body. These methods are intended to correct the balance of Yin and Yang. Immigrants with these beliefs who are sick will often use these methods instead of or as a supplement to treatment by an American physician. They may also pressure their children and grandchildren to do this, too. As an example, a Chinese woman who was a registered nurse "routinely followed her obstetrician's orders, but at the same time, under pressure from her mother and mother-in-law, ate special herbs and foods to insure birth of a healthy baby" (Campbell & Chang, 1981, p. 164).

Religion is an aspect of culture. Many religions in the United States include beliefs that relate to health and illness. For instance, Jehovah's Witnesses reject the use of blood and blood products in medical treatment (Sacks & Koppes, 1986). Christian Scientists reject the use of medicine totally, believing that illnesses are cured only by mental processes in the sick person. As a result, the sick person needs prayer and counsel as treatment to help these processes along (Henderson & Primeaux, 1981). These beliefs are controversial and have led to legal conflicts between the religions and health authorities, particularly when parents reject medical treatments for life-threatening illnesses for their children. In such cases, the physician and hospital can move quickly to seek an immediate judicial decision (Sacks & Koppes, 1986).

Some religions include specific beliefs that promote healthful lifestyles. Seventh-Day Adventists, for example, believe that the body is the "temple of the Holy Spirit." They cite this belief as the reason people should take care of their bodies. Adventists abstain from using tobacco, alcohol, and nonmedically prescribed drugs. In addition, they promote in fellow members a concern for exercise and eating a healthful diet (Henderson & Primeaux, 1981).

RESEARCH METHODS

Contemporary Americans are constantly bombarded with scientific findings by the mass media. Diets high in fiber and low in saturated fats are good for your health. Smoking is not. Dozens of toxic, or poisonous, chemicals have been shown to cause cancer. How do scientists discover these things? What methods do they use?

Scientists do research. Often their research is planned and conducted to test a **theory**—a *tentative explanation* of why and under what circumstances certain phenomena occur. For example, a leading theory of the cause of heart disease is that excess *cholesterol*, a fatty substance in the blood, is deposited on artery walls. Because this substance, like other saturated fats, is not water soluble, it builds up on the walls over time. This buildup hardens and narrows the diameter of the artery, thereby reducing the flow of blood and nutrients and causing tissue damage to the heart or arteries. Cholesterol comes from two sources: Most cholesterol in the blood is manufactured by the body; the rest of it comes from the foods we eat—especially red meats, egg yolks, butter, and most cheeses.

The cholesterol theory is one of several useful theories of heart disease. By "useful" we don't necessarily mean that it is correct. We mean that it

1. Is clearly stated
2. Brings together or organizes known facts
3. Relates information that previously seemed unrelated
4. Enables us to make predictions, such as what would happen if cholesterol levels were reduced

Useful theories play an extremely important role in all sciences. Because of the predictions they provide, they guide research programs by suggesting a sort of "road map" of relationships to study.

As you think about the causes of heart disease, you will realize that both the illness and the theoretical cause—in this case, high levels of cholesterol—can change or vary from one time to another and from one individual to another. That is, the condition of the heart and arteries and the amount of cholesterol in the blood are not constant. Because these things *vary*, they are called *variables*. We will define **variable** as any measurable characteristic of people, objects, or events that may change.

Researchers who study heart disease use a variety of methods to examine variables like the ones we have discussed. The first approach we will consider is the use of *experiments*.

Experiments

An **experiment** is a controlled study in which the researcher manipulates a variable to study its effect on another variable. The manipulated variable is called the *independent variable* because it is varied directly and independently of variables that are not being studied in the experiment. The other variable in the experiment is called the *dependent variable* because its value is *dependent* on the manipulated values of the independent variable. In a well-designed experiment—which is often called a "trial" in health research—other variables are controlled or held constant.

To illustrate the experimental method, let's see how researchers might test the cholesterol theory of heart disease. One prediction, or *hypothesis*, from the theory is that the incidence of heart disease should decrease if the levels of cholesterol in people's blood were reduced. We could test this hypothesis by lowering the cholesterol levels of some people and seeing if they, as a group, develop fewer heart attacks over a suitable period of time than they otherwise would. How can we lower their cholesterol levels? There are two ways, both of which would require the involvement of medical professionals in the research team. One is to alter their diets, and the other is to have them take an anticholesterol drug regularly. We will use the drug approach for our example.

The first thing we need to do is to select a sample of subjects—preferably middle-aged men, because they have a relatively high risk of having a heart attack in the near future. Then we assign these men randomly to the conditions or groups in the experiment. One way to randomly assign them is to put their names on cards in a bowl, mix up the cards, and draw the cards out one at a time. The first name drawn would be assigned to one group, the second name to another group, and so on. By doing this, we distribute other characteristics, such as their personality traits and genetic factors, fairly equally across the groups. As a result, these characteristics will have the same weight or effect for each of the groups.

To test the hypothesis, we will need two groups of subjects. One group receives the experimental treatment, the anticholesterol pills, and is called the *experimental group*. The other group does not receive the treatment, and is called the *control group*. By administering the drug to and lowering the cholesterol level of one group, but not the other, we are manipulating the independent variable. We will then observe the incidence of heart attacks—the dependent variable. If the experimental group has fewer heart attacks than the control group, the hypothesis is supported.

You may be thinking that it is possible that a decrease in heart attacks for the experimental group might not be due to receiving the drug per se, but simply to receiving any medicine-like substance from a medical person. Sometimes people's beliefs or expectations can affect their health (Critelli & Neumann, 1984; Shapiro & Shapiro, 1984). To control for this possibility, we would have a third group of subjects. This group would receive an inert, or inactive, substance or procedure—called a **placebo**—in the form of pills that look like medicine. The placebo group would be given the same instructions as the experimental group, and both would have equal expectations about the effectiveness of the pills.

One other control procedure is needed. Just as the subjects should not know which pills contain the active drug, neither should the person who distributes the pills. Why? This person could inadvertently bias the outcome of the experiment, such as by giving instructions offhandedly to the placebo group and emphatically and precisely to the experimental group. Being unaware of which group is getting the experimental treatment is called being "blind" as to the treatment. Since both the subjects and the person who distributes the pills are unaware, the method we are using is called the **double-blind** procedure.

Now that we have included these control procedures, let's look at the outcome of our hypothetical experiment. As Figure 1.5 shows, the experimental subjects had far fewer heart attacks than subjects who did not. Thus we can conclude that lowering cholesterol levels in the blood causes a decrease in heart disease, as the theory predicts. Notice also in the graph that the men in the placebo group had somewhat

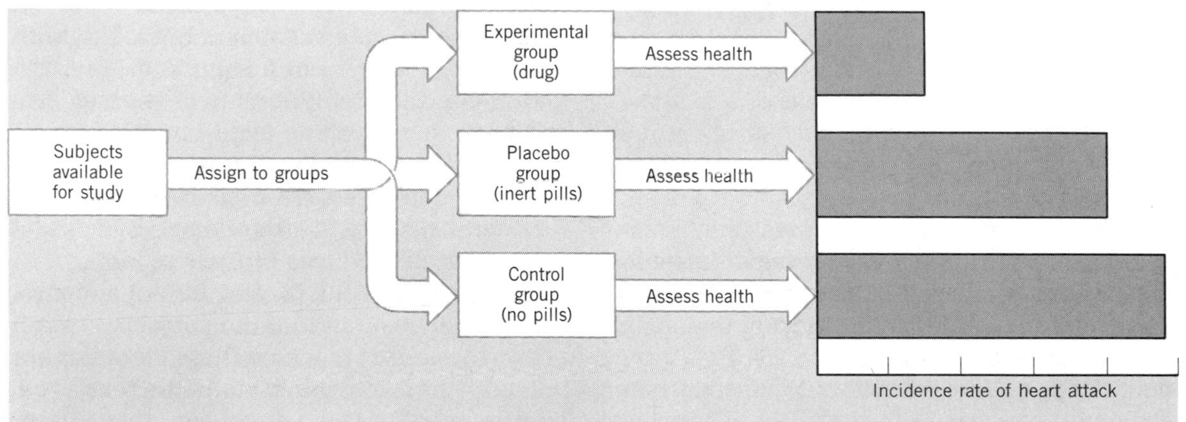

FIGURE 1.5 The left-hand portion of this diagram shows how the study would be carried out. Subjects are assigned to groups and, after a suitable period of time, the researcher checks whether they had heart attacks. The right-hand portion illustrates how the results might appear on a graph: subjects who received the anticholesterol drug had far fewer heart attacks than subjects in the placebo group, who had somewhat fewer attacks than those in the control group.

fewer heart attacks than the control subjects. This suggests that expectancy had some effect on heart disease, but not nearly as much as the active ingredient in the anticholesterol drug.

You may have noticed that our conclusion used the word *causes*: lowering cholesterol "causes" a decrease in heart disease. Because in experiments researchers manipulate the independent variable while controlling variables that are not being studied, they can determine what causes what. This ability generally does not exist when using other, *nonexperimental*, methods.

Research always involves the study of variables. In nonexperimental methods, however, the researcher *does not manipulate an independent variable*. In addition, there is frequently less opportunity for precise measurement and for control of variables not being studied. Consequently, although nonexperimental methods may be used to point out relationships between variables, they do *not* provide direct and unambiguous tests of *cause-effect* relationships.

Nonexperimental methods are nevertheless very valuable and have some important advantages. Sometimes it is simply not possible or feasible to manipulate the variable of interest. We cannot manipulate the past lifestyles of people, for instance; the past has already happened. Nor can we have individuals in one group of a study do harmful things that they would ordinarily not do simply to test an important theory. For instance, it would be unethical to randomly assign people of a sample, some of whom are cigarette smokers, to a group in which all subjects must smoke for the next five years. Even if it were ethical, nonsmokers might refuse to do it. What if we didn't randomly assign the subjects to groups? If we do not randomly assign subjects, the groups are not likely to be equal at the start of the study with respect to characteristics, such as genetics or past lifestyle, that could affect the outcome of the research. In situations like this in which ethical considerations prevent the use of human subjects, animals are sometimes used.

In many cases, the aim of a research project requires only that an association between variables be demonstrated. We may want to know, for instance, which individuals are at greatest risk for a disease so that we may help them avert it. Studies to determine risk factors are examples. This kind of research has revealed that people who are among the most likely to develop heart disease are male and/or over 50 years of age (Susser, Hopper, & Richman, 1983). Obviously the researcher cannot and need not manipulate people's gender or age to arrive at this relationship—and a nonexperimental method is, in fact, the most appropriate technique.

The remainder of our examination of research methods will focus on nonexperimental approaches in research relating to health psychology. We will continue to use the cholesterol theory of heart disease as the basis for research examples. Let's turn to correlational studies as the first of these methods.

Correlational Studies

The term *correlation* refers to the *co* or joint relation that exists between variables—changes in one variable correspond with changes in another variable. Suppose, for example, we did a study of two variables: heart function and people's diets, particularly the amount of cholesterol they consume. A measure of heart function is *cardiac output*, the amount of blood pumped per minute by the heart. Working with a physician, we recruit a sample of, say, 200 middle-aged adults. We contact the subjects and have them keep detailed records of their diets for the two weeks prior to the visit when the physician measures their cardiac output. We then calculate the amount of cholesterol consumed on the basis of their records.

Once we know the cardiac output and cholesterol intake of each of the subjects, we can assess the degree to which these variables are related. This is expressed statistically as a **correlation coefficient**, which can range from +1.00 through .00 to −1.00. The sign (+ or −) of the coefficient indicates the *direction* of the relationship. A plus sign means that the association is "positive": high scores on one variable, say, cardiac output, tend to be associated with high scores on another variable, such as blood pressure. Conversely, a minus sign means that the association is "negative": *high* scores on one variable tend to be associated with *low* scores on another variable. For example, high cardiac output is correlated with low concentrations of red blood cells, because these cells thicken the blood (Guyton, 1985). Thus, there is a negative correlation between cardiac output and concentration of red blood cells.

Disregarding the sign of the correlation coefficient, the absolute value of the coefficient indicates the *strength* of association between variables. The higher the absolute value (that is, the closer to +1.0 or −1.0), the stronger the correlation. As the absolute value decreases, the strength of the relationship declines. A coefficient approximating .00 means that the variables are not related. From the information we have just covered, we can now state a definition: **correlational studies** are nonexperimental investigations of the degree and direction of statistical association between two variables.

Let's suppose that our study revealed a strong negative correlation—a coefficient of −.72—between cardiac output and cholesterol intake. This would support the cholesterol theory because low cholesterol intake should produce less fatty buildup to clog the arteries, thereby allowing the heart to pump more blood per minute. But we cannot say on the basis of our study that these events occurred, and we cannot conclude that low cholesterol intake *causes* high cardiac output. Why? Because we did not manipulate any variable—we simply measured what was there. It may be that some variable that we were not studying was responsible for the correlation. For example, the people with low cholesterol intake may also have had low concentrations of red blood cells, and it may have been this latter factor that was responsible for their high cardiac output. We don't know. As a result, we can only conclude that the two variables have a strong negative relationship.

Correlational studies, despite their inability to determine cause-effect relations, are useful for examining existing relationships and variables that cannot be manipulated, developing hypotheses that may be tested experimentally, and generating predictive information, such as risk factors.

Quasi-Experimental Studies

Sometimes researchers conduct nonexperimental studies by selecting and setting up categories or levels of a variable. Assessment of that variable allows the researcher to categorize individuals in one of two or more groups, such as male or female, for example, or blood cholesterol levels within certain ranges. But notice that the variable—gender or cholesterol level—was not manipulated and the subjects cannot be randomly assigned to the groups. Investigations of this type are called **quasi-experimental studies**—they *look* like experiments because they have separate groups of subjects, but they are not.

We could do a quasi-experimental study relating to the cholesterol theory of heart disease in the following way. Suppose we wanted to see if people's cholesterol level at the time of a heart attack is associated with the severity of the attack. For this study, we could just consult the medical records of heart disease patients, since it is standard practice to assess both variables. We could categorize the patients as having a high or low cholesterol level at the time they were admitted to the hospital. Then we would determine whether the attacks of one group were more severe than those of the other group.

If we found that the high-cholesterol patients had the more severe heart attacks, could we conclude that higher levels of cholesterol in the blood cause more severe attacks? No—for the same reasons we've discussed before. We cannot tell what caused what. In fact, this particular study could have been turned around. We could have categorized the patients on the basis of the severity of their attacks and then compared these groups for cholesterol levels. We would have found the same relationship:

severe heart attacks are associated with a high level of cholesterol in the blood.

In general, the conclusions from quasi-experimental studies are basically correlational. The relationships they reveal do not become causal simply because we categorize subjects. There are many variations to the quasi-experimental method. We will look at a few of the more important ones, beginning with retrospective and prospective approaches.

Retrospective and Prospective Approaches

The prefix *retro* means "back" or "backward," and *spective* comes from the Latin word meaning "to look." Thus, the **retrospective approach** uses procedures that look back in the past histories of subjects—generally people who have a disease. The purpose of this approach is to find commonalities in the histories of these people that may suggest why they developed the disease.

How is the retrospective approach used in a quasi-experimental study? We would identify two groups of individuals. One group would consist of people who have already developed a particular illness, such as heart disease. They would be compared against a control group, consisting of similar people without the disease. We would then examine the two groups for characteristics of their past histories that are common to one group, but not the other. We might find, for example, that the heart disease victims tended to eat higher-cholesterol diets during the past ten years than the control subjects did. Although the retrospective approach is relatively easy to implement, it has a potential shortcoming. When the procedures rely on people's memories, especially of long-past happenings, the likelihood of inaccurate reports increases.

The **prospective approach** uses procedures that look *forward* in the lives of people, by studying subjects repeatedly over a period of time. We could do this to see whether certain characteristics or events in people's lives are associated with their development of one or more diseases. In using the prospective approach, we would start by recruiting a large group of people—say, 2,000—who did not yet have the illness in question, heart disease. Periodically over several years, we would interview them, have a physician examine them, and check their medical records. The interviews would inquire about various events and characteristics, such as cholesterol intake. Then we would categorize the subjects—for instance, as having had or not had a heart attack—and determine whether these groups differed in some aspects of their lives.

What might our study show? We might find that, compared with people who did not have heart attacks, those who did had eaten diets that were much higher in cholesterol. We might also find that *changes* in people's diets, becoming higher or lower in cholesterol content over the years, corresponded with their suffering an attack. That is, those who consumed increasing amounts of cholesterol had more heart attacks than those whose cholesterol intake decreased. Because this is a quasi-experimental study, we cannot be certain that high-cholesterol diets caused the heart disease. But the prospective approach gives greater plausibility to a causal link than the retrospective approach would. This is because the diets, and changes in them, clearly preceded the heart attacks.

The retrospective and prospective approaches were developed by epidemiologists. These approaches have been useful in identifying risk factors for specific illnesses.

Developmental Approaches

We saw earlier that the life-span perspective adds an important dimension to the study of health and illness. An essential research approach in studying life-span development is to examine and compare people at different ages. Of course, the age of the subjects cannot be manipulated; we can assign individuals to groups based on their age, but this assignment is not random. This approach is quasi-experimental, and, therefore, *age* itself cannot be viewed as a cause of health or behavior.

Two basic approaches are used for studying the age variable. In the **cross-sectional approach**, different individuals of different ages are observed at about the same time. Alternatively, the **longitudinal approach** involves the repeated observation of the *same* individuals over a long period of time. The longitudinal approach is a type of prospective method, but it focuses specifically on age as a variable. Let's see how the cross-sectional and longitudinal approaches are used.

Suppose we were interested in examining age-related changes in dietary intake of cholesterol among middle-aged adults. If we use a *cross-sectional* approach, we might evaluate the diets of, say, 50 adults at each of three approximate ages — for example, 35, 45, and 55 years — during the current month. On the other hand, if we use a *longitudinal* approach to examine the same age range, we would evaluate the diets of fifty 35-year-olds during the current month, and again when they are 45 and 55 years of age. This longitudinal study would take 20 years to complete.

Not all longitudinal studies take so long to do. Often a shorter span of ages — sometimes only a few months — is appropriate, depending on the question or issue the researcher wants to resolve. But the longitudinal approach, and the prospective approach in general, is typically more costly in time and money than the cross-sectional approach. Also the longer a study lasts, the greater the likelihood that subjects in the sample will be lost. Some will move away, others will lose interest in participating, and still others may die. Despite these difficulties, it is a valuable research approach that is unique in its ability to examine *change and stability in the lives of individuals* across time. For example, our longitudinal study could tell us whether a person who eats a high-cholesterol diet at 35 years of age will generally continue to do so many years later. In contrast, a cross-sectional approach loses sight of stability and individual changes.

Now, let's suppose that we did our cross-sectional study and found that the cholesterol content of adults' diets decreased with age. We would then like to know why this is so. One possible answer is that people change their diets as they get older because they feel more vulnerable to heart disease. So we asked the oldest group, using the retrospective approach, if they feel more vulnerable and eat less high-cholesterol foods today than they used to. Sure enough, they said yes. But another reason for the current age differences in diet could be that the older adults never ate diets as high in cholesterol as those of the younger adults. So we asked the oldest group to describe the diets they ate 10 or 20 years ago. The diets they described contained less cholesterol than their current diets (which we already knew) *and* the current diets of the 35- and 45-year-olds in our study! This finding reflects the fact that the older subjects grew up at a different time, when food preferences or availability may have been different.

The influence of having been born and raised at a different time is called a **cohort effect**. The term *cohort* refers to a group of individuals who have a demographic factor, such as age or social class, in common. As a result, they share a set of experiences that are distinct from those of adjacent cohorts. In developmental approaches, the meaning of "cohort" is similar to "generation," but the amount of time separating adjacent cohorts can be much shorter than the time separating a generation. For example, a researcher interested in attitudes about war might study 18- to 20-year-olds who served as soldiers in a war that lasted a few years and compare their attitudes with two other cohorts, composed of individuals who were 18- to 20-year-old soldiers shortly before and shortly after the war.

How can research methods take cohort effects into account? One way would be to combine the two developmental approaches to produce a *cross-sectional/longitudinal design* (Buss, 1973; Schaie, 1965). Looking back at our study with middle-aged adults, the combined approach could be carried out by selecting and testing 35-, 45-, and 55-year-olds initially. So far the study is cross-sectional, but we would follow most of these same adults longitudinally and add younger subjects along the way. By doing this in a planned and systematic way, we will have information about cross-sectional differences, changes within each cohort, and differences between cohorts.

Single-Subject Approaches

Sometimes studies are done with just one subject. One type of research that uses this approach is the **case study**, in which a trained researcher constructs a systematic biography from records of the person's history, interviews, and current observation. This kind of research is useful in describing, in depth, the development and treatment of an unusual medical or psychological problem. Earlier in this chapter we saw an excerpt from a case study of a university student who had developed an ulcer.

Another type of research that uses one subject is called the **single-subject design**. This approach is often used for demonstrating the usefulness of a new treatment method for a specific medical or psychological problem. The initial condition of the patient is outlined, treatment is planned and carried out, a comparison of the patient's condition at the beginning and end of therapy is made, and often a follow-up assessment is done months or years later to see if the patient's condition has regressed.

The principal disadvantage of single-subject approaches is that information gained from only one subject, no matter how detailed it is, may not describe what would be found with other individuals. A major purpose of psychological investigations is to collect information that can be applied or generalized to other people. Nevertheless, studies using one subject stimulate the development of new treatment procedures and suggest topics for further research.

Genetics Research

How do psychologists and other scientists determine whether hereditary factors influence people's health and illness? The methods are based on a distinction between two types of twins. *Monozygotic*, or "identical," twins have exactly the same genetic inheritance because they result from the splitting of a single fertilized egg, called a zygote. *Dizygotic*, or "fraternal," twins develop from two separate zygotes, each of which was fertilized by separate sperm. As a result, they are no more genetically similar than any singly born siblings and may, of course, be of different sex.

Most of the research on hereditary factors has focused on the differences in characteristics shown in monozygotic (MZ) twins as compared with dizygotic (DZ) twins. Investigations using this approach are called **twin studies**. The rationale for making these comparisons, although statistically complex, is logically simple. Because a pair of MZ individuals are genetically identical, we can assume that differences between them are environmentally determined. Conversely, the greater the similarity between MZ pairs, the more likely it is that the characteristic is genetically influenced. Differences between DZ pairs, on the other hand, are due to both genetic and environmental factors. If we could assume that both members of each MZ and DZ pair that we study have had equal environmental experiences, then we could measure genetic influence simply by subtracting the differences between MZ pairs from the differences between DZ pairs.

The assumption that both members of each MZ and DZ pair have had equal environmental experiences presents a problem for researchers. As you might expect, environments are more likely to differ for fraternal pairs than for identical pairs. For instance, MZ children more often dress alike, play together, and share the same friends than do same-sex fraternal twins (McClearn, 1968). When this kind of problem exists—and it is hard to avoid totally—it makes the influence of heredity less clear. But some studies have been able to take environmental similarity into account—and when they do, important genetic forces are still found (Scarr & Kidd, 1983).

Another way to examine hereditary influences is to study children adopted at very early ages. **Adoption studies** compare traits of adopted children with those of their natural parents and their adoptive parents. Why?

Adoptive parents contribute greatly to the rearing environment, but are genetically unrelated to the children; the natural parents are genetically related to the children, but play little or no role in rearing them. So, if adopted children are more similar to their natural parents than to their adoptive parents, we then have evidence for heredity's influence.

What conclusions relevant to health psychology have come from twin and adoption studies? Let's look at several. MZs are not only more similar than DZs for physical characteristics, such as height and weight, but also for physiological functions, including heart rate, blood pressure, breathing rate, and skin temperature. In addition, a condition called *hypercholesterolemia*, which produces very high levels of cholesterol in the blood, is known to be caused by a genetic disorder. People with this condition have a very high rate of heart disease, often beginning at very early ages.

In this chapter, we have discussed a variety of research methods that are useful in health psychology. Which one is best? Some scientists might say that the experiment is best because it can uncover cause-effect relationships. But precise control and manipulation do not always yield results that help us understand real-life behavior. For example, studying behavior in experimental settings sometimes involves artificial conditions, such as precisely occurring events and special equipment. To the extent that these conditions are unlike the "real world," the subjects' behavior may be influenced. As a result, when reading about an experiment, it is useful to keep two questions in mind: Does the experimental situation approximate anything the subjects might experience in real life? If the experimental situation is highly "artificial," what specific effect might this have on the outcome of the experiment?

In a sense, all the research methods we discussed are "best," since the investigator must select the most suitable method(s) to answer the specific question(s) under study. This leads us to a final point: it is possible and desirable to use experimental and nonexperimental methods *simultaneously* in one study. Suppose, for instance, we wanted to find out whether reading information about the health effects of excessive cholesterol would induce people to modify their diets. Using experimental methods, we would manipulate the variable in the following way: the experimental group would read the cholesterol information and a control group might read some unrelated material. But isn't it possible that the success of this experiment might depend on a variable that cannot be manipulated, such as the subjects' age or gender? People who are 50 years of age might be more inclined to follow recommendations to lower their cholesterol levels than people who are 20, for example. We could examine both variables by testing experimental and control groups for each of the two ages. Note, however, that the kinds of conclusions yielded by each variable will differ; only the manipulated variable can yield unambiguous causal statements.

SUMMARY

Health and illness are overlapping concepts that exist along a continuum. One end of the continuum is dominated by health—a positive state of physical, mental, and social well-being that varies over time. The other end of the continuum is dominated by illness, which produces signs, symptoms, and disabilities. The patterns of illness affecting people have changed across history, especially in the twentieth century. Compared with earlier times, today people die at later ages and from different causes. Infectious diseases are no longer the principal cause of death in technological societies around the world. Chronic illnesses constitute the main health problem in the United States now.

Ideas about physiology, disease processes, and the mind have changed since the early cultures thousands of years ago, when people apparently believed that illness was caused by evil spirits and the like. Between the years 500 and 300 B.C., Greek philosophers produced the earliest written ideas about health and illness.

They tried to explain how sickness happens and proposed that the mind and body are separate entities. During the Middle Ages, the Church had an enormous influence on ideas about illness, and the belief in mystical causes of disease became strong again. Philosophers and scientists from the seventeenth to the twentieth centuries provided the foundation for the biomedical model as a way to conceptualize health and illness.

The biomedical model has been extremely useful, enabling researchers to make great advances in conquering many infectious diseases through the development of vaccines and treatments. But many researchers today have come to recognize that aspects of individual patients — their histories, social relationships, lifestyles, personalities, mental processes, and biological processes — must be included in a full conceptualization of health and illness. As a result, the biopsychosocial model has emerged as the leading theoretical alternative to the biomedical approach as the fields of psychosomatic medicine, behavioral medicine, and health psychology have developed. This new model proposes a constant interplay of biological, psychological, and social systems — each interrelated with and producing changes in each other. The life-span perspective adds an important dimension to this model by considering the role of the person's development in health and illness.

Health psychology draws upon knowledge from a variety of other subfields in psychology and several nonpsychology fields, such as medicine, biology, social work, epidemiology, public health, sociology, and anthropology. The last four of these fields are especially important in describing the social systems in which health, illness, and the person exist and develop.

The study of important variables in health psychology involves the use of experimental and nonexperimental research methods. Experimental methods usually involve rigorous control and manipulation of variables and lead to cause-effect conclusions. Nonexperimental methods focus on the study of relationships between variables. A correlation describes an association between variables but does not indicate whether it is a causal relation. Quasi-experimental approaches are useful in studying variables that cannot be manipulated, such as the subjects' past history, age, and gender. To study people at different ages, researchers use cross-sectional and longitudinal approaches. The role of heredity in health and illness can be examined through twin and adoption studies.

KEY TERMS

illness/wellness continuum
health
dietary diseases
infectious diseases
chronic diseases
mind/body problem
biomedical model
risk factors
psychosomatic medicine
behavioral medicine
health psychology
biopsychosocial model
system
life-span perspective
mortality
morbidity
prevalence
incidence
epidemic
theory
variable
experiment
placebo
double-blind
correlation coefficient
correlational studies
quasi-experimental studies
retrospective approach
prospective approach
cross-sectional approach
longitudinal approach
cohort effect
case study
single-subject design
twin studies
adoption studies

2

THE BODY'S PHYSICAL SYSTEMS

PROLOGUE

When Tom was born 20 years ago, his parents were thrilled. Here was their first child — a delightful baby with such promise for the future. He seemed to be healthy. His parents were pleased that he began to consume large amounts of milk, often without becoming satiated. They took this as a good sign. But, in this case, it wasn't.

As the weeks went by, Tom's parents noticed that he wasn't gaining as much weight as he should, especially since he was still consuming lots of milk. He started to cough and wheeze a lot and developed one respiratory infection after another. They became concerned, and so did his pediatrician. After a series of tests, the devastating diagnosis was clear: Tom had *cystic fibrosis,* a chronic, progressive, and eventually fatal disease. Cystic fibrosis is an inherited disease of the respiratory system for which there is no cure and no effective treatment.

Tom has had a difficult life, and so has his family. The respiratory infections he had in infancy were just the beginning. His disease causes thick, sticky secretions that constantly block airways, trap air in the lungs, and help bacteria to thrive. Other body systems also become affected, causing additional problems, such as insufficient absorption of food and vitamins. As a result, he was sick often and remained short, underweight, and weak compared with other children. His social relationships have always been limited and strained, and the burden of his illness has taken its toll on his parents.

When Tom was younger and people asked him, "What do you want to be when you grow up?", he would answer, "I'm going to be an angel when I grow up." What other plans could he have had, realistically? At 20, he has reached the age by which half of the victims of cystic fibrosis die. Complications, such as heart damage, that generally afflict several body systems in the last stages of this disease have begun to appear.

We have seen in this story about Tom that biological factors, such as heredity, can affect health and that illness can alter social relationships. We have also seen that interrelated physiological systems of the body all become affected. In this chapter we outline the major physical systems of the body. Our discussion focuses on the normal functions of these systems, but we consider some important problems, too. What determines the degree of paralysis a person suffers after injury to the spine? How does stress affect our body systems? What is a heart attack, and what causes it?

THE NERVOUS SYSTEM

We all know that the nervous system, particularly the brain, in human beings and other animals controls the way we initiate behavior and respond to events in our world. The nervous system receives information about changes in the environment from sensory organs, including the eyes, ears, and nose, and it transmits directions that tell our muscles and other internal organs how to react. The brain also stores information — being a repository for our memory of past events — and provides our capability for thinking, reasoning, and creating.

How the Nervous System Works

The nervous system is constantly integrating the actions of our internal organs — although we are not generally aware of it. Many of these organs, such as the heart and digestive tract, are made of muscle tissues that respond to commands. The nervous system provides these commands through an intricate network of billions of specialized nerve cells, called **neurons.**

Although neurons in different parts of the nervous system have a variety of shapes and sizes, the diagram in Figure 2.1 shows their general features. Projecting from the *cell body* are clusters of branches called *dendrites.* Gen-

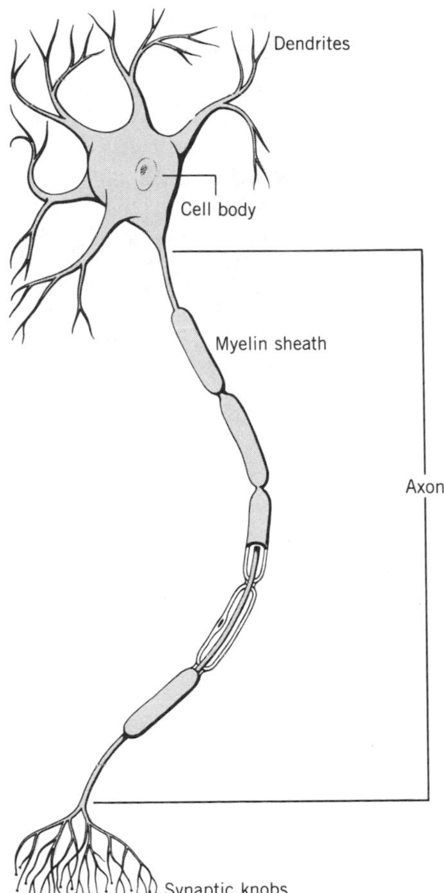

FIGURE 2.1 An idealized diagram of a neuron and some of its major parts. Electrochemical messages received by the dendrites are transmitted to the synaptic knobs. The myelin sheath covers the axon of most neurons.

erally, dendrites function as a receiver for messages from adjacent neurons. These messages then travel through a long, slender projection called the *axon,* which splits into branches at the far end. The tips of these branches have small swellings called *synaptic knobs* that lie close to the dendrites of other neurons. Messages from the knobs cross the gap, or *synapse,* to adjacent neurons, and in this way eventually reach their destination.

The messages neurons send consist of *electrochemical* activity. Within the neuron, the message is an impulse of electrical potential that fires when a dendrite is stimulated. That impulse then travels to the other end of the neuron and stimulates the synaptic knobs to release a chemical called a **neurotransmitter,** which crosses the synapse and reaches the dendrites of an adjacent neuron. Dozens of different neurotransmitters have been identified. Some of them tend to *excite* the receiving neuron, increasing the likelihood that an electrical impulse will be generated. Others tend to *inhibit* the neuron, making an impulse less likely. Some neurotransmitters can have either effect, depending on certain characteristics of the receiving neuron.

What changes occur in the nervous system as a person develops? By the time the typical baby is born, an immature structure has been formed for almost all the neurons this person will have. But the nervous system is still quite immature—for instance, the brain weighs only about 25% of the weight it will have when the child reaches adulthood (Sarafino & Armstrong, 1986). Most of the growth in brain size after birth results from an increase in the number of *glial cells* and the presence of a white fatty substance called *myelin.* The glial cells are thought to service and maintain the neurons. A myelin sheath surrounds the axons of most, but not all, neurons. This sheath is responsible for increasing the speed of nerve impulses and preventing them from being interfered with by adjacent nerve impulses, much like the way insulation is used on electrical wiring. The importance of myelin can be seen in the disease called *multiple sclerosis,* which results when the myelin sheath degenerates. People afflicted with this disease have weak muscles that lack coordination and move spastically (Nelson, 1984).

As the infant grows, the brain forms relatively few new neurons. But the network of dendrites and synaptic knobs to carry messages to and from other neurons expands dramatically, as Figure 2.2 shows. The myelin sheath covering the neurons is better developed initially in the upper regions of the body than in the lower regions. The progress in myelin growth then

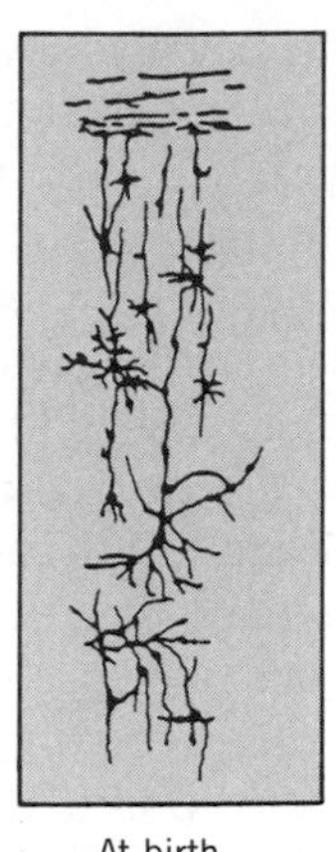

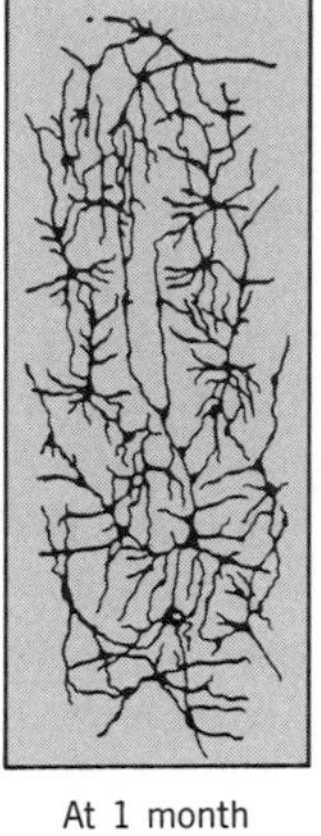

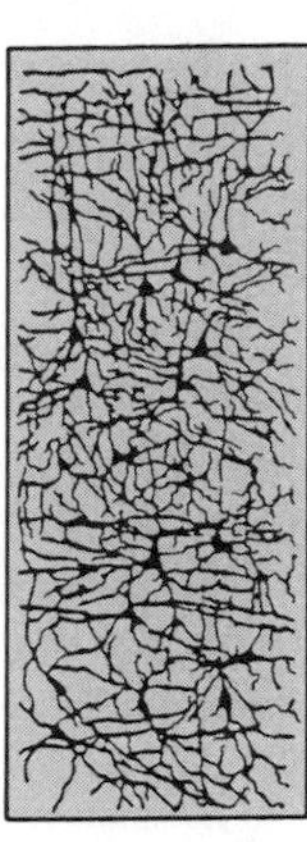

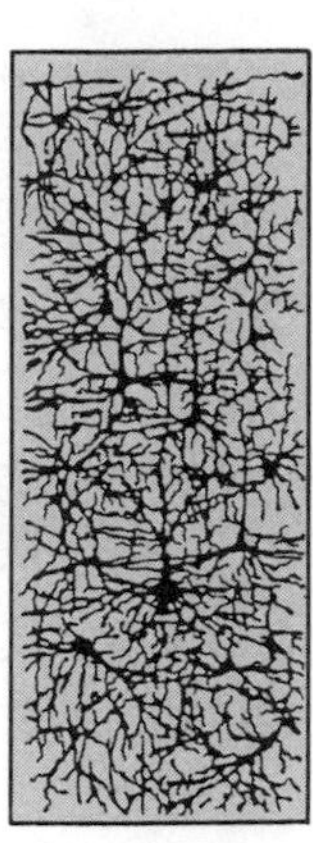

FIGURE 2.2 Drawings showing the neutral structure of a section of the human cortex at four different ages. Notice that the number of cell bodies (dark spots) stays the same, while the network of dendrites expands with age. (Drawings from Lindsey & Norman, 1977, Figure 11-13, based on photographs from Conel, 1939-1963.)

spreads down the body—from the head to shoulders, to the arms and hands, to the upper chest and abdomen, and then the legs and feet. This sequence is reflected in the individual's motor development: the upper parts of the body are brought under control before the lower parts. Studies with animals have found that chronic poor nutrition early in life impairs brain growth by retarding the development of myelin, glial cells, and dendrites. Such impairment can produce long-lasting deficits in a child's motor and intellectual performance (Reinis & Goldman, 1980).

Beginning in early adulthood, the brain tends to lose weight with age (Stevens-Long, 1984). Decreases occur in the number of brain cells, their water and protein content, and in the blood flow to them. At the same time, the chemical composition of the brain changes. For instance, salts and calcium decrease while potassium and phosphorous increase. These alterations in the brain are associated with the declines people often notice in their mental and physical functions after they reach 50 or 60 years of age.

The nervous system is enormously complex. How is it organized? Basically, it has two major divisions—the central nervous system and the peripheral nervous system—that connect to each other. The **central nervous system** consists of the brain and spinal cord. The peripheral nervous system is composed of the remaining network of neurons throughout the body. Each of these major divisions consists of interconnected lower-order divisions or structures. We will examine the nervous system, beginning at the top and working our way down.

The Central Nervous System

The brain and spinal cord race toward maturity early in life. For example, the brain weighs 75% of its adult weight at about 2 years of age, 90% at 5 years, and 95% at 10 years (Tanner, 1970, 1978). The brain is divided into three parts: the *forebrain,* the *cerebellum,* and the *brainstem.* Each of these parts has special functions.

The Forebrain

The forebrain is the uppermost part of the brain. As Figure 2.3 shows, the forebrain consists of two main subdivisions: the *telencephalon,* which consists of the cerebrum and the limbic system, and the *diencephalon,* which includes the thalamus and hypothalamus. As a general rule, areas toward the top and outer regions of the brain are involved in our perceptual, motor, learning, and conceptual activities. Regions toward the center and bottom of the brain are involved mainly in controlling internal and automatic body functions and in transmitting information to and from the telencephalon.

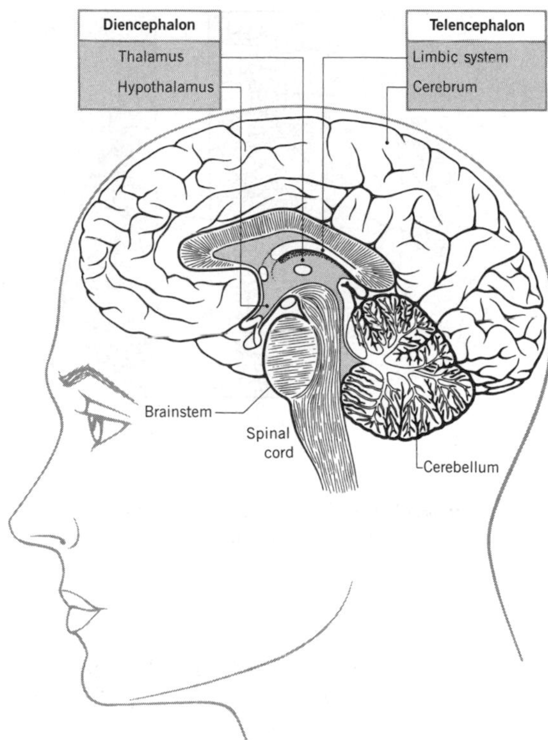

FIGURE 2.3 A side view of the human brain in cross section, sliced through the middle from front to back. The forebrain consists of the telencephalon (cerebrum and limbic system) and the diencephalon (thalamus and hypothalamus). The remaining divisions of the central nervous system—the cerebellum, the brainstem, and the spinal cord—are also labeled.

The **cerebrum** is the upper and largest portion of the human brain and includes the *cerebral cortex,* its outermost layer. The cerebrum controls complex motor and mental activity. It develops rapidly in the first few years of life, becoming larger, thicker, and more convoluted. The cerebrum has two halves—the *left hemisphere* and the *right hemisphere*—each of which looks like the left hemispheres drawn in Figure 2.4.

Although the left and right hemispheres look alike on the surface, they control different types of processes. For one thing, the motor cortex (see Figure 2.4b) of each hemisphere controls motor movements on the opposite side of the body. This is why damage to the motor cortex on, say, the right side of the brain may leave part of the left side of the body paralyzed. The two hemispheres also control different aspects of cognitive and language processes. In most people, the left hemisphere contains the areas that handle language processes, including speech and writing. The right hemisphere usually processes such things as visual imagery, emotions, and the perception of patterns, such as melodies (Geschwind, 1979).

You probably noticed in Figure 2.4 that each hemisphere is divided into a front part, called the frontal lobe, and three back parts: the temporal, occipital, and parietal lobes. The *frontal lobe* is involved in a variety of functions, one of which is motor activity. The back part of the frontal lobe contains the motor cortex, which controls the skeletal muscles of the body. If a patient who is undergoing brain surgery receives stimulation to the motor cortex, some part of the body will move. The frontal lobe is also involved in important mental activities, such as the association of ideas, planning, self-awareness, and emotion. As a result, injury to areas of this lobe can produce personality and emotional reactions, like those described by the physician of Phineas P. Gage:

> He is fitful, irreverant, indulging in the grossest profanity (which was not previously his custom), manifesting but little deference to his fellows, impatient of restraint or advice when it conflicts with his desires, at times . . . obstinate, capricious, and vacillating. . . . His mind was radically changed, so that his friends said he was no longer Gage. (Cited in McClintic, 1985, p. 93.)

Phineas had survived a workplace accident in which a tamping iron was blown through the front of his head.

The *temporal lobe* is chiefly involved in hearing, but also in vision and memory. Damage to this region can impair the person's comprehension of speech and ability to determine the direction from which a sound is coming. The *occipital lobe* contains the principal visual area of the brain. Damage to the occipital lobe can produce blindness or the inability to recog-

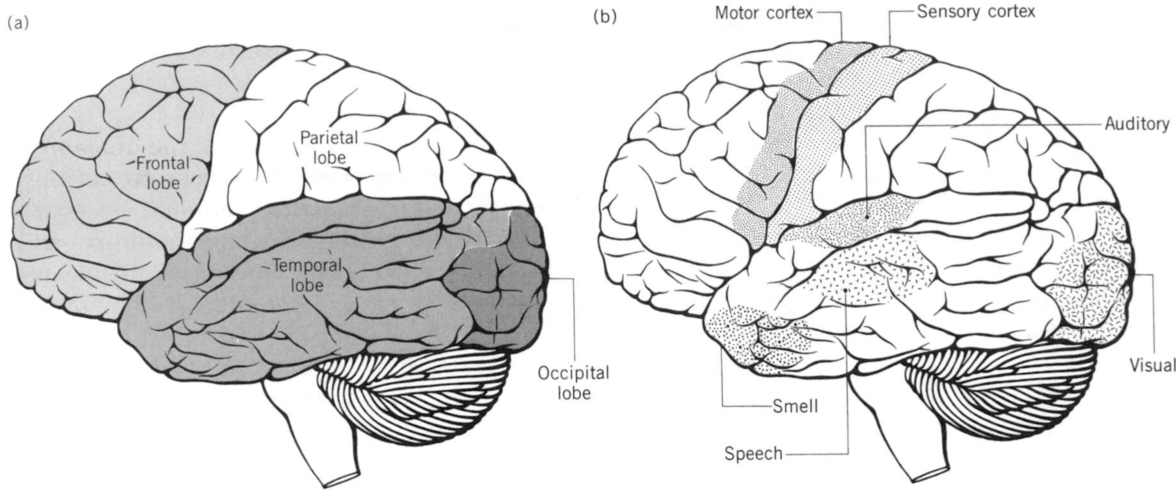

FIGURE 2.4 Two drawings of the surface of the left hemisphere of the cerebrum. The left drawing shows the four parts of the hemisphere, and the right drawing points out the areas associated with specific functions. The right hemisphere has the same four parts and functional areas.

nize an object by sight. The *parietal lobe* is involved mainly in body sensations, such as of pain, cold, heat, touch, and body movement.

The second part of the telencephalon—called the **limbic system**—lies along the innermost edge of the cerebrum, and adjacent to the diencephalon (refer back to Figure 2.3). The limbic system is not well understood yet. It consists of several structures that seem to be important in the expression of emotions, such as fear, anger, and excitement. To the extent that heredity affects a person's emotions, it may do so by determining the structure and function of the limbic system (McClintic, 1985).

The diencephalon includes two structures—the thalamus and hypothalamus—which lie below and are partially encircled by the limbic system. The **thalamus** is a truly pivotal structure in the flow of information in the nervous system. It functions as the chief relay station for directing sensory messages, such as a visual image or pain, to appropriate points in the cerebrum, such as the occipital or parietal lobe. The thalamus also relays commands going out to the skeletal muscles from the motor cortex of the cerebrum.

The **hypothalamus,** a small structure just below the thalamus, plays an important role in people's emotions and motivation. It contains the control centers for eating, drinking, and sexual activity, for instance. Research with animals has shown that if a certain part of the feeding center is destroyed, the animal will eat incessantly; but if a different center is destroyed, the animal refuses to eat. Both of these conditions cause the animal to die (Nelson, 1984). Occasionally people become overweight as a result of a disease that affects the feeding center of this structure.

Another important function of the hypothalamus is to maintain *homeostasis*—a state of balance or normal function among our body systems. Our normal body temperature and heart rate, which are characteristic of healthy individuals, are examples of homeostasis. When our bodies are cold, for instance, we shiver, which produces heat. When we are very warm, we perspire, which cools the body. These adjustments are under the control of the hypothalamus (McClintic, 1985). We will see later that the hypothalamus also plays an important role in our reaction to stress.

The Cerebellum

The **cerebellum** lies at the back of the brain, below the cerebrum. The main function of the cerebellum is in maintaining body balance and coordinating movement. This structure has nerve connections to the motor cortex and most of the sense organs of the body. Although specific movements may be initiated by areas of the cerebrum, the cerebellum makes our actions precise and well-coordinated.

How does the cerebellum do this? There are at least two ways. First, it continuously compares our intent with our performance, ensuring that a movement goes in the right direction, at the proper rate, and with appropriate force. Second, it smoothes our movements. Because of the forces involved in movement, there is an underlying tendency for our motions to go quickly back and forth, as a tremor. The cerebellum damps this tendency (McClintic, 1985). When injury occurs to the cerebellum, the person's actions become jerky and uncoordinated —a condition called *ataxia.* Simple movements, such as walking or touching an object, become difficult and unsteady.

Figure 2.5 shows the location of the cerebellum relative to the brainstem, which is the next section of the brain we will discuss.

The Brainstem

The lowest portion of the brain—called the **brainstem**—has the form of an oddly shaped knob at the top of the spinal cord. The brainstem consists of four parts: the midbrain, reticular system, pons, and medulla.

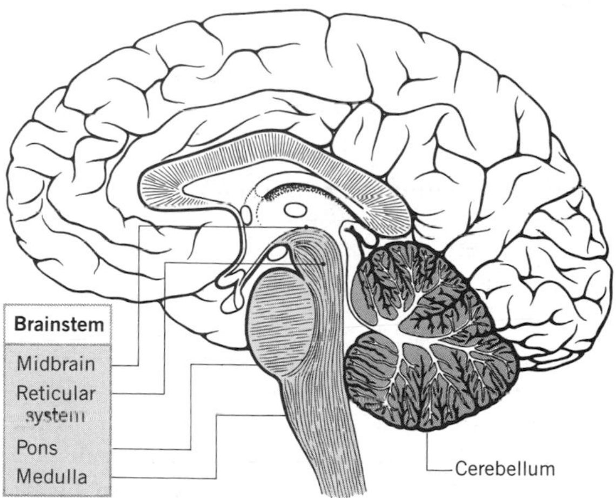

FIGURE 2.5 A side view of the human brain in cross section, showing the cerebellum and the brainstem, which includes the midbrain, reticular system, pons, and medulla.

The **midbrain** lies at the top of the brainstem. It connects directly to the thalamus above it, which relays messages to various parts of the forebrain. The midbrain receives information from the visual and auditory systems and is especially important in muscle movement. The disorder called *Parkinson's disease* results from degeneration of an area of the midbrain (Guyton, 1985). People severely afflicted with this disease have noticeable motor tremors and their neck and trunk posture becomes rigid, so that they walk in a crouch. Sometimes the tremors are so continuous and vigorous that the victim becomes crippled.

The **reticular system** is a network of neurons that extends from the bottom to the top of the brainstem and into the thalamus. The reticular system plays an important role in controlling our states of sleep, arousal, and attention. When people suffer a coma, it is likely that this system is injured or disordered (McClintic, 1985). *Epilepsy,* a condition in which a victim may become unconscious and begin to convulse, seems to result from an abnormality in the reticular system. One type of epileptic seizure called *grand mal* may result from "reverberating cycles" in the reticular system:

> That is, one portion of the system stimulates another portion, which stimulates a third portion, and this in turn restimulates the first portion, causing a cycle that continues for 2 to 3 minutes, until the neurons of the system fatigue so greatly that the reverberation ceases. (Guyton, 1985, p. 356)

Following a grand mal seizure, the person often sleeps at least a few minutes and sometimes for hours.

The **pons** forms a large bulge at the front of the brainstem and is involved in eye movements, facial expressions, and chewing. At the bottom of the brainstem is the **medulla,** which contains vital centers that control breathing, heartbeat rate, and the diameter of blood vessels (which affects blood pressure). Because of the many vital functions it controls, damage to the medulla can be life-threatening. *Polio,* a crippling disease that was once epidemic, sometimes damaged the center that controls breathing. These patients were placed in an iron lung in order to breathe (McClintic, 1985).

The Spinal Cord

Extending down the spine from the brainstem is the **spinal cord,** a major neural pathway that transmits messages between the brain and various parts of the body. It contains neurons that carry impulses away from (the *efferent* direction) and toward (*afferent*) the brain. Efferent commands travel down the cord on their way to produce muscle action; afferent impulses come to the spinal cord from sense organs in all parts of the body.

The organization of the spinal cord parallels that of the body—that is, the higher the region of the cord, the higher the parts of the body to which it connects. As a result, the effect of disease or injury to the spinal cord depends on the location of the damage. For example, if an accident severs the lower portion of the cord, the lower regions of the body are paralyzed—a condition called *paraplegia.* If the upper portion of the spinal cord is severed, paralysis is more extensive. Paralysis of the legs and arms is called *quadriplegia.*

Figure 2.6 depicts the spinal cord and its relation to the brain and the branching network of afferent and efferent neurons throughout the body—the peripheral nervous system.

The Peripheral Nervous System

The **peripheral nervous system** has two parts: the somatic nervous system and the autonomic nervous system. The **somatic nervous system** is involved in both sensory and motor functions, serving mainly the skin and skeletal muscles. The **autonomic nervous system** activates internal organs, such as the lungs and intestines, and reports to the brain the current state of activity of these organs.

In the somatic nervous system, afferent neurons carry messages from sense organs to the spinal cord. Efferent neurons carry messages to, and activate, *striated* (grooved) skeletal muscles, such as those in the face, arms, and legs, that we can move voluntarily. A disorder called *myasthenia gravis* can develop at the junction of these muscles and neurons, weakening muscle function of the head and neck. This produces characteristic symptoms—such as drooping eyelids, blurred vision, and difficulty swallowing and breathing—and can lead to paralysis and death. Although medical treatment is effective in restoring muscle function, some symptoms may recur when the person is under stress (Guyton, 1985; Pillitteri, 1981).

In the autonomic nervous system, neurons carry messages between the spinal cord and the *smooth* muscles of the internal organs, such as the heart, stomach, lungs, blood vessels, and glands. This system itself has two divisions, the sympathetic and parasympathetic, which often act in opposite ways, as Figure 2.7 diagrams. The **sympathetic nervous system** helps us mobilize and expend energy in responding to emergencies, expressing strong emotions, and performing strenuous activity. For instance, suppose you are crossing a street and suddenly notice a speeding car barreling toward you, and its brakes start to squeal. The sympathetic nervous system instantly moves into action, producing several simultaneous changes—for example, it speeds up the heart, dilates certain arteries to increase blood flow to the heart and skeletal muscles, constricts other arteries to decrease blood flow to the skin and digestive organs, decreases salivation, and increases perspiration. These changes, in general, enable you to mobilize energy, and you leap to safety out of the car's path. This system is called "sympathetic" because it acts in agreement with your current emotional state.

What does the parasympathetic division do? The prefix *para* means "alongside of"—this division acts alongside of, and often in opposition to, the sympathetic division. The **parasympathetic nervous system** regulates "quiet" or calming processes, helping our individual organ systems to conserve and store energy. One example of parasympathetic activity can be seen in the digestion of food. When you

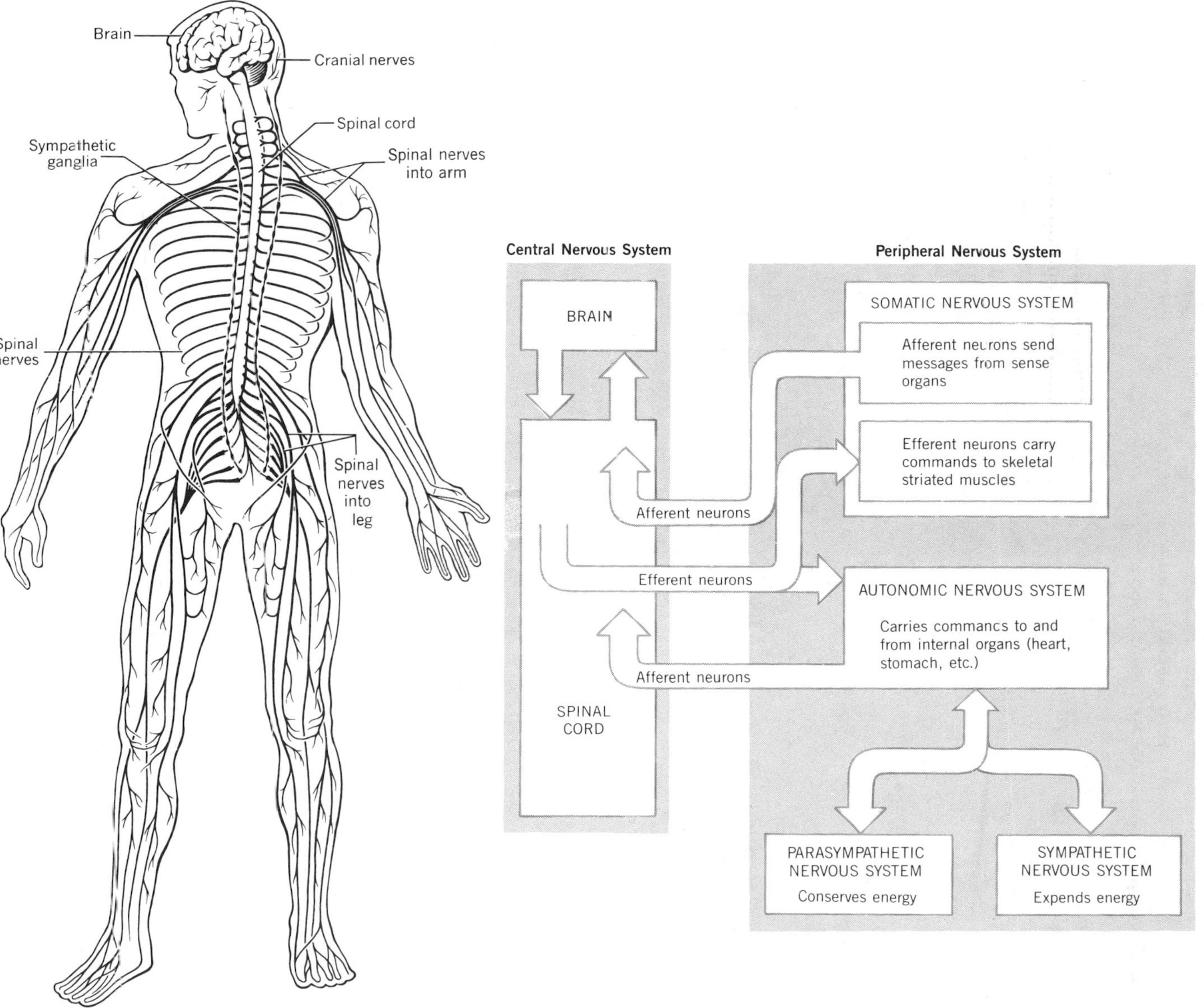

FIGURE 2.6 Diagrams showing the relationship and flow of nerve impulses among the major parts of the nervous system.

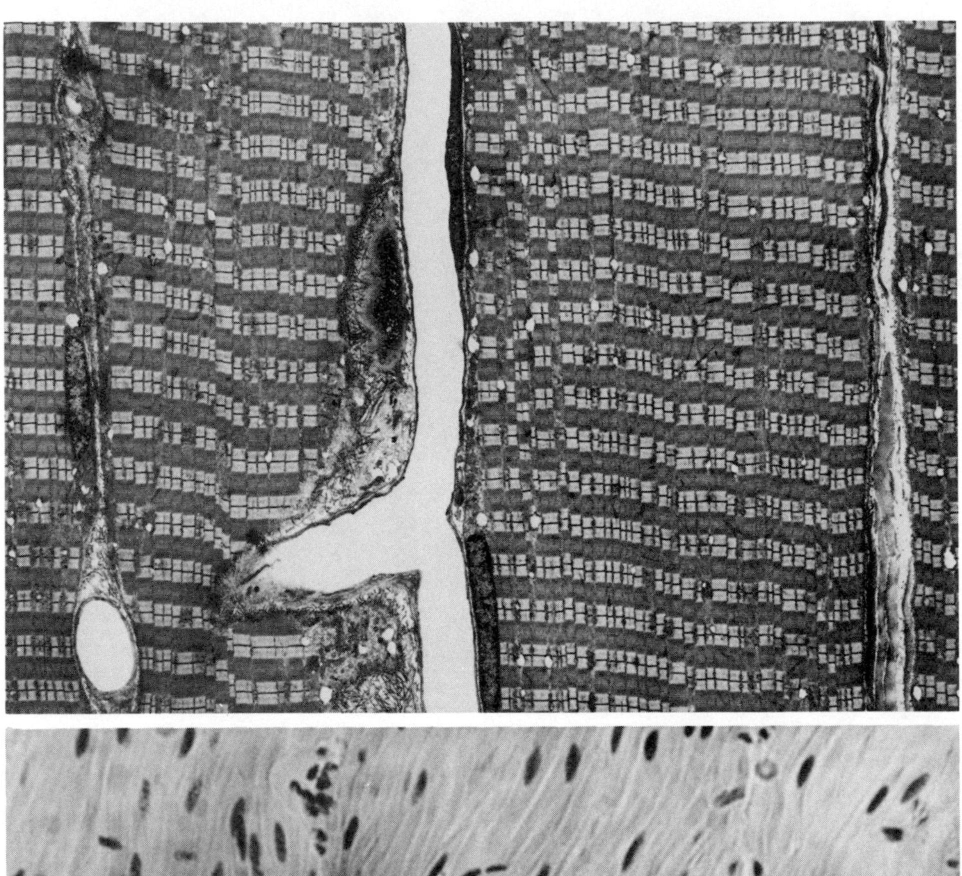

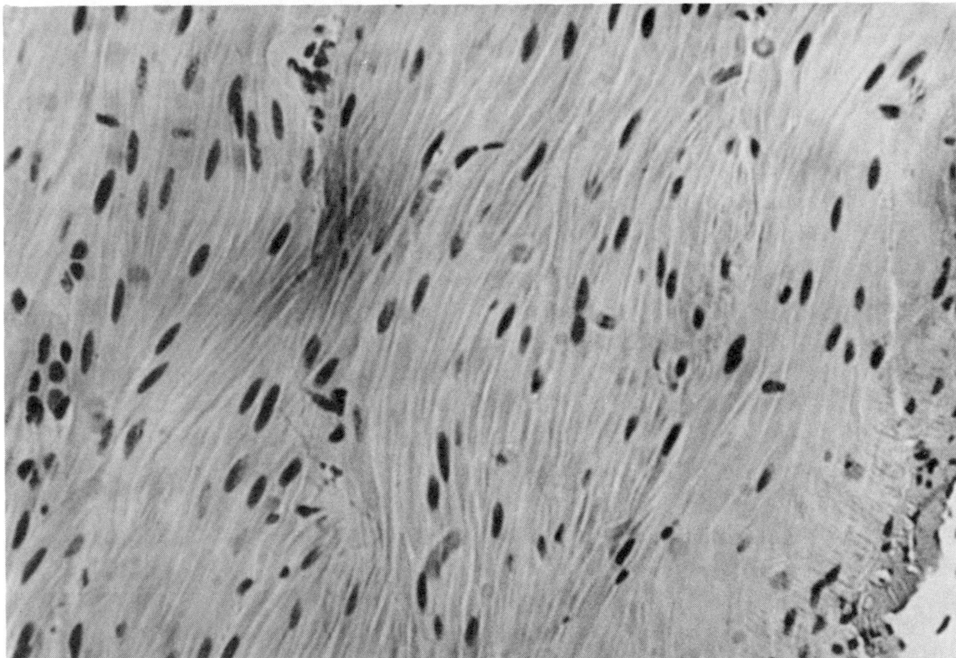

Striated muscles (top), which people can move voluntarily, are structurally different from smooth muscles (bottom) of the internal organs.

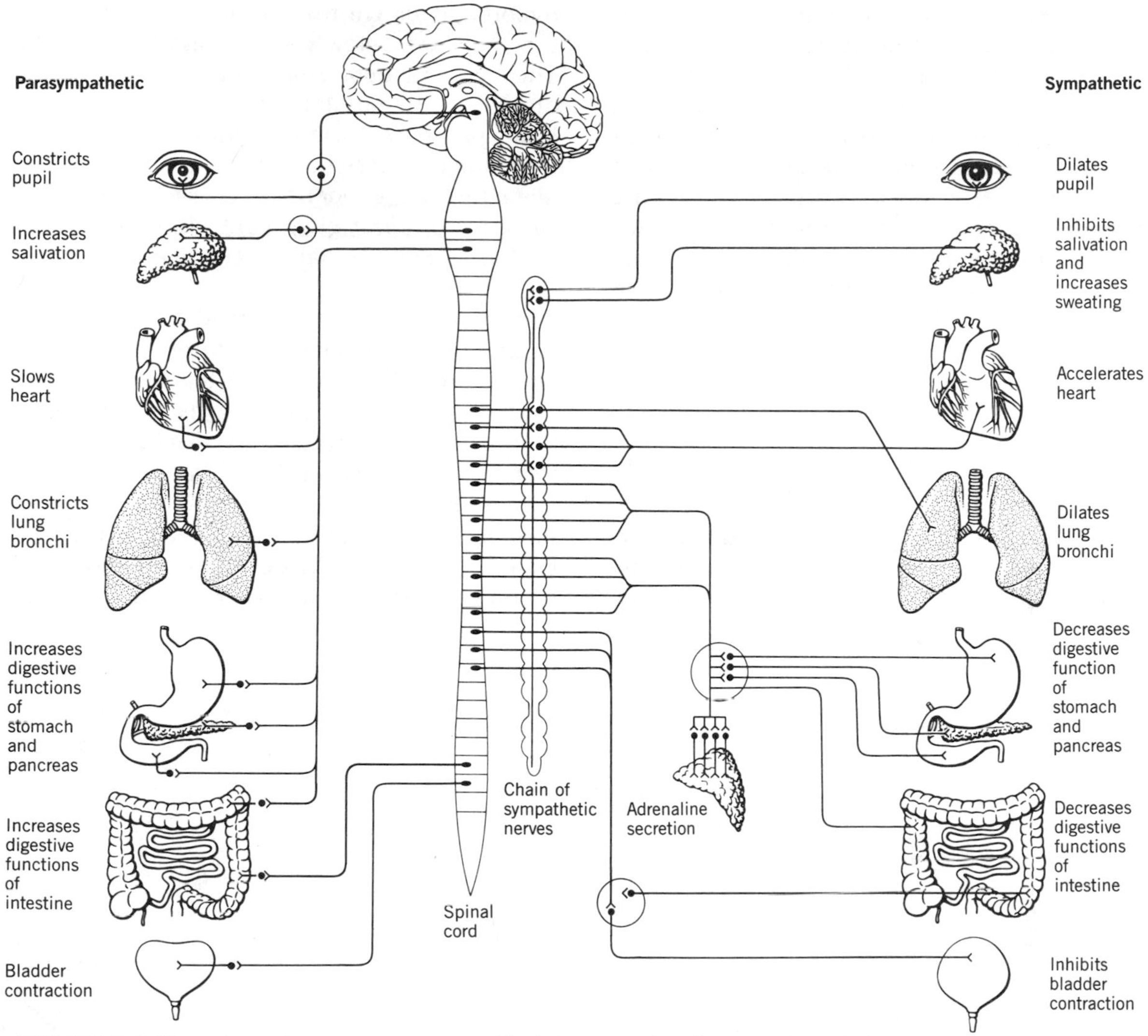

FIGURE 2.7 The autonomic nervous system and its interconnections between the spinal cord and various organs of the body. The function of the parasympathetic division in conserving energy is shown on the left side of the diagram. The function of the sympathetic division in expending energy is shown on the right side. Notice that each organ connects to both divisions.

eat a meal, the parasympathetic nervous system carries messages to regulate each step in the digestive process, such as by increasing salivation and stomach contractions. Another example can be seen in the course of emotional or emergency reactions—when an emergency has passed, the parasympathetic division helps restore your normal body state.

As you now realize, the nervous system is connected to and regulates all of our other body systems, and the brain is the control center. The remainder of this chapter examines these other body systems, beginning with the endocrine system.

THE ENDOCRINE SYSTEM

The **endocrine system** consists of a set of glands that often work in close association with the autonomic nervous system. These systems share an important function: they communicate with various parts of the body. But they do this in somewhat different ways. Whereas the nervous system uses both electrical and chemical messages, the endocrine system communicates only with chemical substances, which are called **hormones.** Each endocrine gland secretes specific hormones directly into the bloodstream, which carries these chemicals to various parts of the body. Figure 2.8 shows where several of the more important endocrine glands are located.

The Endocrine and Nervous Systems Working Together

How are the endocrine and nervous systems associated? The nervous system is linked to the endocrine system by connections between the hypothalamus (in the forebrain) and a gland that lies just below it—the **pituitary gland.** The hypothalamus sends chemical messages directly to the pituitary gland, causing it to release pituitary hormones into the blood. In turn, most of these hormones selectively stimulate the other endocrine glands to secrete. Because the pituitary gland controls the secretion of other endocrine glands, it is called the "master gland."

Researchers have identified dozens of different hormones that course through our veins and arteries. Each hormone has its own specific effects on cells and organs of the body, thereby directly or indirectly affecting psychological and physical functions. Some hormones, such as estrogens and testosterone produced in the *ovaries* and *testes,* are especially important in the development and functioning of female and male reproductive sys-

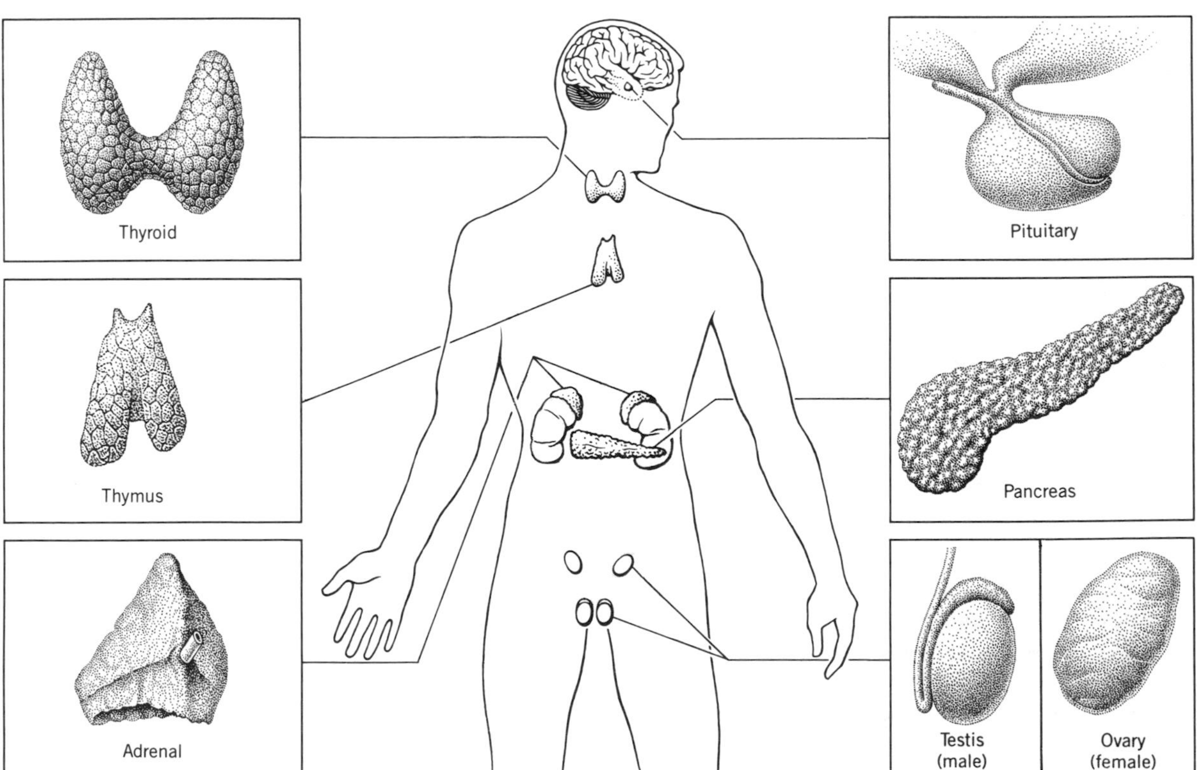

FIGURE 2.8 Some of the endocrine glands and their locations in the body.

tems. Other hormones affect blood pressure, general body growth, and the balance of various chemicals, such as calcium, in the body. Still other hormones help us react to specific situations we encounter in our lives.

We saw earlier that the autonomic nervous system plays an important role in our reaction to an emergency. So does the endocrine system. Let's see how by returning to the incident in which you leaped out of the path of a speeding car. At the same time that the sympathetic nervous system reacts to your emergency, the hypothalamus immediately sends a hormone called corticotropin-releasing factor to the pituitary gland. This causes the pituitary to release ACTH (adrenocorticotropic hormone) into the blood. The ACTH then travels throughout the body and stimulates the release of a variety of hormones — especially those of the adrenal glands — that affect your reaction to the emergency.

Adrenal Glands

The **adrenal glands** are located on top of the kidneys, as Figure 2.8 depicts. These glands release several important hormones in response to emergencies and stress (McClintic, 1985). One of these hormones, *cortisol*, helps to control swelling when we are injured. If when you leaped to avoid being hit by the car you sprained your ankle, this hormone would help reduce swelling. But continued high levels of cortisol and similar hormones over a long time can be harmful to the body. They can lead to high blood pressure and the formation of ulcers, for example.

Two other important adrenal hormones are *epinephrine* and *norepinephrine* (also called adrenalin and noradrenalin). These hormones work in conjunction with the sympathetic nervous system to produce such bodily reactions as speeding up heart and respiration rates and increasing the liver's sugar output for quick energy. After the emergency has passed and sympathetic activity has subsided, some impact of the hormones may continue for a while because they are still in the bloodstream.

The impact of the nervous and endocrine systems' activities in emergency situations differs in the speed and persistence of their effect. The nervous system responds by sending messages that move very rapidly to specific locations; and once they reach their destination, they become inactivated or dissipated. For example, the nervous system also produces and uses epinephrine and norepinephrine, but these chemicals function as neurotransmitters, relaying their commands from neuron to neuron and having a localized effect. The impact of the message stops quickly, and persists only if additional messages are sent. Hormones from the endocrine system move more slowly and more broadly through the body, and their effects can be delayed and long-lasting.

Other Glands

Several other endocrine glands are also important. The *thyroid gland* is located in the neck. It produces hormones that regulate the individual's general activity level and general body growth. Disorders in thyroid production are of two types: *hypothyroidism,* or insufficient secretion of thyroid hormones, and *hyperthyroidism,* or excessive thyroid secretion (Collins & Lipman, 1985). Hypothyroidism leads to low activity levels and weight gain. If the condition is congenital and untreated, dwarfism and mental retardation often result. The condition can be treated medically by having the person take hormone supplements orally. Hyperthyroidism leads to high activity levels, short attention spans, tremors, insomnia, and weight loss. If the person does not receive treatment to reduce thyroid secretions, a disorder called *Graves' disease* may result. People with Graves' disease act in a highly restless, irritable, and confused manner.

The *thymus gland,* which is located in the chest, is quite large in infancy but diminishes in size and efficiency later, particularly after puberty (Batten, 1986). The thymus plays an important role early in life in the development of antibodies and immunities against diseases.

One other endocrine gland is the *pancreas,*

HIGHLIGHT 2A: On Issues
Our Physiological Individuality

Think about some differences between two individuals you know. Probably the first things that come to mind are their physical and behavioral characteristics. One of them is tall and has blond hair, blue eyes, and an outgoing personality; the other is short and has dark hair, dark eyes, and is shy. But what about their internal physiological structure and functions?

We don't usually think about internal physiological differences between people. This is partly because the pictures of internal organs we see in books are always the same. As a result, we get the impression that if you've seen one heart or stomach, you've seen them all. This impression is wrong. Our individuality exists not only in our external features, but in our internal organs and bodily chemistry as well. Examples of some structural variations are given in Figure 2A.1. The aorta is a major blood vessel that "arches," or curves, over and attaches to the heart. The drawing on the left depicts the usual branching that forms at the arch of the aorta, and the other drawings show variations that occur, sometimes quite frequently. Major differences like these occur in virtually all organs (Skolnick, 1986).

Our physiological individuality can have major implications for health and behavior. How? One way is that people's reactions to medicines differ, sometimes quite substantially. Some people may require many times the normal dose of certain drugs before the desired effect occurs. The age and weight of the person contribute to this variability. Heavy people usually require larger doses of a drug than other people do. Infants and the elderly seem to be particularly sensitive to the effects of drugs, and overdoses are a danger (Bennett, 1987; USDHHS, 1981). Blood pressure medication in the elderly may overshoot and lower the pressure too far, for example.

There are gender differences in many organ systems, too. Males generally have larger hearts and lungs, and higher blood pressure, than females do. Their body systems also react to stress differently. We saw earlier that the adrenal glands respond to stress by secreting hormones—two of which are epinephrine and cortisol. When under stress, males secrete more of these hormones than females do (Collins & Frankenhaeuser, 1978; Pollack & Steklis, 1986).

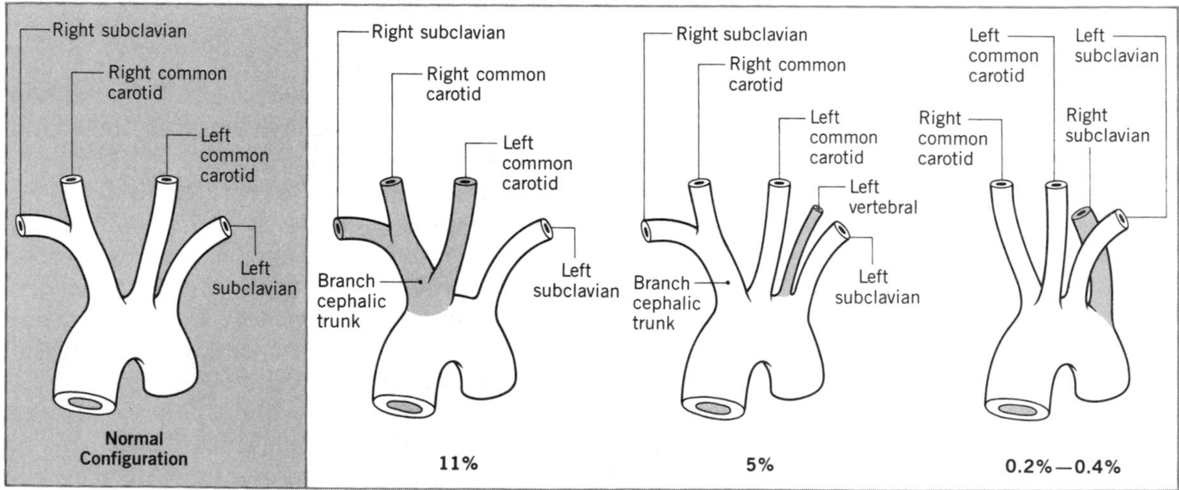

FIGURE 2A.1 Variations in arterial branching of the aortic arch and the approximate percentages of their occurrence. (Drawings adapted are from Grant, 1972, plate 446.4.)

which is located below the stomach. Its main function is to regulate the level of blood sugar, or glucose. The pancreas does this by producing two hormones, *glucagon* and *insulin,* that act in opposition. Glucagon raises the concentration of glucose in the blood, and insulin lowers it (McClintic, 1985). The disorder called *diabetes mellitus* results when the pancreas does not produce sufficient insulin to balance the action of glucagon. This imbalance produces excess blood sugar levels—a condition called *hyperglycemia.* If this condition persists and is untreated, it may cause coma and death. Diabetes can be medically controlled, generally through diet and either medication or daily insulin injections (Kilo & Williamson, 1987; Pohl, Gonder-Frederick, & Cox, 1984).

THE DIGESTIVE SYSTEM

Whether we eat a hamburger, drink some milk, or swallow a pill, our bodies respond in the same general way. The **digestive system** tries to break down what we have ingested, use parts of it, and excrete the rest. The parts that the body uses are absorbed into the bloodstream, which transports them to all of our body cells. Nutrients in the foods we eat provide energy to fuel our activity, body growth, and repair.

Food's Journey through Digestive Organs

Think of the digestive system as a long tube—about 20 feet long—with stations along the way. The journey of food through this tube begins in the *mouth* and ends at the *rectum.* These digestive organs and the major organs in between are shown in Figure 2.9.

How does this system break down food? One way is mechanical: for example, we grind food up when we chew it. Another way is chemical: by the action of **enzymes,** substances that act as catalysts in speeding up chemical reactions in cells. How do enzymes work? You can see the effect of an enzyme by doing the following "experiment." Place a bit of liver in some hydrogen peroxide and watch what happens:

> An enzyme in liver called *catalase* sets off the decomposition of hydrogen peroxide and you'll see a vigorous evolution of oxygen. The frothing seen when hydrogen peroxide is used to disinfect a wound is the same reaction. (Holum, 1987, p. 101)

In most cases, the names for enzymes end in the letters *ase,* and the remainder of each name reflects the substance on which it acts. The following list gives some examples:

- *Carbohydrase* acts on carbohydrates
- *Lactase* acts on lactose (milk)
- *Phosphatase* acts on phosphate compounds
- *Sucrase* acts on sucrose (sugar)

As food is broken down into smaller and smaller units, water molecules become attached to these units. This is the main function of digestion (Nelson, 1984).

When food is in the mouth, there is more digestive action going on than just chewing. Food is moistened with saliva, which contains an enzyme that starts the process of breaking down starches. The salivary glands release saliva in response to commands from the brainstem, which responds primarily to sensory information from taste buds. Simply seeing, smelling, or even thinking about food can produce neural impulses that cause the mouth to water (McClintic, 1985).

The journey of food advances to the *esophagus,* a tube that is normally flattened when food is not passing through it. The esophagus pushes the food down to the stomach by wave-like muscle contractions called *peristalsis.* By the time food enters the esophagus, the stomach has already begun digestive activities by releasing small amounts of gastric juice even before food reaches it. Tasting, smelling, seeing, or thinking about food can initiate this process (Feldman & Richardson, 1986). Once food reaches the stomach, this organ amasses large amounts of gastric juices, including *hydrochloric acid* and *pepsin,* an enzyme that breaks down proteins. (Note that this enzyme name is one of the few that does not end in *ase.*) The stomach also produces a sticky mucus substance to pro-

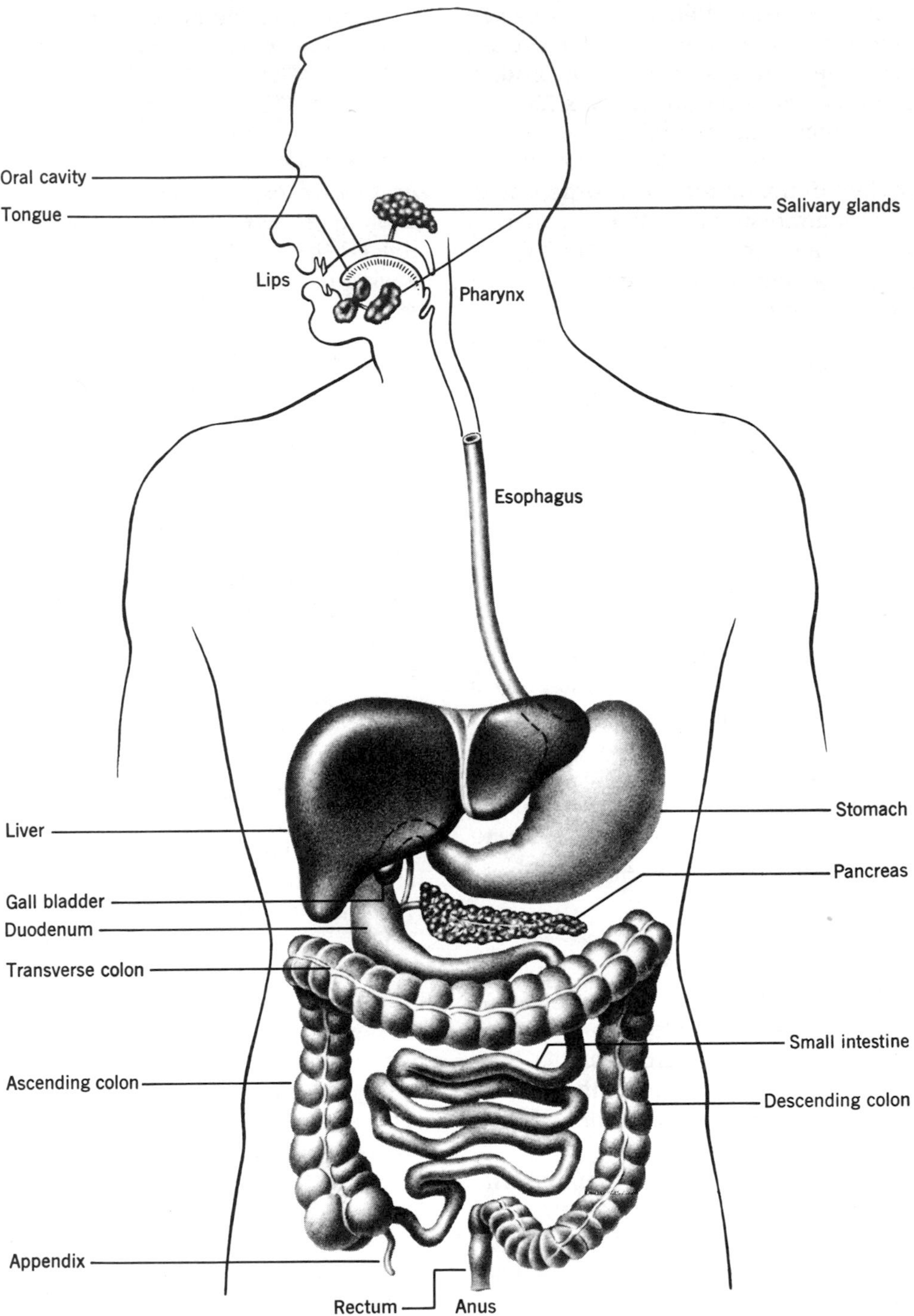

FIGURE 2.9 Major parts of the digestive system.

tect its lining from the highly acidic gastric juices. To prepare the food for the next stage in digestion, the muscular stomach walls produce a churning motion—that we are generally not aware of—which mixes the food particles with the gastric juices.

The mixing action in the stomach continues for three or four hours, producing a semiliquid mixture. Peristalsis in the stomach then moves this mixture on, a little at a time, to the beginning section of the small intestine called the *duodenum.* Several important digestive processes occur in the small intestine (Guyton, 1985; Nelson, 1984). First, the highly acidic food mixture becomes chemically alkaline as a result of substances added from the pancreas, gall bladder, and wall of the small intestine. This is important because the linings of the small intestine and remainder of the digestive tract are not protected from high acidity, as the stomach is.

Second, the process of breaking down food continues. Enzymes secreted by the pancreas into the duodenum break down carbohydrates, proteins, and fats further. The role of the small intestines in the digestion of fats is especially important because fats are not broken down very much before entering the duodenum. The processing of fats in the small intestine is aided by a substance called *bile* that is produced in the liver and stored in the gall bladder. Bile separates fatty materials into tiny particles that enzymes from the pancreas can process efficiently.

The third process that occurs in the small intestine is *absorption.* Most of the ingested substances our bodies use are absorbed into the bloodstream through the lining of the small intestine. The stomach lining normally absorbs very few substances, one of which

> is alcohol, which passes quickly through the stomach walls unless the drinker has previously consumed some fatty materials such as milk, peanuts, or potato chips. Such substances delay the absorption of much of the alcohol until it reaches the small intestine, and the individual doesn't get intoxicated in such a rush. (Nelson, 1984, p. 95)

By the time food is ready to be absorbed through the intestine wall, the digestive process has broken down nutrients into molecules—carbohydrates are broken down into *simple sugars,* fats into *glycerol* and *fatty acids,* and proteins into *amino acids.*

How does absorption occur? The inside of the small intestine is made of a membrane that will allow molecules to pass through. To increase the absorbing surface, the intestine wall has many folds that contain projections, as pictured in Figure 2.10. Each of the many thousands of projections contains a network of structures that will accept the molecules and transport them away to other parts of the body. These structures include tiny blood vessels called *capillaries* and a tube called a *lacteal.* Capillaries absorb amino acids, simple sugars, and water; they also absorb some fatty acids, vitamins, and minerals. Lacteals accept glycerol and the remaining fatty acids and vitamins.

The remaining food material continues its journey to the large intestine, called the *colon.* Although some absorption of nutrients and water takes place here, the main function of the colon is to transport the material and convert it through bacterial action into feces. The feces eventually reach the rectum, where they are stored until defecation occurs.

Judging from the many television commercials we see for stomach and "irregularity" remedies, it seems that people in the United States have a good deal of trouble with their digestive processes. One disorder of the digestive system is *peptic ulcers,* which are open sores in the lining of the stomach or intestine, usually in the duodenum. These sores appear to result from excess gastric juices chronically eroding the lining when there is little or no food in the stomach. Abdominal pain is the chief symptom of the disorder. Although the victims of ulcers are mostly adults, the disorder also occurs in children, particularly boys (Whitehead, 1986). People who experience high levels of stress seem to be more susceptible to ulcers than people who do not.

Hepatitis is a viral disease in which the liver becomes inflamed and unable to function well. The first symptoms often are like those of flu.

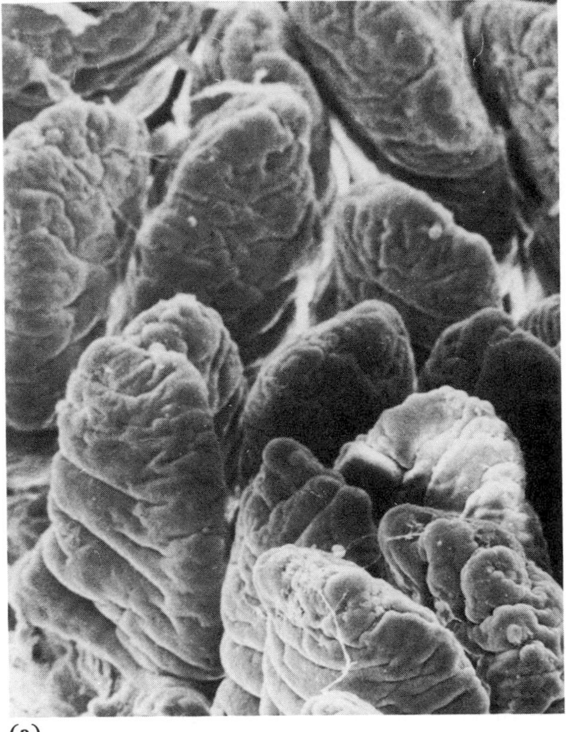
(a)

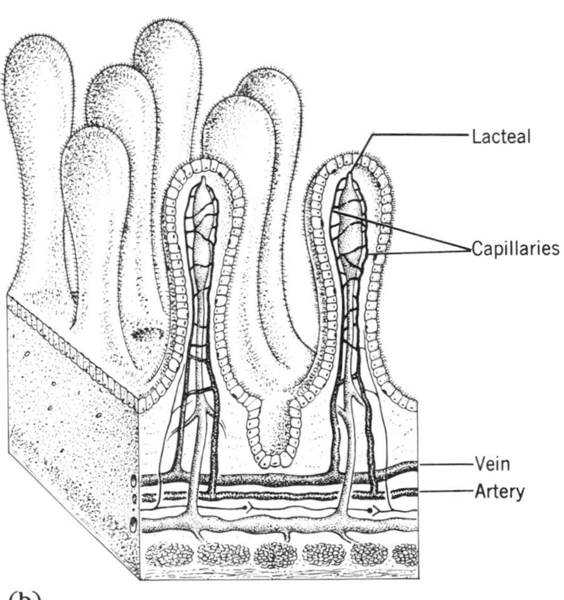

(b)

FIGURE 2.10 The interior wall of the small intestine. (a) The wall has many tiny projections shown greatly magnified in the photograph. (b) The cross-section drawing shows the capillaries and lacteal of each projection.

But the symptoms persist and jaundice, a yellowing of the skin, generally follows. There are two types of hepatitis. *Infectious hepatitis* (often called "hepatitis A") appears to be transmitted through contaminated food, water, and utensils. *Serum hepatitis* ("hepatitis B") is thought to be transmitted by transfusion of infected blood and by the sharing of contaminated needles by drug addicts, but the mode of transmission may be broader. Occasionally, hepatitis leads to permanent liver damage (McClintic, 1985).

Another disease of the liver is called *cirrhosis*. In this disease, liver cells die off and are replaced by a nonfunctional fibrous scar tissue. The scar tissue is permanent—and when it becomes extensive, the liver's normal functions are greatly impaired. As we will see later, the liver is not only important in the digestive process; it also cleanses and regulates the composition of the blood. Cirrhosis can result from several causes, including hepatitis infection and, particularly, alcohol abuse (Nelson, 1984).

Cancer may occur in any part of the digestive tract, especially in the colon and rectum (Levy, 1985; McClintic, 1985). People over 40 years of age have a higher prevalence for cancers of the digestive tract than do younger individuals. Early detection for many of these cancers is possible and greatly improves the person's chances of recovery.

Using Nutrients in Metabolism

The term **metabolism** refers to all chemical reactions that occur in the body's cells (Guyton, 1985; Holum, 1987). Three principal outcomes of metabolism are:

1. *Synthesis* of new cell material from proteins and minerals to build and repair the body.
2. *Regulation* of body processes—by producing enzymes and hormones, for example—through the use of proteins, minerals, and vitamins
3. *Energy* to heat the body and fuel its activities

We will focus on the third outcome, energy production.

Metabolism takes place constantly in the cells of all living things. Without the energy it produces, all of our body systems would cease to function. The energy to fuel our internal functions and our physical actions comes mainly from the metabolism of carbohydrates and fats. Although protein can be converted into energy, little of it is used in this way when other sources of energy are available to the body (McClintic, 1985).

The amount of energy a food contains is measured in *calories*. One calorie is the amount of heat needed to raise one gram of water one degree Celsius. Nutrition researchers measure the calories contained in a given quantity of a food by burning it in a special apparatus. In general, the number of calories per gram of food is more than twice as high for fats than for carbohydrates or proteins, which have about the same calorie content (McClintic, 1985).

How much energy do we use to support our basic bodily functions? The number of calories we burn up when our bodies are at rest—an index called the *basal metabolic rate*—depends on the size of the body (Guyton, 1985). For this reason, the basal metabolic rate is expressed in terms of calories per area of body surface (in square meters) per hour. A person who is 67 inches tall and weighs 132 pounds has a body surface area of about 1.7 square meters, for example. The basal metabolic rate also varies with the person's age and gender: the average rate is higher in males than in females and higher in younger people than in older people, as Figure 2.11 indicates. Thus, a 20-year-old male who is 67 inches tall, weighs 132 pounds, and has a normal metabolic rate burns about 66 calories per hour when at rest ($1.7 \times 39 = 66.3$).

What other factors affect the basal metabolic rate? People who are under stress, live in cold climates, or whose hormone secretion by the thyroid gland is greater than normal tend to have high basal metabolic rates (Guyton, 1985; McClintic, 1985). Factors such as these account for the fact that different people of the same size, age, and gender may have different metabolic rates.

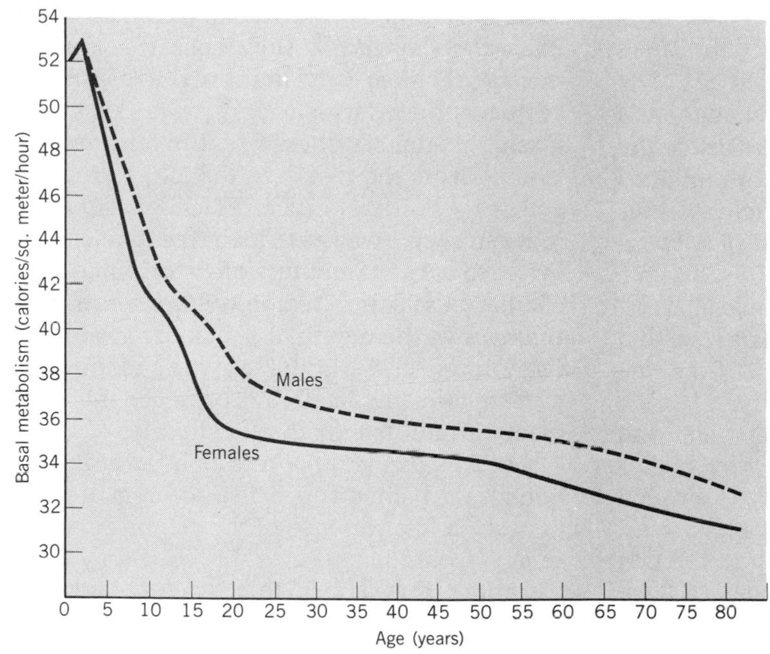

FIGURE 2.11 Normal basal metabolic rate for males and females at different ages in the life span. (Guyton, 1985, Figure 44-2b.)

Activity raises metabolism above the basal rate. Food materials that are not used up by metabolic processes are stored as body fat. This means that people become overweight generally because they regularly consume more calories than their body uses to fuel their internal functions and physical actions. To maintain normal body weight, people who do not metabolize all the calories they consume need to eat less or exercise more, and preferably both.

THE RESPIRATORY SYSTEM

Breathing supplies the body with oxygen—but why do we need oxygen? The chemical reactions in metabolism require oxygen, some of which joins with carbon atoms from food to form *carbon dioxide* (CO_2) as a waste product. So breathing has another function—it lets us get rid of this waste product. We will begin our examination of the **respiratory system** by looking at its structures.

The Respiratory Tract

After air enters the body through the nose or mouth, it travels past the *larynx,* down the *trachea* and *bronchial tubes,* and into the *lungs.* These organs are depicted in Figure 2.12. The bronchial tubes divide into smaller and smaller branches called *bronchioles* inside the lungs. These branches finally end in millions of tiny air sacs called *alveoli.* Each alveolus looks like a minute bubble made of a membrane that is thin enough to allow oxygen, CO_2, and other gasses to pass through. Alveoli are enmeshed in beds of capillaries so that gasses can be transferred to and from the bloodstream quickly and efficiently.

Breathing in is called *inspiration,* and breathing out is called *expiration.* What makes the air go in and out? Inspiration and expiration are caused by diaphragm and rib muscles. When we inhale, the rib muscles draw the ribs up and outward and the diaphragm—a horizontal sheet of muscle below the lungs (see Figure 2.12)—contracts, pulling downward on the bottom of the lungs. These actions pull air in and enlarge the lung chambers (Nelson, 1984). When we exhale, these muscles relax, and the elasticity of the lungs forces the air out, like a balloon.

Respiratory Control and Protective Functions

How do the muscles "know" when it's time to inhale and exhale? The body contains sensors that detect the level of CO_2 in the blood. This information is transmitted to the medulla of the brain, which directs actions of the muscles to cause inspiration and expiration. When the CO_2 level is high, the medulla increases the breathing rate; when the level is low, breathing rate is decreased (Nelson, 1984).

Foreign matter, such as airborne particles and microorganisms, can readily enter the respiratory tract. The respiratory system therefore needs protective mechanisms to prevent foreign matter from reaching the lungs and entering the bloodstream. Two protective mechanisms are *reflexes:* (1) sneezing in response to irritation in nasal passages and (2) coughing in response to irritation in lower portions of the system. Another protective mechanism is the *mucociliary escalator.* How does this mechanism work? Most of the lining of the respiratory system is coated with a sticky mucus that traps foreign matter. Furthermore, the air passages leading from the mouth to the lungs are lined with tiny hairlike structures called *cilia* that move in such a way as to force the mucus coating up toward the mouth. Hence the name "mucociliary escalator." When the mucus reaches the back of the mouth, it is usually swallowed (McClintic, 1985). In this way, the respiratory system cleanses itself and protects the body from harmful matter that we inhale.

The opening story of this chapter is about a young man named Tom who is a victim of cystic fibrosis, a fatal disease of the respiratory system. We will look at several of the many other disorders that attack this system. Some of these disorders mainly affect the alveoli of the

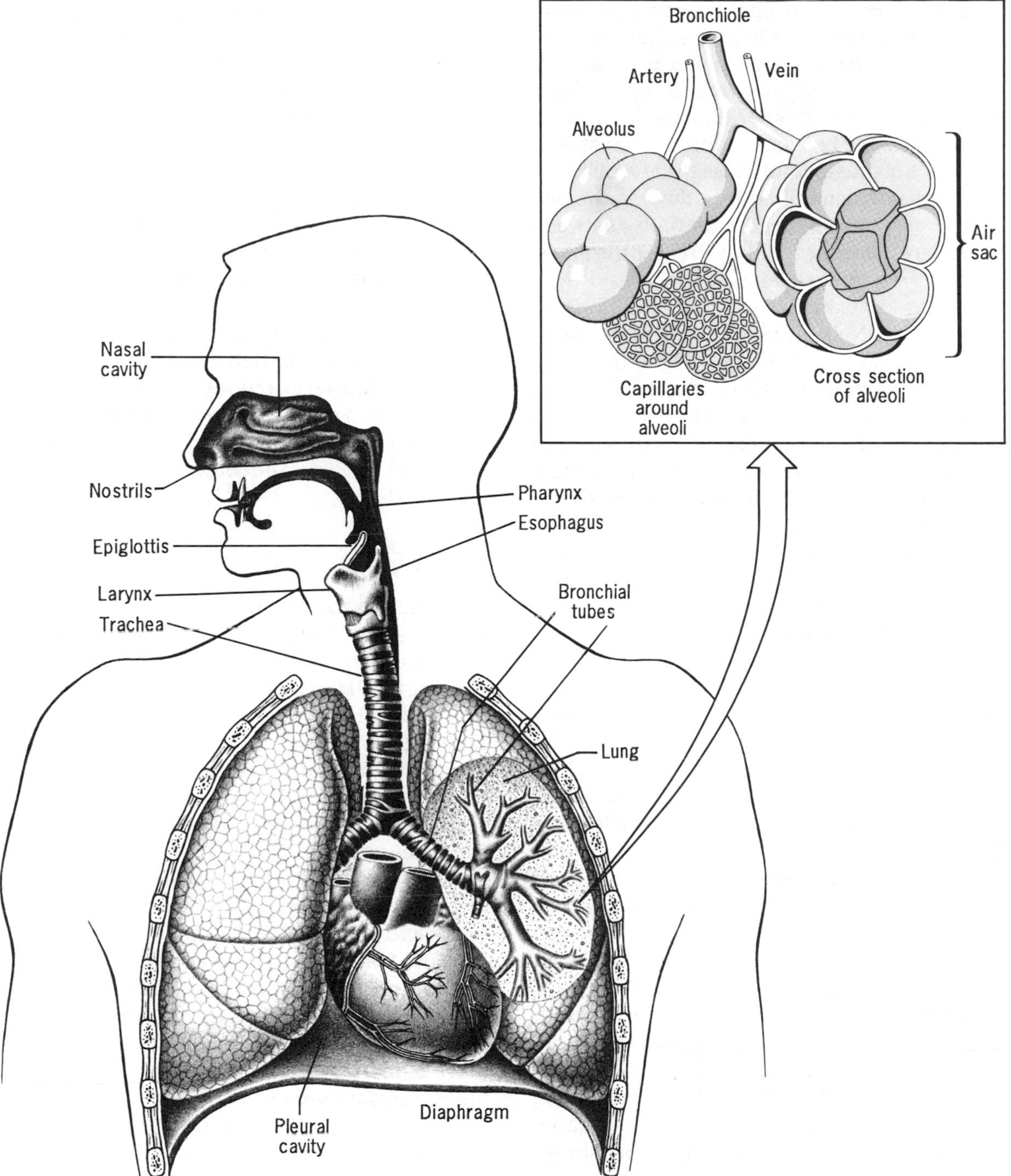

FIGURE 2.12 Major organs of the respiratory (also called pulmonary) system and close-up of alveoli.

lungs, thereby impairing the normal exchange of CO_2 and oxygen. For instance, there are several types of *pneumonia,* which can be caused by either bacterial or viral infection (Burroughs & Dieterle, 1985). Although this disease often affects the bronchial tubes, the most serious types of pneumonia cause the alveoli to become inflamed and filled with fluid. In the disease called *emphysema* the walls between alveoli are destroyed. This decreases the lungs' surface area for exchanging gasses and their elasticity for exhaling CO_2 (Kaplan, Reis, & Atkins, 1985; Nelson, 1984). *Pneumoconiosis* is a disease that afflicts people who chronically inhale air containing high concentrations of dust—generally at their workplaces. The "black lung disease" of coal miners provides an example. Dust that is not removed by protective mechanisms accumulates as thick sheets around the alveoli and bronchioles, damaging these structures and blocking air exchange.

Other disorders of the respiratory system primarily affect the bronchial tubes, usually by narrowing the tubes and reducing air flow. *Asthma* is a disorder in which spasms occur in the muscles of the bronchial tubes usually in response to an irritant, such as an infection or something to which the victim is allergic. The tubes narrow because of the spasms and an oversecretion of mucus. Breathing is very difficult and, in very serious attacks, portions of the lungs may collapse temporarily. In *chronic bronchitis* the bronchial tubes become inflamed and produce excess mucus. The condition may occur several times a year and lasts for two weeks or more each time it occurs (Burg & Ingall, 1985; Kaplan, Reis, & Atkins, 1985).

Lung cancer involves an unrestrained growth of cells, usually in the tissue that lines the bronchial tubes (Nelson, 1984). In its final stages, the diseased cells enter the bloodstream through the capillaries and spread throughout the body. At this point death is almost always near. Many of the respiratory diseases we have discussed can be caused or worsened by smoking cigarettes. This risk factor is also important in diseases of the cardiovascular system.

THE CARDIOVASCULAR SYSTEM

The physical design of every complex organism has to deal with a basic problem: How can the body service its cells—supplying the substances they need to function properly and removing the wastes that metabolism produces? In humans and many other animals, this problem is solved by having a **cardiovascular system** to transport these materials. The blood circulates through blood vessels—capillaries, arteries, and veins—within a closed system, one in which the blood does not directly contact the cells and tissues it services (Nelson, 1984). All transfers of oxygen, nutrients, waste products, and other substances occur through membranes that are separated by fluid-filled spaces. The heart is the center of the cardiovascular system.

The Heart and Blood Vessels

The *heart* is a hollow muscular organ that serves as a pump to circulate the blood throughout the body. The muscular portion of the heart wall is called the *myocardium.* The interior of the heart has four chambers, as the drawing in Figure 2.13 illustrates. The two upper chambers are called atriums, and the two lower ones are called ventricles; the left and right sides are labeled from the body's perspective, not from ours.

Looking at the drawing, we see several blood vessels that connect to the heart. How are arteries and veins different? *Arteries* carry blood *from* the heart, and *veins* carry blood *to* it. You will also notice in the drawing that the shading of some blood vessels is light, and in others the shading is dark. The vessels with light shading carry blood that is laden with CO_2 toward the lungs; the dark vessels carry blood away from the lungs after expelling CO_2 and receiving oxygen.

Now, let's follow the route of blood through the body. The blood that enters the *right atrium* of the heart is laden with CO_2 and deficient in oxygen, which makes blood blue in color. After

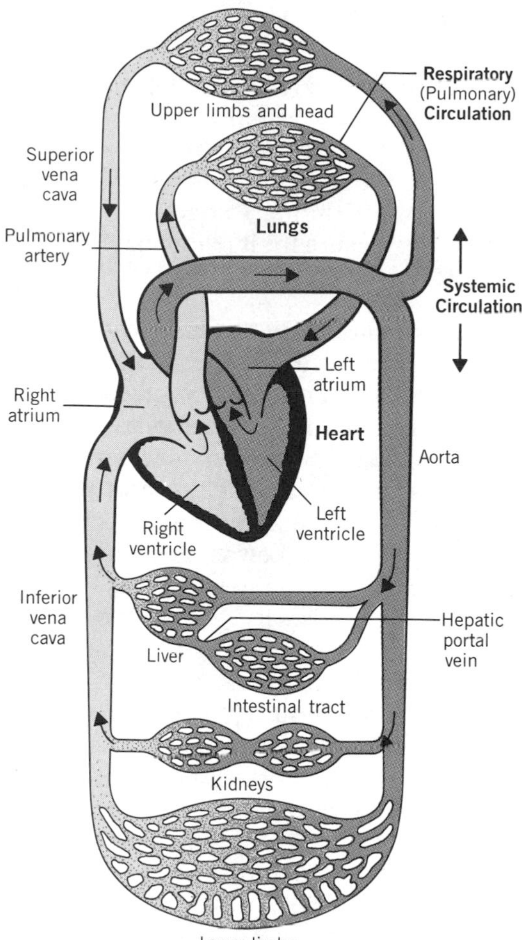

FIGURE 2.13 The circulatory system, including the heart and the loops to respiratory (pulmonary) circulation and systemic circulation. The respiratory loop allows blood to exchange CO_2 for oxygen; the systemic loop transports the blood to and from the rest of the body.

the atrium is filled, the blood passes through a valve to the *right ventricle.* The ventricles provide the main pumping force for circulation, and their valves prevent the blood from going back up to the atriums. From the right ventricle, the blood goes to the lungs, where it becomes oxygenated and, consequently, red in color. The oxygenated blood travels to the *left atrium* of the heart and is passed to the *left ventricle,* which pumps it out through the *aorta.* It then goes to various parts of the body before returning to the heart and beginning the cycle again.

Portions of each quantity of blood pumped by the heart travel through the liver and kidneys, where important functions take place (Guyton, 1985). The *kidneys* receive blood from the general circulatory system, cleanse it of waste products, and pass these wastes on to be eliminated in the urine. The *liver* receives blood from two sources: most of the blood comes from the intestinal tract, and the remainder comes from the general circulatory system. What does the liver do to the blood? It does two things. First, it cleanses the blood of harmful debris, such as bacteria. The liver is "so effective in removing bacteria that probably not one in a thousand escapes through the liver into the general circulation" (Guyton, 1985, p. 467). Second, the liver removes nutrients and stores them. The blood that comes from the intestinal tract after we consume a meal is rich in nutrients, such as simple sugars and amino acids. Large portions of these nutrients are retained in the liver until they are needed by the body. In this way, the ebbs and flows of nutrients in the blood are kept relatively even over time.

Blood Pressure

Imagine you are holding a long balloon that is filled with air and its end is tied off. If you squeeze it in the middle, the rest of it expands. This is what happens when pressure is applied to a closed system. The cardiovascular system is also closed, and the myocardium does the squeezing when it pumps blood from the heart. Like the balloon, the cardiovascular system always has some pressure in it. The squeezing increases the pressure.

Our arteries are elastic—they expand when pressure is applied. **Blood pressure** is the force exerted by blood on the artery walls. The heart is at rest between myocardial contractions, while it fills with blood. The resting force in the arteries that occurs at this time is called *diastolic pressure.* When the heart pumps, each contraction produces a maximum force in the arteries, which is called *systolic pressure.* Blood pressure measurement is expressed with two numbers: a larger number, representing systolic pressure, followed by a smaller number, representing diastolic pressure. Your physician might tell you that your blood pressure is "120 over 80," for example.

Blood pressure varies. It changes from one moment to the next, it is higher in one part of the body than in another, and different people have different blood pressures. What determines blood pressure? We can answer this question in two ways — one involves the laws of fluid dynamics and the other involves factors in people's lives that affect these dynamics. We will start with the first approach and examine five aspects of fluid dynamics that affect blood pressure (McClintic, 1985).

1. *Cardiac output* is the volume of fluid being pumped per minute. Blood pressure increases as cardiac output rises.

2. *Blood volume* refers to the total amount of blood circulating in the system. The greater the volume, the higher the blood pressure needed to move it.

3. *Peripheral resistance* refers to the difficulty fluid encounters in passing through narrow tubes or openings. When you put a nozzle on a hose and turn on the water, the pressure is greater at the nozzle than in the hose. Arteries vary in diameter. *Arterioles* are small arteries that connect larger arteries to capillaries. Peripheral resistance is generally greater in arterioles than in larger arteries. Normally arterioles are highly elastic and can expand or contract readily in response to messages from the nervous and endocrine systems. After we eat a meal, extra blood is needed around the small intestine for the absorption of nutrients. Messages to the arterioles in that region cause them to expand and accept more blood.

4. *Elasticity,* as we have seen, describes the ease in expanding and contracting. When blood vessels become less elastic, blood pressure — especially systolic pressure — rises.

5. *Viscosity* refers to the thickness of the fluid. The viscosity of blood depends on its composition, such as whether it contains high levels of red blood cells. Thicker blood flows less easily than thinner blood and requires more blood pressure for it to circulate through the cardiovascular system.

What factors in people's lives affect these dynamics? In our everyday lives we experience a variety of states that affect blood pressure. The *temperature* of our environment defines one of these states. When the temperature is high, the blood vessels in our skin enlarge and our cardiac output and diastolic pressure fall, which makes us feel drowsy. Low temperatures have the opposite effect. Another factor is *activity.* For example, exercise increases blood pressure during the activity and for some time thereafter. Simply changing our posture can also affect blood pressure. When we go from a lying position to standing, blood flow in the veins that feed the heart slows down because of gravity. This causes a drop in cardiac output and blood pressure. As a result, blood flow to the brain drops, sometimes making us feel dizzy (McClintic, 1985). A third factor is *emotional experience.* When we experience stress, anger, or anxiety, the sympathetic nervous system is activated. This causes a variety of cardiovascular reactions, such as increased cardiac output. Both systolic and diastolic pressure increase when people are emotionally aroused (James et al., 1986).

High blood pressure strains the heart and arteries. Some people have high blood pressure consistently over a period of several weeks or more. This condition is called *hypertension.* How high is "high" blood pressure? People whose pressures are at or above 140 (systolic) over 90 (diastolic) are classified as hypertensives (Herd & Weiss, 1984; USDHHS, 1986a). When systolic pressure reaches 200, the danger is high that a rupture may occur in a blood vessel, particularly in the brain (McClintic, 1985). The rupture of a blood vessel can have serious consequences, including paralysis or death. High diastolic pressure is troubling because the arteries are constantly being strained, even between heartbeats, when they should encounter little pressure.

There are several known risk factors for hypertension. For example, blood pressure shows a positive correlation with body weight, especially in early and middle adulthood (Alexander, 1984). Heavy people have more body mass to move when they are active than lighter people do, and they have a larger volume of blood for the heart to pump. Another factor is age—blood pressure generally rises with age. The percentage of individuals who are hypertensive is more than twice as high among the elderly than among young adults (USDHHS, 1986a). But aging per se may not be responsible for this relationship. Why? As adults get older, for instance, they tend to get heavier, at least in industrialized countries. In a number of primitive societies where adults do not show an increase in body weight as they get older, blood pressure does not seem to increase with age (Herd & Weiss, 1984).

Other risk factors for hypertension among Americans relate to gender, race, and family history (Herd & Weiss, 1984; USDHHS, 1986c). Gender and racial differences in blood pressure do not show up before adulthood (Harlan, 1984). In adulthood, the prevalence rate for hypertension is higher for males than for females, particularly before about 50 years of age. Thereafter, this gender difference disappears. Black adults develop hypertension at a much higher rate than whites do. This is so for both sexes and at virtually every age in adulthood. Family history is important, too. People are more likely to become hypertensive if their parents had high blood pressure.

The reasons for these gender, race, and family history differences in hypertension are not fully clear. Evidence from twin studies suggests that genetics plays a role in blood pressure (Rose, 1986; Smith et al., 1987). Perhaps hereditary factors are responsible for these differences. Body weight may also be important. After 50 years of age, but not before, females are more likely than males to be overweight. In addition, there are racial differences in being overweight: blacks are more likely to be overweight than are whites, and this racial difference is quite pronounced among adult females at all ages (USDHHS, 1986c). Still other factors, such as stress, may play a role—and so may diet, as we will see in the next section.

Blood Composition

Blood is sometimes thought of as a "liquid tissue" because it consists of cells that are suspended in a liquid. The adult's body contains between 4.5 and 6 liters of blood, and males on average have about 10% more blood than females do (McClintic, 1985; Nelson, 1984). Because our bodies can replace blood quickly, we can donate half a liter of blood with no ill effects.

Blood composition can affect blood pressure. As we saw earlier, the thicker the blood, the more pressure is needed to circulate it. What is blood made of, and how does its composition change its thickness? Blood has two components, plasma and formed elements (Landau, 1976; McClintic, 1985). *Plasma* is a liquid substance that comprises about 55% of our blood. About 90% of plasma is water, and the remainder consists of a variety of organic and inorganic elements. We will look at formed elements first.

Formed Elements

Formed elements are the cells and cell-like structures in the blood that constitute about 45% of our blood volume. There are three types of formed elements:

1. *Red blood cells* are the most abundant cells in the blood—there are about five million of them per cubic millimeter of blood. They are formed in the bone marrow and have a lifetime of three or four months. Red blood cells are important mainly because they contain *hemoglobin,* a protein substance that attaches to oxygen and transports this element to body cells and tissues. *Anemia* is a condition in which the level of red blood cells or hemoglobin is below normal (Guyton, 1985; Nelson, 1984).

2. *Leukocytes* are white blood cells. Each of several types of leukocytes serves a special protective function — for example, some engulf or destroy bacteria. White blood cells are produced in the bone marrow and various organs in the body. Leukocytes are the least abundant formed element in the blood. There are normally only 6,000 - 9,000 per cubic millimeter of blood in adulthood. *Leukemia* is a malignant disease in which white blood cells are produced in extremely high quantities, sometimes reaching half a million per cubic millimeter of blood and causing anemia (McClintic, 1985).

3. *Platelets* are granular fragments, produced by the bone marrow, that enable the body to prevent blood loss. They do this by plugging tiny wounds or helping the blood to clot when the wound is larger. *Hemophilia* is a disease in which the platelets do not function properly, thereby reducing the blood's ability to clot (Guyton, 1985; Landau, 1976).

How do formed elements affect the viscosity of blood? The higher the concentration of formed elements suspended in the plasma, the thicker the blood.

Plasma

Besides water, plasma consists of *plasma protein* and various other organic and inorganic elements. Plasma protein is a special element, consisting of molecules that are generally too large to be transferred through capillary walls to body tissue (Landau, 1976). This characteristic is important because this protein is needed within the blood to help other substances pass through capillary walls. Plasma protein increases the thickness of the blood.

Although the remaining elements in plasma constitute only a small percentage of its volume, they are extremely important substances. They include hormones, enzymes, and waste products. They also include the nutrients we derive from digestion — vitamins, minerals, simple sugars, amino acids, and fatty materials.

Fatty materials make up the broad class of substances in the blood called **lipids.** Two of these fatty materials are triglycerides and cholesterol (Landau, 1976; Nelson, 1984). *Triglycerides* are the material we commonly think of as "fat." They are made of glycerol and fatty acid, and are the most abundant lipid in the body. Some of the fatty acids in triglycerides are fully hydrogenated — they cannot take up any more hydrogen — and are called *saturated* for that reason. They are usually solid at room temperature and are mostly derived from animal fat. Other fatty acids are *unsaturated* or *polyunsaturated.* They can take up more hydrogen, are usually liquid at room temperature, and are derived from plants.

Cholesterol is a fatty substance that builds up in patches on artery walls over time and narrows the artery (Ross & Glomset, 1976a, 1976b). Although most of the cholesterol in the blood is manufactured by the body, the rest comes from the foods we eat. Eating fats that are highly saturated tends to increase blood cholesterol levels, thereby adding to the problem. Why is this a problem? The formation of fatty patches, or "plaques," in arteries is a condition called **atherosclerosis.** These plaques tend to harden and reduce the elasticity of the artery — a condition called **arteriosclerosis.** The narrowing and hardening of arteries increase blood pressure (Landau, 1976). Although arteriosclerosis becomes an increasing problem as adults get older, plaque begins to form early in life (Clarkson, Manuck, & Kaplan, 1986). Autopsies on American soldiers killed in Vietnam showed that 45% of these men had some degree of atherosclerosis present in their arteries (McNamara, Molot, Stremple, & Cutting, 1971).

Of the many diseases of the heart and blood vessels, we will describe a few. One of them is *myocardial infarction,* or "heart attack." What does infarction mean? It refers to the death of tissue caused by an obstruction in the supply of blood to it. Thus, a myocardial infarction is the death of heart muscle (myocardium) tissue as a result of arterial blockage, usually resulting from atherosclerosis (Clarkson, Manuck, & Kaplan, 1986). Another form of heart disease is *angina pectoris,* in which the victim feels great pain and tightness in the chest. It is a sign that the heart muscle is not getting enough oxygen because of an obstruction in an artery. Often an attack is brought on by overexercise or stress.

One disorder of the blood vessels is an *aneurysm,* a bulge in a weakened section of an artery or vein. If the bulge is in a major blood vessel and it ruptures, the person may die (Guyton, 1985). Another disorder of the blood vessels—a *stroke*—occurs when the blood supply to a portion of the brain is disrupted. This can be caused by a rupture in a cerebral artery, causing a hemorrhage in the brain, or by a blood clot, called a *thrombosis,* in a cerebral blood vessel. In either case, damage occurs to the brain. The effects of this damage depend on where it occurs and how extensive it is. It may cause paralysis or sensory impairments, for instance, or even death (Guyton, 1985). Aneurysms and strokes can result from atherosclerosis and hypertension.

THE IMMUNE SYSTEM

You may not realize it, but wars are raging inside your body. They happen continuously, every day. Most of the time they are minor skirmishes, and you are unaware of them. When they become major battles, however, you are usually aware something's going on. The "good guys" are the organs and cells that make up your **immune system.** This system fights to defend the body against "foreign" invaders, such as bacteria and viruses.

The immune system is quite remarkable. Scientists knew very little about this intricate and enormously important system until recently. But it is now the subject of major research efforts, and new information about how the immune system functions is emerging rapidly. We know, for instance, that this system is highly sensitive to invasions by foreign matter and is able to distinguish between "self," or normal body constituents, and "not self"—friend and foe.

Antigens

When the body recognizes something as a "not self" invader, the immune system mobilizes body resources and attacks. Any substance that can trigger an immune response is called an **antigen.**

What things trigger an immune response? Some of the first antigens that come to mind are bacteria, fungi, protozoa, and viruses. *Bacteria* are microorganisms that exist in vast numbers throughout the environment—in rivers and oceans, in the air, on and in plants and animals, and in decaying organic matter. Billions of them populate just one pound of rotting garbage. Because they help in breaking down organic matter into simpler units, their activities are essential to the life and growth of all living things. Some bacteria cause illnesses, such as tuberculosis, scarlet fever, and food poisoning. They do this by growing rapidly and competing with our cells for nutrients and by excreting *toxic,* or poisonous, substances that destroy our cells or impair their metabolic processes (Curtis, 1979; Jaret, 1986; Nelson, 1984).

Fungi are organisms, such as molds and yeasts, that attach themselves to an organic host and absorb nutrients from the host. Some of them can cause skin diseases through direct contact, as occurs in ringworm and athlete's foot, and internal diseases through inhalation of contaminated air. Other fungi are very beneficial—for example, penicillin is derived from molds (Curtis, 1979; Richelson, 1982). *Protozoa* are one-celled animals, such as amoebas, that live primarily in water and insects. Drinking contaminated water can cause amoebic dysentery, an intestinal illness, and being bitten by an infected mosquito can cause malaria (Curtis, 1979; Jaret, 1986).

The tiniest of these antigens are *viruses,* particles of protein that are smaller than cells and, strictly speaking, not even alive. They consist of genetic information that allows them to reproduce. A virus functions by attaching to a cell, slipping inside, and taking over by issuing its own genetic instructions. The invaded cell abandons its own metabolic activities and becomes a "factory" for making viruses. In short order, enough viruses can be produced to rupture the cell and spread to infect other cells. Viruses can be quite devious, too, developing new strains and lying dormant in the body for periods of time before becoming infectious. They are responsible for a variety of diseases, including flu, herpes, measles, and polio (Altman, 1986; Curtis, 1979; Jaret, 1986).

The immune system generally recognizes the tissue of an organ transplant as "not self" and treats it as an antigen. This is what physicians mean when they say that the body "rejected" a transplant. There are two basic ways to encourage transplant acceptance. The first is to select the transplant carefully so that the tissues of the donor and the recipient are as similar as possible. The closer the genetic relationship between the two people, the better the match is likely to be. Identical twins provide the best match, of course. The second approach is to suppress the action of the immune system with drugs. A drawback to this approach is that long-term suppression of immune function leaves the patient susceptible to disease (USDHHS, 1985e).

For many people, the immune system mounts an attack against certain harmless substances, such as pollen, tree molds, poison ivy, animal dander, and particular foods. These people suffer from *allergies;* the specific substances that trigger their allergic reactions, such as sneezing and skin rashes, are called *allergens.* Most allergic people react to some, but not all, of the known allergens. Someone with hay fever is not necessarily allergic to poison ivy, for instance. Some allergies can be reduced by administering regular, small doses of the allergen, usually by injection (Guyton, 1985; Jaret, 1986; USDHHS, 1985e).

The Organs of the Immune System

The organs of the immune system are located throughout the body (Curtis, 1979; Guyton, 1985; Nelson, 1984; USDHHS, 1985e). These organs are generally referred to as *lymphatic* or *lymphoid* organs because they have primary involvement in the development and deployment of **lymphocytes,** the white blood cells that are the key functionaries or "soldiers" in our body's defense against invasion by foreign matter. The main lymphatic organs include the bone marrow, thymus, lymph nodes and vessels, and spleen. Let's see what they do.

Lymphocytes originate in *bone marrow,* the soft tissue in the core of all bones in the body. Some of these cells migrate to one of two organs where they mature. One of these organs is the *thymus,* which, as we saw earlier in this chapter, is a gland that lies in the chest. The other organ is not known for certain — although it is probably the liver — but it is thought to have the same function in maturing human lymphocytes that a structure called the "bursa" has in birds (Guyton, 1985). Most of this processing of lymphocytes occurs before birth and in infancy.

The *lymph nodes* are bean-shaped masses of spongy tissue that are distributed throughout the body. Large clusters of them are found in the neck, armpits, abdomen, and groin. What do they do? Each lymph node contains filters that capture antigens and compartments that provide a home base for lymphocytes and other white blood cells. The lymph nodes are connected by a network of *lymph vessels* that contain a clear fluid called *lymph.* These vessels ultimately empty into the bloodstream. Although the lymph nodes and vessels play an important role in cleansing body cells of antigens, they can become a liability in some forms of cancer either by becoming infected with cancer or by distributing cancer cells to other parts of the body.

Lymphocytes and antigens that enter the blood are carried to the *spleen,* an organ in the upper left side of the person's abdomen. The spleen functions like an enormous lymph node except that blood, rather than lymph, travels through it. The spleen filters out antigens and serves as a home base for white blood cells. It also removes ineffective or worn-out red blood cells from the body.

HIGHLIGHT 2B: On Issues

When Immune Functions Are Absent

I can remember reading for the first time many years ago about a child who had to live in a large plastic "bubble" because he was born without virtually all major immune defenses. The condition he had is very rare and is called *severe combined immunodeficiency disease.* He lived in the bubble because it was germ free—exposure to microorganisms in the general environment is soon fatal for such children. Some children have lived for years with this condition, and some have received tissue transplants that have permitted them to develop effective immune systems (USDHHS, 1985e). More common inborn immune deficiencies involve the absence of only part of the system, and can sometimes be treated with injections.

Having little or no immune defense was almost unheard of in the 1960s, and people were not very concerned about immune processes. All that changed in the 1980s as people became aware of the disorder called *acquired immune deficiency syndrome (AIDS).* This disorder is not inborn—it is caused by a virus that is transmitted when an infected person's body fluid, such as blood or semen, contacts the body fluid of an uninfected person. This occurs in three major ways: through sexual activity if the body fluids become exposed to each other, in intravenous drug use if syringes are shared, and from an infected mother to her baby (Francis & Chin, 1987). Receiving contaminated blood in a transfusion was once a major source of the virus, but hospital blood supplies are closely monitored now.

Although AIDS is a fatal disorder, it does not kill directly. It disables or destroys an extremely important component of the immune system—the *helper T-cells*—and leaves the victim defenseless against a variety of diseases, including pneumonia and a form of cancer called Kaposi's sarcoma (Batchelor, 1988; Francis & Chin, 1987; Jaret, 1986). One of these diseases becomes the actual cause of death. Although researchers are working hard to find medical ways to prevent and treat AIDS, none has yet been found.

AIDS is a worldwide epidemic. In the United States alone, tens of thousands of people have been diagnosed with the disorder, many thousands have already died, and perhaps 1½ million people are infected with the virus. So far, most of the victims of AIDS in America have been intravenous drug users and males who practice homosexual sex, particularly anal intercourse (Darrow et al., 1987; Francis & Chin, 1987; Morin, 1988; Specter, 1988). Prevention by changing high-risk behavior is essential, and studies of these changes have found encouraging results. Gay males appear to be reducing their risks by avoiding sex with unfamiliar partners, becoming monogamous, and by using condoms and other methods to decrease the contact of body fluids (Joseph et al., 1987; Stall, Coates, & Hoff, 1988). Intravenous drug users are learning how to use bleach to sterilize their needles and becoming more selective in the people with whom they will share needles (Des Jarlais, Friedman, Casriel, & Kott, 1987). But more progress in preventive efforts is needed in these high-risk groups and among people in the larger population. We will discuss the topic of AIDS again in later chapters.

Soldiers of the Immune System

White blood cells play a key role in the immune system—they serve as soldiers in our counterattack against invading substances in the body. There are two types of white blood cells. Lymphocytes, as we have seen, are one type; phagocytes are the other.

Phagocytes are scavengers that patrol the body and engulf and ingest antigens.

> [They] are not choosy. They will eat anything suspicious that they find in the bloodstream, tissues, or lymphatic system. In the lungs, for instance, they consume particles of dust and other pollutants that enter with each breath. They can cleanse lungs that have been blackened with the contaminants of cigarette smoke, provided the smoking stops. Too much cigarette smoking, over too long a time, destroys phagocytes faster than they can be replenished. (Jaret, 1986, p. 715)

There are two types of phagocytes: *macrophages* become attached to tissues and remain there and *monocytes* circulate in the blood

(Guyton, 1985; USDHHS, 1985e). The fact that phagocytes "are not choosy" means that they are involved in *nonspecific immunity*—they respond to any kind of antigen.

Lymphocytes react in a more discriminating way, being tailored for attacks against specific antigens. The diagram in Figure 2.14 shows that, in addition to the process of nonspecific immunity, there are two types of *specific* immune processes: cell-mediated immunity and antibody-mediated "humoral" immunity (Borysenko, 1984; Braveman, 1987; Guyton, 1985; Jaret, 1986; McClintic, 1985; Rogers, Dubey, & Reich, 1979; USDHHS, 1985e). Let's examine these two specific immune processes and how they interrelate.

Cell-mediated immunity operates at the level of the cell. The soldiers in this process are lymphocytes called **T-cells**—the name of these white blood cells reflects their having matured in the *t*hymus. T-cells are divided into several groups, each with its own important function:

- *Killer T-cells* directly attack and destroy three main targets: transplanted tissue that is recognized as foreign, cancerous cells, and cells of the body that have already been invaded by antigens, such as viruses.
- *Memory T-cells* "remember" previous invaders. At the time of an initial infection, such as with mumps, some T-cells are imprinted with information for recognizing that specific kind of invader—the virus that causes mumps—in the future. Memory T-cells and their offspring circulate in the blood or lymph for long periods of time—sometimes for decades—and enable the body to defend against subsequent invasions more quickly.
- *Delayed hypersensitivity T-cells* have two functions. They are involved in delayed immune reactions, particularly in allergies such as of poison ivy, in which tissue becomes inflamed. They also produce protein substances called *lymphokines* that stimulate other T-cells to grow, reproduce, and attack an invader.
- *Helper T-cells* receive reports of invasions from other white blood cells that patrol the body, rush to the spleen and lymph nodes, and stimulate lymphocytes to reproduce and attack. The lymphocytes they stimulate are from both the cell-mediated and the antibody-mediated immunity processes.
- *Suppressor T-cells* operate in slowing down or stopping cell-mediated and antibody-mediated immunity processes as an infection diminishes or is conquered. Suppressor and helper T-cells serve to regulate cell-mediated and antibody-mediated immune processes.

What is antibody-mediated immunity, and how is it different from the cell-mediated process? **Antibody-mediated immunity** (also called "humoral" immunity) attacks bacteria, fungi, protozoa, and viruses while they are still in body fluids and before they have invaded body cells. Unlike the cell-mediated process of attacking infected cells of the body, the antibody-mediated approach focuses on the antigens directly. The soldiers in this approach are lymphocytes called **B-cells.** Figure 2.14 shows that B-cells give rise to *plasma cells* that produce antibodies. This process is often induced by helper T-cells or inhibited by suppressor T-cells.

How are antibodies involved? **Antibodies** are protein molecules called *immunoglobulins* ("Ig") that attach to the surface of invaders and accomplish three things. First, they slow down the invader, making it an easier and more attractive target for phagocytes to destroy. Second, they recruit other protein substances that puncture the membrane of an invading microorganism, causing it to explode. Third, they form *memory B-cells* for new invaders that operate in the future like memory T-cells do. As you can see, antibodies are like sophisticated weapons in immune system wars. Researchers have identified five classes of antibodies—IgG, IgM, IgA, IgD, and IgE—each with its own special function and "territory" in the body. For example, IgA guards the entrances of the body

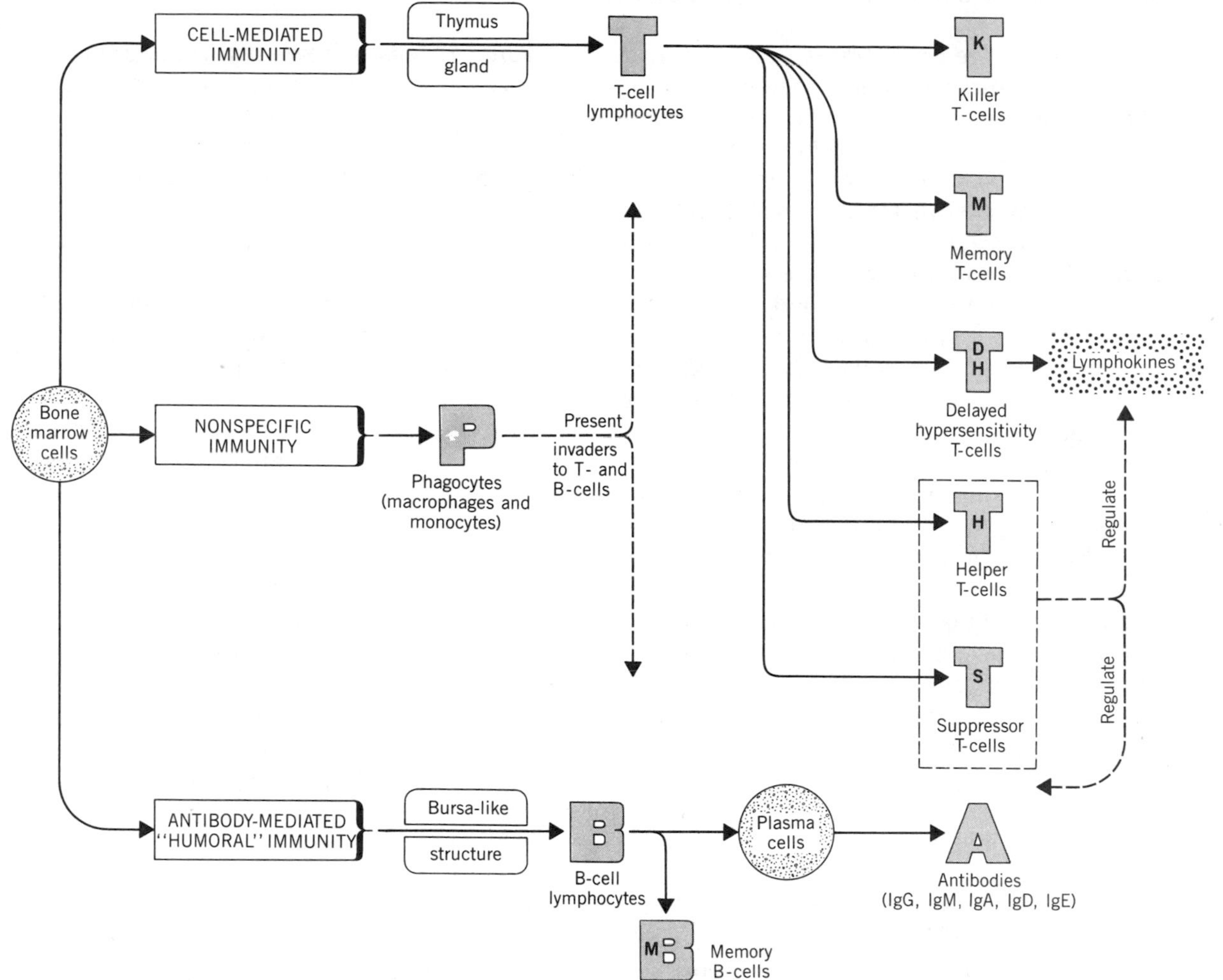

FIGURE 2.14 Development and interrelationships of the immune system. White blood cells produced by bone marrow are of two types—*phagocytes* and *lymphocytes.* There are two kinds of lymphocytes: *T-cells,* which are processed by the thymus gland; and *B-cells,* which are processed by an as yet unknown, bursa-like structure (B-cells were first discovered in the bursa of Facricius structure of birds). See text for description. (Sources: Borysenko, 1984; Braveman, 1987; Guyton, 1985; Jaret, 1986; McClintic, 1985; and USDHHS, 1985e.)

in fluids, such as saliva, tears, and secretions of the respiratory tract.

Defending the Body with an Immune Response

Now that we have seen the soldiers and weaponry of the immune system, let's see how all of this is orchestrated in defending your body. Protection from disease actually involves a series of defenses (Curtis, 1979; Guyton, 1985; Jaret, 1986; McClintic, 1985; USDHHS, 1985e). We will start at the beginning, as the invader tries to enter the body.

Your body's first line of defense is the skin and the mucous membranes that line the respiratory and digestive tracts. Mucous membranes are coated with fluids that contain antibodies and other antimicrobial substances, and the skin serves as a barrier to entry. Even though these defenses are highly effective, large numbers of antigens get through, either by eluding the antibodies or by entering a wound in the skin or the mucous membrane.

Once an antigen penetrates this barrier, it encounters the second line of defense that includes nonspecific and specific immune processes. Phagocytes in your blood and tissues attack and consume invading substances of all types. They also have another important function: They present the antigen to B-cells and helper T-cells, as if to say, "Here's the enemy. Go get 'em!" The B-cells respond to this message and to stimulation from helper T-cells by giving rise to plasma cells that produce the needed antibodies. The role of the phagocytes is especially important if the antigen is new and there are no memory B-cells yet for this substance. Antibodies in body fluids attach to microorganisms, thereby aiding the phagocytes and other protein substances that can kill the invaders.

Antigens that manage to get through and invade body cells encounter the third line of defense in which killer T-cells destroy the invaded cells. Phagocytes often initiate this process by presenting antigens to T-cells, as we have seen. Once again, this is especially important if the antigen is new to the cell-mediated system and there are no memory T-cells for the substance. As the invasion subsides, suppressor T-cells slow down the cell-mediated and antibody-mediated immune responses. Memory B- and T-cells are left in the blood and lymph, ready to initiate the immune response if the same antigen invades the body again.

You may be thinking, "This is a wonderful and complex system that responds when there are antigens in the body, but why do killer T-cells attack cancer cells? Aren't cancer cells basically normal cells that multiply out of control?" Cancer cells have antigens on their surface to which T-cells respond (Curtis, 1979; Jaret, 1986; McClintic, 1985). What scientists don't yet know is why some cancers escape destruction. One possible reason is that the antigen is simply not easy for the immune system to recognize. As a result, the immune response may not be strong enough to stop the cells from multiplying wildly. Some researchers are studying approaches for treating cancer that are designed to strengthen the patient's own immune processes. In one of these approaches, for example, researchers manufacture antibodies that are sensitive to and seek out a specific type of cancer cell. These approaches are not yet perfected, but they are very promising.

Less-Than-Optimal Defenses

If our immune systems always functioned optimally, we would become sick much less often. Why and in what ways do our defenses function less than optimally?

The effectiveness of the immune system changes over the life span, becoming increasingly effective throughout childhood and declining in old age (Rogers, Dubey, & Reich, 1979). Newborns come into the world with relatively little immune defense. They have only one type of antibody (IgG), for example, which they receive prior to birth from their mothers through the placenta (the filterlike organ that permits the exchange of nutrients and certain other substances between the bloodstreams of the mother and baby). Infants who are nursed receive antibodies, particularly IgA, in their mother's milk (Ashburn, 1986).

In early infancy, children in technological societies generally begin a regular schedule of immunization through the use of vaccines. Most vaccines contain dead or disabled disease microorganisms that get the body to initiate an immune response and produce memory lymphocytes, but do not produce the full-blown disease (Nelson, 1984; USDHHS, 1985e). The efficiency and complexity of the immune system develop very rapidly in childhood. As a result, the incidence of illness serious enough to keep children home from school declines with age (Ashburn, 1986).

Throughout adolescence and much of adulthood, the immune system generally functions at a high level. Then, as people approach old age, the effectiveness of the system declines (Braveman, 1987). Although the overall numbers of T-cells, B-cells, and antibodies circulating in the blood do not decrease, their potency diminishes in old age. Compared with the T-cells and B-cells of younger adults, those of el-

HIGHLIGHT 2C: On Research
Stress and the Immune Response

Many people believe that stress and illness are related—and they are right. Research has generally confirmed this belief, showing, for instance, that the incidence of respiratory illnesses increases when people experience high levels of stress (Jemmott & Locke, 1984). Why is this so? A likely answer is that stress suppresses immune functions in some way, leaving the person open to infection. This explanation is consistent with the finding that people who have low levels of the antibody IgA in their saliva—part of the body's first line of defense against respiratory infection—have more respiratory illnesses than people who have high levels of IgA (McClelland, Floor, Davidson, & Saron, 1980).

These findings are provocative, but they do not show a direct relationship between stress and immune function. Psychologist Janice Kiecolt-Glaser and colleagues from a variety of disciplines have done an impressive series of studies to examine this relationship. Let's look at one of their studies in detail (Kiecolt-Glaser et al., 1984). The researchers recruited 75 first-year medical students who were scheduled to take a series of highly stressful final examinations. The study assessed important variables in two sessions: The first session occurred at a time when examination stresses should be relatively low—one month before the finals and one month after their last major examination. The second occurred when stresses should be high, just after the students had taken their first two examinations during the final exam week.

In the first session, the researchers took a sample of blood from the students and had them fill out questionnaires that assessed their experience of loneliness and stress during the past year. In the second session, only a blood sample was taken. Both samples of blood were analyzed for the degree of killer-T-cell activity and concentrations of antibodies. The results showed that, although antibody concentrations were not consistently related to stress variables, killer-T-cell activity was. Killer cell activity was considerably lower in the second (high stress) blood sample than in the first. Moreover, in both blood samples, killer cell activity was lower for students who scored high on the loneliness and stress questionnaires than for those who scored low.

In another study, Kiecolt-Glaser and her coworkers (1987) analyzed blood samples of married and separated or divorced women. Among the married women, those who reported less marital satisfaction showed weaker immune function than those who reported greater satisfaction. Among the separated or divorced women, those who refused to accept the fact of the separation or thought excessively about their ex-spouse had weaker immune function than those who did not. In addition, women who had been separated for relatively short amounts of time showed weaker immune function than married women and women separated for a longer time. The findings of these two investigations provide direct evidence of an association between stress and immunosuppression.

Studies by other researchers support these results, finding, for example, that immune function is suppressed in individuals several weeks following the death of their spouses (Antoni, 1987; Jemmott & Locke, 1984). How does the suppression occur? One way is through the endocrine system. Earlier in this chapter we saw that stress causes the adrenal glands to produce epinephrine and cortisol. These substances affect immune cells (Antoni, 1987; Borysenko, 1984). Epinephrine appears to increase suppressor T-cells and decrease helper T-cells in the blood, at least for a short while. Cortisol inhibits the function of phagocytes and lymphocytes—and if stress is chronic, cortisol causes important lymphoid tissues to wither away.

---

derly people respond weakly to antigens and are less likely to generate the needed supply of lymphocytes and antibodies to fight an invasion.

Poor nutrition can also lead to less-than-optimal immune function (Braveman, 1987; Brody, 1987). Diets deficient in vitamins A and E diminish the production of lymphocytes and antibodies; vitamin C is important in the effectiveness of phagocytes. Being overweight and eating diets that are high in fats and cholesterol seem to impair immune function and increase people's susceptibility to infections.

When your immune system functions optimally, it attacks foreign matter and protects the body. Sometimes this process goes awry, and the immune response is directed at parts of the body it was designed to protect. Several disorders result from this condition—they are called *autoimmune diseases.* One of these diseases is *rheumatoid arthritis,* in which the immune response is directed against tissues and bones at the joints. This causes swelling and pain, and can leave the bones pitted. In *rheumatic fever,* the muscles of the heart are the target. This disease can damage the heart valves permanently. *Multiple sclerosis,* a disease we considered earlier, results when the immune system attacks the myelin sheath of neurons. Another autoimmune disease is *lupus erythematosus,* which affects various parts of the body, including the skin and kidneys. What causes autoimmune diseases? Although we are not certain of the causes, it is likely that heredity and immune responses to prior infections play important roles (Burg & Ingall, 1985; Dix & Koehler, 1985; Gardner, 1983; Jaret, 1986; USDHHS, 1985e).

THE REPRODUCTIVE SYSTEM AND HEREDITY

At one time, many educated people believed that a miniature, completely formed, person was passed on from a man to a woman during sexual intercourse. Then, in the eighteenth century, researchers disproved this and similar ideas and demonstrated that a *sperm* cell from a male had to combine with an egg cell—an *ovum*—from a female before development could begin.

Conception and Prenatal Development

A human being begins to form at conception when a sperm cell unites with an ovum. The resulting single fertilized cell, called a *zygote,* starts to divide, forming new cells. It soon attaches to the wall of the mother's uterus and the *placenta* and umbilical cord develop. These structures allow nourishment, wastes, and other substances to be exchanged between the mother's and offspring's separate bloodstreams.

During the next few weeks, the offspring begins to develop all the body systems we have just examined. By the ninth week of prenatal development, for instance, the fetus has a tiny and incompletely formed heart that pumps blood through minute blood vessels, and the basic structures of the brain, liver, and kidneys have developed. The body systems undergo continuous improvement in organ structure and functioning during the remainder of gestation (Sarafino & Armstrong, 1986).

Pregnancy produces substantial alterations in the mother's anatomy and enormous additional demands on her body systems (Pillitteri, 1981). The most obvious changes result from the size and weight of the fetus and the accompanying structures and fluids. But other, less obvious changes also occur. The mother's blood volume increases by 30%, which places heavy demands on her heart. Furthermore, her usual dietary intake of iron is likely to be inadequate for meeting the combined needs of herself and the fetus. This condition can produce *iron deficiency anemia*—a general physical weakness—in both the mother and baby before and after birth unless she increases her iron intake. Added burdens are also placed on her respiratory and digestive systems.

Genetic Processes in Development and Health

Although researchers in the nineteenth century knew that each person developed from the union of a sperm and an ovum, no one knew what forces or substances inside these cells directed the growth processes. Charles Darwin speculated that unseen particles called "gemmules" were present in the sperm and ovum. Darwin's concept of gemmules formed the basis for the search for genetic materials.

Genetic Materials and Transmission

What did this search yield? By the early twentieth century, researchers discovered threadlike structures called **chromosomes** and proposed that these structures contained units called *genes.* Soon they determined the basic substance common to all genetic material—*deoxyribonucleic acid,* or DNA for short—and described its structure. Today we know that DNA determines our growth patterns and physical structures. We also know that genes are discrete particles of DNA and that strings of genes are organized into chromosomes.

In what form are these genetic materials passed on to the next generation? Each ovum and sperm contains 23 chromosomes. At conception, the 23 chromosomes of the ovum are paired with those of the sperm, yielding 46 chromosomes in the zygote. As the offspring grows, these 46 chromosomes are duplicated and passed on to each newly formed cell of the body. Sperm and ova, which are produced by the reproductive system, are the only cells in the human body that contain just 23 chromosomes. Thus, half of the genetic information contained in each of your body cells comes from each of your parents, and half of their genetic information comes from each of their parents.

Chromosomes can be identified by certain features. Photographs taken through a microscope can be arranged according to the size and shape of chromosome pairs. One pair is called the *sex chromosomes* because they carry the genes that will determine whether an individual will be female or male. The normal sex chromosomes for males consist of one large chromosome (called an X chromosome) and one small chromosome (called a Y chromosome); females have two X chromosomes. Since the mother can only provide an X sex chromosome to her offspring, the child's gender is determined by the information received from the father. If the sperm that fertilizes the ovum carries an X chromosome, the zygote will develop into a female. If the sperm carries a Y chromosome, the child will be a male.

As with chromosomes, genes come in pairs. Some of a person's traits are determined by a single pair of genes. Furthermore, some traits occur in the presence of a single gene, with the paired gene making little or no contribution. Such genes are said to be *dominant.* In humans, dominant genes produce such characteristics as brown eyes and normal color vision. On the other hand, when a trait only occurs if two identical genes make up the pair, these genes are called *recessive.* Recessive characteristics include blue eyes and albinism (lack of coloration in skin, hair, and eyes). When the pair consists of one dominant and one recessive gene—say, one gene for brown eyes and one for blue—the dominant trait appears. This is why it is important to distinguish between the trait we observe, which is called a *phenotype,* and the underlying genetic makeup, which is called the *genotype.*

Not surprisingly, geneticists have discovered that genetic transmission is often far more complicated than the process just described. First of all, paired genes can be *codominant* so that the phenotype will show the influence of both genes. This is the case for the ABO blood type. Also, some genes become dominant at different ages in the life span—changes in hair color and distribution, eruption and loss of teeth, and the production of sex hormones are but a few examples. Second, *mutations* occur that change the chemical or structural composition of a gene. Most mutations are harmful and can be passed on to an offspring as a recessive gene (Gardner, 1983). Such alterations sometimes result from excessive exposure to environmental agents, such as X rays. Finally, it is likely that many behavioral traits, such as intelligence, are partially determined by the process of *polygenic inheritance,* involving the combined interaction of many gene pairs.

The Impact of Genetics on Development and Health

Researchers have identified a vast number of traits—including more than 3,000 diseases—that are affected by heredity. For some diseases, they have even pinpointed the exact gene location. We will look at some of these traits and diseases.

Sickle-cell anemia is a hereditary disease

whose victims are usually black people. In the United States, approximately 10% of the black population carry a recessive gene for this disease and do not have the disorder (Holbrook, 1985). But when a person has two of these genes, large quantities of sickle-shaped red blood cells are manufactured by the body. Compared with normal blood cells, these defective cells carry little oxygen and tend to clump together in the bloodstream—often they cannot pass through capillaries. As a result, the oxygen supply to vital organs becomes inadequate, and tissue damage often occurs. The condition, which usually develops in childhood, leads to progressive organ failure and brain damage.

Another recessive disease is *phenylketonuria* (PKU). In this disease, which occurs more frequently among whites than other racial groups, the baby's body fails to produce a necessary enzyme for metabolizing phenylalanine, a toxic amino acid present in many common foods (Collins & Lipman, 1985). If the disease is not treated, the amino acid builds up and causes brain damage. This can be prevented by placing PKU babies on special diets as soon as possible after birth. When the brain is more fully developed after about 5 years of age, many PKU children can switch to normal diets. PKU provides a good example of an inherited disease that can be controlled by modifying the victim's behavior.

The X chromosome has a special significance beyond determining a person's gender: it sometimes carries genes for a class of disorders that are described as *sex-linked.* These disorders include *color blindness, hemophilia,* and the muscle-wasting disease called *Duchenne's muscular dystrophy* (Sarafino & Armstrong, 1986). For these disorders, if the child has only one X chromosome—as a boy does—and it carries the sex-linked gene, he will have the phenotype. If the child has two X chromosomes—as a girl does—*both* must carry the gene for the phenotype to show up. It is partly for this reason that females can be carriers of a sex-linked disorder but rarely show the phenotype.

Finding specific gene locations on chromosomes to create a "map" of the entire human system of genes is a crucial task of geneticists—and they are well on the way to achieving this goal. They have discovered the specific genes that cause several diseases, such as Duchenne's muscular dystrophy, and can test for the presence of each gene in a fetus early in pregnancy. They are also closing in on certain *oncogenes,* which are structurally abnormal genes that can cause cancer. Researchers have, for example, determined the locations of the oncogenes for certain types of lung and colon cancer (Bodmer et al., 1987; Rodenhuis et al., 1987). These genes are basically mutations that probably result from exposure to harmful environmental agents, such as tobacco smoke. Once the genes are isolated, faster progress can be made in the diagnosis and treatment of these cancers.

Acromegaly is an inherited condition in which excess hormone production by the pituitary gland leads to a gradual thickening of the bones in the head, hands, and feet in adulthood. The photographs of this patient were taken when he was 24, 29, 37, and 42 years of age.

We know that oncogenes can cause cancer. One of the next steps in research will be to increase our knowledge regarding what causes genes to mutate into oncogenes. Assume for a moment that this mutation can result from engaging in certain behaviors, such as smoking cigarettes and eating diets that are high in fats and low in fiber. If this is true, as many researchers believe, we would have additional evidence that behavioral risk factors for cancer constitute major causal links in its development. The case for believing in biopsychosocial determinants of this disease is already strong—it would be ironclad with this evidence.

A biopsychosocial perspective in our examination of heredity is important in another way. Many researchers believe that we often inherit a predisposition or susceptibility—rather than a certainty—for developing a disease (Weiner, 1977; Syme, 1984). This might account in part for the observation that not everyone who is exposed to harmful substances and microorganisms in their environments become sick. People who inherit a high degree of susceptibility to a form of cancer and have relatively little exposure to relevant antigens may be just as likely to develop the illness as someone who has little genetic susceptibility but high antigen exposure. If physicians could determine whether a patient has a genetic predisposition to a specific disease, they could provide the patient with instructions for taking early preventive action.

SUMMARY

To understand health psychology, we need to know how the body systems function. The nervous system provides a communications network for all systems of the body. The central nervous system consists of the brain and spinal cord and is the control center, sending and receiving electrochemical messages through neurons throughout the body. The brain is divided into the forebrain, the cerebellum, and the brainstem. The uppermost regions of the brain are involved in perceptual, motor, learning, and conceptual activities. Areas toward the center and bottom of the brain are important in controlling internal and automatic body functions and the flow of information to and from the brain. The spinal cord is the major neural pathway that connects the brain to the peripheral nervous system.

The peripheral nervous system is a branching network of afferent and efferent neurons throughout the body. It has two divisions, somatic and autonomic. The somatic nervous system is involved in sensory and motor functions. The autonomic nervous system carries messages between the spinal cord and various internal organs, and this system has two parts, sympathetic and parasympathetic. The sympathetic nervous system acts in agreement with our current emotional state and helps us mobilize and expend energy. The parasympathetic nervous system is involved in processes to conserve and store energy and in calming the body following sympathetic arousal.

The endocrine system also communicates with various parts of the body, but does so by sending chemical messages through the bloodstream. This system consists of several glands that secrete hormones. As the "master gland" in this system, the pituitary gland releases hormones that stimulate other glands to secrete. The adrenal glands secrete hormones such as cortisol and epinephrine (adrenalin), which are important in our response to emergencies and stress. Other glands are important in regulating such factors as general body growth and the level of blood sugar.

The digestive and respiratory systems provide the body with essential nutrients, oxygen, and other substances for energy, body growth, and repair. These systems are also involved in removing wastes from the body. The outcomes of the chemical reactions, called metabolism, that occur in our body cells include the synthesis of new cells, the regulation of body processes, and the production of energy to heat the body and fuel its activity.

The cardiovascular system uses the heart to pump blood through an intricate network of blood vessels. The blood's circulation takes it to body cells, where it supplies oxygen and nutrients for metabolism and takes CO_2 and other waste materials away. Systolic and diastolic blood pressure are affected by cardiac output, blood volume, peripheral resistance, elasticity, and viscosity. Blood consists of plasma and formed elements.

The immune system responds to antigens by attacking and eliminating invading substances and microorganisms to protect us from infection and disease. It does this by using white blood cells, including phagocytes and two types of lymphocytes: B-cells, which produce antibodies, and T-cells. The effectiveness of the immune system is impaired by stress and poor nutrition.

The reproductive system and heredity play an important role in development and health by producing a new generation of the species and transmitting genetic information from parents to their offspring. Genetic transmission occurs at conception, when a sperm from the father fertilizes an ovum from the mother. The sperm and ovum each contain 23 chromosomes, which are composed of genes. Each of the body systems that we have examined changes across the life span. In general, they are immature at birth, develop during childhood, function relatively effectively during adolescence and early adulthood, and decline in old age.

KEY TERMS

neurons
neurotransmitter
central nervous system
cerebrum
limbic system
thalamus
hypothalamus
cerebellum
brainstem
midbrain
reticular system
pons
medulla
spinal cord
peripheral nervous system
somatic nervous system
autonomic nervous system
sympathetic nervous system
parasympathetic nervous system
endocrine system
hormones
pituitary gland
adrenal glands
digestive system
enzymes
metabolism
respiratory system
cardiovascular system
blood pressure
lipids
atherosclerosis
arteriosclerosis
immune system
antigen
lymphocytes
phagocytes
cell-mediated immunity
T-cells
antibody-mediated immunity
B-cells
antibodies
chromosomes

part II

STRESS, ILLNESS, AND COPING

3

STRESS—ITS MEANING, IMPACT, AND SOURCES

PROLOGUE

"I've always hated going to the dentist, mostly because of my first visit," says Vicki, remembering back to her first dental checkup 40 years ago. She didn't know what would happen and was fearful of the unfamiliar people, room, and equipment. She began to wimper as the dentist approached her. When he tried to put an instrument in her mouth, Vicki pushed his hand away and began to cry loudly.

How did the dentist handle this situation? Years ago, instead of trying to soothe a fearful child, many dentists tried to force the child to submit to the treatment (Gelfand, 1978). These dentists considered a resistant child to be "willful" and momentarily unable to reason. They tended to agree with the recommendation of a colleague that if a child

> will not listen but continues to cry and struggle . . . hold a folded napkin over the child's mouth . . . and gently but firmly hold his mouth shut. His screams increase his condition of hysteria, but if the mouth is held closed, there is little sound, and he soon begins to reason. (Jordon, cited in Levitas, 1974, p. 178)

Vicki's dentist followed this advice and told her he would not release her until she stopped resisting. Her arms and legs flailed about as she tried to scream through the towel, and her skin flushed from her stressful and exhausting effort. Eventually she submitted. Many dentists still used this approach with resistant children in the 1970s (Levitas, 1974).

Of course, stress is not limited to children in dental settings. We all experience stress in our everyday lives, probably more than we would like. It occurs in a wide variety of situations and settings—in the family, in school, and on the job, for example. Sometimes the stress experience is brief, and sometimes it continues for a long time. Sometimes it is intense, and sometimes it is mild. It varies across time in a particular individual, and it varies between individuals. An experience that is stressful for one person—such as taking a difficult examination—may not be stressful for another, and may even be exciting or challenging for still another person.

In this chapter we discuss what stress is, where it comes from, and the impact it has. As we do, you will find answers to questions you may have about stress. What makes an event stressful? Why does a particular event produce more stress in one person than in another? How does stress affect our bodies and our behavior? Does the experience of stress change across the life span?

EXPERIENCING STRESS IN OUR LIVES

When you hear people say they are "under a lot of stress," you have some idea of what they mean. Usually the statement means that they feel unable to deal with the demands of their environment, and they feel tense and uncomfortable. You understand the meaning because you and they have had similar experiences, which were labeled "stress." Because of the pervasiveness and commonality of these experiences in our lives, you might expect that defining the concept of stress would be simple. But it isn't. Let's see how psychologists have conceptualized stress and what the prevailing definition is today.

What Is Stress?

Stress has been conceptualized in three ways (Coyne & Holroyd, 1982; Stotland, 1987). One approach focuses on the environment, describing stress as a *stimulus.* We see this in people's reference to the source or cause of their discomfort and tension as being an event or set of circumstances—such as having "a high-stress job." Events or circumstances that we perceive as threatening or harmful, thereby producing feelings of tension, are called **stressors**. Researchers who follow this approach study the impact of a wide range of stressors, including (1) catastrophic events, such as tornadoes and earthquakes, (2) major life events, such as the loss of a loved one or a job, and (3) more chronic circumstances, such as living in crowded or noisy conditions.

The second approach treats stress as a *response*, focusing on people's reaction to stressors. We see an example of this approach when people use the word *stress* to refer to their state of tension, and when someone says "I feel a lot of stress when I have to give a speech." The response has two interrelated components. The psychological component involves behavior, thought patterns, and emotions, as when you "feel nervous." The physiological component involves heightened bodily arousal—your heart pounds, your mouth goes dry, your stomach feels tight, and you perspire. The person's psychological and physiological response to a stressor is called **strain.**

The third approach describes stress as a *process* that includes stressors and strains, but adds an important dimension—the relationship between the person and the environment (Cox, 1978; Lazarus & Launier, 1978; Lazarus & Folkman, 1984a, 1984b; Mechanic, 1976). This process involves continuous interactions and adjustments—called **transactions**—between the person and the environment, with each affecting and being affected by the other. According to this view, stress is not just a stimulus or a response, but rather a process in which the person is an active agent who can influence the impact of a stressor through behavioral, cognitive, and emotional strategies. People differ in the amount of stress they experience from the same stressor, such as being stuck in traffic or losing a job. One person who is stuck in traffic and late for an important appointment keeps looking at his watch, honking his horn, and getting angrier by the minute; another person in the same circumstances stays calm, turns on the radio, and listens to music.

To define stress, we will borrow ideas from several sources (Cox, 1978; Lazarus & Folkman, 1984b; Mechanic, 1976; Singer & Davidson, 1986; Stotland, 1987; Trumbull & Appley, 1986). **Stress** is the condition that results when person/environment *transactions* lead the individual to *perceive a discrepancy*—whether real or not—between the *demands* of a situation and the *resources* of the person's biological, psychological, or social systems. Let's look at the four components of this definition, starting at the end.

1. Stress taxes the person's biopsychosocial *resources* for coping with difficult events or circumstances. These resources are limited. We saw an example of limited resources being exhausted when Vicki submitted in her first dental examination. Sometimes the impact is focused mainly on our biological system—for instance, when we tax our physical strength to lift something heavy. More typically, however, the strain impacts on all three systems; in Vicki's stressful experience, her physical, psychological, and social resources were strained and became exhausted. Other stressful encounters that strain our biopsychosocial resources include participating in a competitive athletic event, being injured in an accident, or becoming nauseated before performing in a play.

2. The phrase "*demands* of a situation" refers to the amount of our resources the stressor appears to require. In Vicki's case, the demands of her dental visit were intense.

3. When there is a poor fit, or a mismatch, between the demands of the situation and the resources of the person, a *discrepancy* exists. This generally takes the form of the demands taxing or exceeding the resources, such as when we have too much to do in too short a time. But the opposite discrepancy also occurs—that is, our resources may be underutilized—and this can be stressful, too. A worker who is bored by a lack of challenge in a job may find this situation stressful. An important point to keep in mind is that the discrepancy may be either *real* or just *believed* to exist. Suppose you had to take an exam and wanted to do well, but worried greatly that you would not. If you had procrastinated and did not prepare for the test, the discrepancy you see between the demands

and your resources might be real. But if you had previously done well on similar exams, prepared thoroughly for this one, and scored well on a pretest in a study guide yet still thought you would not do well, the discrepancy you see would not reflect the true state of affairs. People's stresses often result from inaccurate perceptions of discrepancies between environmental demands and their actual resources. Stress is in the eye of the beholder.

4. Our assessments of discrepancies between demands and resources occur through our *transactions* with the environment. These transactions are affected by many factors, including our prior history and aspects of the current situation. Suppose you are on a track team and are running in a race. Relevant transactions for this race actually began long before the race started, such as in your previous wins and losses, your recent training and fitness, and your knowledge of and experience with your competitors. During the race, these prior transactions have an impact on the continuous transactions that occur as you assess your strength and energy reserves, the position you are in relative to the other runners, and the likelihood that another runner will show a surge of speed toward the end of the race.

Appraising Events as Stressful

Transactions that lead to the condition of stress generally involve an assessment process that Richard Lazarus and his coworkers call **cognitive appraisal** (Cohen & Lazarus, 1983; Lazarus & Folkman, 1984b; Lazarus & Launier, 1978). Cognitive appraisal is a mental process by which people assess two factors: (1) whether a demand threatens their well-being and (2) the resources available for meeting the demand. These two factors form the distinction between two types of appraisal—primary and secondary.

Primary and Secondary Appraisal

When we encounter a potentially stressful event, such as the news of an approaching blizzard, we first try to assess the meaning of the situation for our well-being. This assessment process is called **primary appraisal**. In effect this appraisal seeks answers to such questions as "What does this mean to me?" and "Will I be okay or in trouble?" Suppose the blizzard was certain to hit your community tomorrow night. Your primary appraisal regarding the blizzard could yield one of three judgments:

1. *It is irrelevant*—as you might decide if you were leaving on a vacation tomorrow morning, well before the snowstorm will arrive.
2. *It is good* (called "benign-positive")—which might be your appraisal if you were planning to go skiing or wanted a college exam postponed.
3. *It is stressful*—as you might judge if you were fearful of driving in snow and would have to do so.

Events that we appraise as stressful receive further appraisal for three implications: harm-loss, threat, and challenge. *Harm-loss* refers to the amount of damage that has already occurred, as when someone is incapacitated and in pain following a serious injury. *Threat* is the expectation of future harm—for example, when a hospitalized patient contemplates his medical bills, difficult rehabilitation, and loss of income. *Challenge* is the opportunity to achieve growth, mastery, or profit by using more than routine resources to meet a demand. For instance, an offer of a higher-level job might be viewed as stressful by a worker, but also as an opportunity to expand her skills, demonstrate her ability, and make more money.

Sometimes we experience stress even when the stressor does not relate to us directly—that is, the transaction is *vicarious*. If we see other people in stressful circumstances, such as suffering from pain or a life-threatening illness, we may empathize with their feelings and feel vulnerable ourselves. A classic experiment demonstrated empathic appraisal by showing college-student subjects a film called "Subincision" (Speisman, Lazarus, Mordkoff, & Davison, 1964). The film showed a rite of passage for

This woman's face reveals that she appraises the pain in her chest as stressful.

young adolescent boys in a primitive society in which the underside of the penis is cut deeply from the tip to the scrotum, using a sharp stone. Before seeing the film, the subjects were divided into four groups, so that each group would see the film a different way. One of the groups saw the film with no sound track. Another group heard a sound track with a "trauma" narrative that emphasized the pain, danger, and primitiveness of the operation. A third group heard a "denial" narration that denied the pain and potential harm to the boys, describing them as willing participants in a joyful occasion who "look forward to the happy conclusion of the ceremony." The fourth group heard a "scientific" narration that encouraged the viewers to watch in a detached manner—for example, the narrator commented, "As you can see, the operation is formal and the surgical technique, while crude, is very carefully followed."

Did the different sound tracks affect the subjects' appraisals of stress? To evaluate this, the researchers used both physiological and self-report measures of stress. The physiological measures, such as heart rate, were taken continuously during the viewing of the film. The self-report measures were questionnaires that evaluated feelings of stress immediately after the film presentation. The results showed that, compared with the subjects who saw the film with no sound track, those who heard the trauma narration reacted with more stress, particularly during the film; those who heard the denial and scientific narrations reacted with less stress. These results show that people can experience stress vicariously and that their reactions depend on the process of primary appraisal.

Secondary appraisal refers to our ongoing assessment of the resources we have available for coping. Although we generally engage in an assessment of our resources after we appraise an event as stressful, secondary appraisal "does not necessarily follow primary appraisal in time" (Cohen & Lazarus, 1983, p. 609). The two processes are highly interrelated, and sometimes our secondary appraisal of limited resources, or weakness, can lead to primary "appraisals of threat where they would not otherwise occur" (Coyne & Holroyd, 1982, p. 109). Nevertheless, we are probably more aware of secondary appraisal when we judge a situation as potentially stressful and try to determine whether our resources are sufficient to meet the harm, threat, or challenge we face. Examples of secondary appraisal judgments include:

- I can't do it—I know I'll fail.
- I'll try, but my chances are slim.
- I can do it if Ginny will help.
- If this method fails, I can try a few others.
- I can do it if I work hard.
- No problem—I can do it.

The condition of stress that we experience often depends on the outcome of the appraisals we make in our transactions with the environment. When we judge the fit between demands and resources to be close, we may experience little or no stress; but when our appraisals indicate a discrepancy, particularly if we appraise greater demands than resources, we may feel a great deal of stress.

Can stress occur without cognitive appraisals? According to some researchers, it can, particularly in emergency situations. Suppose you are in your car, stopped at a red light. In a split second you hear the squealing of brakes; your body tenses as you say "Oh my God!"; and a car smashes yours in the rear. Your saying "Oh my God!" is not really a cognitive appraisal—it's a reflexive response. But a stress reaction has already begun, as the tensing of your body indicates, and this is "*followed* by 'feelings' and appraisals" (Trumbull & Appley, 1986, p. 34). Often in serious emergencies the stress reaction includes a state of shock in which the person is stunned, dazed, or disoriented (Coleman, 1976). This state may last for minutes or hours, or much longer. Because cognitive functioning is impaired during shock, it is unlikely that appraisal processes play an important role in the stress experienced while in that state.

What Factors Lead to Stressful Appraisals?

Appraising events as stressful depends on two types of factors—those that relate to the person and those that relate to the situation (Cohen & Lazarus, 1983; Lazarus & Folkman, 1984b). Let's begin by looking at how personal factors can affect appraisals of stress.

Personal factors include intellectual, motivational, and personality characteristics. One example has to do with self-esteem: people who have high self-esteem are likely to believe that they have the resources to meet demands that require the strengths they possess. If they perceive an event as stressful, they may interpret it as a challenge rather than a threat (Cohen & Lazarus, 1983). Another example relates to motivation: the more important a threatened goal, the more stress the person is likely to perceive (Paterson & Neufeld, 1987). One other example involves the person's belief system: as the psychologist Albert Ellis has noted, many people have irrational beliefs that increase their stress, for instance:

> "Because I strongly desire to have a safe, comfortable, and satisfying life, the conditions under which I live *absolutely must* be easy, convenient and gratifying (and it is *awful* and *I can't bear it* and *can't be happy at all* when they are unsafe and frustrating)!" (1987, p. 373)

A person who has such a belief is likely to appraise almost any sort of inconvenience as harmful or threatening.

HIGHLIGHT 3A: On Issues
What's "A Disaster?"

A delightful student in one of my classes got a grade of B on an exam and announced that "This grade is a *disaster.*" Although I realized that we tend to use this word broadly, I couldn't help but wonder, "If a grade of B is a disaster, what will we call an airplane crash that kills a hundred people?" Let's see what a disaster is and how disasters vary.

According to Webster's dictionary, a disaster is a happening that results in great trauma, harm, or damage, particularly to life or property. An example of a disaster was the mass kidnapping of 26 schoolchildren and a bus driver by masked bandits in Chowchilla, California, in 1976. The victims were taken on an 11-hour bus ride and then placed in a large truck, which was then buried in a huge pit. After many stressful hours underground, they were able to escape by digging their way to the surface. We will use this episode to illustrate how disasters differ in five ways (Berren, Beigel, & Ghertner, 1986).

1. *Type of disaster.* There are three types of disasters: natural, man-made, and mixed. Disasters caused by nature include tornadoes and earthquakes. Man-made disasters are caused by people, as when an arson starts a major fire or when someone commits a mass murder. Many disasters are caused by both nature and humans—for example, when an airplane crashes because of bad weather and human error. The Chowchilla disaster was obviously perpetrated by people.
2. *Duration of the disaster.* Some disasters last for minutes or several hours, as often happens in earthquakes and major fires. Other disasters continue for days, months, or years—as occurred in the Ethiopian famine in the mid-1980s. The Chowchilla episode lasted for about 27 hours.
3. *Degree of personal impact.* This refers to the amount of harm or damage caused by the disaster and the number of people affected. If two earthquakes of equal magnitude occur, the personal impact would be greater for the one that happened in a city, destroying many buildings and taking many lives, than for the one that happened in an undeveloped area and took no lives. Throughout the Chowchilla episode, the victims suffered tremendous emotional trauma, thought they would die, and had no food and no access to restrooms. Their families also suffered great anguish.
4. *Potential for occurrence or recurrence.* Some disasters are more likely to occur or recur than are others. The likelihood of a hurricane hitting Florida in the fall is fairly high, but the likelihood of a mass kidnapping like the one in Chowchilla is extremely slim.
5. *Control over future impact.* Some disasters can be prevented or their consequences reduced by people's efforts—for example, major floods can sometimes be prevented by building a dam or their damage can be reduced with sandbags. A disaster like the Chowchilla kidnapping would be difficult, if not impossible, to prevent.

Knowing what constitutes a disaster is important for two reasons. First, by using the word "disaster" to refer to a less serious event, people exaggerate its personal impact and increase their feeling of stress (Ellis, 1987). People who do this can be helped to see what they are doing and how to think more realistically about events in their lives. Second, by identifying the actual elements of a disaster after it occurs, people who provide help to the victims can choose the most useful courses of action. As an example, for the children in the Chowchilla kidnapping, the enormous personal impact of the disaster indicated that they needed one-to-one counseling—in some cases, long-term counseling. Many of these children developed extreme fears and nightmares relating to the kidnapping. A 9-year-old girl, for instance, dreamed she was riding in a car with her family when "Men in a van got us, kidnapped us, killed us, and put us in a grave" (Terr, 1986, p. 344). Focusing help on prevention or reduction of future impact would not have been very useful for them. If a disaster produces less personal impact but is preventable, the opposite helping approach might be most appropriate.

What is it about situations that make them stressful? There are several factors. First, events that involve very *strong demands* and are *imminent* tend to be seen as stressful (Cohen & Lazarus, 1983; Paterson & Neufeld, 1987). Thus, patients who expect to undergo a physically uncomfortable or painful medical procedure, such as surgery, tomorrow are likely to view their situation as being more stressful than, say, expecting to have a blood pressure test next week.

Also, *life transitions* tend to be stressful (Moos & Schaefer, 1986; Sarason & Sarason, 1984). Life has many major events that mark the passing from one condition or phase to another and they produce substantial changes and new demands in our lives. These events are called transitions, and include:

- Starting day care or school
- Moving to a new community
- Reaching puberty, with accompanying biological and social changes
- Starting college, especially away from home
- Entering a career
- Getting married
- Becoming a parent
- Losing a spouse through divorce or death
- Retiring from a career

Becoming a parent, for instance, can be stressful before and after the birth (Miller & Sollie, 1986; Quadagno, Dixon, Denney, & Buck, 1986). Stress is experienced before birth for many reasons, including the physiological burden of pregnancy on the mother's body and concerns about the baby's and mother's health. After birth, stress results from the parents' being tied down, having a less orderly and predictable lifestyle, and having their sleep interrupted often, among other things. The stress produced by this transition was expressed by one mother in the following way: "Like many new mothers I am faced with hard decisions about the future of my career since my baby was born. I am full of doubts, and I'm uncertain how to maintain my career and raise my child satisfactorily" (Miller & Sollie, 1986, p. 136).

The *timing* of a life transition can affect the stress it produces. People expect some events, such as marriage or retirement, to occur at certain times in the life span (Neugarten & Neugarten, 1987). Deviations from the expected timetable are stressful. Why? One reason is that

> *having an event happen too early or too late can mean that one is deprived of the support of compatible peers.* Consider a woman whose first child is born when she is 38. The new mothers with whom she might hope to share information about child care, from whom she might seek emotional support regarding the demands of a new baby, or with whom she might like to spend time while walking the baby in the park are likely to be 15 years younger than she. How comfortable will she feel with them and they with her? (Lazarus & Folkman, 1984b, p. 109)

Also, being off schedule may be interpreted as a failure, and this is stressful. Some people who are "late" graduating college or advancing on the job feel as if they have failed.

Ambiguity—a lack of clarity in a situation—can have an effect on stress appraisals. But the effect seems to depend on the type of ambiguity that exists. *Role ambiguity* occurs when the information about a person's function or task is unclear or confusing (Quick & Quick, 1984). In the workplace, for instance, this is reflected in unclear guidelines, standards for performance, and consequences for job-related activities. Role ambiguity often increases people's stress because they are uncertain about their actions and decisions. *Harm ambiguity* occurs when the likelihood of harm or the availability of resources to meet situational demands is unclear. With this kind of ambiguity, the effect on stress is variable and depends heavily on the person's personality, beliefs, and general experience (Lazarus & Folkman, 1984a, 1984b; Paterson & Neufeld, 1987). One person who is seriously ill and has unclear information about the chances of recovery may draw hope from this ambiguity; another person in the same situation may believe that people are deliberately giving ambiguous information because the prognosis is so poor.

Another factor that influences stress appraisals is the *desirability* of the situation. Some events are typically undesirable to a person in most or all respects—losing your house in a fire is an example. Other events, such as selling a house, are usually viewed as desirable. But either selling a house or losing it in a fire can be stressful because they both produce demands that may tax or exceed the individual's resources. Actually, a wide variety of both desirable and undesirable situations can be stressful. These events include the transitions we saw earlier, as well as less momentous circumstances, such as getting a traffic ticket or preparing to throw a party. In general, undesirable events are more likely to be appraised as stressful than are desirable ones (McFarlane et al., 1980; Sandler & Guenther, 1985; Suls & Mullen, 1981; Vinokur & Selzer, 1975).

One other aspect of the situation that affects the appraisal of stress is its *controllability*—that is, whether the person has the real or perceived ability to modify or terminate the stressor. People tend to appraise an uncontrollable event as being more stressful than a controllable event, even if they don't actually do anything to affect it (Miller, 1979; Suls & Mullen, 1981; Thompson, 1981). There are at least two types of control, behavioral and cognitive. In the case of *behavioral control,* we can affect the impact of the event by performing some action. Suppose, for example, you are experiencing intense pain from a headache. If you have the ability to reduce the pain, you are less likely to be stressed by the headache than if you do not have this ability. In the case of *cognitive control,* we can affect the impact of the event by using some mental strategy, such as by distracting our attention from the stressor or developing a plan to overcome a problem.

BIOPSYCHOSOCIAL REACTIONS TO STRESS

In some of the stress experiences we have discussed, we saw that stressors produce strain in the person's biological, psychological, and social systems. Let's examine biopsychosocial reactions to stress more closely.

Biological Aspects of Stress

Anyone who has experienced a very frightening event, such as a near accident or other emergency, knows that there are physiological reactions to stress—for instance, our heartbeat and breathing rates increase immediately and, a little later, our skeletal muscles may tremble, especially in the arms and legs. The body is aroused and motivated to defend itself. As we saw in the preceding chapter, the sympathetic nervous system and the endocrine system cause this arousal to happen. After the emergency has passed, the arousal subsides.

Many years ago the distinguished physiologist Walter Cannon (1929) provided a basic description of how the body reacts to emergencies. He was interested in the physiological reaction people and animals make in response to a perceived danger. This reaction has been called the *fight-or-flight* response because it prepares the organism to attack the threat or to flee. In the fight-or-flight response, the perception of danger causes the sympathetic nervous system to stimulate the adrenal glands of the endocrine system to secrete epinephrine, which arouses the body. Cannon proposed that this arousal could have both positive and negative effects: The fight-or-flight response is adaptive because it mobilizes the organism to respond quickly to danger, but the state of high arousal can be harmful to health if it is prolonged.

General Adaptation Syndrome

What happens to the body when stress is prolonged? Hans Selye studied this issue by subjecting laboratory animals to a variety of stressors—such as very high or low environmental temperatures, X rays, insulin injections, and exercise—over a long period of time. He also observed people who experienced stress from being ill. Through this research, he discovered that the fight-or-flight response is only the first in a series of reactions the body makes when stress is long-lasting (Selye, 1956, 1976, 1985). Selye called this series of physiological reactions the **general adaptation syndrome** (GAS). As Figure 3.1 shows, the GAS consists of three stages:

1. **Alarm reaction.** The first stage of the GAS is like the fight-or-flight response to an emergency—its function is to mobilize the

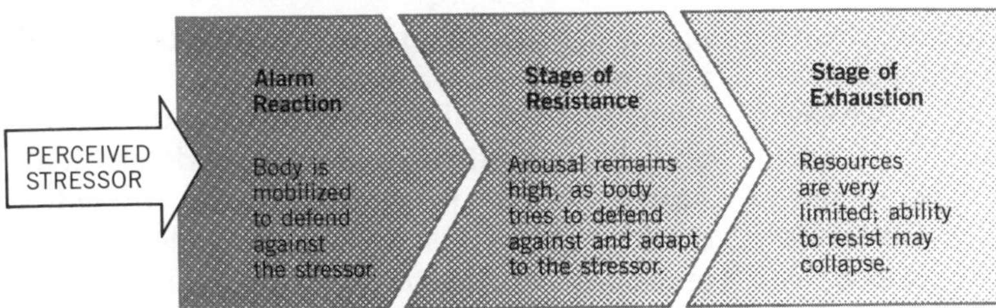

FIGURE 3.1 General Adaptation Syndrome.

body's resources. At the very beginning of the alarm reaction, arousal—as measured by blood pressure, for example—drops below normal for a moment, but then quickly rises to above normal. This fast-increasing arousal results from the release of hormones by the endocrine system: The pituitary gland secretes ACTH, which causes a heightened release of epinephrine, norepinephrine, and cortisol by the adrenal glands into the bloodstream. By the end of this stage in the GAS, the body is fully mobilized to resist the stressor strongly. But the body cannot maintain the intense arousal of the alarm reaction for very long. If the stress is extremely intense and unavoidable, and the alarm reaction continues unabated, the organism may die within hours or days.

2. **Stage of resistance.** If a strong stressor continues but is not severe enough to cause death, the physiological reaction enters the stage of resistance. In this stage, the body tries to adapt to the stressor. Physiological arousal declines somewhat but remains higher than normal, and the body replenishes the hormones released by the adrenal glands. Despite this continuous physiological arousal, the organism may show few outward signs of stress. But the ability to resist new stressors is im-

Physical exertion, such as in athletic competition, is a stressor that produces strain in the body.

paired. According to Selye, one outcome of this impairment is that the organism becomes increasingly vulnerable to health problems he called *diseases of adaptation.* These health problems include ulcers, high blood pressure, asthma, and illnesses that result from impaired immune function.

3. **Stage of exhaustion.** Prolonged physiological arousal produced by severe long-term or repeated stress is costly. It depletes the body's energy reserves until the physical ability to resist is very limited. At this point, the stage of exhaustion begins. If the stress continues, disease and physiological damage become increasingly likely, and death may occur.

Do All Stressors Produce the Same Physical Reactions?

Increases in the secretion of hormones by the adrenal glands have been found in many studies with a wide variety of stressors (Baum, Grunberg, & Singer, 1982; Ciaranello, 1983). These stressors include cold temperatures. noise, pain, failure, athletic competition, taking examinations, flying in an airplane, and being in crowded situations.

Selye believed that the GAS is *nonspecific* with regard to the type of stressor. That is, the series of physiological reactions described by the GAS will occur regardless of whether the stress results from very cold temperature, physical exercise, illness, or the death of a loved one. Although the fact that various stressors increase the secretion of adrenal hormones is consistent with Selye's view, the notion of nonspecificity does not take important psychosocial processes into account. There are at least two reasons why this is a problem.

One reason is that some stressors elicit a stronger *emotional* response than others do. This is important because the amount of hormone released in reaction to a stressor that involves a strong emotional response, as a *sudden* increase in environmental temperature might produce, appears to be different from the amount released with a less-emotional stressor, such as a *gradual* increase in temperature. After conducting extensive studies of various stressors and hormones, John Mason concluded that he and his colleagues "have not found evidence that any single hormone responds to *all* stimuli in *absolutely* nonspecific fashion" (1975, p. 27). He also pointed out that research conducted since Selye first described the GAS has shown that the release of hormones by the pituitary and adrenal glands is highly sensitive

> to psychological and social influences, even of a relatively subtle nature. It is now known that emotional stimuli rank very high among the most potent and prevalent natural stimuli capable of increasing pituitary-adrenal cortical activity. (1975, p. 23)

In other words, stressors are most likely to trigger the release of large amounts of cortisol, epinephrine, and norepinephrine if the individual's response includes a strong element of emotion.

The second reason is that cognitive appraisal processes appear to play a role in people's physiological reaction to stress. This role is suggested by the results of a study by Katherine Tennes and Maria Kreye (1985). The researchers assessed elementary school children's cortisol levels in urine samples taken on regular school days and on days when achievement tests were given. The expected increase in cortisol on test days was found, but not for all children—their intelligence was an important factor. Intelligence test scores were obtained from school records. Cortisol levels increased on test days for children with above average intelligence, but not for children with low to average intelligence. The influence of intelligence suggests that the brighter children were more concerned about academic achievement and, as a result, appraised the tests as more threatening than the other children did.

Psychosocial Aspects of Stress

At this juncture, we can begin to see how interwoven our biological, psychological, and social systems are in the experience of stress. Stress produces physiological changes, but psychosocial factors also play a role. To give a more complete picture of the interplay among these systems, we will now examine the impact of stress on people's cognitive, emotional, and social systems.

Cognition and Stress

Many students have had this experience: While taking a particularly stressful exam in school, they may neglect or misinterpret important information in a question or have difficulty remembering an answer they had studied well the night before. It is infuriating to know that an answer is "on the tip of your tongue," especially since you will probably remember it after the test if over. High levels of stress impair people's memory and attention during cognitive activities (Cohen, Evans, Stokols, & Krantz, 1986).

Noise can be a stressor, and some people live in very noisy environments — next to train tracks or highways, for instance. How does chronic noise affect people's cognitive performance? Many people can deal with this kind of stress by changing the focus of their attention from the noise to relevant aspects of a cognitive task — they "tune out" the noise. Psychologist Sheldon Cohen (1980) has proposed that children who try to tune out chronic noise may develop generalized cognitive deficits because they have difficulty knowing which sounds to attend to and which to tune out. Evidence from several studies supports this position (Cohen, Evans, Stokols, & Krantz, 1986).

One of these studies tested second- to fifth-grade children with normal hearing ability who lived in apartments with different noise levels (Cohen, Glass, & Singer, 1973). The children lived in an apartment complex that was built on bridges spanning a busy highway. The apartments on the lower floors, being closer to the highway, were noisier than those on the upper floors. The children's ability to discriminate between spoken words was tested in a quiet setting by having them listen to pairs of words. The two words were either identical (for example, goat-goat) or similar sounding (house-mouse). The children simply had to indicate whether the two words were the same or different. The results of this study showed a correlation between noise level and ability to discriminate between words. The children who lived in the noisier apartments had more difficulty in the discrimination task than those who lived in quieter apartments. The correlation was especially strong among the children who had lived in the apartment complex a long time. Furthermore, the children from the noisier apartments had poorer reading ability than those from the quieter apartments. These results suggest that children who live in noisy environments become less and less attentive to sounds and that this strategy for adapting to stress impairs their development of important academic abilities.

Emotions and Stress

Long before infants can talk, they display what they feel by their motor, vocal, and facial expressions. You can test this with a little experiment: Place a bit of a bitter food, such as unsweetened chocolate, in a newborn's mouth and watch the baby's face — the eyes squint, brows drop and draw together, mouth opens, and tongue juts out. This is the facial expression for the emotion of disgust.

According to Carroll Izard (1979), a prominent researcher of infant emotions, newborn babies do not display all the emotional expressions they will develop, but they do express several emotions, such as disgust, distress, and interest. To study the facial expression of emotion in infants, Izard runs tests — like the one using bitter food — using stimuli that intuitively should elicit a specific feeling. During the test, he videotapes the infant's expressions, which are assessed later by using a standard scoring system (Izard & Dougherty, 1982). Each emotion has its own pattern of specific features of facial expression. Using this procedure, he and his colleagues studied how infants' emotional reactions to stress develop (Izard, Hembree, Dougherty, & Spizzirri, 1983). The babies were videotaped as they received their regular inoculations when they were about 2, 4, 8, and 19 months of age. Assessment of the expressions they displayed following needle penetration revealed that pain produced two principal responses—distress and anger—in infants of all ages. But distress was the immediate and dominant emotion at the younger ages, and anger the immediate and dominant emotional response at 19 months. The reason anger becomes an increasingly dominant reaction to pain is that infants become more able to try to act for themselves, such as by pushing at the nurse's hand. Anger spurs this kind of defensive action; distress merely signals the need for help.

Emotions tend to accompany stress, and people often use their emotional state to evaluate their stress. Cognitive appraisal processes can influence both the stress and the emotional experience (Maslach, 1979; Schachter & Singer, 1962, 1979; Scherer, 1986). For example, you might experience stress and fear if you came across a snake while walking in the woods, particularly if you recognized it as poisonous. Your emotion would not be joy or excitement, unless you were studying snakes and were looking for this particular type. Both situations would produce stress, but you might experience fear if your appraisal was one of threat, and excitement if your appraisal was one of challenge.

Fear is a common emotional reaction that involves a combination of psychological discomfort and physical arousal in threatening situations. Of the various types and intensities of fears people experience in their everyday lives, psychologists classify many into two categories: phobias and anxiety. *Phobias* are intense and irrational fears that are directly associated with specific events and situations. Some people are afraid of being enclosed in small rooms, for instance, and are described as claustrophobic. *Anxiety* is a vague feeling of uneasiness or apprehension—a gloomy anticipation of impending doom—that often involves a relatively uncertain or unspecific threat. That is, the person may not be aware either of the situations that seem to arouse anxiety or of exactly what the "doom" entails. Patients awaiting surgery or the outcome of diagnostic tests generally experience high levels of anxiety. In other situations, anxiety may result from appraisals of low self-worth and the anticipation of a loss of either self-esteem or the esteem of others.

The specific things people fear are related to their age (Graziano, DeGiovanni, & Garcia, 1979; Sarafino, 1986). During childhood, for example, the things children fear become *less* concrete or tangible and *more* abstract and social as they get older. In infancy and early childhood, many children develop fears of such concrete things as loud noises, strangers, doctors and dentists, and animals. They also become increasingly afraid of imaginary creatures, such as ghosts and monsters, that they hear about in stories or see on television or in movies. Later in childhood, these early fears tend to decline while anxieties relating to school, individual competence, and social relations become pronounced. More and more, children notice differences between each other, and they make comparisons of academic ability, conduct, talents, physical attractiveness, popularity, and so on. Children who see themselves as less able than their age-mates are likely to appraise their own resources as insufficient to meet the demands of stressors.

Stress can also lead to feelings of sadness or *depression*. We all feel depressed at times, although we may call the feeling something else, like "sad," or "blue," or "unhappy." These feelings are a normal part of life for children and adults (Quay & La Greca, 1986; Rosenhan & Seligman, 1984). The difference between "normal" depression and depression as a serious *disorder* is a matter of degree. Depression becomes a psychological disorder when it is severe, frequent, and long-lasting. People with this disorder tend to:

- Have a generally unhappy mood
- Feel hopeless about the future
- Appear listless and passive
- Show disrupted eating and sleeping habits
- Have low self-esteem, often blaming themselves for the troubles that afflict them (Rosenhan & Seligman, 1984)

Having long-term disabling health problems, such as being paralyzed by a stroke, often leads to depressive disorders. Although children do have depressive feelings, the question of whether the type of disorder seen in adults ever develops before adolescence is controversial (Quay & La Greca, 1986). Assessing the severity of depression in children is difficult because they cannot describe their feelings as well as adults can.

Another common emotional reaction to stress is *anger*, particularly when the person perceives the situation as harmful or frustrating. You can see this in the angry response often shown by babies who receive an inoculation, children whose favorite toy was taken away, and adults who are stuck in a traffic jam. Anger has important social ramifications—it can produce aggressive behavior, for instance.

Social Behavior and Stress

Stress changes people's behavior toward one another. In some stressful situations, such as disasters, many people may work together to help each other survive. Perhaps they do this because they have a common goal that requires cooperative effort (Sherif & Sherif, 1953). In other stressful situations, people may become less sociable or caring and more hostile and insensitive toward other individuals.

When stress is accompanied by anger, negative social behaviors tend to increase. Two experiments by Edward Donnerstein and David Wilson (1976) examined the effects of stress and anger on people's aggressive behavior. The first experiment consisted of two phases: (1) the subjects were either angered or not angered by a confederate of the researcher and (2) they were then placed in a situation in which they could behave aggressively toward the confederate. During the second phase, the subjects were exposed to one of two levels of stress produced by unpredictable bursts of noise—half of the angered and nonangered subjects heard loud noise (95 decibels) and half heard mild noise (55 decibels). The results showed that the angered subjects were more aggressive than the nonangered subjects, and the angered subjects were especially aggressive if they were exposed to the loud noise. Anger tends to increase aggression during stressful experiences.

Do the effects of anger and stress continue after the experience is over? The second experiment by Donnerstein and Wilson examined this question in three phases. First, the subjects worked on a math task, during which some of them were exposed to loud noise and others worked in quiet conditions. Then the subjects were either angered or not angered by a confederate. In the third phase of the experiment, the subjects had the opportunity to be aggressive toward the confederate. The subjects who were angered and exposed to loud noise were more aggressive toward the confederate than the subjects in the other conditions of the experiment. Thus, the effects of anger and stress do continue after the experience is over.

The increased aggressive behavior that stress and anger produce has important implications in real life, outside the laboratory. Child abuse is a major social problem that poses a serious threat to children's health, physical development, and psychological adjustment. Studies have found a connection between parental stress and child abuse (Kempe, 1976; Kolbe et al., 1986). Prior to an act of battering, frequently the parent has experienced a stressful crisis, such as the loss of a job. A parent under high levels of stress is at risk of losing control. If, for example, the child runs around the house making a racket, a stressed parent may become very angry, lose control, and start beating the child.

Stress also affects helping behavior. This was shown in an experiment conducted in a shopping center (Cohen & Spacapan, 1978). The researchers manipulated stress in two ways: (1) the subjects either had a difficult shopping task or an easy one and (2) the shopping center was either crowded, which can be stressful, or uncrowded. After completing the shopping task, each subject walked through a deserted hallway to meet with the researcher. In the hallway, the subject encountered a woman who feigned dropping a contact lens—a situation in which the subject could provide help. Those subjects who had just experienced the most stress, having completed the difficult shopping task in crowded conditions, helped less often and for less time than those who had completed the easy task in uncrowded conditions.

We have seen that the effects of stress are wide-ranging, involving an interplay among our biological, psychological, and social systems. Even when the stressor is no longer present, the impact of the stress experience can continue. Some people experience more stress than others do, but we all find stress somewhere in our lives. Stress arises from a countless variety of sources.

SOURCES OF STRESS THROUGHOUT LIFE

Babies, children, and adults all experience stress. The sources of stress may change as people develop, but the condition of stress can occur at any time throughout life. Where does stress come from, and what are its sources? To answer this question, we will divide up a variety of sources on the basis of the systems from which they arise. That is, we will examine sources that arise within the *person*, in the *family*, and in the *community* and *society*.

Sources within the Person

Sometimes the source of stress is within the person. One way stress arises from within the individual is through *illness*. Being ill places demands on the person's biological and psychological systems, and the degree of stress these demands produce depends on the seriousness of the illness and the age of the individual, among other things. Why is the person's age important? For one thing, the ability of the body to fight disease improves in childhood and declines in old age (Rogers, Dubey, & Reich, 1979). Another reason is that the meaning of a serious illness for the individual changes with age. For example, young children have a limited understanding of disease and death. Because of this, their appraisal of stress that arises from their illness is likely to focus on current, rather than future, concerns—such as how well they feel at the moment and whether their activities are impaired (La Greca & Stone, 1985). Stress appraisals by ill adults typically include both current difficulties and concerns for the future, such as whether they may be disabled or may die.

Another way stress arises within the person is through the appraisal of opposing motivational forces, when a state of *conflict* exists. Suppose you were looking in your closet for a sweater to wear for a "really important" social engagement. You find two that you like, each with its own advantages and disadvantages. You can only wear one at a time, of course. Which will you choose? You have a conflict—you are being pushed and pulled in two directions. Many conflicts are more momentous than this one. We may need to choose between two or more job offers, or different medical treatments, or houses we are thinking of buying, for instance. Conflict is a major source of stress.

The pushes and pulls of conflict produce two opposing tendencies: *approach* and *avoidance*. These two tendencies characterize three basic types of conflict (Lewin, 1935; Miller, 1959):

1. *Approach/approach conflict* arises when a person is attracted toward two appealing goals that are incompatible. For example, individuals who are trying to lose weight either to improve their health or appearance experience frequent conflicts when delicious, fattening foods are available. Although people generally resolve an approach/approach conflict fairly easily, the more important they perceive the decision to be, the greater the stress it is likely to produce.

2. *Avoidance/avoidance conflict* occurs when a person is faced with a choice between two undesirable situations. For example, patients with serious illnesses may be faced with a choice between two treatments that will control or cure the disease, but each treatment has very undesirable side effects. People in avoidance/avoidance conflicts usually try to postpone or escape from the decision: a patient might delay or discontinue treatment or change physicians in the hope of getting choices that are more appealing. When delaying or escaping is not possible, people often

vacillate between the two alternatives, changing their minds repeatedly. Sometimes they get someone else to make the decision for them. People generally find avoidance/avoidance conflicts difficult to resolve and very stressful.

3. *Approach/avoidance conflict* arises when a person sees attractive and unattractive features in a single goal or situation. This type of conflict can be stressful and difficult to resolve. Consider, for instance, individuals who smoke cigarettes and want to quit. They may be torn between wanting to improve their health and to avoid the weight gain and cravings they believe will occur.

As you may realize, conflicts can be more complicated than the examples we have considered. People often have to choose between two or more alternatives, while recognizing that each has multiple attractive and unattractive features. Buying a new car provides an example. One car is snazzy-looking, comes in the color you want, and offers some of the optional equipment you are looking for—but it costs more than you should spend, and consumer magazines say it is unreliable and the brakes are poor. Another car is less snazzy, does not come in the color you want, and has some other optional equipment you want—but it costs less and consumer magazines rate it highly. These conflicts can be extremely difficult to resolve because the features are so numerous and may not be comparable. For example, how much "snazziness" compensates for the difference in cost? In general, however, people are likely to find conflict stressful when the choices involve many features, when opposing motivational forces have fairly equal strength, and when the "wrong" choice can lead to very negative and permanent consequences. These conditions often apply when people face major decisions about their health.

Sources in the Family

The behavior, needs, and personality of each member of a family impact on and interact with those of the other members of the family system, sometimes producing stress. Interpersonal conflict can arise from financial problems, from inconsiderate behavior, or from opposing goals. This can be seen when siblings argue over which television program to watch or when a parent confronts an adolescent who plays music at deafeningly loud levels, for example. Living in an overcrowded household increases conflict over privacy and the use of family resources, such as the bathroom. Of the many sources of stress in the family, we will focus on the impact of adding a new family member and of illness, infirmity, and death in the family.

An Addition to the Family

A new child in the family is a joyful event, but it also brings stress—particularly to the mother, of course, during pregnancy and after the birth. But an addition to the family is stressful to other family members, too. For instance, the father may feel the need to earn more money, or worry about his wife's and baby's health, or fear that his relationship with his wife may deteriorate. As one expectant father put it, "I really feel left out" (Shapiro, 1987, p. 42). He felt like "the fifth wheel" in the relationship between his wife and the baby. Although not all fathers feel this way, it is not unusual for fathers to be concerned about how the marital relationship will change (May, 1986).

After the baby is born, parents experience stress from their new responsibilities in caring for the child. An important factor in parental stress relates to the child's personality. Each baby comes into the world with certain personality dispositions, which are called **temperaments** (Buss & Plomin, 1975; Thomas, Chess, & Birch, 1970). Pediatric nurses and physicians, well aware of the unique combinations of temperaments that babies show right from birth, describe infants broadly as "easy" babies and "difficult" ones. These terms do, in fact, capture the general dispositions of most infants fairly accurately on the basis of differences in the way babies react to feeding, cuddling, bathing, and dressing and undressing.

Temperamentally difficult babies tend to cry a great deal—often very loudly—and efforts to

HIGHLIGHT 3B: On Issues
Divorce and Children's Stress

Tony was 6 years old when his father left their family almost a year ago. Since that time, Tony has been whiney and quarrelsome. This morning at breakfast he began to cry uncontrollably when he spilled a little milk and his mother asked him to clean it up. She didn't know that he, like she, is upset because his father has just moved in with a new family. So she shouts "Go to your room"—and as Tony runs off, she collapses in a chair and begins to sob. The emotional stress of the past year has taken its toll on the family.

Children of divorce have many stressful transitions to make. They may move to a new neighborhood, be left with new sitters, or have to take on new chores at home. The custodial parent may not be very available to the children because of work or other preoccupations. Adapting to divorce usually takes several years, and some children never fully adjust. According to Judith Wallerstein (1983, 1986), the adjustment process begins when the child acknowledges the separation and begins to grasp its immediate and realistic consequences. How children react to the stress of divorce depends in part on their age. Very young children may feel responsible for the divorce, worry that the custodial parent will also leave, and develop sleep disturbances. Older children and adolescents tend to react with anger, often siding with one parent and blaming the other.

What measures can help children and parents adapt effectively to divorce? The following five principles provide useful advice:

1. *Tell the children in advance.* Regardless of the children's age, they should be told of the impending separation, preferably as a family unit with both parents there (Formanek & Gurian, 1980). In some cases the children will already suspect a split because they have heard many arguments.
2. *Encourage open communication.* Answer the children's questions truthfully, but sensitively. Try not to give answers that stop communication, such as "You're too young to understand."
3. *Gear explanations to the child's level of understanding.* Young children often believe they must have done something "bad" to make the parent go away. They need to know this idea is incorrect. They also need concrete and accurate information about what will happen to all members of the family. Older children, say, 10 or so, can understand that people and feelings change: one boy explained, "It's like if somebody is in a club, and they decide that they didn't belong in that kind of club anymore" (Neal, 1983, p. 11).
4. *Use support systems.* Children and their parents adjust better when the parents get advice and help from social support systems, such as relatives, counselors, parent organizations, and the children's schools (Hetherington, Cox, & Cox, 1982; Kurdek & Berg, 1983).
5. *Encourage children's contact with both parents.* Children often benefit from a good deal of contact with both parents if all members of the family want it (Steinman, 1981).

soothe them do not seem to work very well. They resist being introduced to new foods, routines, and people, and their patterns of sleep, hunger, and bowel movements are hard to predict from day to day. Although only about 10% of babies are classified as "difficult" and display most or all of these traits fairly consistently, many others show some of these traits at least occasionally. A child who reacts in a very negative manner to minor irritations is very stressful to parents (Cutrona & Troutman, 1986). For these parents, there is bad news and good news: Longitudinal studies have shown that children's temperaments are fairly stable across time—for example, a baby who cried intensely with wet diapers at 2 months of age screamed and kicked when having its temperature taken at 1 year. But, although aspects of these traits tend to continue for many years, many difficult children show changes toward the development of easy traits (Carey & McDevitt, 1978; Thomas, Chess, & Birch, 1970).

The arrival of a new baby can also be stressful to other children in the family (Honig, 1987; Rutter, 1983). This stress seems to be particularly strong among children who are very young, say, 2 or 3 years old, and who may not want to share their parents with the new

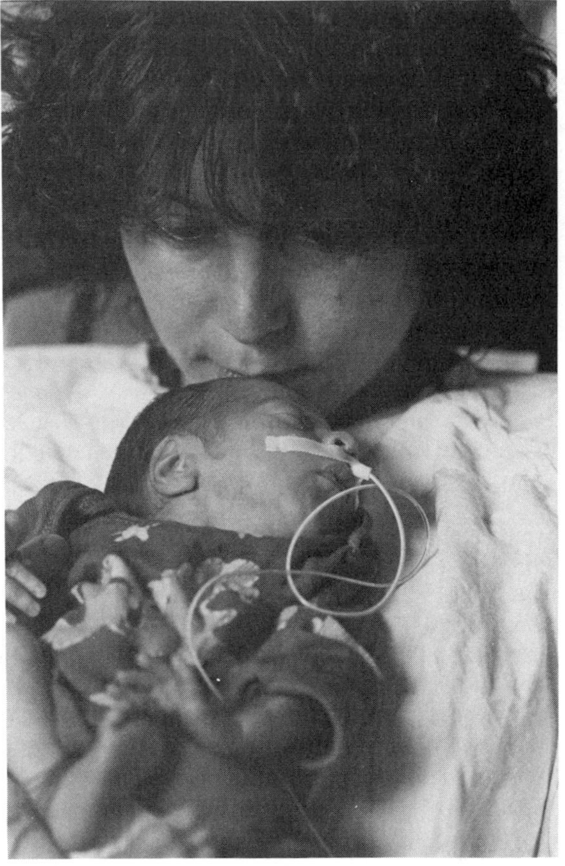

An addition to the family can produce stress, especially if the baby requires special medical attention.

brother or sister. After the baby arrives, these children tend to show increased clinging to the mother, as well as increased sleeping and toileting problems. If the children are older, they are less likely to view the baby as a rival for their parents' attention and their stress seems to relate to changes in the pattern of family interaction, such as when the parents introduce new prohibitions.

Family Illness, Disability, and Death

The following is a very familiar story to many parents: In the middle of a frantic day at work, the parent receives a call from the school nurse, who says, "Your child is sick. You'll have to come and pick him up." Having a sick child adds to the stress in an already stressful day—and chances are the extra stress befalls the mother rather than the father. Even in today's world, if both parents have careers outside the home, the mother usually gets called when their child is sick.

When children have a serious chronic illness, their families must adapt to unique and long-term stresses (Johnson, 1985; Leventhal, Leventhal, & Van Nguyen, 1985). Part of the stress stems from the amount of time needed to care for the child and from the reduced freedom family members have in their schedules. For example, children with the respiratory disease called cystic fibrosis generally need physiotherapy two or three times a day to reduce the mucus that collects in their lungs (Burroughs & Dieterle, 1985). The family also faces many difficult decisions and must learn about the illness and how to care for the child. The medical needs of chronically ill children are expensive, and this burden adds to the family's stress. Relationships between family members may also suffer. The parents are likely to feel that having a chronically ill child reduces the time they have to devote to each other. In addition, other children in the family may feel isolated and deprived of parental attention.

Adult illness or disability is another source of family stress. The strain on their financial resources is especially severe if the sick adult is a principal breadwinner. Having a physically ill or disabled adult in the family restricts the family's time and personal freedom and produces very important changes in interpersonal relationships (Leventhal, Leventhal, & Nguyen, 1985; Michela, 1987; Skelton & Dominian, 1973). For example, when a husband has a heart attack, the wife generally experiences stress from fears that he may have another attack and from his increased irritability and dependency. Although husbands and wives tend to show increased affection for one another during convalescence, their sexual relations are curtailed—often because of fears that sex could induce another attack. And the roles of family members change: The healthy spouse and the children who are old enough take on many of the responsibilities and tasks of the recovering spouse. As the convalescing adult begins to show good physical recovery, the stress generally diminishes in the family.

Does the stress a family experiences when an adult is seriously ill depend on the sick person's age? It can. For instance:

> Cancer in an 80-year-old woman has a quite different meaning than the same disease in a 30-year-old woman with two young children. In the former instance, the illness is likely to be seen as striking at an appropriate or expected time in life, after the individual has lived many years, worked, raised children, enjoyed grandchildren. . . . Cancer in the young mother is asynchronous with her roles and functions: It is a threat to the family unit. . . . Chronic illness that is out of step with family and individual life-course processes is likely to generate powerful frustration and intense distress and anger. (Leventhal, Leventhal, & Van Nguyen, 1985, pp. 132–133)

But if an elderly person who is ill or disabled must live with and be cared for by relatives, the stress for all of those in the household can be severe, especially if the person requires constant care and shows mental deterioration (Robinson & Thurnher, 1986).

Age is also an important factor in the experience of stress when a family member dies. Some children suffer the loss of a parent during the childhood years—one of the most traumatic events a child can face. Children under about 5 years of age seem to grieve for the lost parent less strongly and for a shorter time than older children and adolescents do (Garmezy, 1983; Rutter, 1983). This age difference probably results from their different levels of understanding about the nature of death. Children's concept of death changes between 4 and 8 years of age (Lonetto, 1980; Speece & Brent, 1984). Young children think death is reversible: the person is simply living somewhere else—such as underground—and can come back. By about 8 years of age, most children understand that death is final and involves an absence of bodily functions.

Adults whose child or spouse dies suffer a tremendous loss (Kastenbaum & Costa, 1977; Kosten, Jacobs, & Kasl, 1985). Losing a child creates other losses—for example, bereaved mothers reported that they had lost important hopes and expectations for the future (Edelstein, 1984). Mothers who lose their only child lose their identity and role as a mother, too. When a spouse dies, the surviving spouse also loses important hopes, expectations, and roles—as well as the one companion who made him or her feel loved, wanted, special, and safe. Although the loss of a spouse is difficult at any age, it appears to be especially stressful in early adulthood (Ball, 1976–77).

Sources in the Community and Society

The contacts people make outside the family provide many sources of stress. For instance, children experience stress at school and in competitive events, such as in sports and band performances (Passer, 1982). Many of the stresses adults experience are associated with their occupations, and a variety of environmental situations can be stressful. We will focus on how people's jobs and environments can be sources of stress.

Jobs and Stress

Almost all people at some time in their lives experience stress that relates to their occupations. Often these stressful situations are minor and brief, and have little impact on the person. But for many people, the stress is intense and continues for long periods of time. What factors make jobs stressful?

The *demands of the task* can produce stress in two ways. First, the work load may be too high. Some people work very hard for long hours over long periods of time because they feel required to do so—for example, if they need the money or think their boss would be unhappy if they did not. Studies have found that excessive work loads are associated with increased rates of accidents and health problems (Mackay & Cox, 1978; Quick & Quick, 1984). Second, some kinds of activities are more stressful than others. For example, repetitive jobs that underutilize the worker's abilities can produce stress. As one worker put it:

> I sit by these machines and wait for one to go wrong, then I turn it off, and go and get the supervisor. They don't go wrong very much. Sometimes I think I'd like them to keep going wrong, just to have something to do. . . . It's bloody monotonous. (Mackay & Cox, 1978, p. 159)

Another kind of activity that can produce stress is the evaluation of an employee's job performance—a process that is often difficult for both the supervisor and the employee (Quick & Quick, 1984).

Jobs that involve a *responsibility for people's lives* can be very stressful. Medical personnel have heavy work loads and must deal with life or death situations every day. Making a mistake can have dire consequences. In an intensive care unit of a hospital, emergency situations are common; decisions must be made instantly and carried out immediately and accurately. As part of her job,

> the nurse must reassure and comfort the man who is dying of cancer; she must change the dressings of a decomposing, gangrenous limb; she must calm the awakening disturbed "overdose" patient. . . . It is hard to imagine any other situation that involves such intimacy with the frightening, repulsive, and forbidden. . . . To all this is added the repetitive contact with death. (Hay & Oken, 1985, p. 108)

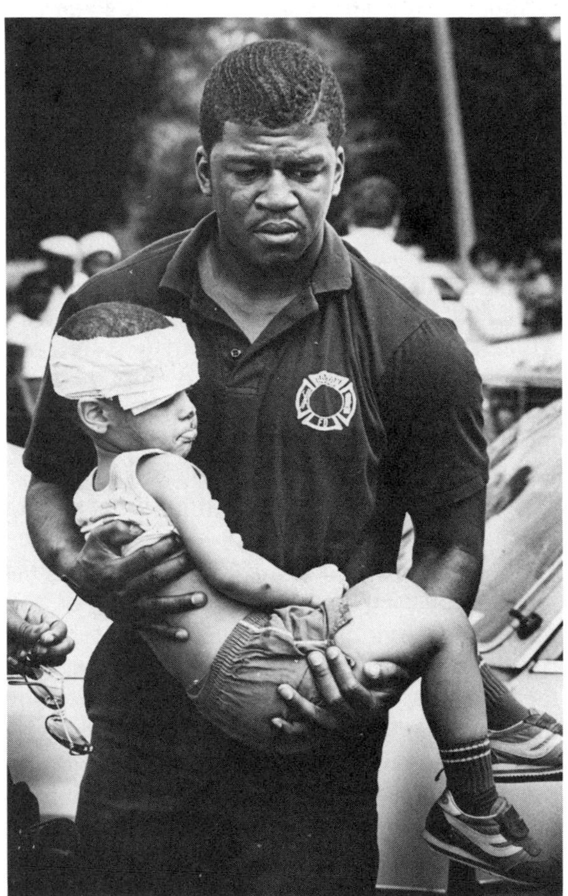

Firefighters have stressful jobs, partly because of their responsibility for people's lives.

These and other conditions of jobs in the health professions take their toll, often leading to feelings of emotional exhaustion and burnout (Maslach & Jackson, 1982). Similar stresses exist in the jobs of police and fire personnel.

Several other aspects of jobs can increase the stress of workers. For example, stress can result from:

1. The *physical environment* of the job. Stress increases when the job involves extreme levels of noise, temperature, humidity, or illumination (Mackay & Cox, 1978; Quick & Quick, 1984).

2. *Perceived insufficient control* over aspects of the job. People experience stress when they have little influence over work procedures or the pace of the work, such as when a machine feeds work to them at a predetermined speed (Cottington & House, 1987).

3. *Poor interpersonal relationships.* People's stress on the job increases when their boss or a coworker is socially abrasive, being insensitive to the needs of others or condescending and overly critical of the work other individuals do (Quick & Quick, 1984).

4. *Perceived inadequate recognition or advancement.* Workers feel stress when they do not get the recognition or promotions they believe they deserve (Cottington, Matthews, Talbott, & Kuller, 1986; Quick & Quick, 1984).

Lastly, people experience stress when they think their job is threatened or when they do not have one. Workers who believe they are likely to be fired or laid off feel a sense of *job insecurity*—and this is stressful, particularly if they have little prospect of finding another job (Cottington, Matthews, Talbott, & Kuller, 1986; Quick & Quick, 1984). The reasons why a person does not have a job can include unemployment—that is, not being able to find one—and retirement. Studies have shown that *unemployment* produces psychological and physiological signs of stress, such as in people's loss of self-esteem and heightened blood pressure (Olafsson & Svensson, 1986).

Many elderly people approach *retirement* with expectations of blissful freedom and leisure. But it does not always turn out that way. Retirees often find that they have lost opportunities for social interaction and an important part of their identity. They may miss the power and influence they once had, the structure and routines of a job, and the feeling of being useful and competent (Bohm & Rodin, 1985; Bradford, 1986). The stress this can produce is reflected in the following excerpt:

> When for the umpteenth time I had complained to my wife about the emptiness in my life, Martha exploded, "I've heard enough of your complaining! You dragged me away from the city and the home I loved best. Do you know why I don't like it here? Do you know why I've gone to the hospital twice this year for checkups, only to find nothing wrong? It was because I was unhappy. Did you consider my life in retirement when you retired?" I hadn't, though I thought we had talked everything over. Maybe I had just talked about *my* retirement. What she said woke me up, and I listened. (Bradford, 1986, p. 212)

Many retirees have the added problem that their income is not sufficient for their needs.

Environmental Stress

Have you ever been at a big noisy event with thousands of people jammed into an arena and felt physiologically aroused, tense, and uncomfortable? Events like these can be stressful partly because noise is a stressor, as we have seen, and also because of the crowded conditions. Why do you feel uncomfortable in crowded conditions? There are three reasons (Karlin, Epstein, & Aiello, 1978). First, you may feel a lack of control over your interpersonal interaction, as when other people can overhear your conversation. Also, you may not like the congestion, that is, your restricted ability to move about freely or your reduced access to resources, such as seats. Third, you may feel that other people are physically closer than you usually prefer people to be—they are intruding into your "personal space" (Sarafino, 1987a). Noise and crowding are two stressors in the environment.

Some environmental conditions are intensely stressful—imagine how you would react to learning that a hazardous substance has seeped into the water supply where you live. How much of it have you and your family already drunk? Has it damaged your bodies already? Will you develop serious illnesses because of it in the future? Can the substance be removed? And after it is, will you believe there is no more danger? Can you sell your house now without suffering a great financial loss? Many people who are exposed to hazardous substances in their environment worry for years about what will happen to them (Baum, 1988).

In the late 1970s, national attention was focused on this type of situation at Love Canal in New York State, where a chemical dump site had contaminated a residential community. In many ways this situation is more stressful than a natural disaster—at least a tornado ends quickly, its damage can be assessed, and much of the damage can be repaired in time. At Love Canal, however, "the nightmare goes on and on" (Holden, 1980). Another example of the psychological effects of living in a hazardous environment comes from the nuclear accident at the Three Mile Island power plant in Pennsylvania. More than a year after the accident, researchers compared the stress of nearby residents to that of people who lived near a different nuclear facility that had not had an accident. This comparison revealed greater psychological and physiological evidence of stress among the residents around Three Mile Island than among those near the other facility (Fleming, Baum, Gisriel, & Gatchel, 1982).

So far in this chapter we have seen that stress involves biopsychosocial reactions, and that all sorts of events or circumstances can be stressors. We saw, for instance, that stressors can include extreme temperatures, noise, taking an exam, being stuck in a traffic jam, having a painful medical test, getting married, and losing a job. The possible stimuli and reactions, and the appraisal processes that link them, make for an interesting question: If you were doing research and needed to know whether different people had experienced different amounts of stress, how could you assess this variable? The next section answers this question.

MEASURING STRESS

Researchers have used several different approaches for measuring stress (Baum, Grunberg, & Singer, 1982). Three of these approaches have been used extensively. They involve assessing people's (1) physiological arousal, (2) life events, and (3) daily hassles.

Physiological Arousal

Stress produces physiological arousal, which is reflected in the functioning of many of our body systems. One way to assess arousal is to use electrical/mechanical equipment to take measurements of blood pressure, heart rate, respiration rate, or galvanic skin response (GSR). Each of these indexes of arousal can be measured separately, or they can all be measured and recorded simultaneously by one apparatus called the **polygraph** (Figure 3.2).

Another way to measure arousal is to assess the secretion of hormones by the adrenal glands by doing a biochemical analysis of blood or urine samples. Using this approach, researchers can test for two classes of hormones: **corticosteroids**, the most important of which is cortisol, and **catecholamines**, which include epinephrine and norepinephrine. The analysis is done by a chemist using special procedures and equipment.

(a)

(b) (c)

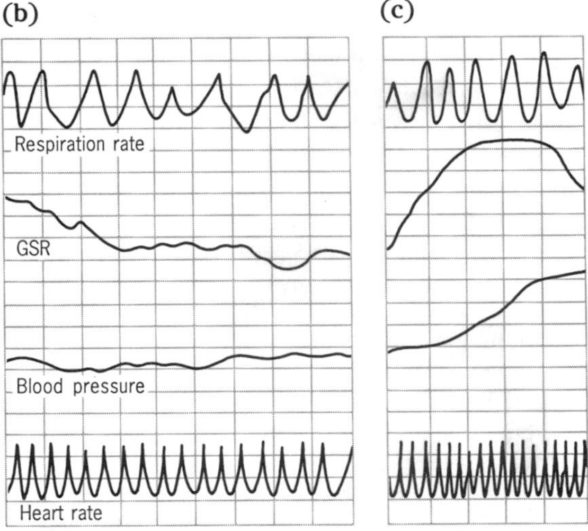

FIGURE 3.2 A typical polygraph (a) makes a graphical record of several indexes of arousal, including blood pressure, heart rate, respiration rate, and the galvanic skin response (the GSR measures skin conductance, which is affected by sweating). A comparison of the two graphs depicts the difference in arousal between someone who is calm (b) and someone who is under stress (c).

There are several advantages to using measures of physiological arousal to assess stress (Baum, Grunberg, & Singer, 1982; Cacioppo, Petty, & Marshall-Goodell, 1985). Physiological

HIGHLIGHT 3C: On Research

Stress and Measures of Physiological Arousal

Marianne Frankenhaeuser and her colleagues have conducted many studies of stress, using measures of physiological arousal. In one of their experiments, they studied male and female engineering students' reactions to stress (Collins & Frankenhaeuser, 1978). Each subject was tested individually in an experimental (stress) and a control session—each of which lasted 100 minutes and occurred in the morning, a few days apart. The researchers had previously asked the subjects not to smoke nor consume any drugs, coffee, or alcohol prior to participating.

At the beginning of each session, the subjects gave a urine sample and then ate a light breakfast provided by the researchers. In the control condition, the subjects relaxed, read magazines and newspapers, and listened to the radio during the remaining hour or so. In the stress condition, the subjects spent about an hour engaged in a difficult and increasingly stressful cognitive/perceptual task. Heart rate was measured for all subjects continuously during each session, and the subjects gave another urine sample at the end. The urine samples were later analyzed for catecholamine (epinephrine and norepinephrine) and corticosteroid (cortisol) concentrations per unit of body weight. The results revealed that heart rate and epinephrine levels increased in both males and females during stress, but other physiological reactions depended on the gender of the subjects.

The outcomes of this and many other studies have led Frankenhaeuser to propose that the pattern of physiological arousal under stress depends on two factors: effort and distress. *Effort* involves the person's interest, striving, and determination, and *distress* involves anxiety, uncertainty, boredom, and dissatisfaction. She has described that:

> *Effort with distress* tends to be accompanied by an increase of both catecholamine *and* cortisol excretion. This is the state typical of daily hassles. . . . In working life, it commonly occurs among people engaged in repetitious, machine-paced jobs on the assembly line or in highly routinized work as, for example, at a computer terminal.
>
> *Effort without distress* is a joyous state, characterized by active and successful coping, high job involvement, and a high degree of personal control. It is accompanied by increased catecholamine secretion, whereas cortisol secretion may be suppressed.
>
> *Distress without effort* implies feeling helpless, losing control, giving up. It is generally accompanied by increased cortisol secretion, but catecholamines may be elevated, too. This is the endocrine profile typical of depressed patients. (1986, p. 107)

Clearly, psychosocial processes play an important role in physiological reactions to stress.

Research on physiological reactions to stress has shown that it is important to measure more than one index of arousal and to examine psychological and social factors, too.

---

measures are reasonably direct and objective, quite reliable, and easily quantified. But there are disadvantages as well. Assessing physiological arousal can be expensive, and the measurement technique may itself be stressful for some people, as may occur when blood is drawn or when electrical devices are attached to the body. The polygraph is a large apparatus that is best suited for use in a laboratory, rather than in everyday life activities. Smaller devices are available for measuring blood pressure (for example, the *sphygmomanometer* your physician uses), and miniaturized instruments are being developed for other indexes. Lastly, measures of physiological arousal are affected by the person's gender, body weight, activity prior to or during measurement, and consumption of various substances, such as caffeine.

Life Events

If you wanted to know whether people were feeling stress, you might simply ask them. Using a self-report method is easy to do. But in doing research, you would probably want to get a more precise answer than, "Yes, I am," or even, "Yes, I'm under a lot of stress." For this reason, a number of different scales have been developed to measure people's stress and assign it a numerical value.

The Social Readjustment Rating Scale

One approach that many scales have used is to develop a list of **life events** — major happenings that can occur in a person's life that require some degree of psychological adjustment. The scale assigns each event a value that reflects its stressfulness. The most widely used scale of life events has been the *Social Readjustment Rating Scale* (SRRS) developed by Thomas Holmes and Richard Rahe (1967). To develop this scale, these researchers constructed a list of events they derived from clinical experience. Then they had hundreds of men and women of various ages and backgrounds rate the amount of adjustment each event would require, using the following instructions:

> *Use all of your experience* in arriving at your answer. This means personal experience where it applies as well as what you have learned to be the case for others. Some persons accommodate to change more readily than others; some persons adjust with particular ease or difficulty to only certain events. Therefore, strive to give your opinion of the average degree of readjustment necessary for each event rather than the extreme. (p. 213)

The researchers used these ratings to assign values to each event and construct the scale shown in Table 3.1.

As you can see, the values for the life events in the SRRS range from 100 points for death of a spouse to 11 points for minor violations of the law. To measure the amount of stress people have experienced, subjects are given a survey form listing these life events and asked to check off the ones that happened to them during a given period of time, usually not more than the past 24 months. The values of the checked items are then summed to give a total stress score.

How commonly do life events like those in the SRRS occur? A study of nearly 2,800 adults used a modified version of the SRRS and found

TABLE 3.1 Social Readjustment Rating Scale

Rank	*Life Event*	*Mean Value*
1	Death of spouse	100
2	Divorce	73
3	Marital separation	65
4	Jail term	63
5	Death of close family member	63
6	Personal injury or illness	53
7	Marriage	50
8	Fired at work	47
9	Marital reconciliation	45
10	Retirement	45
11	Change in health of family member	44
12	Pregnancy	40
13	Sex difficulties	39
14	Gain of new family member	39
15	Business readjustment	39
16	Change in financial state	38
17	Death of close friend	37
18	Change to different line of work	36
19	Change in number of arguments with spouse	35
20	Mortgage over $10,000	31
21	Foreclosure of mortgage or loan	30
22	Change in responsibilities at work	29
23	Son or daughter leaving home	29
24	Trouble with in-laws	29
25	Outstanding personal achievement	28
26	Wife begin or stop work	26
27	Begin or end school	26
28	Change in living conditions	25
29	Revision of personal habits	24
30	Trouble with boss	23
31	Change in work hours or conditions	20
32	Change in residence	20
33	Change in schools	20
34	Change in recreation	19
35	Change in church activities	19
36	Change in social activities	18
37	Mortgage or loan less than $10,000	17
38	Change in sleeping habits	16
39	Change in number of family get-togethers	15
40	Change in eating habits	15
41	Vacation	13
42	Christmas	12
43	Minor violations of the law	11

Source: From Holmes & Rahe (1967).

that 15% of the subjects reported having experienced none of the events during the prior year, and 18% reported five or more (Goldberg & Comstock, 1980). The three most frequent events reported were "took a vacation" (43%), "death of a loved one or other important person" (22%), and "illness or injury" (21%). The number of life events the subjects reported *decreased* with age from early adulthood to old age and *increased* with the number of years of schooling. Single, separated, and divorced people reported a larger number of events than married and widowed individuals did.

Strengths and Weaknesses of the SRRS

When you examined the list of life events included in the SRRS, you probably noticed that many of the events were ones we have already discussed as stressors, such as the death of a spouse, divorce, pregnancy, and occupational problems. One of the strengths of the SRRS is that the items it includes represent a fairly wide range of events that most people do, in fact, find stressful. Also, the values assigned to the events were carefully determined from the ratings of a broad sample of adults. These values provide an estimate of the relative impact of the events, distinguishing fairly well between such stressors as "death of a close family member" and "death of a close friend." Another strength of the SRRS is that the survey form can be filled out easily and quickly.

One of the main uses of the SRRS has been to relate stress and illness. Many studies have addressed this issue by using retrospective approaches—for example, by asking subjects to recall events and illnesses they experienced over the past year. Other studies have combined retrospective and prospective methods—for instance, by having subjects report recent life events and then checking their medical records over the next months. Studies using these approaches have generally found that people's illness and accident rates tend to increase following increases in stress (Holmes & Masuda, 1974; Johnson, 1986; Rahe, 1974, 1987; Rahe & Arthur, 1978). But the correlation between subjects' scores on the SRRS and illness is only about .30—which means that the relationship is not very strong (Dohrenwend & Dohrenwend, 1981). One reason that the relationship is not stronger is that people get sick and have accidents for many reasons other than stress. But another factor is that the SRRS has several weaknesses.

Some researchers have criticized items in the SRRS as being vague or ambiguous (Hough, Fairbank, & Garcia, 1976). For example, "change in responsibilities at work" fails to indicate how much change and whether it involves more or less responsibility. As a result, someone whose responsibility has decreased a little gets the same score as someone whose responsibility has increased sharply. Similarly, "personal injury or illness" does not indicate the seriousness of the illness—someone who had the flu gets the same score as someone who became paralyzed. Vague or ambiguous items reduce the precision of an instrument and the correlation it is likely to have with other variables (Anastasi, 1982).

Another criticism is that the scale does not consider the meaning or impact of an event for the individual (Cohen, Kamarck, & Mermelstein, 1983; Lazarus & Folkman, 1984b). For example, two people who each had a mortgage for $20,000 would get the same score for "mortgage over $10,000" even though one of them made ten times the income of the other. Similarly, the score people get for "death of spouse" is the same regardless of their age, dependence on the spouse, and the length and happiness of the marriage. These items do not take the person's subjective appraisal into account, and this may also reduce the precision of the instrument.

One other problem with the SRRS is that it does not distinguish between desirable and undesirable events. Most people view some events, such as "marriage" or "outstanding personal achievement," as desirable; but "sex difficulties" and "jail term" are undesirable. Other items could be either desirable or undesirable, for example, "change in financial state"; the score people get is the same regardless of whether their finances improved or worsened. This is important because studies have found that undesirable life events are correlated with illness, but desirable events are not (McFarlane, Norman, Streiner, & Roy, 1983; Sarason, Sarason, Potter, & Antoni, 1985).

Given the weaknesses of the SRRS, the correlations between its scores and illness may be considered all the more impressive. Because the overall approach it uses to measure stress is clearly useful, researchers have constructed other life event scales in an effort to develop more precise instruments.

Other Life Events Scales

Among the several life event scales that have attempted to improve on the method of the SRRS are the following:

1. *The Life Experiences Survey* (LES) contains 57 items that are stated relatively precisely, for example, "major change in financial status (a lot better off or a lot worse off)." Subjects rate each event on a 7-point scale, ranging from extremely negative (−3) to extremely positive (+3). The items perceived as positive or as negative can be examined separately or combined for a total change score (Sarason, Johnson, & Siegel, 1978).

2. *The PERI Life Events Scale* contains 102 items that describe events involving either a gain, a loss, or an ambiguous outcome. The items are stated clearly and organized into 11 topic areas, including work, finances, family, and health. For example, an item dealing with work is, "took on a greatly increased work load." Like the SRRS, each item has an assigned value, and the subject simply indicates which events occurred within a given time period (Dohrenwend, Krasnoff, Askenasy, & Dohrenwend, 1978).

3. *The Unpleasant Events Schedule* (UES) contains 320 items and takes an hour to complete (although a shorter, 53-item form is also available). The items are divided into a number of categories, such as sexual / marital / friendship and achievement / academic / job, and stated relatively precisely, for example, "being fired or laid off from work." The subjects rate each item on a 3-point scale twice, first for frequency and then for aversiveness. These two ratings are multiplied, and a total score is summed for the entire schedule (Lewinsohn, Mermelstein, Alexander, & MacPhillamy, 1985.

New scales such as these are being used extensively in research today. Through this research, we should be able to determine which scales are most useful as measures of stress.

The instruments we have discussed so far have been designed to measure stress mainly in adults. Other scales have been developed to measure stress in children and adolescents. The most widely used scale for children is the Life Events Record, which is very similar to the SRRS in its items, format, and scoring (Coddington, 1972a, 1972b). As Table 3.2 shows, separate values have been assigned for children of different age groups: preschool, elementary school, junior high, and senior high. When children are not old enough to respond to the items themselves, their parents complete the scale for them. Because the Life Events Record has many of the same problems as the SRRS, other instruments for children have been developed (Johnson, 1986).

Daily Hassles

Not all of the stress we experience comes from major life events—lesser events can also be stressful, as when we give a speech, misplace our keys during a busy day, or have our quiet disrupted by a loud party next door. These are called **daily hassles**. Some people experience more daily hassles than others do.

Richard Lazarus and his associates have constructed a scale to measure people's experiences with day-to-day unpleasant or potentially harmful events (Kanner, Coyne, Schaefer, & Lazarus, 1981). This instrument—called the *Hassles Scale*—lists 117 of these events that range from minor annoyances, such as "silly practical mistakes," to major problems or difficulties, such as "not enough money for food." The subjects indicate which hassles occurred in the past month and rate each event as having been "somewhat," "moderately," or "extremely" severe. These researchers tested 100 middle-aged adults monthly over a nine-month

TABLE 3.2 Stress Values by Age Group for Items of the Life Events Record (Coddington, 1972a, 1972b)

Life Events	*Preschool*	*Elementary*	*Junior High*	*Senior High*
Beginning nursery school, first grade, seventh grade, or high school	42	46	45	42
Change to a different school	33	46	52	56
Birth or adoption of a brother or sister	50	50	50	50
Brother or sister leaving home	39	36	33	37
Hospitalization of brother or sister	37	41	44	41
Death of brother or sister	59	68	71	68
Change of father's occupation requiring increased absence from home	36	45	42	38
Loss of job by a parent	23	38	48	46
Marital separation of parents	74	78	77	69
Divorce of parents	78	84	84	77
Hospitalization of parent (serious illness)	51	55	54	55
Death of a parent	89	91	94	87
Death of a grandparent	30	38	35	36
Marriage of parent to stepparent	62	65	63	63
Jail sentence of parent for 30 days or less	34	44	50	53
Jail sentence of parent for 1 year or more	67	67	76	75
Addition of third adult to family (e.g., grandparent)	39	41	34	34
Change in parents' financial status	21	29	40	45
Mother beginning to work	47	44	36	26
Decrease in number of arguments between parents	21	25	29	27
Increase in number of arguments between parents	44	51	48	46
Decrease in number of arguments with parents	22	27	29	26
Increase in number of arguments with parents	39	47	46	47
Discovery of being an adopted child	33	52	70	64
Acquiring a visible deformity	52	69	83	81
Having a visible congenital deformity	39	60	70	62
Hospitalization of yourself (child)	59	62	59	58
Change in acceptance by peers	38	51	68	67
Outstanding personal achievement	23	39	45	46
Death of a close friend (child's friend)	38	53	65	63
Failure of a year in school		57	62	56
Suspension from school		46	54	50
Pregnancy in unwed teen-age sister		36	60	64
Becoming involved with drugs or alcohol		61	70	76
Becoming a full-fledged member of a church/synagogue		25	28	31
Not making an extracurricular activity you wanted to be involved in (i.e., athletic team, band)			49	55
Breaking up with a boyfriend or girlfriend			47	53
Beginning to date			55	51
Fathering an unwed pregnancy			76	77
Unwed pregnancy			95	92
Being accepted to a college of your choice				43
Getting married				101

Source: Heisel et al. (1973, Table I).

period. The half-dozen most frequent hassles reported were:

- Concerns about weight
- Health of a family member
- Rising prices of common goods
- Home maintenance
- Too many things to do
- Misplacing or losing things

In the course of developing the Hassles Scale, these researchers proposed that having desirable experiences makes hassles more bearable and reduces their impact on health. So they developed another instrument, the *Uplifts Scale*, which lists 135 events that bring peace, satisfaction, or joy. This instrument was administered along with the Hassles Scale to the same adults, who indicated which uplifts they experienced in the past month and whether each event had been "somewhat," "moderately," or "extremely" strong. The half-dozen most frequently occurring uplifts were:

- Relating well to your spouse or lover
- Relating well with friends
- Completing a task
- Feeling healthy
- Getting enough sleep
- Eating out

Are hassles and uplifts related to health? Several studies have examined this issue. One study tested middle-aged adults, using four instruments: (1) the Hassles Scale; (2) the Uplifts Scale; (3) a life events scale that includes no desirable items; and (4) the Health Status Questionnaire, which contains questions regarding a wide variety of bodily symptoms and overall health (DeLongis et al., 1982). Both hassles scores and life events scores were associated with health status — both correlations were weak, but hassles were more strongly associated with health than life events were. Uplifts scores had virtually no association with health status. Other studies generally support these findings regarding the relationship of hassles and uplifts to health (Gortmaker, Eckenrode, & Gore, 1982; Holahan, Holahan, & Belk, 1984; Weinberger, Hiner, & Tierney, 1987; Zarski, 1984).

To summarize the research on measures of stress, the instruments that have been developed either have shortcomings or have not been sufficiently tested to know how accurate they are. Stress is a difficult concept to define, and it is even more difficult to measure. Judging from the evidence that exists, however, stress seems to have a consistent but moderate relationship to health. Stress is one of many factors that contribute to the development of illness.

CAN STRESS BE GOOD FOR YOU?

Another reason why measures of stress do not correlate very highly with illness may be that not all stress is unhealthy. Is it possible that some types or amounts of stress are neutral or, perhaps, *good* for you? There is reason to believe that this is the case (Seliger, 1986).

How much stress may be good for people? Some theories of motivation and arousal propose that people function best, and feel best, at what is, *for them*, an "optimal" level of arousal (Fiske & Maddi, 1961; Hebb, 1955). People

"I JUST READ THAT A CERTAIN AMOUNT OF STRESS IS GOOD FOR YOU."
Reprinted with special permission of King Features Syndicate, Inc.

differ in the amount of arousal that is optimal, but too much or too little arousal impairs their functioning. Figure 3.3 gives an illustration of how stress, as a form of arousal, relates to the quality of functioning. Let's consider an example of how different levels of stress affect functioning. Imagine that you are in class one day and your instructor passes around a surprise test. If the test would not be collected or count toward your final grade, you might be underaroused and answer the questions carelessly or not at all. But if it would count as 10% of your grade, you might be under enough stress to perform well. And if it would count a lot, you might be overwhelmed by the stress and do poorly.

Are some types of stress better than others for people? Three prominent researchers on stress have taken very similar positions on this question, claiming that there are at least two kinds of stress that differ in their impact. Selye (1974, 1985), for instance, claimed one kind of stress is harmful and damaging, and is called *distress*; another kind is beneficial or constructive, and is called *eustress* (from the Greek *eu*, which means "good"). Similarly, as we saw earlier, Frankenhaeuser (1986) has described two components of stress, *distress* and *effort*. Distress with or without effort is probably more damaging than effort without distress. Lastly, Lazarus has described three types of stress appraisals—*harm-loss, threat*, and *challenge*—and noted:

> Challenged persons are more likely to have better morale, because to be challenged means feeling positive about demanding encounters, as reflected in the pleasurable emotions accompanying challenge. The quality of functioning is apt to be better in challenge because the person feels more confident, less emotionally overwhelmed, and more capable of drawing on available resources than the person who is inhibited or blocked. Finally, it is possible that the physiological stress response to challenge is different from that of threat, so that diseases of adaptation are less likely to occur. (Lazarus & Folkman, 1984, p. 34)

There is a commonality to these three positions: To state it in its simplest form, there is good stress and bad stress—bad stress generally involves a strong negative emotional component. Cognitive appraisal processes play an important role in determining which kind of stress we experience.

Finally, in discussing whether stress is harmful, one other point should be made: individuals seem to differ in their susceptibility to the effects of stress. John Mason (1975) has proposed that these differences are like those that people show to the effects of viruses and bacteria. That is, not all people who are exposed to a disease-causing antigen, such as a flu virus, develop the illness—some individuals are more susceptible than others. Susceptibility to the effects of antigens and to stress varies from one person to the next and within the same individual across time. These differences result from biological variations within and between individuals, and from psychosocial variations, as we will see in the next chapter.

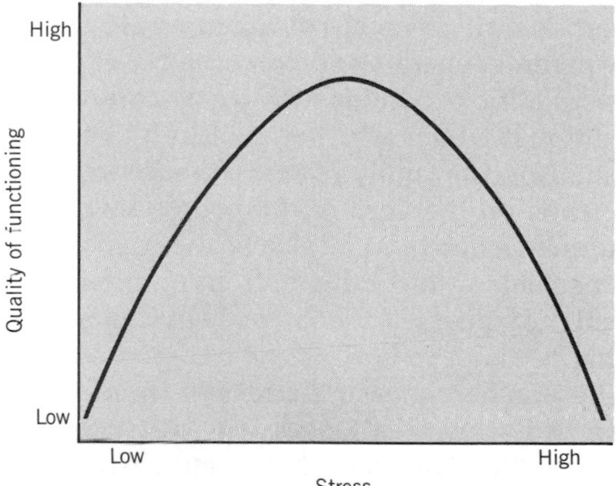

FIGURE 3.3 Quality of functioning at varying levels of stress. Functioning is poor at very low and very high levels of stress, but is best at some moderate, "optimal" level. (Based on material in Hebb, 1955.)

SUMMARY

Researchers have conceptualized stress in three ways. In one approach, stress is seen as a stimulus, and studies focus on the impact of stressors. Another approach treats stress as a response and examines the strains that stressors produce. The third approach views stress as a process that involves continuous interactions and adjustments — or transactions — between the person and the environment. These viewpoints have led to the definition of stress as the condition that results when person/environment transactions lead the individual to perceive a discrepancy between the demands of a situation and the resources of the person's biological, psychological, and social systems.

Transactions that lead to the condition of stress generally involve a process of cognitive appraisal, which takes two forms. One type of appraisal, called primary appraisal, focuses on whether a demand threatens the person's well-being and produces one of three judgments: the demand is irrelevant, it is good, or it is stressful. A stressful appraisal receives further assessment for the amount of harm or loss, the threat of future harm, and the degree of challenge the demand presents. The other type of appraisal, called secondary appraisal, assesses the resources available for meeting the demand. When primary and secondary appraisals indicate that the fit between demands and resources is close, we may experience little stress. But when we appraise a discrepancy — especially if the demands seem greater than our resources — we may feel a substantial amount of stress.

Whether events are appraised as stressful is influenced by two types of factors — those that relate to the person and those that relate to the situation. Factors of the person include intellectual, motivational, and personality characteristics, such as the person's self-esteem and belief system. With regard to situational factors, events tend to be appraised as stressful if they involve strong demands, are imminent, are undesirable and uncontrollable, involve major life transitions, or occur at an unexpected time in the life span.

Stressors produce strain in the person's biological, psychological, and social systems. Emergency situations evoke a physiological fight-or-flight reaction, by which the organism prepares to attack the threat or flee. When stress is strong and prolonged, the physiological reaction goes through three stages: the alarm reaction, the stage of resistance, and the stage of exhaustion. This series of reactions is called the general adaptation syndrome. According to Selye, continuous high levels of stress can make the person vulnerable to health problems called diseases of adaptation, including ulcers and high blood pressure. Psychosocial factors influence the physiological reaction to stress.

Stress can affect psychosocial processes. It can impair cognitive functioning and may lead to generalized cognitive deficits in children. Various emotions can accompany stress — these emotions include fear, anxiety, depression, and anger. When stress is accompanied by anger, aggressive behavior tends to increase and remains at a relatively high level even after the stressful experience is over. Stress also reduces people's helping behavior.

Although the sources of stress may change as people develop, the condition of stress can occur at any time in the life span. Sometimes stress arises from within the person, such as when the person is ill or experiences conflict. The family can be another source of stress, through the behavior, needs, and personality of each of its members. The whole family can experience stress (1) when one of its members is seriously ill, becomes disabled, or dies; (2) if the parents separate or divorce; and (3) if there is an addition to the family, particularly if the addition is a baby who has a difficult temperament. How the family reacts to these stressors depends on the ages of the people involved. The source of stress can also be the community and society — for example, from problems related to people's jobs or environmental hazards.

Researchers measure stress in three ways. One way involves assessing physiological arousal. Blood pressure, heart rate, respiration rate, and galvanic skin response can be measured with an apparatus called the polygraph. Biochemical analyses of blood or urine samples can test for corticosteriods (for example, cortisol) and catecholamines (for example, epinephrine and norepinephrine). Another method of measuring stress is to use an instrument to assess people's life events. The most widely used scale of life events has been the Social Readjustment Rating Scale, but newer instruments have been developed to correct some of its weaknesses. The third method for measuring stress involves assessing the daily hassles people experience. Although stress can contribute to the development of illness, many psychologists believe that not all stress is harmful.

KEY TERMS

stressors
strain
transactions
stress
cognitive appraisal
primary appraisal
secondary appraisal
general adaptation syndrome
alarm reaction
stage of resistance
stage of exhaustion
temperaments
polygraph
corticosteroids
catecholamines
life events
daily hassles

4

STRESS, BIOPSYCHOSOCIAL FACTORS, AND ILLNESS

PROLOGUE

They were best friends, Joan and Sally, on their way to an art museum a year ago when a car accident ended their lives. Their husbands, Bob and Walt, were devastated, not only by their individual loss but for each other's. These men were also friends — both worked as engineers for the same company and shared hobbies and other interests. The four of them used to double-date often, leaving the kids with one babysitter. How did the terrible loss of their wives affect these men?

The initial impact of their loss was similar, but the stresses that followed were different. Bob's stresses were not as severe as Walt's. One thing that helped Bob was that he had an extended family that lived nearby. They provided consolation for his grief, a place to go to get out of the house and to socialize, and help in caring for his children. After school, the kids would go to either Bob's or Joan's parents' house, and Bob would pick them up on his way home from work. Sometimes he and the children would stay there for dinner. This helped save him time and money — both of which were in short supply. How was Bob doing a year later? He had made a good adjustment, had a good relationship with his children, was starting to date, and was in good health.

Walt was not so fortunate. For one thing, he had no family to rely on. Compared to Bob, Walt had little emotional support in his grief, and being a single parent made his work load and financial situation very difficult. Walt had little time or money for socializing, and virtually all of his adult contacts were at work. Although he and Bob often had lunch together, their interests were drifting apart. Unlike Bob, Walt had never been very outgoing, and he felt awkward and insecure in meeting women. A year after Sally died, he was isolated and lonely. His relationship with his children was deteriorating, and so was his health. He had developed migraine headaches, neck problems, and high blood pressure. The stress in Walt's life was taking its toll.

This chapter examines the effects of stress on health. We begin by looking at psychosocial factors that can modify the stress people experience. Then we consider how stress affects health and the development of specific illnesses. And in this chapter we address many questions about stress and illness that are of great concern today. Why can some people experience one traumatic event after another without ill effects, but others cannot? Are hard-driving people more likely to have a heart attack than people who are easygoing? Can people actually "die of a broken heart"? Can stress retard people's recovery from illness?

PSYCHOSOCIAL MODIFIERS OF STRESS

People's reaction to stress varies from one person to the next and from time to time for the same person. These variations often result from psychological and social factors that seem to modify the impact of stressors on the individual. Let's look at some of these modifiers, beginning with the role of social support.

Social Support

We saw in the bereavement experiences of Bob and Walt how important social ties and relationships can be during troubled times. The social support Bob got from his family tempered the impact of his stressful loss and probably helped him adjust. **Social support** refers to the perceived comfort, caring, esteem, or help a person receives from other people or groups (Cobb, 1976; Gentry & Kobasa, 1984; Wallston, Alagna, DeVellis, & DeVellis, 1983; Wills, 1984). This support can come from many different sources — the person's spouse or lover, family, friends, coworkers, physician, or community organizations. According to Sidney Cobb (1976), people with social support believe they are loved and cared for, esteemed and valued, and part of a social network, such as a family or community organization, that can provide goods, services, and mutual defense in times of need or danger.

Types and Determinants of Social Support

What specifically does social support provide to the person? To answer this question, researchers have tried to classify various types of support (Cobb, 1976; Cohen & McKay, 1984; House, 1984; Schaefer, Coyne, & Lazarus, 1981; Wills, 1984). These classifications suggest that there are four basic types of social support:

1. *Emotional support* involves the expression of empathy, caring, and concern toward the person. It provides the person with a sense of comfort, reassurance, belongingness, and of being loved in times of stress. We saw earlier how Bob's family gave him emotional support after the death of his wife.

2. *Esteem support* occurs through people's expression of positive regard for the person, encouragement or agreement with the individual's ideas or feelings, and positive comparison of the person with others, such as people who are less able or worse off. This kind of support serves to build the individual's feeling of self-worth, competence, and of being valued. Esteem support is especially useful during the appraisal of stress, such as when the person assesses whether the demands exceed his or her personal resources.

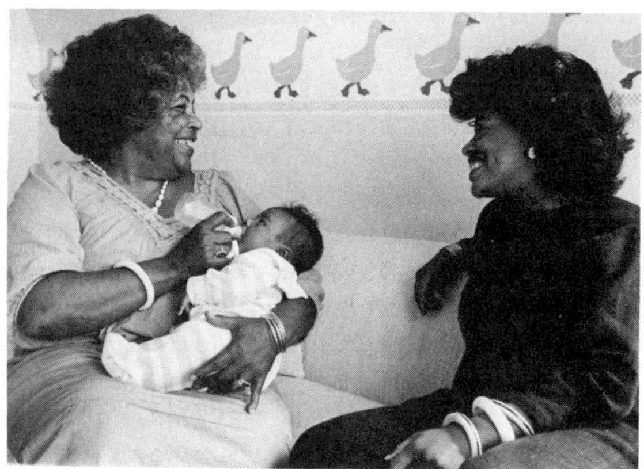

A grandmother feeding her daughter's baby. The family is an important source of social support.

3. *Tangible or instrumental support* involves direct assistance, as when people give or lend the person money or help out with chores in times of stress. Bob's family helped with child care, for example, which reduced the demands on his time and finances.

4. *Informational support* includes giving advice, directions, suggestions, or feedback about how the person is doing. For example, a person who is ill might get information from family or a physician on how to treat the illness. Or someone who is faced with a very difficult decision on the job might receive suggestions or feedback about his or her ideas from coworkers.

The type of support a person receives and needs depends on the stressful circumstances. For instance, emotional and informational support may be particularly important for people who are seriously ill (Wortman & Dunkel-Schetter, 1987).

What type of support do people generally get? Carolyn Cutrona (1986) studied college students' perceptions of different types of social support in their lives. First the students filled out a questionnaire, rating the degree to which their current relationships provided them with different types of support. For example, they rated the statement "I have close relationships that provide me with a sense of emotional security and well-being." Then the students kept a daily record for two weeks, keeping track of two kinds of experiences: (1) stressful events that "left them feeling upset for 2 hours or more" and (2) social interactions "that lasted 10 minutes or more." The daily records revealed a wide range in the number of stressful events they experienced, with the average being one event every two days. Although most of the events in the two weeks were relatively minor, such as having car trouble or an argument with a roommate, one-fifth of the subjects reported a severe event, such as a parent's diagnosis of cancer or the ending of a long-term romantic relationship. As you might expect, the subjects received more social support following stressful events than at less stressful times, and those who initially perceived themselves as having high levels of social support reported receiving more support during the two weeks. Tangible support occurred very infrequently, but emotional, informational, and esteem support occurred often. Although the subjects received emotional and informational support mainly in times of stress, receiving esteem support did not depend on stress. Students who received more frequent esteem support tended to report less depression following stressful experiences, suggesting that esteem may protect people from negative emotional consequences of stress.

Not everyone gets the social support they need. Many factors determine whether people receive support (Broadhead et al., 1983; Wortman & Dunkel-Schetter, 1987). Some factors relate to the potential *recipients* of support. For one thing, people are unlikely to receive support if they don't let others know that they need it. Some people are not assertive enough to ask for help, or feel that they should be independent or not burden others, or feel uncomfortable confiding in others, or don't know whom to ask. Also, sometimes the potential recipient has characteristics that are unappealing or don't invite help, as when a child has a difficult temperament or asks for help in an annoying manner, such as by whining constantly. Other factors relate to the potential *providers* of support. For instance, they may not have the resources needed, or may be under stress and in need of help themselves, or may simply be insensitive to the needs of others.

Whether people receive social support also depends on the composition and structure of their **social network**—that is, the linkages they have with people in their family and community (Mitchell, 1969; Schaefer, Coyne, & Lazarus, 1981). These linkages can vary in *quantity* and *quality*. For instance, social networks differ in *size*—the number of people with whom you have regular contact; *frequency of contact*—how often you see these people; *composition*—whether these people are family, friends, coworkers, and so on; and *intimacy*—the closeness of individual relationships and mutual willingness to confide in each other. People who have a social network with a reasonably high quantity and quality of linkages are likely to have many opportunities to receive social support.

People's need for, sources of, and ability to provide social support change throughout the life span (Antonucci, 1985; Broadhead et al., 1983; Bruhn & Phillips, 1987; Sarafino & Armstrong, 1986). For example, most young children readily ask for and receive help from older people, but their immature cognitive and social skills hamper their ability to recognize other people's needs easily and provide effective help themselves. As children's social contacts expand outside the family, their peers become an increasingly important source of both stress and social support, particularly during the adolescent years. By the end of adolescence, they have strong cognitive and social skills and can provide very effective support, but many teenagers are reluctant to ask for help or confide in others. Adulthood is a time for taking on increasing levels of responsibility in a family, on the job, and in the community. These changes create new stresses, but they also bring new sources for and opportunities to provide social support. The intimacy and caring that usually characterize adult loving relationships, such as in marriage, give adults a continuous source of support. Old age is a time when social support sometimes declines. Although the size of people's social networks does not get smaller in old age, the elderly exchange less support, perhaps because of the loss of a spouse or because they may feel reluctant to ask for help if they become unable to reciprocate.

How can we assess people's social support, given the different types of support and the complex relationships that are involved? Researchers have begun to develop questionnaires to measure social support. Although there are many instruments available, none currently provides a strong measure of all aspects of social support (Heitzmann & Kaplan, 1988; Wortman & Dunkel-Schetter, 1987). One of the more highly regarded instruments is the *Social Support Questionnaire* developed by Irwin Sarason and his colleagues (1983). It consists of 27 items, such as "Who helps you feel that you truly have something positive to contribute to others?" For each item, the respondents list the people they can rely on and then indicate their overall degree of satisfaction with the support available. Using this instrument, these researchers have found that some people report high levels of satisfaction with support from a small number of close friends and relatives, but others seem to need a large social network.

Social Support, Stress, and Health

We have seen that people often receive social support in times of stress. What benefits do people get from this support? To answer this question, we will look at how social support is related to stress and health.

Research findings suggest that social support reduces the stress people experience. A study by James LaRocco, James House, and John French (1980) examined data from questionnaires assessing the job stress and social support of over 2,000 men in a variety of white- and blue-collar occupations. The impact of job stress, such as from high work load and job insecurity, was inferred from measures of psychological strain, as shown by feelings of anxiety, depression, and irritation. The measure of social support included items regarding emotional and tangible or instrumental support, and assessed the support available from three sources: the employee's supervisor; coworkers; and wife, family, and friends. Correlational analyses revealed that the greater the social support available to the employees, the lower the psychological strain they reported. Although social support from home was helpful, reduced job stress of the employees was more strongly related to the support they received from their supervisors and coworkers.

Similar associations between social support and reduced job stress have been found in several other studies (Constable & Russell, 1986; Cottington & House, 1987). Furthermore, social support appears to reduce stress from a variety of other sources, too. For example, research has examined the influence of social support on two other stressors: (1) being a new mother and (2) developing a loss of hearing in adulthood (Turner, 1981). In both circumstances, people with high levels of social support felt less psychological strain than those with low levels of social support. Another study examined the influence of social support on the stress experienced by people living near the damaged nuclear power plant at Three Mile Island (Fleming, Baum, Gisriel, & Gatchel, 1982). Those residents with high levels of emotional support showed less psychological strain and cognitive impairment than those with low levels of support.

Having social support also seems to benefit people's health. This has been shown in the death rates for people who have different amounts of social support. A study by James Lynch (1977), for instance, found that widowed, divorced, and never married individuals have far higher death rates from heart disease than married people do. He argued that being lonely or having a "broken heart" is a risk factor for heart disease. Lisa Berkman and S. Leonard Syme (1979) conducted a prospective study of more than 4,700 men and women between 30 and 69 years of age in California. The subjects were asked about four aspects of social support: marital status, contacts with family and friends, church membership, and formal and informal group associations. Over the next nine years, mortality data on these people were collected. The results showed that the greater the degree of social support the subjects had, the lower the likelihood of their dying during the period of the study. Figure 4.1 shows an example of these findings. In each age category, subjects with few contacts with friends and relatives had higher mortality rates than those with many contacts. In addition, social support was not only associated with deaths from all causes, but also with mortality from several specific diseases, including cancer and heart disease.

The relationship between social support and mortality in these studies is correlational. How do we know whether social support produces better health and lower mortality or whether the causal relationship is the other way around? That is, could the people who had less

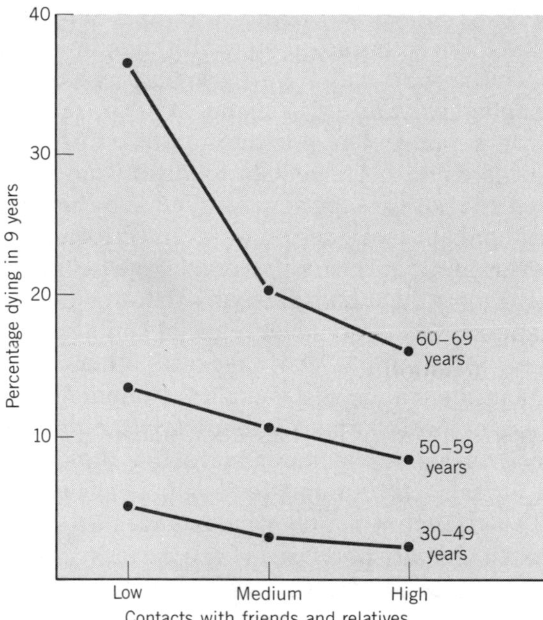

FIGURE 4.1 Percentage of adults who died within nine years as a function of the number of contacts with friends and relatives and the subjects' ages at the start of the study, in 1965. (Data from Berkman & Syme, 1979, Table 2.)

social support be less active socially because they were already sick at the start of the study? Berkman and Syme provided some evidence that this was not the case. For instance, the subjects had been asked about past illnesses at the initial interview, and those with high levels of social support did not differ from those with low levels of support. But better evidence comes from a similar study of more than 2,700 adults in Michigan (House, Robbins, & Metzner, 1982). The subjects in this study were medically examined at the start of the research. These researchers found essentially the same relationship between social support and mortality as Berkman and Syme did, and the initial health of the subjects with low social support was the same as that of those with high support.

Researchers have also studied the association between social support and the likelihood that people will develop illnesses and recover quickly when they do. Some early studies found an association between support and illness or recovery, but others did not (Wallston, Alagna, DeVellis, & DeVellis, 1983). These results were mixed probably because of weaknesses and variations in research methodology, such as in the way support was defined and measured (Friis & Taff, 1986; Wortman & Dunkel-Schetter, 1987). The results of newer research seem to be more consistent in showing that social support can reduce the likelihood of illness and speed recovery. Although social support appears to influence health, it is only one of many psychosocial factors that are involved (Kobasa, Maddi, Puccetti, & Zola, 1985). Social support probably has a strong impact on the health of some individuals, and a weak influence on the health of others.

How Does Social Support Affect Health?

To explain how social support influences health and well-being, researchers have proposed two theories: the "buffering" and the "direct effects" hypotheses. Studies have found evidence consistent with both theories (Cohen & Wills, 1985; Payne & Jones, 1987; Thoits, 1982; Wortman & Dunkel-Schetter, 1987). We will begin with the buffering hypothesis.

We saw in Chapter 3 that prolonged exposure to high levels of stress can lead to illness. According to the **buffering hypothesis**, social support affects health by *protecting* the person against these negative effects of high stress. A graphical illustration of the buffering hypothesis appears in Figure 4.2a. As the graph shows, this protective function is effective only or mainly when the person encounters a strong stressor. Under low-stress conditions, little or no buffering occurs.

How does buffering work? There are at least two ways (Cohen & Wills, 1985). One way involves the process of cognitive appraisal. When people encounter a strong stressor, such as a major financial crisis, those individuals with high levels of social support may be less likely to appraise the situation as stressful than those with low levels of support. Individuals with high social support may expect that someone they know can and will help, such as by lending the needed money or giving advice on how to get it. As a result, they judge that they can meet the demands and decide that the situation is not very stressful. The second way social support can buffer the effects of stress is by modifying people's response to a stressor after they have appraised the situation as stressful. For instance, people with high social support might have someone provide a solution to the problem, convince them that the problem is not very important, or cheer them on to "look on the bright side" or "count their blessings." People with little social support are much less likely to have any of these advantages—so the negative impact of the stress is greater for them than for those with high levels of support.

The **direct effects hypothesis** maintains that social support is beneficial to health and well-being regardless of the amount of stress people experience. According to this hypothesis, the beneficial effects of social support are similar under high and low stressor intensities, as depicted in Figure 4.2b. There are several ways by which direct effects may work (Cohen & Wills, 1985; Wortman & Dunkel-Schetter, 1987). For example, people with high levels of social support may have a greater sense of belongingness and self-esteem than those with little support. The positive outlook this produces could be beneficial to health independently of stress experiences, such as by making individuals more resistant to infection. High levels of support may also encourage people to lead more healthful lifestyles than low social support does. People with social support may feel, for example, that because others care about them and need them, they should exercise, eat well, and seek medical attention before a problem becomes serious.

Does social support always benefit health? No—there are many circumstances in which social ties with people can harm an individual's health (Suls, 1982). One circumstance is when people set a bad example for the person. We see this when smoking and drinking behavior by friends and family lead an adolescent to engage in these behaviors. Friends and family can also set bad examples by *not* engaging in healthful behaviors, such as using seat belts, eating a bal-

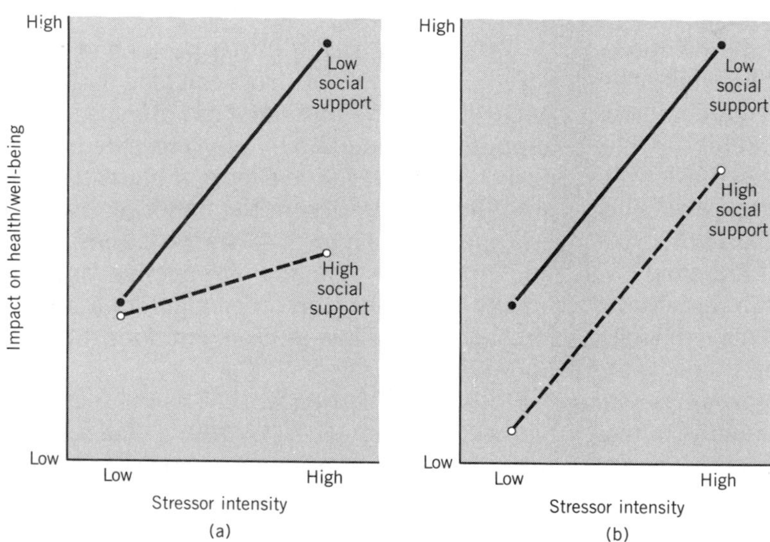

FIGURE 4.2 Illustration of two ways social support may benefit health and well-being. Graph (a) illustrates the *buffering hypothesis*, which proposes that social support modifies the negative health effects of high levels of stress. Graph (b) depicts the *direct effects hypothesis*, which proposes that the health benefits of social support occur irrespective of stress.

anced diet, or exercising. Other circumstances in which social support can be harmful arise when the person has developed a health problem. For instance, someone who is overweight and has high blood pressure may be encouraged by family to eat prohibited foods. They may say "Doctors don't know everything," or "A little more cheesecake can't hurt," or "You can make up for it by dieting next week." Also, when someone suffers a long and serious illness, such as heart disease, families may be overprotective and discourage the patient's desire to become more active or to go back to work. This can interfere with a program of rehabilitation and make the patient increasingly dependent and disabled.

In summary, people receive various types of support from friends, family, and others in their lives. Social support appears to reduce people's stress and generally benefits their health. We turn now to another psychosocial factor that modifies the stress people experience. This factor is the degree of control people feel they have in their lives.

A Sense of Personal Control

People generally like the feeling of having some measure of control over the things that happen in their lives. We choose representatives to work for our point of view through unions or associations in the workplace and through political processes in government. We also take individual action when we want to influence events directly. In doing these things, people strive for a sense of **personal control**—the feeling that they can make decisions and take effective action to produce desirable outcomes and avoid undesirable ones (Rodin, 1986). Several studies have found that having a sense of personal control can reduce the impact of stressors on the individual (Elliott, Trief, & Stein, 1986; Matheny & Cupp, 1983; McFarlane, Norman, Streiner, & Roy, 1983; Suls & Mullen, 1981).

Types of Control

Giving birth is a stressful event, and many pregnant women have excessive fears about the pain they will experience during labor. These women often lack an understanding of the birth process and what they can do to make it go more smoothly. Women who attend natural childbirth classes learn many techniques that enhance their personal control in the birth process. How can personal control reduce the aversiveness and stress they experience in childbirth?

People can influence events in their lives and reduce the stress they experience in many ways (Averill, 1973; Cohen, Evans, Stokols, & Krantz, 1986; Miller, 1979; Thompson, 1981). These ways have been classified into five types of control:

1. **Behavioral control** involves the ability to take concrete action to reduce the impact of a stressor. This action might reduce the intensity of the event or shorten its duration. During childbirth, for example, the mother can use special breathing techniques that reduce the pain of labor.

2. **Cognitive control** is the ability to use thought processes or strategies to modify the impact of a stressor. These strategies can include thinking about the event differently or focusing on a pleasant or neutral thought or sensation. While giving birth, for instance, the mother might think about the event differently by going over in her mind the positive meanings the baby will give to her life. Or she could focus her attention on the sensation of the baby's movements or on an image, such as a pleasant day at the beach.

3. **Decisional control** is the opportunity to choose between alternative procedures or courses of action. The mother and father have many choices to make about the birth process before it occurs. For many of these decisions, the mother usually has the final word—such as in the choice of the obstetrician, whether to use conventional or natural childbirth methods, and whether the birth will occur in a hospital, at home, or at an alternative birth center. In other medical situations, the patient may be given a choice regarding which treatment pro-

cedure to use, when the treatment will occur, and so on.

4. **Informational control** involves the opportunity to get knowledge about a stressful event—what will happen, why, and what the consequences are likely to be. For example, a pregnant woman may get information about the sensations she will experience during labor and delivery, the procedures she can expect to happen, and the range of time the process generally takes. Informational control can help reduce stress by increasing the person's ability to predict and be prepared for what will happen and by decreasing the fear people often have of the unknown.

5. **Retrospective control** pertains to beliefs about what or who caused a stressful event after it has occurred. In the aftermath of misfortune, people seek a sense of meaning for the event in their lives. Although this does not give them control over the event itself, it helps them modify the stress they experience by enabling them to perceive the world as an orderly and meaningful place. Having someone or something to blame—even oneself—sometimes reduces anxiety. And so, when a baby is born with a heart defect, a mother who blames herself because she drank alcohol often during pregnancy may adapt better to this misfortune than a mother who blames the defect on fate.

Each of these types of control can reduce stress, but one of them—cognitive control—seems to have the most consistently beneficial effect (Cohen, Evans, Stokols, & Krantz, 1986; Thompson, 1981).

Beliefs about Oneself and Control

People differ in the degree to which they believe they have control over their lives. Some people believe they have a great deal of control, and others think they have almost none. The latter is shown in the case study of a man named Karl, who was referred to therapy by the Veterans Administration.

> He was sometimes anxious, and a bit distressed from time to time. But his main problem seemed to be an almost total lack of social and interpersonal skills. He had no friends and, aside from his mother with whom he lived, no sustained contact with anyone. He was jobless and living off a small government pension. . . . Therapy turned into a teaching process, with the goals of helping him learn how to find a job, keep a job, talk with a girl, interest her, have dates, and so on. Many therapeutic hours were spent discussing techniques for fulfilling these goals. But progress was painfully slow. . . . After much coaching and discussion, Karl applied for a job and got it. But this did not raise his expectancies of being able to get another job should he have to do so. Indeed, he attributed his success entirely to good fortune. He believed that the employer probably was partial to veterans or just happened to be in a good mood that day. Karl was adamant in his unwillingness to take responsibility for his own success. After several comparable episodes, it began to dawn upon the therapist that here was a person who believed that the occurrence of reinforcement was outside his own personal control. (Phares, 1984, pp. 505–506)

People who believe they have control over their successes and failures are described as possessing an *internal* **locus of control.** That is, the control for these events lies within themselves—they are responsible. Other people, like Karl, who believe that their lives are controlled by forces outside themselves, for example, by luck, have an *external* locus of control (Phares, 1987; Rotter, 1966).

Certainly it is unrealistic for people to assume that everything in their lives is under their control. But the degree to which they attribute responsibility to themselves, versus other forces, determines their locus of control. Julian Rotter (1966) has developed the *I-E Scale*, a test that is used for measuring the degree of internality or externality of a person's beliefs about personal control. This scale presents a series of paired items, such as: "The average citizen can have an influence in government decisions" and "This world is run by a few people in power, and there is not much the little guy can do about it." For each pair of internal/external items, the respondent selects the one with which he or she most agrees. Most people have moderate beliefs about the influence they have on events in their lives. Their locus of control falls in the midrange between being highly internal or external.

There is another aspect of personal control besides internality/externality that is important, too. This aspect is our sense of **self-efficacy**—the belief that we can succeed at something we want to do (Bandura, 1977, 1986). People estimate their chances of success and failure on the basis of their prior observations of the effects that a given activity had for themselves and others. They decide whether to attempt the activity according to their expectations that (1) the behavior, if properly carried out, would lead to a favorable outcome, and (2) they can perform the behavior properly. For example, you may know that by taking and doing well in a series of honors courses in college that you can graduate with some recognition of that accomplishment, such as a special diploma or certificate. But if you estimate the likelihood of achieving that feat as "zilch," you are not likely to try. People with a strong sense of self-efficacy show less psychological and physiological strain in response to stressors than do those with a weak sense of efficacy (Bandura, Reese, & Adams, 1982; Bandura et al., 1985; Holahan, Holahan, & Belk, 1984).

Determinants and Development of Personal Control

On what basis do people judge that they have control over things that happen in their lives? We make these assessments by using a wide variety of information and knowledge that we gain from our experiences throughout life (Bandura, 1986; Phares, 1987; Rodin, 1987a; Schunk & Carbonari, 1984). One of the most important sources is our own performance—the successes and failures we perceive in the activities we attempt. Infants begin to learn about personal control from their own performance as they coordinate their sensory experiences with their motor activity. An example of this is when babies learn that they can make a noise with a rattle by shaking it.

We also assess our personal control through the process of *social learning*, in which we learn by observing the behavior of others (Bandura, 1969, 1986). During early childhood, the family is particularly important in this process, with members serving as models of behavior, as agents of reinforcement, and as standards for comparison. Parents who are caring, encouraging, and consistent in their standards for behavior tend to have children who develop an internal locus of control and a strong sense of efficacy (Harter, 1983). After children enter day care or school, their peers become increasingly important in social learning processes. Children notice differences and they compare themselves against their peers, using the value system of their family and society. They compare themselves for academic ability, naughtiness, talents, popularity, and so on. Adolescents tend to be highly self-conscious during the early teenage years, and the sense of personal control they develop will be strongly affected by, and will in turn affect, their social and sexual relationships and their decisions about higher education and careers.

As people enter adulthood, they are faced with important transitions, such as beginning a career and getting married, that provide new challenges and sources of information about personal control (Bandura, 1986; Rodin, 1987a). Those who reach adulthood with poor intellectual and social skills and many self-doubts tend to find these events and many other aspects of adult life stressful. By middle age, people generally settle into established roles, and their sense of personal control tends to stabilize. Their children are now grown, and they have advanced in their careers about as far as they will go. As people approach old age, their declining physical capacity may be compensated by gains in their skills and knowledge. From adulthood to old age, people's beliefs in self-efficacy become stronger but their locus of control becomes more external—that is, their beliefs that chance and powerful others affect their lives increase (Lachman, 1986). As a result, when elderly individuals develop serious illnesses, they are more inclined than younger people to prefer having professionals make health-related decisions for them (Woodward & Wallston, 1987).

You may have noticed that the information people use in determining their personal control is usually retrospective, can be very complex, and is not always clear-cut. As a result, the judgments we make about our control are not always very objective or based on fact. We sometimes develop what Ellen Langer (1975) calls an *illusion of control*—a belief in our control over what is really an event that is determined by chance. Camille Wortman (1975) demonstrated this illusion in an experiment with college students in a game of chance, using the following materials: a red and a blue marble and a coffee can. In one condition of the experiment, the *researcher* performed all the actions for the game, after telling the subjects: "I will put the two marbles that you hand me in the coffee can, mix them up, reach in without looking, and pull one out." In another condition, the *subjects* performed the actions themselves, after being told: "I would like you to put the two marbles in the coffee can, mix them up, reach in without looking, and pull one out." For both conditions, the color of the marble that was pulled out determined which of two prizes the subjects would get. The subjects then filled out some questions, one of which asked them to rate on a scale (0 = not at all; 20 = very much) how much they felt they could influence which marble they got. Subjects whose marble was picked by the researcher felt they had a little control, but subjects who pulled out the marble themselves felt they had much more control (their average rating of 5.65 was three times that of the other subjects). In reality, none of them had any control.

When People Lack Personal Control

What happens to people who experience high levels of stress over a long period of time and feel that nothing they do matters? They feel helpless. They feel trapped and unable to avoid negative outcomes. A worker who cannot seem to please her boss no matter what she does, a student who cannot perform well on exams, or a patient who is unable to relieve his severe low back pain—each of these examples describes a situation that can produce apathy. As a result, they may stop striving for these goals, come to believe they have no control over these and other events in their lives, and may fail to exert control in situations in which success is possi-

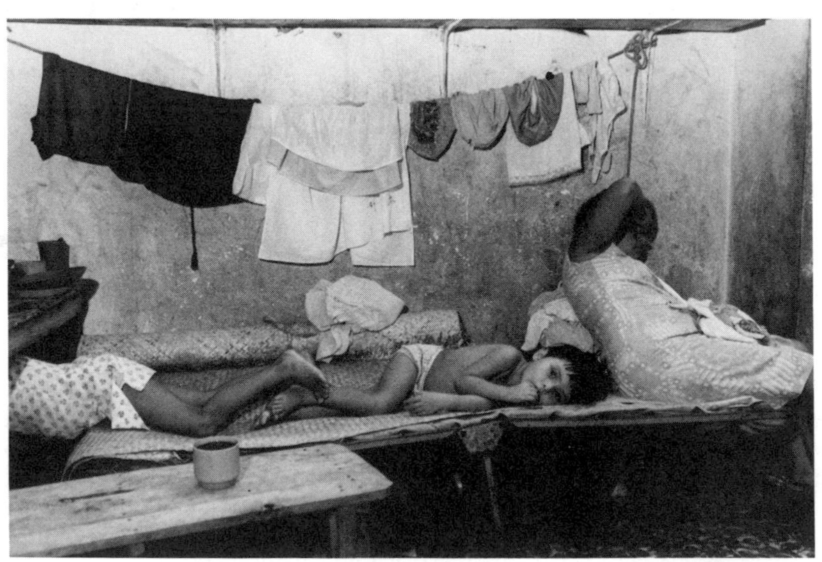

This displaced family in El Salvador probably sees little personal control in their lives and feels very helpless.

ble. This is the condition Martin Seligman (1975) has called **learned helplessness**— which he describes as a principal characteristic of depression.

An experiment by Donald Hiroto and Martin Seligman (1975) demonstrated that people learn to be helpless by being in uncontrollable situations that lead to repeated failure. The researchers assigned college students to one of three training groups that experienced an unpleasant loud noise. In one group, the *controllable-noise* condition, the subjects were told that a noise would come on from time to time and "there is something you can do to stop it." They were given an opportunity to discover that pressing a button on an apparatus would stop it, which they did. The *uncontrollable-noise* group had the same instructions and apparatus, but nothing they did affected the presence of the noise. In a *comparison* group, the subjects were simply told "From time to time a loud tone will come on for awhile. Please sit and listen to it." All the subjects were tested later for helplessness in a uniform way: they were told that a noise would come on and off and that "there is something you can do to stop it." The apparatus was new—it had a sliding knob that, when manipulated correctly, would terminate the noise. In this test, students in the uncontrollable-noise group performed much more poorly than those in the controllable-noise and comparison groups. Learning that the noise is uncontrollable with the push-button apparatus impaired the subjects' discovering how to control the noise with the knob apparatus.

Seligman and his colleagues have extended the theory of learned helplessness to explain two important observations (Abramson, Seligman, & Teasdale, 1978). For one thing, being exposed to uncontrollable negative events does not always lead to learned helplessness. Second, depressed people often report feeling a loss in self-esteem. The theory needed to answer the question of why people would blame themselves for negative events that are beyond their control. The revised theory attempts to deal with these observations by proposing that when people experience uncontrollable negative events, they ask themselves "Why am I unable to affect these events and how long will they continue?" They answer this question through the cognitive process called **attribution**, in which people judge or explain their own or others' actions, motives, feelings, or intentions.

In this process of attribution, people assess the following three dimensions of the situation:

1. *Internal - external.* When feeling trapped and unable to control negative events, people assess whether this situation results from their own personal inability to control outcomes or whether it is due to external causes that are beyond anyone's control. For example, a patient who is receiving physical therapy for a serious injury but cannot seem to meet the goals each week may attribute this failure either to his or her own lack or fortitude or to the rehabilitation program the physical therapist designed. Both attributions may make the person stop trying. But a person who attributes the difficulty to a lack of personal strength is likely to suffer a loss of self-esteem, and a person who attributes the difficulty to external causes is not.

2. *Stable - unstable.* Individuals who experience uncontrollable negative events assess whether the situation results from a cause that is long-lasting (stable) or temporary (unstable). If they determine that it is long-lasting, as when people develop a chronic and disabling disease, they are more likely to feel helpless and depressed than if they think their condition is temporary.

3. *Global - specific.* People in unpleasant situations that they cannot control try to assess whether these events result from factors that have global and wide-ranging effects or specific and narrow effects. Someone who is unable to stop smoking cigarettes and makes a global attribution—for example, "I'm totally no good and weak-willed"—is more likely to feel helpless and depressed than a similar individual who makes a specific attribution, such as "I'm not good at controlling this part of my life."

To summarize, people who tend to attribute negative events in their lives to *stable* and *global* causes are at high risk for feeling helpless and depressed. If their attributions are also *internal*, their depressive thinking is likely to include a loss of self-esteem as well.

Studies have examined the relationships among stress, personal control, attributions, and learned helplessness in real-life situations, such as in college dormitories (Baum, Aiello, & Calesnick, 1978; Baum & Gatchel, 1981; Rodin & Baum, 1978). Stress and control in dormitories were defined on the basis of differences in crowding that result from two types of floor plans: (1) *short-corridor* designs cluster residents in small numbers around shared areas and (2) *long-corridor* designs have large numbers of residents along a long hallway. Surveys of dormitory residents have shown that those who live in long-corridor designs report more stress and less ability to control unwanted social interaction than those in short corridors. Furthermore, these differences are associated with helplessness. When tested in social situations, students who live in long corridors show more evidence of helplessness than those who live in short corridors—for example, long-corridor residents initiate fewer conversations with a stranger and they show less cooperation and a greater tendency to give up in competitive games.

Carol Dweck and her associates have examined attributions and learned helplessness in schoolchildren. In one study, fifth-graders were given multicolored blocks and asked to arrange the blocks to match a pictured design (Dweck & Repucci, 1973). The task was actually impossible—the design could not be made with the blocks given. Children who attributed their failure to stable, uncontrollable factors, such as their own lack of ability, showed poorer performance on subsequent problems than those who attributed failure to unstable, modifiable factors, such as a lack of effort. Thus, the children's attributions were linked to their feelings of helplessness. Another study found evidence that teachers provide feedback that leads girls to feel more helpless than boys (Dweck, Davidson, Nelson, & Enna, 1978). Children acquire feelings of helplessness from their experience.

Personal Control and Health

There are two ways in which personal control and health may be related. First, people who have a strong sense of personal control may be more likely or able to maintain their health and prevent illness than those who have a weak sense of control. Second, once people become seriously ill, those who have a strong sense of control may adjust to the illness and promote their own rehabilitation better than those who have a weak sense of control. Both types of relationships have been examined.

To study these relationships, researchers have used several approaches to measure people's personal control. For instance, some researchers have constructed questionnaires or interviews to assess the degree to which people use specific types of control—such as cognitive, behavioral, or informational control. Others have examined people's locus of control, either by applying the I-E Scale or by using scales developed to assess specifically health-related control. One of the best-developed health-related measures today is called the *Multidimensional Health Locus of Control Scales* (Wallston, Wallston, & DeVellis, 1978). This instrument has 18 items; the person responds to each item with ratings ranging from "strongly agree" to "strongly disagree." These items are divided into three scales:

1. *Internal Health Locus of Control.* This scale measures the degree of internality of the person's beliefs with items such as "The main thing which affects my health is what I myself do."

2. *Powerful-Others' Health Locus of Control,* which assesses the belief that health is controlled by other people, such as physicians. One item for measuring this is "Whenever I don't feel well, I should consult a medically trained professional."

3. *Chance Locus of Control.* This scale measures the belief that health is controlled by luck

or fate, using items such as "Luck plays a big part in determining how soon I will recover from an illness."

As you can see, the powerful-others' and chance scales are directed toward assessing the degree to which people believe that important external sources have control over their health.

Does a strong sense of control help people adjust to becoming seriously ill and promote their recovery? Yes, it does, particularly if the patients perceive their condition as very severe. Patients with illnesses such as kidney failure or cancer who score high on either internal or powerful-others' health locus of control suffer less depression than those with strong beliefs in the role of chance (Devins et al., 1981; Marks, Richardson, Graham, & Levine, 1986). The belief that either they or someone else can influence the course of their illness allows patients to be hopeful about their future. Moreover, patients with strong internal locus of control beliefs probably realize that they have effective ways for controlling their stress.

Some types of control may be more effective than others in helping people adjust to serious illness. One study investigated the relationship between adjustment to breast cancer and the patients' use of different types of control, three of which were cognitive, behavioral, and informational (Taylor, Lichtman, & Wood, 1984). This study found that adjustment was most strongly associated with patients' use of cognitive control, such as by thinking about their lives differently and taking life more easily. Also, patients who used behavioral control—for example, by exercising more than before—showed better adjustment than those who did not. But adjustment was not related to their use of informational control, such as by reading books on cancer. It may be that seeking information about the illness either leads the patient to materials that increase their fears or simply has little influence if the patient has no cognitive or behavioral possibilities for control.

Personal control also affects the efforts patients will make toward their own rehabilitation—in particular, feelings of self-efficacy enhance their efforts. A study demonstrated this with older adult patients who had serious respiratory diseases, such as chronic bronchitis and emphysema (Kaplan, Atkins, & Reinsch, 1984). The patients were examined at a clinic and given individualized prescriptions for exercise, based on their performance on a treadmill exercise test. They also filled out a questionnaire that assessed their self-efficacy with respect to ability to perform certain physical activities, such as walking, lifting objects, and climbing stairs. Each activity was presented as a series of increasingly more difficult gradations. For example, the item for walking had nine gradations, including: "walk 1 block (approximately 5 minutes), walk 2 blocks (10 minutes) . . . walk 3 miles (90 minutes)." The patients indicated the degree of certainty in their ability—that is, their self-efficacy—to perform at each gradation. Correlational analyses revealed that the greater the patients' self-efficacy for the physical activity, the more likely they were to adhere to the exercise prescription.

To summarize the material on personal control, people differ in the degree to which they believe they have control over the things that happen in their lives. People who experience prolonged, high levels of stress and lack a sense of personal control tend to feel helpless. Having a strong sense of control seems to benefit people's health and help them adjust to their sickness when they become seriously ill. A sense of personal control contributes to people's "hardiness," which is the next psychosocial modifier of stress we will examine.

The Hardy Personality

According to researchers Suzanne Kobasa and Salvatore Maddi, individual differences in personal control provide only part of the reason why some people who are under stress get sick whereas others do not. They have proposed that a broader array of personality characteristics—called **hardiness**—differen-

HIGHLIGHT 4A: On Research
Health and Personal Control in Old Age

Here are two things we know about elderly people who live in nursing homes: First, they often show declines in their activity and health after they begin living in a nursing home. Second, residents of nursing homes often have few responsibilities or opportunities to influence their everyday lives. Could it be that the declines in activity and health among nursing-home residents result in part from their dependency and loss of personal control that the routines and procedures of the nursing home seem to encourage?

Ellen Langer and Judith Rodin (1976) studied this issue by manipulating the amount of responsibility allowed residents of two floors of a modern, high-quality nursing home. The residents on the two floors were similar in physical and psychological health and prior socioeconomic status. On one floor, the residents were given opportunities to have responsibilities, for example, they were given small plants to care for themselves and encouragement for making decisions about participating in activities and rearranging furniture. In comparison, the residents of the other floor continued to have little personal control. For example, they were assigned to various activities without choice, and when they were given plants, they were told that the staff would take care of them. Measures of the activity and happiness of the residents revealed that the residents who were given more responsibility became happier and more active and alert than the residents who had little control. A year and a half later the residents who were given responsibility were still happier and more active than those who had little control (Rodin & Langer, 1977). Moreover, comparisons of health data for the residents of the two floors during these 18 months showed that the residents with responsibility were healthier, and only about half as many died.

An experiment by Richard Schulz (1976) with residents of a retirement home also demonstrated the importance of personal control on physical and psychological well-being. Residents who agreed to participate in a study of "daily activities of aged individuals" were randomly assigned to one of four conditions that related to their being visited by university students during a two-month period. Residents in the *regulate-visit* condition determined when visits would occur and how long each meeting would last. Individuals in the *predict-visit* condition were informed when they could expect each visit, but they were not given the opportunity to determine when or how long it occurred. In the *random-visit* condition, subjects were not told when a visit would occur nor given the opportunity to determine its length. In scheduling the predict-visit and random-visit meetings, the researchers made sure that the visits matched the frequency and length of visits for the subjects in the regulate-visit condition. Lastly, residents in the *no-visit* condition were not visited by the students. The results of this study were similar to those of Langer and Rodin—the subjects in the regulate-visit and predict-visit groups became more happy, active, and healthy than those in the random-visit and no-visit conditions.

Once the Schulz experiment was over, the students gradually stopped visiting, and this had an important and dismaying effect on the residents' well-being. Richard Schulz and Barbara Hanusa (1978) conducted a follow-up study of the health and psychological status of the residents over the next 42 months. As Figure 4A.1 shows, the health of subjects who had benefited from the visits in the original experiment—that is, those in the regulate-visit and predict-visit conditions—declined drastically. Although other residents also showed a decline in

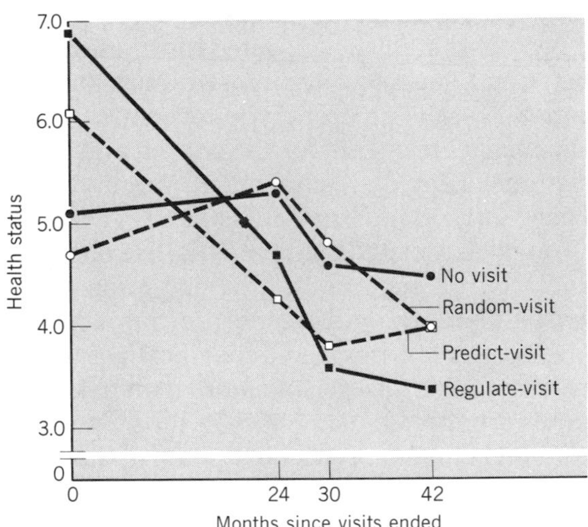

FIGURE 4A.1 Health status of retirement-home residents over the 42 months after student visits ended as a function of the four research conditions: regulate-visit, predict-visit, random-visit, and no-visit. Health status was measured on a 9-point scale, where 9 = "in perfect health" and 1 = "extremely ill." (Adapted from Schulz & Hanusa, 1978, Figure 1.)

their health, it was not nearly as sharp. Similar declines were also found in the subjects' psychological status, such as their "zest for life."

Why was there a difference in the long-term effects of these studies of elderly individuals? The improved happiness, activity, and health of the subjects who were given responsibility in the Langer and Rodin research was maintained over time because efforts and opportunities for personal control probably continued after the original study ended. In the Schulz research, the enhanced opportunities for personal control ended when the students stopped visiting. Those residents who had received visits may subsequently have felt a loss of social support. The results of these studies suggest two important conclusions. First, personal control — even over relatively simple or minor events — can have a powerful effect on people's health and psychological condition. Second, health-care workers and researchers need to consider the nature of the personal control they introduce and what the impact will be if it is removed.

---

tiates people who do and do not get sick under stress (Kobasa, 1979, 1986; Kobasa & Maddi, 1977). Hardiness includes three characteristics:

1. *Control*, or people's belief that they can influence events in their lives — that is, a sense of personal control. Questionnaires to measure hardiness assess control by asking the person to indicate agreement or disagreement with items such as "Most of my activities are determined by what society demands." These items are like those used for measuring locus of control.

2. *Commitment*, or people's sense of purpose or involvement in the events, activities, and people in their lives. This characteristic helps people turn to others for assistance and resist giving up in times of stress. People who have a strong sense of commitment tend to agree with the statement "I often wake up eager to start on the day's projects," and disagree with the statement "Getting close to people puts me at risk of being obligated to them."

3. *Challenge*, or the tendency to view changes as incentives or opportunities for growth rather than threats to security. People who have a strong challenge orientation do not seek safety and stability as their main goals. They are likely to agree with the statement "I would be willing to sacrifice financial security in my work if something really challenging came along," and disagree with the statement "I really don't mind when I have nothing to do."

According to Kobasa (1979), people under stress who have a greater sense of control, commitment, and challenge will remain healthier than those whose personalities are less hardy. This is because hardy people are better able to deal with stressors and are less likely to become anxious and aroused by these events. As a result, the spiraling process that can lead from stress to illness never takes hold.

Other researchers have described similar personality traits that, like hardiness, protect people from the effects of stress. Aaron Antonovsky (1979, 1987) has described the *sense of coherence*, which involves the tendency of people to see their worlds as comprehensible, manageable, and meaningful. Another concept — that of *resilience* — has been applied to children who develop into competent and well-adjusted individuals despite growing up under extremely difficult conditions (Garmezy, 1983; Werner & Smith, 1982). Resilient children bounce back from life's adversities and recover their strength and spirit. The following case shows what this means:

> In the slums of Minneapolis, for example, there is a 10-year-old boy who lives in a dilapidated apartment with his father, an exconvict now dying of cancer, his illiterate mother, and seven brothers and sisters, two of whom are mentally retarded. Yet his teachers describe him as an unusually competent child who does well in his studies and is loved by almost everyone in the school. (Pines, 1979, p. 53)

Other cases have been described of children who flourished or were well-adjusted despite being abused by their parents, or growing up in concentration camps, or living in societies with civil strife and wars (Garmezy, 1983; Hartup, 1983; Werner, 1987).

Studies of resilient children have found that they share important characteristics (Garmezy, 1983; Pines, 1979; Werner, 1987; Werner & Smith, 1982). These children have good social skills, being friendly and at ease with age-mates and adults. Their temperaments tend to be "easy," rather than difficult, and this promotes positive relationships with family and community members. They have strong feelings of self-esteem and personal control, and they are high achievers, generally doing well in the things they undertake.

Why are some children resilient and others not? Part of the answer may lie in their genetic endowments. Resilient children may have inherited traits, such as their relatively easy temperaments, that enable them to cope better with stress and turmoil. Another part lies in their experiences. Resilient children who have a history of stressful events often have compensating experiences and circumstances in their lives, such as special talents or interests that absorb them and give them confidence, and close relationships with friends or teachers. For instance,

> often they make school a home away from home, a refuge from a disordered household. A favorite teacher can become an important model of identification for a resilient child whose own home is beset by family conflict. (Werner, 1987, p. 95)

Sometimes these compensating relationships occur within the family, such as with older siblings or grandparents. Hardiness, resilience, and coherence have a great deal in common, and may be basically the same thing.

Hardiness and Health

To determine the role of hardiness in health, Kobasa (1979) conducted a study of highly stressed men who worked as executives in a large corporation. She began by testing several hundred executives with questionnaires to identify two groups of individuals: one group that had experienced high levels of both stress and illness, and another that had experienced high levels of stress but little illness. The question under investigation was whether hardiness would differentiate the high-illness from the low-illness subjects. She tested this issue by having the two groups fill out several questionnaires to assess their hardiness. Although both groups had experienced equally high levels of stress, their responses revealed that the low-illness executives were hardier than the high-illness executives. The low-illness men reported a greater sense of control, commitment, and challenge than the high-illness men did.

Because personality is not the only psychosocial factor that can modify the effects of stress on health, Kobasa and her colleagues have studied how illness is affected by the combination of hardiness and other factors. One of their studies used retrospective methods to examine the role of hardiness and physical exercise on illness among men who worked as managers for a large company (Kobasa, Maddi, & Puccetti, 1982). These men filled out questionnaires measuring the illnesses and stressful life events they experienced, their hardiness, and the extent to which they exercised. The results showed that illness increased with stress and decreased with greater hardiness and exercise. Those men who had high scores in both hardiness and exercise experienced the least amount of illness; those who had low scores in both hardiness and exercise had the most illness. This suggests that the protective effects of hardiness and of exercise add to each other—that is, people who score high on both are likely to be healthier than people who score high on only one. Moreover, the protective effects of hardiness and of exercise were greater for men with high degrees of stress than for those with little stress.

Another study used both retrospective and prospective methods to examine the degree to which people are protected against illness by three factors: hardiness, exercise, and social support (Kobasa, Maddi, Puccetti, & Zola,

1985). This study focused on male business executives who had reported experiencing a high level of stress in the preceding year. These men filled out questionnaires at the beginning of the study to measure their illnesses in the past year, their hardiness and social support, and the extent to which they exercised. A year later, they completed the survey on illness again, but this time for the intervening year. Both the retrospective and the prospective data revealed protective effects for each of the three factors, with hardiness playing the strongest role. As Figure 4.3 illustrates, the protective effects of each factor add to each other — that is, the likelihood of poor health decreases with each increase in the number of protective factors people have.

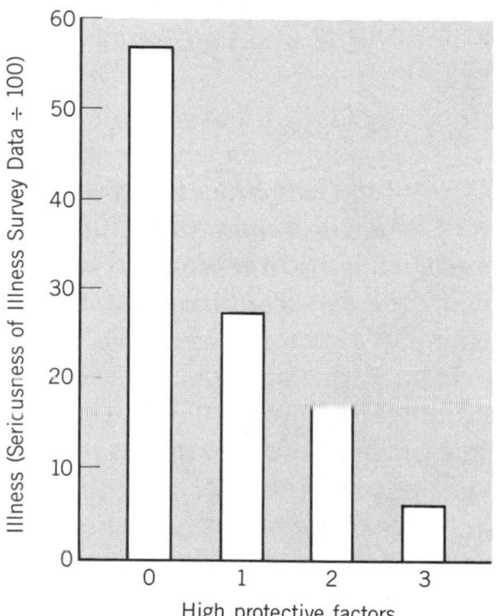

FIGURE 4.3 Prospective data on illness among high-stress business executives who began the study with high scores on 0, 1, 2, or 3 of the following protective factors: hardiness, exercise, and social support. Illness was measured with the Seriousness of Illness Survey, which weights the severity of each physical and mental symptom or illness. The resulting score indicates not just the number of illnesses, but the severity of the health problems experienced. (Data from Kobasa, Maddi, Puccetti, & Zola, 1985, Table I, prospective illness data.)

It is clear that hardiness can play an important role in maintaining health, but the concept of and research regarding hardiness are not without criticism or problems. For one thing, only two of the three characteristics of hardiness — control and commitment — have consistently been associated with health; challenge has not (Gentry & Kobasa, 1984; Hull, Van Treuren, & Virnelli, 1987). Also, research on hardiness has focused mainly on one segment of the population: white, middle-class business and professional men. It is possible that hardiness has different effects for women and people of other age, ethnic, socioeconomic, and occupational groups. Lastly, as psychologists W. Doyle Gentry and Suzanne Kobasa have noted, researchers have concentrated only on one direction of the hardiness/health relationship, that is,

> the effects of hardiness on health and/or illness. This unidirectional focus fails to take into account the possible reverse effects of health-illness on hardiness. One wonders if, for example, illness experienced early in life can result in a failure to develop hardiness, in that persons experiencing such illnesses learn to perceive themselves as being out of control with respect to their health status or are unable to commit themselves to major tasks of daily living because of disability resulting from the illness. Or, on the contrary, can early illness cause one to become hardy by emphasizing . . . the need to remain flexible in the face of potential life-threatening events, including diagnosed illness? (1984, p. 102)

Hardiness in Old Age

As individuals develop, they learn to deal with change by trying and succeeding, failing, or compromising. Setbacks can be difficult, but they teach people patterns of behavior that accumulate throughout life. Old age is a time when some very difficult life events occur, particularly those that involve reduced income, failing health and disability, and the loss of one's spouse and close friends. What are hardy people like in old age, and how did they get that way?

Elizabeth Colerick (1985) studied the personalities of elderly men and women for the quality she called *stamina*, which is similar to hardiness. This research was undertaken to determine how people who do and do not have stamina in later life deal with setbacks, such as the loss of a loved one. By using questionnaires and interviews, she was able to identify two groups: one with high stamina and one with low stamina. She found that stamina in old age is characterized by "a triumphant, positive outlook during periods of adversity," as illustrated by the following interview excerpts from three different high-stamina people:

> The key to dealing with loss is not obvious. One must take the problem, the void, the loneliness, the sorrow and put it on the *back* of your neck and use it as a driving force. Don't let such problems sit out there in front of you, blocking your vision. . . . Use hardships in a positive way. (p. 999)

> I realize that setbacks are a part of the game. I've had 'em, I have them now, and I've got plenty more ahead of me. Seeing this—the big picture—puts it all into perspective, no matter how bad things get. (p. 999)

> Years ago as a student thinking about my career, I thought I was going to teach a year or two here, a year or two there. I was going to see the world, you know. Well, the Depression came along and I never did. Retirement provided an opportunity to finally do those things. Sure you felt cut off from your lifeline for a while but it's all in how you see your options—I saw great beginnings and there were. (p. 1000)

In contrast, low-stamina people described a negative outlook and feelings of helplessness and hopelessness in the face of changes they experienced in old age. One woman who had undergone surgery for colon cancer said:

> I was certain that I would die on the table . . . never wake up. . . . I felt sure it was the end. Then I woke up with a colostomy and figured I have to stay inside the house the rest of my life. Now I'm afraid to go back to the doctor's and keep putting off my check ups. (p. 999)

There is little research available that bears directly on the question of how people become hardy, but the study by Colerick found some interesting relationships. Compared with low-stamina individuals, those with high stamina reported healthier past histories, more years of schooling, and more activities in their current lives involving social service and personal growth, for example, visiting museums and traveling. Some tentative research findings suggest that people can learn to be hardier (Kobasa, 1986). More research is needed on a variety of biopsychosocial factors that are likely to shape hardy personalities.

In summary, hardy people—those who have a strong sense of control, commitment, and challenge—seem to have some protection against the harmful effects of stress on health. The last psychosocial modifier of stress we will consider is people's tendency toward the Type A or B behavioral and emotional style.

Type A and Type B Behavior Patterns

The history of science has many stories about researchers accidently coming upon an idea that changed their focus and led to their making major discoveries. Such was the case for bacteriologist Alexander Fleming, for instance. When the bacteria cultures he was studying developed unwanted molds, he happened to notice some properties of the molds that led to his discovery of penicillin. Serendipity also led to the discovery of the "Type A" behavior pattern by cardiologists Meyer Friedman and Ray Rosenman. They were studying dietary differences in cholesterol intake between male heart disease victims and their wives when one of the wives exclaimed: "If you really want to know what is giving our husbands heart attacks, I'll tell you. It's stress, the stress they receive in their work, that's what's doing it" (Friedman & Rosenman, 1974, p. 56). These researchers began to study this possibility by looking at differences between heart disease patients and similar people who were healthy, focusing on the subjects' stress and related behavioral characteristics. This comparison revealed differences in behavioral and emotional style: the patients were more likely than the nonpatients to display a pattern of behavior we now refer to as Type A.

What is the Type A behavioral and emotional style? The **Type A behavior pattern** consists of three characteristics (Chesney, Frautschi, & Rosenman, 1985; Friedman & Rosenman, 1974):

1. *Competitive achievement orientation.* Type A individuals tend to be very self-critical and to strive toward goals without feeling a sense of joy in their efforts or accomplishments.
2. *Time urgency.* Type A people seem to be in a constant struggle against the clock. Often, they quickly become impatient with delays and unproductive time, schedule commitments too tightly, and try to do more than one thing at a time, such as reading while eating or watching TV.
3. *Anger/hostility.* Type A individuals tend to be easily aroused to anger or hostility, which they may or may not express overtly.

In contrast, the **Type B behavior pattern** is characterized by low levels of competitiveness, time urgency, and hostility. People with the Type B pattern tend to be more easygoing and "philosophical" about life—they are more likely to "stop and smell the roses."

Measuring Type A and Type B Behavior Patterns

Researchers measure people's Type A and Type B behavior either by using a standard interview procedure or by having the people fill out questionnaires. The most widely used interview procedure is called the *Structured Interview,* a standard procedure in which a trained interviewer asks individual subjects a series of questions about their behavioral and emotional style, particularly regarding their competitiveness, impatience, and hostility (Chesney, Eagleston, & Rosenman, 1980; Rosenman, 1978; Rosenman, Swan, and Carmelli, 1988). For instance, they are asked, "When you play games with people your own age, do you play for the fun of it, or are you really in there to win?" Although the specific answers people give to these questions contribute to the assessment of their behavior pattern, their style of interaction with the interviewer also contributes. Some features of the interview are designed to encourage Type A behaviors such as interrupting and talking fast and loudly. For example, the interviewer asks slowly and with hesitations, "Most people who work have to get up fairly early in the morning. In your particular case, uh, what time, uh, do you, uh, ordinarily, uh-uh-uh, get up?" (You can imagine the Type A person saying "Six o'clock!" at the second "uh.") The interviewer also does things to annoy or challenge the subjects, thereby encouraging Type A behavior. This is done by interrupting the subjects often and asking for clarifications in a harsh manner—asking, for instance, "What do you mean by that?" rather than, "Could you tell me a bit more about that?"

Structured Interview sessions are audiotaped or videotaped and scored by a trained rater who knows nothing about the subjects beyond what the tapes present. In the scoring process, the rater considers specific answers given to questions, speech characteristics, and a variety of behaviors that suggest annoyance, for example, sighing frequently or attempting to hurry the interviewer. Videotapes allow the rater to consider other behavioral features also, such as facial expressions, sitting on the edge of the chair, and fidgeting. The rater's overall scores for subjects determine their classification as Type A or B. Interestingly, a study found that measurements with an apparatus that analyzes voice qualities can be as effective as raters who use both speech characteristics and content of the answers in classifying Type A and B subjects in the Structured Interview (Glass, Ross, Isecke, & Rosenman, 1982). This may be because raters' judgments tend to rely very heavily on specific speech characteristics, such as voice emphasis and speed of speaking (Scherwitz, Graham, Grandits, & Billings, 1987). These are aspects of speech that can be measured with electronic devices.

The questions used in the Structured Interview have been adapted to construct a 52-item self-report questionnaire called the *Jenkins Activity Survey* (Jenkins, Zyzanski, & Rosenman, 1979). These items inquire about the person's usual way of responding to situations that can produce stress as a result of, for example, competition, time pressure, or frustration. A sample question is:

> Would people who know you well agree that you tend to do most things in a hurry?
> Definitely yes
> Probably yes
> Probably no
> Definitely no

Other questions ask about the person's speed of eating, tendency to hurry someone who talks slowly, and work habits. This questionnaire was designed to test adults, but versions have also been developed for college students (Yarnold, Bryant, & Grimm, 1987). Another questionnaire for measuring the Type A and B behavior patterns is the *Framingham Type A Scale* (Haynes et al., 1978). It contains only ten items and has slightly different versions for testing students, housewives, and people who are employed (Powell, 1987).

Researchers have also developed methods to measure Type A and B behavior patterns in children and adolescents. Probably the most widely used of these methods is the *Matthews Youth Test for Health* (Matthews & Angulo, 1980). This method uses an instrument that has 17 statements, such as: "This child gets irritated easily," "This child is patient when working with children slower than he/she is," and "It is important to this child to win, rather than to have fun in games or schoolwork." An adult, such as a parent or teacher, who is familiar with the child rates each statement for the degree to which it characterizes the child's behavior, using a 5-point scale that ranges from "extremely characteristic" to "extremely uncharacteristic." These ratings are then combined to yield an overall score that indicates the degree to which the child exhibits the Type A or Type B pattern. Because an adult fills out the instrument, this method can be used for children who are too young to read.

Is one approach for measuring Type A and B behavior better than the others? Each approach has its own strengths and weaknesses (Carver, Diamond, & Humphries, 1985; Matthews, 1982; O'Rourke, Houston, Harris, & Snyder, 1988; Powell, 1984, 1987). The Structured Interview has two important strengths. Its assessment of behavior patterns seems to involve all three Type A characteristics: competitiveness, time urgency, and anger/hostility. In addition, the Type A classification using this method has been associated fairly consistently with health outcomes, particularly heart disease. But the Structured Interview is time-consuming and expensive to use, and the classifications made by different raters can vary widely. Perhaps the use of electronic devices to analyze voice characteristics will help reduce these problems. The strengths of self-report methods rest mainly in their time- and cost-efficiency. But they have three important weaknesses. First, the relationship between health outcomes and Type A classification with existing self-report methods appears to be weak and inconsistent. Second, because characteristics such as impatience and hostility are socially undesirable, people may underreport these behavioral or emotional tendencies. Third, Type A measurements with the Jenkins Activity Survey and Framingham Type A Scale rely very little on and provide poor measures of the anger/hostility dimension of the behavior pattern. Because of the problems with the existing interview and self-report methods, new approaches or instruments to measure Type A and B behavior are needed (Byrne, Rosenman, Schiller, & Chesney, 1985).

Behavior Patterns and Stress

Individuals who exhibit the Type A behavior pattern react differently to stressors than do those with the Type B pattern. That is, Type A individuals respond more quickly and strongly to stress, often interpreting stressors as threats to their personal control (Carver, Diamond, &

Reprinted with special permission of King Features Syndicate, Inc.

Humphries, 1985; Glass, 1977). But the Type A behavior pattern may have another kind of impact on stress: the Type A pattern may actually increase the person's likelihood of encountering stressful events (Byrne & Rosenman, 1986; Smith & Anderson, 1986). For example, Type A individuals tend to seek out demanding situations in their lives. What is more, people who are often in a hurry and impatient with delays—as is the case for Type A individuals—tend to have more accidents than people who are more easygoing (Suls & Sanders, 1988). In these ways the Type A and B patterns can affect the transactions of people in their environment and modify the stress they experience in their lives.

People's response to stress—or strain—includes both psychological and physiological components. The physiological portion of the response to stress is called **reactivity**, which is measured against a baseline, or "resting," level of arousal (Matthews, 1986). Do Type A individuals show greater reactivity to stress than Type Bs? In general, yes. One study examined the reactivity of men who each competed in a video game against an individual who was a confederate of the researchers (Glass et al., 1980). Although the instructions indicated that the winner would receive a prize, the game was rigged so that a subject could never win. The subjects were assigned to two groups, Type A or Type B, on the basis of their performance in the Structured Interview. Half of the men in each group played the game while being harassed and insulted by the confederate; for the remaining subjects, the confederate was silent. Several physiological measures were used, including blood pressure, heart rate, and plasma catecholamine levels. In the absence of harassment, both Type A and Type B subjects showed substantial and equal increases in physiological arousal over their baseline levels. But in the harassment condition, the Type A subjects showed greater reactivity than the Type Bs did.

Many other studies have also compared the reactivity of Type A and Type B people, using male and female subjects and a variety of tasks, ways to induce stress, and measures of Type A and B behavior. Although there are some inconsistencies in their outcomes, most of these studies have found greater reactivity among Type A individuals, especially males (Carver, Diamond, & Humphries, 1985; Contrada & Krantz, 1988; Houston, 1986). Other researchers have examined reactivity in Type A and Type B boys and girls and found results similar to those found with adults (Lawler, Allen, Critcher, & Standard, 1981; Lundberg, 1986; Matthews & Jennings, 1984; Thoresen & Pattillo, 1988). This suggests that the tendency of Type A individuals to be highly reactive to stress may begin in childhood.

Some research suggests the intriguing possibility that people's Type A behavior may, in part, be caused by their physiological responses to stress (Contrada, Krantz, & Hill, 1988; Krantz & Durel, 1983; Krantz, Lundberg, & Frankenhaeuser, 1987). Two lines of evidence seem to support this view. First, research has been conducted with Type A patients who were either taking or not taking *beta-blockers,* a class of drugs that dampens sympathetic nervous system transmission. This research demonstrated that Type A patients who were taking a beta-blocker exhibited less Type A behavior in the Structured Interview than those who were not taking the drug (Krantz et al., 1982). Second, studies have examined the blood pressure of Type A and B patients under general anesthesia at the start of coronary bypass surgery. Compared with Type Bs, Type A patients showed greater blood pressure increases over the pressure measured when they were admitted to the hospital (Kahn et al., 1980). This is important because research showing greater reactivity in Type A than Type B individuals was typically done with subjects who could use conscious appraisal processes to judge the situation as stressful. Since all the bypass patients were unconscious during the operation, the results with these patients indicate that the Type A person's greater reactivity to stress can occur without the role of conscious processes. Taken together, these lines of evidence suggest that physiological reactions to stressors can influence Type A behavior.

The relationships between psychosocial factors and Type A behavior are very complex and seem to involve multiple levels of human experience. To describe these relationships, we can use a systems or "ecological" approach with four levels (Margolis, McLeroy, Runyan, & Kaplan, 1983). The first level is *intrapersonal:* within the person, there are many psychological factors that relate to Type A behavior. One of these factors is personal control. David Glass (1977) has proposed, for example, that Type A behavior may represent an effort by individuals to control stressful experiences in their lives. Research has generally supported this view (Matthews, 1982).

At the *interpersonal* level, social processes and Type A behavior affect each other. The impact of the Type A behavior pattern on social interaction was demonstrated in a study in which paired subjects could either cooperate or compete in a game (Van Egeren, Sniderman, & Roggelin, 1982). The pairs of subjects consisted of either two Type A college students or two Type Bs. The Type A pairs showed more competition and less cooperation than the Type B pairs. Similar results have also been found with children (Spiga, 1986). Other research has demonstrated the reverse effect—that is, that social interaction can affect Type A behavior. For example, a study found that being insulted increases the hostility and aggression of both Type A and Type B subjects, but the effect is much greater for the Type A individuals (Carver & Glass, 1978). In general, people who display Type A behavior tend to elicit reactions from others that create more demands and stimulate more Type A behavior (Smith & Anderson, 1986).

The third level is *institutional,* and includes the experiences of people in educational and occupational settings. There are several ways these experiences can foster Type A behavior. One way involves reward structures that promote aggressive competition, as can happen when many individuals are vying for a small number of rewards, such as job promotions or high grades. Another way involves time or work demands by a boss or teacher that encourage the feeling of time urgency. Research has shown that Type A individuals exhibit greater reactivity to stress than Type Bs during final exams in medical school (Lovallo et al., 1986). Research has also found that employees with high scores on the Jenkins Activity Survey for Type A behavior have longer work hours and less supportive relationships with co-workers than Type B workers do (Sorensen et al., 1987).

The fourth level of relationships between psychosocial factors and Type A behavior is *cultural.* Some cultures place greater emphasis than others on the work ethic, getting ahead, status, and accumulating goods that reflect status. People in cultures that emphasize these values are likely to display more Type A behavior than those who live in cultures that do not (Margolis, McLeroy, Runyan, & Kaplan, 1983).

Type A Behavior and Health

How are people's health and behavior patterns related? To answer this question, researchers have used two approaches. First, studies have examined whether Type A individuals are at greater risk than Type Bs for becoming sick with any of a wide variety of illnesses. One study, for instance, found that Type A people reported having experienced more respiratory symptoms, such as asthma attacks and coughing spells, and more gastrointestinal symptoms, such as ulcers, indigestion, and nausea (Woods & Burns, 1984). Although several other studies have found similar results, the overall evidence for a link between Type A and B behavior and general illnesses is weak and inconsistent (Orfutt & Lacroix, 1988; Suls & Sanders, 1988). The second approach has focused on the Type A pattern as a risk factor for **coronary heart disease** (CHD)—illnesses that result from the narrowing or blocking of the coronary arteries, which supply blood to the heart muscle. These illnesses include *angina, arteriosclerosis,* and *myocardial infarction* (commonly called "heart attack").

Many studies have revealed a clear link between Type A behavior and CHD (Booth-Kewley & Friedman, 1987; Haynes & Matthews, 1988). The most convincing evidence of this link comes from two large-scale prospective studies. The Western Collaborative Group Study determined the health status and behavior patterns (using the Structured Interview) of over 3,000 39- to 59-year-old employed men, most of whom had white-collar jobs (Rosenman et al., 1975; Rosenman, Brand, Sholtz, & Friedman, 1976). A follow-up on these men 8½ years later showed that the Type A subjects were twice as likely as Type Bs to have developed CHD and to have died of CHD. Because of these and similar results, Type A behavior has been called "coronary prone behavior."

The second investigation, called the Framingham Heart Study, followed more than 1,600 men and women for eight years, after assessing their health status and behavior patterns (using the Framingham Type A Scale). This study found that, overall, Type A individuals of both genders were substantially more likely than Type Bs to develop CHD. But when the men's data were separated on the basis of the kind of job they had, the results for men showed an interesting relationship: the Type A pattern sharply increased the risk of CHD for men with white-collar jobs but had no effect for blue-collar workers (Haynes, Feinleib, & Kannel, 1980).

Not all studies have confirmed the link between CHD and behavior patterns. One notable disconfirming investigation comes from a large-scale project called the Multiple Risk Factor Intervention Trial (MRFIT). This study began by identifying over 12,000 middle-aged men who showed no evidence of CHD but still had a moderately strong level of risk for heart disease on the basis of their cigarette smoking, high blood pressure, and so on (Shekelle et al., 1985). The behavior patterns of these men were determined in two ways: all the subjects completed the Jenkins Activity Survey and about one-fourth of them were also tested with the Structured Interview. The Type A and Type B subjects did not differ in the incidence of heart disease over the next seven years. Another study found that of men who were already coronary patients, those with the Type A behavior pattern had a *lower* mortality rate from CHD over a 12-year period than the Type Bs (Ragland & Brand, 1988). Why these studies have not found the expected association between behavior patterns and CHD is unclear, but the reasons may involve differences in procedures used in assessing behavior patterns (Haynes & Matthews, 1988).

Despite these inconsistencies, an overview of the research suggests that Type A women and men, particularly white-collar workers, have a much greater chance of developing CHD than Type B adults do. As we have seen, however, the Type A behavior pattern consists of three components—is one component more damaging than the others? Redford Williams (1986; Williams & Barefoot, 1988) has argued that the anger/hostility component is the most important factor. One of several studies that support this position examined the records of 255 men (Barefoot, Dahlstrom, & Williams, 1983). These men were physicians who had taken a psychological test that included a scale for hostility while they were in medical school 25 years earlier. For the physicians with high scores on the hostility scale, the rates of both CHD and overall mortality during the intervening years were several times higher than for those with low hostility scores. Anger seems to be especially damaging to health when it is turned against the self rather than expressed and when it involves a cynical or suspicious mistrust of others (Dembroski et al., 1985; Williams, 1986; Williams et al., 1980).

Why is the Type A behavior pattern linked to CHD? We don't have a complete answer yet, but part of it seems to involve the relatively high physiological reactivity of Type A people (Carver, Diamond, & Humphries, 1985; Krantz, Lundberg, & Frankenhaeuser, 1987; Wright, 1988). Frequent episodes of high arousal produce a lot of "wear and tear" on the cardiovascular system. One way this may occur is through the hormones that are released during arousal. Research has shown that chronically high levels of hormones, such as epinephrine and norepinephrine, can injure the heart and blood vessels. Another way wear and tear may lead to CHD in Type A people is through blood pressure. Studies have recorded higher blood pressure reactivity among Type A individuals—particularly those who score high on measures of anger and hostility—than among Type Bs during stressful situations (Diamond, 1982; Diamond et al., 1984; Spiga, 1986). High blood pressure strains the heart and arteries.

Behavioral factors may also contribute to the link between Type A behavior and CHD. For instance, Type A individuals drink considerably more alcohol than Type Bs do, and excessive alcohol use is associated with CHD (Carmargo, Vranizan, Thoresen, & Wood, 1986). Another important risk factor for CHD is cigarette smoking. Of adults who smoke, Type A people inhale the smoke for a much longer time than Type Bs do, which provides more time for the lungs to absorb the harmful elements of smoke (Lombardo & Carreno, 1987). And Type A individuals have more difficulty quitting smoking than Type Bs do (Caplan, Cobb, & French, 1975). Lastly, compared with Type Bs, Type A individuals are more likely to suppress or ignore their symptoms of fatigue and exert themselves to their limits despite having been injured (Carver, Coleman, & Glass, 1976; Carver, DeGregorio, & Gillis, 1981; Weidner & Matthews, 1978). It may be that Type A individuals often drive themselves far beyond the point when they should slow down, and that their frequent physical exhaustion leads to illness, such as CHD (Carver, Diamond, & Humphries, 1985).

Behavior Patterns and Development

Research has addressed some important questions relating to the development of Type A and B behavior patterns. For example, do people's behavior patterns change over the life span? Longitudinal studies have found that although people's behavior patterns often change over time, many individuals exhibit the same pattern across many years. This has been shown for both children and adults (Bergman & Magnusson, 1986; Carmelli, Rosenman, & Chesney, 1987; Visintainer & Matthews, 1987). In addition, cross-sectional studies have found that the Type A behavior pattern among Americans becomes more prevalent with age from childhood through middle age or so and then declines (Amos et al., 1987; Moss et al., 1986; Powell, 1987). But it is currently uncertain whether the decline in the prevalence in old age is the result of Type A individuals dying at earlier ages than Type Bs.

Other studies have been conducted to determine the origins of the Type A pattern and factors that influence its development. One promising approach for determining the origins of Type A behavior is to study how its development relates to the early *temperaments* of children. This is because behavior patterns and temperaments involve some similar characteristics, such as the impulsiveness and intensity with which the person reacts and his or her ease in adjusting to changes in the environment. One longitudinal study found that temperament ratings taken in early childhood were related to measures of Type A behavior taken 20 years later (Steinberg, 1985). Another longitudinal study examined this relationship in adults and found an association between measures of temperament and Type A behavior both at the beginning of the study and 10 years later (Carmelli, Rosenman, & Chesney, 1987). These results suggest that adult Type A behavior has roots in the person's early temperament, which remains influential over time in at least some individuals.

Do both biological and psychosocial factors affect the development of Type A and B behavior patterns? It appears that they do. Research with monozygotic (identical) and dizygotic twins has demonstrated a genetic contribution in the development of temperament (Buss & Plomin, 1975, 1986) and of Type A behavior (Carmelli, Rosenman, & Chesney, 1987; Matthews et al., 1984). That is, monozygotic twins are more similar to each other in temperament and behavior patterns than are dizygotic twins.

Research has also examined the influence of various psychosocial factors on Type A behavior. One finding from this research is that children's behavior patterns are related to the parenting styles they experience. For example, compared with Type Bs, Type A boys who are working on a task receive less praise from their mothers and more statements to strive for improvement, such as "That was fine, but next time try harder" (Krantz, Lundberg, & Frankenhaeuser, 1987; Matthews & Woodall, 1988). Other findings relate to work experiences. Research with employed adults has shown that stressful work experiences affect people's behavior patterns. Type A individuals work longer hours and have less supportive relationships with coworkers than Type Bs do (Sorensen et al., 1987). Also, a longitudinal study found that workers exhibit less Type A behavior a year after retirement than they did shortly before retiring (Howard, Rechnitzer, Cunningham, & Donner, 1986). Finally, there seem to be cultural differences in the prevalence of the Type A behavior pattern. For instance, one study found that only a small percentage of Japanese-American men living in Hawaii exhibited the Type A pattern (Cohen, Syme, Jenkins, & Kagan, 1975). Research on psychosocial factors has revealed a wide variety of environmental influences on the development of Type A behavior.

As a summary of the role of psychosocial modifiers of stress, we have seen that social support, personal control, hardiness, and the Type A and B behavior patterns are factors that can modify the impact of stress on health. High levels of social support, personal control, and hardiness are generally associated with reduced stress and resulting illnesses; Type A behavior is associated with increased stress and illness. The remainder of this chapter focuses on health problems that are affected by people's experience of stress. We begin by considering how stress leads to illness.

HOW STRESS AFFECTS HEALTH

What is it about the experience of stress that leads to illness? The causal sequence between stress and illness can involve either of two routes: (1) a direct route, resulting from the changes stress produces in the body's *physiology*, or (2) an indirect route, affecting health through the person's *behavior*. Let's look first at the behavioral route.

Stress, Behavior, and Illness

The behavioral link between stress and illness can be seen in many stressful situations, such as when a family undergoes a divorce. In many cases during the first year following the separation, the parent who has the children is less available and responsive to them than she or he was before—a situation described as "diminished parenting" (Wallerstein, 1983). The parent's change in behavior often makes conditions in the family less healthful, involving haphazard meals and less regular bedtimes, for example. Stress can affect behavior, which, in turn, can impair health.

Research has shown that people who experience high levels of stress tend to perform behaviors that increase their chances of becoming ill or injured (Wiebe & McCallum, 1986). For instance, they consume more alcohol, cigarettes, and coffee than people who experience less stress (Baer et al., 1987; Conway, Vickers, Ward, & Rahe, 1981). Consumption of these substances has been associated with the development of various illnesses. In addition, behavioral factors, such as alcohol use and carelessness, probably play a role in the relatively high accident rates of people under stress. Studies have found that children and adults who experience high levels of stress are more likely to suffer accidental injuries at home, in sports activities, on the job, and while driving a car than individuals under less stress (Johnson, 1986; Quick & Quick, 1984).

Stress, Physiology, and Illness

Stress produces many changes in the body's physical systems that can affect health. The clearest connections between stress and illness involve the release of hormones—particularly catecholamines and corticosteroids—by the endocrine system during arousal. One way in which high levels of these hormones can lead to illness involves their effects on the cardiovascular system. For example, an intense episode of stress with extremely high levels of these hormones can cause the heart to beat erratically and may lead to sudden death. In addition, chronically high levels of catecholamines and corticosteroids appear to increase the growth of plaques (fatty patches) on artery walls (McKinney, Hofschire, Buell, & Eliot, 1984; Schneiderman, 1983). This condition—called atherosclerosis, which we discussed in Chapter 2—narrows the inside diameter of the arteries. As these plaques harden, the narrowing and hardening of arteries increase the blood pressure of the cardiovascular system and the likelihood of a heart attack or stroke.

The release of catecholamines and corticosteroids during arousal affects health in another way: Some of these hormones impair the functioning of the immune system (Jemmott & Locke, 1984; Schleifer, Scott, Stein, & Keller, 1986). For example, increases in cortisol and epinephrine are associated with decreased activity of T-cells and B-cells against antigens. This decrease in lymphocyte activity appears to be important in the development and progression of a variety of diseases, including cancer. Sandra Levy and her coworkers (1985) tested women diagnosed with breast cancer and found that patients with high levels of killer-T-cell activity exhibited less spread of the cancer to surrounding tissue than those with low levels of lymphocyte activity.

Cancer can result from excessive exposure to harmful chemical or physical agents called **carcinogens**, which include radiation, tobacco tars, and some food additives, such as nitrates and saccharine (Nelson, 1984). Carcinogens can damage the DNA in body cells, which may then develop into mutant cells and spread. Fortunately, people's exposure to carcinogens is generally at low levels and for short periods of time, and most DNA changes probably do not lead to cancer (Glazer et al., 1985). When mutant cells develop, the immune system attacks them with killer T-cells. Actually, the body begins to defend itself against cancer even before a cell mutates by using enzymes to destroy chemical carcinogens or to repair damaged DNA. Research has shown that high levels of stress, however, reduce the production of these enzymes and the repair of damaged DNA

HIGHLIGHT 4B: On Issues Sudden or "Voodoo" Death

Can a person die from extreme psychological distress? It seems so, at least on the basis of anecdotal evidence, such as the following case study:

> In 1967 a distraught woman, pleading for help, entered the Baltimore City Hospital a few days before her 23rd birthday. She and two other girls had been born of different mothers assisted by the same midwife in the Okefenokee Swamp on a Friday the 13th. The midwife cursed all three babies, saying one would die before her 16th birthday, another before her 21st birthday, and the third before her 23rd birthday. The first had died in a car crash during her 15th year; the second was accidently shot to death in a nightclub fight on the evening of her 21st birthday. Now she, the third, waited in terror for her own death. The hospital somewhat skeptically admitted her for observation. The next morning two days before her 23rd birthday, she was found dead in her hospital bed—physical cause unknown. (Seligman, cited in Rosenhan & Seligman, 1984, p. 292)

This case provides an example of **sudden death**—the sudden and medically unexplained death of a seemingly healthy person. Sudden death was originally called "voodoo death" (Cannon, 1942), perhaps because many of the cases described were from primitive cultures.

Sudden death usually results from cardiac failure of some sort and appears to involve two factors: a preexisting physical weakness or vulnerability and a severe stressor, such as the loss of a loved one (Newquist, 1985; Reker & Wong, 1985). In a sense, people can die of a "broken heart," and this may happen in two ways (McKinney, Hofschire, Buell, & Eliot, 1984; Schneiderman & Hammer, 1985; Verrier, DeSilva, & Lown, 1983). First, the cardiac episode may result from damage to the myocardium caused by high levels of catecholamines in the blood. Second, the episode probably involves the occurrence of *cardiac arrhythmia*—an abnormal rhythm of the heart's functioning. Arrhythmias can take the form of an extremely high heart rate, called *flutter*, or of uncoordinated heartbeats, called *fibrillation* (McClintic, 1985).

(Glaser et al., 1985; Kiecolt-Glaser & Glaser, 1986; Kiecolt-Glaser et al., 1985).

Psychoneuroimmunology

We have seen in this and earlier chapters that psychological systems, such as the experience of emotion, and biological systems are interrelated—as one system changes, the others are often affected. The recognition of this interdependence and its connection to health and illness led researchers to form a new field of study called **psychoneuroimmunology**. This field focuses on the relationships between psychosocial processes and the activities of the nervous, endocrine, and immune systems (Ader & Cohen, 1985; Buck, 1988). These systems form a *feedback loop*: the nervous and endocrine systems send chemical messages in the form of neurotransmitters and hormones that increase or decrease immune function, and cells of the immune system produce chemicals, such as ACTH, that feed information back to the brain. The brain appears to serve as a control center to maintain a balance in immune function, since too little immune activity leaves the individual open to infection and too much activity may produce autoimmune diseases (Buck, 1988).

People's emotions—particularly stress-related emotions, such as anxiety and depression—play a critical role in the balance of immune functions. Research has shown that both major and minor stressful events can lead to impaired immune function (Zautra et al., 1989). Furthermore, major negative events and their accompanying emotional states tend to suppress immune processes over an extended period of time. This was demonstrated with healthy elderly individuals who were taking part in a longitudinal study of the aging process

(Willis, Thomas, Garry, & Goodwin, 1987). All of the 256 subjects in the study were sent a letter asking them to contact the researchers as soon as they were able if they experienced any major crises, such as the diagnosis of a serious illness in or the death of a spouse or child. Fifteen subjects did so. A month after the crisis, and again several months later, the researchers assessed the subjects' cortisol and lymphocyte blood concentrations, recent diets, weight, and psychological distress. Because the subjects were already participating in the longitudinal study, comparable data were available from a time prior to the crisis. A longitudinal analysis of these data revealed that lymphocyte concentrations, caloric intake, and body weight decreased and cortisol concentrations and psychological distress increased soon after the crisis. By the time of the last assessment several months later, however, all of these measures had returned almost to the precrisis levels.

Research on psychoneuroimmunology with animals has revealed that the influence of psychological processes on immune function is not limited to the effects of stress. The impact may be far more broad and pervasive. Robert Ader and Nicholas Cohen (1975, 1985) have described research showing that immunosuppression can be *conditioned.* In their original research, they were actually studying how animals learn to dislike certain tastes. The procedure used a single conditioning trial: the subjects (rats) received saccharin-flavored water to drink (which they seemed to like) and then got an injection of a drug that induces nausea. To see if the rats' subsequent dislike of the taste depended on its strength, some subjects received more saccharin flavoring than others in this conditioning trial. Over the next several weeks, the drug was *not* used, but the animals continued to receive saccharin-flavored water. During this time, the researchers noticed a curious thing: a number of rats had fallen ill and died—and these animals tended to be the ones that had consumed the greatest amount of saccharin in the conditioning trial.

How did these deaths relate to immunosuppression? Since the nausea-inducing drug used in the conditioning trial was also known to suppress immune function temporarily, Ader and Cohen hypothesized that the continued intake of saccharin water served as a conditioned stimulus, suppressing the ability of the rats to fight infection. Subsequent experiments by these researchers and others confirmed this hypothesis and demonstrated that conditioning can influence both antibody-mediated and cell-mediated immune processes (Ader & Cohen, 1985). Although the extent to which this kind of conditioning impairs immune function is fairly moderate, the effect is clear.

Psychoneuroimmunology is a very new and exciting field of study, and researchers are discovering fascinating connections between biological and psychosocial processes very quickly.

PSYCHOPHYSIOLOGICAL DISORDERS

A study of over 1,500 children and adolescents found that "psychosomatic" illnesses increase during two stressful periods of transition, the early elementary-school and the early adolescence years (Schor, 1986). The word *psychosomatic* has a long history, and was coined to refer to symptoms or illnesses that are caused or aggravated by psychological factors, mainly emotional stress (Lipowski, 1986). Although this term is still commonly used by professionals and the general public, the concept has undergone some changes and now has a new name. The term **psychophysiological disorders** refers to physical symptoms or illnesses that result from the interplay of psychosocial and physiological processes. This definition clearly uses a biopsychosocial perspective.

Which illnesses are considered psychophysiological? Actually all the illnesses we will discuss in the remainder of this chapter could qualify because they are linked with stress. In this section, however, we will briefly discuss several that have been traditionally classified as psychosomatic. Some of these illnesses will be examined in greater detail in later chapters.

Ulcers and Inflammatory Bowel Disease

Both **ulcers** and **inflammatory bowel disease** are illnesses that involve wounds in the digestive tract that may cause pain and bleeding. Ulcers are found in the stomach and the duodenum, or upper section of the small intestine. Inflammatory bowel disease, which includes disorders such as *colitis*, can occur in the colon (large intestine) and the small intestine. Although ulcers and inflammatory bowel disease afflict mostly adults, these illnesses also occur in childhood and adolescence (Peck, 1985; Werry, 1986; Whitehead, 1986).

Researchers generally believe that ulcers are produced by excess gastric juices chronically eroding the lining of the stomach and duodenum when there is little or no food present. But other factors must also be involved since ulcers have occurred in individuals with very low levels of stomach acid (Weiss, 1984). The physical process that produces inflammatory bowel disease is not yet known (Peck, 1985).

Stress seems to be an important psychosocial factor in ulcers and inflammatory bowel disease. In a classic study, a patient (called Tom) agreed to cooperate in a lengthy and detailed examination of gastric function (Wolf & Wolff, 1947). Tom was unique in that many years earlier, at the age of 9, he had had a stomach operation that left an opening to the outside of the body. This opening, which provided the only way he could feed himself, was literally a window through which the inside of his stomach could be observed. When Tom was subjected to stressful situations, causing feelings of hostility and anxiety, his stomach-acid production greatly increased. When he was under emotional tension for several weeks, there was a pronounced reddening of the stomach lining. Another study reported similar effects with a 15-month-old girl, Monica, who had a temporary opening to her stomach. Her highest levels of acid secretion occurred when she experienced rage (Engel, Reichsman, & Segal, 1956).

Asthma

Asthma is a respiratory disorder in which spasms in the muscles of the bronchial tubes lead to difficulty in breathing, accompanied by wheezing or coughing. This ailment is more common in children than adults, and in boys than girls. About 3–5% of the population in the United States suffers from asthma (Cluss & Fireman, 1985; Gergen, Mullally, & Evans, 1988; Werry, 1986).

Asthma appears to result from some combination of the following three factors (Werry, 1986):

1. Specific physical allergies to substances, such as dust, pollen, or food additives
2. Respiratory infections, such as whooping cough or bronchitis
3. Psychological processes, such as stress

Once the condition exists, attacks tend to be triggered by a combination of allergic and psychosocial processes. In some cases, the cause of an attack may be mostly physical; in others, it may be mostly psychological.

Professionals working with hospitalized children have noted an interesting phenomenon that suggests a psychosocial factor in asthma. Many asthmatic children (about one-third) are relieved of their symptoms shortly after admission to the hospital even though their medication is not changed. When they return home, the symptoms reappear (Bakwin & Bakwin, 1972; Purcell, Weiss, & Hahn, 1972). This, of course, does not prove that a psychosocial factor is involved. After all, maybe the children were simply allergic to something in their own houses, such as the dust. This idea was tested in an ingenious study (Long et al., 1958). Without the children knowing, the researchers vacuumed the children's homes and then sprayed the collected dust from each house into their individual hospital rooms. The fascinating result was that *none* of the children had respiratory difficulty when exposed to their home dust. Incidently, most of the children had been diagnosed previously as allergic to house dust on the basis of skin tests. Although this evidence does not point to a specific psychosocial factor, the results of other research suggest that stress can trigger an asthma attack (Cluss & Fireman, 1985; Eiser, 1985).

Chronic Headache

Most people have headaches at least occasionally. Although some headaches result from organic damage, as occurs in concussions or neurological diseases, the great majority do not. Most headaches are psychophysiological in origin.

Many people suffer chronically from intense headaches. There are basically two types of chronic headache: muscle-contraction and migraine (Andrasik, Blake, & McCarran, 1986; Bakal, 1979; Feuerstein & Gainer, 1982). **Muscle-contraction** (or *tension*) **headaches** are caused by persistent contraction of the head and neck muscles, which is a typical feature of people's reaction to stressors. The pain it produces is a dull and steady ache that often feels like a tight band of pressure around the head. Muscle-contraction headaches sometimes occur twice a week or more, and may last for hours, days, or weeks.

Migraine headaches result from the constriction and dilation of blood vessels inside and outside the skull. The pain often begins on one side of the head near the temple, is sharp and throbbing, and lasts for hours or, sometimes, days. One form of migraine, called the "classic migraine," is preceded by an *aura*, a set of symptoms that signal an impending headache. These symptoms usually include sensory phenomena, such as seeing lines or shimmerings in the visual field. This may be accompanied by dizziness, nausea, and vomiting.

Perhaps 15 to 20% of the population suffers from chronic headaches, and muscle-contraction headaches are far more common than migraines (Andrasik, Blake, & McCarran, 1986; Bakal, 1979; Blanchard & Andrasik, 1985). Many children experience their first headaches in the preschool years, and the incidence of headache increases as they get older. Chronic headaches have been reported in boys and girls as young as 6 years of age. By 10 years of age and thereafter, chronic headaches afflict far more females than males. Figure 4.4 presents a drawing by an 11-year-old girl named Meghan to describe her experience of migraine headache pain.

What triggers headaches? Sometimes they are brought on by consuming certain substances, such as wine or chocolate, and by other aspects of people's lifestyles. Research has also shown that stressors—particularly the hassles of everyday living—play an important role in triggering headaches (Andrasik, Blake, & McCarran, 1986; Gannon, Haynes, Cuevas, & Chavez, 1987; Levor et al., 1986). Yet some chronic-headache patients have attacks when they are not under great stress, and others fail to have a headache when they are under stress (Bakal, 1979). Stress appears to be one of many factors that produce headaches, but the full nature of these causes is not yet known.

Other Disorders

There are several other psychophysiological disorders for which stress appears to be involved in triggering or aggravating episodes. One of these illnesses is *rheumatoid arthritis*—a chronic and very painful disease that produces inflammation and stiffness of the small joints, such as in the hands. It afflicts about 1% of the population, and its victims are primarily women (Anderson et al., 1985). Another disorder, called *dysmenorrhea*, affects millions of women. It is characterized by painful menstruation, which may be accompanied by nausea, headache, and dizziness (Calhoun & Burnette, 1983; Schuster, 1986). A third stress-related problem involves skin disorders, such as *hives*, *eczema*, and *psoriasis*, in which the skin develops rashes or becomes dry and flakes or cracks (Grossbart, 1982). In many cases, specific allergies are identified as contributing to

FIGURE 4.4 Drawing by 11-year-old Meghan of her experience of migraine headache pain. The lower left-hand corner has a self-portrait with a dramatic facial expression. When a headache begins, Meghan typically retreats to her bedroom "to ride out the storm," lying down in a darkened room. (From Andrasik, Blake, & McCarran, 1986, Figure 18.1.)

episodes of these skin problems (Burg & Ingall, 1985).

Although current evidence implicates both biological and psychosocial causes for each of the illnesses we have considered, the evidence is sketchy and the nature of the interplay of these factors is unclear. For the remainder of this chapter we will focus on the role of stress in the development of cardiovascular disorders and cancer. These diseases are potentially very serious and the evidence for the role of stress is relatively strong.

STRESS AND CARDIOVASCULAR DISORDERS

Earlier in this chapter, we saw that psychosocial modifiers of stress can affect health. For instance, we saw that people who exhibit the Type A behavior pattern are more likely to develop CHD than those who have the Type B pattern. Such findings indirectly implicate stress as a cause of cardiovascular disorders, the number one cause of death in the United States. Is there more direct evidence for the role of stress? We will examine this question for two types of cardiovascular disorders, hypertension and CHD.

Hypertension

Hypertension—the condition of having high blood pressure consistently over several weeks or more—is a major risk factor for CHD, stroke, and kidney disease (Gorkin, 1987; Schneiderman & Hammer, 1985; Shapiro & Goldstein, 1982; USDHHS, 1986a). About 30% of the adult American population is classified as hypertensive, having blood pressures that consistently exceed 140 (systolic) over 90 (diastolic). The prevalence rates for hypertension increase in adulthood, particularly after about 40 years of age. Fortunately, the percentage of adults with high blood pressure has declined somewhat since 1960 (Dannenberg et al., 1987). Some cases of hypertension are caused by, or are "secondary" to, disorders of other body systems or organs, such as the kidneys or endocrine system. Secondary hypertension can usually be cured by medical procedures. But the vast majority—about 85%—of hypertensive cases are classified as *primary* or **essential hypertension**, in which the mechanisms causing the high blood pressure are unknown.

To say that the causes for essential hypertension are "unknown" is somewhat misleading. In cases of essential hypertension, physicians are unable to identify any biomedical causes, such as infectious agents or organ damage. But a variety of risk factors are associated with the development of hypertension—and there is evidence now implicating several of these risk factors as determinants of hypertension (Shapiro & Goldstein, 1982). These determinants include:

- Obesity
- Dietary elements, such as salt, caffeine, or cholesterol
- Alcohol use
- Physical inactivity
- Family history of hypertension
- Psychosocial factors

The psychosocial factors that have received the most research attention involve emotional behavior—stress, anger, and hostility.

People's occupations provide a source of stress that can impact on their blood pressure. Traffic controllers at airports have an occupation that is often described as stressful. Sidney Cobb and Robert Rose (1973) compared the medical records of thousands of men employed as air traffic controllers or as second-class airmen. Both occupations require yearly physical examinations for renewal of their licenses. The medical records were separated so that comparisons could be made for different age groups, since blood pressure increases with age. These comparisons for each age group revealed prevalence rates of hypertension among the traffic controllers that were several times higher than those among airmen. The researchers also compared the records of traffic controllers who experienced high and low levels of stress, as measured by the traffic density at the air station where they worked. Figure 4.5 depicts the results of this analysis: For each age group, the prevalence rates of hypertension were higher for traffic controllers working at high-stress locations than for those at low-stress sites.

Stress is also related to environmental conditions, such as living in crowded neighborhoods. Researchers have studied whether living in crowded conditions influences blood pressure by comparing cardiovascular reactivity among people who live in crowded and uncrowded neighborhoods (Fleming et al., 1987). The subjects from the two types of neighbor-

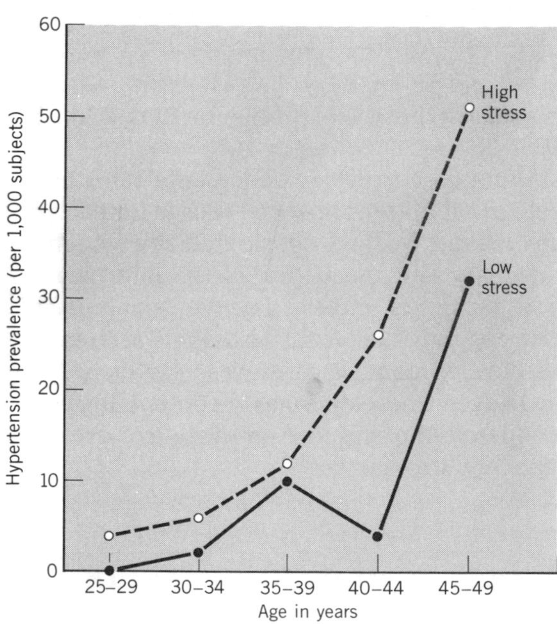

FIGURE 4.5 Prevalence of hypertension per 1,000 air traffic controllers as a function of stress and age. Hypertension rates increase with age and stress. (Data from Cobb & Rose, 1973, Table 3.)

hoods were similar in a variety of important characteristics, such as age, gender, and family income. To assess the subjects' reactivity, their blood pressure and heart rate were measured before and while they worked on a challenging cognitive task. The residents from crowded neighborhoods showed greater increases in heart rate and systolic and diastolic pressure than those from uncrowded neighborhoods. Tentative findings of other research indicate that high cardiovascular reactivity may be a risk factor for, or even a cause of, hypertension (Manuck & Krantz, 1986; Rose & Chesney, 1986). Taken together, the evidence suggests that chronic environmental stress may play an important role in the development of hypertension.

The impact of occupational and environmental stress on hypertension in the United States may be particularly relevant for black people, who have a much higher prevalence rate of high blood pressure than whites do (USDHHS, 1986a). In a study of blacks and whites in Detroit, the highest blood pressure readings found were those of blacks living in "high-stress" areas of the city—neighborhoods that were crowded and had high crime rates and low incomes (Harburg et al., 1973). But blacks and whites who lived in low-stress areas had similar blood pressures. In addition, a study of occupational stressors among black men found that high blood pressure was associated with the subjects' perceptions of low job security, of lack of job success, and of being hindered in their chances of achieving job success because they were black (James, LaCroix, Kleinbaum, & Strogatz, 1984).

Other research on emotional factors in the development of essential hypertension has focused on the role of anger and hostility. Some studies have found that hypertensives are more likely to be chronically hostile and resentful than are *normotensives*—that is, people who have normal blood pressure (Diamond, 1982). Other studies have shown that systolic and diastolic blood pressure increase more when people experience anger and hostility in their everyday lives than when they experience positive emotions, such as happiness (James et al., 1986; Southard et al., 1986). What is more, there is some evidence that people in high-stress jobs who suppress, or hold in, their anger when angry are at greater risk for hypertension than workers who express their anger or have low-stress jobs (Cottington, Matthews, Talbott, & Kuller, 1986). The results of these studies indicate that chronically high levels of anger and hostility may contribute to the high blood pressure of many hypertensives.

Few, if any, cases of essential hypertension are likely to be caused by emotional factors alone (Schneiderman & Hammer, 1985). Most cases of high blood pressure probably involve several of the determinants listed earlier in this section.

Coronary Heart Disease

Epidemiologists have studied the distribution and frequency of CHD over many decades in many different cultures. The data they have collected suggest that CHD is, to some extent, a disease of modernized societies—that is, the incidence rate of heart disease is higher in technologically advanced countries than in other nations (Susser, Hopper, & Richman, 1983).

There are many reasons why modernized societies have higher rates of CHD. For one thing, people in technologically advanced societies live longer than those in less-developed countries, being less likely to die of infectious diseases, such as malaria, for instance. As a result, people in advanced societies live long enough to become victims of CHD, which afflicts mainly older individuals. Also, people in modernized societies are more likely than those in less-developed countries to have certain risk factors for CHD, such as cigarette smoking, obesity, and low levels of physical activity. Lastly, the psychosocial stresses of modernized societies are different from those in other societies and may be more conducive to the development of heart disease.

The link between stress and CHD is clear. For example, studies of occupational stress have shown that high work loads, job responsibility, and job dissatisfaction are associated with a high incidence of CHD (Cottington & House, 1987; Quick & Quick, 1984). Other research has examined the relationship between heart disease and major life stressors, as measured by life events scales. Retrospective studies have found that victims of myocardial infarction tended to have high levels of life events in the months preceding the attack (Garrity & Marx, 1979). Prospective research has also supported the link between stress and CHD. For instance, researchers carried out periodic follow-up assessments over an eight-year period with patients who had recovered from their first myocardial infarction (Theorell & Rahe, 1975). These patients were separated into two groups — those that did and those that did not have a subsequent attack. The group that suffered a subsequent infarction — some of whom died — had experienced a substantial build-up in life events over the year or so preceding the attack. But the group that had no recurrence of heart attack reported no increase in life events during the study.

We have seen that stress increases catecholamine and corticosteroid release by the endocrine glands and that chronically high levels of these hormones can damage the arteries and heart, promote atherosclerosis, and lead to the development of hypertension and arteriosclerosis (hardening of the arteries). Stress can also produce cardiac arrhythmia, which can cause a cardiac episode and sudden death. These are some of the physiological connections between stress and CHD. There are behavioral connections, too. Stress is associated with high levels of cigarette smoking, coffee consumption, and alcohol use, for example, which are behavioral risk factors for CHD (Epstein & Jennings, 1986; Levenson, 1986; Shapiro, Lane, & Henry, 1986).

STRESS AND CANCER

The idea that stress and other psychosocial factors contribute to the development of cancer has a long history. The physician Galen, who practiced in Rome during the second century A.D., believed that individuals who were sad and depressed, or "melancholy," were more likely to develop cancer than those who were happy, confident, and vigorous (Sklar & Anisman, 1981). Similar ideas have appeared in the writings of physicians in later eras.

Cancer is a term that refers to a broad class of disease in which cells multiply and grow in an unrestrained manner. As such, cancer does not refer to a single illness, but to dozens of disease forms that share this characteristic (Burg & Ingall, 1985; Levy, 1985; Nelson, 1984). It includes, for instance, *leukemias*, in which the bone marrow produces excessive numbers of white blood cells, and *carcinomas*, in which tumors form in the tissue of the skin and internal organ linings. Some cancers take a longer time to develop or follow a more irregular course in their development than others do. Because cancer appears in so many different forms, each with its own characteristics, it is very difficult to study the causes of this disease (Fox, 1978). Nevertheless, current evidence tends to support the view that stress plays a role in the beginnings and progression of cancer.

Most of this evidence linking stress and cancer has come from research using retrospective methods (Blaney, 1985; Sklar & Anisman, 1981). These methods generally involve having cancer patients fill out life events questionnaires to assess the stress they experienced during the year or so preceding the diagnosis. The results of these studies have been fairly consistent in showing that the appearance of several forms of cancer in children and adults is associated with their reports of high levels of prior stress. But there are problems with retrospective methods that cloud the interpretation of the results of these studies (Fox, 1978; Sklar & Anisman, 1981). For one thing, the diagnosis of cancer is typically made years after — sometimes many years after — the disease process starts. As a result, the patients' cancers were probably present prior to and during the year for which they reported high levels of stress. Also, the patients' perceptions or recollections of prior stress may have been distorted by their knowledge that they have cancer.

Stronger evidence implicating the role of stress in the development of cancer comes from prospective studies that have measured psychosocial factors and followed up on the subjects' health over time. Some of these studies focused on the incidence of cancer in individuals who were healthy at the start of the research, and other studies examined the progress of the disease in people who were already diagnosed with cancer. Research with initially healthy subjects has found that people who experienced high levels of stress during the intervening years were more likely to develop cancer than those with less stress (Sklar & Anisman, 1981). A study with people already diagnosed with cancer found that patients who adjusted well to their illness were less likely to suffer a relapse within one year than those who adjusted less well (Rogentine et al., 1979).

Although the results of research with human subjects link stress and the development of cancer, we cannot yet conclude that the relationship is causal. One problem is that experimental research with animals has produced inconsistent outcomes (Sklar & Anisman, 1981). As researcher Paul Blaney has noted, "in animals exposed to a carcinogen or implanted with a tumor, stress induction sometimes increases malignant proliferation, sometimes inhibits it, and sometimes has no effect" (1985, p. 545). The effect of stress seems to be influenced by many factors, such as the source or kind of stress, whether the stress is chronic, and whether it is experienced before or after the carcinogen or tumor is introduced. Assuming that stress plays a causal role in the development of cancer, it probably does so by impairing the immune system's ability to combat the disease and by increasing behavioral risk factors, such as smoking cigarettes.

SUMMARY

Researchers have identified several psychosocial factors that modify the impact of stress on the individual. One of these factors is social support—the perceived comfort, caring, esteem, or help a person receives from other people or groups. There are four basic types of support: emotional, esteem, tangible or instrumental, and informational. Whether people receive social support depends on characteristics of the recipients and providers of support and on the composition and structure of the social network.

Social support reduces the stress people experience and generally benefits their health. The greater the degree of support people have, the lower their mortality rates and likelihood of becoming ill. These beneficial effects appear to accrue in two ways. First, social support buffers the person against the negative effects of high levels of stress. Second, social support can be beneficial to health regardless of the level of stress by simply providing encouragement for leading healthful lifestyles, for instance.

Another psychosocial modifier of stress is the sense of personal control people have over the events in their lives. Personal control includes beliefs about the locus of control—that is, whether control is internal or external to the person—and self-efficacy. People acquire a sense of personal control from their successes and failures and through the process of social learning. Individuals who experience prolonged, high levels of stress and have a weak sense of personal control tend to feel helpless. The cognitive process of attribution seems to be important in the development of learned helplessness. A strong sense of personal control tends to benefit people's health and help them adjust to a serious illness if it occurs.

Hardiness is another psychosocial modifier of stress. Hardy individuals have a strong sense of control, commitment, and challenge; they tend to remain healthier when under stress than individuals who are less hardy. The effects of hardiness, social support, and exercise appear to add to each other in protecting people from illness.

One other psychosocial modifier of stress is people's tendency toward the Type A or B behavior pattern. The Type A behavior pattern consists of three characteristics: competitive achievement orientation, time urgency, and anger or hostility. Compared with Type Bs, Type A individuals respond more quickly and strongly to stressors both in their overt behaviors and in their physiological reactivity. The Type A pattern — particularly the anger/hostility component — is associated with the development of coronary heart disease (CHD). Both biological and psychosocial factors affect the development of the Type A and B behavior patterns.

Stress affects health in two ways. First, stress can affect health-related behaviors, such as alcohol and cigarette use. Second, it produces changes in the body's physical systems, as when the endocrine system releases catecholamines and corticosteroids, which can cause damage to the heart and blood vessels and impair immune system functioning. The physiological effects of intense stress can even lead to sudden death. Psychoneuroimmunology is a new field of study that focuses on how psychosocial processes and the nervous, endocrine, and immune systems are interrelated. Stress also plays a role in many psychophysiological disorders, such as ulcers, asthma, chronic headache, rheumatoid arthritis, and several skin disorders. In addition, stress is implicated in the development of hyptertension, CHD, and cancer.

KEY TERMS

social support
social network
buffering hypothesis
direct effects hypothesis
personal control
behavioral control
cognitive control
decisional control
informational control
retrospective control
locus of control
self-efficacy
learned helplessness
attribution
hardiness
Type A behavior pattern
Type B behavior pattern
reactivity
coronary heart disease (CHD)
carcinogens
sudden death
psychoneuro-immunology
psychophysiological disorders
ulcers
inflammatory bowel disease
asthma
muscle-contraction headaches
migraine headaches
hypertension
essential hypertension

5

COPING WITH AND REDUCING STRESS

PROLOGUE

One morning while taking a shower, Cicely felt a small lump on her breast. She was sure it had not been there before. It didn't hurt, but she was momentarily alarmed—her mother had had breast cancer a few years ago. "It could be a pimple or some other benign growth," she thought. Still, it was very worrisome. She decided not to tell her husband or her physician about it yet because "it may not be anything." Over the next several days, she examined the lump daily. This was a very stressful time for her, and she slept poorly and seemed preoccupied. After a week without the lump changing, she decided to take action. She told her husband and made an appointment to see her physician.

Another woman, Beth, had a similar experience. She was also alarmed by finding a lump on her breast, but she didn't deal with the stress as rationally as Cicely did. Beth's initial fright led her to reexamine her breast just once, and in a cursory way. She told herself that "there isn't really a *lump* on the breast, it's just a rough spot." And she convinced herself that she should not touch it because "that will only make it worse." During the next few months, Beth was quite worried about the "rough spot." She studiously avoided touching it, even while washing. She became increasingly moody, slept poorly, and developed many more headaches than usual. She also told her husband that she didn't like him to fondle her breasts in lovemaking. When he asked why she was acting so differently in recent weeks, she denied that anything was wrong. Beth finally mentioned the "rough spot" to a friend who convinced her to have her physician examine it.

People vary in the way they deal with stress. Sometimes people confront a problem directly and rationally, as Cicely did, and sometimes they do not. For these two women, the way they dealt with their stress had the potential for affecting their health. Because Beth did not face up to the reality of the lump she delayed seeking medical attention and experienced high levels of stress for a very long time. If the lump was malignant, delaying treatment would allow the cancer to progress and spread. As we have seen, prolonged stress can have adverse health effects even in healthy people.

In this chapter we discuss the ways people can and do deal with stress. Through this discussion, you will find answers to questions you may have about the methods people use in handling stress. Are some methods for coping with stress more effective than others? How can people reduce the potential for stress in their lives? When people encounter a stressor, how can they reduce the strain it produces?

COPING WITH STRESS

Individuals of all ages experience stress and try to deal with it. Stress arising from fearful situations occurs often in childhood, when a wide variety of fears develop (Sarafino, 1986). One of the more common fears of childhood is of thunderstorms. Psychologist Lois Murphy has described the progress a little girl made in dealing with this fear between the ages of 2 and 5:

1. As a two-year-old, Molly cried many times and was completely terrified during thunderstorms or when a jet plane passed overhead.
2. A year later she was able to get into bed with her older sister during a thunderstorm and accept comfort from her.
3. At about the same time Molly began to reassure herself (and her baby brother), saying, "It's just noise and it really won't hurt you a bit."
4. A month after this storm Molly was again terrified as a jet plane flew unusually low overhead; she cried and clung to her sister for comfort. A few hours later she repeated several times to herself, "Thunder really doesn't hurt you; it just sounds noisy. I'm not scared of planes, only thunder."
5. The next month she opened the door to her parents' room during a thunderstorm, say-

ing that her younger brother was afraid (although he was really fast asleep).

6. Nine months later, at four years and two months, she was awakened from a nap during a thunderstorm, but remained quietly in bed. Afterward she said to her sister, "There was lots of thunder, but I just snuggled in my bed and didn't cry a bit."
7. Four months later, at four and a half years, Molly showed no open fear herself during a storm, and comforted her frightened brother, saying, "I remember when I was a little baby and I was scared of thunder and I used to cry and cry every time it thundered." (1974, p. 76)

Although Molly's progress had some setbacks, such as when the plane flew very low, she became better able to cope effectively with this stressor as she got older. What is more, in the last steps of her progress she showed pride in having mastered her fear.

What is Coping?

Because the emotional and physical strain that accompanies stress is uncomfortable, people are motivated to do things to reduce their stress. These "things" are what is involved in coping.

What is coping? Several definitions of coping exist (Lazarus, 1987; Lazarus & Folkman, 1984b). We will use a definition that is consistent with the way we defined stress earlier. In Chapter 3 we saw that stress involves a *perceived discrepancy* between the demands of the situation and the resources of the person. Since people engage in coping in an effort to neutralize or reduce stress, coping activities are geared toward decreasing the person's appraisal of or concern for this discrepancy. Thus, **coping** is the process by which people try to *manage the perceived discrepancy* between the demands and resources they appraise in a stressful situation.

The word *manage* in this definition is important. It indicates that coping efforts can be quite varied and do not necessarily lead to a solution of the problem. Although coping efforts can—and, some would argue, should—be aimed at correcting or mastering the problem, they may also simply help the person alter his or her perception of a discrepancy, tolerate or accept the harm or threat, and escape or avoid the situation (Lazarus & Folkman, 1984b; Moos & Schaefer, 1986). For example, a child who faces a stressful exam in school might cope by feeling nauseated and staying home.

We cope with stress through the transactions we have with the environment. Suppose you have a job as a sales representative. Your sales have been disappointing, and your boss tells you they must improve. The implied threat is that you may lose your job. This is stressful. How might you cope with this? Some people would cope by seeking information about ways to improve their sales technique. Other people would simply find another job. Others would attribute their disappointing sales to fate or "the will of God" and leave the problem "in His hands." Still others would try to deaden their feelings with alcohol or drugs. People use many different methods to try to manage the appraised discrepancy between the demands of the situation and their resources.

The coping process is not a single event. Because coping involves ongoing transactions with the environment, the process is best viewed as a dynamic series

> of continuous appraisals and reappraisals of the shifting person–environment relationships. Shifts may be the result of coping efforts directed at changing the environment, or coping directed inward that changes the meaning of the event or increases understanding. They may also be the result of changes in the environment that are independent of the person and his or her coping activity. Regardless of its source, any shift in the person–environment relationship will lead to a reevaluation of what is happening, its significance, and what can be done. The reevaluation process, or reappraisal, in turn influences subsequent coping efforts. (Lazarus & Folkman, 1984b, pp. 142–143)

And so, in coping with the job stress of disappointing sales, people who make efforts to improve their performance may receive encouragement and better relationships with the boss. But individuals who resort to alcohol to cope are likely to experience worse and worse relationships. Each shift in one direction or the other is affected by the transactions that preceded it and affects subsequent transactions.

Functions and Methods of Coping

You have probably realized by now that people have an enormous number of ways for coping with stress. Because of this, researchers have attempted to organize coping approaches on the basis of their functions and the methods they employ.

Functions of Coping

According to Richard Lazarus and his colleagues, coping can serve two main functions (Cohen & Lazarus, 1979; Lazarus & Folkman, 1984b; Lazarus & Launier, 1978). It can alter the *problem* causing the stress or it can regulate the *emotional* response to the problem.

Emotion-focused coping is aimed at controlling the emotional response to the stressful situation. People can regulate their emotional response through behavioral and cognitive approaches. Some examples of behavioral approaches are using alcohol or drugs, seeking social support from friends or relatives, and engaging in activities, such as sports or watching TV, that distract one's attention from the problem. Cognitive approaches involve how people think about the stressful situation. One cognitive approach involves changing the meaning of the situation — for example, by deciding that "There are worse things in life than having to change jobs because of my heart condition" or "Now that my girlfriend has left me, I realize that I really didn't need her." Another cognitive approach involves denying unpleasant facts, as Beth did with the lump on her breast.

People tend to use emotion-focused approaches when they believe that they can do nothing to change the stressful conditions (Lazarus & Folkman, 1984b). A clear example of this is when a loved one dies — in this situation, people often seek emotional support and distract themselves with funeral arrangements and chores at home or at work. Other examples can be seen in situations in which individuals believe their resources are not and cannot be adequate to meet the demands of the stressor. A child who tries very hard to be the "straight A" student his or her parents seem to want, but never succeeds, may reappraise the situation and decide that "I don't need their love."

Problem-focused coping is aimed at reducing the demands of the stressful situation or expanding the resources to deal with it. Everyday life provides many examples of problem-focused coping, including quitting a stressful job, negotiating an extension for paying some bills, devising a new schedule for studying (and sticking to it), choosing a different career to pursue, seeking medical or psychological treatment, and learning new skills. People tend to use problem-focused approaches when they believe that their resources or the demands of the situation are changeable (Lazarus & Folkman, 1984b).

Can problem-focused and emotion-focused coping be used together? Yes, and people often

Reprinted with special permission of King Features Syndicate, Inc.

Sometimes people don't cope effectively with stress.

do. Let's look at an example that involves a case in which an employee experienced stress when he was accused by a coworker of not sending out the appropriate letters for a job. In describing how he reacted to this accusation, he said:

> "Well, it burned me up. . . . My immediate first reaction was to confirm . . . that what he was saying was not true, that everything [letters] had gone out. There's always a chance you might be wrong so I checked first. Then I told him. No, everything had gone out. My immediate reaction was to call him on the carpet first. He doesn't have any right to call me on something like this. Then I gave it a second thought and decided that that wouldn't help the situation. (Kahn et al., cited in Lazarus & Folkman, 1984b, p. 155)

This example shows problem-focused coping in confirming that the letters had gone out, and emotion-focused coping in controlling his angry impulse "to call him on the carpet."

Methods of Coping: Skills and Strategies

What types of skills and strategies do people use in altering the problem or regulating their emotional response when they experience stress? We will look at some of the more commonly used methods, which were drawn from three sources (Cohen & Lazarus, 1979; Moos & Schaefer, 1986; Pearlin & Schooler, 1978).

The first of these methods, called **direct action**, involves doing something specifically and directly to cope with a stressor. It includes the approaches we described as problem-focused coping—for example, negotiating or consulting—and other actions, such as arguing, running away, or punishing someone. But even activity that is unrelated to the problem or threat can be helpful in coping during stressful periods (Gal & Lazarus, 1975). For instance, it can help in regulating emotional states by distracting the person from the problem.

Another method, **seeking information**, in-

HIGHLIGHT 5A: On Research
People's Focuses in Coping

To what extent do people use problem-focused and emotion-focused approaches in coping with stress in their lives? This was a basic question in a study by Andrew Billings and Rudolf Moos (1981). The researchers mailed questionnaires to 360 families in the San Francisco Bay Area. For almost 200 of the families, both the husbands and their wives responded—these people were the subjects in the study.

The subjects were asked to indicate a personal crisis or negative life event that happened to them in the past year. Then they answered "yes" or "no" to 19 items regarding how they handled the situation. Some of the items described problem-focused approaches, for example:

- Considered several alternatives for handling the problem
- Tried to find out more about the situation.
- Talked with a professional person (e.g., doctor, clergy, lawyer) about the situation.

Other items described emotion-focused approaches, such as:

- Tried to see the positive side.
- Sometimes took it out on other people when I felt angry or depressed.
- Got busy with other things in order to keep my mind off the problem.

The outcomes of this research revealed some interesting relationships. Both the husbands and the wives used more of the problem-focused approaches than the emotion-focused methods to cope with the stressful event. But the wives reported using more of the emotion-focused approaches than the husbands did. Subjects with higher incomes and educational levels reported greater use of problem-focused coping than those with less income and education. Lastly, the subjects used much less problem-focused coping when the stress involved a death in the family than when it involved other kinds of problems, such as illness or economic difficulties.

---

volves acquiring knowledge about the stressful situation — knowledge that can then be used in promoting problem-focused or emotion-focused coping. For example, women who have been sexually assaulted may seek information about legal procedures, which might be useful in problem-focused activities, such as deciding whether to testify in court. They may also seek information about who is "responsible" for rape. Since many assaulted women blame themselves, knowledge about responsibility may be helpful in regulating their emotional reactions.

Two other methods are called turning to others and resigned acceptance. In **turning to others**, the person seeks help, reassurance, and comfort from family, friends, or other people. The help that is received may be useful in problem-focused coping, as a loan would be when the stressor is a financial crisis. Reassurance and comfort are important in emotion-focused coping. In **resigned acceptance**, the person comes to terms with the problem situation and accepts it as it is. This method is especially suitable in emotion-focused coping, when the basic circumstances of the stressor cannot be changed, such as when the person loses a limb in an accident or suffers the loss of a loved one.

Emotional discharge is a method in which people express their feelings or reduce their tension when under stress. This can include screaming when angry, crying, and "using jokes and gallows humor to help allay constant strain" (Moos & Schaefer, 1986, p. 18). An example of the humor people use in coping comes from a man who jokingly nicknamed himself "Semicolon" after part of his colon was removed in an operation for cancer. The method of emotional discharge can also include using cigarettes, alcohol, and drugs to reduce tension. Research has shown that people use these substances in their efforts toward emotion-focused coping (Wills, 1986).

The last method we will consider, called **intrapsychic processes**, uses cognitive strategies to reappraise a stressful situation. There is a wide variety of such strategies, and they are particularly useful in regulating emotional reactions. *Cognitive redefinition* is a strategy whereby people try to put a good face on a bad situation, such as by noting that things could be worse, making comparisons with individuals who are less well off, or seeing something good growing out of the problem. We can see this approach in the following statements of women with breast cancer (Taylor, 1983):

> What you do is put things into perspective. You find out that things like relationships are really the most important things you have — the people you know and your family — everything else is just way down the line. It's very strange that it takes something so serious to make you realize that. (p. 1163)

> The people I really feel sorry for are these young gals. To lose a breast when you're so young must be awful. I'm 73; what do I need a breast for? (p. 1166)

People who want to redefine a stressful situation can generally find a way to do it since there is almost always *some* dimension or aspect of one's life that can be turned into a positive viewpoint (Taylor, 1983).

Other intrapsychic processes include the cognitive strategies Freud called "defense mechanisms," which involve distorting memory or reality in some way. For instance, when something is too painful to face, the person may deny that it exists. This defense mechanism is called *denial*. In medical situations, individuals who are diagnosed with a terminal disease often use this strategy and refuse to believe they are really ill. Another defense mechanism, called *intellectualization*, consists of dealing with or confronting a stressor on an abstract, intellectual level. Nurses and physicians who have to deal with enormous amounts of human suffering need some way to detach their emotions from these situations. They may intellectualize, for example, by referring to a patient dying of liver cancer as "the liver in 203." One other defense mechanism we will consider is *suppression* — the deliberate effort to put a stressful memory out of one's mind. Here, the person consciously controls painful thoughts, sometimes verbalizing the method: "I won't think about how he's hurt me," for instance. Suppression can be useful in temporarily pushing aside these memories in order to get on with other activities of life.

You may have noticed that some of the methods people use in coping with stress tend to increase the *attention* they give to the problem. Direct action and seeking information generally do this. Other methods, particularly intrapsychic processes, tend to promote *avoidance* of the problem. Both approaches can be beneficial under some circumstances. Intrapsychic processes, such as denial, are beneficial when there is little the person can do about the problem (Cohen & Lazarus, 1979; Lazarus, 1983). For instance, a study examined the coping strategies of women after they had undergone a mastectomy for breast cancer. Patients who avoided thinking about cancer and minimized the impact of their illness showed less evidence of distress than those who did not use avoidance strategies (Meyerowitz, 1983). But if the person *can* do something about the problem, failing to give it attention can be more harmful than helpful, as we saw in Beth's denial of the lump in her breast at the beginning of the chapter.

The time frame for using attention or avoidance strategies is also important. Jerry Suls and Barbara Fletcher (1985) examined and combined the results of a large number of studies. Their analysis led to two conclusions. First, avoidance strategies can benefit coping mainly in the short run, such as during an early stage of a prolonged stress experience. This is the case for individuals who are diagnosed with a serious illness, for instance. Second, as time goes by, attention strategies become more effective than avoidance in the coping process. As a rule of thumb, the effectiveness of avoidance methods seems to be limited to the first couple of weeks of a prolonged stress experience. Thereafter, coping is better served by attention strategies.

Our discussion indicates that there is no one best method of coping. No single method is uniformly applied or effective with all stressful situations (Ilfeld, 1980; Menaghan, 1982; Pearlin & Schooler, 1978). Research has revealed two important patterns in the way people cope. First, individuals tend to be consistent in the way they cope with a particular type of stressor—that is, when faced with the same problem, people tend to use the same methods they used in the past (Stone & Neale, 1984). Second, people seldom use just one method to cope with a stressor. Their efforts typically involve a combination of strategies. Thus, for example, when faced with a stressful situation, most people use attention strategies, such as direct action, along with avoidance methods, such as intellectualization (Holahan & Moos, 1985). The degree to which individuals rely on avoidance strategies may have important health implications. A one-year prospective study compared people who differed in their reported use of avoidance coping approaches. Of the subjects who experienced a high degree of stress during the intervening year, those who had reported a greater tendency to use avoidance methods had, at the end of the study, more psychosomatic symptoms, for example, headaches and acid stomach (Holahan & Moos, 1986).

Developing Methods of Coping

Psychologists have long assumed that coping changes across the life span. But the nature of these changes is unclear because there is little systematic research, especially longitudinal studies, charting these changes (Lazarus & DeLongis, 1983; Lazarus & Folkman, 1984b).

Some aspects of the changes in coping that occur in the early years are known. Infants and toddlers do not cope very effectively with stress. As we saw earlier in the case of Molly, young children develop coping skills that enable them to overcome many of their fears. The skills she acquired often made use of her expanding cognitive abilities, such as in thinking logically and in using language. Marion Hyson (1983) studied the coping behavior of infants and children who ranged from 6 months to 5 years in age at examinations by their pediatricians. Infants and toddlers tended to react to the doctor by trying to stop the examination — by protesting, pushing the doctor's hand away, or kicking the doctor. The older children showed much less protest and allowed the checkup to be completed. But *after* the examination was over, they showed negative behaviors: "This is a naughty shirt," a 5-year-old remarked as she dressed, "I do not like it." The 4- and 5-year-olds seemed to delay their negative reaction and direct it elsewhere ("naughty shirt"), rather than showing immediate and direct resistance.

Over the next several years, children come to rely increasingly on cognitive strategies for coping (Brown, O'Keeffe, Sanders, & Baker, 1985; Miller & Green, 1984). So, for example, they learn to think about something else to distract themselves from stress. More and more, they regulate their emotions with intrapsychic processes, such as cognitive redefinition — for instance, saying to themselves, "I can do it," while preparing to give a speech. But children's improving cognitive abilities do not always lead to reduced stress. Young children's lack of understanding about the concept of death seems to protect them from the grief that older children experience at the death of a loved one, such as their parent (Garmezy, 1983; Rutter, 1983).

Few studies have examined changes in methods of coping from adolescence to old age. One study used interviews and questionnaires to compare the daily hassles and coping methods of middle-aged and elderly men and women (Folkman, Lazarus, Pimley, & Novacek, 1987). The middle-aged men and women used more problem-focused forms of coping, whereas the elderly subjects used more emotion-focused approaches. For example, the middle-aged people were more likely to report coping with stress in a confrontive and direct manner — claiming such actions as "Stood my ground and fought for what I wanted" and "I made a plan of action and followed it." The elderly individuals were more likely to report passive and defensive approaches — claiming such approaches as "Went on as if nothing happened" and "Wished that the situation would go away or somehow be over with."

Why do adults shift from problem-focused to emotion-focused coping as they get older? These changes probably result at least in part from differences in what people must cope with as they age. The elderly subjects in this study were retired from full-time work and reported more stress relating to health and home maintenance than the middle-aged people did; the middle-aged individuals reported more stress relating to work, finances, and family and friends. Direct action and confrontation are probably more effective strategies for coping with the kinds of stressors encountered by middle-aged than by elderly people. But there was also a difference in the outlook of the two age groups: regardless of the source of stress, the elderly people appraised their problems as *less* changeable than the middle-aged subjects did. As we saw earlier, people tend to use problem-focused approaches when they believe the situation is changeable, and rely on emotion-focused coping when they do not.

We have examined many ways people cope with stress. Each method can be effective and adaptive for the individual if it neutralizes the current stressor and does not increase the likelihood of future stressful situations. Sometimes the way people cope can *reduce* the potential impact of stressors they experience. Consider the situation in which a customer receives a phone bill that has an error. Although many people appraise the hassles in this kind of situation as stressful, a person who often uses humor to cope may appraise this situation differently, perhaps finding it almost amusing (Folkman, Lazarus, Pimley, & Novacek, 1987). In the next section, we consider how people can reduce the potential for stress for themselves and for others.

REDUCING THE POTENTIAL FOR STRESS

Can people become "immune" to the impact of stress to some extent? Some aspects of people's lives can reduce the potential for stressors to develop and help individuals cope with problems when they occur. Prevention is the first line of defense against the impact of stress. We will look at several ways people can help themselves and others prevent and cope with stress. The first approach makes use of the beneficial effects of social support.

Enhancing Social Support

We have all turned to others for help and comfort when under stress at some time in our lives. If you have ever had to endure troubled times on your own, you know how important social support can be. But social support is not only helpful after stressors appear, it also can help avert problems in the first place. Consider, for example, the tangible or instrumental support newlyweds receive when they get married. The gifts they receive include many of the things the couple will need to set up a household. Without these things, the couple would be saddled either with the financial burden of buying the items or with the hassles of not having them.

Although there are people in all walks of life who lack the social support they need, some segments of the population seem to have less than others (Antonucci, 1985; Broadhead et al., 1983). For instance:

- Social networks tend to be smaller for men than for women.
- Many elderly individuals live in isolated conditions and have few people on whom to rely.
- Network size is related to social prestige, income, and education: the lower the prestige, income, and education level of individuals, the smaller their social networks tend to be.

Furthermore, the networks of people from lower socioeconomic classes are usually less diverse than those of people from higher classes, that is, lower class networks contain fewer nonkin members. In contemporary American society, the traditional sources of support have shifted to include greater reliance on individuals in social and helping organizations. As Marc Pilisuk has noted, "the geographic proximity and the functions of the modern extended family have changed substantially, and do not typically provide the same protective buffer associated with large families in the preindustrial era" (1982, p. 26).

Social support is a dynamic process. People's needs for, giving of, and receipt of support change over time. Some factors within the individual determine whether he or she will receive or provide social support when it is needed (Broadhead et al., 1983; Wortman & Dunkel-Schetter, 1987). One factor is the person's temperament. People differ in their need for and interest in social contact and affiliation. Those individuals who tend to seek interaction

Many elderly people are isolated and lack the social support they need.

with others are more likely to give and receive support than those who do not. To some extent, these tendencies are determined by the experiences people have. Children who grow up in a caring family and have good relations with peers learn the social skills needed to seek help and give it when needed. But research has found that people who report that they are coping well with stressful events in their lives "are more likely to be regarded as attractive by others and less likely to be avoided than those who indicate that they are having some difficulties coping. The implications of these results are depressing, because they suggest that those in greatest need for social support may be least likely to get it" (Wortman & Dunkel-Schetter, 1987, p. 98).

Efforts to enhance people's ability to give and receive social support can begin in early childhood, particularly at school (Broadhead et al., 1983). One approach teachers can use is to have children engage in cooperative games that promote prolonged interactions with one another. Mara Sapon-Shevin has identified four types of specific behaviors that teachers can help children learn:

1. Talking nicely to classmates: calling classmates only by names they like, noticing and commenting on classmates' strengths rather than weaknesses.
2. Sharing and taking turns.
3. Including children who have been left out; opening one's games or activities to others, finding a part for another child to play.
4. Touching other children gently; helping other children who have fallen down or who are experiencing difficulty. (1980, p. 235)

She also described a variety of suitable games the teacher can use, such as having the children sit in a circle and construct a story, with each child contributing a little piece to it in sequence. Children's storybooks can also be used for having the children point out when someone needs help or comfort and how to provide it.

In adulthood, people can enhance their ability to give and receive social support by joining community organizations, such as social, religious, special interest, and self-help groups. These organizations have the advantage of bringing together individuals with similar problems and interests, which can become the basis for sharing, helping, and friendship. There is a wide variety of nationally known self-help groups, including Alcoholics Anonymous and Parents without Partners, and special interest groups, including the American Association of Retired People and the Gray Panthers. Isolated people of all ages—especially the elderly—can be encouraged to join suitable organizations.

An interesting community education program called *Friends Can Be Good Medicine* was introduced throughout the state of California (Taylor, Lam, Roppel, & Barter, 1984). Its main objectives were to inform the public about the benefits of supportive relationships for mental and physical health and to encourage people to develop social networks. The program distributed educational materials, organized local activities, and arranged for radio and TV discussions and public service announcements to promote these objectives. Telephone interviews to assess the impact of the program on people's knowledge, attitudes, and behavior regarding social relationships revealed positive changes that were maintained over time. Communities can play a clear and valuable role in enhancing people's resources for social support.

Social support in occupational settings is also important, and employers can help improve support systems on the job (Quick & Quick, 1984). They can do this in many ways, such as by organizing workers in teams or work groups, providing facilities for recreation and fitness training during lunch time or other nonwork hours, arranging social events for workers and their families on weekends, and providing counseling services to help employees through troubled times. Some bosses get so caught up in the role of "manager" that they fail to give the personal support their subordinates need. A supportive boss discusses

HIGHLIGHT 5B: On Issues
The Amish Way of Social Support in Bereavement

The Amish people form a conservative religious sect that settled originally in Pennsylvania in the eighteenth century. Amish families generally live in colonies that now exist in about 20 states and Canada. These families have a strongly religious orientation and a serious work ethic that centers around farming. Their way of life is quite distinctive: they wear uniquely simple and uniform clothing; speak mainly a Pennsylvania-German dialect; and reject modern devices, using horse-driven buggies instead of automobiles, for example. Their social lives require their adherence to strict rules of conduct and obedience to patriarchal authority.

One feature of Amish life is that they give assistance to one another in all times of need. Their way of dealing with death provides a good example, as Kathleen Bryer (1986) has studied and described. Before death, a person who is seriously ill receives care from his or her family. This almost always occurs at home, rather than in a hospital. The Amish not only expect to give this care, but see it as a positive opportunity. A married woman who was asked about caring for a dying relative replied, "Oh yes, we had the chance to take care of all four of our old parents before they died. We are both so thankful for this" (p. 251). The experience of death typically occurs at home, in the presence of the family.

Upon the death, the Amish community swings into action. Close neighbors notify other members of the colony, and the community makes most of the funeral arrangements. The family receives visits of sympathy and support from other Amish families, some of whom come from other colonies far away and may not even know the bereaved family. In contrast to the social support most Americans receive in bereavement, Amish supportive efforts do not end shortly after the funeral—they continue at a high level for at least a year. Supportive activities include evening and Sunday visiting, making items and scrapbooks for the family, and organized quilting projects that create fellowship around a common task. Moreover, Amish individuals often give extraordinary help to bereaved family members. For instance, the sister of one widower came to live with him and care for his four children until he remarried. The community encourages widowed individuals to remarry in time, and they often do so.

The Amish provide social support to one another in many ways, as when they build a barn for a member of their colony.

decisions and problems with employees, compliments subordinates and gives them credit for good work, and stands behind reasonable decisions they make (Kobasa, 1986). Less supportive bosses can make a conscious effort to improve these behaviors.

Although social support is generally helpful and appreciated, it isn't always. As we saw in Chapter 4, well-meaning efforts by friends and relatives can undermine good health habits and impair the recovery of people who are ill. Social support can also be ineffective if the recipient interprets it as a sign of inadequacy, feels uncomfortable about not being able to reciprocate, or believes his or her personal control is limited by it (Cohen & McKay, 1983). Providing effective social support requires sensitivity and good judgment.

Improving One's Personal Control and Hardiness

When life becomes stressful, people who lack a strong sense of personal control may stop trying, thinking, "Oh, what's the use." Instead of feeling they have power and control, they feel helpless and afraid that their efforts will lead to failure and embarrassment. This outlook increases people's potential for stress and can have a negative effect on their health. How can a person's sense of control be enhanced? The process can begin very early. Parents, teachers, and other caregivers can show a child their love and respect, provide a stimulating environment, encourage and praise the child's accomplishments, and set reasonable standards of conduct and performance that he or she can regard as challenges, rather than threats.

Adults' personal control can be enhanced, too. Employers can help by giving workers some degree of control over aspects of their jobs (Quick & Quick, 1984). One approach involves having employees work in groups to make certain managerial decisions or solve problems, such as how to improve the quality of the product they manufacture. Other approaches include allowing workers to have some control over their work hours, which tasks to work on, and the order in which they do them. Similarly, nursing homes and families can allow elderly individuals to do things for themselves and have responsibilities, such as in cleaning, cooking, and arranging social activities. One woman described the prospect of living with her children in the following way: "I couldn't stand to live with my children, as much as I love them, because they always want to take over my life" (Shupe, 1985).

Personal control is an important component of hardiness—is it possible to train people to become more hardy? Salvatore Maddi and Suzanne Kobasa have designed a program to do just that (Fischman, 1987; Kobasa, 1986). It consists of three techniques:

- *Focusing.* Because people are so used to the signs of strain in their bodies, such as neck muscle tightness, they may be only vaguely aware of their stress. Focusing on various body sensations can help identify times of stress and, thereby, enable the person to consider what the source might be.
- *Reconstructing stressful situations.* This technique has the person think about a recent stressful situation and make two short lists: ways it could have turned out better and ways it might have turned out worse. Doing this allows the person to examine alternative courses of action and realize that "it could be worse."
- *Compensating through self-improvement.* When people face a stressor that they cannot avoid or change, it may be helpful for them to take on a new challenge that they are likely to master. Doing so reassures them that they can still cope.

Although the evidence for the effectiveness of this program so far is limited, people who have completed it appear to score higher on a test of hardiness, report feeling less distress, and have lower blood pressure than before.

Organizing One's World Better

"Where did I put my keys?" You have probably heard someone ask this frantically while running late to make an appointment. People often feel stress because they are running late or "don't have enough time" to do the tasks of the day. They need to organize their worlds to make things happen efficiently. This can take the form of designating certain places for certain items—"A place for everything, and everything in its place"—or putting materials in alphabetized file folders, for instance. Organizing one's world reduces frustration, wasted time, and the potential for stress.

An important approach for organizing one's time is called **time management**. It consists of three elements (Lakein, 1973). The first element is to *set goals.* These goals should be reasonable or obtainable ones, and they should include long-term goals, such as getting a job promotion next year, and short-term ones, such as meeting a weekly sales quota. The second element involves making daily *To Do* lists with priorities indicated, keeping the goals in mind. These lists should be composed early each morning or late in the preceding day. Each list must be written—trying to keep the list in your head is unreliable and makes setting priorities difficult. The third element is to set up a *schedule* for the day, allocating estimated time periods to each item in the list. If an urgent new task arises during the day, the list should be adjusted to include it.

Exercising to Increase Fitness

You have probably heard from TV, radio, magazine, and newspaper reports that exercise and physical fitness can protect people from the harmful effects of stress on health. These reports cite a wide range of benefits from increased intellectual functioning and personal control to decreased anxiety, depression, hostility, and tension. Do exercise and fitness reduce the potential for stress and its effects on health?

Most studies of this question have used correlational or retrospective methods, and show that people who exercise or are physically fit often report less anxiety, depression, and tension in their lives than do people who do not exercise or are less fit (Blumenthal & McCubbin, 1987; Dishman, 1986). Although these results are consistent with the view that exercise and fitness reduce the potential for stress, they do not tell us what causes what. Do exercise and fitness cause people to feel less stress? Or do people who experience high levels of stress lack the time and motivation to exercise and keep fit? Or are other factors involved? These questions cannot be answered using correlational or retrospective methods. Fortunately, there is stronger evidence for the beneficial effects of exercise and fitness.

An experiment by Bram Goldwater and Martin Collis (1985) examined the effects of exercise on cardiovascular fitness and feelings of anxiety in males between 19 and 30 years of age. The subjects were randomly assigned to one of two groups after they were shown to be in good health by a medical examination. In one group, the subjects worked out five days a week in a vigorous fitness program. Their exercises included swimming and active sports, such as soccer. Subjects in the second group had a more moderate fitness program. They met twice a week and engaged in less demanding exercise activities, such as badminton. Both groups participated in their programs for six weeks and were tested for cardiovascular fitness and anxiety before and after participating. Compared with the subjects in the moderate program, those in the vigorous program showed greater gains in fitness and reductions in anxiety. Other researchers have found similar beneficial effects of exercise on anxiety with middle-aged adults (Blumenthal, Williams, Needles, & Wallace, 1982).

Research has also assessed the effects of exercise on blood pressure and heart rate. Once again, most of the evidence is correlational, revealing that people who exercise or are physically fit show less cardiovascular reactivity to stressors and are less likely to be hypertensive than individuals who do not exercise or are less fit (Dimsdale, Alpert, & Schneiderman, 1986; Martin & Dubbert, 1985). But some studies have used experimental methods. Garry Jennings and his colleagues (1986) conducted an experiment with healthy 19- to 27-year-old individuals who had sedentary occupations and had not regularly engaged in vigorous physical activity in the previous year. Over the next four months, the subjects spent one month at each of four levels of activity: (1) their sedentary normal activity; (2) below-normal activity, which included two weeks of rest in a hospital setting; (3) above-normal activity, which involved their normal activity plus three sessions of vigorous exercise weekly; and (4) much-above-normal activity, consisting of their normal activity plus daily vigorous exercise. Each exercise period lasted 40 minutes. Measurements of heart rate and blood pressure were taken after each month, when the subjects came in to the laboratory and rested before beginning the next activity level. The results demonstrated that regular exercise lowers heart rate and both systolic and diastolic blood pressure—all three measures were lower for subjects following the above-normal and much-above-normal activity months than following the normal and below-normal months.

We need to consider one more link in reviewing the protective effects of exercise and fitness against the impact of stress on health. That is, do exercise and fitness prevent people from developing stress-related illnesses? The results of two studies suggest that they do. One of these studies used retrospective methods with men who reported having experienced either high or low levels of stress in the past three years (Kobasa, Maddi, & Puccetti, 1982). Those men who scored higher on a survey of their exercise practices reported less illness during the three-year period than those who had lower scores on exercise, and these protective effects were greater for subjects with high levels of stress than for those with less stress. The other study used prospective methods by first assessing the subjects' recent life events and fitness, and then having them keep records concerning their health over the next nine weeks (Roth & Holmes, 1985). The results revealed that individuals who reported high levels of stress had poorer subsequent health if they were not fit; stress had little impact on the health of fit subjects.

Preparing for Stressful Events

In this and previous chapters we have discussed a wide variety of stressful events, ranging from being stuck in traffic, to starting day care or school, being overloaded with work, selling a house, going through a divorce, and experiencing a disaster. Can people reduce the potential for stress by preparing in some way for the event?

Irving Janis (1958) pioneered the psychological study of the need to prepare people for stressful events, such as surgery. In one study, he found that patients with moderate levels of anxiety before the surgery showed better adjustment after the operation than did those with either very high or very low anxiety. From this finding, Janis proposed that some degree of anticipatory worry about a stressful event is adaptive because it motivates coping via the process he called the *work of worrying*. He described three steps in this process: The person first receives information about the event, which generates anxiety; then develops expectations by rehearsing the event mentally; and then mobilizes coping techniques in an effort to become reassured of a successful outcome. Patients with too little anxiety are not motivated enough to complete the process, and those with too much anxiety are distracted or immobilized by their fear.

Subsequent research has confirmed some, but not all, of Janis' findings and theory. In particular, this research has shown that low levels of anxiety do not impair patients' success in coping with or recovery from surgery. The overall picture from this research indicates that the higher the *pre*operative fear of patients, the worse their *post*operative adjustment and recovery tend to be (Anderson & Masur, 1983; Johnson, 1983). These postoperative outcomes have been shown for a variety of measures, including:

- The patient's self-reported pain
- Amount of medication taken to relieve pain
- Self-reported anxiety or depression
- Length of hospital stay after surgery
- Ratings by hospital staff of the patient's recovery or adjustment

These poorer postoperative outcomes of patients with high levels of anxiety suggest that helping patients cope with their preoperative concerns could enhance later adjustment and recovery.

Many studies have been done to determine what methods are effective in preparing people psychologically for surgery. Some methods have involved brief *psychotherapy*, in which patients express their worries and receive emotional support and reassurance. But the effectiveness of these approaches is, as yet, unclear (Anderson & Masur, 1983). Other methods have involved *hypnosis*, such as by giving the patient the suggestion under hypnosis that the postoperative pain will not be very severe. These methods seem promising for patients who are hypnotically suggestible, but more research is needed to determine when and how best to apply them (Anderson & Masur, 1983; Barber, 1986).

The most clearly effective methods in preparing people for the stress of surgery are those designed to enhance the patients' feelings of *control* (Anderson & Masur, 1983; Mathews & Ridgeway, 1984). One approach attempts to improve patients' *behavioral control* by teaching them how to reduce discomfort or promote rehabilitation through specific actions they can take, such as by doing leg exercises to improve strength or deep breathing exercises to reduce pain. Another method is designed to enhance patients' *cognitive control*, for instance, by instructing them on ways to concentrate on the pleasant or beneficial aspects of the surgery, rather than the unpleasant aspects. One other method involves *informational control*, in which patients receive information about the procedures and/or sensations they will experience. Each of these and other control-enhancing methods is effective in promoting postoperative adjustment and recovery. (We will examine these methods in greater detail in Chapter 10, when we discuss hospital treatment.)

Although enhanced control can be helpful in reducing the potential for stress, these methods need to be applied carefully to prevent some possible negative effects from occurring. One consideration is that sometimes information that is meant to reassure people and reduce stress can have the opposite effect. As psychologist Suzanne Thompson has described:

> The Los Angeles City Council had placed cards in the city elevators assuring riders that they should stay calm, since "there is little danger of the car dropping uncontrollably or running out of air". . . . A year later the cards had to be removed because of complaints from elevator riders that the message made them anxious. Apparently most people had not worried about these dangers until they read the card meant to reassure them. (1981, p. 96)

Another consideration is whether a person can have *too much* control. There is some evidence that having too much information, for example, can be confusing and actually arouse fear. Young children who receive a great deal of information about the medical procedures they will undergo often become more anxious (Miller & Green, 1984). With children in dental or medical settings, it is generally best not to give a lot of detail, particularly distressing detail. Describing some sensory experiences to expect is especially helpful, such as the sounds of equipment or the tingly feeling from the dental anesthetic.

In summary, we have discussed several methods that are helpful in reducing the potential for stress and, thereby, benefiting health. These methods take advantage of the stress-moderating effects of social support, personal control, exercise, being well organized, and being prepared for an impending stressor. In

HIGHLIGHT 5C: On Issues
Preparing a Child to Start Day Care or School

Beginning day care or school is a major event that is often stressful for children. It represents an important and frequently sudden transition into a new "world" where they must function separately and independently from their parents. Although many children are fearful when they begin, parents can do things to prepare the child and make the transition easier. Here are some ways parents can help (from Sarafino, 1986):

- Maintain a positive attitude about day care and school, and convey this attitude to the child.
- Familiarize the child with the place in advance. Take the child there to play in the yard, pick up an older sibling or neighbor child, or just to see "the place." Try to have the child meet the teacher and see the classroom. Find out some of the games and activities the child will take part in during the first week or two, and do some of them at home.
- Take care of administrative details and paperwork in advance so you can be free to help the child feel comfortable when the separation begins.
- If the child is starting day care, make transportation arrangements in advance. Many children will worry that their parents have abandoned them—if the person who is to pick up the child is late, this worry becomes aggravated.
- If the child is beginning kindergarten, determine how he or she will get there. Familiarize the child with the trip.
- A familiar person who has a positive attitude about beginning day care or school should accompany the child on the first day. Ideally this person would be one of the parents. This companion should stay with the child for a while and encourage the child to take part in the activities. If the child has no difficulty, simply delivering the child to the classroom for the next day or two may be sufficient. If the child shows a little difficulty, the companion should stay with the child for a while, encourage the child to take part in the activities, and spend less and less time there on each of the next few days.
- Parents who expect that their child will have some trouble starting day care or school—the child is very shy or there are problems at home, for example—should discuss this with the teacher or caregiver in advance. These individuals need to know what to expect and can offer helpful suggestions.

Infants and very young children who have had experience playing with age-mates often have an easier time with being separated from their parents than those who have not. Experience with babysitters and other people also helps.

---

the next section, we consider ways to reduce the reaction to stress once it has begun.

REDUCING STRESS REACTIONS: STRESS MANAGEMENT

People acquire coping skills through their experiences, which may involve strategies they have tried in the past or methods they have seen others use. But sometimes the skills they have learned are not adequate for a current stressor because it is so strong, novel, or unrelenting. In some cases, the approaches they have acquired reduce stress in the short run—as alcohol or drug use can do—but are not adaptive and increase stress in the long run. These problems in coping often arise in individuals whose potential for stress is high because of a lack of social support, personal control, and so on; but coping problems also happen among people whose potential for stress is relatively low. When people cannot cope effectively, they need help in learning new and adaptive ways of managing stress.

A variety of techniques are available to help individuals manage stress. Many of these techniques are psychological, but sometimes *pharmacological* approaches are used under medical supervision. Of the several classes of drugs physicians prescribe to help patients manage stress, we will consider two: benzodiazepines and beta-blockers. Both of these drugs reduce physiological arousal and feelings of anxiety (Priest, 1986; Shapiro, Krantz, & Grim, 1986). *Benzodiazepines*, which include drugs with the trade names Valium and Librium, appear to work by activating a neurotransmitter that decreases neural transmission in the central nervous system. *Beta-blockers*, such as Inderal, appear to block the activity of sympathetic neurons in the peripheral nervous system that are stimulated by epinephrine and norepinephrine. Beta-blockers cause less drowsiness than benzodiazepines, probably because their action is peripheral rather than central. Using drugs to manage stress is generally recommended only as a temporary measure, either to help during an acute crisis, such as in the week or two following the death of a loved one, or while the patient learns new psychological methods for coping.

Behavioral and Cognitive Methods

Psychologists have developed methods they can train people to use in coping with stress. Some of these techniques focus mainly on the person's behavior, and some give greater attention to the person's thinking processes. People who use these methods usually find them helpful.

Relaxation and Systematic Desensitization

The opposite of arousal is relaxation — so relaxing should be a good way to reduce stress. "Perhaps so," you say, "but when stress appears, relaxing is easier said than done." Actually, relaxing when under stress is not so hard to do when you know how. People can learn to control their feelings of tension by using a technique called **progressive muscle relaxation**, in which they focus their attention on specific muscle groups while alternately tightening and relaxing these muscles.

The idea of teaching people to relax their skeletal muscles in order to reduce psychological stress was proposed many years ago by Edmund Jacobson (1938). He developed a device to measure electrical activity in muscle fibers. Using this device, he found that subjects would reduce the tension in their muscles when simply asked to "sit and relax." He later found that muscle tension could be reduced much more if the subjects were taught to pay attention to the sensations as they tense and relax individual groups of muscles. The findings of a recent study indicate that one reason muscle relaxation reduces psychological stress is that the technique tends to arouse pleasant thoughts in the person (Peveler & Johnston, 1986).

Although there are various versions of the progressive muscle relaxation technique, they each outline a particular sequence of muscle groups for the person to follow. For example, the sequence might begin with the person relaxing the hands, then the forehead, followed by the lower face, the neck, the stomach, and, finally, the legs. For each muscle group, the person first tenses the muscles for 7 – 10 seconds, and then relaxes them for about 15 seconds, paying attention to how the muscles feel. This is usually repeated for the same muscle group two or three times in a relaxation session, which generally lasts 20 or 30 minutes. The relaxation technique works best in a quiet, nondistracting setting with the person lying down or sitting on comfortable furniture.

Some people seem to think stress management applies only to adults, as if children don't experience stress or have difficulty coping. As we have seen, however, children do experience stress but often lack the skills they need to deal with it effectively. Fortunately, many behavioral and cognitive methods are easy to learn and can be adapted so that an adult can teach a young child to do them. The relaxation procedure provides a good example. An adult could start by showing the child what relaxing is like by lifting and then releasing the arms and legs of a rag doll, allowing them to fall down. Then, as the following brief version of the technique describes, the adult might say:

1. "OK. Let's raise our arms and put them out in front. Now make a fist with both your hands, really hard. Hold the fist tight and you will see

how your muscles in your hands and arms feel when they are tight." (hold for 7-10 seconds)

"That's very good. Now when I say relax, I want the muscles in your hands and arms to become floppy, like the rag doll, and your arms will drop to your sides. OK, relax." (about 15 seconds)

2. Let's raise our legs out in front of us. Now tighten the muscles in your feet and legs, really hard. Make the muscles really tight, and hold it." (7-10 seconds)

   "Very good. Now relax the muscles in your feet and legs, and let them drop to the floor. They feel so good. So calm and relaxed." (15 seconds)

3. "Now let's do our tummy muscles. Tighten your tummy, really hard—and hold it." (7-10 seconds)

   "OK. Relax your tummy, and feel how good it feels. So comfortable." (15 seconds)

4. "Leave your arms at your side, but tighten the muscles in your shoulders and neck. You can do this by moving your shoulders up toward your head. Hold the muscles very tightly in your shoulders and neck." (7-10 seconds)

   "Now relax those muscles so they are floppy, and see how good that feels." (15 seconds)

5. "Let's tighten the muscles in our faces. Scrunch up your whole face so that all of the muscles are tight—the muscles in your cheeks, and your mouth, and your nose, and your forehead. Really scrunch up your face, and hold it." (7-10 seconds)

   "Now relax all the muscles in your face—your cheeks, mouth, nose, and forehead. Feel how nice that is." (15 seconds)

6. "Now I want us to take a very, very deep breath—so deep that there's no more room inside for more air. Hold the air in." (use a shorter time: 6-8 seconds)

   "That's good. Now slowly let the air out. Very slowly, until it's all out. . . . And now breathe as you usually do." (15 seconds) (Sarafino, 1986, pp. 112-113)

When children and adults first learn this technique, they sometimes don't actually relax their muscles when told to do so. Instead of letting their arms and legs *fall* down, they *move* them down. They also sometimes tense more muscles than they are asked to—for example, tightening facial muscles when they are supposed to tense only hand muscles. These errors should be pointed out and corrected.

Often, after individuals have thoroughly mastered the relaxation procedure, they can apply a very quick version of it in times of stress, such as when they are about to give a speech. This quick version might have the following steps: (1) taking a deep breath, and letting it out; (2) saying to oneself, "Relax, feel nice and calm,"; and (3) thinking about a pleasant thought for a few seconds. In this way, relaxation methods can be directly applied to help people cope with everyday stressful events.

Research has demonstrated that progressive muscle relaxation is highly effective in reducing stress (Rimm & Masters, 1979). Although relaxation is often successful by itself in helping people cope, it is frequently used in conjunction with **systematic desensitization**, a useful method for reducing fear and anxiety. This method is based on the view that fears are learned by *classical conditioning*—that is, by associating a situation or object with an unpleasant event. This can happen, for example, if a person associates visits to the dentist with pain, thereby becoming "sensitized" to dentists. *De*sensitization is a classical conditioning procedure that *reverses* this learning by pairing the feared object or situation with either pleasant or neutral events, as Figure 5.1 outlines. According to Joseph Wolpe (1958, 1973), an originator of the desensitization method, the reversal comes about through the process of *counterconditioning*, whereby the "calm" response gradually replaces the "fear" response. Desensitization has been used successfully in reducing a variety of childrens' and adults' fears, such as fear of dentists, animals, high places, public speaking, and taking tests (Gelfand, 1978; Morris & Kratochwill, 1983; Rimm & Masters, 1979).

One of the most important features of the systematic desensitization method is that it uses a *stimulus hierarchy*—a graded sequence of approximations to the conditioned stimulus, the feared situation. The purpose of these ap-

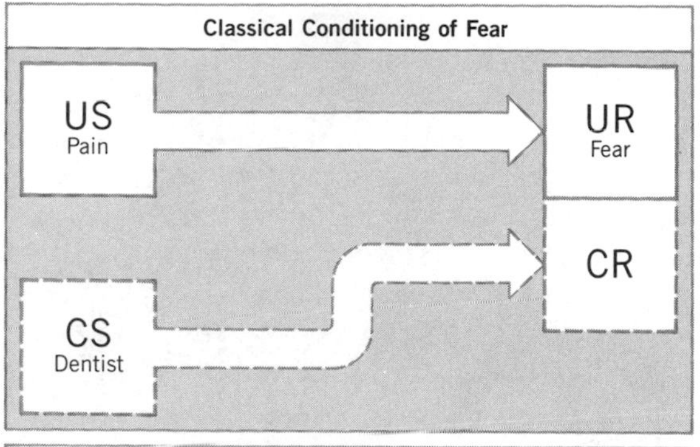

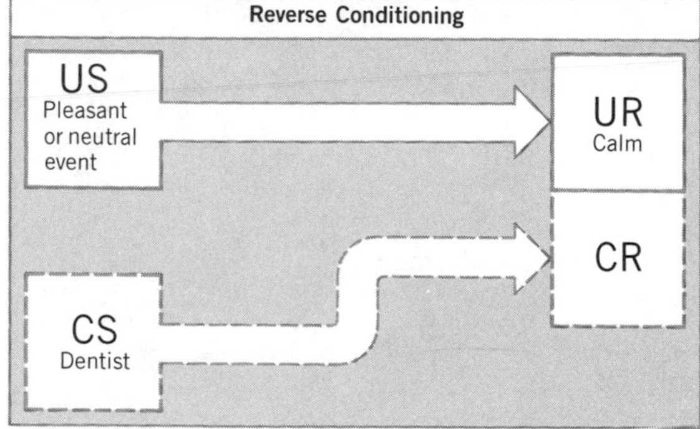

FIGURE 5.1 Classical conditioning in learning to fear dental visits and in reversing this learning. In conditioning the fear, the unconditioned stimulus (US) of pain elicits the unconditioned response (UR) of fear automatically. Learning occurs by pairing the dentist, the conditioned stimulus (CS), with the US so that the dentist begins to elicit fear. The reverse conditioning pairs the feared dentist with a US that elicits calm.

proximations is to bring the person gradually in contact with the source of fear in about 10 or 15 steps. To see how a stimulus hierarchy might be constructed, we will look at one that deals with the fear of dentists. The person would:

1. Think about being in the dentist's waiting room, simply accompanying someone else who is there for an examination.
2. Look at a photograph of a smiling person seated in a dental chair.
3. Imagine this person calmly having a dental examination.
4. Think about calling the dentist for an appointment.
5. Actually call for the appointment.
6. Sit in a car outside the dentist's office without having an appointment.
7. Sit in the dentist's waiting room and hear the nurse say, "The hygienist is ready for you."
8. Sit in the examination room and hear the hygienist say, "I see one tooth the dentist will need to look at."
9. Hear and watch the drill run, without its being brought near the face.
10. Have the dentist pick at the tooth with an instrument, saying, "That doesn't look good."
11. See the dentist lay out the instruments, including a syringe to administer an anesthetic.
12. Feel the needle touch the gums.
13. Imagine having the tooth drilled.
14. Imagine having the tooth pulled.

As you can see, some of the steps involve real-life, or *in vivo*, contacts with the feared situation, and some do not. Two types of non-real-life contacts, of varying degrees, can be included. One uses *imaginal* situations, such as having the person think about calling the dentist. The other involves *symbolic* contacts, such as by showing pictures, films, or models of the feared situation.

In the systematic desensitization procedure, the steps in a hierarchy are presented individually, while the person is calm, relaxed, and comfortable. The steps are presented in a sequence from the least to the most fearful for the individual. Each step may elicit some wariness or fear behavior, but the person is encouraged to relax. Once the wariness at one step has passed and the person is calm, the next step in the hierarchy can be introduced. Completing an entire stimulus hierarchy and reducing a fairly strong fear can be achieved fairly quickly—it is likely to take several hours, divided into several separate sessions. In one study with dental-phobic adults who simply imagined each step in a hierarchy, the procedure successfully reduced their fear in six 1½-hour sessions (Gatchel, 1980). Individual sessions for reducing fears in children are usually much shorter than those used with adults, especially if the child is very young and has a short attention span.

Biofeedback

Biofeedback is a technique in which an electromechanical device monitors the status of a person's physiological processes, such as heart rate or muscle tension, and immediately reports that information back to the individual. This information enables the person to gain voluntary control over these processes through operant conditioning. If, for instance, the person is trying to reduce neck-muscle tension and the device reports that the tension has just decreased, this information reinforces whatever efforts the individual made to accomplish this decrease.

Biofeedback has been used in stress management by helping people learn to relax specific muscles (Quick & Quick, 1984). It has also been employed to treat stress-related health problems. For example, an experiment was conducted with patients suffering from chronic muscle-contraction headaches (Budzynski, Stoyva, Adler, & Mullaney, 1973). Those who were given biofeedback regarding muscle tension in their foreheads later showed less tension in those muscles and reported having fewer headaches than subjects in control groups. What is more, these benefits continued at a follow-up after three months. Biofeedback seems to be about as effective as progressive muscle relaxation methods for treating headache (Blanchard & Andrasik, 1985; Holroyd & Penzien, 1985).

Although biofeedback methods can be useful in treating stress and stress-related illnesses, they have some important limitations (Hatch, Gatchel, & Harrington, 1982). Claims for the effectiveness of biofeedback have sometimes been exaggerated. Moreover, therapists have concerns about whether the benefits of biofeedback outweigh its costs. When successes have been demonstrated in research, they have not always been large enough to justify the cost and complications involved in biofeedback equipment when other effective methods are available. Still, some of the findings from research are encouraging and suggest that some individuals may benefit from biofeedback methods more than others.

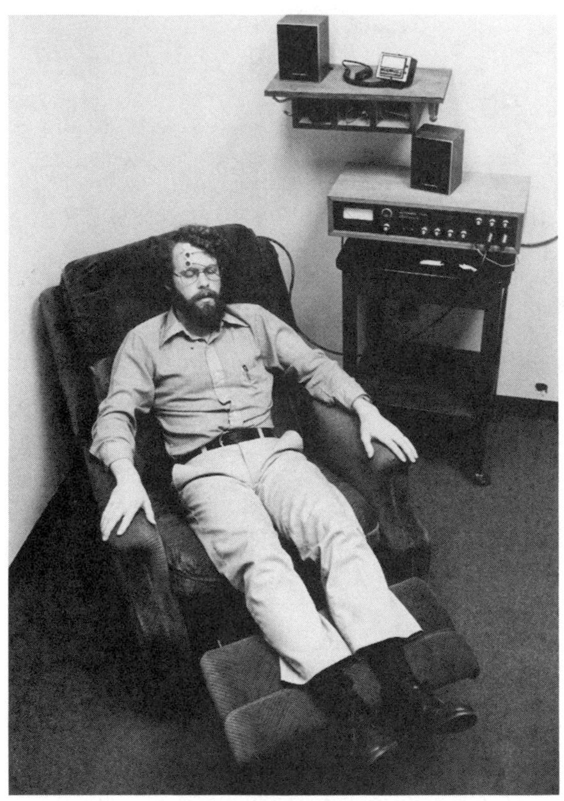

A biofeedback procedure for forehead muscle tensions. One way to give feedback regarding the status of the muscles is with audio speakers, such as by sounding higher tones for higher levels of tension.

According to Virginia Attanasio, Frank Andrasik, and their colleagues (1985), children may be better candidates for biofeedback treatment than adults. In using biofeedback with children and adults who suffer from muscle-contraction headache, these researchers have found that "children exhibit greater self-regulatory abilities than adults, quicker acquisition of the response, and better overall improvement" (p. 135). Why? These researchers have offered some reasons. First, children are generally more enthusiastic about the equipment and procedures than adults, often regarding biofeedback as a game. In fact, some children become so interested and motivated in the "game" that their arousal interferes with relaxation if the therapist does not help them remain calm. But in about 10% of the cases, the children—especially younger ones—may be frightened by the equipment initially. The therapist can usually eliminate these fears by sensitively explaining and demonstrating that the procedure does not hurt and presents no danger. Second, children are usually less skeptical about their ability to succeed in biofeedback training and to benefit from doing so. Adults often say, "Nothing else I've ever tried has worked, so why should biofeedback?" This difference in skepticism probably reflects their differences in past experiences: adults are likely to have had more failure experiences with other treatments than children. Third, children are more likely than adults to practice their training at home, as they are instructed to do.

Although children have many characteristics that make them well-suited to biofeedback methods, they also have some special difficulties (Attanasio et al., 1985). For one thing, children—particularly those below the age of 8—have shorter attention spans than adults. If biofeedback sessions last more than, say, 20 minutes or so, it may be necessary to divide each session into smaller units with brief breaks in between. A related problem is that children sometimes perform disruptive behaviors during a session, disturbing the electrodes and wires or interrupting to talk about tangential topics, for instance. The therapist can reduce the likelihood of these unwanted behaviors, such as by providing rewards for being cooperative. Clearly, the difficulties some children have in biofeedback training can usually be overcome. But research is needed to determine whether children benefit more from biofeedback methods than from other approaches for reducing stress-related illnesses.

Modeling

People learn not just by doing, but also by observing. They see what others do and the consequences of the behavior these models perform. As a result, this kind of learning is called **modeling**, and sometimes "observational" or "social" learning.

People can learn fears and other stress-related behavior by observing fearful behavior in other individuals. In one study, children (with their parents' permission) watched a short film showing a 5-year-old boy's reaction to plastic figures of the cartoon characters Mickey Mouse and Donald Duck (Venn & Short, 1973). In the film when the boy's mother showed him the Mickey Mouse figure, he screamed and withdrew; but when she showed him the Donald Duck figure, he remained calm and displayed no distress. While the subjects watched the film, physiological measures of stress were taken, confirming that the children were more aroused while watching the episode with Mickey Mouse (fearful) than the one with Donald Duck. After the children watched these scenes, they participated in a task that involved the two figures from the film. At this time, they tended to avoid the Mickey Mouse figure (the stressful one) in favor of Donald Duck. This avoidance reaction was pronounced initially—but a day or two later, the children showed no avoidance or preference for either figure.

Since people can learn stressful reactions by observing these behaviors in others, modeling should be effective in reversing this learning and helping people cope with stressors, too. A large body of research has confirmed that it is (Rimm & Masters, 1979; Thelen, Fry, Fehrenbach, & Frautschi, 1979). The therapeutic use of modeling is similar to the method of desensitization: The person relaxes while watching a model calmly perform a series of activities arranged as a stimulus hierarchy—that is, from least to most stressful. The modeling procedure can be presented *symbolically*, using films or videotapes, or *in vivo*, with real-life models and events. Using symbolic presentations, for example, Barbara Melamed and her coworkers have shown that modeling procedures can reduce the stress experienced by hospitalized 4- to 17-year-old children and improve their recovery from surgery (Melamed, Dearborn, & Hermecz, 1983; Melamed & Siegel, 1975). But the child's age and previous experience with surgery were also found to be important considerations in using this approach. Children under the age of 8 who had had previous surgery experienced increased anxiety rather than less. These children may benefit from other methods to reduce stress, such as activities that simply distract their attention.

Cognitive/Behavioral Approaches

Because stress results from cognitive appraisals that are frequently based on a lack of information, misperceptions, or irrational beliefs, cognitive/behavioral methods have been developed to help people cope better with the stress they experience. To accomplish this goal, some cognitive/behavioral methods guide people toward what Arnold Lazarus (1971) has called a "restructuring" of their thought patterns. **Cognitive restructuring** is a process by which stress-provoking thoughts or beliefs are replaced with more constructive or realistic ones that reduce the person's appraisal of threat or harm.

The most widely known approach that focuses on cognitive restructuring is **rational-emotive therapy** (RET), which was developed by Albert Ellis (1962, 1977, 1987). RET is based on the view that stress often arises from faulty or irrational ways of thinking. These ways of thinking affect stress appraisal processes, increasing the appraisal of threat or harm. According to Ellis, some commonly used irrational ways of thinking include *awfulizing* (for example, "It is *awful* if I get turned down when I ask for a date"), *can't-stand-itis* ("I *can't stand* not doing well on a test"), and *musterbating* ("I *must* have people like me, or I'm worthless"). These thoughts exaggerate the person's negative view of a situation and are upsetting. The purpose of RET is to change these thoughts and beliefs.

To illustrate how irrational thoughts can increase stress and lead to psychological problems consider the case of a college baseball player, nicknamed "Bear," who

> was not hitting up to expectations, and was very depressed about his poor performance. In talking with Bear, it quickly became apparent that his own expectations were unrealistic. For instance, Bear wanted to hit the ball so hard that it would literally be bent out of shape (if someone happened to find it in the next county!). After a particularly bad batting session, he would go home and continue to practice until he was immobilized with exhaustion. Simply put, he believed that if an athlete was not performing well, this could only mean he was not trying hard enough. (Rimm & Masters, 1979, p. 40)

Bear's therapy involved progressive muscle relaxation and getting him to realize two important things: First, although motivation and desire do increase performance, they do so only up to a point, after which additional motivation impairs performance. Second, although hitting very well is "nice," hitting moderately well is not "terrible" or "intolerable." These realizations restructured Bear's thinking about his performance, and his batting average increased dramatically.

The procedures used in RET focus on several aspects or stages of the person's thought processes. We can describe these procedures by using the case of a woman we will call Sue, who is in therapy and is upset at having been fired from a job. The basic outline of these procedures can be seen in Ellis's (1977) A-B-C-D-E paradigm:

- *A* stands for the *activating* experience, the event Sue describes as having precipitated her upset: Her boss said, "I've warned you time and again about your lateness and sloppy work. I don't want you to work here anymore. You're fired."
- *B* refers to the *beliefs* and thoughts that go through the person's mind in response to *A*. These thoughts may be rational, as in, "I guess I deserved being fired. I need to be more responsible and careful about my work." But Sue focused on irrational beliefs, thinking, "I can't do anything right. I wish I had behaved better; that was a good job. I'm totally worthless and useless. I can't stand myself and I can't bear facing people and telling them I was fired."

• *C* symbolizes the emotional and behavioral *consequences* of *B*. These consequences may be appropriate, such as feelings of disappointment and a determination to improve in her next job. But Sue's consequences were inappropriate—she felt depressed, ashamed, and helpless, and has not tried to find a new job in the several months since she was fired.

• *D* refers to the *disputing* of irrational beliefs that goes on in therapy. It includes discriminating between true ideas, such as "I wish I had behaved better," and irrational ones, such as "I'm totally worthless." Irrational beliefs are critically and logically examined in RET so that they can be disproven.

• *E* stands for the therapy's *effect*, which consists of a restructured belief system and philosophy. With this effect, Sue should be able to cope with her world more sensibly in the future.

An important feature of RET is that it uses homework assignments—the person might be asked to read some materials about irrational beliefs or do desensitization exercises, for instance.

Research has examined the effectiveness of RET and has generally found it successful in treating anxiety and depression (DiGiuseppe & Miller, 1977; Rimm & Masters, 1979). But the evidence is far from conclusive, and many questions remain as to why it works and whether improvements persist (Patterson, 1986). A newer cognitive/behavioral therapeutic approach—called *cognitive therapy*—has been proposed by Aaron Beck (1976; Beck & Shaw, 1977). Its approach is similar to RET's in attempting to restructure thought patterns, but it focuses mainly on treating depression. Evidence for its success is limited but encouraging (Rimm & Masters, 1979).

Not all cognitive/behavioral approaches for helping people cope with stress have the goal of restructuring irrational thought patterns as the principal focus in therapy. Donald Meichenbaum and his colleagues have developed a procedure called **stress-inoculation training** that is designed to teach people skills for alleviating stress and achieving personal goals (Meichenbaum & Cameron, 1983; Meichenbaum & Turk, 1982). The training program involves three phases:

1. *Conceptualization.* In this phase, the person learns about the nature of stress and how people react to it. This learning occurs through discussions of the person's past stressful experiences; these discussions can be done on an individual basis or in groups, with each member contributing. They consider such questions as: Under what specific circumstances do you experience stress? What did you do to reduce stress, and what do you believe could have been done? What seems to make a problem worse or better? What would you have to do to change the way you deal with stress?

2. *Skills acquisition and rehearsal.* In the second phase, the person learns behavioral and cognitive skills to use in emotion-focused and problem-focused coping. Some of these skills are general ones that all individuals in the program would learn, such as skills in relaxation, desensitization, emotional discharge, turning to others, and cognitive redefinition. Other skills may depend on the individual's personal circumstances and problems. Thus, some people might learn communication skills, or parenting techniques, or study skills, and so on. The person practices the skills he or she has learned under the therapist's supervision.

3. *Application and follow-through.* The last phase involves making the transition to using the learned coping skills in the real world. To achieve this transition, the person responds to stressors that are introduced in the therapy setting in a graded sequence, as in a stimulus hierarchy. A variety of stressors are used to promote effective coping in diverse real-world situations. Follow-up sessions are held periodically during the subsequent year.

The methods used in stress-inoculation training are well thought out and include a number of well-established techniques, such as relaxation, desensitization, and modeling. Although research on the effectiveness of stress-inoculation training in alleviating stress has produced encouraging results, much more evidence is needed to demonstrate its value relative to other approaches (Meichenbaum & Turk, 1982).

Multimodal Therapy

Therapists usually find that an individual who enters therapy has problems that are multidimensional and multifaceted. As a result, one particular technique is not sufficient in treating that person, and the most effective approach usually draws upon many approaches. The method of stress-inoculation training provides an example of therapy that uses a variety of techniques.

In an effort to promote the use of eclectic approaches to therapy, Arnold Lazarus (1981) has introduced the concept of **multimodal therapy**, in which the therapist separates each of the individual's problems into levels and chooses appropriate techniques for each level. The therapist would consider such levels as *behavior* (for example, excessive eating), *affect* (such as frequent anxiety), and *interpersonal relationships* (for instance, manipulative tendencies). As a result, the therapeutic plan for helping an individual cope better with stress would be tailored to the person's specific problems and may make use of any of the methods we have considered, many methods that would take this discussion too far afield, and the methods we are about to examine.

Meditation and Hypnosis

People's mental activity is constantly changing. Some of these changes are quite obvious, such as the shifts in consciousness when we go from wakefulness to sleep or if we drink alcohol. When our mental functioning changes from its ordinary pattern of wakefulness, we are said to be in an *altered state of consciousness.* Variations from our ordinary pattern of wakefulness can occur in several ways other than by going to sleep or drinking alcohol—two of these ways are meditation and becoming hypnotized. Because people generally report that altered states of consciousness affect their arousal, psychologists have examined the usefulness of meditation and hypnosis in stress management.

Meditation

Transcendental meditation is a method in the practice of yoga that was promoted by Maharishi Mahesh Yogi as a means of improving physical and mental health and reducing stress (Benson, 1984; Nystul, 1987). Individuals using this procedure are instructed to practice it twice a day, sitting upright with eyes closed and repeating a word or sound (such as "om"), called a *mantra,* to prevent thoughts from occurring.

Similar meditation methods have been advocated by psychologists and psychiatrists for reducing stress. For example, Herbert Benson has recommended that the person:

> Sit quietly in a comfortable position and close your eyes. . . . Deeply relax all your muscles. . . . Become aware of your breathing. As you breathe out, say the word *one* silently to yourself. . . . Maintain a passive attitude and permit relaxation to occur at its own pace. Expect other thoughts. When these distracting thoughts occur, ignore them by thinking "Oh well" and continue repeating "one." (1984, p. 332)

The purpose of this procedure is to increase the person's ability in the face of a stressor to make a "relaxation response" as an alternative to a stress response. According to Benson, the relaxation response enhances health, such as by reducing blood pressure, and may be achieved in many different ways. For example, a religious person might find that a meditative prayer is the most effective method for bringing forth the relaxation response.

Many people believe that meditation enables the person to reach a state of profound rest, as is claimed by popular self-help books (for example, Forem, 1974). Quasi-experimental studies have examined this issue by comparing meditators and nonmeditators on measures of physiological arousal, such as blood pressure, heart rate, and respiration rate. In these studies, the meditators were asked to meditate and the nonmeditators were asked simply to rest while their arousal was measured. A review of these studies does not support the view that meditation produces an especially profound level of rest, that is, research has revealed no consistent differences in blood pressure, heart rate, or respiration rate between the meditating and the resting subjects (Holmes, 1984). But the quasiexperimental nature of these studies leaves open the possibility that the failure to find consistent differences in arousal may be due to other differences between individuals who do and do not meditate.

Still, the main question of concern for stress management is whether meditation is a useful procedure for alleviating stress. The evidence indicates that it is probably less effective than other methods, such as desensitization and progressive muscle relaxation (Holmes, 1984).

Hypnosis

The modern history of hypnosis began with its being called "animal magnetism" and "Mesmerism" in the eighteenth and nineteenth centuries. The Austrian physician Franz Anton Mesmer popularized its use in treating patients who had symptoms of physical illness, such as paralysis, without having a detectable underlying organic disorder. Today, *hypnosis* is considered to be an altered state of consciousness that is induced by special techniques of suggestion and leads to varying degrees of responsiveness to directions for changes in perception, memory, and behavior (Orne, 1980).

Not everyone can be hypnotized. People differ in their *suggestibility*, or the degree to which they can be hypnotized. Perhaps 15 to 30% of the general population is easily and deeply hypnotizable (Evans, 1987; Hilgard, 1967). Suggestibility appears to change with age, being particularly strong among children between the ages of about 7 and 14, and then declining in adolescence to a level that remains stable throughout adulthood (Hilgard, 1967; Place, 1984). People who are reasonably suggestible can often learn to induce a hypnotic state in themselves — a process called *self-hypnosis*. Usually they learn to do this after they have experienced hypnosis under the supervision of a skilled hypnotist.

Because subjects who have been hypnotized usually claim that it is a relaxing experience, some researchers have examined whether it can help in reducing stress. But there are two interwoven problems with doing therapy and research with hypnosis: most people are not highly suggestible and the success of the treatment depends heavily on how suggestible the subjects are. Despite these problems, studies have found that hypnosis can be helpful in stress management, but it is not necessarily a more effective method than other relaxation techniques (Tapp, 1985; Wadden & Anderton, 1982).

USING STRESS MANAGEMENT TO REDUCE CORONARY RISK

Of the many risk factors that have been identified for CHD, a few of them — such as age and family history — are beyond the control of the individual. But many risk factors for CHD are directly linked to the person's experiences and behavior, particularly stress. It should be possible to modify these risk factors. In the remainder of this chapter, we will consider how stress management techniques can be applied to reduce coronary risk.

Modifying Type A Behavior

When the Type A behavior pattern was first established as a risk factor for CHD, researchers began to study ways to modify Type A behavior in an effort to reduce coronary risk (Roskies, 1983; Suinn, 1982). The task is a difficult one because we don't yet know for certain exactly what makes Type A individuals vulnerable to heart disease.

Ethel Roskies and her colleagues (1978, 1979, 1986) began a research and therapy program in the 1970s to modify Type A behavior. This program — now called the Montreal Type A Intervention Project — has focused, so far, on studying Type A male subjects who are healthy and employed in a professional or managerial capacity. These men were recruited through newspaper advertisement and through the corporations where they worked. In the initial research (Roskies et al., 1978, 1979), potential subjects were assessed for Type A behavior with the Structured Interview method and given a physical examination. The healthy Type A men were randomly assigned to two therapy groups: (1) progressive muscle relaxation and (2) brief psychotherapy, in which a therapist discussed with the men how their childhood experiences may have led to their competitive, hard-driving behavior. A third group was formed from Type A individuals who showed signs of CHD; these men received the progressive muscle relaxation therapy. Each group had weekly therapy sessions over 14 weeks, during which time the subjects were asked to try to maintain their usual dietary, exercise, smoking, or work habits. Several psychological and physiological measures were taken before, immediately after, and six months after the treatment phase began. The results showed that all three groups improved during treatment with respect to their feelings of time pressure, blood cholesterol levels, and blood pressure. During the six-month follow-up period, the two relaxation groups maintained their improvements better than the psychotherapy group did.

Although these results were encouraging, Roskies and her coworkers decided they could increase the impact of the intervention on Type A behavior by using a multimodal approach (Roskies, 1983). They changed the program by adding cognitive/behavioral components to it, so that the revised program included progressive muscle relaxation and most aspects of RET and stress-inoculation training. By doing this, they felt that the program could combat Type A individuals' *physical tension* through relaxation, *emotional outbursts* through RET, and *interpersonal friction* through stress-inoculation training in problem solving and communication skills.

The effectiveness of the revised program was then tested in a study with 107 men who were employed in managerial jobs (Roskies et al., 1986). These men were selected from a pool of potential subjects on the basis of their passing a physical examination and exhibiting the Type A pattern in the Structured Interview. They were then randomly assigned to either the revised multimodal program or to one of two physical exercise groups. One exercise group focused on aerobic training (mostly jogging) and the other followed a weight-training program with Nautilus equipment. Subjects in all three groups attended two or three sessions a week for 10 weeks. At the end of this period, the men were again tested in the Structured Interview, and their blood pressure and heart rate reactivity were assessed in response to stressors, such as doing mental arithmetic, for comparison with measures taken in the initial physical examination. Although none of the three treatments reduced the men's physiological reactivity, the multimodal program was substantially more successful than either of the exercise programs in reducing Type A behavior. The multimodal program was effective in reducing not only *overall* Type A behavior, but each of its components, as well. Its beneficial effect on the subjects' hostility, for example, can be seen in Figure 5.2.

Research by Raymond Novaco (1975, 1978) has also demonstrated the usefulness of stress-inoculation training and relaxation in helping people control their anger. He trained individuals who were both self-identified and clinically assessed as having serious problems controlling anger. In this treatment program, the subjects first learned about the role of arousal and cognitive processes in feelings of anger. Then they learned muscle relaxation and statements—like those in Table 5.1—they could say to themselves at different times in the course of angry episodes, such as at the point of impact and confrontation. Finally, they practiced the techniques while imagining and role-playing realistic anger situations arranged in a hierarchy from least to most provoking. The results showed that this treatment improved the subjects' ability to control anger, as measured by their self-reports and their blood pressure when provoked in the laboratory.

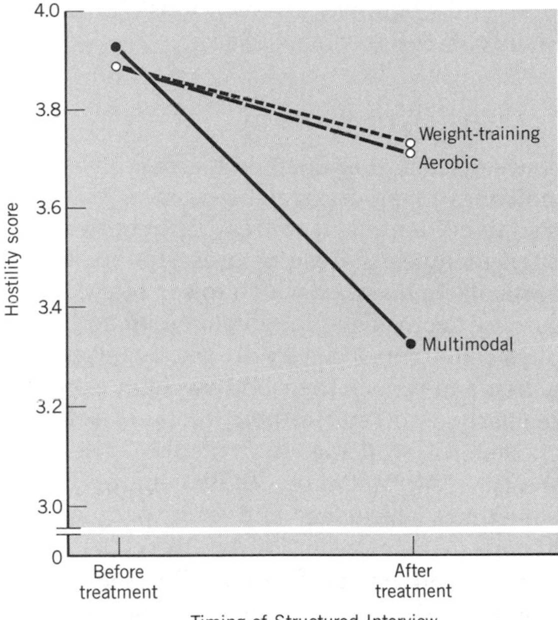

FIGURE 5.2 Hostility of Type A men measured by the Structured Interview method before and after a 10-week multimodal, aerobic exercise, or weight-training treatment program. (Data from Roskies, et al., 1986, Table 4.)

Demonstrating that stress management techniques are effective in modifying Type A behavior in healthy people is an important accomplishment. But does decreasing Type A behavior decrease the incidence of CHD? Meyer Friedman, Lynda Powell, and Carl Thoresen have been working together and with other colleagues in an ambitious intervention program called the Recurrent Coronary Prevention Project to examine this question (Friedman et al., 1986; Powell, 1984; Powell & Friedman, 1986; Powell et al., 1984; Thoresen et al., 1985). The researchers recruited over 1,000 patients who had suffered a myocardial infarction and who agreed to participate in the study for five years. The subjects were primarily married, middle-aged males, and about half were college educated. They were *not* selected on the basis of their exhibiting Type A behavior, and they continued to be treated by their own physicians throughout the study. Over 860 of the subjects were randomly assigned to two intervention groups; the remaining subjects served as a control group, receiving no special intervention.

TABLE 5.1 Examples of Anger Management Self-Statements Rehearsed in Stress-Inoculation Training

Preparing for a Provocation
This could be a rough situation, but I know how to deal with it. I can work out a plan to handle this. Easy does it. Remember, stick to the issues and don't take it personally. There won't be any need for an argument. I know what to do.

Impact and Confrontation
As long as I keep my cool, *I'm* in control of the situation. You don't need to prove yourself. Don't make more out of this than you have to. There is no point in getting mad. Think of what you have to do. Look for the positives and don't jump to conclusions.

Coping with Arousal
Muscles are getting tight. Relax and slow things down. Time to take a deep breath. Let's take the issue point by point. My anger is a signal of what I need to do. Time for problem-solving. He probably wants me to get angry, but I'm going to deal with it constructively.

Subsequent Reflection

a. Conflict unresolved
Forget about the aggravation. Thinking about it only makes you upset. Try to shake it off. Don't let it interfere with your job. Remember relaxation. It's a lot better than anger. Don't take it personally. It's probably not so serious.

b. Conflict resolved
I handled that one pretty well. That's doing a good job. I could have gotten more upset than it was worth. My pride can get me into trouble, but I'm doing better at this all the time.
I actually got through that without getting angry.

Source: From Novaco (1978, p. 150).

The purpose of this study was to determine whether Type A behavior can be modified in a general sample of cardiac patients and whether this modification will lower their subsequent cardiac morbidity and mortality rates.

Subjects in one of the two intervention groups received a program of frequent *cardiac counseling*, which provided information about the causes of myocardial infarction; the importance of altering standard coronary risk factors, such as cigarette smoking (Type A behavior was not discussed); surgical and drug treatment of CHD; and the importance of avoiding activities, such as excessive physical exertion, that may precipitate another attack. The second group—called the *Type A/cardiac* group—had the same cardiac counseling, but also participated in a multimodal program to modify Type A behavior. Type A modification sessions met very frequently at first, and then met monthly for the remainder of the study. The multimodal program included progressive muscle relaxation and cognitive restructuring techniques, as well as several other methods. The outcome of the study demonstrated the importance of modifying Type A behavior, which was measured with the Structured Interview method and questionnaires. The Type A/cardiac subjects showed a much larger decrease in Type A behavior than those in the other groups and had substantially lower rates of cardiac morbidity and mortality (Friedman et al., 1986).

Some researchers have investigated the posibility of using pharmacological approaches to modify Type A behavior, particularly by prescribing beta-blockers. In one experiment, male hypertensive patients were randomly assigned to either a group treated with beta-blockers or a control group (Schmeider et al., 1983). The groups were equivalent in Type A behavior before treatment, but after treatment, the subjects treated with beta-blockers showed less Type A behavior and lower cardiovascular reactivity than the controls. Although the use of beta-blockers may not be the treatment of choice for most Type A individuals, it may be an appropriate alternative for people who are at coronary risk who do not respond to behavioral and cognitive interventions (Chesney, Frautschi, & Rosenman, 1985).

Treating Hypertension

As we discussed in Chapter 4, essential hypertension is an important risk factor for CHD. The traditional approach to treating hypertension often includes the use of prescription drugs, particularly *diuretics*, which lower blood pressure by decreasing blood volume. In addition, physicians generally try to get hypertensive patients to reduce their body weight, exercise regularly, and reduce their intake of sodium, cholesterol, caffeine, and alcohol (Herd & Weiss, 1984; McCaffrey & Blanchard, 1985). Sometimes physicians and other people urge hypertensive patients "to try to relax" when hassles and pressure occur. But there is a danger in this advise: untrained people who make an effort to relax often end up increasing their blood pressure rather than decreasing it (Suls, Sanders, & Labrecque, 1986).

Because the development of essential hypertension has been linked to the amount of stress people experience, researchers have examined the utility of stress management techniques in treating high blood pressure. In general, studies have found that blood pressure can be reduced to some degree through a variety of behavioral and cognitive methods, particularly progressive muscle relaxation (English & Baker, 1983; McCaffrey & Blanchard, 1985; Patel, 1984). Biofeedback and meditation techniques have also had some success. But none of these stress management approaches is as effective as diuretic drugs in controlling blood pressure (McCaffrey & Blanchard, 1985). As a result, psychological approaches for treating hypertension may have value as an adjunct—rather than an alternative—to medical treatment for most patients, allowing them to use fewer drugs or lower doses. Behavioral and cognitive approaches may be recommended as an alternative to drugs for those individuals who cannot tolerate the side effects of diuretics.

Other researchers have examined the usefulness of stress management methods in modifying cardiovascular reactivity. Recall from Chapter 4 that reactivity refers to the physiological response to a stressor, as when blood pressure rises during a confrontation, and that frequent and prolonged high reactivity may lead to CHD. Some studies have shown that biofeedback, progressive muscle relaxation, and cognitive restructuring methods can reduce reactivity, but other studies have produced inconsistent or negative findings (Blanchard et al., 1988; Jacob & Chesney, 1986; Seraganian et al., 1987). The discrepancies in the outcomes of these studies may be the result of differences in their methodological details, such as the duration of the intervention training or therapy, the types and durations of the stressors used, and whether the participants liked or believed in the particular intervention they received (Seraganian et al., 1987).

In an effort to improve the health of employees, many large companies have introduced voluntary stress management programs for their workers. Most studies of these programs have found that they produce improvements in measures of workers' psychological and physiological stress (Alderman, 1984; Sallis et al., 1987). Sometimes the programs are offered specifically for hypertensive employees, and sometimes they are open to anyone who would like to learn techniques for reducing stress. Of course, they are probably more successful in lowering blood pressure with hypertensives than with normotensives.

Despite the success of stress management programs in reducing coronary risk by modifying Type A behavior and lowering blood pressure, they are not yet applied widely. Part of the reason for this is that the evidence supporting the use of these programs is relatively new, and they cost money to run. Other reasons relate to the participants. Although people typically recognize the seriousness of heart disease, Type A individuals probably don't see any connection between CHD and their hard-driving lifestyle (Roskies, 1983). Also, people with high blood pressure either don't know they have it or say they "feel good anyway." For these and other similar reasons, many people who could benefit from a stress management program don't join one when it is available. And many of those who do join drop out before completing the program or don't adhere closely to its recommendations, such as to practice relaxation techniques at home (Alderman, 1984; Hoelscher, Lichstein, & Rosenthal, 1986).

SUMMARY

Coping is the process by which people try to manage the real or perceived discrepancy between the demands and resources they appraise in a stressful situation. We cope with stress through transactions with the environment that do not necessarily lead to a solution to the problem.

Coping serves two types of functions. The function of emotion-focused coping is to regulate the person's emotional response to stress. This regulation occurs through the person's behavior, such as using alcohol or seeking social support, and through cognitive strategies, such as denying unpleasant facts. People tend to rely on emotion-focused coping when they believe they cannot change the stressful conditions. The function of problem-focused coping is to reduce the demands of the stressor or expand the resources to deal with it, such as by learning new skills. People tend to use problem-focused coping when they believe they can change the situation. Adults report using more problem-focused than emotion-focused coping approaches when they experience stress.

People use a wide variety of methods in coping with stress. These methods include direct action, seeking information, turning to others, resigned acceptance, emotional discharge, and intrapsychic processes. The strategies within intrapsychic processes include cognitive redefinition and the defense mechanisms of denial, intellectualization, and suppression. Some of these methods tend to increase the attention the person gives to the problem, and other methods promote avoidance of the problem. There is no one best method of coping, and no method is uniformly applied or effective with all stressors. People tend to use a combination of methods in coping with a stressful situation.

Although coping changes across the life span, the exact nature of these changes is unclear. Young children's coping is limited by their cognitive abilities, which improve throughout childhood. During adulthood, a shift in coping function occurs as people approach old age—they rely less on problem-focused and more on emotion-focused coping. Elderly people seem to regard stressors as less changeable than middle-aged individuals do.

People can reduce the potential for stress in their lives and others' lives in several ways. First, they can increase the social support they give and receive by joining social, religious, and special interest groups. Second, they can improve theirs and others' sense of personal control and hardiness by giving and taking responsibility. Also, they can reduce frustration and waste less time by organizing their world better, such as through time management. And, by exercising and keeping fit, they can reduce the experience of stress and the impact it has on their health. Lastly, they can prepare for stressful events, such as a medical procedure, by improving their behavioral, cognitive, and informational control.

Sometimes the coping skills that individuals have learned are not adequate for dealing with a stressor that is very strong, novel, or unrelenting. A variety of stress management techniques are available to help people who are having trouble coping effectively. One technique is pharmacological, that is, using prescribed drugs, such as beta-blockers. Behavioral and cognitive methods include progressive muscle relaxation, systematic desensitization, biofeedback, modeling, and cognitive/behavioral approaches. Rational-emotive therapy (RET) attempts to modify stress-producing, irrational thought patterns through the process of cognitive restructuring. Stress-inoculation training is designed to teach people skills to alleviate stress and achieve personal goals. Stress-inoculation training is an example of multimodal therapy in that it uses a variety of techniques that are designed to reduce specific components of the person's problems. Beneficial effects have been found for all of the behavioral and cognitive stress management methods, particularly relaxation. The benefits of meditation and hypnosis for reducing stress have not yet been demonstrated unambiguously. Stress management techniques can reduce coronary risk by modifying Type A behavior and by treating hypertension.

KEY TERMS

coping
emotion-focused coping
problem-focused coping
direct action
seeking information
turning to others
resigned acceptance
emotional discharge
intrapsychic processes
time management
progressive muscle relaxation
systematic desensitization
biofeedback
modeling
cognitive restructuring
rational-emotive therapy
stress-inoculation training
multimodal therapy

part III

Enhancing Health and Preventing Illness

6

LIFESTYLES AND HEALTH: HEALTH-RELATED BEHAVIOR AND HEALTH PROMOTION

PROLOGUE

"It's getting worse—those health nuts are all over the place these days, telling me how to live my life," said Joshua as he took a puff from his cigarette. Things were not necessarily "worse," but they had changed. People were now much more health conscious. They were exercising more, eating more healthful diets, and using better hygiene. Does this story describe the contemporary scene in the United States? It could, but it could also describe the mid-1800s. People of today are not the first to be interested in health and fitness.

In the mid-1800s, disease was widespread, epidemics were common, and physicians had few effective methods for preventing or treating illness. As a result, health reformers advocated that people change their lifestyles in order to protect their health (Collins, 1987; Leventhal, Prohaska, & Hirschman, 1985). These reformers were often imbued with patriotic or religious zeal. Some of them advocated vegetarian diets. Others proposed that people chew their food to a watery consistency, or stop drinking and smoking cigarettes, or get more exercise if they lead a sedentary life. Often people who exercised wore loose-fitting gym suits and used a variety of apparatuses, such as rowing machines. It was a lot like today, wasn't it?

This chapter begins our examination of health enhancement and illness prevention. We first consider what health habits people practice, and how their lifestyles affect their health. Then we turn our attention to factors that influence the health-related behaviors that individuals adopt. In the final section of this chapter, we discuss programs to help people lead more healthful lives. As we study these topics, you will find answers to questions you may have about health-related behavior and health promotion. Are people in the United States leading more healthful lives today than in the past? Why is it that some people take better care of themselves than others do? How effective are health promotion programs that try to motivate healthful behavior through fear?

HEALTH AND BEHAVIOR

The role of behavior in health has received increasing attention since the turn of the century, as the causes of death in the United States shifted from infectious and dietary diseases to chronic diseases. Mortality from most of today's ten leading causes of death, shown in Figure 6.1, could be substantially reduced if people would improve a few health-related behaviors, such as by stopping smoking, reducing alcohol consumption, eating more healthful diets, and getting sufficient exercise (Matarazzo, 1984). Knowledge of the important impact of behavior on health led the Secretary of Health, Education and Welfare in 1979 to state:

> We are killing ourselves by our own careless habits.
>
> We are killing ourselves by carelessly polluting the environment.
>
> We are killing ourselves by permitting harmful social conditions to persist—conditions like poverty, hunger and ignorance—which destroy health, especially for infants and children.
>
> You, the individual, can do more for your own health and well-being than any doctor, any hospital, any drug, any exotic medical device. (Califano, 1979, p. viii)

Behavioral risk factors for major chronic diseases can be controlled through modifications in people's lifestyles.

Lifestyles, Risk Factors, and Health

Generally speaking, people's lifestyles include many behaviors that are risk factors for illness and injury. Millions of people in the United States, for instance, smoke cigarettes, drink ex-

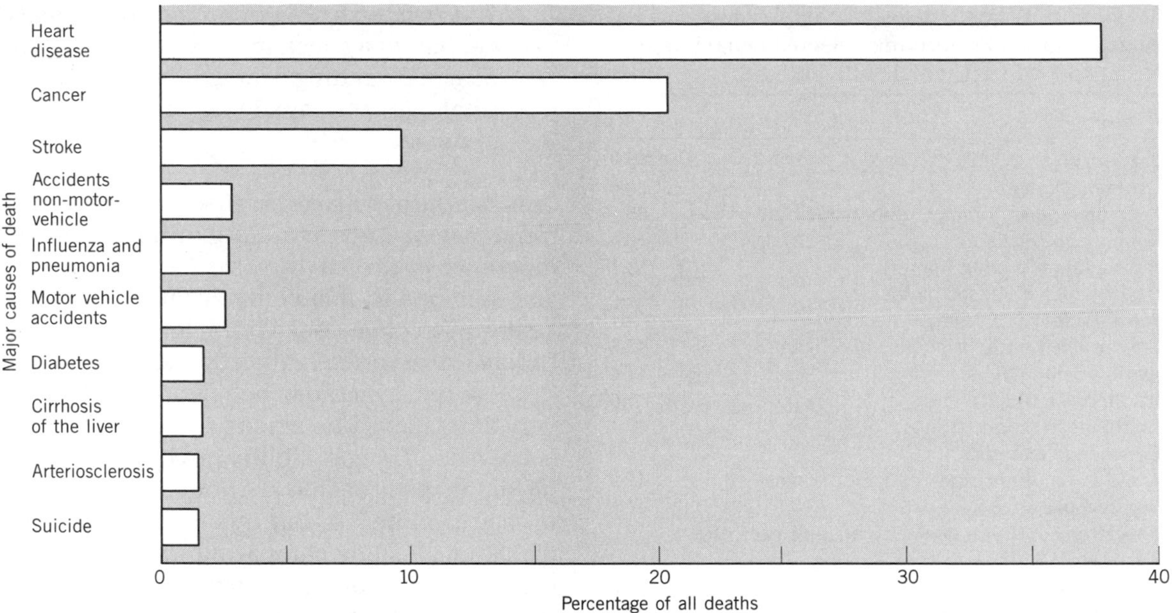

FIGURE 6.1 Percentage of all deaths caused by each of the ten leading causes of death in the United States. (Data from Matarazzo, 1984, Table 1.1.)

cessively, use drugs, eat high-fat and high-cholesterol diets, eat too much and become overweight, have too little physical activity, and behave in unsafe ways, such as by not using seat belts in automobiles. Many people realize the danger these and other risk factors present and adjust their behavior to protect their health.

What do people do to protect their health? To answer this question, Daniel Harris and Sharon Guten (1979) studied a class of behaviors they called **health-protective behavior,** which they defined as "any behavior performed by a person, regardless of his or her perceived health status, in order to protect, promote, or maintain his or her health, whether or not such behavior is objectively effective toward that end" (p. 18). The researchers interviewed hundreds of adults from the general population in the Cleveland area, asking them to indicate which of 30 behaviors they "always or almost always" perform in order to protect their health. As Table 6.1 shows, the three most commonly reported behaviors were eating sensibly, getting enough sleep, and keeping emergency phone numbers near the phone. These behaviors were claimed by about two-thirds of the subjects. Almost all the subjects reported performing at least some of the 30 health-protective behaviors regularly, and most claimed to perform a wide range of these behaviors. Although the results of this study are encouraging, they also reveal a great deal of room for improvement. Less than a majority of these people claimed to practice regularly some very important health-protective behaviors, such as watching their weight, getting enough exercise, not smoking, limiting fats and coffee in their diets, and using seat belts.

Who practices health-protective behavior and why? We are far from a complete answer to this question, but some tentative information is available. One study compared the attitudes and health-protective behavior of licensed practical nurses (LPNs), high school teachers, and college students (Turk, Rudy, & Salovey, 1984). The subjects rated the importance of and frequency with which they practiced each

TABLE 6.1 Percentages of Sample Always or Almost Always Performing Selected Behaviors in Order to Protect Their Health ($N = 842$)

Behavior	%
Eat sensibly	66.0
Get enough sleep	66.0
Keep emergency phone numbers near the phone	65.9
Get enough relaxation	56.4
Have a first aid kit in home	53.1
Destroy old or unused medicines	52.3
See a doctor for a regular checkup	51.1
Pray or live by the principles of religion	47.5
Avoid getting chilled	47.4
Watch one's weight	47.0
Do things in moderation	46.4
Get enough exercise	46.0
Avoid parts of the city with a lot of crime	41.2
Don't smoke	41.1
Check the condition of electrical appliances, the car, etc.	40.0
Don't let things "get me down"	39.3
Fix broken things around home right away	39.2
See a dentist for a regular checkup	36.6
Avoid contact with doctors when feeling okay	35.3
Spend free time out of doors	33.7
Avoid overworking	33.0
Limit foods like sugar, coffee, fats, etc.	31.9
Avoid over-the-counter (OTC) medicines	30.2
Ignore health advice from lay friends, neighbors, relatives	29.0
Take vitamins	24.1
Don't drink	24.0
Wear a seat belt when in a car	22.8
Avoid parts of the city with a lot of pollution	21.5
Discuss health with lay friends, neighbors, relatives	17.1
Use dental floss	15.9
Mean = 40.0; Median = 39.7	

Source: Harris & Guten (1979, Table I).

of the 30 behaviors examined by Harris and Guten, which are listed in Table 6.1. The three behaviors rated as most important overall were eating sensibly, getting enough exercise, and getting enough sleep—in that order. But what behaviors did the subjects actually practice? The three behaviors that had the highest frequency ratings for each group were:

- *LPNs:* keeping emergency numbers near the phone, destroying old or unused medicines, and having a first aid kit in the home.
- *Teachers:* watching one's weight, seeing a dentist for a checkup, and eating sensibly.
- *Students:* getting enough exercise, not smoking, and spending free time out-of-doors.

This sample of behaviors reflects an interesting trend that is representative of the full pattern of differences between the LPNs and the teachers and students in this study. That is, of all the health-protective behaviors examined, the LPNs were more likely than the teachers or students to focus on those behaviors that require very little effort. The reason for this difference is not clear. One possibility might be that people in the medical field are not very committed to their own health. But this is an unlikely explanation. A study comparing the lifestyles of medical and nonmedical students found that the medical students exercised more and were much less likely to smoke cigarettes, drink alcohol excessively, and use drugs (Golding & Cornish, 1987). Perhaps the different focuses of the LPNs, teachers, and students simply reflect the degree to which the behaviors are salient to them.

You probably know some individuals who are highly health-conscious and others who seem to have little concern about their health. Because of these contrasts, some people expect that individuals who practice certain behaviors that benefit their health (1) also practice other healthful behaviors and (2) continue to perform these behaviors over time. Several studies have examined these expectations and found little consistency in people's health habits (Harris & Guten, 1979; Langlie, 1977; Mechanic, 1979). One of these studies, conducted by David Mechanic, provides a good example of this research because it examined both the interrelationships between current health habits and the stability of health-related behaviors over time. The subjects were tested originally when they were children and then again 16 years later. In the original testing and the adulthood testing, the subjects were asked several questions about their health-related behavior, such as whether they were afraid to do things when there was a risk of getting injured. The answers they gave to these questions in childhood were weakly correlated (generally between .1 and .2) with the answers they gave 16 years later. Adulthood testing included additional items concerning their current health habits, such as using seat belts, exercising, smoking, and drinking. Correlational analyses of these current habits revealed only modest correlations (mostly in the .2 to .4 range).

These results indicate three things. First, health-protective behaviors can be quite changeable over time. Second, current health habits are not strongly interdependent—that is, if we know that a person practices one particular health habit, such as using seat belts, we cannot accurately predict that he or she practices another particular habit, such as exercising. Third, health-protective behaviors do not seem to be governed in each person by a single set of attitudes or response tendencies. Thus, a girl who uses seat belts to protect herself from injury may watch her weight to be attractive and not smoke because she is allergic to it.

Why are health habits not more strongly interdependent and stable? One reason people's current health habits are not more *interdependent* is that different habits may serve different purposes. For example, people practice some habits, such as getting enough sleep and eating breakfast, to *promote health* but engage in other health-protective behaviors, such as limiting their use of alcohol and cigarettes, to *avoid health risks* (Leventhal, Prohaska, & Hirschman, 1985). Another reason for the low interdependence of habits is that different behaviors may be influenced differently by various aspects operating in people's lives. For instance, a person may have lots of social encouragement to eat heartily ("You don't like my cooking?") and fatteningly, and, at the same time, to limit drinking and smoking. Reasons for the *low stability* of health-protective behaviors over time include the fact that people change as a result of experience. For example, many people did not avoid smoking until they learned that it is harmful. Another reason for the low stability of habits is that people's life circumstances change. Thus, factors, such as peer pressure, that may have been important in initiating and maintaining exercising or smoking at one time may no longer be present, thereby increasing the likelihood that the habit will change (Leventhal, Prohaska, & Hirschman, 1985).

An important perspective in studying health-related behavior is to consider how it changes with the health status of the individual. Stanislav Kasl and Sidney Cobb have defined the types of behavior that characterize three stages in the progress of disease:

1. **Health behavior** refers to "any activity undertaken by a person believing himself to be healthy, for the purpose of preventing disease or detecting it in an asymptomatic stage" (1966a, p. 246). These activities might include exercising, eating a healthful diet, having a regular dental checkup, and getting vaccinations against diseases.

2. **Illness behavior** involves "any activity, undertaken by a person who feels ill, to define the state of his health and to discover a suitable remedy" (1966a, p. 246). These activities generally include complaining about symptoms and seeking help or advice from relatives, friends, and medical practitioners. A person who feels stomach pains and complains to friends or makes an appointment with a physician is displaying illness behavior.

3. **Sick-role behavior** refers to "the activity undertaken, for the purpose of getting well, by those who consider themselves ill. It includes receiving treatment from appropriate therapists, generally involves a whole range of dependent behaviors, and leads to some degree of neglect of one's usual duties" (1966b, p. 531). A patient who gets a prescription filled, takes it as the physician directed, and stays home from work to recover is exhibiting sick-role behavior.

Health behavior has a preventive function—people engage in it to maintain or improve their current good health and avoid illness. But when people are well, they may not feel in-

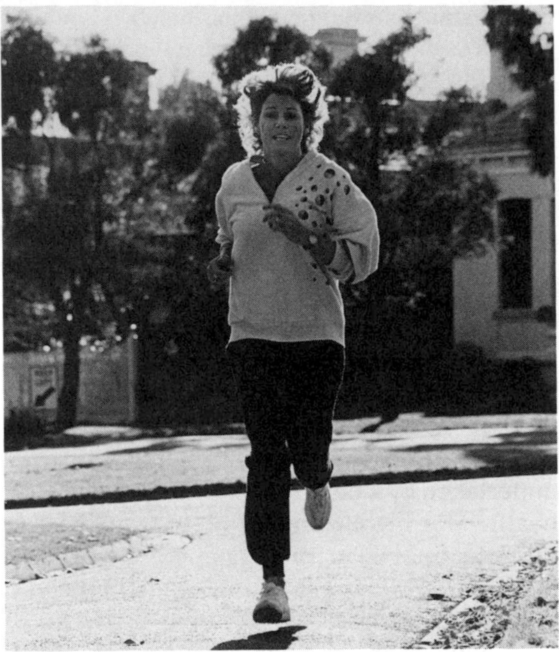

People engage in health behaviors, such as jogging, to maintain or improve their health and avoid illness.

clined to devote the effort and sacrifice that health behavior entails. They may take the view that "If it ain't broke, don't fix it." Thus, whether a person engages in health behavior depends heavily on motivational factors, particularly with regard to the individual's perception of a threat of disease, the value in the behavior in reducing this threat, and the attractiveness of the opposite behavior. Unhealthful behaviors, such as drinking or smoking, are often seen as pleasurable or the "in" thing to do. As a result, many individuals do not resist beginning unhealthful behaviors and may reject efforts or advice to get them to quit. Some people think that health and pleasure are necessarily opposites, feeling that a life that stresses health behavior is doomed to dullness and fear of illness.

People acquire healthful and unhealthful behaviors through learning processes, which occur by way of direct experience and through observing the behavior of others. If the behavior becomes well established, it tends to become *habitual,* that is, the person often performs it automatically and without awareness. For example,

> a confirmed smoker working at his desk may, despite a severe head cold, respond to the sight of an open pack of cigarettes by automatically reaching out, taking one, and starting to smoke without at all being aware of what he has done. Only when the irritation produced in his nose and throat . . . by the smoke "captures his attention" is he likely to disengage in smoking behavior. (Hunt, Matarazzo, Weiss, & Gentry, 1979, p. 115)

Even though the behavior may have been learned because it was reinforced by positive consequences, it is now less dependent on its consequences and more dependent on cues or stimuli in the environment with which it has been associated in the past (Hunt, Matarazzo, Weiss, & Gentry, 1979). This is consistent with such statements as "I have to have a cigarette with my coffee after breakfast," which smokers commonly make. Behaviors that become habitual can be very difficult to change.

Because of the difficulty in changing habitual behaviors, it is important to develop health behaviors as early as possible and eliminate unhealthful activities as soon as they appear. The family system plays a major role in children's learning of health-related behaviors (Baranowski & Nader, 1985). Children observe, for example, the dietary, exercise, and smoking habits of other family members and often receive encouragement to behave in similar ways. Children who observe and receive encouragement for healthful behavior at home are more likely to develop good health habits than children who do not.

Illness behavior has a problem-solving function. The person is concerned about symptoms he or she is experiencing and seeks information and help. People do not always engage in illness behavior when symptoms appear, and some people are more likely to complain and seek help than others are (Kasl & Cobb, 1966a; Rosenstock & Kirscht, 1979). There are many reasons for these differences. For example, some individuals may be more afraid than others of physicians, hospitals, or the serious illness a diagnosis may reveal. Also, some people are more "stoic" or less concerned than others about the aches and pains they experience. In addition, some people simply have less money than others to pay for medical care and, therefore, do not seek help when they need it. We will examine these and other reasons why people do and do not use health care services in more detail in Chapter 9.

Sick-role behavior is what people do when they believe they are ill. The concept of a sick role was first described by sociologist Talcott Parsons (1951, 1964). By adopting the sick role, patients are exempt from their normal obligations and life tasks, such as going to work or school. But a special obligation accompanies this status—that of trying to get well. Most sick-role behaviors are performed by the patient for the purpose of getting well, as in taking medication as directed. Unfortunately, many patients drop out of treatment, particularly if it is inconvenient to continue and impersonally administered (Rosenstock & Kirscht, 1979). Other sick-role behaviors seem to serve emotional functions, as when the patient moans or sighs and receives sympathy.

How people behave when they are sick depends in large measure on what they have learned. As an example, a study of female college students assessed whether they had been encouraged during adolescence to adopt the sick role for menstruation or had observed their mothers exhibit menstrual distress. Compared with students who did not have these experiences, those who *did* reported more menstrual symptoms, disability, and clinic visits for these symptoms as adults (Whitehead, Busch, Heller, & Costa, 1986). Other research has found that there are cultural differences in the way people respond to their symptoms and go about trying to get well (Chrisman & Kleinman, 1983; Zola, 1973). For example, studies in the United States have found differences among groups of immigrants in their willingness to tolerate pain, but these differences diminish in succeeding generations (Chapman & Brena, 1985).

Interdisciplinary Perspectives on Prevention

According to public health expert Lester Breslow, although medical science and technology have made great progress in treating disease, "the principal advances in health have come about through health promotion and disease prevention rather than through diagnosis and therapy" (1983, p. 50). These advances have come about through three approaches: *behavioral* influence for change, *environmental* measures, and *preventive medical* efforts. Using the health problem of tooth decay as an example:

- Behavioral influence has included encouraging and demonstrating good brushing and flossing techniques.
- Environmental measures have involved fluoridating water supplies.
- Preventive medical efforts have included removing calculus from teeth and repairing cavities.

Comprehensive and effective efforts for health promotion and disease prevention consist of some combination of these three approaches. In the United States, the greatest opportunity for health promotion probably lies in influencing behavior (Breslow, 1983). This is because the major fatal illnesses of our time—cancer and cardiovascular diseases—are strongly influenced by behavioral risk factors, such as cigarette smoking, excessive alcohol use, and unhealthful dietary practices.

We usually think of prevention as occurring before an illness takes hold. Actually, there are three levels of prevention, only one of which applies before a disease or injury occurs (Clark, 1981; Leventhal, Prohaska, & Hirschman, 1985; Runyan, 1985). These levels are called *primary, secondary,* and *tertiary* prevention. Each level of prevention can include the efforts of oneself, one's social network, and professionals who are working to promote health.

Primary Prevention

Primary prevention consists of actions taken to avoid disease or injury. In avoiding automo-

HIGHLIGHT 6A: On Issues

Two Health Behaviors: Breast and Testicular Examinations

Breast cancer is one of the leading causes of cancer deaths and of all deaths among women in the United States (American Cancer Society, 1989). One of every 10 American women is likely to have breast cancer at some time in her life, especially after the age of 50. Compared with breast cancer, testicular cancer is much less prevalent, but it is the leading cause of cancer deaths and the second leading cause of all deaths among American men between the ages of 15 and 35 (Friman & Christophersen, 1986; Friman et al., 1986). Its victims are primarily younger rather than older men. Both breast and testicular cancer are effectively treated through some combination of radiation therapy, chemotherapy, and surgery, and both cancers have very high cure rates if treated early.

Individuals can detect cancer of the breast or testicles in its early stages by self-examination. Breast and testicular self-examinations are done with the fingers, searching mainly for abnormal lumps. Figure 6A.1 depicts the most commonly recommended method for breast self-examination (BSE). This method has been used for many years, but there is some evidence that a newer procedure—one that has the hand follow a pattern of vertical strips rather than concentric circles—may produce a more thorough search (Saunders, Pilgrim, & Pennypacker, 1986). The method for testicular self-examination (TSE) is fairly simple. The man first locates the tube-like structures that extend behind the testicle. Then he rotates the entire surface of each testicle between the fingers and thumbs of both hands, looking for lumps.

Do people practice BSEs and TSEs? Most of what we know about the practice of these health behaviors comes from research on BSEs. Almost all American women know of the BSE, and the great majority have tried it at least once. Yet only perhaps one-quarter or one-third of them practice it at the recommended monthly frequency (Craun & Deffenbacher, 1987; Kegeles, 1983; Levy, 1985). This is disheartening because the procedure appears to be effective, and over 90% of breast cancers are detected by the women themselves. Women who do practice BSE on a regular basis tend to come from higher social classes, have more education, and feel more vulnerable to cancer than those who do not (Kegeles, 1983; Levy, 1985; Strauss et al., 1987). Research has revealed several reasons why most women do not practice BSE regularly: some women lack the knowledge or confidence for doing it correctly, do not know how important early detection can be, are afraid that they will find a malignant lump, feel embarrassed or immodest by the method, or simply forget and have no reminders to do it (Alagna & Reddy, 1984; Champion, 1985; Craun & Deffen-

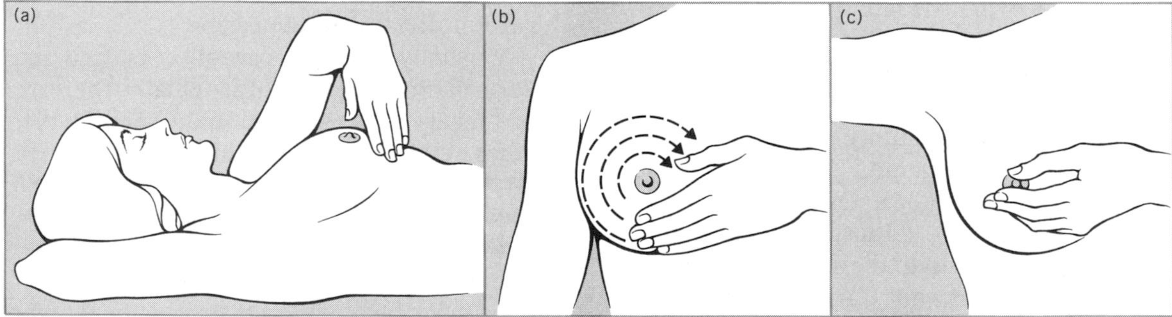

FIGURE 6A.1 Each breast is examined in the following way: (a) Place the arm of the same side of the body as the breast behind your head. With the other hand, fingers flat, press gently in small circular motions, beginning at an outermost point of the breast area. (b) Move the hand, tracing a large concentric circle in one direction (for example, clockwise), continuously making small circular motions. After completing the large circle, trace smaller and smaller circles until you reach the nipple. Breast tissue by nature is not perfectly smooth, so expect to find normal textural inconsistencies. (c) Squeeze the nipple gently, looking for any discharge. Repeat the procedure on the other breast. Report any concerns or abnormalities to your physician.

bacher, 1987; Kegeles, 1983). Similar factors are probably involved in men's practice and nonpractice of TSE (Friman et al., 1986).

How can we encourage the practice of BSE and TSE? One way is through mass communication. Following news reports of breast cancer in prominent women, such as First Ladies Betty Ford and Nancy Reagan, increases in mammograms (breast X-ray tests) and women's concerns about the disease were reported in newspapers. Mass communication can be a very useful avenue for increasing people's knowledge about the importance of early detection. Statistics should be reported for breast and testicular cancer, comparing the very high cure rates (about 90%) when detected in the early stages with the much lower rates when detected later. People also need to know that the treatment for cancer in its early stages is often less extensive, traumatic, and disfiguring than in the later stages. For example, breast cancer in its early stages can often be treated without removing the entire breast.

Another way to encourage these health behaviors is for health practitioners, such as physicians or nurses, to provide information and training through individual and group contacts. This can be done in many settings, such as schools or colleges, worksites, and medical offices. Training is probably more important for BSE than TSE because it is a more complicated procedure. Many women who perform BSEs have received little or no training and do it incorrectly (Kegeles, 1983). But TSEs can be carried out proficiently with just written instructions (Friman et al., 1986). A particularly effective training technique for BSE has the woman perform the examination on a synthetic model (the Betsi Breast model) that has two lumps in each breast, allowing her to learn to discriminate the presence and absence of suspicious masses of different sizes and depths (Craun & Deffenbacher, 1987; Hall et al., 1980).

Finally, having reminders to do examinations greatly increases the frequency with which they are done. This was shown for BSEs with college-aged women who either received or did not receive mailed monthly reminders that simply said, "Remember to practice a breast self-examination this month" (Craun & Deffenbacher, 1987). In some cases, individual women may be able to devise their own systems of reminders, such as by writing them in a calendar.

---

bile injuries, for example, primary prevention activities include our personal use of seat belts, a friend reminding us to use them, and public health reminders on TV to buckle up. Similarly, primary prevention includes actions taken that help people brush and floss their teeth proficiently, resist beginning to smoke, or gain immunity against a contagious disease.

Primary prevention for an individual can begin before he or she is born, or even conceived. Today it is possible to estimate the risks of a child inheriting a genetic disorder and, in some cases, to diagnose genetic abnormalities in the unborn fetus. Through **genetic counseling,** prospective and expectant parents may obtain information to help them make important family planning decisions (Emery & Pullen, 1986; Harper, 1981). If the child has not yet been conceived, the counselor can use several types of information to estimate genetic risks. The ages and biological tests of the parents provide useful data. For some inherited diseases or defects, the incidence increases with the parents' ages; for others, there are biological tests for carriers of the gene (Kopp, 1983). Genetic counselors can also construct a *pedigree,* or family history, using data regarding prior generations to estimate the genetic pattern that produced any inherited diseases or defects. But the outcomes of pedigree analyses must be used cautiously since the data they include are likely to have some inaccuracies because correct information is not always known or recalled precisely by family members. By combining all sources of data, the counselor can provide a rough idea of the risk of conceiving a child who could have the specific health problems assessed.

If conception has already occurred, these same techniques may be used for determining whether biological tests on the fetus are warranted. These tests, *amniocentesis* and *chorion biopsy,* are expensive and may present some degree of risk of injury to the fetus. If the likelihood of the child inheriting a serious health problem greatly exceeds the risk of injury during the test, the procedure is usually recommended. Genetic counseling and biological tests can be applied to determine the risk of many serious and potentially fatal problems, such as the metabolic disorder *Tay-Sachs disease,* the red blood cell disorder *sickle-cell anemia,* and *Duchenne muscular dystrophy.*

Clearly, the use of genetic counseling and biological tests on the fetus can play an important role in primary prevention, allowing prospective and expectant parents to make informed decisions regarding future pregnancies and abortion. These parents can get advice from their physician in selecting a genetic counselor from a list offered by the March of Dimes Foundation. Genetic counselors can provide information, but the decisions the parents may need to make are not easy, either emotionally or cognitively (Emery & Pullen, 1986; Restak, 1975). The information from genetic counseling is complicated and difficult to interpret. Many people do not understand risks expressed as "probabilities," and they may want a decision or specific direction: "Should we have the baby or not?" What is more, the realization that a future child or current fetus could have a genetic disorder can produce anger, guilt, anxiety, and depression.

Another way parents can exercise primary prevention for children is by following the recommended immunization schedule of the American Academy of Pediatrics. Although many prevalent illnesses, such as pneumonia and the common cold, cannot yet be controlled through immunization, several diseases can. These diseases include diphtheria, tetanus, whooping cough, measles, rubella, mumps, and polio. Nevertheless, 40% of American preschool children lack full immunization from currently controllable diseases, and this percentage is much higher among nonwhite children (USBC, 1983; USDHHS, 1986c).

A promising approach to primary prevention involves helping people recognize the need for improvements in their health behaviors by assessing their lifestyles with *health hazard/health risk instruments* (Weiss, 1984). Dozens of questionnaires have been developed for this purpose, and they range from simple self-completed and self-scored tests to elaborate tests that are scored and analyzed by computer. These instruments typically ask an array of questions about the person's past and current health, family history of illness, and personal characteristics, such as age, height and weight, sex, and race. They also ask various questions about the person's lifestyle—personal hygiene, eating habits, use of tobacco and alcohol, stress and relaxation, physical activity, and so on. Then, generally with the help of a health professional, the person's answers are "compared to mortality statistics and epidemiologic data in order to estimate the individual's risk (or probability) of dying by some specified future time. The instruments often also calculate the amount of risk that could be eliminated by making appropriate behavioral changes" (Weiss, 1984, p. 275). These tests can be used for an individual respondent or for groups, and the results are given with a discussion about changing behavior.

Secondary Prevention

In **secondary prevention,** actions are taken to identify and treat an illness or injury early with the aim of stopping or reversing the problem. In the case of someone who has developed an ulcer, for example, secondary prevention activities include the person's illness behavior of seeking medical care for abdominal pain, the physician's prescribing medication and dietary changes, and the patient's sick-role behavior of following the doctor's prescriptions. Instances of secondary prevention for other health problems can be found in many different settings: examination of the mouth and jaw regions for early cancer detection during dental visits, free blood pressure measurements at shopping malls, and assessments of children's vision and hearing at school, to cite a few.

Many physicians and adult patients practice secondary prevention through complete physical examinations each year. These checkups are costly in time and money—they consist of a medical history, examination of the body, assessment of vital signs (blood pressure, heart rate, etc.), and a variety of X-ray and laboratory tests. Because evidence now suggests that several components of the traditional annual physical are not very useful in preventing illness, most medical and public health groups today no longer recommend a complete physical every year (Council on Scientific Affairs, 1983; Shuchman & Wilkes, 1986). Instead, they recommend six to ten specific tests, each with recommended schedules ranging from one to five years, depending on the person's age. For instance, women should have a *mammogram* (breast X ray) annually after the age of 50, but less frequently at younger ages. All adults over the age of 40 should have a *sigmoidoscopy* (colon inspection) every three to five years or so. Individuals who are not healthy or are considered to be at high risk, for example, because of past illnesses, family history, or hazardous work conditions, should be examined more often.

Tertiary Prevention

When a serious injury occurs or a disease progresses beyond the early stages, the condition often leads to lasting or irreversible damage. **Tertiary prevention** involves actions to contain or retard this damage, prevent disability, and rehabilitate the patient. For patients with severe arthritis, for instance, tertiary prevention includes doing exercises for physical therapy and taking medication to control inflammation and pain. In the treatment of incurable forms of cancer, the goal may be simply to keep the patient reasonably comfortable and the disease in remission as long as possible. And people who suffer a disabling injury may undergo intensive long-term physical therapy to regain the use of their limbs or develop other means for independent functioning.

Problems in Efforts for Prevention

The process of preventing illness and injury can be thought of as operating as a system, in which the individual, his or her family, health professionals, and the community each play a role. The effectiveness of each component can be impaired by a wide variety of factors and problems. Let's look at some of these problems, beginning with those associated with the individual.

People who consider ways to protect their own health often face an uphill battle with themselves. One problem is that many healthful behaviors are less pleasurable than their unhealthful alternatives, which may produce a state of conflict. Some people deal with this conflict by maintaining a balance in their lives, setting reasonable limits on the unhealthful behaviors they perform. But most people probably do not — they opt too frequently in favor of pleasure, sometimes vowing to change in the future: "I'll go on a diet next week," for example. Another problem is that prevention generally requires that individuals change long-standing behaviors that have become habitual and may involve an addiction, as in cigarette smoking. Habitual and addictive behaviors are extremely difficult to modify. A third problem is that people who are currently healthy often have little immediate incentive to practice health behavior, particularly if the behavior is unappealing or inconvenient. The positive consequences of health behavior — such as being healthier and more fit — are not immediate, and the negative consequences of not practicing health behavior — that is, developing a serious illness — may never materialize. But even when individuals know they have a health problem, all too frequently they drop out of treatment or fail to follow some of the recommendations of their physician (DiMatteo & DiNicola, 1982; Rosenstock & Kirscht, 1979).

The family also encounters problems in their efforts to prevent illness or injury. These problems often come about because the family is composed of individuals, each with his or her own motivations and habits. Suppose, for instance, that only one member of the family smokes and will not or cannot quit. How can the family protect themselves from the second-hand smoke generated by that one member? Or suppose that a member of a family wants to consume less cholesterol, but no one else is willing to stop eating high-cholesterol foods, such as butter, eggs, and red meats. These kinds of circumstances can create friction in the family and may undermine preventive efforts that the majority of family members support. Similar interpersonal conflicts can undermine prevention efforts among friends, classmates at school or college, and fellow employees at work.

Health professionals face their own unique problems in trying to prevent illness and injury. One problem is that the knowledge professionals need to help people lead more healthful lives is incomplete — they need more information to know when and how to intervene to change unhealthful behaviors effectively. Another problem is that practitioners in the field of medicine have traditionally focused their attention on treating, rather than preventing, illness and injury. But this focus has begun to change, and physicians are becoming increasingly interested in prevention (Breslow, 1983). They are also becoming more accepting of the role psychologists can play in medical settings (Nethercut & Piccione, 1984). Hopefully, physicians in the future will begin to integrate primary prevention activities into their daily practice and use behavioral principles to enhance their current effectiveness in secondary and tertiary prevention.

Lastly, the larger community's role in preventing illness and injury is challenged by an enormous array of problems, such as having insufficient funds for public health projects and research, needing to adjust to and communicate with individuals of very different ages and sociocultural backgrounds, and providing health care services for those who need it most. Among the most difficult problems the community faces is trying to balance public health and economic priorities. For example, in some industries, workers are subjected to potentially unhealthful conditions, such as toxic substances, which may also pose a threat to the community as a whole. Suppose that a company with these conditions exists in a town that depends heavily on that industry for jobs and tax revenue, and that the cost of reducing the potential for harm would force the company out of business. What should the community do? Many dilemmas of this type exist throughout the United States and the world.

WHAT DETERMINES PEOPLE'S HEALTH-RELATED BEHAVIOR?

If people were all like Dr. Spock of the TV show *Star Trek,* the answer to the question of what determines people's health-related behavior would be simple: facts and logic, for the most part. As a result, they would embrace preventive measures to promote their health willingly and without conflicting motivations. In this section we examine the complex factors that affect people's health-related behavior.

General Factors in Health-Related Behavior

The "average" person can describe healthful behaviors and generate quite a complete list: "Don't smoke," "Don't drink too much, and don't drive if you do," "Eat balanced meals, and don't overeat," "Get regular exercise," and so on. But practicing them is another matter. Several factors affect people's practice of health-related behavior.

One factor is *heredity.* Genetic factors appear to influence some health-related behaviors, and excessive alcohol use provides a good example. Twin studies and adoption studies have confirmed that heredity plays a role in the development of alcoholism (Davidson, 1985; Schuckit, 1985). But the exact nature of this role and the relative degree to which genetic and psychosocial factors are involved are unknown.

People also learn health-related behavior, particularly by way of *operant conditioning,* whereby behavior changes because of its consequences. Three types of consequences are important:

- *Reinforcement:* When we do something

that brings a pleasant, wanted, or satisfying consequence, the tendency to repeat that behavior is increased or *reinforced.* A child who receives something she wants, such as a penny, for brushing her teeth at bedtime is more likely to brush again the following night. The penny in this example is a "positive" reinforcer partly because it was wanted and partly because it was *added* to the situation. But reinforcement can also occur in a different way. Suppose you have a headache, you take aspirin, and the headache goes away. In this case, your headache was aversive and your behavior of taking aspirin *removed* it from the situation. The headache is called a "negative" reinforcer because it was *un*wanted or *un*pleasant and it was *taken away* from the situation. In both cases of reinforcement, the end result is a desirable state of affairs from the person's point of view.

- *Extinction:* When the consequences that maintain a behavior are eliminated, the response tendency gradually weakens. The process or procedure of extinction only exists if no alternative maintaining stimuli (reinforcers) for the behavior have supplemented or taken the place of the original consequences. In the above example of toothbrushing behavior, if the money is no longer given, the child may continue brushing if another reinforcer exists, such as praise from her parents or her own satisfaction with the appearance of her teeth.
- *Punishment:* When we do something that brings an aversive consequence, the behavior tends to be suppressed. A child who gets a scolding from his parents for playing with matches is less likely to repeat that behavior, especially if his parents might see him. The influence of punishment on future behavior depends on whether the person expects the behavior will lead to punishment again. Take, for example, people who injure themselves (punishment) jogging—those who think they could be injured again are less likely to resume jogging than those who do not.

We have seen before that people can learn by observing the behavior of others—a process called *modeling,* and sometimes "observational" or "social" learning. In this kind of learning, the consequences the model receives affect the behavior of the observer (Bandura, 1965a, 1965b). If a teenager sees people enjoying and receiving social attention for smoking cigarettes, these people serve as powerful models and increase the likelihood that the teenager will begin smoking, too. But if models receive punishment for smoking, such as being avoided by classmates at school, the teenager may be less likely to smoke. In general, people are more likely to perform the behavior they observe if the model is *similar to themselves,* that is, of the same sex, age, or race, and is a *high-status person,* such as a physically attractive individual, movie star, or well-known athlete (Bandura, 1969, 1986). Advertisers of products such as alcoholic beverages know these things and use them in their commercials.

Many health-related behaviors are affected by or associated with *social* factors (Baranowski & Nader, 1985; Kirscht, 1983). One of these factors is the degree of support or encouragement individuals receive from other people for a health behavior, such as physical activity. American boys have traditionally been more physically active than girls. Although this sex difference may be determined partly by biology, social factors are also important. Right from birth, parents' perceptions of their newborn son or daughter seem to be biased by their expectation of sex differences. In one study, parents of newborns were interviewed on the day of the birth of their child (Rubin, Provenzano, & Luria, 1974). Even though the male and female babies selected in this study were matched for size, weight, and general health, both the fathers and mothers described daughters differently from sons. Daughters were rated as smaller, softer, and less attentive; sons were seen as firmer, stronger, better coordinated, and alert. Other studies reveal that later, in infancy and early childhood, parents see daughters as more fragile or vulnerable than sons (Huston, 1983). These attitudes, in turn, are related to the different ways boys and girls are treated. For instance, parents tend to play more roughly and vigorously with their sons than with their daughters (Block, 1983). These findings show very different patterns of encouragement, leading boys more than girls toward healthful physical activity.

Another factor that affects health-related behavior is the person's *emotional state*, particularly stress. People who experience high levels of stress consume more alcohol, cigarettes, and coffee than those who experience less stress (Baer et al., 1987; Conway, Vickers, Ward, & Rahe, 1981). If you ask people why they smoke, many will say, "To relieve tension." People cite coping with stress as their most important reason for continuing to smoke (Gottlieb, 1983). One source of stress is being unemployed. Studies have shown that unemployed young adults tend to have unhealthful lifestyles that include heavy tobacco, alcohol, and drug use (Olafsson & Svensson, 1986). This is consistent with the findings of research indicating that people often smoke when anxious or bored (Leventhal, Prohaska, & Hirschman, 1985).

People's *perceived symptoms* of illness also influence their health-related behaviors. The way they react varies from ignoring the problem to seeking immediate professional care for it. Certainly when the symptoms are severe— as with excruciating pain, obvious bone fractures, profuse bleeding, or extremely high fever—virtually everyone who has access to a health care system would decide to use it (Rosenstock & Kirscht, 1979). But how do symptoms affect behavior when they are not so severe? Adult subjects in a study were asked to describe their current health and indicate whether they had engaged in illness or sick role behavior recently (Harris & Guten, 1979). On the basis of this information, they were classified into three groups: good, moderate, and poor health. They were also asked to indicate health-protective behaviors they perform. Compared with subjects in good health, a greater percentage of those in poor health reported behaviors such as getting enough relaxation, avoiding chills, doing things in moderation, limiting certain foods, taking vitamins, and not drinking. These results show that many people react to illness in reasonable ways, adjusting their health-related behaviors to meet the needs of their health problems.

Lastly, *cognitive* factors play an important role in the health-related behaviors people perform. People make many judgments that impact on their health. They assess the general condition of their health: Is it good or bad? They also make decisions about other questions, such as: Should I cut back on the cholesterol in my diet? Should I begin an exercise program? Should I stop smoking? And, will I stick with these health behaviors if I start them? But these answers are sometimes based on misconceptions, as when hypertensive patients overestimate their ability to know intuitively when their blood pressure is high (Baumann & Leventhal, 1985; Meyer, Leventhal, & Guttmann, 1985; Pennebaker & Watson, 1988). Hypertensive patients generally report that they can tell when their blood pressure is up, citing symptoms such as headache, warmth or flushing face, dizziness, and nervousness. But research has shown that they are poor estimators of their blood pressure. When hypertensive and normotensive individuals are asked to assess their blood pressure, their assessments correlate strongly with their symptoms and moods, but very modestly with their actual blood pressure.

Can these beliefs of hypertensives affect their health? The potential harm in their erroneous beliefs is that patients often alter their medication-taking behavior, and sometimes drop out of treatment, on the basis of their subjective assessment of their blood pressure. Clearly, beliefs are important determinants of health-related behavior. The next section examines the role of beliefs in people's health.

The Role of Health Beliefs

There is a story that comes from the field of consumer psychology that illustrates how people's thinking is not only an important factor in their behavior, but also can be very hard to anticipate. The Pillsbury Company developed a cake mix in the 1950s that made great-tasting cake and only required the cook to add milk.

With preparation so easy, it would "sell like hot cakes"—or so they thought. But it didn't. Later they found out that it was *too* easy to prepare—people at that time wanted to feel they were "adding value" to a mix (Deutsch, 1987). So Pillsbury changed the mix, requiring the cook to add both milk and an egg, and the product was a success!

People's thinking can affect how people feel. Barbara Fradkin and Philip Firestone (1986) conducted an experiment with 25- to 40-year-old women to determine how women's beliefs about premenstrual symptoms affect how they feel during the premenstrual period. The subjects were assigned to three informational groups: a *control* group, which received no information, and two experimental groups. Both experimental groups received information on premenstrual tension by reading an article on the topic, seeing a videotape of a gynecologist discussing it, and taking part in a discussion group. Each experimental group received information with a different orientation—either biological or psychological. For women in the *biological* group,

> the information strongly endorsed a physiological etiology for universal, unavoidable fluctuations in mood and concentration. Detailed information on hormonal and chemical changes was given, with the intent of enhancing symptom expectations. (p. 249)

In contrast, the women in the *psychological* group received information arguing that

> premenstrual tension was due not to biology but to negative societal myths. The information indicated that self-fulfilling expectations, cognitive bias, misattribution, and the negative labeling of ambiguous physiological arousal combine to create an illusion of premenstrual tension without biological basis. This information was designed to lower symptom expectancy. (p. 249)

The subjects in all three groups filled out a questionnaire on their premenstrual symptoms before and during the month after the information was presented. The symptoms reported by the three groups were equivalent initially, and remained the same for the control and biological groups after the information phase. But the women in the psychological group reported a dramatic decline in their symptoms during the month after receiving the information. The information evidently changed their beliefs, which reduced the symptoms they experienced.

Researchers have also been interested in the role of health beliefs in people's practice and nonpractice of health, illness, and sick-role behaviors. The most widely researched and accepted theory of why people do and do not practice these behaviors is called the health belief model (Becker, 1979; Becker et al., 1977; Becker & Rosenstock, 1984; Rosenstock, 1966). Let's see what this theory proposes.

The Health Belief Model

According to the **health belief model,** the likelihood that individuals will take *preventive action*—that is, perform some health, illness, or sick-role behavior—depends directly on the outcome of two assessments they make. One of these evaluations pertains to the threat of a health problem, and the other weighs the pros and cons of taking the action. What factors go into these assessments?

Figure 6.2 shows that several factors influence people's *perceived threat* of illness or injury. These factors include:

- *Perceived seriousness* of the health problem. People consider how severe the organic and social consequences are likely to be if they develop the problem or leave it untreated. The more serious they believe the effects will be, the more likely they are to take preventive action.
- *Perceived susceptibility* to the health problem. People evaluate the likelihood of their developing the problem. The more vulnerable they perceive themselves to be, the more likely they are to take preventive action.
- *Cues to action.* People who are reminded or alerted about a potential health problem are more likely to take preventive action than are

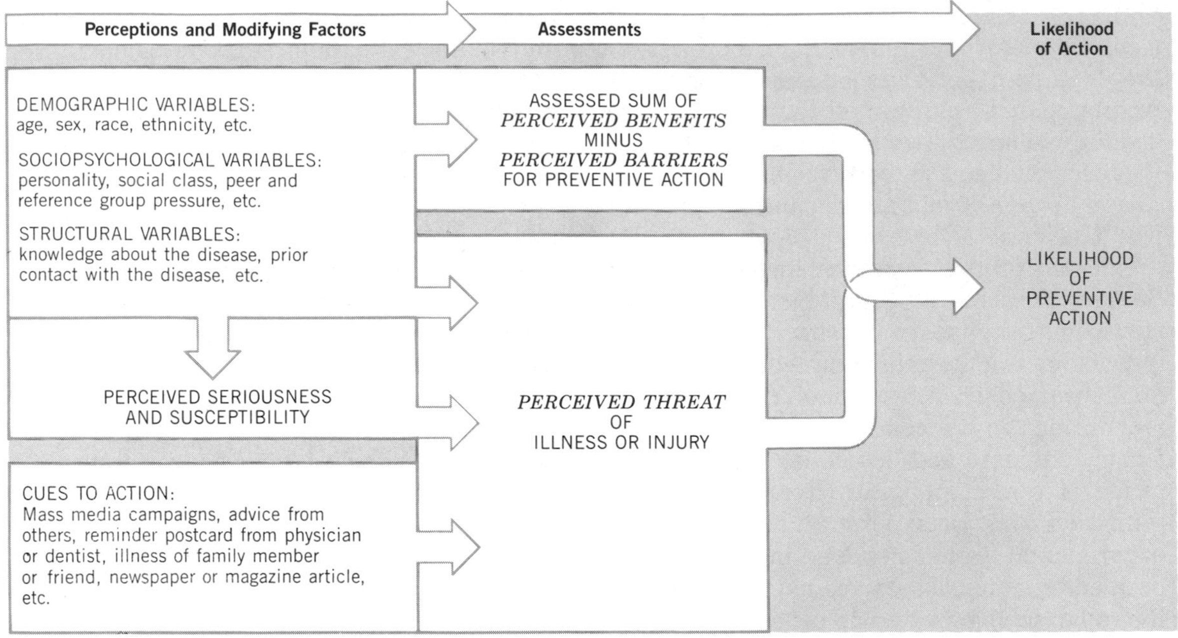

FIGURE 6.2 The health belief model. People's likelihood of taking preventive action is determined by their assessments of the threat of illness and the pros and cons of taking action. Many factors contribute to these assessments. (Adapted from Becker & Rosenstock, 1984, Figure 2.)

those who are not. Cues to action can take many forms, such as a public service announcement of a dangerous storm approaching or a reminder phone call for an upcoming dental appointment.

In addition, three other factors are implicated in people's perceived threat of illness or injury. These factors are: *demographic variables,* which include age, sex, race, and ethnic background; *sociopsychological variables,* including personality traits, social class, and social pressure; and *structural variables,* such as knowledge about or prior contact with the health problem. Thus, for example, elderly individuals whose close friends have developed severe cases of cancer or heart disease are more likely to perceive a personal threat of illness than young adults whose friends are in good health.

In weighing the pros and cons of taking preventive action, people arrive at a decision as to whether the *perceived benefits*—such as being healthier or reducing health risks—of the action exceed its *perceived barriers* or costs. The barriers involved in the health behavior of getting a periodic physical checkup, for instance, might include financial considerations ("Can I afford the bills?"), psychosocial consequences (for example, "People will think I'm getting old if I start having checkups."), and physical considerations (for example, "My doctor's office is across town, and I don't have a car."). As these costs suggest, people's assessments are associated with demographic, sociopsychological, and structural variables. Thus, for example, individuals from the lower classes are more likely than people from higher classes to feel that affording the bills or getting to the doctor's office is very difficult. The connection between these factors and the assessment process can be seen in Figure 6.2. The outcome of weighing the benefits against the barriers is an assessed sum: the extent to which taking the action is more beneficial for them than not taking the action.

The perceived threat of illness or injury combines with the assessed sum of benefits and barriers to determine the likelihood of preventive action. For the health behavior we have been considering, people who feel threatened by an illness and believe that the benefits of having a periodic checkup outweigh the barriers are likely to go ahead with it, taking action for primary prevention. But people who do not feel threatened or assess that the barriers are too strong are unlikely to have the checkup. According to the health belief model, the processes we described for health behavior also determine people's illness behavior in secondary prevention, such as going to the doctor when sick or taking curative medication, and sick-role behavior in tertiary prevention, such as sticking with a rehabilitation program following a stroke.

Has research generally supported the health belief model's explanation of health-related behavior? The model has generated a great deal of research, most of which has upheld its predictions (Becker, 1979; Becker & Rosenstock, 1984; Kirscht, 1983; Rosenstock & Kirscht, 1979). Let's consider the case of primary prevention. Studies have found that compared to people who do *not* get vaccinations, have regular dental visits, get regular breast and cervical cancer tests, and take part in exercise programs, those who *do* are more likely to believe that they are susceptible to the related health problem, that developing the problem would have very serious effects, and that the benefits of preventive action outweigh the barriers. Similar relationships have been found for secondary and tertiary prevention. That is, compared to people who do not take medication as directed and do not stick with prescribed dietary and weight loss programs, those who do are more likely to believe that they are susceptible to a worsening of their health, that the resulting illness would have serious effects, and that the benefits of protective action exceed the costs. Furthermore, studies have shown that cues to action, such as reminders to perform breast self-examinations (Craun & Deffenbacher, 1987), and demographic and sociopsychological variables (Becker, 1979) influence people's practice of preventive measures.

Despite the success that the health belief model has had, it has some shortcomings. One shortcoming is that it does not account for health-related behaviors that people perform habitually, such as toothbrushing—behaviors that probably originated and have continued without the consideration of health threats, benefits, and costs. Another problem is that there is no standard way of measuring its components, such as perceived susceptibility and seriousness. Different studies have used different questionnaires to measure the same factors, thereby making it difficult to compare the results across studies. Lastly, the model's focus on rational decision making ignores other factors, so that

> many important aspects of patients' decisions fall between the cracks. For example, the model does not provide an adequate explanation for the widespread tendency of patients who have painful heart attacks to delay obtaining medical aid. . . . Typically, when the afflicted person thinks of the possibility that it might be a heart attack, he or she assumes that "it couldn't be happening to me." The patients' delay of treatment is not attributable to unavailability of medical aid or transportation delays; approximately 75% of the delay time elapses before a patient decides to contact a physician. . . . The important point is that the health belief model, like other models of rational choice, fails to specify under what conditions people will give priority to avoiding subjective discomfort at the cost of endangering their lives, and under what conditions they will make a more rational decision. (Janis, 1984, pp. 331–332)

These problems do not mean that the theory is wrong, but that it is incomplete. We now turn to another theory that focuses on the role of people's beliefs on their practice of health-related behavior.

The Theory of Reasoned Action

Suppose you are having dinner at a restaurant with a male friend who is overweight, and you

HIGHLIGHT 6B: On Research
Pollyannas about Health

"Compared to other people your age and sex, are your chances of getting lung cancer greater than, less than, or about the same as theirs?" This is the kind of question Neil Weinstein has used in his research to examine how optimistically people view their future health. Through this research, he has shown that people tend to be Pollyannas about their health—they are unrealistically optimistic about their susceptibility to illness.

In one of these studies, Weinstein (1982) had students fill out a questionnaire with a long list of health problems. The subjects were asked to indicate their own risk for developing each problem, relative to other students of the same sex at the university, using the following choices: much below average, below average, slightly below average, average, slightly above average, above average, and much above average. The students believed that they were less likely than others to develop three-quarters of the health problems listed, including:

- Alcoholism
- Arteriosclerosis
- Diabetes
- Drug addiction
- Heart attack
- Lung cancer
- Overweight by 40 pounds
- Skin cancer
- Venereal disease

They believed that they were more susceptible than other students to only one of the health problems, that of ulcers.

In a later study, Weinstein (1987) used a very similar procedure with adults in the general population who ranged from 18 to 65 years of age. The questionnaires were mailed to individuals who had agreed on the telephone to participate. The results revealed that these subjects also believed that they were less likely to develop over three-quarters of the listed health problems, as compared with other adults of their own age and sex. Furthermore, they did not believe they were more susceptible than others for developing any of the problems. What is it about people's thinking that makes them so optimistic? This study found four cognitive factors that affect people's optimism:

> (1) the belief that if the problem has not yet appeared, one is exempt from future risk; (2) the perception that the problem is preventable by individual action; (3) the perception that the hazard is infrequent; and (4) lack of experience with the hazard. If a hazard had such characteristics, people had a strong tendency to conclude that their own risk was less than the risk faced by their peers. (Weinstein, 1987, p. 496)

Note that the thinking described by these factors is not very logical. For instance, the frequency with which a health problem occurs does not affect one's risk relative to that of others.

Do people remain optimistic about their health when they are sick or when a threat of illness is clear? Evidently not. Using a procedure similar to Weinstein's, a study found that university students who were waiting for treatment at the student health center were less optimistic about their future health than were healthy students in a psychology course (Kulik & Mahler, 1987b). Another study was conducted with students in Poland, just after the radioactive cloud reached their community from the explosion of the atomic power plant at Chernobyl in the Soviet Union (Dolinski, Gromski, & Zawisza, 1987). Although these subjects believed they were less likely than others to have a heart attack or be injured in an accident, they believed they were equally likely to develop cancer and *more* likely than others to suffer illness effects of the radiation over the next several years. Thus, in the face of a real threat, they showed "unrealistic pessimism" regarding their health.

Clearly, people's beliefs play a powerful role in their perceptions of health risks, and their beliefs are not always logical. Studies of optimistic and pessimistic beliefs are important because research has shown that people who practice health-protective behaviors tend to feel susceptible to associated health problems (Becker & Rosenstock, 1984).

wondered whether he will order dessert. How could you predict his behavior? That's simple —you could ask what he *intends* to do. According to the **theory of reasoned action,** people decide their intention in advance of most voluntary behaviors, and intentions are the best predictors of what people will do (Ajzen & Fishbein, 1980; Fishbein, 1980, 1982).

What determines people's intentions? Figure 6.3 outlines the theory of reasoned action and indicates that a person's intention to perform a behavior is determined by two attitudes. One attitude is personal in nature—the person's *attitude regarding the behavior,* which is simply a judgment of whether or not the behavior is a good thing to do. This judgment is based on two types of *behavioral beliefs:* beliefs as to the likely outcomes of the behavior and evaluations of whether the outcomes would be rewarding. For example, Elly, who has the attitude that "Using seat belts would be a good thing to do," may have developed that view from the belief that "Using seat belts will protect me in an accident" and the evaluation that "Being safe and avoiding injury is satisfying to me."

The second attitude that determines people's intention to practice a behavior reflects the impact of social pressure or influence. The theory describes this attitude as a *subjective norm*—the perception of and commitment to social standards regarding the behavior's acceptability or appropriateness. As Figure 6.3 shows, subjective norms are based on two *normative beliefs:* beliefs regarding others' opinions about the behavior and the person's moti-

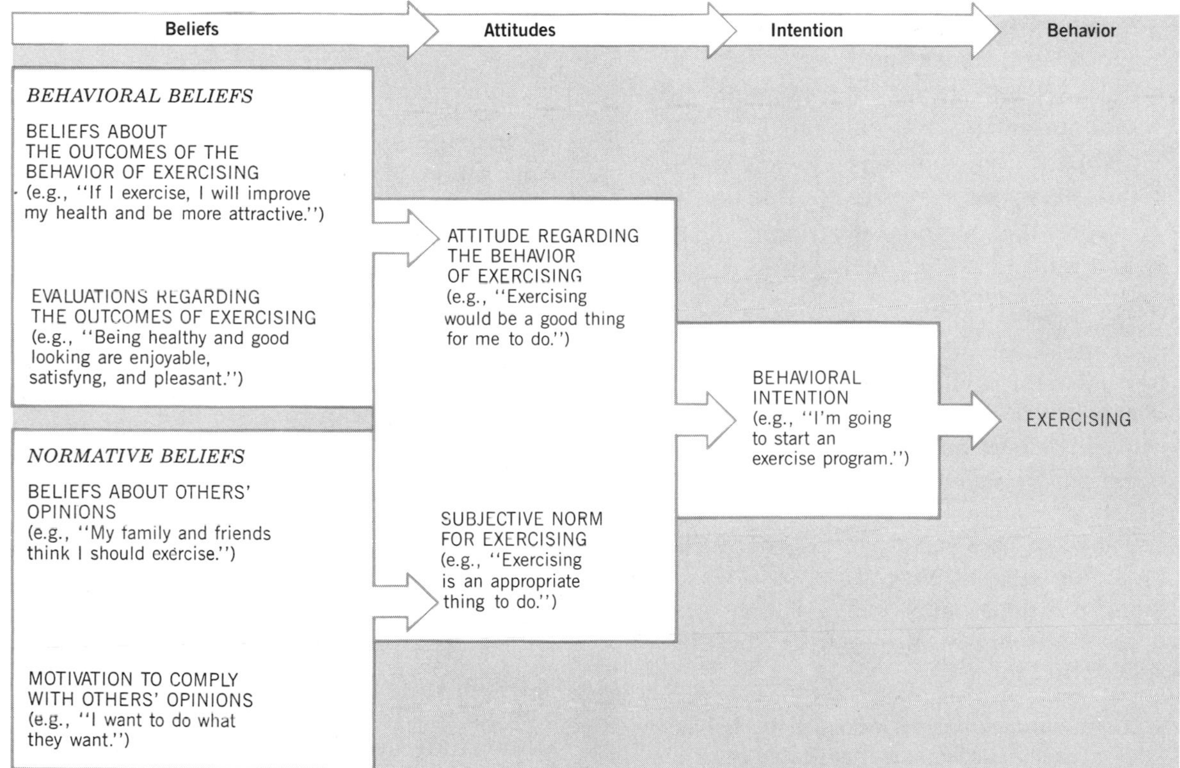

FIGURE 6.3 The theory of reasoned action applied to a specific health behavior: exercising. The behavior follows the intention to do so, which is determined by two attitudes. One of these attitudes pertains to the behavior, and is based on two types of behavioral beliefs. The other attitude is a subjective norm, which is based on two normative beliefs. (From material in Ajzen & Fishbein, 1980, and Fishbein, 1980.)

vation to comply with those opinions. These beliefs answer the questions "What do important other people think I should do?" and "Do I want to do what they want?" Thus, for instance, Elly has the attitude that "Using seat belts is appropriate behavior." She may have arrived at this subjective norm from the belief that "My family and friends think I should use seat belts" and "I value their opinion and want to follow their advice."

The theory of reasoned action proposes that the two attitudes—the subjective norm and the attitude regarding the behavior—combine to produce an intention, which leads to performance of the behavior. Thus, the attitudes Elly generated from her beliefs are likely to produce the intention to start using seat belts, which will, in turn, lead her to do it. Suppose, on the other hand, that she has the following beliefs:

> "Using seat belts is inconvenient and causes more harm than good."
>
> "I suffer enough inconvenience in my life without having to buckle up."
>
> "Nobody I know seems to want me to use seat belts, and they don't buckle up either."
>
> "I value the opinion of my friends and family and want to be like them."

With these beliefs, Elly almost certainly would not generate an intention to use seat belts, and her behavior would reflect this failure.

If people's behavior is ultimately a function of their beliefs, we are left with the following question: What factors determine beliefs? The theory of reasoned action proposes that beliefs are affected by a variety of external variables, including age, sex, education, social class, religion, and personality traits. These variables determine behavior indirectly, rather than directly, that is,

> a person does not perform a given behavior *because* she is a woman or educated or altruistic or religious. . . . Instead, she ultimately performs the behavior *because* she believes that its performance will lead to more "good" than "bad" consequences and/or because she believes that most of her important others (i.e., the individuals she wants most to comply with) think she should perform that behavior. (Fishbein, 1980, p. 103)

Behavior is directly determined by intentions.

The theory of reasoned action was originally formulated to explain a wide variety of behaviors, particularly those of interest to social psychologists. Applying the theory to health psychology has been successful, and research has found support for aspects of the theory in explaining several health-related behaviors. A study by Richard Bagozzi (1981), for example, examined the attitudes, intentions, and behavior of adults regarding donating blood during an annual Red Cross blood drive. In the week prior to the drive, the subjects filled out a questionnaire that asked them to rate the strength of their intentions and their attitudes, such as the degree of pleasantness or unpleasantness, toward giving blood. The Red Cross provided information on whether they actually gave blood. As the theory predicts, attitudes about giving blood influenced the actual behavior through their impact on the subjects' intentions. Other studies have found that people's attitudes and intentions are related to their cigarette smoking (Fishbein, 1982), exercising (Wurtele & Maddux, 1987), and losing weight (Schifter & Ajzen, 1985).

What shortcomings does the theory of reasoned action have? One problem is that, like the health belief model, it does not adequately account for irrational decisions that people often make about their health, such as delaying medical treatment when clear symptoms exist. Another problem is that intentions and behavior are only moderately related—people do not always do what they plan (or *claim* they plan) to do. One final problem is that the theory is incomplete (Fishbein, 1980). An important factor that is not included is the person's prior experience with the behavior. In the blood donation study described, the subjects were also asked about their past behavior in donating or not donating blood (Bagozzi, 1981). Of those subjects who said they intended to give blood, those who had given before were more likely to actually give than those who had not donated in the past. Similarly, other studies have found that people's past history of performing a health-related behavior, such as exercising or using alcohol or drugs, is a strong predictor of their future practice of that behavior (Bentler & Speckart, 1979; Godin, Valois, Shephard, & Desharnais, 1987). Thus, for example, compared to adults who have engaged in little exercise in the past, those who have gotten more exercise are much more likely to carry out their promise to exercise in the future.

The health belief model and the theory of reasoned action each provide valid explanations for parts of the process that determines people's practice of health-related behavior. At their core, both theories assume that people weigh perceived benefits and costs and behave according to the outcome of their analysis. But neither approach is sufficient (Janis, 1984; Kirscht, 1983). Neil Weinstein (1988) has outlined several limitations of these approaches. One weakness in these theories is that they assume people think about risks in a detailed fashion, knowing what diseases are associated with different behaviors and estimating the likelihood of becoming seriously ill. In fact, people may modify their lifestyle, for instance, by reducing coffee consumption, for very vague reasons, such as "My doctor says coffee is bad for you." Also, these approaches do not consider that the benefits and costs of changing a health-related behavior may vary over time. Compare these three examples:

- Switching to a fluoridated toothpaste produces an immediate, constant benefit with a small, constant cost.
- Getting vaccinated for measles in infancy produces an immediate, constant benefit, but the moderate cost occurs immediately and ends.
- Quitting smoking produces gradual, accumulating benefits and the initial cost is high, but may decrease over time.

These differences are likely to affect people's willingness to modify their behavior.

In the next section we examine a theory that focuses on another factor these approaches do not take into account—the role of stress on the cognitive processes that affect people's likelihood of taking preventive action.

The Role of Stress

We have seen that the decisions people make regarding health-related behavior are not always rational. **Conflict theory** presents a model to account for both rational and irrational decision making (Janis, 1984; Janis & Mann, 1977). The model does this by describing a series of *stages* that people use in making important decisions—including health-related decisions—and by introducing the influence of *stress* on cognition.

According to the *conflict theory model,* the process people use in arriving at a stable health-related decision involves a series of five stages. This process starts when an event challenges the individual's current course of action or lifestyle. The challenge can be either a *threat,* such as a symptom of illness or a news story about the dangers of smoking, or an *opportunity,* such as the chance to join a free program at work to quit smoking. Let's see what these five stages are:

1. *Appraising the challenge.* The challenge momentarily points up the negative consequences of the individual's current health-related behavior, and the person tries to dismiss it as being untrue, irrelevant, or inapplicable to his or her circumstances. This stage boils down to the question, "Are the risks serious if I don't change?" If the judgment is "no," the behavior stays the same and the decision-making process ends; but if the answer is "yes," the process moves to the next stage.

2. *Surveying alternatives.* Once the person's complacency with the behavior has been shaken, he or she begins to search for alternatives to examine. For each potential alternative, the person asks, "Is this alternative an acceptable means for dealing with the challenge?" This stage ends with the decision that the available alternatives have been sufficiently surveyed.

3. *Weighing alternatives.* In this stage, the person assesses the pros and cons of each alternative in an attempt to answer two main questions: "Which alternative is best?" and "Could the best alternative meet the essential requirements?" Once the process leads to a tentative decision, the next stage begins.

4. *Deliberating about commitment.* The person focuses on a final choice in this stage and becomes increasingly committed to it. The key question becomes, "Shall I implement the best alternative and allow others to know?"

5. *Adhering despite negative feedback.* After making and beginning to implement a decision, people often have second thoughts about it—often because of negative feedback from others. For example, sometimes individuals in a family complain about changes in their food or extra effort on their part if one of its members decides to go on a diet. The second thoughts that arise become challenges, and give rise to some old questions: "Are the risks serious if I *don't* change?" and "Are the risks serious if I *do* change?" People at this point are generally only temporarily shaken by these challenges, and they tend to continue implementing the decision.

The decision-making process can be aborted at any point. For instance, the person could decide in the second stage that the search was thorough enough and revealed no acceptable alternatives.

Conflict theory proposes that all major decisions, particularly those relating to health, produce stress that arises from the person's conflict about what to do:

> People realize that whichever course of action or inaction they choose could lead to serious material or social losses, such as becoming physically incapacitated or losing the esteem of loved ones. . . . The conflict theory model is based on the assumption that the stress itself is frequently a major cause of errors in decision making. This assumption does not deny the influence of other common causes of misjudgments, such as information overload and the limitations of human information processing, group pressures, blinding prejudice, ignorance, and organizational constraints. . . . It maintains, however, that a major reason for many ill-conceived and poorly implemented decisions has to do with the motivational consequences of decisional conflict, particularly attempts to ward off the stresses generated by agonizingly difficult choices. (Janis, 1984, p. 335)

Since people decide whether or not to perform many health-related behaviors, the way they cope with stress is seen as playing an important role in health, illness, and sick-role behavior.

What determines how effectively they deal with health-related decisions? Conflict theory indicates that people's coping with decisional conflict depends on their perceptions of the presence or absence of three factors: *risks, hope,* and *adequate time.* Different combinations of these three factors produce the following five coping patterns:

- *Unconflicted adherence.* People who perceive no serious risks for maintaining the status quo experience low stress and tend to continue their current behavior.
- *Unconflicted change.* People who see serious risks in their current behavior and no serious risks in an alternative also experience low stress, but they are likely to adopt the alternative behavior.
- *Defensive avoidance.* When people perceive serious risks in both changing and not changing their behavior *and* see no hope of finding a better alternative, they experience a high degree of stress. As long as these conditions prevail, individuals try to evade the conflict by procrastinating, shifting responsibility to someone else, or using intrapsychic processes, such as denial.
- *Hypervigilance.* People sometimes see serious risks in their current behavior and those alternatives they have considered. If they believe they may still find a better solution *but* think they are fast running out of time, they experience high stress. Under these circumstances, people tend to search frantically for a

solution — and may choose an alternative hastily, especially if it promises immediate relief.

• *Vigilance.* People who perceive serious risks in all possibilities they have considered *but* believe they may find a better alternative and have the time to search experience only moderate levels of stress. Under these conditions, people tend to search thoroughly and make rational choices.

According to the theory, vigilant coping is the only consistently adaptive pattern for decision making. When the challenge consists of a physician's warning or obvious symptoms of illness, the other coping patterns can be highly maladaptive. Unconflicted adherence and unconflicted change often arise when the person lacks motivation or concern, thereby failing to consider potential risks that may actually exist in the chosen action. Defensive avoidance obviously delays needed preventive action. And hypervigilance involves a harried decision-making process in which the person may overlook the full range of consequences and choose impulsively.

Although the conflict theory model was developed on the basis of an existing and extensive body of research, studies have not yet directly tested its predictions to the point that its strengths and weaknesses are clear. Still, there is little question but that the impact of stress is an important determinant of preventive action, particularly in people's illness and sick-role behavior.

The Role of Personal Control

In Chapter 4 we examined how a sense of personal control can modify the stress people experience. In this section, we will consider how people's health-related behavior is influenced by two aspects of personal control: *locus of control* and *self-efficacy*.

You might expect that people whose health locus of control is strongly *internal*— as measured by a locus of control scale — would tend to practice behaviors that prevent illness and promote their health. Because these individuals believe they can influence their health, they should practice more healthful behavior than those who score high on external control. To some extent this is so. Compared to people who score high on external control beliefs, those who score high on internal control tend to perform more health-protective behaviors, such as getting physical examinations and dieting for health reasons (Seeman & Seeman, 1983). They also tend to be more successful in reducing cigarette smoking and seek out more information on some health issues, such as high blood pressure (Strickland, 1978; Wallston & Wallston, 1982). But these relationships are not very strong.

Why is locus of control not more strongly associated with health-protective behavior? One reason is that locus of control is just one of many factors that influence the practice of healthful behavior. Another reason is that the belief in internal control is likely to have a greater impact among people who place a high value on their health than among those who do not (Wallston & Wallston, 1982). To examine this possibility, researchers tested female subjects, using a Health Value scale in which individuals rate their agreement with items such as "There is nothing more important than your health" (Lau, Hartman, & Ware, 1986). The subjects also completed a health locus of control scale and provided information about their practice of breast self-examinations. Analysis of these data revealed that the correlation between locus of control and performing breast examinations was substantially higher for the women who valued their health highly than for those who valued their health less.

In some cases, performing a healthful behavior is hard to do, for instance, it may be strenuous or complicated. Therefore, people's belief that they can succeed at something they want to do — or self-efficacy — may be an important determinant of whether they choose to practice specific behaviors (Bandura, 1986). Individuals acquire a sense of efficacy through their own successes and failures, observations of others' experiences, and assessments of their abilities that other people communicate.

When deciding to practice a health-protective behavior, people appraise their efficacy on the basis of the effort required, complexity of the task, and other aspects of the situation, such as whether they are likely to receive help from other people (Schunk & Carbonari, 1984).

Research has found that self-efficacy does influence people's health, illness, and sick-role behavior. Cigarette smokers who believe they are incapable of kicking the habit typically don't try, but smokers who believe they can succeed in quitting often break the habit (DiClemente, Prochaska, & Gilbertini, 1985). Similarly, individuals who believe they can succeed in losing weight are more likely to try and to succeed than those who do not (Schifter & Ajzen, 1985). Moreover, patients with chronic respiratory illnesses who believe they can perform a prescribed program of physical exercises are more likely to adhere to the program than those who have less self-efficacy (Kaplan, Atkins, & Reinsch, 1984).

The practice of health-protective behavior is clearly determined by the complex interplay of many biopsychosocial factors. We next examine the relationships that exist between individuals' lifestyles and three factors—age, sex, and sociocultural background.

DEVELOPMENTAL, GENDER, AND SOCIOCULTURAL FACTORS

It comes as no surprise that people's health changes across the life span, that women and men have some differences in health risks and needs, and that variations in preventive behavior occur between individuals of different social class and ethnic backgrounds. What are some of these changes and differences, and why do they exist? Let's examine these health issues, starting with the role of development.

Development and Health-Related Behavior

As a person develops, many things change within the individual and in his or her environment. These changes affect the preventive action taken to protect that person's health. During the beginning of the life span, and sometimes toward the end, the individual may lack the ability to take needed action, and other people assume that responsibility.

During Gestation and Infancy

Each year in the United States about 250,000 babies—or 7 out of every 100 births—are born with birth defects. These defects range from relatively minimal physical and mental abnormalities to gross deformities. Some of these defects are not apparent until months or years later, and some are fatal. These defects result from genetic abnormalities and harmful factors in the fetal environment.

For the most part, the mother can control the fetal environment through her behavior. Early in gestation, a *placenta* and *umbilical cord* develop and begin to transmit substances to the fetus from the mother's bloodstream. Although these substances consist mostly of nourishment, they can also include hazardous microorganisms and chemicals that happen to be in her blood. We will consider three main hazards. First, the mother may be malnourished, because of inadequate food supplies or knowledge of nutritional needs. Babies born to malnourished mothers tend to be low in birth weight and high in risk of mortality in the first weeks after birth (Korones, 1981; Pilliteri, 1981).

Second, certain infections the mother may contract during pregnancy can also attack her gestating baby, sometimes causing permanent injury or death (LaBarba, 1984; Moore, 1983). For example, infection with *rubella* (German measles) in the first several weeks of pregnancy may cause the baby to die or be severely malformed, and infection with *toxoplasmosis* can cause brain damage or death. Pregnant women can protect the fetus from rubella through vaccination and from toxoplasmosis by avoiding contact with major sources of infection (cats, cat litter, and undercooked meats). Third, various substances the mother uses may enter her bloodstream and harm the

HIGHLIGHT 6C: On Issues
Prevention over the Life Span

The health problems and risk factors that individuals face change throughout life. For instance, middle-aged adults are much more likely than children to be concerned with cholesterol levels of their foods, have hypertension, and suffer from heart disease. Adolescents and young adults are much more likely to die in automobile accidents than are people of other age groups. Because the preventive needs of individuals change with age, Lester Breslow and Anne Somers (1977) have described a wide variety of preventive goals, assigning each to different periods within the life span. Some of these goals are presented in the following lists.

Health Goals of Gestation and Infancy

- To provide the mother a healthy, full-term pregnancy and rapid recovery after a normal delivery.
- To facilitate the live birth of a normal baby, free of congenital or developmental damage.
- To help both mother and father achieve the knowledge and capacity to provide for the physical, emotional, and social needs of the baby.
- To establish immunity against specified infectious diseases.
- To detect and prevent certain other diseases and problems before irreparable damage occurs.

Health Goals of Childhood and Adolescence

- To facilitate the child's optimal physical, emotional, and social growth and development.
- To establish healthy behavioral patterns [in children] for nutrition, exercise, study, recreation, and family life, as a foundation for a healthy lifetime lifestyle.
- To reinforce healthy behavior patterns [in adolescents], and discourage negative ones, in physical fitness, nutrition, exercise, study, work, recreation, sex, individual relations, driving, smoking, alcohol, and drugs.

Health Goals of Adulthood

- To prolong the period of maximum physical energy and to develop full mental, emotional, and social potential.
- To anticipate and guard against the onset of chronic diseases through good health habits and early detection and treatment where effective.
- To detect as early as possible any of the major chronic diseases, including hypertension, heart disease, diabetes, and cancer, as well as vision, hearing, and dental impairments.

Health Goals in Old Age

- To minimize handicapping and discomfort from onset of chronic conditions.
- To prepare in advance for retirement.
- To prolong the period of effective activity and ability to live independently, and avoid institutionalization so far as possible.
- When illness is terminal, to assure as little physical and mental stress as possible and to provide emotional support to patient and family.

These goals broadly identify areas of specific concern for different age groups, based on changing lifestyles, health needs, and problems. The entire health care system—including patients and practitioners—needs such goals in order to keep in mind what health means and requires at different ages and to take the most appropriate preventive action at the right time.

---

baby (LaBarba, 1984). Cigarette smoking is associated with low birth weight, and using drugs can cause addiction in the baby. Drinking alcohol excessively is related to the birth of babies with *fetal alcohol syndrome,* which has the following symptoms: (1) low birth weight and retarded subsequent growth, (2) subnormal intelligence, and (3) physical abnormalities, such as heart defects (Jones, Smith, Ulleland, & Streissguth, 1973; Moore, 1983; Nilsen, Sagen, Kim, & Bergsjo, 1984).

Birth catapults the newborn into a new

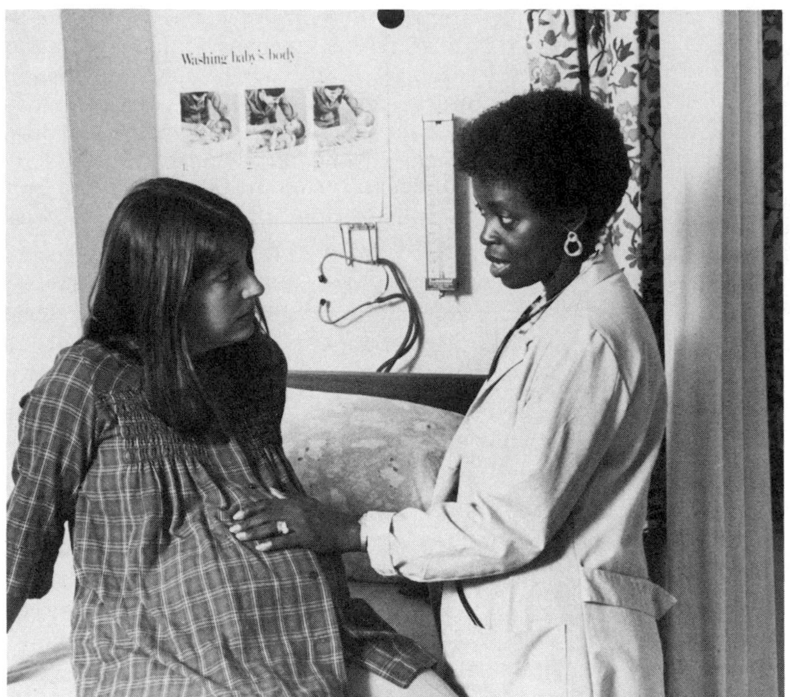

Women who receive and follow medical advice during pregnancy can enhance the healthfulness of their baby's prenatal environment.

world where risks continue. Although the rate of infant mortality in the United States is higher than in several other industrialized countries, it has declined to less than 11 per 1,000 live births for the first year of life (Moore, 1983). Out of these, approximately two-thirds die within the first week. In early infancy, the baby's immunity to disease depends largely on the white blood cells and antibodies passed on by the mother prenatally and in her milk if she breast-feeds. Because of the immunity it gives to the baby, breast milk is sometimes called "nature's vaccine." Parents should arrange for the baby to begin a vaccination program early in infancy for such diseases as diphtheria, whooping cough, and polio.

Childhood and Adolescence

In the second year of life, toddlers are walking and beginning to "get into everything." Although children's advancements in motor development are important, they place children at increasing health risk for accidents around the house, such as with sharp objects and chemicals, and outdoors, such as with swimming pools, cars, and skateboards. Today accidental injury is the leading cause of death during childhood and adolescence (Cataldo et al., 1986; Haggerty, 1986). Parents, teachers, and other caregivers can reduce the likelihood of injury by teaching children safety behaviors, supervising them when possible, and decreasing their access to dangerous situations, such as by keeping chemicals out of reach.

The role of cognitive processes in the practice of health-related behavior has important implications here, since cognitive abilities are immature in early childhood and become increasingly sophisticated as children get older. With these advances, children are more able to engage in health-protective behavior and to assume responsibility for promoting their own health and safety (Burbach & Peterson, 1986;

Maddux, Roberts, Sledden, & Wright, 1986). As part of this ability, children need to understand the relationship between behavior and health. Roger Bibace and Mary Walsh (1979) have described six stages through which this understanding progresses:

1. *Phenomenism:* In children's earliest understandings of the relationship between health and behavior, they tend to define an illness in terms of a single symptom, usually a sensation they associate with it. The cause they cite for the illness is likely to be remote, for example, a 3-year-old might say "the sun" causes heart attacks.

2. *Contagion:* At this stage, children continue to describe an illness in terms of a single symptom, but they know a little more about its cause. They attribute a person's sickness to the proximity of a person or object that is its source—without understanding how the proximity might be important. Thus, if children at this stage say that "people get measles from other people" and you ask how, they might simply answer, "When you walk near them." They cannot explain the link further.

3. *Contamination:* Children at this stage define an illness with multiple symptoms and understand still more about its cause. Most children progress this far by 7 years of age. They state that contact with "dirt or germs" causes illness, and they recognize that behavior can play a role, saying that people catch colds from "taking your jacket off outside." But sometimes they report that certain behaviors, such as "smoking without your mother's permission," can cause illness simply because it's "bad."

4. *Internalization:* At this stage of development, children conceptualize illness in terms of a problem inside the body. They also know that the problem can result from contaminants getting inside when the person swallows or inhales. And they realize the direct effect that behavior can have, such as that people get heart attacks "from lifting heavy stuff and working too hard." Children now view themselves as being "able to prevent illness through proper care" (Bibace & Walsh, 1979, p. 294). This is consistent with the finding that children's beliefs in internal health locus of control increase sharply between 7 and 10 years of age (Perrin & Shapiro, 1985).

5. *Physiological:* Children at this stage can define illness in terms of specific body organs, giving details of how internal functions break down and citing multiple physical causes. Most children are able to do this by about 11 years of age. They might say, for example, "Cancer is when cells grow too fast. It may happen because of air pollution or chemicals."

6. *Psychophysiological:* In the last stage, children realize that illness can result from both physiological and psychological sources. They might state, for instance, that people get headaches "from problems and aggravation."

As individuals enter adolescence, they become more aware of the complex interaction of internal and external factors in health, illness, and recovery (La Greca & Stone, 1985). Caregivers and health professionals need to adjust their explanations and expectations for preventive action in light of young children's cognitive limitations and the progress they make as they get older (Burbach & Peterson, 1986).

Adolescence is a particularly critical time in the development of preventive behavior. Although teenagers have the cognitive ability to make the logical decisions leading to healthful behavior, they face many temptations and forces—especially peer pressure—that lead them in other directions (Brunswick & Merzel, 1986; Jessor, 1984; La Greca & Stone, 1985). This is the time when they stand the greatest chance of starting to have sexual relations, smoke, drink, and use drugs. Teenagers also learn to drive, and too often combine this new skill with drinking and using drugs. The large majority of deaths in adolescence result from accidents and violence. Deaths from automobile accidents rise sharply during the teenage years and account for more than 43% of all deaths among 16- to 17-year-olds. All these newly acquired behaviors involve substantial health risks, which teenagers are highly susceptible to taking. In performing these behaviors, the immediate experience and impressing peers seem to be more important to adolescents than the possible long-term consequences. Public health efforts need to be directed toward changing the behavior, personality, and environment of adolescents to reduce behavioral risks and enhance health-protective behavior.

Adulthood and Aging

When people reach adulthood, they become less likely than they were in adolescence to adopt new behavioral risks to their health. The large majority of adults of all ages practice at least some healthful behaviors with the intention of protecting, promoting, or maintaining their health (Amir, 1987; Harris & Guten, 1979). In general, older adults are more likely than younger ones to engage in various health behaviors, such as eating healthful diets, getting enough sleep, getting medical checkups, and not smoking (Belloc & Breslow, 1972; Leventhal, Prohaska, & Hirschman, 1985).

Do these age-related improvements in health behavior indicate that adults become more concerned about health habits as they get older? Probably, but this is not clear for two reasons. First, developmental research on the practice of health behavior has generally used cross-sectional methods. Age-related increases in the percentages of individuals who practice healthful behaviors may simply reflect an increased rate of survival of people who engage in these habits. Second, older and younger adults have very similar beliefs regarding the effectiveness of these behaviors in preventing such chronic illnesses as high blood pressure, heart attacks, and cancer (Leventhal, Prohaska, & Hirschman, 1985). Still, older adults are likely to perceive themselves as more vulnerable to these illnesses than younger adults, and may engage in preventive acts for that reason.

Old age is not what it used to be. Older people, as a group, are living longer and are in better financial and physical condition than in the past (Horn & Meer, 1987). One health behavior that generally declines as adults get older is regular substantial exercise (Leventhal, Prohaska, & Hirschman, 1985). Many elderly people avoid physical exercise because they tend to exaggerate the danger that exertion poses to their health, underestimate their physical capabilities, and feel embarrassed by their performance of these activities (Woods & Birren, 1984). The importance of developmental factors in promoting health will be examined in the next two chapters.

Gender and Health-Related Behavior

It is general knowledge that women live longer than men. At birth, an average female's expected life span is seven years longer than a male's in the United States. For those who survive to 65 years of age, a woman's remaining life expectancy is four years longer than a man's (USDHHS, 1987b). Why is this so? The answer involves both biological and behavioral factors (Cataldo et al., 1986; Kuller, Meilahn, & Costello, 1983; Verbrugge, 1985; Waldron, 1985; Wingard, 1982). Some of these factors are:

- The sex hormones that women produce in larger quantities than men seem to help protect them biologically from certain health problems, particularly cardiovascular disease, until menopause.
- Males have shorter life expectancies in most developed countries of the world, and boys have higher death rates than girls even in infancy. These findings also suggest that biological factors play a role in gender differences in mortality.
- Behavioral factors are implicated in the fact that boys have higher rates of injury than girls—such as from drowning, bicycling, and pedestrian traffic accidents.
- In adolescence and adulthood, males have higher rates of injury and death from automobile accidents than females.
- Men smoke more and drink more than women do, thereby making men more susceptible to cardiovascular and respiratory diseases, some forms of cancer, and cirrhosis of the liver.
- It may be that men's jobs, household work,

and leisure activities pose greater health hazards than women's, but little or no research has been done on these issues.

One of the few behavioral advantages that men have is that they get more strenuous exercise than women do. The practice of most other health-protective behaviors is similar for men and women.

The longer lives of women do not suggest that they have fewer health problems than men. Actually, the opposite is true (Verbrugge, 1985). Women have far higher rates of acute illnesses, such as respiratory and digestive ailments, and nonfatal chronic diseases, such as arthritis, dermatitis, anemia, and headache. They also use medical drugs and services much more than men do, even when pregnancy and other reproductive conditions are not counted.

Sociocultural Factors and Health-Related Behavior

If you were to ask Americans in the general population to rate the state of their health, you would probably find that most feel they are in pretty good health. A survey of over 200,000 people of all ages and backgrounds found that almost 90% of the males and females claimed to be in "good" to "excellent" health (USDHHS, 1986c). But not all segments of the population had such positive assessments. Compared with the population as a whole, people were much more likely to rate their health as "fair" or "poor" if they were over 45 years of age, or from the lower social classes, or black. As it turns out, these lower assessments reflect real health problems of the individuals who comprise these groups. In this section, we examine how health and health-related behavior are linked to two sociocultural factors—social class and minority group background.

The concept of social class, or socioeconomic status, describes differences in people's resources, prestige, and power within a society (Filsinger, 1987; Fitzpatrick & Scambler, 1984). These differences are reflected in three main characteristics: income, occupational prestige, and education. By almost any gauge of wellness, health correlates with social class (Marmot, Kogevinas, & Elston, 1987). Individuals from the lower classes are more likely than those from higher classes to:

- Be born with very low birth weight.
- Die in infancy or in childhood.
- Die in adulthood before age 65.
- Develop a long-standing illness in adulthood.
- Experience days of restricted activity because of illness.

Not coincidentally, people from the lower classes have poorer health habits and attitudes than those from higher classes; for instance, they smoke more, participate less in active sports, and are less likely to feel that individuals can actively promote their own health (Fitzpatrick & Scambler, 1984; Marmot, Kogevinas, & Elston, 1987). Research has also shown that people from the lower classes have less knowledge about risk factors for disease. They are less likely than individuals from upper classes to know, for example, that people can reduce their cardiovascular risk by controlling their blood pressure, stopping smoking, and eating a low-cholesterol diet (Hossack & Leff, 1987). As you probably know, members of disadvantaged minority groups are disproportionately represented in the lower social classes (USDHHS, 1986c).

Today a baby born in Cuba stands a better chance of reaching the age of one than the average black newborn in the United States (Moore, 1983; USDHHS, 1986c, 1987b). The rate of infant mortality in America is almost twice as high for blacks as for whites. Among babies who survive the first year, the life expectancy for a black baby is about five years shorter than that for a white baby in America. Moreover, regardless of that black baby's gender, he or she is far more likely than a same-sex white baby to contract a major chronic disease in its lifetime, and to die of that disease. Figure 6.4 compares racial mortality data for four major illnesses, revealing that the death rates from these health problems are far higher for blacks than for

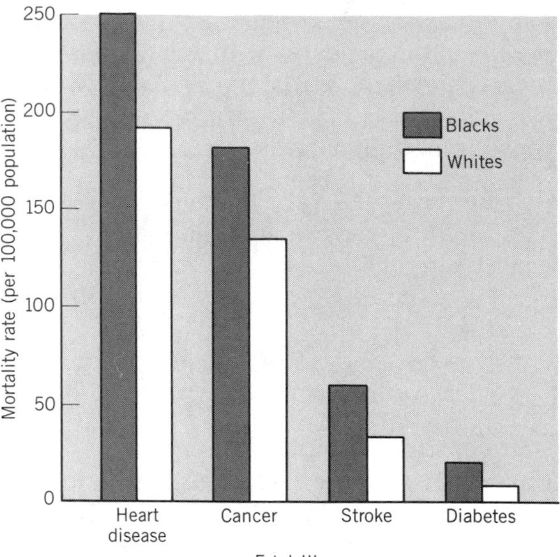

FIGURE 6.4 Death rates (per 100,000 individuals in the population) for whites and blacks in the United States, resulting from four leading chronic diseases. The rates are age-adjusted to take into account the facts that mortality rates increase with age and the average age of blacks is less than that of whites. (Data from USDHHS, 1986c, Table 20.)

whites. Although racial differences in health were much larger at the turn of the century, they are still substantial and remain a dilemma and a national disgrace. Clearly, minority group background is an important risk factor for poor health.

The two minority groups that have the greatest health risks in the United States are blacks and Hispanics. In general, the health problems and risk factors of Hispanics are intermediate, being neither as negative as those of blacks nor as positive as those of whites (USDHHS, 1986c). Many individuals in these minority groups live in environments that do not encourage the practice of health-protective behavior. Blacks and Hispanics also share a vulnerability to two health problems: substance abuse and injury or death from violence (Schinke, Schilling, & Gilchrist, 1986). Thus, they are more likely than whites to smoke, drink heavily, and use drugs. What is more, blacks and Hispanics—especially young males—are several times more likely than their white counterparts to become victims of homicide. These problems are disturbing, and correcting them will take a great deal of time, effort, and social change.

How can society help its members live healthful lives? Communities consist of individuals of different ages, genders, and sociocultural backgrounds. Efforts to promote health and prevent illness need to consider the specific health problems, lifestyles, cognitive abilities and beliefs, and sex-role characteristics of the targeted population. The remainder of the chapter focuses on programs for enhancing health and preventing illness.

PROGRAMS FOR HEALTH PROMOTION

In 1982, fast-food chains in New Orleans began using a gimmick to reverse a dangerous trend: more and more parents were not having their children vaccinated. The gimmick involved offering discount coupons for meals to parents who have their children immunized before the end of the summer. Other creative approaches by public health agencies have been used in other communities for the same purpose. We will begin our discussion of programs for health promotion by looking at some of the methods they use.

Methods for Promoting Health

Programs for health promotion try to encourage the practice of healthful behavior by teaching individuals what these behaviors are and how to perform them and by persuading people to change their current unhealthful habits. An important step in this effort is motivating individuals to *want* to change, and this often requires modifying people's health beliefs and attitudes. What methods do these programs use to encourage health-protective behavior?

Fear-Arousing Warnings

According to the health belief model, people are likely to practice healthful behavior if they believe that by not doing so they are susceptible to serious health problems. In other words, they are motivated by fear to protect their health. Many studies have found that fear-arousing warnings can be effective in motivating people to adopt a variety of more healthful attitudes and behavior, such as regarding dental health, safe driving, and smoking cigarettes (Sutton, 1982; Sutton & Hallett, 1988).

How threatening should the warning be? There is some controversy about this. Irving Janis (1967, 1984) has argued that each person and circumstance has an optimal level of fear arousal to motivate a change in attitude or behavior. Too much fear stimulates the person to use intrapsychic processes to cope — by ignoring, minimizing, or denying the threat. Although some research findings support this view, most studies of warnings do not (Janis, 1984; Sutton, 1982). Appeals that are very upsetting are more likely to induce people to change their attitudes than weaker appeals are. In an experiment demonstrating this, cigarette smokers filled out a questionnaire on their attitudes about smoking and their desire to quit (Leventhal, Watts, & Pagano, 1967). Then they received either a moderate-fear or a high-fear presentation regarding smoking. For both conditions, subjects saw a brief color movie that showed a mechanical "smoking machine" to demonstrate the harmful effects of smoking and some charts that described the link between cigarette sales and deaths from lung cancer. But the high-fear presentation had an added feature: a movie showing an actual operation to remove the diseased lung of a patient with lung cancer. Several subjects watching the film were so upset by this movie that they had to leave the room. After the presentation, the subjects answered the same questions they had answered before. The results showed that the subjects in the high-fear condition reported being more vulnerable to lung cancer and more eager to stop smoking than those in the moderate-fear group. The high-fear appeal was much more effective than the moderate-fear appeal in changing people's attitudes and intentions regarding smoking.

Do these results invalidate Janis' view? Not entirely. Although the high-fear presentation was very upsetting, it may have been feelings of revulsion more than fear that caused subjects to leave the room during the movie showing the operation. Warnings, no matter how intense, may not be as personally and directly threatening as having clear symptoms of a serious illness, as when a woman finds an obvious lump on her breast. When the situation is perceived to be personally and directly threatening, people may be more likely to use intrapsychic processes to cope.

An important problem with using fear-arousing warnings is that the attitude changes they produce often do not lead to behavioral changes. Many people may say they believe smoking causes cancer and they want very much to quit smoking, but still will not quit. Two conditions can enhance the likelihood that people's changed attitudes will lead to changed behavior (Sutton, 1982). First, people are more likely to carry out a new preventive action if they receive specific instructions for performing it. Second, some individuals lack a sense of self-efficacy to carry out a specific plan for health promotion. A program may be more successful in changing people's behavior if it helps bolster their self-confidence before urging them to begin the plan.

Providing Information

People who want to lead a healthful life need information — they need to know what to do and when, where, and how to do it. Consider, for example, the issue of dietary cholesterol. People need to know what cholesterol is and that it can clog blood vessels, which can produce heart disease. They also need to know where they can have their blood tested for cholesterol level, what levels are high, how much cholesterol is in the foods they currently eat, which foods might be good substitutes for ones they should eliminate from their diets, and how to prepare these foods.

Television, radio, newspapers, and magazines can play a useful role in promoting health by presenting warnings and providing information. The mass media have used three approaches in health campaigns, such as to help people avoid or stop smoking (Flay, 1987). One approach is simply to provide information to the general population about the *negative consequences* of an activity — smoking — and try to persuade people not to smoke, as public service announcements often do. This approach seems to have very limited success in affecting behavior (Flay, 1987; Lau et al., 1980). Another method focuses on people who already want to stop an unhealthful habit and tries to get them to *take the first steps* in doing so. In helping people stop smoking, a program using this method might ask smokers to quit for a day, request printed materials or kits with hints on how to stop, or contact a community agency. This method is successful in helping people stop smoking, particularly if it links the person with a community agency. The third approach presents *self-help clinics,* in which a TV audience follows individuals who are trying to change an unhealthful habit as they progress through a self-help program. This is probably the most successful mass media approach (Flay, 1987). Even though only about 20% of the audience of self-help clinics successfully quit smoking for a long period of time, these programs generally have a very large audience and help impressive numbers of people.

Medical settings, particularly physicians' offices, can be and should be a major source for information and warnings to promote preventive behavior. To be maximally effective, this process should be designed as a "lifetime health monitoring program" with particular health goals for each age period in the life span (Breslow & Somers, 1977). The physician or other health care worker would recommend and explain the importance of specific health behaviors and then try to assess the problems the patient may have following these recommendations. As Highlight 6C indicated earlier, the goals include beginning a schedule of vaccinations against infectious diseases in infancy and discouraging cigarette smoking in adolescence and adulthood.

There are advantages and disadvantages in using medical settings as a source of information for health promotion. Two advantages are that many individuals visit a physician at least once a year and respect health care workers as experts. But two disadvantages are that these efforts take up time in already busy practices and medical personnel may not know how to help people overcome the problems they have in following recommendations for prevention. Public health agencies have begun to address these disadvantages in their publications, such as *Clinical Opportunities for Smoking Intervention: A Guide for the Busy Physician* (USDHHS, 1986b). Table 6.2, for example, presents responses that health care workers can use to combat rationalizations smokers commonly give for not quitting.

Behavioral Methods

Behavioral methods focus directly on enhancing people's performance of the preventive act itself. These methods include providing specific instructions or training for performing the behavior, calendars to indicate when to perform infrequent preventive actions, and reminders of appointments. Research has shown that these techniques enhance the effectiveness of programs for health promotion (Kegeles, 1983).

Behavioral methods in health promotion also include manipulating the consequences of people's health-related behavior, particularly by providing reinforcers for practicing preventive action. Although using reinforcers can be useful for increasing health behavior, such as practicing good dental hygiene, the effectiveness of this method depends on many factors, including the type of rewards used, the age and sociocultural background of the individual, and the person's interest in performing the activity (Lund & Kegeles, 1982, 1984; O'Leary, 1984; Sarafino, 1987; Suls, 1984). For instance, people differ in their reward preferences — tickets for a Stevie Wonder concert might be very enjoyable for you, but your friend might prefer hearing a symphony performed by the Philadelphia Orchestra; and attending either of these events might be very unpleasant for someone else. The consequences need to be matched to the person. There is also some evidence that reward preferences change with age: kindergar-

TABLE 6.2 Responses to Common Patient Rationalizations

Rationalization	*Physician Response*
I am under a lot of stress, and smoking relaxes me.	Your body has become accustomed to nicotine, so you naturally feel more relaxed when you get the nicotine you have come to depend on. But nicotine is actually a stimulant that temporarily raises heart rate, blood pressure, and adrenaline level. After a few weeks of not smoking, most ex-smokers feel less nervous.
Smoking stimulates me and helps me to be more effective in my work.	Difficulty in concentrating can be a symptom of nicotine withdrawal, but it is a short-term effect. Over time, the body and brain function more efficiently when you don't smoke, because carbon monoxide from cigarettes is displaced by oxygen in the bloodstream.
I have already cut down to a safe level.	Cutting down is a good first step toward quitting. But smoking at any level increases the risk of illness. And some smokers who cut back inhale more often and more deeply, thus maintaining nicotine dependence. It is best to quit smoking completely.
I only smoke safe, low-tar/low-nicotine cigarettes.	Low-tar cigarettes still contain harmful substances. Many smokers inhale more often or more deeply and thus maintain their nicotine levels. Carbon monoxide intake often increases with a switch to low-tar cigarettes.
I don't have the will power to give up smoking.	It can be hard for some people to give up smoking, but for others it is much easier than they expect. More than 3 million Americans quit every year. It may take more than one attempt for you to succeed, and you may need to try different methods of quitting. I will give you all the support I can.

Source: From USDHHS (1986b).

ten children tend to prefer material rewards (a charm, money, candy) over social rewards such as praise, but this preference seems to reverse by third grade (Witryol, 1971). Other findings indicate that material rewards generally enhance performance of a behavior when the person's interest in practicing it is low, but they can *reduce* motivation when interest is very high (Sarafino & DiMattia, 1978). Programs for health promotion need to consider the point of view of the individual with regard to the preventive action and any consequences that the program introduces to enhance performance of that behavior.

Many types of programs have been carried out to promote health in different settings and with a variety of goals, methods, and populations. We will examine different types of programs, beginning with health education efforts that are designed to reach children and adolescents in schools and establish healthful habits at early ages.

Promoting Health in the Schools

Public and private schools have a unique opportunity for promoting health in the United States. They have access to virtually all individuals in the nation during the years that are probably most critical in the development of health-related behavior. Effective school-based health education teaches children what healthful and unhealthful behaviors are and the consequences of practicing these acts. This can produce two benefits. First, children may avoid developing unhealthful habits at the time when they are most vulnerable to these behaviors taking hold. Second, children may acquire health-protective behaviors that become established or habitual aspects of their beliefs and lifestyles that may stay with them throughout their lives.

Are school programs effective? Some have been. An experiment in 22 Bronx, New York, elementary schools introduced a carefully designed curriculum with emphasis on nutrition and physical fitness (Walter et al., 1985). The schools were randomly assigned so that their students either participated in the program or served as a control group. The researchers compared the two groups after a year. Relative to the control subjects, the children who participated in the program showed improvements in their blood pressure and cholesterol levels. Another study found that more children practiced safety behavior if they were taught about health and safety in a four-year program than if they were not (Parcel, Bruhn, & Cerreto, 1986). But many schools do not provide health education at all or their programs are underfunded, poorly designed, and taught by teachers whose interests and training are in other areas (Kolbe & Iverson, 1984).

Schools can use awards to encourage fitness, as these proud winners show.

Worksite Wellness Programs

There is a new "epidemic" in the health field—wellness programs are spreading rapidly in American workplaces. Some programs award prizes for losing weight, or pay employees for stopping smoking, or give bonuses for staying well. By doing this, employers are helping their workers and saving a great deal of money, too! Workers with poor health habits cost employers substantially more in health benefits and other costs of absenteeism than those with good habits. These extra costs generally exceed the expense of running a wellness program, thus making the program cost-effective (Fielding, 1982).

Worksite wellness programs vary in their aims, but they usually address some or all of the following risk factors: hypertension, cigarette smoking, unhealthful diets and overweight, poor physical fitness, alcohol abuse, and high levels of stress. Housing these programs in workplaces has several advantages:

> (a) Most employees go to the workplace on a regular schedule, facilitating *regular* participation in the programs; (b) contact with coworkers can provide reinforcing social sup-

> port, which is believed by many to be a primary force in sustaining a life-style change; (c) the workplace offers many opportunities for environmental supports, such as healthy food in the cafeteria and office policies regarding smoking; (d) opportunities abound for positive reinforcement for individuals participating in the programs; (e) programs in the workplace are generally less expensive for the employee than comparable programs in the community; and (f) programs in the workplace are convenient. (Cohen, 1985, p. 215).

These advantages suggest that worksite programs can attract high levels of participation and that employees who choose to participate are likely to succeed in improving their health behavior. How successful are worksite wellness programs? We will look at two model programs.

Johnson & Johnson's "Live for Life" Program

Johnson & Johnson is the nation's largest producer of health care products. They began the *Live for Life* program in 1978, and it is one of the largest, best-funded, and most effective worksite programs yet developed (Nathan, 1984). It is offered so far to about 10,000 employees in New Jersey and Pennsylvania, who comprise one-sixth of Johnson & Johnson employees worldwide. The health goal of the program is to help as many employees as possible live healthier lives by making improvements in their health knowledge, stress management, and efforts to exercise, stop smoking, and control their weight.

For each participating employee, Live for Life begins with a *health screen*—a detailed assessment of the person's current health and health-related behavior, which is shared with the individual later. After taking part in a lifestyle seminar, the employee joins *action groups* for specific areas of improvement, such as quitting smoking or controlling weight. Professionals lead sessions of these action groups, focusing on how the employees can alter their lifestyles and maintain these improvements permanently. Follow-up contacts are made with each participant during the subsequent year. The company also provides a work environment that supports and encourages healthful behavior; it has designated no-smoking areas, established exercise facilities, and made nutritious foods available in the cafeteria, for example.

Evaluation of Live for Life involves ongoing assessments, using quasi-experimental research methods. One epidemiological study compares the health and behavior of about 3,000 employees from different Johnson & Johnson companies that either did or did not offer the Live for Life program (Nathan, 1984). All these employees did, however, complete the initial health screen and another one a year later. Compared with the employees at the companies where Live for Life was not offered, those where it *was* implemented showed greater improvements in their physical activity, weight, smoking behavior, self-reported sick days, general well-being, and ability to handle job stress.

Control Data's "Staywell" Program

Control Data Corporation is a major computer manufacturer. This company introduced the *Staywell* worksite program in 1979 and offers it to 22,000 of its employees in 14 cities in the United States. The program has enrolled a large majority of these employees, particularly workers who are women, have higher levels of education, and do not travel a great deal (Naditch, 1984). The goals of this program are very similar to those of Live for Life.

Each Staywell participant completes a *health screening*, receives a resulting confidential health risk profile, and attends a workshop that focuses on interpreting the profile. The person can then join courses taught by professionals that provide information about lifestyle and health and teach the skills needed to change unhealthful behaviors. There are courses in physical fitness, nutrition, weight control, stopping smoking, and stress management. The individual can also join *action teams* that focus on two things: (1) making the work environment more healthful, such as by suggesting more nutritious foods for vending machines or organizing hiking or aerobic dance activities, and (2) forming support groups whereby members help one another in changing their behavior.

Evaluation of the Staywell program uses two approaches. First, because the program was not offered at some locations of Control Data, the health behaviors of workers at these sites could be compared against employee behavior at sites offering the program, using quasi-experimental methods. Second, at worksites with the Staywell program, comparisons could be made of health behaviors practiced by employees with different levels of participation, ranging from not participating at all to enrolling in courses to change unhealthful behaviors. Preliminary evaluations of Staywell using both of these approaches indicate that the program is quite successful in improving employees' health behaviors in weight control, exercise, smoking, nutrition, and stress management (Naditch, 1984).

Communitywide Wellness Programs

Communitywide programs for health promotion are designed to reach large numbers of people and improve their knowledge and performance of preventive behavior. These programs may use any or all of the methods we have considered. They may, for instance, use a media blitz to warn people of the dangers of drinking and driving, or provide information regarding free blood pressure testing, or offer people a chance to win a prize for stopping smoking or getting vaccinations. We will look at large-scale programs that were designed to improve people's health-related behavior and evaluate the effectiveness of the methods used.

The Three Community Study

In the early 1970s, researchers began the Stanford Heart Disease Prevention Program—an ambitious communitywide effort to get people to change their behavior and reduce their risk of cardiovascular disease. This program has conducted many studies since it began.

One of the program's earliest and best-known projects is called the *Three Community Study* (Farquhar et al., 1977; Meyer et al., 1980). For this study, the investigators selected three very similar communities with an average of about 14,000 people in northern California. Two of these towns shared the same TV and radio stations, and were chosen to receive an extensive mass-media campaign. The third town received no campaign and served as a control community because it was relatively distant and isolated from media in the other towns. The media campaign lasted for two years and consisted of warnings and information concerning smoking, diet, and exercise. The media included TV, radio, newspapers, posters, and materials sent through the mail.

To evaluate the success of the campaign, the researchers randomly selected several hundred 35- to 59-year-old men and women from each community and interviewed them annually. The large majority of these people completed the entire study, being interviewed before the media campaign began, again after one year, and then at the end of the campaign. At each interview, the researchers took blood pressure measurements and a sample of blood for analysis; they also assessed the subject's recent health behavior and knowledge about risk factors for heart disease. After the first interview, the researchers identified over 100 of the subjects in one of the two campaign towns as being at high cardiovascular risk; these individuals also received face-to-face health counseling. The researchers calculated each person's *overall risk* of cardiovascular disease by combining data on several risk factors, such as age, blood pressure, blood cholesterol levels, weight, smoking behavior, and so on. The Three Community Study found that people's overall risk increased somewhat in the control community and decreased moderately in the two campaign towns. Face-to-face counseling was particularly effective in getting people to stop smoking.

At about the same time that the Three Community Study was conducted, other researchers did a similar study in Finland and found similar results (Salonen, Heinonen,

Kottke, & Puska, 1981). Although the improvements in risk factors were not dramatic in either study, they showed that communitywide programs offer promising approaches for health promotion (Farquhar, Maccoby, & Solomon, 1984). As a result, subsequent research has focused on finding optimal strategies for changing health-related behavior.

Integrated Communitywide Programs

The success of the Three Community Study led researchers in different areas of the nation to undertake larger-scale and longer-term projects with more advanced methods for reducing cardiovascular risk factors. These projects include:

- *The Minnesota Heart Health Program*—conducted in midwestern cities and towns with a total of more than 350,000 people (Blackburn et al., 1984).
- *The Pawtucket Heart Health Project*—conducted in two New England cities with a total of over 170,000 people (Lasater et al., 1984).
- *The Pennsylvania County Health Improvement Program*—conducted in two Pennsylvania counties having a total of over 220,000 people (Stunkard, Felix, & Cohen, 1985).
- *The Stanford Five City Project*—conducted in five California cities with a total of about 350,000 people (Farquhar et al., 1984; Farquhar, Maccoby, & Solomon, 1984).

Each program involves several years of intervention that includes media campaigns and the extensive participation and integration of community organizations. The Pennsylvania program, for instance, involves a massive media blitz; special efforts by physicians to monitor their patients' control of hypertension and smoking; health promotion activities by social, civic, and religious groups; health education programs in schools, particularly for preventing smoking; and worksite programs to help workers stop smoking and improve their nutrition, weight control, blood pressure, and exercise behavior. All these programs have periodically collected data on their subjects, and preliminary analyses so far point to very favorable outcomes.

Prevention with Specific Targets: Focusing on AIDS

Sometimes prevention programs focus on reducing people's risk of developing a specific health problem and center these efforts on specific segments of the population. One example of this approach is the Multiple Risk Factor Intervention Trial (MRFIT), a project that recruited and provided health promotion programs for thousands of men across the United States who were at substantial risk for heart disease (Caggiula et al., 1981; Shekelle et al., 1985). The advent of the acquired immune deficiency syndrome (AIDS) epidemic has presented a major health crisis around the world and a challenge for public health programs. This disease is presently incurable and fatal. We will focus this section on efforts for the prevention of AIDS.

The magnitude of the AIDS threat is astounding—some public health experts have estimated that by 1988 possibly 10,000,000 people around the world had already been infected with the AIDS virus (HIV). About 100 countries have reported cases of AIDS, but the infection is unevenly distributed worldwide. The largest concentration of infections is in Africa, where the outlook is cataclysmic: estimates indicate that "between five and ten million people in Africa are now infected and by 1991 it is predicted that the number will increase ten-fold" (Osborn, 1988, p. 563). The second largest concentration is in the United States, where as many as 1½ million people are infected (Specter, 1988). Although no one knows for certain, some experts currently estimate that between 75 and 99% of those who are now infected will contract AIDS and die (Batchelor, 1988; Smith, 1988; Specter, 1988).

There is no vaccine against the HIV virus, and there is not likely to be one in the near future. The virus spreads to an uninfected person only through contact of his or her body fluids with that of an infected person, generally either through sexual practices or when intravenous drug users share needles. Infected mothers can also transmit the virus to their babies during gestation, delivery, and later during breast-feeding (Francis & Chin, 1987). Changing people's behavior is virtually the only means of reducing the risk of infection, and efforts for prevention have concentrated on using fear-arousing warnings and providing information. American mass media present warnings and new information about AIDS daily, public health agencies have prepared materials for teachers to present in schools, local health organizations have made speakers available for various community groups and worksites, and so on. These sources convey three basic messages:

1. Use "safe sex" practices by selecting sexual partners carefully, avoiding practices that may injure body tissues, and using condoms in all forms of sexual intercourse with individuals outside of very long term monogamous relationships.
2. Do not share needles or syringes. If you do, make sure they are sterile.
3. Women who could have been exposed to the virus through sexual practices or drug use should have their blood tested for the HIV antibody before becoming pregnant and, if the test is positive, avoid pregnancy.

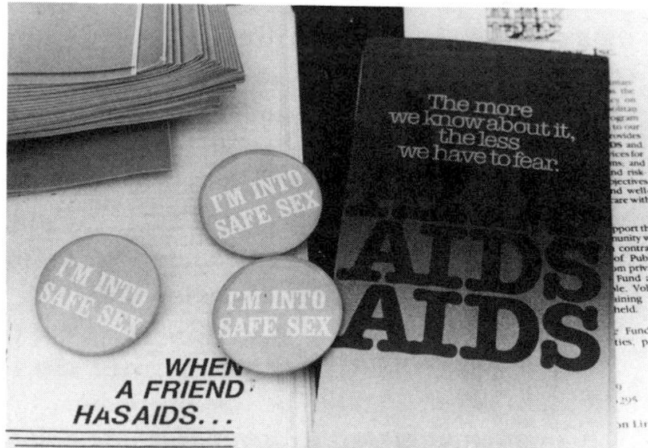

Efforts to prevent the spread of AIDS include the information on this table at a street fair.

Public health agencies also try to correct misconceptions about HIV transmission—for instance, that AIDS can only happen to homosexuals and drug users, that all gay men are infected, that mosquitoes can spread the virus, or that the virus can be transmitted through casual contact, such as by touching or hugging infected individuals or by sharing office equipment or *washed* kitchen utensils they have used (Batchelor, 1988; DiClemente, Zorn, & Temoshok, 1987).

It is true that a large proportion of AIDS victims in the United States have been gay men. This is probably because many gay men have been very promiscuous and have engaged regularly in certain sexual practices, especially anal intercourse, that involve a high risk of transmission (Darrow et al., 1987; Francis & Chin, 1987; Osborn, 1988). But many gay men do not lead high-risk lifestyles, lesbians have a very low incidence of AIDS, and the vast majority of victims in Africa are heterosexuals. A person's sexual orientation is not a guarantee of high or low risk.

Fear-arousing warnings have clearly aroused fear. Have informational efforts helped to change people's knowledge and behavior? Public health campaigns have been directed toward the general population, intravenous drug users and their sexual partners, and gays and bisexuals. Of people in the general population, adolescents and young adults are the age groups most vulnerable to infection because of their relatively high levels of sexual promiscuity and drug use. There is some evidence to suggest that knowledge about AIDS is improving in these age groups and that college students know more about it than high schoolers (Dorman & Rienzo, 1988). But because so many heterosexuals still have incorrect beliefs about the transmission of the virus and their likelihood of infection, they frequently do not take the precautions they should (Hirschorn, 1987).

Research findings with intravenous drug users suggest that over 90% of these people know that sharing needles can transmit AIDS and that most of them are now using sterile needles (Des Jarlais & Friedman, 1987, 1988; Des Jarlais, Friedman, Casriel, & Kott, 1987). But this caution is not extending as readily into their sexual behavior. Few drug users and their sexual partners use condoms (Krajick, 1988). Most drug users are heterosexual men, and their sexual partners often are women who know about the risks but feel powerless and are willing to go along with having unprotected sex.

Perhaps the best-organized efforts to change sexual practices have been directed at gays, particularly in gay communities in large cities. This is partly because many gay social, political, and religious organizations existed before the AIDS epidemic began, and these groups have become actively involved in public health campaigns to prevent the spread of the disease. Studies have found that these efforts have had a substantial impact on gay sexual behavior across the United States — such as in Chicago (Joseph et al., 1987), New York City (Martin, 1987), and San Francisco (Winkelstein et al., 1987). In San Francisco, for instance, gay men significantly reduced several high-risk patterns of sexual behavior between 1982 and 1986, and this greatly decreased the spread of the virus: incidence rates of infection declined during that period from over 18% to about 4% per year. AIDS education and prevention campaigns with gay and bisexual men have produced "the most profound modifications of personal health-related behaviors ever recorded" (Stall, Coates, & Hoff, 1988, p. 878).

Campaigns for reducing the spread of AIDS clearly can be highly effective. Although more needs to be done in gay communities, efforts must be sharply intensified in the general population — especially among adolescents, and particularly among black and Hispanic minority groups that have relatively high rates of intravenous drug use (Brooks-Gunn, Boyer, & Hein, 1988; Mays & Cochran, 1988; Peterson & Marín, 1988).

SUMMARY

People's behavior has an important impact on their health. Mortality from today's leading causes of death could be markedly reduced if people would adopt a few health-protective behaviors, such as not smoking, not drinking excessively, eating healthful diets, and exercising regularly. Although some people think that individuals are generally consistent in their practice of health-related behaviors and these behaviors are stable over time, this idea seems to be false. These behaviors can be quite changeable over time and practicing one habit is not strongly related to other habits. A person's practice of health-protective behaviors does not seem to be governed by a single set of attitudes or response tendencies. A health-related behavior that becomes well established tends to become habitual or automatically performed.

Health problems can be averted through three levels of prevention, one of which applies before a disease or injury occurs. Each level can involve efforts by the individual and by his or her social network, physician, and other health professionals. Primary prevention consists of actions taken to avoid illness or injury. It can include public service announcements, genetic counseling, and a wide variety of health behaviors, such as using seat belts and performing breast or testicular self-examinations. Secondary prevention involves actions taken to identify and stop or reverse a health problem. It includes tests and treatments health professionals may conduct, as well as illness and sick-role behaviors, such as visiting a physician when ill and taking medication as prescribed. Tertiary prevention consists of actions taken to contain or retard damage from a serious injury or advanced disease, prevent disability, and rehabilitate the patient.

People acquire health-related behaviors through modeling and through operant conditioning, whereby behavior changes because of its consequences: reinforcement, extinction, and punishment. Other determinants of these behaviors include genetic, social, emotional, and cognitive factors. Errors in people's perceived symptoms and ideas they have about illnesses can lead to health problems. People's thinking about health and illness is not always logical, and often they are unrealistically optimistic about their health.

Two theories focus on the role of health beliefs to account for people's performance of health-related behavior. The health belief model proposes that people take preventive action on the basis of their assessments of the threat of a health problem and the pros and cons of taking the action. The perception of threat is based mainly on the person's perceived seriousness of and susceptibility to the health problem. Assessing the pros and cons of the action involves weighing its perceived benefits and barriers. These assessments combine to determine the likelihood of preventive action. The theory of reasoned action proposes that people's health-related behavior is determined by their intentions, which are a function of their attitude regarding the behavior (for example, "Is it a good thing to do?") and their subjective norm. Both theories have been supported by research, but both provide incomplete explanations of health-related behavior. Other approaches for explaining health-related behavior include an emphasis on the role of stress (conflict theory) and on the role of personal control.

People's age, sex, and sociocultural background also affect health-related behavior and need to be considered in programs for health promotion. Methods for promoting health include fear-arousing warnings, providing information, and behavioral approaches. Programs for health promotion can be effective in the schools and in worksites. Communitywide wellness programs are designed to reach large numbers of people and improve their knowledge and practice of preventive behavior. The Three Community Study demonstrated that media campaigns can promote health, and subsequent research has also integrated extensive efforts by community organizations toward improving people's preventive actions, such as in stemming the spread of AIDS.

KEY TERMS

health-protective behavior
health behavior
illness behavior
sick-role behavior
primary prevention
genetic counseling
secondary prevention
tertiary prevention
health belief model
theory of reasoned action
conflict theory

7

LIFESTYLE FACTORS AND MODIFICATION I: SUBSTANCE ABUSE

PROLOGUE

The stakes were high when Jim signed an agreement to quit smoking for a year, beginning January 2nd. The contract was with a worksite wellness program at the large company where he was employed as a vice president. It called for money to be given to charity by either Jim or the company, depending on how well he abstained from smoking. For every day he did not smoke, the company would give $20 to the charity; and for each cigarette Jim smoked, he would give $25, with a maximum of $100 for any day.

Jim knew that stopping smoking would not be easy for him—he had smoked more than a pack a day since he began the habit over 20 years ago and he had tried to quit a couple of times before. In the contract, the company could have required that he submit to medical tests to verify that he did in fact abstain, but were willing to trust his word and that of his family, friends, and coworkers. These people were committed to helping him quit, and they agreed to being contacted by someone from the program weekly and giving honest reports. Did he succeed? Yes, but he had a few "lapses" that cost him $325. By the end of the year, Jim had not smoked for eight months continuously.

People voluntarily use many different substances that can harm their health. This chapter focuses on people's use of three of the most common of these substances: tobacco, alcohol, and drugs. For each substance, we examine who uses it and why, how the substance can affect health, and what can be done to help prevent people from using the substance and stop them from abusing it if they start. As these topics suggest, we address many questions in this chapter that are of concern to people who want to enhance their own and others' health. Do people smoke tobacco, drink alcohol, and use drugs more than in the past? Why do people start to smoke, or drink excessively, or use drugs? Why is it so difficult to quit these behaviors? If individuals succeed in stopping smoking, will they gain weight?

SUBSTANCE ABUSE

"I just can't get started in the morning without a cup of coffee and a cigarette—I must be addicted," you may have heard someone say. The term *addicted* used to have a very limited meaning, referring mainly to people's excessive use of alcohol and drugs. In recent years the meaning of the term has broadened, and people are commonly said to be "addicted" to smoking, eating, gambling, buying, and a wide variety of other things. How shall we define addiction?

Addiction is a condition, produced by repeated consumption of a natural or synthetic substance, in which the person has become physically and psychologically dependent on the substance. What are physical and psychological dependence? **Physical dependence** is a state in which the body has adjusted to the presence of a substance and incorporated it into the "normal" functioning of the body's tissues. This state has two characteristics:

- **Tolerance** is the process in which the body increasingly adapts to a substance and requires larger and larger doses of it to achieve the same effect. At some point, these increases level off.
- **Withdrawal** refers to unpleasant physical and psychological symptoms people experience when they discontinue using a substance on which the body has become physically dependent. The symptoms experienced depend on the particular substance used, and can include anxiety, irritability, intense cravings for the substance, hallucinations, nausea, headache, and tremors.

Different substances appear to have different degrees of *potential* for producing physical dependence: the potential is very high for heroin but is lower for other substances, such as amphetamines and LSD.

Psychological dependence is a state in which individuals feel a compulsion to use a substance for the pleasant effect it produces, without necessarily being physically dependent on it. They rely heavily on it—often to help them adjust to life and feel good—and they center many activities around obtaining and using it. Psychological dependence develops with repeated use through the process of learning. People who become addicted to alcohol first become psychologically dependent on it, and later become physically dependent as their body develops a tolerance for it. The potential for producing psychological dependence differs from one substance to another—it seems to be high for heroin and amphetamines and low for LSD.

Whether a person is *abusing*, or overusing, such substances as tobacco, alcohol, and drugs depends on the extent and impact of the use. Psychiatrists and clinical psychologists are concerned primarily with the psychosocial functioning of the person. They diagnose **substance abuse** on the basis of three criteria (Rosenhan & Seligman, 1984):

1. Existence of a clear pattern of pathological use, such as heavy daily use and an inability to stop or decrease using it.
2. Heightened problems in social or occupational functioning resulting from substance use, as when the person loses friends or jobs repeatedly because of it.
3. The existence of pathological use for at least a month.

Individuals meeting all three criteria are diagnosed as abusers. The second criterion clearly applies to alcohol and drug use, and not to tobacco use.

Like clinical psychologists, health psychologists are concerned about people's psychosocial functioning, but the impact of substance use on illness and injury is of great concern, too. As a result, we might want to add the issue of increased risk factors to the second criterion, which would then read: "heightened *risk factors for disease or* problems in social or occupational functioning resulting from substance use." Individuals who meet the three criteria, as revised, would be considered "substance abusers" from a health psychology point of view. Smoking cigarettes on a regular basis would qualify as abuse.

SMOKING TOBACCO

When Columbus explored the Western Hemisphere, he recorded in his journal that the people living here would set fire to leaves—rolled up or in pipes—and draw in the smoke through their mouths (Ashton & Stepney, 1982). The leaves these people used were tobacco, of course. Other early explorers tried smoking and, probably because they liked it, took tobacco leaves back to Europe in the early 1500s, where tobacco was used mainly for "medicinal purposes." Smoking for pleasure spread among colonists and in Europe later in that century. In the 1600s, pipe smoking became popular, and the French introduced *snuff*, powdered tobacco that people consumed chiefly by inserting it in the nose and sniffing strongly. After inventors made a machine for mass-producing cigarettes and growers developed mellower tobacco in the early 1900s for easier inhaling, the popularity of smoking grew rapidly over the next 50 years.

Cigarette smoking reached its greatest popularity in the United States in the mid-1960s, when about 53% of adult males and 34% of adult females smoked regularly (Shopland & Brown, 1985). Among adults between 20 and 45 years of age, smoking was even more prevalent: about 60% of the men and 40% of the women smoked regularly. It was at about that time, however, that the Surgeon General issued a report describing the adverse health effects of smoking, and warnings against smoking began to appear in the media and on cigarette packages. Since that time, the prevalence of adult smokers has dropped fairly steadily. Today, less than 33% of the men and about 28% of the women in America smoke (McGinnis, Shopland, & Brown, 1987).

Do these trends mean that cigarette manufacturers are on the verge of bankruptcy? Not at all—their profit margins are at an all-time high! This is because there are still 50 million smokers in America, the retail price of cigarettes has increased, and manufacturers have sharply increased sales to foreign countries (Stout, 1988). At the same time that smoking has declined in the United States, it has been increasing in Asia, Africa, and Latin America, especially in "third world" nations (Netter, 1987).

Who Smokes?

Although many millions of Americans smoke, most people do not. The adolescent and adult populations of the United States have more than twice as many nonsmokers as smokers. Are some segments of the population more likely to smoke than others?

Smoking varies with age. Very few individuals in the United States begin to smoke regularly before 12 years of age. But the great majority of people who will ever become regular smokers begin the habit before the age of 20 or so (Matarazzo, 1982; McGinnis, Shopland, & Brown, 1987). The habit generally develops gradually, and several years may pass before the individual's rate of smoking reaches its eventual adult level (Pechacek et al., 1984). The percentage of adults in the population who smoke reaches its highest level among individuals between 20 and 45 years of age and declines thereafter (McGinnis, Shopland, & Brown, 1987). Many people stop smoking in adulthood. About 31% of the men and 18% of the women in America today are *former* smokers.

We have mentioned gender differences in smoking, and these differences are significant. Before the 1970s, the prevalence of smoking among American males had always been far greater than that among females, but this gender gap has narrowed considerably for two reasons (McGinnis, Shopland, & Brown, 1987). First, much larger numbers of men than women have stopped smoking after starting. Second, although the percentage of individuals who have started smoking has declined steadily, it has decreased more sharply for males than for females. In every year since the mid-1970s, the percentage of adolescent girls who smoked regularly has exceeded that of boys by substantial margins. One representative example of this difference is for the year 1984: among high school seniors, 20.5% of the females and 16% of the males smoked regularly (McGinnis, Shopland, & Brown, 1987). According to psychologist Joseph Matarazzo, cigarette advertisers played a major part in these gender-related shifts in smoking prevalence by creating clever brand names and slogans. One slogan is

> "You've come a long way, baby," with its strong but still subtle appeal to the women's liberation movement. The "Virginia Slims" brand name artfully takes advantage of the increasingly well-documented research finding that, for many female (and male) smokers, quitting the habit is associated with gaining weight. (1982, p. 6)

There is an important and hopeful thing to keep in mind about the changes we have described in recent smoking behavior: they demonstrate that people can be persuaded to avoid or quit smoking.

Sociocultural factors are also associated with smoking (McGinnis, Shopland, & Brown, 1987). Although the percentages of both blacks and whites who smoke regularly have declined substantially since the 1960s, blacks are still more likely to smoke than whites. Differences in smoking rates are also related to social class. The percentage of people who smoke generally declines with increases in education, income, and job prestige. Thus, the highest rates of smoking are likely to be found among adults who did not graduate high school, have incomes under $10,000, and have blue-collar occupations, such as carpenters, maintenance workers, and truck drivers. In general, racial and social class differences in smoking are more pronounced among males than females.

How Much Smokers Smoke

An examination of cigarette sales figures reveals two curiously contrasting trends (Shopland & Brown, 1985). First, the number of cigarettes sold per adult person in the United States has decreased sharply since the 1960s, which corresponds with the decline in the percentage of smokers. But second, the total amount of cigarettes consumed in America has *increased* considerably during most of that period. These trends seem inconsistent, but they are not really.

There are two reasons why total cigarette consumption has increased. One reason is that the number of adults in the population increased, thereby offsetting the effect that declines in the percentage of adults who smoke would have on the number of smokers. The other reason relates to how much smokers smoke—since the 1960s, the proportion of smokers who smoke *heavily* has increased (McGinnis, Shopland, & Brown, 1987). Figure 7.1 shows how the percentages of male and female smokers who smoked heavily increased from 1965 to 1985. During the same period, the percentages of male and female smokers who were moderate smokers remained fairly stable and the percentages who were light smokers decreased. What this means, of course, is that the people who continue to smoke today are the ones who need to quit the most.

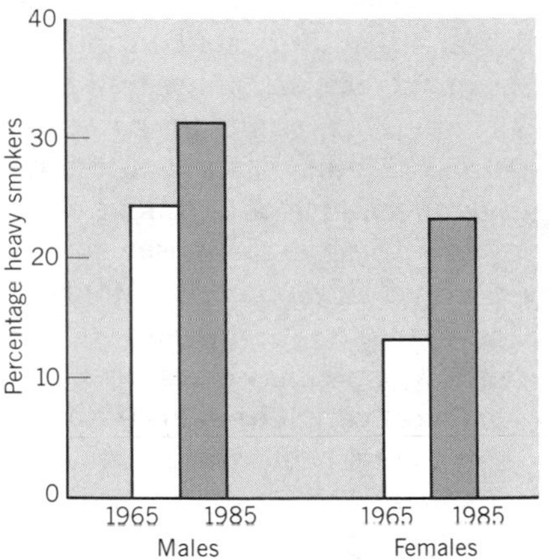

FIGURE 7.1 Percentage of American adult male and female smokers in 1965 and 1985 who were heavy smokers, consuming 25 or more cigarettes a day. (Data from McGinnis, Shopland, & Brown, 1987, Table 5.)

Why People Smoke

Cigarette smoking is a strange phenomenon in some respects. If you ever tried to smoke, chances are you coughed the first time or two, found the taste unpleasant, and, perhaps, even experienced nausea. This is not the kind of outcome that usually makes people want to try something again. But many teenagers do, even though they generally know that smoking is harmful to people's health (Evans, 1984; USDHEW, 1979). Given these circumstances, we might wonder why people start to smoke and why they continue.

Starting to Smoke

Smoking usually starts during the teenage years, and psychosocial factors provide the primary forces that lead adolescents to begin smoking. Several aspects of the social environment are influential in shaping teenagers' attitudes, beliefs, and intentions about smoking. For instance, many studies have found that adolescents are more likely to begin smoking if their parents and friends smoke (Hansen et al., 1987; Mittelmark et al., 1987; Pederson & Lefcoe, 1986; Severson & Lichtenstein, 1986; USDHEW, 1979). And when youngsters try their first cigarette, they typically smoke it in the company of peers, and with the peers' encouragement (Leventhal, Prohaska, & Hirschman, 1985). These findings suggest that modeling and peer pressure are important determinants of smoking.

The "smoker's image" and adolescent rebelliousness also seem to influence whether teenagers begin to smoke. Studies have found that boys and girls between the ages of 11 and 15 often associate smoking with being attractive to and interested in the opposite sex and with being "tough" rather than timid (Barton, Chassin, Presson, & Sherman, 1982; McKennell & Bynner, 1969). As psychologists Howard Leventhal and Paul Cleary have suggested, teenagers

> who are less successful in school . . . , more rebellious, and doing less well in meeting expectations of parents and traditional authorities . . . are more likely to be attracted to smoking at an early age and begin using cigarettes as a means of defining themselves as tough, cool, and independent of authority. (1980, p. 384)

Social images, models, and peer pressure are not easily overlooked by teenagers who are very concerned with how they are viewed by others.

Becoming a Regular Smoker

There is a rule of thumb about beginning to smoke that seems to have some validity: individuals who smoke their *fourth* cigarette are very likely to become regular smokers (Leventhal & Cleary, 1980). Although the vast majority of youngsters try at least one cigarette, most of them never get to the fourth one and don't go on to smoke regularly. Becoming a habitual smoker often develops slowly, sometimes taking a year or more (Ary & Biglan, 1988).

Why is it that some people continue smoking after the first tries, and others don't? Part of the answer lies in the psychosocial influences that got them to start in the first place. A longitudinal study examined the influence of psychosocial factors on the development of smoking by having over 6,000 young adolescents fill out questionnaires in school in two consecutive years (Murray, Swan, Johnson, & Bewley, 1983). The researchers then compared the subjects' reports for the two years to determine whether their social environments and beliefs about smoking were related to changes in their smoking behavior. Increases in smoking tended to occur if the subjects:

- Had at least one parent who smoked.
- Perceived their parents as unconcerned or even encouraging about their smoking.
- Had siblings or friends who smoked.
- Socialized with friends very often.
- Felt peer pressure to smoke, for example, reporting that "Others make fun of you if you don't smoke" and "You have to smoke when you're with friends who smoke."
- Held positive attitudes about smoking, such as "Smoking is very enjoyable" and "Smoking can help people when they feel nervous or embarrassed."
- Did not believe smoking would harm their health, for instance, feeling that "Smoking is dangerous only to older people" and "Smoking is only bad for you if you have been smoking for many years."

Other research has shown that teenagers usually smoke in the presence of other people, especially peers, and that smokers consume more cigarettes when in the company of someone who smokes at a high rate rather than a low rate (Antonuccio & Lichtenstein, 1980; Biglan et al., 1984). Adolescents who smoke also receive many times more offers of a cigarette from friends than nonsmokers do (Ary & Biglan, 1988).

Silvan Tomkins (1966, 1968) has outlined four psychological reasons why people who begin to smoke on a regular basis continue to smoke. One reason focuses on achieving a *positive affect*—smoking for stimulation, relaxation, or pleasure. Another reason centers on reducing *negative affect*, such as to relieve anxiety or tension. The third explanation is that smoking may become a *habitual* or automatic behavior that the person performs without awareness. Fourth, people may develop a *psychological dependence* (which he called "addiction") on smoking to regulate positive and negative emotional states. According to Tomkins, one or another of these reasons is the chief controlling factor in a particular person's smoking behavior. As a result, the person can be categorized as a "positive affect smoker" or a "habitual smoker," and so on.

Research has generally supported Tomkins's model, finding that people can be classified according to the chief controlling reason they express for smoking and that this reason affects their smoking behavior (Leventhal & Cleary, 1980). For example, two studies had smokers complete a questionnaire that assessed their reasons for smoking and then compared the behavior of subjects who scored high on a particular reason with those who scored low on it (Ikard & Tomkins, 1973; Leventhal & Avis, 1976). In one test of their behavior, the subjects smoked their own cigarettes that had been dipped in vinegar, which made the taste less pleasant. The subjects had been told that the study was to test "a special ingredient . . . to counteract some of the negative effects of smoking on lung capacity." Positive affect smokers — that is, those who scored high on the pleasure-taste reason for smoking — consumed fewer of these cigarettes than those who scored low on this reason. In another test, negative affect smokers — those who scored high on smoking to reduce anxiety — smoked more after watching a fear-arousing film than those who scored low on this reason.

Findings of other research also indicate that people use smoking as a means of coping with stress. One study found that smoking among young adolescents is related to the amount of stress in their lives — the greater the stress, the more likely they are to smoke (Wills, 1986). Another study had adult smokers interact in stressful social situations while they either smoked or did not smoke, and then had them fill out a questionnaire regarding their feelings during the interactions (Gilbert & Spielberger, 1987). The subjects reported less anxiety and greater effectiveness in expressing their opinions in the interactions when they smoked than in those when they did not smoke. But this does not mean that smoking is a "good" way to relax and reduce tension. Although smokers often perform better and feel more relaxed in stressful situations when they are allowed to smoke than when they are not, some evidence indicates that they do not perform better or feel more relaxed than nonsmokers do (Schachter, 1980).

Biological factors are also involved in sustaining smoking behavior. The fact that adolescent smoking is strongly associated with parental and sibling smoking shows that smoking runs in families. Certainly part of this relationship results from social learning processes. Does heredity also play a role? Twin and adoption studies have demonstrated that genetic factors have at least a modest influence on people's acquisition and maintenance of smoking (Hughes, 1986). Although researchers do not yet have a clear picture of the specific ways heredity influences smoking, tentative evidence suggests three possible routes. First, genetic factors may underlie certain personality traits, such as rebelliousness, that are associated with smoking. Second, heredity may influence the degree to which a person finds tobacco pleasant or unpleasant. Third, genetic factors may affect the degree to which a person becomes physically dependent on tobacco. As people become regular smokers, they show the phenomenon of tolerance, using increasing amounts of tobacco; and if smokers try to quit, they often suffer withdrawal symptoms (Blakeslee, 1987; Jarvik, 1979).

Physical dependence to tobacco occurs because of the chemical substances the body takes in with each puff. A person who smokes a pack a day takes more than 50,000 puffs a year, with each puff delivering a wide assortment of chemicals into the lungs and bloodstream (Jarvik, 1979; Pechacek, Fox, Murray, & Luepker, 1984; USDHHS, 1986e). These chemicals include carbon monoxide, tars, and nicotine. Cigarette smoke has high concentrations of **carbon monoxide**, a gas that is readily absorbed by the bloodstream and rapidly affects the person's physiological functioning, such as by reducing the oxygen-carrying capacity of the blood. It is possible that these physiological changes influence whether people like or dislike smoking. **Tars** exist as minute particles of residue, suspended in smoke. Although tars have important health effects, there is no evidence that they affect people's desire to smoke. **Nicotine** is the chemical in cigarette smoke that clearly produces rapid and powerful physiological effects that probably lead to physical dependence.

Nicotine is a substance that occurs only in

tobacco. When a person smokes, nicotine can penetrate cell membranes of the mouth and nose even before the smoke reaches the lungs, where alveoli quickly absorb nicotine (Jarvik, 1979; Pechacek, Fox, Murray, & Luepker, 1984). Nicotine is then transmitted to the blood and carried to the brain. There, it triggers the release of catecholamines, which activate both the central and sympathetic nervous systems, and these changes increase heart rate and blood pressure, for instance. In other words, nicotine stimulates or arouses the body. With each cigarette smoked, nicotine increases very rapidly in the blood. But it soon decreases through metabolism—about half of the nicotine inhaled from a cigarette decays after, perhaps, 20 to 60 minutes.

Biological explanations of people's continued cigarette smoking have focused chiefly on the role of nicotine. The most prominent of these explanations is called the **nicotine regulation model**. According to this model, established smokers continue to smoke to maintain a certain level of nicotine in their bodies and to avoid withdrawal symptoms. Stanley Schachter and his associates (1977) conducted an ingenious series of studies with adult smokers that provides strong evidence for this model. In one study, the researchers had subjects smoke low-nicotine cigarettes during one week and high-nicotine cigarettes during another week. As the model predicts, the subjects smoked more low- than high-nicotine cigarettes. This effect was especially strong for heavy smokers, who smoked 25% more of the low- than high-nicotine cigarettes. Consistent with these results, other researchers have found that people who regularly smoke "ultralow"-nicotine cigarettes do not consume less nicotine than those who smoke other cigarettes—ultralow smokers simply smoke more cigarettes (Maron & Fortmann, 1987).

Schachter and his colleagues also devised a set of studies that was based on three facts. First, chemical substances can vary in the degree to which they are acidic or alkaline, as measured on a scale of *pH* values: alkaline substances are high in pH, and acidic substances are low. Second, the body does not metabolize all the nicotine in it; the remainder is excreted in the urine. Third, the rate at which the body excretes nicotine depends on the pH of the urine—the lower the pH (that is, the more acidic it is), the more nicotine is excreted. Using these facts, these researchers manipulated urinary pH levels in adult smokers. During each of several successive weeks, the subjects took pills to govern the pH levels of their urine. Four types of pills were used. The acid-*decreasing* pills consisted of sodium bicarbonate. The acid-*increasing* pills were of two types, vitamin C and Acidulin. Lastly, the placebo pills consisted of cornstarch. The subjects did not know which kind of pill they received. The results were largely as predicted by the nicotine regulation model. Although the acid-decreasing pills had no effect relative to the placebo, the acid-increasing pills increased the subjects' smoking. This increase was about 17%, or four cigarettes a day.

The results of these studies clearly demonstrate that smokers try to regulate nicotine levels in their bodies by smoking. But there are reasons to think that the nicotine regulation model provides only part of the explanation for people's smoking behavior (Leventhal & Cleary, 1980). One reason is that the conditions used in Schachter's research did not have dramatic effects on the subjects' smoking—if nicotine regulation was the only factor, the changes in smoking would have been much larger. Another reason is that people who quit smoking typically continue to crave it, and often return to smoking, long after all the nicotine is gone from their bodies. Researchers today generally recognize that a complete explanation of the development and maintenance of smoking behavior involves the interplay of biological, psychological, and social factors (Ashton & Stepney, 1982; Galizio & Maisto, 1985).

Smoking and Health

"Warning: The Surgeon General has determined that cigarette smoking is dangerous to your health," a pack of cigarettes tells us. Since the late 1960s, cigarette manufacturers have been required by law to place a warning on each pack of cigarettes sold in America. Smoking is responsible for 320,000 deaths in the United States each year (McGinnis, Shopland, & Brown, 1987). It reduces people's life expectancy by several years and increases their risk of many illnesses, particularly cancer and cardiovascular diseases. To what extent do your odds of dying of lung cancer or heart disease increase if you smoke? Figure 7.2 shows that the odds increase greatly, especially for lung cancer (Mattson, Pollack, & Cullen, 1987). The more you smoke, the worse your odds become —and if you quit, your odds improve.

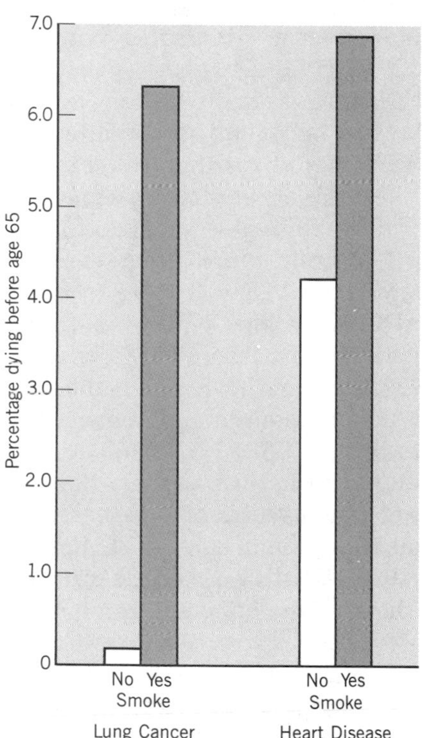

FIGURE 7.2 Probability of a 35-year-old man dying of lung cancer or heart disease before age 65 as a function of smoking heavily or not smoking. Data for women were less complete, but probably would reveal similar risk increases. (Data from Mattson, Pollack, & Cullen, 1987, p. 427.)

Cancer

In the late 1930s, two important studies were done that clearly linked smoking and cancer for the first time (Ashton & Stepney, 1982). One study presented statistics showing that nonsmokers live longer than smokers. In the other study, researchers produced cancer in laboratory animals by administering cigarette tar. By producing cancer with experimental methods, these researchers demonstrated a causal link between cancer and a chemical in tobacco smoke and identified tar as a likely *carcinogen.* Today the evidence is overwhelming that tobacco tars and probably other by-products of tobacco smoke cause cancer (Nelson, 1984; USDHHS, 1986e).

Hundreds of retrospective and prospective studies have consistently demonstrated the link between tobacco use and cancer in humans. Prospective research provides particularly strong evidence for a causal relationship because the subjects' smoking status is established at the start, and then they are followed over a long period of time to see if they develop cancer. According to researcher Sandra Levy, a number of large-scale prospective studies have linked smoking and

> cancers of the lung, mouth, pharynx, esophagus, bladder, and probably pancreas and kidney. Smoking is thought to contribute to bladder and kidney cancer because tobacco smoke contains a variety of chemicals—some of which are mutagenic—that are absorbed into the blood through the lung apparatus and travel to distant body sites. These chemicals have been found in concentrated doses in smokers' urine. (1985, p. 27)

Cancers of the mouth, pharynx, and esophagus can also result from using smokeless tobacco —chewing tobacco or snuff (Gritz, Ksir, & McCarthy, 1985; McGinnis, Shopland, & Brown, 1987). Thus, carcinogenic substances exist not only in smoke, but in tobacco products themselves.

As recently as the 1930s, lung cancer in America was quite uncommon and much less prevalent than many other forms of cancer, such as cancer of the breast, stomach, and prostate (Silverberg & Lubera, 1989). Deaths from lung cancer at that time occurred at an annual rate of about 5 per 100,000 people in the population, whereas mortality rates for breast and stomach cancer were more than five times that high. Over the years, the mortality rates for most forms of cancer have either declined or remained fairly constant, but not for lung cancer. The annual death rate for lung cancer has increased sharply to about 45 per 100,000 population. It is the deadliest form of cancer, being responsible for over 50% more deaths yearly than cancer of the colon or rectum, the second most deadly form. Lung cancer claims more than 100,000 lives in the United States each year, and over 90% of these deaths are related to smoking (Levy, 1985; Nelson, 1984).

The correspondence between the rises in lung cancer deaths and in smoking prevalence since the 1930s is quite striking (McGinnis, Shopland, & Brown, 1987; Shopland & Brown, 1985). The rate of mortality from lung cancer began to rise about 15 or 20 years after the rate of smoking started to rise, and these rates have paralleled each other ever since. During this time, the rates of smoking and of lung cancer were higher for males than for females, but since the mid-1960s, important gender-related changes have occurred. Smoking has decreased among men and increased among women, thus narrowing the gender gap—and corresponding changes in the incidence of lung cancer are now evident. Among men, the incidence of lung cancer may have leveled off or even started to decline, but it has been increasing steadily and alarmingly among women.

How does smoking harm the lungs? When smoke recurrently passes through the bronchial tubes, the lining of the tubes begins to react to the irritation by increasing the number of cells just below the surface. Then,

> the fine, hairlike growths, or cilia, along the surface of the lining, whose function is to clear the lungs of foreign particles, begin to slow or stop their movement. In time, the cilia may disappear altogether, and as a consequence carcinogenic substances remain in contact with sensitive cells in the lining of the bronchi instead of being removed in the mucous. . . . At this stage, a *smoker's cough* may develop. It is a feeble attempt by the body to clear the lungs of foreign particles in the absence of functioning cilia. (La Place, 1984, p. 326)

Lung cancer usually originates in the bronchial tubes. In most cases, it probably develops because of the continual contact of carcinogens with the bronchial lining.

Smoking is a major risk factor for all forms of cancer, but its role is more direct and powerful in lung cancer than in other cancers. People's environments contain many other carcinogens and smoking is not the only cause of these diseases.

Cardiovascular Disease

Cardiovascular disease—including coronary heart disease (CHD) and stroke—is the leading cause of death by far in the United States. It is responsible for almost half of all deaths each year and claims more lives than cancer, accidents, and several other causes combined (Matarazzo, 1984; Russell & Epstein, 1988). When you point out these facts to some smokers, they say, "Well you have to die of *something*." Of course, that's true—but *when* will you die is the real issue. Cardiovascular disease takes many lives early and is the leading cause of death among people between 55 and 65 years of age (USDHHS, 1985b).

Many millions of Americans suffer from CHD and stroke, and about a third of these cases are related to smoking (Bonita et al., 1986; Epstein & Jennings, 1986; USDHHS, 1986d). A prospective study examined the impact of smoking on the incidence of CHD across $8\frac{1}{2}$ years (Rosenman, Brand, Sholtz, & Friedman, 1976). Over 3,000 men participated in the research, beginning when they were 39 to 59 years of age. Compared to nonsmokers, the incidence of CHD was more than 50% higher for men who smoked about a pack a day and over twice as high for those who smoked more than a pack a day. The risks that smoking presents for developing CHD also depend on, or interact with, several other factors (Epstein & Jenkins, 1986; Khaw &

HIGHLIGHT 7A: On Issues
Does Someone Else's Smoking Affect Your Health?

"What do you mean I can't smoke on this plane! I paid for my ticket, and it isn't anybody else's business what I do to my body," the passenger said indignantly to the flight attendant. Some customers of airlines, railroads, and other businesses reacted strongly when smoking was banned in many public places recently. Why were these regulations introduced?

Not all tobacco smoke goes into the smoker's body, and much of that which does comes back out. All this excess smoke gets into the environment for others to consume, and is called *secondhand smoke* or *environmental tobacco smoke.* Breathing secondhand smoke is called **passive smoking** or involuntary smoking. In the mid-1980s, the Surgeon General issued a report on the effects of passive smoking, based on a careful examination of available evidence by dozens of physicians and scientists. This examination led to three conclusions:

1. Involuntary smoking is a cause of disease, including lung cancer, in healthy nonsmokers.
2. The children of parents who smoke compared with the children of nonsmoking parents have an increased frequency of respiratory infections, increased respiratory symptoms, and slightly smaller rates of increase in lung function as the lung matures.
3. The simple separation of smokers and nonsmokers within the same air space may reduce, but does not eliminate, the exposure of nonsmokers to environmental tobacco smoke. (USDHHS, 1986e, p. 7)

The smoke that comes from the burning tip of a cigarette—or *sidestream smoke*—makes up most of environmental tobacco smoke and contains high concentrations of known carcinogens (Eriksen, LeMaistre, & Newell, 1988).

The available evidence of the harmful effects of secondhand smoke is quite substantial. Some of the strongest evidence relates passive smoking to lung cancer (Erikson, LeMaistre, & Newell, 1988; USDHHS, 1986e). Many studies of this relationship have been conducted in a variety of countries around the world. These studies have typically examined the development of cancer in nonsmokers who had spouses who smoked. The large majority of these studies have found at least a modest elevation—ranging from 10 to 300%—in the risk of lung cancer. Given that the dose of smoke inhaled from the environment is less concentrated than that inhaled by smoking a cigarette, these results are very compelling. Research attempting to relate passive smoking to other cancers and cardiovascular disease have produced mixed or inconclusive results so far.

For people with existing cardiovascular conditions, such as angina, and respiratory problems, such as asthma and hay fever, environmental tobacco smoke can bring on attacks or aggravate acute symptoms (Eriksen, LeMaistre, & Newell, 1988). People are becoming increasingly aware of the health effects of secondhand smoke. As a result, nonsmokers have become more vocal in demanding smoke-free environments and the American public shows strong and growing support for efforts to ban smoking in public places and worksites.

Barrett-Connor, 1986; Perkins, 1985). In general, these risks of CHD are especially strong for people who:

- Are males.
- Are 45 to 55 years of age, rather than older.
- Have a family history of heart disease.
- Have high levels of cholesterol in their blood.
- Have high blood pressure.

Two other points are important in the link between smoking and CHD. First, the greater risks for CHD among smokers than nonsmokers may be aggravated by stress, since smoking increases when people are under stress. Second, smokers tend to have lifestyles that include other risk factors for CHD, such as being physically inactive (Castro, Newcomb, McCreary, & Baezconde-Garbanati, 1989).

How does smoking cause cardiovascular disease? Researchers generally believe that the disease process involves several effects that the nicotine and carbon monoxide in cigarette smoke have on cardiovascular functioning (USDHHS, 1986b). Carbon monoxide reduces the availability of oxygen to the heart, which may cause damage and lead to atherosclerosis. Nicotine constricts blood vessels and increases heart rate, cardiac output, and both systolic and diastolic blood pressure.

Other Illnesses

Smoking can lead to a wide variety of other illnesses—particularly emphysema and chronic bronchitis—which are classified together as *chronic obstructive pulmonary disease.* Illnesses of this kind are characterized by reduced airflow while the patient tries to exhale with force. Over 80% of cases of chronic obstructive pulmonary disease in the United States are related to smoking (Parker, 1985; USDHHS, 1986b). As we saw earlier, recurrent smoking irritates and damages respiratory organs. Research has shown that more damage occurs from smoking high-tar than low-tar cigarettes and that regularly smoking "non-tobacco" (marijuana) cigarettes also damages the respiratory system (Bloom et al., 1987; Paoletti, Camilli, Holberg, & Lebowitz, 1985).

Both emphysema and chronic bronchitis can incapacitate their victims, often forcing relatively young individuals to retire from work. These diseases also cause tens of thousands of deaths each year. The mortality rate from these diseases is much higher among smokers than nonsmokers at all ages in adulthood, and the difference in rates increases with age. For every 100,000 Americans between 65 and 75 years of age, for example, the annual number of deaths from emphysema and chronic bronchitis is about 180 for smokers and 16 for nonsmokers (USDHHS, 1986b).

Preventing Smoking

How can we prevent people from smoking? Public health approaches have involved increasing the price of cigarettes through taxation and restricting the purchase of cigarettes by underage adolescents. Other approaches try to help people avoid beginning to smoke. To do this effectively, prevention programs need to consider two important factors: *when* and *why* individuals start to smoke. The first factor is straightforward and easily addressed by prevention programs. People's likelihood of smoking begins to rise during the junior high school years and increases sharply in the high school years. Individuals rarely start to smoke in adulthood. As a result, programs to prevent smoking occur mainly in the schools, and should begin by the time children reach the age of 12 or so (Evans, 1984; Matarazzo, 1982).

Traditional approaches in the schools have focused on giving fear-arousing warnings, focused primarily around the future health consequences of smoking (Evans, 1984; Flay, 1985). These programs failed to take into account the past social experiences and current psychosocial forces that exert very strong influences on teenage behavior. As psychologist Brian Flay has pointed out in his evaluation of these programs,

> most past programs have been based on the premise that if children know why cigarette smoking is bad for them, they should choose to not start smoking. Of those conventional smoking education programs evaluated, many have succeeded in changing students' knowledge, some their beliefs, and some their attitudes, but very few have consistently reduced the onset of smoking behavior. (1985, p. 450)

Although these programs "educated" the students, they were not very effective in achieving their goal—preventing smoking. This failure points up the need of smoking prevention programs to consider more fully *why* children and adolescents begin to smoke.

As we saw earlier, researchers have identified several psychosocial reasons why young people start to smoke. Social influences and associated social skills appear to have stronger effects on teenage smoking than long-range health consequences that seem remote, both in time and in likelihood. Recognizing this, Richard Evans and his colleagues designed and tested a school-based program to deter teenage smoking by addressing psychosocial factors (Evans, 1976, 1984; Evans et al., 1978). The program focused on the immediate consequences of smoking, such as how much it costs and its physiological effects, and used films that had same-age peers as narrators. These peers gave information to help students understand how modeling, peer pressure, and cigarette advertising influence their willingness to smoke and to teach them how to resist these forces. The purpose of the program was to provide a *social inoculation*, whereby the knowledge and skills teenagers learned would "immunize" them against unhealthful forces that lead to smoking. This social inoculation approach produced very encouraging results, and has since served as the basis for developing increasingly effective methods for deterring smoking (Best et al., 1988; Flay, 1985; Severson & Lichtenstein, 1986).

Using the social inoculation approach, studies have tested programs for smoking prevention longitudinally, spanning one to three years (Best et al., 1988; Flay et al., 1985; Johnson, Hansen, Collins, & Graham, 1986; Murray et al., 1988; Murray, Richards, Luepker, & Johnson, 1987; Severson & Lichtenstein, 1986). Although the exact procedures varied somewhat from one study to the next, they were fairly similar. Most of the studies began when the children were in sixth or seventh grade (about age 12). They used a large number of schools, which were assigned to *program* or *control* groups in ways to assure comparability of the schools' size and social class across conditions. The subjects' self-reports of their smoking were verified in all studies, using biochemical analyses of saliva or breath samples.

What did the programs consist of and how effective were they? In one representative study (Flay et al., 1985), the program had the following components:

- Information about the short- and long-term health and social consequences of smoking.
- Discussions and films regarding how peers, family members, and the media influence smoking by teenagers.
- Modeling and role-playing of specific refusal skills, such as saying, "No thank you, I don't smoke."
- Requiring that each student decide his or her intention regarding whether or not to smoke and announce that decision publicly to classmates.

The program in this study was successful. Assessments of smoking after 18 months showed that the control subjects smoked more and were more likely to begin to smoke occasionally than the program subjects. Of the subjects in both groups who smoked regularly, those in the program group smoked less than the control subjects did. Perhaps most importantly, the beneficial effects of the program were strongest for subjects who were at high risk for smoking, that is, these adolescents already smoked occasionally before the program began and they had friends and family models who smoked.

Another school-based psychosocial approach for preventing smoking, called *Life Skills Training*, has been outlined and tested by Gilbert Botvin and his colleagues (Botvin, Renick, & Baker, 1983; Botvin & Wills, 1985). Since many individuals may begin smoking because they lack general social, cognitive, and coping skills, this approach focuses on improving these relatively broad skills with training in three areas:

1. Information about social influences on smoking and the short-term and long-term social and physiological effects of smoking.
2. Personal skills, including critical thinking for making decisions, techniques for coping with anxiety, and basic principles for changing their own behavior.
3. Social skills, including methods for being assertive and making conversation.

This program was tested in several junior high schools over a two-year period. Comparisons of smoking behavior of students in the Life Skills Training program with control subjects showed that the percentage of students who began smoking was lower among those in the program.

Despite the very encouraging results of these psychosocial approaches to prevent smoking, there are two reasons to be cautious about their effectiveness at this time. First, some psychosocial programs have not been successful and have had high subject attrition rates, particularly among smokers and those at high risk of becoming smokers (Biglan et al., 1987). Second, researchers do not yet know what specific skills, information, and methods of presentation are responsible for the success of programs that prevented or reduced smoking (McCaul & Glasgow, 1985; Severson & Lichtenstein, 1986). Still, the successes of many of these programs suggest that psychosocial approaches can be effective and should be applied in schools more widely to prevent smoking (Best et al., 1988).

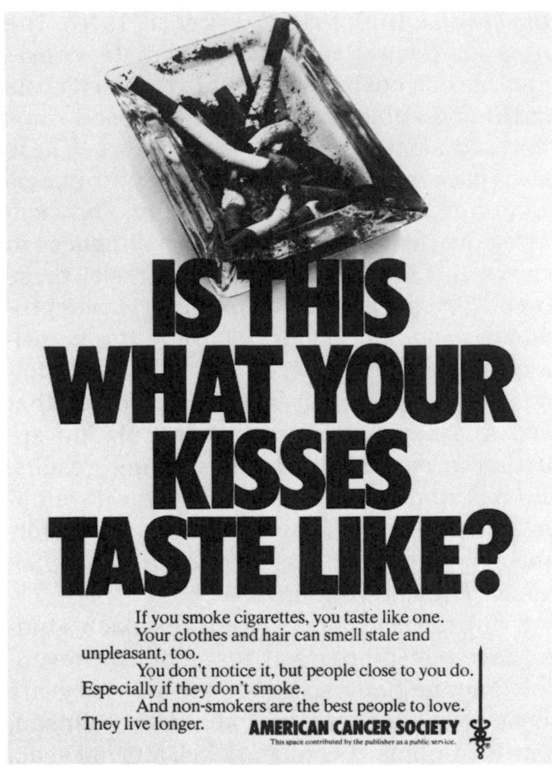

An advertisement by the American Cancer Society that may motivate people to avoid starting or to quit smoking.

Quitting Smoking

People are finding that cigarette smoking is not only harmful to their health, but it has negative social effects, too. Smoking in the United States has become something like a "deviant behavior"—many nonsmokers resent people smoking in their presence, and many smokers feel guilty when they smoke because they know it offends others and believe it is unhealthy, irrational behavior. Smokers today probably want to quit more than smokers ever did before. What methods do they use to quit, and which ones work?

Stopping on One's Own

You probably know people who were smokers —perhaps heavy smokers—who have quit. Chances are they stopped without any sort of professional help. In 1979, the Surgeon General estimated that about 29 million people had quit smoking in the previous 15 years, and that 95% of them had done so on their own. Are people really effective at stopping on their own, and does it take titanic effort?

Stanley Schachter (1982) interviewed about 160 men and women about their experiences in stopping smoking if they had ever smoked cigarettes regularly. The subjects ranged in age from 16 to 79 years and came from two communities: about half of them were residents of a small resort town and the other half were associated with the Columbia University Psychology Department, where he is a professor. Of these individuals, 94 had been or were currently smokers—73 were classified as heavy smokers (smoking at least three-quarters of a pack a day) and the remainder were classified as light smokers. These interviews revealed that over 60% of the smokers in each community who tried to quit had succeeded—virtually all had not smoked in the last three months, and the average length of abstinence was more than seven years. Was it harder for the heavy smokers to quit than the light smokers? Yes, much harder. Nearly half of the heavy smokers who quit reported severe withdrawal symptoms, such as intense cravings, irritability, sleeplessness, and cold sweats; less than 30% reported having no difficulties. In contrast, almost all of the light smokers said quitting had been easy, even if they failed! Interestingly, these differences had no effect on the subjects' success in quitting—63% of the heavy smokers and 65% of the light smokers who tried to stop were currently nonsmokers. A similar study conducted by researchers at another university found very similar results (Rzewnicki & Forgays, 1987).

The results of these studies suggest that most people can stop smoking on their own. Heavy smokers can be just as successful as light smokers at quitting, even though staying abstinent is much more difficult for them. Perhaps heavy smokers succeed as well as light smokers because they are more motivated to stop, perceiving greater social and financial costs and greater susceptibility to illness. What methods do smokers use when trying to quit? To answer this question, researchers interviewed participants in a month-long communitywide stop-smoking contest that had a grand prize of a trip to Disney World (Glasgow, Klesges, Mizes, & Pechacek, 1985). These interviews revealed that:

- The vast majority of the men and women attempted to quit "cold turkey" rather than trying to reduce their smoking gradually before the contest began.
- Most participants used oral substitutes, such as candy or mints, in place of cigarettes.
- Most tried to "go it alone," without involving other people, but many others used a buddy system or made bets with others.
- Most used cognitive strategies, such as telling themselves "I don't need a cigarette" or reminding themselves of the health risks in smoking, the commitment they made to quit, or the possibility of winning a prize.
- A minority of individuals provided themselves with material rewards or punishment for sticking with quitting or for backsliding.

Fifty-five participants—about 40%—remained abstinent throughout the month (which was verified through biochemical saliva or breath analyses). Some methods were more strongly related to successful quitting than others. Although some of the strategies were probably effective in helping particular individuals quit, only a few methods stood out as being effective for many participants. Compared to individuals who failed, those who succeeded tended to quit cold turkey rather than gradually, provide themselves with rewards for abstaining, and use positive cognitive statements to themselves (for example, "Think of the example I'll set by stopping smoking.") rather than negative ones (for example, "Think how weak I'll be if I give in and smoke.").

What about smokers who cannot seem to succeed in stopping on their own even after many attempts? Many of them stop trying to quit and continue to smoke, of course. Many others seek professional help in trying to stop.

Treatment for Stopping Smoking

Of the smokers who are willing to try to stop smoking, the ones who seek help are likely to be very psychologically and physically dependent on smoking. Therapists in clinics use a variety of methods to help.

One approach therapists have tried involves using *drugs* that might combat the conditions that maintain or increase smoking behavior (Blaney, 1985; Kozlowski, 1984). People report many reasons for smoking, including wanting to become aroused or to reduce tension. As a result, therapists have tried using tranquilizers and stimulants to reduce people's smoking, but these drugs have not been effective. Other drugs have been tested to combat the role of nicotine in smoking. For example, sodium bicarbonate has been tested because it alters the pH content of urine, thereby retains nicotine in the smoker's body, and should then reduce the craving for cigarettes. Another drug, lobeline, has been tested because it is like nicotine and might curb the desire to smoke. Current research does not support the use of either of these drugs. Perhaps the most promising drug approach involves having the smoker take nicotine directly, such as by chewing *nicotine-containing gum*. The gum decreases smoking withdrawal symptoms and appears to enhance short-term and long-term quitting success.

Therapists also use many behavioral methods for helping smokers quit. There are basically two categories of behavioral methods for stopping smoking—aversion strategies and self-management strategies—each of these includes several techniques (Kamarck & Lichtenstein, 1985; Lichtenstein & Mermelstein, 1984). **Aversion strategies** involve the use of unpleasant stimuli to discourage behavior—in this case, smoking. Therapists have tried three main types of unpleasant stimuli: electric shock, imagined negative scenes, and cigarette smoke itself. When electric shock is used in aversion methods, the level of shock is usually predetermined by increasing it from a low level until the person feels that it is uncomfortable or somewhat painful (Rimm & Masters, 1979). The shock is then paired with smoking situations. When imagined negative scenes are used, the person thinks about a sequence of events—for instance, getting ready to smoke followed by becoming nauseated and vomiting. Neither imagined scenes nor electric shock is a very effective aversion strategy for controlling smoking (Kamarck & Lichtenstein, 1985).

Using cigarette smoke as the unpleasant stimulus in aversion methods seems to be a more promising approach. One technique for using smoke as an aversive stimulus is called *smoke holding*, in which the person puffs on a cigarette and holds the smoke in his or her mouth for an extended time without inhaling. Another technique is *focused smoking*, whereby the person smokes regularly and pays close attention to the negative stimuli (odors, burning sensations) each puff produces. A third technique, called *satiation*, has the person double or triple his or her usual smoking rate at home for some period of time. These three methods appear to be useful in helping people stop smoking (Lichtenstein & Mermelstein, 1984).

One other approach that uses cigarette smoke as an aversive stimulus is controversial. This is the method of *rapid smoking*, in which the person smokes continually, inhaling every 6 seconds or so, until he or she is no longer able to tolerate more. Although rapid smoking is effective in helping people quit smoking, the procedure has important side effects—for instance, it can produce cardiovascular irregularities that could be dangerous for individuals who have coronary problems (Kamarck & Lichtenstein, 1985; Lichtenstein & Mermelstein, 1984). Rapid smoking may still be an appropriate procedure for young and healthy people who have been screened with a physical examination.

Self-management strategies involve techniques that are designed to help people gain control over environmental conditions that sustain an undesirable behavior, such as smoking (Blaney, 1985; Lichtenstein & Mermelstein, 1984; Rimm & Masters, 1979). Of the many self-management techniques therapists use to help people stop smoking, we will describe four:

1. *Self-monitoring* is a procedure in which people record information pertaining to their problem behavior, such as how often they smoked and the circumstances, places, and times of each instance. To encourage self-monitoring, a pencil and paper can be kept with the smokers' cigarettes. Although this technique by itself can produce a temporary decrease in smoking, its utility is mainly in gathering information to be used in other techniques.

2. *Stimulus control* procedures involve altering elements of the environment that serve as cues and lead individuals to perform the problem behavior. Many smokers report that they regularly have (and "*need* to have") a cigarette in certain situations, such as after meals, or with coffee or alcohol, or when talking on the phone, or while sitting in a favorite chair watching TV. Elements of these environments can be altered in many different ways, for example, by removing smoking cues such as ashtrays and matches or by restricting the time spent watching TV or sitting at the table after meals. Stimulus control procedures by them-

selves are moderately effective in reducing smoking, and are very useful when used with other techniques.

3. *Response substitution* involves replacing a problem behavior with an alternative one, particularly one that is incompatible with or not likely to be performed at the same time as the problem behavior. A smoker who "has to have a cigarette with coffee after breakfast" could skip coffee and take a shower right after breakfast. People are not likely to smoke in the shower (but some smokers do!).

4. *Contingency contracting* is a technique whereby certain conditions and consequences regarding the problem behavior are spelled out in a contract. Contingency contracts usually indicate the conditions under which the behavior may or may not occur and specify what reinforcing and punishing consequences will be applied, and when. Contracts for quitting smoking often have the person deposit a substantial sum of money, which is then meted out if he or she meets certain goals. This technique seems to be effective in controlling smoking, but only while the contingencies are in effect.

Each of these self-management methods is useful in the treatment of smoking. These methods are most effective when they are used together, rather than separately.

Several other therapy techniques have been tested, sometimes receiving a great deal of media attention. But research has not yet demonstrated that they are clearly more effective than control conditions (Blaney, 1985; Glasgow & Lichtenstein, 1987; Hunt & Matarazzo, 1982). These techniques include *hypnosis*, *systematic desensitization*, and *Restricted Environmental Stimulation Therapy* (REST). In the REST technique, the smoker lies on a bed for a 24-hour period in a very dark and quiet chamber, with no objects or stimulation available, but is free to eat, drink, and toilet freely (Suedfeld & Ikard, 1974).

Research has shown that some of the drug methods, aversion strategies, and self-management strategies are useful in controlling smoking, but none is highly effective *alone*. As a result, they are sometimes combined in *multimodal approaches* to improve their effectiveness. One multimodal program, for example, combined rapid smoking and self-management techniques, such as contingency contracting, and was highly successful: 76% of the smokers who received the multimodal program remained abstinent six months later (Lando, 1977). Another multimodal approach combined a variety of behavioral and educational techniques to help over 4,000 men in the MRFIT cardiovascular intervention program stop smoking. Of these men, 46% remained abstinent after four years (Hughes et al., 1981).

Regardless of the particular treatment techniques a program uses, it is more likely to succeed in stopping smoking if it includes three features. First, using biochemical analyses to verify self-reports of smoking and demonstrating these verification procedures at the *beginning* of treatment enhances the success of a program (Glynn, Gruder, & Jegerski, 1986). Second, a brief daily telephone call to the smokers improves their compliance with certain procedures, such as self-monitoring (McConnell, Biglan, & Severson, 1984). Third, people are more likely to decide to quit smoking and stick with it if their physician recommended that they stop (Anda, Remington, Sienko, & Davis, 1987; USDHHS, 1986b).

Succeeding at Quitting and Abstaining for Good

Quitting smoking is one thing — *staying* quit is another. As Mark Twain noted: "To cease smoking is the easiest think I ever did; I ought to know because I've done it a thousand times" (Grunberg & Bowen, 1985). The methods we have considered work well in helping people stop smoking, but preventing backsliding is a major problem.

Regardless of how smokers quit, their likelihood of *relapse* is very high in the first weeks and months after stopping. Most people who quit smoking start again within a year — estimates of relapse rates vary from 50 to 80%, depending on many factors, including the methods used in quitting, how heavily the person smoked, and characteristics of the individual and his or her environment (Brownell, Marlatt, Lichtenstein, & Wilson, 1986; Ossip-Klein et al., 1986). Withdrawal symptoms probably contribute strongly to immediate relapses, but these symptoms decline sharply in the first week or so after stopping (Cummings, Giovino, Jaén, & Emrich, 1985). What factors lead people to return to smoking?

One important factor in smoking relapse is *stress*: people who experience high levels of stress are more likely to start smoking again than those who experience less stress. Early research demonstrated, for example, that former smokers experienced less work stress than current smokers who had comparable jobs (Caplan, Cobb, & French, 1975). More recent research has examined the role of stress in relapse more directly: among individuals who have quit smoking, those who perceive higher levels of stress in their lives are more likely to relapse in the future than those with less stress (Lichtenstein et al., 1986). Acute episodes of anxiety or frustration at work or at home frequently lead ex-smokers to smoke (Shiffman, 1986).

Another factor in smoking relapse is *social support*, which can operate in at least two ways. First, high levels of positive social support can prevent individuals from backsliding by buffering them against stress, as we saw in Chapter 4. Second, social support can directly prevent relapse if people in the ex-smoker's social network encourage the person not to smoke (Colletti & Brownell, 1983). Encouragement can come from the person's family, friends, and coworkers, as well as from buddy systems in self-help support groups. But social support for smokers is not simply being in a social situation—which often encourages a relapse, particularly when the ex-smoker is in a restaurant or bar (Shiffman, 1986). Unfortunately, many people who quit smoking do not have the kind of support they need, and may even be explicitly *dis*couraged from abstinence by others offering them cigarettes or expressing doubt that they will remain abstinent (Sorensen, Pechacek, & Pallonen, 1986).

People's beliefs and attributions about themselves can also affect whether they return to smoking. Research has shown that people with high levels of *self-efficacy* for quitting and remaining abstinent are less likely to relapse than individuals with less self-efficacy (Baer, Holt, & Lichtenstein, 1986; Eiser, van der Pligt, Raw, & Sutton, 1985). Maintaining a sense of self-efficacy for remaining abstinent is not always easy. G. Alan Marlatt and Judith Gordon (1980) have proposed that for many individuals who quit, violating their abstinence—even with just one cigarette— can destroy their confidence in remaining abstinent and precipitate a full relapse. These people tend to interpret their violation as a sign of a personal failure, making them think, for instance, "I don't have any willpower at all and I cannot change." A study of individuals who violated their abstinence has supported this proposal (Curry, Marlatt, & Gordon, 1987).

People who go back to smoking often claim they did so because they were *gaining weight.* Smokers tend to weigh less than nonsmokers, and this difference increases with age and continued smoking (Grunberg & Bowen, 1985; Hofstetter, Schutz, Jéquier, & Wahren, 1986). When individuals stop smoking, most—but not all—do, in fact, tend to gain weight. Why is this so? Judith Rodin (1987) compared the food intake and exercise of individuals who gained weight with those who did not during the two months after they stopped smoking. Although those who gained weight did not consume more calories than the others did, they ate more sugar and engaged in less aerobic activity. But food intake and exercise are not the only reasons for weight changes after quitting smoking. Even when food and activity are unchanged, *not* smoking tends to reduce the overall amount of energy a smoker's body expends in metabolism (Hofstetter, Schutz, Jéquier, & Wahren, 1986). The results of these studies indicate that behavioral and physiological factors contribute to the changes in weight that ex-smokers experience. To prevent weight gain, many ex-smokers may need to control their diets and get more exercise.

The factors that lead an ex-smoker to smoke

again are very powerful; controlling them will be difficult. Some efforts to do this have been tried, but have had mixed success so far (Brandon, Zelman, & Baker, 1987; Glasgow & Lichtenstein, 1987; Hall, Rugg, Tunstall, & Jones, 1984). As you might expect, programs to prevent relapses have been more successful with people who had been lighter smokers than with heavier smokers—the ones who are likely to need help the most.

ALCOHOL USE AND ABUSE

People's use of alcoholic beverages has a very long history, beginning before the eras of ancient Egypt, Greece, and Rome, when the use of wine and beer was very common. Its popularity continued through the centuries and around the world, eventually reaching America in the colonial period. According to Barbara Critchlow,

> Colonial Americans brought with them to the New World the drinking habits and attitudes of the places they left behind. Liquor was viewed as a panacea; even the Puritan minister Cotton Mather called it "the good creature of God." By all accounts, these people drank, and drank hard. (1986, p. 752)

Women in the temperance movement were very assertive, and some went to saloons to keep records of who bought drinks.

But the Puritans also realized that excessive drinking led to problems for society, so they condemned drunkenness as sinful and enforced laws against it.

Over the next two centuries, attitudes about alcohol changed. The American *temperance* movement began in the eighteenth century and pressed for total abstinence from alcohol. By the mid-1800s, the use of alcohol had diminished sharply and so had its reputation: People in the United States at this time generally believed that alcohol destroys morals and creates crime and degenerate behavior (Critchlow, 1986). These attitudes persisted and helped bring about Prohibition, beginning in 1920, when the manufacture, transport, and sale of alcohol became unlawful. After the repeal of Prohibition, the use of alcohol increased, of course, and attitudes of Americans about alcohol softened. People today believe that alcohol has both good and bad effects.

Who Drinks, and How Much?

The casualness of many young people's attitudes today about drinking is reflected in a college yearbook rendition of little Miss Muffet sitting on her tuffet:

Drinking her whiskey and gin,
Along came a spider, and sat down beside her,
Said she, "It's the D.T.s again."
(From Kett, 1977, p. 261)

The "D.T.s" is slang for *delirium tremens*, the withdrawal syndrome commonly seen when alcoholics stop drinking. The symptoms of withdrawal often include intense anxiety, tremors, and frightening hallucinations.

People's experience with drinking alcoholic beverages in the United States typically begins before they leave high school, and sometimes in childhood. In a survey of thousands of students across the country, researchers found that more than 90% had tried alcohol by the end of their senior year (Johnston, Bachman, & O'Malley, 1982). Among high school seniors, males drank more than females: 29% of the boys, versus 15% of the girls, reported using alcohol at least 40 times in the preceding year; and 8.4% of the boys, versus 3.4% of the girls, claimed daily use of alcohol. More than half of the seniors reported that their first use of alcohol occurred prior to the tenth grade. Often the individual's early experience with alcohol occurs in the home with the parents present, such as at a special occasion. But most teenage drinking occurs in different circumstances. Even though it is illegal for most high school and college students to purchase alcohol and to drink without parental supervision, they do anyway.

About two-thirds of American men and women — over 110 million people — drink alcohol at least occasionally (Mayer, 1983; Rosenhan & Seligman, 1984). Most of these people are light-to-moderate drinkers, consuming fewer than, say, 60 drinks a month. Many people drink much more heavily, but not all of these drinkers meet the criteria for substance abuse we described earlier. Some heavy drinkers, for instance, are psychologically dependent on having, say, three drinks late at night to help them sleep, but their social and occupational functioning are not seriously impaired. Of those individuals who develop problems associated with drinking, most — but not all — do so within about five years of starting to drink regularly (Sarason & Sarason, 1984).

How many drinkers meet the criteria for substance abuse? Estimates indicate that more than 10% of all drinkers in the United States — over 11 million people — *abuse* alcohol (Mayer, 1983; Rosenhan & Seligman, 1984; Sarason & Sarason, 1984). People who abuse alcohol drink heavily on a regular basis, are psychologically dependent on it, and suffer social and occupational impairments. These people are called **problem drinkers.** They often get drunk, frequently drink alone, regularly drink during the day or go to work intoxicated, drive under the influence, and so on. Of adults who are problem drinkers, males outnumber females by a ratio of about 3 to 1 (McCrady, 1988). About half of those who abuse alcohol are physically dependent, or addicted, to it, and are classified as **alcoholics.** These people have developed a very high tolerance for alcohol, often suffer blackout periods or substantial memory losses, and experience delirium tremens when they stop drinking. Although alcoholics often drink the equivalent of a fifth of whiskey (about 25 ounces) a day, 8 ounces can sometimes be sufficient to produce addiction in humans (Davidson, 1985).

Who abuses alcohol? Many people have an image of the "typical" alcoholic as a scruffy looking, unemployed derelict with no family or friends. But this image is valid for only a small minority of people who abuse alcohol (Mayer, 1983; McCrady, 1988; Rice, 1984). Most problem drinkers are married, living with their families, and employed. Many women who are problem drinkers are homemakers, and a large proportion of alcoholic women are married to men who drink heavily. Although individuals from the lower social classes are at greater risk than those from higher classes for abusing alcohol, large numbers of problem drinkers come from the higher classes and hold high-status jobs. Problem drinking is very rare in childhood — its prevalence increases in adolescence and early adulthood, and people are more likely to seek treatment for alcoholism during the middle-age years than at any other time in the life span (Davidson, 1985; Rice, 1984; Stevens-Long, 1984). Alcohol abuse is a major social problem that affects substantial numbers of people from almost all segments of society.

Why People Use and Abuse Alcohol

In examining why people use and abuse alcohol, we need to consider why individuals start to drink in the first place. The chief reasons for starting to drink involve social and cultural factors (Bandura, 1986; Jessor, 1984). Children and adolescents learn through watching others that drinking is "fun"—people who are drinking are often boisterous, laughing, and, perhaps, celebrating. These people are typically family members, friends, and celebrities on TV or in movies—all of whom are powerful models. Through social learning processes, children and adolescents acquire *expectancies* about the positive effects of alcohol (Adesso, 1985). Teenagers also learn that drinking is "sociable" and "grown up," two things they generally want very much to be. As a result, when teenagers are offered a drink by their parents or friends, they are likely to see this as a very positive opportunity.

Adolescents continue drinking partly for the same reasons they started, but these factors intensify and new ones come into play. For one thing, the role of peers increases. Although teenagers usually begin drinking under their parents' supervision, drinking at home tends to remain at about the same level throughout adolescence while drinking with peers at parties or in cars increases steadily (NIAAA, 1974). A study of 14- to 17-year-olds found that as teens got older, they reported requiring more alcohol to "get a buzz" and more of them claimed to have friends who had used alcohol often; among the 17-year-olds, one-fourth reported that a close friend had been cited for driving while intoxicated (Schwartz, Hayden, Getson, & DiPaola, 1986). In late adolescence and early adulthood, drinkers drink frequently and almost always socially, with friends at parties or in bars. The social aspect is important in two ways (McCarty, 1985). First, in social drinking, modeling processes affect the behavior—for example, people tend to adjust their drinking rate to match that of their companions. Second, drinking socially creates a subjective norm in individuals that the behavior is appropriate and desirable.

Operant conditioning is another process by

Drinking and celebrating often occur together, and this association conveys the message that drinking is fun.

HIGHLIGHT 7B: On Research
How Does Heredity Lead to Alcohol Abuse?

It's one thing to know that heredity affects the development of alcohol abuse—as twin and adoption studies have shown—and another thing to know *how* it does. To understand how, researchers have been studying the children of alcoholics to determine why these offspring are prone to becoming problem drinkers themselves.

Marc Schuckit is one of the leading researchers in this field. He has conducted a series of studies with the basic approach of comparing individuals who are genetically at *high risk* for becoming alcoholic with those who are at *low risk*, where risk is determined by whether they have close relatives who abuse alcohol (Schuckit, 1985). He matches the high-risk and low-risk subjects on the basis of important demographic variables, such as age, religion, race, and amount of education. A critical feature of these studies is that Schuckit recruits the subjects during the late adolescent or early adulthood years, *before* any of them actually develops a drinking problem. In the research, the subjects receive either an alcoholic drink or a placebo, and are then tested for their reaction to the drink. The alcoholic drink is a pretty strong one—the equivalent of a few drinks—and the placebo looks, smells, and tastes like the alcoholic drink. The subjects in these studies have been males because the reactions of females to alcohol may be affected by their menstrual cycle or birth control pills.

What kinds of reactions to alcohol has Schuckit studied in these subjects, and what has he found? One reaction is their subjective feeling of intoxication, as rated by the subjects an hour or more after taking the drink. Of the individuals who had the alcoholic drink, those in the high-risk group reported less intoxication than those in the low-risk group. Both of these groups reported far higher intoxication levels than those who drank the placebo. In the placebo condition, high-risk and low-risk subjects did not differ in their low ratings of intoxication. Schuckit also studied other reactions to alcohol, as seen in eye-hand coordination and the swaying of the body. In all these tests, he found that the high-risk subjects showed less intense reactions to modest amounts of alcohol than the low-risk individuals.

What do these findings suggest regarding how heredity may lead to alcohol abuse? Schuckit has speculated that people who are genetically prone to becoming problem drinkers may lack the ability to feel the effects of drinking "at the blood concentrations at which most people make a decision to stop drinking" (1985, p. 2616). As a result, people who do not experience the symptoms of drunkenness early enough in each drinking episode may have trouble learning to stop.

---

which people continue or increase their drinking behavior through either positive or negative reinforcement (Davidson, 1985). Individuals may receive *positive* reinforcement for drinking if they like the taste of a drink, for example, or if they think that they succeeded in business deals or social relationships as a consequence of drinking. Having reinforcing experiences with drinking increases individuals' expectancies for desirable consequences when deciding to drink in the future (Adesso, 1985). In the case of *negative* reinforcement, people may use alcohol to reduce stress. Research has shown that people drink more when they experience higher levels, rather than lower levels, of stress (Baer et al., 1987; Marlatt, Kosturn, & Lang, 1975; Wills, 1986). Also, individuals drink to suppress their negative thoughts about themselves (Hull, Young, & Jouriles, 1986). But the effects of alcohol on people's anxiety and tension are not so simple: Although drinkers report that alcohol reduces tension and improves their mood, it only seems to do so with the first few drinks they consume in a series; after people consume many drinks, their anxiety and depression levels usually increase (Adesso, 1985; Davidson, 1985; Hull & Bond, 1986).

Why can most people drink in moderation, but others become problem drinkers? Part of the answer lies in psychosocial differences between these people. Compared to individuals who do not abuse alcohol, those who do are more likely to experience higher levels of stress and come from environments that encourage drinking. But a complete answer also includes biological factors (Galizio & Maisto, 1985; Zucker & Gomberg, 1986). Dozens of twin and adoption studies, as well as research with animals, have clearly demonstrated a genetic influence in the development of problem drinking (Crabbe, McSwigan, & Belknap, 1985; Goodwin, 1986; Schuckit, 1985). Twin studies in general have found that if one member of a same-sex twin pair is alcoholic, the risk of the other member being alcoholic is twice as great if the twins are identical rather than fraternal. Moreover, the results of adoption studies indicate that adopted children of alcoholics are, perhaps, four times as likely to become problem drinkers than other adoptees, irrespective of the drinking habits of their adoptive parents. But the interplay of genetic and psychosocial factors seems to be very complex, and their relative impact depends on the subjects' gender and severity of alcohol abuse.

Drinking and Health

Drinking too much is associated with a wide range of health hazards for the drinker and for people he or she may harm. Drinkers can harm others in several ways. Pregnant women who drink more than two drinks a day place their babies at risk for health problems (Cooper, 1987; LaBarba, 1984). Two to four drinks a day may lead to the baby being born with low birth weight; more than four drinks can produce *fetal alcohol syndrome*, which can involve serious cognitive and physical defects. The likelihood of fetal alcohol syndrome increases with the amount of alcohol consumed, the incidence rate being 0.4 per 1,000 births for the general population and as high as 690 per 1,000 births for babies of alcoholic mothers.

Drinking also increases the chance that individuals will harm themselves and others through accidents of various types, from unintentionally firing a gun to having a boating or skiing mishap (Smith & Kraus, 1988). Drunk driving is a major cause of death in the United States. Almost half of the approximately 50,000 deaths each year in automobile accidents are associated with alcohol use (McGuire, 1982; Press, 1987). Consuming alcohol impairs cognitive, perceptual, and motor performance for several hours, particularly the first two or three hours after drinks are consumed. The degree of impairment that individuals experience can vary widely from one person to the next and depends on the rate of drinking and the person's weight. Figure 7.3 gives the *average* im-

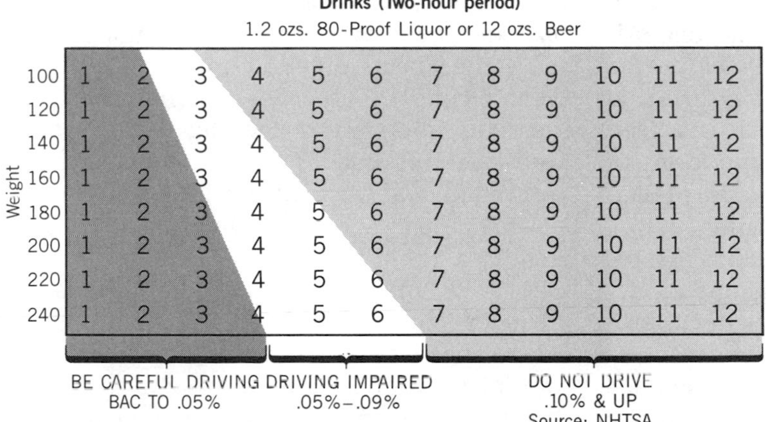

FIGURE 7.3 Chart developed by the National Highway Traffic Safety Administration (NHTSA) showing the *average* effects of blood alcohol concentration (BAC) on driving. Although alcohol impairment varies from one person to the next, three drinks (the equivalent of three 12-ounce bottles of beer) in a two-hour period will make most adults' driving unsafe.

pairment for driving—but for some people, one or two drinks may be too many to drive safely.

Many people have misconceptions about the effects of alcohol, believing that drinking on a full stomach prevents drunkenness or that "I'll be OK as soon as I get behind the wheel," for example. One study had sober college students estimate the effects of alcohol in a variety of drinking scenarios (Jaccard & Turrisi, 1987). The subjects' judgments revealed several misconceptions about alcohol: for instance, they underestimated the impact alcohol has two or three hours after drinking; thought that later drinks in a series have less impact than the first couple; and downplayed the effects of beer relative to wine, and wine relative to mixed drinks. Although beer contains a smaller percentage of alcohol than other liquors, many people seem to interpret this to mean that "beer does not make you as drunk as hard liquor," which is false. Getting drunk just takes a greater volume of beer than hard liquor.

Long-term, heavy drinkers place themselves at risk for developing several health problems. One of the main risks is for a disease of the liver called *cirrhosis.* Heavy drinking over a long period is one of several conditions that can cause liver cells to die off and be replaced by permanent, nonfunctional scar tissue. When this scar tissue becomes extensive, the liver is less able to cleanse the blood and regulate its composition. Cirrhosis causes thousands of deaths each year (USDHHS, 1985a). Heavy drinking also presents other health risks: it has been linked to the development of some forms of *cancer* (Levy, 1985), *high blood pressure* (Gleiberman & Harburg, 1986; MacMahon, 1987), and *brain damage* (Goldman, 1983; Parsons, 1986). The brain damage many alcoholics develop impairs their cognitive functions, producing perceptual disorders, severe memory deficits, and disorientation. These functions generally recover gradually over time after the person stops drinking, but some impairments may persist for many years or never disappear.

Some people believe that drinking in moderation—having, say, a drink or two a day—is *good* for their health, and they may be right. Several large-scale longitudinal studies, following many thousands of people across many years, have found that people who drink light or moderate amounts of alcohol each month have lower morbidity and mortality rates than individuals who drink heavily or who do not drink at all (Friedman & Kimball, 1986; Gordon & Doyle, 1987; Gordon & Kannel, 1984; Klatsky, Friedman, & Siegelaub, 1974, 1981). Does moderate drinking cause better health? We cannot be sure because of the quasi-experimental nature of these studies. If it does, the greatest benefit may be in reducing coronary heart disease. Although the reason alcohol may protect people from heart disease is not yet clear, there is evidence supporting two possibilities (Bennett, 1988; Levenson, 1986). First, alcohol affects the body's response to stress, reducing cardiovascular and endocrine (for example, catecholamine production) reactions. Second, alcohol promotes the production of one or more substances in the blood that protect the blood vessels from cholesterol. Still, we do not know enough about the effects of alcohol to recommend it for heart attack prevention.

Preventing Alcohol Abuse

Ever since the repeal of Prohibition, individuals and agencies concerned with public health have tried many different approaches to prevent alcohol abuse. We will classify these methods into three categories: public policy and legal approaches, health promotion and education, and early intervention approaches.

Public policy and legal approaches for preventing alcohol abuse are designed to reduce per capita consumption of alcohol by creating "barriers" to drinking (Ashley & Rankin, 1988). These approaches include limiting the number of outlets where alcoholic beverages can be bought and restricting the times when they are on sale. These two methods do not seem to be very effective in reducing drinking. A more effective method is to prohibit underage individuals from buying or consuming alcohol. This method reduces alcohol consumption and related automobile accidents among individuals in the late adolescent and early adulthood years. One of the most effective methods for reducing per capita alcohol consumption and preventing alcohol-related health problems is to increase the price of alcoholic beverages through taxation.

Health promotion and education approaches for preventing alcohol abuse provide information and training to help people avoid drinking heavily. Most of these programs have been directed at children and adolescents in schools and colleges. Unfortunately, the great majority of programs introduced before the late 1970s either were poorly conceived or did not provide a means for evaluating their success (Engstrom, 1984; Nathan, 1985; Pandina, 1986). More recent programs have demonstrated that *social inoculation* methods, like those we considered for preventing smoking, can be effective in controlling drinking among adolescents. The worksite should be a good place for preventing alcohol abuse because most individuals who abuse alcohol have jobs, and drinking is often related to stresses on the job (Mayer, 1983).

Another reason for using worksites for prevention programs is that some jobs or work environments encourage drinking, as when executives or sales representatives conduct business at "three-martini" lunches. Researchers discovered a more extreme situation among heavy-drinking, blue-collar workers at an industrial plant who

> drank on the job, during lunch breaks, and after work in parking lots, nearby bars, or in selected homes where cohort drinking was tolerated by wives. Many of those who worked nights began their drinking with their car pools on the way to work. Alcohol was often brought into the plant in lunch box thermos jugs or stored in lockers. . . . By their own reports, and that of their wives, most of the heavy drinkers had a routine weekday cycle of drinking by day in the work environment, and recovering or sleeping it off at home. (Ames & Janes, 1987, p. 952)

Unfortunately, wellness programs at worksites rarely include specific efforts to prevent employees from beginning to drink heavily (Nathan, 1985).

Early intervention approaches for preventing alcohol abuse focus on detecting the beginning stages of heavy drinking and providing information and help to reverse the individual's pattern of drinking (Ashley & Rankin, 1988; Engstrom, 1984). These efforts have been directed mainly at three populations: drinking drivers, employees, and medical patients. Efforts with drinking drivers have been disappointing—several very different approaches have been tested and shown to be successful *only* with people who are relatively *light* drinkers, not with heavy drinkers (McGuire, 1982). Indeed, heavy drinkers who receive intervention often have *worse* subsequent records of alcohol-related accidents and driving violations than heavy drinkers who receive no treatment.

For early intervention approaches with drinking employees and medical patients, however, the picture is brighter (Ashley & Rankin, 1988; Engstrom, 1984). Detection of emerging drinking problems can be accomplished in hospitals through laboratory tests and questionnaires, and in the workplace through the employee's job performance. If the drinking problem is detected very early, successful intervention may simply involve providing information and advice, and the person may be able to reduce his or her drinking pattern to one of moderation (Ashley & Rankin, 1988). If the problem is detected after addiction has set in, the treatment must be more intensive and the person may not be able to return to drinking at all. Many employers and unions provide *employee assistance programs* ("EAPs") to help individuals who have personal problems, such as with drinking or stress.

Treatments for Alcohol Abuse

In psychology and medicine, the term *spontaneous remission* refers to the disappearance of symptoms or problems without the benefit of formal treatment. Many people who abuse alcohol stop or markedly reduce their drinking on their own, without treatment. To some extent the phenomenon of reduced drinking is age-related: heavy drinking in the United States occurs more often in early adulthood than later, and

> the highest frequency of alcohol-related problems occurs in persons aged 25–45. . . . From ages 45–60, the frequency of alcoholism in the general population decreases. This has been called the "maturing out" phenomenon. Because of this age relation, it is expected that any reports of spontaneous change or treatment success will be smaller at younger ages. (Davidson, 1985, p. 393)

What proportion of people who abuse alcohol recover on their own? The best estimates available are based on data from a small number of studies of treatment effectiveness in which some problem drinkers were randomly assigned to control groups that received no treatment. Using the data on the control subjects, William Miller and Reid Hester (1980) calculated that spontaneous remission—stopping or markedly reducing drinking—occurs in about 19% of alcohol abuse cases.

Because of the physical dependence alcoholics have when they enter treatment, the first step in their recovery is **detoxification**—the "drying out" process of getting an addicted person safely through the period of withdrawal from a substance. This is an essential step for all addicted individuals before treatment can proceed. Because withdrawal symptoms can be very severe, sometimes even causing death, detoxification has typically taken place in hospitals under medical supervision. But improvements in assessment procedures and detoxification methods have reduced the need for direct medical supervision during alcohol withdrawal today (Miller & Hester, 1985). It is now possible to identify those alcoholics who are likely to need medical supervision and those who do not. About half of alcoholics who seek treatment can undergo detoxification at home if they receive careful assistance and support from trained individuals.

Where Should Treatment Occur, and What Should Be the Goals and Criteria for Success?

Professionals have applied many different treatments for problem drinking that have been based on a variety of philosophies and conducted in very different settings. In designing a treatment program, one of the many decisions the treatment team needs to make is where it should be carried out. Sometimes treatment occurs in residential settings, such as hospitals; in other cases, treatment is given through halfway houses or on an outpatient basis. Is residential treatment more effective than nonresidential treatment? In general, current evidence indicates that it is not (Miller & Hester, 1985). Problem drinkers can usually receive all or most of their treatment as outpatients.

The treatment team also needs to decide on procedures for assessing whether the program is effective. If treatment for alcohol abuse is effective, its rate of success should be greater than would be expected through spontaneous remission and its effects should be long-lasting. Ideally, treatment should "cure" the person's drinking problem forever, of course, but at what point can the team expect that their assessments of the success of treatment are likely to reflect durable effects? On this issue, there is considerable agreement among researchers: they generally recommend and use a minimum follow-up interval of 12–18 months to determine the success of treatment (Emrick & Hansen, 1983; Nathan, 1986). Many programs today also attempt to verify self-reports of drinking behavior through other sources—through reports by the ex-drinker's spouse or through blood or breath tests, for instance—and measure other outcomes of treatment, such as physical health, employment status, and legal problems encountered.

Another issue the treatment team needs to resolve is what the goal of treatment should be, that is, whether the program should aim to have all of its problem drinkers become *permanently abstinent* or whether some can return gradually to *controlled drinking*. The issue of whether recovered problem drinkers can ever drink again generated a bitter controversy in the 1980s (Marlatt, 1983; Peele, 1984). Research findings had indicated earlier that some problem drinkers—including alcoholics—can learn to drink in moderation after first becoming abstinent (Armor, Polich, & Stambul, 1978; Davies, 1962; Polich, Armor, & Braiker, 1981; Sobel & Sobel, 1976, 1978). Other researchers strongly attacked some of this research and the concept that people who abuse alcohol may be able to control their drinking (Block, 1976; Pendery, Maltzman, & West, 1982). Although the controversy is not completely resolved, it does appear that *some* problem drinkers can learn through treatment to drink in moderation. Several factors seem to be important in predicting which problem drinkers may succeed at controlled drinking (Miller & Hester, 1980; Peele, 1984). Individuals who have the best prospects:

- Are relatively young.
- Are socially stable, that is, married or employed.
- Have had a relatively brief history of alcohol abuse.
- Have *not* suffered severe withdrawal symptoms while becoming abstinent.
- Prefer trying to drink in moderation, and have *not* made a personal commitment to abstinence as a goal.

In other words, individuals who have the best chances of succeeding in controlled drinking are those who have the least resemblance to chronic alcoholics. For long-term alcoholics today, pursuing the goal of controlled drinking is unrealistic and probably not in their best interests (Nathan, 1986).

Alcoholics Anonymous

Alcoholics Anonymous (AA) is a widely known and used self-help program for quitting drinking that was founded in the 1930s by people with drinking problems (Robertson, 1988). The program now has thousands of chapters throughout the United States and around the world, and has set up organizations to help alcoholics' families: *Al-Anon* for the spouses of alcoholics and *Alateen* for their adolescent children. The AA philosophy includes two basic views. First, people who abuse alcohol are "alcoholics" and remain alcoholics for life, even if they never take another drink. Second, taking one drink after becoming abstinent can be enough to set off an alcoholic binge and, therefore, must be avoided. As a result, AA is committed to the goal of permanent and total abstinence, and their approach is aimed at helping their members resist even one drink.

Because the AA philosophy has its roots in evangelical Protestantism, the program emphasizes the individual's needs for spiritual awakening, public confession, and contrition (Peele, 1984; Robertson, 1988). This philosophy can be seen in the Twelve Steps AA uses to help drinkers quit—for example, one step is "Admitted to God, to ourselves, and to another human being the exact nature of our wrongs." Most members attend about four AA meetings a week, which use the Twelve Steps to promote frank discussions about the members' experiences with alcohol and difficulties resisting drinking. An important feature of the AA approach is that its members develop friendships with other ex-drinkers and get encouragement from each other and from knowing individuals who have succeeded.

Does AA work, and is it more effective than other approaches for helping drinkers quit? AA claims a very high rate of success: for example, one AA report claimed that 75% of those "who really tried" became abstinent (Miller & Hester, 1980). But AA's overall effectiveness is actually unknown because its membership is "anonymous" and the organization does not keep systematic information about people who attend. One way to compare the AA program against other approaches would be to randomly assign a pool of problem drinkers to different programs, as one experiment did (Brandsma, Maultsby, & Welsh, 1980). The subjects—most of whom had been referred by the courts because of their drinking problems—were assigned to either an AA program, one of three other treatment programs, or a control group. The results revealed greater improvement among those who received treatment than those who did not, and the subjects in the AA program showed somewhat less improvement than those in other treatments. It may be, however, that AA is the best approach for certain types of problem drinkers, particularly those who need an authoritarian structure and the intensive social support of other problem drinkers (Miller & Hester, 1980).

Insight-Oriented Psychotherapy

Many approaches to psychotherapy are designed to help the person achieve *insight*—an understanding of the roots of his or her problem. The rationale for these approaches is that insight is necessary for the person to "work through" and solve the problem (Sarason & Sarason, 1984). Although the nature of psychotherapy can vary widely and depends on the theoretical orientation of the therapist, most types of *insight-oriented psychotherapy* involve some form of counseling and have similar goals for the treatment of drinking problems. These goals include helping drinkers to accept that they need help, believe that they are worthwhile individuals, understand the factors that led to their drinking problem, and cope effectively with these factors.

Insight-oriented psychotherapy can be conducted with individual clients or with groups, and sometimes both approaches are used within one program for treating alcohol abuse. Studies have found that individual and group methods are each modestly effective in treating drinking problems (Miller & Hester, 1980). Since these two methods are equally successful with problem drinkers, conducting the therapy in groups has the advantage of being more cost-effective.

Behavioral and Cognitive Methods

Drinking excessively and smoking cigarettes heavily have a great deal in common—these behaviors can lead to addiction and they are difficult to quit, for example. As a result, variations of the methods we considered in the section on treatment for stopping smoking may apply to stopping drinking, too.

Aversion strategies—using unpleasant stimuli to discourage behavior—have been applied as treatment for alcohol abuse. One aversion strategy involves pairing drinking with electric shock, but this method has not been very successful in stopping people's problem drinking (Miller & Hester, 1980). A much more effective aversion strategy has been to pair drinking with a drug that induces nausea, as **emetine** does. (Another drug called *Antabuse* has been used, but it has several drawbacks.) Using this method, the person receives an injection of emetine, drinks alcoholic beverages, and very soon becomes nauseated and vomits. This process is generally repeated in a session for about half an hour (Miller & Hester, 1980). The person undergoes several of these sessions, typically as an inpatient in a hospital, and then receives "booster" sessions periodically after discharge. A study of hundreds of problem drinkers who received emetine therapy revealed that 63% of the men and women remained abstinent during the 12 months after treatment, and half of these individuals remained abstinent for the next two years (Wiens & Menustik, 1983). Other studies using emetine therapy have also demonstrated high rates of success (Miller & Hester, 1980).

Because *self-management strategies* are useful in helping people stop smoking, you might expect them to aid in quitting drinking—and they do (Lang & Marlatt, 1982; Miller & Hester, 1980). Successful treatment programs have used:

- Self-monitoring to help problem drinkers determine the situations that elicit and maintain drinking behavior.
- Stimulus control procedures to change or eliminate environmental cues that promote drinking, for example, by socializing with people who don't drink.
- Response substitution, such as finding someone to talk to instead of drinking when upset.
- Contingency contracting to help structure a set of rewards for abstinence and punishers for drinking.

The problem drinker's family can play an important role in self-management. Research has found that training family members, such as the alcoholic's spouse, in these strategies enables them to help in the drinker's self-management efforts, rather than undermining these efforts (Sisson & Azrin, 1986).

Two other methods seem to be useful in helping people quit drinking (Miller & Hester, 1980). One method involves training problem drinkers in *relaxation* and *systematic desensitization* techniques for coping with stress. This approach has value because feelings of anxiety and tension increase people's drinking behavior. The other method involves training in *social and problem-solving skills* to resist the urge to return to drinking. In one study, researchers focused on helping hospitalized alcoholics deal with realistic situations that can elicit drinking (Chaney, O'Leary, & Marlatt, 1978). As an example, the problem drinker imagined the following scene: being at a restaurant with friends, each friend orders a drink, and it is now the problem drinker's turn to order. The alcoholics were randomly assigned to skill training and control conditions. The results showed that drinkers who received training in dealing with difficult situations, such as the one in our example, were far more successful in maintaining improvements in their drinking behavior after a year than were drinkers who did not get this training.

Treatment Success and the Relapse Problem

The success of treatment for alcohol abuse depends on characteristics of the program and of the person. We have seen that many techniques are effective in helping people overcome drinking problems. Current research indicates that combining these techniques in a *multimodal* program generally offers the strongest promise for success, at least in the first year or two after treatment begins (Moos & Finney, 1983). Research by Raymond Costello and his colleagues has identified several components of programs that, when combined, seem to produce the greatest success (Costello, 1975; Costello, Baillargeon, Biever, & Bennett, 1980). These components include intensive inpatient treatment for several weeks, use of aversion strategies, continued outpatient treatment after release, application of self-management strategies, and active involvement of the person's relatives and employer.

Who succeeds when treated for alcohol abuse? Generally speaking, problem drinkers who function the best at the start of treatment are the most likely ones to succeed (Nathan, 1986). Thus,

> high socioeconomic status, a stable marriage or relationship, a steady and supportive employment milieu, higher education (12 years or more), a stable residential setting, and no criminal record (or few convictions) have all been related to a good prognosis irrespective of the type of treatment employed. (Caddy & Block, 1985, p. 353)

But many people drop out of treatment for alcohol abuse—and of those who complete a program, less than a majority maintain their improvement in drinking behavior beyond the first year or so. This seems to be the case regardless of the treatment characteristics, even when the more successful multimodal approaches are used (Costello, Baillargeon, Biever, & Bennett, 1980; Nathan, 1986).

The problem of *relapse* is at least as severe in efforts to stop drinking as it is in quitting smoking. Many of the more successful treatment approaches for alcohol abuse produce very high rates of success initially, but these rates decline sharply by the end of the first year and again during the next two years (Nathan, 1986). Studies of problem drinkers who relapsed have found that the circumstances preceding the relapse generally involve *negative emotional states*, such as depression or anxiety, and *social influences*, such as anger or social pressure (Abrams et al., 1986; Marlatt & Gordon, 1980). The method we saw earlier of training in social and problem-solving skills seems to be helpful in reducing relapse rates (Chaney, O'Leary, & Marlatt, 1978). In addition, social support systems, like those in AA programs, are likely to help ex-drinkers avoid relapse (Colletti & Brownell, 1983). Discovering effective methods of preventing relapse among problem drinkers has become a major focus of research.

DRUG USE AND ABUSE

Although the word *drug* can refer to an enormous variety of substances, including medicine, that people may take into their bodies, we will limit the term to refer to *illegal* substances that alter the person's *mood* and cause physical or psychological dependence. Like smoking and drinking, the use of drugs has a long history—for example, the Chinese evidently used marijuana 27 centuries B.C. In the United States, addiction to narcotics was widespread among people of all ages in the nineteenth century. Many "patent medicines" in those days contained opium and were sold without government regulation. As a result, large numbers of people became addicted at early ages (Kett, 1977). Laws were enacted in the early 1900s against the use of narcotics in America.

Who Uses Drugs, and Why?

We have seen that smoking and drinking are more likely to begin in adolescence than at any other time in the life span. This developmental pattern is true for using drugs, too. Using drugs also tends to begin during adolescence. For example, people's use of the most popular drug, marijuana, rarely begins before the seventh grade, and individuals who eventually try it are likely to do so for the first time before they reach the eleventh grade. Most teenagers try marijuana before they graduate high school (Johnston, Bachman, & O'Malley, 1982). Use of other drugs tends to begin somewhat later and is less prevalent. Whether a person progresses from a less serious drug, such as marijuana, to a more serious drug, such as cocaine, is related to how heavily the earlier drug was used (Kandel & Faust, 1975; Newcomb & Bentler, 1986). Heavy users of a less serious drug are more likely to begin using more serious drugs than light users are.

Why do adolescents use marijuana and other drugs? They do for many of the same reasons that they drink or smoke cigarettes (Hansen et al., 1987; Stein, Newcomb, & Bentler, 1987). Probably the strongest factor in determining initial and early stages of drug use is social learning: What behaviors and attitudes regarding drug use does the teenager perceive among peers and important adults, such as parents and celebrities? Studies have shown that adolescents are more likely to use marijuana and other drugs if their parents and friends use mood-altering substances, such as alcohol and marijuana (Brook, Whiteman, & Gordon, 1983; Jessor & Jessor, 1977; Stein, Newcomb, & Bentler, 1987). Teenagers' marijuana use seems to be affected more by their friends' than their parents' substance use, and the first introduction of most youths to marijuana is through a friend (Kandel, 1974).

After people start using drugs, they tend to continue if they like the experience—that is, if the drug makes them "feel good" or helps them feel *better* than they felt before taking it (Barrett, 1985; Rice, 1984). Many people claim that taking drugs reduces their anxiety and tension. In other words, drugs have reinforcing effects. Because people often use drugs in the presence of friends and other peers, social pressure and encouragement also tend to maintain and increase drug use. Why do some individuals progress from drug use to *drug abuse*? Personality traits seem to affect whether people abuse drugs. Compared to individuals who use drugs occasionally, those who go on to abuse drugs tend to be *more* rebellious, impulsive, accepting of illegal behavior, and oriented toward sensation seeking; and they tend to be *less* socially conforming and committed to a religion (Brook, Whiteman, Gordon, & Cohen, 1986; Cox, 1985; Newcomb, Maddahian, & Bentler, 1986; Stein, Newcomb, & Bentler, 1987).

Drug Use, Abuse, and Health

The effects of drug use and abuse on people's health are not as well documented as those of drinking and cigarette smoking. This is because drug use only became widespread since

HIGHLIGHT 7C: On Issues
Types and Effects of Drugs

"Oh, I feel so light, like a feather," said Dolores, after taking several "hits" from a "joint." That lightness of feeling is a common effect people get from smoking a marijuana cigarette. Each drug has its own set of general psychological and physiological effects. Some drugs are highly addictive, and others have little potential for producing physical dependence. Drugs are usually classified into four categories: stimulants, depressants, hallucinogens, and narcotics.

Stimulants are chemicals that produce physiological and psychological arousal, keeping the user awake and making the world seem to race by. This category of drugs includes *amphetamines* and *cocaine.* Chronic use of stimulants can produce mental confusion, exhaustion, and weight loss—and can lead to psychological dependence (Rice, 1984). The degree to which amphetamines and cocaine are addictive is debated, but people generally do not experience severe withdrawal symptoms when they abruptly stop using these drugs (Bardo & Risner, 1985).

Depressants decrease arousal and increase relaxation. People use these drugs to reduce anxiety and induce sleep. Depressants include *methaqualone* ("Quaaludes") and a variety of *tranquilizers* and *barbiturates.* Alcohol also causes depressant effects, but it is not illegal for adults to use. Excessive and chronic use of depressants interferes with motor and emotional stability and produces psychological *and* physical dependence.

Hallucinogens produce perceptual distortions, such as when the body or mind feels light. The most commonly used drug of this type is *marijuana,* which people use for the relaxation and intoxication it causes. Other hallucinogens, such as *mescaline, LSD* (lysergic acid diethylamine), and *PCP* (phencyclidine), often produce a feeling of exhilaration. Hallucinogens have a low potential for causing physical dependence, but chronic use of some of these drugs—especially marijuana—can lead to psychological dependence (Rice, 1984).

Narcotics or *opiates* are sedatives that relieve pain. In many people, but not all, they produce a euphoric and relaxed feeling. The narcotics include *morphine, codeine,* and *heroin.* These drugs, especially heroin, generally cause intense physical *and* psychological dependence with continued use (Bardo & Risner, 1985).

The effects of drugs can vary. The same dose of a drug may produce quite different reactions in different people and in the same person on different occasions (Bardo & Risner, 1985). Why? Physiological processes, such as metabolism and absorption by tissues, vary from one person to the next and within each individual over time. Partly because very young people and the elderly have lower rates of metabolism than others do, they tend to experience relatively strong reactions to drugs. Stress can also influence the effects of a drug. Being under stress causes physiological changes that may increase a drug's impact.

---

the early 1960s, it is still much less prevalent than drinking and smoking, and many drug users are unwilling to admit to researchers that they use drugs—a criminal offense—for fear of being prosecuted. Nevertheless, some health effects are known. For example, drugs taken by women during pregnancy cross the placenta and may harm the fetus; and babies born to addicted mothers are likely to be addicted, too (Moore, 1983). Also, smoking marijuana damages the user's lungs (Bloom et al., 1987). Furthermore, drug use is implicated in many automobile accidents each year (Jessor, 1984).

The health effects of cocaine are becoming increasingly clear, particularly with regard to the cardiovascular system (Altman, 1988). Taking cocaine causes the person's blood vessels to constrict, heart rate to speed up, and blood pressure to increase suddenly. It can also trigger cardiac arrhythmia. Any of these conditions can cause angina or myocardial infarction. Sometimes damage to the heart muscle can occur without pain or other clear symptoms and leave streaks of permanent, nonfunctional cells that cause the heart to beat irregularly. All these cardiovascular conditions can lead to death. Cocaine also produces harmful conditions in other parts of the body: it can destroy cells in the liver, cause brain seizures, and damage cells in the nose when it is sniffed.

Preventing and Stopping Drug Abuse

Public health efforts to prevent drug abuse have been directed mainly at children and adolescents through educational programs and campaigns in the schools and mass media. Before the 1980s, these efforts focused on presenting information about the negative consequences of drug use and were not very successful (Des Jarlais, Friedman, Casriel, & Kott, 1987). Prevention today tends to focus on teaching children and adolescents how to resist starting to use drugs, using programs based on the *social inoculation* and *Life Skills Training* methods we considered in preventing cigarette smoking. Preliminary research has shown these approaches to be much more effective than earlier methods in preventing drug use (Botvin & Wills, 1985).

Drug abuse involves entrenched behaviors that are difficult to stop, particularly if physical dependence has developed. Most of the approaches that have been tried for treating drug abuse are similar to those we considered for stopping drinking. Although the recent research literature on treating drug abuse is sparse, it seems to point to two conclusions (Bardo & Risner, 1985; Callahan, 1980; Parloff, London, & Wolfe, 1986). First, the more promising treatment approaches include behavioral and cognitive methods, such as self-management techniques. Second, for cases of narcotic addiction, effective treatment programs also use chemical agents to block the euphoric effects of heroin, morphine, or codeine. The most widely used agent is called **methadone**, a chemical that has physiological effects that are similar to those of opiates, except for two things: (1) it does not produce euphoria and (2) when it is taken regularly, it prevents euphoria from occurring if the person then takes an opiate. Methadone is usually taken orally. Having a narcotics addict take methadone—or a similar agent, *levoalpha acetylmethadyl* (LAAM)—regularly as a substitute for the opiate is called *methadone maintenance.*

Although methadone maintenance can be very effective in reducing the addict's craving for opiates, preventing withdrawal symptoms, and enabling the person to function in society, it also has some drawbacks (Callahan, 1980; Sarason & Sarason, 1984). For one thing, methadone is a form of narcotic, too—and the person becomes physically dependent on it. Taking methadone may also lead to weight gain and increased alcohol use, and sometimes produces involuntary muscle jerking. One other problem of methadone maintenance programs

A demonstration against the use of "crack," a form of cocaine.

is that many addicts in these programs would continue to use other drugs, such as cocaine. But this problem seems to have been solved: Programs often stipulate that before addicts get their next dose of methadone, they must submit to a urine test, which must find no evidence of drug taking. This approach has been very effective in stopping the use of nonnarcotic drugs (Callahan, 1980).

In our discussions of stopping smoking and drinking, we noted that relapse is a persistent and important problem. It is also a problem in stopping drug abuse, although methadone maintenance approaches have reduced the relapse rates for ex-opiate users. To prevent relapse with regard to all the substances we have considered in this chapter, programs for quitting will need to (1) enhance substance abusers' motivation to quit; (2) develop ways to match individuals to particular methods that are most likely to succeed for them; (3) teach them critical skills early in the program for avoiding relapse; and (4) have an aftercare program that involves continued monitoring of their behavior, provides helpful social support, and helps them adjust to a general lifestyle change (Brownell, Marlatt, Lichtenstein, & Wilson, 1986).

SUMMARY

People's use of tobacco, alcohol, and drugs can affect their health, particularly if the substance is abused. Addiction is a condition in which individuals have become psychologically and physically dependent on the substance. People who are physically dependent on a substance have developed a tolerance for it and suffer withdrawal symptoms when they abruptly stop using it. Substance abuse exists when a person has shown a clear pattern of pathological use for at least a month with resulting problems in social and occupational functioning.

Smoking tobacco preceded colonization in America, but did not become very popular until after the early 1900s. It reached its greatest popularity in the mid-1960s, and then declined after the Surgeon General released a report describing its harmful health effects. Most people who become cigarette smokers begin the habit in adolescence. Although a larger percentage of men than women smoke, this gap has decreased in recent years and a larger percentage of adolescent girls than boys smoke today. People are more likely to smoke if they are black rather than white and are from the lower rather than the higher social classes. Psychosocial factors influence whether individuals will start to smoke.

Whether people go on to smoke on a regular basis is determined by biopsychosocial factors. The likelihood of individuals becoming regular smokers increases if they have peer and adult models of smoking, experience peer pressure to smoke, and find that smoking helps them relax and have less tension. Cigarette smoke contains tars and carbon monoxide, as well as nicotine, a chemical that appears to produce physical dependence. The nicotine regulation model proposes that established smokers continue to smoke to maintain a certain level of nicotine in their bodies and avoid withdrawal. Research has shown that heredity also plays a role in people's becoming smokers. Smoking reduces the person's life expectancy and increases the risk of lung cancer, other cancers, cardiovascular disease, and chronic obstructive pulmonary disease. Breathing secondhand smoke is called passive smoking and is also harmful to people's health.

Programs to prevent smoking attempt to address relevant psychosocial factors by providing information and teaching important social skills. These programs teach children and adolescents about the immediate and long-term consequences of smoking, the ways modeling and peer pressure influence their tendency to smoke, and the ways they can resist these forces. Some programs also teach general social, cognitive, and coping skills. Once people become regular smokers, many of them — even those who are heavy smokers — are able to quit on their own, but many others are not. For those who have trouble stopping, therapists use several approaches that help. These approaches include having the smoker take nicotine directly; using aversion strategies, such as smoke holding, focused smoking, and satiation; and having the smoker learn and apply self-management strategies, such as self-monitoring and contingency contracting. Combining effective methods in a multimodal approach improves treatment success. Many people who quit eventually return to smoking. Relapse can result if the person experiences high levels of stress, does not have helpful social support, lacks self-efficacy, and begins to gain weight.

Americans drank alcohol at extremely high rates prior to the mid-1800s, when the temperance movement changed people's views about drinking and eventually led to Prohibition. After the repeal of Prohibition, alcohol use began to increase gradually. Most American adults drink at least occasionally. More than 10% of those who drink abuse alcohol and are classified as problem drinkers. About half of the problem drinkers are physically dependent on alcohol and are classified as alcoholics. People who are addicted to alcohol suffer withdrawal symptoms called delirium tremens when they quit drinking. Psychosocial factors —such as modeling, social pressure, and reinforcement—have a very powerful influence on drinking. Heredity plays an important role in the development of alcohol abuse.

Heavy drinking is related to a variety of health problems, including fetal alcohol syndrome in babies of drinking mothers, automobile accidents, and such diseases as cirrhosis of the liver, cancer, high blood pressure, and brain damage. The most promising programs for preventing alcohol abuse involve public policy and legal approaches, health promotion and education approaches, and early intervention approaches. For people who become problem drinkers, the first step in their recovery is detoxification. Treatment approaches for stopping drinking include Alcoholics Anonymous, insight-oriented psychotherapy, and a variety of behavioral and cognitive methods, such as aversion and self-management strategies, systematic desensitization, and training in social and problem-solving skills.

Many people use and abuse drugs that can be classified as stimulants, depressants, hallucinogens, and narcotics. Drugs differ in their potential for producing physical and psychological dependence. Drug abuse is related to a number of psychosocial factors, such as modeling, social pressure, reinforcement, and personality traits. The health effects of drug use and abuse are becoming increasingly clear. For example, using cocaine produces cardiovascular reactions that can cause a potentially fatal myocardial infarction. Prevention efforts today focus on social inoculation methods, like those used in preventing smoking and drinking. The most effective programs for treating drug abuse involve behavioral and cognitive methods; treatments for narcotic addiction often use drugs, such as methadone, that block the euphoric effects of opiates. Relapse is a critical problem in treatment programs for all of the substances discussed in this chapter.

KEY TERMS

addiction
physical dependence
tolerance
withdrawal
psychological dependence
substance abuse
carbon monoxide
tars
nicotine
nicotine regulation model
passive smoking
aversion strategies
self-management strategies
problem drinkers
alcoholics
detoxification
emetine
stimulants
depressants
hallucinogens
narcotics
methadone

8

LIFESTYLE FACTORS AND MODIFICATION II: NUTRITION, WEIGHT CONTROL AND DIET, EXERCISE, AND SAFETY

PROLOGUE

"Let's share something with each other," said the health expert to the members of a community workshop. "What excuses do we find ourselves using for not eating more healthfully, not exercising regularly, and not behaving in other ways that promote health, such as using seat belts? I'll start it off," she said, "by confessing that I sometimes skip exercising because I run out of time. What excuses do you use?" The answers came quickly:

"I never seem to have the energy to exercise."

"My wife sprained her ankle jogging, and I know lots of other people who injured themselves exercising."

"I don't have the time to prepare healthful meals."

"My grandparents ate high-fat diets and lived past 85."

"My kids hate vegetables and my husband insists on having meat for dinner."

"Seat belts are uncomfortable to use and wrinkle my clothes."

"I've had my habits for so long—it's hard to change."

People cite many reasons for not leading more healthful lifestyles. Some of the obstacles they describe can be overcome fairly easily, but others are more difficult. In most cases, people could find ways to overcome obstacles to healthful behavior if they believed it was important and were motivated to do so.

In this chapter, we discuss how nutrition, weight control, exercise, and safety measures are important to people's health. We also examine what people do and do not do in these areas of their lifestyles, as well as why they behave as they do and how they can change unhealthful behaviors. As we study these lifestyle factors, we will consider important questions and problems people have in leading a healthy life. Which foods are healthful, and which are not? What determines the preferences people have for different foods, such as sweets? Why do overweight individuals have such a hard time losing weight and keeping it off? What kinds of exercise benefit health? What hazards exist in our environments, and how can we protect ourselves from them?

NUTRITION

"You are what you eat," as the saying goes. This saying has at least two meanings. The most common meaning is that the quality of your diet can determine how you look, act, and feel. Another meaning is that

> food and the human body are made up of the same classes of chemicals: water, carbohydrates, fats, proteins, vitamins, and minerals. . . . Each of these classes makes identifiable contributions to the metabolic processes of all cells in the body. (Greenfield, 1985, pp. 293–294)

In this section, we will examine aspects of both meanings, beginning with the components of food and their importance in metabolic processes.

Components of Food

Healthful diets provide optimal amounts of all essential nutrients for the body's metabolic needs. In addition to water, food contains five types of chemical components that provide specific nutrients for body functioning (Greenfield, 1985; Holum, 1987; Nelson, 1984; Suitor & Hunter, 1980). The five types of components and their roles in metabolism are:

1. *Carbohydrates* include simple and more complex sugars that constitute major sources of energy for the body. Simple sugars include *glucose*, which is found in foods made of animal products, and *fructose*, which is found in fruits and honey. Diets may also provide more complex sugars, such as *sucrose* (table sugar), *lactose* in milk products, and *starch* in many plants.

2. *Lipids* or "fats" also provide energy for the body. Lipids include saturated and polyunsaturated fats, as well as cholesterol.

3. *Proteins* are important mainly in the body's synthesis of new cell material. They are composed of organic molecules called *amino acids*; about half of the 20 or so known amino acids are essential for body development and functioning and must be provided by the diet.

4. *Vitamins* are organic chemicals that regulate metabolism and functions of the body. They are used in converting nutrients to energy, producing hormones, and breaking down waste products and toxins. Some vitamins (A, D, E, and K) are *fat-soluble*—they dissolve in fats and are stored in the body's fatty tissue. The remaining vitamins are *water-soluble*—the body stores very little of these vitamins and excretes excess quantities as waste.

5. *Minerals* are inorganic substances—such as calcium, phosphorus, potassium, sodium, iron, iodine, and zinc—and each is important in body development and functioning. For example, calcium and phosphorus are components of bones and teeth, potassium and sodium are involved in nerve transmission, and iron is important in transporting oxygen in the blood.

Food also contains *fiber*, which is not considered a nutrient because it is not used in metabolism but is still needed in the process of digestion.

People can get all the nutrients and fiber they need by eating diets that consist of a variety of foods from four basic groups: grains, fruits and vegetables, milk products, and meats and fish (Nelson, 1984; Suitor & Hunter, 1980). Breads and cereals made of whole grains have more fiber than those made of grains that are "enriched" or "fortified" with nutrients. Most people who eat healthfully do not need to supplement their diets with vitamins and other nutrients—one carrot, for instance, provides enough vitamin A to last four days. Women who are pregnant have greater needs of all nutrients; although most of the extra nutrients can come from adjustments in their diets, they should also take recommended supplements, such as of iron (Hegsted, 1984; St. Jeor, Sutnick, & Scott, 1988). For people with balanced diets, supplements are usually a waste of time and

Reading labels informs the consumer of the food's content.

money. Some people who do take supplements have an attitude of "the more the better." But it is possible to overdo taking nutrients, leading to a form of "poisoning" if they accumulate in the body. For example, large doses of the fat-soluble vitamins A and D pose serious health hazards to the liver and kidneys, respectively.

Unprocessed foods are generally more healthful than processed foods, which often contain additives that benefit the food industry more than the consumer. These additives include: *preservatives* that lengthen the shelf life of the food, *emulsifiers* to enable oil and water to mix, *thickeners* and *stabilizers* that improve or maintain the texture of foods, and *flavor enhancers* that heighten the natural taste of foods (Klockenbrink, 1987). Although most additives are not dangerous to people's health, some are being questioned as possible carcinogens. Some additives are known to be harmful to specific groups of individuals; for example, the flavor enhancer disodium guanylate should be avoided by people who have gout. Children may be especially vulnerable to the effects of additives because their body systems are still forming and maturing rapidly and, pound-for-pound, they eat more than adults.

What People Eat

For most of this century, American diets have shown a fairly consistent trend: people have been consuming more and more sugar, animal fats, and animal proteins, while consuming less and less fiber (Winikoff, 1983). This trend is partly the result of people eating fewer vegetables, fruits, cereals, and potatoes, while consuming more meats and sugary foods, such as soft drinks and processed goods. But the way food is prepared also affects people's diets. Consider the potato, for example. A raw, baked, or boiled potato by itself

> has 0.5 percent of its calories as fat, and 11 percent of its calories as protein. When french-fried, the same potato has 42 percent of its calories as fat and 6 percent as protein. When made into a potato chip, on the other hand, 60 percent of the calories are fat and only 3.6 percent are protein. (Winikoff, 1983, p. 88)

People's increased use of processed and fast foods has contributed over the years to the changes seen in American diets, too.

How healthful are people's diets in the United States? One dimension of this question involves their consumption of sugars and animal fats, which is far too high. Nutritionists and others concerned with people's health have been recommending that Americans reduce these components in their diets. Are Americans beginning to follow these recommendations? Preliminary data from the Agriculture Department indicate that they are (Fisher, 1987). In recent years, people's consumption of sugar has declined, and they are switching from whole to low-fat milk and from red meats to fish and poultry. These data are encouraging. Another dimension of the healthfulness of Americans' diets involves the consumption of proteins, vitamins, and minerals. Data on the consumption of these nutrients can be compared against the high standards of the Recommended Dietary Allowances. These comparisons indicate that most Americans at all ages consume sufficient amounts of almost all the essential nutrients (Hegsted, 1984). However, women and the elderly may not be consuming sufficiently high levels of calcium, iron, magnesium, and vitamin B_6—and supplements of these nutrients may be warranted.

Why do people eat what they eat? Diets are determined by biopsychosocial factors (Rozin, 1984). Most people around the world—even newborn babies—like sweet tastes and avoid bitter tastes. These preferences appear to have a biological basis, perhaps benefitting survival since poisonous substances are often bitter tasting. But individuals also acquire preferences as a result of experience. For instance, people sometimes develop aversions to a food if ingesting that food is followed by nausea, even if they know that the food did not cause the illness. Temporary food aversions often develop in cancer patients when they first receive a chemotherapy treatment that produces nausea (Mattes, Arnold, & Boraas, 1987a, 1987b).

Sociocultural factors have a major influence on the tastes children acquire for foods (Rozin, 1984; Wadden & Brownell, 1984). Children receive certain foods, but not others, depending on cultural and economic conditions—and simply being exposed to a food may increase people's liking of it. Children also observe in person and through TV commercials how other people respond to a food and tend to become more attracted to it if they see that others eat it and like it. Through social experiences, individuals develop ideas about foods they have never even tried: Suppose you saw TV commercials for two new chocolate candies, one with "a special fruit filling" and the other filled with cockroaches. How would you feel about trying these products?

Enormous numbers of children around the world simply do not have nutritious diets available to them for proper growth and development. Figure 8.1 gives the average heights for 9-year-olds in different parts of the world. The cultural comparisons reflected in the figure show that the smallest children tend to live in highly impoverished areas, and the tallest in wealthier locations. Notice that the tallest children live in the Netherlands, a prosperous, well-fed, and healthy nation. In contrast, the shortest children live in rural India and Thailand, where poverty, famine, and disease are relatively common. The figure also shows contrasts between children from rich and poor families living in the same area. Upper-class Chinese 9-year-olds living in Hong Kong are 2.2 inches taller, on average, than their lower-class counterparts (Meredith, 1978). But these same upper-class Chinese are 3.9 inches shorter than upper-class children living in the Netherlands. Such regional and social class differences in bodily growth are due to many variables, including genetics, nutrition, and disease.

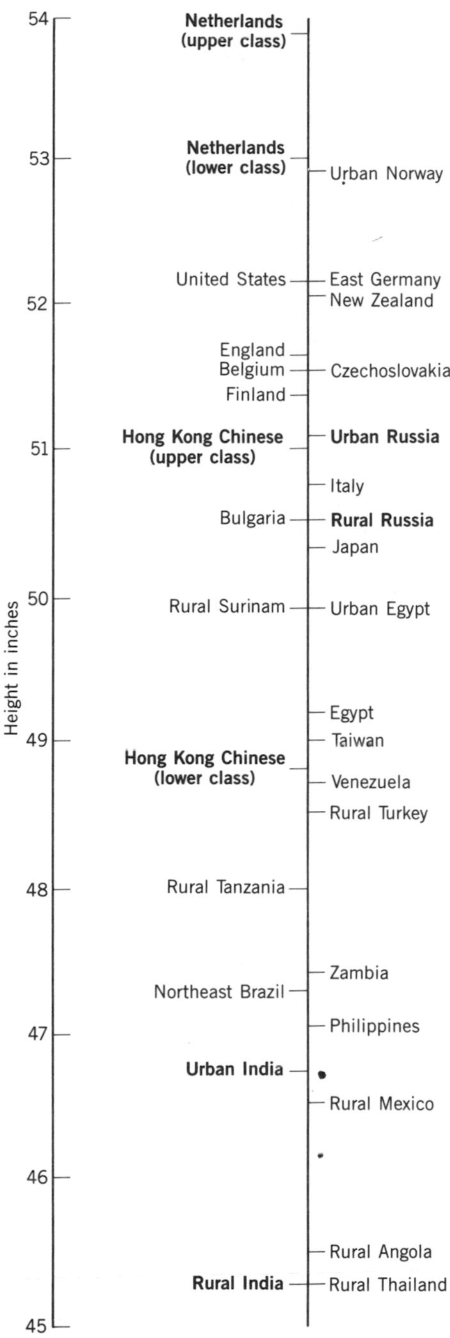

FIGURE 8.1 Average heights of 9-year-olds of both sexes from around the world. Locations in boldface show social class and rural/urban comparisons. (From Sarafino & Armstrong, 1986, Figure 6.3; based on data from Meredith, 1978.)

Nutrition and Health

The mass media announce almost daily that American diets are not as healthful as they should be. Some individuals have responded by using foods and substances sold at "health food stores." Although some of these products —such as whole grains—are clearly beneficial, many supplements and other products are of dubious worth (Nelson, 1984; Suitor & Hunter, 1980). Some people attempt to improve their diets by becoming *vegetarians.* There are degrees of vegetarianism, ranging from simply avoiding red meats to strictly using only plant foods and no animal products whatsoever. When people avoid all animal products, they must plan very carefully to assure that their diets, and especially their children's, contain a balance of proteins and sufficient amounts of essential vitamins and minerals (Suitor & Hunter, 1980). The most widespread culprits in American diets are those associated with the development of atherosclerosis, hypertension, and cancer.

Diet and Atherosclerosis

Cholesterol is the main dietary culprit in atherosclerosis, the deposit of fatty plaques in our blood vessels. As we saw in Chapter 2, cholesterol is a fatty substance—our bodies produce most of the cholesterol in the blood, and our diets provide the remainder. Whether cholesterol forms plaques in our blood vessels depends on the presence of different types of cholesterol-carrying proteins called **lipoproteins**. There are three types of lipoproteins: **low-density lipoprotein** (LDL) and **very-low-density lipoprotein** (VLDL) are associated with *increased* cholesterol deposits, but **high-density lipoprotein** (HDL) is associated with *decreased* likelihood of plaque buildup (Cooper, 1988). Some researchers believe that LDL and VLDL carry cholesterol *toward* the body cells, whereas HDL carries cholesterol *away* from the cells to be processed or removed by the liver.

How much cholesterol in the blood is too much? Normal levels of cholesterol increase with age in adulthood, and are measured in milligrams of cholesterol per 100 milliliters of blood serum. Americans at about 30 years of age have average cholesterol levels of about 200 mg, and those between 45 and 65 have about 228 mg (USDHHS, 1986f). Although experts generally agree that long-term high levels of cholesterol in the blood can lead to heart disease and stroke, there is some disagreement as to the specific levels that present serious risk. Probably most experts accept the guidelines of the American Heart Association:

- *Adults in their 30s* who have serum cholesterol levels of 220-240 mg are at *moderate risk*, and those with over 240 are at *high risk.*
- *Adults over 40* years of age with levels of 240-260 mg are at *moderate risk*, and those with over 260 are at *high risk.*

Middle-aged adults whose blood tests indicate over 260 mg have cholesterol levels that are in the top 20% or so of people in that age group. A prospective study followed the health of over 350,000 adults for six years and found that, within any age group, the higher the subjects' cholesterol levels at the start of the study, the greater their risk of mortality from heart disease or stroke (Stamler, Wentworth, & Neaton, 1986). The risk for individuals with cholesterol levels over 245 mg was 3.4 times as high as for those with levels under 180.

People's cholesterol levels are determined partly by heredity (Rona et al., 1985) and partly by the foods they eat. Some foods, such as eggs, many milk products, and fatty meats, contain very high concentrations of cholesterol. The American Heart Association has developed guidelines for the maximum amounts of cholesterol adults should consume. These guidelines are based on the measured cholesterol levels of the person: Individuals at *high risk* should consume less than 150 mg of cholesterol per day, those at *moderate risk* should have less than 250 mg, and those with less risk may consume up to 300 mg. Physicians may prescribe medication to lower the high cholesterol levels of some patients because changes in their diets could not lower the levels enough. Children after the preschool years should follow diets like those recommended for adults. Atherosclerosis can begin in childhood, and children need to develop good eating habits early so that they don't have entrenched habits

HIGHLIGHT 8A: On Research
Interventions to Reduce Cholesterol Intake

People can lower their cholesterol intake markedly if they will modify their eating habits, sometimes by making very simple changes. For example, a person whose cholesterol intake averages 400 mg per day can lower this amount to 251 mg by substituting low-cholesterol foods, such as cereals, for just four eggs per week—an egg contains about 260 mg of cholesterol. Other ways to reduce cholesterol intake include reducing the amounts and changing the types of meats in the diet, broiling or baking foods instead of frying, using low-cholesterol vegetable fats for cooking, and using low-fat dairy products. Most cereals, breads, fruits, nuts, and vegetables contain little or no cholesterol. But people should be wary of some processed foods that do not specify the kind of "vegetable oil" they use—these products often contain saturated fats (coconut or palm oils) rather than the more expensive polyunsaturated fats, such as corn or soybean oils. Oils that derive from certain plants, such as olives, consist of *monounsaturated* fats that contain no cholesterol and may actually work to *lower* serum cholesterol (Cooper, 1988).

Because Americans consume high levels of cholesterol, researchers have tested intervention programs to help people lower their intake levels. One of these programs was part of the Multiple Risk Factor Intervention Trial (MRFIT) and was designed to modify the diets of thousands of men over a period of six years (Caggiula et al., 1981; Dolecek et al., 1986; Gorder et al., 1986). The subjects were between 35 and 57 years of age at the start of the study and were at risk of coronary heart disease because of high serum cholesterol levels, high blood pressure, and cigarette smoking. Before they entered the study, they had already made self-initiated changes to reduce saturated fats in their diets. The subjects were randomly assigned to two groups, so that half of the men participated in the intervention program and the remainder were simply referred to their physicians as a "usual care" control group. All the subjects returned each year for a medical examination and to report the diets they consumed during the prior 24 hours. Those men who received the intervention provided dietary reports three times a year. These men received counseling on an individual basis each year after the initial few months of the intervention, when they and "their homemakers" participated in a series of group meetings that provided information about the benefits of and methods for modifying their diets.

The MRFIT program was successful in modifying the diets and lowering the serum cholesterol levels of the men. At the start of the study, the intervention and control subjects were consuming an average of 450 mg of cholesterol a day. During the study, the daily cholesterol intake of the intervention subjects dropped to 267 mg, whereas that of the controls declined only to 425 mg. The improved diet of the intervention subjects was reflected in their lowered serum cholesterol levels, most of which occurred in the first year. As Figure 8A.1 shows, the higher the initial serum cholesterol levels of the intervention subjects, the greater the reduction they achieved in these levels by the end of the study. This means that the men who most needed to modify their diets tended to do so and achieved the greatest gains.

Although the MRFIT program improved the men's diets substantially, the improvements fell short of the program's goals and the guidelines of the American Heart Association. Other researchers have tried to determine ways to make dietary inter-

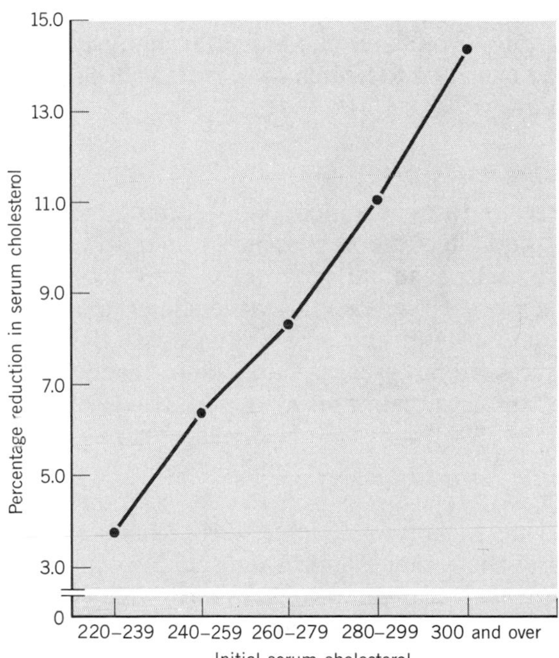

FIGURE 8A.1 Percentage by which intervention subjects reduced their serum cholesterol levels as a function of their level of cholesterol at the start of the study. (Data from Dolecek et al., 1986, Table 7.)

ventions more successful by comparing the effectiveness of different methods. One study compared three approaches with 255 male and female adult volunteers from the general population—that is, they were *not* selected for being at high risk for health problems (Foreyt, Scott, Mitchell, & Gotto, 1979). The subjects were randomly assigned to three conditions: One group simply received a *booklet* describing a low-cholesterol diet program; another group attended a series of *nutrition education* classes; and a third group received a *behavioral/education* program that combined the nutrition education classes with behavioral methods, such as self-monitoring and contingency management. Assessments of serum cholesterol levels were made at the start of the study and after 3, 6, and 12 months. These assessments showed that the cholesterol levels dropped sharply at 3 months for all three groups. At 6 months, cholesterol levels in the behavioral/education group dropped again (a total drop of 8.5%), but those in the other two groups increased. At 12 months, the cholesterol levels of all three groups increased. These findings indicate that using behavioral methods and nutritional education was the most effective approach, but that a follow-up program may be needed to maintain improved diets. The success of this approach is especially impressive because the subjects did not have very high serum cholesterol levels to begin with.

Effective intervention to reduce high serum cholesterol levels is likely to involve behavioral and educational programs for the patient, training and cooperation by other members of the patient's household, support groups, and a long-term follow-up program (Carmody et al., 1982). Devising successful interventions to lower serum cholesterol is clearly very important. Researchers have demonstrated that large reductions in serum cholesterol, produced through combined dietary and drug treatment, retard and in some cases *reverse* the development of atherosclerosis (Blankenhorn et al., 1987).

---

to overcome later (Cooper, 1988; Wadden & Brownell, 1984). Americans have been reducing their intake of cholesterol recently, but still consume far too much—an average of 450 mg a day.

Diet and Hypertension

Of all the substances in people's diets that could affect blood pressure, *sodium*—such as in salt (sodium chloride)—may play the strongest role. Studies have shown that consuming high levels of sodium increases people's blood pressure and their reactivity in stressful situations (Falkner & Light, 1986; Kaplan, 1986). A teaspoon of salt contains about 2,000 mg of sodium, and between 1,100 and 3,300 mg a day is considered "safe and adequate" (Suitor & Hunter, 1980; Zamula, 1987). But the average American probably consumes 7,000 mg of sodium daily, some of which comes from the person adding salt to foods. The rest comes mainly from eating foods that already contain high levels of sodium, as do many processed meats, potato chips, and cereals, for example. Because sodium can elevate blood pressure, physicians often place hypertensive patients on low-sodium diets. These diets help some, but not all, of these people—the reduction in blood pressure that results from decreasing dietary sodium is greatest in older patients and those with relatively high blood pressure levels (Grobbee & Hofman, 1986; Kaplan, 1986).

Caffeine is another dietary substance that affects blood pressure. Most of the caffeine people consume generally comes from drinking caffeinated coffee, strong tea, and cola beverages. Caffeine increases people's reactivity to stress and raises their blood pressure at least temporarily, and may be implicated in the development of hypertension and coronary heart disease (France & Ditto, 1988; Lane & Williams, 1987; Shapiro, Lane, & Henry, 1986). A prospective study followed the health of over 1,900 men for 19 years and found that subjects who drank six or more cups of coffee a day had much higher mortality rates from coronary heart disease than those who drank less (LeGrady et al., 1987).

Diet and Cancer

Diets high in fat and low in fiber are associated with the development of cancer, particularly cancer of the colon (Bristol, Emmett, Heaton, &

Williamson, 1985; Levy, 1985). Although some people believe individuals can "protect" themselves against cancer by increasing the fiber content of their diets, evidence for this belief is not yet clear (Levy, 1985). The diets of most Americans do not conform to the recommendations of the American Cancer Society. A survey of over 11,000 adults found that they were far more likely to eat foods that pose a higher risk of cancer—such as red meats, bacon, and lunch meats—than to eat foods that pose a lower risk, such as fruits, certain vegetables, and high-fiber breads and cereals (Patterson & Block, 1988).

Another possible protective component of diets is vitamin A. Many fruits and vegetables are rich in *beta-carotene*, which the body converts to vitamin A. These foods include spinach, broccoli, lettuce, tomatoes, and several yellow/orange-colored fruits and vegetables, such as cantaloupe, apricots, carrots, and sweet-potatoes. A study comparing the diets of lung cancer patients with those of healthy individuals found that diets rich in vitamin A were associated with lower risk of cancer (Byers et al., 1987). On the basis of findings like these, some people have begun to supplement their diets with vitamin A tablets. Nutritionists recommend against this approach because vitamin A builds up in the body, and it is too easy to overdose.

What people include in their diets is clearly related to their risk of developing several major chronic diseases. Other dietary problems that affect health arise from consuming unhealthful amounts of food, as we are about to see.

WEIGHT CONTROL AND DIET

Americans are very "weight conscious," and often start being concerned about their weight in childhood, particularly if they are overweight and are teased and excluded from social groups (Brownell, 1986b). When children reach the teenage years, they become greatly preoccupied with their physical appearance and would like to change how they look (Conger & Petersen, 1984). They frequently express concerns about skin problems and wanting to have a better figure or more athletic body, to be taller or shorter, and to be the "right" weight.

Being the "wrong" weight affects people's self-esteem, especially if they are females. A study of overweight 10- to 16-year-olds found that the girls' self-esteem declined sharply and consistently through those years, but the boys' self-esteem only declined during the early years (Mendelson & White, 1985). Perhaps as overweight boys get older, some degree of bulk is considered "manly." Another study surveyed high schoolers and found that 63% of the girls and 16% of the boys were trying to *lose* weight, and 9% of the girls and 28% of the boys were trying to *gain* weight (Rosen & Gross, 1987). The greater concern among females than males about their weight—especially about being overweight—continues in adulthood (Forman et al., 1986). *Whether* individ-

Many teenagers and adults become preoccupied with their body appearance and go to great lengths to make it "perfect."

uals do anything about their weight and *what* they do can have important implications for their health.

Overweight and Obesity

No matter how fit we are, our bodies have some fat—and they should. Having fat only becomes a problem when we have too much. The question is: How much is too much? Determining how much fat a person's body has is not as easy as it may seem. Bulk or stockiness alone can be misleading since some stocky people simply have larger skeletal frames than other people do, or their bodies are more muscular. As a result, researchers often use complex methods for accurately measuring the amount of body fat an individual has (Weltman, 1984). They then calculate an index mathematically for classifying the person as being overly fat.

A more common and simple approach for assessing whether someone is overly fat is based on data regarding *desirable weights* of men and women, determined through studies of mortality rates. The Metropolitan Life Insurance Company has developed a chart of desirable weights, presented in Table 8.1, which has become a standard for assessing overweight. The table gives specific ranges of weights for people of different sex, heights, and body types—that is, whether the frame is small, medium, or large. For example, a man with a medium frame who is 5′10″ tall (with shoes) has a desirable weight range of 151-163 pounds, including an allowance for clothing. People are classified as **overweight** if their weight exceeds this range by 10 to 20%, and **obese** if their weight exceeds the range by more than 20% (Suitor & Hunter, 1980). If the man in our example weighed 180 pounds (with clothes), he would be overweight; if he weighed 197 or more, he would be obese.

Why People Become Overly Fat

Tens of millions of American adults, adolescents, and children are overweight or obese (Weltman, 1984; Werry, 1986). The prevalence of overly fat people varies with nationality, sociocultural factors, gender, and age. For example, the United States has a higher percentage of overweight and obese adults than Britain and Canada do (Millar & Stephens, 1987). In the United States, higher percentages of adult blacks and Hispanics than whites are overweight or obese (Forman et al., 1986; USDHHS, 1986c). And among men, the prevalence rate of being too heavy increases until about age 50; among women, the prevalence rate increases into old age (Millar & Stephens, 1987; USDHHS, 1985b). Research has also revealed a disturbing trend—the proportion of children in the United States who are overly fat has increased substantially since the 1960s (Gortmaker, Dietz, Sobol, & Wehler, 1987).

People add fat to their bodies because they consume more calories than they burn up through metabolism. The body stores excess calories as fat in *adipose tissue*, which consists of cells that vary in number and size (Suitor & Hunter, 1980). According to researcher Margaret Straw, the

> growth of adipose tissue throughout childhood and adolescence involves both an increase in cell size and in cell number. Thereafter, it appears that growth in adipose tissue is initially associated with an increase in cell size; if cell size becomes excessive, new adipose tissue is generated through an increase in the number of cells. (1983, p. 223)

A major reason why adults tend to gain weight as they get older is that metabolism and physical activity decline with age (Smith, 1984). To maintain their younger weight levels, people need to exercise and take in fewer calories as they get older.

Because the metabolic rates of individuals can differ greatly, some thin people consume many more calories than some heavy people do and still stay slim. Fat tissue is less metabolically active than lean tissue, "so fatness itself can directly lower metabolic rate if fat tissue begins to replace lean tissue" (Rodin, 1981, p. 362). This may be one of the reasons why many individuals who have become obese no longer overeat, as they did while they were gaining weight. Not all heavy people eat a great deal—

TABLE 8.1 Desirable Weights from the 1983 Metropolitan Height and Weight Tables for Men and Women: Ages 25–59

*Height (in shoes)**		*Weight in Pounds (in indoor clothing)*†		
Feet	*Inches*	*Small Frame*	*Medium Frame*	*Large Frame*
			MEN	
5	2	128–134	131–141	138–150
5	3	130–136	133–143	140–153
5	4	132–138	135–145	142–156
5	5	134–140	137–148	144–160
5	6	136–142	139–151	146–164
5	7	138–145	142–154	149–168
5	8	140–148	145–157	152–172
5	9	142–151	148–160	155–176
5	10	144–154	151–163	158–180
5	11	146–157	154–166	161–184
6	0	149–160	157–170	164–188
6	1	152–164	160–174	168–192
6	2	155–168	164–178	172–197
6	3	158–172	167–182	176–202
6	4	162–176	171–187	181–207
			WOMEN	
4	10	102–111	109–121	118–131
4	11	103–113	111–123	120–134
5	0	104–115	113–126	122–137
5	1	106–118	115–129	125–140
5	2	108–121	118–132	128–143
5	3	111–124	121–135	131–147
5	4	114–127	124–138	134–151
5	5	117–130	127–141	137–155
5	6	120–133	130–144	140–159
5	7	123–136	133–147	143–163
5	8	126–139	136–150	146–167
5	9	129–142	139–153	149–170
5	10	132–145	142–156	152–173
5	11	135–148	145–159	155–176
6	0	138–151	148–162	158–179

Source: Metropolitan Life Foundation (1983).
*Shoes with 1-inch heels.
†Indoor clothing weighing 5 pounds for men and 3 pounds for women.

indeed, studies have found that obese and normal-weight individuals do not differ in the amount or type of food they report having consumed recently, such as in the last 24 hours (Berkowitz, 1983; Braitman, Adlin, & Stanton, 1985). It is possible, however, that heavy and normal-weight people may differ in the accuracy of their reports; for example, heavy people may underestimate their food intake. More research is needed to clarify this issue.

Many people believe that individuals become obese because of "glandular problems." Although malfunctioning endocrine glands can cause extreme weight gains, this occurs in only a small percentage of obese people (Robinson & Lawler, 1977). Are other biological processes important in the development of obesity? Yes—for one thing, heredity clearly plays a role (Epstein & Cluss, 1986). Twin studies have shown that identical twins reared apart or together are much more alike in their degree of overweight than are same-sex fraternal twins (Börjeson, 1980; Stunkard, Foch, & Hrubec, 1986). Adoption studies have found that children's being overweight is much more strongly related to the weight of their biological parents than their adoptive parents (Price, Cadoret, Stunkard, & Troughton, 1987; Stunkard et al., 1986). Relationships have also been noted between the fatness of parents in general and that of their offspring. About 7% of the offspring of normal-weight parents are obese. But among families with one obese parent, 40% of the children are likely to be obese; and if both parents are obese, the figure may jump to 80% (Mayer, 1975, 1980). These parent/child similarities may not be the result only of genetic factors—for instance, children learn many of their eating habits and food preferences from their parents.

How does heredity affect our weight? Part of the answer seems to be described in **set-point theory**, which proposes that each person's body has a certain or "set" weight that it strives to maintain (Bennett & Gurin, 1982; Keesey, 1986; Keesey & Powley, 1975; Nisbett, 1972). The body tries to maintain its weight near the set-point by means of a thermostatlike mechanism in the hypothalamus of the brain. When a person's weight departs from the set-point, the body takes corrective measures, such as by increasing or decreasing metabolism. Research with animals has shown that damage to specific parts of the hypothalamus causes weight to change and eventually level off, suggesting that a new set-point has been established. If the damage is in the *lateral* region of the hypothalamus, the new set-point is for a lower weight; damage to the *ventromedial* region leads to obesity. One way the hypothalamus might regulate body weight is by monitoring some aspect of fat cells. One study found, for instance, that when adipose tissue was surgically removed from young rats, their bodies later replaced it quite precisely (Faust, Johnson, & Hirsch, 1977). The role of heredity in weight control might be in determining the set-point or other weight-related processes controlled by the hypothalamus.

Another way the hypothalamus may affect the process of weight control is by regulating the level of insulin in the person's blood (Keesey & Powley, 1975). **Insulin** is a hormone, produced by the pancreas, that speeds the conversion of sugar (glucose) to fat and promotes the storage of fat in adipose tissue (Rodin, 1981, 1985). Obese individuals tend to have high serum levels of insulin—a condition called *hyperinsulinemia*. Eating increases insulin secretion, and this response can become classically conditioned so that just seeing or thinking about food can raise a person's insulin level. People who exhibit this conditioned response show a greater tendency to gain weight than those who do not. Furthermore, elevations in serum insulin levels increase the person's sensations of hunger, perceived pleasantness of sweet tastes, and food consumption. Taken together, these findings indicate that weight gain results from a biopsychosocial process in which physiological factors interact with psychological and environmental factors (Rodin, 1985).

It seems likely that the setting and function of the set-point in regulating a person's weight depend on the number and size of fat cells in the body. Psychologist Kelly Brownell (1986b) has suggested that people whose weights are above the set-point may be able to reduce fairly readily until the fat cells reach their lower limit in *size*. The body weight at which this level is reached would depend on the *number* of fat cells in the body. Since the number of fat cells increases mainly in childhood and adolescence, the diets of individuals during that time in the life span are likely to be very important. Obese children between 2 and 10 years of age have fat cells that are as large as those of adults (Knittle et al., 1981). As these children gain weight, they do so mainly by increasing the number of their fat cells. Fat cell size for normal-weight children does not reach adult levels until age 12, and the number of their fat cells does not increase very much between 2 and 10 years of age.

How does adding fat cells to the body affect people's ability to control their weight? Evidence indicates that the number of fat cells can increase, but *not* decrease (Brownell, 1982). Individuals who develop too many fat cells—a condition called *fat-cell hyperplasia*—may be doomed to a difficult struggle against a high set-point for the rest of their lives. When fat-cell-hyperplastic adults try to lose weight, their fat cells shrink and

> send out metabolic signals similar to those during food deprivation. As a result, bodily mechanisms respond as though the person were starving, resulting in, among other things, an increase in hunger and a decrease in basal metabolism so that energy stores (i.e., fat) are maintained more efficiently. This system is clearly useful when food is scarce . . . but in a food-rich environment it leads to obesity that is extremely resistant to change. In fact, dieting may actually compound the problem by slowing basal metabolism, thus converting energy that should fuel metabolism into fat and indirectly sapping strength and vigor, encouraging a sedentary life-style. (Buck, 1988, p. 467)

This suggests that the diets children eat may be critical in determining whether they become overly fat. It may be possible to help prevent obesity by providing children with nutritious diets that do not lead to hyperplasia (Brownell, 1986b). Once the person's set-point becomes established, however, changing it appears to be very difficult. Although some researchers have suggested that set-points may be changed through exercise, drugs, and other methods, there is little evidence for these possibilities so far (Brownell, 1986a).

The factors in weight control that we have discussed so far are mainly *internal*, or inside the person. But *external*, environmental factors are important, too. Obese people tend to be more sensitive or responsive to food-related cues in the environment than nonobese people are (Schachter, 1971). For example, they eat more than normal-weight people do when the food tastes good, but eat less than normal-weight individuals when it tastes bad. This stronger responsiveness to food cues suggests that obese individuals may be more susceptible than nonobese people to, say, the influence of a "sales pitch" when deciding whether to have a dessert. A study tested this possibility in a restaurant by having the waitress describe or display a dessert to her diners (Herman, Olmstead, & Polivy, 1983). The results showed that obese diners were more influenced by the description or display of the dessert than nonobese diners were. Because of this susceptibility to food-related cues, obese children are likely to have a difficult time controlling their eating at home. Studies examining family behaviors at mealtimes have shown that parents give more encouragement for eating and offer food more often to heavier children than to slimmer ones (Baranowski & Nader, 1985).

For many people, keeping their weight at a desired level is a struggle in which they constantly worry about what they eat and try to resist eating what they want. These people have been described as *restrained* eaters (Herman & Mack, 1975; Herman & Polivy, 1980; Ruderman, 1986). At the other end of the spectrum are *unrestrained* eaters who eat freely, as the desire strikes them. This distinction forms the basis of **restraint theory**, which proposes that restrained eaters tend to develop abnormal eating patterns marked by vacillating between inhibited consumption, such as dieting, and overindulgence. According to this theory, the inhibited eating behavior of restrained eaters often becomes temporarily "disinhibited," or released, by certain events, and this produces a bout of overeating.

Research has supported the idea of disinhibition by comparing the behavior of individuals assessed as restrained or unrestrained eaters on the basis of their responses to a questionnaire (Ruderman, 1986; Weber, Klesges, & Klesges, 1988). One type of event that appears to disinhibit restrained eaters is the perception that they have already violated their diet, as might happen at a dinner party that begins with a fattening first course. After eating this course, restrained eaters may think, "I've blown it now — I might as well eat what I want." Dieting is an all-or-none thing for them, and simply *anticipating* violating their diet may sometimes be enough to lead restrained eaters to give up trying to inhibit their eating for the moment. Another type of event that leads restrained eaters to overindulge is experiencing negative emotional states, such as anxiety or depression. Lastly, social influence through modeling can affect the food consumption of both restrained and unrestrained eaters.

It is tempting to think that obese people are simply unrestrained eaters, but we have already seen that obese and nonobese individuals do not differ very much in their food consumption. A very different view comes from restraint theory, which proposes that obese individuals face an especially difficult struggle with weight, feel higher levels of restraint, and are more susceptible to disinhibiting events than the nonobese are. But research has not supported this view (Ruderman, 1986). Although disinhibiting events affect the food consumption of restrained and unrestrained eaters differently, the relationship between these effects and obesity is unclear. Studies attempting to relate dietary restraint to obesity have focused on adult subjects so far. Perhaps the role of restraint would be clearer in childhood, as obesity is developing.

Overweight and Health

In a study of overweight and normal-weight men and women, subjects were asked to rate their own health on a 10-point scale, where 1 equaled the "worst health" and 10 equaled the "best health" they could imagine (Laffrey, 1986). The ratings of the overweight and normal-weight individuals were about the same, averaging in the mid-7s. Are overweight and normal-weight people equally healthy?

To answer this question, we need to consider two factors, one of which is the *degree of overweight.* Research has clearly demonstrated that obesity is associated with high cholesterol levels and the development of hypertension, coronary heart disease, and diabetes (Alexander, 1984; Bray, 1984; Brownell, 1982; Hubert, 1986). The greater the severity of obesity, the greater the person's risk of developing and dying from heart disease and diabetes. Thus, a person whose weight exceeds the desirable weight by 50% has a much greater risk of heart disease and diabetes morbidity and mortality than someone whose weight is 20% over. But the risk of dying from these diseases for someone whose weight is less than, say, 10% over the desirable weight is almost as low as for someone at the desirable weight. One thing to keep in mind, however, is that people of ideal weight

Compared with individuals of normal weight, an obese person is at greater risk of developing heart disease and diabetes.

are not necessarily at low risk themselves—recall from the previous chapter that individuals who smoke cigarettes tend to weigh less than those who do not.

The second factor in assessing the health risks of being heavy involves the *distribution of fat* on the body. Whereas heavy men tend to have much of their fat concentrated in the abdominal region, heavy women have more of their fat on the thighs, hips, and buttocks (Brownell, 1986a). Since men have a higher prevalence of cardiovascular disorders than women, these and other health problems may be related to having bodies that are "rounded in the middle." The results of a study of over 30,000 women support this possibility (Hartz, Rupley, & Rimm, 1984). Subjects whose *ratio of waist to hip girth*—that is, their waist measurements compared to their hip measurements—was large had a higher incidence of hypertension and diabetes than those whose ratio was small. Other studies with women and with men have also found higher risks of hypertension and diabetes, as well as of coronary heart disease, among people with higher, rather than lower, ratios of waist to hip girth (Gillum, 1987a, 1987b; Welin et al., 1987). These are recent discoveries, and the reasons for the influence of fat distribution on health are unclear.

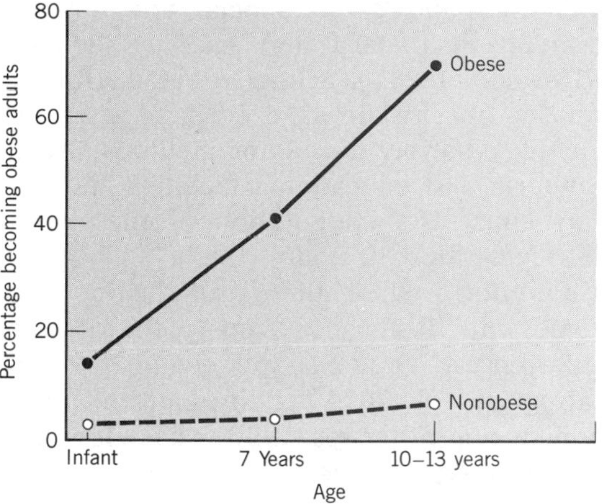

FIGURE 8.2 Percentage of obese and nonobese children who eventually become obese adults, as a function of age when weight status is assessed. (Data of Epstein, reported in Brownell, 1986b, p. 313.)

Preventing Overweight

Being obese presents disadvantages to the person's health and social relationships in childhood and adulthood (Bray, 1984; Brownell, 1986b). Is it true, as many people believe, that children tend to "outgrow" weight problems, or that they will find it easy to lose weight when they are interested in dating? Probably neither belief is true for most children (Brownell, 1986b; Woodall & Epstein, 1983). Losing weight after becoming obese is not easy at any age, and this is one reason why it is important to try to prevent overweight.

Preventing overweight should begin in childhood (Brownell, 1986b; Woodall & Epstein, 1983). Beginning fairly early is important for two reasons. First, obesity in childhood is likely to continue into adult life. As Figure 8.2 depicts, this likelihood depends on the age of the child—although only 14% of obese infants become obese adults, 70% of obese 10- to 13-year-olds do. Few normal-weight children become obese adults. Another reason to begin early is to prevent fat-cell hyperplasia, which develops in childhood and adolescence. Obese adults who were fat in childhood have the double burden of dealing with bigger fat cells and more of them.

Most children will not require special preventive efforts to control their weight. Those who will need these efforts are likely either to have a family history of obesity or to have become overweight already (Woodall & Epstein, 1983). Efforts to help children control their weight need to focus on both diet and physical activity. Health and physical education programs in schools provide excellent opportunities to promote healthful eating and exercise habits in all schoolchildren. Studies have shown, for example, that children who receive instruction on healthful diets begin to bring healthier lunches to school and throw fewer healthy foods away (Striegel-Moore & Rodin, 1985; Wadden & Brownell, 1984). Children who are at risk of becoming obese on the basis of family history or current overweight can be identified and given special attention and training in dietary and exercise behavior (Brownell, 1986b). School programs for preventing obesity are most effective when they include a variety of training methods, involve cafeteria and educational facilities and staff, and enlist the cooperation of the parents (Striegel-Moore & Rodin, 1985).

Parents provide almost all the food that comes into the house and most of the food their children eat. They also model and encourage eating and physical activity patterns. Nutritionists and other researchers have identified several ways parents can help their children avoid becoming overly fat (Striegel-Moore & Rodin, 1985; Suitor & Hunter, 1980). These recommendations include:

- Encourage regular physical activity and discourage excessive TV watching.
- Don't use material rewards for eating a nonpreferred food (e.g., "You may have dessert if you eat your peas."); use praise as the reward instead.
- Decrease buying high-cholesterol and sugary foods of all kinds—have less of them in the house.
- Use fruits, nuts, and other healthful foods as regular desserts, and reserve rich cakes and other less-healthful desserts for special occasions or once-a-week treats.
- Make sure the child eats a healthful breakfast (with few eggs) each day and does not have high-calorie snacks at night. Calories consumed early in the day tend to be used as fuel; metabolism generally decreases later in the day, and calories consumed at night often become fat.
- Monitor the child's weight on a regular basis and compare it against a chart of desirable weights. Consult a pediatrician about the diet periodically.

Childhood is probably the ideal time to establish activity and dietary habits to prevent individuals from becoming overly fat. Parents, schools, and the mass media can play important roles in helping people control their weight.

Dieting and Treatments to Lose Weight

Many millions of Americans are trying to lose weight on any given day of the year, especially in the spring when they are getting ready to bare their bodies in the summer. Although some individuals try to lose weight because they are concerned about the health risks of being overly fat, many others are motivated by how they look and what other people think of them.

By American tastes, fatness is considered unattractive, particularly for females—and this confers important disadvantages for heavy people in social situations, such as dating. There is also a social stigma to being very heavy because many people *blame* heavy individuals for their condition, believing that they "simply lack will power." Experiments by William DeJong (1980) had high school girls rate whether they thought they would like girls they did not know. The subjects gave lower ratings for an obese girl than for a normal-weight girl unless the obese girl described an acceptable reason for her weight, such as a "thyroid condition," or indicated that she had recently lost a good deal of weight. The social aspects of overweight can be distressing to those who see themselves as being too heavy, and this often motivates them to try to lose weight.

Most people try to reduce their weight on their own, by "going on a diet." Does this approach work? Losing weight and keeping it off is difficult for most people. Individuals are more likely to succeed if they have a high degree of self-efficacy or confidence that they can do it and if they have constructive social support from their family and others in their social network (Coletti & Brownell, 1983; Edell et al., 1987). Many people go on frequent diets, losing several pounds or more successfully and gaining it right back. Kelly Brownell (1988) has described repeated cycles of weight loss and gain as *yo-yo dieting*. Evidence is accumulating that each time individuals lose weight and gain it back, losing weight in the future becomes harder. The reason for this effect is not yet clear, but it may be that dieting lowers the person's metabolism for a substantial time thereafter. The best approach to dieting involves making permanent lifestyle changes that the person and his or her family can accept and maintain.

Overweight and obese people are likely to have a great deal of difficulty making and sticking with the lifestyle changes needed to lose weight, but it appears that many of them can do it successfully. In the previous chapter, we examined a study by Stanley Schachter (1982) of people who stopped smoking on their own. That study also investigated whether people who had a history of overweight (at least 15% above the desirable weight) were successful in reducing on their own. Of the 46 subjects who had a history of overweight, 40 had attempted to lose weight—26 tried only on their own and 14 had sought the help of physicians, therapists, or weight-loss programs. Of the 40 who tried, 25 (62.5%) succeeded, reducing to their desirable weight or within 10% of it. Furthermore, they had maintained the lower weight over many years—at the time of the interview, the men who succeeded were about 39 pounds under their prediet weight, and the women were still 29 pounds under. Of those who tried to reduce without seeking help, 18 (69%) were successful; and of the 14 who sought help, half were successful. A later study replicated Schachter's procedure with a smaller sample of people who had a history of overweight and found that some succeeded in losing weight, but most did not (Rzewnicki & Forgays, 1987).

Although many people can lose weight on their own and keep it off, others feel they need help. Probably all of those who seek help have tried to reduce on their own at some time—perhaps numerous times—and either failed to reduce or could not maintain the new weight. What kinds of help do people seek, and what works?

Commercial Diet Plans: Fad Diets

One kind of help millions of people try is the latest "miracle diet," which is often "guaranteed" to work in a short time. There never seems to be a shortage of these "crash" *fad diets*—many of which are not only ineffective, but are nutritionally unsound and often produce unpleasant side effects, such as diarrhea (La Place, 1984). Some of these fad diets prescribe a strict dietary regimen with virtually no deviations permitted—the "Scarsdale Diet" outlined a specific breakfast, for example, that the dieter was to eat each day. Other fad diets have people eat a single type of food, such as only fruit, as in the "Beverly Hills Diet." Still other approaches, called "low-carbohydrate diets," have the person drastically reduce carbohydrate intake while eating unlimited amounts of high-protein foods. No crash diet is a substitute for adopting a healthful lifestyle of exercise and moderately sized, balanced meals.

Exercise

Some people think that exercising is self-defeating when they try to control their weight because they associate exercising with large appetites (Suitor & Hunter, 1980). They have heard, for instance, that some football players eat enormous meals. But these players generally have huge bodies and they are trying to maintain their weight, not lose weight. For some positions in football, bulk is a great advantage.

Physical activity is an important component in controlling weight. One of its benefits is that it increases metabolism, thereby helping the body to burn off an increased number of calories. Unfortunately, dieters often fail to exercise as part of reducing because they notice that it takes a lot of exercise to use up a few hundred calories—for instance, they would have to jog about half an hour to burn off the 400 or so calories in a milkshake. But studies of dieting obese individuals have revealed a variety of benefits of exercise in weight control, and these advantages seem to accumulate over time. The main benefit of exercise in the first couple of months of weight reduction is that it focuses the reduction mostly on body fat, while preserving lean tissue (Hill, Sparling, Shields, & Heller, 1987). Over the next several months, combining exercise with reduced caloric intake leads to greater weight losses than dieting alone (Epstein, Wing, Penner, & Cress, 1985). Thereafter, compared to dieters who do not exercise, those who do exercise are better able to maintain their reduced weight, probably because their improved fitness makes being physically active increasingly easy for them (Epstein, Wing, Valoski, & DeVos, 1988).

Behavioral Techniques

People who try to lose weight usually find that changing their eating patterns is very hard to do. Why? A major reason is that they don't know how to gain control over environmental conditions that maintain their eating patterns. Behavioral techniques have been developed to help dieters gain the control they need. Richard Stuart (1967) conducted a pioneering study of the utility of behavioral techniques, such as self-monitoring and stimulus control, in helping several obese women lose weight over a 12-month period. The results were quite impressive: Each of the eight women who stayed with the program lost weight fairly consistently throughout the year, losing from 26 to 47 pounds.

The dramatic success of Stuart's program prompted dozens of other researchers to study the usefulness of behavioral techniques in weight control. The outcome of these studies suggests the following conclusions (Brownell, 1982; Straw, 1983; Wilson, 1984): First, behavioral techniques are generally helpful in losing weight, but they do not work with all patients. Second, behavioral programs have very low dropout rates, and people who complete a program lose an average of about 11 pounds in the first three months. Third, the more the patients weigh at the start of treatment and the longer the program, the more weight they lose. Fourth, behavioral methods are more effective in helping people lose weight than any other approach, except certain medical treatments. Fifth, a clear majority of individuals who complete a behavioral program for weight control maintain their lower weight for at least a year. Although most studies of behavioral programs have used adult subjects, research has shown that these techniques are also effective with children of various ages (Epstein & Wing, 1987).

What techniques do behavioral programs for weight loss use? Although the specific techniques vary somewhat from one program to the next, they typically include the following components (Straw, 1983; Stunkard, 1987; Stunkard & Berthold, 1985; Wilson, 1984):

- *Nutrition and exercise counseling.*
- *Self-monitoring* by keeping careful records of the foods eaten, when, where, with whom, and under what circumstances.
- *Stimulus control* techniques, such as shopping for food with a list, storing food out of sight, and eating at home in only one room.
- *Altering the act of eating*, for example, by chewing the food very thoroughly before swallowing and putting utensils down on the table between mouthfuls.
- *Contingency contracting*, or setting up a system of rewards for sticking to the diet.

Another technique behavioral programs often use is *cognitive restructuring*, in which the patient learns counterarguments to pessimistic thoughts they have about dieting. For example, a person who thinks, "Everyone in my family has a weight problem. It's in my genes," would learn to counter this thought with "That just makes it harder, not impossible. If I stick with this program, I will succeed" (Stunkard, 1987). Many programs in the early 1970s used aversive strategies, such as pairing eating certain foods with unpleasant stimuli, but aversive methods have for the most part been abandoned for treating weight problems (Straw, 1983).

Because behavioral approaches stress the processes of data collection, planning, and feedback, some programs have begun to use computers to make these processes more effective. In one program, several obese subjects were trained to use a computer, which was small enough for them to carry throughout their normal daily routines during the eight weeks of treatment (Agras, 1987; Burnett, Taylor, & Agras, 1985). They used the computer for their self-monitoring activities regarding physical activity and calorie intake, and could get feedback on their progress toward daily goals at any time. They could also use the computer to *plan* their behavior, for example, by seeing in advance what effect eating a food would have on their progress. These subjects had been randomly assigned to the computer condition; other equally obese subjects were assigned to a control group that used similar behavioral techniques, but without computer assistance. The results showed that the subjects who used the computers lost more than twice as much weight as the controls by the end of the treatment. Furthermore, during the following eight months when *none* of the subjects was using the computers, those who had used the computers in their treatment continued to lose weight, but the controls did not.

Self-Help Groups and Worksite Weight-Loss Programs

Although there are dozens of self-help organizations for weight control, *Weight Watchers* is the most widely known of these groups and is attended by more than 500,000 people each week (Brownell, 1986a). The Weight Watchers approach uses several behavioral techniques, such as self-monitoring, along with nutritional information and group meetings for social support. Different self-help organizations have their own mix of methods to help people lose weight. *Take Off Pounds Sensibly* (TOPS), for example, uses few behavioral techniques even though research has demonstrated that the program might be more effective if it did (Chesney, 1984). Unfortunately, very little research has been done to evaluate the success of self-help groups because they have been "notoriously unwilling to permit external evaluation" of their effectiveness (Brownell, 1986a, p. 525). Current evidence suggests, however, that dropout rates for self-help groups are extremely high. Researchers have assessed attrition rates in a few groups and found that over 50% of the members drop out in the first six weeks alone (Stunkard, 1987).

Worksite weight-loss programs have been introduced and evaluated in a variety of businesses and industries. Although these programs have typically used behavioral techniques for weight control, they have not been very successful — having high dropout rates and producing small weight losses (Brownell, 1986a). The reason for the lack of success of these programs seems to be the subjects' lack of motivation. To overcome this problem, Kelly Brownell and his colleagues (1984) introduced three *weight-loss competitions* in different businesses and industries. In the first competition, the presidents of three banks issued challenges to each others' banks for a weight loss contest over a three-month period. All participating employees from each bank comprised a team. Each participant was given a weight-loss goal based on the difference between his or her actual weight and desirable weight, with a 20-pound maximum. To discourage crash dieting, losses greater than the person's goal were not counted. The prize for the team that achieved the greatest percentage of its weight loss goal was a pool of money to which each participant contributed $5. The only "program" they received to help them reduce was a series of weekly manuals that gave information about such factors as nutrition, exercise, self-monitoring, stimulus control, and reinforcement.

The researchers also conducted two similar competitions within two manufacturing companies, and the participants from each company were randomly assigned to teams. The three competitions had a total of 277 participants, but the research results focused on the 213 who were overweight by 10% or more at the start of the contest. Only one of these overweight or obese individuals dropped out of the contest, and the average weight loss of these subjects was 12 pounds — about a pound a week. Furthermore, a follow-up of the bank employees six months later showed that the overweight and obese individuals kept off 80% of the weight they lost in the competition. Clearly, the focus of this approach on the *motivation* of dieters is very promising and needs to receive further research.

Medically Supervised Approaches

Some approaches for losing weight involve medical procedures or require the supervision of a physician. One approach that requires medical supervision involves placing the patient on a *very-low-calorie diet* (VLCD) regimen. VLCDs contain fewer than 800 calories per day —and often have only 500 or so (Agras, 1987; Brownell, 1988; Wilson, 1984). Some VLCDs are unsafe to use because they are deficient in protein and potassium, but others—called "protein sparing" diets—are safe if the patient's health is monitored regularly. Although VLCDs produce rapid and substantial weight losses, they have unpleasant side effects, such as constipation and fatigue. Furthermore, relapse rates are high in the months following VLCDs, but relapses can be reduced by combining the diet with behavioral techniques (Wadden & Stunkard, 1986). VLCDs are currently recommended mainly for obese patients who are more than 50 pounds overweight, have failed to control their weight with behavioral techniques, and whose obesity poses an unusually high health risk (Agras, 1987).

Another medical approach for losing weight involves the use of drugs. At one time, *amphetamines* seemed to be useful because they suppress appetite and increase metabolism. They have since been abandoned because they produce psychological and, perhaps, physical dependence. The preferred prescription diet drug today is *fenfluramine*, an appetite suppressant that does not seem to cause dependence (Agras, 1987). Although drugs can be very effective in helping people to lose weight initially, they are not recommended for long-term weight control, and relapse rates are high after the patient stops taking them (Straw, 1983; Wilson, 1984). Some research indicates that relapse rates are lower if the use of drugs is combined with behavioral techniques in a weight-loss program (Agras, 1987).

The most drastic medical approaches for losing weight involve surgery, particularly to the stomach or intestines. In one surgical approach called *gastric restriction*, the size of the stomach is reduced by literally stapling part of it up; a less commonly used method is to remove part of the intestines to reduce the amount of nutrients absorbed from the digestive system. Although these approaches effectively reduce weight, they entail some surgical risk and may produce unpleasant side effects —for example, some patients who have undergone gastric restriction surgery experience nausea, vomiting, and abdominal pain after eating. As a result, these methods are recommended only for patients who are more than 100% overweight and have failed to lose weight by less drastic means (Straw, 1983; Stunkard, Stinnett, & Smoller, 1986). The surgical procedure called *liposuction*, in which adipose tissue is torn from the body and sucked out with a tube, is not really a weight reduction method—its function is strictly cosmetic (Henig, 1988). It is used for removing only a few pounds of fat from a specific region of the body, such as the thighs or abdomen, and it entails risks during the procedure and may have unpleasant aftereffects.

Relapse after Weight Loss

The problem of relapse after completing treatment to lose weight is similar to that which many people experience after receiving treatment to quit smoking, drinking, or using drugs (Brownell, Marlatt, Lichtenstein, & Wilson, 1986). Although most individuals who lose weight in behavioral programs maintain their lower weight for at least a year without follow-up treatment programs, many do not (Straw, 1983).

Michael Perri and his colleagues (1988) have demonstrated that follow-up treatment programs can be effective in reducing the relapse problem in weight control. In this study, obese men and women lost weight in a program that included exercise training and behavioral techniques such as self-monitoring, reinforcement, stimulus control, and cognitive restructuring. The subjects were then randomly assigned (with restrictions to balance degree of overweight) to five groups: one control group and four follow-up treatment conditions. The follow-up conditions all included regular meetings with a behavioral therapist, but incorporated different degrees of exercise and social influence. Weight measurements taken 18 months after the original treatment revealed that the subjects who received follow-up treatment were far more successful at maintaining their lower weights than the control subjects were. Analysis showed that the different follow-up treatments were about equally effective and that there seemed to be two critical components in their success: (1) frequent therapist meetings to deal with specific problems individuals were having in maintaining their weight and (2) social influences of other members of a treatment group. These findings are very encouraging and suggest that many obese individuals who have lost weight would benefit from having continued meetings with a therapist, relapse "hot lines" to call, and support groups.

Anorexia Nervosa and Bulimia

Although overeating is a very common weight control problem with psychosocial relationships, it is not considered to be a psychiatric disorder. In contrast, two relatively unusual eating disorders—*anorexia nervosa* and *bulimia*—are viewed as psychiatric disorders. These two disorders have been receiving a great deal of attention recently. Anorexia nervosa is illustrated in the following case study of 12-year-old Jim, who was hospitalized following a

> loss of weight from 100 to 67 pounds over a period of 18 months, associated with refusal to eat, irritability, and hostile controlling behavior in relation to his parents. . . . The frantic parents then became panicky in their struggle to get him to eat, for he had decreased his meager rations until he was restricting himself to the sugar content of the gum he chewed excessively. (Falstein, Feinstein, & Judas, 1956, pp. 754–755)

Not only did Jim's weight drop by a third, but this occurred at a time in development when weight and height normally increase. This case is especially unusual because the patient is a male—anorexia nervosa occurs 10 or 15 times more frequently in females than males (Polivy & Thomsen, 1988; Werry, 1986).

As Jim's case shows, **anorexia nervosa** is an eating disorder that involves a drastic reduction in food intake and an unhealthy loss of weight. This disorder is characterized by a weight loss of at least 25% and an intense fear of becoming fat, which continues despite the extreme loss of weight (Agras, 1987). The severity of the weight loss may be so extreme as to cause or contribute to the person's death (Sarason & Sarason, 1984). The incidence of anorexia nervosa increases during the adolescent years and probably declines in early adulthood (Polivy & Thomsen, 1988). The disorder afflicts about 1 of every 250 adolescent girls, is more prevalent in upper-class than lower-class individuals, and appears to have become more prevalent since the 1960s (Lacey & Birtchnell, 1986; Polivy & Thomsen, 1988). Anorexia nervosa is especially common among dance students, models, and athletes who feel pressured to control their weight (Werry, 1986).

Bulimia is an eating disorder that is characterized by recurrent episodes of *binge eating*, generally followed by *purging* by self-induced vomiting, laxative use, or other means to prevent gaining weight (Fairburn, 1987; Lacey & Birtchnell, 1986; Werry, 1986). This disorder can lead to medical complications, such as rectal bleeding and unhealthful levels of electrolytes (for example, sodium and potassium) in the body. Bulimic individuals are aware that their eating pattern is abnormal, are fearful of having lost control of their eating, and tend to be depressed and self-critical after a bulimic episode.

Bulimia was not recognized as a distinct syndrome until the late 1970s. As a result, there is still some controversy regarding the most appropriate criteria to be used in its diagnosis, and less is known about this disorder than about anorexia nervosa (Agras, 1987; Fairburn, 1987). Bulimia is far more prevalent among females than males and is more likely to occur in adolescence and early adulthood than at other times in the life span. This disorder seems to be more prevalent than anorexia nervosa—afflicting perhaps 1 to 3% of female adolescents—and there is some evidence that the incidence of bulimia may be increasing (Agras, 1987; Schotte & Stunkard, 1987). Many individuals exhibit some bulimic behaviors, such as purging, but are not classified as bulimics because they engage in these behaviors infrequently.

Why People Become Anorexics and Bulimics

What causes the eccentric eating habits of anorexia nervosa and bulimia? The answer is still unclear, and researchers have suggested biological, psychological, and cultural factors that may be involved. Evidence for biological factors in these eating disorders is quite limited and centers on genetic and physiological links to anorexia nervosa (Lacey & Birtchnell, 1986). For example, some research findings indicate that the hypothalamus of anorexics may function abnormally (Gold et al., 1986).

Cultural factors may provide the answer to two obvious questions about these eating disorders: Why is the prevalence of anorexia nervosa and bulimia so much greater among females, and why has it increased in recent years? Beauty plays a central role in the sex-role stereotype of women in Western cultures, and these cultures have witnessed recent changes in their ideals about female beauty (Polivy & Thomsen, 1988; Striegel-Moore, Silberstein, & Rodin, 1986). These changes are evident in the body proportions of models and beauty pageant contestants. Years ago, the "ideally beautiful woman" had a figure that was more rounded, with larger bust and hip measurements. After 1960 or so, the ideal figure of a woman has become much thinner, and the social pressures on women to be slender have increased. As we saw earlier, females are more likely than males to wish they were thinner and to diet.

The role of psychological factors is suggested by circumstances that relate to the onset of these eating disorders. For one thing, most adolescents—especially females—try to control their weight by adjusting their eating habits in a normal manner. But the methods many dieters use for weight control tend to become more extreme, involving occasional fasting or purging. A study of over 1,700 15-year-old male and female high school students, for instance, revealed that about 13% of them had engaged in some for of purging behavior, with the rate for females being twice as high as for males (Killen et al., 1986). Most of these purging behaviors occurred infrequently—on a monthly basis or less. Individuals who develop anorexia nervosa and bulimia typically start out dieting normally, and then begin using more extreme methods (Polivy & Thomsen, 1988). They may come to rely on these methods because they feel that they "work." Because bulimics are restrained eaters, they may binge as a result of becoming disinhibited by events, such as feelings of anxiety.

Why do these eating patterns become so compulsive? People who are extremely con-

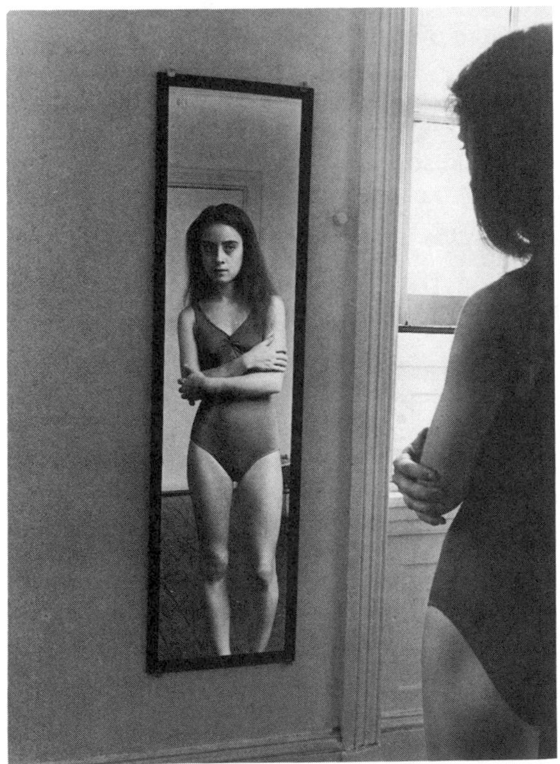

Anorexics tend to see themselves as "too fat" despite their thinness.

cerned about their weight tend to see themselves as round-faced and pudgy, even when others do not. Studies using ingenious apparatuses, such as special projectors, have shown that the great majority of women overestimate their size and generally perceive themselves to be one-fourth larger than they really are (Thompson, 1986). Although men make similar errors, they do so to a much lesser degree—and, unlike women, many of these men may *want* to be larger. Body size overestimations are particularly pronounced among anorexics and bulimics. Among anorexics, for example, the idea that they are overweight persists long after they have become slim. When they are reduced to skin and bones, anorexics still claim to be "too fat" and greatly overestimate their size (Askevold, 1975; Crisp & Kalucy, 1974).

Treatments for Anorexics and Bulimics

Because anorexia nervosa involves a severe and health-threatening underweight condition, the first priority in treating this disorder is to restore the person's body weight and nutrition to as near normal as possible. This is usually done in a hospital setting, and several approaches that include behavioral techniques and drug therapy are effective for putting weight on (Agras, 1987; Werry, 1986). Keeping the weight on is difficult; about half of previously treated anorexics continue to have eating problems and often show other social and emotional difficulties, such as depression. Follow-up treatment is essential and tends to focus on the person's distorted body image, continued desire to restrict food intake, and various interpersonal and job-related problems.

Treatment for bulimia appears to be more successful than that for anorexia nervosa (Agras, 1987; Lacey & Birtchnell, 1986). The use of *antidepressant drugs* can generally be a useful first step in the treatment of bulimics (Agras & McCann, 1987). Other effective approaches for treating bulimia involve behavioral and cognitive techniques, such as self-monitoring, reinforcement, relaxation training, and cognitive restructuring (Agras, 1987; Wilson & Smith, 1987). Few studies have assessed the long-term success of these treatments for bulimia, and the relapse rates found have been quite variable. A promising approach for preventing relapse was tested with bulimic women. The treatment used cognitive restructuring and a procedure to help the women "disconfirm, on the basis of their own experience, their fears about losing control, being swept away by irresistible urges to vomit and uncontrollably gaining weight" (Wilson, Rossiter, Kleifield, & Lindholm, 1986, p. 281). Following this treatment, the therapist contacted each woman monthly by phone—and in an interview at the end of a year, all the women who had completed the treatment reported that they had not binged and purged since being treated. This evidence is encouraging, but should be regarded as tentative because the sample size was small and the researchers did not have an independent source to confirm the subjects' reports.

We have discussed the problems people have in controlling their weight through adjustments in their diets. We have also seen that exercise can play an important role in reducing body fat and, thereby, can enhance people's health. The next section examines exercise as a means of becoming fit and keeping well.

EXERCISE

A "fitness boom" seems to have occurred across the United States since the early 1960s. The proportion of Americans who exercise has doubled since then, and about three-fifths of individuals over 18 years of age engage in some type of regular exercise (Serfass & Gerberich, 1984). Joggers and bicyclists can be seen on roads and paths in cities and out in the country, and fitness clubs have sprung up everywhere. We have all heard that "exercise is healthy." We will see why in this section.

The Health Effects of Exercise

If you asked fitness conscious people why they exercise, they would probably give a variety of reasons: "Exercising helps me keep my weight

HIGHLIGHT 8B: On Issues
Types and Amounts of Healthful Exercise

All physical activities—even just fidgeting—use energy and burn calories. *Exercise* is a special class of physical activity in which people exert their bodies for the sake of health or body development. There are several types of exercise, each with its own form of activity and physical goals. Let's see what these types of exercise are and what pattern of activities experts recommend to benefit most people's health.

Isotonics, Isometrics, and Isokinetics

The distinctions between isotonic, isometric, and isokinetic exercise are based on the degree to which:

- The activity enhances strength or endurance.
- Muscle contractions in the activity overcome an object's resistance to move.
- Exertion is required in more than one direction.

The term **isotonic exercise** refers to a type of activity that builds strength *and* endurance by the person moving a heavy object, exerting most of the muscle force in one direction. This type of exercise includes weight lifting and many calisthenics. In doing push-ups, for example, most of the exertion occurs in raising the body.

Isometric exercise, in contrast, builds mainly strength rather than endurance, and the person exerts muscle force against an *immovable* object. An example of an isometric exercise is the "chair lift": the person sits in a standard unupholstered chair, grasps the sides of the seat with both hands, and pulls upward, straining the arm muscles. The pulling doesn't move the seat. **Isokinetic exercise** builds strength *and* endurance by the person exerting muscle force in more than one direction in the course of moving an object. An example would be in exerting substantial force to push a bar forward and to pull it back. Isokinetic exercise typically requires special equipment, such as Nautilus machines.

Aerobics

The word *aerobics* literally means "with oxygen." What does oxygen have to do with exercise? When we exert ourselves in physical activity, the energy for it comes from the metabolic process of burning fatty acids and glucose in the presence of oxygen. Continuous exertion at high intensity over many minutes requires a great deal of oxygen. Being "in shape" means that the person consumes a high *volume of oxygen* (VO_2) per heartbeat during physical exertion.

The term **aerobic exercise** refers to energetic physical activity that requires high levels of oxygen over an extended number of minutes, say, half an hour. Aerobic activities generally involve rhythmical action that move the body over a distance or against gravity—as occurs in running, bicycling, swimming, or certain calisthenics (Haskell, 1984, 1985). Performing this kind of activity with sufficient intensity and duration on a regular basis increases the body's ability to extract oxygen from the blood and generate energy efficiently. The intensity of the exercise must be great enough to raise the heart rate to within a moderately high range. In the process of becoming aerobically fit, individuals increase their physical endurance because their efficient use of oxygen allows the body to burn fatty acids and glucose more completely. This is the main goal of aerobic exercise.

A Healthful Exercise Program

How much and what kinds of exercise do experts recommend to promote fitness? To answer this question, we need to recognize that any specific program would depend on the individual's age, current health and physical capacity, goals, interests, and opportunities, such as whether facilities or partners are available (Haskell, 1985; Ribisl, 1984). Almost all individuals need to begin with a moderate *starter program* and progress in a gradual manner toward fitness. People who are elderly or less fit at the beginning of an exercise program typically need to progress more slowly than others do. Progressing gradually avoids muscle soreness and injury, and allows the body systems to adapt to increasing demands that are being made on them, such as in the use of oxygen. Heavy exercise without sufficient oxygen simply causes the muscles to fatigue.

Individuals should aim for a program that involves about an hour of exercise three or four times a week. Each hour would consist of three phases (Haskell, 1985; Ribisl, 1984):

1. *Warm-up.* The first 20 minutes or so of each session is devoted to warming-up activities in preparation for aerobics. These activities generally include stretching and flexibility exercises for various major muscle groups, such as of the neck, back,

shoulders, abdomen, and legs. They also include strength and endurance exercises, such as sit-ups, push-ups, and pull-ups.

2. *Aerobics.* The next 20 to 40 minutes consists of rhythmical exercise of large muscle groups, performed vigorously enough to raise the heart (pulse) rate to a moderately high "target range." The easiest way to estimate the target range for an adult is to use a formula based on the person's age: The *minimum* heart rate would be 160 pulse beats per minute minus the person's age; the *maximum* is 200 minus age (LaPlace, 1984). Thus, 30-year-olds would maintain their heart rate between 130 and 170 beats per minute during aerobics. A more accurate estimate of the range can be calculated by a complex procedure using the individual's resting and peak heart rates (Ribisl, 1984). Examples of aerobic exercises include aerobic dancing, bicycling, canoeing, handball, rope skipping, swimming, and jogging.

3. *Cool-down.* Just as the warm-up period prepares the body for vigorous aerobics, the last several minutes of exercise should be devoted to gradually returning the body to its normal state. This is especially important for the cardiovascular system (Ribisl, 1984). The exercises performed during the cool-down phase can include calisthenics or walking, and should taper off in intensity.

Although these recommendations seem fairly rigid, there is room for flexibility. For instance, people who exercise at the upper end of their target range can use fewer or shorter exercise periods each week (Simons-Morton et al., 1988). Also, because of the variety of possible exercises that can be performed during each phase, the program can be tailored to the goals and interests of the individual. Someone who likes variety can jog on one day, canoe on another, swim on another, and so on. Someone who wants to firm his or her abdomen can focus on appropriate activities during the warm-up and cool-down phases.

---

down," "I like it when I'm in shape—and so does my boyfriend," "It helps me unwind and relieves my tension," "Being in shape keeps me sharp on my job," "I don't get sick as often when I'm fit," and "It makes people's hearts stronger, so they live longer." These answers describe several psychosocial and physical health benefits of exercising and are, for the most part, correct.

Three psychosocial benefits of exercise have received considerable research support. First, engaging in regular vigorous exercise reduces people's feelings of *stress* and anxiety, as we discussed in Chapter 5. Second, people who get involved in fitness programs report that their *work performance* and attitudes improve —they make fewer errors, for instance (Folkins & Sime, 1981). Third, participating in regular exercise appears to enhance the *self-concepts* of individuals, especially children (Dishman, 1986; Folkins & Sime, 1981). These improvements in the self-concept occur because individuals who exercise are better able to control their weight, maintain an attractive appearance, and engage successfully in various physical activities and sports—all of which help these people to feel a heightened sense of esteem and to receive the many social advantages that accrue with being fit.

Of the many physiological effects that physical activity produces, one effect is especially intriguing: exercise seems to increase the body's production of *endorphins,* which are morphinelike chemical substances. Studies have shown that endorphin levels in the blood are higher after exercise than before (Carr et al., 1981). Some researchers claim that the euphoric "runner's high" that many individuals feel after a very vigorous aerobic workout results from high levels of endorphins reaching the brain. These researchers have also proposed that these higher endorphin levels may be responsible for decreases in both the stress and sensations of pain many people feel during or after vigorous exercise. But the results of research so far do not appear to confirm these possibilities (Hopson, 1988; Sime, 1984).

Exercise can enhance many aspects of people's physical fitness throughout the life span. But as adults get older, they generally show a gradual decline in their physical work capacity —as reflected in their muscle flexibility, strength, and endurance (Serfass & Gerberich, 1984). This decline occurs partly because individuals get less exercise as they get older. An 18-year longitudinal study examined the physical work capacity of men who were over 50 years of age at the start of the study and who engaged in aerobic exercise regularly (Kasch, Wallace, & Van Camp, 1985). The work capacity of these men decreased only slightly across the 18 years, whereas individuals in the general population tend to show a 1 to 2% decrease per year. Also, the percentage of body fat and resting blood pressure of these men did not show the increases that usually occur during these years. These results indicate that engaging in aerobic exercise curbs the usual decline in fitness that people experience as they get older.

The physical benefits people gain from vigorous and regular exercise are reflected not only in their improved work capacity but also in their health. The main health benefits of exercise relate to preventing cardiovascular problems (Haskell, 1984, 1985). Many studies have demonstrated that individuals who regularly engage in vigorous physical activity are less likely to develop and die from coronary heart disease (CHD) than those who lead relatively sedentary lives (Powell, Thompson, Caspersen, & Kendrick, 1987). Although no experimental research has been done in which human subjects were randomly assigned to exercise and nonexercise conditions, research with animals and prospective studies with humans indicate that the link between physical activity and reduced risk of CHD may be causal.

How does engaging in regular vigorous activity protect individuals against CHD? The role of exercise in reducing blood pressure is especially clear. Studies have shown that children and adults who are physically active have lower systolic and diastolic blood pressure than those who are not (Haskell, 1984; Hofman, Walter, Connelly, & Vaughn, 1987; Panico et al., 1987). Furthermore, the results of an experimental study indicate that vigorous "exercise performed three times a week lowers blood pressure and should reduce cardiovascular risk" (Jennings et al., 1986, p. 30). Researchers have also proposed other ways that exercise may prevent CHD, for example, that physical activity may retard or reverse atherosclerosis or it may reduce the incidence of arrhythmic heartbeats (Haskell, 1984). But these possibilities have only limited support so far.

Not all effects of exercise are beneficial—there can be hazards as well. One hazard occurs when people jog or bicycle in traffic, of course, risking a collision. But the most common problems that arise involve injury to bones or muscles from other kinds of accidents and from overstraining the body (Haskell, 1985). Many injuries happen to people who do not exercise regularly or are beginners. The main dangers to these people come from overtaxing their bodies and from unsafe exercise conditions, such as having improper shoes. Exercising too long in very hot weather can lead to heat exhaustion—with symptoms of dizziness, rapid and weak pulse, and headache—or a more severe condition called heat stroke, which can be fatal. An infrequent but extremely serious hazard of exercise is in precipitating cardiac arrest. A study of autopsy reports for individuals who had died in association with exercising revealed that almost all these people died of cardiac arrest, and most of them had cardiovascular problems that existed prior to the attack (Northcote, Flannigan, & Ballantyne, 1986). Most of these problems could have been detected by medical screening, and the deaths of these people might have been avoided through medical counseling. Special exercise programs and recommendations are available for individuals who have specific health problems, such as diabetes and CHD (Ribisl, 1984).

Conclusions regarding the health effects of exercise are fairly clear. Practicing vigorous exercise on a regular basis is psychologically and physically healthful, particularly for preventing heart disease. People who begin an exercise program should guard against overtaxing their bodies, exercise under safe conditions with proper skills, and have periodic medical examinations to determine whether any underlying risks exist. Although more people exercise today than was the case years ago, most adults probably do not get enough regular and energetic physical activity to gain substantial cardiovascular benefits (Dishman, Sallis, & Orenstein, 1985; Oldridge, 1984).

Who Gets Enough Exercise, Who Does Not—and Why?

Some people have lifestyles that provide regular, vigorous, and sustained activity naturally, without actually doing "exercises" (Oldridge, 1984). They may, for example, commute to work by bicycle or have a job that involves energetic work, as farmers, laborers, and homemakers often do. These people can get enough exercise as long as the sustained vigorous activity occurs at least three times a week. But most people in the United States have relatively sedentary life circumstances (Dishman, Sallis, & Orenstein, 1985), and many individuals who could be physically active in their normal lifestyles choose not to be—they may take rest breaks rather than sustaining an activity or opt to use a machine instead of doing a task manually. Because little is known about people's everyday physical activities, we will focus our discussion on factors associated with doing and not doing exercises.

Rod Dishman and his colleagues have reviewed a large number of studies and described some factors that distinguish individuals who exercise from those who do not (Dishman, 1982; Dishman, Sallis, & Orenstein, 1985). Those who *do* exercise tend to be young and well-educated adults, members of upper socioeconomic groups, and individuals who have participated in exercise in the past. People who do *not* exercise tend to be blue-collar workers, older individuals, and people who are at relatively high risk for developing CHD, such as by being overweight or smoking cigarettes. From the standpoint of performing health-protective behavior, those whose health would benefit most from physical activity seem to be the most resistant to starting or maintaining an exercise program.

Whether or not people exercise is also related to the social influences in their lives and to their health beliefs. Social influences on exercise behavior involve modeling, encouragement, and reinforcement by peers and family. Studies have found that adults who exercise tend to have spouses who encourage them to do so, and children and adolescents who exercise or engage in sports tend to have friends or family who also do so (Dishman, Sallis, & Orenstein, 1985; Gottlieb & Baker, 1986; Sallis et al., 1988). The role of health beliefs on exercise behavior has been demonstrated in research in which subjects received information describing their level of fitness or indicating they might be susceptible to health problems that could be prevented through exercise (Godin, Desharnais, Jobin, & Cook, 1987; Wurtele & Maddux, 1987). Compared to subjects who did not get such information, those who did were more likely to start exercising.

When Americans are asked why they don't exercise, the most common reason they give is that they cannot find the time (Dishman, Sallis, & Orenstein, 1985). Actually, of course, people generally do have the time but choose to use it in other ways. People also report not exercising because they have no convenient place to do it or because the weather or other environmental conditions make it unpleasant or impossible. Another factor is age—as adults get older,

> they gradually disengage from participating in physical activities due less, it appears, to decrements in physiological functioning ability than to cultural and psychosocial factors which persuade them that vigorous exercise is not appropriate for the elderly. Sedentary social role models, distorted body image, exaggerated notions of risk, expectations of disapproval, fear of failure, misinformation and limited previous involvement in physical activities all conspire to limit the elderly's desire to be active. (Vertinsky & Auman, 1988, p. 16)

These forces against exercise are particularly strong among today's elderly women, whose past sex-role experiences have taught them that men are more socially and physically suited to vigorous activity than females. Although both male and female older people tend to underrate their physical capabilities and exaggerate their health risks in performing energetic exercise after middle age, women are especially prone to these beliefs (Vertinsky & Auman, 1988; Woods & Birren, 1984). Health care workers and organizations for the elderly have many opportunities to dispel incorrect beliefs about health risks, change sex-role stereotypes regarding exercise, and encourage older individuals to develop more active lifestyles.

Promoting Exercise Behavior

A person who spends time watching youngsters play is likely to have the impression that children are innately very active—running, jumping, and climbing—and that they do not need to be encouraged to exercise, as older individuals do. Although children are generally more active than adults, and about three-fifths of schoolchildren and adolescents get healthful levels of exercise throughout the year, many other children are not active enough (Simons-Morton et al., 1988). People of all ages could benefit from school, park, and worksite recreation programs and facilities to promote exercise.

Researchers have outlined several strategies that are important in promoting exercise behavior (Dishman, Sallis, & Orenstein, 1985; Oldridge, 1984; Ribisl, 1984; Serfass & Gerberich, 1984). These strategies can be grouped into the following categories:

- *Preassessment:* Before people begin an exercise program, they need to determine their purposes for exercising and the benefits they can expect. They should also assess their health status, preferably through a medical checkup.
- *Exercise selection:* The exercises included in the program should be tailored to meet the health needs of the individual and his or her interests and purposes, such as firming up certain parts of the body. People are more likely to stick with the program if it includes exercises that they enjoy doing.
- *Exercise conditions:* Before people start an exercise program, they should determine when and where they will exercise and arrange to get any equipment they will need. Some people seem to adhere to a program if they pick a fixed time for exercising and refuse to schedule anything else at that

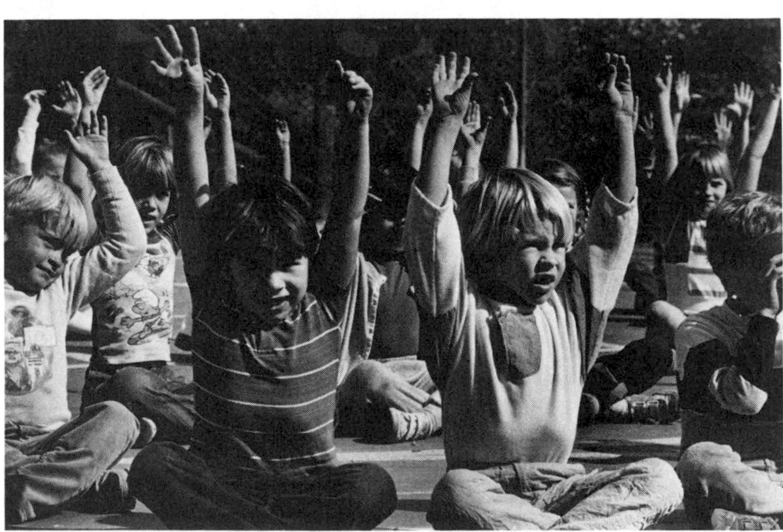

People of all ages can benefit from exercise programs. These children are participating in a "Jazzercise" class.

time; others can be more flexible and still make sure to exercise about every other day. The exercise conditions should be safe and convenient.

- *Goals and contingencies:* Most people adhere to a program more closely if they write out a specific sequence of goals and consequences for exercise behavior in a contingency contract. The goals should be graduated, beginning at a modest level. They should also be measurable—as body weight or number of push-ups would be—rather than vague, such as "to feel good." Some individuals may need tangible reinforcers to maintain their exercise behavior in the early stages of the program. After these people get in shape, many will find that the enjoyment of exercise and the physical benefits are sufficient rewards.
- *Social influence:* People are more likely to start and stick with an exercise program if these efforts have the support and encouragement of family and friends. Exercising with a partner or in groups sometimes enhances people's motivation to continue in a program.
- *Record keeping:* People can enhance their motivation to exercise by keeping records of their weight and performance. Seeing on paper how far they have progressed can be very reinforcing.

To obtain the full health benefits of physical activity, people need to continue doing exercises or being very active in their normal lifestyles throughout their lives. Few Americans achieve this ideal. Of those individuals who are already exercising regularly at any given time, about half will quit in the coming year (Dishman, Sallis, & Orenstein, 1985). Although the strategies we have just examined improve people's adherence to exercise programs, the dropout and relapse rates are too high even in well-designed and supervised programs introduced for students in college and for employees at their worksites (Bélisle, Roskies, & Lévesque, 1987; Oldridge, 1984).

SAFETY

Unsafe conditions threaten people's health in virtually all environments, such as in traffic, at home, on the job, and at the beach. These conditions produce huge numbers of illnesses, injuries, and deaths each year. In most cases, these health problems could have been avoided if the victim or other people had taken reasonable safety precautions. Let's see what is known about the hazards people face and how to help people live safer lives.

Accidents

In a typical hour of an average day in the United States, over 1,000 injuries occur that require medical attention (Christophersen, 1989). Some of these injuries are serious enough to cause long-term disability or death. More than 90,000 Americans die each year from unintentional injuries in accidents. By far the most frequent of these accidental fatalities involve traffic mishaps—followed by falls, drownings, fires, poisonings, and firearms (Waller, 1987). More than 3,000 people die at their jobs each year, and thousands of other workers are seriously injured. Industries with the highest mortality rates include mining and construction businesses, and industries with the highest injury rates include meatpacking, heavy manufacturing (mobile and prefabricated homes, vending machines, and structural wood), rubber recycling, and sawmill companies (USDL, 1987). Government data reveal that accidental injury is:

- The fourth most frequent cause of death in the American population as a whole.
- The leading cause of death of individuals under age 45.
- Responsible for over half of all deaths of children and adolescents (Cataldo et al., 1986; Haggerty, 1986; Waller, 1987).

Another way to see the relative impact of injury versus disease on life is to estimate the years of life lost by the victims of these causes of death. We could, for instance, use the age of

65 as a standard, subtract the age of death of each person who dies earlier, and then total all the years lost to injuries separately from those lost to disease. Calculations like these reveal that the total number of years lost from the combination of unintentional and intentional (that is, homocide or suicide) injuries is about the same as from the combination of heart disease, cancer, and stroke — the three most frequent causes of death in America (Christophersen, 1984; Robertson, 1983; Waller, 1987). About two-thirds of injury deaths are unintentional.

How can accidental injuries be prevented? In discussing this question, we will focus on injuries in traffic mishaps for two reasons: (1) they account for about half of all accidental deaths and (2) researchers have done many studies on methods to prevent traffic injuries. The death rates for motor vehicle accidents increase dramatically during adolescence, as depicted in Figure 8.3, and males are about 2½ times more likely to die in a traffic mishap than females between 15 and 19 years of age (Matarazzo, 1984). Because of the high rates of traffic fatalities in adolescence, special safe-driving programs have been directed toward teenagers. One approach has involved providing driver training in high schools, and early quasi-experimental research showed that students who take a driver education course subsequently have fewer accidents than those who do not. But later studies revealed that the course itself was *not* the cause of this relationship; for some reason, students who elect to take driver education simply drive less than those who do not (Robertson, 1986). Similarly, driver education for adults — for example, as a condition for employment or in response to traffic violations — also seems to have little effect on accidents.

Other ways to reduce traffic accidents have been more effective than driver training. One

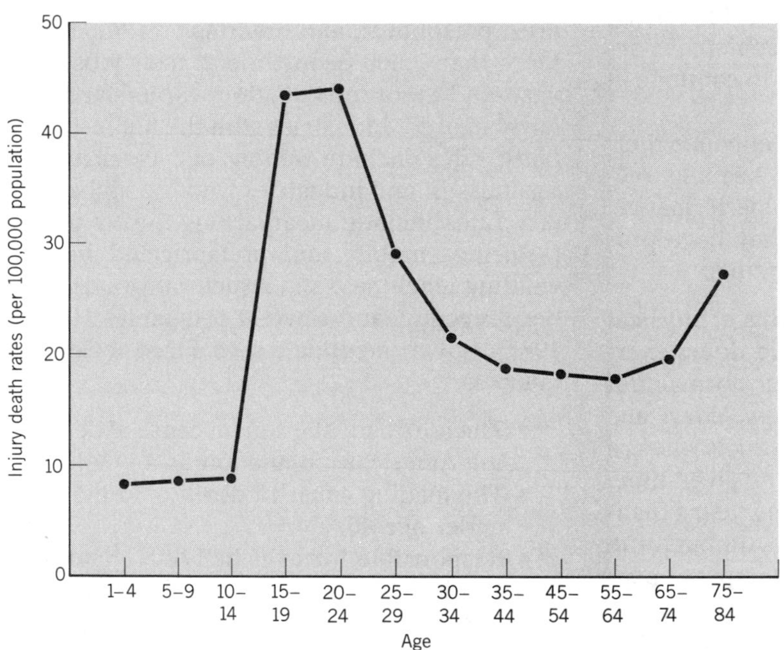

FIGURE 8.3 The relationship between age and traffic-injury death rates. (Data from Waller, 1987, Table 3.) Note, however, that the dramatic increase during adolescence primarily reflects the deaths of individuals who are *occupants* of motor vehicles; the upswing in old age mainly reflects deaths of individuals who are *pedestrians* (Cataldo et al., 1986).

approach capitalizes on research findings regarding drivers' perceptual and reaction abilities, with the goal of reducing their errors and enhancing their reaction time. Public health researcher Leon Robertson has described two examples:

> An extra brake light mounted in the center of the vehicle above the trunk resulted in a 50% reduction in rear-end collisions when the front vehicle was braking, compared to randomly assigned control cars in the same fleets.
>
> Stripes across a road at an exponentially decreasing distance creates the illusion of acceleration when crossing at a constant speed. . . . Installation of such stripes at high speed approaches to traffic circles in England resulted in an average 66% reduction in crashes at such sites. (1986, pp. 22–23)

Findings such as these have led to changes in automobile design and highway markings, which should reduce traffic injuries. Another approach that is quite effective in reducing traffic deaths is not very popular with teenagers; it involves raising the legal driving age (Robertson, 1986).

Injuries and deaths can also be prevented if drivers and passengers will use protective equipment, such as seat belts in cars and helmets when riding a motorcycle (Latimer & Lave, 1987; Robertson, 1986; Waller, 1987). But after seat belts were installed as standard equipment in cars, few people opted to use them. As a result, researchers began to study a wide variety of methods to promote the use of protective equipment in cars. Some of these studies were conducted to improve car safety for children by providing instruction and information to parents through hospitals and pediatricians. These programs have had mixed success (Cataldo et al., 1986; Christophersen, 1984, 1989). A successful hospital-based program provided computer-assisted video instruction on using an infant safety seat to mothers before leaving the hospital after giving birth (Hletko, Robin, Hletko, & Stone, 1987). A parking lot attendant at the hospital subsequently assessed the use of a safety seat when the mother brought the baby back for a checkup four months later. Nearly 65% of these mothers had their infants correctly restrained — a rate that was substantially higher than the 53% observed with untrained mothers.

Some programs to increase seat belt use have been directed at the child, rather than the parent. One study presented a two-week passenger safety curriculum to children in several preschools, using a theme character called "Bucklebear" (Chang, Dillman, Leonard, & English, 1985). Two of the curriculum's main messages were that "buckling up" for every ride is a good thing for everyone to do and that the best seat in the car is the back seat. Some of the parents also took part in a workshop and other activities to promote seat belt use. The children in several other preschools served as a control group who were matched to the experimental subjects for their prior seat belt use. Follow-up observations in the preschool parking lots three weeks after the program was completed revealed that over 44% of the "Bucklebear" children and only about 22% of the control children were using seat belts. Another program used rewards to encourage seat belt use by children (Roberts & Fanurik, 1986). Before the rewards were introduced, about 5% of the children used the belts; after the rewards were introduced, about 70% used the belts. As you might expect, follow-up observations 2½ months after the program and rewards ended revealed that seat belt use declined — but between 10 and 20% of the children were still using the belts.

Less than 15% of Americans were using seat belts by the early 1980s, despite public health announcements and other programs to promote this behavior (Latimer & Lave, 1987). As a result, many states began to pass laws requiring adults and children to use protective equipment in cars. Seat belt and safety seat use has generally increased sharply and traffic fatalities have decreased after these laws went into effect (Latimer & Lave, 1987; Robertson, 1986; Wagenaar & Webster, 1986; Waller, 1987). But many people begin to revert to not using the equipment after a while, and probably less than half of the people comply with the law by the time a year has passed. Although such laws are helpful, they may not be sufficient.

Environmental Hazards

A 1987 newspaper poll in New Jersey asked people, "Do you use sunscreen in the summer?" One young man answered, "No. I don't use anything—never have, never will," and a young woman said, "Never, because the sun's not too hot in New Jersey." Another young woman said she uses only the weakest sunscreen because "I want to have a gorgeous tan." Ever since the French fashion designer Coco Chanel made tanning fashionable, people in many parts of the world have come to believe that tans are attractive and "healthful."

Today we know that excessive exposure to the sun's ultraviolet rays makes the skin age and can cause skin cancers, particularly in people who are fair skinned and burn easily (Levy, 1985). Although most cases of skin cancer can be easily treated and cured, others cannot, especially if they are discovered late. Dermatologists and other health care practitioners recognize that most people will not stay out of the sun and that many strive for a "healthy" and attractive tan. As a result, these practitioners recommend that most people use sunscreens when exposed to the sun for more than, say, an hour or so. A study of adult California sunbathers found that those who use sunscreens tend to be females rather than males and know about skin cancer risks (Keesling & Friedman, 1987).

Ultraviolet radiation from the sun is only one of many environmental hazards people need to guard against. Many harmful chemicals and gasses can be found in people's households, worksites, and general communities.

- *Household hazards:* American homes contain a wide assortment of household cleaning chemicals and pesticides that, for the most part, present little risk when kept out of children's reach and used with proper ventilation. Other substances present greater risks, however. *Lead* poisoning presents a serious health problem for developing embryos and children, and can damage their nervous systems and impair intelligence and hearing (Harvey, 1984). Children may ingest lead in many ways, such as by mouthing objects painted with lead-based paints, drinking water from a plumbing system with poorly soldered lead joints, or drinking acidic beverages from lead-glazed ceramics. Pregnant women who ingest leaded water or beverages may pass the substance on to their developing babies. Another hazardous household substance is a radioactive gas called *radon*, which may be present at dangerously high levels in hundreds of thousands of homes throughout the United States (Monmaney, Hager, & Emerson, 1988). The chief risk of breathing radon is in developing lung cancer—breathing air with moderately high levels of radon for many hours each day presents the same cancer risk as smoking one or two packs of cigarettes a day. Because radon enters the house from the ground, the usual way for reducing radon pollution is to ventilate the basement.
- *Worksite hazards:* Millions of people have jobs that can bring them in contact with hazardous substances, some of which are toxic or carcinogenic (Anderson, 1982; Baker, 1988; Clever & Omenn, 1988; Levy, 1985; USDHHS, 1985d). For example, people who come in regular contact with *asbestos* risk developing lung cancer—similarly, excessive exposure to *benzine* is linked to bone marrow cancer; *vinyl chloride*, with liver cancer; *aromatic amines*, with bladder cancer; and *cadmium*, with prostate cancer. People who work with hazardous materials need to know what the substances are, what dangers they pose, and how to use them safely. Some states have enacted "Right to Know" laws that require employers to notify and train employees regarding the safe use of hazardous materials.
- *Community hazards:* The air, water, and ground have become polluted with harm-

ful chemicals and gasses in communities throughout the United States. Some "Right to Know" laws apply to communities and require agencies to provide information about the exposure of residents to hazardous materials. If people know that a danger exists, they can try to take protective action (for example, by drinking bottled water), become involved in community change, and notify their physician so that appropriate tests can be done periodically as secondary prevention.

People are becoming increasingly concerned about the chemicals and gasses that pervade our lives. They should be vigilant—but they should also be aware of three things: First, not every chemical or gas is harmful. Second, exposure to toxic or carcinogenic substances poses little risk when the contact is infrequent and the dosage is very small. Third, some harmful substances may have benefits that outweigh their dangers. For example, chlorinating water has all but erased many of the waterborne infections that once threatened enormous numbers of lives. But chlorinated water often has very small amounts of the carcinogen *chloroform* in it. Given these circumstances, the benefits of chlorination appear to outweigh the risks.

SUMMARY

In addition to water, food contains five types of chemical components: carbohydrates, lipids or "fats," proteins, vitamins, and minerals. People can get all the nutrients and fiber they need by eating diets that include grains, fruits and vegetables, milk products, and meats and fish. Until recently, the trend in American diets was toward consuming more and more sugar, animal fats, and animal proteins, while consuming less and less fiber. People's food preferences are determined by biological and psychosocial factors.

Diet is associated with the development of atherosclerosis, hypertension, and cancer. Cholesterol is the main dietary culprit in atherosclerosis. Whether plaques form in our blood vessels depends on the presence of three types of lipoproteins: low-density lipoprotein, very-low-density lipoprotein, and high-density lipoprotein. People's serum cholesterol levels are determined by genetic factors and by the foods they eat. Although Americans have been reducing their intake of cholesterol recently, they still consume more than 50% too much. Intervention programs can be effective in helping people reduce dietary cholesterol substantially. High blood pressure can result from consuming too much sodium and caffeine. Diets high in fat and low in fiber increase people's risk of cancer, especially cancer of the colon.

Americans are very conscious of and concerned about their weight. Most concerns are with being too fat, rather than too thin, particularly among females. One method for determining whether individuals are too heavy is to compare their weights against the desirable weights given in standard tables. People are classified as overweight if their weight exceeds their desirable weight by 10%; they are considered obese if their weight is more than 20% above the desirable weight. People become fat because they consume more calories than they burn up through metabolism. The excess calories are stored as fat in adipose tissue, which contains cells that can increase in size and number, especially in childhood and adolescence. Heredity plays a role in weight control, probably by affecting the set-point for body weight. Psychosocial factors also affect weight control. Restraint theory proposes that individuals who struggle constantly to keep their weight down develop abnormal eating patterns of inhibition and disinhibition.

Obesity is associated with the development of hypertension, coronary heart disease, and diabetes. These health risks depend on two factors. First, these risks increase with the degree of obesity. Second, individuals whose fat is concentrated in the abdominal region have greater health risks than those whose fat is mostly in the thighs, hips, and buttocks. Prevention of overweight should begin in childhood to avoid fat-cell hyperplasia. Schools and parents can play important roles in this effort.

Most heavy people try to reduce their weight on their own by going on a diet. Although overweight and obese individuals are likely to have difficulty adopting a lifestyle that maintains a lower weight, many of them can do it successfully. Heavy people who are not able to lose weight on their own often seek help through fad diets, exercise programs, behavioral techniques, self-help groups, and worksite weight-loss programs. Behavioral programs are more effective than other approaches. In relatively extreme cases, drastic procedures with medical supervision may be warranted; these procedures include placing the patient on a very-low-calorie diet, using appetite-suppressing drugs, or performing surgery. Although most people who lose weight in behavioral programs maintain their lower weight, others do not. Obese individuals who complete a behavioral program are less likely to relapse if the program includes frequent follow-up meetings with their weight-control therapist and social influences of other members in a treatment group.

Anorexia nervosa is an eating disorder that results in an unhealthy and extreme loss of weight. Bulimia is an eating disorder that involves recurrent episodes of binge eating and purging. Both of these disorders occur mainly in adolescence and early adulthood, and are much more prevalent in females than males. Treatment for anorexia nervosa is more difficult and less successful than that for bulimia.

More people are exercising today than years ago. Three types of exercise are isotonic, isometric, and isokinetic. Aerobic exercise refers to energetic physical activity that involves rhythmical movement of large muscle groups and requires high levels of oxygen over a period of half an hour or so. A healthful program of exercise would include a warm-up phase, an aerobic exercise phase, and a cool-down phase. Engaging regularly in vigorous exercise reduces stress, improves work performance, and enhances the person's self-concept. It also protects people against coronary heart disease, partly because it reduces blood pressure. People who exercise tend to be young and well-educated adults from the upper social classes. Individuals whose health would benefit most from physical activity seem to be the most resistant to starting and maintaining exercising.

Tens of thousands of people die each year in accidents involving traffic mishaps, falls, drownings, fires, poisonings, and firearms. The death rates for motor vehicle accidents increase dramatically during adolescence. There are many environmental hazards that people need to guard against. These include excessive exposure to sunlight and harmful chemicals and gasses.

KEY TERMS

lipoproteins
low-density lipoprotein
very-low-density lipoprotein
high-density lipoprotein
overweight
obese
set-point theory
insulin
restraint theory
anorexia nervosa
bulimia
isotonic exercise
isometric exercise
isokinetic exercise
aerobic exercise

Becoming Ill and Getting Medical Treatment

9

USING HEALTH SERVICES

PROLOGUE

Jo's life had just undergone major changes—she had been promoted by her employer and relocated to a new town with her two children. Then she noticed that a mole had developed on her shoulder. Uncertain whether the mole was a sign of something serious and harried by her current pressures, she decided to wait before doing anything about it. Then, soon after she found a new family physician, her youngest child became ill with the flu. Jo made an appointment for 10-year-old Mary with Dr. Armstrong and thought, "If I get a chance, I'll mention the mole to the doctor when we go, and have him look at it." But she wondered if he would be like their last physician who would sweep into the examining room, hurriedly ask very specific short-answer questions, dominate the conversation, and rush on to the next patient.

Fortunately, Dr. Armstrong was not like their last doctor. He started the visit by chatting a little with Mary to learn more about her and to establish a friendly relationship. Then he asked her about her health problem, did some physical tests, and discussed with her and Jo what they needed to do to treat the illness. At the end of that discussion, he switched the focus to Jo, asking about her job and general life situation to assess possible risk factors. When he asked, "How has your health been recently?", she anxiously told him about the mole, which he inspected. He told her that it looked harmless—as most moles are. He added, "People who have a mole should inspect it periodically, once a month or so. If it changes color, bleeds, grows, or changes in any other way please have me examine it without delay. Some moles develop into a skin cancer called melanoma, which can be treated effectively if we catch it early. I'll give you some information about moles before you leave."

Jo left the office very much relieved that the doctor had examined the mole and pronounced it harmless. She also noted that if the mole had been the beginnings of melanoma, they would have caught it early. She felt secure in having found a competent and caring physician whom she and her children could talk to easily and trust.

In this chapter, we will see that the relationship the patient and health care practitioner develop can influence the actions they take in primary, secondary, and tertiary prevention. The importance of this relationship will become clear as we discuss the kinds of health services available to people, how patients decide when to use these services, and why some patients use health services effectively whereas others do not. As we examine these topics, you will find answers to questions you may have about people's use of health services. How do people decide they are sick and may need medical attention? Why do some individuals seek health care more readily than others do? How can patients influence their health care? Do patients follow medical advice—and if not, why don't they comply?

TYPES OF HEALTH SERVICES

The system of medical care delivery and management in the United States is extremely complex, consisting of an enormous variety of health services. We can see the complex nature of this system by looking at three dimensions of its delivery and management: the *specialized functions* of health care workers and whether the care involves *inpatient treatment* or *office-based treatment.*

Specialized Functions of Practitioners

The American medical care system is staffed by several million health care workers who differ greatly in their roles and specialties. This system includes physicians of many types—general practitioners, pediatricians, cardiologists, neurosurgeons, dermatologists, gynecologists, psychiatrists, and so on—as well as nurses, dentists, optometrists, respiratory therapists, physical therapists, medical social workers, and dietitians, to name only a small number. Each type of practitioner provides a different type of health service, using specialized knowledge and skills.

Because each of these services involves an enormous amount of knowledge and skill that grows and changes very rapidly, individual practitioners cannot perform the services of several specialties simultaneously with a high degree of skill. The advantage in organizing the health care system into specialties is that patients can receive the greatest expertise available for each aspect of the treatment of each health problem. But this great advantage is not without drawbacks. For instance, the many health care practitioners working with a particular patient do not always communicate with each other effectively, so that the physician in charge of the treatment may not have a full picture of the person's condition or progress. Also, because many practitioners work with a patient very briefly—performing just a few medical tests, for example—the contact these practitioners have with patients is often impersonal.

Inpatient Treatment

People with serious illnesses who require medical attention either on a continuous basis or with complex equipment or procedures generally receive treatment as inpatients in hospitals and nursing homes. *Hospitals* are the most complex medical facilities in the medical care system, employing highly sophisticated equipment and skilled practitioners from almost all specialty areas. As a result, they can provide a wide variety of services, ranging from emergency care, to diagnostic testing, to curative treatment, to rehabilitation and social services (Easterbrook, 1987). Some hospitals have specialized missions, such as in providing care for children or for certain health problems—cancer, eye diseases, or orthopedic problems, for instance.

Nursing homes provide care for patients who need relatively long-term medical and per-

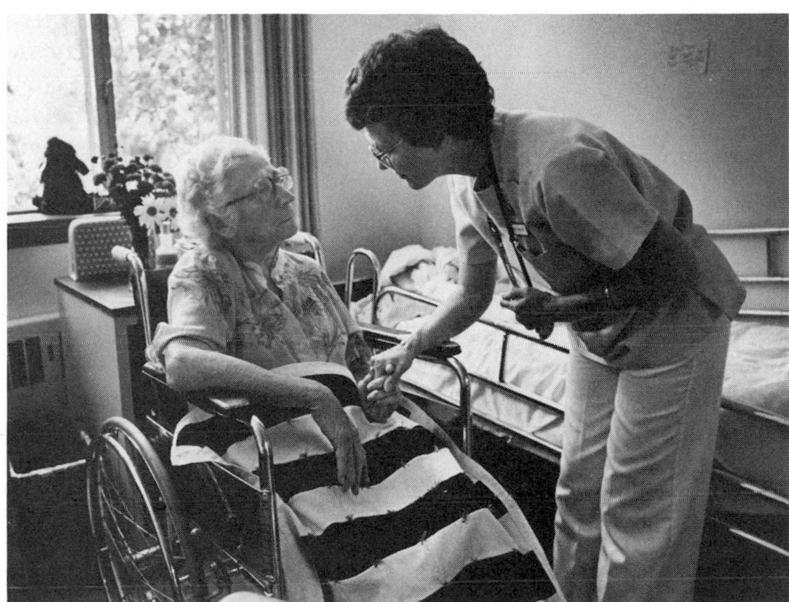

Most patients in nursing homes are elderly individuals who need long-term medical and personal care.

sonal care, particularly if the patients or their families cannot provide this care (Lawrence & Gaus, 1983; Shanas & Maddox, 1985; Vladeck, 1983). The large majority of patients in nursing homes are very frail, elderly individuals who often need help in day-to-day activities such as dressing and bathing themselves. The typical nursing home is a relatively small facility, having only about 75 or 80 beds. But because the United States has many more nursing homes than hospitals, on any given day nursing homes serve almost twice as many patients as hospitals do. Some nursing homes are designed and staffed to provide skilled nursing and rehabilitative services, whereas others are designed to treat mainly patients who require lesser degrees of health-related care and services. Although most nursing homes provide high-quality care, many others do not and have been cited for having unsanitary conditions, failing to follow doctors' instructions for giving drugs, and abusing patients (Tolchin, 1988).

Patients with long-term health problems have been relying less and less on inpatient services in recent years, opting instead for *home health care* (Freudenheim, 1988; Shanas & Maddox, 1985). The shift toward home care has occurred because of the fast-rising costs of hospital and nursing home services and because technological advances have made it possible to maintain medical treatment with outpatients. An example of a widely used technological device that provides treatment on an outpatient basis is the *pacemaker*, which sends electrical pulses to regulate heartbeat. Many patients with pacemakers can even transmit electrocardiograms by telephone to their physicians' offices. Another device is a pocket-size pump that can deliver precise amounts of medication on a specific schedule. Patients who use home care usually begin their treatment on an inpatient basis, but they are then discharged in the care of a home health care service.

Home health care offers some advantages over inpatient care (Freudenheim, 1988). For one thing, home care is likely to be less expensive. Also, patients usually prefer being at home, and can often return to work or school while receiving outpatient treatment. But for some patients—particularly the elderly—home health care can present problems if they lack needed help from family or friends and do not have a means of transportation to make periodic visits to their physicians (Shanas & Maddox, 1985).

Office-Based Treatment

When Americans get sick and seek professional treatment, the first place they usually go is to their family physician at his or her office. Several decades ago, office-based medical treatment in the United States was given only by private-practice practitioners who charged a fee for each service. Recently, however, other systems for delivering and managing office-based treatment have become widely available (Easterbrook, 1987). In one of these systems—called the *preferred provider organization* (PPO)—a group insurance plan negotiates with specific hospitals and physicians for discounted fee-for-service rates to provide health care for members of the plan, who are usually employees of large companies or organizations. Member patients may go to any physician or doctor who is affiliated with the PPO.

A small but growing percentage of Americans today receive office-based medical care through prepaid group plans. The most common type of group plan is the *health-maintenance organization* (HMO), in which members pay an annual fee and are entitled to use the services whenever they want with little or no additional charges (Easterbrook, 1987; Luft, 1983). Members seeking medical care go to a clinic run by the HMO and receive treatment by a physician who is a salaried employee. If necessary, this physician can arrange for the patient to be referred to a specialist or admitted to a hospital. The HMO pays for all treatments it arranges or recommends. Some HMOs provide financial incentives to their physicians for cost-saving behaviors, such as seeing a large number of patients per hour or sending a small number of patients to hospitals (Easterbrook, 1987). HMOs that use these kinds of incentives may encourage less-than-optimal care.

Is the medical care provided by HMOs as

good as that given by private physicians? Harold Luft (1983) reviewed the research on this question and noted some important problems in arriving at a clear answer. For one thing, HMOs vary greatly in their policies and structures. Also, the research comparing HMO and private-physician care has used quasi-experimental methods, and most of the HMOs studied have been large, well-established plans, rather than newer, developing ones. With these cautions in mind, Luft offered the following tentative conclusions regarding the medical care provided by HMOs and private-practice physicians:

- Both approaches appear to provide similar types and quality of services.
- The use of preventive services by patients in HMOs is very similar to that of patients who have conventional insurance plans and use private physicians; but private physicians' patients who have little or no insurance are less likely to use preventive services.
- A higher proportion of HMO than private-practice patients see their physicians at least once a year.
- Hospital admissions rates are lower for HMO than for private-practice patients, but the reason for this difference is unclear.
- HMO patients often express less satisfaction with their physicians than private-practice patients do.

Are HMO patients really less satisfied with their physicians than are private-practice patients? Some people argue that physicians in large HMOs are less concerned with satisfying their patients because the HMO pays their salaries, not the patients. If so, these physicians may spend less time with their patients and may not show as much interest in their patient's needs and problems (Mechanic, 1975). Although this possibility could be true, another factor may account for the lower satisfaction researchers have found among HMO patients: The results of a study comparing mothers' satisfaction with their children's private-practice and HMO pediatricians suggest that differences in patients' ratings may depend on the *timing* of the assessment (Ross, Wheaton, & Duff, 1981). The researchers identified and contacted 71 pediatricians in the New Haven, Connecticut, area, and 61 agreed to participate; 26% of them were employed by large prepaid group plans. Part of the study involved interviewing hundreds of the children's mothers, which revealed interesting changes in their satisfaction with their pediatricians over time: Of the mothers who had used the practitioner for less than a year or so, those with HMO physicians were less satisfied than those with private-practice physicians. But mothers who had used the practitioner for several years showed the opposite opinion, being more satisfied with the HMO than the private-practice pediatricians.

Another part of the study involved interviewing the physicians and observing the care they gave. Compared with the private-practice physicians, the HMO pediatricians spent more time with their patients, knew the family better, related more positively to the children, and responded better to the mothers' questions. On the basis of both sets of findings, the researchers suggested that the patients begin HMO affiliation with

> images of the impersonal "clinic" doctor, a doctor who treats the poor, and who is uncaring and rushed. These images are generally held and they produce negative expectations about the care received in "clinics." These expectations produce relative dissatisfaction in clients who have recently joined a large prepaid group. However, as positive experiences in these groups accumulate, satisfaction increases. (p. 252)

Patients' expectations and satisfaction regarding private-practice physicians are relatively high initially, and then tend to either remain the same or decline over time, perhaps because of negative experiences with their medical care.

These findings are provocative, but conclusions about them should be made cautiously. All the cautions we discussed earlier apply to this study. For example, the HMO physicians were all employed by just three large and well-established organizations. Also, all the practitioners were pediatricians. Practitioners from other specialties and employed by other HMOs may relate differently with their patients. Lastly, the researchers did not compare the HMO and private-practice physicians with respect to demographic characteristics, such as age and gender, which may be relevant variables. Still, it is clear that the timing of satisfaction assessments is an important variable that needs to be examined further.

Because the American medical care system is so complex and offers so many alternatives, using these services can be intimidating to some people. A critical step in the process of seeking medical attention is finding a regular physician to contact when we are sick. He or she can either cure our illness or help us find other help within the system. Now, suppose someone who has a regular physician develops some symptoms—say, nausea and a 100° fever. Will the person go to the doctor? An important step in using health services involves deciding when we are sick enough to require medical attention in the first place. This is the topic of the next section.

PERCEIVING AND INTERPRETING SYMPTOMS

If you came down with a case of strep throat as a child, chances are the symptoms you experienced were obvious to you and your parents. You had a very sore throat, fever, and headache, for instance. Your physician asked about your symptoms, took your temperature and did some tests, and prescribed a curative course of action. From experiences of this type, you learned that symptoms accompany illness—and when they go away, you are well again. You also learned that certain symptoms reliably signal certain illnesses, and that some symptoms are more serious than others. As an adult, you decide whether to visit your physician on the basis of the symptoms you perceive and what they mean to you.

Perceiving Symptoms

Perceiving symptoms of illness is more complicated than it may seem. It is true that we perceive internal states on the basis of physical sensations, and we are more likely to notice strong sensations than weak ones. But we do not assess our internal states very accurately. For example, people's estimates of their own heart rate and degree of nasal congestion correlate poorly with physiological measures of these states (Pennebaker, 1983; Skelton & Pennebaker, 1982). Partly because of people's low degree of accuracy in these assessments, the point at which people notice a symptom can differ from one individual to the next and within the same person from one time to the next. Furthermore, people do not always notice a symptom—even a strong one—when it is there, and they may sometimes perceive a symptom that has no actual physical basis. Let's see what factors affect our perception of symptoms.

Individual Differences

You may have heard someone say, "He's such a big baby; he notices every little ache and pain." Why do some individuals report more symptoms than others do? One reason is that some people simply *have* more symptoms than others, of course. Another possibility is that people could differ in the sensation they experience from the same symptom, such as a specific intensity of a painful stimulus. But research has cast doubt on this possibility. For instance, studies testing large numbers of normal individuals with stimuli of different temperatures have found that people seem to have a uniform threshold at which heat becomes painful—"almost all persons begin to feel pain when the tissue temperature rises to a level between 44°C and 46°C" (Guyton, 1985, p. 302). On the other hand, individuals differ in the degree of pain they will tolerate before doing something about it, such as taking medication (Karoly, 1985; Melzack & Wall, 1982).

Some individuals seem to pay more attention to their internal states than others do

(Pennebaker, 1983). They show a heightened awareness of or sensitivity to their body sensations. As a result, these people notice changes more quickly than individuals who tend to focus their attention on external happenings. But this does not mean that internally focused individuals are more *accurate* in their perceptions of internal changes—indeed, research has found that they are more likely than externally focused people to overestimate changes in their bodily functions, such as heart rate (Pennebaker, 1983). Other research has shown that among patients who seek medical treatment for symptoms, those who are internally focused tend to have less severe illnesses and perceive their recovery as slower than those who pay less attention to their internal states (Miller, Brody, & Summerton, 1987). These findings suggest that many internally focused individuals may pay *too much* attention to their internal states and, in so doing, magnify departures from normal bodily sensations.

Competing Environmental Stimuli

You may have heard anecdotes about athletes who were unaware of a major injury they had suffered during a competition until after the sporting event was over— *then* it hurt! The extent to which people pay attention to internal stimuli at any given time depends partly on the nature or degree of environmental stimuli that are present at that time.

When the environment contains a great deal of sensory information or is highly exciting, people become less likely to notice internal sensations. James Pennebaker (1983) has described several findings from research that are consistent with this view. For example,

> people are far more likely to report a variety of physical symptoms and sensations when the external environment is boring or lacking in information than when they must be attentive to the environment. . . . Similarly, individuals are more likely to notice itching or tickling sensations in their throats and emit coughs during boring parts of movies than during interesting portions. (p. 191)

Also, people who hold boring jobs or live alone tend to report more physical symptoms and use more aspirin and sleeping pills than those who hold interesting jobs or live with other people.

Psychosocial Influences

Because people are not very accurate in assessing their actual internal physical states, their perception of body sensations can be heavily influenced by cognitive, social, and emotional factors (Skelton & Pennebaker, 1982). One way researchers have demonstrated the role of cognitive factors in symptom perception is in the effects of *placebos*, which are inert substances or sham treatments (Melzack & Wall, 1982; Shapiro & Shapiro, 1984). For example, people who receive a placebo "drug" to reduce their pain, not knowing that it is inert, often report that it relieves their symptoms or sensations.

Another demonstration of the role of cognitive factors in symptom perception focused on the symptoms women experience just before the onset of menstrual periods. Diane Ruble (1977) gave women a physiological "test" that she falsely described as being highly accurate in pinpointing the timing of their next menstruation. Using these false test results, she told randomly selected women that they were within a couple of days of beginning menstruation; other women were told their menstruation was a week or more away. In fact, the beginning of menstruation was an average of about a week away for women in both conditions. The subjects then filled out a questionnaire that asked about premenstrual symptoms they were experiencing. Those women who were led to believe they were near menstruation reported more premenstrual symptoms—such as water retention and pain—than the other women. These findings indicate that the premenstrual symptoms that women experience result not only from the physiological changes that occur in their bodies but from their beliefs, too.

The combined roles of cognitive, social, and emotional factors in symptom perception can be seen in two interesting phenomena. The first is called *medical student's disease.* As medical students learn about the symptoms of various diseases, more than two-thirds of them come to believe incorrectly that they have contracted one of these illnesses at one time or another (Mechanic, 1972). The second phenomenon, called *mass psychogenic illness,* involves widespread symptom perception among a large group of individuals, even though tests indicate that their symptoms have no medical basis either in their bodies or in the environment, such as from toxic substances. Michael Colligan and his associates (1979) have described a case of mass psychogenic illness that began one summer morning at an electronics plant in a midwestern city. A female production worker became faint, and another female worker who came to her aid also fainted. Soon, many other workers began reporting dizziness, headache, nausea, and difficulty breathing; 20 workers were taken to the hospital; and the building was evacuated. Two similar episodes occurred days later after the plant reopened. Medical and environmental tests after each episode revealed no abnormalities that could account for the symptoms the workers experienced.

Why do such phenomena occur? Researchers have described several reasons (Colligan et al., 1979; Mechanic, 1972, 1980; Skelton & Pennebaker, 1982). The symptoms perceived by individuals with medical student's disease and mass psychogenic illness often involve common physiological sensations, such as headache or dizziness, that are vague and highly subjective in nature. Cognitive factors come into play when the person exaggerates these sensations and attaches to them more importance than they warrant. Modeling is a social factor that undoubtedly contributes to the contagion in mass psychogenic illness; and the symptoms experienced in medical student's disease often seem to be modeled after those of a patient the students have seen. An important emotional factor in these phenomena is stress—that is, medical student's disease and mass psychogenic illness tend to occur when individuals have been experiencing high levels of anxiety, heavy work loads, or disturbing interpersonal conflicts. In some cases, stress may cause or exaggerate the sensations the people perceive, as when nausea or headache are the symptoms the person notices.

In summary, people's perception of a symptom depends on the strength of the underlying physical sensation, their tendency to pay attention to their internal states, the degree to which external stimuli compete for their attention, and a variety of cognitive, social, and emotional processes. What individuals *do* when they perceive symptoms is the topic of the next section.

Interpreting and Responding to Symptoms

George Engel (1980) described the case of a 55-year-old man whom he called Mr. Glover, who suffered his second heart attack six months after his first. He was at work, alone at his desk, when

> he began to experience general unease and discomfort and then during the next minutes growing "pressure" over his mid-anterior chest and an aching sensation down the left arm to the elbow. The similarity of those symptoms to those of his heart attack six months earlier immediately came to mind. . . . but he dismissed this in favor of "fatigue," "gas," "muscle strain," and, finally, "emotional tension." But the negation itself, "*not* another heart attack," leaves no doubt that the idea "heart attack" was very much in his mind despite his apparent denial. Behaviorally, he alternated between sitting quietly to "let it pass," pacing about the office "to work it off," and taking Alka Selzer. (p. 539)

When Mr. Glover's boss noticed his strange behavior and sick appearance, she convinced him to let her take him to the hospital.

People's prior experiences affect their interpretation of and response to the symptoms they perceive. The knowledge individuals extract from their experiences plays an important role in their decisions about what the symp-

HIGHLIGHT 9A: On Research
People's Ideas about Illness

Do you believe that disease is caused by germs, that all diseases have noticeable symptoms, or that we are cured when the symptoms disappear? From our direct experiences and the things we read and hear about illnesses throughout our lives, we develop ideas and expectations about disease. Some of these ideas are correct, and some are not. We use this information to construct *cognitive representations* or **common-sense models** of different illnesses, and these models affect our health-related behavior. Researchers have studied common-sense models of illnesses and discovered several basic components of how people think about disease (Lau & Hartman, 1983; Meyer, Leventhal, & Gutman, 1985).

Illness Identity

One component in these common-sense models is the illness *identity*, which consists of the name and symptoms of the disease. A study by George Bishop and Sharolyn Converse (1986) examined the knowledge college students have about the actual symptoms of nine different illnesses: chicken pox, flu, hay fever, heart attack, mumps, pneumonia, strep throat, stroke, and ulcer. The subjects were given a questionnaire that contained vignettes describing sets of symptoms people experienced. After reading each vignette, the subjects indicated whether the set of symptoms the person had corresponded to a particular illness, and, if so, to name the disease.

The questionnaire was designed and administered in such a way that the subject could make judgments using symptom sets that differed in the degree to which they corresponded to each illness. For example, the vignette with symptoms having a *high* correspondence with the actual symptoms of *hay fever* was:

> This afternoon your friend Bob mentions that for the last few days he has been sneezing quite a bit, his sinuses have been inflamed, and he has had an itchy nose. Also he has had nasal congestion with teary eyes and nasal discharge.

All the symptoms mentioned in this set are typical of hay fever. In contrast, the following set of symptoms for *strep throat* had a *low* correspondence with the actual symptoms of that illness:

> Yesterday when you were talking, your friend Bill mentioned that recently he has had trouble remembering things. He also mentioned that he has had a sore throat and some difficulty swallowing, along with some pain over his heart. He also noticed a swollen wrist and burning in his eyes.

Only the sore throat and difficulty swallowing in this set are typical symptoms of strep throat.

The results of this study showed that college students have a good deal of knowledge about the symptoms of different illnesses. As you might expect, the subjects made their judgments on the basis of the degree of correspondence between the symptoms and the disease and were much more likely to identify the illness correctly if the symptom set was highly typical of the malady than if it was not. Still, the subjects' knowledge was far from perfect: Even when the symptoms were highly typical, the subjects either gave no answer or a completely unrelated answer for about one-third of the illness judgments they made.

Causes and Underlying Pathology

"I got a cold because a girl sneezed her germs in my face," someone might say. Or a patient who is diagnosed as having high blood pressure might think, "It's just because I've been eating too much salt." A person's common-sense model of an illness also includes ideas about its *causes* and *underlying pathology*. Some of these ideas are likely to be correct, and some are not.

One study examined the ideas and understanding mothers had about the underlying pathology of their infants' congenital heart disease (Kaden, McCarter, Johnson, & Ferencz, 1985). The researchers asked 285 mothers about their babies' heart defects and recorded their responses verbatim. Although most of the mothers could give a reasonably good description of their baby's disorder or knew the correct name for it, more than a third of the mothers either said they did not know what the problem was, showed a complete misunderstanding of it, or had only a vague idea of it. For instance, one mother thought her baby's heart had an "extra opening in a valve," when the actual diagnosis was *truncus arteriosus.* This disease has two major features: (1) the wall that should completely separate the ventricles has an opening which connects these two lower chambers of the heart and (2) a single artery receives blood from both ventricles, so that oxygenated and oxygen-depleted blood mix.

Some of the mothers with little or no knowledge about their child's disorder claimed that "the doctor never said" what the problem was, but most simply did not understand the physician's explanation. Demographic and sociocultural factors were associated with the degree of knowledge the mothers had. Compared with mothers who had a good understanding of their baby's disease, those who did not tended to be very young women who had not been married and had relatively little education.

Prognosis and Cure

Other components of people's common-sense model of an illness relate to its *prognosis* and *cure*—that is, the consequences, seriousness, duration, and treatment of the disease. Many people mistakenly believe, for instance, that the diagnosis of breast cancer is a death sentence, that the disease is painful, and that the women must lose the breast.

People determine their ideas about the prognosis and cure of an illness from various types of information from many sources. One type of information people seem to use in judging the seriousness of an illness, for example, is its prevalence. John Jemmott and his colleagues have reported a series of studies showing that people tend to believe that rare diseases are more serious than common ones (Jemmott, Croyle, & Ditto, 1988; Jemmott, Ditto, & Croyle, 1986). In the first of these studies, the researchers recruited college students for a "Health Awareness Project," in which the subjects filled out questionnaires about their health and individually underwent several medical tests, such as for blood pressure and eyesight.

One of the medical tests the subjects took was fictitious—it was called the "Thioamine Acetylase Saliva Reaction Test" and purportedly assessed an enzyme deficiency that could lead to a disorder of the pancreas. Each subject was shown the results of the test, indicating that he or she had the deficiency, and told either that the deficiency was rare or that it was prevalent. The subjects then completed a questionnaire that included items asking them to rate the seriousness of various diseases, including "thioamine acetylase deficiency." (The subjects were debriefed immediately so they would understand that they were not ill, the disease was fictitious, and the test results were fabricated.) Those subjects who were led to believe that the deficiency was rare rated the disease as being more serious than those who were told the deficiency was prevalent.

People's common-sense models of illness can affect their health, illness, and sick-role behaviors. The influence on sick-role behavior can be seen in the findings of research described by Howard Leventhal (1982). Cancer patients whose tumors had responded most quickly to chemotherapy were *more* distressed by the treatment than those whose tumors responded more slowly. Why? Subsequent interviews revealed that the distressed patients had incorrect ideas about symptoms and cures. These ideas related to the fact that the patients were still receiving chemotherapy after the tumor was gone. They were upset for two reasons: First, some patients thought that the tumor's disappearance meant they were cured and should not have to endure the discomfort of the treatment anymore. Second, some patients were afraid that the continued treatment meant that the cancer had spread to other parts of their bodies.

---

toms reflect and whether they warrant professional attention. Probably most often, this knowledge helps people make appropriate judgments. A study found, for instance, that prior experience—that is, whether the child or a relative had had a similar problem in the past—is one of the strongest factors in mothers' correct decisions to seek medical care for their children (Turk, Litt, Salovey, & Walker, 1985). But sometimes people's prior experiences and expectations can lead them to incorrect interpretations of their symptoms. For example, many elderly individuals assume that tiredness and weakness are symptoms of old age rather than signs of illness (Leventhal & Prohaska, 1986; Prohaska, Keller, Leventhal, & Leventhal, 1987). Although this assumption may be correct when these symptoms are mild, it may lead elderly people to ignore more severe symptoms that do, in fact, need treatment.

In the case of Mr. Glover, his prior experience did not help him interpret and respond to the symptoms appropriately. His reaction to the classic heart attack symptoms he was having was governed by emotion, probably elicited by his earlier attack. Although fear can motivate a person toward health-protective behavior, it can also motivate maladaptive avoidance behavior. As we saw in Chapter 6, *conflict theory* proposes that stress can interfere with rational decision making (Janis, 1984; Janis & Mann, 1977). In Mr. Glover's case, he perceived severe risks in both seeking and not seeking medical care. He tried to deny the meaning of the symptoms, but that didn't seem to work, and the real meaning was still on his mind. As conflict theory predicts in these circumstances, he used a *hypervigilant* coping pattern: He believed he was fast running out of time and began to search frantically for a solution, as when he tried sitting quietly, pacing, and taking Alka Selzer.

Mr. Glover finally decided to go to the hospital after his boss persuaded him that his symptoms needed treatment. Before people decide to seek medical attention for their symptoms, they typically get advice from friends, relatives, or coworkers (Sanders, 1982; Scambler & Scambler, 1984). These "advisors" form a **lay referral system**, an informal network of nonpractitioners who provide their own information and interpretations regarding the person's symptoms (Freidson, 1961). People in the lay referral system provide information or advice when the person requests it, or even if he or she simply looks sick or mentions the symptoms. Close family or friends are generally the first people consulted for lay referral, and they might:

- Help interpret a symptom—such as "Jim and his sister Lynn both had rashes like that. They were just allergic to a new soap their mother had bought."
- Give advice about seeking medical attention—as in "MaryLou had a dizzy spell like the one you just had, and it was a mild stroke. You'd better call your doctor."
- Recommend a remedy—such as "A little chicken soup, some aspirin, and bed rest, and you'll be fine in no time."
- Recommend consulting another lay referral person—as in "Pat had the same problem. You should give him a call."

Although the lay referral system often provides good advice, laypersons are, of course, far more likely than practitioners to recommend actions that worsen the condition or delay the person's use of appropriate and needed treatment (Sanders, 1982).

People with a health problem often consult a pharmacist for an over-the-counter remedy before seeing their physician.

USING AND *MIS*USING HEALTH SERVICES

The pharmacist is often the first health professional that people consult when they have a health problem. A customer might ask, "My hands get these red patches that peel, and hand creams don't do any good. Do you have anything that will help?" When pharmacists suggest an over-the-counter remedy, they usually recommend that the person see a physician if it doesn't work.

Most prospective patients clearly try hard to avoid contacting their physicians. But despite these avoidant efforts, Americans consult their doctors' offices either in person or by telephone over a billion times a year for medical advice or treatment (USDHHS, 1987a). This comes to about five contacts per person per year. What are the most frequent *acute* and *chronic* conditions discussed in these contacts? The acute conditions are flu, common cold, fractures or dislocations, sprains or strains, wounds, and ear infections; the chronic conditions are hypertension, orthopedic problems, arthritis, diabetes, asthma, and heart disease. Of course, these illnesses are not evenly distributed over the American population—and as you might expect, some segments of the population who become ill are more likely to use health services than are others.

Who Uses Health Services?

Public health researchers have outlined several demographic and sociocultural factors that are related to the use of health services in America. One of these factors is *age*. In general, young children and the elderly contact their physicians more often each year than adolescents and young adults do (USDHHS, 1986g, 1987a). Young children visit physicians for general checkups and vaccinations, and they develop a variety of infectious "childhood" diseases. As we saw in Chapter 2, children's immune systems are relatively weak at birth, but develop rapidly in the early years. Physician contacts decline in late childhood and remain relatively infrequent in early adulthood, but increase in the middle-age and elderly years as the incidence of chronic diseases rises.

Figure 9.1 depicts how physician contacts vary with age and with another important factor, the patient's *gender*. Women have a higher rate of physician contacts than men (USDHHS, 1987a). This gender difference does not exist in childhood, but begins to appear during adolescence. Much of the gender difference in physician contacts in early adulthood certainly results from the medical care women require when they become pregnant. But even when physician visits for pregnancy and childbirth are not counted, women still use medical services more than men (Cleary, Mechanic, & Greenley, 1982; Verbrugge, 1985). The reasons for this difference in use of medical care are unclear, but researchers have offered several possible explanations (Verbrugge, 1980, 1985). One obvious explanation is that women may simply develop more illnesses that require medical attention. Although men are more likely than women to develop fatal chronic diseases, women show higher rates of medical drug use and illness from both acute conditions, such as respiratory infections, and from nonfatal chronic diseases, such as arthritis and migraine headache. Another explanation re-

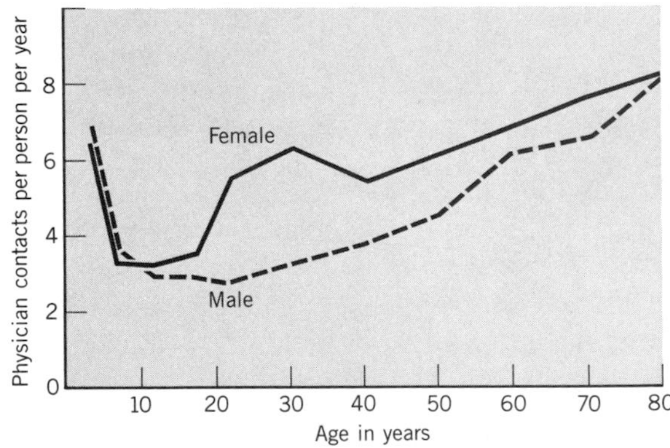

FIGURE 9.1 Average number of physician contacts (in person and by telephone) per person per year as a function of age and gender. (From USDHHS, 1987a, Figure 3.)

lates to the fact that men are more hesitant than women to admit having symptoms and to seek medical care for the symptoms they experience. This difference in responding to symptoms probably reflects sex-role stereotypes; that is, American society encourages men more than women to ignore pain and to be "tough" and independent.

The United States Department of Health and Human Services conducts periodic large-scale surveys to determine the degree to which different segments of the population use health services. The results of these surveys lead to the following conclusions (USDHHS, 1986c, 1987a):

- The percentage of patients who seek medical care at a physician's office or by telephone increases with their family income.
- Blacks and other people with low family incomes are far more likely than whites and others with higher incomes to use outpatient clinics and hospital emergency rooms for medical care. A major reason for this is that disadvantaged people are less likely to have a regular physician.
- The annual number of physician contacts by adults increases with number of years of education they have completed.
- The annual number of physician contacts per person decreases with family size.
- Of different occupational groups, white-collar workers have the highest annual number of physician contacts per person, those in service and farming occupations have an intermediate number of contacts, and blue-collar workers have the lowest number.

Although there is clearly a gap between social classes in utilization of health services, it has narrowed since the mid-1960s when the government introduced two health insurance programs: *Medicare* for the elderly and *Medicaid* for low-income individuals. These programs are responsible for much of the 25% increase in physician visits that occurred between 1968 and 1972 (USDHHS, 1985b). Despite the help Medicare and Medicaid provide, the costs that patients must bear for medical treatment can still be substantial because public and private insurance programs generally do not cover all the expenses. Some kinds of treatment are excluded, and patients typically must pay part of the costs for those treatments that are covered.

The expense of medical care still makes it difficult for low-income Americans to get the treatment they need today, but this reason is a less prominent cause of the gap between social classes in using health services than it used to be. What other reasons account for social class differences in medical care use? A survey of several hundred adults by Thomas Rundall and John Wheeler (1979) revealed two reasons. First, individuals from the lower classes tend to perceive themselves as being less susceptible to illness than those from the higher classes do —as a result, low-income people are less likely to seek out preventive care. Second, people with low incomes are less likely to have a regular source of health care than those with higher incomes. Often this situation develops because low-income areas of cities and states are unable to attract physicians to provide health services there. In addition, people in the lower classes may feel less welcomed by and trustful of the health care system than those in higher classes. These and many other factors tend to reduce the likelihood that low-income individuals will use health services for preventive care and when they are ill.

The relatively infrequent use of health services by individuals from the lower classes is especially troubling because, as we saw in Chapter 6, these people have more health problems and poorer health habits than those from the middle and upper classes. Public health efforts need to focus on breaking down cultural barriers that impede the use of these services. As community health researchers Lee Crandall and R. Paul Duncan have noted, for example, the

> failure of many parents to carry out immunization schedules for their children even when these services are provided in free neighborhood clinics demonstrates that appropriate use of health services cannot be guaranteed

> simply through the removal of financial and geographic barriers. Efforts to remove "subjective" and cultural barriers to the use of physicians' services seem necessary in order to ensure that poor persons receive the services needed to prevent and cure illness. In this regard, the use of "health guides," the development of community health education programs, and the implementation of formal training in self-health care for low-income persons seem to be necessary steps toward improving the nation's health. (1981, p. 73)

The title of this section was Who Uses Health Services? To answer this question, we can construct two portraits—one of the users and one of the nonusers of these services. The users of health services tend to be young children, women, and elderly individuals from the higher social classes. The nonusers are likely to be members of the lower classes and minority groups, particularly those who are males in adolescence and early adulthood. But virtually all Americans use health services at some time, and many upper-class individuals fail to get medical treatment when they should. Thus, although these portraits give us an image of *who* uses health services, they do not provide a full explanation of *why* (Wolinsky, 1978).

Why People Use, Don't Use, and Delay Using Health Services

"Remember how the medicine Buddy's doctor gave him made him sicker? I don't trust doctors," the ailing man said while considering whether to seek treatment for his symptoms. Sometimes patients develop health problems as a *result* of medical treatment, and these problems are called **iatrogenic conditions**. The condition can result either from a practitioner's error or as a normal side effect or risk of the treatment, as may occur when patients undergo surgery or begin to take a new medication. Stories we hear of patients developing iatrogenic conditions may weigh against the decision to use medical services. Health psychologists and others who study health care have discovered many factors that influence whether and when the individuals decide to seek medical care. Some of these factors involve people's health beliefs.

Health Beliefs and Seeking Medical Care

In Chapter 6, we examined the role of health beliefs in taking preventive action, such as adopting healthful habits. We saw that the *health belief model* provides a useful framework for explaining why people do and do not practice health-related behaviors. How does the health belief model apply to people's seeking medical care when they notice symptoms?

According to the health belief model, symptoms initiate a decision-making process about seeking medical care. Part of this process involves assessing the *perceived threat* suggested by the symptoms (Becker & Rosenstock, 1984; Rosenstock & Kirscht, 1979). The degree of threat individuals perceive depends mainly on three factors. First, the symptoms themselves serve as a *cue to action*, arousing concern. Other cues to action may include advice sick people receive in lay referral and information they acquire through the mass media, such as descriptions of cancer symptoms. Then the two other factors—*perceived susceptibility* and *perceived seriousness*—come into play. These factors modify the concern aroused by the symptoms; that is, the threat people feel intensifies with increases in the perceived susceptibility to the particular illness and the perceived seriousness of the physical and social consequences of contracting the disease.

The health belief model also proposes that people assess whether the *perceived benefits* of getting treatment outweigh the *perceived barriers* in doing so. Individuals assess the benefits of seeking medical care on the basis of their beliefs about the effectiveness of treatment. People who believe that treatment can cure the symptoms or arrest the progression of the illness are more likely to seek medical care than those who believe otherwise. In assessing the barriers to medical care, people bring into play their expectations of whether the treatment will have unpleasant side effects and will be costly, painful, and difficult to obtain. The assessed sum of benefits and barriers combines with the perceived threat to determine the likelihood of seeking care. People who feel threatened by their symptoms and believe that the benefits of receiving treatment outweigh the barriers are likely to visit a practitioner. But individuals who do not feel threatened or assess that the barriers are too strong are likely to decide to delay treatment or avoid it altogether.

The results of research suggest that the factors described by the health belief model do influence people's decisions to use health services (Becker & Rosenstock, 1984; Rosenstock & Kirscht, 1979). One study found, for example, that the greater people's belief in the effectiveness of medical care, the more likely they were to use health services (Crandall & Duncan, 1981). Other research has examined whether factors in the health belief model relate to people's delay in seeking a diagnosis for cancer symptoms. These studies have found that individuals who are aware of the symptoms of cancer *and* believe that cancer cannot be treated effectively or cured are likely to delay seeking medical care much longer than individuals who know the symptoms *but* believe treatment can be successful (Antonovsky & Hartman, 1974). However, some studies have found only a weak relationship between factors in the health belief model and people's likelihood to use health services, which suggests that other variables are also important in decisions to seek treatment (Harris & Guten, 1979; Langlie, 1977).

Social and Emotional Factors and Seeking Medical Care

Social and emotional factors can play important roles in people's decisions about seeking treatment for their symptoms. Let's see how by examining the role of emotions first.

Earlier, we considered the case of Mr. Glover, who delayed medical treatment for clear symptoms of a heart attack. Strong emotional reactions to symptoms sometimes impede people's use of health services. Individuals may perceive a disease to be so serious that they are reluctant to seek medical attention for their symptoms because of the extreme anxiety and fear their perceptions generate. As a result, the threat these individuals perceive does not increase their likelihood of using health services, but may decrease it. Interviews with hundreds of adults, for instance, revealed that people perceive cancer as an extremely painful disease, and 18% of these people said they might be reluctant to seek medical care for cancer symptoms because of their fear of the physical pain they associate with the disease and its treatment (Levin, Cleeland, & Dar, 1985). Expectations of pain probably also play a strong role in people's fear of dental care—about 5% of Americans are so fearful that they avoid all kinds of dental treatment (Gatchel, 1980).

Social factors influence people's tendency to seek medical care for their symptoms, such as through the process of lay referral. According to Irving Zola (1973), the decision to seek treatment can be prompted by several types of "triggers," three of which are social in nature. He described one of these social triggers as *perceived interference* of the symptoms with individuals' interpersonal relations or activities. For example, a man with an ulcer experienced pain when he would consume certain foods and beverages, such as beer. One day after one of these painful episodes, he decided to seek treatment, saying, "if you can't drink beer with friends, what the hell" (Zola, 1973, p. 684). Similarly, symptoms that interfere with work may spur a person to seek care. An *interpersonal crisis* can also serve as a trigger, particularly if the person uses medical treatment as a means of resolving or escaping the crisis. Zola described an example of a woman who was having serious problems with her relatives while she was on vacation. She decided to enter a hospital and have a benign cyst removed so that her relatives would "stop bothering" her. The third type of social trigger is called *sanctioning*, in which someone asks or insists that the person have the symptoms treated. For instance, a man who had been having problems with his vision for a while finally went to a doctor after his wife prodded him to do so. Sometimes overt prodding isn't even necessary—sick individuals who simply believe that significant others want them to seek treatment are more likely to do so than those who believe others think they should wait (Timko, 1987).

Stages in Delaying Medical Care

When symptoms of a potentially serious illness develop, seeking treatment promptly is imperative. **Treatment delay** refers to the time that elapses between when a person first notices a symptom until he or she enters medical care. In medical emergencies, such as severe injury or a heart attack, people often seek help in a matter of minutes or hours, as Mr. Glover did. What determines how long people wait?

On the basis of extensive interviews with patients at a clinic, Martin Safer and his colleagues discovered that treatment delay occurs as a sequence of three stages (Safer, Tharps, Jackson, & Leventhal, 1979). As the diagram in Figure 9.2 illustrates, the three stages are:

1. *Appraisal delay*—the time a person takes to interpret a symptom as a sign of illness.
2. *Illness delay*—the time taken after recognizing a sign of illness until deciding to seek medical attention.
3. *Utilization delay*—the time after deciding to seek medical care until actually going in to use that health service.

The researchers also assessed the patients' reasons for delaying treatment and found that different factors were important for different stages of delay. During the appraisal delay stage, the sensory experience of the symptom had the greatest impact on delay—for instance, patients recognized the symptom as a sign of illness more quickly if they experienced severe pain or bleeding than if they did not.

In the illness delay stage, thoughts about the symptom had the greatest impact. Thus, patients decided to seek medical attention more quickly if (1) the symptom was new than if it had been experienced many times before and if (2) they spent little time thinking about the symptom and its implications than if they spent a lot of time doing so. During the utilization delay stage, perceptions of benefits and barriers were important—delay was shortest for those patients who were less concerned about the cost of treatment, had severe pain, and felt that their symptoms could be cured. In addition, the researchers found that having a major nonillness problem or life event, such as a marriage or divorce, was an important factor that increased the *total* treatment delay.

How long did these people wait before going in for medical care after first noticing a symptom? For half of these patients, treatment delay was about a week or less, but many of the others waited two months or more. Some of these people may have delayed a long time because they were not experiencing pain. As we just dis-

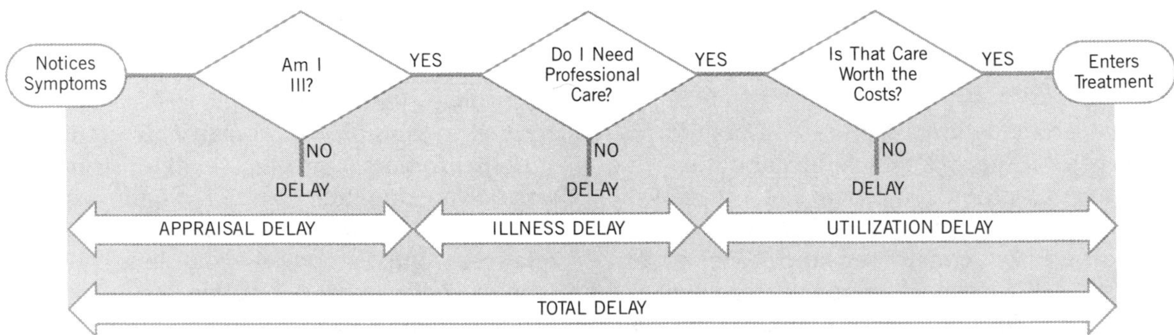

FIGURE 9.2 Treatment delay is conceptualized as having three stages: appraisal delay, illness delay, and utilization delay. (From Safer, Tharps, Jackson, & Leventhal, 1979, Figure 1.)

cussed, *not having pain* is a major factor in delaying. This factor is potentially very important because pain is *not* a major symptom of many very serious diseases, such as hypertension. Pain is also not one of the main warning signs of cancer, which are:

- *C*hange in bowel or bladder habits.
- *A* sore that does not heal.
- *U*nusual bleeding or discharge.
- *T*hickening or lump in the breast or elsewhere.
- *I*ndigestion or difficulty swallowing.
- *O*bvious change in a wart or mole.
- *N*agging cough or hoarseness. (American Cancer Society, 1989)
  (Notice that the first letters spell "caution.")

Most people who notice one of these warning signs wait at least a month before visiting a physician, and between 35 and 50% delay for more than three months (Antonovsky & Hartman, 1974). People need to know what the symptoms of serious diseases are and realize that some illnesses do not have the signs people often rely on in deciding whether to seek medical care.

Misusing Health Services

In a sense, delaying medical care is a misuse of health services, but a more obvious *mis*use is *over*use—that is, using health services repeatedly when there is no need. People in the general population commonly refer to patients who overuse medical care as "hypochondriacs" and think that these patients are either malingering or imagining symptoms, so that the illness is "all in their heads."

But this common view is inaccurate. Although some patients do imagine symptoms and some malinger to get various benefits of the sick role, *hypochondriacs* tend to interpret real but benign bodily sensations as symptoms of illness—deciding, for example, that their gastric pains are signs of a serious disease rather than of eating spicy foods (Barsky & Klerman, 1983; Skelton & Pennebaker, 1982). They may also amplify minor sensations, such as muscle soreness or twinges, and perceive them as very painful. Because of these characteristics, psychologists and psychiatrists use the term **hypochondriasis** to refer to the tendency for individuals to worry excessively about their own health, monitor their bodily sensations closely, make frequent unfounded medical complaints, and believe they are ill despite reassurances by physicians that they are not (Barsky & Klerman, 1983; Costa & McCrae, 1985; Kellner, 1985, 1987; Skelton & Pennebaker, 1982).

Paul Costa and Robert McCrae (1980, 1985) have demonstrated an important link between hypochondriasis and emotional maladjustment, or *neuroticism*, which they defined as:

> a broad dimension of normal personality that encompasses a variety of specific traits, including self-consciousness, inability to inhibit cravings, and vulnerability to stress as well as the tendency to experience anxiety, hostility, and depression. (1985, p. 21)

These researchers tested about 1,000 normal adults in one study, using two self-report scales: (1) the Cornell Medical Index to assess the subjects' "somatic complaints," that is, medical conditions or symptoms, and (2) the Emotional Stability Scale to measure neuroticism. The subjects were in generally good health and ranged in age from under 20 to over 90. Analysis of the questionnaire responses showed that somatic complaints increased with neuroticism—individuals who scored high on neuroticism reported two to three times as many somatic complaints as those who scored low on neuroticism.

Does this association mean that neuroticism causes more complaints or that having many illnesses causes neuroticism? Although either causal direction is possible, some of the clearest research findings so far suggest that "neuroticism appears to lead to complaints" (Costa & McCrae, 1985, p. 23). A prospective study, for example, assessed hypochondriasis in several hundred patients who had suffered an episode of chest pain, but had minimal or no coronary disease (Wielgosz et al., 1984). The absence of coronary disease was determined by a test called a *coronary angiography*, which measures whether the coronary arteries are constricted. A year later, each patient was interviewed regarding his or her health and asked about the frequency and severity of chest pain during the last six weeks. The researchers evaluated the relationship between the patients' recent pain and several factors, such as the severity of pain they had experienced in their initial episodes. But the factor that was most predictive of continued pain was hypochondriasis: Patients who were greatly preoccupied with personal somatic complaints after the initial episode reported far more continued and unimproved pain a year later than those who were not so hypochondriacal.

Many people believe that hypochondriasis increases in old age. Costa and McCrae (1980, 1985) have presented evidence that this belief is incorrect. For one thing, neuroticism does not increase with age. Second, although older individuals have more somatic complaints and use health services more than younger adults do, the greater somatic complaints of the elderly are mainly related to sensory, cardiovascular, and genitourinary problems, which are known to increase in old age. If elderly people were prone to hypochondriasis, we would expect them to report more complaints with regard to other body systems, too. But they do not. This indicates that the elderly use health services more than younger individuals simply because they are less healthy. The proportion of people who are hypochondriacs appears to be no higher in old age than in earlier adult periods.

To summarize, there is an enormous variety of reasons why people use, don't use, overuse, and delay using health services. These reasons include the nature of the symptoms people perceive, the health beliefs they hold, and social and emotional factors. Another factor that effects people's decisions about using health services is the quality of the relationship they have with their physician. This important relationship is the subject of the next section.

THE PATIENT/PRACTITIONER RELATIONSHIP

A woman who had been receiving treatment for cancer at a clinic on a regular basis began to procrastinate about going in for periodic examinations and care. When her family asked why she had not gone in on schedule, she replied, "They gave me a new doctor, and he's not very nice. He treats me like a number, and I don't feel comfortable talking to him — he talks down to me when I ask him questions." Many patients have stories about negative experiences with practitioners, and these experiences can lead patients to delay or stop getting the medical attention they need. These stories often involve the practitioner's hurried manner, insensitivity, lack of responsiveness, failure to explain the medical problem or the treatment, or unwillingness to involve the patient in planning the treatment.

Patient Preferences for Participation in Medical Care

When patients visit a physician about a health problem, do they just want to be "cured" or do they also want to know what the illness is, what caused it, what the prognosis is, and how to treat it? How involved do they want to be in decisions and activities in their treatment? Physicians often misjudge their patients' answers to these kinds of questions (Kindelan & Kent, 1987). Correctly judging the amount and type of participation that patients prefer can be important — patient/practitioner relationships depend to some extent on the compatibility between what the patient wants and what the practitioner provides.

Patients differ in the participation they want in their medical care. Although almost all patients want to know what their illness is and exactly how to treat it, some want more details and involvement in decisions than others do. A study found, for example, that elderly patients are more likely than younger adults to want health professionals to make health-related decisions for them (Woodward & Wallston, 1987). In an effort to assess the degree of participation patients want, researchers have developed the Health Opinion Survey (Krantz, Baum, & Wideman, 1980). This instrument has 16 items to measure preferences regarding three areas of participation by patients:

- Preference for information about their health care—as illustrated by the item "I usually ask the doctor or nurse lots of questions about the procedures during a medical exam."
- Preference for self-care—as in "If it costs the same, I'd rather have a doctor or nurse give me treatments than to do the same treatments myself."
- Preference for involvement in decisions about their health—as illustrated by the item "I'd rather have doctors and nurses make decisions about what's best than for them to give me a whole lot of choices."

Studies have found that providing the amount and type of participation that patients want enhances their adjustment to and satisfaction with medical treatment (Auerbach, Martelli, & Mercuri, 1983; Martelli, Auerbach, Alexander, & Mercuri, 1987).

Just as patients differ in the information and involvement they want regarding their health, practitioners differ in the participation they are inclined to provide. For instance, research has shown that some physicians are more inclined than others to share their authority and decision making even among colleagues (Eisenberg, Kitz, & Webber, 1983). What happens in the patient/practitioner relationship when the patient wants a different level of participation than the practitioner is willing to give? A study by Marie Haug and Bebe Lavin (1981) involved a large-scale survey in which patients and physicians described their own attitudes and behavior regarding the participation of patients in health care. The subjects' responses suggest three conclusions. First, although both the patients and the physicians expressed the attitude that patients should participate in activities and decisions pertaining to their health, neither the patients nor the physicians behaved in this way very often. Second, when the patient wants a high level of participation but the practitioner wants to take total responsibility, conflict can be expected. As a result, the patient either finds or is told to find another doctor. Third, when a patient wants the doctor to take charge but the physician wants the patient to participate, both may feel uncomfortable. This may lead to the doctor taking charge or the patient finding a "take charge" physician.

These findings indicate that a mismatch between the patient's and the practitioner's ideas about participation can impair their relationship. The results of other research indicate that mismatches of this type can increase the stress patients experience during unpleasant medical procedures (Auerbach, Martelli, & Mercuri, 1983; Miller & Mangan, 1983). In deciding how much information and involvement to provide each patient, practitioners clearly need to assess and consider how much the patient wants.

The Practitioner's Behavior and Style

Imagine this "test": You recently completed medical training and have just started a position in an HMO clinic as a general practitioner. Your next patient this morning is waiting in an examination room, which you are preparing to enter. Your task will be to decide whether this patient has one or more of the more than 1,300 disease entities known to medicine (Mentzer & Snyder, 1982). Or maybe the patient has no physical problem at all. You have 20 minutes.

Diagnosing and treating health problems are difficult tasks which different physicians undertake with their own behaviors and styles of interacting with patients. Patrick Byrne and Barrie Long (1976) identified different styles of interacting by analyzing about 2,500 tape-recorded medical consultations with physicians in several countries, including England, Ireland, Australia, and Holland. Each physician tended to use a consistent style for all patients being treated. Most of the styles were classified

HIGHLIGHT 9B: On Issues
Fighting for Your Life

Not all victims of serious diseases who are getting medical care receive the most effective treatments available (Kolata, 1989). Although this situation sometimes occurs because a doctor is overworked or not competent, several other factors are far more likely to cause it. A major factor that interferes with patients getting the most effective treatment is that advances in medical knowledge occur so rapidly that each physician cannot always keep up with new research findings. Another factor is that many doctors are conservative in their approach to medicine, being reluctant to switch from a procedure that works reasonably well to one that may work better. What can patients do to get the best possible treatment?

Patients and/or people close to them can join the fight for their lives by taking an active interest in their illness and health care (Laszlo, 1987; Paulson, 1988). Let's consider a hypothetical case of a man named Alan who has a life-threatening illness, such as cancer. Once he receives the diagnosis, he and his family can swing into action by getting information immediately about the disease and the usual courses of treatment. Information about cancer is readily available in books he can purchase in bookstores or consult through public, college, and medical school libraries. The next step would be for him to make a list of questions to ask the physician who is handling his case. If possible, Alan should have a relative or friend accompany him to discussions with his physician concerning treatment options. One of them should take notes during the meeting, and they should ask to know all possible treatment options and determine what each treatment involves, what the risks are, and the likelihood of success.

At this point, Alan may want to broaden his sources of information. Two national organizations—the National Cancer Institute and the American Cancer Society—have toll-free phone numbers he can call for publications and information about cancer support groups, treatment methods, treatment centers, and oncologists—that is, internists who specialize in treating various forms of cancer. At least one of the specialists he consults regarding treatment options should be a certified medical oncologist, preferably one "who is affiliated with a major university, cancer center or teaching hospital and is involved in or in close touch with ongoing research" (Paulson, 1988, p. 106). Many patients consult only the original physician who handles their case, and this is a mistake. It is important to get the points of view of at least two experts on the best course of treatment. By using a variety of reputable information sources, Alan can also find out about very new medical procedures (and even some risky "experimental" ones). Even though many newer approaches may provide the most effective treatment, not all physicians know about them or feel comfortable about recommending them.

Patients who have other serious illnesses can join the fight for their lives in similar ways. When patients and people close to them take an active interest in their health care they can play an informed role in decision making and increase the likelihood that all options for treatment will be considered. These patients can also be comforted by knowing that they are getting the best treatment available and by strengthening their sense of efficacy in themselves and in their physician.

---

as **doctor-centered**, in which the physician asked questions that required only brief answers—generally "yes" or "no"—and focused mainly on the first problem the patient mentioned. These physicians tended to ignore attempts by a patient to discuss other problems he or she might have had. Doctor-centered physicians seemed to be intent on establishing a link between the initial problem and some organic disorder, without being sidetracked. In contrast, physicians who used the opposite, **patient-centered** style took a less controlling role. They tended to ask open-ended questions, such as "Can you describe the situations when the pain occurs?", that allow the patient to relate more information and introduce new facts that may be pertinent. They also tended to avoid using medical jargon and to allow the patient to participate in some of the decision making.

The patient/practitioner relationship depends on the ability of the two participants to communicate with each other. But physicians sometimes impede communication by using *medical jargon* or technical terms. For example, telling hypertensive patients to "reduce sodium intake" is an accurate recommendation, but will they know what it means? Some patients will know exactly what sodium is, others won't have any idea, and others will think it only means table salt, not realizing that there are other sources of dietary sodium. Studies have found that most patients, particularly those from lower-class backgrounds, fail to understand many of the terms used by their physicians—such terms as "incubation period," "secretions," "sutures," and "glucose," for instance (DiMatteo & DiNicola, 1982; McKinlay, 1975). Although jargon is useful for accuracy and for communicating among medical professionals, practitioners who use medical and technical terms in talking with a patient without explaining the terms or checking comprehension can create confusion, incorrect ideas, and dissatisfaction in the patient.

John McKinlay (1975) conducted a study to assess lower-class patients' understanding of 13 terms used with them by their physicians in a maternity ward. Although over two-thirds of the women understood the terms "breach" and "navel," almost none understood "protein" and "umbilicus"—and on the average, each of the 13 words was understood by only about 39% of the patients. McKinlay also had the physicians indicate for each word whether they thought "average lower working-class women" would understand the term. The physicians expected even *less* comprehension than the patients showed, yet they used these terms often with these women.

Why would physicians use terms with a patient when they do not expect the person to understand? Sometimes they may do this "out of habit," that is, the terms are so familiar to them that they forget that the patient is less medically sophisticated. Or they may feel—perhaps in a patronizing way—that the patient "doesn't need to know." Other reasons for using jargon may involve their perceptions of what would benefit the patient or the medical staff (DiMatteo & DiNicola, 1982; McKinlay, 1975). How might using jargon benefit the patient? Sometimes physicians may feel that the patient is "better off" not knowing exactly what the disease or its treatment may entail; knowing may produce too much stress or interfere with treatment, they may think. And how may using jargon with a patient benefit the medical staff? For one thing, using medical terms without explanations keeps interactions between the patient and practitioners short. It may also reduce the likelihood that the patient will react emotionally to the information, or ask questions about the treatment, or discover if errors have been made. Finally, using "big words" that the patient does not understand elevates the status of practitioners.

First and foremost, patients prefer to have a practitioner they think is competent. But there are other factors that are important in the patient/practitioner relationship, too—especially the *sensitivity, warmth*, and *concern* the patient perceives in the practitioner's behavior. Studies have demonstrated that most patients prefer and evaluate highly dentists and physicians who seem friendly and interested in the patient as a person, show empathy for the patient's feelings, project a feeling of reassurance, and present a calm and competent image (Ben-Sira, 1980; Corah et al., 1988; DiMatteo, Linn, Chang, & Cope, 1985). In contrast, practitioners who seem emotionally "neutral" are often evaluated less positively, perhaps because they appear detached and unconcerned. Patients assess these characteristics not just by the words the practitioner says, but by his or her "body language"—facial expressions, eye contact, and body positions (DiMatteo, 1985; DiMatteo, Friedman, & Taranta, 1979; Thompson, 1984). With regard to body positions, for instance, Americans tend to perceive a person who stands or sits a moderate distance away, leans toward them, gestures and nods, and has a relaxed posture as being relatively warm and friendly.

The behavior and style of practitioners can have important implications for them and their patients. Research has shown that patients

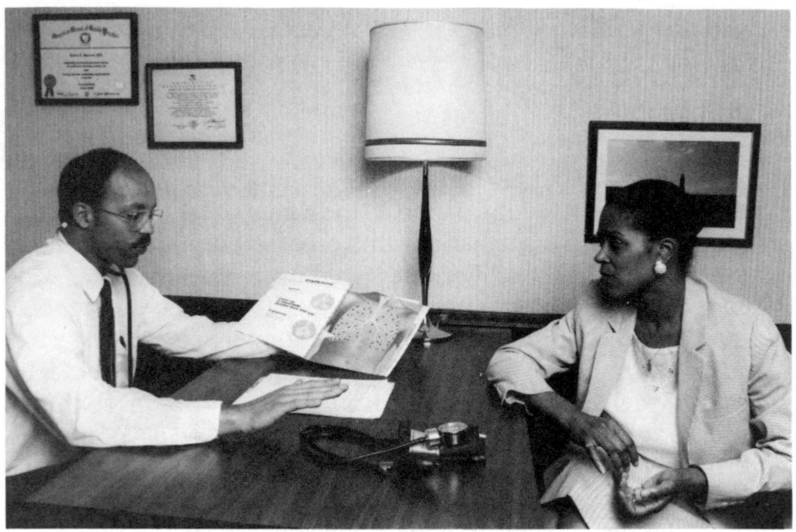

Patients tend to prefer a physician who gives clear explanations about illnesses and treatments, encourages them to ask questions, and conveys a feeling of concern for them.

tend to express greater satisfaction for physicians who give patients a chance to talk, take the time to listen, give clear explanations about illnesses and treatments, and project a feeling of concern and reassurance than for doctors who do not (Feletti, Firman, & Sanson-Fisher, 1986). The greater satisfaction these patients feel may translate into a higher likelihood that they will keep appointments with their doctors. A study found that physicians who were more sensitive to others' emotions had fewer cancellations of appointments that were not rescheduled than doctors who were less sensitive (DiMatteo, Hays, & Prince, 1986).

Perhaps the most important implication of physicians' styles relates to the diagnostic information they receive from their patients. A study by Debra Roter and Judith Hall (1987) found that physicians vary greatly in their ability to elicit significant diagnostic details from their patients. Those physicians who asked more open- and closed-ended questions, gave more information about the cause and prognosis of the illness, and discussed more details about prevention and treatment received more diagnostic facts from their patients than those doctors who did less of these things. The additional facts these doctors received were not trivial ones, but ones that other physicians judged to be important in diagnosing the patient's illness. Findings like these have led medical schools to introduce programs to educate future physicians regarding psychosocial factors in treating patients—Harvard's "New Pathway" program is an example (Wallace, 1986).

The Patient's Behavior and Style

It takes two to tango, as the saying goes. Although the practitioner's behavior plays an important role in the relationship he or she forms with a patient, the patient's behavior and style are important, too. Physicians reported in a survey, for instance, that patients sometimes do things that can be very troubling or unsettling for a doctor (Smith & Zimny, 1988). Some of these behaviors include:

- Expressing criticism or anger toward the physician.

- Ignoring or not listening to what the doctor is trying to say.
- Insisting on laboratory tests, medications, or procedures the physician thinks are unnecessary.
- Requesting that the doctor certify something, such as a disability, that he or she thinks is untrue.
- Making sexually suggestive remarks or behaviors toward the physician.

If behaviors such as these lead to a breakdown in the relationship between the patient and practitioner, the quality of the medical care the patient receives may conceivably suffer.

Sometimes patients' *manner or focus in describing symptoms* impairs patient/practitioner communication. This can be seen in patients' different descriptions of the symptoms they experience for the same health problem. As an example, two women who had developed *hyperopia* (farsightedness) went to their physicians for medical care (Zola, 1973). In response to the practitioner's question, "What seems to be the trouble?", one patient simply said, "I can't see to thread a needle or read the paper." The other patient answered, "I have a constant headache and my eyes seem to get all red and burny." Neither patient expanded her description with significant facts when asked if she had anything to add.

Why do patients describe their symptoms for the same health problem so differently? One reason may lie in the way they perceive or interpret different symptoms. As we saw earlier, people differ in the attention they pay to internal states and the degree to which they associate different sensations with health problems. Also, individuals form different commonsense models of illness. When reporting symptoms to a doctor, patients may describe only or mainly those problems they think are "important," based on their own commonsense models (Bishop & Converse, 1986). Lastly, patients may try to either emphasize or downplay a symptom they believe may reflect a serious illness. For example, hypochondriacs may try to maximize the physician's attention to a sensation they are worried about, whereas other patients may describe a worrisome symptom very casually or offhandedly in the hope that the doctor will agree that "it's nothing."

Another communication problem can occur in medical situations when patients cannot describe their symptoms in terms that the doctor can clearly understand. This often occurs when the patient is very young. For instance, a child at 2 years of age may describe the problem as "my head hurts," but may not be able to describe the type of pain and its intensity or location very accurately. Similar communication difficulties can occur when the patient and practitioner have different primary languages. The United States, for example, has always had large numbers of immigrants from many parts of the world who do not speak English well. If these people must describe their problem in English because they do not have a practitioner who speaks their primary language, their descriptions are likely to be inaccurate and incomplete (Marcos, Urcuyo, Kesselman, & Alpert, 1981). These people are also unlikely to understand fully what their illness is or what they need to do to treat it.

One thing to keep in mind with respect to the way patient/practitioner relationships develop is that practitioners don't always get feedback regarding their work. Probably people in all occupations don't get all the positive feedback they should when they do good work, but medical workers may be less likely than other workers to receive negative feedback. Patients who are dissatisfied with the care they receive may be reluctant to complain because they feel intimidated by the status and knowledge of health care workers or by the possibility that the care they receive in the future may be diminished. Also, although a patient may have follow-up visits if symptoms persist or if the illness is serious or long term, physicians cannot be certain that *not* hearing from a patient means that a diagnosis was correct or that the treatment was effective. Furthermore, as we are about to see, practitioners usually cannot be sure to what extent a patient is following the medical *regimen*—the treatment or lifestyle change—they recommended.

COMPLIANCE: ADHERING TO MEDICAL ADVICE

"Now don't tell the doctor, but I don't always take my medicine when I'm supposed to," one patient whispered to another in their physician's waiting room. Patients don't always *adhere to*, or *comply with*, their practitioner's advice. **Adherence** and **compliance** are terms that refer to the degree to which patients carry out the behaviors and treatments their practitioners recommend. Most researchers have used these terms interchangeably, and we will, too. But *adherence* is a more satisfactory term because the dictionary definition of the word *compliance*—"giving in to a request or demand" or "acquiescence"—suggests that the practitioner uses an authoritarian style and that the patient obeys reluctantly (DiMatteo & DiNicola, 1982; Turk, Salovey, & Litt, 1986). The remainder of this chapter examines the extent to which patients fail to follow medical advice, why they do and do not comply, and what can be done to increase their adherence.

Extent of the Nonadherence Problem

How widespread is the problem of noncompliance? Answering this question is actually more difficult than it may seem (Cluss & Epstein, 1985; Epstein & Cluss, 1982). First of all, failures to adhere may occur for many different types of medical advice—for instance, patients may fail to take their medication as directed, not show up for a recommended appointment, skip or stop doing rehabilitation exercises, or "cheat a little" in following a specific diet or other lifestyle change advised by a practitioner. Second, patients can violate each of these types of advice in many different ways. In failing to take their medication as directed, for example, they might omit some doses, use a drug for the wrong reasons, take medication in the wrong amount or at the wrong time, or discontinue the drug before the prescribed course of therapy ends. Finally, there is the problem of determining whether a patient has or has not complied—What is the most accurate and practical way to assess compliance?

Researchers assess patient adherence to medical recommendations in several different ways, and each way has advantages and disadvantages (Cluss & Epstein, 1985; DiMatteo & DiNicola, 1982; Epstein & Cluss, 1982). One of the easiest approaches for measuring compliance is to *ask a practitioner* who works with the patient to estimate it. As it turns out, however, practitioners do not really know; they generally overestimate their patients' compliance and are poor at estimating which patients adhere better than others. Another simple approach is to *ask the patient.* But patients tend to overreport their adherence, perhaps because they know they should "follow the doctor's orders." These two methods are very subjective and open to various forms of bias, including lying and wishful thinking. As a result, researchers who use these approaches today usually supplement them with reports of family members or medical personnel and with other methods that are more objective.

There are three relatively objective approaches for assessing adherence to using medication. One of these methods is a *pill or quantity accounting,* in which the remaining medication is measured, such as by counting the number of pills left, and then compared against the quantity that should be left at that point in treatment if the patient has been following the directions correctly. Of course, this method does not reveal whether the patient used the medication at the right times, and patients who expect an accounting and want to conceal their noncompliance can discard some of the contents. Another method involves using *medication dispensers* with mechanical or electromechanical recording devices that can count and record the time when the dispenser is used. Although this approach is expensive to implement, it assesses compliance accurately as long as the patient does not deliberately create a ruse. If patients know about the device and want to avoid taking the medicine, they can operate the dispenser at the right time and discard the drug. The third objective method for assessing adherence involves *biochemical tests*, such as of the patient's blood or urine. This approach can accurately assess recent medication use, but it can also be very time-consuming and expensive to implement.

Despite the complexities in assessing adherence, we can provide some general answers to the question we started with: How widespread is the problem of noncompliance? Speaking in very broad terms, the average rate of patient noncompliance to medical advice is about 40%, that is, *two of every five patients fail to adhere* reasonably closely to their regimens (DiMatteo, 1985). Conversely, the overall rate of *adherence* is about 60%. Adherence varies considerably, depending on the type of medical advice, the duration of the recommended regimen, and whether its purpose is to prevent an illness from occurring or to treat or cure an illness that has developed. An overview of the findings of research on compliance indicates the following conclusions (Cluss & Epstein, 1985; Sackett & Snow, 1979):

- The average adherence rate for taking medicine to treat acute illnesses with short-term treatment regimens is about 78%; for chronic illnesses with long-term regimens, the rate drops to about 54%.
- The average adherence rates for taking medicine to prevent illness is roughly 60% for both short-term and long-term regimens.
- Patients adherence to scheduled appointments with a practitioner is much higher if the patient initiated the appointment than if the practitioner did.
- Adherence to recommended changes in lifestyle, such as stopping smoking or altering one's diet, is generally quite variable and often very low.

But keep in mind two things about these conclusions. First, the percentages given may *over*estimate compliance. This is because studies generally

> include in their sample only those patients who are willing to participate in a research project. It is reasonable to assume that this subgroup of volunteers may be different in motivational or other characteristics, making them more likely to comply as a group than others who are not willing to participate. (Cluss & Epstein, 1985, p. 410)

Second, the rates we cited do not reflect the range of noncompliance by patients: some adhere exactly to a medical regimen, others do not comply at all, and probably most comply at some "in between" level.

Why Patients Do and Do Not Adhere to Medical Advice

We have seen that practitioners do not generally know how well their patients adhere to medical advice. What do physicians think when they learn that their patients have not followed their advice? They are concerned about the effects of noncompliance on the patient's health, of course, and they tend to attribute most of the "blame" to characteristics of the patients—their "uncooperative" personalities, inability to understand the advice, or difficult life situations (Davis, 1966). But research has shown that patients' personality traits do not play a major role in their noncompliance and that both the practitioners and their patients influence adherence (DiMatteo & DiNicola, 1982; Ley, 1982).

Researchers have studied dozens of factors to determine their relationship to adherence. Reviews of these studies suggest that there is little or no association between compliance in general and patients' specific personal and demographic characteristics, such as their age, gender, social class, race, and religion (Cluss & Epstein, 1985; Haynes, 1976). Does this mean that these factors are never linked to compliance? Probably not. For one thing, although each of these factors is not *by itself* strongly related to adherence, when they are *joined*—for example, gender plus age plus social class—their combination shows a stronger association to compliance (Korsch, Fine, & Negrete, 1978). Furthermore, some of these factors may be related to adherence in some circumstances but not others. Consider the factor of *age*, for instance. Children become increasingly responsible for their own medical treatment as they get older (La Greca & Stone, 1985). Adolescents may be less likely than patients from other age groups to comply with long-term treatments that single them out or make them different from peers. And the elderly are more likely than other age groups to suffer from visual, hearing, and other impairments that may lead to noncompliance (Amaral, 1986).

Many other factors seem to have more general effects on whether patients do and do not comply with medical regimens. In our examination of these factors, we will divide them into three categories: characteristics of the regimen and illness, psychosocial aspects of the patient, and interactions between the patient and practitioner.

Medical Regimens and Illness Characteristics

The medical regimens that practitioners advise can differ in many ways, such as in their complexity, duration, cost, side effects, and the degree to which they require changes in the patient's habits. Let's see whether and how each of these factors relates to compliance.

Some regimens require patients to *change long-standing habits*—for example, to begin and maintain exercising regularly, reduce the calories or certain components in their diets, stop smoking cigarettes, or cut down on drinking alcoholic beverages. We have seen in previous chapters that these changes can be very difficult for people to make. Recommendations by physicians can induce many patients to make changes in such habits, particularly if the patients are at high risk for serious illness (Dolecek et al., 1986; Pederson, 1982). But studies have consistently found that patients are much less likely to adhere to medical advice for changes in personal habits than for taking medication (Haynes, 1976).

Some treatment regimens are more *complex* than others—such as by requiring the patient to take two or more drugs, each with its own special instructions: "Take one of these pills after meals, and two of these other pills at bedtime, and one of these other pills every eight hours." As you might expect, the greater the number of drugs and the more complex the medication schedule and dosage, the greater the likelihood the patient will make an error, thereby failing to adhere to the regimen (Haynes, 1976; Kirscht & Rosenstock, 1979). Regimens also become complicated by having the patient do a variety of tasks; for example, patients suffering from kidney failure must have their blood filtered through *dialysis*, take medications and vitamin supplements, and restrict their dietary intake of sodium, potassium, protein, and fluids (Finn & Alcorn, 1986; Swigonski, 1987). In general, the more a patient is required to do, the more likely compliance will suffer (Kirscht & Rosenstock, 1979).

Many people believe that the duration, expense, and side effects of a medical regimen are major factors in whether patients adhere to their practitioner's advice. Studies have confirmed the role of *duration*—compliance tends to decline over time (Parrish, 1986; Varni & Babani, 1986). Short-term regimens are usually prescribed for acute illnesses and show beneficial effects fairly quickly and dramatically, but long-term regimens usually apply to chronic health problems and have slower and less obvious beneficial effects. Do the *expense* and *side effects* of treatment also affect adherence? The evidence regarding these factors is not very consistent (DiMatteo & DiNicola, 1982; Haynes, 1976). Some studies have found that the expense and side effects of treatment seem to distinguish between patients who comply and those who do not, but other studies have not confirmed these findings. It may be that the sick-role behaviors of most patients are not strongly affected by these factors—for these patients, the treatment expense may not prevent them from adhering because they have sufficient incomes to pay for it, or they have insurance to cover the costs, or they feel that the benefits of the treatment are essential despite the cost. Similarly, most drugs do not have noticeable or worrisome side effects. But what happens, for instance, when individuals cannot afford their medicine or its side effects do become a problem? Some patients may reduce the dosage of the drug or discontinue using it entirely. The expense and side effects of treatment can impair adherence for some patients.

Many people also think that individuals who have health problems that could disable them or threaten their lives are more likely to adhere to their treatment regimens than individuals who have less serious illnesses. But whether this idea is correct seems to depend on whose perspective of the severity of the health problem we consider — the patient's or the practitioner's. When illness severity is judged by *physicians*, patients with serious illnesses are no more likely to adhere than those with milder health problems (Becker & Rosenstock, 1984; Haynes, 1976). Perhaps this is because many very serious health problems, such as hypertension and atherosclerosis, have no symptoms that worry people greatly or interfere with their functioning; on the other hand, many less serious illnesses do have such symptoms. In contrast, when illness severity is judged by *patients* who have the health problem, adherence increases with severity. Those patients who perceive their illness as relatively serious generally show better adherence to their treatment regimens than those who perceive their illness to be less severe (Becker & Rosenstock, 1984).

Psychosocial Aspects of the Patient

We have just seen that the seriousness of an illness and the costs of its treatment can affect compliance, depending on the point of view of the patient. Perceived seriousness and perceived costs and benefits are two psychosocial factors that should have a familiar ring by now — we have examined them more than once before as components in the *health belief model*. The components of the health belief model are just as important in explaining why people do and do not adhere to medical advice as they are in explaining other health-related behaviors, such as whether people are likely to adopt health behaviors or use health services (Becker, 1979; Becker & Rosenstock, 1984; Rosenstock & Kirscht, 1979). Thus, patients who feel threatened by an illness and believe that the benefits of the recommended regimen outweigh the barriers are likely to adhere to their practitioner's advice. But individuals who do not feel threatened by the health problem or assess that the barriers of the regimen outweigh the benefits are unlikely to comply.

According to Howard Leventhal (1982), patients' *common-sense models* about their illness can interfere with adherence to their practitioner's recommendations. As an example, hypertensive patients often erroneously believe they can tell when their blood pressure is high. Patients who have definite ideas about their health problem may adjust their treatment, thinking that they know something their doctor doesn't about "how my own illness should be treated." Of course, they probably don't tell their doctor what they are thinking for several reasons:

> They may feel awkward about arguing or afraid they will look foolish. They may not wish to express the fears they have about their interpretations of their illness. Or they may simply not want to challenge the doctor's authority, fearing loss of his or her support. (Leventhal, 1982, p. 55)

These patients recognize that their ideas are contrary to their physician's — and if they are caught in their failure to comply, they may invent a "little white lie" to explain, for example, why they have more pills left than they should.

Patients' adherence to medical advice is often affected by *cognitive and emotional* factors operating at the time they receive the recommendations. These factors are illustrated in the following summary of research findings:

1. Patients forget much of what the doctor tells them.
2. Instructions and advice are more likely to be forgotten than other information.
3. The more a patient is told, the greater the proportion he or she will forget.

4. Patients will remember: (a) what they are told first and (b) what they consider most important.
5. Intelligent patients do not remember more than less intelligent patients.
6. Older patients remember just as much as younger ones.
7. Moderately anxious patients recall more of what they are told than highly anxious patients or patients who are not anxious.
8. The more medical knowledge a patient has, the more he or she will recall. (Cassata, cited in DiMatteo & DiNicola, 1982, p. 45

In order for patients to comply with a treatment regimen, they must understand and remember what they are to do. The directions they receive are often complex and given at a time when they may not be listening as carefully as they should.

Another psychosocial factor that is associated with adherence is *social support.* Generally speaking, people who feel they receive the comfort, caring, and help they need from other individuals or groups are more likely to follow medical advice than patients who have less social support (DiMatteo & DiNicola, 1982). This support can come from the patient's family, friends, or support groups, such as the many organizations to help people deal with specific illnesses. The support that patients receive seems to be most beneficial to regimen adherence when it specifically involves help and encouragement in caring for the health problem (Carmody et al., 1982; Stanton, 1987). But social relationships can sometimes lead to noncompliance. Mary Swigonski (1987) studied kidney disease patients whose complex treatment regimen included restricting fluid intake and found that the more social support the patients had, the greater the likelihood of nonadherence for fluids. As she pointed out, social gatherings often occur with food and beverages present—in meetings for lunch, dinner, drinks, or just a cup of coffee, for instance. Engaging in many social activities like these makes it difficult for patients to restrict their fluid consumption.

Patient/Practitioner Interactions

The dictionary tells us that the word "doctor" comes from the Latin *docere,* which means "to teach." Two features of good teaching involve explaining information in a clear and organized fashion and assessing whether the learner has learned or understands. Some medical practitioners are good teachers, and others are not—

> for example, there are documented cases of men consuming contraceptive drugs intended for their wives. The idea may be amusing, but the fact of an unwanted child was not. (Hunt & MacLeod, 1979, p. 315)

This example illustrates that physicians do not always make sure the patient understands what they have said. Successful communication in patient/practitioner interactions is essential if the patient is to adhere to the advice.

Communicating with Patients

If your physician told you to "take one pill every six hours," does that mean you should wake up in the middle of each night to take one? Or would it be OK simply to take four pills a day, equally spaced during your waking hours? Would you ask? Sometimes the information patients get from practitioners is not very clear. You might argue that the advice *was* clear: every six hours, on the dot. But practitioners need to anticipate unspoken questions—saying, for instance, "You'll need to wake up to take one because the infection may recover if the medicine wears off." If practitioners don't do this, patients usually answer these questions themselves, often incorrectly.

Many patients leave their doctor's office not knowing how to follow their treatment regimen. Bonnie Svarstad (1976) reported the results of research in which she interviewed patients at a community health center and checked their medication containers after they visited their physicians. She also recorded the actual verbal interactions between the physicians and their patients. The results of this research demonstrated four things. First, the patients' knowledge about their treatment was seriously deficient—for example, half of the patients did not know how long they should continue taking their medication, and about one-fifth of them did not know the purpose of or how often to take the prescribed drugs. Second, an important reason for the patients' poor knowledge was that the physicians often did not provide the needed information. For most of the prescriptions, for example, the physicians failed to give explicit instructions on how regularly or how often to use the medication—for that matter, some of the drugs were never discussed at all during the visit. Third, the patients asked very few questions during the visits. Fourth, the more explicit the physicians' directions, the greater the patients complied, which Svarstad measured by pill counts at the patients' homes about a week later.

Physicians spend very little time giving information to patients during a visit. Howard Waitzkin and John Stoeckle (1976) recorded the interactions between hundreds of patients and their physicians in office and hospital visits. They found that during these visits, which lasted an average of about 20 minutes, the physicians spent only about one minute, or 5% of the time, communicating information to the patients about their illness or treatment. Interestingly, the physicians themselves reported a very different picture of their interactions: When asked how much time they spent giving information, the doctors gave estimates that were several times higher than the records showed. Other researchers have conducted similar studies and found doctors spending somewhat more time communicating with their patients. Averaging across these studies, it appears that doctors spend perhaps 10% of the time in consultations giving patients information (DiMatteo, 1985).

A patient's adherence to medical advice depends on the practitioner's communicating information. Good communication takes time and is much more likely to occur when the practitioner's style is more patient-centered than doctor-centered.

Adherence and the Patient/Practitioner Relationship

As we have seen, patients generally prefer medical care that involves a patient-centered style in which the practitioner is warm and caring, listens to the patient, and discusses and explains the patient's illness and treatment clearly. Research has shown that patients who have this kind of relationship with their physician are more likely to adhere to the medical advice he or she gives (DiMatteo, 1985; Garrity, 1981; Ley, 1982).

Barbara Korsch and her colleagues have examined the link between patients' satisfaction with medical care and compliance (Francis, Korsch, & Morris, 1969; Freemon, Negrete, Davis, & Korsch, 1971; Korsch, Gozzi, & Francis, 1968). The research methodology involved tape-recording several hundred pediatric consultations at a walk-in clinic and then interviewing the mothers immediately after they left the doctor's office. Although most of the mothers reported being at least moderately satisfied with the visit, nearly one-fifth of the mothers said they did not receive a clear statement of what was wrong with their child and about half did not know what caused the illness. The most common complaint of the mothers was that the physician did not seem to respond warmly or sympathetically to their anxiety about their child. One mother, for instance, felt the doctor did not pay attention to her concern that the convulsions her child experienced might damage his brain.

This research also assessed whether compliance was related to the mothers' satisfaction with their visit. A week or two after the medical consultation, the researchers visited the mothers to determine their adherence with the recommended regimens. This assessment was done through the mothers' reports and, when possible, through pill counts or contacts with the pharmacy. The results revealed that those mothers who were very satisfied with the physician's warmth, concern, and communication of information were three times more likely to adhere closely to the regimen than those who were dissatisfied. In other words, the doctors who were most successful in fostering compliance were those who used a patient-centered style.

To summarize, the reasons why patients do and do not adhere to medical advice include some factors that are associated mainly with the patients, some with the practitioners, and some with the way these people interrelate. While reading this material, you may have thought, "Couldn't many of the circumstances that lead to nonadherence be changed to enhance compliance?" The next section examines this question.

Increasing Patient Adherence

Implicit in our interest in enhancing adherence is the assumption that doing so is important—that it would benefit the patient's health. How important is adherence to the patient's health? If it is very important, should health care workers aim for each patient to comply perfectly to his or her regimen, or would a lesser degree of adherence be acceptable? We will address these questions briefly before considering ways to increase compliance.

Noncompliance and Health Outcomes

By not adhering to regimens recommended by their physicians, patients increase their risk of developing health problems they don't already have or of prolonging or worsening their current illnesses. Estimates suggest that 20% of hospital admissions probably result from patients' noncompliance with medication regimens (Ley, 1982).

But failing to follow a practitioner's orders exactly is not always detrimental to the patient's health. One reason is that some treatments are harmful and have side effects that produce iatrogenic conditions. Patients should notify their physicians when a treatment causes problems. Another reason is that doctors sometimes prescribe unnecessary drugs or other procedures with nonmedical goals in mind, such as to avoid risking a malpractice suit. Of course, in the great majority of cases, the doctor's recommendations are correct and are in the patient's best interests. Yet even when medically sound advice is given, some patients who follow their doctors' orders closely show little benefit from the treatment, whereas other patients who are much less compliant show substantial improvements in their health (Cluss & Epstein, 1985).

The importance of following medical advice closely seems to depend on the particular health problem and the treatment prescribed. For hypertensive patients, for instance, consuming 80% of the medication prescribed to reduce their blood pressure is probably the minimum level of compliance needed to treat hypertension effectively. For other health problems, "however, an 80% rate of compliance may be unnecessary" (Epstein & Cluss, 1982, p. 952). As an example, following the usual regimen of penicillin for treating rheumatic fever at only a 50% rate may be sufficiently effective. Unhealthful noncompliance might therefore be defined as "the point below which the desired preventive or therapeutic result is unlikely to be achieved with the medication prescribed" (Parrish, 1986, p. 456). Unfortunately, however, compliance cutoff points still need to be established for individual illnesses and treatments.

Although more research is needed to determine compliance cutoff points, two things should be clear. First, *perfect* adherence may not be necessary in many cases. Second, the current adherence levels of patients are very far from perfect and need to be improved.

Methods for Enhancing Compliance

Probably most physicians in the past who have dealt with the compliance problem at all did so after the fact. Rather than trying to prevent noncompliance, they tried to correct it if and when they learned about it. How did they try to correct it? A study examined this question and found that the first step physicians used when a patient failed to adhere was to give a "thorough explanation of the regimen and repeat it so that the patient understands" (Davis, 1966). As we have seen, explaining the regimen and making sure the patient understands can prevent noncompliance in the first place.

Getting practitioners to improve their *style of communicating* with patients is not necessarily difficult to accomplish. In one study, for instance, researchers designed a brief program to instruct physicians about the kinds of reasons hypertensive patients have for not adhering to their regimens and about ways to detect and improve low compliance (Inui, Yourtee, & Williamson, 1976). The physicians who participated in the study were treating hypertensive patients at a hospital clinic. On the basis of their work schedules, about half of the doctors were assigned to an experimental group, which received the instructional program. The remaining physicians served as controls. Subsequent assessments demonstrated that the program was quite effective in changing the physicians' behavior and in benefitting their patients' health. Compared to the control doctors, the physicians who received the program spent more time giving information during patient visits—and, more importantly, their patients subsequently showed more knowledge about their regimen and illness, greater adherence in taking medications, and better blood pressure control. How long such changes last is uncertain, but results like these have spurred medical schools to provide training in doctor/patient relationships, communications skills, and sociocultural issues (Wallace, 1986).

Because patients often misunderstand or forget medical recommendations, practitioners are also being taught specific *techniques for presenting medical information.* Several methods are particularly effective (Ley, 1982; Parrish, 1986; Rosenstock, 1985; Schraa & Dirks, 1982). These methods include:

- Simplifying instructions by using clear and straightforward language and sentences.
- Using specific and concrete statements—such as, "You should walk a mile a day for the first week, and two miles after that" instead of "You should get daily exercise."
- Breaking down a complicated or long-term regimen into smaller segments. The patient might begin the regimen by doing only part of it and then adding to it later. Or the regimen might involve a series of smaller goals that the patient believes he or she can achieve.
- Emphasizing key information by stating why it is important and presenting it early in the presentation.
- Using written instructions.
- Having the patient repeat the instructions or state them in his or her own words.

These techniques appear to be more effective in improving compliance with short-term regimens than with long-term regimens (Haynes, 1982).

Another approach that appears to promote adherence at least for short-term regimens is to have the person state explicitly that he or she will comply. An experiment by James Kulik and Patricia Carlino (1987) demonstrated this in a pediatric setting with the parents of children who were suffering from acute infections. The researchers randomly assigned the subjects to two groups: Parents in the experimental group were simply asked by the physician, "Will you promise me you'll give all the doses?", and all agreed; parents in the control condition were not asked for this commitment. When the patients returned for a follow-up visit about 10 days later, their recovery was medically evaluated and compliance was assessed both by interviewing the parent and by doing an analysis of the child's urine. Compared with the control group, those in the experimental condition showed higher compliance rates and greater recovery from their illnesses.

Social and motivational forces in patients' lives can have important effects on adherence, particularly when the regimen is long term or requires lifestyle changes. One approach that makes use of social and motivational factors is for the practitioner or patient to recruit constructive sources of *social support* (Jenkins, 1979; Peck & King, 1985; Rosenstock, 1985). Family and friends who are committed to the regimen can promote compliance by having a positive attitude about the treatment activities and making sure they occur. Patients who receive encouragement, praise, reminders, and assistance in carrying out the regimen are more likely to comply than those who do not. Effective social support can also come from self-help groups, patient groups, and organizations to help with specific health problems. These groups can give information and assistance, provide a sense of comfort and belongingness, and bolster the patient's sense of esteem. Practitioners can help patients make contact with appropriate groups.

Several *behavioral methods* are also effective in enhancing patients' motivation to adhere to their treatment regimens (DiMatteo & DiNicola, 1982; Epstein & Cluss, 1982; Haynes, 1982; Jenkins, 1979). These methods include:

- *Tailoring the regimen*, in which activities in the treatment are designed to be compatible with the patient's habits and rituals. For example, taking a pill at home at breakfast or while preparing for bed is easier to do and remember for most people than taking it in the middle of the day.
- *Prompts and reminders*, which serve as cues to perform recommended activities. These cues can include reminder phone calls for appointments or notes that remind the patient to exercise. Innovative drug packaging can also help—for instance, some drugs today come in dispensers with dated compartments or built-in reminder alarms.
- *Self-monitoring*, in which the patient keeps a written record of regimen activities, such as the foods eaten each day.
- *Contingency contracting*, whereby the practitioner and patient negotiate a series of treatment activities and goals in writing and specify rewards the patient will receive for succeeding.

A major advantage of these methods is that the patient becomes actively involved in their design and execution (Turk, Salovey, & Litt, 1986). Furthermore, the patient can carry them out alone or with the aid of the practitioner, family, or friends.

The procedures we have examined for increasing patient compliance often involve the practitioner in much more constructive interactions with the patient than just giving brief instructions. Although some of these methods are easy to incorporate into existing ways of interacting with patients, others are complicated and time-consuming to arrange and involve skills that are outside the expertise of most medical workers. When patients have treatment regimens that are difficult for them to adhere to, the skills of health care workers who are trained in psychological principles may be needed to enhance the patients' treatment compliance and, thereby, their health.

SUMMARY

The American system for the delivery and management of medical care is extremely complex, consisting of millions of health care workers with a wide variety of specialized functions who provide inpatient and office-based treatment. Inpatient treatment for people with serious illnesses occurs in hospitals; nursing homes provide care primarily for elderly individuals who need long-term medical and personal care. Practitioners give office-based treatment in private practice and in prepaid group plans, such as health-maintenance organizations. These two office-based treatment approaches appear to provide similar types and quality of service.

People decide that they are sick and in need of medical attention mainly on the basis of the symptoms they perceive. The point at which people notice a symptom differs from one individual to the next and within the same person from one time to another. Some people seem to pay closer attention to their internal states than other individuals do and are, therefore, more likely to notice changes in physical sensations and to perceive these sensations as symptoms. People are less likely to notice internal sensations when the environment contains a great deal of sensory information or is very exciting than when it has few external stimuli to compete for their attention. Because people generally do not assess their internal states very accurately, psychosocial factors can have a strong influence on the perception of symptoms and may produce two interesting phenomena: medical student's disease and mass psychogenic illness. People's health-related behaviors are influenced by common-sense models they develop of different illnesses. A common-sense model consists of information about the illness identity, its causes and underlying pathology, and its prognosis and cure.

Many factors affect how individuals interpret and respond to the symptoms they perceive. The knowledge people extract from their experience with symptoms generally helps them to make appropriate decisions about seeking medical attention. Sometimes people's prior experiences and their emotions, such as intense fear or anxiety, can lead them to interpret their symptoms incorrectly and delay seeking care. Before individuals decide to seek medical attention, they typically get advice from their lay referral system, which consists of relatives, friends, and coworkers.

Certain demographic characteristics are associated with the use of health services. Young children and the elderly use health services more than adolescents and young adults do, and women use more medical drugs and have higher rates of illness from acute and nonfatal chronic illnesses than men do. Individuals from the lower social classes are less likely to use health services than are people from higher classes. This class difference is especially troubling because individuals from the lower classes have higher rates of health problems and poorer health habits than those from higher classes.

The health belief model has been useful in helping to explain why people use, don't use, and delay using health services. People's ideas about iatrogenic conditions may also affect whether they decide to seek medical care. Treatment delay appears to involve three stages—appraisal delay, illness delay, and utilization delay—each of which is affected by different factors. Many individuals wait several months before seeking attention for symptoms of serious illnesses, such as cancer. In contrast, some people overuse health services. Hypochondriasis involves the tendency for a person to interpret real but benign bodily sensations as symptoms of illness despite reassurances by a doctor that they are harmless. Studies have shown that hypochondriasis is linked to emotional maladjustment, but it is not more common in old age than at other ages.

Patients generally express high levels of satisfaction with the care they receive from physicians who communicate with a patient-centered rather than a doctor-centered style. Patient-centered physicians tend to ask open-ended questions, avoid using medical jargon or technical terms, and allow patients to participate in some of the decision making regarding the treatment of their illness. These doctors are also likely to project a feeling of concern and reassurance and to give clear explanations about illnesses and treatments. Of course, patients vary in their behaviors and styles, too, and may impair communication with their doctor because of the manner or focus they use in describing their symptoms.

Patient compliance with or adherence to medical advice varies greatly, and noncompliance is very common. About two of every five patients fail to adhere reasonably closely to the medical regimens their doctor prescribes. Patients tend to be less compliant for long-term regimens to treat chronic diseases than for short-term regimens to treat acute illnesses, and they are particularly unlikely to comply with recommendations to change long-standing habits. Also, the more complicated the regimen, the more likely adherence will suffer. Adherence is affected by various psychosocial factors, including the patients' health beliefs, the social support they have, and several cognitive and emotional conditions operating at the time they receive the medical advice. Many patients leave their physician's office not knowing how to follow the prescribed regimen. Patients tend to adhere closely to their regimens when their practitioner is warm and caring, gives them opportunities to talk, and explains their illness and treatment clearly. A variety of behavioral and communication-enhancing methods can help to improve patients' adherence to medical advice.

KEY TERMS

common-sense models
lay referral system
iatrogenic conditions
treatment delay
hypochondriasis
doctor-centered
patient-centered
adherence
compliance

10

IN THE HOSPITAL: THE SETTING, PROCEDURES, AND EFFECTS ON PATIENTS

PROLOGUE

"I had a fast-growing conviction that a hospital was no place for a person who was seriously ill," a patient once wrote. This patient was Norman Cousins, the former editor of *Saturday Review*, whom we described in Chapter 1 as having developed and recovered from a typically incurable and fatal crippling disease. The symptoms he experienced began with a fever and general achiness — the kinds of sensations we usually associate with minor illnesses. Within a week, however, his condition worsened, and he began to have difficulty moving his neck, legs, arms, and hands. He was soon hospitalized for the diagnostic tests that pinpointed his disease.

What experiences did Cousins have that led to his negative view of hospitals? One example he described is:

> I was astounded when four technicians from four different departments took four separate and substantial blood samples on the same day. That the hospital didn't take the trouble to coordinate the tests, using one blood specimen, seemed to me inexplicable and irresponsible. When the technicians came the second day to fill their containers with blood for processing in separate laboratories, I turned them away and had a sign posted on my door saying that I would give just one specimen every three days and that I expected the different departments to draw from it for their individual needs. (Cousins, 1985, pp. 55–56)

He also criticized other hospital practices, such as awakening patients from sleep to carry out regular routines. In his view, sleep in the hospital is an "uncommon blessing" that should not be interrupted casually.

Few patients enjoy being hospitalized, even under the best of circumstances. Although most patients probably have more positive feelings about their hospital experiences than those Cousins had, some have even worse impressions. We have all heard stories of mistakes being made or other situations that produced more serious health problems than those with which the patient was admitted to the hospital. This chapter focuses on the patient's experience of hospitalization. First we examine the hospital — its history, setting, and procedures — as well as the roles and points of view of the staff. Then we consider what being hospitalized is like from the patient's perspective, and what can be done to assess and provide help for the psychological needs of patients. As we study these topics, we will consider important questions that are of great concern to patients, their families, and practitioners. For instance, working in a hospital is very difficult — what impact does this have on the staff? How do patients adjust to being hospitalized? What special needs do children have as patients, and how can hospitals and parents help? How can practitioners reduce the stress patients experience with unpleasant, painful, and surgical procedures?

THE HOSPITAL — ITS HISTORY, SETTING, AND PROCEDURES

Hospitals in industrialized countries around the world are typically large institutions with separate wards or buildings for different kinds of health problems and treatment procedures. These institutions have changed in their long history, and so have people's attitudes about them. People in the United States today are more likely than people years ago to view hospitals as a place to go to get well rather than to die, even though most Americans are in a hospital when they die (Easterbrook, 1987). Let's see how hospitals began and evolved.

How the Hospital Evolved

The concept of having special places to care for the ill did not always exist. One of the earliest roots of this concept can be seen in the ancient Greeks' establishment of temples where sick people would pray and receive a cure or advice from the god Aesculapius (Anderson & Gevitz, 1983). But the idea of having special facilities to house and treat the sick probably began with the Roman military, who established separate barracks for their ill and disabled soldiers.

The first institutions established to care for the sick were associated with Christian monasteries and had a broad charitable purpose—that of helping the less fortunate members of society. As a result, these facilities housed not only sick people, but also orphans, the poor, and even travelers who needed lodging. One of the earliest of these hospitals, the Hôtel-Dieu of Lyons in present-day France, was established in A.D. 542 (Anderson & Gevitz, 1983). The charitable purposes of hospitals in Western Europe continued with little change until the eighteenth and nineteenth centuries, when these institutions became more specialized in two ways.

> First, the conventional approach of lumping all types of dependents into the same facility was gradually discarded as hospitals became repositories for the poor sick. Not all of the medically incapacitated were admitted, though—only the "worthy poor," i.e., those lower class individuals adjudged by administrators and sponsors to be potentially useful citizens capable of making a contribution to the commonweal. Others, namely the aged, the very young, the physically handicapped, and the mentally deficient . . . were confined to abysmally kept poorhouses, irrespective of whether they were in need of medical attention. The second change was that hospitals became more medically specialized. Wards were established for different illness categories. . . . By keeping patients with the same or seemingly related ailments together, one could readily make far more detailed comparisons and thus advance learning. (Anderson & Gevitz, 1983, p. 307)

The American colonies used similar approaches to those used in Europe for the care

Typical of European hospitals prior to the twentieth century, this seventeenth-century hospital in Paris had many beds close together in a huge room.

of the sick. In 1751, Pennsylvania Hospital opened in Philadelphia as the first institution in the colonies devoted exclusively to treating disease. It was built as a result of a citizens' campaign led by Benjamin Franklin.

Until the twentieth century, hospitals had always had a well-deserved bad reputation as a place that gave miserable care and ministered exclusively to poor people, who often died from infections they did not have when they entered. Sick people from the upper and middle classes were treated at home. But this situation quickly changed with advances in medical knowledge and technology in the late 1800s. In 1873, there were only 178 hospitals in the United States; in 1909, there were over 4,300, and the increase in the number of hospital beds was seven times that which would be expected on the basis of population growth alone (Anderson & Gevitz, 1983). American hospitals in the early twentieth century gained a much more positive reputation and were attracting patients from all social classes. Nowadays, the nation's hospitals admit about 40 million people as inpatients each year (USDHHS, 1985b).

Hospitals today involve a wider variety of functions than ever before—they are institutions for curing disease and repairing injury, preventing illness, conducting diagnostic tests, aiding patients' rehabilitation and life situation after being discharged, conducting research, and teaching current and future medical personnel. To carry out these complex and varied functions, hospitals require an organized hierarchy of personnel with specific roles and lines of authority, as we are about to see.

The Organization and Functioning of Hospitals

The organizational structure of hospitals in the United States differs from structures used in most other countries. The American structure begins with a board of trustees, whose members are generally upper-level business and professional people from the community (Anderson & Gevitz, 1983). Most boards limit their role mainly to long-range planning and fund-raising. At the next level of authority, the chain of command splits into two parallel lines of responsibility: The hospital *administrators* are mainly in charge of the day-to-day business of the institution, such as in purchasing equipment and supplies, keeping records and accounts, and providing food and maintenance services. These functions often affect the medical care patients receive. The *medical staff* are responsible for patient care. Each of these two lines has its own hierarchy of authority; but we will focus on the medical staff because of their direct impact on the health of the patients.

The head of the medical staff is a physician who generally has the title "Medical Director" or "Chief of Staff." The next level of authority consists of the staff (or "attending") physicians. In the majority of American hospitals, most staff physicians are not actually employed or paid by the institution. They are employed in private practice or affiliated with a private clinic or group health plan, and they provide services at the hospital for their patients from these sources (Anderson & Gevitz, 1983; Easterbrook, 1987). Those doctors who are in private practice get paid for their hospital services by billing each of their patients; the remaining doctors are paid a salary by their employer. To become a staff physician, a doctor must receive *admission privileges*, generally by applying to a committee of physicians at the hospital. As a condition for granting privileges, most hospitals require staff physicians to do certain tasks, such as teaching or providing emergency or clinic service. The main exception to this system of staff physicians occurs at "teaching hospitals," which are affiliated with medical schools. Although teaching hospitals grant admission privileges, they also have a large staff of doctors who are employed and paid by the hospital or medical school; these doctors include (1) *residents*, who are medical school graduates, and (2) full-fledged physicians, whose duties include supervising the residents.

Nurses form the next rung in the hierarchy of medical staff in hospitals. Although many physicians think of nurses as their assistants, nurses are actually salaried employees of the hospital who have two functions: caring for patients and managing the ward (Aiken, 1983). Because the former function is medical and the latter is administrative, nurses may receive directives from physicians and administrators. Sometimes the orders that nurses receive from these two sources are incompatible and cause conflict, such as when a physician orders an action that the administration has banned as a cost-cutting measure. Whose directives should the nurse follow? The answer isn't always clear. Other conflicts and difficulties that nurses experience stem from their relatively low pay and the discrepancy between their high level of training and low involvement in medical decision making (Aiken, 1983, Easterbrook, 1987). Nurses are, of course, as important as doctors to a patient's recovery, and they spend more time with the patient, often explaining medical regimens and procedures when physicians do not.

The medical staff also includes a great variety of allied health workers, such as physical therapists, respiratory therapists, laboratory technicians, pharmacists' assistants, and dietitions (Ginsburg, 1983). These workers often have less authority than nurses. At the bottom of the medical staff hierarchy are orderlies and other workers whose roles require less advanced skills than those of the allied health workers.

Roles, Goals, and Communication

As the ambulance crew wheels the victim of an automobile accident into the emergency room, the medical staff swings into action. Their specific actions and roles are dictated by the presenting health problems of the patient and would be different if the patient had suffered serious burns in a fire or symptoms of a heart attack, for instance. Quick assessments and decisions need to be made regarding tests to perform, medications to administer, and procedures to apply to control the damage, stabilize the patient's body functions, and set the stage for recovery. Nurses and orderlies know the usual procedures for patients with the presenting problems and begin to perform their roles without specific instruction—for example, a nurse may prepare to take a blood sample and an orderly may wheel a piece of equipment into place. The physician is, of course, in charge and either conducts needed actions directly or orders others to do them.

Years ago, the typical hospital patient received services from a small team of physicians and nurses who worked side by side in close communication throughout the patient's stay (Benoliel, 1977). This situation rarely exists today. Instead, assessment and treatment procedures for a hospitalized patient involve a wide array of personnel who have different specializations and carry out their roles separately, often with little contact with each other and with the patient. The danger in the current approach is that the patient's care can become *fragmented*, or uncoordinated. Hospitals attempt to minimize this danger by giving a particular staff position—usually a nursing position—responsibility for coordinating the care of each patient in a ward (Aiken, 1983; Benoliel, 1977; Kneut, 1982). This person tries to make sure that relevant information is communicated among the many personnel involved in the patient's treatment.

Communication among medical personnel is also important because hospitals contain many health hazards for personnel and patients. These hazards include chemicals that are used in treatment and various other hospital procedures (Clever & Omenn, 1988; USDHHS, 1985d). One substance called *ethylene oxide*, for example, is widely used as a sterilizing agent for medical supplies and equipment. Long-term high-level exposure to this chemical has been linked with the development of several forms of cancer. Although hospital workers' exposure to ethylene oxide is typically short term and at low levels, sometimes high exposure levels occur when sterilizing equipment is malfunctioning or improperly designed. Hospitals need to inform their workers about the dangers and safe use of the substances they work with, monitor the environment for levels of these substances, provide necessary ventilation and devices to minimize exposure to harmful chemicals, and keep records of the amount of time personnel work where these substances are used. Hospitals also need to protect patients from unsafe exposure to various chemicals used in their treatment.

Another hazard in hospitals is the potential exposure of personnel and patients to disease-causing microorganisms. As we saw earlier, hospitals prior to the twentieth century were places where infection spread quickly and widely, and patients often died of diseases they did not have when they entered. Although the spreading of infection in hospitals has been greatly reduced, it has not been eliminated. Researchers have estimated that perhaps 5% of patients in American hospitals—or 2,000,000 people each year—acquire a **nosocomial infection**, an infection that a patient contracts while in the hospital setting. About 15,000 of these patients die from the infections they acquire in the hospital (Raven & Haley, 1982). To combat this problem, national guidelines for hospital infection control have been developed and widely adopted. According to these guidelines, each hospital should have an Infection Control Committee headed by an epidemiologist to establish policies to control the spread of disease. Furthermore, the medical staff should include an Infection Control Nurse (ICN) with experience in a clinical setting and training in epidemiology and infectious diseases. The ICN has the most direct role in curbing the spread of disease, being responsible for detecting and recording instances of nosocomial infections and taking measures to prevent them.

Hospitals have attempted to reduce nosocomial infections by establishing regulations regarding such issues as when medical workers must wash their hands or wear masks. But hospital personnel sometimes break these rules, and physicians seem to be the worst offenders. Bertram Raven and Robert Haley (1982) surveyed about 8,000 hospital personnel at hundreds of hospitals in the United States to determine whether medical workers adhere to infection control regulations and what is done when they do not. The survey sample consisted of over 7,000 nurses, almost 350 ICNs, and over 400 epidemiologists. The results revealed—with reports by nurses and epidemiologists being in agreement—that hospital workers showed very good compliance with the rules, but doctors were considerably less likely to comply than were nurses and laboratory technicians. To find out how the ICNs would handle violations of the rules by physicians, nurses, and technicians, the ICNs were also asked:

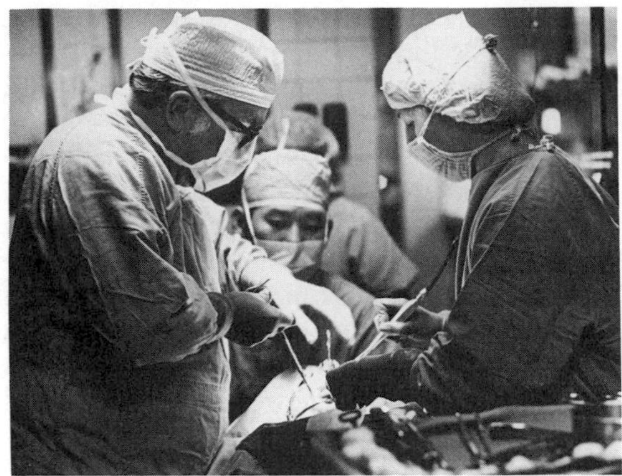

Hospitals try to reduce the spread of infection by establishing rules about medical staff wearing clean masks, clothing, and gloves.

> On your rounds you may have observed members of the staff not following good infection control practices. How often would you say something to the staff member about the following incidents? . . . Entering a strict isolation room without masking; discarding an unprotected hypodermic needle in a waste basket; after handling a contaminated dressing or article, proceeding to a "clean" procedure without first washing . . . hands. (Raven & Haley, 1982, p. 422)

Their responses indicated that ICNs generally correct infection control violations by nurses and technicians, but they are much less likely to correct violations by physicians.

Although nosocomial infection continues to be a serious problem in hospitals, role relationships among medical personnel seem to impair the communication needed to reduce the spread of disease. In general, personnel feel much less comfortable giving advice or corrective feedback to an individual whose status is higher than their own than to someone whose status is equal to or lower than theirs. Hospitals need to find constructive ways to enable a staff member at a lower level of the medical staff hierarchy to give feedback to individuals at higher levels regarding their nonadherence to infection control regulations.

The Impact of the "Bottom Line"

The costs of medical services were probably expensive when hospitals first began to charge patients, and the costs are still high. The Medicare system has probably helped to contain these costs in recent years, but it initially made the situation worse because

> payment was pass-along. Hospitals forwarded their invoices to Washington, physicians claimed their "customary" fee, a phrase that came to mean almost anything a doctor wanted it to mean. The more the health-care system ran up the bill, the more it could profit. (Easterbrook, 1987, p. 43).

The incentives encouraged keeping patients in the hospital and performing many tests and procedures. Maintaining a hospital's financial solvency was a relatively easy job for administrators.

But this situation soon changed as a result of a payment mechanism called the *prospective-payment system* (PPS) that was adopted by Medicare (Easterbrook, 1987; Kiesler & Morton, 1988). With the PPS approach, health problems are classified into "diagnosis related groups," and a hospital that is treating a patient who has a particular health problem receives a predetermined fixed fee. This fee reflects the average cost of treating patients in the corresponding diagnostic-related group, based on past recovery rates for similar patients. If the patient's condition does not respond to the treatment as readily as expected and requires extra care, the hospital usually bears the cost beyond the PPS allowance. But if the patient's condition responds better than expected, the hospital keeps the excess payment. The combination of the spiraling costs of medical care and hospital administrators' concern for the "bottom line" has contributed to changes in hospital procedures in recent years.

How have hospital procedures changed? Although some institutions in the United States focus on treating patients who require long-term care, the great majority of hospitals were established to treat people quickly and discharge them in good health (Lawrence & Gaus, 1983; USDHHS, 1985b). Most hospitals keep patients for an average of less than 30 days, and are classified as *short-stay hospitals.* As Figure 10.1 depicts, the rate at which short-stay hospitals admit and discharge patients has been increasing, while the length of stay in the hospital has been decreasing since the late 1960s. The decreased stays in hospitals reflect two important changes. First, medical procedures are becoming increasingly efficient. For example, new surgical methods for correcting orthopedic injuries entail little or no cutting of healthy tissue, so that recovery time and pain are greatly diminished. Second, patients are being released at earlier stages of recovery, so that a larger part of their recovery time is spent at home while receiving care as outpatients. Although some critics worry that people are being released too quickly from hospitals, the evidence suggests that patients have not been harmed by these procedures (Easterbrook, 1987).

Patients typically prefer being released from the hospital as early as possible. Being hospitalized is in many ways a negative experience—financially, physically, socially, and emotionally. The next section considers how being hospitalized impacts on the patient.

BEING HOSPITALIZED

Although being sick is unpleasant and being seriously ill is worse, being hospitalized adds many other negative dimensions to a person's

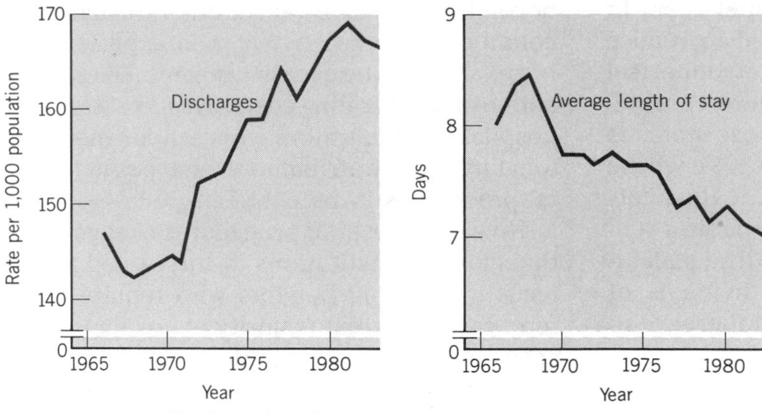

FIGURE 10.1 Yearly United States hospital utilization from 1966 to 1983, as indicated by patient discharge rate and length of stay at non-Federal "short-stay" hospitals. (From USDHHS, 1985b, Figure 30.)

sick-role experience. Hospitalization drastically disrupts the individual's lifestyle, involves a high degree of dependency on others, and presents many events that can be extremely distressing. The unpleasantness may begin at admission, such as when a clerk asks questions about the patient's ability to pay for the medical services the hospital will provide. As this example suggests, part of the unpleasantness of being hospitalized relates to the interactions between the patient and the hospital staff.

Relations with the Hospital Staff

When patients enter the hospital, they typically do so with a clear social role—that of being dependent for their very lives on the medical staff who have most of the knowledge, authority, and power in their relationship (Rodin & Janis, 1979; Taylor, 1979). The patient is a stranger in the hospital community and is likely to be unfamiliar with its structure, procedures, and terminology. These conditions often make the patient feel uneasy in an already worrisome situation.

Anxiety is probably the most common and pervasive emotion of hospitalized patients (Newman, 1984a). If their health problem has not yet been diagnosed, they worry about what the problem is, what the prognosis will be, and how the illness will influence their lives. If the diagnosis has been made, they worry about many things, such as what the treatment will be like and the degree to which it will be successful. Many of the worries patients have stem from uncertainties that result from a lack of information. Although the lack of information may occur because tests have not yet been completed, frequently it occurs because no one has taken the time to inform the patient. One hospital patient, for example, gave the following description of experiences with a physician:

> He'll say well, we'll talk about it next time. And next time he'll talk fast, he out-talks you—and rushes out of the room and then when he's out of the room you think, well, I was supposed to ask him what he's going to do about my medicine . . . you run in the hall and he has disappeared that fast. (Tagliacozzo & Mauksch, 1972, p. 177)

Hospitals are busy places, but the limited time of medical personnel is only one reason for their failure to provide the information patients may need. Practitioners sometimes withhold information or disguise it with jargon because they expect that the patient will misunderstand it or be alarmed by it (McKinlay, 1975).

Many patients react to not being informed by their doctors by gathering information from other patients, asking orderlies and nurses, and eavesdropping. As one patient put it:

> Well, I ask the nurses about the blood pressure and if they don't tell me, I go to my chart and look at it. It's six of one and half-a-dozen of the other. When the doctor comes by, I listen to him. I get some information from him when he's speaking about me to the students, although he doesn't know he's giving it to me. (McKinlay, 1975, p. 9)

People are resourceful, but it seems fairly likely that the information patients receive in these indirect ways will be incorrect or misleading. The resulting beliefs these patients develop may impair compliance with the advice of the medical staff or lead to unnecessary emotional suffering. Thus, withholding information may produce, rather than prevent, misunderstandings and alarm in patients.

Another common characteristic of the way practitioners interact with patients is called **depersonalization**, or treating the patient as though he or she were either not present or not a person. Sociologist Erving Goffman referred to this characteristic as "non-person treatment" and described the practitioner's behavior in the following way: "the patient is greeted with what passes as civility, and said farewell to in the same fashion, with everything in between going on as if the patient weren't there as a person at all, but only as a possession someone has left behind" (1961, pp. 341–342). A psychologist has described the following example of depersonalization from his own experience as a patient:

> Recently when I was being given emergency treatment for an eye laceration, the resident surgeon abruptly terminated his conversation with me as soon as I lay down on the operating table. Although I had no sedative, or anesthesia, he acted as if I were no longer conscious, directing all his questions to a friend of mine —questions such as, What's his name?, What occupation is he in? . . . As I lay there, these two men were speaking about me as if I were not there at all. The moment I got off the table and was no longer a cut to be stitched, the surgeon resumed his conversation with me, and existence was conferred upon me again. (Zimbardo, 1970, p. 298)

Why do practitioners treat patients as nonpersons? One reason, according to Goffman (1961), is that nonperson treatment helps practitioners deal with the fact that the body they are working on is attached to a thinking and worried patient—a person who can observe what is going on, ask questions, and behave in ways that can interfere with their work. He contrasted this situation with that of mechanics who repair a car or appliance in a shop without the owner present. The implication of Goffman's view is that medical workers try to save themselves and the patient a lot of trouble, awkwardness, and anxiety by acting as if the person had dropped off the defective body at the hospital for repair and would pick it up when it was ready.

There are also many emotional factors that lead hospital workers to treat patients in a depersonalized manner. Hospital jobs can be very hectic, particularly when many emergencies punctuate the day. Furthermore, practitioners' jobs entail heavy responsibilities and, sometimes, risks to their own health, as when they work with hazardous chemicals or patients with serious contagious illnesses (Clever & Omenn, 1988; O'Donnell et al., 1987). Quite literally, the activities and decisions of hospital workers have life-or-death implications for their patients and themselves. These features can create high levels of stress, which may lead workers to give less personalized care. Sometimes practitioners who are under prolonged stress may even begin to blame patients for their health problems, thinking, for instance, "You wouldn't have this illness if you had taken care of yourself and not smoked" (Maslach & Jackson, 1982). Lastly practitioners need ways to protect themselves emotionally when patients take a turn for the worse or die (Benoliel, 1977; Kneut, 1982). The death of a patient can be a crushing experience. Depersonalization probably helps practitioners be relatively de-

HIGHLIGHT 10A: On Research
Burnout among Health Care Professionals

Hour after hour, day after day, people who work with people who are suffering and distressed must cope with the stress these encounters produce. All jobs have stressful conditions of some kind, such as heavy work loads, deadlines, and interpersonal conflicts. But workers in certain professions — for example, police work, social work, and health care — have the added emotional burden of working continuously in emotionally charged situations that involve feelings of anxiety, fear, embarrassment, and hostility. This burden makes the risk of "burnout" greater in these professions than in most others. **Burnout** is an "erosion of the human spirit" that results from chronic exposure to high levels of occupational stress (Baron, 1986). Workers who experience burnout tend to show low levels of job satisfaction and high levels of absenteeism, job turnover, and alcohol and drug abuse.

What psychological characteristics contribute to the erosion of the human spirit of burned-out workers? Christina Maslach and Susan Jackson (1982) have developed the Maslach Burnout Inventory (MBI) and used it to study burnout among health care workers. This instrument assesses three psychosocial components of burnout:

1. *Emotional exhaustion*—the feeling of being drained of emotional resources and being unable to help others on a psychological level. People who feel this way are likely to agree with the MBI item, "Working with people all day is really a strain for me."
2. *Depersonalization*—a lack of personal regard for others, as shown by treating people as objects, having little concern for and sensitivity to their needs, and developing callous attitudes toward them. Workers with this characteristic tend to agree with the statement, "I worry that this job is hardening me emotionally."
3. *Perceived inadequacy of professional accomplishment*—the feeling of falling short of personal expectations for work performance. Workers who feel this way are likely to *disagree* with the MBI item, "I feel I'm positively influencing other people's lives through my work."

Maslach and Jackson administered the MBI to a large sample of workers in a variety of helping professions and to separate samples of nurses and physicians.

This research produced several important findings. First, the nurses, physicians, and workers in various helping professions reported fairly similar, high levels of emotional exhaustion. Second, some differences were found among the three occupations for the two other components of burnout. Specifically, of the occupational groups, the nurses showed the lowest degree of depersonalization and the physicians reported the least dissatisfaction with their sense of accomplishment in their work. The researchers suggested that the low degree of depersonalization among nurses may reflect a sex difference in empathy toward people since the females consistently showed less depersonalization than the males in the helping professions sample, and almost all the nurses but few of the physicians were females. The relatively high sense of accomplishment among doctors may be the result of such factors as their higher pay and status in the medical staff hierarchy. Finally, Maslach and Jackson found that the more time health care workers spent in direct care of patients, the greater was their risk of emotional exhaustion. For instance, physicians who spent almost all their time in direct care reported greater emotional exhaustion than those who spent some of their time in teaching or administrative duties.

What can hospitals do to help health care workers avoid or cope with burnout? We can describe two ways (Baron, 1986; Maslach & Jackson, 1982). First, hospitals can provide opportunities for workers to mix direct care for patients and other tasks in their daily activities whenever possible. Second, hospitals can help establish support groups for their health care workers. Meetings of these groups can provide opportunities for workers to share the difficulties they are experiencing and help each other cope.

tached and less emotionally affected when death occurs.

Of course, the relations between patients and practitioners in the hospital are not only affected by the behavior of the medical staff, but by the patient's behavior, too. As we are about to see, patients differ in their adjustment to the hospital environment and the way they behave there, and this can affect their interactions with the staff and the care they receive.

Sick-Role Behavior in the Hospital

Being hospitalized complicates patients' psychosocial transition to the sick role (Kasl & Cobb, 1966b). For many patients, the unfamiliar and strange environment of a hospital requires psychological and social adjustments that are difficult to make. They must get used to a lack of privacy, strict rules and time schedules, having their activities restricted, having little control over events around them, and being dependent on others. How are patients supposed to behave in the hospital?

When patients enter the hospital, they have ideas about how they should behave. Judith Lorber (1975) studied these ideas and the sick-role behavior of over 100 patients who entered a hospital for elective surgery. The large majority of these subjects were over 40 years of age; they were selected to represent patients having surgeries ranging from routine, to moderately serious, to very serious. Lorber interviewed the patients at the beginning of their hospital stay, asking them to indicate their degree of agreement or disagreement with several statements, such as: "The best thing to do in the hospital is to keep quiet and do what you're told," "I cooperate best as a patient when I know the reason for what I have to do," and "When I'm sick, I expect to be pampered and catered to." The patients' responses to such items indicated whether they thought patients should be *active* or *passive*. Subjects' agreement with the first of these items and disagreement with the second two, for example, would indicate that they believe patients should be passive, or "conforming."

One purpose of this study was to determine whether patients' ideas about the sick role are related to their behavior in the hospital. To assess the patients' behavior during their stay in the hospital, Lorber interviewed them just before they were discharged. As expected, patients' sick-role beliefs predicted their reported hospital behavior. Thus, for example, patients who had passive beliefs when they entered were less likely than those with active beliefs to argue with the staff and complain about minor discomforts.

Another purpose of this study was to examine the reactions of the medical staff to the patients' sick-role behaviors. At the end of each patient's stay, the medical staff rated the individual as a "good patient," "average patient," or "problem patient." They were also asked to provide verbal descriptions of the patient's behavior and their reactions when the behavior occurred. In general, the individuals rated as *good patients* were those who were cooperative, uncomplaining, and stoical; those rated as *problem patients* were seen as uncooperative, constantly complaining, overemotional, and dependent. One example of a problem patient was a 74-year-old man who had his gallbladder removed and had postoperative psychological and medical complications. He

> was labeled a problem patient by the surgeon, resident, intern, and day staff nurse. In the questionnaire, the resident said the patient's uncooperativeness made it difficult to perform routine procedures on him. The surgeon wrote that the patient was "lachrymose, combative, and generally impossible" . . . the surgeon added that the patient had called him names, lied, and generally carried on. (Lorber, 1975, p. 218)

But the opposite behavior of patients—being overly passive or "too considerate"—can present problems, too. One very sick patient "didn't want to bother" the nurses, even when she should have. As a result, the nurses' routines were disrupted by having to check on her status very frequently to make sure she was all right.

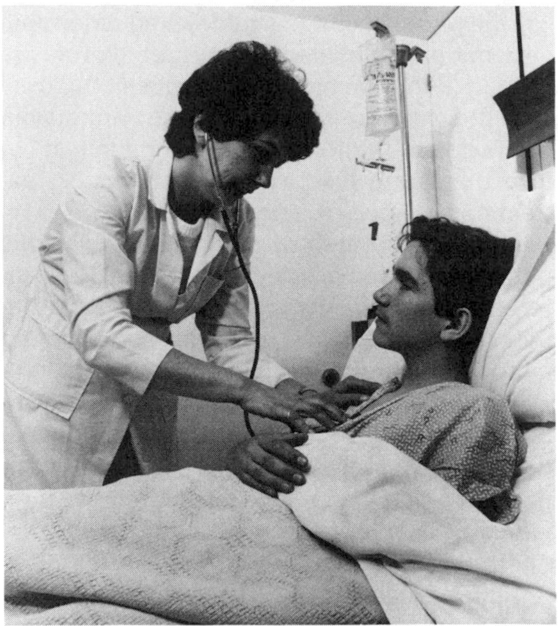

"Good patients" are cooperative, calm, and attentive in discussions with medical staff.

For some problem patients, their difficult behavior is understandable because of their severe medical condition. The staff recognized this and distinguished between two types of problem patients. One type consists of patients who are very seriously ill, having severe complications or a poor prognosis. Although these patients show problem behaviors and require a lot of attention, the staff often "forgives" their behavior because of their medical condition. The second type consists of patients who are not seriously ill but take up more time and attention than is warranted by their condition—they frequently argue, complain, or fail to cooperate with the staff. Why do patients who are not seriously ill behave so disruptively? One possibility is that this behavior is their reaction to being angry at their loss of freedoms and control (Taylor, 1979). For instance, a patient may not be allowed to walk for a while because of a leg injury, or watch television late because it would disturb other patients, or have visitors at certain times because their presence might make the work of the medical staff more difficult. People's angry response to being controlled or believing their freedom is threatened is called **reactance** (Brehm, 1966).

Psychologist Shelley Taylor has described how hospital patients sometimes show reactance in their

> petty acts of mutiny such as making passes at nurses, drinking in one's room, smoking against medical advice, and wandering up and down the halls. Such minor incidents tend to irritate nursing and custodial staff, but rarely do any damage. However, petty acts of mutiny can turn into self-sabotage, such as failing to take medications which are essential to recovery, or engaging in acts which have potentially fatal consequences. Coupled with these mutinous acts against the hospital routine and treatment regimen are frequent demands upon the staff for attention, treatment, and medication, and frequent complaints regarding the quality of same. (1979, p. 172)

How does the hospital staff deal with problem patients? In many cases, hospital workers respond in a pleasant manner, for example, by providing reassurance or explanations (Lorber, 1975). In other cases, the response is not so positive. Staff members sometimes scold patients, or begin to "tune out" or ignore their problem behavior, or respond less quickly to their calls for attention. In addition, hospital personnel often deal with problem patients by administering sedatives and, in highly problematic cases, even by arranging for premature discharge.

Fortunately, the large majority of patients are not problem patients (Lorber, 1975). Most patients try to be considerate, recognizing that medical workers have difficult jobs. One patient compared being in a hospital with being at a hotel:

> If it is a hotel you won't hesitate to pick up a phone or to complain; in a hospital you think twice about it—you figure maybe they are busy or shorthanded. . . . It's a much more human thing, the hospital . . . it's more personal. (Tagliacozzo & Mauksch, 1972, p. 175)

Others behave as "good patients" because they are wary of the consequences of being disliked by the staff. These patients do not want to appear to be "troublemakers," by being too demanding or too dependent. They may think that an angered staff may "refuse to answer your bell" or "refuse to make your bed," for instance. As a result, these patients may anxiously watch the clock when their medication does not arrive on time, rather than reminding the nurse (Tagliacozzo & Mauksch, 1972).

The sick-role behavior of hospitalized patients is affected by many factors in addition to the seriousness of their illness, their ideas about how they should behave, and their reaction to their restricted freedoms. As we have seen before, social interactions in a medical setting involve a "two-way street" in which both the patient's and the practitioner's behavior are important. Patients respond differently to medical staff who grumble or frown when asked to do something than to staff who carry out requests cheerfully and seem to want to help (Tagliacozzo & Mauksch, 1972). Finally, sick-role behavior depends on how well patients cope with their medical condition and the medical treatment procedures they experience in the hospital.

EMOTIONAL ADJUSTMENT IN THE HOSPITAL

Being hospitalized with a serious illness or painful injury produces enormous stress and anxiety to which the patients must adjust, and they generally do so gradually. For example, most surgical patients experience anxiety levels that are especially high when they are admitted, remain quite high prior to the operation, and then decline steadily during the week or two after surgery (Newman, 1984a). But sometimes the anxiety levels of patients increase with time, as happened with a 25-year-old man who had suffered serious burns over 30% of his body:

> In his third postburn week he became increasingly uncooperative and demanding. He complained of pain despite adequate analgesia, to the point that he would not let anyone near him for dressing changes. . . . The staff reacted angrily to his conduct, which in turn led to a perpetuation and increase in his complaints and demands. In a series of brief interviews the motivation for his conduct was elucidated. He had a very exaggerated view of the nature of his injury, expecting it would render him a cripple for life and unable to support himself or him family. He feared discharge and the subsequent demands of his family. (Steiner & Clark, 1977, p. 138)

The way patients adjust to their health problem and treatment in the hospital depends on a wide variety of factors, such as their age and gender and characteristics of the illness or injury (Moos, 1982). For instance, young adults often have a more difficult time coping with serious illness than older individuals do. Also, men tend to be more distressed than women by illnesses that reduce their vigor and physical abilities, but women often have an especially difficult time adjusting to a facial injury or the loss of a breast.

Coping Processes in Hospital Patients

In Chapter 5, we noted that people with stress and anxiety use coping processes to achieve two main goals: to alter the problem causing the stress or to regulate the emotional response to the problem. Some of the situations that produce stress in the hospital can be altered by the patient's taking action, such as by asking for medication to reduce pain or by reading information about recovery from his or her health problem. Because these actions can reduce the demands of the stressor or expand the patient's resources for dealing with it, they are examples of *problem-focused coping.*

Patients in the hospital experience many stressors they believe they cannot change. In some cases these beliefs are correct, as when a patient whose spinal cord was severed in an accident must cope with not being able to walk; but in other cases they are incorrect, as when a patient does not realize that alternate medications can be used if a drug produces discomfort or other side effects. People who believe they can do nothing to change the stressful conditions usually try to cope by regulating their emotional response to the situation, using methods classified as *emotion-focused coping*. One way patients may try to regulate their emotions is by engaging in certain behaviors, such as seeking social support or performing a distracting activity. Research has consistently shown that social support aids patients' recovery from and adjustment to illness (Wallston, Alagna, DeVellis, & DeVellis, 1983). Patients also try to control their emotions by using cognitive processes to change the way they think about their situation, such as by denying unpleasant facts.

One cognitive process many patients engage in after becoming ill or injured is attributing *blame*—trying to answer the question, "Who's at fault for my condition?" They often grapple with this issue while in the hospital. Some patients blame mainly themselves, others blame someone else, and others attribute their condition to "luck" or "God's will." Does the way people attribute blame affect their success in coping with their condition? We might expect, for instance, that people who blame themselves would have intense feelings of guilt and self-recrimination and, therefore, have more difficulty adjusting to their condition than those who blame someone else. On the other hand, blaming someone else may induce intense feelings of anger and bitterness, which would impair adjustment. Research has examined this issue and found that the more blame for their condition that patients attribute to other people, the poorer their adjustment tends to be (Bulman & Wortman, 1977; Taylor, Lichtman, & Wood, 1984). Although it is unclear why adjustment is so difficult when patients blame someone else, the reason may be that these people feel an added sense of injustice if the person they blame did not suffer severe consequences, too. These feelings are reflected in such statements as, "I'm paralyzed, but the driver only broke his leg" or "I can't walk now, but the guy who shot me is now walking free" (Bulman & Wortman, 1977, p. 360).

But the relation between *self-blame* and adjustment is unclear. One study found that self-blame was associated with good adjustment (Bulman & Wortman, 1977), another found it was associated with poor adjustment (Kiecolt-Glaser & Williams, 1987), and another found no relationship between self-blame and adjustment (Taylor, Lichtman, & Wood, 1984). The influence of self-blame on adjustment may depend on the type or seriousness of the patient's illness or injury, whether adjustment is assessed early or late in the coping process, or on the person's age, gender, or background. The studies of self-blame differed in all these ways. Furthermore, the cognitive processes people use in ascribing blame can be quite convoluted, as in

> a case in which a young man bought gasoline from a service station owned by his father-in-law. He used the gasoline to set himself on fire at the service station. He attributed all the blame for the incident to his father-in-law, saying he acted as he did because his father-in-law had said disparaging things about him. (Kiecolt-Glaser & Williams, 1987, p. 191)

This example raises a question for researchers: Should reasonable and unreasonable attributions of blame be examined separately for their relation to adjustment? Lastly, we must keep in mind that all this research on the role of blame has been correlational. Thus, it may be that variations in both blame and adjustment are caused by some other factor.

Another cognitive process that patients engage in involves the assessment of their personal control. Patients enter the hospital with the expectation of losing some degree of personal control, either from the effects of the illness itself or from being dependent on the actions of the medical staff. Hospital environments encourage patients to believe that their involvement in the treatment process is irrelevant—that they are *helpless*. Patients often express this feeling, saying "when you are really sick, you are at the mercy of the hospital staff" or "trying to change things is futile and won't get you anywhere" (Tagliacozzo & Mauksch, 1972). Those patients who feel this way are likely to behave like "good patients" (Taylor, 1979). Some patients enter the hospital feeling quite helpless right from the start, but others try to exert control and sometimes show angry reactance behavior when these efforts fail. Through repeated failures in exerting control, many patients learn to be helpless in the hospital, eventually making no effort to initiate changes when control is actually possible. One study found, for instance, that patients' helplessness and feelings of depression increased with time in the hospital, even as their health improved (Raps, Peterson, Jonas, & Seligman, 1982).

The connection between "good patient" behavior, helplessness, and depression can be seen in the case of a 50-year-old divorced man who had suffered burns over 40% of his body. When he returned to the hospital six months later for a follow-up visit, his hands were still stiff and he was having many psychological problems. He had

> moved in with his daughter and her husband in hopes that he would be able to take care of repair work that needed doing around the house. When it became clear that he was not able to do any of these things to his satisfaction, he became increasingly depressed. His depression persisted despite the fact that his daughter and her husband remained very supportive and accepting of him and sought to alleviate his distress in many ways. . . . On reviewing his case it turned out that he had indeed been a very "good" patient, quiet and cooperative. He never asked any questions about the details or the implications of his illness. (Steiner & Clark, 1977, p. 139)

This case is consistent with Taylor's (1979, p. 171) view that "the so-called 'good patient' is often actually in a state of helplessness," which may eventually lead to feelings of depression.

One circumstance in the hospital that seems to help patients adjust to their illness and impending treatment is sharing a room with a patient who is recovering after undergoing a similar medical procedure. James Kulik and Heike Mahler (1987a) conducted an experiment with patients who began their stay in the hospital two days before having an operation. All the subjects were men, 46 to 69 years of age, who were scheduled for coronary bypass surgery. Upon admission, each subject was assigned a roommate, based on room availability, for the two days prior to surgery. About half of the men shared a room with a patient who was also awaiting an operation, and the remaining subjects shared a room with a patient who already had an operation and was recovering. Assessments were made of the subjects' anxiety the evening before their surgery, physical activity during the week after the operation, and speed of recovery. The results revealed beneficial effects for surgical patients who had a roommate who was recovering from surgery: Compared to the other subjects, those with a roommate who had already undergone surgery were far less anxious before their operation, engaged in much more physical activity after surgery, and were able to leave the hospital an average of 1.4 days sooner.

Although patients entering a hospital for surgery typically prefer having a roommate who is already recovering from an operation, they rarely have a choice in the matter (Kulik & Mahler, 1987a). The logistics of admissions procedures would make it extremely difficult to honor such requests. In addition, more research is needed on this issue before recommending that hospitals seek ways to match presurgery patients with recovering patients. This approach seems to have promise in helping patients cope with stressful medical procedures.

Preparing Patients for Stressful Medical Procedures

Preparing patients psychologically for surgery has important implications for their recovery. As we discussed in Chapter 5, the more anxiety patients feel before surgery, the more difficult their adjustment and recovery are likely to be after the operation. Thus, patients with high preoperative anxiety tend to report more pain, use more medication for pain, stay in the hospital longer, and report more anxiety and depression during their recovery than patients with less preoperative fear (Anderson & Masur, 1983; Johnson, 1983). This knowledge led researchers to find ways to reduce the stress patients experience in conjunction with medical procedures.

Psychological Preparation for Surgery

Although several methods seem to be useful in helping people cope with impending surgery, the most effective of these approaches are those that enhance patients' sense of *control* over the situation or the recovery process (Anderson & Masur, 1983; Mathews & Ridgeway, 1984; Thompson, 1981). These approaches are generally designed to give the patient one or more of the following types of control:

- *Behavioral control*—being able to reduce discomfort or promote recovery during or after the medical procedure by performing certain actions, such as special breathing or coughing exercises.
- *Cognitive control*—knowing how to focus on the benefits of the medical procedure and not its unpleasant aspects.
- *Informational control*—gaining knowledge about the events and/or sensations to expect during or after the medical procedure.

Patients can acquire the knowledge for these types of control in many ways, such as through discussion with practitioners, reading, listening to tape recordings, or watching film or video recordings.

An example of an approach to enhance *cognitive control* comes from an experiment with patients who were in the hospital to undergo major elective surgery (Langer, Janis, & Wolfer, 1975). The types of surgery the patients were scheduled to have, for example, hernia repairs and hysterectomies, typically have favorable prognoses. The researchers assigned the subjects to groups on a random basis, but also tried to equate the groups for several characteristics, such as age, sex, and seriousness of the operation. One of the groups received training in cognitive control. Through instruction and discussion with a psychologist, these patients learned how paying attention to negative aspects of an experience increases stress but focusing on positive thoughts decreases it. They generated examples of these effects from their everyday lives, discussed what the positive aspects of their impending surgery would be, and were asked to think about these positive aspects when feeling distressed by the surgical experience. A comparison (control) group spent an equal amount of time with the psychologist, but they only engaged in general conversation about the hospital experience. To evaluate the effects of the psychological preparation, nurses on the surgical ward rated the stress behavior of the subjects in the different groups before and after the surgery and kept track of the patients' requests for pain relievers and sedatives. These data revealed important benefits of training in cognitive control: the patients who received this training showed greater reductions in preoperative stress behavior, less postoperative stress, and fewer requests for medication after surgery than the subjects in the comparison group.

Several other studies have demonstrated beneficial effects of enhancing surgical patients' *informational* and *behavioral control* (Anderson, 1987; Andrew, 1970; Felton, Huss, Payne, & Srsic, 1976; Johnson, Rice, Fuller, & Endress, 1978; Vernon & Bigelow, 1974). One experiment was conducted by Erling Anderson with 60 adult male cardiac patients who were scheduled for coronary bypass surgery. The researcher randomly assigned the subjects to three groups. One group had a general conversation with the researcher and received the *standard preparation* of the hospital, in which the patient and a nurse discussed two pamphlets that outlined the procedures related to the upcoming surgery. A second group received the standard preparation plus training to enhance *informational control*, which delivered procedural and sensory information in two ways: the patients (1) watched a videotape called "Living Proof," which presents interviews with recovered bypass patients and follows a patient from admission through various preoperative tests and exercises, preparation for surgery, recovery, and discharge; and (2) they were given an audiotape, describing sensations they might experience, that they could play in their rooms. The third group received training in both *informational and behavioral control.* These subjects had the same preoperative training as the informational control group, but were also taught how to perform various behaviors, such as coughing exercises and ways to turn in bed, that they would need to do after the operation.

Anderson used a variety of measures to assess the effects of these methods of psychological preparation on the patients' adjustment and recovery. For example, the patients filled out a questionnaire (the State-Trait Anxiety Inventory) to measure their distress at three times: when they were admitted, the evening before surgery, and one week after the operation. As Figure 10.2 depicts, the subjects' anxiety levels in the three groups were almost identical on admission, but then diverged after the different preparation methods were conducted. Both types of psychological preparation reduced the patients' anxiety substantially before and after the operation. Assessments were also made of the patients' use of pain medication and length of stay in the hospital, but the three groups did not differ on these measures. Finally, the patients' blood pressures were monitored closely because dangerous levels of acute hypertension occur very commonly during the first 12 hours following bypass surgery. For this critical measure, psychological preparation had a very beneficial effect. Of the patients who received the standard preparation, 75% developed acute hypertension and required medication to dilate their blood vessels. In contrast, only 45% of patients in the informational control group and 40% of those in the informational and behavioral control group had an episode of acute hypertension.

The studies we have examined clearly demonstrate the value of psychological preparations that increase patients' sense of control when awaiting an operation. One thing to keep in mind about providing information to patients about medical procedures is that unclear information can lead to misconceptions and anxiety and be more harmful than good (Wallace, 1986). Patients need to receive straightforward and clear materials and instructions, and they need to discuss this information with medical practitioners. Of course, surgery is only one of many types of stressful medical procedures that may occur in the hospital, and patients often dread experiencing each of them.

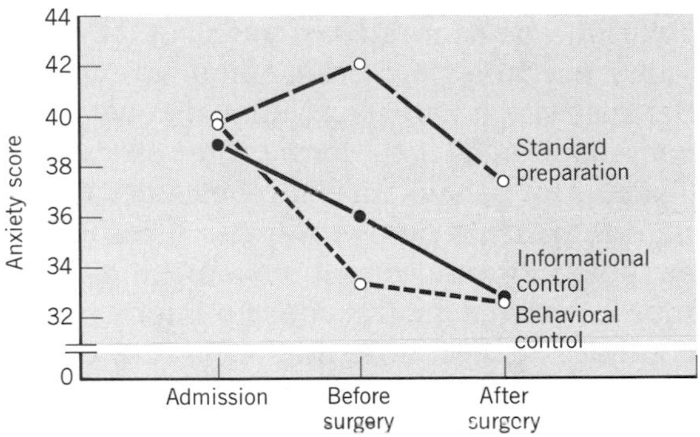

FIGURE 10.2 Anxiety levels of cardiac surgery patients as a function of the psychological preparation they received. Anxiety was measured by the State-Trait Anxiety Inventory at three times: on admission, the evening before surgery, and one week after the operation. (Adapted from Anderson, 1987, Figure 1.)

Psychological Preparations for Nonsurgical Procedures

How would you like to be awake while a physician inserts a thin, hollow tube called a *catheter* into one of your blood vessels, gently threads it toward your heart, and then injects dye through the catheter? This is a procedure called *cardiac catheterization,* which is used with patients who show signs of cardiovascular disorders, such as damage to a major blood vessel or heart valve. The dye enables practitioners to see the damage with the aid of X-ray or other radiological devices. By using this procedure, physicians can determine whether to recommend other medical procedures, such as bypass or open-heart surgery. Patients undergoing cardiac catheterization receive tranquilizing medication and a local anesthetic for the area where the tube enters the body. Although this procedure is not painful, it is quite unpleasant and produces strange and frightening sensations, such as "hot flashes" when dye is injected into the heart.

How might patients and hospital staff benefit by the use of psychological preparations for patients undergoing cardiac catheterization? Preparing them for unpleasant medical procedures should help to reduce patients' anxiety and disruptive behavior during the procedures, for example, and their general level of stress prior to surgery. Philip Kendall and his associates (1979) examined the effects of psychological preparation for cardiac catheterization on the anxiety experienced by male patients, about two-thirds of whom had undergone the procedure at least a year earlier. The subjects were randomly assigned to four groups. One group received training in *cognitive control* methods from a therapist, learning how to recognize signs of their own anxiety and ways to cope when these signs occur. Another group received preparation to enhance their *informational control*, learning about the procedures and sensations to expect through printed materials and a discussion with a therapist.

Two other groups served as comparison (control) conditions. In one of these conditions, subjects received only a general conversation with a therapist. If a patient asked questions about the catheterization procedure, he was told that his cardiologist could answer these questions. Subjects in the other comparison condition received the standard hospital preparation, consisting of "a brief description of the catheterization provided by the cardiologist during rounds and the courteous reassurances of the physicians and nurses involved in the catheterization procedure." The anxiety of the patients in each of the four groups was assessed by having (1) the subjects fill out a questionnaire called the State-Trait Anxiety Inventory before the catheterization, (2) the physicians and other hospital workers rate the tension and behavior each subject showed during the procedure, and (3) the patients fill out a modified form of the anxiety inventory after the procedure to describe their anxiety during it. Analyses of these three measures showed that both the cognitive and the informational control preparations effectively reduced patients' anxiety; subjects who received these preparations experienced less anxiety than those in the two comparison groups before and during catheterization.

As you may have surmised, the catheterization procedure requires that the patient be inactive. There are no actions the patient can take to make the process occur more smoothly or pleasantly—that is, the patient has little or no behavioral control. This is true of many but not all aversive medical procedures. One medical procedure in which patients can perform useful actions is called an *endoscopy*, which is used in diagnosing ulcers and other disorders of the digestive tract. The most aversive aspect of an endoscopic examination is that a long, flexible, fiber-optic tube, almost half an inch in diameter, must be passed through the patient's mouth and down to the stomach and intestine. This tube remains in the digestive tract, transmitting images of the lining, for about 15 to 30 minutes. During this procedure, the patient is awake, but has received tranquilizing medication and the throat has been swabbed with a local anesthetic.

In an experiment with patients who had never undergone an endoscopy before, Jean Johnson and Howard Leventhal (1974) provided psychological preparation to enhance the behavioral and informational control the subjects could use during the procedure. Training for behavioral control included teaching the patients helpful ways to breathe and swallow while the throat is swabbed and the tube is inserted. Instructions for informational control involved descriptions of the procedures and sensations the patients could expect during the examination. Some patients received instruction for either behavioral control or informational control, some had both types of preparation, and others served as a comparison group, receiving no psychological preparation. All patients, however, received a standard

HIGHLIGHT 10B: On Issues
Lamaze Training as a Method of Psychological Preparation for a Medical Procedure

During much of the twentieth century, Americans generally accepted two ideas about childbirth: (1) the mother will experience intense and prolonged pain unless she is given tranquilizing and pain-reducing drugs, and (2) the use of drugs is best for the mother and her baby. But these beliefs have changed since the 1960s for two reasons. First, research has shown that drugs given to the mother during childbirth pass through the placenta and can harm the baby, for instance, by impairing the newborn's spontaneous breathing (Bowes, Brackbill, Conway, & Steinschneider, 1970). Second, anthropologists have reported that women in cultures where childbirth is regarded as an easy and open process have shorter and less complicated labors than women in cultures where birth is regarded as fearful and private (Mead & Newton, 1967). Could it be that part of the difficulty many American mothers have in childbirth is the result of the inadequate psychological preparation they receive?

Because of these considerations, many prospective parents opt for preparation involving "natural childbirth" methods, such as **Lamaze training**. Natural childbirth methods generally involve three components: preparation, participation, and minimal medication (Parfitt, 1977). Birth is essentially a process in which the muscles of the uterus contract in a rhythmical pattern to push the baby out. A fearful woman is likely to tighten her muscles, which then act against the natural muscular contractions and make labor more painful. A main purpose of natural childbirth methods is to prepare the woman to be more relaxed and better able to control her breathing and muscular activity to help in the process at each stage.

Margaret Wideman and Jerome Singer (1984) have analyzed Lamaze training and described the psychological mechanisms it includes. In addition to the social support women in Lamaze training get from the baby's father and the people in the training meetings, the method is designed to enhance the mother's sense of control. Lamaze training includes features that promote:

- Informational control, such as by providing descriptions of the physiological processes in birth and the procedures and sensations to expect during labor and delivery.
- Behavioral control, for example, through instruction and practice in muscle relaxation and special breathing techniques.
- Cognitive control, such as by teaching the woman to visually focus on an object in the room or to concentrate on images or phrases during the birth process.

Most obstetricians today recommend natural childbirth preparation and almost all hospitals cooperate with the medical procedures the method describes, such as having the father present (Wideman & Singer, 1984).

Is Lamaze preparation beneficial? Although the results of studies suggest that it is, the evidence is not yet very clear (Wideman & Singer, 1984). Research has found, for instance, that women who receive Lamaze training use less painkilling drugs during delivery and are less anxious about the birth procedure than those who do not; but these studies have used quasi-experimental designs and self-report methods. Part of the difficulty in interpreting these findings is that women who choose natural childbirth are different from those who do not; for example, they tend to be from higher social classes and report lower anxiety levels even before receiving the training.

---

explanation of the endoscopic procedure from a physician. The researchers found that patients in the comparison group showed much more emotional behavior and gagging during the procedure than those who received psychological preparation, particularly if this preparation included instruction for both informational and behavioral control.

In summary, psychological preparation can enhance patients' sense of control and their adjustment to nonsurgical medical procedures. Generally speaking, when these procedures offer little opportunity for the patient to take helpful action, psychological preparation to promote informational and cognitive control may be especially effective. But when patients will undergo procedures in which they can take direct action to facilitate the process and reduce their own discomfort, preparation should usually include approaches to enhance behavioral control.

Coping Styles and Psychological Preparation

People use many different styles in coping with stress, as we discussed in Chapter 5. When faced with stressful medical procedures, for instance, some individuals tend to cope by using *avoidance* strategies to minimize the impact of the situation. They may deny that a threat exists; refuse to seek or attend to threatening information, perhaps saying, "I don't want to know"; or suppress unpleasant thoughts. In contrast, other individuals tend to use *attention* or "vigilant" strategies, seeking detailed information about the situation (Newman, 1984a). Some studies have found that patients who use avoidance strategies often show better emotional adjustment to medical procedures, such as blood donation or dental surgery, than those who use attention strategies (Kaloupek, White, & Wong, 1984; Kiyak, Vitaliano, & Crinean, 1988). If this is so, how do patients who use avoidance strategies react to psychological preparations that enhance their control?

Researchers have examined this question by using approaches to enhance informational control with patients who were classified as using avoidance or attention styles. One of these studies was conducted by Suzanne Miller and Charles Mangan (1983) with women who were scheduled to undergo an unpleasant but painless diagnostic test for gynecological cancer. The subjects were classified as using avoidance or attention styles on the basis of their responses in a questionnaire. By random assignment, half of the avoidance subjects (called "blunters") and the attention subjects ("monitors") received extensive information regarding the procedures and sensations they would experience during the examination; the remaining subjects got very little information about the examination. Measures of the patients' distress were taken at three times: before receiving the information, after getting the information but before the examination, and after the examination. Figure 10.3 presents the results of this research, using the patients' pulse rates as the measure of distress. These findings indicate that monitors who receive very little information and blunters who receive extensive information react negatively to the amount of information they receive, as

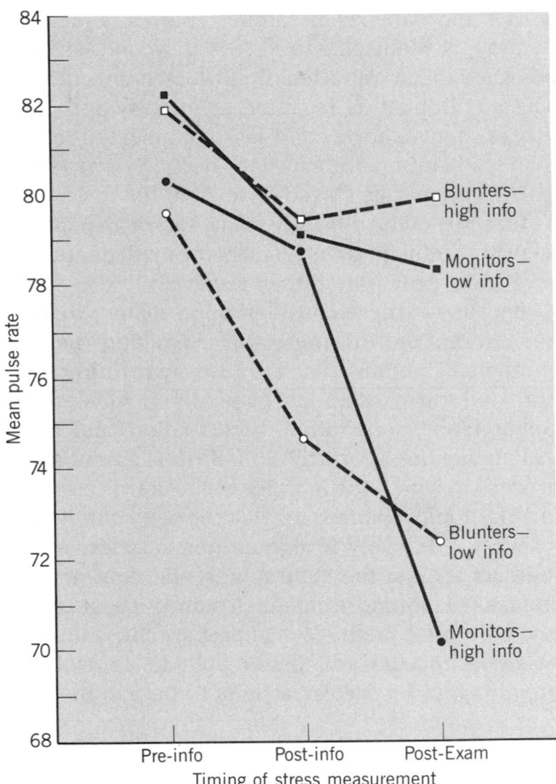

FIGURE 10.3 Effects of extensive information versus little information regarding an impending medical examination on the stress experienced by patients who use avoidance coping strategies (the "blunters") or attention strategies (the "monitors"). Pulse rate, the measure of stress, was taken for each subject at three times: before receiving the information, after the information, and after the examination. High pulse rate indicates more distress. (From Miller & Mangan, 1983, Figure 7.)

shown by their continued high pulse rates after the examination.

Although these results suggest that patients who tend to use avoidance coping strategies might be better off not receiving much information about the medical procedures they will experience, there is reason to delay reaching this conclusion. The number of times patients see the information seems to affect the amount of stress they experience. In one study, patients awaiting an endoscopic examination filled out a questionnaire that assessed their coping styles and then watched a videotape that showed the procedures and sensations they could expect during their own endoscopies (Shipley, Butt, Horwitz, & Farbry, 1978). Some patients watched the informational tape only once, and others viewed it three times. A comparison group watched an irrelevant tape. Measures of the patients' anxiety during their endoscopies included heart rate and questionnaire assessments by the patients and practitioners after the examinations. The study found that avoidance copers who saw the informational tape only once experienced more anxiety than those who saw it three times and those who watched the irrelevant tape. For the patients with attention coping strategies, those who watched the irrelevant tape experienced the most anxiety and those who viewed the informational tape three times had the least anxiety.

The benefits of psychological preparations for medical procedures seem to depend on the patients' coping styles, and it may be that different preparations are more helpful for patients using avoidance strategies than for those using attention strategies. Although being exposed to information about impending medical procedures more than once appears to help all patients, it may be particularly beneficial to patients who tend to cope by using avoidance strategies.

When the Hospitalized Patient Is a Child

Nearly 3.7 million individuals who are admitted to short-stay hospitals in the United States each year are under 15 years of age, and about 30% of these children are from 1 to 4 years old (USDHHS, 1984). We have seen that adults become distressed by pain and illness, think hospitals are big and frightening places, and become anxious when undergoing unpleasant or painful medical procedures. So do children, but their level of psychosocial development may make some aspects of the hospital experience particularly difficult for them. For one thing, children are less able than adults to influence and understand what is happening to them. Children at young ages may also feel abandoned or unloved by being without their families, and they may even believe that they were put in the hospital as punishment for misbehavior. What special adjustments do children need to make when they are hospitalized, and how well do they cope? Answers to these questions depend partly on the child's age.

Hospitalization in the Early Years of Childhood

The experience of being hospitalized is distressing for children of all ages, but the reasons for their distress tend to change as they get older (La Greca & Stone, 1985; Sarafino, 1986). For children in toddlerhood and the preschool years—who are rarely inactive when healthy—a hospital experience that involves being immobilized can be very stressful. These children may protest loudly and struggle against medically necessary devices that restrain their movement (Smith & Autman, 1985). But the most salient source of stress of young children in the hospital is being separated from their parents.

Separation distress is the normal reaction of being upset and crying that young children exhibit when they are separated from their parents, particularly in unfamiliar surroundings (Ainsworth, 1973, 1979). Late in the first year of life, most infants begin showing this reaction, even in everyday short separations of a few minutes or hours. As Figure 10.4 illustrates, the tendency of children to show distress in situations of short-term separation peaks at roughly 15 months of age. This is true of children from a wide variety of cultures around the world. After

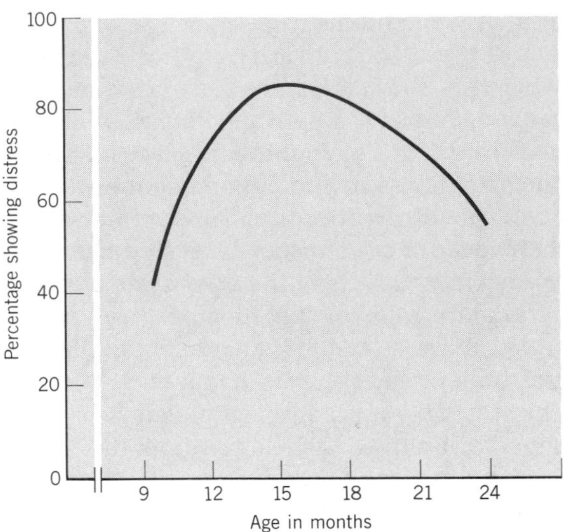

FIGURE 10.4 Illustration of children's tendency to exhibit separation distress when tested with short-term separations at different ages. (From Sarafino & Armstrong, 1986, Figure 5.3.) The graph represents approximate percentages at each age, averaged across cultures—for example, the reaction occurs in about 90% of American working-class infants and 70–80% of Guatemalan babies at 15 months (Super, 1981).

that age, the percentage of children showing distress with short-term separations declines universally (Super, 1981). But hospitalization can involve prolonged periods of separation, with little parent/child contact for days, weeks, or longer. How well do toddlers and preschool-age children cope with long-term separation?

Prolonged separation produces dramatic and, perhaps, long-lasting reactions in young children. During hospitalization, children's conduct often "regresses" sharply, reverting back to forms of behavior they may have used at younger ages. Thus, they may become less sociable and start wetting the bed and having temper tantrums again (Ramsey, 1982). John Bowlby (1969, 1973) has described the behavioral and psychological consequences that unfold during the first weeks of prolonged separation. The initial reaction is one of *protest*, in which the child displays excessive crying, calling, and searching for his or her parents, typically the mother. Following this period, the child's reaction appears to be one of *despair*, usually reflected in reduced activity, withdrawal, and feelings of hopelessness. Finally, if separation from the parents is quite long or permanent, such as if they died, the child enters the final period of *detachment*. The child appears on the surface to be "back to normal" but, if the parents return, the child seems to reject them, no longer seeking interaction or contact with them.

After a prolonged or difficult stay in the hospital, young children often display anxious behavior at home. They may continue their regressive behaviors, begin having nightmares, or become very clinging and unwilling to let their mothers out of their sight. One child named Sara, for instance, had attended nursery school and was becoming quite independent for her age before having a difficult hospital experience that included receiving 22 injections in just two days. After she returned home, she was highly anxious. Her mother reported:

> She follows me everywhere! I can't even go to the bathroom alone. She wakes up screaming five or six times at night, shaking and crying, "The nurses are giving me shots! I can't run away! They're tying me down" . . . and when I approach her, she backs away and shakes like a hurt puppy! (Ramsey, 1982, p. 332)

Sara's hospital experience was very traumatic. Subsequently, she seemed to be afraid that if she was separated from her mother, she would again be left alone and unprotected.

Preschoolers do not yet think very logically and, as a result, may have many misconceptions about their health problems and why things happen in the hospital (Eiser, 1985; Ramsey, 1982; Smith & Autman, 1985). They may, for example, believe that their illness or the treatments they receive are punishments for having been bad. These ideas probably come from two sources: (1) young children's general belief that breaking rules leads to inevitable punishment and (2) adults' statements that link disobedience with getting sick or injured—such statements as, "You'll catch cold if you don't wear your coat," "You'll fall and hurt yourself if you climb trees," or "You'll get an upset stomach if you eat too much candy." Some adults even threaten children with going to the doctor or having an operation if they continue to disobey (Eiser, 1985). In the hospital, young children sometimes become worried by seeing other patients with disfigurements, such as an amputation or extensive scars. These children may think that one of these conditions may happen to themselves in the hospital.

Hospitalized School-Age Children

Advances in school-age children's psychosocial development enable them to cope with some aspects of hospitalization better than younger patients can. For instance, although prolonged separation from their parents can be difficult for older children, they can usually tolerate it more easily than preschoolers can. The cognitive ability of school-age children progresses rapidly, but they sometimes retain earlier misconceptions about their illness or develop new ones. An older child's incorrect ideas can be seen in the following report by a nursing student:

> My patient, a 10-year-old hemophiliac, seemed to know everything about his disease. When I asked him what happened when he bled, he said, "Oh . . . there's a hemophiliac bug eating his way in and out of my blood vessels, and that's what makes me bleed." And when asked what caused his disease, he answered, "Well, it's 'cause I ate too much candy after my mom told me not to." (Ramsey, 1982, pp. 335–336).

Clearly, the idea that illness is a punishment can continue long after early childhood.

Four aspects of hospitalization seem to become increasingly difficult for children as they get older (Ramsey, 1982; Smith & Autman, 1985). One aspect relates to their feelings of personal control. As children get older and their greater cognitive and social abilities strengthen their sense of control, the limited independence and influence they experience in the hospital may become very irritating and distressing. Second, the increased cognitive abilities of school-age children allow them to think about and worry about the outcomes of their illness or treatment, such as whether they will be physically harmed or even die. Third, being away from friends and schoolmates can lead to feelings of loneliness, boredom, and concern about losing friends or status in their social groups. Fourth, as children get older—particularly when they are entering puberty—they tend to become more embarrassed by exposing their bodies to strangers or needing help with "private" activities, such as toileting.

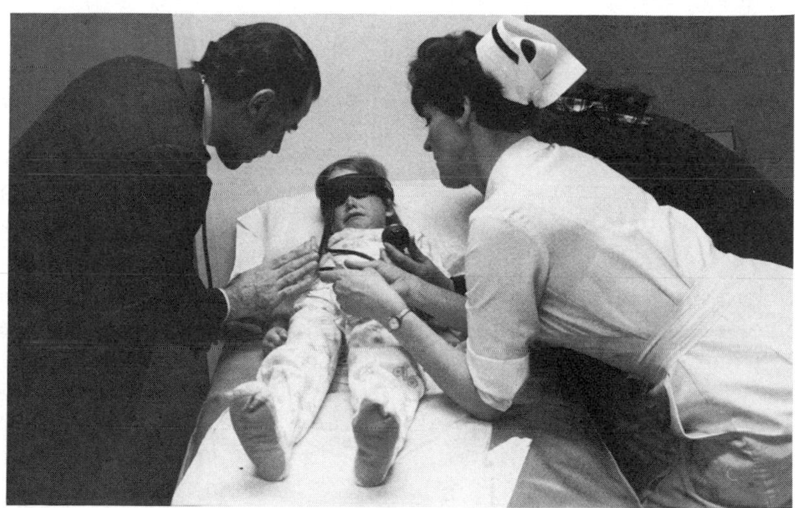

Medical procedures and equipment are often very frightening to young children.

Helping Children Cope with Being Hospitalized

Studies conducted in the 1950s revealed that most children who were hospitalized were very poorly prepared for the experience (Eiser, 1985). Perhaps three-fourths of them, for instance, were either told nothing about why they were there, or received only vague reasons, or learned why by overhearing others' conversations. This situation has changed since then, and today children are much better prepared for stays in the hospital (La Greca & Stone, 1985).

Ideally, psychological preparation should begin before the child enters the hospital, if at all possible. Research has shown that children cope better with medical procedures if their parents give them information about their illness and treatment and try to allay their fears than if the parents do not (Melamed & Bush, 1985). Parents can help their child cope with an impending hospital stay in several ways (Sarafino, 1986). They can:

- Explain the reason for the stay and what it will be like.
- Give the child opportunities to ask questions, answering them carefully and in a way he or she can understand.
- Read with the child a children's book that describes a child's hospital experience.
- Take the child to the hospital and explain some of the hospital routines, such as what to do about going to the bathroom and how he or she will be awakened in the morning and have breakfast in bed.
- Describe when the parents will be with the child.
- Maintain a calm and confident manner, thereby conveying the message that there is no need to be very frightened.

Parents who appear highly agitated and anxious about their child's welfare before medical treatment seem to transmit their fear and be unable to allay their child's anxiety effectively. Studies have found that children with highly anxious parents do not cope as well with medical procedures as those with parents who are relatively calm (Bush, Melamed, Sheras, & Greenbaum, 1986; Melamed & Bush, 1985).

When the child is admitted to the hospital, one or both of the parents (or another very familiar adult) should accompany and remain with the child at least until he or she is settled into the room. Many parents stay much longer, taking advantage of opportunities hospitals provide today for a parent to "room in" with the child, especially when the patient is very young or very seriously ill (Olivet, 1982). As psychologists Barbara Melamed and Joseph Bush have noted, rooming-in opportunities have spread rapidly in the United States:

> According to a survey by a parent advocacy group, Children in Hospitals, only 16% of the 54 hospitals surveyed in 1973 permitted open visiting; the rest had restrictions. Although 42% had rooming in, this option was often restricted to parents of nursing babies and critically ill, dying, or handicapped children. In 1982, however, 100% of the 80 hospitals surveyed had 24-hour visiting and rooming in. In addition, over 20% permitted parents in the anesthesia room during induction, and 30% permitted parents in the recovery room. (1985, p. 186)

Most pediatric hospitals today also provide psychological preparation for their patients (Melamed & Bush, 1985). Some of these changes have come about as a result of governmental action.

What kinds of psychological preparation do hospitals provide? Basically, four approaches have been used, all of which are designed to furnish information to the parents and/or the child (Eiser, 1985). One approach simply involves distributing leaflets to the parents to share with the child. The leaflets contain information about hospital routines and medical procedures the child is likely to experience. In another approach, hospital personnel discuss the routines and procedures with the parents and child. Often this is done at home, before admission. The third method involves using puppets in a play activity to demonstrate medical procedures, such as surgery or cardiac catheterization. This approach may be especially appropriate for preschoolers and younger school-age children. These three methods are probably the most commonly used approaches by hospitals to help children cope with medical procedures (La Greca & Stone, 1985).

The fourth approach uses a video presentation. This method was evaluated in an experiment by Barbara Melamed and Lawrence Siegel (1975) with 4- to 12-year-old children who were in the hospital for elective surgery, such as for hernias or tonsillectomies. The researchers assigned the children to two groups, matching the subjects for age, sex, race, and type of operation. One group saw a film that was relevant to having surgery, and the other group saw a film about a boy who goes on a nature trip in the country. The relevant film, entitled "Ethan Has an Operation," portrays the hospital experience of a 7-year-old boy,

> showing various events that most children encounter when hospitalized for elective surgery from the time of admission to time of discharge including the child's orientation to the hospital ward and medical personnel such as the surgeon and anesthesiologist; having a blood test and exposure to standard hospital equipment; separation from the mother; and scenes in the operating and recovery rooms. In addition to explanations of the hospital procedures provided by the medical staff, various scenes are narrated by the child, who describes his feelings and concerns. (Melamed & Siegel, 1975, p. 514)

Although Ethan exhibits visible apprehension initially, he overcomes his fear and has the operation without serious distress.

To assess the emotional adjustment of the children in the two groups the evening before surgery and at a follow-up visit about three weeks after the operation, the researchers used three types of measures: the children's hand sweating, questionnaire self-reports of fear, and ratings of their emotional behavior by trained observers. The results with all three measures revealed that the children who saw the film about Ethan's operation experienced less anxiety before and after surgery than those who saw the irrelevant film. Several studies have found similar benefits in reducing children's medical fears with video presentations (Eiser, 1985; Miller & Green, 1984). What is more, video preparations for surgery are cost-effective: A study of children in the hospital for elective surgery found that those who received a video preparation recovered more quickly than those who did not. The savings from being released from the hospital sooner amounted to several times the cost of providing the preparation (Pinto & Hollandsworth, 1989).

Although most children benefit from information about impending medical procedures presented by any of the methods we have considered, not all children do—and some are actually made *more* anxious by the preparation. Studies have shown that the effects of the preparation depend on its timing and on the child's age, coping style, and previous medical experience (Dahlquist et al., 1986; Melamed & Bush, 1985; Melamed, Dearborn, & Hermecz, 1983; Miller & Green, 1984). More specifically, children younger than age 7 or so seem to profit from information presented shortly before the medical procedure, whereas older children are more likely to benefit from information presented several days before. In addition, young children more so than older ones may be made more anxious by information if they have had prior difficult experiences with medical procedures. Also, although the evidence is slim, children who tend to use avoidance strategies to cope with stressful events probably derive less benefit from information about medical procedures than those who use attention strategies.

Hospitals and medical workers usually try to make a child's stay as pleasant as they can. Pediatric nurses, for instance, receive training in the special needs of children and ways to introduce tests and equipment in a nonthreatening manner (Ramsey, 1982). When preparing to take the child's blood pressure with a sphygmomanometer, for example, the nurse might demonstrate its use on someone else and say, "When I squeeze this ball, the thing on the arm just becomes tight, like a belt. It doesn't hurt—it just gets tight. . . . Now when I'm done, I make it get loose and take it off." Hospital pediatric wards also arrange for children to play together when possible and try to have entertainment, such as a clown show, for their patients. For most hospitalized children who have positive health outcomes today, the stress of their hospital experience tends to be temporary and does not seem to produce serious long-term emotional problems (La Greca & Stone, 1985).

Patients of all ages can have difficulty coping with hospitalization and medical procedures. Psychological interventions can help promote positive emotional adjustment among patients and reduce the psychological problems that may be associated with their medical condition.

PSYCHOLOGICAL PROBLEMS OF HOSPITALIZED PATIENTS

Some patients in hospitals have illnesses that are partly caused by psychological factors, and some patients develop psychological problems because of their illness and hospitalization. In the former case, health psychologists are interested in correcting the factors that produced the disease in order to help these patients recover and prevent recurrences of their illness. In the latter case, health psychologists try to help patients cope with their illness, treatment regimen, possible disability or deformity, and, if their condition is terminal, with their impending death.

The role of psychologists in the overall treatment program for hospitalized patients has expanded in recent years. As psychologist Theodore Millon has noted,

> psychologists are not only finding themselves increasingly accepted as members of the health team but their participation is being actively sought by physicians who have come to appreciate the significant contributions they can make to a variety of diverse problems that range from presurgical counseling to posthospital medication compliance. . . . The specialties of internal medicine—especially cardiology, gastroenterology, obstetrics and gynecology, rehabilitation and physical medicine, pediatrics, family medicine, oncology, and surgery—have been adding psychologists to their service teams at a rapid rate. Hospital-affiliated pain clinics . . . almost invariably include a psychologist as an integral therapy team member. (1982, p. 10)

In order to provide help effectively and efficiently to those patients who need and want it, psychologists try to determine the needs and problems of these individuals in several ways, such as by interviewing them, observing their behavior, or administering psychological tests.

Tests for Psychological Assessment of Medical Patients

Psychologists have developed hundreds of instruments to assess a wide variety of psychological characteristics of people, including personality traits and intellectual ability. Some instruments are particularly useful for assessing the needs and problems of medical patients. We will describe a few of these instruments.

The Minnesota Multiphasic Personality Inventory

One approach that psychological tests use for assessing the needs and problems of individuals is to ask them questions about themselves to reveal aspects of their personality. The most widely used personality test is the **Minnesota Multiphasic Personality Inventory** (MMPI), which was originally developed in the 1930s and later revised (Hathaway & McKinley, 1967). This test has the person respond in a true/false format to over 500 statements, such as "I would rather win than lose a game" and "I am worried about sex matters." The items in the test cover a great variety of topics.

Although the MMPI was developed to characterize the personalities that underlie or correspond with specific psychiatric disorders, portions of the test can supply important information about the emotional adjustment of medical patients. The instrument contains 10 scales, each of which measures a different psychiatric personality trait. Three of these scales are especially relevant toward providing psychological help for medical patients. These scales are:

- *Hypochondriasis,* which assesses people's preoccupation with and complaints about their physical health.

- *Depression,* which measures people's feelings of unhappiness, pessimism, and hopelessness.
- *Hysteria,* which assesses people's tendency to cope with problems by using avoidance strategies and developing physical symptoms.

The scores patients obtain on these scales can suggest significant issues for the therapist to explore further. For one thing, individuals who score high on these three scales are prone to developing psychophysiological disorders, such as ulcers and chronic headaches (Gilberstadt & Duker, 1965). Also, patients with serious illnesses, such as cancer or heart disease, may fail to comply with their treatment regimens because of intense feelings of depression, which might be revealed by their scores on the depression scale of the MMPI (Green, 1985).

The MMPI can be usefully applied in the psychological treatment in medical settings, but it has two important drawbacks: it takes about 1½ hours to complete and it measures many traits that are not pertinent to the treatment of most medical patients. In recent years, psychologists have developed new tests that are specifically designed to assess psychological characteristics associated with physical illness. These tests include instruments that we considered in Chapters 3 and 4, which measure people's stress and their Type A and Type B behavior patterns—two characteristics that are associated with heart disease, for instance. As we saw in Chapter 5, psychological methods can be applied effectively to reduce people's stress and modify their Type A behavior, thereby lowering their risk of heart attack. We turn now to a discussion of other psychological tests that were designed specifically for medical populations.

The Millon Behavioral Health Inventory

The **Millon Behavioral Health Inventory** (MBHI) is a self-report questionnaire that was developed to assess specific psychosocial factors and decision-making issues that are known to be relevant for medical patients (Green, 1985; Millon, Green, & Meagher, 1982). It consists of 150 true/false items that provide health care workers with information regarding the patient's:

- *Basic coping style,* or the way the patient tends to approach difficult life situations and interact with other people.
- *Psychogenic attitude,* which includes assessments of the patient's experience of stress, tendency toward helplessness and hopelessness, social support, and hypochondriacal tendencies.

The MBHI also attempts to assess the patient's reaction to his or her illness and predict difficulties with the treatment regimen.

Although the MBHI is being used in a variety of medical settings, such as in pain treatment centers and cancer units, and it should prove to be a valuable tool, more research is needed to establish its utility. Some evidence for its usefulness in medical settings has begun to appear (Gatchel et al., 1986).

The Psychosocial Adjustment to Illness Scale

Another psychological test designed specifically for use with medical patients is the **Psychosocial Adjustment to Illness Scale** (PAIS), which was developed by Leonard Derogatis (1977, 1986). The PAIS consists of just 46 items, and the patient responds to each item on a 4-point scale, such as "not at all," "mildly," "moderately," or "markedly." This test is available in two forms—one that patients can fill out on their own and one that is administered by an interviewer.

The PAIS was designed to assess seven psychosocial aspects of the patient's life, each of which is known to be associated with adjustment to medical illness. These aspects are:

- *Health care orientation,* which refers to the nature of the patient's attitudes about health care in general, views regarding health care professionals, and expectancies about his or her health problem and its treatment.
- *Vocational environment,* which reflects the impact of the health problem on such

issues as the patient's vocational performance and satisfaction.

- *Domestic environment,* which deals with the difficulties the health problem will present for the patient and his or her family in the home environment.
- *Sexual relationships,* which involves modifications in sexual activity as a result of the health problem.
- *Extended family relationships,* which reflects disruptions in relationships between the patient and family members outside of his or her immediate family.
- *Social environment,* which refers to the impact of the health problem on the patient's socializing and leisure time activities.
- *Psychological distress,* which reflects the effect of the health problem on such factors as the patient's self-esteem and feelings of depression, anxiety, and hostility.

The results of several studies appear to confirm the ability of the PAIS to measure adjustment problems accurately in patients with a variety of serious illnesses, such as kidney disease, hypertension, and cancer (Derogatis, 1986).

The Medical Compliance Incomplete Stories Test

The last psychological test we will discuss is noteworthy because of its very specific purpose: to assess the likelihood of patients with cystic fibrosis to adhere to their treatment regimen. This instrument, called the **Medical Compliance Incomplete Stories Test** (M-CIST), consists of five incomplete stories in which the focal character faces a dilemma regarding whether to follow specific medical advice. When taking this test, the patient furnishes the ending to each story in his or her own words. The therapist can then use specified criteria to evaluate the patient's responses and assign an overall score. The developers of the M-CIST have reported research indicating that patients' scores on this test correlate very strongly with their subsequent compliance (Czajkowski & Koocher, 1986, 1987).

In summary, psychologists have begun to develop instruments specifically for the purpose of assessing the psychological needs and problems of medical patients. These tests, and those yet to be developed, offer considerable promise for aiding health psychologists and other health care workers in promoting the health and adjustment of their patients.

Promoting Patients' Health and Adjustment

The first step in promoting the health and adjustment of patients in the hospital is to identify what help they need. Once this has been determined through various methods of psychological assessment, specific therapeutic techniques can be applied to address particular difficulties.

As we have seen in previous chapters, behavioral and cognitive methods have been applied with some degree of success—sometimes with great success—in a wide variety of primary, secondary, and tertiary prevention efforts. These techniques are useful in helping people improve their eating and exercise habits, stop smoking and curb their drinking, and reduce the stress and other negative emotional states they experience, for instance. Other therapeutic techniques, such as group-discussion approaches and psychotherapy, have also had some success. But all the methods developed to date still have important limitations, particularly in their continued effectiveness over long periods of time and in preventing relapse. Overcoming these limitations constitutes a major challenge for health psychologists in the future.

SUMMARY

The huge hospitals of today evolved from institutions in Europe that were established to give help to people with various needs—the sick, the poor, orphans, and even travelers who needed lodging. By the nineteenth century, hospitals became separate from poorhouses, but still provided health care only to people who were poor. Well-to-do individuals received better care at home. In the early twentieth century, hospitals gained a much better reputation and began to attract patients from all social classes.

The hospital medical staff has a typical hierarchy of authority with physicians at the top, followed by nurses and various allied health workers. Years ago, patients received care from hospital personnel who worked together as a team. Today, the great variety of hospital personnel with different specializations function more separately, which can lead to fragmented health care. Good communication among hospital personnel not only improves the treatment patients receive but can help protect patients and health care workers from potential hazards in the hospital, such as from toxic substances and nosocomial infection. The system of payment for medical care in the United States has changed since Medicare was introduced, and this has led to decreases in the length of time patients stay in the hospital.

Being hospitalized is unpleasant because of the disruptions it produces in the patients' lifestyles, the high degree of dependency patients have on others, the experience of aversive medical procedures, and the many worries patients have about their condition, treatment, and future. Many of these worries develop because patients do not always receive the information they need. Also, sometimes the treatment patients receive is characterized by depersonalization, which may result from practitioners wanting to be efficient in handling heavy work loads or to protect themselves emotionally when patients take a turn for the worse. Working in emotionally charged situations can lead to burnout among health care professionals, especially those who spend almost all of their time providing direct care to patients.

Some patients enter the hospital with the idea that the sick role involves being passive. These patients are generally described by hospital staff as "good patients," being relatively cooperative, uncomplaining, and stoical. Other patients believe they should be more active in their sick-role behavior. Some of these patients are described as "problem patients," showing little cooperation, voicing many complaints, and being very dependent and emotional. When problem patients are very seriously ill, their difficult behavior is usually understandable to the medical staff. But other problem patients take up more time and attention than their condition seems to warrant, and may display angry reactance behavior in response to having their freedoms or control curtailed. Patients and practitioners contribute to the relationship they develop with each other in the hospital.

Patients engage in problem-focused and emotion-focused coping techniques to adjust to the stress and anxiety they experience in the hospital. Some of their anxiety stems from their impending surgery and from nonsurgical medical procedures, such as cardiac catheterization and endoscopy. High levels of anxiety before surgery, for instance, appear to impair patients' physical recovery after the operation. Reducing the anxiety connected with medical procedures can be accomplished through methods of psychological preparation that provide patients with behavioral, cognitive, and informational control. Lamaze training for childbirth seems to provide these kinds of preparation.

Although most patients benefit from methods of psychological preparation that enhance control, some benefit more than others. One factor that seems to affect the success of these methods is whether the patient's coping style tends toward avoidance rather than attention strategies. Children's separation distress in the hospital can be reduced if parents visit often or room in. Children can also benefit from psychological preparation for medical procedures, but the success of providing children with information depends on its timing and on their age, coping style, and previous medical experience.

The role of psychologists in the overall treatment effort for hospitalized patients has increased in recent years, particularly in preparing patients for surgery and other medical procedures, helping them adjust to their medical condition, and enhancing their adherence to treatment regimens after discharge. To identify the needs and problems of patients, psychologists use the Minnesota Multiphasic Personality Inventory and other instruments developed specifically for use with medical patients, such as the Millon Behavioral Health Inventory, the Psychosocial Adjustment to Illness Scale, and the Medical Compliance Incomplete Stories Test.

KEY TERMS

nosocomial infection
depersonalization
burnout
reactance
Lamaze training
separation distress
Minnesota Multiphasic Personality Inventory
Millon Behavioral Health Inventory
Psychosocial Adjustment to Illness Scale
Medical Compliance Incomplete Stories Test

part V

PHYSICAL SYMPTOMS: PAIN AND DISCOMFORT

11

THE NATURE AND SYMPTOMS OF PAIN

PROLOGUE

"Wouldn't it be wonderful never to experience pain," many people have thought when they or others they have known were suffering. Pain hurts, and people typically dislike it and try to avoid it. But being able to sense pain is critical to our survival—without it, how would we know when we are injured? We could have a sprained ankle or an ulcer, for instance, without realizing it, and not seek treatment. And how would we know we are about to be injured, such as when we approach a hot flame without seeing it? Pain serves as a signal to take protective action.

Are there people who do not feel pain? Yes—several disorders can reduce or eliminate the ability to sense pain. People with a condition called *congenital insensitivity to pain,* which is present from birth, may report only a "tingling" or "itching" sensation when seriously injured. A young woman with this disorder

> seemed normal in every way, except that she had never felt pain. As a child she had bitten off the tip of her tongue while chewing food, and had suffered third-degree burns after kneeling on a hot radiator to look out of a window. When examined by a psychologist . . . in the laboratory, she reported that she did not feel pain when noxious stimuli were presented. She felt no pain when parts of her body were subjected to strong electric shock, to hot water at temperatures that usually produce reports of burning pain, or to a prolonged ice-bath. Equally astonishing was the fact that she showed no changes in blood pressure, heart rate, or respiration when these stimuli were presented. Furthermore, she could not remember ever sneezing or coughing, the gag reflex could be elicited only with great difficulty, and the cornea reflexes (to protect the eyes) were absent. (Melzack, quoted in Bakal, 1979, p. 141)

This disorder contributed to her death at the age of 29. People with congenital insensitivity to pain often die young because injuries or illnesses, such as acute appendicitis, go unnoticed (Chapman, 1984; Manfredi et al., 1981).

Health psychologists study pain because it influences whether individuals seek and comply with medical treatment and because being in pain can be very stressful, particularly when it is intense or enduring. In this chapter we examine the nature and symptoms of pain, and the effects it has on its victims when it is severe. As we consider these topics, you will find answers to questions you may have about pain. What is pain, and what is the physical basis for it? Can people feel pain when there is no underlying physical disorder? Do psychosocial factors affect our experience of pain? Since pain is a subjective experience, how do psychologists assess how much pain a person feels?

WHAT IS PAIN?

Pain is the sensory and emotional experience of discomfort, which is usually associated with actual or threatened tissue damage or irritation (Sanders, 1985). Virtually all people experience pain and at all ages—from the pains of birth for mother and baby, to those of colic and teething in infancy, to those of later injuries and illnesses, and those that become chronic, such as the pain of arthritis, problems of the lower back, migraine headache, and cancer.

People's experience with pain is important for several reasons. For one thing, no medical complaint is more common than pain. According to researcher Paul Karoly, pain is the "most pervasive symptom in medical practice, the most frequently stated 'cause' of disability, and the single most compelling force underlying an individual's choice to seek or avoid medical care" (1985, p. 461). As we saw in Chapter 9, people are more likely to seek medical treatment without delay if they feel pain. Also, severe and prolonged pain can come to dominate the lives of its victims, impairing their general functioning, ability to work, social relationships, and emotional adjustment. Lastly, pain has enormous social and economic effects on all societies of the world. At any given time, about a third of Americans suffer from one or more continuous or recurrent painful conditions that require medical care, and tens of millions of these people are partially or completely disabled by their condition (Sanders, 1985; Turk, Meichenbaum, & Genest, 1983). Each year in the United States, tens of billions of dollars are spent on pain-related expenses, such as for treatment, loss of income, disability payments, and litigation.

The Qualities and Dimensions of Pain

Our sensations of pain can be quite varied and have many different qualities. We might describe some pains as "sharp" and others as "dull," for example—and sharp pains can have either a stabbing or pricking feel. Some pains involve a burning sensation, and others have a cramping, itching, or aching feel. And some pains are throbbing, or constant, or shooting, or pervasive, or localized. Often the feeling we experience depends on the kind of irritation or damage that has occurred and its location. For instance, when damage occurs deep within the body, individuals usually report feeling a "dull" or "aching" pain; but damage produced by a brief noxious event to the skin is often described as "sharp" (McClintic, 1985; Schiffman, 1976).

The painful conditions people experience also differ according to the origin of the pain and the duration of the condition. We will consider two dimensions that describe these differences, beginning with the degree to which the origin of the pain can be traced to existing tissue damage.

Organic versus Psychogenic Pain

People who suffer a physical injury, such as a serious burn, experience pain that is clearly related to tissue damage. When discomfort is caused mainly by tissue damage, it is described as *organic pain*. For other pains, no tissue damage appears to exist—at least, medical examinations fail to find an organic basis. The discomfort involved in these pains seems to result primarily from psychological processes. For this reason, this type of discomfort is described as *psychogenic pain*. Extreme examples of psychogenic pain are sometimes seen in the hallucinations of psychotic individuals: I once talked with a schizophrenic man who claimed —and *really* looked like—he was "feeling" the stings from being "shot by enemy agents with ray guns."

Not long ago, researchers considered organic and psychogenic pain to be separate entities, with psychogenic pain not involving "real" sensations. As pain researcher Donald Bakal has noted, a practitioner's reference to pain as "psychogenic"

> was taken to mean "due to psychological causes," which implied that the patient was "imagining" his pain or that it was not really pain simply because an organic basis could not be found. Psychogenic pain is not experienced differently, however, from that arising from physical disease or injury. Psychogenic and organic pain both hurt. (1979, p. 167)

Researchers now recognize that virtually all pain experiences involve an interplay of both physiological and psychological factors. As a result, the dimension of pain involving organic and psychogenic causes is viewed as a continuum rather than a dichotomy. Different pain experiences simply involve different mixtures of organic and psychogenic factors. A mixture of these factors seems clear in, for example, cases of muscle-contraction headache, which results from sustained muscle tension that occurs when people experience stress (Weisenberg, 1977). But some pain patients experience chronic discomfort that is predominantly psychogenic in origin, and psychiatrists classify this condition as a *somatoform disorder* (Sarason & Sarason, 1984). Unfortunately, many health care workers still think pain that has no demonstrated physical basis is purely psychogenic, and their patients struggle to prove that "the pain isn't just in my head, Doc" (Karoly, 1985).

Acute versus Chronic Pain

Experiencing pain either continuously or frequently over a period of many months or years is different from having occasional and isolated short-term bouts with pain. The length of experience individuals have had with their painful condition is an important dimension in describing their pain.

Most of the painful conditions people experience are temporary—the pain arrives and then subsides in a matter of minutes, days, or even weeks, often with the aid of painkillers or other treatments prescribed by a physician. If a similar painful condition occurs in the future, it is not connected in a direct way to the earlier experience. This is the case for most everyday headaches, for instance, and for the pain typically produced by such conditions as toothaches, muscle strains, accidental wounds, and surgeries. **Acute pain** refers to the discomfort people experience with temporary painful conditions that last less than six months or so (Turk, Meichenbaum, & Genest, 1983).

Patients with acute pain often have high levels of anxiety while the pain exists, but their distress subsides as their condition improves and their pain decreases (Fordyce & Steger, 1979). When a painful condition lasts for more than a few months, patients remain highly anxious and tend to develop feelings of hopelessness and helplessness because various medical treatments have failed to alleviate their condition. Pain can come to dominate their lives. This is what often happens when pain becomes *chronic,* as reflected in the following passage:

> Pain patients frequently say that they could stand their pain much better if they could only get a good night's sleep. . . . They feel worn down, worn out, exhausted. They find themselves getting more and more irritable with their families, they have fewer and fewer friends, and fewer and fewer interests. Gradually, as time goes by, the boundaries of their world seem to shrink. They become more and more preoccupied with their pain, less and less interested in the world around them. Their world begins to center around home, doctor's office, and pharmacy. (Sternbach, quoted in Bakal, 1979, p. 165)

People's experience of pain is very different when the condition is chronic than when it is acute. Furthermore, many chronic sufferers leave their jobs for emotional and physical reasons and must live on a reduced income at the same time that their medical bills are piling up.

People's experience with chronic pain also depends on two factors: (1) whether the underlying condition is *benign* or is *malignant* and worsening and (2) whether the discomfort exists *continuously* or occurs in frequent and intense *episodes.* Using these factors, Dennis Turk, Donald Meichenbaum, and Myles Genest (1983) have described three types of chronic pain:

- **Chronic/recurrent pain** stems from benign causes and is characterized by repeated and intense episodes of pain separated by periods without pain. Two examples of chronic/recurrent pain are migraine headaches and muscle-contraction (tension) headaches; another example is *myofascial pain,* a syndrome that typically involves shooting or radiating, but dull, pain in the muscles and connective tissue of the head and neck, and, sometimes, the back (Hare & Milano, 1985; Turk, Meichenbaum, & Genest, 1983).
- **Chronic/intractable/benign pain** refers to discomfort that is typically present all of the time, with varying levels of intensity, and is not related to an underlying malignant condition. Chronic low back pain often has this pattern.
- **Chronic/progressive pain** is characterized by continuous discomfort, is associated with a malignant condition, and becomes increasingly intense as the underlying condition worsens. Two of the most prominent malignant conditions that frequently produce chronic/progressive pain are rheumatoid arthritis and cancer.

As we shall see later in this chapter and the next one, the type of pain that people experience influences their psychosocial adjustment and the treatment they receive to control their discomfort.

Perceiving Pain

Of the several perceptual senses the human body uses, the sense of pain has three important and unique properties (Chapman, 1984;

HIGHLIGHT 11A: On Issues
Acute Pain in Burn Patients

Almost every day we hear or read about people being seriously burned, such as in a fire or through scalding. Each year in the United States, over two million individuals become victims of burn injuries that require medical attention (Tarnowski, Rasnake, & Drabman, 1987; Winters, 1985). Those victims whose burns are serious enough to require hospitalization number about 130,000 individuals—one-third of whom are children. These people suffer acute pain both from their injuries and from the treatment procedures that must be performed.

Medical workers describe the severity of a burn on the basis of its location and with two measures of its damage (Pillitteri, 1981). One measure estimates the amount of skin *area* affected in terms of the percentage of the body surface burned; the other assesses the *depth* of the burn, expressed in three "degrees":

1. *First-degree burns* involve damage restricted to the epidermis, or outermost layer of skin. The skin turns red, but does not blister—as, for example, in most cases of sunburn.
2. *Second-degree burns* are those that include damage to the dermis, the layer below the epidermis. These burns are quite painful, often form blisters, and can result from scalding and fire.
3. *Third-degree burns* destroy the epidermis and dermis down to the underlying layer of fat, and may extend to the muscle and bone. These burns usually result from fire. Because the nerve endings are generally damaged in third-degree burns, there is generally no pain sensation in these regions initially.

Practitioners assess the depth of a burn by its appearance and the sensitivity of the region to pain.

Hospital treatment for patients with severe burns progresses through three phases (Wernick, 1983; Winters, 1985). The first few days after the burn is called the *emergency phase*, during which medical staff assess the severity of the burn and work to maintain the patient's body functions and defenses, such as in preventing infection and keeping a balance of fluids and electrolytes. The *acute phase* extends from the end of the emergency phase until the burned area is covered with new skin. This process can take from several days to several months, depending on the severity of the burn. The pain is constant during most or all of this phase, particularly when nerve endings begin to regenerate in third-degree burns. Suffering is generally

> greatest during "tankings," in which the patient is lowered on a stretcher into a large tub. The old dressings are removed and the patient is gently scrubbed to remove encrusted medication. Debridement, which is usually necessary during the early weeks of hospitalization, involves the vigorous cutting away of dead tissue in burned areas. The process, which may last for more than an hour and involve several people working on different parts of the body simultaneously, ends when fresh medication and new dressings are applied. (Wernick, 1983, p. 196)

These and many other painful medical procedures occur very frequently, and burn patients must also do exercises for physical or occupational therapy. Lastly, the *rehabilitation phase* begins at about the time of discharge from the hospital and continues until the scar tissue has matured. Although the pain has now subsided, itching in the healed area (which should not be scratched) can be a source of discomfort, as can using devices and doing exercises to prevent scarring and contractures (skin shrinkage that can restrict the person's range of motion).

Analgesic medication is the main approach for controlling acute pain in the hospital (Kanner, 1986). But psychological approaches can also help burn patients cope with their pain so that they need less medication. Robert Wernick (1983) used a program of psychological preparation with adult severe-burn patients. This preparation was designed to enhance the patients' sense of informational, behavioral, and cognitive control over their discomfort, especially with regard to the tanking and debridement procedures. Although these patients were not specifically asked to reduce their use of drugs, they subsequently requested much less medication than patients in a comparison (control) group who received the standard hospital preparation. Similar preparation methods have also been successful with children (Tarnowski, Rasnake, & Drabman, 1987).

Melzack & Wall, 1982). First, although nerve fibers in the body sense and send signals of tissue damage, the receptor cells for pain are different from those of other perceptual systems, such as vision. Whereas the visual system contains specific receptor cells that transmit only messages about a particular type of stimulation—light—there are no *specific* receptor cells in the body that transmit *only* information about pain. Second, the body senses pain in response to many types of noxious stimuli, such as physical pressure, lacerations, and intense heat or cold. Third, the perception of pain almost always includes a strong emotional component. As we are about to see, perceiving pain involves a complex interplay of physiological and psychological processes.

The Physiology of Perceiving Pain

To describe the physiology of perceiving pain, we will trace the bodily reaction to tissue damage, as when the body receives a cut or burn. The noxious stimulation immediately triggers chemical activity at the site of injury, releasing chemicals called **algogenic substances** that exist naturally in the tissue (Chapman, 1984). These chemicals—which include *serotonin, histamine,* and *bradykinin*—function to promote immune system activity, cause inflammation at the injured site, and activate endings of nerve fibers in the damaged region, signaling injury.

The signal of injury is transmitted by afferent neurons of the peripheral nervous system to the spinal cord, which carries the signal to the brain. The afferent nerve endings in a damaged region of the body that respond to pain stimuli and signal injury are called **nociceptors** (Bakal, 1979; Chapman, 1984). These fibers

> have no special structure for detecting injury; they are simply free nerve endings. They may be found in skin, blood vessels, subcutaneous tissue, muscle, . . . joints, and other structures. When activated, these end organs, like other receptors, generate impulses that are transmitted along peripheral fibers to the central nervous system. (Chapman, 1984, p. 1261)

There are several types of afferent peripheral fibers, and pain signals are carried by only two types: A-delta and C fibers. *A-delta fibers* are coated with myelin, a fatty substance that enables neurons to transmit impulses very quickly. These fibers are associated with sharp, well-localized, and distinct pain experiences. *C fibers* transmit impulses more slowly—because they are not coated with myelin—and seem to be involved in experiences of diffuse dull, burning, or aching pain sensations (Bakal, 1979; Chapman, 1984; Melzack & Wall, 1982).

Signals from A-delta and C fibers follow different paths when they reach the brain (Bloom, Lazerson, & Hofstadter, 1985; Guyton, 1985). A-delta signals, which reflect sharp pain, pass through specific areas of the thalamus on their way to motor and sensory areas of the cerebral cortex. This suggests that signals of sharp pain receive special attention in our sensory awareness, probably so that we can respond to them quickly. On the other hand, C fiber signals, which reflect burning or aching pain, terminate mainly in the brainstem and lower portions of the forebrain, such as the limbic system, thalamus, and hypothalamus. The remaining C fiber impulses spread to many areas of the brain by connecting with a diffuse network of neurons. Signals of dull pain are less likely to command our immediate attention than those of sharp pain, but are more likely to affect our mood, general emotional state, and motivation.

So far, the description we have given of physiological reactions to tissue damage makes it seem as though the process of perceiving pain is rather straightforward. But it actually isn't. One phenomenon that complicates the picture is that pains originating from internal organs are often perceived as coming from other parts of the body, usually near the surface of the skin. This is called **referred pain** (Guyton, 1985; McClintic, 1985; Melzack & Wall, 1982). The pain people experience in a heart attack provides one of the most widely known examples of this phenomenon: the pain is referred to the shoulders, pectoral area of the chest, and the arms. Other examples of referred pain include:

- Pain perceived to be in the shoulder that results from inflammation of the diaphragm.
- Pain in the upper-middle abdomen during the first stages of appendicitis (the appendix is deep in the lower right side).
- Pain in the ear or in the wrong area of the mouth that results from a toothache.

Referred pain results when sensory impulses from an internal organ and the skin use the same pathway in the spinal cord. Because people are more familiar with sensations from the skin than from internal organs, they tend to perceive the spinal cord impulses as coming from the skin (Guyton, 1985). Another issue that complicates our understanding of pain perception is that people feel pains that have no apparent physical basis, as the next section discusses.

Pain without Apparent Physical Basis

Some pains people experience are quite mysterious, since they occur with no apparent "reason"—for instance, no noxious stimulus is present. Most of these pain experiences belong to one of three syndromes: neuralgia, causalgia, and phantom limb pain. These syndromes often begin with an injury, but the pain (1) persists long after healing is complete, (2) may spread and increase in intensity, and (3) may become stronger than the pain experienced with the initial injury (Melzack & Wall, 1982).

Neuralgia is an extremely painful syndrome in which the patient experiences recurrent episodes of intense shooting or stabbing pain along the course of a nerve (Chapman, 1984; McClintic, 1985; Melzack & Wall, 1982). In one form of this syndrome called *trigeminal neuralgia,* excruciating spasms of pain occur along the trigeminal nerve that projects throughout the face. Episodes of neuralgia occur very suddenly and without any apparent cause. Curiously, attacks of neuralgia can be provoked more readily by innocuous stimuli than by noxious ones. For instance, drawing a cotton ball across the skin can trigger an attack, but a pin prick does not.

Another mysterious pain syndrome is *causalgia,* which is characterized by recurrent episodes of severe burning pain (Melzack & Wall, 1982; Weisenberg, 1977). A patient with causalgia might report, for instance, that the pain feels "like my arm is pressed against a hot stove." In this syndrome, the pain feels as though it originates in a region of the body where the patient had at some earlier time been seriously wounded, such as by a gunshot or stabbing. Curiously, only a small minority of severely wounded patients develop causalgia—but for those who do, the pain persists long after the wound has healed and damaged nerves have regenerated. Episodes of causalgia often occur spontaneously and

> may take minutes or hours to subside, but may occur repeatedly each day for years after the injury. The frequency and intensity of the spontaneous pain-attacks may increase over the years, and the pain may even spread to distant areas of the body. (Melzack, quoted in Bakal, 1979, p. 142)

Like neuralgia, attacks of causalgia can be triggered by minor stimuli, such as a gentle touch or a puff of air.

Phantom limb pain is an especially puzzling phenomenon because the patient—an amputee or someone whose peripheral nervous system is irreparably damaged—feels pain in a limb that either is no longer there or has no functioning nerves (Chapman, 1984; Melzack & Wall, 1982). After an amputation, for instance, most patients claim to have sensations of their limb still being there—such as by feeling it "move"—and many of these individuals report feeling pain, too. In about 5 or 10% of amputees, the perception of pain in the phantom limb persists, is severe, and often becomes worse over time (Bakal, 1979). These patients may experience either recurrent or continuous pain and may describe it as shooting, burning, or cramping. For example, many patients who feel pain in a phantom hand report sensing that the hand is tightly clenched and its fingernails are digging into the palm.

Why do people feel pain when no noxious

stimulation is present? Perhaps the answer relates to the neural damage that precedes the development of causalgia and phantom limb pain—and perhaps even neuralgia involves neural damage, albeit of a less obvious nature, such as from infection (Hare & Milano, 1985). But then why is it that the large majority of patients who suffer obvious neural damage do not develop these curious pain syndromes? Although the puzzle is far from being solved, the explanation will almost surely involve both physiological and psychological factors.

The Role of the "Meaning" of Pain

Some people evidently "like" pain—at least under some, usually sexual, circumstances—and are described as *masochists.* For them, the meaning of pain seems to be different from that of most other people. Some psychologists believe that individuals may come to like pain through classical conditioning, that is, by participating in or viewing activities that associate pain with pleasure in a sexual context (Wincze, 1977). Most of the evidence for the view that the meaning of pain can change by its association with pleasure comes from research with animals. For example, Ivan Pavlov (1927) demonstrated that the dogs' negative reaction to aversive stimuli, such as electric shocks or skin pricks, changed if the stimuli repeatedly preceded presentation of food. Eventually, the dogs would try to approach the aversive stimuli, which now signaled that food, not danger, was coming.

Henry Beecher (1956) described a dramatic example of how the meaning of pain affects people's experience of it. During World War II, he had examined soldiers who had recently been very seriously wounded and were in a field hospital for treatment. Of these men, only 49% claimed to be in "moderate" or "severe" pain and only 32% requested medication when asked if they "wanted something to relieve it." Some years later, Beecher conducted a similar examination—this time with civilian men who had just undergone surgery. Although the surgical wounds were in the same body regions as those of the soldiers, the soldiers' wounds had been more extensive. Nevertheless, 75% of the civilians claimed to be in "moderate" or "severe" pain and 83% requested medication. (The painkillers used in both groups were narcotics.)

Why did the soldiers—who had more extensive wounds—perceive less pain than the ci-

For many wounded soldiers, their pain seemed to be reduced by the knowledge that they were going home.

HIGHLIGHT 11B: On Research
Inducing Pain in Laboratory Research

To conduct an experiment dealing with pain, researchers sometimes need to create a physically painful situation for human subjects. How can they accomplish this in a standard way without harming the subjects? Several approaches have been used safely; two of the more common methods are the *cold-pressor procedure* and the *muscle-ischemia procedure* (Turk, Meichenbaum, & Genest, 1983). Let's look at these two methods and some example research.

The Cold-Pressor Procedure

The cold-pressor procedure basically involves immersing the subject's hand and forearm in ice water for a few minutes. A special apparatus is used, like the one illustrated in Figure 11B.1, so that the researcher can maintain a standard procedure across all subjects. The apparatus consists of an armrest mounted on an ice chest filled with water, which is maintained at a temperature of 2°C (35.6°F). Water at this temperature produces a continuous pain that subjects describe as "aching" or "crushing." A pump vigorously circulates the water to prevent it from warming in local areas around the arm.

Before using the apparatus, the subject's arm is immersed in a bucket of room-temperature water for one minute. The researcher also explains the cold-pressor procedure, solicits questions, and indicates that some temporary discoloration of the arm is common. When the procedure is over and the subject's arm is removed from the apparatus, the researcher notes that the discomfort will decrease rapidly but that it sometimes increases first for a short while (Turk, Meichenbaum, & Genest, 1983). When using this procedure, the subject's pain may be assessed in several ways, such as by self-ratings or by the length of time he or she is willing to endure the discomfort.

An experiment by Michel Girodo and Douglas Wood (1979) used the cold-pressor procedure to examine the role of coping methods on pain perception. The subjects were randomly assigned to several conditions, with each subject undergoing the cold-pressor procedure twice. Before the second procedure, subjects in different groups received different types of training for coping with pain. We will focus on two groups. One group was trained to cope by making positive *self-statements;* they were taught a list of 20 statements, such as "No matter how cold it gets, I can handle it" and "It's not the worst thing that can happen." For the other group, training involved the same self-statements, but they also received an *explanation* of how using these statements can enhance their personal control and help them cope with the pain. Immediately after each cold-pressor procedure, the subjects rated their experi-

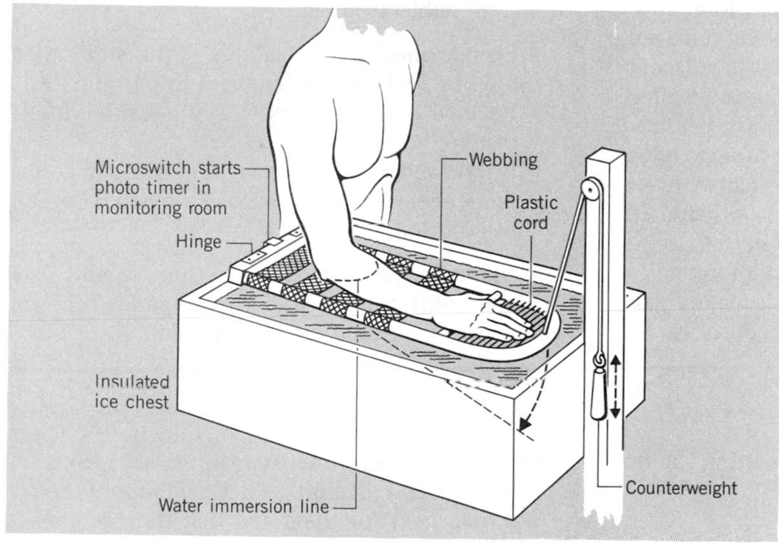

FIGURE 11B.1 Apparatus for cold-pressor procedure.

ence of pain on an 11-point scale, ranging from "no pain felt" to "worst pain ever felt." Analysis of the change in pain ratings from the first to the second procedure indicated that the experience of pain *decreased* for subjects who received the explanation for making the statements and *increased* for those who did not receive the explanation. These results suggest that people's experience of pain is affected by their beliefs about the purpose of using self-statements.

The Muscle-Ischemia Procedure

The condition of *ischemia*—or insufficient blood flow—is an important stimulus for the experience of pain when damage occurs to internal organs (Guyton, 1985). The pain people experience in a heart attack, for instance, results from poor blood flow in the blood vessels to the heart muscle.

The muscle-ischemia procedure for inducing pain involves reducing blood flow to the muscles of the arm. This is accomplished by wrapping the cuff of a sphygmomanometer (blood pressure testing device) around the arm, inflating it, and maintaining the pressure at a high level—240 mm Hg (Turk, Meichenbaum, & Genest, 1983). This pressure produces pain without causing damage and can be applied safely for 50 minutes or so. Before the procedure begins, the arm is raised over the subject's head for one minute to drain excess venous blood. The researcher also informs the subject that the procedure is safe and harmless, but that it is uncomfortable and may produce temporary numbness, throbbing, changes in arm temperature, and discoloration of the arm and hand. When the cuff is being removed, the researcher informs the subject that the discomfort will continue for a short while before subsiding. The subject then raises the arm over his or her head (sometimes with the aid of the other arm) to allow blood flow to return gradually and comfortably—a process taking three to five minutes. As with the cold-pressor procedure, measures of muscle-ischemia pain can include self-ratings and endurance.

Another way to measure muscle-ischemia pain involves a modification to the procedure we described; that is, the cuff is only inflated to the point when the subject first reports discomfort. This approach provides an assessment of the individual's pain *threshold.* Researchers used this approach to examine the effects of laughter and relaxation experiences on people's discomfort thresholds (Cogan, Cogan, Waltz, & McCue, 1987). The researchers randomly assigned subjects to four conditions, each involving a different type of experience immediately preceding assessment of discomfort. The *laughter* group listened to a comedy recording by Lily Tomlin, and every subject did in fact laugh out loud; the *relaxation* group listened to a tape designed to induce progressive muscle relaxation; the *narrative* group listened to a tape of a lecture on ethics and sociology; and a control group did not listen to any recording. Subsequent threshold assessments provided data regarding the cuff pressure at which the subjects reported discomfort. This pressure was more than 50% higher for individuals in the laughter and relaxation groups than for those in the narrative and control groups.

Pain Research and Ethical Standards

When conducting any kind of research with human subjects, psychologists are obliged to follow the ethical standards set forth by the American Psychological Association (separate guidelines apply for animal studies). Some of the standards are especially pertinent for research with aversive stimuli. First of all, researchers should make certain that any aversive stimulus they use is not actually harmful. In addition, all subjects should:

- Be informed of any features of the study that might affect their willingness to participate.
- Receive clear answers to any questions they have.
- Be allowed to choose freely, and without undue influence, whether to participate and whether to quit at any point.

If the subjects are children, researchers should also obtain consent for each child's participation from an appropriate guardian, usually a parent.

---

vilians? Beecher described the meaning the injuries had for the soldiers:

> the men studied had been subjected to almost uninterrupted fire for weeks. Notable in this group of soldiers was their optimistic, even cheerful, state of mind. . . . They thought the war was over for them and that they would soon be well enough to be sent home. It is not difficult to understand their relief on being de-

> livered from this area of danger. The battlefield wound marked the end of disaster for them. (1956, p. 1069)

For the civilian surgical patients, however, the wound marked the *start* of a personal disaster and their condition represented a major disruption in their lives.

We discussed in Chapter 9 how people's perceptions of body sensations are influenced by cognitive, social, and emotional factors—for instance, that they are less likely to notice pain when they are distracted by competing environmental stimuli, such as while participating in competitive sports. Psychological factors play an important role in perceiving pain, and theories of pain need to take these factors into account.

THEORIES OF PAIN

You have probably seen demonstrations in which hypnotized people were instructed that they would not feel pain—they were then stuck by a pin and did not react. When people under hypnosis do not react to noxious stimulation, do they still perceive the pain—only "it doesn't matter" to them? Similarly, do patients who seem relaxed while under the influence of painkillers actually perceive their pain? Some theories of pain would answer "yes" to these questions (Karoly, 1985). Let's look at two of these theories as we begin to examine how to explain pain perception.

Specificity and Pattern Theories of Pain

In the early 1900s, the dominant theories of pain took a very "mechanistic" view of pain perception, proposing that if a receptor is activated by an appropriate stimulus, the signal travels to the spinal cord and then the brain, and sensation results (Melzack & Wall, 1965, 1982; Schneider & Tarshis, 1975; Weisenberg, 1977).

Specificity theory provided one of these early viewpoints. This theory argued that the body has a separate sensory system for perceiving pain—just as it does for hearing and vision—and this system contains its own special receptors for detecting pain stimuli, its own peripheral nerves and pathway to the brain, and its own area of the brain for processing pain signals. When a noxious event stimulates a pain receptor, a signal travels to the pain center in the brain.

In contrast, *pattern theory* proposed that there is no separate system for perceiving pain, and the receptors for pain are shared with other senses, such as of touch. According to this view, people feel pain when certain patterns of neural activity occur, such as when appropriate types of activity reach excessively high levels in the brain. These patterns occur only with intense stimulation. Because strong and mild stimuli of the same sense modality produce different patterns of neural activity, being hit hard feels painful, but being caressed does not.

Although both of these theories contain features that have received research support, neither theory adequately explains pain perception (Melzack & Wall, 1982). We will cite just a few of their shortcomings. One problem with specificity theory is that the pain area of the brain it proposed does not exist. A difficulty with pattern theory stems from its requirement that the stimuli triggering pain must be intense. Thus, it cannot account for the fact that innocuous stimuli can trigger episodes of causalgia and neuralgia. Perhaps the most serious problem with both theories is that neither attempts to explain why the experience of pain is affected by psychological factors, such as the person's ideas about the meaning of pain, beliefs about the likelihood of pain, and attention to (or distraction from) noxious events. Partly because these theories overlook the role of psychological factors, they incorrectly predict that a person must feel just as much pain when hypnotized as when not hypnotized, even though he or she does not show it. Research findings indicate that people who are instructed not to feel pain actually do feel less pain when deeply hypnotized than when in the normal waking state (Hilgard & Hilgard, 1983).

The Gate-Control Theory of Pain

In the 1960s, Ronald Melzack and Patrick Wall (1965, 1982) introduced the **gate-control theory** of pain perception. This theory improved on the conceptions from the specificity and pattern theories in several ways, particularly by describing a physiological mechanism by which psychological factors can affect people's experience of pain. As a result, the gate-control theory can account for many phenomena in pain perception that have vexed earlier theories. For instance, it does not have to predict that hypnotized people must feel noxious stimulation (Karoly, 1985).

At the heart of the gate-control theory is a neural "gate" that can be "opened" or "closed" in varying degrees, thereby modulating incoming pain signals before they reach the brain. The theory proposes that the *gating mechanism* is located in the spinal cord—more specifically, in the *substantia gelatinosa* of the *dorsal horns,* which are part of the *gray matter* that runs the length of the core of the spinal cord. Figure 11.1 depicts how the gate-control process works. You can see in both diagrams of the figure that signals of noxious stimulation enter the substantia gelatinosa of the spinal cord from small-diameter *pain fibers,* A-delta and C fibers. After these signals pass through the gating mechanism, they activate *transmission cells,* which send impulses to the brain. When the output of signals from the transmission cells reaches a critical level, the person perceives pain; the greater the output beyond this level, the greater the pain intensity.

The two diagrams in the figure outline how the gating mechanism controls the output of impulses by the transmission cells. When pain signals enter the spinal cord and the gate is open, the transmission cells send impulses freely; but to the extent that the gate is closed, the output of the transmission cells is inhibited. What controls the opening and closing of the gate? The gate-control theory proposes that three factors are involved:

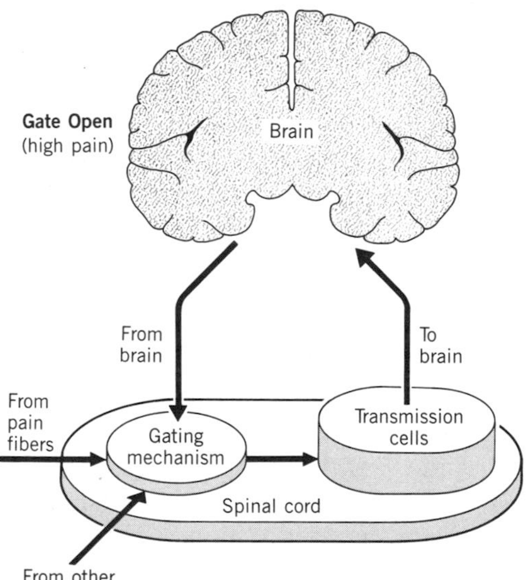

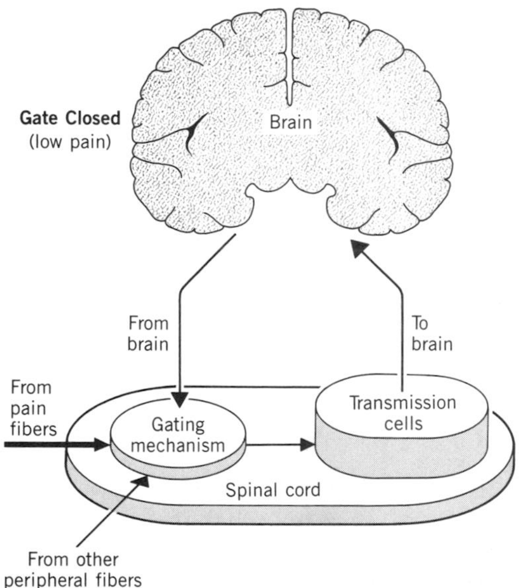

FIGURE 11.1 Two diagrams to illustrate gate-control theory predictions when strong pain signals arrive at the spinal cord, along with signals from other peripheral fibers and the brain. The diagram on the left depicts what conditions might exist when the gate is *open,* and the person feels strong pain; the one on the right shows a scenario when the gate is *closed,* and the person feels little pain. The thick arrows indicate conditions that increase the likelihood of perceiving pain, and the thin ones indicate the opposite effect. Pain signals enter the spinal cord and pass through a gating mechanism before activating transmission cells, which send impulses to the brain. (From information in Melzack & Wall, 1965, 1982.)

1. *The amount of activity in the pain fibers.* Activity in these fibers tends to open the gate. The stronger the noxious stimulation, the more active the pain fibers.

2. *The amount of activity in other peripheral fibers*—that is, those fibers that carry information about harmless stimuli or mild irritation, such as touching, rubbing, or lightly scratching the skin. These are large-diameter fibers called *A-beta fibers.* Activity in A-beta fibers tends to close the gate, inhibiting the perception of pain when noxious stimulation exists. This would explain why gently massaging or applying heat to sore muscles decreases the pain.

3. *Messages that descend from the brain.* Neurons in the brainstem and cortex have efferent pathways to the spinal cord, and the impulses they send can open or close the gate. The impact produced by some brain processes, such as those in anxiety or excitement, probably have a general effect, opening or closing the gate for *all* inputs from *any* areas of the body. But the impact of other brain processes may be very specific, applying to only some inputs from certain parts of the body. The idea that brain impulses influence the gating mechanism helps to explain why people who are hypnotized or distracted by competing environmental stimuli may not notice the pain of an injury.

The theory proposes that the gating mechanism responds to the combined effects of these three factors. As Melzack and Wall have stated, "the degree to which the gate increases or decreases sensory transmission is determined by the relative activity in large-diameter (A-beta) and small-diameter (A-delta and C) fibers and by descending influences from the brain" (1982, p. 222). Table 11.1 presents a wide variety of conditions in people's lives that seem to open or close the gate. For instance, anxiety and boredom are conditions that tend to open the gate, and positive emotions and distraction tend to close it.

TABLE 11.1 Conditions That Can Open or Close the Pain Gate

Conditions That Open the Gate
Physical conditions
Extent of the injury
Inappropriate activity level
Emotional conditions
Anxiety or worry
Tension
Depression
Mental conditions
Focusing on the pain
Boredom; little involvement in life activities
Conditions That Close the Gate
Physical conditions
Medication
Counterstimulation (e.g., heat or massage)
Emotional conditions
Positive emotions (e.g., happiness or optimism)
Relaxation
Rest
Mental conditions
Intense concentration or distraction
Involvement and interest in life activities

Source: Based on material by Karol et al., cited in Turk, Meichenbaum, & Genest (1983).

The gate-control theory has stimulated a great deal of research and has received strong support from the findings of many, but not all, of these studies (Melzack & Wall, 1982; Winters, 1985). One study, for instance, confirmed the prediction from gate-control theory that impulses from the brain can inhibit the perception of pain. David Reynolds (1969) conducted this study with rats as subjects. He first implanted an electrode in the midbrain portion of each rat's brainstem, varying the exact location from one rat to the next. Then he made sure they could feel pain by applying a clamp to their tails—and all reacted. Several days later, he tested whether stimulation through the electrode would block pain. While providing continuous, mild electrical stimulation, he again applied the clamp. Although most of the subjects did show a pain reaction, those with electrodes in a particular region of the midbrain—the **periaqueductal gray** area—did not. The electrical stimulation had produced a state of not being able to feel pain, or *analgesia,* in these rats. Then Reynolds used these few rats for a dramatic demonstration: he performed abdominal surgery on them while they were awake and with only the analgesia produced through electrode stimulation. Subsequent studies by other researchers have confirmed that stimulation to the periaqueductal gray area can induce analgesia in animals and in humans. Moreover, they have determined that morphine works as a painkiller by activating the brainstem to send impulses down the spinal cord (Chapman, 1984; Melzack & Wall, 1982; Winters, 1985).

Other research findings have not supported some of the details of the theory. But, as one reviewer has noted,

> regardless of the specific wiring diagrams involved, the gate-control theory of pain has been the most influential and important current theory of pain perception. It ties together many of the puzzling aspects of pain perception and control. It has had profound influence on pain research and the clinical control of pain. It has generated new interest in pain perception, stimulating a multidisciplinary view of pain for research and treatment. It has been able to demonstrate the tremendous importance of psychological variables. (Weisenberg, 1977, p. 1012).

The gate-control theory clearly takes a biopsychosocial perspective in explaining how people perceive pain. You will see many features of this theory as you read the material in the next section.

BIOPSYCHOSOCIAL ASPECTS OF PAIN

Why does electrical stimulation to the periaqueductal gray area of the brain produce analgesia? The search for an answer to this question played an important part in major discoveries about the neurochemical bases of pain. We will begin this section by examining some of these discoveries and seeing that the neurochemical substances that underlie acute pain are linked to psychosocial processes. Then we will consider how psychosocial factors are related to the experience of chronic pain.

Neurochemical Transmission and Inhibition of Pain

The phenomenon whereby stimulation to the brainstem produces insensitivity to pain has been given the name **stimulation-produced analgesia** (SPA). To understand how SPA occurs, we need to see how transmission cells are activated to send pain signals to the brain. This activation is triggered by a neurotransmitter called *substance P* that is secreted by small-diameter pain fibers and crosses the synapse to the transmission cells (Bloom, Lazerson, & Hofstadter, 1985; Chapman, 1984). SPA occurs when another chemical blocks the pain fibers' release of substance P. Let's see how this happens and what this other chemical is.

Electrical stimulation to the periaqueductal gray area starts a neurochemical chain reaction that seems to take the course shown in Figure 11.2. The impulse travels down the brainstem to the spinal cord, where the neurotransmitter *serotonin* activates nerve cells called "inhibitory interneurons." Impulses in these interneurons then cause the release of the neurotransmitter *endorphin* at the synapse with pain fibers; endorphin inhibits these fibers from releasing substance P (Bloom, Lazerson, & Hofstadter, 1985; Winters, 1985). Endorphin is a chemical belonging to a class of opiatelike substances called **endogenous opioids** that the body produces naturally; *enkephalin* is another of these chemicals. (*Endogenous* means "developing from within" and *oid* is a suffix meaning "resembling.") Endogenous opioids and opiates (morphine and heroin) appear to function in much the same way as painkillers (Snyder, 1977; Winters, 1985). Many neurons in the central nervous system have receptors that are sensitive to both opiates and opioids and allow these chemicals to bind to them.

Researchers have studied the action of opiates and endogenous opioids by using the drug *naloxone,* which acts in opposition to opiates and opioids and prevents them from working as painkillers (Bloom, Lazerson, & Hofstadter, 1985; Winters, 1985). In fact, physicians administer naloxone to counteract the ef-

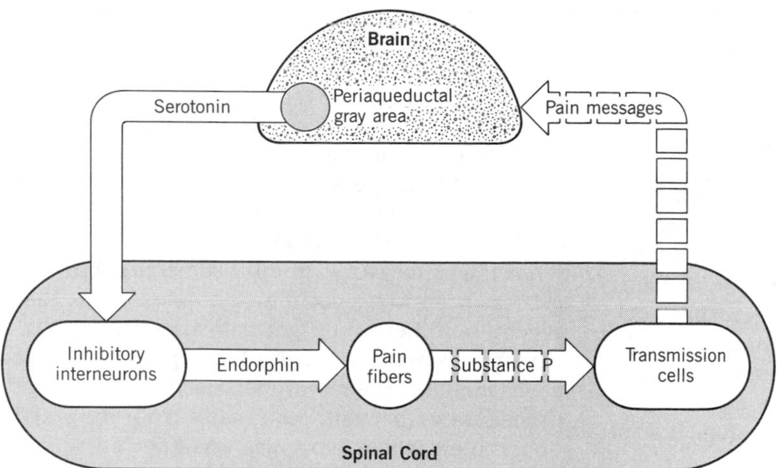

FIGURE 11.2 Illustration of the chain of activity involved in SPA. Stimulation to the periaqueductal gray area of the brain starts a sequence of electrochemical reactions, eventually leading to inhibition (shown by dashed arrows) of the pain fibers' release of substance P, thereby reducing pain messages from the transmission cells to the brain.

fects of heroin in addicts who have taken an overdose of the narcotic. In studying the action of opioids, researchers have examined whether these chemicals are involved in the phenomenon of SPA and found that naloxone blocks the analgesic effects of electrical stimulation to the periaqueductal gray area. One study, for instance, found that when animals received naloxone prior to brainstem stimulation, they continued to feel pain—they felt a noxious stimulus and reacted strongly. But if they did not receive naloxone, analgesia occurred, and they did not react to the noxious stimulus (Akil, Mayer, & Liebeskind, 1976). Furthermore, research with humans found that injecting naloxone in patients who have undergone tooth extractions increases their pain (Levine, Gordon, & Fields, 1978). These findings indicate that endogenous opioids are involved in producing SPA.

The body clearly contains its own natural painkilling substances, but the mechanisms by which they reduce pain are more complicated than they once appeared. For one thing, studies have found that naloxone does not always block SPA; the effect of naloxone may depend on exactly where the electrode delivers stimulation in the periaqueductal gray area (Cannon, Prieto, Lee, & Liebeskind, 1982). As Melzack and Wall have noted:

> It soon became apparent that there was not one but several descending control systems, and that some are sensitive to naloxone and others are not. Furthermore, a host of non-opioid transmitters—such as noradrenalin, acetylcholine and dopamine—are also involved in analgesia. . . . The role of endorphins and enkephalins—despite their undoubted existence—is becoming more hazy. They play a role in pain and analgesia, but the nature of that role is poorly understood. It is possible that they are involved in sudden stress or sudden injury to prevent the animal or person from being overwhelmed by pain, but there is little evidence that they play a role beyond that. (1982, p. 174)

Part of the reason for questioning the extent to which endogenous opioids influence pain is that research on these chemicals has focused mainly on their role in momentary pain that generally lasts only seconds or minutes. A newer technique for inducing longer-lasting

HIGHLIGHT 11C: On Issues
Placebos and Pain

You have probably heard of physicians prescribing a medicine that actually consisted of "sugar pills" when they could not find a physical cause for a patient's complaints or did not know of any medication that would help. You may also have heard that this "treatment" sometimes works—the patient claims that the symptoms are reduced. An inert substance or procedure that produces an effect is called a *placebo.* Studies have shown that placebos can often be effective in treating a wide variety of ailments, including coughs, nausea, and hypertension, at least on a temporary basis (Agras, 1984).

Placebos can also be effective in treating pain (Melzack & Wall, 1982). They do not always work, but they seem to produce substantial relief in about half as many patients as does a real drug, such as aspirin or morphine. The effect of placebos depends on the patient's belief that they will work—for instance, they are more effective:

- With large "doses"—such as more capsules or larger ones—than with smaller doses.
- When injected than when taken orally.
- When the practitioner indicates explicitly and strongly that they will work.

Unfortunately, however, the effectiveness of placebos tends to decline with repeated use.

Why do placebos reduce pain? One explanation is that the patient's expectation that the treatment will work triggers the release of endogenous opioids in the body, thereby inhibiting the transmission of pain signals (Fields & Levine, 1984). An experiment with dental patients who had had impacted wisdom teeth removed found evidence that this is the case (Levine, Gordon, & Fields, 1978). Patients who volunteered to participate in the study all received nitrous oxide anesthetic at the start of surgery. Two hours later they received an injection, and three hours after that they received another injection. The subjects were told that the substance in each injection might increase, decrease, or have no effect on the pain. These injections contained either naloxone or a placebo and were randomly assigned, using the following pattern: One group of subjects got the placebo as their first injection, and naloxone as their second; another group got naloxone first and the placebo second; and a third group received placebos for both. The researchers used a double-blind procedure so that neither the subject nor the practitioner knew which substance was injected.

To determine the effects of these treatments, the researchers had the subjects rate the intensity of their pain several times during the study. The results revealed two important findings: First, the patients reported much more pain when given naloxone than when given the placebo. Second, of the subjects who got the placebo first and then naloxone, those who reported pain relief with the placebo reported increased pain with the naloxone, but those who did not respond to the placebo showed no change in their pain with the naloxone. Because the effects of naloxone occurred mainly among subjects who had gotten relief from the placebo, these findings suggest that placebos relieve pain by activating endogenous opioids. The role of opioids in the placebo effect of relieving pain has been confirmed by other researchers, using the cold-pressor procedure to induce pain (Bandura et al., 1987).

The effects of placebos are fascinating and important, but they also present major ethical dilemmas for practitioners. Is it appropriate to use placebo drugs or procedures to treat symptoms and illnesses—and if so, when and under what circumstances?

---

acute pain in animals involves injecting a substance called *formalin* under the skin, which produces pain of moderate intensity—like that of a bee sting—for about two hours. Some research findings suggest that the role of different neurotransmitters may be different for momentary pain than for longer-lasting pain. Furthermore, when morphine is given to control pain, tolerance to the drug occurs quickly for momentary pain but does *not* seem to occur for formalin-induced pain and for chronic severe pain, such as that experienced by some cancer patients. These patients, for example, "show little evidence of tolerance to morphine" so that "the same dose maintains its effectiveness" during months or years of use

(Melzack & Wall, 1982, p. 176). Just why these differences in tolerance occur is unclear.

Although researchers do not have a full understanding of the mechanisms by which endogenous opioids work, it seems clear that having internal pain-relieving chemicals serves an adaptive function. It enables people to regulate the pain they experience to some extent so that they can attend to other matters, such as taking immediate action to survive serious injuries. Pain activates this analgesic system (Winters, 1985). But most of the time, high levels of endogenous opioid activity are not needed and would be maladaptive since chronic analgesia would undermine the value of pain as a warning signal. Perhaps because emotions are an important component of pain, studies have found that psychological stress can trigger endogenous opioid activity (Bloom, Lazerson, & Hofstadter, 1985; Winters, 1985). The release of endogenous opioids in times of stress may help to explain how injured athletes in competition and soldiers on the battlefield continue to function with little or no perception of pain. The connection between stress and opioid activity points up the interplay between biological and psychosocial factors in people's experience of pain.

Personal and Social Experiences and Pain

Imagine this scene: Little Stevie is a year old and is in the pediatrician's office to receive a standard immunization shot, as he has done before. As the physician approaches with the needle, Stevie starts to cry and tries to kick the doctor. He is reacting in anticipation of pain—something he learned through *classical conditioning* when he had received vaccinations before.

We learn to associate many things with pain, especially if the pain is severe and repeated, as it usually is with chronic pain. Many individuals who suffer from migraine headaches, for example, often can tell when a headache is on the way because they experience symptoms, such as dizziness, that precede the pain. These symptoms become conditioned stimuli that tend to produce distress, a conditioned response, and may heighten the perception of pain when it arrives. Also, words or concepts that describe the pain people have experienced can become conditioned stimuli and produce conditioned responses. A study demonstrated this with migraine sufferers and nonsufferers by measuring their physiological arousal in response to pain-related words, such as "throbbing," "sickening," "stabbing," "scalding," and "itching" (Jamner & Tursky, 1987). The migraine sufferers displayed much stronger physiological reactions to these words—especially the words that described their own experience with migraine pain—than the nonsufferers did.

Learning also influences the way people behave when they are in pain. People in pain behave in characteristic ways—they may moan, or grimace, or limp, for instance. These actions are referred to as **pain behaviors.** Researchers have identified four types of pain behaviors (Turk, Wack, & Kerns, 1985):

- *Facial/audible expression of distress,* as when people clench their teeth, moan, or grimace.
- *Distorted ambulation or posture,* such as moving in a guarded or protective fashion, stooping while walking, or rubbing or holding the painful area.
- *Negative affect,* such as being irritable.
- *Avoidance of activity,* as when people lie down frequently during the day, stay home from work, or refrain from motor or strenuous behavior.

Pain behaviors are a part of the sick role, and sometimes people in pain begin to exaggerate these behaviors because "No one believes me" (Hendler, 1984). Regardless of why the behaviors start, they are often strengthened or maintained by reinforcement in *operant conditioning,* as Wilbert Fordyce has pointed out (1976; Fordyce & Steger, 1979). When pain persists and becomes chronic, these behaviors often become part of the person's habits and lifestyle. People with entrenched patterns of pain behavior usually feel powerless to change.

How are pain behaviors reinforced? Although being sick or in pain is unpleasant, it sometimes has benefits, or "secondary gains." Someone who is in pain may be relieved of certain chores around the house or of going to work, for instance. Also, when an individual has a painful condition that flares up in certain circumstances, such as when lifting heavy objects, he or she may begin to avoid these activities. In both of these situations, pain behavior is reinforced if the person does not like doing these activities in the first place—thus, getting out of doing them is rewarding. Another way pain behavior and other sick-role behaviors may be reinforced is if the person receives disability payments. Studies conducted with injured or ill patients who either do or do not get disability compensation have shown that those who do receive payments tend to remain hospitalized longer and take longer to return to work (Block, Kremer, & Gaylor, 1980b; Chapman & Brena, 1985). This may reflect a willingness of those receiving compensation to take more time to recover and try to prevent a relapse. Patients who do and do not receive disability compensation may still show similar benefits from rehabilitation programs (Trabin, Rader, & Cummings, 1987).

People who suffer with pain also receive attention, care, and affection from family and friends, which provide social reinforcement for pain behavior. Researchers have demonstrated this relationship with both child and adult patients. Karen Gil and her colleagues (1988) conducted a study of parents' reactions to the pain behavior of their children who suffered from a chronic skin disorder that causes severe itching. Practitioners discourage scratching the itch since it can cause peeling and infection. The researchers videotaped the behavior of each child and his or her parent in the child's hospital room. As you might expect, the parents paid attention to the scratching, perhaps because of the harm it can do. But what effect did the attention have? An analysis of the children's behaviors revealed that parent attention to their scratching appeared to *increase* it, rather than decrease it. The results also indicated that paying attention to the children when they were *not* scratching seemed to reduce their scratching behavior.

Research has also examined how the reactions of spouses affect their husbands' or wives' pain behavior. One study used questionnaire reports by pain patients and their spouses to assess how the patients' behaviors were related to their spouses' being solicitous, that is, reacting to pain behaviors by giving attention and care (Flor, Kerns, & Turk, 1987). Higher levels of solicitousness by the spouse were associated with patients showing more pain behavior and less activity, such as in visiting friends or going shopping. In another study, patients with chronic pain reported their perceptions of their spouses' solicitousness regarding their pain behavior (Block, Kremer, & Gaynor, 1980a). Each patient was also interviewed in two meetings, in which they were aware of being observed through a one-way mirror and who was observing. In one interview, the observer was the patient's spouse; in the other, the observer was identified as a hospital employee. All patients were asked to describe their pain in each interview. The interesting finding was that the degree of pain they reported varied, depending on two factors: (1) whether the spouse or the employee was observing and (2) whether the patient thought the spouse was solicitous. Patients who felt their spouses were solicitous reported *more* pain when their spouses watched than when the employee did. In contrast, patients who felt their spouses were not solicitous reported *less* pain when their spouses watched than when the employee did.

The findings of research on parents' and spouses' reactions to chronic pain behavior illustrate the impact of each family member's behavior on each other's behavior within the family system (Flor, Kerns, & Turk, 1987; Flor & Turk, 1985; Gil, Keefe, Crisson, & Van Dalfsen, 1987). Showing care and concern when people are in pain is, of course, important and constructive. But when family members are highly solicitous to pain behavior without encouraging other behaviors, particularly those that allow the patient to become increasingly active, they are likely to promote sick-role behavior. This situation may then develop into a vicious circle of solicitousness leading to more pain behavior, which elicits more solicitousness, and so on. The patient's diminished activity may also lead to physical deterioration, such as through muscle atrophy, and lead to progressively more pain and less activity. These social processes in the family system of pain patients are gradual and insidious—they tend to increase the patients' dependency and decrease their self-efficacy and self-esteem.

Emotions, Coping Processes, and Pain

Pain and emotion are intimately linked, and cognitive processes mediate this link. In a study of these relationships, Gerry Kent (1985) had dental patients fill out a brief dental anxiety scale while waiting for their appointment. Then they rated the pain they expected in their visit. After the appointment, the patients rated the pain they actually experienced, and rated it again by mail three months later. The results revealed that anxiety played a role in their expectations of pain and in their memories of it three months later. The patients with high dental anxiety expected *and* later remembered four times as much pain as they experienced. In contrast, the low-anxiety patients expected and remembered less than twice as much pain as they experienced. These findings suggest that high-anxiety patients' memories of pain are determined more by what they expect than by what they feel.

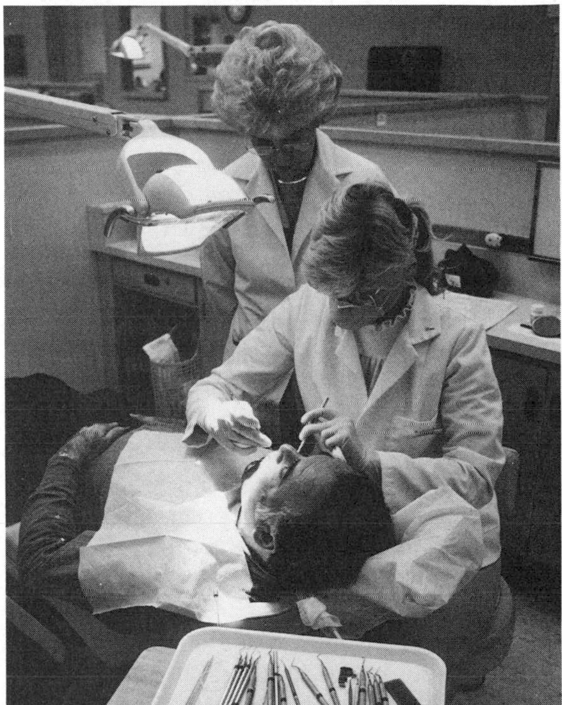

Many dental patients feel uneasy about going to the dentist because they associate it with pain.

Does emotion affect pain? One study compared the anxiety and stress levels of children who suffered from migraine headache with those of their best friends, and then had the migraine sufferers keep diaries of their headaches over the next four months. Although the scores on tests of anxiety and stress were about the same for the two groups and were within the normal range, migraine sufferers with high levels of anxiety had more frequent and severe headaches than those with lower anxiety (Cooper, Bawden, Camfield, & Camfield, 1987). Other investigations using self-report methods have found that migraine headaches tend to occur after periods of heightened stress and that Type A individuals have more frequent migraine and muscle-contraction headaches than others do (Levor et al., 1986; Woods et al., 1984). These studies clearly indicate that stress and headache are related. Has any research shown that stress causes headaches?

Convincing evidence that stress can cause headaches comes from a study with three groups of adult subjects, balanced for gender and age (Gannon, Haynes, Cuevas, & Chavez, 1987). One group consisted of chronic sufferers of migraine headache, the second group was composed of chronic sufferers of muscle-contraction headache, and the third consisted of individuals who had only occasional headaches. Before testing a subject, researchers attached sensors to the person's body to take several physiological measurements, such as of heart rate and electrical activity of muscles. A researcher also told the subjects that they "might or might not" experience headache pain in the procedures and that they would rate their perception of pain several times during the study. The study then proceeded in three phases: (1) In the baseline phase, the subjects sat quietly for 15 minutes. (2) In the stress phase, they were given arithmetic problems, such as 349 + 229, every 15 seconds for an hour. In addition, they were told that a buzzer would sound if their performance fell below a norm. Actually, the buzzer sounded periodically regardless of their performance. (3) In the recovery phase, the subjects sat quietly for 10 minutes. How did the subjects react to these conditions? More than two-thirds of the chronic headache sufferers and only one-fourth of the occasional sufferers reported developing headaches during the stress phase. Ratings of headache pain increased throughout the stress phase for all three groups, and then decreased during the recovery phase. The headaches tended to resemble muscle-contraction headaches and be preceded by sustained physiological arousal. These are important findings that indicate that stress can cause headaches.

Stress is also related to other kinds of pain, but whether stress causes the pain is still in question. Research has demonstrated, for instance, that people who suffer from recurrent low back pain have chronically higher levels of anxiety and tension than pain-free control subjects do, but these mood states do not worsen during 24 hours or so preceding pain attacks (Feuerstein, Carter, & Papciak, 1987). What is clear, however, is that pain is very stressful and that many people with chronic pain consider their discomfort—the actual pain and the physical limitations it produces—to be the most prominent stressor in their lives (Turner, Clancy, & Vitaliano, 1987). Part of the stress that chronic pain patients experience stems from their common belief that they have little personal control over their pain, aside from avoiding activities they believe can trigger an attack or make it worse. As a result, they tend to deal with their stress by using emotion-focused coping strategies. That is, rather than trying to alter the problem itself, they try to regulate their emotional response to it. Some of the more common coping methods that chronic pain patients use include hoping or praying the pain will get better someday, telling themselves that they can be brave and carry on despite their discomfort, and diverting their attention, such as by counting numbers or running a song through their heads (Keefe & Dolan, 1986; Rosenstiel & Keefe, 1983). The effectiveness of such approaches in reducing chronic pain is very limited.

How effectively do people cope with pain? One way researchers have tried to answer this question involves assessing pain patients' emotional adjustment with psychological tests, particularly the Minnesota Multiphasic Personality Inventory (MMPI). This test contains several scales, three of which are especially relevant for medical patients. These three scales assess: *hypochondriasis,* the tendency toward being preoccupied with physical symptoms and health; *depression,* feelings of unhappiness, pessimism, and hopelessness; and *hysteria,* the tendency to cope with problems by developing physical symptoms and using avoidance methods, such as denial. Because the MMPI is given and scored in a standardized manner and the test has been administered to large samples of people, norms exist that allow psychologists to compare an individual's scores on the different scales with those of the general population. For instance, a score of 70 or above on any scale occurs in less than 5% of the population and is considered extreme and clinically significant (Anastasi, 1982). Psychologists generally refer to hypochondriasis, depression, and hysteria as the "neurotic triad" because psychiatric patients with neurotic disorders often have high scores on these three scales.

Studies using the MMPI with pain patients have found some fairly consistent outcomes (Cox, Chapman, & Black, 1978; Rappaport, McAnulty, Waggoner, & Brantley, 1987; Rosen,

Grubman, Bevins, & Frymoyer, 1987). These outcomes lead to three conclusions. First, individuals who suffer from various types of chronic pain, such as severe headache and low back pain, show a characteristic MMPI profile that includes extremely high scores on all three of the neurotic triad scales. But their scores on the remaining MMPI scales tend to be well within the normal range. Second, this pattern appears to hold regardless of whether their pain has a known organic source. In other words, individuals whose pain might be classified as "psychogenic" by a physician tend to show similar problems of adjustment on the MMPI as those whose pain has a clear organic basis. Third, individuals with acute pain, such as patients recovering from an injury, sometimes have moderately elevated scores on the neurotic triad scales, but these scores and those for the remaining MMPI scales are generally well within the normal range. These findings make sense and reflect the differential psychological impact of pain that patients expect will end soon versus pain they fear will never end.

It is clear that being in frequent, severe discomfort is related to having high scores on the MMPI neurotic triad scales, but does chronic pain cause maladjustment? One school of thought is that the causal sequence may be the other way around—that is, that some individuals have a "pain-prone" personality that predisposes them to experience chronic pain (Blumer & Heilbronn, 1982). According to this view, chronic pain may be a symptom of a psychological disorder, such as depression, that preceded the pain syndrome. But there is currently little support for this position (Anderson et al., 1985; Turk & Holzman, 1986). The evidence points in the other direction—indicating, for instance, that people in chronic pain become depressed because of the stress they experience without being able to change their situation. They develop a sense of helplessness, which leads to depression. As Melzack and Wall have noted:

> Perhaps the most convincing evidence that chronic pain is usually the cause rather than the result of neurotic symptoms derives from studies of patients who are eventually relieved of their pain. . . . In one study, it was found that patients who had pain of more than six months' duration—due to spinal injuries, post-herpetic neuralgia and other problems—showed significant decreases in several indices of psychological disturbance when their pain was abolished by successful surgery. . . . Similarly, patients suffering several forms of chronic pain—including headache, colitis and abdominal pain—were found to have lower self-esteem than pain-free control groups. However, after these patients underwent several therapeutic procedures that significantly reduced their pain, they showed a striking improvement in their self-esteem ratings. (1982, p. 49)

Of course, this does not mean that psychological factors cannot lead to physical pain—as we have seen, stress can cause headaches. Pain and maladjustment involve interacting processes, with each feeding on the other over time. In cases of chronic pain, however, the pain syndrome usually precedes the maladjustment.

To summarize, the process by which people perceive pain involves a complex chain of physiological and neurochemical events. These events can be affected by a variety of psychosocial processes, such as people's beliefs about whether a drug will reduce their discomfort. Pain also affects and can be influenced by people's learning, cognition, social experiences, and stress. Although people can indicate through their behavior that they are feeling pain, the pain they perceive is actually a private and subjective experience. How can researchers and clinicians who work with patients who have painful symptoms assess the level and type of pain these individuals perceive? We turn now to answering this question.

ASSESSING PEOPLE'S PAIN

Researchers and clinicians have developed a variety of techniques for assessing people's pain. Although virtually all these methods can be applied both in research and in treating pain patients, some techniques are used more often in research, whereas others are more likely to be used in clinical practice. We will organize our discussion of techniques for measuring people's pain by classifying them into three groups: self-report methods, behavioral assessment approaches, and psychophysiological measures.

Self-Report Methods

Perhaps the most obvious approach to measuring people's pain is to ask them to describe their discomfort, either in their own words or by filling out a rating scale or questionnaire. In treating a patient's pain, health care workers ask where the pain is, what it feels like, how strong it is, and when it tends to occur. With chronic pain patients, medical and psychological professionals often incorporate this kind of questioning within the structure of a clinical interview.

Interview Methods in Assessing Pain

To treat chronic pain effectively, professionals need more information than just a description of the pain. Interviews with the patient and key others, such as family members and coworkers, provide a rich source of background information in the early phases of treatment (Karoly, 1985; Turk, Meichenbaum, & Genest, 1983). These discussions ordinarily focus on such issues as:

- The history of the pain problem, including when it started, how it progressed, and what approaches have been used for controlling it.
- The patient's emotional adjustment, currently and before the pain syndrome began.
- The patient's lifestyle—recreational interests, exercise patterns, diet, and so on—before the pain condition began.
- The pain syndrome's impact on the patient's current lifestyle, interpersonal relations, and work.
- The social context of pain episodes, such as happenings in the family before an attack and how family members respond when the pain occurs.
- Factors that seem to trigger attacks or make them worse.
- How the patient typically tries to cope with the pain.

The information obtained in these interviews can also be supplemented by having the patient and key others fill out questionnaires (Turk, Meichenbaum, & Genest, 1983).

Rating Scales

One of the most direct, simple, and commonly used ways to assess pain is to have individuals rate some aspect of their discomfort on a scale (Chapman et al., 1985; Karoly, 1985; Pearce, 1986). This approach is used very often to measure pain intensity, and there are basically two types of pain rating scales. One type is the *visual analog scale,* which uses a 10-centimeter-long line with markings or labels only at each end—for example, "no pain" at one end and "worst pain ever" at the other. The person marks a point on the line that describes the pain's intensity. The visual analog scale is very easy for people to use and can be used with children as young as 5 years of age (Karoly, 1985). The second type of rating scale—the *category scale*—also uses a line, but it is divided into sections with labels, such as "no pain," "mild," "discomforting," "distressing," "horrible," and "excruciating." The person marks the section that corresponds to the pain experienced.

Because rating scales are so easy and quick to use, people can rate their pain frequently. Repeated ratings would reveal how their pain changed over time, such as during everyday activities or during the course of an experiment. As an example, Dennis Turk and his colleagues have described how this approach can be used with chronic pain patients (Turk, Meichenbaum, & Genest, 1983). Each hour of a day, the patients rate their pain on an index card, which has a separate category scale for each hour. They do this for, say, two weeks, also indicating whenever they take pain medication. Before starting this procedure, they learn what to say if someone sees them filling out the card and asks what they are doing, ways to remind themselves to do each hourly rating, and what to do if they forget. One use of repeated ratings is in showing the ebbs and flows of pain intensity that patients often experience. For instance, one patients' wife

> believed that her husband was experiencing incapacitating and severe pain every waking hour of his life. This belief contributed to her preventing him from participating in any but the simplest chores around the house. Their social life had deteriorated, and the couple had grown increasingly depressed over the course of 4 years. Upon hearing that her husband experienced only moderate pain most of the time, that he indeed felt capable of various tasks, and that he actually resented his wife's efforts at pampering him, she was helped to alter her behavior. (Turk, Meichenbaum, & Genest, 1983, pp. 218–219)

Repeated ratings during each day may also reveal patterns in the timing of severe pain. Is the pain most severe in the evening, or on certain days? If so, are there environmental factors that may be responsible and, perhaps, changeable?

Pain Questionnaires

Pain is only partly described by the intensity of the discomfort people feel—the experience of pain has many qualities and dimensions. Ronald Melzack began to recognize the multidimensional nature of pain through his interactions with pain patients. He described in an interview how this realization emerged from talks he had with a woman who suffered from phantom limb pain. She

> would describe burning pains that were like a red-hot poker being shoved through her toes and her ankle. She would cry out from the pain in her legs. Of course, there were no legs. Well, that made me realize the utter subjectivity of pain—no objective physical measure is very likely to capture that. . . . I began to write down the words she used to describe her pain. I realized that the words describing the *emotional-motivational* component of her pain—"exhausting, sickening, terrifying, punishing"—were very different from those for the *sensory* component—"shooting, scalding, splitting, cramping." Later I came to see there was also an *evaluative* component, such as "it's unbearable" or "it's annoying." I wrote down the words other patients used, too, but I didn't know what to do with them. (Warga, 1987, p. 53, italics added)

Melzack determined that pain involves three broad dimensions—*affective* (emotional-motivational), *sensory,* and *evaluative*—by conducting a study in which subjects sorted over 100 pain-related words into separate groups of their own making (Melzack & Torgerson, 1971).

Melzack's research also indicated that each of the three dimensions consisted of subclasses. For instance, the sensory dimension included a subclass with the words "hot," "burning," "scalding," and "searing"—words relating to temperature. Notice that these four words connote increasingly hot temperatures, with searing being the hottest. Similarly, the affective dimension included a subclass of three words relating to fear: "fearful," "frightful," "terrifying." Then, by determining the degree of pain reflected by each word, Melzack (1975)—a professor at McGill University—was able to construct an instrument to measure pain. This test is called the **McGill Pain Questionnaire** (MPQ).

The MPQ basically presents a list of words that describe pain, separated into a total of 20 subclasses. The test instructs the person to select from each subclass the best word to describe his or her pain. Each word in each class has an assigned value based on the degree of pain it reflects. Let's look, for instance, at the subclass that ranges from "hot" to "searing." Selecting "searing" would contribute the highest number of points from this subclass to the person's pain score ("hot" would contribute the lowest number). The sum of these points across the 20 subclasses is called the *pain rating index*. The MPQ also contains a category rating scale, yielding a separate score called the *present pain intensity*.

The MPQ appears to have many strengths as an instrument for assessing chronic pain, both for research and for clinical purposes. For one thing, research has generally confirmed that the experience of pain is multidimensional, involving between two and four dimensions (Brennan, Barrett, & Garretson, 1987). Also, individuals with similar pain syndromes tend to choose the same patterns of words to describe their pain. But people suffering from very different types of pain — for example, toothache, arthritis, cancer, and phantom limb pain — choose different patterns of words in the MPQ to describe their experience (Melzack & Wall, 1982). The main limitation of the MPQ is that it requires that the patient have a fairly strong English vocabulary (Chapman et al., 1985; Karoly, 1985). For instance, it includes a few words, such as "taut" and "lancinating," that many people may not know. Moreover, sometimes respondents must make very fine distinctions between words, as with "throbbing," "beating," and "pounding." As a result, the MPQ may not be useful across all cultural and subcultural groups and cannot be used with individuals under about 12 years of age.

The MPQ is the best-known and most widely used pain questionnaire today. Researchers have recently developed other pain questionnaires, such as the *West Haven - Yale Multidimensional Pain Inventory* (Kerns, Turk, & Rudy, 1985). Although some of these tests seem very promising, they have not been studied very thoroughly yet.

Behavioral Assessment Approaches

Because people tend to exhibit pain behaviors when they are in discomfort, it should be possible to assess their pain by observing and assessing their behavior. A person with intense pain is likely to behave differently from someone with moderate pain. An individual with headache pain tends to behave differently from a person with low back pain. And a chronic pain sufferer is likely to have somewhat different patterns of pain behavior if the pain is recurrent than if it is intractable. Psychologists have developed procedures for assessing pain behavior in two types of situations: in *everyday activities* and in *structured clinical sessions*.

Assessing Pain Behavior in Structured Clinical Sessions

Procedures are now available whereby health care workers can assess the pain behavior of patients in structured clinical sessions. These sessions are usually conducted in hospital settings and are structured by the specific pain behaviors to be assessed and the tasks the patient is asked to perform. One approach of this kind has been developed into a pain assessment instrument — the *UAB Pain Behavior Scale* — for use by nurses during their standard routines, such as in early morning rounds (Richards, Nepomuceno, Riles, & Suer, 1982). The nurse has the patient perform several activities and rates each of 10 behaviors, such as the patient's mobility and use of medication, on a 3-point scale: "none," "occasional," and "fre-

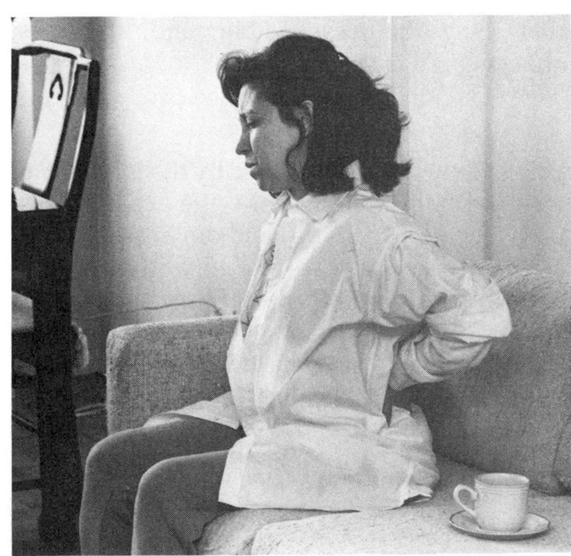

This woman's pain behavior can be used in assessing her discomfort.

quently." These ratings are converted into numerical values and summed for a total score.

Some investigations using structured clinical sessions have focused on assessing discomfort in patients suffering from low back pain (Follick, Ahern, & Aberger, 1985; Keefe & Block, 1982; Kleinke & Spangler, 1988). Each investigation had patients perform a standard set of activities. In the study by Chris Kleinke and Arthur Spangler, for example, the patients were asked to walk, pick up an object on the floor, remove their shoes while sitting, and perform several exercises, such as trunk rotations, toe touching, and sit-ups. The patients in each investigation were videotaped, and trained assessors rated their performance for several pain behaviors, such as guarded movement, rubbing the pain area, grimacing, and sighing. These studies have shown that these pain behaviors can be assessed easily and reliably and that behavioral assessments correlate well with patients' self-ratings of pain.

Assessing Pain Behavior in Everyday Activities

How does the pain patient behave in everyday activities, especially at home? Does the patient spend much of his or her time in bed, complain of discomfort a lot, seek help frequently in moving, or walk with a limp most of the time? How much of these behaviors does the person exhibit? These are the kinds of behavioral assessments that can be made regarding the everyday activities of a patient.

Family members or key others in the patient's life are usually the best people to make these everyday assessments of pain behavior. These people must, of course, be willing to help and be trained to make careful observations and keep accurate records. Pain researcher Wilbert Fordyce (1976) has recommended a procedure whereby the assessor — say, the patient's spouse — compiles a list of five to ten behaviors that generally signal when the patient is in pain. Then the spouse receives training in watching for these behaviors and keeping track of the amount of time the patient exhibits them. Finally, the spouse is trained to monitor how people, including the assessor, react to the patient's pain behavior. This procedure is useful not only in assessing the patient's pain experiences but in determining their impact on his or her life and the social context that may maintain pain behaviors.

Several modifications or supplements to Fordyce's procedure have been described by other researchers (Turk, Meichenbaum, & Genest, 1983). For one thing, the assessor — usually the patient's spouse — may fill out a rating scale periodically to measure the intensity of the pain, as reflected by the patient's behavior. Also, the spouse may keep track of the patient's pain experiences for, say, a couple of weeks by means of a *pain diary.* The diary is designed to record episodes when the spouse is aware that the patient's pain is very severe. In keeping a pain diary, the spouse records the date and time, as well as where the episode occurred, such as in the car or at home in bed. Then the spouse describes what he or she:

- Noticed as behaviors that suggested the patient was in pain.
- Thought and felt during the episode.
- Did in order to help, along with a rating of the action's effectiveness, ranging on a scale from "did not help at all" to "seemed to stop the pain completely."

These supplemental procedures provide additional data that can be of value in dealing with interpersonal issues that influence the pain experience.

Psychophysiological Measures

Another approach for assessing pain involves taking measurements of physiological activity, since pain has both sensory and emotional components that can produce changes in bodily functions. *Psychophysiology* is the study of mental or emotional processes as reflected by changes they produce in physiological activity (Lykken, 1987).

One psychophysiological measure researchers have used for assessing pain uses an apparatus called an *electromyograph* (EMG) to measure the electrical activity in muscles, which reflects their tension. Because *muscle tension* is associated with various pain states, such as headaches and low back pain, we might expect EMG recordings to be different between pain patients and pain-free controls. Studies have compared EMG recordings of headache and low back pain patients while *not* in pain with recordings of pain-free subjects and have generally not confirmed this expectation (Blanchard & Andrasik, 1985; Chapman et al., 1985). But the findings of other research suggest that differences between pain patients and controls may exist when the subjects' muscles are active (Chapman et al., 1985). Also, headache patients show different EMG patterns when they have headaches than when they do not (Blanchard & Andrasik, 1985). More research is needed, however, to verify that EMG measurements provide a useful measure of pain.

Researchers have also attempted to assess people's pain with measures of *autonomic activity*, such as of heart rate and skin conductance. A study by John Dowling (1983) used these two measures of autonomic activity before, during, and after college students underwent a cold-pressor procedure. Before the procedure, measurements of skin conductance and heart rate were taken during a *warning* period, as the subjects awaited a signal to immerse the hand in the ice-cold water; after the procedure, measurements were taken during a *resting* period, when the subjects knew that they would not experience further pain. The results showed that autonomic activity during *both* the warning period and immersion correlated moderately with the length of time the subjects left their hands in the water. Finding that pain tolerance correlated with autonomic activity during the warning period is interesting and illustrates a limitation to this measure of pain—that is, changes in autonomic activity readily occur in the absence of the sensation of pain. Although some measures of autonomic activity may be useful in assessing the emotional component of pain, they are not likely to be useful beyond that role (Chapman et al., 1985).

The last psychophysiological measure of pain we will consider involves the electrical activity of the brain, as measured by the *electroencephalograph* (EEG). When a person's sensory system detects a stimulus, such as a clicking sound, the signal to the brain produces a change in EEG voltage. Electrical changes produced by stimuli are called *evoked potentials* and show up in EEG recordings as sharp surges or peaks in the graph. Research has demonstrated that pain stimuli produce evoked potentials that vary in magnitude—the amplitudes of the surges increase with the intensity of the stimuli, decrease when subjects take analgesics, and correlate with people's subjective reports of pain (Chapman et al., 1985).

Even though psychophysiological measures provide objective assessments of bodily changes that occur in response to pain, these changes may also be affected by other factors, such as attention, diet, and stress. In clinical situations, measures of muscle tension, autonomic activity, and evoked potential are probably best used as supplements to self-report and behavioral assessment approaches (Chapman et al., 1985).

PAIN IN CHILDREN

We have focused in this chapter mainly on the experience of pain by adults, and we have mentioned many different types of discomfort and pain syndromes. Virtually every pain condition we have considered is experienced by children, too (Lavigne, Schulein, & Hahn, 1986b; Varni & Thompson, 1986). Children suffer acute pain from illnesses and injury, often being victims of burns and fractures, for instance. They also experience pain associated with chronic diseases, such as arthritis and cancer, and suffer from a wide range of painful conditions that do not have known physical bases—conditions such as recurrent abdominal pain, causalgia, and migraine and muscle-contraction headache. Indeed, some children suffer from a curious painful condition—unique to their age group—that involves pain deep in the arms or legs but not near a joint. The condition is sometimes called "growing pains," which may be a misnomer because it is most prevalent among 8- to 12-year-olds, a time when growth is relatively slow for children (Lavigne, Schulein, & Hahn, 1986b).

Much less is known about the pain people experience in childhood than at other times in their lives (Bush, 1987; Jeans, 1983). In fact, there is still some controversy about the age at which children begin to feel pain strongly, with some practitioners believing that infants under about 3 months of age feel relatively little pain. This belief derives from (1) the knowledge that babies' nervous systems are very immaturely developed and (2) the results of early studies which found, for instance, that newborns did not respond to a pinprick to the arm or leg by pulling the limb away. Because of the belief that very young infants are insensitive to pain, physicians in the past often performed surgery on babies using only a mild anesthetic or muscle relaxant. Minor operations, such as circumcision, were commonly done on infants with little or no anesthesia. But this situation changed rapidly in the 1980s as a result of new research. Let's see what is known today about pain in children.

Pain and Children's Sensory and Cognitive Development

Although the issue of whether babies are as sensitive as adults to pain is not yet resolved, one thing is clear: newborn babies feel pain. The fact that they typically cry when slapped on the rump if they do not start to breathe after birth certainly suggests that they feel pain. Is clearer evidence available?

Better evidence that young babies perceive pain comes from studies with newborns as they underwent noxious medical procedures, such as when the foot is pierced to draw a blood sample. One of these studies found that babies' reactions to the noxious stimulus included a "pain" facial expression: they had their eyes squeezed, brows contracted, tongue taut, and mouth open (Grunau & Craig, 1987). This pattern is comparable to the expression adults display when in pain. Another study found that the pattern of newborns' crying varied with the intensity of the noxious procedure they experienced (Porter, Miller, & Marshall, 1986). Highly noxious procedures elicited cries with certain characteristics, such as relatively high pitched peak tones, that adults judged as indicating "urgency." If newborns feel pain, why didn't the babies in the early research withdraw their limbs when stuck by a pin? The answer probably has to do with the pain behavior measured: withdrawing the limb requires that the subjects coordinate sensory events with their motor responses—a cognitive operation that babies do poorly during their first weeks of life.

One difficulty young children have in expressing their experience of pain is that their language abilities are very limited. Toddlers may know the word "hurt," but they do not usually have many other words to describe their pain (Jeans, 1983; McGrath, 1987). Instead of telling adults of their pain, they may display other pain behaviors, such as rubbing the affected area or clenching their lips. Mary Ellen Jeans (1983) interviewed 5- to 13-year-old children to determine their knowledge about pain. When asked to describe pain, the 5-year-olds used only an average of five different adjectives in their descriptions. But the children's use of different adjectives increased with age, with the 13-year-olds using an average of 26. The strategies the children gave for coping with pain also changed as they got older. Children under age 10 reported physical strategies, such as rubbing the painful area, almost exclusively. In contrast, the 13-year-olds cited more varied strategies, and 35% of their descriptions reflected psychological coping strategies, such as distracting their attention.

Assessing Pain in Children

When a patient has symptoms that include pain, the physician usually needs to know its location, intensity, quality, duration, and temporal patterning. This information helps in

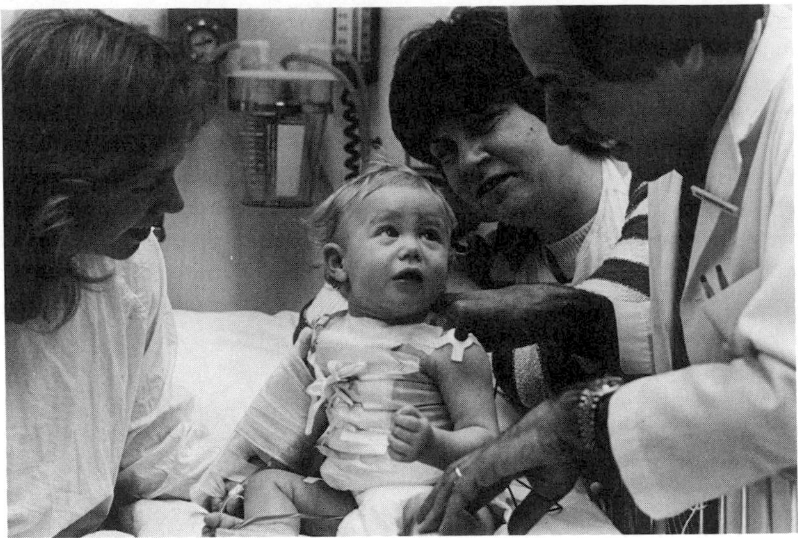

Very young children in acute pain do not have sufficient language to express what they are feeling and need special efforts to reduce their distress.

making an accurate diagnosis. But children's ability to provide this information is quite limited, especially if they are young.

Although researchers are currently working to develop questionnaires and other self-report procedures to assess children's pain, physicians today must rely mainly on interviews and behavioral assessment approaches (Bush, 1987; Lavigne, Schulein, & Hahn, 1986a; McGrath, 1987). Effectively interviewing children requires a great deal of skill in developing rapport with them, asking the right questions in ways they can understand, and knowing what their answers mean. Behavioral assessment approaches probably provide the most valuable source of information about the pain younger children experience. The most obvious of these approaches simply involves having the parents report pain behaviors they have observed. Other behavioral assessments involve structured clinical sessions in which health care workers rate or record the occurrence of pain behavior.

What kinds of self-report methods for assessing children's pain are researchers developing? Much of the research has been directed at finding effective ways for children to describe the intensity of their pain (Lavigne, Schulein, & Hahn, 1986a; McGrath, 1987). It appears that children as young as 5 years of age can understand and use visual analog scales correctly and reliably. They can also use category scales if the sections are labeled in ways they can understand, such as with faces indicating graded degrees of distress. But more research is needed to determine how accurately the ratings children give reflect their actual pain. Lastly, two pain questionnaires are being developed: one is the Pediatric Pain Questionnaire (Varni & Thompson, 1986) and the other is the Children's Comprehensive Pain Questionnaire (McGrath, 1987). Both instruments are designed to measure multiple dimensions of the pain experiences of children from about 4 years of age to adolescence. An adult may help the children fill out portions of the questionnaires when they lack needed reading skills.

Children's pain experiences are undoubtedly affected by a wide variety of psychosocial factors, particularly the social environment in which pain occurs (Bush, 1987). Parents serve as models and agents of reinforcement for the pain behavior of their children. But little is known about the personality and family characteristics of children that may contribute to the intensity and frequency of their pain. The vast majority of studies on pain have focused on adult subjects, not on children, and the studies conducted with children have generally produced unclear results because they were often poorly designed and carried out (Jeans, 1983; Lavigne, Schulein, & Hahn, 1986b). In addition, researchers need to overcome the difficulties in assessing children's pain so that they can do the kind of high-quality research that is needed.

SUMMARY

Although pain is typically unpleasant, it is a critical sense for survival because it warns us of actual or threatened tissue damage. It is the most frequent medical complaint of patients and the most commonly stated reason for disability. Pain includes both sensory and emotional components, and it has many different qualities. Sometimes pain feels sharp, and other times it's dull; sometimes it's localized, and other times it's pervasive; sometimes it has a burning sensation, and other times it has a cramping or aching feel.

Pain experiences also vary along a continuum, ranging from those that are mostly organic in origin to those that are mostly psychogenic. Virtually all pain experiences involve an interplay of both physiological and psychological processes, but the mixture of organic and psychogenic factors varies. Most painful experiences involve acute pain, which eventually disappears. They may last just a moment or as long as a few months, as with a very serious burn. Other pain conditions last for more than a few months, and are described as chronic. Long-lasting pain can be classified as chronic/recurrent, chronic/intractable/benign, and chronic/progressive pain.

The body's tissues contain algogenic substances that are released at the site where an injury occurs, thereby activating nociceptors, which are afferent free nerve endings. Pain signals are carried toward the central nervous system by two types of afferent peripheral fibers: (1) A-delta fibers carry signals of sharp and well-localized pain rapidly through the thalamus to motor and sensory areas of the cortex. These signals probably receive special attention in our sensory awareness, permitting a quick response. (2) C fibers carry information about dull and diffuse pain. These signals travel relatively slowly and terminate mainly in the brainstem and lower portions of the forebrain.

The process of pain perception involves three curious and fascinating types of phenomena. The first type is called referred pain, whereby pain originating from internal organs is perceived as coming from other parts of the body. The second type involves pain with no apparent physical basis. Neuralgia, causalgia, and phantom limb pain are syndromes that involve intense pain even though no noxious stimulus is present. In the third type of phenomenon, the "meaning" of pain affects people's experience of it. Individuals for whom pain means that a personal disaster is almost over and better things are coming seem to perceive less pain than do individuals with similar wounds who believe the personal disaster is just beginning.

The gate-control theory of pain proposes that neural signals of pain pass through a gate that can modulate the signals before they reach the brain. The degree to which the gate is open or closed depends on three factors: the amount of activity in the pain fibers, the amount of activity in other peripheral fibers, and messages that descend from the brain. This theory allows for the influence of psychological factors in pain perception. The phenomenon of stimulation-produced analgesia supports this theory, demonstrating that stimulation to the periaqueductal gray area of the brainstem can block the sensation of noxious stimulation elsewhere in the body. The findings of research with a drug called naloxone indicate that this phenomenon depends on the action of endogenous opioids—a class of neurochemicals that includes endorphin and enkephalin. The effect of placebos in reducing pain also depends on opioids.

Psychological processes play an important

role in the experience of pain. People in pain generally display pain behaviors, such as moaning, guarded movement, or avoidance of activity. These behaviors are often reinforced—for instance, when they result in the person being relieved of doing disliked activities or receiving special attention, care, and affection. Pain and stress are intimately linked: pain is stressful, and stress can produce pain—at least headache pain. People often have a difficult time coping with chronic pain, which can lead to psychological maladjustment.

A person's pain can be assessed in several ways. Self-report methods include interviews, rating scales, and pain questionnaires. The McGill Pain Questionnaire assesses three dimensions of pain: affective, sensory, and evaluative. Behavioral assessment approaches can measure pain in the person's everyday activities and in structured clinical sessions. Psychophysiological measures of pain assess muscle tension, autonomic activity, and evoked potentials of the brain. Children can perceive pain when they are born, but assessing pain in children is extremely difficult because of their limited language development.

KEY TERMS

pain
acute pain
chronic/recurrent pain
chronic/intractable/benign pain
chronic/progressive pain
algogenic substances
nociceptors
referred pain
gate-control theory
periaqueductal gray
stimulation-produced analgesia
endogenous opioids
pain behaviors
McGill Pain Questionnaire

12

MANAGING AND CONTROLLING CLINICAL PAIN

PROLOGUE

"Ouch! My foot hurts," the little girl cried as she tried to walk. The nurse responded quickly, saying, "I'm sorry it hurts. Show me where it hurts. . . . Let's get some exercise some other time." This 3-year-old girl was a patient who had had a difficult life. She was in her tenth month of hospitalization after receiving second- and third-degree burns to her legs and buttocks from having been immersed in scaldingly hot water. There was some evidence that the burn had been deliberately inflicted, and that she was a victim of child abuse.

After all these months this little girl's discomfort was not over. She still needed physical therapy and operations for plastic surgery, and she still had to wear uncomfortable knee-extension splints to prevent contractures. But her therapy was not going well. What had become clear was that the hospital staff was inadvertently reinforcing her pain behavior by comforting her and allowing her to avoid disliked activities. James Varni and Karen Thompson have described how this situation was not in the child's long-term best interests, having disrupted her physical, social, and emotional rehabilitation:

> Physical therapy was essentially terminated because of the patient's interfering pain behaviors. Two patterns emerged when the patient was placed in her bedroom in the crib with knee extension splints on. First, the child would struggle until she had removed the splints, resulting in further contractures and the need for additional plastic surgery. Second, if she failed to remove the splints, her crying would intensify to the point of screaming. At times she would fall asleep, exhausted, and continue sobbing well into the naptime hour. Other times, she would continue screaming until, in consideration of the other children, the nursing staff would remove her to a separate room for the remainder of the hour. (1986, p. 382)

Her interactions with adults and other children were being limited because of her behavior, and she was clearly not coping with her situation in constructive ways.

What can be done to help patients who, like this girl, have developed chronic pain behaviors that interfere with their rehabilitation? We will examine in this chapter how she was helped, and what methods are effective in reversing chronic pain behaviors. We will also discuss a variety of techniques and programs for treating and helping patients control the pain experience. As we study these issues, we will try to answer other questions you may have about dealing with pain. Do effective treatments for acute pain also work with chronic pain? What role do drugs have in treating pain, and how can patients decrease drug use? Do such methods as hypnosis and acupuncture really work in reducing pain? What are "pain clinics," and are they effective in treating pain?

CLINICAL PAIN

Not all of our pain experiences receive professional treatment, and not all of them require it. The term **clinical pain** refers to any pain that receives or requires professional treatment. The pain may be either acute or chronic and may result from known or unknown causes (Sanders, 1985). Clinical pain calls for treatment in and of itself, and not only because it may be a symptom of a progressive disease, such as arthritis or cancer. Relieving pain is important for humanitarian reasons, of course —and doing so also produces medical and psychosocial benefits for the patient (Chapman, 1984). Let's look at medical and psychosocial issues that are associated with controlling pain, beginning with acute pain.

Acute Clinical Pain

By using techniques to prevent or relieve acute pain, practitioners make medical procedures go more smoothly, reduce patients' stress and anxiety, and help them recover more quickly. Much of the acute pain people experience in today's world has little survival value (Chapman, 1984). What survival value would there be in feeling the pain as a dentist drills a tooth or a surgeon removes an appendix? How would people's survival be enhanced by feeling the intense pain that accompanies normal healing while resting in a hospital during the days after surgery?

When competent medical care is available, these pains are not useful. Yet during recovery after surgery in the United States, 30% of patients experience mild pain, 30% have moderate pain, and 40% suffer severe or very severe pain (Chapman, 1984). The level of pain varies, depending on the type of surgery involved and a wide variety of psychosocial factors, such as the patients' past medical experience, anxiety prior to the operation, and knowledge about the sensations they can expect. Postoperative pain that is not adequately reduced can cause abnormal physiological reactions that can lead to medical complications and even death. For instance, inadequately relieved pain and muscle spasms that may arise from abdominal and chest surgery can prevent patients from breathing deeply and coughing, thereby allowing bacterial infections to take hold in the lungs and cause pneumonia (Chapman, 1984).

Chronic Clinical Pain

When pain persists and becomes chronic, patients begin to perceive its nature differently. Whereas in the acute phase the pain was very aversive, the patients expected it to end and did not see it as a permanent part of their lives. As the pain persists, patients tend to become discouraged and angry, and are likely to seek the opinions of various physicians. This can be constructive. But when this is not successful and as patients come to see less and less connection between their discomfort and any known or treatable disorder, hopelessness and despair may lead them to resort to consulting quacks (Chapman, 1984).

The transition from acute to chronic pain is a critical time when these patients tend to develop pervasive feelings of helplessness (Keefe, 1982). The neurotic triad—hypochondriasis, depression, and hysteria—often becomes a dominant aspect of their personalities, especially if the pain is severe and disabling (Bradley & Van der Heide, 1984; Rosen, Grubman, Bevins, & Frymoyer, 1987). These changes typically parallel alterations in the patients' lifestyles, employment status, and family lives—as the following letter from a wife to her husband's therapist reflects:

> Whether or not I will be able to visit you again because of my working nights, I don't know but that perhaps if I could explain my husband's attitudes it might help you understand his problems. . . . The questionnaire you gave him to complete and send back became a tremendous ordeal for him. Why, I'll never know, because the questions were simple, but in the state of mind he is in, everything gets to be a chore. . . . Since his back operation five years ago he has become increasingly impatient and progressively slower with no ambition at all to even try to help himself. He had made himself an invalid and it has become very difficult for me or my family to tolerate his constant complaining. He blames me, blames our two sons, who he says don't help him around the house when in fact he does little or nothing to help himself. He does exactly the same things day after day with projects he starts and never completes and always because of his health. . . . To dwell on his illness is what he wants and only that he will do, believe me. He needs psychiatry of some kind. (Flor & Turk, 1985, p. 268)

Chronic pain often creates a broad array of long-term psychosocial problems and impaired interrelationships, which distinguish its victims from those of acute pain.

Individuals who receive treatment for their pain after it has progressed and become chronic tend to exhibit certain physical and psychosocial symptoms that characterize a "chronic pain syndrome." According to psychologist Steven Sanders (1985), these symptoms include:

- Associated tissue damage or irritation, which may be minor or major.
- Persistent pain complaints and other pain behaviors, such as grimacing or guarded movement, when in discomfort.

- Disrupted daily activity patterns, characterized either by a general reduction or by recurrent large fluctuations.
- Disrupted social, marital, employment, and recreational activities.
- Excessive use of drugs or repeated use of surgical procedures to relieve their pain.
- Disturbed sleep patterns.
- Increased anxiety and depression.

Chronic pain patients usually exhibit the first two symptoms and at least one of the remaining ones. Generally speaking, the more symptoms the patient presents, the greater the impact the pain has had and the greater the maladjustment it has produced.

Because of the differences between acute pain and chronic pain in their duration and the effects they have on their victims, these conditions usually require different treatment methods. Health care professionals need to distinguish between acute and chronic pain conditions and provide the most appropriate pain relief techniques for the patient's needs. Failing to do so can make the condition worse (Chapman, 1984). Keeping this caution in mind, we will turn our attention for the remainder of this chapter to the wide variety of medical, psychological, and physical techniques available to help control patients' pain.

MEDICAL TREATMENTS FOR PAIN

A few centuries ago, peasants in Western cultures commonly treated pain by piercing the affected area of the body with a "vigorous" twig of a tree, believing that the twig would absorb the pain from the body (Turk, Meichenbaum, & Genest, 1983). Then, to prevent anyone from getting the pain from that twig, they buried it deep in the ground. Other early practices for controlling pain were not so farfetched, but they were crudely applied, even by physicians. In nineteenth-century America, alcoholic beverages and "medicines" laced with opium were readily available (Critchlow, 1986; Kett, 1977). Many people used these substances to alleviate pain, and physicians commonly employed

Readily available elixirs in nineteenth-century America often contained such substances as opium and cocaine.

them as anesthetics for surgery before the mid-1800s, when ether was introduced. Today when patients suffer from pain, physicians try to reduce the discomfort in two ways—chemically and surgically.

Surgical Methods for Treating Pain

Treating pain with surgical methods is a relatively radical approach, and some surgical procedures are more useful than others. In some procedures, the surgery removes or disconnects portions of the peripheral nervous system or the spinal cord, thereby preventing pain signals from reaching the brain. These are extreme procedures—and if they are successful, they produce numbness and, sometimes, paralysis in the region of the body served by the affected nerves. But these procedures seldom provide long-term relief from the pain, which is often replaced after some days or months by pain and other sensations that are worse than the original condition (Hare & Milano, 1985; Melzack & Wall, 1982). Because of the poor prospects of permanent relief and the risks involved in these surgical procedures, they are rarely used today.

Other surgical procedures for relieving pain do not remove or disconnect nerve fibers and are much more successful. One example is the *synovectomy,* a technique whereby a surgeon removes membranes that become inflamed in arthritic joints. Physicians consider using this procedure for an arthritis patient when inflammation persists in only a few joints and other treatment methods have failed (Anderson et al., 1985). Despite the effectiveness of some surgical procedures for controlling pain, physicians and patients typically prefer other medical approaches, such as chemical methods.

Chemical Methods for Treating Pain

Medical research has led to many advances in treating pain since the 1800s, but this progress has been slow. The field of medicine has been much more concerned with developing methods for curing disease than with reducing pain (Melzack & Wall, 1982). The most common medical approaches for treating pain today involve the use of various chemicals. As we will see, there are basically four types of chemicals for treating pain.

Types of Pain-Relieving Chemicals

One category of painkilling pharmaceuticals consists of *peripherally acting analgesics* (Aronoff, Wagner, & Spangler, 1986). As the name implies, these drugs reduce pain by their action in the peripheral nervous system, such as by inhibiting the synthesis of neurochemicals that sensitize nociceptors to algogenic substances released at the site of tissue damage. *Aspirin,* which was first manufactured in the late 1800s, is by far the best-known and most widely used drug in this class. Americans take about 19 billion aspirins a year (Winters, 1985). Aspirin is a remarkable drug, being a very effective analgesic for mild-to-moderate pain, while also reducing fever and inflammation. Using aspirin on an occasional basis appears to have no adverse effects, but heavy use can cause irritation of the stomach lining. Other peripherally acting analgesics include *acetaminophen* (brand names Tylenol and Datril) and *ibuprofen* (Advil and Nuprin).

Another type of painkilling medication consists of *centrally acting analgesics*—narcotics that act by binding to opiate receptors in the central nervous system (Aronoff, Wagner, & Spangler, 1986). These narcotics are either derived directly from the opium poppy—as are codeine and morphine—or they are synthetic substances, such as heroin, methadone, and the brand name drugs Percodan and Demerol. Narcotics are highly effective in reducing severe pain, and they are far more potent when administered by injection than orally (Kanner, 1986; Winters, 1985). The chief reservation physicians and patients have in using narcotics for pain relief is the potential these drugs have for producing tolerance, in which the individual requires increasingly large doses, and for causing addiction. Some patients fear becoming or being thought of as a "junkie" and may fail to take a prescribed painkilling drug for that reason. There is currently some controversy about the risks of narcotic tolerance and addiction in pain patients (compare, for example, Aronoff, Wagner, & Spangler, 1986; and Melzack & Wall, 1982). We will look at this issue again shortly.

Local anesthetics, such as novocaine, lidocaine, and bupivacaine, make up the third category of chemicals for relieving pain (Melzack & Wall, 1982; Winters, 1985). Although local anesthetics can be applied topically, they are much more potent when injected at the site where the pain originates, as a dentist does before drilling or pulling a tooth. These chemicals work by blocking nerve cells in the region from generating impulses—and they often continue to relieve pain for hours or days after the chemical action has worn off (Hare & Milano, 1985). Local anesthetics offer great promise in controlling discomfort, but they have two important drawbacks (Melzack & Wall, 1982). First, they do not just block impulses in pain fibers, but in all nerves in the region—including motor neurons. As a result, the muscles are paralyzed as long as the drug is active. Second, these drugs seem to prevent the transport of substances needed to maintain the integrity of the nerve and related organs. As a result, continuous use is not recommended.

The fourth type of chemical used in treating

pain includes various drugs that may help by *indirect action.* These drugs include sedatives, tranquilizers, antidepressants, and anticonvulsants (Aronoff, Wagner, & Spangler, 1986; Foley, 1985). *Sedatives,* such as barbiturates, and *tranquilizers,* such as diazepam (Valium), are "depressants"—they depress bodily functions by decreasing the transmission of impulses throughout the central nervous system. Although pain patients often claim that sedatives and tranquilizers help them, there is no clear evidence that these drugs alleviate pain as much as they reduce anxiety and help patients sleep. The danger with using depressants for pain relief is that chronic use produces psychological and physical dependence. Drugs classified as *antidepressants,* such as doxepin, appear to help pain patients in two ways: (1) they reduce several symptoms of psychological depression that accompany chronic pain and (2) they affect the activity of pain-related neurotransmitters, particularly serotonin and norepinephrine. *Anticonvulsants* are drugs that are used in treating epilepsy; because they seem to inhibit random nerve impulses, they also seem to be useful in controlling some types of pain.

Using Chemicals for Acute and Chronic Pain

Each type of pharmaceutical we have discussed can be effective and appropriate for treating acute pain. In choosing the specific drug, physicians consider many factors, such as how intense the pain is and its location and cause. There is some evidence to suggest that another factor—whether the patient is a child—sometimes enters into the decision about the type and amount of painkiller to use. Research findings show that children are much more likely to be *under*medicated than adults who have the same medical condition (Bush, 1987; Schechter, Allen, & Hanson, 1986). When the patient is a child, practitioners tend to administer painkilling medication less frequently, give doses below the recommended level, and discontinue it earlier. The reason why this occurs is unclear—it may be, for instance, that practitioners believe children feel less pain than adults. Or children may simply request less medication, perhaps because they dislike injections more than adults do.

The conventional method practitioners use in administering chemicals to relieve severe acute pain involves giving injections or pills either on a schedule or at the patient's request, but two other methods are available today (Chapman, 1984; Kanner, 1986; Melzack & Wall, 1982). In one of these methods—called an *epidural block*—practitioners inject narcotics or local anesthetics epidurally, that is, near the membrane that surrounds the spinal cord. These chemicals then prevent pain signals from being transmitted to the brain. The second technique is called *patient-controlled analgesia.* This procedure allows the patient to determine how much painkiller, such as morphine, he or she needs, and get it without delay. The patient simply pushes a button to activate a computerized pump that dispenses a preset dose of the chemical through a needle that remains inserted continuously. Practitioners monitor the patient's use of the drug and set limits on the rate of its use.

Do patients abuse the opportunity to control their use of narcotics for pain control? Current evidence suggests that the risk of abuse may be low for most patients, at least under certain circumstances (Melzack & Wall, 1982). A study by Marc Citron and his colleagues (1986) examined this issue with hospitalized cancer patients. The patients were eight male volunteers in severe pain, ranging from 54 to 62 years of age. They were placed on a patient-controlled analgesia procedure for a little over two days, on average. A physician preset for each patient the dosage of morphine the pump would deliver and a lockout time, that is, the interval after a dose when no more morphine would be available. The average lockout time was about 30 minutes. The results revealed that the patients' rate of morphine use *declined* rather than increased, being far more heavily used in the first few hours rather than later. During the first four hours, the subjects took about one dose per hour, on average, consuming morphine at a rate of 4 milligrams an hour. But their use dropped sharply after the initial high use

—for the remainder of the two days, their rate of morphine use was less than 40% of the earlier rate. These patients were free to take much more medication, but they did not.

Many health care practitioners have long advocated using narcotics for the relief of severe pain in cancer patients, and narcotic analgesics are commonly prescribed when these patients are dying (Dugan, 1984; Foley, 1985). In some cases of cancer, severe pain becomes chronic and is associated with the progression of the disease. Because of the intensity of the pain and the terminal nature of the disease, practitioners generally view the options for pain relief in these patients differently from those who have other types of chronic/progressive pain. For example, chemical methods for relieving the discomfort in patients with rheumatoid arthritis generally focus on reducing the painful inflammation that occurs in their joints and other tissues (Anderson et al., 1985; Hollander, 1984). Physicians rarely prescribe narcotic analgesics for arthritis sufferers and tend to reserve these drugs for only the most severe cases.

Are narcotics ever used in treating chronic/recurrent and chronic/intractable/benign pain? Medical researchers tested the utility of drug therapy, combining methadone and an antidepressant, over a two-year period for patients with severe phantom limb pain (Urban et al., 1986). The subjects included three men and two women, ranging in age from 53 to 77. They reported having had the pain syndrome for an average of five years, being in pain almost constantly, having limited their lifestyles because of it, and having used a wide variety of treatments for pain relief in the past, including narcotics. The drug therapy began in a hospital, at which time the researchers gradually adjusted the drugs to produce the most analgesia from the smallest dose, thereby keeping side effects to a minimum. The subjects reported at discharge that their pain had been reduced by about two-thirds, and this level of pain reduction continued throughout the next two years with very low daily maintenance doses of each drug.

Findings such as these, indicating that narcotics in low doses can provide effective pain relief without requiring progressively larger doses or leading to addiction, are important, but they do not yet indicate that these drugs should be used more widely for chronic pain. More research is needed for at least three reasons. First, the research findings we have described need to be confirmed with a greater variety of subjects and types of pain conditions. Despite the low risk that drug abuse appears to have for most pain patients, it probably poses a high risk for *some* patients. Second, studies need to determine specifically how patients' lives and functioning are altered by taking daily doses of narcotics. Third, researchers need to find out why tolerance and addiction to narcotics are less likely when taken for pain relief. Is it because the doses are so small, for instance, or that the practitioners monitor and set limits on the drug use, or that the patients believe they may lose their painkillers if they use them too much?

Although future research findings may lead to a wider application of narcotics for pain sufferers—particularly some who suffer disabling chronic/intractable/benign pain—it seems unlikely that these drugs will prove to be a valuable component of treatment for the vast majority of chronic pain patients. The nonnarcotic chemicals we described earlier are used extensively as part of the treatment programs for chronic pain sufferers. For example:

- Aspirin and other peripherally acting analgesics provide substantial pain relief for a wide variety of pain conditions, especially arthritis and other conditions that involve inflammation (Anderson et al., 1985; Kanner, 1986).
- Local anesthetics are often effective when injected at the site of localized pain, such as in the stump of an amputated limb (Melzack & Wall, 1982).
- Antidepressants are useful in treating many types of chronic painful conditions (Aronoff, Wagner, & Spangler, 1986).
- Anticonvulsants appear to be helpful in treating some forms of neuralgia, especially trigeminal neuralgia (Aronoff,

Wagner, & Spangler, 1986; Melzack & Wall, 1982).

Even though pharmaceutical methods can help in relieving chronic pain, health care professionals often prefer not to rely on them for long-term pain control for two reasons. First, drugs often have undesirable side effects and can lead to psychological and, sometimes, physical dependence. Second, chemical methods are usually not sufficient for controlling pain by themselves. Other approaches are also needed—as physician Ronald Kanner has noted, "there is no *single* answer to pain" (1986, p. 2113).

The need for other approaches can be seen in the findings of research on drugs currently used for treating migraine and muscle-contraction headache. These drugs include a wide variety of analgesics, tranquilizers, and chemicals that constrict blood vessels (Andrasik, Blake, & McCarran, 1986; Feuerstein & Gainer, 1982). Research has investigated the effectiveness of these drugs by using a double-blind procedure and giving some subjects a placebo. These studies have shown that although many headache patients claim to experience substantial relief when taking one drug or another, so do many who take the placebo. Because placebo effects result from psychological processes, we might expect that treatments using psychological methods might also relieve pain. As we saw in Chapter 11 when considering the gate-control theory of pain, separating physiological and psychosocial aspects of a person's pain experience is artificial.

Because psychosocial factors are so important in people's experience of chronic pain, many medical practitioners treat pain patients by joining forces with psychologists and other health care professionals, such as social workers and physical and occupational therapists. When introducing a "team" approach to chronic pain patients, physicians need to describe the rationale for it and the functions each professional can provide. As psychologists Roy Cameron and Larry Shepel have noted, for instance,

> pain patients might balk at the suggestion that they see a psychologist. They typically believe, generally quite correctly, that their problems have a physical basis. Hence, the relevance of a psychological consultation may not be evident to the patient. The meaning of the referral also may be unclear. The patient may infer that the physician making the referral believes the problem to be somehow less than real, or believes the patient to be seriously maladjusted psychologically. Patients who interpret the referral this way are likely to be guarded with the psychologist. (1986, p. 242)

The physician should state clearly that (1) he or she realizes the patient is "obviously living in a great deal of pain," (2) patients can help themselves control their pain by working with these other professionals, and (3) that the physician will be an active part of the team.

To summarize, medical treatments of pain focus mainly on using chemical approaches to reduce discomfort. For chronic pain patients, these approaches can be enhanced when combined with pain control methods that other health care professions provide. Physicians usually want to minimize the use of medication by their patients, especially when drugs would be taken on a long-term basis. Reducing the patient's drug consumption is one of the goals in using other methods of pain control with chronic pain patients.

BEHAVIORAL AND COGNITIVE METHODS FOR TREATING PAIN

Gate-control theory changed the way many health care workers conceptualize pain by proposing that pain can be controlled not only by biochemical methods that alter sensory input directly, but by modifying motivational and cognitive processes, too. This theory provided the rationale for psychologists to develop techniques with two purposes: reducing patients' reliance on drugs for pain control and helping patients cope more effectively with the pain they experience. Some of the methods psychologists developed involve behavioral and cognitive techniques, and we will examine three of these approaches in this section. The first approach focuses on changing patients' pain behavior through techniques of operant conditioning.

The Operant Approach

At the start of this chapter, we described the case of a 3-year-old girl whose rehabilitation after suffering severe burns months earlier was hampered by her pattern of pain behaviors. The help therapists provided was successful. It used an *operant approach,* in which therapists apply operant conditioning techniques to modify patients' behavior.

The approach the therapists used in changing this girl's behavior involved extinction procedures for her pain behavior and reinforcement for appropriate, or "well," behavior (Varni, Jay, Masek, & Thompson, 1986; Varni & Thompson, 1986). Initial observations of the child's social environment revealed that her pain behaviors — crying, complaining of pain, resisting the nurse's efforts to put her splints on, and so forth — were maintained by the hospital staff giving attention to those behaviors and allowing her to avoid uncomfortable or disliked activities, such as physical therapy. To change this situation, the therapists instructed the hospital staff to:

- Ignore the pain behaviors they paid attention to in the past.
- Provide rewards for compliant behavior — telling her, for instance, "If you don't cry while I put your splints on, you can have some cookies when I'm finished" or "If you do this exercise, we can play a game."
- Praise her if she helps in putting on the splints, sleeps through naptime, goes for a period of time without complaining, or does an exercise.

Changing the consequences of her behavior in these ways had a dramatic effect: her pain behaviors decreased sharply, and she began to comply with requests to do exercises, make positive comments about her accomplishments, and assist in putting on her splints.

The operant approach to treating pain can be adapted for use with individuals of all ages, in hospitals and at home — and elements of the operant approach may even be introduced before pain behavior becomes chronic. But treatment programs using this approach are usually applied with patients whose chronic pain has already produced serious difficulties in their lives. These programs typically have two main goals: the first is to reduce the patient's reliance on medication. This can be achieved with the patient's approval, using a technique described by Wilbert Fordyce (1976). One feature of this technique is that the medication is given on a fixed schedule, such as every four hours, rather than whenever the patient requests it. This makes receiving the painkiller independent of requesting it, thereby eliminating any reinforcing effect the drug may have on that pain behavior. In addition, the medication is mixed with a flavored syrup to mask its taste. Then, over a period of several weeks, the dosage of medication in this "pain cocktail" is gradually reduced until the syrup contains little or no drugs.

The second goal of the operant approach is to reduce the disability that generally accompanies chronic pain conditions. This is accomplished by altering the consequences for behavior so that they promote "well" behavior and discourage pain behavior, as we just saw in the program with the young burn patient. The chief feature of this approach is that the therapist trains people in the patient's social environment to monitor and keep a record of pain behaviors, try not to reinforce them, and systematically reward physical activity. The reinforcers may be of any kind — attention, praise and smiles, candy, money, or the opportunity to watch TV, for example — and may be formalized within a contingency contract (Fordyce, 1976; Roberts, 1986). The therapist periodically reviews the record of pain behavior to determine whether changes in the program are needed.

Is the operant approach effective? Studies have shown that operant techniques can successfully increase patients' activity levels and decrease medication use (Bradley, 1983; Linton, 1982; Roberts, 1986; Turk, Meichenbaum, & Genest, 1983). Although these findings are promising, some reservations should be mentioned. First, most of the studies have not included control groups, so that it is difficult to know whether changes in the patients' behavior in these studies resulted specifically from the operant methods or from other factors, such as simply being in a hospital. Second, not all chronic pain patients are likely to benefit from the operant approach. For one thing, the goals of this approach seem more appropriate for patients with chronic/recurrent or chronic/intractable/benign pain than with chronic/progressive pain, such as in cancer patients. Also, patients are less likely to show behavioral improvements if they or people in their social environment are unwilling to participate and if they receive disability compensation (Fordyce, 1976). Despite these reservations, it seems clear that the operant approach can be a very useful component in treatment programs for many chronic pain patients.

Relaxation and Biofeedback

Many people experience chronic episodes of pain that result from underlying physiological processes, and these processes are often triggered by stress. If these patients could control their stress or the physiological processes that cause pain, they should be able to decrease the frequency or intensity of discomfort they experience. Headache provides a good example of the way stress and physiological arousal may influence pain, and Figure 12.1 diagrams how this may occur. In some cases, stress causes cephalic arteries to dilate, and migraine headaches may develop. In other cases, stress causes muscles of the scalp, neck, and shoulders to contract, and muscle-contraction headaches may result.

Because of the connection of stress and physiological processes in producing pain, therapists have applied the methods of progressive muscle relaxation and biofeedback in helping patients control their pain. These forms of treatment are usually conducted in weekly sessions that span about two or three months (see, for example, Blanchard et al., 1986). We saw in Chapter 5 that patients using

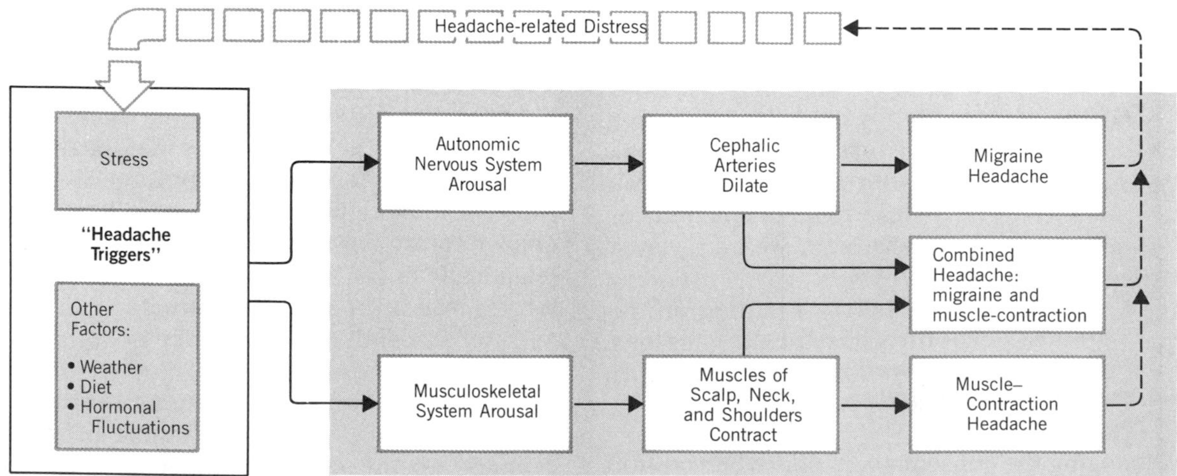

FIGURE 12.1 "Headache triggers" (stress and other factors) and physiological events that may lead to migraine, muscle-contraction, and combined headache. (Adapted from Andrasik, 1986, Figure 13.1.)

the technique of *progressive muscle relaxation* focus their attention on specific muscle groups while alternately tightening and relaxing these muscles. Patients who receive training in relaxation to control pain are urged to use this technique to reduce feelings of stress, particularly if they feel a pain episode coming on. Figure 12.1 shows why reducing stress might be effective in controlling headache pain.

In *biofeedback* procedures, patients learn to exert voluntary control over a bodily function, such as heart rate, by receiving information about changes in that function. Of the many physiological processes people can learn to control through biofeedback, two have received particular attention in the treatment of pain. One of these processes focuses on muscle activity and is used for muscle-contraction headaches. Patients learn to control the tension of specific muscle groups — such as those in the scalp and neck — by receiving biofeedback from an electromyograph (EMG) device, which measures electrical activity in the muscles. The other process is used for migraine headaches. It focuses on controlling the constriction and dilation of arteries — such as those in the head — which can be measured indirectly on the basis of the temperature of the skin in the region of the target blood vessels. Patients learn to control arterial dilation through temperature biofeedback — as the arteries dilate and contain more blood, the region becomes warmer. Therapists urge patients who learn to control muscle tension or arterial dilation to practice this skill at home and use it when they feel a pain episode beginning. Figure 12.1 shows why using one or the other of these biofeedback skills might reduce headache pain.

Do relaxation and biofeedback procedures help in relieving pain? Yes, they do. This broad conclusion comes from reviews of many studies that were conducted to examine the effectiveness of these procedures (Andrasik, Blake, & McCarran, 1986; Belar & Kibrick, 1986; Blanchard, 1987; Feuerstein & Gainer, 1982; Holroyd & Penzien, 1985; Linton, 1982; Turk, Meichenbaum, & Berman, 1979). But several points need to be made to clarify this conclusion. The first point is that the large majority of studies testing relaxation and biofeedback treatments have focused on headache pain. Although a few studies have demonstrated that these treatments can help alleviate other types of pain, such as arthritic and phantom limb pain (Bradley, 1983), current knowledge about the effectiveness of these procedures is based mainly on their ability to relieve headache pain.

Second, relaxation and biofeedback treatments are about equally effective in relieving headache pain — relaxation is somewhat more effective with migraine headache, and biofeedback is somewhat more effective with muscle-contraction headache (Andrasik, Blake, & McCarran, 1986; Holroyd & Penzien, 1985). Studies have examined the success of these procedures by (1) assessing whether the patients' daily records at the end of treatment showed improvements in the headache pain, as measured by its frequency, intensity, and duration, and (2) comparing the headache pain of patients who received these treatments with those who were in control groups. In one type of control group, the subjects receive no training but "monitor" their headache pain with daily records; in another type of control condition, subjects keep records and receive a "placebo" treatment, such as by taking sham medication or by receiving biofeedback sessions that give false feedback about changes in the subjects' bodily functions. Generally speaking, relaxation and biofeedback treatments are about twice as effective in relieving pain as placebo conditions, which are more effective than just monitoring headache pain. Figure 12.2 depicts these effects for muscle-contraction headache sufferers, averaged across subjects in many studies.

Third, the graph in Figure 12.2 suggests that muscle-contraction headache sufferers get slightly more pain relief with biofeedback than with relaxation treatment, and that they seem to gain even more relief when these treatments are combined. This may be the case and may be important for clinical purposes, but these dif-

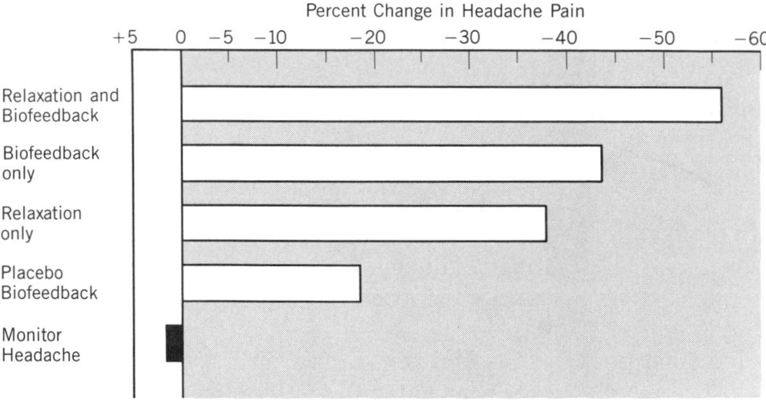

FIGURE 12.2 Percentage change in headache pain, pretreatment to posttreatment, across many studies with patients suffering from chronic *muscle-contraction* (tension) headaches. Treatments consisted of EMG biofeedback, or relaxation, or EMG biofeedback and relaxation combined. Control conditions consisted of placebo biofeedback or simply monitoring headache pain. (Data from Holroyd & Penzien, 1985, Table IV.)

ferences are not reliable because patients vary greatly in the amount of benefit they get from these treatments. For instance, among subjects who received relaxation treatment, the percentage by which their pain improved ranged from 17 to 94%; among those who had the combined treatment, improvements ranged from 29 to 88% (Holroyd & Penzien, 1985). This variability is important for two reasons. One reason is that it reflects the fact that many pain patients—especially middle-aged and elderly ones—seem to gain relatively little relief with these treatments (Blanchard & Andrasik, 1985; Holroyd & Penzien, 1985). The other reason is that biofeedback treatment is relatively expensive to conduct, and the likelihood of improvement beyond just using relaxation for many pain conditions may not justify its expense (Turk, Meichenbaum, & Berman, 1979). However, it may be possible to predict who will benefit most from biofeedback treatment. Tentative evidence suggests, for example, that children and individuals who show certain psychophysiological patterns, such as a high correlation between their pain and EMG levels, may be better candidates for biofeedback treatment than other individuals (Attanasio et al., 1985; Keefe & Gil, 1985).

Fourth, although the pain relief that patients experience with relaxation or biofeedback treatment may result from the specific skills they learned for controlling physiological processes, other psychological factors also seem to play a role. Consider, for instance, the fact that placebo conditions often produce more relief than simply monitoring headache pain (Andrasik, 1986). Why is this? The patients' thoughts, beliefs, and spontaneous cognitive strategies probably account for the success of placebo conditions and contribute to part of the success of relaxation and biofeedback treatments in controlling pain (Turk, Meichenbaum, & Genest, 1983).

Relaxation and biofeedback techniques are very helpful in controlling the discomfort many chronic pain patients experience, but these treatments do not provide all the pain relief most patients need. Because chronic pain involves a complex interplay of sensory and psychosocial factors, therapists generally use these techniques along with several other approaches, especially cognitive therapies that address the thought patterns that occur when people experience pain.

Cognitive Techniques

What do people think about when they experience pain? In an acute pain situation, some peo-

HIGHLIGHT 12A: On Research
How Durable Are the Effects of Relaxation and Biofeedback Treatments for Pain?

After a patient completes the treatment for chronic pain, how long do the effects of the treatment last? Do the effects wear off in a few weeks or months? This is an issue of great importance in health psychology—as we saw in earlier chapters, psychological interventions do not always last, such as in cases of alcohol abuse, and relapse often occurs. Edward Blanchard, Frank Andrasik, and their associates have attempted to address this issue by conducting a five-year follow-up investigation on chronic headache patients who completed training for either relaxation or for both relaxation and biofeedback in the early 1980s (Blanchard et al., 1986; Blanchard, Andrasik, et al., 1987; Blanchard, Appelbaum, et al., 1987).

The subjects in this research were patients chronically suffering either from muscle-contraction headache or from "vascular" headache, which includes both migraine and combined (migraine plus muscle-contraction) headache. They ranged in age from 25 to 68 years and had suffered their headache conditions for an average of nearly 18 years. All patients received relaxation training in 10 sessions, spanning eight weeks. Those patients whose headache pain had not improved by at least 60% were offered additional treatment: 12 sessions of biofeedback training, with muscle-contraction sufferers receiving EMG biofeedback and vascular sufferers getting temperature biofeedback. All subjects had an audiotape to guide their practice of relaxation, and those who received training in temperature biofeedback were given a temperature-monitoring device to use at home. All subjects kept daily "headache diaries" that included four ratings each day of their headache pain. Psychological assessment of these subjects before the treatment and again a few months after treatment revealed that their feelings of depression and anxiety improved substantially (Blanchard et al., 1986).

Of the subjects who completed the treatment and continued to be available for the study, the researchers attempted to follow only those whose headache pain had been improved by at least 50% at the end of treatment. These subjects, nearly three-fourths of whom were women, consisted of 14 muscle-contraction patients and 24 vascular patients. During the first six months after treatment, the subjects continued to keep their daily headache diaries, were interviewed by a therapist monthly, and received a treatment booster session at these interviews if they desired it. Thereafter, patients who continued to participate in the study met with a therapist yearly, starting with the first anniversary of the end of their original treatment. The subjects were contacted about a month before each annual meeting and received a supply of headache diary materials to fill out daily during this month. They were paid for participating in the annual follow-ups.

A major difficulty in doing longitudinal research is that the number of original subjects who are available and willing to participate declines over time. At the time of the fifth annual follow-up, only 21 of the 38 subjects could be located and agreed to participate. These individuals consisted of 9 muscle-contraction patients and 12 vascular patients. To assess the continued success of the treatments, the researchers used the ratings these subjects made four times each day in their headache diaries. The patients made their ratings on a five-point scale, ranging from "no headache" to "intense, incapacitating headache." The researchers averaged the ratings for each subject across each of seven four-week periods, which occurred at pretreatment, posttreatment, and years one through five in the follow-up. As Figure 12A.1 shows, the treatment effects were quite durable for the patients who continued in the study.

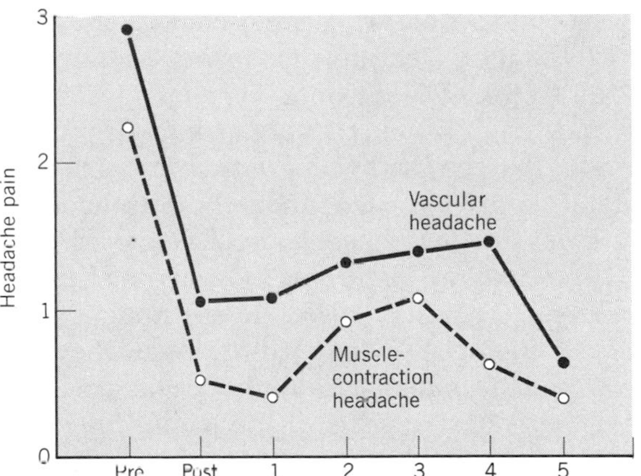

FIGURE 12A.1 Averaged ratings of headache pain for muscle-contraction and vascular (migraine and combined) headache patients who successfully completed treatment and continued to participate in the follow-up. The graphs depict these ratings at pretreatment, posttreatment, and follow-up years one through five. (Data from Blanchard, Appelbaum, et al., 1987, Table 1.)

What about the 17 patients who did not continue through the five-year follow-up—were their treatments durable? Although there is no way of knowing for sure, there is reason to believe they were (Blanchard, Andrasik, et al., 1987; Blanchard, Appelbaum, et al., 1987). Most of these patients simply could not be located, but five were contacted and did not indicate that they were having pain problems when they declined to participate. Moreover, most of those who dropped out during the five years had reported very successful pain relief in the last follow-up they completed, which suggests that they dropped out for reasons other than a relapse in pain. The results of several other follow-up studies confirm that headache treatments consisting of relaxation training or relaxation followed by biofeedback training provide durable relief for at least two years (Blanchard, 1987).

---

ple focus on the ordeal and how uncomfortable and miserable they are, but others do not (Turk & Rudy, 1986). For example, researchers asked children and adolescents what they think about when getting an injection at their dentist's office (Brown, O'Keeffe, Sanders, & Baker, 1986). Over 80% of the subjects reported thoughts that focused on negative emotions and pain, such as "This hurts, I hate shots," "I'm scared," and "My heart is pounding and I feel shaky." One-fourth of the subjects had thoughts of escaping or avoiding the situation, as in "I want to run away." These types of thoughts focus the person's attention on the unpleasant aspects of the experience and make the pain worse (Turk, Meichenbaum, & Genest, 1983; Turk & Rudy, 1986).

Not all people who experience acute pain focus on the ordeal and discomfort—many use cognitive strategies to modify their experience. For instance, by 10 years of age, many children report that they try to cope with pain in a dental situation by thinking about something else or by saying to themselves such things as "It's not so bad" or "Be brave" (Brown, O'Keeffe, Sanders, & Baker, 1986). Even though children's coping skills tend to improve as they get older, many patients in adulthood still exaggerate the fearful aspects of the painful medical procedures they experience (Chaves & Brown, 1987). As you might expect, many cognitive strategies are effective in helping people cope with acute pain. These strategies can be classified into three basic types: *attention-diversion, imagery,* and *redefinition* (Fernandez, 1986; McCaul & Malott, 1984). After we examine these cognitive techniques, we will consider their usefulness for people with chronic pain.

Attention-Diversion

At your dentist's office, do the examination rooms have colorful pictures or large windows with nice views on all the walls a patient can see while in the dental chair? My dentist's rooms do, and I use the pictures and windows to divert my attention when I feel the need. **Attention-diversion from pain** is the technique of focusing on a nonpainful stimulus in the immediate environment in order to be distracted from discomfort (Fernandez, 1986). Attention-diversion can be either *passive,* such as looking at a picture or listening to a song on the radio, or *active,* such as singing a song, counting ceiling tiles, playing a video game, or doing mathematics problems.

Not all efforts at attention-diversion are likely to work in relieving pain. Research on acute pain has shown that these strategies are more effective if the pain is mild or moderate than if it is strong, and if the technique attracts a high degree of attention or involvement than if it does not (McCaul & Malott, 1984). Doing moderately difficult mathematics problems, for example, is likely to be more effective than doing very simple ones. Another factor in whether attention-diversion relieves pain is whether the technique seems credible to the person. A study demonstrated this by having college students undergo the cold-pressor procedure while listening to distracting stimuli through earphones (Melzack, Weisz, & Sprague, 1963). During the cold-pressor test, the subjects in one condition listened to a clearly noticeable sound, such as music, after having been told that they could control its volume and that dentists had found that loud sound helps reduce pain. Subjects in another condition were treated in the same way, but they were not told that the sound would help them tolerate the pain. And subjects in a third condition listened to a low-intensity hum, described to them as an "ultrasonic sound, beyond the range of frequencies audible to the human ear." They were also told that they could control the intensity of the hum and that dentists found it reduces pain when set at its highest levels. The results of the cold-pressor test showed that subjects got the greatest benefit toward tolerating pain if they heard the noticeable sound and were told it would help. Subjects got the least benefit if they heard the hum and were told it would help.

Why was the hum condition less effective than the others? It attracted less attention, and the subjects probably did not believe it would work. Because of the role that credibility can play in using attention-diversion methods, therapists may need to help patients understand how these techniques can work. One therapist described the following approach for doing this:

> First, I ask the patient to be aware of the sensations in his thighs as he sits in his chair. I note that those sensations are real, and they have a physical basis, but they are not normally experienced because other things occupy his attention. Then I suggest that he think of a TV set: he could block out the channel 9 signal by tuning in channel 11; the channel 9 signal is still there, but not being tuned in. I suggest that while his pain signals are real, he can learn to "tune them out". . . . A number of pain patients have reported that they frequently think of the TV metaphor when experiencing pain and take appropriate action to "tune out." (Cameron, quoted in Turk, Meichenbaum, & Genest, 1983, p. 284)

By providing plausible explanations for a recommended technique, therapists can increase its effectiveness and the likelihood that the patient will use it.

Attention-diversion strategies are especially useful for reducing acute pain, such as that experienced in some medical or dental procedures. Distraction can also provide relief for chronic pain patients in some circumstances. Singing a song or staring intently at a stimulus can divert the person's attention for a short while—and this may be a great help, such as for an arthritis sufferer who experiences heightened pain when climbing stairs. People with moderate levels of continuous pain may get longer-lasting relief through attention-diversion by engaging in an extended engrossing activity, such as watching a movie or reading a book.

Imagery

Sometimes when children are about to receive an injection, their parents will say something like, "It'll be easier if you think about something nice, like the fun things we did at the park." **Nonpain imagery**—sometimes called *guided imagery*—is a strategy whereby the person tries to alleviate discomfort by conjuring up a mental scene that is unrelated to or incompatible with the pain (Fernandez, 1986). The most common type of imagery people use involves a scene that is pleasant to them — they think of "something nice." This scene might involve being at the beach or in the country, for instance, and the person is usually encouraged to include aspects of a variety of senses: vision, hearing, taste, smell, and touch. As an example, the scene at the beach could include the sight and smell of the ocean water, the sound of the waves, and the warm, grainy feel of the sand. Other types of imagery for controlling pain are not necessarily pleasant—they can involve such themes as having an argument with someone or replacing the feeling of pain with another sensation, such as a tingling feeling. The person generally tries to keep the imagined event in mind as long as possible.

The imagery technique is in many ways like attention-diversion. The main difference is that imagery is based on the person's imagination rather than on real objects or events in the environment. As a result, individuals who use imagery do not have to depend on the environment to provide a suitably distracting stimulus. They can develop one or more scenes that work reliably, which they "carry" around in their heads. They can then call one of these scenes up for pain relief whenever they need it. Like attention-diversion, imagery works best when it attracts high levels of the person's attention or involvement, and it is likely to work better with mild or moderate pain than with strong pain (McCaul & Malott, 1984; Turk, Meichenbaum, & Genest, 1983). Although imagery clearly helps in reducing acute pain, the extent of this technique's usefulness with longer-lasting pain episodes is unclear. One limitation with using imagery in pain control is that some individuals are less adept in imagining scenes than others (Melzack & Wall, 1982).

Redefinition

The third type of cognitive strategy for reducing discomfort is **pain redefinition,** in which the person substitutes constructive or realistic thoughts about the pain experience for ones that arouse feelings of threat or harm (Fernandez, 1986; McCaul & Malott, 1984). Therapists can help people redefine their pain experience in several ways. For one thing, providing information about the sensations to expect in medical procedures can reduce the pain patients experience when undergoing these procedures (Anderson & Masur, 1983). Since many patients have misconceptions or exaggerated expectations about the discomfort they will feel, providing realistic information helps them redefine the experience before it occurs.

Another approach we have discussed before that can be helpful in redefining pain experiences involves engaging in an internal dialogue, using positive self-statements. There are basically two kinds of self-statements for controlling pain (Fernandez, 1986): *Coping statements* emphasize the person's ability to tolerate the discomfort, as when people say to themselves, "It hurts, but you're in control" or "Be brave—you can take it." *Reinterpretative statements* are designed to negate the unpleasant aspects of the discomfort, as when people think, "It's not so bad," "It's not the worst thing that could happen," or "It hurts, but think of the benefits of this experience." This last statement can be particularly appropriate when undergoing painful medical procedures.

A third approach for redefining pain experiences involves helping the patients see that some of their beliefs are illogical and are making the discomfort worse. We see how this process can work in the following dialogue between a therapist and "Mrs. D," a 56-year-old patient who worried that her chronic/recurrent head pain was actually caused by a tumor, which repeated neurological tests had failed to reveal. The therapist suggested that they examine those thoughts, and she replied:

Mrs. D.: Yes, I know they're not true but I cannot help it.

Therapist: You don't think you have control over your thoughts?

Mrs. D.: Yes, they just come to me.

T.: Well, let's come back to the idea that your thoughts are automatic. First, let's break down your flood of negative thoughts and look at each part separately. Do you really think that you have a tumor

Mrs. D.: I don't know. I guess not (pause) but it's hard not to worry about it. My head hurts so bad.

T.: Yes, I know. So how do you convince yourself that you don't have a tumor or something else seriously wrong?

Mrs. D.: Well, as you know I've been examined many times by the best neurologists around. They say I'm OK. Also, my pain always goes away and I've never had any other neurological problems. My only problem is the pain. But, it's hard to remember these facts when my pain is so awful.

T.: It's much easier to be positive about your condition when you're not suffering. Nevertheless, rationally, you really are convinced that there's nothing seriously wrong.

Mrs. D.: I guess so. If only I could remember that when my pain starts coming on.

T.: So the goal of our work today could be to figure out a strategy to increase the likelihood that you'll remember the positive thoughts during a pain episode.

Mrs. D.: Yes, that sounds good.

T.: Let's start by generating a list of accurate statements about your pain. Then we can talk about ways you can cue yourself to remember the list when you begin to feel pain. You already mentioned a couple of beliefs about your pain; that is, that there's nothing seriously wrong, that the pain always goes away, and that, other than the pain, you feel pretty healthy. Can you think of other accurate and positive thoughts? (Holzman, Turk, & Kerns, 1986, pp. 45–46)

In this example, the therapist helped the patient examine the logic of her thought patterns and generate a list of ideas she believed that were incompatible with her irrational fears. They later rehearsed these beliefs so that she could use them as self-statements when pain episodes occurred.

The Value of Cognitive Strategies in Controlling Pain

Studies have tested the effectiveness of different cognitive strategies in reducing acute pain. The findings of these studies suggest that attention-diversion and imagery are particularly useful with mild or moderate pain, and that redefinition appears to be more effective with strong pain (McCaul & Malott, 1984). There is also some evidence that redefinition is more effective in relieving chronic pain than attention-diversion is. A study compared these two techniques in reducing the chronic pain of patients who were receiving physical rehabilitation for a variety of medical problems, including arthritis, amputation, and spinal cord injury (Rybstein-Blinchik, 1979). Although both techniques were effective, patients who received redefinition training reported less pain and exhibited less pain behavior than those who were trained in attention-diversion.

Because each type of cognitive strategy can be helpful in treating clinical pain, programs to help chronic pain sufferers control their pain generally combine different types of strategies. In one study, for instance, arthritis sufferers received a five-week pain control program that included training in attention-diversion, imagery, and redefinition (O'Leary, Shoor, Lorig, & Holman, 1988). The program gave special emphasis to having the patients use these techniques in specific painful activities, such as carrying groceries, climbing stairs, and mopping floors. A control group simply received a self-help book for arthritis sufferers. Assessments made just before and just after the program was conducted revealed that it was very effective. The control group showed little or no improvement during that time period. In contrast, the treated group reported having less pain, greater self-efficacy, less depression, and improved sleep patterns.

Another study used a program that combined imagery, redefinition, and relaxation training to treat chronic low back pain patients (Turner, 1982). Some subjects received this program, others received a program of only relaxation training, and a third group served as controls. Compared with the control subjects, the patients in both programs reported much less pain, depression, and disability by the end of treatment—and these improvements were similar for the patients in both programs. A follow-up on the patients in the two programs more than a year and a half later revealed that the benefits of the treatments were maintained, as measured by the subjects' ratings of pain and reports of health care use. But the patients who received the program combining cognitive strategies and relaxation also showed a marked improvement in their employment, working 60% more hours per week than those who had the program of relaxation only.

To summarize, several behavioral and cognitive methods are effective in helping people control acute and chronic pain. These methods include operant techniques, relaxation and biofeedback, and the cognitive strategies of attention-diversion, imagery, and redefinition. Behavioral and cognitive methods seem to be most helpful when used in combination.

HYPNOSIS AND INSIGHT-ORIENTED PSYCHOTHERAPY

You may have noticed that the behavioral and cognitive methods we just described for relieving pain sound familiar—and they should. For the most part, they involve psychological procedures derived from the stress reduction techniques we considered in Chapter 5. Because people's experience of pain includes an emotional component and is stressful, and because behavioral and cognitive methods are effective in reducing stress, psychologists have adapted these techniques to help people control their pain. Other psychological approaches have also been applied to relieve pain. These approaches include hypnosis and insight-oriented psychotherapy.

Hypnosis as a Treatment for Pain

In the mid-1800s before ether was discovered, dramatic reports began to appear of physicians performing major surgery on individuals, using hypnosis as the sole method of analgesia (Bakal, 1979; Barber, 1986). In one case, a surgeon made an incision halfway across the chest of a woman with breast cancer and removed the tumor as well as several enlarged glands in her armpit. During the procedure, the woman conversed with the surgeon and showed no signs of feeling pain. Another physician reported having done hundreds of major surgeries with hypnosis as the only analgesic, and argued that the patients experienced no pain. Were all of these operations painless? Probably not—although many patients *claimed* to feel no pain, some showed other pain behaviors, such as with facial expressions suggesting they were suppressing their agony (Bakal, 1979). Nevertheless, hypnosis does appear to reduce the intensity of pain that some individuals experience (Hilgard & Hilgard, 1983).

How and why does hypnosis reduce pain? First of all, we should note that hypnosis is not effective for all people—in fact, it produces a high degree of analgesia in only a minority of individuals (Hilgard & Hilgard, 1983; Melzack & Wall, 1982). People vary in their ability to be hypnotized, and those who can be hypnotized very easily and deeply seem to gain more pain relief from hypnosis than those who are less hypnotically susceptible. The mechanisms underlying the pain relief that some individuals get from hypnosis are not clear (Barber, 1986). Part of the mechanism may involve the relaxation people experience when hypnotized—as we saw earlier, relaxation can help relieve pain. Cognitive factors also seem to be involved (Barber, 1986; Turk, Meichenbaum, & Genest, 1983). Hypnosis often produces states of heightened attention to internal images and "inattention" to environmental stimuli. For instance, while under hypnosis, people may experience "positive" hallucinations, in which they either perceive objects and events that are not really there, or "negative" hallucinations, in which they fail to perceive things they ordinarily would. Because hypnosis may produce analgesia somewhat like placebos do, researchers have looked for neurophysiological mechanisms that may underlie hypnotic pain relief. Although research has apparently disconfirmed the role of endorphins, findings for other neurochemicals seem more promising (Barber, 1986).

Hypnosis has always been viewed as an odd phenomenon, and its role in pain relief has not changed that view. When it produces analgesia, it can do so very quickly and dramatically. Furthermore, patients who experience hypnotic analgesia sometimes do not even believe they were hypnotized, perhaps because they have unrealistic ideas about "what it feels like" to be hypnotized. One patient, for example, underwent a normally painful dental procedure with only hypnosis as an anesthetic. He claimed to the dentist that he was not hypnotized "because I can't be hypnotized" and that the reason he did not feel pain was that "you didn't do anything to me that would hurt" (Barber, 1986).

In some cases these patients' claims that they were not hypnotized may actually be right. According to Theodore Barber (1982), laboratory research on acute pain, induced by cold-pressor or muscle-ischemia procedures, has found that:

- Hypnosis can reduce pain.
- When hypnotized, the people who gain the most pain relief from suggestions of analgesia tend to be those who are highly responsive to other suggestions, such as that their arm is becoming light.
- Whether under hypnosis or not, individuals who are told to try not to feel pain tend to use attention-diversion and redefinition techniques.
- Contrary to the common myths about hypnosis, people usually show as much pain reduction using cognitive strategies, such as imagery and redefinition, as they do under hypnosis.

It may be that some patients who were supposedly hypnotized actually were not, and they may have applied cognitive strategies to reduce the pain.

Can hypnosis also help relieve chronic pain? Although some research has found support for the effectiveness of hypnosis in treating chronic headache, low back pain, and cancer pain, almost all these studies either lacked appropriate control groups or they simply provided descriptions of individual cases (Barber, 1982; Melzack & Wall, 1982). As a result, there is little clear evidence that hypnosis provides any better relief for chronic pain than a placebo drug or sham treatment would. The success of hypnosis with acute pain suggests that it might be effective with chronic pain, but better research is needed to demonstrate this clearly. Even if this research is eventually done and confirms its usefulness, hypnosis is not likely to serve as the sole treatment approach. As Barber has noted,

> many people turn to hypnosis with the expectation that it is a magic treatment for chronic pain, just as many regard it as a sole treatment to cure compulsive problems, sexual problems, or anxiety. It cannot. To be effective for such complex problems, hypnosis must be wisely incorporated into a broader psychotherapeutic intervention. (1986, p. 151)

The "psychotherapeutic intervention" Barber mentions might include any of the behavioral and cognitive methods we have examined, as well as the psychotherapies we are about to discuss that involve "insight-oriented" approaches in individual and group counseling for treating pain.

Insight-Oriented Psychotherapies for Pain

Many approaches to psychotherapy involve helping individuals achieve insights into the roots of their problems. In the case of chronic pain patients, these insights often relate to the feelings these patients and their families have about the pain condition, the way they deal with pain behaviors, and the changes that have developed in the interpersonal relationships of these people. The insights these people achieve can provide the first step in helping them cope more effectively with the pain condition and to reduce feelings of depression. Insight-oriented approaches can be used in individual therapy and in groups.

One insight-oriented approach involves showing patients how their pain behavior is part of "pain games" they play with other people (Szasz, cited in Bakal, 1979). In these games, individuals with chronic pain seem to take on a role in which they continually seek to confirm their identity as a suffering person, maintain their dependent lifestyle, and receive various secondary gains, such as attention and sympathy. These patients are probably not aware of what is actually happening in these games, and the purpose of this psychotherapeutic approach is to make them aware. The assumption is that once patients gain an insight into how their behavior patterns are affecting their lives, they can give up the games if they want to and are shown how. Studies with chronic pain patients have found that treatment programs that include an insight-oriented component can successfully reduce pain, but the specific value of insight as part of the programs was not assessed (Turk, Meichenbaum, & Genest, 1983).

Conducting psychotherapy for chronic pain patients within a group format has several advantages in helping patients cope with their pain and disability. According to psychologists W. Doyle Gentry and Daniel Owens (1986), the benefits of *pain groups* over individual therapy include:

1. *Efficiency.* Although each patient has unique problems, chronic pain sufferers also face common difficulties, such as depression and addiction to medication. As a result, they often need similar types of advice and information. Group meetings use the therapist's time more efficiently.
2. *Reduced isolation.* Chronic pain sufferers are typically isolated from extended social contact. This situation can lead to a sense of alienation, which involves feelings of being different from others and of anger and suspicion toward them. Group meetings can help to overcome these feelings.
3. *Credible feedback for patients.* Pain patients often resist feedback or advice from therapists, saying such things as "You don't know what it's like to live with pain 24 hours a day!" In their eyes, the type of feedback other patients can give may be more believable.
4. *A new reference group for patients.* Patients in a pain group develop a new social network of individuals who are comparable to themselves and who can provide social pressure to conform to the realities and constructive "rules" of living with pain and physical limitations.
5. *A different perspective for the therapist.* Watching the patient relate to other individuals in a group provides the therapist with certain kinds of information that may aid in identifying specific problems therapy should address, such as maladaptive coping styles.

The pain group provides a forum for talking about their worst fears and conflicts to people who share these concerns and understand. Patients often say, "I'm afraid the pain will get worse," "I was beginning to believe I was imagining the pain," and "I can't do things because of the pain and I feel guilty, helpless, frustrated, and angry" (Hendler, 1984). Patients in the group may answer, for instance, "You hurt whether you go shopping or not; so the choice isn't between having pain or not, it's a choice between whether you go shopping or stay home!" (Gentry & Owens, 1986). These people can say things to each other that others could not, without seeming cruel. Group members can also disconfirm each other's misconceptions, share their own ways for managing pain on a day-to-day basis, give each other hope and social support, and detect and confront each others' pain games.

Insight-oriented approaches can also help chronic pain patients and their families understand the problems they experience in their relationships within the family system (Flor & Turk, 1985; Roy, 1985). For instance, when a spouse suffers from chronic pain, both spouses experience feelings of frustration, anger, helplessness, and guilt that they often do not communicate openly to each other. These feelings can result from changes in their roles, general style of communication, and sexual relationship. The following excerpt shows how a therapist was able to help a pain patient, John Cox, and his wife gain insights about their feelings and behavior. Mr. and Mrs. Cox were discussing a pain episode that occurred while they watched TV together, and the therapist asked the wife how she reacted when she realized he was in pain:

Mrs. Cox: I really felt sorry for John, but I didn't know what to do. I just tried to watch the show and not say anything to him. At those times I feel . . . so helpless.

Therapist: Mr. Cox, it sounds as if your wife tried to avoid talking about your pain. She sounds sort of helpless and frustrated. . . . How did you feel about her response?

Mr. Cox: I think I got kind of mad at her because she seemed to be ignoring me, not really caring how I was feeling.

Therapist: Mr. Cox, what do you think she should have done at that time?

Mr. Cox: I don't really know.

Therapist: Mr. Cox, do you think there was anything she could have done to make you feel better?

Mr. Cox: Not really.

Therapist: . . . Perhaps at such times ignoring your pain may be the most she can do. . . .

Mr. Cox: Perhaps.

Therapist: Perhaps?

Mr. Cox: Well maybe she did know how I was feeling, but I felt upset that she didn't tell me. (Turk, Meichenbaum, & Genest, 1983, pp. 244-245)

Insights such as these help family members understand each others' feelings and points of view, and this understanding can help to break down the long-standing confusion and conflicts that have developed over time. The resulting improvements in their relationships may then enable the therapist to get all or most of the family's cooperation in the treatment process.

In summary, hypnosis and insight-oriented approaches to psychotherapy offer promising techniques in the treatment of chronic pain. Although both approaches can probably enhance the success of pain control programs for many patients, there is currently little experimental research to confirm this belief. Thus far in our discussion of methods for reducing pain we have considered a variety of medical and psychological techniques. In the next section, we will see how physical therapy and certain skin stimulation methods can also play important roles in controlling pain.

PHYSICAL AND STIMULATION THERAPIES FOR PAIN

Anthropologists and medical historians have noted that most, if not all, cultures in recorded history have learned that people can "fight pain with pain" (Melzack & Wall, 1982). One pain can cancel another—a brief or moderate pain can cancel a longer-lasting or stronger one. For example, you might reduce the pain of an injection by pressing your thumbnail into your forefinger as the shot is given. Reducing one pain by creating another is called **counter-irritation.** People in ancient cultures developed a counter-irritation procedure called *cupping* to relieve headaches, backaches, and arthritic pain. In this procedure, one or more heated glass cups are inverted and pressed on the skin. As the air in the cup cools, it creates a vacuum, causing the skin to be bruised as it is drawn up into the cup. This method is still used in some parts of the world today (Melzack & Wall, 1982).

The principle of counter-irritation is the basis for present-day stimulation therapies for reducing pain. After examining these pain control methods, we will discuss the important role other physical approaches can play in reducing pain.

Stimulation Therapies

Why does counter-irritation relieve pain? One reason is that people actively divert their attention from the stronger pain to the milder one. Another explanation comes from gate-control theory. Recall that activity in the peripheral fibers that carry signals about mildly irritating stimuli tend to close the gate, thereby inhibiting the transmission cells from sending pain signals to the brain. Counter-irritation, such as massaging a sore muscle, activates these peripheral fibers, and this may close the gate and soothe the pain.

This gate-control view of how counter-irritation works led to the development of a pain control technique called **transcutaneous electrical nerve stimulation** (TENS). This technique involves placing electrodes on the skin near where the patient feels pain and stimulating that area with mild electric current, which is supplied by a small portable device. TENS can be effective in reducing acute muscular and postoperative pain in most patients (Chapman, 1984; Hare & Milano, 1985). In a dramatic example of its effectiveness, a 9-year-old boy began receiving TENS while still unconscious after kidney surgery. When he awoke, the hospital staff asked repeatedly if he felt pain in his belly, and he said, "No, it doesn't hurt." The startling thing about this example is that he did not even realize the surgery already occurred—after the surgeon left the room, the boy talked

> casually with the others in the room. When asked whether there was anything he feared, he began to cry and confessed his terror of the expected operation that would remove his kidney. His surprised nurse tried to reassure him that the surgery had already been done, and that there was nothing to worry about. He refused to believe her. "But don't you remember?" she contended, "That's why they put you to sleep this morning—so they could do the operation." The little boy looked very threatened. "It's not true!" he shouted, "It's not true!" When asked why it couldn't be true, he asserted confidently, "Because I haven't got any bandages." We asked him to feel his belly, since his hands were outside of the bedclothes. When he did, an expression of astonishment came over his face. (Chapman, 1984, p. 1265)

Now he claimed to feel pain and began to cry.

TENS has also been used in treating chronic pain, but its success has been mixed. When TENS does relieve discomfort for some chronic conditions, such as phantom limb pain, its effects are often short-lived (Bradley, 1983; Hare & Milano, 1985). But for patients with arthritis, TENS often produces substantial and long-lasting pain relief (Johnson, 1984; Melzack & Wall, 1982). Moreover, for other chronic pain conditions, such as certain forms of neuralgia, TENS sometimes produces long-lasting pain relief in patients who have gotten little or no relief from various other methods (Melzack & Wall, 1982).

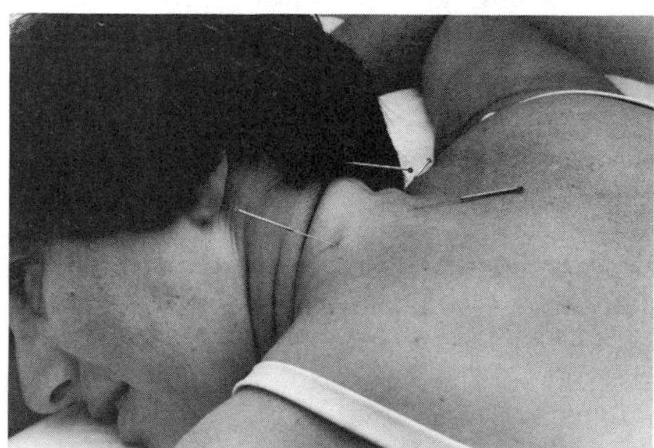

Acupuncture can be effective in reducing pain in some individuals.

Another counter-irritation method that is used today for reducing pain is **acupuncture,** a technique in which fine metal needles are inserted under the skin at special locations and then twirled or electrically charged to create stimulation. Acupuncture has been used in China for at least the past 2,000 years and was originally based on the idea that pain occurred when the life forces of Yin and Yang are out of balance (Bakal, 1979; Melzack & Wall, 1982). Although acupuncturists generally do not believe this rationale any longer, many, but not all, still determine the placement of the needles on the basis of charts that show hundreds of insertion points. These acupuncturists believe that stimulation at several specific points relieves pain in associated parts of the body. On the nose and ear, for example, certain points are associated with the small intestine, whereas other points are associated with the kidney, or heart, or abdomen.

Does acupuncture work? Its ability to produce high levels of analgesia in some individuals has been clearly and dramatically demonstrated—for instance, surgeons have performed major surgery on patients with only acupuncture anesthesia. But research findings point to several conclusions about its effects and its limitations (Bakal, 1979; Chapman, 1984; Melzack & Wall, 1982):

- Even in China, physicians perform only a small percentage (less than 10%) of surgeries with acupuncture analgesia, and these operations are straightforward ones with little likelihood of complications. Patients must volunteer for the procedure, and then their physicians select appropriate candidates very carefully and make sure these patients are well indoctrinated.
- Acupuncture is rarely effective for surgical patients in Western cultures.
- Laboratory studies have shown that acupuncture produces only mild analgesia in most people.

- The degree of analgesia acupuncture produces depends on the intensity of the stimulation, and not on being applied at the exact points described on acupuncture charts.
- Pain patients who benefit most from acupuncture tend to be those who are also easily and deeply hypnotizable.
- Acupuncture does not appear to provide long-term relief for chronic pain patients.

It is tempting to conclude from these findings that acupuncture works simply through suggestion or distraction effects, but this seems unlikely because the technique also produces analgesia in animals, such as monkeys and mice (Melzack & Wall, 1982). Psychological factors cannot provide a full explanation. Perhaps gate-control theory can account for the effects of acupuncture: stimulation through the needles may activate peripheral fibers that close the gate (Bakal, 1979). Stimulation therapies are clearly useful in programs for treating pain, as are several other approaches for physical therapy.

Physical Therapy

Physical therapists use a wide variety of approaches to help reduce pain in patients who suffer from many acute and chronic conditions. A common feature of physical therapy is an exercise program designed to rehabilitate damaged or weakened muscle and joint tissue through stretching and strengthening activities (Hare & Milano, 1985; Wickersham, 1984). The therapist and patient generally plan the program together, setting daily or weekly goals that promote very gradual but steady progress. The progress is tailored to the patient's needs, being fast enough to promote a feeling of accomplishment but slow enough to prevent overexertion or failure. In cases of acute injury, such as serious damage to the knee, the exercise program may span several months. The rationale for using exercise to control pain depends on the type of health problem the patient has—with arthritis, for instance, exercise helps by maintaining the flexibility of the joints and preventing them from becoming deformed (Wickersham, 1984). Other approaches in

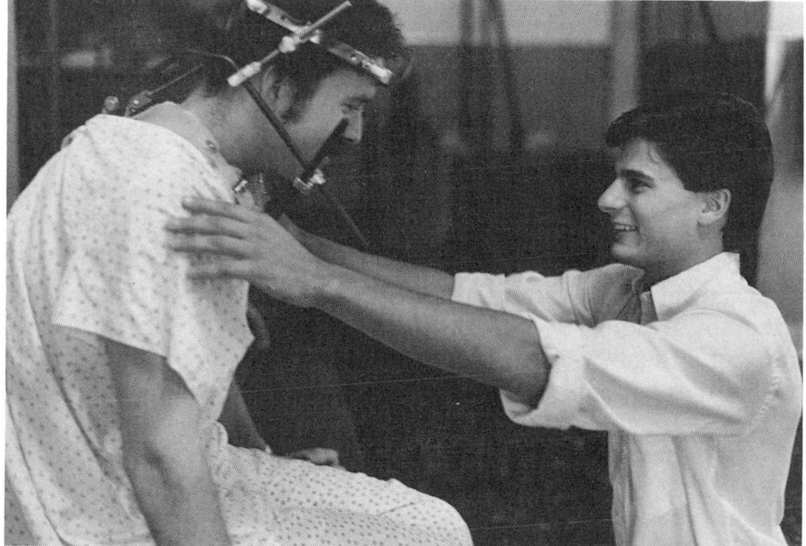

Physical therapy not only promotes rehabilitation for this patient suffering from a back injury but may also help in reducing his pain.

physical therapy involve massage, traction, and applying heat or cold to the painful area of the body (Melzack & Wall, 1982).

Exercise, massage, traction, and the application of heat and cold are also used in reducing pain in some chronic conditions, such as arthritis and low back pain (Banwell, 1984; Hare & Milano, 1985; Swezey, 1984; Wickersham, 1984). A study by Richard Heinrich and his colleagues (1985) compared the effectiveness of physical therapy with that of a program of behavioral and cognitive methods for patients with chronic low back pain. Both therapy groups had subjects whose average age was in the late 40s, about three-quarters of whom were male and married. About half of the patients were employed and none was drug dependent or involved in litigation connected to their back problem. Both therapy programs met for 10 weeks for two hours each week.

The physical therapy in this study consisted of a program of exercise and information and demonstrations about the causes of back pain, proper posture, and maneuvers to protect the back from strain. The behavioral/cognitive program consisted of information and demonstrations to promote psychosocial adjustment as well as training in several pain control techniques, including relaxation, imagery, and positive self-statements. Assessments of pain and of physical and psychosocial functioning were made prior to, at the end of, and six months after the program. The study revealed two main findings. First, during the programs both groups experienced similar reductions in pain, which they maintained in the following months. Second, each group showed improvements that were specific to the programs they received: At the end of the programs and at follow-up, subjects in the physical therapy group showed better physical functioning, and those in the behavioral/cognitive group showed better psychosocial adjustment. These findings suggest that chronic pain patients might benefit from receiving both types of treatment.

We have described many different types of treatment, including medical, psychological, and physical therapies, in this chapter, and we have seen that each method can help to alleviate clinical pain. Some methods seem to be more effective than others, especially for particular types of pain conditions. Typically, no single approach is sufficient by itself. Therefore, therapists who provide treatment in "pain clinics" often apply several methods in combination.

PAIN CLINICS

Before the 1970s, if people's pain lingered and their physician could not determine its cause or find a remedy for the discomfort, these patients were left with virtually no reasonable treatment alternatives. In desperation, they could try extreme medical approaches that might lead to drug addiction or irreversible nerve damage, or they could turn to "quacks" for "help." Although many people with chronic pain still use ill-conceived, desperate measures to gain relief from their discomfort, effective alternatives are available today, as we have seen. Effective pain control treatments can now be obtained through **pain clinics** or "pain centers," which are institutions or organizations that have been developed specifically for the treatment of chronic pain conditions.

The concept of having special institutions for treating pain originated with John Bonica, an anesthetist who founded the first pain clinic at the University of Washington Medical School (Fordyce, 1976; Melzack & Wall, 1982). Soon other professionals followed suit, and today there are well over a thousand pain clinics in the United States alone (Newman & Seres, 1986). The structure and approaches of pain clinics vary widely: Many pain clinics are private organizations, whereas others are affiliated with medical schools, university departments of behavioral medicine, and hospitals; many provide inpatient treatment, and others focus on outpatient care; and many incorporate a variety of treatment methods, whereas others provide basically one approach, such as acupuncture, hypnosis, biofeedback, or TENS (Follick, Ahern, Attanasio, & Riley, 1985; Kanner, 1986; Newman & Seres, 1986).

HIGHLIGHT 12B: On Issues
Physical Activity and Back Pain

The spine has an intricate structure, with each of its many sections of bone, called *vertebrae*, being cushioned from adjacent sections by rubbery *disks* of connective tissue. Each vertebra is connected to adjacent ones by antler-shaped *facet joints* that enable the vertebrae to pivot against one another (Guyton, 1985). But the spine depends on the muscles of the back and abdomen for support, without which it would just topple over. When all these muscles are strong and in good working order, they balance each other's action and keep the body's weight centered on the spine. But when these muscles are weak or the back muscles are under excessive or prolonged tension—sometimes due to emotional stress—back problems tend to occur.

A 10-year longitudinal study of men and women found evidence suggesting that low back pain progresses over time through a vicious circle: poor muscle function may lead to low back disorders, which lead to poorer muscle function, and so on (Leino, Aro, & Hasan, 1987). Although back pain can arise from such conditions as arthritis and "ruptured" disks, this occurs in only a small proportion of patients. Medical examinations do not find evidence of underlying physical causes in two-thirds to three-quarters of back pain cases (Chapman, 1984; Melzack & Wall, 1982). Most backaches seem to arise from muscle or ligament strains, lack of proper exercise, and normal wear and tear on facet joints. These problems tend to increase with age for many reasons—for instance, people's muscular conditioning usually declines as they get older, the effects of wear and tear accumulate, and the disks gradually dry out and provide less cushioning for the vertebrae. People whose jobs require frequent heavy lifting are more likely than other workers to develop low back pain (Kelsey & Hochberg, 1988). Exercise can help protect people from back problems, but it needs to consist of *proper* activities. People who do the wrong kinds of exercises do not get this protection, and those who overexert themselves can precipitate back pain.

What kinds of physical activity can help protect against back problems? Proper exercise involves a program of back-strengthening and stretching activities, along with abdominal exercises. Many different exercises are available for these purposes, and Figure 12B.1 presents a few. What should people do when they develop a backache? Medical advice in the past called for getting lots of bed rest, applying heat, and taking aspirin. But this advice has changed as a result of new research (Monmaney, 1988). Most backaches resolve themselves in a few days or weeks with or without medical attention. Physicians today recommend that the person apply *cold* packs instead of heat and *become active as soon as possible*—walking and exercising cautiously—even if it hurts a little. People with back pain should consult their doctor when the pain is:

- Associated with a known injury, such as from a fall.
- Severe enough to disable the sufferer and awaken him or her at night.
- Not relieved by changing position or lying down.
- Accompanied by nausea, fever, difficulty or pain in urinating, loss of bladder or bowel control, numbness or weakness in a leg or foot, or pain that shoots down the leg.

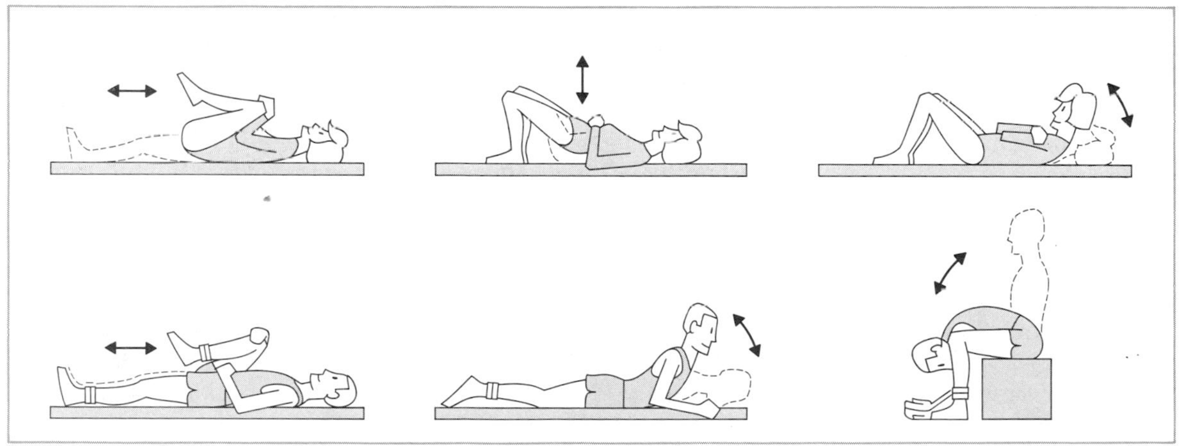

FIGURE 12B.1 Six stretching and strengthening exercises to protect from low back pain.

Multidisciplinary Programs

A theme that has appeared more than once in this chapter is that no single method for treating chronic pain is likely to succeed. In fact, one physician has advised that "monomodality clinics should be avoided" (Kanner, 1986, p. 2113). *Multidisciplinary pain clinics*—those that combine and integrate several effective approaches—are likely to succeed for the largest percentage of patients and provide the greatest pain relief for each individual. Clinics that use multidisciplinary programs generally include medical, psychosocial, physical therapy, occupational therapy, and vocational elements in *both* the assessment and treatment procedures for each patient (Follick, Ahern, Attanasio, & Riley, 1985; Newman & Seres, 1986).

Assessment procedures are used in determining the factors that are contributing to the patient's condition and in identifying the specific ones that need to be addressed in the program. Although the goals and objectives of different multidisciplinary programs vary, they typically include:

- Reducing the patient's experience of pain.
- Improving physical and lifestyle functioning.
- Decreasing or eliminating drug intake.
- Enhancing social support and family life.
- Reducing the patient's use of medical services.

Multidisciplinary programs generally integrate specific treatment components to achieve each goal (Follick, Ahern, Attanasio, & Riley, 1985). These programs include, for example, procedures to decrease the patient's reliance on medication and physical exercises to increase the person's strength, endurance, flexibility, and range of motion. They provide counseling to improve family relationships and to enable the patient to find full-time employment when possible. And they offer a wide range of psychological services to reduce the experience of pain, decrease pain behavior, and improve the patient's psychosocial adjustment to the pain condition.

Evaluating the Success of Pain Clinics

How effective are multidisciplinary pain clinics? We will examine the procedures and results of two pain programs. Each program (1) was conducted by a hospital-affiliated pain clinic, (2) provided treatment on an inpatient basis for four weeks with weekends off, and (3) treated several patients at a time. Each program also used a variety of treatment techniques and had staff to provide medical, psychological, physical, and occupational therapy.

The first of these programs took place at the Miller-Dwan Hospital Pain Control Center in Minnesota (Cinciripini & Floreen, 1982). The subjects were 121 men and women with an average age of 44 years. They had suffered intractable pain for at least a year and were unemployed because of their pain condition. All of these patients' conditions had resulted from a known injury or a disease, such as arthritis. All subjects received the full program, which consisted of a medication reduction procedure, physical therapy, relaxation and biofeedback training, self-monitoring, contingency contracting, cognitive/behavioral group therapy, and family involvement and training. The researchers assessed the patients' behavior and functioning at the start and at the end of the program, and in follow-ups 6 months and 12 months after.

By the end of the Miller-Dwan treatment program, the patients' activity levels had increased and their pain experiences, pain behaviors, and drug use had decreased sharply—indeed, 90% of the patients were now free of analgesic medication. About two-thirds of the subjects participated in the follow-up assessments, which revealed that they continued to be active and about half were employed. Moreover, their pain continued to diminish: before treatment their average pain rating was 4.6 on a 10-point scale, by the end of the program it was 2.2, and after a year it was 1.2.

The second program was conducted at the University of Nebraska Pain Management Center (Guck, Skultety, Meilman, & Dowd, 1985). This study compared a *treatment group* that completed the program with a *control group* that met all the criteria for acceptance into the program but declined to participate solely because they lacked insurance coverage. The two groups were similar in age, gender composition, marital status, employment status, educational level, use of drugs, length of pain history, and prior hospitalization history. The treatment program included a medication reduction procedure, physical therapy, relaxation and biofeedback training, group and individual therapy, family therapy, and vocational counseling.

Comparisons between the treatment group and the control group in this study were based on follow-up contacts with the subjects one to five years after they were originally evaluated for treatment. These comparisons showed that the treatment group had experienced far less pain in the prior month and were less depressed than the controls; the treatment group also reported less interference from pain in various activities, such as household chores, socializing, sexual relations, exercise, and sleep. Almost two-thirds of the treatment group and only one-fifth of the controls were employed, and far fewer treatment subjects used painkilling drugs.

The outcomes of these two studies clearly demonstrate that well-designed multidisciplinary pain clinics achieve the kinds of goals they set out to accomplish and can provide enormous and lasting benefits for their patients. Programs that provide medical, psychosocial, physical, and occupational therapy can improve chronic pain patients' psychosocial and physical functioning and reduce their pain, pain behavior, and drug use.

SUMMARY

Pain that receives or requires professional attention is called clinical pain. Practitioners are concerned about reducing acute clinical pain for humanitarian reasons and to enable medical procedures to be carried out smoothly, reduce patients' stress, and help patients recover quickly and without complications. Relieving chronic pain is important because of the severe and pervasive impact it can have on almost every aspect of patients' lives. Although the medical treatment for pain may involve surgery if all other methods have failed, it usually involves pharmaceuticals selected from four types: peripherally acting analgesics; centrally acting analgesics; local anesthetics; and sedatives, tranquilizers, antidepressants, and anticonvulsants. These chemical methods are used extensively for relieving acute pain, and they are sometimes administered by an epidural block or a patient-controlled analgesia technique. Health care professionals usually try not to rely on pharmaceutical methods for reducing chronic pain.

One of the main goals of behavioral and cognitive methods for treating chronic pain is to reduce the patient's drug consumption. The operant approach focuses on reducing pain behaviors through extinction procedures and increasing "well" behavior through reinforcement. Therapists apply methods of progressive muscle relaxation and biofeedback to reduce the stress and muscle tension that can cause or aggravate patients' pain experiences. Research mainly with headache patients has shown that relaxation and biofeedback training appear to produce effective and long-lasting pain relief. Cognitive techniques focus on changing thought patterns that increase the intensity or frequency of pain experiences. Attention-diversion from pain and nonpain imagery appear to be effective methods chiefly for mild or moderate acute pain or for brief episodes of heightened chronic pain. Pain redefinition can involve clarifying what a pain experience will be like, using positive self-statements, and correcting faulty beliefs and logic. Redefinition appears to be helpful in reducing strong pain and chronic pain.

Hypnosis seems to relieve pain to the extent that the person can be deeply hypnotized, and it provides a high degree of analgesia in only a minority of individuals. In general, people can reduce their pain as effectively with cognitive strategies in the waking state as with hypnosis. Insight-oriented psychotherapies are designed to help people achieve insights into the roots of their problems. For pain patients, this may involve making them aware of what is happening in the pain games they play or of how others feel about their pain condition. These insights can occur in pain groups or in individual and family therapy.

Counter-irritation is a procedure whereby a brief or moderate pain cancels a longer-lasting or stronger one. A pain control technique that is based on this procedure is called transcutaneous electrical nerve stimulation, in which mild electrical stimulation is applied to the skin at the painful region. This technique is effective for relieving acute pain and some types of chronic pain. Acupuncture is an ancient Oriental procedure for reducing pain that appears to produce high levels of analgesia for acute pain in some patients, but not in most. It does not seem to be useful in treating chronic pain. Physical therapy includes such approaches as exercise, massage, traction, and the application of heat and cold to painful regions. These methods help to reduce chronic pain and rehabilitate damaged or weakened tissue in muscles and joints. Proper exercise can protect individuals from low back pain.

Pain clinics are institutions developed specifically for treating chronic pain. Although some of these clinics focus on applying essentially one technique, such as hypnosis or biofeedback, others use programs that integrate medical, psychosocial, physical, and occupational therapy. Multidisciplinary pain clinics provide highly effective and long-lasting pain relief, while also rehabilitating their patients physically, psychologically, socially, and vocationally.

KEY TERMS

clinical pain
attention-diversion from pain
nonpain imagery
pain redefinition
counter-irritation
transcutaneous electrical nerve stimulation
acupuncture
pain clinics

CHRONIC AND TERMINAL HEALTH PROBLEMS

13

LIVING WITH SERIOUS AND DISABLING CHRONIC HEALTH PROBLEMS

PROLOGUE

"It's not fair," 12-year-old Joe complained. "Why can't I eat the stuff I like? Other kids can. Why do I have to check my blood every day and take shots? Nobody else has to do that." He voiced these complaints as he left the emergency room after suffering severe stomach cramps because he was not adhering to his medical regimen. Hospital tests recently determined that Joe has diabetes, and he was not adjusting well to the regimen his physician instructed him to follow. His parents tried to explain that not following the regimen could have serious health consequences, but Joe thought, "I'll do some of the things they say I should do, and that'll be enough. I feel fine—so those problems won't happen to me." It wasn't until his noncompliance caused him to lapse into a coma for a couple of days that he finally believed the warnings he received, and he began to adhere closely to his regimen.

Different individuals react differently to developing a chronic illness. Their reactions depend on many factors, such as their coping skills and personality, the social support they have, the nature and consequences of the illness, and the impact of the illness on their daily functioning. At the very least, having a chronic condition entails frequent impositions on the patients and their families. These patients may suffer periodic episodes of feeling poorly and need to have regular medical checkups, restrict their diets or other aspects of their lifestyles, or administer daily treatment, for instance. Many chronic conditions entail more than just impositions — they produce frequent pain or lead to disability or even death. Although the prospect of developing a chronic health problem is unappealing, most of us will develop at least one of these illnesses in our lifetimes, and one of them will probably take our lives.

This chapter and the next examine how people react to and cope with chronic health problems and what can be done to help these people cope effectively. In contrast to the next chapter, which focuses on illnesses that have high rates of mortality and on processes relating to dying and death, the present chapter concentrates on health problems that are less likely to result in death but often lead to disability. This chapter begins by discussing people's initial reactions to having a chronic condition, then examines the experiences and needs of individuals living with various health problems, and ends by considering patients' long-term adaptation to their condition. These discussions address many questions that are of great concern to patients, their families and friends, and probably to you. How do patients tend to react after their initial shock of learning that they have a chronic illness? What kinds of health problems usually involve the most difficult adjustments for patients? How do patients' chronic conditions impact on their families? What can families, friends, and therapists do to help patients adapt effectively to their chronic condition?

ADJUSTING TO A CHRONIC CONDITION: THE FIRST PHASES

"I felt like I'd been hit in the stomach by a sledgehammer" — this is how many patients describe their first reaction upon learning that they have a disabling or life-threatening illness. Questions without immediate answers flash through their minds: How disabled will I be, and will I die? Will I be disfigured or in pain? How soon will these consequences happen? What will happen to my family? Do I have adequate medical and life insurance? Learning of a chronic health problem usually comes as a great shock, and this is often the first reaction patients experience when the physician tells them the diagnosis.

Initial Reactions to Having a Chronic Condition

By observing patients in rehabilitation and health settings, Franklin Shontz (1975) has described a sequence of reactions patients tend to exhibit following the diagnosis of a serious illness. The first reaction in this sequence—*shock*—occurs to some degree in any crisis situation that people experience, but it is likely to be most pronounced when the crisis comes without warning. Shock appears to be an emergency reaction, marked by three characteristics: (1) being stunned or bewildered, (2) behaving in an automatic fashion, and (3) feeling a sense of detachment from the situation. In describing these feelings of detachment, individuals often claim that the experience is more like being an observer rather than a participant in the events that occur. The shock phase may last a short while or may continue for weeks.

The second phase in responding to the diagnosis is an *encounter* reaction, which is characterized by disorganized thinking and feelings of loss, grief, helplessness, and despair. During this phase, patients often feel overwhelmed by reality and seem unable to reason or plan effectively in efforts to solve problems that arise and to improve their situation. Because encounter reactions are intensely stressful, patients begin to cope by using avoidance strategies, particularly denial. This marks the start of the third phase, which Shontz calls *retreat.* During the retreat phase, individuals tend to deny either the existence of the health problem or its implications. But this state of affairs generally cannot last, and reality begins to intrude—the condition does not go away, additional diagnoses confirm the original one, the symptoms get worse, and the patients get reminders from people that the illness exists and adjustments need to be made. Using retreat as a "base of operation," patients begin to contact reality a little at a time until they adjust fully to the health problem and its implications.

People use avoidance strategies to control their emotional response to stressful conditions, especially when they believe they can do nothing to change the situation (Lazarus & Cohen, 1979; Lazarus, 1983). This approach can be useful, within limits. Evidence from research indicates that patients can benefit psychologically from using avoidance strategies early in the process of coping with their health problems (Suls & Fletcner, 1985). But excessive avoidance can soon become maladaptive to patients' physical and psychological well-being. For example, when hospitalized patients receive information about their condition and future risk factors, those individuals who use avoidance strategies heavily gain less information about their condition than those who use these strategies to a lesser degree (Shaw, Cohen, Doyle, & Palesky, 1985). Patients often need to make major decisions about their immediate treatment—How can they make these decisions rationally if they fail to take in the information practitioners present? Later, they may need to take action to promote their rehabilitation, reduce the likelihood of future health problems, and adjust their lifestyles, social relationships, and means of employment. According to Shontz, the retreat phase gives way to reality as patients make progress toward adapting successfully to their condition.

Do all individuals react in the ways that Shontz has described when they are faced with such crises as being diagnosed with a serious illness? No, but probably most do. For instance, when faced with a crisis, most people react with shock initially, but other individuals may be "cool and collected" and others may be "paralyzed" with anxiety or may become "hysterical" (Silver & Wortman, 1980). Similarly, although many patients with a serious illness feel extremely helpless and overwhelmed after the initial shock, others do not. And many patients do not rely heavily on avoidance strategies to cope with the stress caused by having a health problem. What factors influence how people react to their health problem? The next section provides some answers to this question.

Processes in Coping with a Health Crisis

Healthy people tend to take their health for granted. They expect to be able to carry out their daily activities and social roles from one day to the next without substantial disruptions due to illness. When a serious illness or injury occurs, their everyday life activities are disrupted. Regardless of whether the condition is temporary or chronic, the first phases in coping with it are similar. But there is an important difference: in contrast to the short-term disruptions that temporary illnesses cause, chronic health problems usually require that patients and their families make permanent behavioral, social, and emotional adjustments.

When patients learn that they have a chronic health problem, the diagnosis changes the way they view themselves and their lives instantly. The plans they had for tomorrow and for the next days, weeks, and years may be affected. Major plans and minor ones may change: Did they plan to go on a trip this weekend? They may change their minds now. Did they plan to complete a college education, or enter a specific career field, or get married and have children, or move to a new community when they retire? All these ideas for the future may evaporate within minutes after the diagnosis. As psychologists Frances Cohen and Richard Lazarus have noted, because the idea of

> being healthy, able, and having a normal physique is central to most people's image and evaluation, becoming ill can be a shock to a person's sense of security and to his or her self-image. Not only does it threaten the customary view of oneself, but it further underscores that one is indeed vulnerable . . . , that life is uncertain, that one may have little control over events, and that one's life may be changed in major respects. As a result, adjustment to an illness or injury which is life-threatening or potentially disabling may require considerable coping effort. (1979, p. 218)

Potentially disabling or life-threatening conditions leave patients and their families with many uncertainties. Often no one can tell for certain exactly what the course of the illness will be.

Why do some individuals cope differently from others after learning they have a chronic health problem? Rudolf Moos (1982; Moos & Schaefer, 1986) has proposed the **crisis theory**, which describes a variety of factors that influence how people adjust during the first phases of a crisis, such as having an illness. Figure 13.1 presents his conceptual model, showing that the outcome of the crisis —or the adjustment the person makes— depends on the coping process, which depends on three contributing influences: *illness-related* factors, *background and personal* factors, and *physical and social environmental* factors. We will look first at the three contributing influences, and then see how they affect the coping process the patient uses.

Illness-Related Factors

Some health problems present a greater threat to the person than others do—they may be more disabling, disfiguring, painful, or life-threatening, for example. As you might expect, the greater the threat patients perceive for any of these factors, the more difficult time they are likely to have coping with their condition (Cohen & Lazarus, 1979; Diamond, 1983; Moos, 1982). Being disfigured can be extremely difficult to adjust to, particularly when it involves

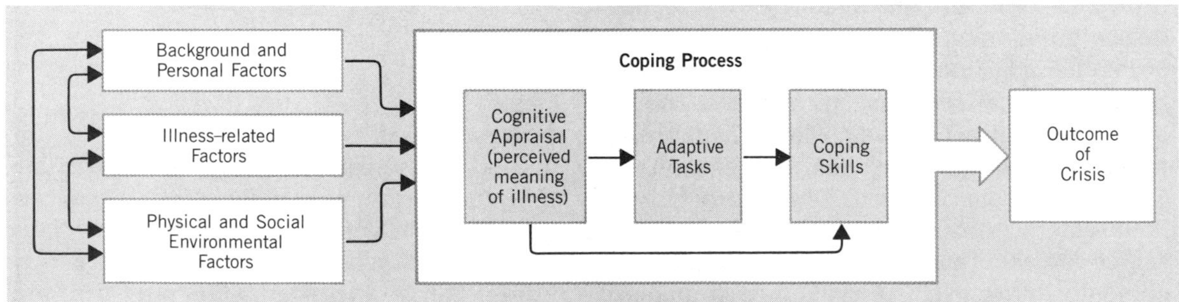

FIGURE 13.1 A diagram of crisis theory's description of factors and the coping process patients use in the first phases of adjusting psychologically to a serious illness. (Adapted from Moos, 1982, Figure 1.)

the person's face. Patients whose faces are badly scarred often withdraw from social encounters, sometimes completely. Their disfigurements are noticeable to anyone, and usually cannot be hidden. People who see the disfigurement tend to react awkwardly, and may even show a feeling of revulsion. Even children react more negatively to people's facial disfigurements than to injuries to other parts of the body, such as when people are crippled or missing a limb (Richardson, Goodman, Hastorf, & Dornbusch, 1961).

Patients also have difficulty coping with illness-related factors that involve annoying or embarrassing changes in bodily functioning or that draw attention to their condition (Diamond, 1983). People with some illnesses, for instance, may need artificial devices for excreting fecal or urinary wastes. These devices may be noticeable either visibly or by their odors, and many patients have exaggerated impressions of the social impact such devices have. Other patients must treat their conditions with ointments that may have odors or equipment that is visible or makes noise. Still others may experience periodic seizures or muscle spasms that can be embarrassing. Many people with chronic illnesses feel self-conscious about their health problems—or even "stigmatized" by it—and want to hide it from others (Scambler, 1984).

Background and Personal Factors

The way individuals cope with a chronic health problem also depends on a variety of background and personal factors, such as their age, gender, social class, philosophical or religious commitments, emotional maturity, and self-esteem (Moos & Schaefer, 1986). With respect to gender differences, for instance, men are more likely than women to be "threatened by the decreases in ambition, vigor, and physical prowess that often result from serious illness because, by comparison with women, they are confident in the stability of their physical abilities and bodily functioning" (Moos, 1982, p. 132). Having a chronic illness often means that the individual must take on a dependent and passive role for a long period of time. For men, this can be especially difficult since it is inconsistent with the assertive and independent roles they generally occupy in most societies of the world.

The timing of a health problem in the life cycle affects the way it impacts on patients. In the case of very young children, their limited cognitive abilities prevent them from understanding fully the nature of their illness, the treatment regimen they must follow, and the long-term implications of their condition (Bibace & Walsh, 1979; Burbach & Peterson, 1986). Their concerns are likely to focus on any restrictions that are imposed on their lifestyles and activities, the frightening medical procedures they experience, and possible separations from their parents. As children get older and their comprehension improves, they may be able to participate in making some decisions about their treatment. Adolescents can understand information about their illness and treatment, but their need to be like and feel accepted by their peers can lead to difficulties in coping with their health problems (La Greca & Stone, 1985). Because of these motivations, adolescents may deny important aspects of their condition and neglect their medical care to avoid appearing "different" from their friends.

In adulthood, too, the difficulties individuals have in coping with chronic health problems change with age (Mages & Mendelsohn, 1979; Moos, 1982). When a disabling or life-threatening illness or injury occurs during the adolescent and early adulthood years, patients tend to resent their not having had the chance to develop their lives in the direction they planned—to get married, have children, or to enter a particular career. In contrast, middle-aged patients may have problems adjusting to the disruption of established roles and lifestyles and to not being able to finish tasks they started, such as building up a business. In old age, patients may resent not being able to enjoy the leisure they feel they earned in their lifetime of work and self-sacrifice.

Another personal factor that affects how individuals cope with a chronic health problem is the set of beliefs they have about health and illness. Suppose a patient believes, for instance, that "Nothing is seriously wrong if you don't feel any pain." This person is not likely to be very concerned when he or she develops a condition that has no clear symptoms, as happens with hypertension. In Chapter 9, we saw that people form a common-sense model of each health problem on the basis of their direct experiences with the illness or injury and things they have heard or read about it. Oftentimes these beliefs are wrong, and sometimes these misconceptions can add to the stress of having a chronic health problem. For example, an 18-year-old girl who was diagnosed as being diabetic enrolled in a therapy group because she was having difficulty coping with her condition. As it turned out, she believed incorrectly that she now could not attend college, that she "would constantly look drunk and crazy," and that no one would want to be near her (Roback, 1984). By attending the therapy group with other diabetic patients, she was able to see that she could pursue her life goals much as she had planned before learning of her condition.

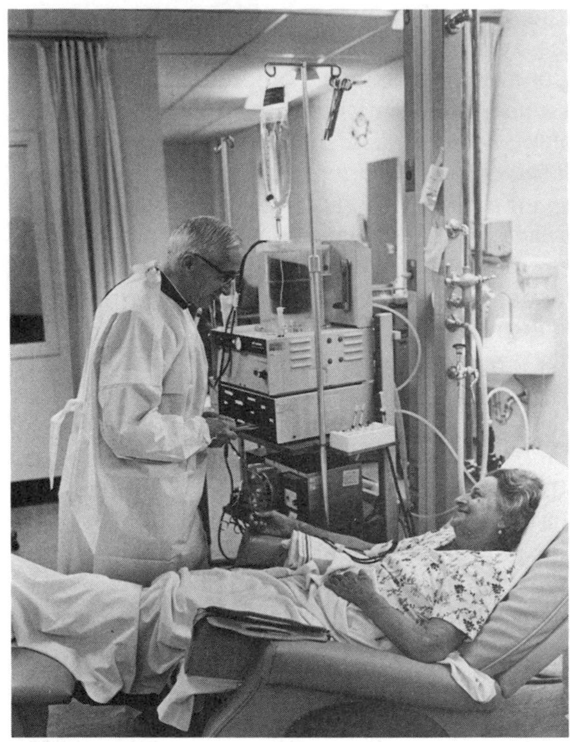

Sources of social support for patients can include their families, friends, and people from support groups and religious organizations.

Physical and Social Environmental Factors

Many physical and social features of patients' environments can affect the way they adjust to a chronic health problem (Moos, 1982). The presence of social support, for example, generally helps patients cope with their illness. Individuals who live alone and have few friends or who have poor relationships with the people they live with tend to adjust poorly to chronic health conditions (Gentry & Kobasa, 1984; Wallston, Alagna, DeVellis, & DeVellis, 1983). Sometimes, however, people in a patient's social network may undermine effective coping by providing bad examples or poor advice (Suls, 1982).

The primary source of social support for children and most adults who are ill typically comes from their immediate families, of course. But people in old age whose spouses are either deceased or unable to help are likely to receive support mainly from their children —especially their daughters—and from siblings, friends, and neighbors (Cantor & Little, 1985). At almost any age, patients may join *support groups* for people with specific medical problems. As we saw in the example of the diabetic girl, these groups can provide informational and emotional support. Patients with specific health problems can get information about the availability of support groups in their geographical area through their physician or through national organizations for the particular illness they have.

Physical aspects of a patient's environment can also affect how well he or she copes with the condition. The hospital environment, for instance, is usually very dull and confining for patients, thereby depressing their general morale and mood (Moos, 1982). For some patients, the home environment may not be much better. Many patients have difficulty getting around their houses or performing self-help tasks, such as buttoning clothes or opening food containers. These patients' adjustment to their health problems can be impaired if they do not have special tools or equipment to help them be more self-sufficient.

As Figure 13.1 depicts, the three contributing influences are interrelated and can modify each other. The patient's social class or cultural background, for instance, may affect the threat presented by the health problem and his or her access to special tools and equipment to promote self-sufficiency. These contributing factors combine to influence the coping process the patient uses to deal with the crisis.

The Coping Process

The coping process begins with the patient's *cognitive appraisal* of the meaning or significance of the health problem to his or her life. The outcome of this appraisal leads the patient to formulate an array of *adaptive tasks* and to apply various *coping skills* to deal with these tasks. Let's see what these tasks and skills are.

According to Moos (1982), patients need to formulate several adaptive tasks in the coping process, some of which relate directly to their illness and treatment whereas others pertain to their general psychosocial functioning. With respect to tasks related to the illness or injury, there are three major types of adaptive tasks. Patients must learn to:

1. Deal with the symptoms and incapacitation caused by the illness or injury itself. This includes adjusting to being laid up and having pain and other symptoms, such as dizziness or paralysis.
2. Adjust to the hospital environment and the medical procedures needed to treat the health problem. This includes learning and adhering to a medical regimen.
3. Develop and maintain adequate relationships with their practitioners.

If patients are to achieve a highly adaptive outcome to their health crisis, they must adjust effectively to their illness, incapacitation, treatment, and health care providers.

An additional set of four adaptive tasks applies to patients' general psychosocial functioning. Patients must strive to:

1. Maintain a reasonable emotional balance by controlling the negative feelings that the health problem arouses and retaining some hope or positive outlook for the future.
2. Preserve a satisfactory self-image and sense of competence and mastery by coming to terms with changes in their appearance or body functioning.
3. Maintain positive relationships with family and friends.
4. Prepare for an uncertain future.

Achieving these goals can be very difficult for patients, particularly when their health problems may lead to disability, disfigurement, or death. Still, many patients with poor prognoses for their health manage to adapt successfully and make the most of their new life circumstances.

Crisis theory proposes that patients encounter all seven adaptive tasks in any health problem they experience. But the relative importance or salience of each task for each illness or injury depends on

> the nature of the disease, the personality of the individual involved, and the unique set of environmental circumstances. For the person suddenly rendered blind, the physical discomfort may be minor while the difficulty of restoring social relations can be overwhelming. . . . A woman who has had a mastectomy may find that accepting her new self-image is her most significant task. Someone who is physically active, like a professional athlete or a construction worker, probably will experience more difficulty adjusting to a wheelchair than a person with a more sedentary occupation. (Moos, 1982, p. 137)

Family members must make similar adjustments, and these individuals are critically important in helping patients achieve each goal. Patients are likely to adapt successfully to their chronic condition if they have family members who participate actively in their treatment regimen, encourage them to be self-sufficient, and respond to their needs in a caring and sensitive manner.

What coping skills do patients and their families employ to deal with these adaptive tasks? There are several strategies that they commonly use. One strategy simply involves denying or minimizing the seriousness of the situation. As we saw earlier, this approach can be beneficial in the early phases of adjusting to a health problem. Patients may also benefit from this approach by using it selectively to "isolate or dissociate" their emotions temporarily, thereby rescuing them "from being overwhelmed or provide the time needed to garner other personal coping resources" (Moos, 1982, p. 138). A second approach is to seek information about the health problem and treatment procedures. In another strategy, patients learn how to provide their own medical care, such as in giving themselves insulin shots. With this approach, patients gain a sense of control and personal effectiveness with respect to their condition.

A fourth coping strategy for mastering the adaptive tasks of a crisis involves maintaining regular routines as well as possible and setting concrete, limited goals, such as in exercising or in attending shows or social gatherings. By doing this, patients have things to look forward to and opportunities to achieve goals they consider meaningful. In another coping approach, patients recruit help and emotional support from family, friends, and practitioners by expressing their needs and feelings. A sixth coping strategy involves thinking about and discussing possible future events and stressful circumstances in order to know what lies ahead and to be prepared for unexpected difficulties. The last type of coping skill entails putting the health problem and its treatment into a manageable perspective by finding a long-term "purpose" or "meaning" for the experience. Patients often do this by applying religious beliefs or by recognizing how they have been changed in positive ways by the experience.

Each of these coping skills can be useful in achieving the goals of the various adaptive tasks and in leading to a positive outcome of the crisis. Is one approach "best?" Generally speaking, although moderate or temporary use of any specific skill can be beneficial, using any single skill exclusively may undermine the coping process (Moos, 1982). Some coping skills may be more appropriate for dealing with some tasks than with others. As a result, patients generally use these skills selectively, often in combination. For instance, patients who have had a leg amputated might (1) seek information about activities they can do to strengthen their other limbs and (2) then set reasonable goals for doing these exercises. By using these two coping skills, these patients can help reduce their incapacitation, develop good relationships with their families and practitioners, and bolster their self-image. Once patients have adjusted successfully to the crisis, they are ready to deal effectively with subsequent phases in their adjustment to their health problem.

To summarize, most people tend to react to becoming seriously ill with shock, followed by a period of disorganized thinking and feelings of loss and helplessness. Avoidance strategies, such as denial, constitute one of several types of coping skills patients use in order to deal with the adaptive tasks they identify through the process of cognitive appraisal. The importance of each adaptive task depends on the patient's personality, the physical and social environment, and the specific chronic health problem to which he or she must adjust.

LIVING WITH AN ENDOCRINE/ CIRCULATORY DISEASE: DIABETES AND KIDNEY DISEASE

Beginning with this section, we will consider what it is like to live with specific chronic medical conditions. The particular health problems we will examine were selected to illustrate widely different adjustment difficulties. Some of these health problems tend to develop at much earlier ages than others; some require much more complex treatment regimens than others; and some produce more pain and disability than others. Although the medical problems we will discuss in this chapter include some that can be life-threatening, none of these chronic conditions is among the most deadly ones people in the United States often develop —those of heart disease, cancer, stroke, and AIDS—which we will examine in the next chapter.

The health problems are arranged according to the main body system involved. We will start by considering two endocrine and circulatory conditions: diabetes and kidney disease. Of the diseases we will consider in this chapter, these two pose the greatest threat to life.

Diabetes

"Too much of a good thing is wonderful," the late actress Mae West once said. Although her rule might possibly apply for some good things, glucose in the blood is not one of them. The body needs glucose to fuel metabolic processes, but too much of it in the blood over a long period of time—a condition called *hyperglycemia*—is the mark of *diabetes mellitus*. The body normally controls blood sugar levels with the hormone *insulin*, which the pancreas produces. In the disorder of diabetes, however, abnormal levels of glucose accumulate in the blood because the pancreas does not produce sufficient insulin (Kilo & Williamson, 1987; Pohl, Gonder-Frederick, & Cox, 1984).

Diabetes is among the most common chronic conditions in the United States, where it afflicts nearly 5% of the population. There are about 5½ million American patients diagnosed with the disorder and probably an equal number of diabetics who have not yet been diagnosed (Turk & Speers, 1983; USDHHS, 1985b, 1986d). The prevalence rate for diabetes is somewhat higher for females than males and increases with age throughout the life span, being many times higher among middle-aged and elderly individuals than among children and adolescents. Furthermore, this age difference is widening—the prevalence rates of diabetes in the United States have been increasing steadily for many years among middle-aged and older people, but not among children and adolescents, as Figure 13.2 shows (USDHHS, 1985b).

The Types and Causes of Diabetes

Diabetes is not a single disease—it occurs in two major patterns that require different kinds of treatment and may have somewhat different causes. The two forms of diabetes are:

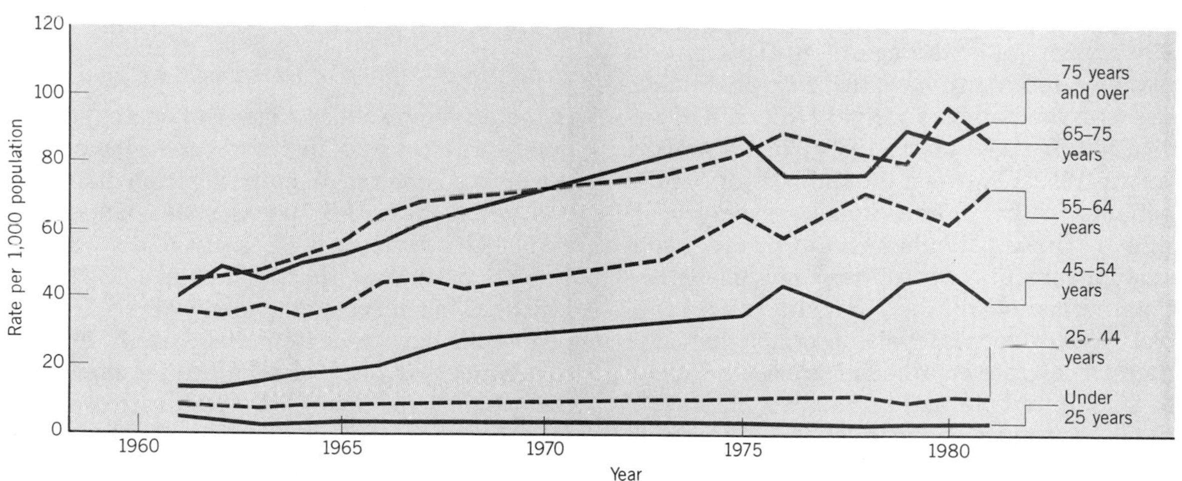

FIGURE 13.2 Prevalence rates of diagnosed diabetes in the United States from 1961 to 1981 as a function of age. (From USDHHS, 1985b, Figure 17.)

• *Type I.* This form of diabetes typically develops in childhood or adolescence and accounts for only 5 to 10% of diabetes cases. It is called **insulin-dependent diabetes mellitus** (IDDM) because the pancreas produces virtually no insulin and patients afflicted with IDDM require insulin injections to prevent acute and very serious complications (Collins & Lipman, 1985; Kilo & Williamson, 1987; Pohl, Gonder-Frederick, & Cox, 1984). The main acute complication that occurs without insulin in IDDM is called *ketoacidosis*, in which high levels of fatty acids in the blood lead to kidney malfunctions, thereby causing wastes to accumulate and poison the body. The symptoms of ketoacidosis generally begin with very frequent thirst and urination, followed by nausea, vomiting, abdominal pain, and labored breathing. About one-third of new IDDM cases are diagnosed after these symptoms appear. If left untreated, ketoacidosis can lead to coma and death in a matter of days or weeks.

• *Type II.* The vast majority of diabetics have the second form of this disease, which is called **non-insulin-dependent diabetes mellitus** (NIDDM) because the pancreas does produce at least some insulin and treatment often does not require insulin injections. Most, but not all, patients with NIDDM can manage their glucose levels without taking insulin by carefully following a special diet and taking medication. Although NIDDM can develop at any age, it usually appears after the age of 40. This type of diabetes appears to have two *subtypes* that depend on the patient's weight (Kilo & Williamson, 1987; Turk & Speers, 1983; Wing, Nowalk, & Guare, 1988). Between 60 and 90% of NIDDM patients in the United States are very overweight. These patients seem to produce substantial amounts of insulin—sometimes more than normal quantities—but still cannot control their glucose levels, probably because their fat cells are enlarged and resist the action of insulin. In contrast, normal-weight NIDDM patients produce reduced levels of insulin. In either case, hyperglycemia results.

What causes the pancreas to reduce its production of insulin? Although the causes are not well understood, twin studies have demonstrated that genetic factors are involved in both IDDM and NIDDM (Kilo & Williamson, 1987; Pohl, Gonder-Frederick, & Cox, 1984; Wing, Nowalk, & Guare, 1988). The great majority of diabetics probably inherit some form of susceptibility to the effects of environmental conditions that could affect insulin production, and then experience those conditions. In the case of IDDM, the environmental conditions—probably virus infections of pancreas cells—seem to trigger an immune response that destroys those cells. In NIDDM, the environmental factors are essentially unknown, but one possibility may be overeating, which

> stimulates insulin production by the pancreas leading to elevated blood levels of insulin, which may cause two things to occur. First, cells or tissues which normally respond to insulin may become resistant to the action of this hormone as a result of long standing exposure to excessive amounts. Second, in the face of long standing overstimulation, the insulin producing cells in the pancreas may become damaged or exhausted leading to insufficient insulin production. (Pohl, Gonder-Frederick, & Cox, 1984, p. 4)

At this time, however, the nature of the susceptibility to diabetes and the types of environmental conditions that are involved are quite unclear and, for the most part, speculative.

Health Implications of Diabetes

Diabetes can be a direct cause of death. Fortunately, as a result of improved management of the disease, the rate of mortality from diabetes has declined in the United States since the early 1970s from over 14 to just under 10 per 100,000 people in the population (USDHHS, 1986c). This means that today about 25,000 people die each year from diabetes. An upsetting aspect of these deaths is that many of them—perhaps one-third—result from acute complications, such as ketoacidosis, that "are usually preventable by appropriate medical care" (Wing, Nowalk, & Guare, 1988, p. 246). Few diabetics die of acute complications if they follow the recommended medical regimens for controlling glucose levels (Santiago, 1984).

But the deaths that are caused directly by diabetes constitute only part of the serious health effects of this disease (Kilo & Williamson, 1987; Pohl, Gonder-Frederick, & Cox, 1984; Turk & Speers, 1983). Diabetes is implicated in the development of a variety of disabling health problems and contributes indirectly to about 100,000 deaths each year. One health problem diabetes can lead to is *neuropathy*, or nerve disease. High blood glucose levels appear to cause chemical reactions that can destroy the myelin sheath that insulates nerve fibers. When this occurs in peripheral fibers, such as in the feet, the patient may lose sensation in the affected area or have abnormal sensations, such as chronic pain. When the damage occurs in autonomic nerve fibers, the symptoms may include chronic dizziness, urinary incontinence, and sexual impotence (in males).

Diabetes can also lead to the development of other serious health problems. Physicians Charles Kilo and Joseph Williamson have noted that compared to individuals who are not diabetic, people who have diabetes are:

- 6.8 times more likely to become blind,
- 11.3 times more likely to develop kidney disease,
- 29.9 times more likely to get gangrene,
- 4.6 times more likely to develop heart disease, and
- 5.4 times more likely to have a stroke. (1987, p. 54)

The way diabetes contributes to these health problems is through its effects on the vascular system (Kilo & Williamson, 1987; Pohl, Gonder-Frederick, & Cox, 1984; Wing, Nowalk, & Guare, 1988). High levels of glucose in the blood lead to a thickening of arterial walls as a result of atherosclerosis. This can occur in large blood vessels, such as those in the legs and near the heart, causing gangrene in a limb or heart disease. It can also occur in small blood vessels and capillaries, such as those in the eyes, kidneys, and brain.

The long-term health risks of diabetes are extremely serious, and patients and their families worry about them greatly (Holmes, 1986; Wilkinson, 1987). They worry about the possibilities of, for instance, dying prematurely, becoming blind, losing a limb if gangrene cannot be controlled, and being unable to perform sexually. The patients who are at greatest risk for these problems are those whose disease requires insulin in its treatment and starts in childhood, adolescence, or early adulthood (Cameron, 1986). But these risks can be reduced if patients receive appropriate medical care and carefully follow prescribed treatment regimens (Kilo & Williamson, 1987; Santiago, 1984).

Managing Diabetes

The main approach for managing diabetes entails a "balancing act" with medication, diet, and exercise under medical supervision. But researchers have discovered that the biochemical processes in diabetes are also affected by another important factor: stress (Hanson, Henggeler, & Burghen, 1987; Surwit, Feinglos, & Scovern, 1983). When people are under stress, the adrenal glands release epinephrine and cortisol into the bloodstream. *Epinephrine* causes the pancreas to decrease insulin production; *cortisol* causes the liver to increase glucose production and body tissues to decrease their use of glucose. These biochemical reactions to stress clearly worsen the glucose regulation problems of diabetics. Studies have shown, however, that training in progressive muscle relaxation can help diabetic patients manage their stress and their blood glucose levels (Surwit, Feinglos, & Scovern, 1983; Wing, Epstein, Nowalk, & Lamparski, 1986).

To what extent can patients with diabetes reduce their long-term health risks by keeping their blood glucose levels within the normal range? Research has demonstrated that long-term complications occur much later and less often among individuals who show better control over their blood glucose levels than those who show less control (Kilo & Williamson, 1987; Santiago, 1984). But the *extent* of the reduced risk is unclear. One reason the full bene-

HIGHLIGHT 13A: On Issues
Medical Regimens for Diabetes

Ideally, the treatment for diabetes would enable the body to perform or simulate the normal biochemical activities for processing and maintaining normal levels of glucose. Medical regimens available today approximate this ideal, but they do not enable the body to function exactly as it normally does, such as in continuously monitoring the need for insulin and secreting this hormone in precisely needed bursts. Physicians generally prescribe somewhat different regimens for IDDM and NIDDM patients and tailor the treatment for individual needs (Kilo & Williamson, 1987; Pohl, Gonder-Frederick, & Cox, 1984; Wing, Nowalk, & Guare, 1988). These treatments require the patient to perform several self-care activities that focus mainly on four components: self-monitoring of blood glucose, taking insulin or other medication, diet, and exercise.

Self-Monitoring Blood Glucose

The traditional method by which patients estimate the sugar content of their blood has been by testing their urine. But many patients now use a more accurate procedure to monitor blood glucose that involves assessing sugar levels in the blood itself. In this procedure, patients prick their finger to get a drop of blood, put the blood on a chemically treated strip of paper that changes color in reaction to glucose, and wipe the blood off after a minute or so (Gonder-Frederick, Cox, Pohl, & Carter, 1984; Kilo & Williamson, 1987). They can then assess the sugar content either by comparing the color on the strip visually against a color chart or by inserting the strip into a small meter that displays a digital glucose reading. Although this procedure may sound simple, its accuracy depends on how precisely it is carried out. Waiting too long to wipe the blood off the strip or to assess the color can change the reading. Treatment regimens usually require NIDDM patients to monitor blood glucose once a day and IDDM patients to do it four times: before each meal and at bedtime (Pohl, Gonder-Frederick, & Cox, 1984).

Taking Insulin and Oral Medication

In the early 1920s, a physician named Frederick Banting devised a method that made it possible to extract insulin from the pancreas glands of slaughtered pigs and cattle. These animals are the chief sources of insulin for treating diabetes today (Kilo & Williamson, 1987; Pohl, Gonder-Frederick, & Cox, 1984). Over the years, refinements have been made to the insulin extracted, and forms of the hormone are available that last for different lengths of time. Most diabetics who need to take insulin inject it twice a day—morning and evening (Kilo & Williamson, 1987). But many patients need to take it more frequently to ensure better glucose control (Pohl, Gonder-Frederick, & Cox, 1984; Wing, Nowalk, & Guare, 1988). Some diabetics are able to use a device called an "insulin pump" that can be implanted in the body and delivers small amounts of insulin continuously, with extra doses at mealtimes.

One of the problems in using insulin is knowing how much to inject—taking too much may be as dangerous as taking too little. Using too much insulin can produce *hypo*glycemia, the condition of having too little sugar in the blood. Severe hypoglycemia can cause "insulin shock," in which the patient lapses into a coma (Kilo & Williamson, 1987). When hypoglycemia is somewhat less severe, it can markedly impair cognitive and emotional functioning, making the person excited, irritable, confused, and, sometimes, violent (Holmes, 1986). Patients dread these episodes, and so do their families (Wilkinson, 1987). Today's relatively precise methods for assessing blood glucose should help patients to reduce these episodes and to maintain glucose levels within the normal range by adjusting their insulin doses more accurately (Gonder-Frederick, Cox, Pohl, & Carter, 1984). Adjusting doses can be a complicated task, and patients usually need careful training to do it correctly.

Many diabetics use medication to control their blood glucose levels. Different types of drugs work different ways—for instance, some drugs increase insulin production in functioning pancreatic cells whereas others reduce the liver's production of glucose (Kilo & Williamson, 1987). Physicians typically do periodic blood tests in these patients because these drugs sometimes become less effective in controlling glucose levels over time.

Diet and Exercise

The diets physicians recommend for diabetics are designed to accomplish four things (Kilo & Williamson, 1987; Wing, Epstein, & Nowalk, 1984):

- Drastically reduce the intake of foods that contain sugar and some other carbohydrates that lead to high blood glucose levels.

- Reduce cholesterol consumption.
- Achieve and maintain the desirable body weight for the patient's height and frame.
- Maintain a balanced intake of nutrients, especially to promote normal growth and development when the patient is a child.

Patients who must take insulin are required to maintain consistency in the timing of their meals and, usually, in their calorie intake each day. Once they take their insulin, they generally need to eat within a range of time thereafter to prevent an episode of hypoglycemia.

Because physical activity burns up glucose as fuel, exercise is an important component in the treatment of diabetes, too. Research has shown that engaging in physical activity after meals inhibits glucose production by the liver and increases glucose use by the muscles (Zinman, 1984). Regular exercise also complements dietary efforts to reduce body weight and maintain overall fitness. But unplanned vigorous activity can cause an episode of hypoglycemia. People with diabetes who expect to engage in vigorous activity should eat a sufficient number of calories to last through the event (Kilo & Williamson, 1987). As a precaution, diabetics can quickly self-monitor their blood glucose and carry packets of medication that quickly adjusts their blood sugar.

Following a regimen to treat diabetes is not easy and can be complicated, but the risks of not doing so are serious. It takes a good deal of planning, strong efforts to maintain the routine with only occasional departures, and the confidence of patients and their families that they can do it.

---

fits of keeping blood glucose levels in the normal range are unclear is that the long-term complications of diabetes take many years or decades to develop. To know the full extent of reduced risk, researchers would have to follow the health of these patients closely for at least 20 years. Second, patients have not always been able to keep their blood glucose levels consistently in the normal range even when they tried conscientiously to do so. The methods for treating diabetes today allow patients to have better control over their blood sugar than in the past, but these new methods are still not perfect. Third, even when patients have a regimen that could provide good control over their blood glucose, many do not adhere to it closely.

Noncompliance with the treatment regimen is a major problem in managing diabetes. According to researchers who have reviewed studies on this issue, the most thorough survey of patients' adherence to diabetes regimens found that:

> - 80% of patients administered insulin in an unhygienic manner.
> - 58% administered the wrong dose of insulin.
> - 77% tested their urine incorrectly or interpreted the results "in a manner likely to be detrimental to their treatment."
> - 75% did not eat the prescribed foods.
> - 75% did not eat with sufficient regularity. (Wing, Epstein, Nowalk, & Lamparski, 1986, p. 78)

Diabetes patients generally do *try* to adhere to their regimens, but they do not always succeed. One reason they fail may be that they rely on symptoms they perceive, such as dizziness or emotional states, in assessing their glucose levels (Diamond, Massey, & Covey, 1989; Gonder-Frederick, Cox, Bobbitt, & Pennebaker, 1989). Although many patients can make crude estimates of their actual glucose levels on the basis of perceived symptoms, these judgments are usually not very accurate.

Research with IDDM patients, ranging from about 12 years of age to old age, found that they have more difficulty following dietary and exercise advice than the more "medical" aspects of their regimens—doing their glucose testing and taking their insulin on time (Glasgow, McCaul, & Schafer, 1986, 1987). These patients' self-reports indicated they had complied fairly closely to their insulin and testing regimens. However, self-report data can be misleading. In two studies, for instance, researchers secretly inserted memory chips in blood glucose testing devices of adult and adolescent diabetics but also had the subjects keep records of their testing (Mazze et al., 1984; Wilson & Endres, 1986). The results showed that many subjects' records were inaccurate — at least according to the memory chips' "memory." The records did *not* contain data for some tests the subjects had done and *did* contain data for tests that they did not actually perform.

Why don't diabetes patients adhere more closely to their regimens? As we saw in Chapter 9, compliance to medical recommendations generally tends to be low when the regimen is complex, must be followed for a long period of time, requires changes in the patient's lifestyle, and is designed to prevent rather than cure illness. Treatment regimens for diabetes have all of these characteristics. In addition, psychosocial factors in patients' lives are related to compliance. A study of over 200 middle-aged and elderly NIDDM patients found that subjects' self-reports of adherence to dietary, exercise, and glucose testing aspects of their regimens increased with their perceived social support (Wilson et al., 1986). The patients' health beliefs were also related to their self-reports of adherence, but neither social support nor health beliefs was related to actual glucose control, as measured by biochemical analysis of blood samples.

Other research has shown that interfering circumstances arise in the everyday lives of diabetic patients (Glasgow, McCaul, & Schafer, 1986). They may find it embarrassing to test their glucose levels at work or school, or forget to take their testing materials with them, or have difficulty getting up on weekend mornings to take their injections on time, or make mistakes in judgments about what they can eat, for example. Also, because diabetes is not itself a painful condition, patients may not always feel that following the regimen closely matters very much (Kilo & Williamson, 1987).

One other psychosocial situation that can lead to noncompliance is when the patient and the physician have different goals of treatment. A study demonstrated this by having doctors and the parents of diabetic children serve as subjects and asking them to assess hypothetical glucose test profiles (Marteau, Johnston, Baum, & Bloch, 1987). The researchers presented the subjects with several different test results, including one each reflecting a normal glucose level, hypoglycemia, and three degrees of hyperglycemia. The doctors were asked to pick the one profile they would be "happiest to see" for a child at their clinic; the parents were asked to pick the one they would be "happiest to see" for *their* own child. The results showed that the vast majority of physicians, but only about half of the parents, chose the profile reflecting the normal glucose level. More than a third of the parents chose either the mild or the moderate *hyper*glycemic profile. This suggests that the main focus of doctors is on preventing long-term complications from developing. In comparison, parents seem to be more interested in preventing *hypo*glycemic episodes and in promoting the day-to-day well-being and activity of their child. Not surprisingly, the children's actual glucose levels more closely matched the goals of their parents than those of physicians. Because much smaller deviations from normal blood sugar levels result in symptoms of hypoglycemia than hyperglycemia, parents and patients may choose to err on the side of higher glucose levels (Varni & Babani, 1986).

When the Diabetic Is a Child or Adolescent

Parents react to the diagnosis of diabetes in their child at first with shock, anxiety, and guilt, wondering whether they are to blame in some way. But these emotions tend to subside after the treatment regimen is in effect and seems to be controlling the child's glucose levels, and most families cope well with the disease (Eiser, 1985; Turk & Speers, 1983). Some family stressors remain, however, and stem from having to deal with occasional diabetic crises, take the child in for periodic medical examinations, give the glucose tests and injections, and make dietary adjustments, either by making special meals for the patient or by modifying the whole family's diet. Parents also worry more than the child about future health complications.

Diabetic children younger than, say, 8 or 10 years of age have little knowledge or understanding about their condition, possible long-term health problems, and why aspects of their regimen are necessary. They also do not see themselves as being very different from other children. As researcher Christine Eiser (1985) has noted, unlike children with other medical conditions, those with diabetes do not look different from other children and do not experience regular and painful medical procedures. The things that set diabetic children apart from others are their rigid eating patterns and dietary restrictions, their need to balance their intake of food carefully in relation to exercise, and, of course, the daily glucose monitoring and insulin injections. These are the kinds of things children dislike most about having diabetes (Eiser, 1985). Most of these activities can be done at home or privately.

Maintaining the diabetes treatment regimen during childhood is essentially the parents' responsibility. When can children do some of the treatment activities on their own? Children's cognitive and motor abilities allow most of them to learn to select appropriate foods by 8 years of age, give themselves injections by 9 or 10, and perform glucose testing by 12 (Eiser, 1985). Moreover, adolescent and preadolescent diabetics generally think that children are able to manage their own diabetes care at around 12 years of age. Parents tend to agree—and as adolescence approaches, they allow their children more and more responsibility for managing the diabetes regimen. But research has shown that the quality of diabetes care is often lower in early adolescence than in the preadolescent years. Compliance with glucose monitoring and diet is lower, and adolescents are less likely than their parents to make the adjustments in insulin dosage they were trained to do (Ingersoll, Orr, Herrold, & Golden, 1986; Jacobson et al., 1987). Although the psychosocial immaturity of patients in early adolescence is probably responsible for many of these compliance problems, another possibility is that the hormonal changes that occur during adolescence make the task of controlling blood glucose more difficult (Eiser, 1985).

By the time children with diabetes reach adolescence, they have the cognitive abilities to understand the disease and its long-term implications. Instead of feeling confident in their future—as other teenagers do—they may see a cloudy and vulnerable life ahead, and feel angry and cheated (Holmes, 1986). Compared to teen-aged patients who show relatively poor psychosocial adjustment, those who have high levels of self-esteem, social competence, and parental support adhere more closely to the diabetes regimen (Hanson, Henggeler, & Burghen, 1987; Jacobson et al., 1987). Teenagers who feel less sure of themselves are more likely to neglect their self-care activities partly because they may feel a greater need to avoid appearing "different" from their peers.

How can compliance to diabetes care be increased? In Chapter 9, we discussed a variety of methods that are effective in enhancing adherence to medical regimens. Some of these methods involve improving the way practitioners present information about the procedures and the importance of following the treatment. Other approaches use behavioral methods, such as tailoring the regimen to make it as compatible as possible with patients' habits, using prompts and reminders, having patients keep records of their self-care activities, and providing a system of rewards through the method of contingency contracting. Research has shown that various approaches can be useful in improving compliance with different aspects of the diabetes regimen (Wing, Epstein, Nowalk, & Lamparski, 1986). One study, for instance, introduced a series of behavioral methods in an eight-week program to improve regimen adherence in three noncompliant 16- to 18-year-old IDDM patients: Kathy, Tom, and Kim (Shafer, Glasgow, & McCaul, 1982). Both Kathy and Tom showed substantial improvements in their adherence and glucose control. Kim's self-care did not improve, probably because she came from a family with severe marital and family problems that therapy had failed to resolve. Family problems can have an overriding influence and undermine efforts to improve compliance.

Kidney Disease

The kidney is a highly complex organ. Although its basic function is to cleanse the blood, it does much more than that. When blood arrives at the kidneys, structures called *nephrons* remove water, nutrients, ions, and waste products from it. The waste products and portions of the other materials are excreted in the urine, but the nephrons return the remaining materials to the blood as the body needs them. The kidneys also activate vitamin D and produce hormones that help to regulate blood pressure (Cameron, 1986).

The kidneys can sustain permanent damage from a wide variety of medical conditions, including diabetes, hypertension, and many different kidney, or *renal,* diseases (Cameron, 1986; Guyton, 1985; McClintic, 1985; Polise, 1985). One class of kidney diseases—called **nephritis**—is characterized by inflammation of kidney tissue and destruction of nephrons. These diseases can occur as acute conditions, or they can become chronic. In one of these diseases, called *pyelonephritis,* an infection of the kidneys develops and either directly or indirectly causes nephron damage. In another of these diseases, *glomerulonephritis,* an infection occurs and leads to an immune reaction that destroys kidney tissue. An acute episode of nephritis can be severe enough to cause extensive damage, shut down the kidneys, and require intensive hospital care. Chronic nephritis tends to entail recurrent, milder episodes, with symptoms that may include body swelling, increased blood pressure, and blood in the urine. Chronic kidney diseases that cause permanent damage can occur at any age, and some are inborn—but their prevalence increases with age and are most common among the elderly (Cameron, 1986; Polise, 1985; USDHHS, 1986b).

The damage to nephrons produced by kidney diseases accumulates over time, thereby involving larger and larger proportions of kidney tissue. What is surprising about this accumulated injury is that the person generally does not notice any obvious symptoms of the damage until it is quite extensive, involving perhaps two-thirds or more of the nephrons in the two kidneys (Cameron, 1986; Guyton, 1985). Why are there no symptoms? Evidently, individual nephrons can process blood at a far greater rate than they normally do. When some nephrons are lost, the remaining ones compensate by increasing their activity. At some point, of course, the damage becomes so extensive that the kidneys cannot handle the load, and symptoms of fatigue, weight loss, and frequent thirst occur. At this point, *chronic renal failure* is already under way, and the kidneys slowly and progressively deteriorate (Polise, 1985). In the last stage in this process—called **end-stage renal disease** (ESRD)—the kidneys barely function and cannot support life. Glomerulonephritis and pyelonephritis are by far the leading causes of chronic renal failure and are the principal causes of nearly 60% of ESRD cases (Cameron, 1986).

Medical Treatments for Renal Failure

Once chronic renal failure begins, little can be done to prevent its relentless progression (Cameron, 1986; Polise, 1985). The condition may take months or many years to reach ESRD, and the patient and practitioner typically use the intervening time to prepare for that eventuality. What happens when the condition reaches ESRD? Until around 1960, there was no way to save the lives of these patients (Armstrong, 1984). They would lapse into a coma and die. But today there are three life-saving medical options. One of these treatments is *hemodialysis,* a procedure in which the patient's blood is shunted from an artery to an apparatus—commonly called an "artificial kidney"—and returned to a vein. Hemodialysis processes the blood, removing wastes and adjusting the amounts of other substances, such as sodium and potassium. The apparatus is available in portable units, and some are even disposable, but no practical wearable unit is yet available. Hemodialysis treatment generally requires three sessions a week, each lasting about four to six hours, during which time the patient may either sleep or engage in a sedentary activity, such as reading. The United States has over 90,000 ESRD patients, and about 70% of them are being treated with hemodialysis (Cameron, 1986).

Another approach to treating ESRD is called *continuous ambulatory peritoneal dialysis* (CAPD); about 10% of American ESRD patients use this method (Cameron, 1986). To understand how CAPD works, you need to know that the *peritoneum* is a large, tough membrane that lines the abdominal cavity, forming a sac that can hold liquid. Because it has a rich blood supply, it can be used as a structure to exchange substances to and from the blood (Cameron, 1986). Using this structure requires access to it with a catheter that is implanted through the skin surgically. In performing CAPD, the patient connects the catheter to a tube that leads to a plastic bag that contains a dialysis solution. Gravity feeds the solution into the peritoneum where it remains to exchange substances with the blood through the membrane. After several hours, the patient drains the used solution and replaces it with a fresh batch. Although most patients do four exchanges a day, others need only three.

The third treatment for ESRD is *kidney transplantation*, which requires finding a suitable transplant organ—usually either from a relative or, more commonly, from a person who recently died—and installing it surgically (Benvenisty & Hardy, 1986; Cameron, 1986). Finding an organ that is genetically well matched is often very difficult, but the medical procedure with such organs is highly successful: about 95% of transplanted kidneys continue to function after a year. The main problem for the patients who receive a transplant is that, unless the donor was an identical twin, they must take drugs thereafter to suppress rejection of the organ by the immune system. These drugs have two important side effects. First, because the patients' immune systems are suppressed, they face the constant threat of infections,

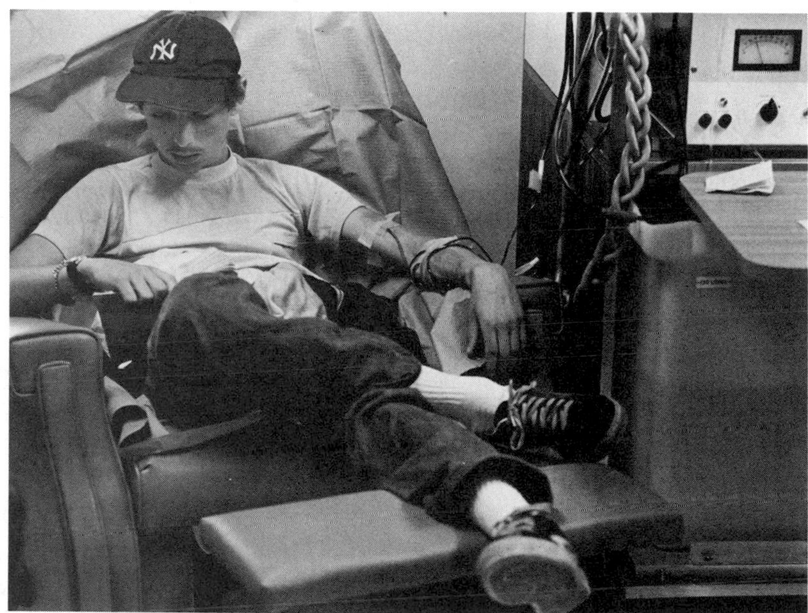

Although a hemodialysis session takes several hours, patients can read or engage in other sedentary activities.

some of which can be life-threatening. Second, these patients also face a somewhat increased risk of developing various chronic illnesses, such as cancer. But transplantation as a treatment for ESRD also has many advantages — for instance, it is less expensive in the long run than hemodialysis, and the patient has a real kidney and can lead a life with few constraints of medical regimens, except for taking pills each day. Some patients today have had their transplants for over 20 years so far (Cameron, 1986).

What are the pros and cons of the two dialysis approaches? Hemodialysis is a very demanding treatment regimen (Cameron, 1986; Finn & Alcorn, 1986; Nehemkis & Gerber, 1986; Swigonski, 1987). Although some patients can perform the treatment at home, usually with the assistance of a family member, most go to a clinic for it. This can restrict the person's lifestyle severely and is very time-consuming and expensive. These patients must also eat very restricted diets and take large quantities of medication and vitamins — sometimes involving dozens of pills a day — while, at the same time, limiting fluid intake to only about two cups a day. Many patients find that adhering closely to their dietary restrictions is not feasible. The treatment itself can produce muscle cramps and nausea and often leaves patients feeling "washed out" and tired. The following day patients usually feel good, but by the time the next session arrives, they feel lethargic. Moreover, long-term hemodialysis patients are at risk for developing hepatitis, duodenal ulcers, and various other ailments. The procedure keeps the patients alive, and some have been using it for over 20 years, but their lives are very difficult.

CAPD is a relatively new procedure that was introduced in the late 1970s (Polise, 1985). It seems to be a very promising technique, but it does not yet have a long-term track record of either success or failure. The main risk medical workers have identified so far is of infection in connection with the catheter, which occurs often enough in some patients that they must abandon CAPD. Although the procedure does not restrict patients' lifestyles as severely as hemodialysis does, CAPD takes up a few hours each day, and the patient must be seated during that time. But it has the advantages of having no complex apparatus and being an inexpensive procedure that can be done easily at home or in a private location elsewhere, such as at work during lunch hour. Compared with hemodialysis, CAPD has fewer dietary restrictions and seems to be less stressful for patients, physically and, perhaps, emotionally (Cameron, 1986; House, 1987; Nehemkis & Gerber, 1986; Polise, 1985). Also, tentative research results indicate that child patients show better growth when treated with CAPD than with hemodialysis (Polise, 1985). As a result, CAPD may become the treatment of choice for children who are too young to receive a transplant.

How effective is medical treatment in saving the lives of ESRD patients? It is difficult to answer this question because successful treatments have only been available since the early 1960s and the patients have differed in their age and the extent to which other illnesses impaired their survival. These factors are important in three ways. First, more than half of hemodialysis patients in the United States are over 50 years of age, and one-third are over 60 (Appel & Cahill, 1986; Swigonski, 1987). As you might expect, long-term survival is better for younger than older patients. For instance, among patients who received hemodialysis at home in Europe, survival at five years declined from 81% for 15- to 34-year-olds to 58% for 55- to 64-year-olds (Cameron, 1986). Second, age and the presence of other diseases affect medical decisions: ESRD patients who are under 3 years of age, or are over 65, or have complicating illnesses are generally considered poor candidates for a transplant (Benvenisty & Hardy, 1986). Patients who cannot have a transplant or are waiting for one receive dialysis. Third, treatment procedures have improved over the years. In the case of transplants, for example, mortality rates have decreased as a result of having better kidneys to transplant and better immunosuppressant drugs (Cameron, 1986).

Psychosocial Factors in Renal Failure

Of course, survival is not the only criterion for evaluating the success of treatment — the quality of life is extremely important, too. Patients' quality of life is usually far superior with kidney transplantation than with years of hemodialysis. Transplant patients have more energy, require less medical care, can eat a more varied diet, and have much more freedom in their lives. Although the great majority of adult ESRD patients with transplant or hemodialysis treatment are physically able to work, those who receive dialysis at a clinic are far less likely to do so (Cameron, 1986). Home dialysis offers more freedom than clinic dialysis, thereby enabling patients to travel and work more freely. But dialysis of any kind, including CAPD, places more restrictions on patients' lives than transplants do. When deciding which type of treatment to pursue, patients need to weigh many factors relating to their health and lifestyle.

Because hemodialysis is such a demanding and stressful medical regimen, many researchers have studied how well patients adjust to this treatment. With cases of childhood ESRD, hemodialysis is generally used only temporarily while they await kidney transplantation or CAPD (Polise, 1985). For most adult patients, hemodialysis is considered a long-term or permanent treatment. Studies of these patients have found that they often feel a sense of helplessness and hopelessness and experience high levels of depression (Armstrong, 1984; Devins et al., 1981; Swigonski, 1987). Many hemodialysis patients are unable to maintain their prior jobs and fail to find alternative work, particularly if they had held blue-collar jobs. Sexual difficulties are also common among hemodialysis patients. Adjusting to these problems is difficult for patients and their families. ESRD patients have good prospects for psychological adjustment if they are physically able to engage in activities and they receive high levels of social support, especially in the first year or two of treatment (Carney, Wetzel, Hagberg, & Goldberg, 1986; Siegal, Calsyn, & Cuddihee, 1987).

In summary, both diabetes and kidney disease threaten the lives of their victims. The treatment regimens for each of these diseases can save, or at least prolong, the lives of its victims. But the diabetes and hemodialysis regimens are very complex and involve major lifestyle changes. As a result, many patients fail to adhere to the treatment requirements. In the next section, we will examine the experiences of individuals who suffer from asthma — a respiratory disorder.

LIVING WITH A RESPIRATORY DISORDER: ASTHMA

We all experience respiratory disorders at one time or another. If we are fortunate, these disorders are limited to occasional bouts with winter colds and the flu. But tens of millions of people are not so fortunate, and they suffer from a wide variety of chronic respiratory problems. In some cases, these problems involve constant breathing impairments that vary in intensity from one day to the next. In other cases, the victims breathe normally most of the time but suffer recurrent episodes of impaired breathing. Some chronic respiratory illnesses, such as *emphysema*, result largely from environmental causes, such as cigarette smoking. Others do not. Some chronic respiratory disorders become severe enough to disable its victims and may even claim their lives. This can happen with *asthma*.

What is Asthma?

Imagine being at home reading one evening and noticing that a slight whistling, wheezing sound starts to accompany each breath you take. Soon the sound becomes louder and your breathing becomes labored. You try opening your mouth to breathe, but very little air goes in or out. When your chest begins to contract from the effort and your heart pounds rapidly, you are quite frightened and worry, "Will my next gasp for air be my last?" This is what a major asthma attack is like. Victims of extreme attacks may begin to turn blue and look as if they are about to die, and some do die.

About nine million Americans — 3 - 5% of the population — suffer from asthma, and the prevalence rates are much higher for children, especially boys, than for adults (Cluss & Fireman, 1985; Gergen, Mullally, & Evans, 1988). Although the disorder may emerge at any age, about 80% of asthmatics experience their first episode by their fifth birthday. Fortunately, most childhood cases of asthma become less severe over time (Burg & Ingall, 1985), and 25 - 50% of the children who develop asthma no longer have symptoms by the time they reach adulthood (Cluss & Fireman, 1985; Eiser, 1985). Each year, nearly 4,000 asthmatics in the United States die from asthma attacks (Blakeslee, 1988). The death rates from attacks are higher among the elderly than younger individuals, and higher among blacks than whites. Because black people have lower incomes than whites and are less likely to have a regular physician, they tend to use hospital emergency rooms as their main source of treatment for asthma and seek help mainly when the attack is severe.

Asthma is a leading cause of short-term disability in the United States (USDHHS, 1986d). Each year, it results in millions of restricted-activity days in which patients either remain in bed or are unable to carry out their usual major activities, such as going to work or school. In childhood alone, asthma results in:

- 28 million restricted-activity days a year.
- 2.2 million physician visits, making it the tenth most frequent reason.
- Many hospitalizations, which have increased sharply since the 1960s. (Gergen, Mullally, & Evans, 1988)

Asthma is clearly a major health problem. Let's see what causes asthma attacks.

The Physiology, Causes, and Effects of Asthma

Most asthma episodes are, at least in part, allergic reactions in which the immune system detects and attacks allergens — harmless substances, such as pollen and molds. Allergens may enter the body in several ways and produce different types of allergic reactions (Burg & Ingall, 1985). These substances may be:

- *Inhaled*, as pollen and dust are, and produce bouts of hay fever or asthma.
- *Ingested*, as foods and drugs are, and lead to various types of reactions, such as asthmatic attacks, skin rashes, abdominal pain, and diarrhea.
- *Injected*, as drugs and vaccines are, and show up as rashes.
- *Contacted* through the skin, as with ointments, soaps, cosmetics, and clothing fibers, and produce rashes.

The immune system responds by producing antibodies that cause the body's tissues in the affected area to release a chemical called *histamine*. This chemical makes it easier for white blood cells of the immune system to pass through the capillary walls in the area. In the case of hay fever, for example, inhaled allergens release histamine in the nose, producing irritation in the nasal membranes.

When allergens trigger an asthmatic attack, the site of irritation is in the smooth muscles of the bronchial tubes (Burg & Ingalls, 1985). The muscles develop spasms and the walls of the tubes constrict and produce mucus, which tends to plug the airway. This reaction lasts, perhaps, an hour or two (Blakeslee, 1988). Then, a few hours later, asthmatics often experience a second phase of the attack that involves the white blood cells. When the white blood cells reach the area, they release chemicals that can inflame and damage the tissues, thereby increasing the likelihood of more frequent and severe future attacks. This second phase may last hours or even days, and its symptoms may be more severe than those of the first phase.

Researchers demonstrated the important role of the immune system in allergic reactions with a study involving transplanted bone marrow, the tissue that produces white blood cells (Agosti et al., 1988). The subjects were cancer patients who needed the transplants as part of their treatment. Each of the subjects and the donors was given skin tests with 17 allergen extracts — including house dust, cat hair, penicillin, mites, and ragweed—before the transplant and one year after. In some of the pretransplant tests, the donor showed a positive allergic reaction but the patient did not. When testing was done a year later, the patients now showed reactions in 44.5% of these tests. In other pretransplant tests, neither the donor nor the patient showed an allergic reaction. This situation served as a control condition—and a year later the patients showed reactions in only 3% of these tests. These findings indicate that the bone marrow contains allergen-specific antibodies and that the donors' allergies were passed on to the patients. This research also produced evidence of asthma being transmitted from donors to patients who previously had no history of asthma.

Allergies appear to play a greater role in triggering attacks in some asthmatics than in others (Burg & Ingall, 1985; Creer, 1983). At one end of the continuum are patients suffering from *extrinsic asthma*, in which attacks tend to occur in the presence of specific allergens that are "extrinsic" to the body. These patients' attacks are related to allergies they are known to have, such as to dust or certain foods. Asthmatics who are allergic only to a certain pollen, for example, may have attacks during the season when that pollen is prevalent and not at other times of the year. At the other end of the continuum are patients with *intrinsic asthma*, in which attacks do not seem to depend on the presence of allergens. For these patients, their condition probably results from respiratory infections or from other physiological factors that are "intrinsic" to the body. Unlike patients with extrinsic asthma, these individuals may suffer attacks at any time of the year. As Figure 13.3 diagrams, in the middle range of the continuum are asthmatics of a "mixed" type whose attacks can be triggered by either intrinsic or extrinsic factors, or both.

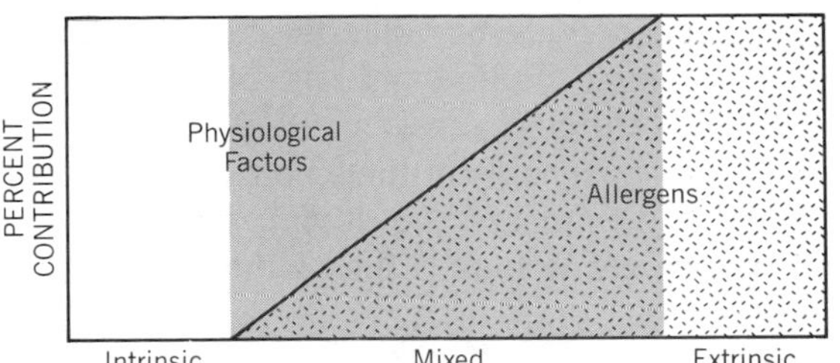

FIGURE 13.3 Diagram illustrating the contributions of physiological factors and allergens to the asthma attacks of patients with intrinsic, mixed, and extrinsic asthma.

Psychosocial Factors in Asthma

Allergens are not the only triggers of asthma attacks, there are five others: chemical irritants, infections, weather changes, exercise, and psychosocial factors (Burg & Ingalls, 1985). In Chapter 4, we noted that psychosocial factors, including stress, can produce or aggravate an asthmatic episode. Studies have also shown that *suggestion* can induce symptoms in asthmatic subjects. In one study, researchers had the subjects inhale several doses of a placebo solution, with each succeeding dose labeled as containing an increasingly strong dose of an allergen (Luparello, Lyons, Bleecker, & McFadden, 1968). Nearly half of the subjects developed symptoms, either as full asthmatic attacks or as spasms of the bronchial muscles. Another study confirmed this effect, finding that subjects who were told that the placebo solution they were inhaling was an irritant developed asthmatic symptoms (Butler & Steptoe, 1986). But this research also showed that the asthmatic reaction could be negated if the subjects were first given another placebo that was described as a new asthma drug. In other words, the first suggestion blocked the second one.

Not all investigations have succeeded in producing symptoms in asthmatic patients by using placebos and suggestion, but several have (Butler & Steptoe, 1986; Cluss & Fireman, 1985). Many other studies have shown other links between asthma and psychosocial factors, such as emotions (Creer, 1983; Eiser, 1985). Although there is little question that psychosocial factors can influence asthma attacks, we do not know how these factors work and which asthmatics are more affected by them. It is possible that psychosocial factors make asthmatics more sensitive to the allergens that produce their attacks. On the other hand, the symptoms of individuals suffering from extrinsic asthma—those for whom asthmatic reactions are clearly allergen related—may be less strongly influenced by psychological factors than are the symptoms of people with intrinsic asthma (Cluss & Fireman, 1985).

Managing Asthma

Medical approaches provide the cornerstone of treatment for asthma (Burg & Ingall, 1985; Cluss & Fireman, 1985; Werry, 1986). Asthma regimens consist of three components, the first being to *avoid known triggers* of attacks. The second component involves medication. To treat an acute attack, patients may use two types of drugs: *bronchodilators*, which open up constricted airways, and inhaled *steroids*, which reduce inflammation during the second phase of the attack. Because steroids can have undesirable side effects, they are usually reserved for people with severe asthma and used sparingly. Other drugs, particularly *cromolyn sodium*, prevent attacks by blocking the release of histamine and other chemicals that cause bronchial spasms. When patients use cromolyn, they are usually advised to inhale it three or four times a day.

The third component of asthma regimens involves *exercise*. In the past, physicians advised many asthmatics to avoid exercise because it could induce an attack (Stockton, 1988). But it now appears that the less these patients exercise, the worse their conditions get. Many physicians today recommend treatment regimens that carefully combine fitness training and the use of medication. Asthma's potential for producing disability and, sometimes, death makes it important that patients adhere to their regimen. Research has shown that patients who comply with their regimens experience far fewer attacks and incidents of wheezing, for example (Cluss & Epstein, 1985). But many asthmatics do not adhere closely, often failing to take medication to prevent attacks and using medication during an attack incorrectly (Cluss & Fireman, 1985; Creer, 1983).

Because of the role of stress in asthma, psychologists have trained patients to use stress management techniques—especially progressive muscle relaxation, biofeedback, and systematic desensitization—to help reduce the frequency and intensity of attacks. Although these techniques show some promise, studies demonstrating their success have usually used small numbers of subjects, failed to use appropriate control groups, and failed to assess success in long-term follow-ups (Cluss & Fireman, 1985). Psychologists have also been involved in developing self-management programs for asthmatics that include a variety of behavioral and counseling techniques to improve compliance, enhance self-esteem, and reduce stress (Cluss & Fireman, 1985; Parker, 1985). These programs show promise, too.

Asthma attacks are frightening for the patient and family alike, and frequent episodes are costly to the family and disrupt these people's lives and functioning (Cluss & Fireman, 1985). Living with this disorder adds to the stress that patients and their families experience, and studies have found that asthma is sometimes related to maladjustment in patients and their families (Werry, 1986). This relationship probably involves two causal directions: (1) living with asthma sometimes leads to emotional problems and (2) maladjustment in the family increases asthmatic episodes. Some asthmatics are chronically short of breath and have frequent attacks, and others have long attack-free periods. The psychosocial impact of asthma is likely to depend on how severe and disabling the condition is. In the next section, we will examine highly disabling disorders that affect the muscles and skeleton of the body.

LIVING WITH A MUSCULOSKELETAL DISORDER: ARTHRITIS AND SPINAL CORD INJURIES

Disorders of the musculoskeletal system include a wide range of medical conditions, such as arthritis, low back problems, amputation,

HIGHLIGHT 13B: On Research
Beliefs about Illness: Fear of the Unknown?

Before people actually experience a specific chronic illness in their family, they have some ideas about how serious the health problem is. How do they feel about an illness after someone in the family develops it? Is it worse than they expected, or not as bad, or about the same? The answers to these questions should have a bearing on how well the family adjusts to health problems.

Theresa Marteau and Marie Johnston (1986) conducted a study with parents whose children had one of four health statuses, having either diabetes, asthma, epilepsy, or no chronic illness. The researchers selected the subjects from a large sample in order to equate the four groups for the children's ages and length of illness, if any. The parents of 93 children made up the final sample. On average, the children with each health status were about 6 or 7 years of age and had experienced their illness, if any, for about three years. The researchers had the parents rate how serious each of several health problems would be if their child were to develop it (or had it now). The health problems included diabetes, asthma, and epilepsy, and the parents rated the various illnesses on a six-point scale that had the following end points: 1 = "not at all serious" and 6 = "extremely serious."

Table 13B.1 presents averages of the ratings the parents gave for diabetes, asthma, and epilepsy, separated on the basis of the health condition of their child. Notice that in each of the three illness columns, the lowest ratings the parents gave were for the health problem their own child had. Moreover, parents whose child did not have a chronic illness rated each of the health problems as being rather serious. Clearly, parents who live with a chronic illness in their child have a less negative view of the health problem than parents whose child does not have that illness.

What do these results mean? They could mean that the parents were using avoidance strategies to cope with their child's illness and denying the seriousness of it. But this possibility is not supported by other ratings the parents made. For example, parents with a diabetic child who also had another relative with diabetes rated the likelihood that their child would develop complications in the future. If the parents perceived the relative to be in poor health, they were more pessimistic about their child's future health than if they thought the relative was in good health. This suggests that the parents did not avoid the unpleasant information about their other relative's health and that this information influenced their judgments about their child's future health. A more likely meaning of the ratings in the table is that people are frightened of the prospects of health problems but tend to adjust well to the reality of an illness when it actually occurs.

TABLE 13B.1 Ratings of Perceived Seriousness of Three Diseases by Parents of Children with One of These Illnesses or with No Chronic Illness

	Child's Health Condition			
Rated Illness	*Diabetes*	*Asthma*	*Epilepsy*	*No Illness*
Diabetes	3.45	4.64	4.05	4.81
Asthma	4.55	3.29	3.79	4.11
Epilepsy	4.96	5.23	3.51	5.01

Source: Ratings calculated on the basis of data in Tables I and II in Marteau & Johnston (1986).

and various paralyzing conditions. These disorders are among the most prevalent chronic health problems of Americans and are responsible for an enormous amount of temporary and permanent disability and functional impairment (USDHHS, 1986d). Large-scale studies in the United States have found that about 10% of the population have chronic or permanent musculoskeletal conditions that regularly decrease or eliminate their ability to perform important functions and that about half of adults either have musculoskeletal defects or a history of chronic muscle or skeletal symptoms (Kelsey & Hochberg, 1988). We will discuss two very different musculoskeletal disorders, arthritis and spinal cord injuries.

Arthritis

Disorders of the bones and joints have probably always plagued humans and almost all other animals — archaeologists have found evidence of arthritis in the fossil bones of dinosaurs and prehistoric bears, for instance. These disorders

> are found in some form in all creatures having a skeleton. The exceptions are animals that hang upside down such as bats or sloths — a strange bit of trivia that may ultimately be of some importance in understanding the etiological mysteries of the musculoskeletal disorders. (Achterberg-Lawlis, 1988, p. 222)

Musculoskeletal disorders that affect the joints of the body and connective tissues near the joints are called *rheumatic diseases* (Burg & Ingall, 1985; Crain, 1971). Most cases of rheumatic disease are classified as **arthritis** — a category of over 100 conditions that involve inflammation of the joints, pain, stiffness, and, sometimes, swelling (Achterberg-Lawlis, 1988; Kelsey & Hochberg, 1988). By far the most common arthritic condition is osteoarthritis, followed by rheumatoid arthritis and then gout.

The Types and Causes of Arthritis

Osteoarthritis is a disease in which the joints degenerate, mainly as a result of wear and tear. People's risk of developing this condition increases with age and body weight, and is associated with certain occupations in which particular joints are subjected to repeated heavy use (Kelsey & Hochberg, 1988). For instance, weavers and cotton pickers often develop osteoarthritis of the hands, whereas ballet dancers tend to have the condition in their feet. *Gout* can affect any of the body's joints. In this disease, the body produces more uric acid than the kidneys can process, and the excess acid circulates in the blood and leaves crystalline deposits at the joints (Crain, 1971).

Rheumatoid arthritis is a disease that involves extreme inflammation of joint tissues and also affects the heart, blood vessels, and lungs when it reaches advanced stages (Achterberg-Lawlis, 1988; Kelsey & Hochberg, 1988). It is potentially the most serious arthritic condition, being the most crippling and painful type. It often spreads to all of the body's joints. Although the mechanisms that lead to rheumatoid arthritis are unclear, they seem to involve an immune response that attacks the tissues and bones of the joints (Anderson et al., 1985; Burg & Ingall, 1985). All three types of arthritis run in families, and evidence exists for hereditary factors in each condition (Crain, 1971). Some research has found evidence linking stress and rheumatoid arthritis, finding that patients reported that major stressful events often preceded the onset of the disease and its flare-ups (Achterberg-Lawlis, 1988; Anderson et al., 1985).

About 30 million Americans suffer from arthritis (USDHHS, 1986d). Although the condition can appear at any age, it becomes far more prevalent as people get older. As Figure 13.4 depicts, arthritis afflicts nearly half of Americans over 65 years of age and occurs more often among females than males. But three points should be made about the data in the figure. First, they probably underestimate the actual number of people who have the disorder because mild cases often do not come to the attention of health agencies (Kelsey & Hochberg, 1988). Second, the figure does not show that, whereas the female-to-male ratio is 3:2 for osteoarthritis and 2.5:1 for rheumatoid arthritis, the sex ratio for gout is reversed — being 1:7 (Achterberg-Lawlis, 1988). Third, of the three disorders, rheumatoid arthritis is the most common type in childhood. Tens of thousands of American children have *juvenile rheumatoid arthritis*, and, like the adult form, it occurs more often in girls than boys (Achterberg-Lawlis, 1988; McCormick, Stemmler, & Athreya, 1986). Researchers have estimated that between 70 and 90% of children who develop juvenile rheumatoid arthritis will *not* suffer serious disability in their adult lives (Burg & Ingall, 1985).

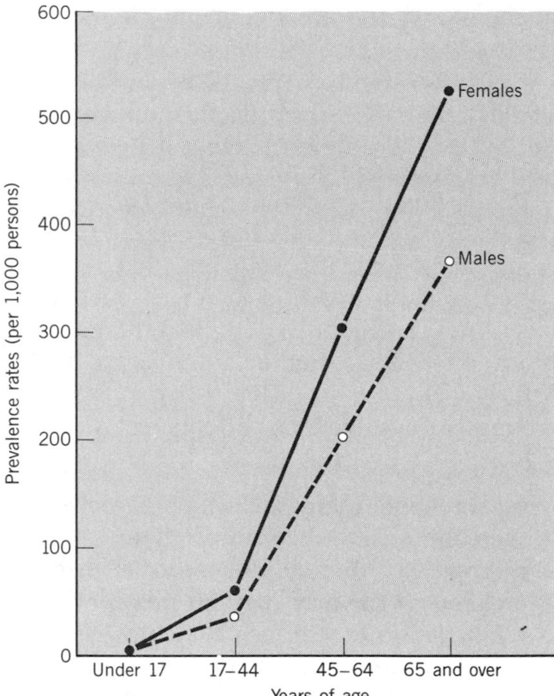

FIGURE 13.4 Prevalence rates of arthritis per 1,000 males and females in the United States at each age range. (Data from USDHHS, 1986d, Tables 18 and 19.)

The Effects and Management of Arthritis

Of the major chronic diseases that afflict people in the United States, arthritis is the leader each year in causing people to cut down on their usual activities, such as going to work. Moreover, it is second, behind heart disease, in causing people to stay in bed most or all of the day (USDHHS, 1986d). Any type of arthritis can disable its victims on a short-term or long-term basis, and the course of the disease is highly variable.

In the case of rheumatoid arthritis, some patients experience only mild episodes of inflammation and pain in a few joints; other patients, however, suffer intense pain in many joints, often showing the following progression:

- The lubricating fluid leaks out of the joints, usually in the knees, ankles, shoulders, elbows, and wrists.
- Cartilage is destroyed and joint function is reduced.
- The conversion of organic matter into minerals for bones decreases near the joints.
- Bone erosions take place near the joints.
- Joints become dislocated and sometimes fused, producing deformities. (Anderson et al., 1985)

Some of the patients whose rheumatoid arthritis progresses to the later stages show associated damage to other organ systems, developing vascular or heart valve diseases, for example.

Severe arthritis often has a substantial psychosocial impact on the patients and their families. For children with severe juvenile rheumatoid arthritis, their illness causes them to miss dozens of school days each year and engage in less play and social activities with family and friends (Billings, Moos, Miller, & Gottlieb, 1987; McCormick, Stemmler, & Athreya, 1986). The greater the degree of physical care these children need, the greater the stress their condition produces in the family. Studies of adult arthritis patients have shown that those whose conditions are severe are much more likely to feel helpless and seriously depressed than those with milder conditions (Anderson et al., 1985). One study, for instance, examined over 200 patients' disability and feelings of helplessness about their condition over a one-year period (Nicassio et al., 1985). Their self-reports showed that their feelings of helplessness correlated with changes in their ability to perform daily activities, such as dressing, turning faucets on and off, and getting in and out of a car.

Of course, not all individuals with severe arthritis experience serious emotional difficulties. Some severely ill patients feel a greater sense of personal control over their condition than others do, and this difference relates to their emotional adjustment. In a study examining this relationship, researchers interviewed adult rheumatoid arthritis patients regarding their mood states and their perceptions of personal control over their illness (Affleck, Tennen, Pfeiffer, & Fifield, 1987). These interviews revealed three main findings. First, the patients generally thought their practitioner had greater control over the *course* of the disease than they did themselves. Second, of the subjects who had relatively active symptoms, those who believed they could control their *daily symptoms* reported less mood disturbance than those who did not. Third, the patients who saw themselves as *active partners* in decisions about their medical care and treatment showed better adjustment to their illness. These findings are also important because patients who understand their treatment and believe it can help are more likely to adhere closely to their medical regimens than those patients who do not (Jette, 1984).

What treatments can be used in managing the pain and functional impairment of arthritis? Patients with arthritis typically take some form of pain-relieving medication, especially aspirin and other drugs, such as ibuprofen, that reduce inflammation (Anderson et al., 1985; Crain, 1971). For relatively severe cases, two types of medication are often prescribed. *Steroids* are fast-acting drugs that tend to reduce inflammation, stiffness, and swelling in a matter of hours. *Gold compounds* are salts that are soluble in liquid. Although most patients who are treated with gold get at least moderate relief, it usually takes weeks or months for patients to notice improvements, and the action of this drug is not well understood. But both steroids and gold compounds have serious negative side effects, such as gastrointestinal problems and kidney damage. Studies of compliance with taking medication have shown that patients adhere closely to recommendations for the more powerful drugs, but not for milder ones, such as aspirin (Anderson et al., 1985).

In extreme cases when other medical approaches have not helped, surgeons replace affected joints with artificial ones. Other approaches for managing arthritic pain and impairment involve maintaining proper body weight and, especially for gout patients, limiting certain foods and alcohol (Crain, 1971). Physical therapy is very important and includes exercise, applying heat or cold, and using devices to prevent joint damage and assist patients in performing daily activities (Banwell, 1984; Crain, 1971; Schweidler, 1984; Seeger, 1984; Wickersham, 1984). Patients appear to comply less closely with physical therapy aspects of their regimens than with taking medication (Anderson et al., 1985).

Public health researcher Kate Lorig (1984; see also McLeod, 1986) has described a program called Arthritis Self-Help that was designed to help arthritis sufferers cope with their illness and comply with their treatment. It is now offered across the United States by the Arthritis Foundation. The program involves group meetings in which patients receive training in:

- Exercising, including which exercises to do and exactly how to do them.
- Protecting their joints, such as through changing the way they lift heavy objects.
- Relaxation techniques to control stress.
- Appropriate diets for their illness.
- Self-monitoring and contingency contracting to promote their complying with regimen activities.

The program lasts about 12 weeks and is often conducted by a layperson who has arthritis. Educational approaches such as the Arthritis

Physical therapy for a patient with arthritic hands can involve enjoyable activities that exercise the affected joints.

Self-Help program do appear to help arthritis patients to reduce pain and enhance their health status (Lorig, 1984; Mullen, Laville, Biddle, & Lorig, 1987).

Spinal Cord Injuries

Prior to the 1940s, medical practitioners knew almost nothing about treating patients who suffered a severe injury to the spinal cord (Hendrick, 1985). In World War I, 80% of the soldiers who received such injuries died within two weeks. People who survived severe spinal cord injuries had a poor prognosis for their future health, which was characterized by major health complications and a short life span. As a result, patients and practitioners had a defeatist attitude, and little attempt was made toward rehabilitation. In World War II, however, England established special medical units to develop and provide comprehensive care and rehabilitation techniques for patients with spinal cord injuries. These medical units served as a model for others to be developed in countries around the world.

The Prevalence, Causes, and Physical Effects of Spinal Cord Injuries

The term **spinal cord injury** refers to neurological damage in the spine that results in the loss of motor control, sensation, and reflexes in associated body areas. The damage may be caused by disease or by an injury that compresses, tears, and severs the cord (Brucker, 1983; Hendrick, 1985). When the cord is badly torn or severed, the damage is permanent because little or no nerve tissue will regenerate; but if the cord is compressed or has an abrasion, some function may be recovered when the pressure is removed or healing occurs. As we saw in Chapter 2, the degree to which the patient's function is impaired depends on the amount of damage and its location. If the cord is completely severed in the neck region, *quadriplegia* results; if a lower portion is severed, *paraplegia* results. If the cord is not completely severed, partial function remains.

The United States has more than 250,000 people living with spinal cord injuries, and about 10,000 new cases occur each year (Brucker, 1983). Most of these people suffer neck injuries and are quadriplegics. The great majority of Americans who receive spinal cord injuries are males, and most of them are between 10 and 30 years of age at the time. About half of these injuries result from automobile and motorcycle accidents, and the remainder result mainly from falls, sporting activities, and wounds, such as from a gunshot or stabbing (Brucker, 1983; Hendrick, 1985).

The physical effects that patients experience after a spinal cord injury change over time and progress through two stages:

1. *Short-term effects.* The immediate physiological reaction is called "spinal shock," which usually lasts between a few days and three months (Hendrick, 1985; Nash & Smith, 1982). In spinal shock, neural function is devastated either by the cord being severed or by inflammation at the site of lesser damage. The result is that the body cannot regulate blood pressure, temperature, respiration, and bladder and bowel function. Medical personnel must intervene to control these functions. Usually, the shorter the period of spinal shock, the better the prognosis of recovery.
2. *Long-term effects.* The full extent of spinal cord damage may not be clear for some time, and long-term predictions are difficult to make during the first six months or so (Hendrick, 1985). If the cord is not severed, considerable functional recovery may occur over a long period of time. If the cord is severed, some autonomic functions will recover, but other functions will not. Severe damage to the higher regions of the cord often leave the person totally paralyzed and unable to breathe without a respirator.

The initial care these patients receive typically focuses on their medical needs, with little or no attention to their psychological reactions (Brucker, 1983). They receive very little information about their prognosis because it is so hard to predict and the medical staff want to avoid the depression their speculations might produce. Once the condition of these patients has stabilized, the process of rehabilitation begins. Almost all spinal cord injury patients enter rehabilitation expecting to regain total function and are not prepared to cope with the reality of permanent functional losses.

Physical Rehabilitation

The process of physical rehabilitation for patients with spinal cord injuries is geared toward helping them (1) regain as much physical function as the neurological damage will allow and (2) become as independent in their functioning as possible (Brucker, 1983). This process focuses initially on training the patients to develop bladder and bowel control and on assisting them in moving paralyzed limbs to maintain their range of motion (Hendrick, 1985). Although many patients will eventually be able to control their bladder functions, others will not and will need to use a catheter or other device. Hygienic bladder care is extremely important because the most common cause of death in these patients after the spinal shock period is renal failure from repeated infections (Hendrick, 1985; Nash & Smith, 1982).

The next phase of rehabilitation extends the focus of physical therapy toward maintaining and improving the function of muscles over which the patient has some control (Hendrick, 1985). For example, quadriplegics receive special attention toward improving respiration; paraplegics do exercises to strengthen the upper body. When some neural connection to affected parts of the body remains, therapy may include biofeedback to "reeducate" the muscles in those areas. The last phase of physical rehabilitation extends the therapy as much as possible to include activities of daily living. Those patients who have regained sufficient function learn how to perform self-care activities independently and to use devices to compensate for permanent physical losses. Some devices today are highly sophisticated and use computers, allowing paralyzed individuals to turn on lights, answer the telephone, and operate a computer keyboard with voice commands.

Rehabilitation programs for individuals with spinal cord injuries involve an interdisciplinary team of professionals — physicians, nurses, physical and occupational therapists, psychologists, social workers, vocational counselors, and recreational therapists — working in an integrated manner toward the overall goals of rehabilitation (Brucker, 1983). Psychologists have the important role in this process of helping each patient cope with the psychosocial implications of his or her physical losses and using behavioral and cognitive principles to enhance the patient's participation in and adherence to the therapeutic regimen.

Psychosocial Aspects of Spinal Cord Injury

Patients with spinal cord injuries face a long life ahead — an average of over 30 years after the injury (Brucker, 1983). Their main challenge is to make the most of their remaining abilities and lead as full a life as possible. Some patients handle this challenge better than others. What can health care workers, family, and friends do to help?

One way to help is to use behavioral methods to enhance the process of physical rehabilitation. Several studies have demonstrated that reinforcement techniques are highly effective in improving the performance of therapeutically beneficial behaviors by patients (Brucker, 1983). These behaviors include:

- Increasing daily fluid intake to prevent urinary tract infections.
- Changing one's sitting or lying position frequently to reduce the occurrence of bed sores.
- Using orthopedic devices to improve limb functioning.
- Performing exercises to increase strength and endurance.

One successful approach, for instance, involves praising patients for each measurable improvement, such as in arm strength, and periodically updating each patient's graph that charts these improvements.

Family and friends can help by providing social support without being overprotective and "taking over" when the patient has difficulty performing self-help tasks. Having a disabled individual in the household increases the stresses of all family members. They need to make many adjustments in daily living and, while doing so, try not to make the patient feel like a burden. If the patient is a husband or wife, his or her spouse faces very difficult adjustments (Hendrick, 1985). Role changes occur immediately—at least for a while, and perhaps permanently. The healthy spouse, with or without the help of other family members, must suddenly take on full responsibility for providing the family's income, maintaining the household, caring for the children, and caring for the patient. Sexual problems brought on by the patient's injury may become a major source of stress in the marital relationship.

Many people believe that all individuals who become paralyzed below the waist lose all sexual function and interest. This belief is not correct (Brucker, 1983; Hendrick, 1985). Males usually lose their fertility. But although they initially lose the ability to have an erection, they often regain it to some degree. Females generally retain their fertility after paralysis, but they only rarely achieve orgasm and their sensory impairment reduces the pleasure of sexual activity. The most serious barriers to sexual function in people with spinal cord injuries appear to be psychosocial rather than physical. These patients and their sexual partners can overcome many of these barriers through counseling and education, such as in ways to position themselves during sex acts and to heighten the degree of stimulation they achieve.

Disabled people also experience many unpleasant thoughts about themselves, their future, their relations with other people in general, and physical barriers in society (Eisenberg, 1984). They find that many places they once liked to go to are inaccessible by wheelchair, for example. Furthermore, people in general act strangely toward them—staring, or quickly averting their eyes, or behaving awkwardly or uncomfortably in their presence. These experiences tend to reduce the self-esteem of disabled people, many of whom have intense feelings of depression (Frank et al., 1987).

Group therapy approaches can help many individuals with spinal cord injuries understand and cope with their thoughts and feelings. For example, one hospitalized quadriplegic man who became difficult to deal with each night revealed in group therapy that

> he found nighttime very frightening, because at night he felt particularly vulnerable and helpless. As a result, he worried excessively about himself and his future. This led to his making constant requests of the staff, which kept him distracted and reduced his anxiety. In the group, other patients further along in the adjustment process expressed having experienced similar feelings. Through this group experience, the patient learned that his feelings of fright and powerlessness were not unusual. . . . After hearing other members express concerns similar to his own and receiving helpful feedback, this patient reported feeling more able to confront his disability and to solve the problems created by it. (Eisenberg, 1984, p. 115)

Group therapy has also been used in sexual counseling and in helping families gain insights into the thoughts, needs, and problems each member faces.

To summarize, both arthritis and spinal cord injury involve musculoskeletal disorders that can produce disability. Arthritis is a progressive and painful disorder that afflicts older more than younger individuals, and females more than males. Spinal cord injury usually arises suddenly in the years from late childhood to early adulthood, and its victims are usually males. Each of these disorders can lead to severe emotional difficulties in the victims and their families.

LIVING WITH A BRAIN DISORDER: EPILEPSY AND ALZHEIMER'S DISEASE

Disorders of the brain can have profound, direct effects on the person's emotions, cognitive functions, and general behavior. These effects make brain disorders very different from the other health problems we have discussed in this chapter. What are these direct effects, and how do brain disorders affect the lives of their victims? We will examine the effects of two brain disorders—epilepsy and Alzheimer's disease—and see what living with them is like for the patients and their families.

Epilepsy

Because individuals having an epileptic episode lose control of their behavior and "act strange," their condition stigmatizes them among people who do not understand it (Scambler, 1984). This stigma is clear in the experience of a college freshman named Kurt when he witnessed a severe epileptic attack for the first time:

> In the center of my college dining hall, a young man who worked in the kitchen had collapsed in a convulsion. Four students quickly piled on top of him. His arms and legs jerked violently and, in the process of trying to hold him down, the students seemed to be smothering him. The young man's face, twisted and red, made him appear to be in great pain and, somehow, inhuman. Yet I could see myself in his place—I had just found out that I had epilepsy.
>
> I did not want to say anything, but I thought the four students, in their panic, might kill the young man. So I told the largest of them, who by then had a headlock on the kitchen worker, to let go. The student brushed off my concern and seemed irritated that I should bother him at such a time. I paused, then repeated my statement in louder tones. The student was angry. "Look, kid, I'm a pre-med. I know what I'm doing. What makes you think you know so much?" I opened my mouth, but no words came out. Instead, I walked to a corner and leaned against a wall. As the young man's convulsions grew more violent, I whispered an apology to him and began to cry.
>
> Just four weeks before, back home in Dallas, a neurologist had diagnosed my epilepsy. The doctor warned me—and so did members of my family soon afterward—that if I did not keep my epilepsy a secret, people would fear me and I would be subject to discrimination. (Eichenwald, 1987, p. 30)

Many centuries ago, people believed that individuals with epilepsy were possessed by the devil, and many of its victims became social outcasts (Kaplan & Wyler, 1983). Today, epileptic attacks often arouse fear and horror in people who witness them.

What Is Epilepsy?

Epilepsy is a condition marked by recurrent, sudden seizures that result from electrical disturbances of the cerebral cortex (Chelune, 1987; Hobdell, 1985; Kaplan & Wyler, 1983). Although the seizures that epileptics may experience can vary greatly, the two most common types are the:

- *Grand mal*, or "tonic-clonic," attack, which is the most severe form and entails three phases. It begins with a very brief "tonic" phase, in which the person loses consciousness and stops breathing. It then progresses to a longer "clonic" phase that includes muscle spasms and twitching. In the last phase, the person relaxes and drifts into a comatose state until awakening. Sometimes before a grand mal attack epileptics experience an *aura*, which consists of unexplained sounds, smells, or other sensations.
- *Petit mal*, or "absence," attack, which involves diminished consciousness, and in which the person stares blankly for a short while and may show slight facial twitching. When the spell ends, the person simply resumes whatever he or she was doing, sometimes not even being aware that the episode happened. Petit mal attacks occur mainly in childhood and usually disappear by adulthood.

Estimates of the prevalence of epilepsy vary somewhat, but there are probably about a million diagnosed cases of epilepsy in the United States and perhaps as many undiagnosed and untreated cases (Eickenwald, 1987; Kerns & Curley, 1985; USDHHS, 1986d). The great majority of epileptics experience their first seizure by 20 years of age. The prevalence rate for epi-

HIGHLIGHT 13C: On Issues
What to Do for a Seizure

People react negatively to a grand mal attack for many reasons, one of which may be that they do not know what to do to help. Actually, there is little one *can* do other than to remain calm and try to protect the epileptic from injury as he or she falls or flails about during the tonic or clonic phases. If you witness a seizure, the following five actions are recommended (Eichenwald, 1987; Kaplan & Wyler, 1983):

1. Prevent injury from falls or flailing. Break the fall if possible and provide a cushion, such as a coat, between the person's head and the ground.
2. Do *not* put anything in the person's mouth. Many people believe they must put a spoon or other object in the mouth to prevent the epileptic from swallowing his or her tongue, which actually cannot happen. Loosen tight clothing around the neck. If the epileptic is salivating profusely, turn the person on his or her side so that the saliva does not obstruct breathing.
3. Do *not* restrain the person. If you believe the epileptic could be injured while flailing near a hard object, try to move the object.
4. If the person does not come out of the attack in five or ten minutes, call an ambulance.
5. After the person wakes up, describe what happened and see if he or she needs help when ready to leave. Epileptics are often disoriented after an attack.

For the most part, the role of the bystander requires calm and patient caring and common sense.

---

lepsy peaks in the early adulthood years and declines thereafter. Sometimes physicians find a specific neurological defect that is the cause of a patient's disorder, but usually they do not (Hobdell, 1985).

Aside from the reactions their attacks produce in people, what other problems do epileptics face as a result of their illness? People who have had seizures within the past year cannot obtain a driver's license in most states in America and provinces in Canada (Kaplan & Wyler, 1983). Many jobs are closed to epileptics, as is military service. An example of the discrimination epileptics sometimes experience comes from the case of Kurt, the freshman we just discussed. Because of his condition, he was dismissed from the prestigious college he attended. As it turned out, however, he was reinstated after the United States Department of Health and Human Services advised him that dismissal on the basis of a handicapping condition is discriminatory. He graduated in 1983.

Managing Epilepsy

Anticonvulsant drugs provide the main medical treatment for epilepsy (Chelune, 1987; Kaplan & Wyler, 1983; Sterman, 1986). But these medications do not work for all patients and have undesirable side effects, such as drowsiness and, possibly, long-term cognitive impairments. Patients whose seizures result from a clear neurological defect sometimes have the option of surgical treatment, particularly if they have frequent, severe attacks and medication does not work or the side effects are a problem. After surgery, about 30% of the patients no longer have seizures and 50% experience markedly reduced attacks (Kaplan & Wyler, 1983).

Another approach for managing epileptic attacks uses EEG biofeedback techniques (Hatch, Gatchel, & Harrington, 1982; Kaplan & Wyler, 1983; Sterman, 1986). Patients receive intensive training in using EEG feedback to control their electrical brain activity. Although not all patients benefit from this approach, many do. Which patients are likely to benefit? One of the main problems in using biofeedback to reduce seizures is that there is no good way yet to determine in advance who will benefit from this approach and who will not. This is an important issue because the procedure is very costly. Epileptic patients who receive biofeedback therapy generally require many hours of one-to-one training with a psychologist or other highly trained individual, using expensive equipment and computer analyses.

What psychosocial impact does epilepsy have on patients and their families, and how well do they adjust to the disorder? Less is known about the impact of epilepsy than of the other illnesses we have discussed. Some evidence suggests that the mothers of child epileptics may be more controlling than other mothers and that child epileptics suffer reduced self-esteem, being more likely than other children to agree with such statements as "I cause trouble to my family" and "My family is disappointed in me" (Kerns & Curley, 1985). Many of the adjustment problems that epileptics face can be reduced through counseling when the diagnosis is made and through the work of support groups, such as the Epilepsy Foundation of America and Epilepsy Canada (Kaplan & Wyler, 1983).

Alzheimer's Disease

The term *dementia* refers to a progressive loss of cognitive functions, usually in old age (Rosenman & Seligman, 1984). By far, the most common form of dementia is **Alzheimer's disease**, a brain disorder characterized by a deterioration of attention, memory, and personality. Prevalence estimates indicate that 6% of individuals 65 years of age and older have Alzheimer's disease—but the percentage increases with age, and 20% of people at 85 and older have the disorder (Heckler, 1985). Some individuals show early stages of the disease in their late 40s (Thorne, 1987).

The cognitive functions in Alzheimer patients do not disappear all at once. Perhaps the most critical functions to go at first are *attention* and *memory*. Peter Vitaliano and his colleagues (1986) conducted a two-year follow-up study of Alzheimer patients with mild impairment and found that their main deficits initially were in their attentive and memory abilities. The extent of these deficits was strongly associated with the degree of their impairment two years later. As the disease progresses over several years, the effects of the disorder become more pronounced (Heckler, 1985). Personality changes may emerge, with the victims becoming less spontaneous and more apathetic and withdrawn. Self-care deteriorates and behavior problems appear, as when these individuals wander and become lost. At some point, they may become frequently disoriented with regard to time, their location, and their identity.

The Causes and Treatment of Alzheimer's Disease

What causes Alzheimer's disease? Researchers have found that the brains of Alzheimer patients are different from those of other elderly individuals: Alzheimer brains contain much higher concentrations of abnormal protein deposits and of gnarled and tangled nerve fibers, for instance (Thorne, 1987). Although the cause of this disorder is currently unknown, researchers are studying several promising ideas (Crook & Miller, 1985; Heckler, 1985). For one thing, the outcomes of some studies suggest that heredity plays a role and that Alzheimer patients have a higher frequency of Down's syndrome and blood disorders in their families than other individuals do. Other studies have found a link between the development of Alzheimer's disease and high concentrations of aluminum traces in the brain. Particles of aluminum can be found in the air, drinking water, foods, and many products people use, such as deodorant. These particles probably only reach the brain in individuals who have a defect or disease that allows aluminum to penetrate the body's protective barriers.

Although no treatment exists yet to prevent or stop the progression of Alzheimer's disease, family members and others can help maximize the patient's functioning in the early stages of the disease (Crook & Miller, 1985). But as patients lose more and more of their cognitive function, their inability to do simple tasks and remember everyday things causes them great frustration and leads to feelings of helplessness and depression. Their frequent, increasingly problematic behavior produces great stress in the family as the disease progresses. The patients may, for instance, accuse a family member of hiding things they cannot find, develop sleep disturbances and stay awake most of the night, get lost after wandering out of the house, or become bedridden. The demands in caring for Alzheimer patients can become physically and emotionally overwhelming, particularly when the caregivers are elderly spouses in failing health or grown children who have many career and family pressures of their own. Support groups for Alzheimer families can help by providing information, giving sensitive emotional support, and sharing their own experiences and ways of dealing with everyday problems and difficult decisions, such as whether to place the patient in a nursing home (Heckler, 1985; Kapust & Weintraub, 1984; Kerns & Curley, 1985).

We have examined in this chapter what it is like to live with each of a wide variety of chronic health problems. Some of these disorders are more visible to people than others are, some begin earlier in the life span than others, some involve more difficult treatment regimens than others, and some are more painful, or disabling, or life-threatening than others. Each of these differences is important in determining patients' and their families' initial adjustment and long-term adaptation to the health problem.

LONG-TERM ADAPTATION TO CHRONIC HEALTH PROBLEMS

As we have seen, a chronic disorder can last for a very long time—and patients and their families need to adapt to it. The term **adaptation** refers to the changes individuals make toward useful and successful adjustments to the circumstances in their lives. For chronically ill individuals and their families, the adaptive adjustments they make enhance the patient's quality of life by promoting effective physical, psychological, and social functioning (Cohen & Lazarus, 1983; Diamond, 1983). A great variety of factors affect how well people adapt to chronic health problems. We will discuss some of these factors briefly, classifying them into three categories: aspects of the illness and treatment, the individual's psychological resources, and the social environment.

Aspects of the Illness and Treatment

Although all chronic conditions present their own special problems for people to adapt to, some conditions present more severe problems than others. Generally speaking, people have a difficult time adapting to disorders that are visible and cause pain and disability. One study in Canada examined the impact of chronic illness and disability on children's psychosocial adjustment (Cadman, Boyle, Szatmari, & Offord, 1987). The researchers surveyed parents about the health of their children. Of the approximately 3,000 children in the sample, 110 had a chronic illness that disabled them, 418 had a chronic illness without disability, and the remainder were healthy. Assessments were also made of the children's psychosocial adjustment through reports of the parents and either the child or his or her teacher. The results revealed that chronic illness was associated with increased risk for maladjustment, particularly if the illness was accompanied by disability.

Various aspects of treatment regimens can make adaptation very difficult. Some treatments are painful or involve medications that produce serious side effects—either by leading to additional health problems or by interfering with the patient's daily functioning, such as by making the person drowsy. Other regimens, such as hemodialysis at a clinic, may require schedules and time commitments that make it difficult for the patient to find a job. Some regimens require patients and their families to make substantial changes in their lifestyles, which they often resent and fail to carry out. Each of these factors can impair adaptation.

The Individual's Psychological Resources

People who are able to adapt to a chronic health problem have the psychological and behavioral resources to "resolve the chronicity or 'long-termness' of the situation, balance hope against despair, and find purpose and quality in life" (Diamond, 1983, p. 683). Often, these people have hardy or resilient personalities that allow them to see "a good side" in difficult situations. As an example, a 16-year-old boy named Ralfie, whose body had wasted away to 50 pounds from a rare spinal-muscular disease, stated:

> When I take a bath and look at myself naked, I think, "God Jesus." I'm disappointed when it comes to my body, but when it comes to my inside, my personality, my sense of humor, I'm proud of the way I am. I think I'm a nicer person. The girls always tell me, "You're very special. You're different than the other guys." (Hurley, 1987, p. 34)

People with chronic diseases who are like Ralfie can often find purpose and quality in their lives, maintain their self-esteem, and resist feeling helpless and hopeless.

Individuals who show effective long-term adaptation to chronic illness often have psychological resources that enable them to apply appropriate coping strategies to deal with the problems they face. When chronically ill patients can expect to live for many years, they need to make many decisions, such as career selections, that involve examining their options based on a realistic assessment of their condition. People who continue to rely heavily on avoidance coping strategies, such as denial, are less likely to adapt effectively than those who use strategies that allow them to consider their situation more carefully and objectively (Suls & Fletcher, 1985).

The Social Environment

Adaptation to chronic health problems is also enhanced by having an effective system of social support (Wallston, Alagna, DeVellis, & DeVellis, 1983). Patients with chronic medical conditions usually receive this support from family or friends, but it can also come from support groups.

Sometimes, however, family and friends can interfere with the efforts of patients to adapt. John Adams and Erich Lindemann (1974) described and contrasted case studies of two young men, 17 and 18 years of age, who had suffered spinal cord injuries that rendered them quadriplegic. One adapted successfully, and the other did not. The patient who adapted well was able to accept the injury and abandon the part of his self-concept that was associated with his being a fine athlete. He then turned his energies toward academic pursuits and eventually became a history teacher. He also coached a local basketball team from his wheelchair.

The other patient provides a striking contrast. He was never able to accept the injury or the permanence of his condition. He became extremely withdrawn and depressed—at one point he was spending "much time in bed with the curtains drawn and frequently with the sheet over his head." A few years later, he was readmitted to the hospital after taking an overdose of medication. At last contact, he was living at home, still clinging to the hope that he would walk again.

Why did these young men adapt so differently to their similar physical conditions? Adams and Lindemann noted the strikingly different ways these patients' families and friends responded to their condition. In the case of the patient who adapted well to his condition, his parents and friends also accepted his paralysis and provided an environment in which he could redefine his self-concept. For instance, his parents installed ramps in their home and widened doorways to accommodate a wheelchair. The other patient's family and friends were not able to accept his condition or provide the support he needed to help him adapt.

SUMMARY

The initial reactions of individuals when diagnosed with a chronic illness tend to follow three phases, beginning with shock, in which they are bewildered and behave in an automatic fashion. This phase is followed by an encounter reaction, characterized by feeling overwhelmed and helpless. The third phase involves a retreat reaction, in which people use avoidance coping strategies, such as denial, particularly if they believe they can do nothing to change the situation.

Crisis theory provides a model that describes how patients adjust to learning they have a chronic health problem. According to this model, their adjustment depends on the coping processes they use, which, in turn, depend on illness-related factors, background and personal factors, and physical and social environmental factors. Patients begin the coping process with a cognitive appraisal of the meaning or significance of the health problem to their lives. This appraisal leads to their formulating adaptive tasks, such as adjusting to their symptoms or maintaining positive relations with family or friends, and applying various coping skills to deal with these tasks. These coping skills include denying or minimizing the implications of their condition, learning how to provide their own treatment, maintaining regular routines as well as possible, and discussing the future.

Diabetes is a chronic disease in which the blood contains high levels of glucose. Some patients with this disorder have insulin-dependent diabetes mellitus and must inject insulin daily to prevent very serious acute and long-term health complications. But the vast majority of diabetics have non-insulin-dependent diabetes mellitus, and most of these patients can use medication and diet to control their blood sugar. Another chronic condition is kidney disease, which includes nephritis—an inflammation that destroys the kidney nephrons. This damage accumulates over time and may lead to chronic renal failure, culminating in end-stage renal disease. Medical treatments for end-stage renal disease include hemodialysis, continuous ambulatory peritoneal dialysis, and kidney transplantation. Both chronic renal failure and diabetes are life-threatening diseases that require complicated and demanding medical regimens.

Asthma is a respiratory disorder that produces periodic attacks in which the bronchial tubes constrict and develop spasms, resulting in extremely labored breathing. For patients with extrinsic asthma, attacks are associated with allergies these individuals are known to have; for patients with intrinsic asthma, attacks do not seem to depend on the presence of allergens and probably result from infections and other physiological factors. Asthma attacks can be triggered by allergens, chemical irritants, infections, weather changes, exercise, and psychosocial factors. Although asthma is treated mainly with medication to prevent and combat attacks, exercise and stress management may also be useful.

Musculoskeletal disorders that affect the joints and connective tissues are called rheumatic diseases. A class of rheumatic diseases that produces painful inflammation and stiffness of the joints is arthritis; the three most common types are osteoarthritis, rheumatoid arthritis, and gout. Although each type can lead to disability, rheumatoid arthritis is usually the most crippling and painful of the three. Treatment is mainly through drugs, but also includes maintaining proper body weight and physical therapy. Other musculoskeletal disorders involve spinal cord injuries, which are generally caused by accidents and render the person paraplegic or quadriplegic. Intensive rehabilitation programs are geared toward helping these patients regain as much physical function and independence as possible.

Epilepsy is a disorder in which electrical disturbances in the brain produce seizures that vary in intensity. In grand mal attacks, the epileptic loses consciousness and exhibits muscle spasms. Sometimes specific neurological defects are identified as causing the disorder. Drugs provide the main form of treatment, but sometimes surgery and biofeedback are useful. Another brain disorder is Alzheimer's disease, which involves a progressive deterioration of the person's cognitive functions, beginning with attention and memory. Since there is no effective treatment for this disorder, therapy focuses on maximizing the patient's functioning and helping the family cope. Long-term adaptation to chronic health problems occurs when the patient and his or her family make adjustments that enhance the patient's quality of life by promoting effective physical, psychological, and social functioning.

KEY TERMS

crisis theory
insulin-dependent diabetes mellitus
non-insulin-dependent diabetes mellitus
nephritis
end-stage renal disease
arthritis
spinal cord injury
epilepsy
Alzheimer's disease
adaptation

14

LIVING WITH HIGH-MORTALITY ILLNESSES AND LOSS

PROLOGUE

Deep down, in the "wishing" part of his mind, Jack thought he was immortal. Oh, he acknowledged that "I'll die someday," but that day would *forever* be a long way off, he seemed to believe. He lived his life accordingly, even though he had almost every known major risk factor for heart disease. He was 30 pounds overweight, ate high-cholesterol food with abandon, smoked two packs a day, got little exercise, experienced a lot of anger that he had trouble expressing, and his father died of a heart attack at the age of 48. Jack felt especially invulnerable two years ago on his 49th birthday, almost believing that, if he lived past his father's age of death, the grim reaper would somehow never find him.

Jack's beliefs were jolted a couple of months ago—he had a heart attack that put him in the hospital for three weeks, including a week in the coronary care unit. He was stunned at first. "This can't be happening to *me*," he thought. Soon it sank in that it *was* happening to him, and he felt anger and a sense of grief and helplessness. He was not prepared for this. He tried to deny and minimize the problem, but his physical weakness made it clear to him that he is, after all, vulnerable. Although this realization was depressing to him for a while, he had always taken pride in his "fighting spirit." A month later Jack announced, "I'm gonna change my life," and he did! He gave up smoking, changed his diet, and started an exercise program. Just as important, he changed his outlook on life. He realized how much the people in his life mean to him and how important he is to them, and he is actively working to get closer to them.

Although many people react to having a high-mortality chronic illness in positive and constructive ways, not all do. In this chapter we will examine how patients and their families react to and cope with a health problem that has a high likelihood of taking their lives. We will also see the psychosocial adjustments these people make when the illness is terminal. As we study these difficult circumstances, we will consider many important issues and try to provide answers to questions you may have. What is it like to live with heart disease, cancer, stroke, and AIDS? How do these illnesses affect the patient's functioning and what treatment regimens do they entail? What special problems exist when the patient is a child? What can be done to help terminally ill patients and their loved ones cope?

COPING WITH AND ADAPTING TO HIGH-MORTALITY ILLNESS

Many healthy individuals who want to estimate how much longer they are likely to live look up the statistical life expectancy for people their age and gender and probably adjust that figure on the basis of the longevity of other people in their family. But estimates of a person's life expectancy are very imprecise, and this is true even for patients with health conditions that seriously threaten their lives. Public opinion aside, having a high-mortality disease—even cancer or AIDS—does not usually mean the patient will die in a matter of several weeks or months. Many cancer patients, for instance, survive for 10 or 20 years before the disease takes their lives, and some are totally cured. Still, no one can tell for sure what the course of the disease will be, and these patients and their families must adapt to this uncertainty.

Adapting While the Prospects Seem Good

Since none of us knows for sure what lies ahead for us, we all live with some degree of uncertainty. But for patients with high-mortality illnesses, the uncertainty for them and their families is more real and urgent. Even though the patients may have good prospects for the future, either in the short run or more permanently, the diagnosis changes them.

Mortality is the main issue of concern to patients in the first few months of convalescence with a seriously life-threatening illness. During this time, patients often show an optimistic attitude, hope they will be cured, but begin to view their plans for the future more tentatively (Moos, 1982; Weisman, 1979). They also tend to switch from using mainly avoidance coping strategies to using active problem-focused approaches. Jack, the man we described who had a heart attack, showed these adjustments when he changed his lifestyle and his outlook regarding the people in his life. As patients' recovery progresses, they are able to return more and more to a regular routine, often gaining great satisfaction by once again being able to do simple household or self-help activities. Although convalescing patients tend to be optimistic about their health, they are very watchful for symptoms and changes in their condition.

Having activities to occupy the day is important to convalescing patients, particularly those with chronic high-mortality health problems. These activities give them some respite from thinking about their condition. Patients often try to "isolate" the disease from the rest of their lives by focusing on other things, such as preparing to do projects around the house or to return to work. Sometimes these plans and preparations can lead to problems, however, if patients overestimate what they can do. For example, a patient named Clay who suffered a serious stroke described how he started making plans the day he left the hospital:

> That was a glorious day. I started planning all the things I could do with the incredible amount of free time I was going to have. Chores I put off, museums and galleries to visit, friends I had wanted to meet for lunch. It was not until several days later that I realized I simply couldn't do them. I didn't have the mental or physical strength, and I sank into depression. (Dahlberg, 1977, p. 124)

Patients need to be encouraged to develop reasonable plans and to carry them out, especially with regard to going back to work or getting training to enter a new job, if necessary. Patients' efforts to isolate the disease from the rest of their lives is likely to be even more effective when they finally resume most of their normal life activities.

Sometimes the helplessness that chronically ill patients feel and the nurturance that their families give lead to a cycle of continued dependence that persists when the patients are able to begin doing things for themselves. This was starting to happen with Clay after his stroke, and his wife realized it. As she described the situation:

> As time went on and he was gradually improving, I occasionally was concerned about his dependency on me, which seemed unnecessary. . . . It can easily become a habit after the need no longer exists. Gradually, I started asking him to do certain things, leaving things undone which were previously his domain, acting indecisively, and leaving decisions up to him. At first he was surprised, and then did what was needed. He gradually took over more and more, giving up his "stroke personality." (Dahlberg, 1977, p. 128)

Gentle nudges by family members, like those from Clay's wife, can help patients become more self-sufficient, thereby making them feel useful and bolstering their self-esteem.

In the process of adapting to a high-mortality illness over a long period of time, people make many important cognitive adjustments. By interviewing women who had had surgery for breast cancer a few years earlier, researchers found that these adjustments center on three themes (Taylor, 1983; Taylor, Lichtman, & Wood, 1984). First, patients try to *find meaning* in their illness experience, either by determining why it happened or by rethinking their attitudes and priorities. One woman said, for instance,

> I have much more enjoyment each day, each moment. I am not so worried about what is or isn't or what I wish I had. All those things you get entangled with don't seem to be part of my life right now. (1983, p. 1163)

Second, patients try to *gain a sense of control* over the illness, such as by engaging in activities that reduce their risk of the illness getting worse or increase their knowledge about their care. A spouse said of his wife:

> She got books, she got pamphlets, she studied, she talked to cancer patients, she found out everything that was happening to her, and she fought it. She went to war with it. She calls it taking in her covered wagons and surrounding it. (1983, p. 1164)

Third, they try to *restore their self-esteem*, often by comparing themselves with less fortunate people. In one example, a woman said:

> If I hadn't been married, I think this thing would have really gotten to me. I can't imagine dating or whatever knowing you have this thing and not knowing how to tell the man about it. (1983, p. 1166)

These cognitive adjustments seem to promote adaptation and probably help patients achieve or, in some cases, exceed their previous level of psychosocial functioning.

Adapting in a Recurrence or Relapse

One thing that makes high-mortality diseases so dangerous is that the deadly medical conditions they produce have high rates of recurrence or relapse. Among stroke victims, for instance, 30–40% develop another stroke within five years (Flinn, Dalsing, & White, 1986). Patients correctly recognize their heightened vulnerability and worry about it, and so do their families.

A recurrence or relapse of the condition presents another crisis for patients and their families, which may be harder to cope with than the first (Moos, 1982; Weisman, 1979). They rightly perceive this event as a bad sign —it typically indicates that the prognosis is now worse than before, since additional damage has occurred. Patients focus again on the illness, being concerned about controlling its progression and forestalling a deterioration in their general functioning and quality of life. They undergo a new round of hospitalization, medical procedures, and, perhaps, surgery. In coping with setbacks in their condition, patients and their families go through the kinds of coping processes they experienced in the initial phases of their reaction to the original diagnosis. But they are likely to be less hopeful than they were before.

In summary, patients and their families must cope with the uncertainties that a life-threatening illness presents for the future and try to come to terms with the patient's mortality. One way they cope is by diverting their attention to other things. In the process of adapting over time, they make cognitive adjustments by finding meaning in their illness experience, gaining a sense of control over their condition, and restoring their self-esteem. When patients experience a setback in their condition, they face a new crisis that may be more difficult to cope with than the original crisis. Living with any high-mortality disease can be quite stressful, but each disease creates a pattern of stresses that is unique.

FOUR HIGH-MORTALITY HEALTH PROBLEMS

Although the death rate for heart disease has declined by more than a third since 1950, it is still the number one killer by far in the United States; cancer is second, and stroke is third (USDHHS, 1986c, 1986d). People know these are the leading causes of death — and for many patients and their families, being diagnosed with one of these diseases *means* death. AIDS emerged in the 1980s as a major killer, and public attention has focused on how it is spread, the large numbers of people infected with the virus, and the sharply increasing numbers of AIDS victims who die each year. As we examine how people adapt to living with high-mortality health problems, we will focus on heart disease, cancer, stroke, and AIDS.

Heart Disease: Adapting after Myocardial Infarction

Coronary heart disease refers to illnesses that result from the narrowing or blocking of the coronary arteries, which enmesh the heart and supply it with oxygen-rich blood. As we saw in Chapter 2, blood vessels become narrowed and blocked as plaques build up in the condition called *atherosclerosis*. If the blockage of oxygenated blood to the heart is only brief or incomplete, the person may develop a painful cramp called **angina pectoris** in the chest and arm. Little or no permanent damage occurs if the blockage ends quickly. But if the blockage is severe or prolonged, a portion of the muscle tissue of the heart (myocardium) may be destroyed—a condition called **myocardial infarction**, or "heart attack." According to the American Heart Association, each year about 1½ million Americans suffer a heart attack; more than a third of the victims die, usually before they reach a hospital (Clark, 1988; Krantz & Deckel, 1983; Langosch, 1984).

Are some segments of the population more likely than others to develop heart disease? Age and gender seem to be the main differentiating factors. The prevalence rates for heart disease increase as people get older, particularly after about 45 years of age. In the years prior to old age, far more men than women develop and die from heart disease (Mattson & Herd, 1988; USDHHS, 1982). Even though women are less likely than men to have a heart attack, they are more likely to die from it if they have one. Although myocardial infarctions can occur at any time in a 24-hour day, they are most likely to occur in the morning hours from 7 to 11 A.M. and least likely to occur during sleep at night (Muller et al., 1987). This increased risk in the morning hours seems to result from biochemical changes and rising blood pressure that are associated with getting up and becoming active.

Initial Medical Treatment for Heart Attack

When heart attack patients enter the hospital, they receive emergency medical treatment to prevent or limit damage to the myocardium. Part of this treatment generally involves using *clot-dissolving medication* to free blocked arteries. Most patients are then placed in a *coronary care unit*, where medical staff can closely monitor their physiological functioning. The risk of another attack is high during the first few days. Medical assessments indicate whether certain other procedures are also needed. One of these procedures is called *balloon angioplasty*, in which a tiny balloon is inserted in the blocked artery and inflated to open the blood vessel. Another procedure—called *bypass surgery*—entails replacing the diseased section of artery with a healthy vessel taken from another part of the body.

As you might expect, most cardiac patients experience extremely high levels of anxiety in the first day or two of coronary care. Many of these people cope with this crisis through denial, and those who do tend to be less anxious in the first few days than those who do not (Froese, Hackett, Cassem, & Silverberg, 1974). Regardless of whether cardiac patients use denial, their anxiety levels soon start to decline. After about the fourth day or so, the anxiety levels of those who do and do not use denial are about the same, but still higher than normal. These fairly high anxiety levels tend to persist for the remainder of the hospital stay (Cay, Philip, & Dugard, 1972; Froese, Hackett, Cassem, & Silverberg, 1974). The cardiac patients who have the greatest difficulty coping are not necessarily the ones who are the most seriously ill—instead, they tend to be those who were experiencing distress and social problems before the heart attack.

Many patients anticipate psychosocial problems ahead, particularly in relation to their work. A program for rehabilitation generally begins after the first week, when heart attack patients are transferred to a general ward.

Rehabilitation of Cardiac Patients

The program of rehabilitation after myocardial infarction begins by providing the patients with information on such topics as the symptoms and restrictions they can expect, medications they should take to reduce symptoms and blood pressure, and risk factors for having another heart attack (Cromwell & Levenkron, 1984). Many patients will experience recurrent angina pectoris episodes for many months or even years after discharge (Langosch, 1984;

Lavey & Winkle, 1979). These episodes can be very frightening to them and their families. Sometimes the chest pain requires medical attention, but often patients can simply take medication to control it. To reduce the likelihood of another infarction, most coronary patients receive advice on lifestyle changes, such as quitting smoking, losing weight, and reducing their dietary cholesterol and alcohol consumption. They also receive training and supervision in a program of exercise and, often, in stress management (Langosch, 1984). Many heart attack victims who make healthful changes in their lifestyles and attitudes live longer than comparable people who have not had an infarction.

Some cardiac patients find it easy to follow the medical regimen—but others do not, and may resent the restrictions their condition imposes. One patient said of his doctor's advice:

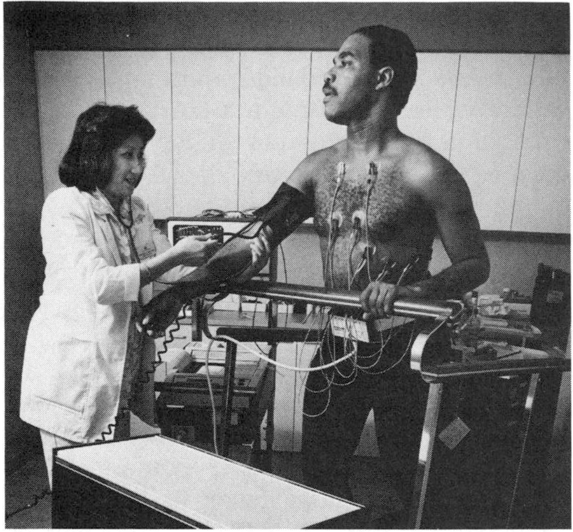

The treadmill test is used in assessing the ability of heart patients to engage in strenuous exercise.

> If he tells you you must stay in bed, well, how come this sudden change? I don't want to stay in bed, and if he tells you that you cannot walk upstairs, he is telling you that you are weak, that you are no longer strong. He has taken something away from you—ah, your pride. You suddenly want to do what you are not supposed to do, what you have been doing all your life and that you have every right to do. (Tagliacozzo & Mauksch, 1972, p. 178)

Coronary patients who perceive little social support in their lives are less likely to adhere to the regimen than those who have high levels of social support from family and friends (Friis & Armstrong, 1986; Moos, 1985).

Exercise is a very important component of the medical regimen for cardiac patients. A program of physical activity needs to be introduced gradually and tailored to each patient's physical condition. It begins in the hospital with supervised short-distance walking. In the following weeks, the physical activities become more and more vigorous and long-lasting and are likely to include long-distance walking, calisthenics, and often jogging, bicycling, or swimming. Adhering to the exercise program produces substantial physical and psychosocial benefits to coronary patients (Roviaro, Holmes, & Holmsten, 1984; Thompson & Thompson, 1987). Patients who follow the exercise program show much greater improvements in a variety of physiological measures than do those who do not adhere—for example, they show lower resting heart rates, lower diastolic blood pressure while at rest, lower systolic blood pressure during exercise, and greater treadmill endurance.

Cardiac patients who adhere to the exercise program also show better psychosocial adjustment, as reflected in their self-concept, perceived health, sexual activity, and involvement in and enjoyment of active leisure activities. Unfortunately, about 50% of patients who begin an exercise program discontinue it within the first six months (Dishman, 1982; Dishman, Sallis, & Orenstein, 1985). Those patients who drop out of exercise programs are likely to be those who smoke cigarettes, work in blue-collar occupations, and begin the program with poorer cardiovascular function, higher body weight, more sedentary lifestyles, and greater anxiety and depression (Blumenthal et al., 1982; Dishman, 1981; Oldridge & Spencer, 1985). Compliance is likely to be higher if the program provides a special facility for the patients to do their exercising, instead of having them exercise on their own.

Cardiac patients may also have a difficult time making other lifestyle changes, particularly in their diets and in stopping smoking. Dietary changes are often hard to make because they impact on family life and, in some cases, may not be economically feasible (Croog, 1983). With respect to stopping smoking, studies have found that only perhaps 40% of individuals who suffer a myocardial infarction quit or substantially reduce their smoking (Burling et al., 1984; Ockene et al., 1985). Those who continue to smoke are in many ways like those who do not exercise. That is, compared to patients who quit, those who do not quit tend to be more anxious and from lower occupational and educational groups. Patients who continue to smoke also tend to smoke heavily and have fewer negative attitudes about smoking.

We saw in Chapters 4 and 5 that heart disease has been linked to stress and the Type A behavior pattern. We also saw that cardiac patients who use stress management techniques to reduce stress and modify Type A behavior subsequently show lower rates of mortality and morbidity from heart disease. Because of these benefits, training in stress management is becoming an increasingly recommended component in cardiac rehabilitation programs (Langosch, 1984). Stress management approaches seem to be particularly effective when they include discussions to help the patient recognize situations that are stressful for him or her and training in a variety of stress-reducing techniques, such as progressive muscle relaxation and cognitive restructuring (Friedman et al., 1986; Langosch, 1984; Powell et al., 1984; Razin, 1984).

The Long-Term Impact of a Heart Attack

The medical prognosis for a patient after a myocardial infarction depends on several factors, especially the extent of arterial damage and the condition of the heart's ventricles (Langosch, 1984). If the ventricles are functioning well, the survival rates after ten years are: 97% when the damage involves one coronary blood vessel, 79% when it involves two vessels, and 66% for three vessels. But if ventricular functioning is impaired, these survival rates drop to 85%, 58%, and 40%, respectively.

One of the physical problems many cardiac patients must deal with is recurrent chest pain, which, for some patients, can be quite severe and even disabling (Lavey & Winkle, 1979; Wielgosz et al., 1984). Although these pains are troubling, the patients do not seem to suffer tissue damage with the pain nor do they face a greater risk of subsequent myocardial infarction than other cardiac patients. Often, medical tests reveal no physical basis for the pain—that is, there is no substantial coronary blockage or ventricle impairment—but the pain persists. One study found that of those patients whose pain was severe enough to require hospital tests, about half reported they were unemployed because of their symptoms (Lavey & Winkle, 1979).

Being able to work has a special meaning to individuals who suffer from chronic health problems. Cardiac patients, for instance, often view returning to work as an important sign that they are recovering (Croog, 1983). Although physicians generally recommend that patients with uncomplicated coronary conditions return to work after about 60 days, new research has found that these patients can resume working about two weeks earlier without increasing their risk of another cardiac episode (Dennis et al., 1988). Physicians often advise that cardiac patients cut back on the amount of physical effort and stress they experience on the job. Following this advice may mean finding a new job, which may be difficult to do, particularly for patients over age 50 or so. Patients who are near retirement age may simply leave the work force if they can. Nevertheless, most cardiac patients do go back to work, often with jobs that require less productivity or shorter hours than they previously had worked. Studies have found that roughly 85% of cardiac patients who were previously employed return to some type and amount of work within the year following the heart attack (Doehrman, 1977). Compared to patients who do not return to work, those who do return tend to be younger, in better physical condition, better educated, and employed in white-collar jobs. Delaying or failing to go back to work is often associated with having long-lasting emotional distress and depression (Krantz & Deckel, 1983).

Sometimes cardiac patients' work restrictions cause them to experience interpersonal problems with coworkers and heightened work stress. Sydney Croog has described the case of a 55-year-old clerical worker in a small company whose doctor tells him that

> he could carry out all usual activities, except, "Avoid lifting. Don't pick up heavy boxes at the office." In the first weeks of work return, he finds a sympathetic attitude among co-workers and pleasant relationships. As the occasion arises, he calls upon one or another to lift heavy boxes for him. Co-workers assist him, most willingly, in the first days after his return to work. Eventually, the tone in the office changes, and resentment stirs among those who are called upon to interrupt their own work and lift the occasional heavy boxes.
>
> Yet he has received doctor's orders on lifting, and he is unwilling to risk his health or his life by picking up boxes. Occasional mild chest pain and shortness of breath remind him that he is not the man he used to be. One day he asks a fellow worker to lift a box for him. The response comes, "Why don't you go ahead and drop dead, you lazy son-of-a-bitch!" The solutions are limited for this 55-year-old man. Transferring to another department is not possible, as the company is a small one. Leaving for another job is not possible for many reasons. . . . So picking up the heavy boxes seems like the easiest solution — but for how long can he continue? What will be the eventual effects on his heart? (Croog, 1983, pp. 300–301)

Going back to work usually contributes to the long-term well-being of patients. But as this example illustrates, the work situation can also create problems that may impair cardiac patients' physical and psychosocial condition.

Cardiac illness and family relationships are closely interrelated. Studies have found that prior to the heart attack many coronary patients were experiencing family difficulties — such as quarreling over financial and sexual problems — and that these difficulties often become worse after the infarction (Croog & Fitzgerald, 1978; Swan, Carmelli, & Rosenman, 1986). The illness adds to the original difficulties, such as by making the financial and sexual problems worse. What also seems to happen in these families is that a "cycle of guilt and blame" tends to develop (Croog, 1983). For example, a husband who suffers a myocardial infarction may blame his wife or children for his condition, and they may agree and feel guilty. But even when harmonious relations exist before the attack, the illness adds to the stress of all members of the family. One marital difficulty that arises after a heart attack relates to sexual activity, which often never returns to the level that existed prior to the attack (Krantz & Deckel, 1983; Michela, 1987). Either or both spouses may fear that having sex could precipitate another attack. The marital satisfaction of both partners generally benefits by having little or no sex initially and then increasing its frequency gradually, with the advice of the patients' doctor (Michela, 1987).

Families have an enormous impact on the process of cardiac rehabilitation, and the danger exists that the family will promote *cardiac invalidism,* in which the patient becomes increasingly dependent and helpless (Krantz & Deckel, 1983). Research has shown that the beliefs a spouse has about the patient's physical capabilities can aid or retard rehabilitation. A study of this process examined the beliefs that wives held about their husbands' physical abilities several weeks after these men suffered a myocardial infarction (Taylor et al., cited in Bandura, 1986). Each wife evaluated her husband's cardiac and physical ability before and after one of three conditions: she either *observed* him perform vigorously on a treadmill, *participated* on the treadmill herself after watching him perform, or was *uninvolved* in the treadmill situation. Analysis of the wives' evaluations revealed that the beliefs of the wives who were uninvolved in the treadmill situation or had simply observed their husbands' performance did not change — these wives continued to give low assessments of their husbands' physical abilities, even after receiving medical counseling to the contrary. In contrast, the wives who participated on the treadmill after watching their husbands perform raised their evaluations of their husbands' physical ability. These results suggest that family members need to see and personally experience the physical feats the cardiac patient can perform. By doing so and receiving medical counseling, they can provide more effective encouragement for the patient to become increasingly active.

What are the long-term emotional consequences of heart disease on patients? Most cardiac patients experience higher than normal levels of anxiety and depression during the first weeks or months after the heart attack, but their distress declines during the next year or two (Doehrman, 1977). In a sense, the emotions of the first few months may be like grieving after any major loss — in the case of cardiac patients, the loss is to their self-esteem, independence, and health. If very high levels of anxiety and depression continue beyond a few months, however, these emotions become signs of poor adaptation and are likely to decrease compliance with the cardiac regimen and lead to a deterioration in the patient's physical condition.

Several types of interventions can enhance patients' long-term adaptation to having heart disease. One intervention uses a technological approach. Researchers equipped patients with an electrocardiogram (ECG, or "EKG") monitor that could transmit an analysis of their heart function to a hospital nurse by telephone (Follick et al., 1988). The patients called the nurse and transmitted the ECG analysis on a periodic schedule and whenever they felt certain symptoms. If the analysis indicated medical action was needed, the nurse dispatched a rescue squad and instructed the patient to take a drug. Compared with patients who received the standard cardiac care, those with the ECG system were far less depressed during the next several months.

Other types of interventions involve psychological methods. One intervention program provided patients with information about their condition and treatment, training in relaxation, and counseling for their fears and anxieties while they were still in the hospital (Oldenberg, Perkins, & Andrews, 1985). Patients who received this intervention showed far better psychosocial adjustment during the next year than those who received standard care. Another approach, which involves group therapy after discharge from the hospital, can be helpful if it focuses on discussing specific problems that cardiac patients face in their daily lives and providing specific skills in stress management (Razin, 1984). Finally, many communities have self-help and support groups, such as Heart Clubs, that coronary patients can attend (Croog, 1983).

To summarize, recovery after a heart attack presents difficult physical and psychosocial challenges for patients and their families. Cardiac rehabilitation programs require patients to adhere to regimens of exercise, diet control, medication taking, and stress management. The long-term impact of the illness often involves emotional, vocational, and marital problems that may require therapeutic interventions to enhance adaptation.

Adapting to Cancer

Cancer is probably the disease most people fear the most — the word "cancer" itself scares many Americans, and they often overestimate the deaths that cancer causes (Burish, Meyerowitz, Carey, & Morrow, 1987). Practitioners recognize how people feel about the disease and are reluctant to discuss it and its effects with their patients. In a study some years ago of cancer patients who had begun radiation treatment, most reported that their physician had not told them they had cancer (Peck, 1972). Some even claimed their doctor said the condition was benign — such as a wart — but 80% of the patients said they knew it was cancer anyway. Doctors today are far more likely than in the past to share the "bad news" about serious medical conditions with their patients, but some probably still withhold distressing information about the patient's diagnosis and prognosis (Blaney, 1985; Laszlo, 1987; Shuchman & Wilkes, 1989).

The Prevalence and Types of Cancer

A basic characteristic of life and growth is that cells of the body reproduce in an orderly and controlled fashion. Although we know little about the process that maintains the proper number of different types of cells in the body, we do know what the normal pattern of tissue growth looks like (Guyton, 1985). Irregularities in this process can cause unrestricted cell growth, usually forming a tumor called a *neoplasm* (Burg & Ingall, 1985). Some neoplasms are harmless, or benign, but others are malignant.

Cancer is a disease of the cells and is characterized by unrestricted cell proliferation that usually forms a malignant neoplasm. We have seen in earlier chapters that cancer is caused by the interplay of genetic and environmental factors, and that stress can promote the development and progression of the disease. Environmental factors include smoking tobacco, diet, ultraviolet radiation, and household and worksite chemical hazards. Some research has also found a link between certain viral infections and the development of cervical cancer (Levy, 1985; Laszlo, 1987). The viruses are probably transmitted to the women during intercourse. Because not all women who are exposed to the viruses develop cancer, it seems likely that the effects of the infections depend on or combine with genetic and environmental factors to produce the disease.

Although there are more than 200 varieties of cancer, the great majority of cancers are of four types (Burg & Ingall, 1985; Levy, 1985; Nelson, 1984). These four types are:

- *Carcinomas*, which are malignant neoplasms of the skin cells and cells lining many body organs, such as the digestive, respiratory, and reproductive tracts. About 85% of human cancers are carcinomas.
- *Lymphomas*, or cancers of the lymphatic system.
- *Sarcomas*, which are malignant neoplasms of the muscle, bone, or connective tissue.
- *Leukemias*, or cancers of the blood-forming organs, such as the bone marrow, that lead to an extreme proliferation of white blood cells.

An important characteristic of cancer cells is that they do not adhere to each other as strongly as normal cells do (Guyton, 1985; Laszlo, 1987). As a result, they may separate and spread to other parts of the body through the blood or lymph systems. This migration is called *metastasis*, and the new neoplasms are known as *metastases*.

Cancer is the second most frequent cause of death in the United States, and the mortality rates for the disease have been increasing by 1–2% per year since 1950 (American Cancer Society, 1989; Laszlo, 1987; USDHHS, 1986c). These increases may be due in part to the decline in deaths from heart disease during the same period. The mortality and morbidity figures for cancer are sobering: Each year cancer takes more than 500,000 American lives and over a million new cases are diagnosed. About half of the individuals who develop cancer can expect to live for at least five years—most of these patients will be *cured*, having virtually the same life expectancy as someone who never had the disease. Although cancer can strike virtually any area of the body, as Figure 14.1 shows, almost all of the increase in cancer death rates since 1950 is attributed to neoplasms in one body site: the lung.

The Sites and Effects of Cancer

What are the physical effects of cancer, and how does it kill? Cancer progresses by spreading to different sites and growing at each site. As the disease progresses, it also produces pain, often because the tumor creates pressure or blocks the flow of body fluids (Melzack & Wall, 1982). Substantial pain afflicts many patients even in the early stages of the disease and more than two-thirds of those with advanced cancer (Foley, 1985; Greenwald, Bonica, & Bergner, 1987; Laszlo, 1987). The disease

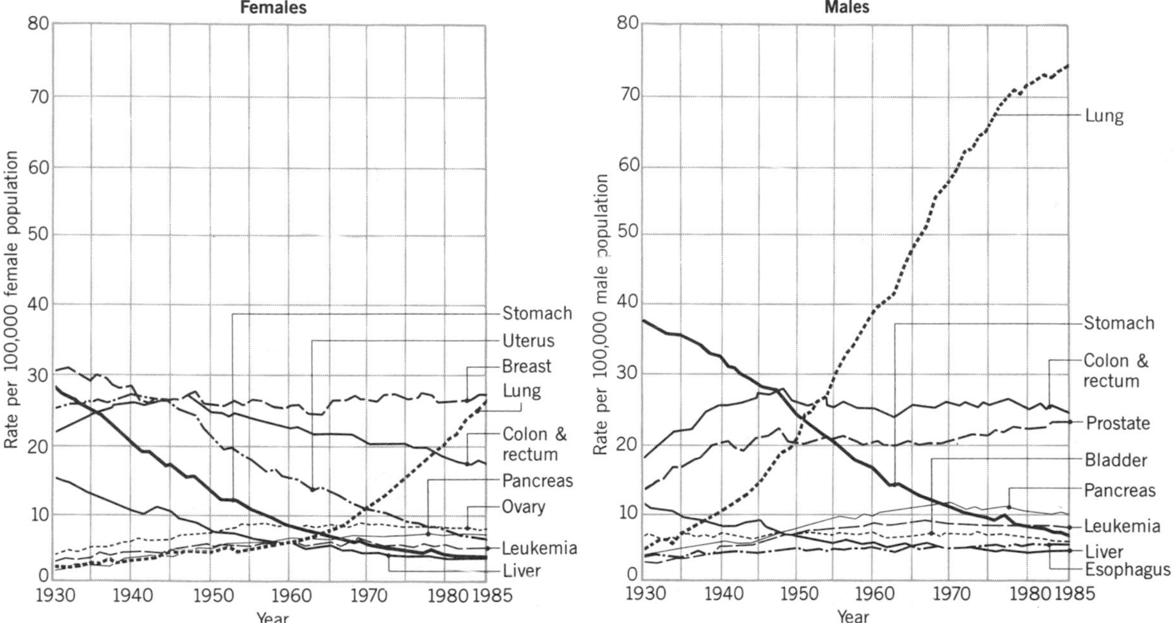

FIGURE 14.1 Age-adjusted death rates for selected cancer sites per 100,000 males and females in the United States between 1930 and 1985. (From Silverberg & Lubera, 1989, pp. 10–11.) Notice two things: First, mortality rates for most forms of cancer have either declined or remained fairly constant; lung cancer is the dramatic exception. Second, the increases in lung cancer deaths for males and females correspond to gender differences in the prevalence of cigarette smoking.

leads to death in direct and indirect ways. In the direct route, the cancer spreads to a vital organ—such as the liver or lungs, competes for and takes most of the nutrients the organ tissues need to survive, and thereby causes the organ to fail. Cancer kills indirectly in two ways: the disease itself weakens the victims and both the disease and the treatment can impair the patient's appetite and ability to fight infection (Laszlo, 1987).

The prognosis for cancer depends on how early it is detected and its site (American Cancer Society, 1989; Battista & Grover, 1988; Laszlo, 1987; Stevens, 1984). We will consider several of the more common sites, listed in order of their yearly incidence in the United States. These sites are:

- *Skin cancer.* With over 500,000 cases diagnosed each year, the skin is the organ with the highest cancer incidence by far in the United States. The vast majority of these cancers are *basal cell* and *squamous cell carcinomas*, and cure is almost assured with early detection. But about 5% of skin cancers are *melanomas*, which form in the pigment-carrying skin cells and are more serious because they metastasize quickly. Still, over 80% of melanoma patients survive at least five years.

- *Lung cancer.* Over 150,000 new cases of lung cancer are diagnosed annually, and the incidence is far greater among males than females, probably because of men's higher smoking rates in the past. The five-year survival rate is only 13% overall, but it is 2½ times as high if the disease is discovered while still localized. In lung cancer, neoplasms tend to metastasize while still small and, for this reason, they generally have already spread by the time they are discovered.

- *Colo-rectal cancer.* Neoplasms of the colon or rectum account for about 150,000 cancer diagnoses each year. These cancers can be detected early—and if they are, 80% of the patients survive at least five years.

• *Breast cancer.* About 10% of women will develop breast cancer at some time in their lives, and its incidence is about 140,000 cases a year. Early detection permits 90% of breast cancer patients to survive at least five years.

• *Uterine and cervical cancer.* Neoplasms of the uterus or cervix of the female reproductive system have an incidence of about 100,000 cases a year. Fortunately, about half of these cases are discovered very early with Pap tests, when the neoplasms are classified as *carcinomas in situ*, which are usually fully curable. Of the remaining cases, the five-year survival rate may be as high as 90%, depending on how early the diagnosis is made.

• *Prostate cancer.* Each year, about 100,000 diagnoses are made of neoplasms of the prostate gland in the male reproductive system. Although prostate cancer can be detected in its early stages, survival rates are unclear because the disease usually becomes evident after the men are over 70 years of age.

For almost all of these sites, the risk of developing cancer increases with age, especially from the middle-age years onward. The main exception is cervical cancer, which often develops in young adult women. For all types of cancer combined, incidence rates for the disease quadruple from 40 to 80 years of age (Mor et al., 1985).

Diagnosing and Treating Cancer

The process for diagnosing cancer can involve three medical procedures (Laszlo, 1987). First, *blood tests* are useful for suggesting the presence of cancer by revealing telltale signs, such as unusual levels of certain hormones or enzymes. Second, *radiological imaging*, through X-ray and other techniques, allows physicians to see the structure of internal organs and whether a tumor exists. Third, the physician does a *biopsy* by taking out a piece of suspicious tissue and having it analyzed. Even when the tissue is deep within the abdomen, it can generally be removed with minor surgical procedures and a local anesthetic.

The ideal goal of cancer treatment is to cure

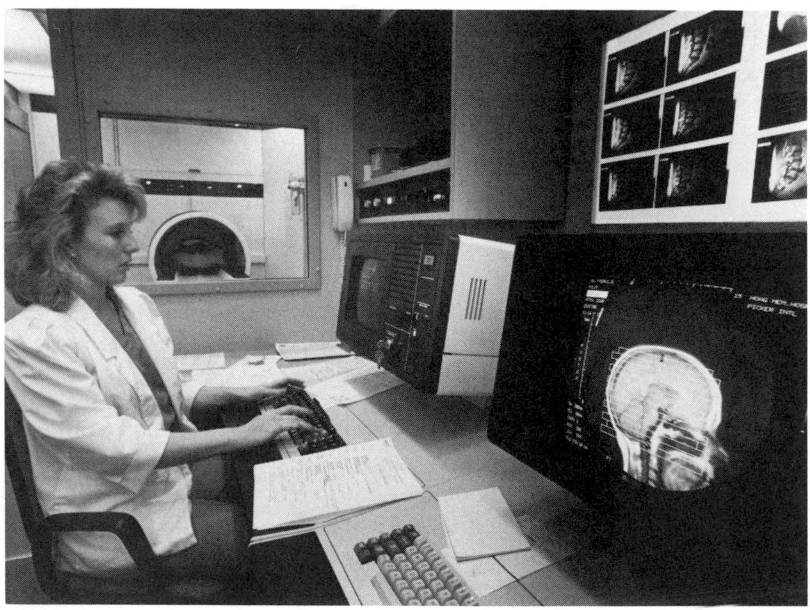

While the patient lies on a table in a large apparatus in the background, a radiological image of his brain appears on the monitor.

the disease — to free the patient from it forever. This ideal is possible when all the neoplasms are found and eliminated (Guyton, 1985; Laszlo, 1987). If not all of the cancer was eliminated, the patient's symptoms may disappear for a time — or "go into remission" — only to return at a later date. Sometimes physicians can be reasonably certain that all of the cancer was removed, but often they cannot be sure. This is why they use the patient's survival for at least five years as a gauge of a treatment's success. There are basically three types of treatment for cancer — surgery, radiation, and chemotherapy — that may be used singly or in combination. When choosing the treatment components, patients and practitioners consider many factors, such as the size and site of the neoplasm, whether it has metastasized, and how the treatment will affect the patient's quality of life. One factor that seems to affect the treatment choice, sometimes inappropriately, is the patients' age. A study using the medical records of nearly 1,900 deceased adult cancer patients found that, among patients with similar stages and sites of neoplasms, those over age 60 or so were much less likely than those under 60 to have received radiation or chemotherapy in their treatment (Mor et al., 1985).

From a medical standpoint, *surgery* is frequently the preferred treatment for eliminating a neoplasm, such as in breast or colo-rectal cancer (Laszlo, 1987; Pack & Lynds, 1984). If the cancer is localized, surgery can be completely effective by itself; if the cancer has spread, surgery may be useful in removing large clusters of cancerous cells, leaving the remainder for radiation or chemotherapy treatment. Sometimes the surgeon removes large portions of tissue near the neoplasm because of the possibility that the cancer has spread to them, too. In patients with colo-rectal cancer, for example, the surgeon may remove a long section of the colon even though the neoplasm seems to be restricted to a small area. But the practice of removing large amounts of nearby tissue is changing, particularly in the treatment of breast cancer: Research has shown that a *mastectomy*— the removal of the entire breast —is not necessary in many, if not most, cases (Laszlo, 1987). Instead, women may choose to have a *lumpectomy*, in which just the tumor is removed, followed by radiation treatment.

Radiation in high doses alters body cells in such a way that they are either destroyed or cannot reproduce (Holum, 1987). In treating cancer, radiation is used in two ways (Burish & Lyles, 1983; Laszlo, 1987; McNaull, 1984). One approach, *external beam therapy*, involves directing a beam of intense radiation at the malignant tissue for a period of seconds or minutes. This is the most commonly used method and the one most people picture when the term "radiation therapy" is used. External beam therapy is usually given several times in a week, and may be continued for up to several weeks. The second approach is called *internal radiation therapy* and involves placing a radioactive substance inside the body, near or into the tumor by surgery or injection. Although radiation therapy is painless, it can have problematic side effects, depending on the area of the body radiated and the dose. Because radiation affects both healthy and malignant cells, the affected area may suffer irritation, burns, or hair loss, for example. Nausea, vomiting, loss of appetite, sterility, and reduced bone marrow function may occur, particularly if the radiated area is large or is in the abdomen. In the day or two before undergoing radiation treatment, cancer patients often worry about these side effects and report heightened anxiety, similar to that of patients awaiting surgery (Andersen, Karlsson, Anderson, & Tewfik, 1984).

In *chemotherapy*, patients receive powerful drugs, usually orally or by injection, that circulate through the body to kill cells that divide very rapidly (Burish & Lyles, 1983; Nevidjon, 1984; Laszlo, 1987). The intended targets, of course, are cancerous cells, most of which reproduce rapidly. Some forms of cancer respond more readily than others to the drugs currently available; cancer of the testicles and some types of leukemia are very responsive, but cancers of the brain and pancreas are not. One problem with chemotherapy is that the drugs also kill certain types of normal cells that divide rapidly—for example, cells of the bone marrow, mouth and intestinal lining, and hair follicles, especially those of the scalp. Programs of chemotherapy often continue for a long time and can have several very adverse side effects, including reduced immunity to infection, sores in the mouth, hair loss, nausea and vomiting, and damage to internal organs (Navidjon, 1984; USDHHS, 1983a).

For many patients, the most unpleasant side effects of chemotherapy are the periods of nausea and vomiting they experience during and after each treatment. These periods can be so aversive and prolonged that some patients have even discontinued treatment, knowing that doing so could shorten their lives (Burish & Redd, 1983). Furthermore, after two or three treatments, some patients who are about to receive the drug begin vomiting before it is given—they develop *anticipatory nausea*—and may even become nauseated and throw up when they arrive at the hospital or while thinking about the upcoming treatment at home the night before.

Anticipatory nausea appears to develop in about a third of chemotherapy patients who have received the treatment for several months (Burish & Redd, 1983; Nerenz, Leventhal, Easterling, & Love, 1986). These patients probably learn this reaction through classical conditioning, whereby the drug itself is the unconditioned stimulus that reflexively produces the unconditioned response of nausea. Through association, other related events, such as seeing the hospital or thinking about the procedure, become conditioned stimuli and can elicit nausea in the absence of the drug. Researchers have tried to help reduce patients' anticipatory nausea by training them in behavioral techniques such as progressive muscle relaxation and biofeedback. Although many patients benefit from these techniques, not all do—and for some patients, the training seems to make the problem worse (Burish & Lyles, 1983; Carey & Burish, 1985; Lyles, Burish, Krozely, & Oldham, 1982).

Not only can cancer treatment be unpleasant, it can also be complex and demanding. Most cancer patients must take medications at home, and many must return to the clinic frequently for laboratory tests, keep diaries of their food intake, or adhere to dietary and alcohol restrictions. Because of these conditions, we might expect cancer patients to show poor compliance with their treatment regimens. Few studies have investigated adherence to cancer regimens so far, and their findings have been mixed (Levy, 1985; Nehemkis & Gerber, 1986; Richardson et al., 1987; Tebbi et al., 1986). Although adults in general seem to adhere very closely to cancer regimens, adolescents and minority group individuals from the lower classes do not. Compliance to medical regimens depends on and influences a variety of psychosocial factors in patients' lives.

The Psychosocial Impact of Cancer

Like all chronic illnesses, cancer involves a series of threats and difficulties that change, often getting worse over time. But cancer creates unique stresses for patients and their families. These patients have a disease they recognize as a "real killer," and one that can lead to intense pain, disability, and disfigurement. Even among patients who go into remission and adapt well during the first months or years, the threat of a recurrence looms—and if the disease flares up, some individuals become psychologically paralyzed by their fear (Mages & Mendelsohn, 1979). In addition, some patients experience medical procedures that, for them, can be more aversive than the disease itself. How well patients adapt to having cancer can have medical consequences and affect the progression of the disease. Individuals who experience high levels of stress and do not cope well show poor immune system activity (Kiecolt-Glaser & Glaser, 1986; Levy, 1985; Levy et al., 1985).

Given all of the stress associated with having cancer, most patients show a remarkable amount of resilience and adapt reasonably well. Even among hospitalized cancer patients, studies have generally found that less than half show significant emotional difficulties, and

HIGHLIGHT 14A: On Research
Chemotherapy and Learned Food Aversions

When patients begin chemotherapy, they commonly experience a loss of appetite that can lead to excessive weight loss. This can create problems in their medical treatment and in their home life. The families of patients who are not eating well become concerned about this situation—and eating turns into a constant battle, with patients feeling "hounded" to eat (Nevidjon, 1984). Part of the reason for the loss of appetite these patients experience may be that they develop a distaste for foods they once liked. Cancer patients who receive chemotherapy or radiation therapy often report that this happens to them (Mattes, Arnold, & Boraas, 1987a, 1987b). Developing a dislike for foods they previously liked a lot, such as chocolate desserts or a morning cup of coffee, is very demoralizing to cancer patients, who are likely to feel that their quality of life has suffered enough.

Why do these patients come to dislike foods they had liked? Since chemotherapy produces nausea and vomiting in many patients, these symptoms may become associated with one or more foods the patients ingest before or after the symptoms occur. A **learned food aversion** is a phenomenon in which a food becomes distasteful because the individual associates it with symptoms of illness or physical discomfort. Richard Mattes, Cathy Arnold, and Marcia Boraas (1987a, 1987b) studied learned food aversions in 76 adult cancer patients who were beginning a program of chemotherapy. The subjects had no other physical conditions, such as diabetes, that might relate to their food preferences. The study began by interviewing the patients during the hour preceding their first treatment. The patients provided information about themselves and their medical histories, described all foods they had consumed during the prior 24 hours, and listed any food aversions they already had. They also rated each of the foods recently eaten, using a 9-point scale that ranged from "I would eat this every opportunity I had" to "I would eat this only if I were forced to." The subjects were then given a form to fill out at home and return by mail. The form had the subjects list and rate all foods eaten during the 24 hours after the treatment.

At the next scheduled visit and at other visits during the next six months of treatment, the patients provided information about their food preferences and any side effects they experienced from the treatment. The results revealed several interesting findings. First, 55% of the patients developed aversions to foods consumed within the 24 hours preceding and following treatments. Second, many of these aversions formed after only one treatment, and subsequent treatments produced fewer and fewer new dislikes. Third, the amount of time (up to 24 hours) between eating the food and receiving the treatment did not affect whether an aversion would develop. Fourth, patients whose side effects included vomiting developed more learned food aversions than those whose side effects did not, but receiving drugs to prevent vomiting did not help prevent aversions from forming. Fifth, the aversions generally lasted less than a month and included many of the foods the patients previously ate frequently and liked a great deal.

Can something be done to prevent cancer patients from learning to dislike foods they normally eat? One promising approach involves having patients consume a strongly flavored, unfamiliar food between their last meal and the chemotherapy treatment. Why? The purpose is to create a "scapegoat"—that is, to direct the learning process to this new food and allow it to become disliked, instead of foods in the patient's normal diet. Research has shown that this approach works for many adult and child cancer patients (Broberg & Bernstein, 1987; Mattes, Arnold, & Boraas, 1987b). Patients who form an aversion to the scapegoat food are much less likely to develop a dislike to foods in their normal diets.

most of these involve relatively transient problems—chiefly anxiety and depressed mood—that are usually responsive to psychological therapy (Burish, Meyerowitz, Carey, & Morrow, 1987). This incidence of emotional problems may seem high, but there are a few points to keep in mind. First, these studies were done with hospitalized patients, and hospitalization itself elevates anxiety and depression. Second, among patients hospitalized for all reasons, perhaps one-fourth have emotional disorders, and often these problems developed before the illness. Patients' emotional problems result from many factors other than their disease, such as experiencing other major stressful events and not having social support in their lives. Lastly, psychologists often consider it "'normal' for cancer patients to have some elevations in depression and anxiety. Given the life circumstances of these patients, it is often a difficult and quite arbitrary decision as to when to consider these responses appropriate and when to consider them dysfunctional" (Burish, Meyerowitz, Carey, & Morrow, 1987, p. 144).

Although adaptation to cancer can be very difficult for patients during the first several months and when their condition worsens, their ability to adjust to their illness appears to improve with time during remission or after a cure (Burish, Meyerowitz, Carey, & Morrow, 1987). By two years or so, their psychosocial functioning stabilizes at levels similar to those they had prior to the diagnosis. One study administered questionnaires regarding psychosocial adjustment to over 130 breast cancer patients and 260 women from the general population (Craig, Comstock, & Geiser, 1974). All the subjects with breast cancer had been diagnosed and treated more than nine months prior to the study. The patients and controls showed very similar levels of depression, happiness, optimism for the future, and perceived health.

Adaptation among cancer patients depends on many aspects of their illness and psychosocial situation. With respect to the illness, the emotional adjustment that patients achieve depends on their physical condition. For example, the most severely depressed patients tend to be those who are physically disabled by the disease or in pain (Burish, Meyerowitz, Carey, & Morrow, 1987). The site of the cancer is also important, and its impact often depends on the patient's age. Norman Mages and Gerald Mendelsohn have contrasted the situations of two men with testicular cancer, each of whom had been made sterile by their treatment but had good medical prognoses:

> The first, a young man in his late twenties, had begun to live with an older woman two years before his cancer and had shortly thereafter received a position in a moderately high-level technical occupation. Both the relationship and the position were secure and held much promise for the future, but were, of course, of fairly recent origin. The second, a man of forty-eight, was a very accomplished and well-regarded professional, married for about twenty-five years and with grown children. It is surely not surprising that the younger man was far more deeply distressed by his cancer than the older. His sterility was particularly painful for it meant that he could never have children of his own and, perhaps unrealistically, raised doubts about a future marriage and his sexual competence. The cancer, moreover, seemed especially disruptive and unjust to someone who had, later than most and only recently, assumed an adult role and established his independence. The older man, in contrast, was relatively little affected by his disease. Though he too had to face the issue of a potentially shortened life span, he had long since established a stable and satisfying adult existence and was securely embedded in a supportive social network. (1979, p. 277)

A similar pattern of concerns also affects women with cancer of the breast, cervix, and uterus, but their difficulties may be compounded if surgery seriously disfigures their bodies or alters their physical ability to function sexually (Andersen & Hacker, 1983; Burish & Lyles, 1983). As you might expect, sexual problems very frequently occur among men and women patients with cancers in sex-related organs, but many patients with cancers in other sites may also experience sexual problems as a result of their medical regimen, such as when chemotherapy causes fatigue (Burish, Meyerowitz, Carey, & Morrow, 1987; Nevidjon, 1984).

Many cancer patients experience psychosocial problems that stem from changes in their relationships with family members and friends. In some cases, patients may begin to withdraw from social contact because they feel socially awkward or embarrassed by their condition, especially if their bodies have become noticeably disfigured (Mages & Mendelsohn, 1979). Perhaps more commonly, friends and family begin to avoid the patient. Although this sometimes occurs as a result of fear and ignorance, such as when people believe that cancer is contagious, other reasons are often involved (Wortman & Dunkel-Schetter, 1979). For example, friends and family may experience conflicts between wanting to be cheerful and optimistic with the patient, while at the same time feeling very sad and personally vulnerable in his or her presence. They may also worry that they will "break down," or "betray their feelings," or "say the wrong thing" in front of the patient. When these people and the patient do get together, everyone may behave awkwardly.

Because of the social problems that cancer patients face, they and their families may benefit from group therapy and support groups (Jerse, Whitman, Gustafson, 1984; Wortman & Dunkel-Schetter, 1979). In one study, cancer patients in a support group received counseling sessions, training in relaxation, and information about diet, exercise, and their illness (Cain et al., 1986). Subsequent comparisons with control subjects revealed that those in the support group were less depressed and anxious, had fewer sexual problems, and participated more in leisure activities. The American Cancer Society sponsors about 3,000 local units that provide a variety of patient services, rehabilitation programs, and support groups, some of which focus on specific types of cancer or on helping families with children who have cancer (Laszlo, 1987).

Childhood Cancer

Cancer strikes about 6,000 children each year in the United States, and *leukemia* is the most common form of the disease in individuals under 15 years of age (Eiser, 1985; Laszlo, 1987; Herman & Smith, 1984; Stevens, 1984). Improved treatment methods have reduced the death rate from cancer in childhood by about half since 1950. Chemotherapy is the main form of treatment, but radiation may be used to prevent the disease from developing in the brain. These treatments produce much the same side effects in children as in adults, including chronic nausea and vomiting. Losing their hair can be a very traumatic and embarrassing experience to most children and teenagers even though it does grow back eventually (Spinetta, 1982). But if a child receives treatment and a relapse does not occur in the first five years after diagnosis, the chances are very high that the leukemia will never recur (Laszlo, 1987).

The treatment program for leukemia begins on an inpatient basis with an "induction" phase, in which the patients receive combinations of drugs in high doses to produce a full remission (Eiser, 1985; Herman & Smith, 1984). Because of the high risk of relapse without continued treatment during the next three years, the program continues with a "maintenance" phase on an outpatient basis. During this time, patients receive chemotherapy, weekly or biweekly blood tests, and frequent bone marrow examinations to check for the presence of cancer cells. One of these examinations—called a *bone marrow aspiration*—is extremely painful. It involves inserting a large needle into the child's hip bone, and then suctioning out a sample of marrow. The whole procedure is painful, but the most excruciating pain occurs as the marrow is withdrawn. Although painkilling drugs help somewhat, the patients still feel intense pain. Researchers have found that these children's pain and distress can be reduced with psychological methods, such as showing them a film of a child coping realistically with the procedure and teaching them to use techniques to distract their attention from the pain (Jay, Elliot, Katz, & Siegel, 1987; Jay et al., 1985).

What are the psychosocial effects of having cancer on childhood patients and their families? In an overall sense, the effects are like those with adult patients. The initial trauma is extremely difficult, but their adjustment tends to improve over time (Eiser, 1985; Koocher, O'Malley, Gogan, & Foster, 1980). Two factors that are important in children's psychosocial adaptation to cancer are the age at the onset of the disease and the time since the diagnosis.

HIGHLIGHT 14B: On Issues
Can Patients "Will Away" Their Cancer?

The mind is a powerful instrument, and what people think can affect their health. How powerful is this instrument? Could cancer patients use it to recruit the soldiers of the immune system to seek and destroy malignant cells? The notion that the mind could do this forms the basis of a controversial approach for helping cancer patients control their disease.

O. Carl Simonton developed a therapy program in which patients receive group counseling and training in muscle relaxation while also receiving medical treatment (Simonton & Simonton, 1975; see also Scarf, 1980). The main feature of the program is an "imaging" exercise in which the patients imagine that they can see their white blood cells attack and destroy cancer cells. One patient, for instance, imagined her white cells were sharks that would chase her cancer cells (small fish) "and then pounce upon them, rending them to bits with their long, jagged teeth and destroying them" (Scarf, 1980, p. 40).

Does this therapy program work? There is currently little or no evidence to support the notion that the imaging exercise helps in curing cancer (Blaney, 1985; Laszlo, 1987). But other aspects of the program seem more promising. As adjuncts to medical treatment, counseling and relaxation can benefit patients' psychosocial adjustment, which may enhance their immune function, improve their quality of life, help them become more involved in their treatment, and encourage them to maintain a "fighting spirit."

The earlier the diagnosis and treatment occurred in the children's lives and the longer the patients survive in remission, the better their long-term adjustment tends to be. Another psychosocial issue in childhood cancer is that these patients often lag behind other children in academic skills, particularly during the first few years of school (Allen & Zigler, 1986; Eiser, 1985). These deficits probably result from their missing many school days and the psychosocial and physical effects of their medical treatment.

Adapting after a Stroke

Sitting at the breakfast table, Neil began to feel faint and weak, and the right side of his body seemed numb and tingly. As he realized he was having a stroke, he tried to say so, but the words would not come out. Soon he lost consciousness. A **stroke** is a condition in which damage occurs in some area of the brain when the blood supply to that area is disrupted. Of the major causes of death in the United States, stroke ranks third—half a million strokes occur each year and claim about 200,000 lives (Glick & Cerullo, 1986; Newman, 1984b). The incidence of stroke is very low prior to the middle-age years and increases sharply thereafter.

The disruption in blood supply that causes strokes occurs in two ways. In some cases, damage results from an *infarction* when the blood supply in a cerebral artery is sharply reduced or cut off, either when a blood clot (a *thrombus*) forms or a piece of plaque (an *embolus*) becomes lodged in that area of the artery. In other cases, damage results from a *hemorrhage*, in which a blood vessel ruptures and bleeds into the brain. A stroke caused by a hemorrhage generally occurs rapidly and causes the person to lose consciousness; most of the damage it produces happens in a few minutes. In contrast, a stroke caused by an infarction tends to occur more slowly, and the person is less likely to lose consciousness. Strokes from hemorrhages occur much less frequently but are much more likely to cause extensive damage and death than those from infarctions (Glick & Cerullo, 1986; Newman, 1984b). The medical procedures—drugs and surgery—for treating a stroke can vary greatly, depending on its cause and the size and location of the damage (Caplan, 1986).

The Physical Effects of Stroke

Many strokes are very severe, but some can be quite mild. People who survive a moderate or severe stroke generally suffer some degree of motor, sensory, learning, or speech impairment as a result of the brain damage. If enough cells are affected, the functions controlled by the damaged area of the brain can be severely disrupted. The extent and type of impairment depends on the amount and location of the damage. The following discussion assumes that the stroke was at least moderately severe.

Although the initial deficits that stroke victims experience can be permanent, patients often show considerable improvement over time. Medical treatment and physical, occupational, and speech therapy can help patients regain some of the functions they lost. Some evidence suggests that younger stroke patients may show somewhat better recovery than older ones, and the functional impairments caused by hemorrhages are more easily overcome than those caused by infarction (Hier, 1986). Hemorrhages often impair functioning partly by creating pressure on neurons. If that pressure is relieved by the blood being reabsorbed by the body, the patient may gradually recover some of the lost functioning.

The most common deficits that stroke patients experience involve motor action (Gordon & Diller, 1983; Newman, 1984b). For these patients, some degree of paralysis occurs immediately, and the person usually cannot move the arm and leg on one side of the body. Which side becomes paralyzed depends on which half of the brain is damaged: The left hemisphere of the brain controls movement of the right side of the body and the right hemisphere controls movement on the left side. As a result, the paralysis occurs on the side of the body opposite to the hemisphere that sustained damage in the stroke. Because of the paralysis, these patients cannot walk, dress themselves, or perform many usual self-help activities. After about six weeks of physical rehabilitation, about half of these patients can perform activities of daily living independently and the great majority can get around on their own, but often with the aid of a cane or other device (Gordon & Diller, 1983).

Other common deficits that many stroke patients face involve cognitive functions—language, learning, and perception. The specific type of impairment they have depends on which side of the brain was damaged. In most people, the left hemisphere contains the areas that handle language processes, including speech and writing (Geshwind, 1979). Thus, damage on the left side often causes language and learning deficits. A common language disorder in stroke patients is *aphasia*, which is marked by difficulty in understanding or using words. There are two kinds of aphasia: *receptive aphasia* refers to a difficulty in understanding verbal information, and *expressive aphasia* involves a problem in producing language, even though the person can make the component sounds. For example, the patient may not be able to differentiate between two verbalized words, such as "coal" and "cold." Or the patient may have difficulty remembering a sequence of things he or she is told to do—such as, "Touch your right ear with your left hand and touch your left eyebrow with your right hand."

What deficits are associated with damage on the right side of the brain? The right hemisphere usually processes visual imagery, emotions, and the perception of patterns, such as melodies (Geshwind, 1979). As a result, visual disorders are common with right-brain damage (Gordon & Diller, 1983). In one of these disorders, stroke patients fail to process information on the left side of the normal visual field—for example, they may fail to notice food on the left side of a tray, items on the left side of a menu, or a minus sign in an arithmetic task (see Figure 14.2). This problem also impairs their ability to perceive distances correctly and causes them to bump into objects or door frames on the left side of the visual field, making them "accident-prone." Sometimes patients with this disorder feel they are "going crazy" when they hear someone speaking but cannot see the person because he or she is standing in the left side of the visual field. The discrepancy between what they are hearing and what they are seeing makes them wonder if they are hallucinating.

7	6	28	31	96	74
+4	−2	+11	−10	−29	+18
11	8	39	41	125	92

FIGURE 14.2 An illustration of arithmetic errors (circled items) that a stroke patient with a visual disorder might make at the start of rehabilitation. In this case, the patient fails to scan to the left and assumes all of the problems involve addition. Rehabilitation can help patients overcome this deficit.

Like people in general, stroke patients with this visual disorder take for granted that what they see reflects the full size of their normal visual field. Because they think they see the whole field, they need to have their visual deficit clearly demonstrated. According to rehabilitation therapists Wayne Gordon and Leonard Diller, one effective approach involves placing folding money

> on the table in front of the patient. The large bills are purposely put on the impaired side. The patient is asked to pick up all of the money on the table. Naturally, a large sum of money remains on the table after the patient says that he or she has completed the task. Having the patient turn his or her head to see all the money that was left on the table is one way to begin to teach the patient that . . . this difficulty can be overcome by turning the head. (1983, p. 119)

Rehabilitation then proceeds by training the patients to use head turning automatically. A good way to start this training is to use an apparatus that has the patients track an object as it moves from the right to the left side of the visual field (Gordon & Diller, 1983). Once patients master this task, they can begin training with paper and pencil tasks, such as learning to look for plus and minus signs in arithmetic problems.

The specific location of damage in the brain also may determine emotional disorders that stroke patients show. Some studies have found associations between (1) specific left-hemisphere damage and patients' degree of depression and (2) specific right-hemisphere damage and patients' ability to interpret and express affect (Bleiberg, 1986; Gordon & Diller, 1983; Newman, 1984b). An example of an emotional disorder some stroke patients have is called *pseudobulbar lability of affect*, which can occur in varying degrees:

> The essential features of the disorder are that the patient laughs or cries either on the basis of no provocation or minor provocation and that the patient is surprised and sometimes distressed by the discrepancy between how he feels and the emotions that he is displaying. In milder versions of the disorder, the emotional display is in the same direction as the patient's mood but simply is excessive given the intensity of the patient's mood. For example, the patient is thinking mildly sad thoughts that normally would not elicit tears and winds up in a state of wrenching sobbing. . . . In severer versions of the disorder, the emotional display may be the opposite of the patient's inner mood. Thus, a patient's inner feelings of sadness may precipitate bouts of raucous laughter and a patient perceiving something as humorous and about to laugh may suddenly burst into tears. (Bleiberg, 1986, p. 222)

In other emotional disorders, stroke patients may be unable to interpret other people's emotions correctly and may react oddly to them.

The Psychosocial Impact of Stroke

Recovery from a severe stroke is a long and arduous process. The initial physical and cognitive deficits are extremely frightening, but many patients are heartened by early gains in their functioning. Because of these gains, patients may become overly optimistic about the speed and degree of recovery to expect. One stroke patient noted that his physician

> warned me that the first days of recovery are the fastest, and that improvement continues much more slowly later. I was happy as a clam, and I didn't give a damn. Giving a damn came a few weeks later. (Dahlberg, 1977, p. 122)

Although patients with all chronic illnesses often rely on avoidance strategies to cope during the early phases of convalescence, denial seems to be more common among patients who have had a stroke than those with heart disease or cancer (Krantz & Deckel, 1983). Stroke patients who continue to deny their current or possible future limitations often retard their progress in rehabilitation.

When a stroke produces physical or cognitive deficits, the emotional adjustments can be very difficult. Stroke patients are very prone to depression (Bleiberg, 1986; Krantz & Deckel, 1983; Newman, 1984b). Sometimes the brain damage itself can cause depression, as we mentioned earlier. But in all stroke cases that involve long-term impairment, psychosocial factors affect the success of patients' adaptation. As patients see the gains in recovery slowing down and begin to realize the extent of their impairment, feelings of hopelessness and helplessness may develop, leading to depression. Although stroke usually afflicts individuals who are beyond retirement age, many of its victims are employed when the illness occurs and suffer impairments that prevent them from returning to work. The results of follow-up studies suggest that less than half of stroke patients eventually resume working, but the rate tends to be higher among younger patients (Krantz & Deckel, 1983; Newman, 1984b). Some stroke victims who do not return to work are old enough to take advantage of early retirement opportunities, but others must leave the work force under less favorable circumstances, which can be financially and emotionally trying.

The impairments produced by stroke have important social effects on patients and their families, particularly when the patients are severely paralyzed or have aphasia (Newman, 1984b). Some families adjust to the patient's condition reasonably well, as in the following case:

> Mrs. M. had always taken charge of bookkeeping and running the family. When her husband had a stroke, she adapted very well to his aphasia, inventing ways to communicate with him. When he developed cancer five years later, she helped him keep track of his medications by putting them in little cups at the beginning of the day, with coded instructions on how many to take and when to take them. In this way, Mr. M., who worried that he hadn't taken his medication, could keep track of it when she wasn't there. (Gervasio, 1986, p. 115)

But other families do not adjust well to the changing role relationships, and marital harmony often declines. In addition, the social contacts and leisure activities with friends also drop off for both the stroke patient and his or her spouse (Newman, 1984b). Although the decrease in social and leisure activities increases with the extent of the patient's impairment, it is often substantial even when the patient has made a good recovery. Group therapy is the most commonly used approach for helping stroke patients and their families adapt (Krantz & Deckel, 1983).

In summary, stroke is a high-mortality illness that involves neurological damage as a result of a disruption of blood flow to the brain. Survivors of stroke often suffer substantial physical and cognitive impairments, but medical treatment and physical, occupational, and speech therapy can help patients regain many of their lost abilities. The more severe the remaining deficits after rehabilitation, the more likely patients will experience psychosocial problems.

Adapting to AIDS

Acquired immune deficiency syndrome—AIDS—is a very different high-mortality chronic illness from the others we have discussed. For one thing, AIDS is a new disease and was virtually unknown before 1980. Also, it is an infectious disease that is caused by a "human immunodeficiency virus" (HIV) and is spread through the shared contact of blood and semen. Moreover, the number of people who have died from AIDS in each of the last several years is only a small fraction of the number who have died of stroke, the third most deadly illness. But AIDS is an epidemic, its annual mortality statistics are skyrocketing, many millions of people around the world are already infected with the virus, and the great majority of these people will probably eventually die as a result of AIDS (Osborn, 1988).

The process of adapting to AIDS often begins long before the person is officially diagnosed with the disease. This is because the diagnosis of AIDS is made only once the victim has developed one of several "opportunistic" diseases that are associated with the loss of immune function. These illnesses include *Pneumocystis carinii pneumonia* and *Kaposi's sarcoma*, a form of cancer previously rare in the United States. Years before reaching this diagnostic criterion, however, the victim may have learned from a blood test that he or she was infected with HIV (Tross & Hirsch, 1988). Furthermore, between the time of infection and the AIDS diagnosis, the victim's immune system begins to falter, producing a variety of recurrent symptoms, such as spiking fever, night sweats, diarrhea, fatigue, and swollen lymph glands. At this stage, the victim is classified as having **AIDS-Related Complex** (ARC), and may develop AIDS within a few years.

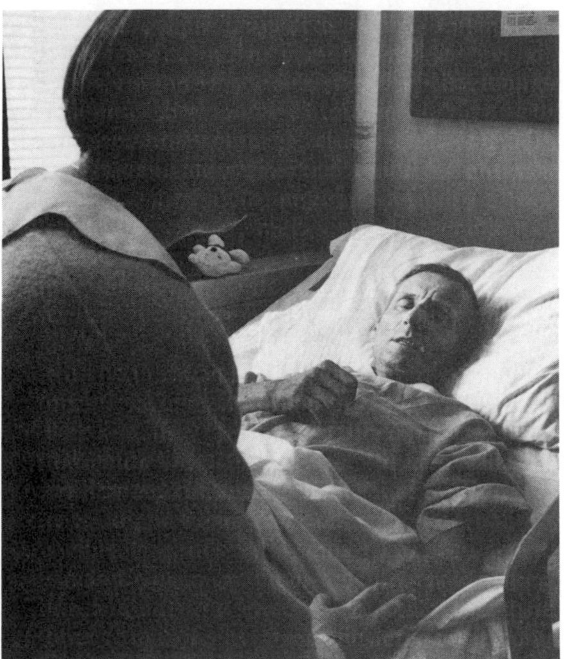

A social worker talks with an AIDS patient who has become blinded as a result of the disease.

The Medical Effects and Treatment of AIDS

Before developing ARC, individuals infected with HIV have no symptoms of the disease. The only way they can tell they are infected is by having a blood test. By the time they are diagnosed with AIDS, their immune system is severely and chronically weakened. From that point on, the disease progresses with repeated bouts of opportunistic diseases.

Most of these opportunistic diseases can be treated successfully with medications, such as antibiotics, but sometimes victims become hypersensitive, or allergic, to the medications, and no therapy is available that their bodies will tolerate. For patients who survive repeated bouts of diseases, the prognosis is still poor (Osborn, 1988; Tross & Hirsch, 1988). Their bodies become severely weakened and they gradually waste away. Many AIDS patients develop a brain disorder when the HIV invades the central nervous system. This invasion causes the brain to deteriorate—a condition called *encephalopathy.* The early behavioral signs of this condition include depression, forgetfulness, and poor concentration. As the encephalopathy worsens, patients gradually lose their cognitive functions and become disoriented and confused. They may also become mute and have seizures. Eventually, they lapse into a coma.

There is no cure for AIDS. Medical treatment relies on an extremely expensive drug called *azidothymidine* (AZT), which slows HIV reproduction but this does not cure the disease (Osborn, 1988; Young, 1987). AZT prolongs survival substantially, prevents encephalopathy, and enables the patient to gain weight, but it does not reduce the incidence of opportunistic diseases. The main side effect identified so far is severe anemia, making frequent blood transfusions necessary.

AIDS is fatal to virtually all of its victims, and most patients die within one or two years of its diagnosis. A minority of patients survive more than three years, and some are still living and active more than five years after the diagnosis

(Gavzer, 1988). Why do some AIDS patients survive so much longer than most others? No one really knows why for sure. A major part of the answer must involve biological differences between those who do and do not continue to survive, and some psychosocial relationships have been discovered. George Solomon and Lydia Temoshok (1987) conducted a long-term follow-up study of patients who filled out questionnaires to assess a variety of psychosocial factors soon after being diagnosed with AIDS or ARC. Longer survival was associated with higher scores on measures of personal control, problem-focused coping, and social support. Because AIDS is such a new disease, most of the little knowledge that exists about patients' treatment and survival is very tentative. Research has begun to move quickly now, after a slow start.

The Psychosocial Impact of AIDS

Every epidemic arouses fear—but when so little is known about the disease except that it is so deadly, people tend to react in extreme ways to protect themselves and the people they love. In 1983, a young man in San Francisco who was diagnosed with AIDS told his housemates of his condition. Soon after, he arrived home one evening and found that the door locks had been changed. He knocked, but no one answered. A few days later, he found that everything in his room had been thrown out—clothes, bed linens, toothbrush, books, curtains, carpeting, and even the wallpaper (Gavzer, 1988). The news media in the mid-1980s had frequent stories of AIDS patients being fired from their jobs, children with AIDS not being allowed to attend school, families with an AIDS patient being driven from their homes, and health care workers refusing to treat AIDS patients.

These stories seem to have disappeared. Perhaps panic has mellowed to caution, as it should. But assaults and other hate crimes against lesbians and gay males seem to have increased in recent years (Herek, 1989) and some degree of irrationality is likely to continue, even among people who are well informed. A beautifully written and sensitive example of this comes from Buffie Kaufman, a medical editor who joined a volunteer group to help AIDS patients, but had not yet met a patient:

> Then I met Tom. It was during a volunteer training session . . . [and] I knew that a person with AIDS was coming to talk with us. Of course they'll send someone in the early stages of the disease, I thought, someone who doesn't look sick. I could handle that.
>
> I was shocked—Tom was literally skin and bones. He walked slowly, unsteadily, and sat down very gingerly on a cushioned chair that was brought in especially for him. He saw the large bowl of jelly beans that I had brought for the group and said, "Great! I have no appetite anymore, but I can always eat candy." "Be my guest," I replied, not looking directly at him. Would I eat anymore jelly beans after he had his hand in the bowl? . . .
>
> Tom has had *Pneumocystis carinii* pneumonia twice, and almost died the second time. Currently he has a fungus infection, tuberculosis, and Kaposi's sarcoma. The tuberculosis isn't contagious; yet, when he coughed, I hoped he wouldn't do it again. . . . There were several moments when I thought I was going to have to leave the room. I felt an overwhelming anxiety, which peaked and diminished often throughout the presentation. I had to control it; I didn't want to offend him by walking out. I concentrated on appearing more comfortable than I was. Part of me wanted to hug this man; part of me wanted to leave. Can you be compassionate from a distance?
>
> After the presentation was over and Tom had left, all the group members sat in a circle on the floor to discuss what had just transpired. I needed to talk. I felt anxious, sad, angry, and emotionally depleted. I told the others that "this was the hardest thing I had ever done." I was referring to just staying in the room. AIDS was now a reality to me. I had seen its devastating effects in a person sitting just a few feet away. Intellectually, I knew I was in no danger, yet I was nervous when he coughed. I didn't eat anymore jelly beans. (1988, pp. 31–32)

If people recognize the irrationality of their feelings, as Ms. Kaufman did, and are willing to discuss those feelings, they can overcome them. Of course, AIDS patients realize the fears other people have of them and must cope with people treating them "like a leper."

Because of the fears about AIDS in society and because the disease is associated with homosexuality and drug abuse, AIDS patients and their families and lovers often feel stigmatized (Flaskerud, 1988; Herek & Glunt, 1988). One of the first questions they consider is "Should we tell our friends, and if so, which ones?" They worry that they will be rejected by their friends, neighbors, and coworkers. This may lead to their being secretive and withdrawn, thereby cutting off the social support they will need as the disease progresses. For some families, learning of the AIDS diagnosis comes at the same time they first learn that the patient—their child or spouse—is gay, or bisexual, or a drug abuser. Moreover, spouses or lovers fear that the patient has already infected them, too. All of these factors add to the shock family and friends experience when they learn the diagnosis. Sometimes the stigma associated with the disease or the anger these people feel causes them to abandon the patient.

For AIDS patients, the anxieties are enormous. They fear being abandoned by those they love and suffering pain, debilitation, and disfigurement (Flaskerud, 1988). Sometimes their treatment requires isolation for periods of time, leaving them without the love and support they need. The cycles of disease recurrences and remissions arouse feelings of hopelessness, helplessness, and depression. Their families, lovers, and friends can help by maintaining a reasonably cheerful but realistic outlook, talking about their feelings and worries, and enlisting the aid of a social network. There are many organizations and support groups around the United States today to help AIDS patients and their families and lovers cope.

In this chapter, we have examined what it is like to live with and adapt to four very different high-mortality health problems. Each of these diseases can disable its victims and progress to the point that the patients and their loved ones are aware that the disease is terminal and death is imminent.

ADAPTING TO A TERMINAL ILLNESS

When people talk about the hypothetical prospects of dying, you will often hear them say, "I hope I go quickly and without pain." Some people might argue that there are no "good" ways to die, but almost everyone would agree that a slow and painful death is not one of them. By definition, a terminal illness entails a slow death. The patient typically suffers a progressive deterioration in the feeling of well-being and ability to function, and may also experience chronic pain. Although this process generally takes several weeks, it sometimes takes as little as a few days or as long as several months (Hinton, 1984). One factor that affects how people adapt to a terminal illness is the age of the patient.

The Patient's Age

"Tragic" and "untimely" are words people often use to describe a young person's terminal illness or death. Psychiatrist Avery Weisman (1976) has outlined several distinctions between *timely* and *untimely* deaths, one of which is whether death is "appropriate" to the person's age. An 80-year-old's death is more appropriate than a 20-year-old's. Let's consider how people adapt to terminal illness in patients at different times in the life span.

A Terminally Ill Child

Do children know what dying means? Death is a very abstract concept and, as such, it is not well understood by young children (Lonetto, 1980; Speece & Brent, 1984). Prior to about 5 years of age, children think death is like living in another place and the person can come back. They may also believe that people can avoid death. For instance, a child might conceive of death as a monster and argue that "You won't die if you run faster than the monster or trick it." By about 8 years of age, most children understand that death happens to everyone, is final, and involves the absence of bodily functions.

Most children at early ages have some experience with dying—for instance, in the death of a close person, such as a grandparent or neighbor, or of a pet. Dying is not an easy topic for many adults to discuss, and they usually try to "spare" children from knowing the realities of death, saying that the dead person "has gone away," or "is in heaven, with Jesus," or "is only sleeping" (Koch, 1977; Sarafino, 1986). When a child has a terminal illness, parents sometimes decide not to tell him or her so that the child will have less emotional suffering. But dying school-age children seem to realize the seriousness of their illness even when they are not told, and they exhibit far greater anxiety than seriously ill children who are not dying (Spinetta, 1974).

Terminally ill children's awareness that they are dying develops gradually: at first, these children recognize they are seriously ill but believe they will recover; later, they realize they are continuously ill and will not get better; and then, when they learn of the death of a peer, especially one with a similar illness, they realize that they are, in fact, dying, too (Bluebond-Langner, 1977). Child specialists today generally believe that children should know as much about the illness as they can comprehend. Because preschool-age children do not understand the meaning of death, there is little need to discuss death with them; the important thing is to allay their concerns about separation from their parents. With older children, an open, honest, and sensitive approach seems to reduce their anxiety and maintain a trusting relationship with their parents (La Greca & Stone, 1985).

A Terminally Ill Adolescent or Young Adult

Although some adolescents and young adults, particularly those of the lower classes, think that their odds of dying at a young age are fairly high, they envision their death as being sudden and violent (Kastenbaum & Costa, 1977). If they develop a terminal illness at this time of life, they realize how unlikely their circumstance is and feel angry by the "senselessness" and "injustice" of it and by not having a chance to develop their lives. As one dying college student put it, 'Now a perfectly good person with an awful lot to give is going to die. A young person is going die. His death is going to be senseless" (Shneidman, 1977, p. 77).

This young man was having a very difficult time coping with his impending death, and his shouting and quarrelsome behavior were creating problems on the hospital ward. Edwin Shneidman, a therapist whom the patients' physician called in, has described their meetings:

> When I first saw him, he was sitting up in bed, behaving in a rather feisty and imperious way to the others in the room. I greeted him at the outset by saying that I had heard that he had been misbehaving. He seemed to like that approach, and we hit it off quite well from the beginning. In my own heart I decided to see him because I felt that he was in for a rough time, and with his own defenses and alienating behavior, he might turn people away from him and have an unnecessarily psychologically painful death. I began to see him almost every day, alone, just he and I. It developed that he was an only child, his father was dead, and his relationship with his mother for the past several years could be characterized as a running verbal hostile fight. The content of our sessions grew more serious as he became increasingly ill. He sobered and matured enormously in a matter of weeks. (1977, p. 75)

During this time this young man's relationship with his mother became very close, and he noted, "I have let her love me. I have let her be a mother. She has been so beautiful. I get more comfort from her than anybody else" (p. 76).

Having a terminal illness seems especially "untimely" when patients have young children. This condition is a threat to the family unit, and the patients feel guilty at not being able to care for their children and cheated out of the joys of seeing them develop. Because of the untimeliness of death at this point in the life span, young adults appear to experience more anger and emotional distress when they have a life-threatening illness than older patients do (Leventhal, Leventhal, & Van Nguyen, 1985).

Terminal Illness in Middle-Aged and Older Adults

As people develop beyond the early adulthood years, the likelihood of contracting a high-mortality chronic illness—especially heart disease, cancer, or stroke—increases sharply. Although dying may not be easy at any point in the life span, it seems to become less difficult as people progress from middle age to old age. Studies have found, for instance, that adults become less and less afraid of death as they get older (Bengston, Cuellar, & Ragan, 1977; Kalish & Reynolds, 1976). Why is this?

Researcher Richard Kalish (1985) has outlined several reasons why the elderly have an easier time than younger individuals in facing impending death. As people get older, developing a terminal illness becomes less unexpected, less of a shock. The elderly know their remaining years are few, they realize that they will probably die of a chronic illness, and they think and talk more about poor health and death than most younger people do. Most of their peers are suffering from declining health or have died. They often have made financial preparations, and some have even made plans or given instructions regarding the terminal care they would prefer and their funeral arrangements. They also

> have had many more death-related experiences than younger people. They have virtually always experienced the deaths of both parents; they have experienced the deaths of more family members and friends; they have attended more funerals and visited more people who were dying; and they are more likely to have had one or more personal encounters with their own possible death. (Kalish, 1985, p. 154)

In addition, older individuals have had a longer past than younger people, which has allowed them the time to achieve more. Patients who have reviewed their past and believe they have accomplished important things and lived their lives well tend to have less difficulty adapting to a terminal illness than those who do not (Mages & Mendelsohn, 1979).

Psychosocial Adjustments to Terminal Illness

As we have seen, most patients with life-threatening chronic illnesses manage to adapt reasonably well to their condition over time after the initial crisis, and so do the closest people in their lives. But when their condition worsens and progresses to a terminal phase, a new crisis emerges that requires intense coping efforts.

How People Cope with Terminal Illness

How do terminally ill patients and their families cope, and what stresses do they experience? The principal coping mechanism people use during the phase of terminal illness is denial (Hackett & Weisman, 1985; Hinton, 1984). As we saw in Chapter 5, emotion-focused coping is especially useful when the individuals cannot do anything to change the situation. Unfortunately, when people mutually deny the reality of the imminent death, they may not discuss with each other how they feel or have any way to "say their goodbyes."

Psychiatrist John Hinton (1984) has described three types of stresses that terminal patients experience. First, they must cope with the physical effects of their worsening condition, such as pain, difficulty breathing, sleeplessness, or loss of bowel control. Second, their condition severely alters their style of living, restricting their activity and making them highly dependent on others. Perhaps two-thirds of dying people are restricted in their activities during the last three months of their lives, and one-fifth of these patients are confined to bed. Third, they typically realize that the end of their life is near, even when not told. If they are in the hospital, as most dying people are, they may think about never going home again or no longer being able to experience the intimacy they used to have with those they love.

Thinking about someone who is dying typically arouses feelings of sadness in people. According to Hinton (1984), healthy individuals who are unaccustomed to serious illness or the declining abilities of age may not realize how well many terminally ill patients come to face and accept dying. He has noted by comparison that people with diminished lives—such as many elderly, disabled, and bereaved individuals—still get pleasure from their lives

> despite any earlier view that such an existence would be intolerable. The same applies to people who have only a very limited life left. If their obvious stresses are relieved, they may still be capable of enjoyment. It helps if there is a sense of fulfillment; that sense depends on the individual's own values. People may derive their greatest satisfaction from their past family life, their career or the children they are leaving behind. . . . Some have the sense that they need struggle no longer and they can now find peace or believe that their life is now reasonably complete. There may be the conviction that they will rejoin a loved person in immortal existence. . . . With good care many people do achieve a positive acceptance of dying and have a peaceful death. (p. 245)

Patients who are most likely to adapt to dying with the least amount of anger or depression are those individuals who are in little pain, receive sensitive and caring social support, feel satisfied with their lives, and have a history of coping well with life's problems and crises (Carey, 1975; Hinton, 1984; Kalish, 1985). Often, the patient adapts better than his or her loved ones. Support groups can be of great help to dying patients and their families.

Does Adapting to Dying Happen in "Stages"?

"Time changes things," as the saying goes. Since time passes in the process of dying from a terminal illness, we might expect that patients' reactions would change as they come to terms with their impending death. Do these changes occur in a predictable pattern, as a series of stages?

On the basis of interviews with over 200 terminally ill patients, Elisabeth Kübler-Ross (1969) proposed that people's adjustment to dying usually follows a predictable pattern, passing through a sequence of *five stages.* These stages are:

1. *Denial.* The first reaction to the prognosis of death involves refusing to believe it is true. Terminally ill patients say, "No, it can't be true," or "There must be some mistake," or "The lab reports must have gotten mixed up." Denial can be a valuable first reaction by giving patients time to mobilize other coping strategies and motivation to get a second opinion. According to Kübler-Ross, denial soon fades in most patients and is replaced by anger.
2. *Anger.* The patients now realize, "Oh, yes, it is me, it was not a mistake," and are outraged and irate, asking "Why me?" or "Why couldn't it have been that miserable no-good guy down the street?" They resent others who are healthy and may show their anger in outbursts toward almost anyone—nurses, doctors, and family.
3. *Bargaining.* At this point, patients try to change their circumstances by offering to "make a deal." Most of the bargains they try to negotiate are with God, for example, thinking, "Oh, God, I promise to be a better person if you'll just make me well."
4. *Depression.* When bargaining no longer helps and patients feel that their time is running out, hopelessness and depression set in. They grieve for things they had in the past and for things they will miss in the future. According to Kübler-Ross, even though depression is painful and may last for a prolonged period, it is helpful because part of the grieving process involves becoming detached from the things in their world. Being detached enables the last stage—acceptance—to occur.
5. *Acceptance.* Patients who live long enough may reach the last stage in which they are no longer depressed, but feel a quiet calm and readiness for death.

Not all the patients she interviewed showed this pattern—a few, for example, continued to deny that they were dying to the very last. But the pattern of adjustments seemed sufficiently regular for Kübler-Ross to propose that coping in most dying patients begins with denial and advances through the stages in order.

Do Kübler-Ross's stages correctly reflect the emotional reactions most dying patients experience as they cope with a terminal illness? Although many people believe that most patients adjust to dying with a predictable and orderly sequence of coping reactions, the evidence from subsequent research does not support this belief (Hinton, 1984; Kalish, 1985; Silver & Wortman, 1980). An overview of this evidence indicates the following conclusion:

> Some individuals do follow a sequence of such reactions when dying, but there is by no means an inevitable smooth passage through a series of predictable stages. Fatal illnesses are often irregular in their progress. Certain emotions or attitudes may be conspicuous in some but absent in others. People can fluctuate to and fro in their reactions, even when the disease or circumstances appear relatively unchanged. (Hinton, 1984, p. 240)

Some terminal patients seem to go through a particular stage, such as anger, more than once during their adjustment; others experience more than one emotional reaction simultaneously; and some seem to skip stages.

Despite these shortcomings, Kübler-Ross's work has had many positive effects. For one thing, it has been influential in stimulating people's awareness and discussion of the dying process and the needs of terminal patients. It has also led to important and very beneficial changes in the care and treatment of dying patients, thereby improving the quality of the last weeks and days of their lives.

THE QUALITY OF LIFE IN DEATH

The medical community and patients' families face one dilemma after another in trying to do "what's best" for a dying patient. Medical technology has made it possible to keep some patients alive only in a legal sense, and society has begun to question whether these patients are alive in a humane sense. The news media describe patients lying in a coma for years, dependent on life-support systems to stay alive, but with virtually no likelihood of recovery. An artificial respirator can make the patient breathe and other devices can keep the heart going. The vast majority of American physicians favor withdrawing life-support systems from hopelessly ill or irreversibly comatose individuals if the patients or their families request it (Shogren, 1988). In many states, patients who anticipate these circumstances may issue a "living will" that instructs practitioners not to use extraordinary life-support measures.

A principal issue that enters into people's judgments about maintaining life support is the patient's quality of life. This is actually an issue that is relevant to all terminally ill patients, not just the extreme cases. What kind of medical and psychological care do dying patients need? Who should be responsible for that care, and where should it be given? These are the main issues we consider in this section.

Medical and Psychological Care of Dying Patients

The terminal phase of care begins when medical judgment indicates that the patient's condition is worsening and no treatment is available to reverse or arrest the progress toward death (Abrams, 1966; Benoliel, 1977). At this point, medical treatment is mainly *palliative*, that is, it focuses on reducing pain and discomfort. This phase of treatment can be very distressing to medical personnel, who entered the medical field to save lives. In some cases today in the United States, terminal care for a patient may include the specific instruction *not* to interfere with the process of death. Many states have laws allowing the instruction "Do Not Resuscitate" to be adopted for a patient, with the consent of courts, the patient, or his or her family (Easterbrook, 1987). When this instruction is entered on a terminally ill patient's hospital chart and he or she begins to die—for instance, if the patient's heart stops beating—the medical staff is not to interfere.

People who work with dying patients on a daily basis must come to grips with the feelings of failure and loss they experience when patients die (Benoliel, 1977; Maguire, 1985). In an effort to protect themselves from this pain and to perform efficiently in their heavy work loads, medical staff often distance themselves psychologically from terminal patients. By doing this, doctors and nurses avoid dealing with the psychological problems these patients are having. How do staff members distance themselves? They may simply not ask about the patient's feelings or adjustment, or they may provide false reassurance, saying, "I'm sure you'll feel better soon," when they believe otherwise. The staff may also use selective attention, as illustrated in the following interaction:

> **Surgeon:** Well, how are you today?
>
> **Patient** (dying of breast cancer): I'm very worried about what is happening to me. I'm beginning to think I'm not going to get better this time. The pain in my hip is getting worse.
>
> **Surgeon:** Tell me more about this pain in your hip. (Maguire, 1985, p. 1711)

Although this patient mentioned both physical and psychological difficulties, the physician followed up only on the physical one. This may lead the patient to conclude that it is not appropriate to discuss psychological problems with medical staff.

Should terminal patients be told they are dying? This is a controversial question, and medical personnel often face the dilemma of believing patients have the right to know and being instructed by the patient's family not to tell (Maguire, 1985). Physician Laurens White has argued strongly that this information should be given to the patient and family together:

> I make it a point to try not to discuss diagnosis and prognosis with the family without the patient being present. In this way everybody knows at the same time what everybody else knows, but, more importantly, everybody knows that everybody knows, and that different stories are not being given to different people. (White, 1977, p. 99)

Psychiatrist Avery Weisman (1977) has taken a similar position, proposing that the issue of whether to tell the patient is moot, since terminal patients generally realize they are dying. In his view, physicians should be "compassionately candid" for medical reasons, to give the patient the right to choose or refuse treatments, and to encourage "the patient and family to initiate bereavement, without waiting for death to take them seemingly by surprise" (p. 117).

Although many patients are able to approach death with a feeling of acceptance and peacefulness, others become very troubled. What can be done to help dying patients cope? In some cases, hospitals may provide individual psychotherapy for those patients who are clearly having difficulty (Shneidman, 1977). Health care workers may also be able to provide information about support groups, such as Make Today Count, that have developed specifically to improve the quality of life for patients with terminal illnesses. In addition, professionally led group therapy appears to be effective in helping terminal patients face their impending death with less anxiety and depression and a greater sense of control over their remaining period of life (Levy, 1983; Solomon & Temoshok, 1987).

A Place to Die—Hospital, Home, or Hospice?

Most people in the United States die in hospitals. Although hospitals can provide a great deal of expertise, technical equipment, and efficient caretaking, they are usually not "psychologically comfortable" places for patients. The environment there is unfamiliar, and often it is mechanical and impersonal. Patients have little control over their daily routine and activities, and they lack access to such things as photo albums and musical recordings that they have relied on in the past for enjoyment and to enrich their experiences. Moreover, most of the people there are strangers, not family or friends. As a result, many terminal patients would rather die at home. Is this a reasonable alternative?

Home Care for the Dying Patient

Whether home care is a reasonable alternative for a dying patient depends on the patient's condition and the quality of care he or she can get at home. Some patients who are incontinent or in extreme pain, for example, may be better off at the hospital (Garfield, 1978). Can patients receive good terminal care at home? Yes, they can. Studies have found that terminally ill patients who have regular contact at home with a medical team and whose family members are trained receive very good care (Malkin, 1976; Zimmer, Juncker, & McCusker, 1985). Unfortunately, many dying patients may not have the option of home care because they lack family members who are able to provide the care they need.

Caring for a terminally ill patient at home can be a very physically and emotionally exhausting experience (Hinton, 1984). There may be only one individual at home who can provide the care, and all of the burden falls on that person's shoulders. If the patient requires continuous attention, the life of that one caretaker may become limited to coping with the dying patient's needs. This may go on for weeks or, sometimes, months. Even when there is more than one person available to help, their lives are to some extent restricted. Some terminally ill patients are bedridden and need to be fed and bathed, for instance. Despite these hardships, however, many people who have cared for a dying patient at home claim that it is extremely rewarding to know that they have done everything they could to make the last days or weeks as pleasant as possible for someone they love.

Hospice Care for the Dying Patient

Is it possible to combine the strengths of a professional support system with the warm and loving care one can get at home, thereby helping terminal patients die comfortably and with dignity? This question led to the development of the concept of **hospice care**, which involves a medical and social support system to provide an enriched quality of life — through physical, psychosocial, and spiritual care — for terminal patients and their families (Cioppa, 1984). In the hospice approach, the staff consists of a medically supervised team of professionals and volunteers. Much of the physical care the staff provides is designed to reduce discomfort and pain, often with the use of drugs.

The hospice care approach to caring for dying patients originated in Great Britain, largely through the efforts of physician Cicely Saunders, who was originally trained as a nurse and social worker (Saunders, 1977; Torrens, 1985). After working at a hospice in Ireland, she

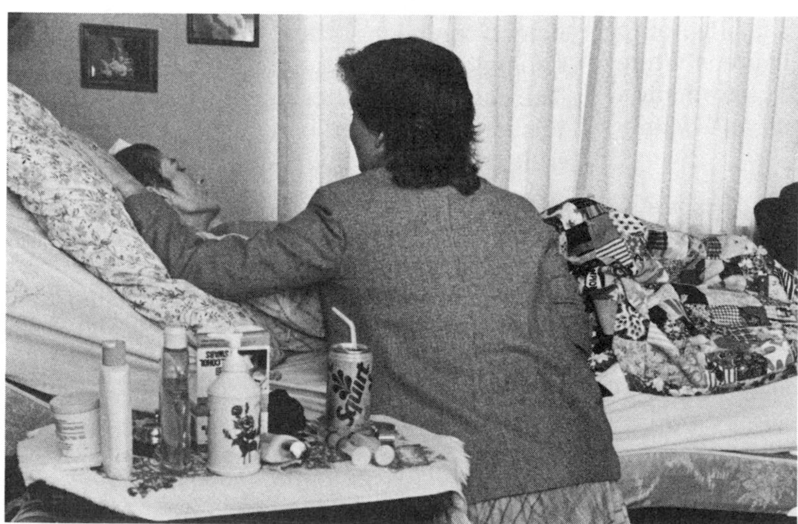

A hospice nurse attends a terminally ill patient. Hospice care can be given at home or in inpatient facilities that look more like a home than a hosiptal.

founded St. Christopher's Hospice near London in 1967. Originally, hospices were designed as separate institutions for the purpose of caring for dying patients on an inpatient basis. But as the philosophy of hospice care spread to the United States and Canada, the organizational structure for delivering this care began to broaden. Hospice services in North America are available today both *at home* and at hundreds of *inpatient facilities*, many of which are housed in hospitals or nursing homes. When home hospice care is used, services are provided on a part-time, regularly scheduled basis and staff are available on-call 24 hours a day, seven days a week (Cioppa, 1984).

Inpatient facilities generally try to make the environment as much like home as possible. If the facility is in a hospital, existing policies need to be adjusted to satisfy the goals of the program. These adjustments often include:

- Flexibility in visiting hours, including regulations that permit children and pets to visit.
- Freedom to wear one's own clothes.
- Provision of alcoholic beverages and meals prepared by family members.
- Expertise in palliative care and management of symptoms, especially the relief of pain.
- Psychologic and spiritual counseling for patients as well as family members.
- Arrangements with family members for assisting patients and their families in completing unfinished business. (Cioppa, 1984, p. 597)

In the hospice care approach, the patient and his or her family are considered to be the "unit of care." What this means is that all of these people together form a system, with each individual affecting each other and each needing hospice attention. Therefore, patients and their families actively participate in the development of a plan for the care of the whole unit (Cioppa, 1984). Cicely Saunders (1986) has outlined several "essential elements" in the hospice approach, some of which deal with psychosocial issues. First, patients should be in a *place of choice* as they end their lives. They and their families should decide whether that place should be at home or in an inpatient setting. Second, the care given during the terminal phase should enable patients to *maximize their potential*, so that they perform to the limits of their physical, cognitive, and social potential, particularly as an active member of their family. Third, the care should *address all family members' needs*, which may involve help resolving interpersonal discord and feelings of anxiety, guilt, and depression. Fourth, *follow-up care* is available, and family members can continue to receive help through the period of bereavement.

Does hospice care help patients and their families cope better with the dying process than conventional care does? The testimonials from patients and family members are massive and glowing, describing the programs as enormously supportive and enriching. But few carefully controlled studies have been done comparing hospice and conventional care (Torrens, 1985). The little research that is available has compared inpatient hospice and hospital care and found similar pain control and daily activities of the patients, but hospice patients showed less anxiety and greater satisfaction with their care.

THE SURVIVORS: AND LIFE GOES ON

Whether a person dies suddenly and unexpectedly or with warning over a long period of time, there are survivors who must now come to terms with the death and eventually pick up the pieces of their lives. The state of having lost someone through death is called *bereavement*, and this state is characterized by feelings of *grief* and the expression of these feelings in *mourning*. People adapt to their bereavement in many different ways—this process takes time, usually at least a year, but it does not seem to follow any particular pattern or stages and there is no rule of thumb for predicting how long it will take (Joyce, 1984; Silver & Wortman, 1980). Each grieving person needs to adjust at his or her own pace, and urgings to "start living again" may be both insensitive and unproductive when they occur early in the adjustment process.

Some people think that coming to terms with the loss of someone we love means that we forget that person—he or she no longer means anything to us. This is not so. People who eventually adapt to the loss may feel recurrent moments or periods of sadness years later, especially on anniversaries or other significant dates (Joyce, 1984). A mother who lost her infant child years ago wrote:

> *My mind does not mourn yesterday*
> *It mourns today*
> *The images that pass before my eyes*
> *Do not recall the infant son*
> *But see you running through my house*
> *A teenage child in search of food and gym shoes and maybe me.*
> *I do not mourn you for what you were,*
> *But for what can't be . . .*
> *(Anonymous, cited in Silver & Wortman, 1980)*

The death of a child is one of the most tragic events that can happen to a family, and parents often experience grief for many years after the loss (Knapp, 1987).

When a parent dies, the surviving children in their early or later childhood years need special attention and understanding. Often the surviving parent is so caught up in his or her own shock and grief that the children's emotional needs are not adequately addressed. Many surviving parents say little about the death and exclude their children from the mourning process. It is not unusual for children to show little sense of loss or outward grief when a close family member dies (Koch, 1977; Sarafino, 1986). Young children do not understand fully what death is, and this may account for their seeming lack of concern. Older children may be so confused and shocked by the tragedy that they are simply numbed emotionally. Their outward calmness should not be mistaken as a sign that they do not love the dead person. Sometimes their grief comes out later, and sometimes it happens privately.

During the first weeks after the death of a spouse, the surviving husband or wife usually receives a great deal of attention from friends and relatives. But soon this changes, and the bereaved person may feel isolated in efforts to organize his or her life and make decisions alone. A widow or widower must gradually become involved again in work and leisure activities, in maintaining old friendships and developing new ones, and, perhaps, in finding a new mate. One man described his experience as a widower in the following way:

> Having to "date" in the early 40s, or older, and after long years of marriage is, for many, an unnerving experience. I suggest there is something even worse—not getting out and having companionship.
>
> How the widower chooses to begin his new social and sex life depends, of course, on his personality, his philosophy, and the sort of companionship he wants. Some widowers prefer to join Parents Without Partners, where they are sure to meet people with common interests. Like the majority of widowers, I had friends and relatives who put forward suggestions and invited me to dinner parties. I found most of these either tedious or painful. One night. . . . however, I did meet a beautiful woman. She was a widow, with one child. . . . We are a complete household again and throughout the home there once again is the sound of laughter, of music and, best of all, the rich sound of meaningful conversation between children and their parents. (Lindeman, 1976, pp. 285–286)

Of course, not all stories of people's coping with the loss of someone they love have happy endings. Some bereaved individuals never adjust to the loss. But with the help and support of others and a determined drive on their own part, most people can build a new and once again enriching life. The social support that bereaved people need can come from family and friends, but support groups may be especially helpful.

SUMMARY

People with high-mortality illnesses do not know for sure what the course of their disease will be or if or when they will die. But their lives are threatened, and they and their families must adapt to living with uncertainty. Convalescing patients tend to be optimistic about their future health, but watchful for symptoms and changes in their condition. Families can help patients adapt by encouraging them to develop reasonable plans and to carry them out, rather than encouraging helplessness and dependence. In adapting to the illness over a long period of time, patients make cognitive adjustments by finding meaning in their illness experience, gaining a sense of control over their illness, and restoring their self-esteem. A recurrence or relapse of the condition creates a new, and often very difficult, crisis.

Heart disease is the leading cause of death in the United States; cancer is second, and stroke is third. Coronary heart disease may show up in an episode of angina pectoris or of myocardial infarction. The prevalence rate for heart disease is greater in men than women and increases with age. Cardiac rehabilitation involves the use of medication, a program of exercise, stress management, and changes in diet and other aspects of lifestyle, especially if the patient smokes, drinks too much, or is overweight. Many heart patients fail to comply with the exercise program and lifestyle changes. Most cardiac patients who were employed before the illness eventually return to work, often in less demanding jobs. Some cardiac patients need special interventions to enhance adaptation.

Although there are many varieties of cancer, they can be classified into four types: carcinomas, lymphomas, sarcomas, and leukemias. Untreated neoplasms eventually metastasize and spread to other parts of the body. The most common sites of cancer are the skin, lungs, colon or rectum, breast, uterus or cervix, and prostate gland. Medical treatment consists of surgery, radiation, and chemotherapy, each of which has important drawbacks. Chemotherapy, in particular, causes nausea and vomiting that is associated with learned food aversions. Despite the great stress individuals experience with cancer, most patients show a remarkable ability to adapt with time during remission or after a cure. Some, however, become very depressed and withdraw from social contact. Leukemia is the most common form of cancer in childhood.

A stroke can cause damage to the brain through either an infarction or a hemorrhage. Depending on the amount and location of neurological damage, patients may suffer functional deficits. Some impairments recover with time and rehabilitation, but others are permanent. Deficits may involve motor action, aphasia, visual disorders, and emotional disorders. Stroke patients are very prone to depression. AIDS and its precursor, ARC, are caused by HIV infection, which impairs the immune system, leaving the victims subject to opportunistic diseases. Most AIDS victims die within one or two years of the diagnosis. Because AIDS is an infectious disease, many people have reacted to its outbreak with alarm and discrimination, making adaptation all the more difficult.

If and when a chronic condition deteriorates and no cure is likely, the illness is considered terminal. One factor that affects how people adapt to terminal illness is the age of the patient. Adults see the death of a young person as particularly tragic and untimely. Young children have little understanding of the meaning of death; by about 8 years of age, children's understanding is fairly complete. Adolescents and young adults react to their impending death with very strong feelings of anger and emotional distress. As adults get older, they become less fearful of death. Dying patients may react to their condition with denial, anger, bargaining, depression, and acceptance. The hospice care approach provides physical, psychosocial, and spiritual care for dying patients and their families during the terminal phase and in bereavement.

KEY TERMS

angina pectoris
myocardial infarction
cancer
learned food aversion
stroke
acquired immune deficiency syndrome
AIDS-Related Complex
hospice care

glossary

acquired immune deficiency syndrome (AIDS) An infectious disease that disables the immune system. The diagnosis of AIDS is reserved for individuals who have contracted one of several opportunistic diseases.

acupuncture A pain control technique in which fine metal needles are inserted under the skin at certain locations and then activated.

acute pain The discomfort patients experience with temporary medical conditions, lasting less than about six months.

adaptation The changes people undergo in making positive adjustments to circumstances in their lives.

addiction The condition of physical and psychological dependence on using a substance.

adherence The degree to which patients follow the medical recommendations of practitioners. Also called *compliance.*

adoption studies Research with subjects adopted at very early ages, comparing their characteristics with corresponding traits of their adoptive and natural parents in order to assess the influence of heredity.

adrenal glands Endocrine glands that secrete several hormones, such as cortisol, epinephrine, and norepinephrine, that are involved in stress reactions.

aerobic exercise Sustained and energetic physical activity in which the body uses high volumes of oxygen over many minutes.

AIDS-Related Complex (ARC) A stage in the development of AIDS in which the immune system begins to falter and some symptoms appear.

alarm reaction The first stage in the general adaptation syndrome when the body's resources are mobilized.

alcoholics People who drink alcohol heavily and are addicted to it.

algogenic substances Chemicals released at the site of tissue damage that cause inflammation and signal injury.

Alzheimer's disease A chronic and progressive brain disorder marked by a loss of cognitive functions, such as memory.

angina pectoris A condition marked by chest pain that generally results from a brief or incomplete blockage of the blood supply to heart tissue.

anorexia nervosa An eating disorder marked by self-starvation and an extreme and unhealthy loss of weight.

antibodies Protein molecules created to protect against specific antigens in body fluids.

antibody-mediated immunity The immune process that employs antibodies to attack antigens while they are still in body fluids and before they have invaded the cells.

antigen Any substance that can trigger the immune system to respond.

arteriosclerosis A condition in which fatty patches have accumulated and hardened on artery walls, thereby reducing their elasticity.

arthritis A category of painful and potentially disabling chronic conditions that involve inflammation of the joints.

asthma A psychophysiological disorder of the respiratory system characterized by bronchial spasms and difficulty in breathing.

atherosclerosis The condition in which fatty patches (plaques) form on artery walls.

attention diversion from pain A pain management technique in which individuals distract their focus to a nonpain stimulus in the environment.

attribution The process by which people attempt to judge or explain their own or others' behavior.

autonomic nervous system A division of the peripheral nervous system that carries messages between the central nervous system and the internal organs. It has two parts: the sympathetic and parasympathetic nervous systems.

aversion strategies Methods that use unpleasant stimuli to discourage an undesirable behavior.

B-cells Lymphocytes that lead to the formation of antibodies.

behavioral control A form of personal control involving the ability to reduce the impact of a stressor by taking concrete action.

behavioral medicine An interdisciplinary field introduced in the early 1970s to study the relations between behavior and health.

biofeedback A process by which individuals can acquire voluntary control over a physiological function by monitoring its status.

biomedical model The view that illness results from physical causes, such as infection or injury; psychosocial processes are not viewed as causal factors.

biopsychosocial model The view that health and illness involve the interplay of biological, psychological, and social factors in people's lives.

blood pressure The force of the blood against the inner walls of the arteries.

brainstem The lowest portion of the brain, located at the top of the spinal cord, consisting of the midbrain, reticular system, pons, and medulla.

buffering hypothesis The view that the health benefits of social support come from its reducing the negative health effects of high stress levels.

bulimia An eating disorder marked by repeated binge eating, usually followed by purging.

burnout An emotional and behavioral impairment resulting from exposure to high levels of occupational stress.

cancer A class of malignant diseases in which cells proliferate in an unrestricted manner, usually forming a tumor.

carbon monoxide A gas that is a constituent of cigarette smoke.

carcinogens Chemical or physical agents that can cause cancer.

cardiovascular system A network of organs that circulates blood to supply oxygen and nutrients to the body's cells and remove wastes and other substances.

case study A nonexperimental method in which a researcher uses interviews, past records, and current observations to construct a biography of a single subject.

catecholamines A class of hormones, including epinephrine and norepinephrine, secreted by the adrenal glands.

cell-mediated immunity The immune process that operates at the cellular level, using T-cells to attack infected cells.

central nervous system That part of the nervous system consisting of the brain and spinal cord.

cerebellum A large portion of the brain that coordinates motor activities and maintains body balance.

cerebrum The upper and largest portion of the human brain. It has primary control over motor and mental activity.

chromosomes Threadlike structures in the nucleus of each cell that contain genes that carry hereditary information.

chronic diseases Illnesses that persist and generally get worse over a long period of time.

chronic/intractable/benign pain Long-term continuous, but variable, discomfort stemming from benign causes.

chronic/progressive pain Long-term continuous discomfort that worsens as the underlying malignant condition progresses.

chronic/recurrent pain Long-term repeated and intense episodes of discomfort stemming from benign causes.

clinical pain Any pain symptoms that receive or require professional treatment.

cognitive appraisal The mental process people use in assessing whether a demand is threatening and what resources are available to meet the demand.

cognitive control A form of personal control involving the ability to reduce the impact of a stressor by using thought processes.

cognitive restructuring A therapeutic process for replacing thoughts that provoke stress with ones that do not.

cohort effect The influence of different subjects having been born and raised in different eras.

common-sense models Cognitive representations people develop regarding specific illnesses.

compliance See *adherence.*

conflict theory An explanation of health-related behavior that includes both rational and emotional factors.

coping The process by which people try to manage the stress they experience.

coronary heart disease (CHD) A class of illnesses that result when a narrowing or blockage of the coronary arteries restricts the blood supply to the heart muscle (myocardium).

correlation coefficient A statistic that reflects

the degree and direction of relationship between two variables; it can range from +1.00, through .00, to −1.00.

correlational studies Nonexperimental research conducted to determine the degree and direction of relationship between variables.

corticosteroids A class of hormones, including cortisol, secreted by the adrenal glands.

counter-irritation A technique whereby one pain is reduced by creating another one.

crisis theory A model describing the factors that affect people's adjustment to having a serious illness. The theory proposes that coping processes are influenced by three types of factors: illness-related, background and personal, and physical and social environmental.

cross-sectional approach Method of studying developmental trends by observing different groups of subjects of different ages within a relatively short period of time.

daily hassles Everyday annoyances or unpleasant events.

decisional control A form of personal control involving the ability to reduce the impact of a stressor by choosing between alternative courses of action.

depersonalization A behavioral style of some practitioners that involves treating a patient as if he or she were not there or not a person.

depressants Drugs that induce relaxation and sleep.

detoxification The process of getting an addicted individual safely through withdrawal after discontinuing the use of a substance.

dietary diseases Illnesses that result from poor nutrition.

digestive system The network of organs that processes ingested food by breaking it down for the body's use and excreting the remains.

direct effects hypothesis The view that the health benefits of social support accrue regardless of whether people experience high or low levels of stress.

doctor-centered The behavioral style of some physicians in which interactions with patients are highly controlled by the practitioner and focus on the symptoms or treatment rather than the person.

double blind An experimental procedure whereby neither the subject nor the researcher knows which research treatment the subject is receiving.

emetine A drug that induces nausea; it is paired in an aversion strategy with drinking alcohol.

emotion-focused coping Approaches people use for managing stress aimed at regulating their emotional response.

endocrine system An array of glands that secrete hormones into the bloodstream.

endogenous opioids Opiatelike substances the body produces naturally that reduce the sensation of pain.

end-stage renal disease (ESRD) The last stage in chronic kidney disease in which kidney function is not sufficient to support life.

enzymes Substances that increase the speed of chemical reactions in cells.

epidemic The situation in which the occurrence of a health problem has increased rapidly.

epilepsy A chronic condition of the nervous system that produces recurrent seizures.

essential hypertension Persistent high blood pressure with no known organic cause.

experiment A controlled study in which variables are manipulated and observed in order to assess cause–effect relationships.

gate-control theory An explanation of pain perception that proposes that a neural gate in the spinal cord can modulate incoming pain signals. The opening and closing of the gate is influenced by messages that descend from the brain and by the amount of activity in pain fibers and in other peripheral fibers.

general adaptation syndrome (GAS) The sequence of physiological reactions to prolonged and intense stress. The sequence consists of the alarm reaction, the stage of resistance, and the stage of exhaustion.

genetic counseling A service whereby prospective and expectant parents may get information regarding their risks of giving birth to a child with genetic defects.

hallucinogens Drugs that can produce perceptual and cognitive distortions.

hardiness An array of personality characteristics that enables individuals to withstand stress and not succumb to its negative health effects.

health A positive state of physical, mental, and social well-being that changes in degree over time.

health behavior Activity undertaken by people who believe they are healthy in order to prevent future health problems.

health belief model An explanation of people's health-related behavior based on their perception of the threat of illness or injury and the pros and cons of taking action.

health-protective behavior Any behavior people perform with the intention of promoting or maintaining well-being regardless of the state of their health.

health psychology A field of psychology introduced in the late 1970s to examine the causes of illnesses and to study ways to promote and maintain health, prevent and treat illness, and improve the health care system.

high-density lipoprotein (HDL) A cholesterol-carrying protein that is associated with decreased cholesterol deposits in blood vessels.

hormones Chemical substances secreted by endocrine glands that affect body functions and behavior.

hospice care A philosophy and procedure for enriching the quality of life of terminally ill patients and their families.

hypertension The condition of persistent high blood pressure.

hypochondriasis The tendency of some individuals to be excessively concerned and vigilant regarding their health and body sensations.

hypothalamus A part of the forebrain that contains control centers for many body functions, such as eating, drinking, and sexual activity.

iatrogenic conditions Health problems that develop as a result of medical treatment.

illness behavior Activity by people who feel ill with the purpose of determining the state of their health or finding a remedy.

illness/wellness continuum A model that describes health and sickness as overlapping concepts that vary in degree, rather than being separate categories.

immune system The organs and structures that protect the body against harmful substances, such as bacteria and viruses.

incidence The number of *new* cases reported during a given period of time, such as the previous year.

infectious diseases Illnesses caused by the body being invaded by microorganisms, such as bacteria or viruses.

inflammatory bowel disease A psychophysiological disorder involving wounds in the large or small intestine.

informational control A form of personal control involving the ability to reduce the impact of a stressor by acquiring knowledge about impending events.

insulin A hormone secreted by the pancreas that speeds the conversion of blood sugar to fat.

insulin-dependent diabetes mellitus (IDDM) The health problem of having chronically elevated blood sugar levels because the pancreas produces little or no insulin. IDDM patients typically require daily insulin supplements.

isokinetic exercise A type of activity that involves exerting muscle force in more than one direction while moving an object.

isometric exercise A type of activity that involves exerting muscle force against an object that does not move.

isotonic exercise A type of activity that involves exerting most of the muscle force in one direction.

Lamaze training An educational and procedural program for natural childbirth that involves preparation, participation, and minimal medication.

lay referral system An informal network of individuals who provide advice or information regarding a person's symptoms and health.

learned food aversions A phenomenon in which a food becomes disliked as a result of being associated with symptoms of illness.

learned helplessness A condition of apathy or inactivity that results from repeated experiences with unavoidable stress.

life events Major occurrences in people's lives that require some degree of psychological adjustment.

life-span perspective The viewpoint that considers the individual's prior development, current level of development, and likely development in the future.

limbic system A set of structures in the forebrain that seems to play a role in emotional expression.

lipids Fatty materials, such as the cholesterol found in blood.

lipoproteins Proteins that transport cholesterol in the blood.

locus of control A generalized belief people have about the causes of events in their lives—whether the causes are within or outside their control.

longitudinal approach Method of studying developmental changes in the same subjects by making repeated observations over a long period of time.

low-density lipoproteins (LDL) A cholesterol-carrying protein that is associated with increased cholesterol deposits in blood vessels.

lymphocytes Various types of white blood cells that have several important functions in the body's immune response.

McGill Pain Questionnaire (MPQ) A self-report instrument for assessing people's pain.

Medical Compliance Incomplete Stories Test (M-CIST) A test that assesses the likelihood of adherence to a regimen for a specific illness, cystic fibrosis.

medulla A part of the brainstem that contains control centers for such vital functions as breathing and heartbeat rate.

metabolism The chemical reactions of the body's cells that synthesize new cell material, regulate body processes, and create energy.

methadone A chemical agent used in treating narcotic addiction that blocks the euphoric effects of opiates.

midbrain A portion of the brainstem that plays an important role in vision, hearing, and muscle movement.

migraine headache Recurrent head pain that results from the constriction and dilation of blood vessels in the head.

Millon Behavioral Health Inventory (MBHI) A test that assesses several relevant characteristics of medical patients, such as their basic coping style and hypochondriacal tendencies.

mind/body problem The issue in psychology and philosophy regarding the relationship between processes and functions of the mind and of the body.

Minnesota Multiphasic Personality Inventory (MMPI) A lengthy test that assesses a variety of psychological problems, such as hypochondriasis, depression, and hysteria.

modeling Learning by watching the behavior of other people.

morbidity The condition of illness, injury, or disability.

mortality Death, usually with reference to large populations.

multimodal therapy An eclectic strategy for therapy whereby the therapist tailors a treatment program that includes specific methods to deal with each aspect of the person's problems.

muscle-contraction headache Recurrent head pain that results from persistent muscle tension in the head and neck. Also called *tension* headache.

myocardial infarction Damage to the heart muscle (myocardium) that results from severe or prolonged blockage of blood supply to the tissue. Commonly called a *heart attack*.

narcotics Drugs that relieve pain, act as sedatives, and may produce euphoria. These substances are also called *opiates* and usually lead to addiction with continued use.

nephritis A class of diseases in which kidney tissue becomes inflamed and may be permanently damaged; if the damage becomes extreme, kidney failure results.

neurons Specialized cells that provide for communication within the nervous system.

neurotransmitter A chemical involved in the transmission of impulses across the synapse from one neuron to another.

nicotine A chemical in cigarette smoke that appears to produce physical dependence.

nicotine regulation model An explanation of continued cigarette smoking based on the body's dependence on nicotine.

nociceptors Afferent nerve endings that respond to pain stimuli in the damaged region of the body.

non-insulin-dependent diabetes mellitus (NIDDM) The health problem of having chronically elevated blood sugar levels even though the pancreas does produce at least some insulin. Most NIDDM patients can manage their condition without insulin supplements.

nonpain imagery A pain management method that involves picturing a mental scene that is unrelated to or incompatible with feeling discomfort.

nosocomial infection An infection a patient acquires while in the hospital.

obese The weight classification of individuals whose weight exceeds their desirable range by more than 20%.

overweight The weight classification of individuals whose weight exceeds their desirable range by 10–20%.

pain The sensory and emotional discomfort, usually related to actual or threatened tissue damage.

pain behaviors Characteristic ways people behave when they are in pain.

pain clinics Centers specializing in the treatment of chronic pain.

pain redefinition A pain management technique in which thoughts about pain that arouse a sense of threat are replaced with other thoughts that are more constructive or realistic.

parasympathetic nervous system A division of the autonomic nervous system that helps the body conserve energy and restore the normal body state after arousal.

passive smoking Breathing the smoke in the

environment from someone else's cigarette or other smoking product.

patient-centered The behavioral style of some physicians in which their interactions encourage patients to share information and participate in medical decisions.

periaqueductal gray A region of the midbrain that plays a major role in the perception of and reaction to pain stimuli.

peripheral nervous system The network of nerve fibers that carry messages between the central nervous system and the skin, skeletal muscles, and internal organs. This network has two parts: the somatic and autonomic nervous systems.

personal control The feeling people have that they can make decisions and take action to produce favorable events and avoid unfavorable ones.

phagocytes Certain types of white blood cells that engulf and ingest any kind of invading particles.

physical dependence A state in which the body has become accustomed to the presence of a substance in its physiological functioning.

pituitary gland An endocrine gland that has connections to the brain and secretes hormones that stimulate other endocrine glands to secrete.

placebo An inactive substance or procedure that may cause a change in an individual's behavior or health.

polygraph An electromechanical device that assesses the body's arousal by measuring and recording several physiological indexes, such as blood pressure and respiration rate, simultaneously.

pons A portion of the brainstem involved in the control of eye movements and facial expressions.

prevalence The total number of cases existing at a given moment in time.

primary appraisal The cognitive process people use in assessing the meaning of a demand for their well-being.

primary prevention Actions undertaken to avoid health problems before they occur.

problem drinkers People who are psychologically dependent on alcohol and drink heavily.

problem-focused coping Approaches people use for managing stress aimed at reducing the discrepancy between their resources and the demands of the situation.

progressive muscle relaxation A stress reduction technique in which people are trained to alternately tighten and relax specific muscle groups.

prospective approach A research strategy whereby characteristics of subjects are measured and later examined for their relation to future conditions, such as health problems.

psychological dependence A state in which people feel compelled to use a substance for the pleasant effect it produces.

psychoneuroimmunology A field of study focusing on relationships between psychosocial processes and nervous, endocrine, and immune system functioning.

psychophysiological disorders Physical symptoms or illnesses resulting from some combination of psychosocial and physiological processes.

Psychosocial Adjustment to Illness Scale (PAIS) A test of several psychosocial aspects of a patient's life that are related to adjustment to medical illness.

psychosomatic medicine A field introduced in the 1930s to study the relations between people's symptoms of illness and their emotions.

quasi-experimental studies Nonexperimental research in which subjects are categorized or separated into two or more groups on the basis of existing characteristics and then compared regarding other variables.

rational-emotive therapy (RET) A therapeutic approach for replacing irrational thought patterns that provoke stress with thought patterns that are more realistic.

reactance People's angry response to restrictions on their freedom of action or choice.

reactivity The physiological component of the response to stress.

referred pain The experience of discomfort as coming from an area of the body other than where the injury exists.

respiratory system A network of organs that supply oxygen for metabolism and expel carbon dioxide.

restraint theory An explanation of eating regulation that proposes that people who constantly try to resist eating what they want tend to develop abnormal eating patterns in which they vacillate between inhibited and disinhibited consumption.

reticular system A portion of the brainstem that contains control centers for sleep, arousal, and attention.

retrospective approach A research strategy whereby the past histories of subjects are examined for their relation to recent conditions, such as health problems.

retrospective control A form of personal control involving the ability to reduce the impact of a stressor by developing beliefs about the cause or meaning of an unfavorable event that occurred.

risk factors Characteristics or conditions that occur more often among individuals who develop a disease or injury than among those who do not.

secondary appraisal The cognitive process people use in assessing the resources they have to meet demands.

secondary prevention Actions undertaken to identify or treat a health problem early with the aim of arresting or reversing the condition.

self-efficacy People's belief that they can succeed at something they want to do.

self-management strategies Methods used in helping people gain control over the conditions in their environment that encourage an undesirable behavior.

separation distress Emotional upset often shown by infants and young children when separated from their primary caretaker, typically their parent.

set-point theory An explanation of weight regulation that proposes that each person has a "set" physiologically based weight level that the body strives to maintain.

sick-role behavior Activity by individuals who consider themselves to be ill for the purpose of becoming well.

single-subject design A research approach in which a variable is observed in one individual during two or more research conditions.

social network A person's linkages with other people, as assessed by various qualitative and quantitative measures of social contacts.

social support The perceived comfort, caring, esteem, or help an individual receives from other people or groups.

somatic nervous system A division of the peripheral nervous system that transmits sensory and motor impulses.

spinal cord The major neural pathway that carries impulses between the brain and the peripheral nervous system.

spinal cord injury Neurological damage in the spine that impairs motor and sensory function.

stage of exhaustion The third stage in the general adaptation syndrome, when the body's energy reserves are severely depleted.

stage of resistance The second stage in the general adaptation syndrome, when the body tries to adapt to the stressor.

stimulation-produced analgesia (SPA) A phenomenon whereby stimulation to the brainstem causes insensitivity to pain.

strain The psychological and physiological response to a stressor.

stress The condition that results when person/environment transactions lead the individual to perceive a discrepancy between the demands of a situation and the person's resources.

stress-inoculation training A cognitive/behavioral approach for stress management that teaches people a variety of skills for alleviating stress and achieving personal goals.

stressors Events or circumstances a person perceives as threatening or harmful.

stimulants Drugs that activate the nervous system, producing physiological and psychological arousal.

stroke A condition involving brain damage that results from a disruption in the blood supply to that region.

substance abuse The prolonged overuse of a substance, involving a clear pattern of pathological use and heightened social and occupational problems.

sympathetic nervous system A division of the autonomic nervous system that enables the body to mobilize and expend energy during physical and emotional arousal.

system A continuously changing entity that consists of constantly interrelated components.

systematic desensitization A classical conditioning technique for reducing fear or anxiety by replacing it with a calm response.

tars Tiny particles in cigarette smoke.

T-cells A class of lymphocytes; some attack antigens directly and some work to regulate other immune functions.

temperaments Basic personality characteristics or dispositions that individuals show right from birth, allowing many of them to be classified broadly as "easy" or "difficult."

tertiary prevention Actions undertaken to contain or slow the progress of damage from a serious or established health problem.

thalamus A structure in the forebrain that serves as a relay station for sensory impulses to and commands from the cerebrum.

theory A tentative explanation of phenomena.

theory of reasoned action An explanation of people's health-related behavior. Their behavior depends on their intention, which is based on their attitudes and beliefs regarding the behavior and the subjective norm.

time management Methods for managing stress that involve organizing one's time.

tolerance A gradual decrease in the body's response to a drug, thereby requiring larger and larger doses to achieve the same effect.

transactions The continuous interplay and adjustments of the person and environment.

transcutaneous electrical nerve stimulation (TENS) A counter-irritation pain control technique that involves electrically stimulating an area near where the patient feels pain.

treatment delay The elapsed time between noticing a symptom and getting medical care.

twin studies Research to assess the influence of heredity in determining a characteristic by focusing on differences between identical and fraternal twins.

Type A behavior pattern A behavioral or emotional style characterized by high levels of competitiveness, time urgency, and anger or hostility.

Type B behavior pattern A behavioral or emotional style characterized by low levels of competitiveness, time urgency, and anger or hostility.

ulcers A psychophysiological disorder involving wounds to the stomach or upper section of the small intestine.

variable A measurable characteristic of people, objects, or events that may change in quantity or quality.

very-low-density lipoproteins (VLDL) A cholesterol-carrying protein that is associated with increased deposits of cholesterol in blood vessels.

withdrawal Physical and psychological symptoms that occur when people stop taking a substance on which the body has become physically dependent.

references

ABRAMS, D. B., NIAURA, R. S., CAREY, K. B., MONTI, P. M., & BINKOFF, J. A. (1986). Understanding relapse and recovery in alcohol abuse. *Annals of Behavioral Medicine, 8*(2-3), 27-32.

ABRAMS, R. D. (1966). The patient with cancer—His changing pattern of communication. *New England Journal of Medicine, 274,* 317-322.

ABRAMSON, L. Y., SELIGMAN, M. E. P., & TEASDALE, J. D. (1978). Learned helplessness in humans: Critique and reformulation. *Journal of Abnormal Psychology, 87,* 49-74.

ACHTERBERG-LAWLIS, J. (1988). Musculoskeletal disorders. In E. A. Blechman & K. D. Brownell (Eds.), *Handbook of behavioral medicine for women.* New York: Pergamon.

ADAMS, J. E., & LINDEMANN, E. (1974). Coping with long-term disability. In G. V. Coelho, D. A. Hamburg, & J. E. Adams (Eds.), *Coping and adaptation.* New York: Basic Books.

ADER, R., & COHEN, N. (1975). Behaviorally conditioned immunosuppression. *Psychosomatic Medicine, 37,* 333-340.

ADER, R., & COHEN, N. (1985). CNS-immune system interactions: Conditioning phenomena. *Behavioral and Brain Sciences, 8,* 379-395.

ADESSO, V. J. (1985). Cognitive factors in alcohol and drug use. In M. Galizio & S. A. Maisto (Eds.), *Determinants of substance abuse: Biological, psychological, and environmental factors.* New York: Plenum.

ADLER, N. E., & STONE, G. C. (1979). Social science perspectives on the health system. In G. C. Stone, F. Cohen, & N. E. Adler (Eds.), *Health psychology—A handbook.* San Francisco: Jossey-Bass.

AFFLECK, G., TENNEN, H., PFEIFER, C., & FIFIELD, J. (1987). Appraisals of control and predictability in adapting to a chronic disease. *Journal of Personality and Social Psychology, 53,* 273-279.

AGOSTI, J. M., SPRENGER, J. D., LUM, L. G., WITHERSPOON, R. P., FISHER, L. D., STORB, R., & HENDERSON, W. R. (1988). Transfer of allergen-specific IgE-mediated hypersensitivity with allogenic bone marrow transplantation. *New England Journal of Medicine, 319,* 1623-1628.

AGRAS, W. S. (1984). The behavioral treatment of somatic disorders. In W. D. Gentry (Eds.), *Handbook of behavioral medicine.* New York: Guilford.

AGRAS, W. S. (1987). *Eating disorders: Management of obesity, bulimia, and anorexia nervosa.* New York: Pergamon.

AGRAS, W. S., & MCCANN, U. (1987). The efficacy and role of antidepressants in the treatment of bulimia nervosa. *Annals of Behavioral Medicine, 9*(4), 18-22.

AIKEN, L. H. (1983). Nurses. In D. Mechanic (Ed.), *Handbook of health, health care, and the health professions.* New York: Free Press.

AINSWORTH, M. D. S. (1973). The development of infant-mother attachment. In B. M. Caldwell & H. N. Ricciuti (Eds.), *Review of child development research* (Vol. 3). Chicago: University of Chicago Press.

AINSWORTH, M. D. S. (1979). Infant-mother attachment. *American Psychologist, 34,* 932-937.

AJZEN, I., & FISHBEIN, M. (1980). *Understanding attitudes and predicting social behavior.* Englewood Cliffs, NJ: Prentice-Hall.

AKIL, H., MAYER, D. J., & LIEBESKIND, J. C. (1976). Antagonism of stimulation-produced analgesia by naloxone, a narcotic antagonist. *Science, 191,* 961-962.

ALAGNA, S. W., & REDDY, D. M. (1984). Predictors of proficient technique and successful lesion detection in breast self-examination. *Health Psychology, 3,* 113-127.

ALDERMAN, M. H. (1984). Worksite treatment of hypertension. In J. D. Matarazzo, S. M. Weiss, J. A. Herd, N. E. Miller, & S. M. Weiss (Eds.), *Behavioral health: A handbook of health enhancement and disease prevention.* New York: Wiley.

ALEXANDER, F. (1939). Psychological aspects of medicine. *Psychosomatic Medicine, 1,* 7-18.

ALEXANDER, F. (1950). *Psychosomatic medicine: Its principles and applications.* New York: Norton.

ALEXANDER, J. A. (1984). Blood pressure and obesity. In J. D. Matarazzo, S. M. Weiss, J. A. Herd, N. E. Miller, & S. M. Weiss (Eds.), *Behavioral health: A handbook of health enhancement and disease prevention.* New York: Wiley.

ALLEN, L., & ZIGLER, E. (1986). Psychosocial adjustment of seriously ill children. *Journal of the American Academy of Child Psychiatry, 25,* 708-712.

ALTMAN, L. K. (1986, September 28). Viruses: Still a mystery after all these years. *New York Times Magazine* (Part 2), pp. 16-61.

ALTMAN, L. K. (1988, January 26). Cocaine's many dangers: The evidence mounts. *New York Times,* p. C1.

AMARAL, P. L. (1986). The special case of compliance in the elderly. In K. E. Gerber & A. M. Nehemkis (Eds.), *Compliance: The dilemma of the chronically ill.* New York: Springer.

AMERICAN CANCER SOCIETY (1989). *Cancer facts and figures — 1989.* Atlanta: American Cancer Society.

AMES, G. M., & JANES, C. R. (1987). Heavy and problem drinking in an American blue-collar population: Implications for prevention. *Social Science and Medicine, 25,* 949-960.

AMIR, D. (1987). Preventive behaviour and health status among the elderly. *Psychology and Health, 1,* 353-377.

AMOS, C. I., HUNTER, S. M., ZINKGRAF, S. A., MINER, M. H., & BERENSON, G. S. (1987). Characterization of a comprehensive Type A measure for children in a biracial community: The Bogalusa Heart Study. *Journal of Behavioral Medicine, 10,* 425-439.

ANASTASI, A. (1982). *Psychological testing* (5th ed.). New York: Macmillan Co.

ANDA, R. F., REMINGTON, P. L., SIENKO, D. G., & DAVIS, R. M. (1987). Are physicians advising smokers to quit? The patient's perspective. *Journal of the American Medical Association, 257,* 1916-1919.

ANDERSEN, B. L., & HACKER, N. F. (1983). Treatment for gynecologic cancer: A review of the effects on female sexuality. *Health Psychology, 2,* 203-221.

ANDERSEN, B. L., KARLSSON, J. A., ANDERSON, B., & TEWFIK, H. H. (1984). Anxiety and cancer treatment: Response to stressful radiotherapy. *Health Psychology, 3,* 535-551.

ANDERSON, A. (1982, July). Neurotoxic follies. *Psychology Today, 16,* pp. 30-42.

ANDERSON, E. A. (1987). Preoperative preparation for cardiac surgery facilitates recovery, reduces psychological distress, and reduces the incidence of acute postoperative hypertension. *Journal of Consulting and Clinical Psychology, 55,* 513-520.

ANDERSON, K. O., BRADLEY, L. A., YOUNG, L. D., MCDANIEL, L. K., & WISE, C. M. (1985). Rheumatoid arthritis: Review of psychological factors related to etiology, effects, and treatment. *Psychological Bulletin, 98,* 358-387.

ANDERSON, K. O., & MASUR, F. T. (1983). Psychological preparation for invasive medical and dental procedures. *Journal of Behavioral Medicine, 6,* 1-40.

ANDERSON, O. W., & GEVITZ, N. (1983). The general hospital: A social and historical perspective. In D. Mechanic (Ed.), *Handbook of health, health care, and the health professions.* New York: Free Press.

ANDRASIK, F. (1986). Relaxation and biofeedback for chronic headaches. In A. D. Holzman & D. C. Turk (Eds.), *Pain management: A handbook of psychological treatment approaches.* New York: Pergamon.

ANDRASIK, F., BLAKE, D. D., & MCCARRAN, M. S. (1986). A biobehavioral analysis of pediatric headache. In N. A. Krasnegor, J. D. Arasteh, & M. F. Cataldo (Eds.), *Child health behavior: A behavioral pediatrics perspective.* New York: Wiley.

ANDREW, J. M. (1970). Recovery from surgery with and without preparatory instruction for three coping styles. *Journal of Personality and Social Psychology, 15,* 223-226.

ANTONI, M. H. (1987). Neuroendocrine influences in psychoimmunology and neoplasia: A review. *Psychology and Health, 1,* 3-24.

ANTONOVSKY, A. (1979). *Health, stress, and coping.* San Francisco: Jossey-Bass.

ANTONOVSKY, A. (1987). *Unraveling the mystery of health: How people manage stress and stay well.* San Francisco: Jossey-Bass.

ANTONOVSKY, A., & HARTMAN, H. (1974). Delay in the detection of cancer: A review of the literature. *Health Education Monographs, 2,* 98-128.

ANTONUCCI, T. C. (1985). Personal characteristics, social support, and social behavior. In R. H. Binstock & E. Shanas (Eds.), *Handbook of aging and the social sciences* (2nd ed.). New York: Van Nostrand-Reinhold.

ANTONUCCIO, D. O., & LICHTENSTEIN, E. (1980). Peer modeling influences on smoking behavior of heavy and light smokers. *Addictive Behaviors, 5,* 299-306.

APPEL, G. B., & CAHILL, L. (1986). Dialysis in the elderly—Another look. In M. A. Hardy, G. B. Appel, J. M. Kiernan, A. H. Kutscher, M. L. Orr, C. S. Torres, & L. Parsonnet (Eds.), *Positive approaches to living with end stage renal disease.* New York: Praeger.

ARMOR, D. J., POLICH, J. M., & STAMBUL, H. B. (1978). *Alcoholism and treatment.* New York: Wiley.

ARMSTRONG, S. (1984). End-stage renal disease. In H. B. Roback (Ed.), *Helping patients and their families cope with medical problems.* San Francisco: Jossey-Bass.

ARONOFF, G. M., WAGNER, J. M., & SPANGLER, A. S. (1986). Chemical interventions for pain. *Journal of Consulting and Clinical Psychology, 54,* 769-775.

ARY, D. V., & BIGLAN, A. (1988). Longitudinal changes in adolescent cigarette smoking behavior: Onset and cessation. *Journal of Behavioral Medicine, 11,* 361-382.

ASHBURN, S. S. (1986). Biophysical development of the toddler and the preschooler. In C. S. Schuster & S. S. Ashburn (Eds.), *The process of human development: A holistic life-span approach* (2nd ed.). Boston: Little, Brown.

ASHLEY, M. J., & RANKIN, J. G. (1988). A public health approach to the prevention of alcohol-related health problems. In L. Breslow, J. E. Fielding, & L. B. Lave (Eds.), *Annual review of public health* (Vol. 9). Palo Alto, CA: Annual Reviews.

ASHTON, H., & STEPNEY, R. (1982). *Smoking: Psychology and pharmacology.* London: Tavistock.

ASKEVOLD, F. (1975). Measuring body image. *Psychotherapy and Psychosomatics, 26,* 71-77.

ATTANASIO, V., ANDRASIK, F., BURKE, E. J., BLAKE, D. D., KABELA, E., & MCCARRAN, M. S. (1985). Clinical issues in utilizing biofeedback with children. *Clinical Biofeedback and Health, 8,* 134-141.

AUERBACH, S. M., MARTELLI, M. F., & MERCURI, L. G. (1983).

Anxiety, information, interpersonal impacts, and adjustment to a stressful health care situation. *Journal of Personality and Social Psychology, 44,* 1284-1296.

AVERILL, J. R. (1973). Personal control over aversive stimuli and its relationship to stress. *Psychological Bulletin, 80,* 286-303.

BAER, J. S., HOLT, C. S., & LICHTENSTEIN, E. (1986). Self-efficacy and smoking reexamined: Construct validity and clinical utility. *Journal of Consulting and Clinical Psychology, 54,* 846-852.

BAER, P. E., GARMEZY, L. B., MCLAUGHLIN, R. J., POKORNY, A. D., & WERNICK, M. J. (1987). Stress, coping, family conflict, and adolescent alcohol use. *Journal of Behavioral Medicine, 10,* 449-466.

BAGOZZI, R. P. (1981). Attitudes, intentions, and behavior: A test of some key hypotheses. *Journal of Personality and Social Psychology, 41,* 606-627.

BAKAL, D. A. (1979). *Psychology and medicine: Psychological dimensions of health and illness.* New York: Springer.

BAKER, E. L. (1988). Organic solvent neurotoxicity. In L. Breslow, J. E. Fielding, & L. B. Lave (Eds.), *Annual review of public health* (Vol. 9). Palo Alto, CA: Annual Reviews.

BAKWIN, H., & BAKWIN, R. M. (1972). *Behavior disorders in children.* Philadelphia: Saunders.

BALL, J. F. (1976-1977). Widow's grief: The impact of age and mode of health. *Omega, 7,* 307-333.

BANDURA, A. (1965a). Influence of model's reinforcement contingencies on the acquisition of imitative responses. *Journal of Personality and Social Psychology, 1,* 589-595.

BANDURA, A. (1965b). Vicarious processes: A case of no-trial learning. In L. Berkowitz (Ed.), *Advances in experimental social psychology* (Vol. 2). New York: Academic Press.

BANDURA, A. (1969). *Principles of behavior modification.* New York: Holt, Rinehart & Winston.

BANDURA, A. (1977). Self-efficacy: Toward a unifying theory of behavioral change. *Psychological Review, 84,* 191-215.

BANDURA, A. (1986). *Social foundations of thought and action: A social cognitive theory.* Englewood Cliffs, NJ: Prentice-Hall.

BANDURA, A., O'LEARY, A., TAYLOR, C. B., GAUTHIER, J., & GOSSARD, D. (1987). Perceived self-efficacy and pain control: Opioid and nonopioid mechanisms. *Journal of Personality and Social Psychology, 53,* 563-571.

BANDURA, A., REESE, L., & ADAMS, N. E. (1982). Microanalysis of action and fear arousal as a function of differential levels of perceived self-efficacy. *Journal of Personality and Social Psychology, 43,* 5-21.

BANDURA, A., TAYLOR, C. B., WILLIAMS, S. L., MEFFORD, I. N., & BARCHAS, J. D. (1985). Catecholamine secretion as a function of perceived coping self-efficacy. *Journal of Consulting and Clinical Psychology, 53,* 406-414.

BANWELL, B. F. (1984). Therapeutic heat and cold. In G. K. Riggs & E. P. Gall (Eds.), *Rheumatic diseases: Rehabilitation and management.* Boston: Butterworth.

BARANOWSKI, T., & NADER, P. R. (1985). Family health behavior. In D. C. Turk & R. D. Kerns (Eds.), *Health, illness, and families: A life-span perspective.* New York: Wiley.

BARBER, J. (1986). Hypnotic analgesia. In A. D. Holzman & D. C. Turk (Eds.), *Pain management: A handbook of psychological treatment approaches.* New York: Pergamon.

BARDO, M. T., & RISNER, M. E. (1985). Biochemical substrates of drug abuse. In M. Galizio & S. A. Maisto (Eds.), *Determinants of substance abuse: Biological, psychological, and environmental factors.* New York: Plenum.

BAREFOOT, J. C., DAHLSTROM, W. G., & WILLIAMS, R. B. (1983). Hostility, CHD incidence and total mortality: A 25-year follow-up study of 255 physicians. *Psychosomatic Medicine, 45,* 559-563.

BARON, R. A. (1986). *Behavior in organizations: Understanding and managing the human side of work* (2nd ed.). Boston: Allyn & Bacon.

BARRETT, R. J. (1985). Behavioral approaches to individual differences in substance abuse. In M. Galizio & S. A. Maisto (Eds.), *Determinants of substance abuse: Biological, psychological, and environmental factors.* New York: Plenum.

BARSKY, A. J., & KLERMAN, G. L. (1983). Overview: Hypochondriasis, bodily complaints, and somatic styles. *American Journal of Psychiatry, 140,* 273-283.

BARTON, J., CHASSIN, L., PRESSON, C. C., & SHERMAN, S. J. (1982). Social image factors as motivators of smoking initiation in early and middle adolescence. *Child Development, 53,* 1499-1511.

BATCHELOR, W. F. (1988). AIDS 1988: The science and the limits of science. *American Psychologist, 43,* 853-858.

BATTEN, M. (1986). Life spans. In M. G. Walraven & H. E. Fitzgerald (Eds.), *Annual Editions: Psychology 86/87.* Guilford, CT: Dushkin.

BATTISTA, R. N., & GROVER, S. A. (1988). Early detection of cancer: An overview. In L. Breslow, J. E. Fielding, & L. B. Lave (Eds.), *Annual review of public health* (Vol. 9). Palo Alto, CA: Annual Reviews.

BAUM, A. (1988, April). Disasters, natural & otherwise. *Psychology Today, 22,* pp. 56-60.

BAUM, A., AIELLO, J. R., & CALESNICK, L. E. (1978). Crowding and personal control: Social density and the development of learned helplessness. *Journal of Personality and Social Psychology, 36,* 1000-1011.

BAUM, A., & GATCHEL, R. J. (1981). Cognitive determinants of reaction to uncontrollable events: Development of reactance and learned helplessness. *Journal of Personality and Social Psychology, 40,* 1078-1089.

BAUM, A., GRUNBERG, N. E., & SINGER, J. E. (1982). The use of physiological and neuroendocrinological measurements in the study of stress. *Health Psychology, 1,* 217-236.

BAUMANN, L.J., & LEVENTHAL, H. (1985). "I can tell when my blood pressure is up, can't I?" *Health Psychology, 4,* 203-218.

BECK, A. T. (1976). *Cognitive therapy and the emotional disorders.* New York: International Universities Press.

BECK, A. T., & SHAW, B. F. (1977). Cognitive approaches to depression. In A. Ellis & R. Grieger (Eds.), *Handbook of rational-emotive therapy.* New York: Springer.

BECKER, M. H. (1979). Understanding patient compliance: The contributions of attitudes and other psychosocial factors. In S. J. Cohen (Ed.), *New directions in patient compliance.* Lexington, MA: Heath.

BECKER, M. H., MAIMAN, L. A., KIRSCHT, J. P., HAEFNER, D. P., & DRACHMAN, R. H. (1977). The health belief model and prediction of dietary compliance: A field experiment. *Journal of Health and Social Behavior, 18,* 348-366.

BECKER, M. H., & ROSENSTOCK, I. M. (1984). Compliance with medical advice. In A. Steptoe & A. Mathews (Eds.), *Health care and human behaviour.* London: Academic Press.

BEECHER, H.K. (1956). Relationship of significance of wound to pain experienced. *Journal of the American Medical Association, 161,* 1609-1613.

BELAR, C. D., & KIBRICK, S. A. (1986). Biofeedback in the treatment of chronic back pain. In A. D. Holzman & D. C. Turk (Eds.), *Pain management: A handbook of psychological treatment approaches.* New York: Pergamon.

BÉLISLE, M., ROSKIES, E., & LÉVESQUE, J. (1987). Improving adherence to physical activity. *Health Psychology, 6,* 159-172.

BELLOC, N. B., & BRESLOW, L. (1972). Relationship of physical health status and health practices. *Preventive Medicine, 1,* 409-421.

BENGSTON, V. L., CUELLAR, J. B., & RAGAN, P. K. (1977). Stratum contrasts and similarities in attitudes toward death. *Journal of Gerontology, 32,* 76-88.

BENNETT, W., & GURIN, J. (1982). *The dieter's dilemma: Eating less and weighing more.* New York: Basic Books.

BENNETT, W. I. (1987, December 13). Monitoring drugs for the aged. *New York Times Magazine,* pp. 73-74.

BENNETT, W. I. (1988, January 10). The drink-a-day lore. *New York Times Magazine,* pp. 55-56.

BENOLIEL, J. Q. (1977). Nurses and the human experience of dying. In H. Feifel (Ed.), *New meanings of death.* New York: McGraw-Hill.

BEN-SIRA, Z. (1980). Affective and instrumental components in the physician-patient relationship: An additional dimension of interaction theory. *Journal of Health and Social Behavior, 21,* 170-180.

BENSON, H. (1984). The relaxation response and stress. In J. D. Matarazzo, S. M. Weiss, J. A. Herd, N. E. Miller, & S. M. Weiss (Eds.), *Behavioral health: A handbook of health enhancement and disease prevention.* New York: Wiley.

BENTLER, P. M., & SPECKART, G. (1979). Models of attitude-behavior relations. *Psychological Review, 86,* 452-464.

BENVENISTY, A. I., & HARDY, M. A. (1986). Renal transplantation: An overview. In M. A. Hardy, G. B. Appel, J. M. Kiernan, A. H. Kutscher, M. L. Orr, C. S. Torres, & L. Parsonnet (Eds.), *Positive approaches to living with end stage renal disease.* New York: Praeger.

BERGMAN, L. R., & MAGNUSSON, D. (1986). Type A behavior: A longitudinal study from childhood to adulthood. *Psychosomatic Medicine, 48,* 134-142.

BERKMAN, L. F., & SYME, S. L. (1979). Social networks, host resistance, and mortality: A nine-year follow-up study of Alameda County residents. *American Journal of Epidemiology, 109,* 186-204.

BERKOWITZ, R. I. (1983). Physical activity, eating style, and obesity in children: A review. *Behavioral Medicine Update, 5*(1), 9-14.

BERREN, M. R., BEIGEL, A., & GHERTNER, S. (1986). A typology for the classification of disasters. In R. H. Moos (Ed.), *Coping with life crises: An integrated approach.* New York: Plenum.

BERTALANFFY, L. VON (1968). *General systems theory.* New York: Braziller.

BEST, J. A., THOMSON, S. J., SANTI, S. M., SMITH, E. A., & BROWN, K. S. (1988). Preventing cigarette smoking among school children. In L. Breslow, J. E. Fielding, & L. B. Lave (Eds.), *Annual review of psychology* (Vol. 9). Palo Alto, CA: Annual Reviews.

BIBACE, R., & WALSH, M. E. (1979). Developmental stages in children's conceptions of illness. In G. C. Stone, F. Cohen, & N. E. Adler (Eds.), *Health psychology—A handbook.* San Francisco: Jossey-Bass.

BIGLAN, A., MCCONNELL, S., SEVERSON, H. H., BAVRY, J., & ARY, D. (1984). A situational analysis of adolescent smoking. *Journal of Behavioral Medicine, 7,* 109-114.

BIGLAN, A., SEVERSON, H., ARY, D., FALLER, C., GALLISON, C., THOMPSON, R., GLASGOW, R., & LICHTENSTEIN, E. (1987). Do smoking prevention programs really work? Attrition and the internal and external validity of an evaluation of a refusal skills training program. *Journal of Behavioral Medicine, 10,* 159-171.

BILLINGS, A. G., & MOOS, R. H. (1981). The role of coping responses and social resources in attenuating the stress of life events. *Journal of Behavioral Medicine, 4,* 139-157.

BILLINGS, A. G., MOOS, R. H., MILLER, J. J., & GOTTLIEB, J. E. (1987). Psychosocial adaptation in juvenile rheumatic disease: A controlled evaluation. *Health Psychology, 6,* 343-359.

BIRREN, J. E., & ZARIT, J. M. (1985). Concepts of health, behavior, and aging. In J. E. Birren & J. Livingston (Eds.), *Cognition, stress, and aging.* Englewood Cliffs, NJ: Prentice-Hall.

BISHOP, G. D., & CONVERSE, S. A. Illness representations: a prototype approach. *Health Psychology, 5,* 95-114.

BLACKBURN, H., LUEPKER, R., KLINE, F. G., BRACHT, N., CARLAW, R., JACOBS, D., MITTELMARK, M., STAUFFER, L., & TAYLOR, H. L. (1984). The Minnesota Heart Health Program: A research and demonstration project in cardiovascular disease prevention. In J. D. Matarazzo, S. M. Weiss, J. A. Herd, N. E. Miller, & S. M. Weiss (Eds.), *Behavioral health: A handbook of health enhancement and disease prevention.* New York: Wiley.

BLAKESLEE, S. (1987, March 29). Nicotine: Harder to kick than heroin. *New York Times Magazine,* pp. 22-23, 49-53.

BLAKESLEE, S. (1988, March 24). Asthma doctors puzzled as the death rate rises despite improved drugs. *New York Times,* p. B6.

BLANCHARD, E. B. (1987). Long-term effects of behavioral treatment of chronic headache. *Behavior Therapy, 18,* 375-385.

BLANCHARD, E. B., & ANDRASIK, F. (1985). *Management of*

chronic headaches: A psychological approach. New York: Pergamon.

BLANCHARD, E. B., ANDRASIK, F., APPELBAUM, K. A., EVANS, D. D., MYERS, P., & BARRON, K. D. (1986). Three studies of the psychologic changes in chronic headache patients associated with biofeedback and relaxation therapies. *Psychosomatic Medicine, 48,* 73-83.

BLANCHARD, E. B., ANDRASIK, F., GUARNIERI, P., NEFF, D. F., & RODICHOK, L. D. (1987). Two-, three-, and four-year follow-up on the self-regulatory treatment of chronic headache. *Journal of Consulting and Clinical Psychology, 55,* 257-259.

BLANCHARD, E. B., APPELBAUM, K. A., GUARNIERI, P., MORRILL, B., & DENTINGER, M. P. (1987). Five year prospective follow-up on the treatment of chronic headache with biofeedback and/or relaxation. *Headache, 27,* 580-583.

BLANCHARD, E. B., MCCOY, G. C., WITTROCK, D., MUSSO, A., GERARDI, R. J., & PANGBURN, L. (1988). A controlled comparison of thermal biofeedback and relaxation training in the treatment of essential hypertension: II. Effects on cardiovascular reactivity. *Health Psychology, 7,* 19-33.

BLANEY, N. T. (1985). Smoking: Psychophysiological causes and treatments. In N. Schneiderman & J. T. Tapp (Eds.), *Behavioral medicine: The biopsychosocial approach.* Hillsdale, NJ: Erlbaum.

BLANEY, P. H. (1985). Psychological considerations in cancer. In N. Schneiderman & J. T. Tapp (Eds.), *Behavioral medicine: The biopsychosocial approach.* Hillsdale, NJ: Erlbaum.

BLANKENHORN, D. H., NESSIM, S. A., JOHNSON, R. L., SANMARCO, M. E., AZEN, S. P., & CASHIN-HEMPILL, L. (1987). Beneficial effects of combined colestipol-niacin therapy on coronary atherosclerosis and coronary venous bypass grafts. *Journal of the American Medical Association, 257,* 3233-3240.

BLEIBERG, J. (1986). Psychological and neuropsychological factors in stroke management. In P. E. Kaplan & L. J. Cerullo (Eds.), *Stroke rehabilitation.* Boston: Butterworth.

BLOCK, A. R., KREMER, E., & GAYLOR, M. (1980a). Behavioral treatment of chronic pain: The spouse as a discriminative cue for pain behavior. *Pain, 9,* 243-252.

BLOCK, A. R., KREMER, E., & GAYLOR, M. (1980b). Behavioral treatment of chronic pain: Variables affecting treatment efficacy. *Pain, 8,* 367-375.

BLOCK, J. H. (1983). Differential premises arising from differential socialization of the sexes: Some conjectures. *Child Development, 54,* 1335-1354.

BLOCK, M. A. (1976). Don't place alcohol on a pedestal. *Journal of the American Medical Association, 235,* 2103-2104.

BLOOM, F. E., LAZERSON, A., & HOFSTADTER, L. (1985). *Brain, mind, and behavior.* New York: Freeman.

BLOOM, J. W., KALTENBORN, W. T., PAOLETTI, P., CAMILLI, A., & LEBOWITZ, M. D. (1987). Respiratory effects of non-tobacco cigarettes. *British Medical Journal, 295,* 1516-1518.

BLUEBOND-LANGNER, M. (1977). Meanings of death to children. In H. Feifel (Ed.), *New meanings of death.* New York: McGraw-Hill.

BLUMENTHAL, J. A., & MCCUBBIN, J. A. (1987). Physical exercise as stress management. In A. Baum & J. E. Singer (Eds.), *Handbook of psychology and health* (Vol. 5). Hillsdale, NJ: Erlbaum.

BLUMENTHAL, J. A., WILLIAMS, R. S., NEEDLES, T. L., & WALLACE, A. G. (1982). Psychological changes accompany aerobic exercise in healthy middle-aged adults. *Psychosomatic Medicine, 44,* 529-536.

BLUMENTHAL, J. A., WILLIAMS, R. S., WALLACE, A. G., WILLIAMS, R. B., & NEEDLES, T. L. (1982). Physiological and psychological variables predict compliance to prescribed exercise therapy in patients recovering from myocardial infarction. *Psychosomatic Medicine, 44,* 519-527.

BLUMER, D., & HEILBRONN, M. (1982). Chronic pain as a variant of depressive disease: The pain-prone disorder. *Journal of Nervous and Mental Disease, 170,* 381-406.

BODMER, W. F., BAILEY, C. J., BODMER, J., BUSSEY, H. J. R., ELLIS, A., GORMAN, P., LUCIBELLO, F. C., MURDAY, V. A., RIDER, S. H., SCAMBLER, P., SHEER, D., SOLOMON, E., & SPURR, N. K. (1987). Localization of the gene for familial adenomatous polyposis on chromosome 5. *Nature, 328,* 614-616.

BOFFEY, P. M. (1987, April 16). Gains against cancer since 1950 are overstated, Congress is told. *New York Times,* pp. A1, B10.

BOHM, L. C., & RODIN, J. (1985). Aging and the family. In D. C. Turk & R. D. Kerns (Eds.), *Health, illness, and families: A life-span perspective.* New York: Wiley.

BONITA, R., SCRAGG, R., STEWART, A., JACKSON, R., & BEAGLEHOLE, R. (1986). Cigarette smoking and risk of premature stroke in men and women. *British Medical Journal, 293,* 6-8.

BOOTH-KEWLEY, S., & FRIEDMAN, H. S. (1987). Psychological predictors of heart disease: A quantitative review. *Psychological Bulletin, 101,* 343-362.

BÖRJESON, M. (1980). The etiology of obesity in children. In P. J. Collipp (Ed.), *Childhood obesity* (2nd ed.). Littleton, MA: PSG Publishing.

BORYSENKO, J. (1984). Stress, coping, and the immune system. In J. D. Matarazzo, S. M. Weiss, J. A. Herd, N. E. Miller, & S. M. Weiss (Eds.), *Behavioral health: A handbook of health enhancement and disease prevention.* New York: Wiley.

BOTVIN, G. J., RENICK, N. L., & BAKER, E. (1983). The effects of scheduling format and booster sessions on a broad-spectrum psychosocial approach to smoking prevention. *Journal of Behavioral Medicine, 6,* 359-379.

BOTVIN, G. J., & WILLS, T. A. (1985). Personal and social skills training: Cognitive-behavioral approaches to substance abuse prevention. In C. S. Bell & R. Battjes (Eds.), *Prevention research: Deterring drug abuse among children and adolescents* (NIDA Research Monograph 63). Washington, DC: U.S. Government Printing Office.

BOWES, W. A., BRACKBILL, Y., CONWAY, E., & STEINSCHNEIDER, A. (1970). The effects of obstetrical medication on fetus and infant. *Monographs of the Society for Research in Child Development, 35* (4, Whole No. 137).

BOWLBY, J. (1969). *Attachment and loss. Vol. 1: Attachment.* New York: Basic Books.

BOWLBY, J. (1973). *Attachment and loss. Vol. 2: Separation.* New York: Basic Books.

BRADFORD, L. P. (1986). Can you survive retirement? In R. H. Moos (Ed.), *Coping with life crises: An integrated approach.* New York: Plenum.

BRADLEY, L. A. (1983). Coping with chronic pain. In T. G. Burish & L. A. Bradley (Eds.), *Coping with chronic disease: Research and applications.* New York: Academic Press.

BRADLEY, L. A., & VAN DER HEIDE, L. H. (1984). Pain-related correlates of MMPI profile subgroups among back pain patients. *Health Psychology, 3,* 157-174.

BRAITMAN, L. E., ADLIN, E. V., & STANTON, J. L. (1985). Obesity and caloric intake: The National Health and Nutrition Examination Survey of 1971-1975 (HANES I). *Journal of Chronic Diseases, 9,* 727-732.

BRANDON, T. H., ZELMAN, D. C., & BAKER, T. B. (1987). Effects of maintenance sessions on smoking relapse: Delaying the inevitable? *Journal of Consulting and Clinical psychology, 55,* 780-782.

BRANDSMA, J. M., MAULTSBY, M. C., & WELSH, R. J. (1980). *Outpatient treatment of alcoholism: A review and comparative study.* Baltimore: University Park Press.

BRAVEMAN, N. S. (1987). Immunity and aging: Immunologic and behavioral perspectives. In M. W. Riley, J. D. Matarazzo, & A. Baum (Eds.), *Perspectives in behavioral medicine: The aging dimension.* Hillsdale, NJ: Erlbaum.

BRAY, G. A. (1984). The role of weight control in health promotion and disease prevention. In J. D. Matarazzo, S. M. Weiss, J. A. Herd, N. E. Miller, & S. M. Weiss (Eds.), *Behavioral health: A handbook of health enhancement and disease prevention.* New York: Wiley.

BREHM, J. W. (1966). *A theory of psychological reactance.* New York: Academic Press.

BRENNAN, A. F., BARRETT, C. L., & GARRETSON, H. D. (1987). The utility of McGill Pain Questionnaire subscales for discriminating psychological disorder in chronic pain patients. *Psychology and Health, 1,* 257-272.

BRESLOW, L. (1983). The potential of health promotion. In D. Mechanic (Ed.), *Handbook of health, health care, and the health professions.* New York: Free Press.

BRESLOW, L. & SOMERS, A. R. (1977). The lifetime health-monitoring program. *New England Journal of Medicine, 296,* 601-608.

BRISTOL, J. B., EMMETT, P. M., HEATON, K. W., & WILLIAMSON, R. C. N. (1985). Sugar, fat, and the risk of colorectal cancer. *British Medical Journal, 291,* 1467-1470.

BROADHEAD, W. E., KAPLAN, B. H., JAMES, S. A., WAGNER, E. H., SCHOENBACH, V. J., GRIMSON, R., HEYDEN, S., TIBBLIN, G., & GEHLBACH, S. H. (1983). The epidemiologic evidence for a relationship between social support and health. *American Journal of Epidemiology, 117,* 521-537.

BROBERG, D. J., & BERNSTEIN, I. L. (1987). Candy as a scapegoat in the prevention of food aversions in children receiving chemotherapy. *Cancer, 60,* 2344-2347.

BRODY, J. E. (1987, March 11). Personal health. *New York Times,* p. C10.

BROOK, J. S., WHITEMAN, M., & GORDON, A. S. (1983). Stages in drug use in adolescence: Personality, peer, and family correlates. *Developmental Psychology, 19,* 269-277.

BROOK, J. S., WHITEMAN, M., GORDON, A. S., & COHEN, P. (1986). Dynamics of childhood and adolescent personality traits and adolescent drug use. *Developmental Psychology, 22,* 403-414.

BROOKS-GUNN, J., BOYER, C. B., & HEIN, K. (1988). Preventing HIV infection and AIDS in children and adolescents. *American Psychologist, 43,* 958-964.

BROWN, J. M., O'KEEFFE, J., SANDERS, S. H., & BAKER, B. (1986). Developmental changes in children's cognition to stressful and painful situations. *Journal of Pediatric Psychology, 11,* 343-357.

BROWNELL, K. D. (1982). Obesity: Understanding and treating a serious, prevalent, and refractory disorder. *Journal of Consulting and Clinical Psychology, 50,* 820-840.

BROWNELL, K. D. (1986a). Public health approaches to obesity and its management. In L. Breslow, J. E. Fielding, & L. B. Lave (Eds.), *Annual review of public health* (Vol. 7). Palo Alto, CA: Annual Reviews.

BROWNELL, K. D. (1986b). Social and behavioral aspects of obesity in children. In N. A. Krasnegor, J. D. Arasteh, & M. F. Cataldo (Eds.), *Child health behavior: A behavioral pediatrics perspective.* New York: Wiley.

BROWNELL, K. D. (1988, January). Yo-yo dieting. *Psychology Today, 22,* pp. 20-23.

BROWNELL, K. D., COHEN, R. Y., STUNKARD, A. J., FELIX, M. R. J., & COOLEY, N. B. (1984). Weight loss competitions at the work site: Impact on weight, morale and cost-effectiveness. *American Journal of Public Health, 74,* 1283-1285.

BROWNELL, K. D., MARLATT, G. A., LICHTENSTEIN, E., & WILSON, G. T. (1986). Understanding and preventing relapse. *American Psychologist, 41,* 765-782.

BRUCKER, B. S. (1983). Spinal cord injuries. In T. G. Burish & L. A. Bradley (Eds.), *Coping with chronic disease: Research and applications.* New York: Academic press.

BRUHN, J. G., & PHILLIPS, B. U. (1987). A developmental basis for social support. *Journal of Behavioral Medicine, 10,* 213-229.

BRUNSWICK, A. F., & MERZEL, C. R. (1986). Biopsychosocial and epidemiologic perspectives on adolescent health. In N. A. Krasnegor, J. D. Arasteh, & M. F. Cataldo (Eds.), *Child health behavior: A behavioral pediatrics perspective.* New York: Wiley.

BRYER, K. B. (1986). The Amish way of death: A study of family support systems. In R. H. Moos (Ed.), *Coping with life crises: An integrated approach.* New York: Plenum.

BUCK, R. (1988). *Human motivation and emotion* (2nd ed.). New York: Wiley.

BUDZYNSKI, T. H., STOYVA, J. M., ADLER, C. S., & MULLANEY, D. J. (1973). EMG biofeedback and tension headache: A controlled outcome study. *Psychosomatic Medicine, 35,* 484-496.

BULMAN, R. J., & WORTMAN, C. B. (1977). Attributions of blame and coping in the "real world": Severe accident victims react to their lot. *Journal of Personality and Social Psychology, 35,* 351-363.

BURBACH, D. J., & PETERSON, L. (1986). Children's concepts of physical illness: A review and critique of the cognitive-developmental literature. *Health Psychology, 5,* 307-325.

BURG, I. N., & INGALL, C. G. (1985). The immune system. In L. L. Hayman & E. M. Sporing (Eds.), *Handbook of pediatric nursing.* New York: Wiley.

BURISH, T. G., & LYLES, J. N. (1983). Coping with the adverse effects of cancer treatments. In T. G. Burish & L. A. Bradley (Eds.), *Coping with chronic disease: Research and applications.* New York: Academic Press.

BURISH, T. G., MEYEROWITZ, B. E., CAREY, M. P., & MORROW, G. R. (1987). The stressful effects of cancer in adults. In A. Baum & J. E. Singer (Eds.), *Handbook of psychology and health* (Vol. 5). New York: Erlbaum.

BURISH, T. G., & REDD, W. H. (1983). Behavioral approaches to reducing conditioned responses to chemotherapy in adult cancer patients. *Behavioral Medicine Update, 5*(2 & 3), 12-16.

BURLING, T. A., SINGLETON, E. G., BIGELOW, G. E., BAILE, W. F., & GOTTLIEB, S. H. (1984). Smoking following myocardial infarction: A critical review of the literature. *Health Psychology, 3,* 83-96.

BURNETT, K. F., TAYLOR, C. B., & AGRAS, W. S. (1985). Ambulatory computer-assisted therapy for obesity: A new frontier for behavior therapy. *Journal of Consulting and Clinical Psychology, 53,* 698-703.

BURROUGHS, B. R., & DIETERLE, P. (1985). The respiratory system. In L. L. Hayman & E. M. Sporing (Eds.), *Handbook of pediatric nursing.* New York: Wiley.

BUSH, J. P. (1987). Pain in children: A review of the literature from a developmental perspective. *Psychology and Health, 1,* 215-236.

BUSH, J. P., MELAMED, B. G., SHERAS, P. L., & GREENBAUM, P. E. (1986). Mother-child patterns of coping with anticipatory medical stress. *Health Psychology, 5,* 137-157.

BUSS, A. H., & PLOMIN, R. (1975). *A temperamental theory of personality development.* New York: Wiley.

BUSS, A. H., & PLOMIN, R. (1986). The EAS approach to temperament. In R. Plomin & J. Dunn (Eds.), *The study of temperament: Changes, continuities and challenges.* Hillsdale, NJ: Erlbaum.

BUSS, A. R. (1973). An extension of developmental models that separate ontogenetic changes and cohort differences. *Psychological Bulletin, 80,* 466-479.

BUTLER, C., & STEPTOE, A. (1986). Placebo responses: An experimental study of psychophysiological processes in asthmatic volunteers. *British Journal of Clinical Psychology, 25,* 173-183.

BYERS, T. E., GRAHAM, S., HAUGHEY, B. P., MARSHALL, J. R., & SWANSON, M. K. (1987). Diet and lung cancer risk: Findings from the Western New York Diet Study. *American Journal of Epidemiology, 125,* 351-363.

BYRNE, D. G., & ROSENMAN, R. H. (1986). The Type A behaviour pattern as a precursor to stressful life-events: A confluence of coronary risks. *British Journal of Medical Psychology, 59,* 75-82.

BYRNE, D. G., ROSENMAN, R. H., SCHILLER, E., & CHESNEY, M. A. (1985). Consistency and variation among instruments purporting to measure the Type A behavior pattern. *Psychosomatic Medicine, 47,* 242-261.

BYRNE, P. S., & LONG, B. E. L. (1976). *Doctors talking to patients.* London: Her Majesty's Stationery Office.

CACIOPPO, J. T., PETTY, R. E., & MARSHALL-GOODELL, B. (1985). Physical, social, and inferential elements of psychophysiological measurement. In P. Karoly (Ed.), *Measurement strategies in health psychology.* New York: Wiley.

CADMAN, D., BOYLE, M., SZATMARI, P., & OFFORD, D. R. (1987). Chronic illness, disability, and mental and social well-being: Findings of the Ontario Child Health Study. *Pediatrics, 79,* 805-813.

CAGGIULA, A. W., CHRISTAKIS, G., FARRAND, M., HULLEY, S. B., JOHNSON, R., LASSER, N. L., STAMLER, J., & WIDDOWSON, G. (1981). The Multiple Risk Intervention Trial (MRFIT): IV. Intervention on blood lipids. *Preventive Medicine, 10,* 443-475.

CAIN, E. N., KOHORN, E. I., QUINLAN, D. M., LATIMER, K., & SCHWARTZ, P. E. (1986). Psychosocial benefits of a cancer support group. *Cancer, 57,* 183-189.

CALHOUN, K. S., & BURNETTE, M. M. (1983). Etiology and treatment of menstrual disorders. *Behavioral Medicine Update, 5*(4), 21-26.

CALIFANO, J. A. (1979). *Healthy people: The Surgeon General's report on health promotion and disease prevention.* Washington, DC: U.S. Government Printing Office.

CALLAHAN, E. J. (1980). Alternative strategies in the treatment of narcotic addiction: A review. In W. R. Miller (Ed.), *The addictive behaviors: Treatment of alcoholism, drug abuse, smoking, and obesity.* New York: Pergamon.

CAMERON, R., & SHEPEL, L. F. (1986). The process of psychological consultation in pain management. In A. D. Holzman & D. C. Turk (Eds.), *Pain management: A handbook of psychological treatment approaches.* New York: Pergamon.

CAMERON, S. (1986). *Kidney disease: The facts* (2nd ed.). Oxford: Oxford University Press.

CAMPBELL, T., & CHANG, B. (1981). Health care of the Chinese in America. In G. Henderson & M. Primeaux (Eds.), *Transcultural health care.* Menlo Park, CA: Addison-Wesley.

CANNON, J. T., PRIETO, G. J., LEE, A., & LIEBESKIND, J. C. (1982). Evidence for opioid and non-opioid forms of stimulation-produced analgesia in the rat. *Brain Research, 243,* 315-321.

CANNON, W. B. (1929). *Bodily changes in pain, hunger, fear and rage* (2nd ed.). New York: Appleton.

CANNON, W. B. (1942). Voodoo death. *American Anthropologist, 44,* 169-181.

CANTOR, M., & LITTLE, V. (1985). Aging and social care. In R. H. Binstock & E. Shanas (Eds.), *Handbook of aging and the social sciences.* New York: Van Nostrand-Reinhold.

CAPLAN, L. R. (1986). Care of the patient with acute stroke. In P. E. Kaplan & L. J. Cerullo (Eds.), *Stroke rehabilitation.* Boston: Butterworth.

CAPLAN, R. D., COBB, S., & FRENCH, J. R. P. (1975). Relationships of cessation of smoking with job stress, personality, and social support. *Journal of Applied Psychology, 60,* 211-219.

CAREY, M. P., & BURISH, T. G. (1985). Anxiety as a predictor of behavioral therapy outcome for cancer chemotherapy patients. *Journal of Consulting and Clinical Psychology, 53,* 860-865.

CAREY, R. G. (1975). Living until death: A program of service and research for the terminally ill. In E. Kübler-Ross (Ed.), *Death: The final stage of growth.* Englewood Cliffs, NJ: Prentice-Hall.

CAREY, W. B., & MCDEVITT, S. C. (1978). Stability and change in individual temperament diagnoses from infancy to early childhood. *Journal of the American Academy of Child Psychiatry, 17,* 331-337.

CARMARGO, C. A., VRANIZAN, K. M., THORESEN, C. E., & WOOD, P. D. (1986). Type A behavior pattern and alcohol intake in middle-aged men. *Psychosomatic Medicine, 48,* 575-581.

CARMELLI, D., ROSENMAN, R. H., & CHESNEY, M. A. (1987). Stability of the Type A Structured Interview and related questionnaires in a 10-year follow-up of an adult cohort of twins. *Journal of Behavioral Medicine, 10,* 513-525.

CARMODY, T. P., FEY, S. G., PIERCE, D. K., CONNOR, W. E., & MATARAZZO, J. D. (1982). Behavioral treatment of hyperlipidemia: Techniques, results, and future directions. *Journal of Behavioral Medicine, 5,* 91-116.

CARNEY, R. M., WETZEL, R. D., HAGBERG, J., & GOLDBERG, A. P. (1986). The relationship between depression and aerobic capacity in hemodialysis patients. *Psychosomatic Medicine, 48,* 143-147.

CARR, D. B., BULLEN, B. A., SKRINAR, G. S., ARNOLD, M. A., ROSENBLATT, M., BEITINS, I. Z., MARTIN, J. B., & MCARTHUR, J. W. (1981). Physical conditioning facilitates the exercise-induced secretion of beta-endorphin and beta-lipotropin in women. *New England Journal of Medicine, 305,* 560-563.

CARVER, C. S., COLEMAN, A. E., & GLASS, D. C. (1976). The coronary-prone behavior pattern and the suppression of fatigue on a treadmill test. *Journal of Personality and Social Psychology, 33,* 460-466.

CARVER, C. S., DEGREGORIO, E., & GILLIS, R. (1981). Challenge and Type A behavior among intercollegiate football players. *Journal of Sport Psychology, 3,* 140-148.

CARVER, C. S., DIAMOND, E. L., & HUMPHRIES, C. (1985). Coronary prone behavior. In N. Schneiderman & J. T. Tapp (Eds.), *Behavioral medicine: The biopsychosocial approach.* Hillsdale, NJ: Erlbaum.

CARVER, C. S., & GLASS, D. C. (1978). Coronary-prone behavior pattern and interpersonal aggression. *Journal of Personality and Social Psychology, 36,* 361-366.

CASTRO, F. G., NEWCOMB, M. D., MCCREARY, C., & BAEZ-CONDE-GARBANATI, L. (1989). Cigarette smokers do more than just smoke cigarettes. *Health Psychology, 8,* 107-129.

CATALDO, M. F., DERSHEWITZ, R. A., WILSON, M., CHRISTOPHERSEN, E. R., FINNEY, J. W., FAWCETT, S. B., & SEEKINS, T. (1986). Childhood injury control. In N. A. Krasnegor, J. D. Arasteh, & M. F. Cataldo (Eds.), *Child health behavior: A behavioral pediatrics perspective.* New York: Wiley.

CAY, E. L., PHILIP, A. E., & DUGARD, P. (1972). Psychosocial status during recovery from an acute heart attack. *Journal of Psychosomatic Research, 16,* 425-435.

CHAMPION, V. L. (1985). Use of health belief model in determining frequency of breast self-examination. *Research in Nursing and Health, 8,* 373-379.

CHANEY, E. F., O'LEARY, M. R., & MARLATT, G. A. (1978). Skill training with alcoholics. *Journal of Consulting and Clinical Psychology, 46,* 1092-1104.

CHANG, A., DILLMAN, A. S., LEONARD, E., & ENGLISH, P. (1985). Teaching car passenger safety to preschool children. *Pediatrics, 76,* 425-428.

CHAPMAN, C. R. (1984). New directions in the understanding and management of pain. *Social Science and Medicine, 19,* 1261-1277.

CHAPMAN, C. R., CASEY, K. L., DUBNER, R., FOLEY, K. M., GRACELY, R. H., & READING, A. E. (1985). Pain measurement: An overview. *Pain, 22,* 1-31.

CHAPMAN, S. L., & BRENA, S. F. (1985). Pain and society. *Annals of Behavioral Medicine, 7*(3), 21-24.

CHAVES, J. F., & BROWN, J. M. (1987). Spontaneous cognitive strategies for the control of clinical pain and stress. *Journal of Behavioral Medicine, 10,* 263-276.

CHELUNE, G. J. (1987). Epilepsy. In R. J. Corsini (Ed.), *Concise encyclopedia of psychology.* New York: Wiley.

CHESNEY, M. A. (1984). Behavior modification and health enhancement. In J. D. Matarazzo, S. M. Weiss, J. A. Herd, N. E. Miller, & S. M. Weiss (Eds.), *Behavioral health: A handbook of health enhancement and disease prevention.* New York: Wiley.

CHESNEY, M. A., EAGLESTON, J. R., & ROSENMAN, R. H. (1980). The Type A Structured Interview: A behavioral assessment in the rough. *Journal of Behavioral Assessment, 2,* 255-272.

CHESNEY, M. A., FRAUTSCHI, N. M., & ROSENMAN, R. H. (1985). Modifying Type A behavior. In J. C. Rosen & L. J. Solomon (Eds.), *Prevention in health psychology.* Hanover, NH: University Press of New England.

CHRISMAN, N. J., & KLEINMAN, A. (1983). Popular health care, social networks, and cultural meanings: The orientation of medical anthropology. In D. Mechanic (Ed.), *Handbook of health, health care, and the health professions.* New York: Free Press.

CHRISTOPHERSEN, E. R. (1984). Preventing injuries to children: A behavioral approach to child passenger safety. In J. D. Matarazzo, S. M. Weiss, J. A. Herd, N. E. Miller, & S. M. Weiss (Eds.), *Behavioral health: A handbook of health enhancement and disease prevention.* New York: Wiley.

CHRISTOPHERSEN, E. R. (1989). Injury control. *American Psychologist, 44,* 237-241.

CIARANELLO, R. D. (1983). Neurochemical aspects of stress. In N. Garmezy & M. Rutter (Eds.), *Stress, coping, and development in children.* New York: McGraw-Hill.

CINCIRIPINI, P. M., & FLOREEN, A. (1982). An evaluation of a behavioral program for chronic pain. *Journal of Behavioral Medicine, 5,* 375-389.

CIOPPA, A. L. (1984). Hospice care. In S. N. McIntire & A. L. Cioppa (Eds.), *Nursing care: A developmental approach.* New York: Wiley.

CITRON, M. L., JOHNSTON-EARLY, A., BOYER, M., KRASNOW, S. H., HOOD, M., & COHEN, M. H. (1986). Patient-controlled analgesia for severe cancer pain. *Archives of Internal Medicine, 146,* 734-736.

CLARK, D. W. (1981). A vocabulary for preventive and community medicine. In D. W. Clark & B. MacMahon (Eds.),

Preventive and community medicine (2nd ed.). Boston: Little, Brown.

CLARK, M. (1988, February 8). Heart attacks. *Newsweek.* pp. 50-54.

CLARKSON, T. B., MANUCK, S. B., & KAPLAN, J. R. (1986). Potential role of cardiovascular reactivity in atherogenesis. In K. A. Matthews, S. M. Weiss, T. Detre, T. M. Dembroski, B. Falkner, S. B. Manuck, & R. B. Williams (Eds.), *Handbook of stress, reactivity, and cardiovascular disease.* New York: Wiley.

CLEARY, P. D., MECHANIC, D., & GREENLEY, J. R. (1982). Sex differences in medical care utilization: An empirical investigation. *Journal of Health and Social Behavior, 23,* 106-119.

CLEVER, L. H., & OMENN, G. S. (1988). Hazards for health care workers. In L. Breslow, J. E. Fielding, & L. B. Lave (Eds.), *Annual review of public health* (Vol. 9). Palo Alto, CA: Annual Reviews.

CLUSS, P. A., & EPSTEIN, L. H. (1985). The measurement of medical compliance in the treatment of disease. In P. Karoly (Ed.), *Measurement strategies in health psychology.* New York: Wiley.

CLUSS, P. A., & FIREMAN, P. (1985). Recent trends in asthma research. *Annals of Behavioral Medicine, 7*(4), 11-16.

COBB, S. (1976). Social support as a moderator of stress. *Psychosomatic Medicine, 38,* 300-314.

COBB, S., & ROSE, R. M. (1973). Hypertension, peptic ulcer, and diabetes in air traffic controllers. *Journal of the American Medical Association, 224,* 489-492.

CODDINGTON, R. D. (1972a). The significance of life events as etiological factors in the diseases of children—I: A survey of professional workers. *Journal of Psychosomatic Research, 16,* 7-18.

CODDINGTON, R. D. (1972b). The significance of life events as etiological factors in the diseases of children—II: A study of a normal population. *Journal of Psychosomatic Research, 16,* 205-213.

COGAN, R., COGAN, D., WALTZ, W., & MCCUE, M. (1987). Effects of laughter and relaxation on discomfort thresholds. *Journal of Behavioral Medicine, 10,* 139-144.

COHEN, F., & LAZARUS, R. S. (1979). Coping with the stresses of illness. In G. C. Stone, F. Cohen, & N. E. Adler (Eds.), *Health psychology—A handbook.* San Francisco: Jossey-Bass.

COHEN, F., & LAZARUS, R. S. (1983). Coping and adaptation in health and illness. In D. mechanic (Ed.), *Handbook of health, health care, and the health professions.* New York: Free Press.

COHEN, J. B., SYME, S. L., JENKINS, C. D., & KAGAN, A. (1975). The cultural context of type A behavior and the risk of CHD. *American Journal of Epidemiology, 102,* 434 (abstract).

COHEN, S. (1980). Aftereffects of stress on human performance and social behavior: A review of research and theory. *Psychological Bulletin, 88,* 81-108.

COHEN, S., EVANS, G. W., STOKOLS, D., & KRANTZ, D. S. (1986). *Behavior, health, and environmental stress.* New York: Plenum.

COHEN, S., GLASS, D. C., & SINGER, J. E. (1973). Apartment noise, auditory discrimination, and reading ability in children. *Journal of Experimental Social Psychology, 9,* 407-422.

COHEN, S., KAMARCK, T., & MERMELSTEIN, R. (1983). A global measure of perceived stress. *Journal of Health and Social Behavior, 24,* 385-396.

COHEN, S., & MCKAY, G. (1984). Social support, stress and the buffering hypothesis: A theoretical analysis. In A. Baum, S. E. Taylor, & J. E. Singer (Eds.), *Handbook of psychology and health.* Hillsdale, NJ: Erlbaum.

COHEN, S., & SPACAPAN, S. (1978). The aftereffects of stress: An attentional interpretation. *Environmental Psychology and Nonverbal Behavior, 3,* 43-57.

COHEN, S., & WILLS, T. A. (1985). Stress, social support, and the buffering hypothesis. *Psychological Bulletin, 98,* 310-357.

COHEN, W. S. (1985). Health promotion in the workplace: A prescription for good health. *American Psychologist, 40,* 213-216.

COLEMAN, J. C. (1976). *Abnormal psychology in modern life* (5th ed.). Glenview, IL: Scott, Foresman.

COLERICK, E. J. (1985). Stamina in later life. *Social Science and Medicine, 21,* 997-1006.

COLLETTI, G., & BROWNELL, K. D. (1983). The physical and emotional benefits of social support: Application to obesity, smoking, and alcoholism. In M. Hersen, R. M. Eisler, & P. M. Miller (Eds.), *Progress in behavior modification.* New York: Academic Press.

COLLIGAN, M. J., URTES, M., WISSEMAN, C., ROSENSTEEL, R. E., ANANIA, T. L., & HORNUNG, R. W. (1979). An investigation of apparent mass psychogenic illness in an electronics plant. *Journal of Behavioral Medicine, 2,* 297-309.

COLLINS, A., & FRANKENHAEUSER, M. (1978). Stress responses in male and female engineering students. *Journal of Human Stress, 4,* 43-48.

COLLINS, C., & LIPMAN, T. H. (1985). The endocrine system. In L. L. Hayman & E. M. Sporing (Eds.), *Handbook of pediatric nursing.* New York: Wiley.

COLLINS, G. (1987, April 29). Keeping fit wasn't easy in 1837, either. *New York Times,* pp. C1, 12.

CONEL, J. L. (1939-1963). *The postnatal development of the human cerebral cortex* (Vols. 1-7). Cambridge, MA: Harvard University Press.

CONSTABLE, J. F., & RUSSELL, D. W. (1986). The effect of social support and the work environment upon burnout among nurses. *Journal of Human Stress, 12,* 20-26.

CONTRADA, R. J., & KRANTZ, D. S. (1988). Stress, reactivity, and Type A behavior: Current status and future directions. *Annals of Behavioral Medicine, 10,* 64-70.

CONTRADA, R. J., KRANTZ, D. S., & HILL, D. R. (1988). Type A behavior, emotion, and psychophysiologic reactivity: Psychological and biological interactions. In B. K. Houston & C. R. Snyder (Eds.), *Type A behavior pattern: Research, theory, and intervention.* New York: Wiley.

CONWAY, T. L., VICKERS, R. R., WARD, H. W., & RAHE, R. H. (1981). Occupational stress and variation in cigarette, coffee, and alcohol consumption. *Journal of Health and Social Behavior, 22,* 155-165.

COOPER, K. H. (1988). *Controlling cholesterol.* New York: Bantam.

COOPER, P. J., BAWDEN, H. N., CAMFIELD, P. R., & CAMFIELD, C. S. (1987). Anxiety and life events in childhood migraine. *Pediatrics, 79,* 999-1004.

COOPER, S. (1987). The fetal alcohol syndrome. *Journal of Child Psychology and Psychiatry, 28,* 223-227.

CORAH, N. L., O'SHEA, R. M., BISSELL, G. D., THINES, T. J., & MENDOLA, P. (1988). The dentist-patient relationship: Perceived dentist behaviors that reduce patient anxiety and increase satisfaction. *Journal of the American Dental Association, 116,* 73-76.

COSTA, P. T., & MCCRAE, R. R. (1980). Somatic complaints in males as a function of age and neuroticism: A longitudinal analysis. *Journal of Behavioral Medicine, 3,* 245-257.

COSTA, P. T., & MCCRAE, R. R. (1985). Hypochondriasis, neuroticism, and aging. *American Psychologist, 40,* 19-28.

COSTELLO, R. M. (1975). Alcoholism treatment and evaluation: In search of methods. *International Journal of the Addictions, 10,* 251-275.

COSTELLO, R. M., BAILLARGEON, J. G., BIEVER, P., & BENNETT, R. (1980). Therapeutic community treatment for alcohol abusers: A one-year multivariate outcome evaluation. *International Journal of the Addictions, 15,* 215-232.

COTTINGTON, E. M., & HOUSE, J. S. (1987). Occupational stress and health: A multivariate relationship. In A. Baum & J. E. Singer (Eds.), *Handbook of psychology and health* (Vol. 5). Hillsdale, NJ: Erlbaum.

COTTINGTON, E. M., MATTHEWS, K. A., TALBOTT, E., & KULLER, L. H. (1986). Occupational stress, suppressed anger, and hypertension. *Psychosomatic Medicine, 48,* 249-260.

COUNCIL ON SCIENTIFIC AFFAIRS (1983). Medical evaluations of healthy persons. *Journal of the American Medical Association, 249,* 1626-1633.

COUSINS, N. (1979). *Anatomy of an illness.* New York: Norton.

COUSINS, N. (1985). Anatomy of an illness (as perceived by the patient). In A. Monat & R. S. Lazarus (Eds.), *Stress and coping: An anthology* (2nd ed). New York: Columbia University Press.

COX, G. B., CHAMPMAN, C. R., & BLACK, R. G. (1978). The MMPI and chronic pain: The diagnosis of psychogenic pain. *Journal of Behavioral Medicine, 1,* 437-443.

COX, T. (1978). *Stress.* Baltimore: University Park Press.

COX, W. M. (1985). Personality correlates of substance abuse. In M. Galizio & S. A. Maisto (Eds.), *Determinants of substance abuse: Biological, psychological, and environmental factors.* New York: Plenum.

COYNE, J. C., & HOLROYD, K. (1982). Stress, coping, and illness: A transactional perspective. In T. Millon, C. Green, & R. Meagher (Eds.), *Handbook of clinical health psychology.* New York: Plenum.

CRABBE, J. C., MCSWIGAN, J. D., & BELKNAP, J. K. (1985). The role of genetics in substance abuse. In M. Galizio & S. A. Maisto (Eds.), *Determinants of substance abuse: Biological, psychological, and environmental factors.* New York: Plenum.

CRAIG, T. G., COMSTOCK, G. W., & GEISER, P. B. (1974). The quality of survival in breast cancer: A case-control comparison. *Cancer, 33,* 1451-1457.

CRAIN, D. C. (1971). *The arthritis handbook* (2nd ed.). New York: Arco.

CRANDALL, L. A., & DUNCAN, R. P. (1981). Attitudinal and situational factors in the use of physician services by low-income persons. *Journal of Health and Social Behavior, 22,* 64-77.

CRAUN, A. M., & DEFFENBACHER, J. L. (1987). The effects of information, behavioral rehearsal, and prompting on breast self-exams. *Journal of Behavioral Medicine, 10,* 351-365.

CREER, T. L. (1983). Respiratory disorders. In T. G. Burish & L. A. Bradley (Eds.), *Coping with chronic disease: Research and applications.* New York: Academic Press.

CRISP, A. H., & KALUCY, R. S. (1974). Aspects of the perceptual disorder in anorexia nervosa. *British Journal of Medical Psychology, 47,* 349-361.

CRITCHLOW, B. (1986). The powers of John Barleycorn: Beliefs about the effects of alcohol on social behavior. *American Psychologist, 41,* 751-764.

CRITELLI, J. W., & NEUMANN, K. F. (1984). The placebo: Conceptual analysis of a construct in transition. *American Psychologist, 39,* 32-39.

CROOG, S. H. (1983). Recovery and rehabilitation of heart patients: Psychosocial aspects. In D. S. Krantz, A. Baum, & J. E. Singer (Eds.), *Handbook of psychology and health* (Vol. 3). Hillsdale, NJ: Erlbaum.

CROOG, S. H., & FITZGERALD, E. F. (1978). Subjective stress and serious illness of a spouse: Wives of heart patients. *Journal of Health and Social Behavior, 19,* 166-178.

CROOK, T. H., & MILLER, N. E. (1985). The challenge of Alzheimer's disease. *American Psychologist, 40,* 1245-1250.

CUMMINGS, K. M., GIOVINO, G., JAÉN, C. R., & EMRICH, L. J. (1985). Reports of smoking withdrawal symptoms over a 21-day period of abstinence. *Addictive Behaviors, 10,* 373-381.

CURRY, S., MARLATT, G. A., & GORDON, J. R. (1987). Abstinence violation effect: Validation of an attributional construct with smoking cessation. *Journal of Consulting and Clinical Psychology, 55,* 145-149.

CURTIS, H. (1979). *Biology* (3rd ed.). New York: Worth.

CUTRONA, C. E. (1986). Behavioral manifestations of social support: A microanalytic investigation. *Journal of Personality and Social Psychology, 51,* 201-208.

CUTRONA, C. E., & TROUTMAN, B. R. (1986). Social support, infant temperament, and parenting self-efficacy: A mediational model of postpartum depression. *Child Development, 57,* 1507-1518.

CZAJKOWSKI, D. R., & KOOCHER, G. P. (1986). Predicting medical compliance among adolescents with cystic fibrosis. *Health Psychology, 5,* 297-305.

CZAJKOWSKI, D. R., & KOOCHER, G. P. (1987). Medical compliance and coping with cystic fibrosis. *Journal of Child Psychology and Psychiatry, 28,* 311-319.

DAHLBERG, C. C. (1977, June). Stroke. *Psychology Today, 10,* pp. 121-128.

DAHLQUIST, L. M., GIL, K. M., ARMSTRONG, F. D., DELAWYER, D. D., GREENE, P., & WUORI, D. (1986). Preparing children for medical examinations: The importance of previous medical experience. *Health Psychology, 5,* 249-259.

DANNENBERG, A. L., DRIZD, T., HORAN, M. J., HAYNES, S. G., & LEAVERTON, P. E. (1987). Progress in the battle against hypertension: Changes in blood pressure levels in the United States from 1960 to 1980. *Hypertension, 10,* 226-233.

DARROW, W. W., ECHENBERG, D. F., JAFFE, H. W., O'MALLEY, P. M., BYERS, R. H., GETCHELL, J. P., & CURRAN, J. W. (1987). Risk factors for human immunodeficiency virus (HIV) infections in homosexual men. *American Journal of Public Health, 77,* 479-483.

DAVIDSON, R. S. (1985). Behavioral medicine and alcoholism. In N. Schneiderman & J. T. Tapp (Eds.), *Behavioral medicine: The biopsychosocial approach.* Hillsdale, NJ: Erlbaum.

DAVIES, D. L. (1962). Normal drinking in recovered alcohol addicts. *Quarterly Journal of Studies on Alcohol, 23,* 94-104.

DAVIS, M. S. (1986). Variations in patients' compliance with doctors' orders: Analysis of congruence between survey responses and results of empirical investigations. *Journal of Medical Education, 41,* 1037-1048.

DEJONG, W. (1980). The stigma of obesity: The consequences of naive assumptions concerning the causes of physical deviance. *Journal of Health and Social Behavior, 21,* 75-87.

DELONGIS, A., COYNE, J. C., DAKOF, G., FOLKMAN, S., & LAZARUS, R. S. (1982). Relationship to daily hassles, uplifts, and major life events to health status. *Health Psychology, 1,* 119-136.

DEMBROSKI, T. M., MACDOUGALL, J. M., WILLIAMS, R. B., HANEY, T. L., & BLUMENTHAL, J. A. (1985). Components of Type A, hostility, and anger-in: Relationship to angiographic findings. *Psychosomatic Medicine, 47,* 219-233.

DENNIS, C., HOUSTON-MILLER, N., SCHWARTZ, R. G., AHN, D. K., KRAEMER, H. C., GOSSARD, D., JUNEAU, M., TAYLOR, C. B., & DEBUSK, R. F. (1988). Early return to work after uncomplicated myocardial infarction: Results of a randomized trial. *Journal of the American Medical Association, 260,* 214-220.

DEROGATIS, L. R. (1977). *Psychological Adjustment to Illness Scale.* Baltimore: Clinical Psychometric Research.

DEROGATIS, L. R. (1986). The Psychological Adjustment to Illness Scale (PAIS). *Journal of Psychosomatic Research, 30,* 77-91.

DES JARLAIS, D. C., & FRIEDMAN, S. R. (1987). Target groups for preventing AIDS among intravenous drug users. *Journal of Applied Social Psychology, 17,* 251-268.

DES JARLAIS, D. C., & FRIEDMAN, S. R. (1988). The psychology of preventing AIDS among intravenous drug users: a social learning conceptualization. *American Psychologist, 43,* 865-870.

DES JARLAIS, D. C., FRIEDMAN, S. R., CASRIEL, C., & KOTT, A. (1987). AIDS and preventing initiation into intravenous (IV) drug use. *Psychology and Health, 1,* 179-194.

DEUTSCH, C. H. (1987, November 8). What do people want, anyway? *New York Times,* p. F8.

DEVINS, G. M., BINIK, Y. M., HOLLOMBY, D. J., BARRÉ, P. E., & GUTTMANN, R. D. (1981). Helplessness and depression in end-stage renal disease. *Journal of Abnormal Psychology, 90,* 531-545.

DIAMOND, E. L. (1982). The role of anger and hostility in essential hypertension and coronary heart disease. *Psychological Bulletin, 92,* 410-433.

DIAMOND, E. L., MASSEY, K. L., & COVEY, D. (1989). Symptom awareness and blood glucose estimation in diabetic adults. *Health Psychology, 8,* 15-26.

DIAMOND, E. L., SCHNEIDERMAN, N., SCHWARTZ, D., SMITH, J. C., VORP, R., & PASIN, R. D. (1984). Harassment, hostility, and Type A as determinants of cardiovascular reactivity during competition. *Journal of Behavioral Medicine, 7,* 171-189.

DIAMOND, M. (1983). Social adaptation of the chronically ill. In D. Mechanic (Ed.), *Handbook of health, health care, and the health professions,* New York: Free Press.

DIAZ-GUERRERO, R. (1984). Behavioral health across cultures. In J. D. Matarazzo, S. M. Weiss, J. A. Herd, N. E. Miller, & S. M. Weiss (Eds.), *Behavioral health: A handbook of health enhancement and disease prevention.* New York: Wiley.

DICARA, L. V., & MILLER, N. E. (1968). Changes in heart rate instrumentally learned by curarized rats as avoidance responses. *Journal of Comparative and Physiological Psychology, 65,* 8-12.

DICLEMENTE, C. C., PROCHASKA, J. O., & GILBERTINI, M. (1985). Self-efficacy and the stages of self-change of smoking. *Cognitive Therapy and Research, 9,* 181-200.

DICLEMENTE, R. J., ZORN, J., & TEMOSHOK, L. (1987). The association of gender, ethnicity, and length of residence in the Bay Area to adolescents' knowledge and attitudes about acquired immune deficiency syndrome. *Journal of Applied Social Psychology, 17,* 216-230.

DIGIUSEPPE, R. A., & MILLER, N. J. (1977). A review of outcome studies on rational-emotive therapy. In A. Ellis & R. Grieger (Eds.), *Handbook of rational-emotive therapy.* New York: Springer.

DIMATTEO, M. R. (1985). Physician-patient communication: Promoting a positive health care setting. In J. C. Rosen & L. J. Solomon (Eds.), *Prevention in health psychology.* Hanover, NH: University Press of New England.

DIMATTEO, M. R., & DINICOLA, D. D. (1982). *Achieving patient compliance: The psychology of the medical practitioner's role.* New York: Pergamon.

DIMATTEO, M. R., FRIEDMAN, H. S., & TARANTA, A. (1979). Sensitivity to bodily nonverbal communication as a factor in practitioner-patient rapport. *Journal of Nonverbal Behavior, 4,* 18-26.

DIMATTEO, M. R., HAYS, R. D., & PRINCE, L. M. (1986). Relationship of physicians' nonverbal communication skill to patient satisfaction, appointment noncompliance, and physician workload. *Health Psychology, 5,* 581-594.

DIMATTEO, M. R., LINN, L. S., CHANG, B. L., & COPE, D. W. (1985). Affect and neutrality in physician behavior: A study of patients' values and satisfaction. *Journal of Behavioral Medicine, 8,* 397–409.

DIMSDALE, J. E., ALPERT, B. S., & SCHNEIDERMAN, N. (1986). Exercise as a modulator of cardiovascular reactivity. In K. A. Matthews, S. M. Weiss, T. Detre, T. M. Dembroski, B. Falkner, S. B. Manuck, & R. B. Williams (Eds.), *Handbook of stress, reactivity, and cardiovascular disease.* New York: Wiley.

DISHMAN, R. K. (1981). Biologic influences on exercise adherence. *Research Quarterly for Exercise and Sport, 52,* 143–159.

DISHMAN, R. K. (1982). Compliance/adherence in health-related exercise. *Health Psychology, 1,* 237–267.

DISHMAN, R. K. (1986). Mental health. In V. Seefeldt (Ed.), *Physical activity and well-being.* Reston, VA: American Alliance for Health, Physical Education, Recreation, and Dance.

DISHMAN, R. K., SALLIS, J. F., & ORENSTEIN, D. R. (1985). The determinants of physical activity and exercise. *Public Health Reports, 100,* 158–171.

DIX, J. & KOEHLER, J. A. (1985). The cardiovascular system. In L. L. Hayman & E. M. Sporing (Eds.), *Handbook of pediatric nursing.* New York: Wiley.

DOEHRMAN, S. R. (1977). Psycho-social aspects of recovery from coronary heart disease: A review. *Social Science and Medicine, 11,* 199–218.

DOHRENWEND, B. S., & DOHRENWEND, B. P. (1981). Life stress and illness: Formulation of the issues. In B. S. Dohrenwend & B. P. Dohrenwend (Eds.), *Stressful life events and their contexts.* New York: Prodist.

DOHRENWEND, B. S., KRASNOFF, L., ASKENASY, A. R., & DOHRENWEND, B. P. (1978). Exemplification of a method for scaling life events: The PERI Life Events Scale. *Journal of Health and Social Behavior, 19,* 205–229.

DOLECEK, T. A., MILAS, N. C., VAN HORN, L. V., FARRAND, M. E., GORDER, D. D., DUCHENE, A. G., DYER, J. R., STONE, P. A., & RANDALL, B. L. (1986). A long-term nutrition experience: Lipid responses and dietary adherence patterns in the Multiple Risk Factor Intervention Trial. *Journal of the American Dietetic Association, 86,* 752–758.

DOLINSKI, D., GROMSKI, W., & ZAWISZA, E. (1987). Unrealistic pessimism. *Journal of Social Psychology, 127,* 511–516.

DONNERSTEIN, E., & WILSON, D. W. (1976). Effects of noise and perceived control on ongoing and subsequent aggressive behavior. *Journal of Personality and Social Psychology, 34,* 774–781.

DORMAN, S. M., & RIENZO, B. A. (1988). College students' knowledge of AIDS. *Health Values, 12*(4), 33–38.

DOWLING, J. (1983). Autonomic measures and behavioral indices of pain sensitivity. *Pain, 16,* 193–200.

DUGAN, S. O. (1984). Pain. In S. N. McIntire & A. L. Cioppa (Eds.), *Cancer nursing: A developmental approach.* New York: Wiley.

DWECK, C. S., DAVIDSON, W., NELSON, S., & ENNA, B. (1978). Sex differences in learned helplessness: II. The contingencies of evaluative feedback in the classroom, and III. An experimental analysis. *Developmental Psychology, 14,* 268–276.

DWECK, C. S., & REPUCCI, N. D. (1973). Learned helplessness and reinforcement responsibility in children. *Journal of Personality and Social Psychology, 25,* 109–116.

EASTERBROOK, G. (1987, January 26). The revolution. *Newsweek,* pp. 40–74.

EDELL, B. H., EDINGTON, S., HERD, B., O'BRIEN, R. M., & WITKIN, G. (1987). Self-efficacy and self-motivation as predictors of weight loss. *Addictive Behaviors, 12,* 63–66.

EDELSTEIN, L. (1984). *Maternal bereavement: Coping with the unexpected death of a child.* New York: Praeger.

EICHENWALD, K. (1987, January 11). Braving epilepsy's storm. *New York Times Magazine,* pp. 30–36.

EISENBERG, J. M., KITZ, D. S., & WEBBER, R. A. (1983). Development of attitudes about sharing decision-making: A comparison of medical and surgical residents. *Journal of Health and Social Behavior, 24,* 85–90.

EISENBERG, M. G. (1984). Spinal cord injuries. In H. B. Roback (Ed.), *Helping patients and their families cope with medical problems.* San Francisco: Jossey-Bass.

EISER, C. (1985). *The psychology of childhood illness.* New York: Springer-Verlag.

EISER, J. R., VAN DER PLIGT, J., RAW, M., & SUTTON, S. R. (1985). Trying to stop smoking: Effects of perceived addiction, attributions for failure, and expectancy of success. *Journal of Behavioral Medicine, 8,* 321–341.

ELLIOTT, D. J., TRIEF, P. M., & STEIN, N. (1986). Mastery, stress, and coping in marriage among chronic pain patients. *Journal of Behavioral Medicine, 9,* 549–558.

ELLIS, A. (1962). *Reason and emotion in psychotherapy.* New York: Lyle Stuart.

ELLIS, A. (1977). The basic clinical theory of rational-emotive therapy. In A. Ellis & R. Grieger (Eds.), *Handbook of rational-emotive therapy.* New York: Springer.

ELLIS, A. (1987). The impossibility of achieving consistently good mental health. *American Psychologist, 2,* 364–375.

EMERY, A. E. H., & PULLEN, I. M. (1986). A contemporary approach to genetic counseling. In M. J. Christie & P. G. Mellett (Eds.), *The psychosomatic approach: Contemporary practice of whole-person care.* New York: Wiley.

EMRICK, C. D., & HANSEN, J. (1983). Assertions regarding effectiveness of treatment for alcoholism. *American psychologist, 38,* 1978–1088.

ENGEL, G. L. (1977). The need for a new medical model: A challenge for biomedicine. *Science, 196,* 129–136.

ENGEL, G. L. (1980). The clinical application of the biopsychosocial model. *American Journal of Psychiatry, 137,* 535–544.

ENGEL, G. L., REICHSMAN, R., & SEGAL, H. L. (1956). A study of an infant with a gastric fistula: I. Behavior and the rate of total hydrochloric acid secretion. *Psychosomatic Medicine, 18,* 374–398.

ENGLISH, E. H., & BAKER, T. B. (1983). Relaxation training and cardiovascular response to experimental stressors. *Health Psychology, 2,* 239–259.

ENGSTROM, D. (1984). A psychological perspective of prevention in alcoholism. In J. D. Matarazzo, S. M. Weiss, J.

A. Herd, N. E. Miller, & S. M. Weiss (Eds.), *Behavioral health: A handbook of health enhancement and disease prevention.* New York: Wiley.

EPSTEIN, L. H., & CLUSS, P. A. (1982). A behavioral medicine perspective on adherence to long-term medical regimens. *Journal of Consulting and Clinical Psychology, 50,* 950–971.

EPSTEIN, L. H., & CLUSS, P. A. (1986). Behavioral genetics of childhood obesity. *Behavior Therapy, 17,* 324–334.

EPSTEIN, L. H., & JENNINGS, J. R. (1986). Smoking, stress, cardiovascular reactivity, and coronary heart disease. In K. A. Matthews, S. M. Weiss, T. Detre, T. M. Dembroski, B. Falkner, S. B. Manuck, & R. B. Williams (Eds.), *Handbook of stress, reactivity, and cardiovascular disease.* New York: Wiley.

EPSTEIN, L. H., & WING, R. R. (1987). Behavioral treatment of childhood obesity. *Psychological Bulletin, 101,* 331–342.

EPSTEIN, L. H., WING, R. R., PENNER, B. C., & KRESS, M. J. (1985). Effect of diet and controlled exercise on weight loss in obese children. *Journal of Pediatrics, 107,* 358–361.

EPSTEIN, L. H., WING, R. R., VALOSKI, A., & DEVOS, D. (1988). Long-term relationship between weight and aerobic-fitness change in children. *Health Psychology, 7,* 47–53.

ERIKSEN, M. P., LEMAISTRE, C. A., & NEWELL, G. R. (1988). Health hazards of passive smoking. In L. Breslow, J. E. Fielding, & L. B. Lave (Eds.), *Annual review of public health* (Vol. 9). Palo Alto, CA: Annual Reviews.

EVANS, F. J. (1987). Hypnosis. In R. J. Corsini (Ed.), *Concise encyclopedia of psychology.* New York: Wiley.

EVANS, R. I. (1976). Smoking in children: Developing a social psychological strategy of deterrence. *Preventive Medicine, 5,* 122–127.

EVANS, R. I. (1984). A social inoculation strategy to deter smoking in adolescents. In J. D. Matarazzo, S. M. Weiss, J. A. Herd, N. E. Miller, & S. M. Weiss (Eds.), *Behavioral health: A handbook of health enhancement and disease prevention.* New York: Wiley.

EVANS, R. I., ROZELLE, R. M., MITTELMARK, M. B., HANSEN, W. B., BANE, A. L., & HAVIS, J. (1978). Deterring the onset of smoking in children: Knowledge of immediate physiological effects and coping with peer pressure, media pressure, and parent modeling. *Journal of Applied Social Psychology, 8,* 126–135.

FAIRBURN, C. G. (1987). The definition of bulimia nervosa: Guidelines for clinicians and research workers. *Annals of Behavioral Medicine, 9*(4), 3–7.

FALKNER, B., & LIGHT, K. C. (1986). The interactive effects of stress and dietary sodium on cardiovascular reactivity. In K. A. Matthews, S. M. Weiss, T. Detre, T. M. Dembroski, B. Falkner, S. B. Manuck, & R. B. Williams (Eds.), *Handbook of stress, reactivity, and cardiovascular disease.* New York: Wiley.

FALSTEIN, E. I., FEINSTEIN, S. C., & JUDAS, I. (1956). Anorexia nervosa in the male child. *American Journal of Orthopsychiatry, 26,* 751–769.

FARQUHAR, J. W., FORTMANN, S. P., MACCOBY, N., WOOD, P. D., HASKELL, W. L., TAYLOR, C. B., FLORA, J. A., SOLOMON, D. S., ROGERS, T., ADLER, E., BREITROSE, P., & WEINER, L. (1984). The Stanford Five City Project: An overview. In J. D. Matarazzo, S. M. Weiss, J. A. Herd, N. E. Miller, & S. M. Weiss (Eds.), *Behavioral health: A handbook of health enhancement and disease prevention.* New York: Wiley.

FARQUHAR, J. W., MACCOBY, N., & SOLOMON, D. S. (1984). Community applications of behavioral medicine. In W. D. Gentry (Ed.), *Handbook of behavioral medicine.* New York: Guilford.

FARQUHAR, J. W., MACCOBY, N., WOOD, P. D. ALEXANDER, J. K., BREITROSE, H., BROWN, B. W., HASKELL, W. L., MCALISTER, A. L., MEYER, A. J., NASH, J. D., & STERN, M. P. (1977, June 4). Community education for cardiovascular health. *Lancet,* 1192–1195.

FAUST, I. M., JOHNSON, P. R., & HIRSCH, J. (1977). Adipose tissue regeneration following lipectomy. *Science, 197,* 391–393.

FELDMAN, M., & RICHARDSON, C. T. (1986). Role of thought, sight, smell, and taste of food in the cephalic phase of gastric acid secretion in humans. *Gastroenterology, 90,* 428–433.

FELETTI, G., FIRMAN, D., & SANSON-FISHER, R. (1986). Patient satisfaction with primary-care consultations. *Journal of Behavioral Medicine, 9,* 389–399.

FELTON, G., HUSS, K., PAYNE, E. A., & SRSIC, K. (1976). Preoperative nursing intervention with the patient for surgery: Outcomes of three alternative approaches. *International Journal of Nursing Studies, 13,* 83–96.

FERNANDEZ, E. (1986). A classification system of cognitive coping strategies for pain. *Pain, 26,* 141–151.

FEUERSTEIN, M., CARTER, R. L., & PAPCIAK, A. S. (1987). A prospective analysis of stress and fatigue in recurrent low back pain. *Pain, 31,* 333–344.

FEUERSTEIN, M., & GAINER, J. (1982). Chronic headache: Etiology and management. In D. M. Doleys, R. L. Meredith, & A. R. Ciminero (Eds.), *Behavioral medicine: Assessment and treatment strategies.* New York: Plenum.

FIELDING, J. E. (1982). Effectiveness of employee health improvement programs. *Journal of Occupational Medicine, 24,* 907–916.

FIELDS, H. L., & LEVINE, J. D. (1984). Placebo analgesia—A role for endorphins? *Trends in Neurosciences, 7,* 271–273.

FILSINGER, E. E. (1987). Social class. In R. J. Corsini (Ed.), *Concise encyclopedia of psychology.* New York: Wiley.

FINN, P. E., & ALCORN, J. D. (1986). Noncompliance to hemodialysis dietary regimens: Literature review and treatment recommendations. *Rehabilitation Psychology, 31,* 67–78.

FISCHMAN, J. (1987, December). Getting tough. *Psychology Today, 21,* pp. 26–28.

FISHBEIN, M. (1980). A theory of reasoned action. Some applications and implications. In M. M. Page (Ed.), *Nebraska symposium on motivation, 1979.* Lincoln, NB: University of Nebraska Press.

FISHBEIN, M. (1982). Social psychological analysis of smoking behavior. In J. R. Eiser (Ed.), *Social psychology and behavioral medicine.* New York: Wiley.

FISHER, L. M. (1987, June 14). How America eats. *New York Times*, p. D5.

FISKE, D. W., & MADDI, S. R. (1961). A conceptual framework. In D. W. Fiske & S. R. Maddi (Eds.), *Functions of varied experience.* Homewood, IL: Dorsey.

FITZPATRICK, R., & SCAMBLER, G. (1984). Social class, ethnicity, and illness. In R. Fitzpatrick, J. Hinton, S. Newman, G. Scambler, & J. Thompson (Eds.), *The experience of illness.* London: Tavistock.

FLASKERUD, J. H. (1988). AIDS: Psychosocial aspects. *Health Values, 12*(4), 44-52.

FLAY, B. R. (1985). Psychosocial approaches to smoking prevention: A review of findings. *Health Psychology, 4,* 449-488.

FLAY, B. R. (1987). Mass media and smoking cessation: A critical review. *American Journal of Public Health, 77,* 153-160.

FLAY, B. R., RYAN, K. B., BEST, J. A., BROWN, K. S., KERSELL, M. W., D'AVERNAS, J. R., & ZANNA, M. P. (1985). Are social-psychological smoking prevention programs effective? The Waterloo Study. *Journal of Behavioral Medicine, 8,* 37-59.

FLEMING, I., BAUM, A., DAVIDSON, L. M., RECTANUS, E., & MCARDLE, S. (1987). Chronic stress as a factor in physiologic reactivity to challenge. *Health Psychology, 6,* 221-237.

FLEMING, R., BAUM, A., GISRIEL, M. M., & GATCHEL, R. J. (1982). Mediating influences of social support on stress at Three Mile Island. *Journal of Human Stress, 8,* 14-22.

FLINN, W. R., DALSING, M. C., & WHITE, J. V. (1986). Carotid endarterectomy: Indications, technique, and results. In P. E. Kaplan & L. J. Cerullo (Eds.), *Stroke rehabilitation.* Boston: Butterworth.

FLOR, H., KERNS, R. D., & TURK, D. C. (1987). The role of spouse reinforcement, perceived pain, and activity levels of chronic pain patients. *Journal of Psychosomatic Research, 31,* 251-259.

FLOR, H., & TURK, D. C. (1985). Chronic illness in an adult family member: Pain as a prototype. In D. C. Turk & R. D. Kerns (Eds.), *Health, illness, and families: A life-span perspective.* New York: Wiley.

FLYNN, J. E., & MABRY, E. R. (1986). Biophysical development of later adulthood. In C. L. Schuster & S. S. Ashburn (Eds.), *The process of human development: A holistic life-span approach.* Boston: Little, Brown.

FOLEY, K. M. (1985). The medical treatment of cancer pain. *New England Journal of Medicine, 313,* 84-95.

FOLKINS, C. E., & SIME, W. E. (1981). Physical fitness training and mental health. *American Psychologist, 36,* 373-389.

FOLKMAN, S., LAZARUS, R. S., PIMLEY, S., & NOVACEK, J. (1987). Age differences in stress and coping processes. *Psychology and Aging, 2,* 171-184.

FOLLICK, M. J., AHERN, D. K., & ABERGER, E. W. (1985). Development of an audiovisual taxonomy of pain behavior: Reliability and discriminant validity. *Health Psychology, 4,* 555-568.

FOLLICK, M. J., AHERN, D. K., ATTANASIO, V., & RILEY, J. F. (1985). Chronic pain programs: Current aims, strategies, and needs. *Annals of Behavioral Medicine, 7*(3), 17-20.

FOLLICK, M. J., GORKIN, L., SMITH, T. W., CAPONE, R. J., VISCO, J., & STABLEIN, D. (1988). Quality of life post-myocardial infarction: Effects of a transtelephonic coronary intervention system. *Health Psychology, 7,* 169-182.

FORDYCE, W. E. (1976). *Behavioral methods for chronic pain and illness.* St. Louis: Mosby.

FORDYCE, W. E., & STEGER, J. C. (1979). Behavioral management of chronic pain. In O. F. Pomerleau & J. P. Brady (Eds.), *Behavioral medicine: Theory and practice.* Baltimore: Williams & Wilkins.

FOREM, J. (1974). *Transcendental meditation.* New York: Dutton.

FOREYT, J. P., SCOTT, L. W., MITCHELL, R. E., & GOTTO, A. M. (1979). Plasma lipid changes in the normal population following behavioral treatment. *Journal of Consulting and Clinical Psychology, 47,* 440-452.

FORMAN, M. R., TROWBRIDGE, F. L., GENTRY, E. M., MARKS, J. S., & HOGELIN, G. C. (1986). Overweight adults in the United States: The behavioral risk factor surveys. *American Journal of Clinical Nutrition, 44,* 410-416.

FORMANEK, R., & GURIAN, A. (1980). *Why? Children's questions.* Boston: Houghton Mifflin.

FOX, B. H. (1978). Premorbid psychological factors as related to cancer incidence. *Journal of Behavioral Medicine, 1,* 45-133.

FOX, B. H. (1982). Endogenous psychosocial factors in cross-national cancer incidence. In J. R. Eiser (Ed.), *Social psychology and behavioral medicine.* New York: Wiley.

FRADKIN, B., & FIRESTONE, P. (1986). Premenstrual tension, expectancy, and mother-child relations. *Journal of Behavioral Medicine, 9,* 245-259.

FRANCE, C., & DITTO, B. (1988). Caffeine effects on several indices of cardiovascular activity at rest and during stress. *Journal of Behavioral Medicine, 11,* 473-482.

FRANCIS, D. P., & CHIN, J. (1987). The prevention of acquired immunodeficiency syndrome in the United States: An objective strategy for medicine, public health, business, and the community. *Journal of the American Medical Association, 257,* 1357-1366.

FRANCIS, V., KORSCH, B. M., & MORRIS, M. J. (1969). Gaps in doctor-patient communication. *New England Journal of Medicine, 280,* 535-540.

FRANK, R. G., UMLAUF, R. L., WONDERLICH, S. A., ASKANAZI, G. S., BUCKELEW, S. P., & ELLIOTT, T. R. (1987). Differences in coping styles among persons with spinal cord injury: A cluster-analytic approach. *Journal of Consulting and Clinical Psychology, 55,* 727-731.

FRANKENHAEUSER, M. (1986). A psychobiological framework for research on human stress and coping. In M. H. Appley & R. Trumbull (Eds.), *Dynamics of stress: Physiological, psychological, and social perspectives.* New York: Plenum.

FREEMON, B., NEGRETE, V. F., DAVIS, M., & KORSCH, B. M. (1971). Gaps in doctor-patient communication: Doctor-patient interaction analysis. *Pediatric Research, 5,* 298-311.

FREIDSON, E. (1961). *Patients' views of medical practice.* New York: Russell Sage Foundation.

FREUDENHEIM, M. (1988, May 2). The boom in home health care. *New York Times,* pp. D1, 3.

FRIEDMAN, H. S., & BOOTH-KEWLEY, S. (1987). The "disease-prone" personality. *American Psychologist, 42,* 539–555.

FRIEDMAN, L. A., & KIMBALL, A. W. (1986). Coronary heart disease mortality and alcohol consumption in Framingham. *American Journal of Epidemiology, 124,* 481–489.

FRIEDMAN, M., & ROSENMAN, R. H. (1974). *Type A behavior and your heart.* New York: Knopf.

FRIEDMAN, M., THORESEN, C. E., GILL, J. J., ULMER, D., POWELL, L. H., PRICE, V. A., BROWN, B., THOMPSON, L., RABIN, D. D., BREALL, W. S., BOURG, E., LEVY, R., & DIXON, T. (1986). Alteration of Type A behavior and its effect on cardiac recurrences in post myocardial infarction patients: Summary results of the Recurrent Coronary Prevention Project. *American Heart Journal, 112,* 653–665.

FRIIS, R., & TAFF, G. A. (1986). Social support and social networks, and coronary heart disease and rehabilitation. *Journal of Cardiopulmonary Rehabilitation, 6,* 132–147.

FRIMAN, P. C., & CHRISTOPHERSEN, E. R. (1986). Biobehavioral prevention in primary care. In N. A. Krasnegor, J. D. Arasteh, & M. F. Cataldo (Eds.), *Child health behavior: A behavioral pediatrics perspective.* New York: Wiley.

FRIMAN, P. C., FINNEY, J. W., GLASSCOCK, S. G., WEIGEL, J. W., & CHRISTOPHERSEN, E. R. (1986). Testicular self-examination: Validation of a training strategy for early cancer detection. *Journal of Applied Behavior Analysis, 19,* 87–92.

FROESE, A., HACKETT, T. P., CASSEM, N. H., & SILVERBERG, E. L. (1974). Trajectories of anxiety and depression in denying and nondenying acute myocardial infarction patients during hospitalization. *Journal of Psychosomatic Research, 18,* 413–420.

GAL, R., & LAZARUS, R. S. (1975). The role of activity in anticipating and confronting stressful situations. *Journal of Human Stress, 1,* 4–20.

GALIZIO, M., & MAISTO, S. A. (1985). Toward a biopsychosocial theory of substance abuse. In M. Galizio & S. A. Maisto (Eds.), *Determinants of substance abuse: Biological, psychological, and environmental factors.* New York: Plenum.

GANNON, L. R., HAYNES, S. N., CUEVAS, J., & CHAVEZ, R. (1987). Psychophysiological correlates of induced headaches. *Journal of Behavioral Medicine, 10,* 411–423.

GARDNER, E. J. (1983). *Human heredity.* New York: Wiley.

GARFIELD, C. (1978). *Psychosocial care of the dying patient.* New York: McGraw-Hill.

GARMEZY, N. (1983). Stressors of childhood. In N. Garmezy & M. Rutter (Eds.), *Stress, coping, and development in children.* New York: McGraw–Hill.

GARRITY, T. F. (1981). Medical compliance and the clinician–patient relationship: A review. *Social Science and Medicine, 15,* 215–222.

GARRITY, T. F., & MARX, M. B. (1979). Critical life events and coronary disease. In W. D. Gentry & R. B. Williams (Eds.), *Psychological aspects of myocardial infarction and coronary care* (2nd ed.). St. Louis: Mosby.

GATCHEL, R. J. (1980). Effectiveness of two procedures for reducing dental fear: Group-administered desensitization and group education and discussion. *Journal of the American Dental Association, 101,* 634–638.

GATCHEL, R. J., MAYER, T. G., CAPRA, P., DIAMOND, P., & BARNETT, J. (1986). Millon Behavioral Health Inventory: Its utility in predicting physical function in low back pain patients. *Archives of Physical Medicine and Rehabilitation, 67,* 878–882.

GAUL, G. M. (1986, November 30). Despite curbs, health-care spending escalates. *Philadelphia Inquirer,* pp. E1–2.

GAVZER, B. (1988, September 18). Why do some people survive AIDS? *Parade Magazine,* pp. 4–7.

GELFAND, D. M. (1978). Social withdrawal and negative emotional states: Behavior therapy. In B. B. Wolman, J. Egan, & A. O. Ross (Eds.), *Handbook of treatment of mental disorders in childhood and adolescence.* Englewood Cliffs, NJ: Prentice–Hall.

GENTRY, W. D. (1984). Behavioral medicine: A new research paradigm. In W. D. Gentry (Ed.), *Handbook of behavioral medicine.* New York: Guilford.

GENTRY, W. D., & KOBASA, S. C. O. (1984). Social and psychological resources mediating stress–illness relationships in humans. In W. D. Gentry (Ed.), *Handbook of behavioral medicine.* New York: Guilford.

GENTRY, W. D., & OWENS, D. (1986). Pain groups. In A. D. Holzman & D. C. Turk (Eds.), *Pain management: A handbook of psychological treatment approaches.* New York: Pergamon.

GERACE, R. A., & VORP, R. (1985). Epidemiology and behavior. In N. Schneiderman & J. T. Tapp (Eds.), *Behavioral medicine: The biopsychosocial approach.* Hillsdale, NJ: Erlbaum.

GERGEN, P. J., MULLALLY, D. I., & EVANS, R. (1988). National survey of prevalence of asthma among children in the United States, 1976 to 1980. *Pediatrics, 81,* 1–7.

GERVASIO, A. H. (1986). Family relationships and compliance. In K. E. Gerber & A. M. Nehemkis (Eds.), *Compliance: The dilemma of the chronically ill.* New York: Springer.

GESCHWIND, N. (1979, September). Specializations of the human brain. *Scientific American, 241,* 180–199.

GIL, K. M., KEEFE, F. J., CRISSON, J. E., & VAN DALFSEN, P. J. (1987). Social support and pain behavior. *Pain, 29,* 209–217.

GIL, K. M., KEEFE, F. J., SAMPSON, H. A., MCCASKILL, C. C., RODIN, J., & CRISSON, J. E. (1988). Direct observation of scratching behavior in children with atopic dermatitis. *Behavior Therapy, 19,* 213–227.

GILBERSTADT, H., & DUKER, J. (1965). *A handbook for clinical and actuarial MMPI interpretation.* Philadelphia: Saunders.

GILBERT, D. G., & SPIELBERGER, C. D. (1987). Effects of smoking on heart rate, anxiety, and feelings of success during social interaction. *Journal of Behavioral Medicine, 10,* 629–638.

GILLUM, R. F. (1987a). The association of body fat distribution with hypertension, hypertensive heart disease, coronary heart disease, diabetes and cardiovascular risk factors in men and women aged 18-79 years. *Journal of Chronic Diseases, 40,* 421-428.

GILLUM, R. F. (1987b). The association of the ratio of waist to hip girth with blood pressure, serum cholesterol and serum uric acid in children and youths aged 6-17 years. *Journal of Chronic Diseases, 40,* 413-420.

GINZBERG, E. (1983). Allied health resources. In D. Mechanic (Ed.), *Handbook of health, health care, and the health professions.* New York: Free Press.

GIRODO, M., & WOOD, D. (1979). Talking yourself out of pain: The importance of believing that you can. *Cognitive Therapy and Research, 3,* 23-33.

GLASER, R., THORN, B. E., TARR, K. L., KIECOLT-GLASER, J. K., & D'AMBROSIO, S. M. (1985). Effects of stress on methyltransferase synthesis: An important DNA repair enzyme. *Health Psychology, 4,* 403-412.

GLASGOW, R. E., KLESGES, R. C., MIZES, J. S., & PECHACEK, T. F. (1985). Quitting smoking: Strategies used and variables associated with success in a stop-smoking contest. *Journal of Consulting and Clinical Psychology, 53,* 905-912.

GLASGOW, R. E., & LICHTENSTEIN, E. (1987). Long-term effects of behavioral smoking cessation interventions. *Behavior Therapy, 18,* 297-324.

GLASGOW, R. E., MCCAUL, K. D., & SCHAFER, L. C. (1986). Barriers to regimen adherence among persons with insulin-dependent diabetes. *Journal of Behavioral Medicine, 9,* 65-77.

GLASGOW, R. E., MCCAUL, K. D., & SCHAFER, L. C. (1987). Self-care behaviors and glycemic control in Type I diabetes. *Journal of Chronic Diseases, 40,* 399-412.

GLASS, D. C. (1977). *Behavior patterns, stress, and coronary heart disease.* Hillsdale, NJ: Erlbaum.

GLASS, D. C., KRAKOFF, L. R., CONTRADA, R., HILTON, W. F., KEHOE, K., MANNUCCI, E. G., COLLINS, C., SNOW, B., & ELTING, E. (1980). Effect of harassment and competition upon cardiovascular and plasma catecholamine responses in Type A and Type B individuals. *Psychophysiology, 17,* 453-463.

GLASS, D. C., ROSS, D. T., ISECKE, W., & ROSENMAN, R. H. (1982). Relative importance of speech characteristics and content of answers in the assessment of behavior pattern A by the Structured Interview. *Basic and Applied Social Psychology, 3,* 161-168.

GLEIBERMAN, L., & HARBURG, E. (1986). Alcohol usage and blood pressure: A review. *Human Biology, 58,* 1-31.

GLICK, R., & CERULLO, L. J. (1986). Subarachnoid and parenchymal hemorrhage. In P. E. Kaplan & L. J. Cerullo (Eds.), *Stroke rehabilitation.* Boston: Butterworth.

GLYNN, S. M., GRUDER, C. L., & JEGERSKI, J. A. (1986). Effects of biochemical validation of self-reported cigarette smoking on treatment success and on misreporting abstinence. *Health Psychology, 5,* 125-136.

GODIN, G., DESHARNAIS, R., JOBIN, J., & COOK, J. (1987). The impact of physical fitness and health-age appraisal upon exercise intentions and behavior. *Journal of Behavioral Medicine, 10,* 241-250.

GODIN, G., VALOIS, P., SHEPHARD, R. J., & DESHARNAIS, R. (1987). Prediction of leisure-time exercise behavior: A path analysis (LISREL V) model. *Journal of Behavioral Medicine, 10,* 145-158.

GOFFMAN, E. (1961). *Asylums.* Garden City, NY: Doubleday.

GOLD, P. W., GWIRTSMAN, H., AVGERINOS, P. C., NIEMAN, L. K., GALLUCCI, W. T., KAYE, W., JIMERSON, D., EBERT, M., RITTMASTER, R., LORIAUX, L., & CHROUSOS, G. P. (1986). Abnormal hypothalamic-pituitary-adrenal function in anorexia nervosa: Pathophysiologic mechanisms in underweight and weight-corrected patients. *New England Journal of Medicine, 314,* 1335-1342.

GOLDBERG, E. L., & COMSTOCK, G. W. (1980). Epidemiology of life events: Frequency in general populations. *American Journal of Epidemiology, 111,* 736-752.

GOLDING, J. F., & CORNISH, A. M. (1987). Personality and life-style in medical students: Psychopharmacological aspects. *Psychology and Health, 1,* 287-301.

GOLDMAN, M. S. (1983). Cognitive impairment in chronic alcoholics. *American Psychologist, 38,* 1045-1054.

GOLDWATER, B. C., & COLLIS, M. L. (1985). Psychologic effects of cardiovascular conditioning: A controlled experiment. *Psychosomatic Medicine, 47,* 174-181.

GONDER-FREDERICK, L. A., COX, D. J., BOBBITT, S. A., & PENNEBAKER, J. W. (1989). Mood changes associated with blood glucose fluctuations in insulin-dependent diabetes mellitus. *Health Psychology, 8,* 45-59.

GONDER-FREDERICK, L., COX, D. J., POHL, S. L., & CARTER, W. (1984). Patient blood glucose monitoring: Use, accuracy, adherence, and impact. *Behavioral Medicine Update, 6*(1), 12-16.

GOODWIN, D. W. (1986). Heredity and alcoholism. *Annals of Behavioral Medicine, 8*(2-3), 3-6.

GORDER, D. D., DOLECEK, T. A., COLEMAN, G. G., TILLOTSON, J. L., BROWN, H. B., LENZ-LITZOW, K., BARTSCH, G. E., & GRANDITS, G. (1986). Dietary intake in the Multiple Risk Factor Intervention Trial (MRFIT): Nutrient and food group changes over 6 years. *Journal of the American Dietetic Association, 86,* 744-751.

GORDON, T., & DOYLE, J. T. (1987). Drinking and mortality: The Albany Study. *American Journal of Epidemiology, 125,* 263-270.

GORDON, T., & KANNEL, W. B. (1984). Drinking and mortality: The Framingham Study. *American Journal of Epidemiology, 120,* 97-107.

GORDON, W. A., & DILLER, L. (1983). Stroke: Coping with a cognitive deficit. In T. G. Burish & L. A. Bradley (Eds.), *Coping with chronic disease: Research and applications.* New York: Academic Press.

GORKIN, L. (1987). Behavioral medicine research in the etiology of essential hypertension: Bridging the cardiovascular reactivity and renal dysfunction paradigms. *Behavioral Medicine Abstracts, 8,* 159-162.

GORTMAKER, S. L., DIETZ, W. H., SOBOL, A. M., & WEHLER, C. A. (1987). Increasing pediatric obesity in the United States. *American Journal of Diseases of Children, 141,* 535-540.

GORTMAKER, S. L., ECKENRODE, J., & GORE, S. (1982). Stress and the utilization of health services: A time series and cross-sectional analysis. *Journal of Health and Social Behavior, 23,* 25-38.

GOTTLIEB, N. H. (1983). The effect of health beliefs on the smoking behavior of college women. *Journal of American College Health, 31,* 214-221.

GOTTLIEB, N. H., & BAKER, J. A. (1986). The relative influence of health beliefs, parental and peer behaviors and exercise program participation on smoking, alcohol use and physical activity. *Social Science and Medicine, 22,* 915-927.

GRANT, J. C. B. (1972). *An atlas of anatomy.* Baltimore: Williams & Wilkins.

GRAZIANO, A. M., DEGIOVANNI, I. S., & GARCIA, K. A. (1979). Behavioral treatment of children's fears: A review. *Psychological Bulletin, 86,* 804-830.

GREEN, C. J. (1985). The use of psychodiagnostic questionnaires in predicting risk factors and health outcomes. In P. Karoly (Ed.), *Measurement strategies in health psychology.* New York: Wiley.

GREENFIELD, D. (1985). Nutritional basis of health and disease. In N. Schneiderman & J. T. Tapp (Eds.), *Behavioral medicine: The biopsychosocial approach.* Hillsdale, NJ: Erlbaum.

GREENWALD, H. P., BONICA, J. J., & BERGNER, M. (1987). The prevalence of pain in four cancers. *Cancer, 60,* 2563-2569.

GRITZ, E. R., KSIR, G., & MCCARTHY, W. J. (1985). Smokeless tobacco use in the United States: Present use and future trends. *Annals of Behavioral Medicine, 7*(2), 24-27.

GROB, G. N. (1983). Disease and environment in American history. In D. Mechanic (Ed.), *Handbook of health, health care, and the health professions.* New York: Free Press.

GROBBEE, D. E., & HOFMAN, A. (1986). Does sodium restriction lower blood pressure? *British Medical Journal, 293,* 27-29.

GROSSBART, T. A. (1982, February). Bringing peace to embattled skin. *Psychology Today, 16,* pp. 55-60.

GRUNAU, R. V. E., & CRAIG, K. D. (1987). Pain expression in neonates: Facial action and cry. *Pain, 28,* 395-410.

GRUNBERG, N. E., & BOWEN, D. J. (1985). Coping with the sequelae of smoking cessation. *Journal of Cardiopulmonary Rehabilitation, 5,* 285-289.

GUCK, T. P., SKULTETY, F. M., MEILMAN, P. W., & DOWD, E. T. (1985). Multidisciplinary pain center follow-up study: Evaluation with a no-treatment control group. *Pain, 21,* 295-306.

GUYTON, A. C. (1985). *Anatomy and physiology.* Philadelphia: Saunders.

HACKETT, T. P., & WEISMAN, A. D. (1985). Reactions to the imminence of death. In A. Monat & R. S. Lazarus (Eds.), *Stress and coping: An anthology* (2nd ed.). New York: Columbia University Press.

HAGGERTY, R. J. (1986). The changing nature of pediatrics. In N. A. Krasnegor, J. D. Arasteh, & M. F. Cataldo (Eds.), *Child health behavior: A behavioral pediatrics perspective.* New York: Wiley.

HALL, D. C., ADAMS, C. K., STEIN, G. H., STEPHENSON, H. S., GOLDSTEIN, M. K., & PENNYPACKER, H. S. (1980). Improved detection of human breast lesions following experimental training. *Cancer, 46,* 408-414.

HALL, S. M., RUGG, D., TUNSTALL, C., & JONES, R. T. (1984). Preventing relapse to cigarette smoking by behavioral skill training. *Journal of Consulting and Clinical Psychology, 52,* 372-382.

HANSEN, W. B., GRAHAM, J. W., SOBEL, J. L., SHELTON, D. R., FLAY, B. R., & JOHNSON, C. A. (1987). The consistency of peer and parent influences on tobacco, alcohol, and marijuana use among young adolescents. *Journal of Behavioral Medicine, 10,* 559-579.

HANSON, C. L., HENGGELER, S. W., & BURGHEN, G. A. (1987). Social competence and parental support as mediators of the link between stress and metabolic control in adolescents with insulin-dependent diabetes mellitus. *Journal of Consulting and Clinical Psychology, 55,* 529-533.

HARBURG, E., ERFURT, J. C., HAUENSTEIN, L. S., CHAPE, C., SCHULL, W. J., & SCHORK, M. A. (1973). Socio-ecological stress, suppressed hostility, skin color, and black-white male blood pressure: Detroit. *Psychosomatic Medicine, 35,* 276-296.

HARE, B. D., & MILANO, R. A. (1985). Chronic pain: Perspectives on physical assessment and treatment. *Annals of Behavioral Medicine, 7*(3), 6-10.

HARLAN, W. R. (1984). Rationale for intervention on blood pressure in childhood and adolescence. In J. D. Matarazzo, S. M. Weiss, J. A. Herd, N. E. Miller, & S. M. Weiss (Eds.), *Behavioral health: A handbook of health enhancement and disease prevention.* New York: Wiley.

HARPER, P. S. (1981). *Practical genetic counselling.* Baltimore: University Park Press.

HARRIS, D. M., & GUTEN, S. (1979). Health-protective behavior: An exploratory study. *Journal of Health and Social Behavior, 20,* 17-29.

HARTER, S. (1983). Developmental perspectives on the self-system. In P. H. Mussen (Ed.), *Handbook of child psychology* (4th ed., Vol. 4). New York: Wiley.

HARTUP, W. W. (1983). Peer relations. In P. H. Mussen (Ed.), *Handbook of child psychology* (4th ed., Vol. 4). New York: Wiley.

HARTZ, A. J., RUPLEY, D. C., & RIMM, A. A. (1984). The association of girth measurements with disease in 32,856 women. *American Journal of Epidemiology, 119,* 71-80.

HARVEY, P. G. (1984). Lead and children's health — Recent research and future questions. *Journal of Child Psychology and Psychiatry, 25,* 517-522.

HASKELL, W. L. (1984). Overview: Health benefits of exercise. In J. D. Matarazzo, S. M. Weiss, J. A. Herd, N. E. Miller, & S. M. Weiss (Eds.), *Behavioral health: A handbook of health enhancement and disease prevention.* New York: Wiley.

HASKELL, W. L. (1985). Exercise programs for health promotion. In J. C. Rosen & L. J. Solomon (Eds.), *Prevention in health psychology.* Hanover, NH: University Press of New England.

HATCH, J. P., GATCHEL, R. J., & HARRINGTON, R. (1982). Biofeedback: Clinical applications in medicine. In R. J. Gatchel, A. Baum, & J. E. Singer (Eds.), *Handbook of psychology and health* (Vol. 1). Hillsdale, NJ: Erlbaum.

HATHAWAY, S. R., & MCKINLEY, J. C. (1967). *The Minnesota Multiphasic Personality Inventory Manual.* New York: Psychological Corporation.

HAUG, M. R., & LAVIN, B (1981). Practitioner or patient—Who's in charge? *Journal of Health and Social Behavior, 22,* 212-229.

HAY, D., & OKEN, D. (1985). The psychological stresses of intensive care unit nursing. In A. Monat & R. S. Lazarus (Eds.), *Stress and coping* (2nd ed.). New York: Columbia University Press.

HAYNES, R. B. (1976). A critical review of the "determinants" of patient compliance with therapeutic regimens. In D. L. Sackett & R. B. Haynes (Eds.), *Compliance with therapeutic regimens.* Baltimore: Johns Hopkins University Press.

HAYNES, R. B. (1982). Improving patient compliance: An empirical review. In R. B. Stuart (Ed.), *Adherence, compliance, and generalization in behavioral medicine.* New York: Brunner/Mazel.

HAYNES, S. G., FEINLEIB, M., & KANNEL, W. B. (1980). The relationship of psychosocial factors to coronary heart disease in the Framingham Study: III. Eight-year incidence of coronary heart disease. *American Journal of Epidemiology, 111,* 37-58.

HAYNES, S. G., LEVINE, S., SCOTCH, N., FEINLEIB, M., & KANNEL, W. B. (1978). The relationship of psychosocial factors to coronary heart disease in the Framingham Study: I. Methods and risk factors. *American Journal of Epidemiology, 107,* 362-383.

HAYNES, S. G., & MATTHEWS, K. A. (1988). Review and methodological critique of recent studies on Type A behavior and cardiovascular disease. *Annals of Behavioral Medicine, 10,* 47-59.

HEBB, D. O. (1955). Drives and the C.N.S. (conceptual nervous system). *Psychological Review, 62,* 243-254.

HECKLER, M. M. (1985). The fight against Alzheimer's disease. *American Psychologist, 40,* 1240-1244.

HEGSTED, D. M. (1984). What is a healthful diet? In J. D. Matarazzo, S. M. Weiss, J. A. Herd, N. E. Miller, & S. M. Weiss (Eds.), *Behavioral health: A handbook of health enhancement and disease prevention.* New York: Wiley.

HEINRICH, R. L., COHEN, M. J., NALIBOFF, B. D., COLLINS, G. A., & BONNEBAKKER, A. D. (1985). Comparing physical and behavior therapy for chronic low back pain on physical abilities, psychological distress, and patients' perceptions. *Journal of Behavioral Medicine, 8,* 61-78.

HEISEL, J. S., REAM, S., RAITZ, R., RAPPOPORT, M., & CODDINGTON, R. D. (1973). The significance of life events as contributing factors in the diseases of children. *Journal of Pediatrics, 83,* 119-123.

HEITZMANN, C. A., & KAPLAN, R. M. (1988). Assessment of methods for measuring social support. *Health Psychology, 7,* 75-109.

HENDERSON, G., & PRIMEAUX, M. (1981). Religious beliefs and healing. In G. Henderson & M. Primeaux (Eds.), *Transcultural health care.* Menlo Park, CA: Addison-Wesley.

HENDLER, N. H. (1984). Chronic pain. In H. B. Roback (Eds.), *Helping patients and their families cope with medical problems.* San Francisco: Jossey-Bass.

HENDRICK, S. S. (1985). Spinal cord injury and neuromuscular reeducation. In N. Schneiderman & J. T. Tapp (Eds.), *Behavioral medicine: The biopsychosocial approach.* Hillsdale, NJ: Erlbaum.

HENIG, R. M. (1988, February 28). The high cost of thinness. *New York Times Magazine,* pp. 41-42.

HERD, J. A., & WEISS, S. M. (1984). Overview of hypertension: Its treatment and prevention. In J. D. Matarazzo, S. M. Weiss, J. A. Herd, N. E. Miller, & S. M. Weiss (Eds.), *Behavioral health: A handbook of health enhancement and disease prevention.* New York: Wiley.

HEREK, G. M. (1989). Hate crimes against lesbians and gay men. *American Psychologist, 44,* 948-955.

HEREK, G. M., & GLUNT, E. K. (1988). An epidemic of stigma: Public reactions to AIDS. *American Psychologist, 43,* 886-891.

HERMAN, C. P., & MACK, D. (1975). Restrained and unrestrained eating. *Journal of Personality, 43,* 647-660.

HERMAN, C. P., OLMSTEAD, M. P., & POLIVY, J. (1983). Obesity, externality, and susceptibility to social influence: An integrated analysis. *Journal of Personality and Social Psychology, 45,* 926-934.

HERMAN, C. P., & POLIVY, J. (1980). Restrained eating. In A. J. Stunkard (Ed.), *Obesity.* Philadelphia: Saunders.

HERMAN, S. B., & SMITH, M. H. (1984). Children—Section 1. Cancer of the blood: Leukemia. In S. N. McIntire & A. L. Cioppa (Eds.), *Cancer nursing: A developmental approach.* New York: Wiley.

HETHERINGTON, E. M., COX, M., & COX, R. (1982). Effects of divorce on parents and children. In M. E. Lamb (Ed.), *Nontraditional families: Parenting and child development.* Hillsdale, NJ: Erlbaum.

HIER, D. B. (1986). Recovery from behavioral deficits after stroke. In P. E. Kaplan & L. J. Cerullo (Eds.), *Stroke rehabilitation.* Boston: Butterworth.

HILGARD, E. R. (1967). Individual differences in hypnotizability. In J. E. Gordon (Ed.), *Handbook of clinical and experimental hypnosis.* New York: Macmillan Co.

HILGARD, E. R., & HILGARD, J. R. (1983). *Hypnosis in the relief of pain* (rev. ed.). Los Altos, CA: Kaufmann.

HILL, J. O., SPARLING, P. B., SHIELDS, T. W., & HELLER, P. A. (1987). Effects of exercise and food restriction on body composition and metabolic rate in obese women. *American Journal of Clinical Nutrition, 46,* 622-630.

HINTON, J. (1984). Coping with terminal illness. In R. Fitzpatrick, J. Hinton, S. Newman, G. Scambler, & J. Thompson (Eds.), *The experience of illness.* London: Tavistock.

HIROTO, D. S., & SELIGMAN, M. E. P. (1975). Generality of learned helplessness in man. *Journal of Personality and Social Psychology, 31,* 311-327.

HIRSCHORN, M. W. (1987, April 29). AIDS is not seen as a major threat by many heterosexuals on campuses. *Chronical of Higher Education,* pp. 1, 32-34.

HLETKO, P. J., ROBIN, S. S., HLETKO, J. D., & STONE, M. (1987). Infant safety seat use: Reaching the hard to reach. *American Journal of Diseases in Children, 141,* 1301-1304.

HOBDELL, E. F. (1985). The neurologic system. In L. L. Hayman & E. M. Sporing (Eds.), *Handbook of pediatric nursing.* New York: Wiley.

HOELSCHER, T. J., LICHSTEIN, K. L., & ROSENTHAL, T. L. (1986). Home relaxation practice in hypertension treatment: Objective assessment and compliance induction. *Journal of Consulting and Clinical Psychology, 54,* 217-221.

HOFMAN, A., WALTER, H. J., CONNELLY, P. A., & VAUGHN, R. D. (1987). Blood pressure and physical fitness in children. *Hypertension, 9,* 188-191.

HOFSTETTER, A., SCHUTZ, Y., JÉQUIER, E., & WAHREN, J. (1986). Increased 24-hour energy expenditure in cigarette smokers. *New England Journal of Medicine, 314,* 79-82.

HOLAHAN, C. J., & MOOS, R. H. (1985). Life stress and health: Personality, coping, and family support in stress resistance. *Journal of Personality and Social Psychology, 49,* 739-747.

HOLAHAN, C. J., & MOOS, R. H. (1986). Personality, coping, and family resources in stress resistance: A longitudinal analysis. *Journal of Personality and Social Psychology, 51,* 389-395.

HOLAHAN, C. K., HOLAHAN, C. J., & BELK, S. S. (1984). Adjustment in aging: The roles of life stress, hassles, and self-efficacy. *Health Psychology, 3,* 315-328.

HOLBROOK, T. (1985). The hematopoietic system. In L. L. Hayman & E. M. Sporing (Eds.), *Handbook of pediatric nursing.* New York: Wiley.

HOLLANDER, J. L. (1984). Rheumatoid arthritis. In G. K. Riggs & E. P. Gall (Eds.), *Rheumatic diseases: Rehabilitation and management.* Boston: Butterworth.

HOLMES, D. M. (1986). The person and diabetes in psychosocial context. *Diabetes Care, 9,* 194-206.

HOLMES, D. S. (1984). Mediation and somatic arousal reduction. *American Psychologist, 39,* 1-10.

HOLMES, T. H., & MASUDA, M. (1974). Life change and illness susceptibility. In B. S. Dohrenwend & B. P. Dohrenwend (Eds.), *Stressful life events: Their nature and effects.* New York: Wiley.

HOLMES, T. H., & RAHE, R. H. (1967). The Social Readjustment Rating Scale. *Journal of Psychosomatic Research, 11,* 213-218.

HOLROYD, K. A., & PENZIEN, D. B. (1985). Client variables and the behavioral treatment of recurrent tension headache: A meta-analytic review. *Journal of Behavioral Medicine, 9,* 515-536.

HOLUM, J. R. (1987). *Elements of general and biological chemistry* (7th ed.). New York: Wiley.

HOLZMAN, A. D., & TURK, D. C. (Eds.) (1986). *Pain management: A handbook of psychological treatment approaches.* New York: Pergamon.

HOLZMAN, A. D., TURK, D. C., & KERNS, R. D. (1986). The cognitive-behavioral approach to the management of chronic pain. In A. D. Holzman & D. C. Turk (Eds.), *Pain management: A handbook of psychological treatment approaches.* New York: Pergamon.

HONIG, A. S. (1987). Stress and coping in children. In H. E. Fitzgerald & M. G. Walraven (Eds.), *Annual editions: Human development 87/88.* Guilford, CT: Dushkin.

HORN, J. C., & MEER, J. (1987, May). The vintage years. *Psychology Today, 21,* pp. 76-84, 89-90.

HOSSACK, K. F., & LEFF, N. B. (1987). Influence of education and work history on patient perception of cardiovascular risk factors. *Journal of Cardiopulmonary Rehabilitation, 7,* 540-546.

HOUGH, R. L., FAIRBANK, D. T., & GARCIA, A. M. (1976). Problems in the ratio measurement of life stress. *Journal of Health and Social Behavior, 17,* 70-82.

HOUSE, A. (1987). Psychosocial problems of patients on the renal unit and their relation to treatment outcome. *Journal of Psychosomatic Research, 31,* 441-452.

HOUSE, J. S. (1984). Barriers to work stress: I. Social support. In W. D. Gentry, H. Benson, & C. de Wolff (Eds.), *Behavioral medicine: Work, stress, and health.* The Hague: Martinus Nijhoff.

HOUSE, J. S., ROBBINS, C., & METZNER, H. L. (1982). The association of social relationships and activities with mortality: Prospective evidence from the Tecumseh Community Health Study. *American Journal of Epidemiology, 116,* 123-140.

HOUSTON, B. K. (1986). Psychological variables and cardiovascular and neuroendocrine reactivity. In K. A. Matthews, S. M. Weiss, T. Detre, T. M. Dembroski, B. Falkner, S. B. Manuck, & R. B. Williams (Eds.), *Handbook of stress, reactivity, and cardiovascular disease.* New York: Wiley.

HOWARD, J. H., RECHNITZER, P. A., CUNNINGHAM, D. A., & DONNER, A. P. (1986). Change in Type A behavior a year after retirement. *The Gerontologist, 26,* 643-649.

HUBERT, H. B. (1986). The importance of obesity in the development of coronary risk factors and disease: The epidemiologic evidence. In L. Breslow, J. E. Fielding, & L. B. Lave (Eds.), *Annual review of public health* (Vol. 7). Palo Alto, CA: Annual Reviews.

HUGHES, G. H., HYMOWITZ, N., OCKENE, J. K., SIMON, V., & VOGT, T. M. (1981). The Multiple Risk Factor Intervention Trial (MRFIT). V. Intervention on smoking. *Preventive Medicine, 10,* 476-500.

HUGHES, J. R. (1986). Genetics of smoking: A brief review. *Behavior Therapy, 17,* 335-345.

HULL, J. G., & BOND, C. F. (1986). Social and behavioral consequences of alcohol consumption and expectancy: A meta-analysis. *Psychological Bulletin, 99,* 347-360.

HULL, J. G., VAN TREUREN, R. R., & VIRNELLI, S. (1987). Hardiness and health: A critique and alternative approach. *Journal of Personality and Social Psychology, 53,* 518-530.

HULL, J. G., YOUNG, R. D., & JOURILES, E. (1986). Applications of the self-awareness model of alcohol consumption: Predicting patterns of use and abuse. *Journal of Personality and Social Psychology, 51,* 790-796.

HUNT, W. A., & MATARAZZO, J. D. (1982). Changing smoking behavior: A critique. In R. J. Gatchel, A. Baum, & J. E.

Singer (Eds.), *Handbook of psychology and health* (Vol. 1). Hillsdale, NJ: Erlbaum.

Hunt, W. A., Matarazzo, J. D., Weiss, S. M., & Gentry, W. D. (1978). Associative learning, habit, and health behavior. *Journal of Behavioral Medicine, 2,* 111-124.

Hurley, D. (1987, August). A sound mind in an unsound body. *Psychology Today, 21,* pp. 34-43.

Huston, A. C. (1983). Sex-typing. In P. H. Mussen (Ed.), *Handbook of child psychology* (4th ed., Vol. 4). New York: Wiley.

Hyson, M. C. (1983). Going to the doctor: A developmental study of stress and coping. *Journal of Child Psychology and Psychiatry, 24,* 247-259.

Ikard, F. F., & Tomkins, S. (1973). The experience of affect as a determinant of smoking behavior: A series of validity studies. *Journal of Abnormal Psychology, 81,* 172-181.

Ilfeld, F. W. (1980). Coping styles of Chicago adults: Description. *Journal of Human Stress, 6,* 2-10.

Ingersoll, G. M., Orr, D. P., Herrold, A. J., & Golden, M. P. (1986). Cognitive maturity and self-management among adolescents with insulin-dependent diabetes mellitus. *Journal of Pediatrics, 108,* 620-623.

Inui, T. S., Yourtee, E. L., & Williamson, J. W. (1976). Improved outcomes in hypertension after physician tutorials. *Annals of Internal Medicine, 84,* 646-651.

Izard, C. E. (1979). Emotions as motivations: An evolutionary developmental perspective. In H. E. Howe & R. A. Dienstbier (Eds.), *Nebraska Symposium on Motivation 1978* (Vol. 27). Lincoln, NB: University of Nebraska Press.

Izard, C. E., & Dougherty, L. M. (1982). Two complementary systems for measuring facial expressions in infants and children. In C. E. Izard (Ed.), *Measuring emotions in infants and children.* Cambridge, England: Cambridge University Press.

Izard, C. E., Hembree, E. A., Dougherty, L. M., & Spizzirri, C. C. (1983). Changes in facial expressions of 2- to 19-month-old infants following acute pain. *Developmental Psychology, 19,* 418-426.

Jaccard, J., & Turrisi, R. (1987). Cognitive processes and individual differences in judgments relevant to drunk driving. *Journal of Personality and Social Psychology, 53,* 135-145.

Jacob, R. G., & Chesney, M. A. (1986). Psychological and behavioral methods to reduce cardiovascular reactivity. In K. A. Matthews, S. M. Weiss, T. Detre, T. M. Dembroski, B. Falkner, S. B. Manuck, & R. B. Williams (Eds.), *Handbook of stress, reactivity, and cardiovascular disease.* New York: Wiley.

Jacobson, A. M., Hauser, S. T., Wolfsdorf, J. I., Houlihan, J., Milley, J. E., Herskowitz, R. D., Wertlieb, D., & Watt, E. (1987). Psychologic predictors of compliance in children with recent onset of diabetes mellitus. *Journal of Pediatrics, 110,* 805-811.

Jacobson, E. J. (1938). *Progressive relaxation.* Chicago: University of Chicago Press.

James, G. D., Yee, L. S., Harshfield, G. A., Blank, S. G., & Pickering, T. G. (1986). The influence of happiness, anger, and anxiety on the blood pressure of borderline hypertensives. *Psychosomatic Medicine, 48,* 502-508.

James, S. A., LaCroix, A. Z., Kleinbaum, D. G., & Strogatz, D. S. (1984). John Henryism and blood pressure among black men. II. The role of occupational stressors. *Journal of Behavioral Medicine, 7,* 259-274.

Jamner, L. D., & Tursky, B. (1987). Syndrome-specific descriptor profiling: A psychophysiological and psychophysical approach. *Health Psychology, 6,* 417-430.

Janis, I. L. (1958). *Psychological stress.* New York: Wiley.

Janis, I. L. (1967). Effects of fear arousal on attitude change: Recent developments in theory and experimental research. In L. Berkowitz (Ed.), *Advances in experimental social psychology* (Vol. 3). New York: Academic Press.

Janis, I. L. (1984). The patient as decision maker. In W. D. Gentry (Ed.), *Handbook of behavioral medicine.* New York: Guilford.

Janis, I. L., & Mann, L. (1977). *Decision making: A psychological analysis of conflict, choice, and commitment.* New York: Free Press.

Jaret, P. (1986). Our immune system: The wars within. *National Geographic, 169,* 702-735.

Jay, S. M., Elliott, C. H., Katz, E., & Siegel, S. E. (1987). Cognitive-behavioral and pharmacologic interventions for children's distress during painful medical procedures. *Journal of Consulting and Clinical Psychology, 55,* 860-865.

Jay, S. M., Elliott, C. H., Ozolins, M., Olson, R. A., & Pruitt, S. D. (1985). Behavioral management of children's distress during painful medical procedures. *Behavior Research and Therapy, 23,* 513-520.

Jeans, M. E. (1983). Pain in children—A neglected area. In P. Firestone, P. J. McGrath, & W. Feldman (Eds.), *Advances in behavioral medicine for children and adolescents.* Hillsdale, NJ: Erlbaum.

Jemmott, J. B., Croyle, R. T., & Ditto, P. H. (1988). Commonsense epidemiology: Self-based judgments from laypersons and physicians. *Health Psychology, 7,* 55-73.

Jemmott, J. B., Ditto, P. H., & Croyle, R. T. (1986). Judging health status: Effects of perceived prevalence and personal relevance. *Journal of Personality and Social Psychology, 50,* 899-905.

Jemmott, J. B., & Locke, S. E. (1984). Psychosocial factors, immunologic mediation, and human susceptibility to infectious diseases: How much do we know? *Psychological Bulletin, 95,* 78-108.

Jenkins, C. D. (1979). An approach to the diagnosis and treatment of problems of health related behaviour. *International Journal of Health Education, 22*(Suppl. 2), 1-24.

Jenkins, C. D., Zyzanski, S. J., & Rosenman, R. H. (1979). *The Jenkins Activity Survey for Health Prediction.* New York: The Psychological Corporation.

Jennings, G., Nelson, L., Nestel, P., Esler, M., Korner, P., Burton, D., & Bazelmans, J. (1986). The effects of changes in physical activity on major cardiovascular risk factors, hemodynamics, sympathetic function, and glucose utilization in man: A controlled study of four levels of activity. *Circulation, 73,* 30-40.

JERSE, M. A., WHITMAN, H. H., & GUSTAFSON, J. P. (1984). Cancer in adults. In H. B. Roback (Ed.), *Helping patients and their families cope with medical problems*. San Francisco: Jossey-Bass.

JESSOR, R. (1984). Adolescent development and behavioral health. In J. D. Matarazzo, S. M. Weiss, J. A. Herd, N. E. Miller, & S. M. Weiss (Eds.), *Behavioral health: A handbook of health enhancement and disease prevention*. New York: Wiley.

JESSOR, R., & JESSOR, S. L. (1977). *Problem behavior and psychosocial development: A longitudinal study of youth*. New York: Academic Press.

JETTE, A. M. (1984). Understanding and enhancing patient cooperation with arthritis treatments. In G. K. Riggs & E. P. Gall (Eds.), *Rheumatic diseases: Rehabilitation and management*. Boston: Butterworth.

JOHNSON, B. G. (1984). Biofeedback, transcutaneous electrical nerve stimulation, acupuncture, and hypnosis. In G. K. Riggs & E. P. Gall (Eds.), *Rheumatic diseases: Rehabilitation and management*. Boston: Butterworth.

JOHNSON, C. A., HANSEN, W. B., COLLING, L. M., & GRAHAM, J. W. (1986). High-school smoking prevention: Results of a three-year longitudinal study. *Journal of Behavioral Medicine, 9,* 439-452.

JOHNSON, J. E. (1983). Psychological interventions and coping with surgery. In A. Baum, S. E. Taylor, & J. E. Singer (Eds.), *Handbook of psychology and health* (Vol. 4). Hillsdale, NJ: Erlbaum.

JOHNSON, J. E., & LEVENTHAL, H. (1974). Effects of accurate expectations and behavioral instructions on reactions during a noxious medical examination. *Journal of Personality and Social Psychology, 29,* 710-718.

JOHNSON, J. E., RICE, V. H., FULLER, S. S., & ENDRESS, M. P. (1978). Sensory information, instruction in a coping strategy, and recovery from surgery. *Research in Nursing and Health, 1,* 4-17.

JOHNSON, J. H. (1986). *Life events as stressors in childhood and adolescence*. Newbury Park, CA: Sage.

JOHNSON, S. B. (1985). The family and the child with chronic illness. In D. C. Turk & R. D. Kerns (Eds.), *Health, illness, and families: A life-span perspective*. New York: Wiley.

JOHNSTON, L. D., BACHMAN, J. G., & O'MALLEY, P. M. (1982). *Student drug use in America 1975-1981* (DHHS Publication No. ADM 82-1221). Washington, DC: U.S. Government Printing Office.

JONES, K. L., SMITH, D. W., ULLELAND, C. N., & STREISSGUTH, A. P. (1973). Pattern of malformation in offspring of chronic alcoholic mothers. *Lancet,* 1267-1271.

JOSEPH, J. G., MONTGOMERY, S. B., EMMONS, C., KESSLER, R. C., OSTROW, D. G., WORTMAN, C. B., O'BRIEN, K., ELLER, M., & ESHLEMAN, S. (1987). Magnitude and determinants of behavioral risk reduction: Longitudinal analysis of a cohort at risk for AIDS. *Psychology and Health, 1,* 73-96.

JOYCE, C. (1984, November). A time for grieving. *Psychology Today, 18,* pp. 42-46.

KADEN, G. G., MCCARTER, R. J., JOHNSON, S. F., & FERENCZ, C. (1985). Physician-patient communication: Understanding congenital heart disease. *American Journal of Diseases in Children, 139,* 995-999.

KAHN, J. P., KORNFELD, D. S., FRANK, K. A., HELLER, S. S., & HOAR, P. F. (1980). Type A behavior and blood pressure during coronary artery bypass surgery. *Psychosomatic Medicine, 42,* 407-414.

KALOUPEK, D. G., WHITE, H., & WONG, M. (1984). Multiple assessment of coping strategies used by volunteer blood donors: Implications for preparatory training. *Journal of Behavioral Medicine, 7,* 35-60.

KALISH, R. A. (1985). The social context of death and dying. In R. H. Binstock & E. Shanas (Eds.), *Handbook of aging and the social sciences*. New York: Van Nostrand-Reinhold.

KALISH, R. A., & REYNOLDS, D. K. (1976). *Death and ethnicity: A psychocultural study*. Los Angeles: University of Southern California Press.

KAMARCK, T. W., & LICHTENSTEIN, E. (1985). Current trends in clinic-based smoking control. *Annals of Behavioral Medicine, 7*(2), 19-23.

KANDEL, D. (1974). Inter- and intragenerational influences of adolescent marijuana use. *Journal of Social Issues, 30,* 107-135.

KANDEL, D., & FAUST, R. (1975). Sequence and stages in patterns of adolescent drug use. *Archives of General Psychiatry, 32,* 923-932.

KANE, R. A. (1983). Social work as a health profession. In D. Mechanic (Ed.), *Handbook of health, health care, and the health professions*. New York: Free Press.

KANNER, A. D., COYNE, J. C., SCHAEFER, C., & LAZARUS, R. S. (1981). Comparison of two modes of stress measurement: Daily hassles and uplifts versus major life events. *Journal of Behavioral Medicine, 4,* 1-39.

KANNER, R. (1986). Pain management. *Journal of the American Medical Association, 256,* 2110-2114.

KAPLAN, B. J., & WYLER, A. R. (1983). Coping with epilepsy. In T. G. Burish & L. A. Bradley (Eds.), *Coping with chronic disease: Research and applications*. New York: Academic Press.

KAPLAN, N. M. (1986). Dietary aspects of the treatment of hypertension. In L. Breslow, J. E. Fielding, & L. B. Lave (Eds.), *Annual review of public health* (Vol. 7). Palo Alto, CA: Annual Reviews.

KAPLAN, R. M., ATKINS, C. J., & REINSCH, S. (1984). Specific efficacy expectations mediate exercise compliance in patients with COPD. *Health Psychology, 3,* 223-242.

KAPLAN, R. M., REIS, A., & ATKINS, C. J. (1985). Behavioral issues in the management of chronic obstructive pulmonary disease. *Annals of Behavioral Medicine, 7*(4), 5-10.

KAPUST, L. R., & WEINTRAUB, S. (1984). Living with a family member suffering from Alzheimer's disease. In H. B. Roback (Ed.), *Helping patients and their families cope with medical problems*. San Francisco: Jossey-Bass.

KARLIN, R. A., EPSTEIN, Y. M., & AIELLO, J. R. (1978). A setting-specific analysis of crowding. In A. Baum & Y. M. Epstein (Eds.), *Human response to crowding*. Hillsdale, NJ: Erlbaum.

KAROLY, P. (1985). The assessment of pain: Concepts and

procedures. In P. Karoly (Ed.), *Measurement strategies in health psychology.* New York: Wiley.

KASCH, F. W., WALLACE, J. P., & VAN CAMP, S. P. (1985). Effects of 18 years of endurance exercise on the physical work capacity of older men. *Journal of Cardiopulmonary Rehabilitation, 5,* 308-312.

KASL, S. V., & COBB, S. (1966a). Health behavior, illness behavior, and sick role behavior: I. Health and illness behavior. *Archives of Environmental Health, 12,* 246-266.

KASL, S. V., & COBB, S. (1966b). Health behavior, illness behavior, and sick role behavior: II. Sick role behavior. *Archives of Environmental Health, 12,* 531-541.

KASTENBAUM, R., & COSTA, P. T. (1977). Psychological perspectives on death. In M. R. Rosenzweig & L. W. Porter (Eds.), *Annual review of psychology* (Vol. 28). Palo Alto, CA: Annual Reviews.

KAUFMAN, B. (1988). A distant compassion. *Health Values, 12*(4), 31-32.

KEEFE, F. J. (1982). Behavioral assessment and treatment of chronic pain: Current status and future directions. *Journal of Consulting and Clinical Psychology, 50,* 896-911.

KEEFE, F. J., & BLOCK, A. R. (1982). Development of an observation method for assessing pain behavior in chronic low back pain patients. *Behavior Therapy, 13,* 363-375.

KEEFE, F. J., & DOLAN, E. (1986). Pain behavior and pain coping strategies in low back pain and myofascial pain dysfunction syndrome patients. *Pain, 24,* 49-56.

KEEFE, F. J., & GIL, K. M. (1985). Recent advances in the behavioral assessment and treatment of chronic pain. *Annals of Behavioral Medicine, 7*(3), 11-16.

KEESEY, R. E. (1986). A set point theory of obesity. In K. D. Brownell & J. P. Foreyt (Eds.), *The physiology, psychology, and treatment of the eating disorders.* New York: Basic Books.

KEESEY, R. E., & POWLEY, T. L. (1975). Hypothalamic regulation of body weight. *American Scientist, 63,* 558-565.

KEESLING, B., & FRIEDMAN, H. S. (1987). Psychosocial factors in sunbathing and sunscreen use. *Health Psychology, 6,* 477-493.

KEGELES, S. S. (1983). Behavioral methods for effective cancer screening and prevention. *Behavioral Medicine Update, 5*(2 & 3), 36-44.

KELLNER, R. (1985). Functional somatic symptoms and hypochondriasis: A survey of empirical studies. *Archives of General Psychiatry, 42,* 821-833.

KELLNER, R. (1987). Hypochondriasis and somatization. *Journal of the American Medical Association, 258,* 2718-2722.

KELSEY, J. L., & HOCHBERG, M. C. (1988). Epidemiology of chronic musculoskeletal disorders. In L. Breslow, J. E. Fielding, & L. B. Lave (Eds.), *Annual review of public health* (Vol. 9). Palo Alto, CA: Annual Reviews.

KEMPE, C. H. (1976). Child abuse and neglect. In N. B. Talbot (Ed.), *Raising children in modern America: Problems and prospective solutions.* Boston: Little, Brown.

KENDALL, P. C., WILLIAMS, L., PECHACEK, T. F., GRAHAM, L. E., SHISSLAK, C., & HERZOFF, N. (1979). Cognitive-behavioral and patient education interventions in cardiac catheterization procedures: The Palo Alto Medical Psychology Project. *Journal of Consulting and Clinical Psychology, 47,* 49-58.

KENT, G. (1985). Memory of dental pain. *Pain, 21,* 187-194.

KERNS, R. D., & CURLEY, A. D. (1985). A biopsychosocial approach to illness and the family: Neurological diseases across the life span. In D. C. Turk & R. D. Kerns (Eds.), *Health, illness, and families: A life-span perspective.* New York: Wiley.

KERNS, R. D., TURK, D. C., & RUDY, T. E. (1985). The West Haven-Yale Multidimensional Pain Inventory. *Pain, 23,* 345-356.

KETT, J. F. (1977). *Rites of passage: Adolescence in America 1790 to present.* New York: Basic Books.

KHAW, K., & BARRETT-CONNOR, E (1986). Family history of heart attack: A modifiable risk factor? *Circulation, 74,* 239-244.

KIECOLT-GLASER, J. K., FISHER, L. D., OGROCKI, P., STOUT, J. C., SPEICHER, C. E., & GLASER, R. (1987). Marital quality, marital disruption, and immune function. *Psychosomatic Medicine, 49,* 13-34.

KIECOLT-GLASER, J. K., GARNER, W., SPEICHER, C., PENN, G. M., HOLLIDAY, J., & GLASER, R. (1984). Psychosocial modifiers of immunocompetence in medical students. *Psychosomatic Medicine, 46,* 7-14.

KIECOLT-GLASER, J. K., & GLASER, R. (1986). Psychological influences on immunity. *Psychosomatics, 27,* 621-624.

KIECOLT-GLASER, J. K., STEPHENS, R. E., LIPETZ, P. D., SPEICHER, C. E., & GLASER, R. (1985). Distress and DNA repair in human lymphocytes. *Journal of Behavioral Medicine, 8,* 311-320.

KIECOLT-GLASER, J. K., & WILLIAMS, D. A. (1987). Self-blame, compliance, and distress among burn patients. *Journal of Personality and Social Psychology, 53,* 187-193.

KIESLER, C. A., & MORTON, T. L. (1988). Psychology and public policy in the "health care revolution." *American Psychologist, 43,* 993-1003.

KILO, C., & WILLIAMSON, J. R. (1987). *Diabetes: The facts that let you regain control of your life.* New York: Wiley.

KINDELAN, K., & KENT, G. (1987). Concordance between patients' information preferences and general practitioners' perceptions. *Psychology and Health, 1,* 399-409.

KIRSCHT, J. P. (1983). Preventive health behavior: A review of research and issues. *Health Psychology, 2,* 277-301.

KIRSCHT, J. P., & ROSENSTOCK, I. M. (1979). Patients' problems in following recommendations of health experts. In G. C. Stone, F. Cohen, & N. E. Adler (Eds.), *Health psychology—A handbook.* San Francisco: Jossey-Bass.

KIYAK, H. A., VITALIANO, P. P., & CRINEAN, J. (1988). Patients' expectations as predictors of orthognathic surgery outcomes. *Health Psychology, 7,* 251-268.

KLATSKY, A. L., FRIEDMAN, G. D., & SIEGELAUB, A. B. (1974). Alcohol consumption before myocardial infarction: Results from the Kaiser-Permanente epidemiological study of myocardial infarction. *Annals of Internal Medicine, 81,* 294-301.

KLATSKY, A. L., FRIEDMAN, G. D., & SIEGELAUB, A. B. (1981).

Alcohol and mortality: A ten-year Kaiser-Permanente experience. *Annals of Internal Medicine, 95,* 139-145.

KLEINKE, C. L., & SPANGLER, A. S. (1988). Psychometric analysis of the audiovisual taxonomy for assessing pain behavior in chronic back-pain patients. *Journal of Behavioral Medicine, 11,* 83-94.

KLOCKENBRINK, M. (1987, September 27). How to read a label. *New York Times Magazine,* pp. 67-72.

KNAPP, R. J. (1987, July). When a child dies. *Psychology Today, 21,* pp. 60-67.

KNEUT, C. M. (1982). Legal, ethical, and moral considerations in pediatric nursing. In M. J. Smith, J. A. Goodman, N. L. Ramsey, & S. B. Pasternack (Eds.), *Child and family: Concepts of nursing practice.* New York: McGraw-Hill.

KNITTLE, J., MERRITT, R. J., DIXON-SHANIES, D., GINSBERG-FELLNER, F., TIMMERS, K. I., & KATZ, D. P. (1981). Childhood obesity. In R. M. Suskind (Ed.), *Textbook of pediatric nutrition.* New York: Raven Press.

KNOWLES, J. H. (1977). The responsibility of the individual. In J. H. Knowles (Ed.), *Doing better and feeling worse: Health in the United States.* New York: Norton.

KOBASA, S. C. (1979). Stressful life events, personality, and health: An inquiry into hardiness. *Journal of Personality and Social Psychology, 37,* 1-11.

KOBASA, S. C. O. (1986). How much stress can you survive? In M. G. Walraven & H. E. Fitzgerald (Eds.), *Annual editions: Human development 86/87.* Guilford, CT: Dushkin.

KOBASA, S. C., & MADDI, S. R. (1977). Existential personality theory. In R. Corsini (Ed.), *Current personality theories.* Itasca, IL: Peacock.

KOBASA, S. C., MADDI, S. R., & PUCCETTI, M. C. (1982). Personality and exercise as buffers in the stress-illness relationship. *Journal of Behavioral Medicine, 5,* 391-404.

KOBASA, S. C. O., MADDI, S. R., PUCCETTI, M. C., & ZOLA, M. A. (1985). Effectiveness of hardiness, exercise and social support as resources against illness. *Journal of Psychosomatic Research, 29,* 525-533.

KOCH, J. (1977, August). When children meet death. *Psychology Today, 10,* pp. 64-66, 79-80.

KOLATA, G. (1989, April 16). Vital opinions. *New York Times Magazine,* p. 46.

KOLBE, L. J., GREEN, L. FOREYT, J., DARNELL, L., GOODRICK, K., WILLIAMS, H., WARD, D., KORTON, A. S., KARACAN, I., WIDMEYER, R., & STAINBROOK, G. (1986). In N. A. Krasnegor, J. D. Arasteh, & M. F. Cataldo (Eds.), *Child health behavior: A behavioral pediatrics perspective.* New York: Wiley.

KOLBE, L. J., & IVERSON, D. C. (1984). Comprehensive school health education programs. In J. D. Matarazzo, S. M. Weiss, J. A. Herd, N. E. Miller, & S. M. Weiss (Eds.), *Behavioral health: A handbook of health enhancement and disease prevention.* New York: Wiley.

KOOCHER, G. P., O'MALLEY, J. E., GOGAN, J. L., & FOSTER, D. J. (1980). Psychological adjustment among pediatric cancer survivors. *Journal of Child Psychology and Psychiatry, 21,* 163-173.

KOPP, C. B. (1983). Risk factors in development. In P. H. Mussen (Ed.), *Handbook of child psychology* (4th ed., Vol. 2). New York: Wiley.

KORONES, S. B. (1981). *High-risk newborn infants* (3rd ed.). St. Louis: Mosby.

KORSCH, B. M., FINE, R. N., & NEGRETE, V. F. (1978). Noncompliance in children with renal transplants. *Pediatrics, 61,* 872-876.

KORSCH, B. M., GOZZI, E. K., & FRANCIS, V. (1968). Gaps in doctor-patient communication: I. Doctor-patient interaction and patient satisfaction. *Pediatrics, 42,* 855-871.

KOSTEN, T. R., JACOBS, S. C., & KASL, S. V. (1985). Terminal illness, bereavement, and the family. In D. C. Turk & R. D. Kerns (Eds.), *Health, illness, and families: A life-span perspective.* New York: Wiley.

KOZLOWSKI, L. T. (1984). Pharmacological approaches to smoking modification. In J. D. Matarazzo, S. M. Weiss, J. A. Herd, N. E. Miller, & S. M. Weiss (Eds.), *Behavioral health: A handbook of health enhancement and disease prevention.* New York: Wiley.

KRAJICK, K. (1988, May). Private passions and public health. *Psychology Today, 22,* pp. 50-58.

KRANTZ, D. S., BAUM, A., & WIDEMAN, M. V. (1980). Assessment for preferences for self-treatment and information in health care. *Journal of Personality and Social Psychology, 39,* 977-990.

KRANTZ, D. S., & DECKEL, A. W. (1983). Coping with coronary heart disease and stroke. In T. G. Burish & L. A. Bradley (Eds.), *Coping with chronic disease: Research and applications.* New York: Academic Press.

KRANTZ, D. S., & DUREL, L. A. (1983). Psychobiological substrates of the Type A behavior pattern. *Health Psychology, 2,* 393-411.

KRANTZ, D. S., DUREL, L. A., DAVIA, J. E., SHAFFER, R. T., ARABIAN, J. M., DEMBROSKI, T. M., & MACDOUGALL, J. M. (1982). Propranolol medication among coronary patients: Relationship to Type A behavior and cardiovascular response. *Journal of Human Stress, 8,* 4-12.

KRANTZ, D. C., LUNDBERG, U., & FRANKENHAEUSER, M. (1987). Stress and Type A behavior: Interactions between environmental and biological factors. In A. Baum & J. E. Singer (Eds.), *Handbook of psychology and health* (Vol. 5). Hillsdale, NJ: Erlbaum.

KÜBLER-ROSS, E. (1969). *On death and dying.* New York: Macmillan Co.

KULIK, J. A., & CARLINO, P. (1987). The effect of verbal commitment and treatment choice on medication compliance in a pediatric setting. *Journal of Behavioral Medicine, 10,* 367-376.

KULIK, J. A., & MAHLER, H. I. M. (1987a). Effects of preoperative roommate assignment on preoperative anxiety and recovery from coronary-bypass surgery. *Health Psychology, 6,* 525-543.

KULIK, J. A., & MAHLER, H. I. M. (1987b). Health status, perceptions of risk, and prevention interest for health and nonhealth problems. *Health Psychology, 6,* 15-27.

KULLER, L. H., MEILAHN, E. N., & COSTELLO, E. J. (1983). Relationship of menopause to cardiovascular disease. *Behavioral Medicine Update, 5*(4), 35-49.

KURDEK, L. A., & BERG, B. (1983). Correlates of children's adjustment to their parents' divorces. In L. A. Kurdek (Ed.), *Children and divorce.* San Francisco: Jossey-Bass.

LABARBA, R. C. (1984). Prenatal and neonatal influences on behavioral health development. In J. D. Matarazzo, S. M. Weiss, J. A. Herd, N. E. Miller, & S. M. Weiss (Eds.), *Behavioral health: A handbook of health enhancement and disease prevention.* New York: Wiley.

LACEY, J. H., & BIRTCHNELL, S. A. (1986). Abnormal eating behavior. In M. J. Christie & P. G. Mellett (Eds.), *The psychosomatic approach: Contemporary practice of wholeperson care.* New York: Wiley.

LACHMAN, M. E. (1986). Personal control in later life: Stability, change, and cognitive correlates. In M. M. Baltes & P. B. Baltes (Ed.), *The psychology of control and aging.* Hillsdale, NJ: Erlbaum.

LAFFREY, S. C. (1986). Normal and overweight adults: Perceived weight and health behavior characteristics. *Nursing Research, 35,* 173-177.

LA GRECA, A. M., & STONE, W. L. (1985). Behavioral pediatrics. In N. Schneiderman & J. T. Tapp (Eds.), *Behavioral medicine: The biopsychosocial approach.* Hillsdale, NJ: Erlbaum.

LANDO, H. (1977). Successful treatment of smokers with a broad-spectrum behavioral approach. *Journal of Consulting and Clinical Psychology, 45,* 361-366.

LANDAU, B. R. (1976). *Essential human anatomy and physiology.* Glenview, IL: Scott, Foresman.

LANE, J. D., & WILLIAMS, R. B. (1987). Cardiovascular effects of caffeine and stress in regular coffee drinkers. *Psychophysiology, 24,* 157-164.

LANG, A. R., & MARLATT, G. A. (1982). Problem drinking: A social learning perspective. In R. J. Gatchel, A. Baum, & J. E. Singer (Eds.), *Handbook of psychology and health* (Vol. 1). Hillsdale, NJ: Erlbaum.

LANGER, E. J. (1975). The illusion of control. *Journal of Personality and Social Psychology, 32,* 311-328.

LANGER, E. J., JANIS, I. L., & WOLFER, J. A. (1975). Reduction of psychological stress in surgical patients. *Journal of Experimental Social Psychology, 11,* 155-165.

LANGER, E. J., & RODIN, J. (1976). The effects of choice and enhanced personal responsibility for the aged: A field experiment in an institutional setting. *Journal of Personality and Social Psychology, 34,* 191-198.

LANGLIE, J. K. (1977). Social networks, health beliefs, and preventive health behavior. *Journal of Health and Social Behavior, 18,* 244-260.

LANGOSCH, W. (1984). Behavioural interventions in cardiac rehabilitation. In A. Steptoe & A. Mathews (Eds.), *Health care and human behaviour.* London: Academic Press.

LA PLACE, J. (1984). *Health* (4th ed.). Englewood Cliffs, NJ: Prentice-Hall.

LASATER, T., ABRAMS, D., ARTZ, L., BEAUDIN, P., CABRERA, L., ELDER, J., FERREIRA, A., KNISLEY, P., PETERSON, G., RODRIGUES, A., ROSENBERG, P., SNOW, R., & CARLTON, R. (1984). Lay volunteer delivery of a community-based cardiovascular risk factor change program: The Pawtucket experiment. In J. D. Matarazzo, S. M. Weiss, J. A. Herd, N. E. Miller, & S. M. Weiss (Eds.), *Behavioral health: A handbook of health enhancement and disease prevention.* New York: Wiley.

LASZLO, J. (1987). *Understanding cancer.* New York: Harper & Row.

LATIMER, E. A., & LAVE, L. B. (1987). Initial effects of the New York State auto safety belt law. *American Journal of Public Health, 77,* 183-186.

LAU, R. R., & HARTMAN, K. A. (1983). Common sense representations of common illnesses. *Health Psychology, 2,* 167-185.

LAU, R. R., HARTMAN, K. A., & WARE, J. E. (1986). Health as a value: Methodological and theoretical considerations. *Health Psychology, 5,* 25-43.

LAU, R., KANE, R., BERRY, S., WARE, J., & ROY, D. (1980). Channeling health: A review of the evaluation of televised health campaigns. *Health Education Quarterly, 7,* 56-89.

LAVEY, E. B., & WINKLE, R. A. (1979). Continuing disability of patients with chest pain and normal coronary arteriograms. *Journal of Chronic Diseases, 32,* 191-196.

LAVIGNE, J. V., SCHULEIN, M. J., & HAHN, Y. S. (1986a). Psychological aspects of painful medical conditions in children. I. Developmental aspects and assessment. *Pain, 27,* 133-146.

LAVIGNE, J. V., SCHULEIN, M. J., & HAHN, Y. S. (1986b). Psychological aspects of painful medical conditions in children. II. Personality factors, family characteristics and treatment. *Pain, 27,* 147-169.

LAWLER, K. A., ALLEN, M. T., CRITCHER, E. C., & STANDARD, B. A. (1981). The relationship of physiological responses to the coronary-prone behavior pattern in children. *Journal of Behavioral Medicine, 4,* 203-216.

LAWRENCE, D. B., & GAUS, C. R. (1983). Long-term care: Financing and policy issues. In D. Mechanic (Ed.), *Handbook of health, health care, and the health professions.* New York: Free Press.

LAZARUS, A. A. (1971). *Behavior therapy and beyond.* New York: McGraw-Hill.

LAZARUS, A. A. (1981). *Multimodal therapy.* New York: Guilford.

LAZARUS, R. S. (1983). The costs and benefits of denial. In S. Bresnitz (Ed.), *Denial of stress.* New York: International Universities Press.

LAZARUS, R. S. (1987). Coping. In R. J. Corsini (Ed.), *Concise encyclopedia of psychology.* New York: Wiley.

LAZARUS, R. S., & DELONGIS, A. (1983). Psychological stress and coping in aging. *American Psychologist, 38,* 245-254.

LAZARUS, R. S., & FOLKMAN, S. (1984a). Coping and adaptation. In W. D. Gentry (Ed.), *Handbook of behavioral medicine.* New York: Guilford.

LAZARUS, R. S., & FOLKMAN, S. (1984b). *Stress, appraisal, and coping.* New York: Springer.

LAZARUS, R. S., & LAUNIER, R. (1978). Stress-related transactions between person and environment. In L. A. Pervin & M. Lewis (Eds.), *Perspectives in interactional psychology.* New York: Plenum.

LEAHEY, T. H. (1987). *A history of psychology: Main currents in psychological thought* (2nd ed.). Englewood Cliffs, NJ: Prentice-Hall.

LEGRADY, D., DYER, A. R., SHEKELLE, R. B., STAMLER, J., LIU, K., PAUL, O., LEPPER, M., & SHRYOCK, A. M. (1987). Coffee consumption and mortality in the Chicago Western Electric Company Study. *American Journal of Epidemiology, 126,* 803-812.

LEINO, P., ARO, S., & HASAN, J. (1987). Trunk muscle function and low back disorders: A ten-year follow-up study. *Journal of Chronic Diseases, 40,* 289-296.

LEVENSON, R. W. (1986). Alcohol, reactivity, and the heart: Implications for coronary health and disease. In K. A. Matthews, S. M. Weiss, T. Detre, T. M. Dembroski, B. Falkner, S. B. Manuck, & R. B. Williams (Eds.), *Handbook of stress, reactivity, and cardiovascular disease.* New York: Wiley.

LEVENTHAL, E. A., & PROHASKA, T. R. (1986). Age, symptom interpretation, and health behavior. *Journal of the American Geriatrics Society, 34,* 185-191.

LEVENTHAL, H. (1982, January). Wrongheaded ideas about illness. *Psychology Today, 16,* pp. 48-55, 73.

LEVENTHAL, H., & AVIS, N. (1976). Pleasure, addiction, and habit: Factors in verbal report or factors in smoking behavior. *Journal of Abnormal Psychology, 85,* 478-488.

LEVENTHAL, H., & CLEARY, P. D. (1980). The smoking problem: A review of research and theory in behavioral risk modification. *Psychological Bulletin, 88,* 370-405.

LEVENTHAL, H., LEVENTHAL, E. A., & VAN NGUYEN, T. (1985). Reactions of families to illness: Theoretical models and perspectives. In D. C. Turk & R. D. Kerns (Eds.), *Health, illness, and families: A life-span perspective.* New York: Wiley.

LEVENTHAL, H., PROHASKA, T. R., & HIRSCHMAN, R. S. (1985). Preventive health behavior across the life span. In J. C. Rosen & L. J. Solomon (Eds.), *Prevention in health psychology.* Hanover, NH: University Press of New England.

LEVENTHAL, H., WATTS, J. C., & PAGANO, F. (1967). Effects of fear and instructions on how to cope with danger. *Journal of Personality and Social Psychology, 6,* 313-321.

LEVIN, D. N., CLEELAND, C. S., & DAR, R. (1985). Public attitudes toward cancer pain. *Cancer, 56,* 2337-2339.

LEVINE, J. D., GORDON, N. C., & FIELDS, H. L. (1978, September 23). The mechanism of placebo analgesia. *Lancet,* 654-657.

LEVITAS, T. C. (1974, May-June). HOME—Hand over mouth exercise. *Journal of Dentistry for Children, 42,* 178-182.

LEVOR, R. M., COHEN, M. J., NALIBOFF, B. D., MCARTHUR, D., & HEUSER, G. (1986). Psychosocial precursors and correlates of migraine headache. *Journal of Consulting and Clinical Psychology, 54,* 347-353.

LEVY, S. M. (1983). The process of death and dying: Behavioral and social factors. In T. G. Burish & L. A. Bradley (Eds.), *Coping with chronic disease: Research and applications.* New York: Academic Press.

LEVY, S. M. (1985). *Behavior and cancer.* San Francisco: Jossey-Bass.

LEVY, S. M., HERBERMAN, R. B., MALUISH, A. M., SCHLIEN, B., & LIPPMAN, M. (1985). Prognostic risk assessment in primary breast cancer by behavioral and immunological parameters. *Health Psychology, 4,* 99-113.

LEWIN, K. (1935). *A dynamic theory of personality.* New York: McGraw-Hill.

LEWINSOHN, P. M., MERMELSTEIN, R. M., ALEXANDER, C., & MACPHILLAMY, D. J. (1985). The Unpleasant Events Schedule: A scale for the measurement of aversive events. *Journal of Clinical Psychology, 41,* 483-498.

LEY, P. (1982). Satisfaction, compliance, and communication. *British Journal of Clinical Psychology, 21,* 241-254.

LICHTENSTEIN, E., & MERMELSTEIN, R. J. (1984). Review of approaches to smoking treatment: Behavior modification strategies. In J. D. Matarazzo, S. M. Weiss, J. A. Herd, N. E. Miller, & S. M. Weiss (Eds.), *Behavioral health: A handbook of health enhancement and disease prevention.* New York: Wiley.

LICHTENSTEIN, E., WEISS, S. M., HITCHCOCK, J. L., LEVETON, L. B., O'CONNELL, K. A. , & PROCHASKA, J. O. (1986). Task Force 3: Patterns of smoking relapse. *Health Psychology, 5*(Supplement), 29-40.

LINDEMAN, B. (1976). Widower, heal thyself. In R. H. Moos (Ed.), *Human adaptation: Coping with life crises.* Lexington, MA: Heath.

LINDSAY, P. H., & NORMAN, D. A. (1977). *Human information processing: An introduction to psychology* (2nd ed.). New York: Academic Press.

LINTON, S. J. (1982). A critical review of behavioural treatments for chronic benign pain other than headache. *British Journal of Clinical Psychology, 21,* 321-337.

LIPOWSKI, Z. J.((1986). WHAT DOES THE WORD "PSYCHOSOMATIC" REALLY MEAN? A HISTORICAL AND SEMANTIC INQUIRY. IN M. J. CHRISTIE & P. G. MELLETT (EDS.), *The psychosomatic approach: Contemporary practice and whole-person care.* New York: Wiley.

LOMBARDO, T., & CARRENO, L. (1987). Relationship of Type A behavior pattern in smokers to carbon monoxide exposure and smoking topography. *Health Psychology, 6,* 445-452.

LONETTO, R. (1980). *Children's conceptions of death.* New York: Springer.

LONG, R. T., LAMONT, J. H., WHIPPLE, B., BANDLER, L., BLOM, G. E., BURGIN, L., & JESSNER, L. (1958). A psychosomatic study of allergic and emotional factors in children with asthma. *American Journal of Psychiatry, 114* 890-899.

LORBER, J. (1975). Good patients and problem patients: Conformity and deviance in a general hospital. *Journal of health and Social Behavior, 16,* 213-225.

LORIG, K. (1984). Arthritis patient education. In G. K. Riggs & E. P. Gall (Eds.), *Rheumatic diseases: Rehabilitation and management.* Boston: Butterworth.

LOVALLO, W. R., PINCOMB, G. A., EDWARDS, G. L., BRACKETT,

D. J., & WILSON, M. F. (1986). Work pressure and the Type A behavior pattern exam stress in male medical students. *Psychosomatic Medicine, 48,* 125-133.

LUFT, H. S. (1983). Health-maintenance organizations. In D. Mechanic (Ed.), *Handbook of health, health care, and the health professions.* New York: Free Press.

LUND, A. K., & KEGELES, S. S. (1982). Increasing adolescents' acceptance of long-term personal health behavior. *Health Psychology, 1,* 27-43.

LUND, A. K., & KEGELES, S. S. (1984). Rewards and adolescent health behavior. *Health Psychology, 3,* 351-369.

LUNDBERG, U. (1986). Stress and Type A behavior in children. *Journal of the American Academy of Child Psychiatry, 25,* 771-778.

LUPARELLO, T. J., LYONS, H. A., BLEECKER, E. R., & MCFADDEN, E. R. (1968). Influences of suggestion on airway reactivity in asthmatic subjects. *Psychosomatic Medicine, 30,* 819-825.

LYKKEN, D. T. (1987). Psychophysiology. In R. J. Corsini (Ed.), *Concise encyclopedia of psychology.* New York: Wiley.

LYLES, J. N., BURISH, T. G., KROZELY, M. G., & OLDHAM, R. K. (1982). Efficacy of relaxation training and guided imagery in reducing the aversiveness of cancer chemotherapy. *Journal of Consulting and Clinical Psychology, 50,* 509-524.

LYNCH, J. J. (1977). *The broken heart: The medical consequences of loneliness.* New York: Basic Books.

MACMAHON, S. (1987). Alcohol consumption and hypertension. *Hypertension, 9,* 111-121.

MADDUX, J. E., ROBERTS, M. C., SLEDDEN, E. A., & WRIGHT, L. (1986). Developmental issues in child health psychology. *American Psychologist, 41,* 25-34.

MAGES, N. L., & MENDELSOHN, G. A. (1979). Effects of cancer on patients' lives: A personological approach. In G. C. Stone, F. Cohen, & N. E. Adler (Eds.), *Health psychology —A handbook.* San Francisco: Jossey-Bass.

MAGUIRE, P. (1985). Barriers to psychological care of the dying. *British Medical Journal, 291,* 1711-1713.

MALKIN, S. (1976). Care of the terminally ill. *Canadian Medical Association Journal, 115,* 129-130.

MANFREDI, M., BINI, G., CRUCCU, G., ACCORNERO, N., BERADELLI, A., & MEDOLAGO, L. (1981). Congenital absence of pain. *Archives on Neurology, 38,* 507-511.

MANUCK, S. B., & KRANTZ, D. S. (1986). In K. A. Matthews, S. M. Weiss, T. Detre, T. M. Dembroski, B. Falkner, S. B. Manuck, & R. B. Williams (Eds.), *Handbook of stress, reactivity, and cardiovascular disease.* New York: Wiley.

MARCOS, L. R., URCUYO, L., KESSELMAN, M., & ALPERT, A. (1981). The language barrier in evaluating Spanish-American patients. In G. Henderson & M. Primeaux (Eds.), *Transcultural health care.* Menlo Park, CA: Addison-Wesley.

MARGOLIS, L. H., MCLEROY, K. R., RUNYAN, C. W., & KAPLAN, B. H. (1983). Type A behavior: An ecological approach. *Journal of Behavioral Medicine, 6,* 245-258.

MARKS, G., RICHARDSON, J. L., GRAHAM, J. W., & LEVINE, A. (1986). Role of health locus of control beliefs and expectations of treatment efficacy in adjustment to cancer. *Journal of Personality and Social Psychology, 51,* 443-450.

MARLATT, G. A. (1983). The controlled-drinking controversy: A commentary. *American Psychologist, 38,* 1097-1110.

MARLATT, G. A., & GORDON, J. R. (1980). Determinants of relapse: Implications for the maintenance of behavior change. In P. O. Davidson & S. M. Davidson (Eds.), *Behavioral medicine: Changing health lifestyles.* New York: Brunner/Mazel.

MARLATT, G. A., KOSTURN, C. F., & LANG, A. R. (1975). Provocation to anger and opportunity for retaliation as determinants of alcohol consumption in social drinkers. *Journal of Abnormal Psychology, 84,* 652-659.

MARMOT, M. G., KOGEVINAS, M., & ELSTON, M. A. (1987). Social/economic status and disease. In L. Breslow, J. E. Fielding, & L. B. Lave (Eds.), *Annual review of public health* (Vol. 8). Palo Alto, CA: Annual Reviews.

MARON, D. J., & FORTMANN, S. P. (1987). Nicotine yield and measures of cigarette smoke exposure in a large population: Are lower-yield cigarettes safer? *American Journal of Public Health, 77,* 546-549.

MARTEAU, T. M., & JOHNSTON, M. (1986). Determinants of beliefs about illness: A study of parents of children with diabetes, asthma, epilepsy, and no chronic illness. *Journal of Psychosomatic Research, 30,* 673-683.

MARTEAU, T. M., JOHNSTON, M., BAUM, J. D., & BLOCH, S. (1987). Goals of treatment in diabetes: A comparison of doctors and parents of children with diabetes. *Journal of Behavioral Medicine, 10,* 33-48.

MARTELLI, M. F., AUERBACH, S. M., ALEXANDER, J., & MERCURI, L. G. (1987). Stress management in the health care setting: Matching interventions with patient coping styles. *Journal of Consulting and Clinical Psychology, 55,* 201-207.

MARTIN, J. E., & DUBBERT, P. M. (1985). Exercise in hypertension. *Annals of Behavioral Medicine, 7*(1), 13-18.

MARTIN, J. L. (1987). The impact of AIDS on gay male sexual behavior patterns in New York City. *American Journal of Public Health, 77,* 578-581.

MARX, M. H., & HILLIX, W. A. (1963). *Systems and theories in psychology.* New York: McGraw-Hill.

MASLACH, C. (1979). Negative emotional biasing in unexplained arousal. *Journal of Personality and Social Psychology, 37,* 953-969.

MASLACH, C., & JACKSON, S. E. (1982). Burnout in health professions: A social psychological analysis. In G. S. Sanders & J. Suls (Eds.), *Social psychology of health and illness.* Hillsdale, NJ: Erlbaum.

MASON, J. W. (1975). A historical view of the stress field. *Journal of Human Stress, 1,* 22-36.

MATARAZZO, J. D. (1982). Behavioral health's challenge to academic, scientific, and professional psychology. *American Psychologist, 37,* 1-14.

MATARAZZO, J. D. (1983). Education and training in health

psychology: Boulder or bolder? *Health Psychology, 2,* 73-113.

MATARAZZO, J. D. (1984). Behavioral health: A 1990 challenge for the health sciences professions. In J. D. Matarazzo, S. M. Weiss, J. A. Herd, N. E. Miller, & S. M. Weiss (Eds.), *Behavioral health: A handbook of health enhancement and disease prevention.* New York: Wiley.

MATHENY, K. B., & CUPP, P. (1983). Control, desirability, and anticipation as moderating variables between life changes and illness. *Journal of Human Stress, 9,* 14-23.

MATHEWS, A., & RIDGEWAY, V. (1984). Psychological preparation for surgery. In A. Steptoe & A. Mathews (Eds.), *Health care and human behaviour.* London: Academic Press.

MATTES, R. D., ARNOLD, C., & BORAAS, M. (1987a). Learned food aversions among cancer chemotherapy patients. *Cancer, 60,* 2576-2580.

MATTES, R. D., ARNOLD, C., & BORAAS, M. (1987b). Management of learned food aversions in cancer patients receiving chemotherapy. *Cancer Treatment Reports, 71,* 1071-1078.

MATTHEWS, K. A. (1982). Psychological perspectives on the Type A behavior pattern. *Psychological Bulletin, 91,* 293-323.

MATTHEWS, K. A. (1986). Summary, conclusions, and implications. In K. A. Matthews, S. M. Weiss, T. Detre, T. M. Dembroski, B. Falkner, S. B. Manuck, & R. B. Williams (Eds.), *Handbook of stress, reactivity, and cardiovascular disease.* New York: Wiley.

MATTHEWS, K. A., & ANGULO, J. (1980). Measurement of the Type A behavior pattern in children: Assessment of children's competitiveness, impatience-anger, and aggression. *Child Development, 51,* 466-475.

MATTHEWS, K. A., & JENNINGS, J. R. (1984). Cardiovascular responses of boys exhibiting the Type A behavior pattern. *Psychosomatic Medicine, 46,* 484-497.

MATTHEWS, K. A., ROSENMAN, R. H., DEMBROSKI, T. M., HARRIS, E. L., & MACDOUGALL, J. M. (1984). Familial resemblance in components of the Type A behavior pattern: A reanalysis of the California Type A Twin Study. *Psychosomatic Medicine, 46,* 512-522.

MATTHEWS, K. A., & WOODALL, K. L. (1988). Childhood origins of overt Type A behaviors and cardiovascular reactivity to behavioral stressors. *Annals of Behavioral Medicine, 10,* 71-77.

MATTSON, M. E., & HERD, J. A. (1988). Cardiovascular disease. In E. A. Blechman & K. D. Brownell (Eds.), *Handbook of behavioral medicine for women.* New York: Pergamon.

MATTSON, M. E., POLLACK, E. S., & CULLEN, J. W. (1987). What are the odds that smoking will kill you? *American Journal of Public Health, 77,* 425-431.

MAY, K. A. (1986). Three phases of father involvement in pregnancy. In R. H. Moos (Ed.), *Coping with life crises: An integrated approach.* New York: Plenum.

MAYER, J. (1975). *A diet for living.* New York: David McKay.

MAYER, J. (1980). The best diet is exercise. In P. J. Collipp (Ed.), *Childhood obesity* (2nd ed.). Littleton, MA: PSG Publishing.

MAYER, W. (1983). Alcohol abuse and alcoholism: The psychologist's role in prevention, research, and treatment. *American Psychologist, 38,* 1116-1121.

MAYS, V. M., & COCHRAN, S. D. (1988). Issues in the perception of AIDS risk and risk reduction activities by black and Hispanic/Latina women. *American Psychologist, 43,* 949-957.

MAZZE, R. S., SHAMOON, H., PASMANTIER, R., LUCIDO, D., MURPHY, J., HATMAN, K., KUYKENDALL, V., & LOPATIN, W. (1984). Reliability of blood glucose monitoring by patients with diabetes mellitus. *American Journal of Medicine, 77,* 211-217.

MCCAFFREY, R. J., & BLANCHARD, E. B. (1985). Stress management approaches to the treatment of essential hypertension. *Annals of Behavioral Medicine, 7*(1), 5-12.

MCCARTY, D. (1985). Environmental factors in substance abuse: The microsetting. In M. Galizio & S. A. Maisto (Eds.), *Determinants of substance abuse: Biological, psychological, and environmental factors.* New York: Plenum.

MCCAUL, K. D., & GLASGOW, R. E. (1985). Preventing adolescent smoking: What have we learned about treatment construct validity? *Health Psychology, 4,* 361-387.

MCCAUL, K. D., & MALOTT, J. M. (1984). Distraction and coping with pain. *Psychological Bulletin, 95,* 516-533.

MCCLEARN, G. E. (1968). Behavioral genetics: An overview. *Merrill-Palmer Quarterly, 14,* 9-14.

MCCLELLAND, D. C., FLOOR, E., DAVIDSON, R. J., & SARON, C. (1980). Stressed power motivation, sympathetic activation, immune function, and illness. *Journal of Human Stress, 6,* 11-19.

MCCONNELL, S., BIGLAN, A., & SEVERSON, H. H. (1984). Adolescents' compliance with self-monitoring and physiological assessment of smoking in natural environments. *Journal of Behavioral Medicine, 7,* 115-122.

MCCORMICK, M. C., STEMMLER, M. M., & ATHREYA, B. L. (1986). The impact of childhood rheumatic diseases on the family. *Arthritis and Rheumatism, 29,* 872-879.

MCCRADY, B. S. (1988). Alcoholism. In E. A. Blechman & K. D. Brownell (Eds.), *Handbook of behavioral medicine for women.* New York: Pergamon.

MCFARLANE, A. H., NORMAN, G. R., STREINER, D. L, & ROY, R. G. (1983). The process of social stress: Stable, reciprocal, and mediating relationships. *Journal of Health and Social Behavior, 24,* 160-173.

MCFARLANE, A. H., NORMAN, G. R., STREINER, D. L., ROY, R., & SCOTT, D. J. (1980). A longitudinal study of the influence of the psychosocial environment on health status: A preliminary report. *Journal of Health and Social Behavior, 21,* 124-133.

MCGINNIS, J. M., SHOPLAND, D., & BROWN, C. (1987). Tobacco and health: Trends in smoking and smokeless tobacco consumption in the United States. In L. Breslow, J. E. Fielding, & L. B. Lave (Eds.), *Annual review of public health* (Vol. 8). Palo Alto, CA: Annual Reviews.

MCGRATH, P. A. (1987). An assessment of children's pain: A

review of behavioral, physiological and direct scaling techniques. *Pain, 31,* 147-176.

McGuire, F. L. (1982). Treatment of the drinking driver. *Health Psychology, 1,* 137-152.

McKennell, A. C., & Bynner, J. M. (1969). Self images and smoking behavior among school boys. *British Journal of Educational Psychology, 39,* 27-39.

McKinlay, J. B. (1975). Who is really ignorant—Physician or patient? *Journal of Health and Social Behavior, 16,* 3-11.

McKinney, M. E., Hofschire, P. J., Buell, J. C., & Eliot, R. S. (1984). Hemodynamic and biochemical responses to stress: The necessary link between Type A behavior and cardiovascular disease. *Behavioral Medicine Update, 6*(4), 16-21.

McLeod, B. (1986, October). Rx for health: A dose of self-confidence. *Psychology Today, 20,* pp. 46-50.

McNamara, J. J., Molot, M. A., Stremple, J. F., & Cutting, R. T. (1971). Coronary artery disease in combat casualties in Vietnam. *Journal of the American Medical Association, 216,* 1185-1187.

McNaull, F. W. (1984). Radiation therapy. In S. N. McIntire & A. L. Cioppa (Eds.), *Cancer nursing: A developmental approach.* New York: Wiley.

Mead, M., & Newton, N. (1967). Cultural patterning of perinatal behavior. In S. A. Richardson & A. F. Guttmacher (Eds.), *Childbearing: Its social and psychological aspects.* Baltimore: Williams & Wilkins.

Mechanic, D. (1972). Social psychologic factors affecting the presentation of bodily complaints. *New England Journal of Medicine, 286,* 1132-1139.

Mechanic, D. (1975). The organization of medical practice and practice orientations among physicians in prepaid and nonprepaid primary care settings. *Medical Care, 13,* 189-204.

Mechanic, D. (1976). Stress, illness, and illness behavior. *Journal of Human Stress, 2,* 2-6.

Mechanic, D. (1979). The stability of health and illness behavior: Results from a 16-year follow-up. *American Journal of Public Health, 69,* 1142-1145.

Mechanic, D. (1980). The experience and reporting of common physical complaints. *Journal of Health and Social Behavior, 21,* 146-155.

Meichenbaum, D., & Cameron, R. (1983). Stress inoculation training: Toward a general paradigm for training coping skills. In D. Meichenbaum & M. E. Jaremko (Eds.), *Stress reduction and prevention.* New York: Plenum.

Meichenbaum, D., & Turk, D. (1982). Stress, coping, and disease: A cognitive-behavioral perspective. In R. W. J. Neufield (Ed.), *Psychological stress and psychopathology.* New York: McGraw-Hill.

Melamed, B. G., & Bush, J. P. (1985). Family factors in children with acute illness. In D. C. Turk & R. D. Kerns (Eds.), *Health, illness, and families: A life-span approach.* New York: Wiley.

Melamed, B. G., Dearborn, M., & Hermecz, D. A. (1983). Necessary conditions for surgery preparation: Age and previous experience. *Psychosomatic Medicine, 45,* 517-525.

Melamed, B. G., & Siegel, L. J. (1975). Reduction of anxiety in children facing hospitalization and surgery by use of filmed modeling. *Journal of Consulting and Clinical Psychology, 43,* 511-521.

Melzack, R (1975). The McGill Pain Questionnaire: Major properties and scoring methods. *Pain, 1,* 277-299.

Melzack, R., & Torgerson, W. S. (1971). On the language of pain. *Anesthesiology, 34,* 50-59.

Melzack, R., & Wall, P. D. (1965). Pain mechanisms: A new theory. *Science, 150,* 971-979.

Melzack, R., & Wall, P. D. (1982). *The challenge of pain.* New York: Basic Books.

Melzack, R., Weisz, A. Z., & Sprague, L. T. (1963). Strategems for controlling pain: Contributions of auditory stimulation and suggestion. *Experimental Neurology, 8,* 239-247.

Menaghan, E. (1982). Measuring coping effectiveness: A panel analysis of marital problems and coping efforts. *Journal of Health and Social Behavior, 23,* 220-234.

Mendelson, B. K., & White, D. R. (1985). Development of self-body-esteem in overweight youngsters. *Developmental Psychology, 21,* 90-96.

Mentzer, S. J., & Snyder, M. L. (1982). The doctor and the patient: A psychological perspective. In G. S. Sanders & J. Suls (Eds.), *Social psychology of health and illness.* Hillsdale, NJ: Erlbaum.

Meredith, H. V. (1978). *Human body growth in the first ten years of life.* Columbia, SC: The State Printing Company.

Metropolitan Life Foundation (1983). 1983 Metropolitan Height and Weight Tables. *Statistical Bulletin, 64*(1), 2-9.

Meyer, A. J., Nash, J. D., McAlister, A. L., Maccoby, N., & Farquhar, J. W. (1980). Skills training in a cardiovascular health education campaign. *Journal of Consulting and Clinical Psychology, 48,* 129-142.

Meyer, D., Leventhal, H., & Guttman, M. (1985). Common-sense models of illness: The example of hypertension. *Health Psychology, 4,* 115-135.

Meyerowitz, B. E. (1983). Postmastectomy coping strategies and quality of life. *Health Psychology, 2,* 117-132.

Michela, J. L. (1987). Interpersonal and individual impacts of a husband's heart attack. In A. Baum & J. E. Singer (Eds.), *Handbook of psychology and health* (Vol. 5). Hillsdale, NJ: Erlbaum.

Millar, W. J., & Stephens, T. (1987). The prevalence of overweight and obesity in Britain, Canada, and the United States. *American Journal of Public Health, 77,* 38-41.

Miller, B. C., & Sollie, D. L. (1986). Normal stresses during the transition to parenthood. In R. H. Moos (Ed.), *Coping with life crises: An integrated approach.* New York: Plenum.

Miller, N. E. (1959). Liberalization of basic S-R concepts: Extensions to conflict behavior, motivation, and social learning. In S. Koch (Ed.), *Psychology: A study of a science* (Vol. 2). New York: McGraw-Hill.

MILLER, N. E. (1978). Biofeedback and visceral learning. In M. R. Rosenzweig & L. W. Porter (Eds.), *Annual review of psychology* (Vol. 29). Palo Alto, CA: Annual Reviews.

MILLER, N. E., & BANUAZIZI, A. (1968). Instrumental learning by curarized rats of a specific visceral response, intestinal or cardiac. *Journal of Comparative and Physiological Psychology, 65,* 1-7.

MILLER, N. E., & DICARA, L. V. (1967). Instrumental learning of heart-rate changes in curarized rats: Shaping, and specificity to discriminative stimulus. *Journal of Comparative and Physiological Psychology, 63,* 12-19.

MILLER, S. M. (1979). Controllability and human stress: Method, evidence and theory. *Behaviour Research and Therapy, 17,* 287-304.

MILLER, S. M., BRODY, D. S., & SUMMERTON, J. (1987). Styles of coping with threat: Implications for health. *Journal of Personality and Social Psychology, 54,* 142-148.

MILLER, S. M., & GREEN, M. L. (1984). Coping with stress and frustration: Origins, nature, and development. In M. Lewis & C. Saarni (Eds.), *Origins of behavior* (Vol. 5). New York: Plenum.

MILLER, S. M., & MANGAN, C. E. (1983). Interacting effects of information and coping style in adapting to gynecologic stress: Should the doctor tell all? *Journal of Personality and Social Psychology, 45,* 223-226.

MILLER, W. R., & HESTER, R. K. (1980). Treating the problem drinker: Modern approaches. In W. R. Miller (Ed.), *The addictive behaviors: Treatment of alcoholism, drug abuse, smoking, and obesity.* New York: Pergamon.

MILLER, W. R., & HESTER, R. K. (1985). Inpatient alcoholism treatment: Who benefits? *American Psychologist, 41,* 794-805.

MILLON, T. (1982). On the nature of clinical health psychology. In T. Millon, C. Green, & R. Meagher (Eds.), *Handbook of clinical health psychology.* New York: Plenum.

MILLON, T., GREEN, C., & MEAGHER, R. (1982). *Millon Behavioral Health Inventory Manual.* Minneapolis: National Computer Systems.

MITCHELL, J. C. (Ed.) (1969). *Social networks in urban situations.* Manchester, England: Manchester University Press.

MITTELMARK, M. B., MURRAY, D. M., LUEFKER, R. V., PECHACEK, T. F., PIKIE, P. L., & PALLONEN, U. E. (1987). Predicting experimentation with cigarettes: The Childhood Antecedents of Smoking Study (CASS). *American Journal of Public Health, 77,* 206-208.

MONMANEY, T. (1988, October 24). Bouncing back from bad backs. *Newsweek,* p. 69.

MONMANEY, T., HAGER, M., & EMERSON, T. (1988, September 26). The risk from radon. *Newsweek,* p. 69.

MOORE, M. L. (1983). *Realities of childbearing* (2nd ed.). Philadelphia: Saunders.

MOOS, R. H. (1982). Coping with acute health crises. In T. Millon, C. Green, & R. Meagher (Eds.), *Handbook of clinical health psychology.* New York: Plenum.

MOOS, R. H. (1985). Evaluating social resources in community and health care contexts. In P. Karoly (Ed.), *Measurement strategies in health psychology.* New York: Wiley.

MOOS, R. H., & FINNEY, J. W. (1983). The expanding scope of alcoholism treatment evaluation. *American Psychologist, 38,* 1036-1044.

MOOS, R. H., & SCHAEFER, J. A. (1986). Life transitions and crises: A conceptual overview. In R. H. Moos (Ed.), *Coping with life crises: An integrated approach.* New York: Plenum.

MOR, V., MASTERSON-ALLEN, S., GOLDBERG, R. J., CUMMINGS, F. J., GLICKSMAN, A. S., & FRETWELL, M. D. (1985). Relationships between age at diagnosis and treatments received by cancer patients. *Journal of the American Geriatrics Society, 33,* 585-589.

MORIN, S. F. (1988). AIDS: The challenge to psychology. *American Psychologist, 43,* 838-842.

MORRIS, R. J., & KRATOCHWILL, T. R. (1983). *Treating children's fears and phobias: A behavioral approach.* New York: Pergamon.

MOSS, G. E., DIELMAN, T. E., CAMPANELLI, P. C., LEECH, S. L., HARLAN, W. R., VAN HARRISON, R., & HORVATH, W. J. (1986). Demographic correlates of SI assessments of Type A behavior. *Psychosomatic Medicine, 48,* 564-574.

MULLEN, P. D., LAVILLE, E. A., BIDDLE, A. K., & LORIG, K. (1987). Efficacy of psychoeducational interventions on pain, depression, and disability in people with arthritis: A meta-analysis. *Journal of Rheumatology, 14*(Supplement), 33-39.

MULLER, J. E., LUDMER, P. L., WILLICH, S. N., TOFLER, G. H., AYLMER, G., KLANGOS, I., & STONE, P. H. (1987). Circadian variation in the frequency of sudden cardiac death. *Circulation, 75,* 131-138.

MURPHY, L. B. (1974). Coping, vulnerability, and resilience in childhood. In G. V. Coelho, D. A. Hamburg, & J. E. Adams (Eds.), *Coping and adaptation.* New York: Basic Books.

MURRAY, D. M., DAVIS-HEARN, M., GOLDMAN, A. I., PIRIE, P., & LUEPKER, R. V. (1988). Four- and five-year follow-up results from four seventh-grade smoking prevention strategies. *Journal of Behavioral Medicine, 11,* 395-405.

MURRAY, D. M., RICHARDS, P. S., LUEPKER, R. V., & JOHNSON, C. A. (1987). The prevention of cigarette smoking in children: Two- and three-year follow-up comparisons of four prevention strategies. *Journal of Behavioral Medicine, 10,* 595-611.

MURRAY, M., SWAN, A. V., JOHNSON, M. R. D., & BEWLEY, B. R. (1983). Some factors associated with increased risk of smoking by children. *Journal of Child Psychology and Psychiatry, 24,* 223-232.

NIAAA (NATIONAL INSTITUTE ON ALCOHOL ABUSE AND ALCOHOLISM) (1974). *Alcohol and health* (Publication No. 017-024-00399-9). Washington, DC: U. S. Government Printing Office.

NADITCH, M. P. (1984). The Staywell Program. In J. D. Matarazzo, S. M. Weiss, J. A. Herd, N. E. Miller, & S. M. Weiss (Eds.), *Behavioral health: A handbook of health enhancement and disease prevention.* New York: Wiley.

NASH, S. S., & SMITH, M. J. (1982). Perception and coordination. In M. J. Smith, J. A. Goodman, N. L. Ramsey, & S. B. Pasternack (Eds.), *Child and family: Concepts in nursing practice.* New York: McGraw-Hill.

NATHAN, P. (1984). Johnson & Johnson's Live for Life: A comprehensive positive lifestyle change program. In J. D. Matarazzo, S. M. Weiss, J. A. Herd, N. E. Miller, & S. M. Weiss (Eds.), *Behavioral health: A handbook of health enhancement and disease prevention.* New York: Wiley.

NATHAN, P. E. (1985). Prevention of alcoholism: A history of failure. In J. C. Rosen & L. J. Solomon (Eds.), *Prevention in health psychology.* Hanover, NH: University Press of New England.

NATHAN, P. E. (1986). Outcomes of treatment for alcoholism: Current data. *Annals of Behavioral Medicine, 8*(2-3), 40-46.

NATIONAL SAFETY COUNCIL (1983). *Accident facts—1983 edition.* Chicago: National Safety Council.

NEAL, J. H. (1983). Children's understanding of their parents' divorces. In L. A. Kurdek (Ed.), *Children and divorce.* San Francisco: Jossey-Bass.

NEHEMKIS, A. M., & GERBER, K. E. (1986). Compliance and the quality of survival. In K. E. Gerber & A. M. Nehemkis (Eds.), *Compliance: The dilemma of the chronically ill.* New York: Springer.

NELSON, G. E. (1984). *Biological principles with human perspectives* (2nd ed.). New York: Wiley.

NERENZ, D. R., LEVENTHAL, H., EASTERLING, D. V., & LOVE, R. R. (1986). Anxiety and drug taste as predictors of anticipatory nausea in cancer chemotherapy. *Journal of Clinical Oncology, 4,* 224-233.

NETHERCUT, G., & PICCIONE, A. (1984). The physician perspective of health psychologists in medical settings. *Health Psychology, 3,* 175-184.

NETTER, T. W. (1987, January 25). W.H.O. increasing anti-smoking fund. *New York Times,* p. 15.

NEUGARTEN, B. L., & NEUGARTEN, D. A. (1987, May). The changing meanings of age. *Psychology Today, 21,* pp. 29-33.

NEVIDJON, B. M. (1984). Chemotherapy. In S. N. McIntire & A. L. Cioppa (Eds.), *Cancer nursing: A developmental approach.* New York: Wiley.

NEWCOMB, M. D., & BENTLER, P. M. (1986). Cocaine use among adolescents: Longitudinal associations with social context, psychopathology, and use of other substances. *Addictive Behaviors, 11,* 263-273.

NEWCOMB, M. D., MADDAHIAN, E., & BENTLER, P. M. (1986). Risk factors for drug use among adolescents: Concurrent and longitudinal analyses. *American Journal of Public Health, 76,* 525-531.

NEWMAN, R. I., & SERES, J. (1986). The interdisciplinary pain center: An approach to the management of chronic pain. In A. D. Holzman & D. C. Turk (Eds.), *Pain management: A handbook of psychological treatment approaches.* New York: Pergamon.

NEWMAN, S. (1984a). Anxiety, hospitalization, and surgery. In R. Fitzpatrick, J. Hinton, S. Newman, G. Scambler, & J. Thompson (Eds.), *The experience of illness.* London: Tavistock.

NEWMAN, S. (1984b). The psychological consequences of cerebrovascular accident and head injury. In R. Fitzpatrick, J. Hinton, S. Newman, G. Scambler, & J. Thompson (Eds.), *The experience of illness.* London: Tavistock.

NEWQUIST, D. D. (1985). Voodoo death in the American aged. In J. E. Birren & J. Livingston (Eds.), *Cognition, stress, and aging.* Englewood Cliffs, NJ: Prentice-Hall.

NICASSIO, P. M., WALLSTON, K. A., CALLAHAN, L. F., HERBERT, M, & PINCUS, T. (1985). The measurement of helplessness in rheumatoid arthritis: The development of the Arthritis Helplessness Index. *Journal of Rheumatology, 12,* 462-467.

NILSEN, S. T., SAGEN, N., KIM, H. C., & BERGSJO, P. (1984). Smoking, hemoglobin levels, and birth weights in normal pregnancies. *American Journal of Obstetrics and Gynecology, 148,* 752-758.

NISBETT, R. E. (1972). Hunger, obesity, and the ventromedial hypothalamus. *Psychological Review, 79,* 433-453.

NORTHCOTE, R. J., FLANNIGAN, C., & BALLANTYNE, D. (1986). Sudden death and vigorous exercise—A study of 60 deaths associated with squash. *British Heart Journal, 55,* 198-203.

NOVACO, R. W. (1975). *Anger control: The development and evaluation of an experimental treatment.* Lexington, MA: Heath.

NOVACO, R. W. (1978). Anger and coping with stress: Cognitive behavioral interventions. In J. P. Foreyt & D. P. Rathjen (Eds.), *Cognitive behavior therapy: Research and application.* New York: Plenum.

NYSTUL, M. S. (1987). Transcendental meditation. In R. J. Corsini (Ed.), *Concise encyclopedia of psychology.* New York: Wiley.

OCKENE, J. K., HOSMER, D., RIPPE, J., WILLIAMS, J., GOLDBERG, R. J., DECOSIMO, D., MAHER, P. M., & DALEN, J. E. (1985). Factors affecting cigarette smoking status in patients with ischemic heart disease. *Journal of Chronic Diseases, 38,* 985-994.

O'DONNELL, L., O'DONNELL, C. R., PLECK, J. H., SNAREY, J., & ROSE, R. M. (1987). Psychosocial responses of hospital workers to acquired immune deficiency syndrome (AIDS). *Journal of Applied Social Psychology, 17,* 269-285.

OHKURA, K. (1981). Diseases of the Japanese. In H. Rothschild (Ed.), *Biocultural aspects of disease.* New York: Academic Press.

OLAFSSON, O., & SVENSSON, P. (1986). Unemployment-related lifestyle changes and health disturbances in adolescents and children in the Western countries. *Social Science and Medicine, 22,* 1105-1113.

OLDENBURG, B., PERKINS, R. J., & ANDREWS, G. (1985). Controlled trial of psychological intervention in myocardial infarction. *Journal of Consulting and Clinical Psychology, 53,* 852-859.

OLDRIDGE, N. B. (1984). Adherence to adult exercise fitness programs. In J. D. Matarazzo, S. M. Weiss, J. A. Herd, N. E. Miller, & S. M. Weiss (Eds.), *Behavioral health: A handbook of health enhancement and disease prevention.* New York: Wiley.

OLDRIDGE, N. B., & SPENCER, J. (1985). Exercise habits and

perceptions before and after graduation of dropout from supervised cardiac exercise rehabilitation. *Journal of Cardiopulmonary Rehabilitation, 5,* 313-319.

O'LEARY, A., SHOOR, S., LORIG, K., & HOLMAN, H. R. (1988). Cognitive-behavioral treatment for rheumatoid arthritis. *Health Psychology, 7,* 527-544.

O'LEARY, K. D. (1984). Commentary on rewards and adolescent health behavior. *Health Psychology 3,* 377-379.

OLIVET, L. W. (1982). Basic needs of the hospitalized child. In M. J. Smith, J. A. Goodman, N. L. Ramsey, & S. B. Pasternack (Eds.), *Child and family: Concepts of nursing practice.* New York: McGraw-Hill.

ORFUTT, C, & LACROIX, J. M. (1988). Type A behavior pattern and symptom reports: A prospective investigation. *Journal of Behavioral Medicine, 11,* 227-237.

ORNE, M. T. (1989). On the construct of hypnosis: How its definition affects research and its clinical application. In G. D. Burrows & L. Dennerstein (Eds.), *Handbook of hypnosis and psychosomatic medicine.* Amsterdam: Elsevier.

O'ROURKE, D. F., HOUSTON, B. K., HARRIS, J. K., & SNYDER, C. R. (1988). In B. K. Houston & C. R. Snyder (Eds.), *Type A behavior pattern: Research, theory, and intervention.* New York: Wiley.

OSBORN, J. E. (1988). The AIDS epidemic: Six years. In L. Breslow, J. E. Fielding, & L. B. Lave (Eds.), *Annual review of public health* (Vol. 9). Palo Alto, CA: Annual Reviews.

OSSIP-KLEIN, D. J., BIGELOW, G., PARKER, S. R., CURRY, S., HALL, S., & KIRKLAND, S. (1986). Task Force 1: Classification and assessment of smoking behavior. *Health Psychology, 5*(Supplement), 3-11.

PACK, R., & LYNDS, B. G. (1984). Surgical intervention. In S. N. McIntire & A. L. Cioppa (Eds.), *Cancer nursing: A developmental approach.* New York: Wiley.

PANDINA, R. J. (1986). Methods, problems, and trends in studies of adolescent drinking practices. *Annals of Behavioral Medicine, 8*(2-3), 20-26.

PANICO, S., CELENTANO, E., KROGH, V., JOSSA, F., FARINARO, E., TREVISAN, M., & MANCINI, M. (1987). Physical activity and its relationship to blood pressure in school children. *Journal of Chronic Diseases, 40,* 925-930.

PAOLETTI, P., CAMILLI, A. E., HOLBERG, C. J., & LEBOWITZ, M. D. (1985). Respiratory effects in relation to estimated tar exposure from current and cumulative cigarette consumption. *Chest, 88,* 849-855.

PARCEL, G. S., BRUHN, J. G., & CERRETO, M. C. (1986). Longitudinal analysis of health and safety behaviors among school children. *Psychological Reports, 59,* 265-266.

PARFITT, R. R. (1977). *The birth primer.* Philadelphia: Running Press.

PARKER, S. R. (1985). Future directions in behavioral research related to lung diseases. *Annals of Behavioral Medicine, 7*(4), 21-25.

PARLOFF, M. B., LONDON, P., & WOLFE, B. (1986). Individual psychotherapy and behavior change. In M. R. Rosenzweig & L. W. Porter (Eds.), *Annual review of psychology* (Vol. 37). Palto Alto, CA: Annual Reviews.

PARRISH, J. M. (1986). Parent compliance with medical and behavioral recommendations. In N. A. Krasnegor, J. D. Arasteh, & M. F. Cataldo (Eds.), *Child health behavior: A behavioral pediatrics perspective.* New York: Wiley.

PARSONS, O. A. (1986). Alcoholics' neuropsychological impairment: Current findings and conclusions. *Annals of Behavioral Medicine, 8*(2-3), 13-19.

PARSONS, T. (1951). *The social system.* New York: Free Press.

PARSONS, T. (1964). *Social structure and personality.* London: Collier-Macmillan & Co.

PASSER, M. W. (1982). Psychological stress in youth sports. In R. A. Magill, M. J. Ash, & F. L. Smoll (Eds.), *Children in sport* (2nd ed.). Champaign, IL: Human Kinetics.

PATEL, C. (1984). A relaxation-centered behavioral package for reducing hypertension. In J. D. Matarazzo, S. M. Weiss, J. A. Herd, N. E. Miller, & S. M. Weiss (Eds.), *Behavioral health: A handbook of health enhancement and disease prevention.* New York: Wiley.

PATERSON, R. J., & NEUFELD, R. W. J. (1987). Clear danger: Situational determinants of the appraisal of threat. *Psychological Bulletin, 101,* 404-416.

PATTERSON, B. H., & BLOCK, G. (1988). Food choices and the cancer guidelines. *American Journal of Public Health, 78,* 282-286.

PATTERSON, C. H. (1986). *Theories of counseling and psychotherapy* (4th ed.). New York: Harper & Row.

PAULSON, M. C. (1988, October). Fighting for your life. *Changing Times,* pp. 100-106.

PAVLOV, I. P. (1927). *Conditioned reflexes.* New York: Oxford University Press.

PAYNE, R. L., & JONES, J. G. (1987). Measurement and methodological issues in social support. In S. V. Kasl & C. L. Cooper (Eds.), *Stress and health: Issues in research methodology.* New York: Wiley.

PEARCE, S. (1986). Chronic pain: A biobehavioural perspective. In M. J. Christie & P. G. Mellett (Eds.), *The psychosomatic approach: Contemporary practice of whole-person care.* New York: Wiley.

PEARLIN, L. I., & SCHOOLER, C. (1978). The structure of coping. *Journal of Health and Social Behavior, 19,* 2-21.

PECHACEK, T. F., FOX, B. H., MURRAY, D. M., & LUEPKER, R. V. (1984). Review of techniques for measurement of smoking behavior. In J. D. Matarazzo, S. M. Weiss, J. A. Herd, N. E. Miller, & S. M. Weiss (Eds.), *Behavioral health: A handbook of health enhancement and disease prevention.* New York: Wiley.

PECHACEK, T. F., MURRAY, D. M., LUEPKER, R. V., MITTELMARK, M. B., JOHNSON, C. A., & SHUTZ, J. M. (1984). Measurement of adolescent smoking behavior: Rationale and methods. *Journal of Behavioral Medicine, 7,* 123-140.

PECK, A. (1972). Emotional reactions to having cancer. *American Journal of Roentgenology, Radium Therapy, and Nuclear Medicine, 114,* 591-599.

PECK, C. L., & KING, N. J. (1985). Compliance and the doctor-patient relationship. *Drugs, 30,* 78-84.

PECK, S. N. (1985). The gastrointestinal system. In L. L. Hayman & E. M. Sporing (Eds.), *Handbook of pediatric nursing.* New York: Wiley.

PEDERSON, L. L. (1982). Compliance with physician advice

to quit smoking: A review of the literature. *Preventive Medicine, 11,* 71-84.

PEDERSON, L. L., & LEFCOE, N. M. (1986). Change in smoking status among a cohort of late adolescents: Prediction and explanation of initiation, maintenance and cessation. *International Journal of Epidemiology, 15,* 519-526.

PEELE, S. (1984). The cultural context of psychological approaches to alcoholism: Can we control the effects of alcohol? *American Psychologist, 39,* 1337-1351.

PENDERY, M. L., MALTZMAN, I. M., & WEST, L. J. (1982). Controlled drinking by alcoholics? New findings and a reevaluation of a major affirmative study. *Science, 217,* 169-175.

PENNEBAKER, J. W. (1983). Accuracy of symptom perception. In A. Baum, S. E. Taylor, & J. Singer (Eds.), *Handbook of psychology and health* (Vol. 4). Hillsdale, NJ: Erlbaum.

PENNEBAKER, J. W., & WATSON, D. (1988). Blood pressure estimation and beliefs among normotensives and hypertensives. *Health Psychology, 7,* 309-328.

PERKINS, K. A. (1985). The synergistic effect of smoking and serum cholesterol on coronary heart disease. *Health Psychology, 4,* 337-360.

PERRI, M. G., MCALLISTER, D. A., GANGE, J. J., JORDAN, R. C., MCADOO, W. G., & NEZU, A. M. (1988). Effects of four maintenance programs on the long-term management of obesity. Manuscript submitted for publication.

PERRIN, E. C., & SHAPIRO, E. (1985). Health locus of control beliefs of healthy children, children with a chronic physical illness, and their mothers. *Journal of Pediatrics, 107,* 627-633.

PETERSON, J. L., & MARÍN, G. (1988). Issues in the prevention of AIDS among black and Hispanic men. *American Psychologist, 43,* 871-877.

PEVELER, R. C., & JOHNSTON, D. W. (1986). Subjective and cognitive effects of relaxation. *Behaviour Research and Therapy, 24,* 413-419.

PHARES, E. J. (1984). *Introduction to personality.* Columbus, OH: Merrill.

PHARES, E. J. (1987). Locus of control. In R. J. Corsini (Ed.), *Concise encyclopedia of psychology.* New York: Wiley.

PILISUK, M. (1982). Delivery of social support: The social inoculation. *American Journal of Orthopsychiatry, 52,* 20-31.

PILLITTERI, A. (1981). *Child health nursing: Care of the growing family* (2nd ed.). Boston: Little, Brown.

PINES, M (1979, January). Superkids. *Psychology Today, 13,* pp. 53-63.

PINTO, R. P., & HOLLANDSWORTH, J. G. (1989). Using videotape modeling to prepare children psychologically for surgery: Influence of parents and costs versus benefits of providing preparation services. *Health Psychology, 8,* 79-95.

PLACE, M. (1984). Hypnosis and the child. *Journal of Child Psychology and Psychiatry, 25,* 339-347.

POHL, S. L., GONDER-FREDERICK, L., & COX, D. J. (1984). Diabetes mellitus: An overview. *Behavioral Medicine Update, 6*(1), 3-7.

POLICH, J. M., ARMOR, D. J., & BRAIKER, H. B. (1980). *The course of alcoholism: Four years after treatment.* New York: Wiley.

POLISE, K. (1985). The renal system. In L. L. Hayman & E. M. Sporing (Eds.), *Handbook of pediatric nursing.* New York: Wiley.

POLIVY, J., & THOMSEN, L. (1988). Dieting and other eating disorders. In E. A. Blechman & K. D. Brownell (Eds.), *Handbook of behavioral medicine for women.* New York: Pergamon.

POLLACK, A. C., & STEKLIS, H. D. (1986). Urinary catecholamines and stress in male and female police cadets. *Human Biology, 58,* 209-220.

PORTER, F. L., MILLER, R. H., & MARSHALL, R. E. (1986). Neonatal pain cries: Effects of circumcision on acoustic features and perceived urgency. *Child Development, 57,* 790-802.

POWELL, K. E., THOMPSON, P. D., CASPERSEN, C. J., & KENDRICK, J. S. (1987). Physical activity and the incidence of coronary heart disease. In L. Breslow, J. E. Fielding, & L. B. Lave (Eds.), *Annual review of public health* (Vol. 8). Palo Alto, CA: Annual Reviews.

POWELL, L. H. (1984). The Type A behaviour pattern: An update on conceptual, assessment, and intervention research. *Behavioral Medicine Update, 6*(4), 7-10.

POWELL, L. H. (1987). Issues in the measurement of the Type A behaviour pattern. In S. V. Kasl & C. L. Cooper (Eds.), *Stress and health: Issues in research methodology.* Chichester, England: Wiley.

POWELL, L. H., & FRIEDMAN, M. (1986). Alteration of Type A behaviour in coronary patients. In M. J. Christie & P. G. Mellett (Eds.), *The psychosomatic approach: Contemporary practice of whole-person care.* New York: Wiley.

POWELL, L. H., FRIEDMAN, M., THORESEN, C. E., GILL, J. J., & ULMER, D. K. (1984). Can the Type A behavior pattern be altered after myocardial infarction? A second year report from the Recurrent Coronary Prevention Project. *Psychosomatic Medicine, 46,* 293-313.

PRESS, A. (1987, December 21). The menace on the road. *Newsweek,* pp. 42-43.

PRICE, R. A., CADORET, R. J., STUNKARD, A. J., & TROUGHTON, E. (1987). Genetic contributions to human fatness: An adoption study. *American Journal of Psychiatry, 144,* 1003-1008.

PRIEST, R. G. (1986). Benzodiazepines: The search for tranquility. In M. J. Christie & P. G. Mellett (Eds.), *The psychosomatic approach: Contemporary practice of whole-person care.* New York: Wiley.

PROHASKA, T. R., KELLER, M. L., LEVENTHAL, E. A., & LEVENTHAL, H. (1987). Impact of symptoms and aging attribution on emotions and coping. *Health Psychology, 6,* 495-514.

PURCELL, K., WEISS, J., & HAHN, W. (1972). Certain psychosomatic disorders. In B. B. Wolman (Ed.), *Manual of child psychopathology.* New York: McGraw-Hill.

QUADAGNO, D. M., DIXON, L. A., DENNEY, N. W., & BUCK, H. W. (1986). Postpartum moods in men and women. *American Journal of Obstetrics and Gynecology, 154,* 1018-1023.

QUAY, H. C., & LA GRECA, A. M. (1986). Disorders of anxiety, withdrawal, and dysphoria. In H. C. Quay & J. S. Werry (Eds.), *Psychopathological disorders of childhood* (3rd ed.). New York: Wiley.

QUICK, J. C., & QUICK, J. D. (1984). *Organizational stress and preventive management.* New York: McGraw-Hill.

RAGLAND, D. R., & BRAND, R. J. (1988). Type A behavior and mortality from coronary heart disease. *New England Journal of Medicine, 318,* 65-69.

RAHE, R. H. (1974). The pathway between subjects' recent life changes and their near-future illness reports: Representative results and methodological issues. In B. S. Dohrenwend & B. P. Dohrenwend (Ed.), *Stressful life events: Their nature and effects.* New York: Wiley.

RAHE, R. H. (1987). Recent life changes, emotions, and behaviors in coronary heart disease. In A. Baum & J. E. Singer (Eds.), *Handbook of psychology and health* (Vol. 5). Hillsdale, NJ: Erlbaum.

RAHE, R. H., & ARTHUR, R. J. (1978). Life change and illness studies: Past history and future directions. *Journal of Human Stress, 4,* 3-15.

RAMSEY, N. L. (1982). Effects of hospitalization on the child and family. In M. J. Smith, J. A. Goodman, N. L. Ramsey, & S. B. Pasternack (Eds.), *Child and family: Concepts of nursing practice.* New York: McGraw-Hill.

RAPPAPORT, N. B., MCANULTY, D. P., WAGGONER, C. D., & BRANTLEY, P. J. (1987). Cluster analysis of Minnesota Multiphasic Personality Inventory (MMPI) profiles in a chronic headache population. *Journal of Behavioral Medicine, 10,* 49-60.

RAPS, C. S., PETERSON, C., JONAS, M., & SELIGMAN, M. E. P. (1982). Patient behavior in hospitals: Helplessness, reactance, or both? *Journal of Personality and Social Psychology, 42,* 1036-1041.

RAVEN, B. H., & HALEY, R. W. (1982). Social influence and compliance of hospital nurses with infection control policies. In J. R. Eiser (Ed.), *Social psychology and behavioral medicine.* New York: Wiley.

RAZIN, A. M. (1984). Coronary artery disease. In H. B. Roback (Ed.), *Helping patients and their families cope with medical problems.* San Francisco: Jossey-Bass.

REINIS, S., & GOLDMAN, J. M. (1980). *The development of the brain: Biological and functional perspectives.* Springfield, IL: Charles C. Thomas.

REKER, G. T., & WONG, P. T. P. (1985). Personal optimism, physical and mental health. In J. E. Birren & J. Livingston (Eds.), *Cognition, stress, and aging.* Englewood Cliffs, NJ: Prentice-Hall.

RESTAK, R. (1975, September). The danger of knowing too much. *Psychology Today, 9,* pp. 21-23, 88, 92-93.

REYNOLDS, D. V. (1969). Surgery in the rat during electrical anesthesia induced by focal brain stimulation. *Science, 164,* 444-445.

RIBISL, P. M. (1984). Developing an exercise prescription for health. In J. D. Matarazzo, S. M. Weiss, J. A. Herd, N. E. Miller, & S. M. Weiss (Eds.), *Behavioral health: A handbook of health enhancement and disease prevention.* New York: Wiley.

RICE, F. P. (1984). *The adolescent: Development, relationships, and culture* (4th ed.). Boston: Allyn & Bacon.

RICHARDS, J. S., NEPOMUCENO, C., RILES, M., & SUER, Z. (1982). Assessing pain behavior: The UAB Pain Behavior Scale. *Pain, 14,* 393-398.

RICHARDSON, J. L., MARKS, G., JOHNSON, C. A., GRAHAM, J. W., CHAN, K. K., SELSER, J. N., KISHBAUGH, C., BARRANDAY, Y., & LEVINE, A. M. (1987). Path model of multidimensional compliance with cancer therapy. *Health Psychology, 6,* 183-207.

RICHARDSON, S. A., GOODMAN, N., HASTORF, A. H., & DORNBUSCH, S. M. (1961). Cultural uniformity in reaction to physical disabilities. *American Sociological Review, 26,* 241-247.

RICHELSON, L. (1982). Infectious processes. In M. J. Smith, J. A. Goodman, N. L. Ramsey, & S. B. Pasternack (Eds.), *Child and family: Concepts of nursing practice.* New York: McGraw-Hill.

RIMM, D. C., & MASTERS, J. C. (1979). *Behavior therapy: Techniques and empirical findings* (2nd ed.). New York: Academic Press.

ROBACK, H. B. (1984). Introduction: The emergence of disease-management groups. In H. B. Roback (Ed.), *Helping patients and their families cope with medical problems.* San Francisco: Jossey-Bass.

ROBERTS, A. H. (1986). The operant approach to the management of pain and excess disability. In A. D. Holzman & D. C. Turk (Eds.), *Pain management: A handbook of psychological treatment approaches.* New York: Pergamon.

ROBERTS, M. C., & FANURIK, D. (1986). Rewarding elementary schoolchildren for their use of safety belts. *Health Psychology, 5,* 185-196.

ROBERTSON, L. S. (1983). Injury epidemiology and the reduction of harm. In D. Mechanic (Ed.), *Handbook of health, health care, and the health professions.* New York: Free Press.

ROBERTSON, L. S. (1986). Behavioral and environmental interventions for reducing motor vehicle trauma. In L. Breslow, J. E. Fielding, & L. B. Lave (Eds.), *Annual review of public health* (Vol. 7). Palo Alto, CA: Annual Reviews.

ROBERTSON, N. (1988, February 21). The changing world of Alcoholics Anonymous. *New York Times Magazine,* pp. 40-47, 57, 92.

ROBINSON, B., & THURNHER, M. (1986). Taking care of aged parents: A family cycle transition. In R. H. Moos (Ed.), *Coping with life crises: An integrated approach.* New York: Plenum.

ROBINSON, C. H., & LAWLER, M. R. (1977). *Normal and therapeutic nutrition* (15th ed.). New York: Macmillan Co.

RODENHUIS, S., VAN DE WETERING, M. L., MOOR, W. J., EVERS, S. G., VAN ZANDWIJK, N., & BOS, J. L. (1987). Mutational activation of the K-ras oncogene. *New England Journal of Medicine, 317,* 929-935.

RODIN, J. (1981). Current status of the internal-external hypothesis for obesity: What went wrong? *American Psychologist, 36,* 361-372.

RODIN, J. (1985). Insulin levels, hunger, and food intake: An example of feedback loops in body weight regulation. *Health Psychology, 4,* 1-24.

RODIN, J. (1986). Health, control, and aging. In M. M. Baltes & P. B. Baltes (Eds.), *The psychology of control and aging.* Hillsdale, NJ: Erlbaum.

RODIN, J. (1987a). Personal control throughout the life course. In R. P. Abeles (Ed.), *Life-span perspectives and social psychology.* Hillsdale, NJ: Erlbaum.

RODIN, J. (1987b). Weight change following smoking cessation: The role of food intake and exercise. *Addictive Behaviors, 12,* 303-317.

RODIN, J., & BAUM, A. (1978). Crowding and helplessness: Potential consequences of density and loss of control. In A. Baum & Y. M. Epstein (Eds.), *Human response to crowding.* Hillsdale, NJ: Erlbaum.

RODIN, J., & JANIS, I. L. (1979). The social power of health-care practitioners as agents of change. *Journal of Social Issues, 35,* 60-81.

RODIN, J., & LANGER, E. J. (1977). Long-term effects of a control-relevant intervention with the institutionalized aged. *Journal of Personality and Social Psychology, 35,* 897-902.

ROGENTINE, G. N., VAN KAMMEN, D. P., FOX, B. H., DOCHERTY, J. P., ROSENBLATT, J. E., BOYD, S. C., & BUNNEY, W. E. (1979). Psychological factors in the prognosis of malignant melanoma: A prospective study. *Psychosomatic Medicine, 41,* 647-655.

ROGERS, M. P., DUBEY, D., & REICH, P. (1979). The influence of the psyche and the brain on immunity and disease susceptibility: A critical review. *Psychosomatic Medicine, 41,* 147-164.

RONA, R. J., ANGELICO, F., ANTONINI, R., ARCA, M., BRENCI, G., DEL BEN, M., GEDDA, L., HAYWARD, D., HELLER, R. F., LEWIS, B., MONTALI, A., PANDOZI, C., RICCI, G., & URBINATI, G. C. (1985). Plasma cholesterol response to a change in dietary fat intake: A collaborative twin study. *Journal of Chronic Diseases, 38,* 927-934.

ROSE, R. J. (1986). Familial influences on cardiovascular reactivity to stress. In K. A. Matthews, S. M. Weiss, T. Detre, T. M. Dembroski, B. Falkner, S. B. Manuck, & R. B. Williams (Eds.), *Handbook of stress, reactivity, and cardiovascular disease.* New York: Wiley.

ROSE, R. J., & CHESNEY, M. A. (1986). Cardiovascular stress reactivity: A behavior-genetic perspective. *Behavior Therapy, 17,* 314-323.

ROSEN, J. C., & GROSS, J. (1987). Prevalence of weight reducing and weight gaining in adolescent boys and girls. *Health Psychology, 6,* 131-147.

ROSEN, J. C., GRUBMAN, J. A., BEVINS, T., & FRYMOYER, J. W. (1987). Musculoskeletal status and disability of MMPI profile subgroups among patients with low back pain. *Health Psychology, 6,* 581-598.

ROSENHAN, D. L., & SELIGMAN, M. E. P. (1984). *Abnormal psychology.* New York: Norton.

ROSENMAN, R. H. (1978). The interview method of assessment of the coronary-prone behavior pattern. In T. M. Dembroski, S. M. Weiss, J. L. Shields, S. G. Haynes, & M. Feinleib (Eds.), *Coronary-prone behavior.* New York: Springer-Verlag.

ROSENMAN, R. H., BRAND, R. J., JENKINS, C. D., FRIEDMAN, M., STRAUS, R., & WURM, M. (1975). Coronary heart disease in the Western Collaborative Group Study: Final follow-up experience of $8\frac{1}{2}$ years. *Journal of the American Medical Association, 233,* 872-877.

ROSENMAN, R. H., BRAND, R. J., SHOLTZ, R. I., & FRIEDMAN, M. (1976). Multivariate prediction of coronary heart disease during 8.5 year follow-up in the Western Collaborative Group Study. *American Journal of Cardiology, 37,* 903-910.

ROSENMAN, R. H., SWAN, G. E., & CARMELLI, D. (1988). Definition, assessment, and evolution of the Type A behavior pattern. In B. K. Houston & C. R. Snyder (Eds.), *Type A behavior pattern: Research, theory, and intervention.* New York: Wiley.

ROSENSTIEL, A. K., & KEEFE, F. J. (1983). The use of coping strategies in chronic low back pain patients: Relationship to patient characteristics and current adjustment. *Pain, 17,* 33-44.

ROSENSTOCK, I. M. (1966). Why people use health services. *Millbank Memorial Fund Quarterly, 44,* 94-127.

ROSENSTOCK, I. M. (1985). Understanding and enhancing patient compliance with diabetic regimens. *Diabetes Care, 8,* 610-616.

ROSENSTOCK, I. M., & KIRSCHT, J. P. (1979). Why people seek health care. In G. C. Stone, F. Cohen, & N. E. Adler (Eds.), *Health psychology—A handbook.* San Francisco: Jossey-Bass.

ROSKIES, E. (1983). Stress management for Type A individuals. In D. Meichenbaum & M. E. Jaremko (Eds.), *Stress reduction and prevention.* New York: Plenum.

ROSKIES, E., KEARNEY, H., SPEVACK, M., SURKIS, A., COHEN, C., & GILMAN, S. (1979). Generalizability and durability of treatment effects in an intervention program for coronary-prone (Type A) managers. *Journal of Behavioral Medicine, 2,* 195-207.

ROSKIES, E., SERAGANIAN, P., OSEASOHN, R., HANLEY, J. A., COLLU, R., MARTIN, N., & SMILGA, C. (1986). The Montreal Type A Intervention Project: Major findings. *Health Psychology, 5,* 45-69.

ROSKIES, E., SPEVACK, M., SURKIS, A., COHEN, C., & GILMAN, S. (1978). Changing the coronary-prone (Type A) behavior pattern in a nonclinical population. *Journal of Behavioral Medicine, 1,* 201-216.

ROSS, C. E., WHEATON, B., & DUFF, R. S. (1981). Client satisfaction and the organization of medical practice: Why time counts. *Journal of Health and Social Behavior, 22,* 243-255.

ROSS, R., & GLOMSET, J. A. (1976a). The pathogenesis of atherosclerosis (first of two parts.). *New England Journal of Medicine, 295,* 369-377.

ROSS, R., & GLOMSET, J. A. (1976b). The pathogenesis of atherosclerosis (second of two parts). *New England Journal of Medicine, 295,* 420-425.

ROTER, D. L., & HALL, J. A. (1987). Physicians' interviewing styles and medical information obtained from patients. *Journal of General Internal Medicine, 2,* 325-329.

ROTH, D. L., & HOLMES, D. S. (1985). Influence of physical fitness in determining the impact of stressful life events on physical and psychologic health. *Psychosomatic Medicine, 47,* 164-173.

ROTTER, J. B. (1966). Generalized expectancies for the internal versus external control of reinforcement. *Psychological Monographs, 90*(1), 1-28.

ROVIARO, S., HOLMES, D. S., & HOLMSTEN, R. D. (1984). Influence of a cardiac rehabilitation program on the cardiovascular, psychological, and social functioning of cardiac patients. *Journal of Behavioral Medicine, 7,* 61-81.

ROY, R. (1985). Chronic pain and marital difficulties. *Health and Social Work, 10,* 199-207.

ROZIN, P. (1984). The acquisition of food habits and preferences. In J. D. Matarazzo, S. M. Weiss, J. A. Herd, N. E. Miller, & S. M. Weiss (Eds.), *Behavioral health: A handbook of health enhancement and disease prevention.* New York: Wiley.

RUBIN, J. Z., PROVENZANO, F. J., & LURIA, Z. (1974). The eye of the beholder: Parents' views on sex of newborns. *American Journal of Orthopsychiatry, 44,* 512-519.

RUBLE, D. N. (1977). Premenstrual symptoms. A reinterpretation. *Science, 197,* 291-292.

RUDERMAN, A. J. (1986). Dietary restraint: A theoretical and empirical review. *Psychological Bulletin, 99,* 247-262.

RUNDALL, T. G., & WHEELER, J. R. C. (1979). The effect of income on use of preventive care: An evaluation of alternative explanations. *Journal of Health and Social Behavior, 20,* 397-406.

RUNYAN, C. W. (1985). Health assessment and public policy within a public health framework. In P. Karoly (Ed.), *Measurement strategies in health psychology.* New York: Wiley.

RUSSELL, P. O., & EPSTEIN, L. H. (1988). Smoking. In E. A. Blechman & K. D. Brownell (Eds.), *Handbook of behavioral medicine for women.* New York: Pergamon.

RUTTER, M. (1983). Stress, coping, and development: Some issues and some questions. In N. Garmezy & M. Rutter (Eds.), *Stress, coping, and development in children.* New York: McGraw-Hill.

RYAN, R. S., & TRAVIS, J. W. (1981). *The wellness workbook.* Berkeley, CA: Ten Speed Press.

RYBSTEIN-BLINCHIK, E. (1979). Effects of different cognitive strategies on chronic pain experience. *Journal of Behavioral Medicine, 2,* 93-101.

RZEWNICKI, R., & FORGAYS, D. G. (1987). Recidivism and self-cure of smoking and obesity: An attempt to replicate. *American Psychologist, 42,* 97-100.

SACKETT, D. L., & SNOW, J. C. (1979). The magnitude of compliance and noncompliance. In R. B. Haynes, D. W. Taylor, & D. L. Sackett (Eds.), *Compliance in health care.* Baltimore: Johns Hopkins University Press.

SACKS, D. A., & KOPPES, R. H. (1986). Blood transfusion and Jehovah's Witnesses: Medical and legal issues in obstetrics and gynecology. *American Journal of Obstetrics and Gynecology, 154,* 483-486.

SAFER, M. A., THARPS, Q. J., JACKSON, T. C., & LEVENTHAL, H. (1979). Determinants of three stages of delay in seeking care at a medical clinic. *Medical Care, 17,* 11-29.

SALLIS, J. F., PATTERSON, T. L., BUONO, M. J., ATKINS, C. J., & NADER, P. R. (1988). Aggregation of physical activity habits in Mexican-America and Anglo families. *Journal of Behavioral Medicine, 11,* 31-41.

SALLIS, J. F., TREVORROW, T. R., JOHNSON, C. C., HOVELL, M. F., & KAPLAN, R. M. (1987). Worksite stress management: A comparison of programs. *Psychology and Health, 1,* 237-255.

SALONEN, J. T., HEINONEN, O. P., KOTTKE, T. E., & PUSKA, P. (1981). Change in health behaviour in relation to estimated coronary heart disease risk during a community-based cardiovascular disease prevention programme. *International Journal of Epidemiology, 10,* 343-354.

SANDERS, G. S. (1982). Social comparison and perceptions of health and illness. In G. S. Sanders & J. Suls (Eds.), *Social psychology of health and illness.* Hillsdale, NJ: Erlbaum.

SANDERS, S. H. (1985). Chronic pain: Conceptualization and epidemiology. *Annals of Behavioral Medicine, 7*(3), 3-5.

SANDLER, I. N., & GUENTHER, R. T. (1985). Assessment of life stress events. In P. Karoly (Ed.), *Measurement strategies in health psychology.* New York: Wiley.

SANTIAGO, J. V. (1984). Effect of treatment on the long term complications of IDDM. *Behavioral Medicine Update, 6*(1), 26-31.

SAPON-SHEVIN, M. (1980). Teaching cooperation in early childhood settings. In G. Cartledge & J. F. Milburn (Eds.), *Teaching social skills to children: Innovative approaches.* New York: Pergamon.

SARAFINO, E. P. (1986). *The fears of childhood: A guide to recognizing and reducing fearful states in children.* New York: Human Sciences Press.

SARAFINO, E. P. (1987a). Personal space. In R. J. Corsini (Ed.), *Concise encyclopedia of psychology.* New York: Wiley.

SARAFINO, E. P. (1987b). Rewards and intrinsic interest. In R. J. Corsini (Ed.), *Concise encyclopedia of psychology.* New York: Wiley.

SARAFINO, E. P. (1988). Undergraduate health psychology courses. *Health Psychologist, 10*(3), 2.

SARAFINO, E. P., & ARMSTRONG, J. W. (1986). *Child and adolescent development* (2nd ed.). St. Paul, MN: West.

SARAFINO, E. P., & DIMATTIA, P. A. (1978). Does grading undermine intrinsic interest in a college course? *Journal of Educational Psychology, 70,* 916-921.

SARASON, I. G., JOHNSON, J. H., & SIEGEL, J. M. (1978). Assessing the impact of life changes: Development of the Life Experiences Survey. *Journal of Consulting and Clinical Psychology, 46,* 932-946.

SARASON, I. G., LEVINE, H. M., BASHAM, R. B., & SARASON, B. R. (1983). Assessing social support: The Social Support Questionnaire. *Journal of Personality and Social Psychology, 44,* 127-139.

SARASON, I. G., & SARASON, B. R. (1984). *Abnormal psychology* (4th ed.). Englewood Cliffs, NJ: Prentice-Hall.

SARASON, I. G., SARASON, B. R., POTTER, E. H., & ANTONI, M. H. (1985). Life events, social support, and illness. *Psychosomatic Medicine, 47,* 156-163.

SAUNDERS, C. (1977). Dying they live: St. Christopher's Hospice. In H. Feifel (Ed.), *New meanings of death.* New York: McGraw-Hill.

SAUNDERS, C. (1986). A philosophy of terminal care. In M. J. Christie & P. G. Mellett (Eds.), *The psychosomatic approach: Contemporary practice of whole-person care.* New York: Wiley.

SAUNDERS, K. J., PILGRIM, C. A., & PENNYPACKER, H. S. (1986). Increased proficiency of search in breast self-examination. *Cancer, 58,* 2531-2537.

SCAMBLER, G. (1984). Perceiving and coping with stigmatizing illness. In R. Fitzpatrick, J. Hinton, S. Newman, G. Scambler, & J. Thompson (Eds.), *The experience of illness.* London: Tavistock.

SCAMBLER, G., & SCAMBLER, A. (1984). The illness iceberg and aspects of consulting behaviour. In R. Fitzpatrick, J. Hinton, S. Newman, G. Scambler, & J. Thompson (Eds.), *The experience of illness.* London: Tavistock.

SCARF, M. (1980, September). Images that heal: A doubtful idea whose time has come. *Psychology Today, 14,* pp. 33-46.

SCARR, S., & KIDD, K. K. (1983). Developmental behavior genetics. In P. H. Mussen (Ed.), *Handbook of child psychology* (4th ed., Vol. 2). New York: Wiley.

SCHACHTER, S. (1971). Some extraordinary facts about obese humans and rats. *American Psychologist, 26,* 129-144.

SCHACHTER, S. (1980). Urinary pH and the psychology of nicotine addiction. In P. O. Davidson & S. M. Davidson (Eds.), *Behavioral medicine: Changing health lifestyles.* New York: Brunner/Mazel.

SCHACHTER, S. (1982). Recidivism and self cure of smoking and obesity. *American Psychologist, 37,* 436-444.

SCHACHTER, S., SILVERSTEIN, B., KOZLOWSKI, L. T., PERLICK, D., HERMAN, C. P., & LIEBLING, B. (1977). Studies of the interaction of psychological and pharmacological determinants of smoking. *Journal of Experimental Psychology: General, 106,* 3-40.

SCHACHTER, S., & SINGER, J. E. (1962). Cognitive, social, and physiological determinants of emotional state. *Psychological Review, 69,* 379-399.

SCHACHTER, S., & SINGER, J. E. (1979). Comments on the Maslach and Marshall-Zimbardo experiments. *Journal of Personality and Social Psychology, 37,* 989-995.

SCHAEFER, C., COYNE, J. C., & LAZARUS, R. S. (1981). The health-related functions of social support. *Journal of Behavioral Medicine, 4,* 381-406.

SCHAFER, L. C., GLASGOW, R. E., & MCCAUL, K. D. (1982). Increasing the adherence of diabetic adolescents. *Journal of Behavioral Medicine, 5,* 353-362.

SCHAIE, K. W. (1965). A general model for the study of developmental problems. *Psychological Bulletin, 64,* 92-107.

SCHECHTER, N. L., ALLEN, D. A., & HANSON, K. (1986). Status of pediatric pain control: A comparison of hospital analgesic usage in children and adults. *Pediatrics, 77,* 11-15.

SCHERER, K. R. (1986). Voice, stress, and emotion. In M. H. Appley & R. Trumbull (Eds.), *Dynamics of stress: Physiological, psychological, and social perspectives.* New York: Plenum.

SCHERWITZ, L., GRAHAM, L. E., GRANDITS, G., & BILLINGS, J. (1987). Speech characteristics and behavior-type assessment in the Multiple Risk Factor Intervention Trial (MRFIT) Structured Interviews. *Journal of Behavioral Medicine, 10,* 173-195.

SCHIFFMAN, H. R. (1976). *Sensation and perception: An integrated approach.* New York: Wiley.

SCHIFTER, D. E., & AJZEN, I. (1985). Intention, perceived control, and weight loss: An application of the theory of planned behavior. *Journal of Personality and Social Psychology, 45,* 843-851.

SCHINKE, S. P., SCHILLING, R. F., & GILCHRIST, L. D. (1986). Hispanic and black adolescents, prevention, and health promotion. *Behavioral Medicine Abstracts, 7,* 109-114.

SCHLEIFER, S. J., SCOTT, B., STEIN, M., & KELLER, S. E. (1986). Behavioral and developmental aspects of immunity. *Journal of the American Academy of Child Psychiatry, 26,* 751-763.

SCHMEIDER, R., FRIEDRICH, G., NEUS, H., RÜDEL, H., & VON EIFF, A. W. (1983). The influence of beta-blockers on cardiovascular reactivity and Type A behavior pattern in hypertensives. *Psychosomatic Medicine, 45,* 417-423.

SCHNEIDER, A. M., & TARSHIS, B. (1975). *An introduction to physiological psychology.* New York: Random House.

SCHNEIDERMAN, N. (1983). Animal behavior models of coronary heart disease. In D. S. Krantz, A. Baum, & J. E. Singer (Eds.), *Handbook of psychology and health* (Vol. 3.) Hillsdale, NJ: Erlbaum.

SCHNEIDERMAN, N., & HAMMER, D. (1985). Behavioral medicine approaches to cardiovascular disorders. In N. Schneiderman & J. T. Tapp (Eds.), *Behavioral medicine: The biopsychosocial approach.* Hillsdale, NJ: Erlbaum.

SCHOR, E. L. (1986). Use of health care services by children and diagnoses received during presumably stressful life transitions. *Pediatrics, 77,* 834-841.

SCHOTTE, D. E., & STUNKARD, A. J. (1987). Bulimia vs bulimic behaviors on a college campus. *Journal of the American Medical Association, 258,* 1213-1215.

SCHRAA, J. C., & DIRKS, J. F. (1982). Improving patient recall and comprehension of the treatment regimen. *Journal of Asthma, 19,* 159-162.

SCHUCKIT, M. A. (1985). Genetics and the risk for alcoholism. *Journal of the American Medical Association, 254,* 2614-2617.

SCHULZ, R. (1976). Effects of control and predictability on the physical and psychological well-being of the institutionalized aged. *Journal of Personality and Social Psychology, 33,* 563-573.

SCHULZ, R., & HANUSA, B. H. (1978). Long-term effects of control and predictability-enhancing interventions: Findings and ethical issues. *Journal of Personality and Social Psychology, 36,* 1194-1201.

SCHUNK, D. H., & CARBONARI, J. P. (1984). Self-efficacy models. In J. D. Matarazzo, S. M. Weiss, J. A. Herd, N. E. Miller, & S. M. Weiss (Eds.), *Behavioral health: A hand-*

book of health enhancement and disease prevention. New York: Wiley.

SCHUSTER, C. S. (1986). Biophysical development of the adolescent. In C. L. Schuster & S. S. Ashburn (Eds.), *The process of human development: A holistic life-span approach.* Boston: Little, Brown.

SCHWARTZ, G. E. (1982). Testing the biopsychosocial model: The ultimate challenge facing behavioral medicine? *Journal of Consulting and Clinical Psychology, 50,* 1040-1053.

SCHWARTZ, R. H., HAYDEN, G. F., GETSON, P. R., & DIPAOLA, A. (1986). Drinking patterns and social consequences: A study of middle-class adolescents in two private pediatric practices. *Pediatrics, 77,* 139-143.

SCHWEIDLER, H. (1984). Assistive devices, aids to daily living. In G. K. Riggs & E. P. Gall (Eds.), *Rheumatic diseases: Rehabilitation and management.* Boston: Butterworth.

SEEGER, M. W. (1984). Splints, braces, and casts. In G. K. Riggs & E. P. Gall (Eds.), *Rheumatic diseases: Rehabilitation and management.* Boston: Butterworth.

SEEMAN, M., & SEEMAN, T. E. (1983). Health behavior and personal autonomy: A longitudinal study of the sense of control in illness. *Journal of Health and Social Behavior, 24,* 144-160.

SELIGER, S. (1986). Stress can be good for you. In M. G. Walraven & H. E. Fitzgerald (Eds.), *Annual editions: Psychology 86/87.* Guilford, CT: Dushkin.

SELIGMAN, M. E. P. (1975). *Helplessness: On depression, development, and death.* San Francisco: Freeman.

SELYE, H. (1956). *The stress of life.* New York: McGraw-Hill.

SELYE, H. (1974). *Stress without distress.* Philadelphia: Lippincott.

SELYE, H. (1976). *Stress in health and disease.* Reading, MA: Butterworth.

SELYE, H. (1985). History and present status of the stress concept. In A. Monat & R. S. Lazarus (Eds.), *Stress and coping* (2nd ed.). New York: Columbia University Press.

SERAGANIAN, P., ROSKIES, E., HANLEY, J. A., OSEASOHN, R., & COLLU, R. (1987). Failure to alter psychophysiological reactivity in Type A men with physical exercise and stress management programs. *Psychology and Health, 1,* 195-213.

SERFASS, R. C., & GERBERICH, S. G. (1984). Exercise for optimal health: Strategies and motivational considerations. *Preventive Medicine, 13,* 79-99.

SEVERSON, H. H., & LICHTENSTEIN, E. (1986). Smoking prevention programs for adolescents: Rationale and review. In N. A. Krasnegor, J. D. Arasteh, & M. F. Cataldo (Eds.), *Child health behavior: A behavioral pediatrics perspective.* New York: Wiley.

SHANAS, E., & MADDOX, G. L. (1985). Health, health resources, and the utilization of care. In R. H. Binstock & E. Shanas (Eds.), *Handbook of aging and the social sciences.* New York: Van Nostrand-Reinhold.

SHAPIRO, A. K., & SHAPIRO, E. (1984). Patient-provider relationships and the placebo effect. In J. D. Matarazzo, S. M. Weiss, J. A. Herd, N. E. Miller, & S. M. Weiss (Eds.), *Behavioral health: A handbook of health enhancement and disease prevention.* New York: Wiley.

SHAPIRO, A. P., KRANTZ, D. S., & GRIM, C. E. (1986). Pharmacologic agents as modulators of stress. In K. A. Matthews, S. M. Weiss, T. Detre, T. M. Dembroski, B. Falkner, S. B. Manuck, & R. B. Williams (Eds.), *Handbook of stress, reactivity, and cardiovascular disease.* New York: Wiley.

SHAPIRO, D, & GOLDSTEIN, I. B. (1982). Biobehavioral perspectives on hypertension. *Journal of Consulting and Clinical Psychology, 50,* 841-858.

SHAPIRO, D., LANE, J. D., & HENRY, J. P. (1986). Caffeine, cardiovascular reactivity, and cardiovascular disease. In K. A. Matthews, S. M. Weiss, T. Detre, T. M. Dembroski, B. Falkner, S. B. Manuck, & R. B. Williams (Eds.), *Handbook of stress, reactivity, and cardiovascular disease.* New York: Wiley.

SHAPIRO, J. L. (1987, January). The expectant father. *Psychology Today, 21,* pp. 36-42.

SHAW, R. E., COHEN, F., DOYLE, B., & PALESKY, J. (1985). The impact of denial and repressive style on information gain and rehabilitation outcomes in myocardial infarction patients. *Psychosomatic Medicine, 47,* 262-273.

SHEKELLE, R. B., HULLEY, S. B., NEATON, J. D., BILLINGS, J. H., BORHANI, N. O., GERACE, T. A., JACOBS, D. R., LASSER, N. L., MITTELMARK, M. B., & STAMLER, J. (1985). The MRFIT Behavior Pattern Study: II. Type A behavior and incidence of coronary heart disease. *American Journal of Epidemiology, 122,* 559-570.

SHERIF, M., & SHERIF, C. W. (1953). *Groups in harmony and tension.* New York: Harper.

SHIFFMAN, S. (1986). A cluster-analytic classification of smoking relapse episodes. *Addictive Behaviors, 11,* 295-307.

SHIPLEY, R. H., BUTT, J. H., HORWITZ, B., & FARBRY, J. E. (1978). Preparation for a stressful medical procedure: Effect of amount of stimulus preexposure and coping style. *Journal of Consulting and Clinical Psychology, 46,* 499-507.

SHNEIDMAN, E. S. (1977). The college student and death. In H. Feifel (Ed.), *New meanings of death.* New York: McGraw-Hill.

SHOGREN, E. (1988, June 3). Physicians favor death with "dignity." *Philadelphia Inquirer,* p. D14.

SHONTZ, F. C. (1975). *The psychological aspects of physical illness and disability.* New York: Macmillan Co.

SHOPLAND, D. R., & BROWN, C. (1985). Changes in cigarette smoking prevalence in the U.S.: 1955 to 1983. *Annals of Behavioral Medicine, 7*(2), 5-8.

SHUCHMAN, M., & WILKES, M. (1986, September 28). Challenging the annual physical. *New York Times Magazine,* pp. 36-40.

SHUCHMAN, M., & WILKES, M. S. (1989, February 12). Asking—And telling. *New York Times Magazine,* pp. 45-46.

SHUPE, D. R. (1985). Perceived control, helplessness, and choice: Their relationship to health and aging. In J. E. Birren & J. Livingston (Eds.), *Cognition, stress, and aging.* Englewood Cliffs, NJ: Prentice-Hall.

SIEGAL, B. R., CALSYN, R. J., & CUDDIHEE, R. M. (1987). The relationship of social support to psychological adjustment in end-stage renal disease patients. *Journal of Chronic Diseases, 40,* 337-344.

SILVER, R. L., & WORTMAN, C. B. (1980). Coping with undesirable life events. In J. Garber & M. E. P. Seligman (Eds.), *Human helplessness: Theory and applications.* New York: Academic Press.

SILVERBERG, E., & LUBERA, J. A. (1989). Cancer statistics, 1989. *Ca—A Cancer Journal for Clinicians, 39*(1), 3-20.

SIMONS-MORTON, B. G., PARCEL, G. S., O'HARA, N. M., BLAIR, S. N., & PATE, R. R. (1988). Health-related physical fitness in childhood: Status and recommendations. In L. Breslow, J. E. Fielding, & L. B. Lave (Eds.), *Annual review of public health* (Vol. 9). Palo Alto, CA: Annual Reviews.

SIMONTON, O. C., & SIMONTON, S. S. (1975). Belief systems and the management of emotional aspects of malignancy. *Journal of Transpersonal Psychology, 7,* 29-47.

SINGER, J. E., & DAVIDSON, L. M. (1986). Specificity and stress research. In M. H. Appley & R. Trumbull (Eds.), *Dynamics of stress: Physiological, psychological, and social perspectives.* New York: Plenum.

SISSON, R. W., & AZRIN, N. H. (1986). Family-member involvement to initiate and promote treatment of problem drinkers. *Journal of Behavior Therapy and Experimental Psychiatry, 17,* 15-21.

SKELTON, J. A., & PENNEBAKER, J. W. (1982). The psychology of physical symptoms and sensations. In G. S. Sanders & J. Suls (Eds.), *Social psychology of health and illness.* Hillsdale, NJ: Erlbaum.

SKELTON, M., & DOMINIAN, J. (1973). Psychological stress in wives of patients with myocardial infarction. *British Medical Journal, 2,* 101-103.

SKLAR, L. S., & ANISMAN, H. (1981). Stress and cancer. *Psychological Bulletin, 89,* 369-406.

SKOLNICK, A. S. (1986). *The psychology of human development.* San Diego: Harcourt Brace Jovanovich.

SMITH, E. L. (1984). Special considerations in developing exercise programs for the older adult. In J. D. Matarazzo, S. M. Weiss, J. A. Herd, N. E. Miller, & S. M. Weiss (Eds.), *Behavioral health: A handbook of health enhancement and disease prevention.* New York: Wiley.

SMITH, F. (1988, March 13). 75% with virus will get AIDS, study says. *Philadelphia Inquirer,* p. A3.

SMITH, G. S., & KRAUS, J. F. (1988). Alcohol and residential, recreational, and occupational injuries: A review of the epidemiologic evidence. In L. Breslow, J. E. Fielding, & L. B. Lave (Eds.), *Annual review of public health* (Vol. 9). Palo Alto, CA: Annual Reviews.

SMITH, J. B., & AUTMAN, S. H. (1985). The experience of hospitalization. In L. L. Hayman & E. M. Sporing (Eds.), *Handbook of pediatric nursing.* New York: Wiley.

SMITH, R. C., & ZIMNY, G. H. (1988). Physicians' emotional reactions to patients. *Psychosomatics, 29,* 392-397.

SMITH, T. W., & ANDERSON, N. B. (1986). Models of personality and disease: An interactional approach to Type A behavior and cardiovascular risk. *Journal of Personality and Social Psychology, 50,* 1166-1173.

SMITH, T. W., TURNER, C. W., FORD, M. H., HUNT, S. C., BARLOW, G. K., STULTS, B. M., & WILLIAMS, R. R. (1987). Blood pressure reactivity in adult male twins. *Health Psychology, 6,* 209-220.

SNOW, L. F. (1981). Folk medical beliefs and their implications for care of patients: A review based on studies among black Americans. In G. Henderson & M. Primeaux (Eds.), *Transcultural health care.* Menlo Park, CA: Addison-Wesley.

SNYDER, S. H. (1977). Opiate receptors and internal opiates. *Scientific American, 236,* 44-56.

SOBEL, M. B., & SOBEL, L. C. (1976). Second-year treatment outcome of alcoholics treated by individualized behavior therapy: Results. *Behavior Research and Therapy, 14,* 195-215.

SOBEL, M. B., & SOBEL, L. C. (1978). *Behavioral treatment of alcohol problems.* New York: Plenum.

SOLOMON, G. F., & TEMOSHOK, L. (1987). A psychoneuroimmunologic perspective on AIDS research: Questions, preliminary findings, and suggestions. *Journal of Applied Social Psychology, 17,* 286-308.

SORENSEN, G., JACOBS, D. R., PIRIE, P., FOLSOM, A., LUEPKER, R., & GILLUM, R. (1987). Relationships among Type A behavior, employment experiences, and gender: The Minnesota Heart Survey. *Journal of Behavioral Medicine, 10,* 323-336.

SORENSEN, G., PECHACEK, T., & PALLONEN, U. (1986). Occupational and worksite norms and attitudes about smoking cessation. *American Journal of Public Health, 76,* 544-549.

SOUTHARD, D. R., COATES, T. J., KOLODNER, K., PARKER, F. C., PADGETT, N. E., & KENNEDY, H. L. (1986). Relationship between mood and blood pressure in the natural environment: An adolescent population. *Health Psychology, 5,* 469-480.

SPECTER, M. (1988, June 3). AIDS virus will kill all it infects, federal researchers say for 1st time. *Philadelphia Inquirer,* p. A10.

SPEECE, M. W., & BRENT, S. B. (1984). Children's understanding of death: A review of three components of a death concept. *Child Development, 55,* 1671-1686.

SPEISMAN, J. C., LAZARUS, R. S., MORDKOFF, A., & DAVISON, L. (1964). Experimental demonstration of stress based on ego-defense theory. *Journal of Abnormal and Social Psychology, 68,* 367-380.

SPIGA, R. (1986). Social interaction and cardiovascular response of boys exhibiting the coronary-prone behavior pattern. *Journal of Pediatric Psychology, 11,* 59-69.

SPINETTA, J. J. (1974). The dying child's awareness of death: A review. *Psychological Bulletin, 81,* 256-260.

SPINETTA, J. J. (1982). Behavioral and psychological research in childhood cancer. *Cancer, 50,* 1939-1943.

STALL, R. D., COATES, T. J., & HOFF, C. (1988). Behavioral risk reduction for HIV infection among gay and bisexual men: A review of results from the United States. *American Psychologist, 43,* 878-885.

STAMLER, J., WENTWORTH, D., & NEATON, J. D. (1986). Is relationship between serum cholesterol and risk of premature death from coronary heart disease continuous and graded? Findings in 356,222 primary screenees of the Multiple Risk Factor Intervention Trial (MRFIT). *Journal of the American Medical Association, 256,* 2823-2828.

STANTON, A. L. (1987). Determinants of adherence to medical regimens by hypertensive patients. *Journal of Behavioral Medicine, 10,* 377-394.

STEIN, J. A., NEWCOMB, M. D., & BENTLER, P. M. (1987). An 8-year study of multiple influences on drug use and drug use consequences. *Journal of Personality and Social Psychology, 53,* 1094-1105.

STEINBERG, L. (1985). Early temperamental antecedents of adult Type A behaviors. *Developmental Psychology, 21,* 1171-1180.

STEINER, H, & CLARK, W. R. (1977). Psychiatric complications of burned adults: A classification. *Journal of Trauma, 17,* 134-143.

STEINMAN, S. (1981). The experience of children in a joint-custody arrangement: A report of a study. *American Journal of Orthopsychiatry, 51,* 403-414.

STERMAN, M. B. (1986). Epilepsy and its treatment with EEG feedback therapy. *Annals of Behavioral Medicine, 8*(1), 21-25.

STEVENS, R. E. (1984). Cancer and nursing. In S. N. McIntire & A. L. Cioppa (Eds.), *Cancer nursing: A developmental approach.* New York: Wiley.

STEVENS-LONG, J. (1984). *Adult life: Developmental processes* (2nd ed.). Palo Alto, CA: Mayfield.

ST. JEOR, S. T., SUTNICK, M. R., & SCOTT, B. J. (1988). Nutrition. In E. A. Blechman & K. D. Brownell (Eds.), *Handbook of behavioral medicine for women.* New York: Pergamon.

STOCKTON, W. (1988, March 7). Fresh research tells asthmatics to stay active. *New York Times,* p. C9.

STONE, A. A., & NEALE, J. M. (1984). New measure of daily coping: Development and preliminary results. *Journal of Personality and Social Psychology, 46,* 892-906.

STONE, G. C. (1979). Health and the health system: A historical overview and conceptual framework. In G. C. Stone, F. Cohen, & N. E. Adler (Eds.), *Health psychology—A handbook.* San Francisco: Jossey-Bass.

STOTLAND, E. (1987). Stress. In R. Corsini (Ed.), *Concise encyclopedia of psychology.* New York: Wiley.

STOUT, H. (1988, June 12). Cigarettes: Still big business. *New York Times,* p. D4.

STRAUSS, L. M., SOLOMON, L. J., COSTANZA, M. C., WORDEN, J. K., & FOSTER, R. S. (1987). Breast self-examination practices and attitudes of women with and without a history of breast cancer. *Journal of Behavioral Medicine, 10,* 337-350.

STRAW, M. K. (1983). Coping with obesity. In T. G. Burish & L. A. Bradley (Eds.), *Coping with chronic disease: Research and applications.* New York: Academic Press.

STRICKLAND, B. R. (1978). Internal-external expectancies and health-related behaviors. *Journal of Consulting and Clinical Psychology, 6,* 1192-1211.

STRIEGEL-MOORE, R., & RODIN, J. (1985). Prevention of obesity. In J. C. Rosen & L. J. Solomon (Eds.), *Prevention in health psychology.* Hanover, NH: University Press of New England.

STRIEGEL-MOORE, R. H., SILBERSTEIN, L. R., & RODIN, J. (1986). Toward an understanding of risk factors for bulimia. *American Psychologist, 41,* 246-263.

STUART, R. B. (1967). Behavioral control of overeating. *Behavior Research and Therapy, 5,* 357-365.

STUNKARD, A. J. (1987). Conservative treatments for obesity. *American Journal of Clinical Nutrition, 45,* 1142-1154.

STUNKARD, A. J., & BERTHOLD, H. C. (1985). What is behavior therapy? A very short description of behavioral weight control. *American Journal of Clinical Nutrition, 41,* 821-823.

STUNKARD, A. J., FELIX, M. R. J., & COHEN, R. Y. (1985). Mobilizing a community to promote health: The Pennsylvania County Health Improvement Program (CHIP). In J. C. Rosen & L. J. Solomon (Eds.), *Prevention in health psychology.* Hanover, NH: University Press of New England.

STUNKARD, A. J., FOCH, T. T., & HRUBEC, Z. (1986). A twin study of human obesity. *Journal of the American Medical Association, 256,* 51-54.

STUNKARD, A. J., SORENSEN, T. I. A., HANIS, C., TEASDALE, T. W., CHAKRABORTY, R., SCHULL, W. J., & SCHULSINGER, F. (1986). An adoption of human obesity. *New England Journal of Medicine, 314,* 193-198.

STUNKARD, A. J., STINNETT, J. L., & SMOLLER, J. W. (1986). Psychological and social aspects of the surgical treatment of obesity. *American Journal of Psychiatry, 143,* 417-429.

SUEDFELD, P., & IKARD, F. F. (1974). Use of sensory deprivation in facilitating the reduction of cigarette smoking. *Journal of Consulting and Clinical Psychology, 42,* 888-895.

SUINN, R. M. (1982). Intervention with Type A behavior. *Journal of Consulting and Clinical Psychology, 50,* 933-949.

SUITOR, C. W., & HUNTER, M. F. (1980). *Nutrition: Principles and application in health promotion.* Philadelphia: Lippincott.

SULS, J. (1982). Social support, interpersonal relations, and health: Benefits and liabilities. In G. S. Sanders & J. Suls (Eds.), *Social psychology of health and illness.* Hillsdale, NJ: Erlbaum.

SULS, J. (1984). Levels of analysis and efforts to modify adolescent health behavior: A commentary on Lund and Kegeles. *Health Psychology, 3,* 371-375.

SULS, J., & FLETCHER, B. (1985). The relative efficacy of avoidant and nonavoidant coping strategies: A meta-analysis. *Health Psychology, 4,* 249-288.

SULS, J., & MULLEN, B. (1981). Life change and psychological distress: The role of perceived control and desirability. *Journal of Applied Social Psychology, 11,* 379-389.

SULS, J., & SANDERS, G. S. (1988). Type A behavior as a general risk factor for physical disorder. *Journal of Behavioral Medicine, 11,* 210-226.

SULS, J., SANDERS, G. S., & LABRECQUE, M. S. (1986). Attempting to control blood pressure without systematic instruction: When advice is counterproductive. *Journal of Behavioral Medicine, 9,* 567-576.

SUPER, C. N. (1981). Cross-cultural research on infancy. In H. C. Trandis & A. Heron (Eds.), *Handbook of cross-cul-*

tural psychology: Developmental psychology (Vol. 4). Boston: Allyn & Bacon.

SURWIT, R. S., FEINGLOS, M. N., & SCOVERN, A. W. (1983). Diabetes and behavior: A paradigm for health psychology. *American Psychologist, 38,* 255-262.

SUSSER, M., HOPPER, K., & RICHMAN, R. (1983). Society, culture, and health. In D. Mechanic (Ed.), *Handbook of health, health care, and the health professions.* New York: Free Press.

SUTTON, S. R. (1982). Fear-arousing communications: A critical examination of theory and research. In J. R. Eiser (Ed.), *Social psychology and behavioral medicine.* New York: Wiley.

SUTTON, S., & HALLETT, R. (1988). Understanding the effects of fear-arousing communications: The role of cognitive factors and the amount of fear aroused. *Journal of Behavioral Medicine, 11,* 353-360.

SVARSTAD, B. (1976). Physician-patient communication and patient conformity with medical advice. In D. Mechanic (Ed.), *The growth of bureaucratic medicine.* New York: Wiley.

SWAN, G. E., CARMELLI, D., & ROSENMAN, R. H. (1986). Spouse-pair similarity on the California Psychological Inventory with reference to husband's coronary heart disease. *Psychosomatic Medicine, 48,* 172-186.

SWEZEY, R. L. (1984). Manual mobilization and traction. In G. K. Riggs & E. P. Gall (Eds.), *Rheumatic diseases: Rehabilitation and management.* Boston: Butterworth.

SWIGONSKI, M. E. (1987). *Bio-psycho-social factors affecting coping and compliance with the hemodialysis treatment regimen.* University Microfilms International. (Order No. 8803518).

SYME, S. L. (1984). Sociocultural factors and disease etiology. In W. D. Gentry (Ed.), *Handbook of behavioral medicine.* New York: Guilford.

TAGLIACOZZO, D. L., & MAUKSCH, H. O. (1972). The patient's view of the patient's role. In E. G. Jaco (Ed.), *Patients, physicians, and illness* (2nd ed.). New York: Free Press.

TANNER, J. M. (1970). Physical growth. In P. H. Mussen (Ed.), *Carmichael's manual of child psychology* (3rd ed.). New York: Wiley.

TANNER, J. M. (1978). *Foetus into man.* Cambridge, MA: Harvard University Press.

TAPP, J. T. (1985). Multisystems interventions in disease. In N. Schneiderman & J. T. Tapp (Eds.), *Behavioral medicine: The biopsychosocial approach.* Hillsdale, NJ: Erlbaum.

TAPP, J. T., & WARNER, R. (1985). The multisystems view of health and disease. In N. Schneiderman & J. T. Tapp (Eds.), *Behavioral medicine: The biopsychosocial approach.* Hillsdale, NJ: Erlbaum.

TARNOWSKI, K. J., RASNAKE, L. K., & DRABMAN, R. S. (1987). Behavioral assessment and treatment of pediatric burn injuries: A review. *Behavior Therapy, 18,* 417-441.

TAYLOR, R. L., LAM, D. J., ROPPEL, C. E., & BARTER, J. T. (1984). Friends can be good medicine: Excursion into mental health promotion. *Community Mental Health Journal, 20,* 294-303.

TAYLOR, S. E. (1979). Hospital patient behavior: Reactance, helplessness, or control? *Journal of Social Issues, 35,* 156-184.

TAYLOR, S. E. (1983). Adjustment to threatening events: A theory of cognitive adaptation. *American Psychologist, 38,* 1161-1173.

TAYLOR, S. E. (1987). The progress and prospects of health psychology: Tasks of a maturing discipline. *Health Psychology, 6,* 73-87.

TAYLOR, S. E., LICHTMAN, R. R., & WOOD, J. V. (1984). Attributions, beliefs about control, and adjustment to breast cancer. *Journal of Personality and Social Psychology, 46,* 489-502.

TEBBI, C. K., CUMMINGS, K. M., ZEVON, M. A., SMITH, L., RICHARDS, M., & MALLON, J. (1986). Compliance of pediatric and adolescent cancer patients. *Cancer, 58,* 1179-1184.

TENNES, K., & KREYE, M. (1985). Children's adrenocortical responses to classroom activities and tests in elementary school. *Psychosomatic Medicine, 47,* 451-460.

TERR, L. C. (1986). Psychic trauma in children: Observations following the Chowchilla school-bus kidnapping. In R. H. Moos (Ed.), *Coping with life crises: An integrated approach.* New York: Plenum.

THELEN, M. H., FRY, R. A., FEHRENBACH, P. A., & FRAUTSCHI, N. M. (1979). Therapeutic videotape and film modeling: A review. *Psychological Bulletin, 86,* 701-720.

THEORELL, T., & RAHE, R. H. (1975). Life change events, ballistocardiography, and coronary death. *Journal of Human Stress, 1,* 18-24.

THOITS, P. A. (1982). Conceptual, methodological, and theoretical problems in studying social support as a buffer against life stress. *Journal of Health and Social Behavior, 23,* 145-159.

THOMAS, A., CHESS, S., & BIRCH, H. G. (1970, August). The origin of personality. *Scientific American,* pp. 102-109.

THOMPSON, J. (1984). Communicating with patients. In R. Fitzpatrick, J. Hinton, S. Newman, G. Scambler, & J. Thompson (Eds.), *The experience of illness.* London: Tavistock.

THOMPSON, J. K. (1986, April). Larger than life. *Psychology Today, 20,* pp. 38-44.

THOMPSON, S. C. (1981). Will it hurt less if I can control it? A complex answer to a simple question. *Psychological Bulletin, 90,* 89-101.

THOMPSON, W. R., & THOMPSON, D. L. (1987). Effects of exercise compliance on blood lipids in post-myocardial infarction patients. *Journal of Cardiopulmonary Rehabilitation, 7,* 332-341.

THORESEN, C. E. (1984). Overview. In J. D. Matarazzo, S. M. Weiss, J. A. Herd, N. E. Miller, & S. M. Weiss (Eds.), *Behavioral health: A handbook of health enhancement and disease prevention.* New York: Wiley.

THORESEN, C. E., FRIEDMAN, M., POWELL, L. H., GILL, J. J., & ULMER, D. K. (1985). Altering the Type A behavior pattern in postinfarction patients. *Journal of Cardiopulmonary Rehabilitation, 5,* 258-266.

THORESEN, C. E., & PATTILLO, J. R. (1988). Exploring the Type A behavior pattern in children and adolescents. In

B. K. Houston & C. R. Snyder (Eds.), *Type A behavior pattern: Research, theory, and intervention.* New York: Wiley.

THORNE, B. M. (1987). Alzheimer's disease. In R. J. Corsini (Ed.), *Concise encyclopedia of psychology.* New York: Wiley.

TIMKO, C. (1987). Seeking medical care for a breast cancer symptom: Determinants of intentions to engage in prompt or delay behavior. *Health Psychology, 6,* 305–328.

TOLCHIN, M. (1988, December 2). U.S. study faults nursing home care over medications. *New York Times,* pp. A1, B7.

TOMKINS, S. (1966). Psychological model for smoking behavior. *American Journal of Public Health, 56*(12, Supplement), 17–20.

TOMKINS, S. (1968). A modified model of smoking behavior. In E. F. Borgatta & R. R. Evans (Eds.), *Smoking, health and behavior.* Chicago: Aldine.

TORRENS, P. R. (1985). Hospice care: What have we learned? In L. Breslow, J. E. Fielding, & L. B. Lave (Eds.), *Annual review of public health* (Vol. 6). Palo Alto, CA: Annual Reviews.

TOTMAN, R. (1982). Psychosomatic theories. In J. R. Eiser (Ed.), *Social psychology and behavioral medicine.* New York: Wiley.

TRABIN, T., RADER, C., & CUMMINGS, C. (1987). A comparison of pain management outcomes for disability compensation and non-compensation patients. *Psychology and Health, 1,* 341–351.

TROSS, S., & HIRSCH, D. A. (1988). Psychological distress and neuropsychological complications of HIV infection and AIDS. *American Psychologist, 43,* 929–934.

TRUMBULL, R., & APPLEY, M. H. (1986). A conceptual model for examination of stress dynamics. In M. H. Appley & R. Trumbull (Eds.), *Dynamics of stress: Physiological, psychological, and social perspectives.* New York: Plenum.

TURK, D. C., & HOLZMAN, A. D. (1986). Commonalities among psychological approaches in the treatment of chronic pain: Specifying the meta-constructs. In A. D. Holzman & D. C. Turk (Eds.), *Pain management: A handbook of psychological treatment approaches.* New York: Pergamon.

TURK, D. C., LITT, M. D., SALOVEY, P., & WALKER J. (1985). Seeking urgent pediatric treatment: Factors contributing to frequency, delay, and appropriateness. *Health Psychology, 4,* 43–59.

TURK, D. C., MEICHENBAUM, D. H., & BERMAN, W. H. (1979). Application of biofeedback for the regulation of pain: A critical review. *Psychological Bulletin, 86,* 1322–1338.

TURK, D. C., MEICHENBAUM, D., & GENEST, M. (1983). *Pain and behavioral medicine: A cognitive-behavioral perspective.* New York: Guilford.

TURK, D. C., & RUDY, T. E. (1986). Assessment of cognitive factors in chronic pain: A worthwhile enterprise? *Journal of Consulting and Clinical Psychology, 54,* 760–768.

TURK, D. C., RUDY, T. E., & SALOVEY, P. (1984). Health protection: Attitudes and behaviors of LPNs, teachers, and college students. *Health Psychology, 3,* 189–210.

TURK, D. C., SALOVEY, P., & LITT, M. D. (1986). Adherence: A cognitive-behavioral perspective. In K. E. Gerber & A. M. Nehemkis (Eds.), *Compliance: The dilemma of the chronically ill.* New York: Springer.

TURK, D. C., & SPEERS, M. A. (1983). Diabetes mellitus: A cognitive-functional analysis of stress. In T. G. Burish & L. A. Bradley (Eds.), *Coping with chronic disease: Research and applications.* New York: Academic Press.

TURK, D. C., WACK, J. T., & KERNS, R. D. (1985). An empirical examination of the "pain-behavior" construct. *Journal of Behavioral Medicine, 8,* 119–130.

TURNER, J. A. (1982). Comparison of group progressive-relaxation training and cognitive-behavioral group therapy for chronic low back pain. *Journal of Consulting and Clinical Psychology, 50,* 757–765.

TURNER, J. A., CLANCY, S., & VITALIANO, P. P. (1987). Relationships of stress, appraisal and coping, to chronic low back pain. *Behavior Research and Therapy, 25,* 281–288.

TURNER, R. J. (1981). Social support as a contingency in psychological well-being. *Journal of Health and Social Behavior, 22,* 357–367.

USBC (UNITED STATES BUREAU OF THE CENSUS) (1983). *Statistical abstract of the United States: 1984* (104th ed.). Washington, DC: U.S. Government Printing Office.

USDA (UNITED STATES DEPARTMENT OF AGRICULTURE) (1986). *U.S. demand for food: Household expenditures, demographics, and projections* (Publication No. 490-920-40042). Washington, DC: U.S. Government Printing Office.

USDHEW (UNITED STATES DEPARTMENT OF HEALTH, EDUCATION, & WELFARE) (1979). *Smoking and health: A report of the Surgeon General* (Publication No. 79-50066). Washington, DC: U.S. Government Printing Office.

USDHHS (UNITED STATES DEPARTMENT OF HEALTH AND HUMAN SERVICES) (1981). *Medicines and you* (Publication No. NIH 81-2140). Washington, DC: U.S. Government Printing Office.

USDHHS (UNITED STATES DEPARTMENT OF HEALTH AND HUMAN SERVICES) (1982). *Changes in mortality among the elderly: United States, 1940–78* (Publication No. PHS 82-1406). Washington, DC: U.S. Government Printing Office.

USDHHS (UNITED STATES DEPARTMENT OF HEALTH AND HUMAN SERVICES) (1983a). *A nurse's guide for teaching patients undergoing cancer chemotherapy* (Publication No. NIH 83-2484). Washington, DC: U.S. Government Printing Office.

USDHHS (UNITED STATES DEPARTMENT OF HEALTH AND HUMAN SERVICES) (1983b). *Dietary intake and cardiovascular risk factors, Part II. Serum urate, serum cholesterol, and correlates* (Publication No. PHS 83-1677). Washington, DC: U.S. Government Printing Office.

USDHHS (UNITED STATES DEPARTMENT OF HEALTH AND HUMAN SERVICES) (1984). *Adjustment of hospital utilization rates: United States, 1965–1980* (Publication No. PHS 85-1742). Washington, DC: U.S. Government Printing Office.

USDHHS (UNITED STATES DEPARTMENT OF HEALTH AND HUMAN SERVICES) (1985a). *Alcohol research: Meeting the challenge* (Publication No. DHHS 85-1392). Washington, DC: U.S. Government Printing Office.

USDHHS (UNITED STATES DEPARTMENT OF HEALTH AND HUMAN SERVICES) (1985b). *Charting the nation's health: Trends since 1960* (Publication No. PHS 85-1251). Washington, DC: U.S. Government Printing Office.

USDHHS (UNITED STATES DEPARTMENT OF HEALTH AND HUMAN SERVICES) (1985c). *Hospitalization of persons under 65 years of age: United States, 1980-81* (Publication No. PHS 85-1580). Washington, DC: U.S. Government Printing Office.

USDHHS (UNITED STATES DEPARTMENT OF HEALTH AND HUMAN SERVICES) (1985d). *NIOSH pocket guide to chemical hazards* (Publication No. DHEW 85-114). Washington, DC: U.S. Government Printing Office.

USDHHS (UNITED STATES DEPARTMENT OF HEALTH AND HUMAN SERVICES) (1985e). *Understanding the immune system* (Publication No. NIH 85-529). Washington, DC: U.S. Government Printing Office.

USDHHS (UNITED STATES DEPARTMENT OF HEALTH AND HUMAN SERVICES) (1986a). *Blood pressure levels in persons 18-74 years of age in 1976-80, and trends in blood pressure from 1960-1980 in the United States* (Publication No. PHS 86-1684). Washington, DC: U.S. Government Printing Office.

USDHHS (UNITED STATES DEPARTMENT OF HEALTH AND HUMAN SERVICES) (1986b). *Clinical opportunities for smoking intervention: A guide for the busy physician* (Publication No. NIH 86-2178). Washington, DC: U.S. Government Printing Office.

USDHHS (UNITED STATES DEPARTMENT OF HEALTH AND HUMAN SERVICES) (1986c). *Health status of the disadvantaged: Chartbook 1986* (Publication No. HRS-P-DV86-2). Washington, DC: U.S. Government Printing Office.

USDHHS (UNITED STATES DEPARTMENT OF HEALTH AND HUMAN SERVICES) (1986d). *Prevalence of selected chronic conditions: United States, 1979-81* (Publication No. PHS 86-1583). Washington, DC: U.S. Government Printing Office.

USDHHS (UNITED STATES DEPARTMENT OF HEALTH AND HUMAN SERVICES) (1986e). *The health consequences of involuntary smoking: A report of the Surgeon General* (Publication No. CDC 87-8398). Washington, DC: U.S. Government Printing Office.

USDHHS (UNITED STATES DEPARTMENT OF HEALTH AND HUMAN SERVICES) (1986f). *Total serum cholesterol levels of adults 20-74 years of age: United States, 1976-80* (Publication No. PHS 86-1686). Washington, DC: U.S. Government Printing Office.

USDHHS (UNITED STATES DEPARTMENT OF HEALTH AND HUMAN SERVICES) (1986g). *Use of selected preventive care procedures: United States, 1982* (Publication No. PHS 86-1585). Washington, DC: U.S. Government Printing Office.

USDHHS (UNITED STATES DEPARTMENT OF HEALTH AND HUMAN SERVICES) (1987a). *Physician contacts by sociodemographic and health characteristics: United States, 1982-83* (Publication No. PHS 87-1589). Washington, DC: U.S. Government Printing Office.

USDHHS (UNITED STATES DEPARTMENT OF HEALTH AND HUMAN SERVICES) (1987b). *Vital statistics of the United States, 1984: Life tables* (Publication No. PHS 87-1104). Washington, DC: U.S. Government Printing Office.

USDL (UNITED STATES DEPARTMENT OF LABOR) (1985). *How to prepare for workplace emergencies* (Publication No. OSHA 3088, rev.). Washington, DC: U.S. Government Printing Office.

USDL (UNITED STATES DEPARTMENT OF LABOR) (1986). *Dietetics, nursing, pharmacy, and therapy occupations* (Publication No. BLS 2250-8). Washington, DC: U.S. Government Printing Office.

USDL (UNITED STATES DEPARTMENT OF LABOR) (1987). *Occupational injuries and illnesses in the United States by industry, 1985* (Publication No. BLS 2278). Washington, DC: U.S. Government Printing Office.

URBAN, B. J., FRANCE, R. D., STEINBERGER, E. K., SCOTT, D. L., & MALTBIE, A. A. (1986). Long-term use of narcotic/antidepressant medication in the management of phantom limb pain. *Pain, 24,* 191-196.

VAN EGEREN, L. F., SNIDERMAN, L. D., & ROGGELIN, M. S. (1982). Competitive two-person interactions of Type-A and Type-B individuals. *Journal of Behavioral Medicine, 5,* 55-66.

VARNI, J. W., & BABANI, L. (1986). Long-term adherence to health care regimens in pediatric chronic disorders. In N. A. Krasnegor, J. D. Arasteh, & M. F. Cataldo (Eds.), *Child health behavior: A behavioral pediatrics perspective.* New York: Wiley.

VARNI, J. W., JAY, S. M., MASEK, B. J., & THOMPSON, K. L. (1986). Cognitive-behavioral assessment and management of pediatric pain. In A. D. Holzman & D. C. Turk (Eds.), *Pain management: A handbook of psychological treatment approaches.* New York: Pergamon.

VARNI, J. W., & THOMPSON, K. L. (1986). Biobehavioral assessment and management of pediatric pain. In N. A. Krasnegor, J. D. Arasteh, & M. F. Cataldo (Eds.), *Child health behavior: A behavioral pediatrics perspective.* New York: Wiley.

VENN, J. R., & SHORT, J. G. (1973). Vicarious classical conditioning of emotional responses in nursery school children. *Journal of Personality and Social Psychology, 28,* 249-255.

VERBRUGGE, L. M. (1980). Sex differences in complaints and diagnoses. *Journal of Behavioral Medicine, 3,* 327-355.

VERBRUGGE, L. M. (1985). Gender and health: An update on hypotheses and evidence. *Journal of Health and Social Behavior, 26,* 156-182.

VERNON, D. T. A., & BIGELOW, D. A. (1974). Effect of information about a potentially stressful situation on responses to stress impact. *Journal of Personality and Social Psychology, 29,* 50-59.

VERRIER, R. L., DESILVA, R. A., & LOWN, B. (1983). Psychological factors in cardiac arrhythmias and sudden death. In D. S. Krantz, A. Baum, & J. E. Singer (Eds.), *Handbook of psychology and health* (Vol. 3). Hillsdale, NJ: Erlbaum.

VERTINSKY, P., & AUMAN, J. T. (1988). Elderly women's barriers to exercise, Part I: Perceived risks. *Health Values, 12*(4), 13-19.

VINOKUR, A., & SELZER, M. L. (1975). Desirable and undesirable life events: Their relationship to stress and mental distress. *Journal of Personality and Social Psychology, 32,* 329-337.

VISINTAINER, P. F., & MATTHEWS, K. A. (1987). Stability of overt Type A behaviors in children: Results from a two- and five-year longitudinal study. *Child Development, 58* 1586-1591.

VITALIANO, P. P., RUSSO, J., BREEN, A. R., VITIELLO, M. V., & PRINZ, P. N. (1986). Functional decline in the early stages of Alzheimer's disease. *Journal of Psychology and Aging, 1,* 41-46.

VLADECK, B. C. (1983). Nursing homes. In D. Mechanic (Ed.), *Handbook of health, health care, and the health professions.* New York: Free Press.

WADDEN, T. A., & ANDERTON, C. H. (1982). The clinical use of hypnosis. *Psychological Bulletin, 91,* 215-243.

WADDEN, T. A., & BROWNELL, K. D. (1984). The development and modification of dietary practices in individuals, groups, and large populations. In J. D. Matarazzo, S. M. Weiss, J. A. Herd, N. E. Miller, & S. M.Weiss (Eds.), *Behavioral health: A handbook of health enhancement and disease prevention.* New York: Wiley.

WADDEN, T. A., & STUNKARD, A. J. (1986). Controlled trial of very-low-calorie diet, behavior therapy, and their combination in the treatment of obesity. *Journal of Consulting and Clinical Psychology, 54,* 482-488.

WAGENAAR, A. C., & WEBSTER, D. W. (1986). Preventing injuries to children through compulsory automobile safety seat use. *Pediatrics, 78,* 662-672.

WAITZKIN, H., & STOECKLE, J. D. (1976). Information control and the micropolitics of health care: Summary of an ongoing research project. *Social Science and Medicine, 10,* 263-276.

WALDRON, I. (1985). Why do women live longer than men?: Part I. In M. Bloom (Ed.), *Life span development: Bases for preventive and interventive helping* (2nd ed.). New York: Macmillan Co.

WALLACE, A. (1986, December 21). Teaching the humane touch. *New York Times Magazine,* pp. 23, 52, 55, 72.

WALLACE, L. M. (1986). Communication variables in the design of pre-surgical preparatory information. *British Journal of Clinical Psychology, 25,* 111-118.

WALLER, J. A. (1987). Injury: Conceptual shifts and preventive implications. In L. Breslow, J. E. Fielding., & L. B. Lave (Eds.), *Annual review of public health* (Vol. 8). Palo Alto, CA: Annual Reviews.

WALLERSTEIN, J. S. (1983). Children of divorce: Stress and developmental tasks. In N. Garmezy & M. Rutter (Eds.), *Stress, coping, and development in children.* New York: McGraw-Hill.

WALLERSTEIN, J. S. (1986). Children and divorce: The psychological tasks of the child. In R. H. Moos (Ed.), *Coping with life crises: An integrated approach.* New York: Plenum.

WALLSTON, B. S., ALAGNA, S. W., DEVELLIS, B. M., & DEVELLIS, R. F. (1983). Social support and physical illness. *Health Psychology, 2,* 367-391.

WALLSTON, K. A., & WALLSTON, B. S. (1982). Who is responsible for your health? The construct of health locus of control. In G. S. Sanders & J. Suls (Eds.), *Social psychology of health and illness.* Hillsdale, NJ: Erlbaum.

WALLSTON, K. A., WALLSTON, B. S., & DEVELLIS, R. (1978). Development of the Multidimensional Health Locus of Control (MHLC) Scales. *Health Education Monographs, 6,* 161-170.

WALTER, H. J., HOFMAN, A., CONNELLY, P. A., BARRETT, L. T., & KOST, K. L. (1985). Primary prevention of chronic disease in children: Changes in risk factors after one year of intervention. *American Journal of Epidemiology, 122,* 772-781.

WARGA, C. (1987, August). Pain's gatekeeper. *Psychology Today, 21,* pp. 50-56.

WEBER, J. M., KLESGES, R. C., & KLESGES, L. M. (1988). Dietary restraint and obesity: Their effects on dietary intake. *Journal of Behavioral Medicine, 11,* 185-199.

WEIDNER, G., & MATTHEWS, K. A. (1978). Reported physical symptoms elicited by unpredictable events and the Type A coronary-prone behavior pattern. *Journal of Personality and Social Psychology, 36,* 1213-1220.

WEINBERGER, M., HINER, S. L., & TIERNEY, W. M. (1987). In support of hassles as a measure of stress in predicting health outcomes. *Journal of Behavioral Medicine, 10,* 19-31.

WEINER, H. (1977). *Psychobiology and human disease.* New York: Elsevier.

WEINSTEIN, N. D. (1982). Unrealistic optimism about susceptibility to health problems. *Journal of Behavioral Medicine, 5,* 441-460.

WEINSTEIN, N. D. (1987). Unrealistic optimism about susceptibility to health problems: Conclusions from a community-wide sample. *Journal of Behavioral Medicine, 10,* 481-500.

WEINSTEIN, N. D. (1988). The precaution adoption process. *Health Psychology, 7,* 355-386.

WEISENBERG, M. (1977). Pain and pain control. *Psychological Bulletin, 84,* 1008-1044.

WEISMAN, A. D. (1976). Coping with untimely death. In R. H. Moos (Ed.), *Human adaptation: Coping with life crises.* Lexington, MA: Heath.

WEISMAN, A. D. (1977). The psychiatrist and the inexorable. In H. Feifel (Ed.), *New meanings of death.* New York: McGraw-Hill.

WEISMAN, A. D. (1979). *Coping with cancer.* New York: McGraw-Hill.

WEISS, J. M. (1984). Behavioral and psychological influences on gastrointestinal pathology: Experimental techniques and findings. In W. D. Gentry (Ed.), *Handbook of behavioral medicine.* New York: Guilford.

WEISS, S. M. (1984). Health hazard/health risk appraisals. In J. D. Matarazzo, S. M. Weiss, J. A. Herd, N. E. Miller, & S. M. Weiss (Eds.), *Behavioral health: A handbook of health enhancement and disease prevention.* New York: Wiley.

WELIN, L., SVÄRDSUDD, K., WILHELMSEN, L., LARSSON, B., & TIBBLIN, G. (1987). Analysis of risk factors for stroke in a cohort of men born in 1913. *New England Journal of Medicine, 317,* 521-526.

WELTMAN, A. (1984). Exercise and diet to optimize body

composition. In J. D. Matarazzo, S. M. Weiss, J. A. Herd, N. E. Miller, & S. M. Weiss (Eds.), *Behavioral health: A handbook of health enhancement and disease prevention.* New York: Wiley.

WERNER, E. E. (1987). Resilient children. In H. E. Fitzgerald & M. G. Walraven (Eds.), *Annual editions: Human development 87/88.* Guilford, CT: Dushkin.

WERNER, E. E., & SMITH, R. S. (1982). *Vulnerable but invincible: A study of resilient children.* New York: McGraw-Hill.

WERNICK, R. I. (1983). Stress inoculation in the management of clinical pain: Applications to burn pain. In D. Meichenbaum & M. E. Jaremko (Eds.), *Stress reduction and prevention.* New York: Plenum.

WERRY, J. S. (1986). Physical illness, symptoms, and allied disorders. In H. C. Quay & J. S. Werry (Eds.), *Psychopathological disorders of childhood* (3rd ed.). New York: Wiley.

WHITE, L. P. (1977). Death and the physician: Mortus vivos docent. In H. Feifel (Ed.), *New meanings of death.* New York: McGraw-Hill.

WHITEHEAD, W. E. (1986). Pediatric gastrointestinal disorders. In N. A. Krasnegor, J. D. Arasteh, & M. F. Cataldo (Eds.), *Child health behavior: A behavioral pediatrics perspective.* New York: Wiley.

WHITEHEAD, W. E., BUSCH, C. M., HELLER, B. R., & COSTA, P. T. (1986). Social learning influences on menstrual symptoms and illness behavior. *Health Psychology, 5,* 13-23.

WICKERSHAM, B. A. (1984). The exercise program. In G. K. Riggs & E. P. Gall (Eds.), *Rheumatic diseases: Rehabilitation and management.* Boston: Butterworth.

WIDEMAN, M. V., & SINGER, J. E. (1984). The role of psychological mechanisms in preparation for childbirth. *American Psychologist, 39,* 1357-1371.

WIEBE, D. J., & MCCALLUM, D. M. (1986). Health practices and hardiness as mediators in the stress-illness relationship. *Health Psychology, 5,* 425-438.

WIELGOSZ, A. T., FLETCHER, R. H., MCCANTS, C. B., MCKINNIS, R. A., HANEY, T. L., & WILLIAMS, R. B. (1984). Unimproved chest pain in patients with minimal or no coronary disease: A behavioral phenomenon. *American Heart Journal, 108,* 67-72.

WIENS, A. N., & MENUSTIK, C. E. (1983). Treatment outcome and patient characteristics in an aversion therapy program for alcoholism. *American Psychologist, 38,* 1089-1096.

WILKINSON, G. (1987). The influence of psychiatric, psychological and social factors on the control of insulin-dependent diabetes mellitus. *Journal of Psychosomatic Research, 31,* 277-286.

WILLIAMS, R. (1986). An untrusting heart. In M. G. Walraven & H. E. Fitzgerald (Eds.), *Annual editions: Human development 86/87.* Guilford, CT, Dushkin.

WILLIAMS, R. B., & BAREFOOT, J. C. (1988). Coronary-prone behavior: The emerging role of the hostility complex. In B. K. Houston & C. R. Snyder (Eds.), *Type A behavior pattern: Research, theory, and intervention.* New York: Wiley.

WILLIAMS, R. B., HANEY T. L., LEE, K. L., KONG, Y-H., BLUMENTHAL, J. A., & WHALEN, R. E. (1980). Type A behavior, hostility, and coronary atherosclerosis. *Psychosomatic Medicine, 42,* 539-549.

WILLIS, L., THOMAS, P., GARRY, P. J., & GOODWIN, J. S. (1987). A prospective study of response to stressful life events in initially healthy elders. *Journal of Gerontology, 42,* 627-630.

WILLS, T. A. (1984). Supportive functions of interpersonal relationships. In S. Cohen & L. Syme (Eds.), *Social support and health.* New York: Academic Press.

WILLS, T. A. (1986). Stress and coping in early adolescence: Relationships to substance use in urban school samples. *Health Psychology, 5,* 503-529.

WILSON, D. P., & ENDRES, R. K. (1986). Compliance with blood glucose monitoring in children with type 1 diabetes mellitus. *Behavioral Pediatrics, 108,* 1022-1024.

WILSON, G. T. (1984). Weight control treatments. In J. D. Matarazzo, S. M. Weiss, J. A. Herd, N. E. Miller, & S. M. Weiss (Eds.), *Behavioral health: A handbook of health enhancement and disease prevention.* New York: Wiley.

WILSON, G. T., ROSSITER, E., KLEIFIELD, E. I., & LINDHOLM, L. (1986). Cognitive-behavioral treatment of bulimia nervosa: A controlled evaluation. *Behaviour Research and Therapy, 24,* 277-288.

WILSON, G. T., & SMITH, D. (1987). Cognitive-behavioral treatment of bulimia nervosa. *Annals of Behavioral Medicine, 9*(4), 12-17.

WILSON, W., ARY, D. V., BIGLAN, A., GLASGOW, R. E., TOOBERT, D. J., & CAMPBELL, D. R. (1986). Psychosocial predictors of self-care behaviors (compliance) and glycemic control in non-insulin-dependent diabetes mellitus. *Diabetes Care, 9,* 614-622.

WINCZE, J. P. (1977). Sexual deviance and dysfunction. In D. C. Rimm & J. W. Somervill (Eds.), *Abnormal psychology.* New York: Academic Press.

WING, R. R., EPSTEIN, L. H., & NOWALK, M. P. (1984). Dietary adherence in patients with diabetes. *Behavioral Medicine Update, 6*(1), 17-21.

WING, R. R., EPSTEIN, L. H., NOWALK, M. P., & LAMPARSKI, D. M. (1986). Behavioral self-regulation in the treatment of patients with diabetes mellitus. *Psychological Bulletin, 99,* 78-89.

WING, R. R., NOWALK, M. P., & GUARE, J. C. (1988). Diabetes mellitus. In E. A. Blechman & K. D. Brownell (Eds.), *Handbook of behavioral medicine for women.* New York: Pergamon.

WINGARD, D. L. (1982). The sex differential in mortality rates: Demographic and behavioral factors. *American Journal of Epidemiology, 115,* 205-216.

WINIKOFF, B. (1983). Nutritional patterns, social choices, and health. In D. Mechanic (Ed.), *Handbook of health, health care, and the health professions.* New York: Free Press.

WINKELSTEIN, W., SAMUEL, M., PADIAN, N. S., WILEY, J. A., LANG, W., ANDERSON, R. E., & LEVY, J. A. (1987). The San Francisco Men's Health Study: III. Reduction in human immunodeficiency virus transmission among homosexual/bisexual men, 1982-1986. *American Journal of Public Health, 76,* 685-689.

WINTERS, R. (1985). Behavioral approaches to pain. In N. Schneiderman & J. T. Tapp (Eds.), *Behavioral medicine: The biopsychosocial approach.* Hillsdale, NJ: Erlbaum.

WITRYOL, S. L. (1971). Incentives and learning in children. In H. W. Reese (Ed.), *Advances in child development and behavior* (Vol. 6). New York: Academic Press.

WOLF, S., & WOLFF, H. G. (1947). *Human gastric function* (2nd ed.). New York: Oxford University Press.

WOLINSKY, F. D. (1978). Assessing the effects of predisposing, enabling, and illness-morbidity characteristics on health service utilization. *Journal of Health and Social Behavior, 19,* 384-396.

WOLPE, J. (1958). *Psychotherapy by reciprocal inhibition.* Stanford, CA: Stanford University Press.

WOLPE, J. (1973). *The practice of behavior therapy* (2nd ed.). New York: Pergamon.

WOODS, A. M., & BIRREN, J. E. (1984). Late adulthood and aging. In J. D. Matarazzo, S. M. Weiss, J. A. Herd, N. E. Miller, & S. M. Weiss (Eds.), *Behavioral health: A handbook of health enhancement and disease prevention.* New York: Wiley.

WOODS, P. J., & BURNS, J. (1984). Type A behavior and illness in general. *Journal of Behavioral Medicine, 7,* 411-415.

WOODS, P. J., MORGAN, B. T., DAY, B. W., JEFFERSON, T., & HARRIS, C. (1984). Findings on a relationship between Type A behavior and headaches. *Journal of Behavioral Medicine, 7,* 277-286.

WOODWARD, N. J., & WALLSTON, B. S. (1987). Age and health care beliefs: Self-efficacy as a mediator of low desire for control. *Psychology and Aging, 2,* 3-8.

WORTMAN, C. B. (1975). Some determinants of perceived control. *Journal of Personality and Social Psychology, 31,* 282-294.

WORTMAN, C. B., & DUNKEL-SCHETTER, C. (1979). Interpersonal relationships and cancer: A theoretical analysis. *Journal of Social Issues, 35,* 120-155.

WORTMAN, C. B., & DUNKEL-SCHETTER, C. (1987). Conceptual and methodological issues in the study of social support. In A. Baum & J. E. Singer (Eds.), *Handbook of psychology and health* (Vol. 5). Hillsdale, NJ: Erlbaum.

WRIGHT, L. (1988). The Type A behavior pattern and coronary artery disease. *American Psychologist, 43,* 2-14.

WURTELE, S. K., & MADDUX, J. E. (1987). Relative contributions of protection motivation theory components in predicting exercise intentions and behavior. *Health Psychology, 6,* 453-466.

YARNOLD, P. R., BRYANT, F. B., & GRIMM, L. G. (1987). Comparing the long and short forms of the student version of the Jenkins Activity Survey. *Journal of Behavioral Medicine, 10,* 75-90.

YOUNG, F. E. (1987, September). Special AIDS issue. *FDA Drug Bulletin, 17*(2).

ZAMULA, E. (1987). *A primer on high blood pressure* (HHS Publication No. FDA 87-3162). Washington, DC: U.S. Government Printing Office.

ZARSKI, J. J. (1984). Hassles and health: A replication. *Health Psychology, 3,* 243-251.

ZAUTRA, A. J., OKUN, M. A., ROBINSON, S. E., LEE, D., ROTH, S. H., & EMMANUAL, J. (1989). Life stress and lymphocyte alterations among patients with rheumatoid arthritis. *Health Psychology, 8,* 1-14.

ZIMBARDO, P. G. (1970). The human choice: Individuation, reason, and order versus deindividuation, impulse, and chaos. In W. J. Arnold & D. Levine (Eds.), *Nebraska symposium on motivation, 1969.* Lincoln, NB: University of Nebraska Press.

ZIMMER, J. G., JUNCKER, A. G., & MCCUSKER, J. (1985). A randomized controlled study of a home health care team. *American Journal of Public Health, 75,* 134-141.

ZINMAN, B. (1984). Diabetes mellitus and exercise. *Behavioral Medicine Update, 6*(1), 22-25.

ZOLA, I. K. (1973). Pathways to the doctor — From person to patient. *Social Science and Medicine, 7,* 677-689.

ZUCKER, R. A., & GOMBERG, E. S. L. (1986). Etiology of alcoholism reconsidered: The case for a biopsychosocial process. *American Psychologist, 41,* 783-793.

source notes

Page 5 *Figure 1.1* From R. Ryan & J. Travis (1981). *The wellness workbook.* Berkeley, CA: Ten Speed Press. Copyright © 1981, 1988 by John Travis.

Page 9 *Figure 1.3* From R. Melzack & P. Wall (1965). Pain mechanisms: A new theory. *Science, 150,* 971-979. Copyright © 1965 by the American Association for the Advancement of Science.

Page 38 *Figure 2.2* Drawings from P. H. Lindsay & D. A. Norman (1977, Figure 11-13). *Human information processing: An introduction to psychology* (2nd ed.). Copyright © 1977 by Harcourt Brace Jovanovich, Inc.; reprinted by permission of the publisher. Drawings based on photographs from J. L. Conel (1939-1963). *The postnatal development of the human cerebral cortex* (Vols. 1-7). Reproduced by permission of Harvard University Press.

Page 48 *Figure 2A.1* From J. C. B. Grant (1972). *An atlas of anatomy.* Copyright © 1972 by Williams & Wilkins Co.

Page 53 *Figure 2.11* From A. Guyton (1985, Figure 44-2B). *Anatomy and physiology.* Copyright © 1984 by Saunders College Publishing, a division of Holt, Rinehart & Winston, Inc.; reprinted by permission of the publisher.

Page 98 *Table 3.1* From T. Holmes & R. Rahe (1967). The Social Readjustment Rating Scale. *Journal of Psychosomatic Research, 11,* 213-218.

Page 101 *Table 3.2* From J. S. Heisel, S. Ream, R. Raitz, M. Rappoport, & R. D. Coddington (1973). The significance of life events as contributing factors in the diseases of children. *Journal of Pediatrics, 83,* 119-123.

Page 120 *Figure 4A.1* From R. Schulz & B. H. Hanusa (1978). Long-term effects of control and predictability-enhancing interventions: Findings and ethical issues. *Journal of Personality and Social Psychology, 36,* 1194-1201. Copyright © 1978 by the American Psychological Association; adapted by permission of the author.

Page 137 *Figure 4.4* From F. Andrasik, D. D. Blake, & M. S. McCarran (1986). A biobehavioral analysis of pediatric headache. In N. A. Krasnegor, J. D. Arasteh, & M. F. Cataldo (Eds.), *Child health behavior: A behavioral pediatrics perspective.* Copyright © 1986 by John Wiley & Sons, Inc.

Page 169 *Table 5.1* From R. W. Novaco (1978). Anger and coping with stress: Cognitive and behavioral interventions. In J. P. Foreyt & D. P. Rathjen (Eds.), *Cognitive behavior therapy: Research and application.* Copyright © 1978 by Plenum Press.

Page 177 *Figure 6.1* From D. M. Harris & S. Guten (1979). Health-protective behavior: An exploratory study. *Journal of Health and Social Behavior, 20,* 17-29.

Page 190 *Figure 6.2* Adapted from M. H. Becker & I. M. Rosenstock (1984). Compliance with medical advice. In A. Steptoe & A. Mathews (Eds.), *Health care and human behaviour.* Copyright © 1984 by Academic Press.

Page 255 *Figure 8.1* From E. P. Sarafino & J. W. Armstrong (1986). *Child and adolescent development* (2nd ed.). St. Paul, MN: West Publishing Co.; copyright © 1986 by Edward P. Sarafino and James W. Armstrong.

Page 259 *Table 8.1* From Metropolitan Life Foundation (1983). 1983 Metropolitan Height and Weight Tables. *Statistical Bulletin, 64*(1), 2-9. Courtesy of the Metropolitan Life Insurance Co.

Page 300 *Figure 9.2* From M. A. Safer, Q. J. Tharps, T. C. Jackson, & H. Leventhal (1979). Determinants of three stages of delay in seeking care at a medical clinic. *Medical Care, 17,* 11-29.

Page 335 *Figure 10.2* Adapted from E. A. Anderson (1987). Preoperative preparation for cardiac surgery facilitates recovery, reduces psychological distress, and reduces the incidence of acute postoperative hypertension. *Journal of Consulting and Clinical Psychology, 55,* 513-520. Copyright © 1987 by the American Psychological Association; adapted by permission of the author.

Page 338 *Figure 10.3* From S. M. Miller & C. E. Mangan (1983). Interacting effects of information and coping style in adapting to gynecologic stress: Should the doctor tell all? *Journal of Personality and Social Psychology, 45,* 223-236. Copyright © 1983 by the American Psychological Association; reprinted by permission of the author.

Page 340 *Figure 10.4* From E. P. Sarafino & J. W. Armstrong (1986). *Child and adolescent development* (2nd ed.). St. Paul, MN: West Publishing Co.; copyright © 1986 by Edward P. Sarafino and James W. Armstrong.

Page 390 *Figure 12.1* Adapted from F. Andrasik (1986). Relaxation and biofeedback for chronic headaches. In A. D. Holzman & D. C. Turk (Eds.), *Pain management: A handbook of psychological treatment approaches.* Copyright © 1986 by Pergamon Press PLC.

Page 414 *Figure 13.1* Adapted from R. H. Moos (1982). Coping with acute health crises. In T. Millon, C. Green, & R. Meagher (Eds.), *Handbook of clinical health psychology.* Copyright © 1982 by Plenum Press.

Page 457 *Figure 14.1* From E. Silverberg & J. A. Lubera (1989). Cancer statistics, 1989. *Ca—A Cancer Journal for Clinicians, 39*(1), 3–20. Reproduced with permission of the American Cancer Society.

photo credits

Chapter 1
Page 6: The Bettmann Archive. *Page 8:* The University Museum; University of Pennsylvania. *Page 18:* Alan Carey/The Image Works.

Chapter 2
Page 44: (*top*) Peggy Simsarian Striegel/Graphic Design; (*bottom*) Carolina Biological Supply Company. *Page 52:* Peggy Simsarian Striegel/Graphic Design.

Chapter 3
Page 79: Tom Kelly/The Mercury. *Page 84:* Mark Antman/The Image Works. *Page 92:* Alan Carey/The Image Works. *Page 94:* Jim Mahoney/The Image Works. *Page 96:* Courtesy of Lafayette Instrument Company. *Page 102:* Reprinted with special permission of King Features Syndicate, Inc.

Chapter 4
Page 108: Elizabeth Crews. *Page 116:* Sarah Putnum/The Picture Cube. *Page 127:* Reprinted with special permission of King Features Syndicate, Inc.

Chapter 5
Page 146: Reprinted with special permission of King Features Syndicate, Inc. *Page 151:* Frank Siteman/The Picture Cube. *Page 153:* Richard Reinhold/EKM-Nepenthe. *Page 162:* Ken Robert Buck, University Hospital, Boston/The Picture Cube.

Chapter 6
Page 180: Bill Bachman/Photo Researchers. *Page 200:* Billy E. Barnes/Stock, Boston. *Page 208:* Robert Kalman/The Image Works. *Page 212:* Martha Tabor/Working Images.

Chapter 7
Page 228: Courtesy American Cancer Society. *Page 233:* The Bettemann Archive. *Page 235:* Alan Carey/The Image Works. *Page 246:* UPI/Bettmann Newsphotos.

Chapter 8
Page 251: Cary Wolinsky/Stock, Boston. *Page 257:* Richard Sobol/Stock, Boston. *Page 262:* Richard Falco/Photo Researchers. *Page 270:* Susan Rosenberg/Photo Researchers. *Page 277:* Ellis Herwig/Stock, Boston.

Chapter 9
Page 287: EKM-Nepenthe. *Page 295:* Martha Tabor/Working Images. *Page 306:* Blair Seitz/Photo Researchers.

Chapter 10
Page 321: The Bettmann Archive. *Page 324:* Alan Carey/The Image Works. *Page 330:* Billy E. Barnes. *Page 341:* Jack Spratt/The Image Works.

Chapter 11
Page 358: The Bettmann Archive. *Page 369:* David Powers/Stock, Boston. *Page 374:* Dion Ogust/The Image Works. *Page 378: Richard Wood/The Picture Cube.*

Chapter 12
Page 384: The New York Historical Society. *Page 402:* Judy S. Gelles/Stock, Boston. *Page 403:* Richard Wood/The Picture Cube.

Chapter 13

Page 416: Alan Carey/The Image Works. *Page 427:* Alan Carey/The Image Works. *Page 436:* James Prince/Photo Researchers.

Chapter 14

Page 452: David Powers/Stock, Boston. *Page 458:* Spencer Grant/The Picture Cube. *Page 468:* John Griffin/The Image Works. *Page 476:* Tim Jewett/EKM-Nepenthe.

index